Contemporary
Literary Criticism

Guide to Gale Literary Criticism Series

When you need to review criticism of literary works, these are the Gale series to use:

If the author's death date is:	You should turn to:

After Dec. 31, 1959
(or author is still living)

CONTEMPORARY LITERARY CRITICISM

for example: Jorge Luis Borges, Anthony Burgess,
William Faulkner, Mary Gordon,
Ernest Hemingway, Iris Murdoch

1900 through 1959

TWENTIETH-CENTURY LITERARY CRITICISM

for example: Willa Cather, F. Scott Fitzgerald,
Henry James, Mark Twain, Virginia Woolf

1800 through 1899

NINETEENTH-CENTURY LITERATURE CRITICISM

for example: Fedor Dostoevski, Nathaniel Hawthorne,
George Sand, William Wordsworth

1400 through 1799

LITERATURE CRITICISM FROM 1400 TO 1800
(excluding Shakespeare)

for example: Anne Bradstreet, Daniel Defoe,
Alexander Pope, François Rabelais,
Jonathan Swift, Phillis Wheatley

SHAKESPEAREAN CRITICISM

Shakespeare's plays and poetry

Antiquity through 1399

CLASSICAL AND MEDIEVAL LITERATURE CRITICISM

for example: Dante, Homer, Plato, Sophocles, Vergil,
the Beowulf Poet

Gale also publishes related criticism series:

CHILDREN'S LITERATURE REVIEW

This series covers authors of all eras who write for the preschool through high school audience.

SHORT STORY CRITICISM

This series covers the major short fiction writers of all nationalities and periods of literary history.

ISSN 0091-3421

Volume 48

Contemporary Literary Criticism

Excerpts from Criticism of the
Works of Today's Novelists, Poets,
Playwrights, Short Story Writers, Scriptwriters,
and Other Creative Writers

Daniel G. Marowski
Roger Matuz
EDITORS

Sean R. Pollock
Robyn V. Young
ASSOCIATE EDITORS

Gale Research Company
Book Tower
Detroit, Michigan 48226

STAFF

Daniel G. Marowski, Roger Matuz, *Editors*

Sean R. Pollock, Robyn V. Young, *Associate Editors*

Jane C. Thacker, Thomas J. Votteler, Bruce Walker, *Senior Assistant Editors*

Kent Graham, Michele R. O'Connell, David Segal, *Assistant Editors*

Jean C. Stine, *Contributing Editor*

Jay P. Pederson, Debra A. Wells, *Contributing Assistant Editors*

Jeanne A. Gough, *Production & Permissions Manager*
Lizbeth A. Purdy, *Production Supervisor*
Kathleen M. Cook, *Production Coordinator*
Cathy Beranek, Suzanne Powers, Kristine E. Tipton, Lee Ann Welsh, *Editorial Assistants*
Linda M. Pugliese, *Manuscript Coordinator*
Maureen A. Puhl, *Senior Manuscript Assistant*
Donna Craft, Jennifer E. Gale, Rosetta Irene Simms, *Manuscript Assistants*

Victoria B. Cariappa, *Research Supervisor*
Maureen R. Richards, *Research Coordinator*
Mary D. Wise, *Senior Research Assistant*
Joyce E. Doyle, Kevin B. Hillstrom, Karen D. Kaus, Eric Priehs,
Filomena Sgambati, Laura B. Standley, *Research Assistants*

Janice M. Mach, *Text Permissions Supervisor*
Kathy Grell, *Text Permissions Coordinator*
Mabel E. Gurney, Josephine M. Keene, *Senior Permissions Assistants*
Eileen H. Baehr, H. Diane Cooper, Anita L. Ransom,
Kimberly F. Smilay, *Permissions Assistants*
Melissa A. Kamuyu, Martha A. Mulder, Lisa M. Wimmer, *Permissions Clerks*

Patricia A. Seefelt, *Picture Permissions Supervisor*
Margaret A. Chamberlain, *Picture Permissions Coordinator*
Pamela A. Hayes, Lillian Tyus, *Permissions Clerks*

Since this page cannot legibly accommodate all the copyright notices,
the Appendix constitutes an extension of the copyright notice.

Contents

Preface   vii

Authors Forthcoming in *CLC*   xi

Appendix   431

Literary Criticism Series Cumulative Author Index   443

CLC Cumulative Nationality Index   503

CLC-48 Title Index   513

Preface

Literary criticism is, by definition, "the art of evaluating or analyzing with knowledge and propriety works of literature." The complexity and variety of the themes and forms of contemporary literature make the function of the critic especially important to today's reader. It is the critic who assists the reader in identifying significant new writers, recognizing trends in critical methods, mastering new terminology, and monitoring scholarly and popular sources of critical opinion.

Until the publication of the first volume of *Contemporary Literary Criticism (CLC)* in 1973, there existed no ongoing digest of current literary opinion. *CLC,* therefore, has fulfilled an essential need.

Scope of the Work

CLC presents significant passages from published criticism of works by today's creative writers. Each volume of *CLC* includes excerpted criticism on about forty authors who are now living or who died after December 31, 1959. Nearly 2,000 authors have been included since the series began publication. The majority of authors covered by *CLC* are living writers who continue to publish; therefore, criticism on an author frequently appears in more than one volume. There is, of course, no duplication of reprinted criticism.

Authors are selected for inclusion for a variety of reasons, among them the publication of a critically acclaimed new work, the reception of a major literary award, or the dramatization of a literary work as a film or television screenplay. For example, the present volume includes Richard Wright, whose 1940 novel *Native Son* continues to be read as a searing indictment of racial persecution; Nicolás Guillén, since 1961 the National Poet of Cuba; and Susan Cheever, whose book *Home before Dark* provides an intimate portrait of her father, acclaimed novelist and short story writer John Cheever. Perhaps most importantly, authors who appear frequently on the syllabuses of high school and college literature classes are heavily represented in *CLC;* Carson McCullers and Ezra Pound are examples of writers of this stature in the present volume. Attention is also given to several other groups of writers—authors of considerable public interest—about whose work criticism is often difficult to locate. These are the contributors to the well-loved but nonscholarly genres of mystery and science fiction, as well as literary and social critics whose insights are considered valuable and informative. Foreign writers and authors who represent particular ethnic groups in the United States are also featured in each volume.

Format of the Book

Altogether there are about 600 individual excerpts in each volume—with approximately fifteen excerpts per author—taken from hundreds of literary reviews, general magazines, scholarly journals, and monographs. Contemporary criticism is loosely defined as that which is relevant to the evaluation of the author under discussion; this includes criticism written at the beginning of an author's career as well as current commentary. Emphasis has been placed on expanding the sources for criticism by including an increasing number of scholarly and specialized periodicals. Students, teachers, librarians, and researchers frequently find that the generous excerpts and supplementary material provided by the editors supply them with vital information needed to write a term paper, analyze a poem, or lead a book discussion group. However, complete bibliographical citations facilitate the location of the original source and provide all of the information necessary for a term paper footnote or bibliography.

A *CLC* author entry consists of the following elements:

- The **author heading** cites the author's full name, followed by birth date, and death date when applicable. The portion of the name outside parentheses denotes the form under which the author has most commonly published. If an author has written consistently under a pseudonym, the pseudonym will be listed in the author heading and the real name given on the first line of the biographical and critical introduction. Also located at the beginning of the introduction to the author entry are any important name variations under which an author has written. Uncertainty as to a birth or death date is indicated by question marks.

- A **portrait** of the author is included when available.

- A brief **biographical and critical introduction** to the author and his or her work precedes the excerpted criticism. However, *CLC* is not intended to be a definitive biographical source. Therefore, *cross-references* have been included to direct the reader to these useful sources published by Gale Research: *Contemporary Authors,* which includes detailed biographical and bibliographical sketches on nearly 90,000 authors; *Children's Literature Review,* which presents excerpted criticism on the works of authors of children's books; *Something about the Author,* which contains heavily illustrated biographical sketches of writers and illustrators who create books for children and young adults; *Dictionary of Literary Biography,* which provides original evaluations and detailed biographies of authors important to literary history; *Contemporary Authors Autobiography Series,* which offers autobiographical essays by prominent writers; and *Something about the Author Autobiography Series,* which presents autobiographical essays by authors of interest to young readers. Previous volumes of *CLC* in which the author has been featured are also listed in the introduction.

- The **excerpted criticism** represents various kinds of critical writing—a particular essay may be descriptive, interpretive, textual, appreciative, comparative, or generic. It may range in form from the brief review to the scholarly monograph. Essays are selected by the editors to reflect the spectrum of opinion about a specific work or about an author's literary career in general. The excerpts are presented chronologically, adding a useful perspective to the entry. All titles by the author featured in the entry are printed in boldface type, which enables the reader to easily identify the works being discussed. Publication information (such as publisher names and book prices) and parenthetical numerical references (such as footnotes or page and line references to specific editions of a work) have been deleted at the editor's discretion to provide smoother reading of the text.

- A complete **bibliographical citation** designed to help the user find the original essay or book follows each excerpt.

Other Features

- A list of **Authors Forthcoming in** *CLC* previews the authors to be researched for future volumes.

- An **Appendix** lists the sources from which material in the volume has been reprinted. It does not, however, list every book or periodical consulted during the preparation of the volume.

- A **Cumulative Author Index** lists all the authors who have appeared in *CLC, Twentieth-Century Literary Criticism, Nineteenth-Century Literature Criticism, Literature Criticism from 1400 to 1800,* and *Classical and Medieval Literature Criticism,* with cross-references to these Gale series: *Short Story Criticism, Children's Literature Review, Authors in the News, Contemporary Authors, Contemporary Authors Autobiography Series, Contemporary Authors Bibliographical Series, Dictionary of Literary Biography, Something about the Author, Something about the Author Autobiography Series,* and *Yesterday's Authors of Books for Children.* Readers will welcome this cumulated author index as a useful tool for locating an author within the various series. The index, which lists birth and death dates when available, will be particularly valuable for those authors who are identified with a certain period but whose death date causes them to be placed in another, or for those authors whose careers span two periods. For example, Ernest Hemingway is found in *CLC,* yet a writer often associated with him, F. Scott Fitzgerald, is found in *Twentieth-Century Literary Criticism.*

- A **Cumulative Nationality Index** alphabetically lists all authors featured in *CLC* by nationality, followed by numbers corresponding to the volumes in which they appear.

- A **Title Index** alphabetically lists all titles reviewed in the current volume of *CLC.* Titles are followed by the corresponding page numbers where they may be located. In cases where the same title is used by different authors, the authors' surnames are given in parentheses after the title, e.g., *Collected Poems* (Berryman), *Collected Poems* (Eliot). For foreign titles, a cross-reference is given to the translated English title. Titles of novels, novellas, dramas, films, record albums, and poetry, short story, and essay collections are printed in italics, while all individual poems, short stories, essays, and songs are printed in roman type within quotation marks; when published separately (e.g., T.S. Eliot's poem *The Waste Land*), the title will also be printed in italics.

• In response to numerous suggestions from librarians, Gale has also produced a **special paperbound edition** of the *CLC* title index. This annual cumulation, which alphabetically lists all titles reviewed in the series, is available to all customers and will be published with the first volume of *CLC* issued in each calendar year. Additional copies of the index are available upon request. Librarians and patrons will welcome this separate index: it saves shelf space, is easily disposable upon receipt of the following year's cumulation, and is more portable and thus easier to use than was previously possible.

Acknowledgments

No work of this scope can be accomplished without the cooperation of many people. The editors especially wish to thank the copyright holders of the excerpted essays included in this volume, the permissions managers of many book and magazine publishing companies for assisting us in securing reprint rights, and the photographers and other individuals who provided portraits of the authors. We are grateful to the staffs of the Detroit Public Library, the Library of Congress, the University of Detroit Library, the University of Michigan Library, and the Wayne State University Library for making their resources available to us. We also wish to thank Anthony Bogucki for his assistance with copyright research.

Suggestions Are Welcome

The editors welcome the comments and suggestions of readers to expand the coverage and enhance the usefulness of the series.

Authors Forthcoming in *CLC*

Contemporary Literary Criticism, Volumes 49 and 51, will feature critical excerpts on a number of authors not previously listed as well as criticism on newer works by authors included in earlier volumes. Volume 50 will be a yearbook devoted to an examination of the outstanding achievements and trends in literature during 1987.

To Be Included in Volume 49

Richard Aldington (English poet, novelist, short story writer, critic, and autobiographer)—Regarded as one of the most significant poets of the Imagist movement, Aldington is also recognized for his later verse, in which he explored romantic love, modern warfare, and historical themes.

Gwendolyn Brooks (American poet, novelist, autobiographer, and author of children's books)—The first black author to win a Pulitzer Prize, Brooks is distinguished for blending elevated speech and colloquial dialect in lyrical, inventive verse that objectively addresses the injustices confronted by contemporary urban black Americans.

Humberto Costantini (Argentinian novelist, dramatist, poet, and short story writer)—In his novels *The Gods, The Little Guys, and the Police* and *The Long Night of Francisco Sanctis,* Costantini employs black humor and satire to depict political oppression in Argentina during the 1970s.

H. L. Davis (American novelist, short story writer, poet, essayist, and critic)—Davis's works, set primarily in the American West during the nineteenth and early twentieth centuries, explore such universal concerns as initiation, alienation, the nature of love, and the relationship between past and present. The recent reissue of *Honey in the Horn,* his 1936 Pulitzer Prize-winning novel, has generated renewed interest in Davis's career.

Spalding Gray (American performance artist, dramatist, and actor)—Gray has won acclaim for his humorous dramatic monologues in which he transforms personal stories and anecdotes into larger reflections on contemporary society. His entry will cover *Sex and Death to the Age 14,* a collection of monologues, and *Swimming to Cambodia,* which relates Gray's experiences in Thailand during the filming of *The Killing Fields.*

Tommaso Landolfi (Italian novelist, short story writer, critic, poet, dramatist, essayist, and translator)—Among the most innovative stylists in modern Italian fiction, Landolfi demonstrated a surreal vision and a preoccupation with language similar to those of Franz Kafka and Italo Calvino. His most respected books include *The Moon Stone* and *The Two Spinsters.*

Elmer Rice (American dramatist, novelist, scriptwriter, editor, and autobiographer)—A prolific and diverse dramatist whose career spanned more than fifty years, Rice is best remembered for such plays as *The Adding Machine* and the Pulitzer Prize-winning *Street Scene,* which contributed to the development of a socially conscious American theater.

Vladimir Voinovich (Russian-born novelist, short story writer, essayist, and nonfiction writer)—A Russian exile since 1980, Voinovich is well known for his satires of life in the Soviet Union. Recent works to be covered in his entry include *The Anti-Soviet Soviet Union,* a collection of prose pieces, and *Moscow 2042,* a futuristic novel.

Terence de Vere White (Irish novelist, short story writer, biographer, nonfiction writer, memoirist, and editor)—In such novels as *An Affair with the Moon, Lucifer Falling,* and *The Distance and the Dark,* White combines mild social commentary with sophisticated humor to satirize the conventions of Irish gentility and explore the changes that have occurred in his country's social structures since the demise of British rule.

W. S. Wilson (American short story writer and novelist)—Best known for his short story collection *Why I Don't Write Like Franz Kafka,* Wilson imbues his fiction with scientific and philosophical language and methodology to explore such topics as human relationships, epistemology, and the nature of fiction.

Chinua Achebe (Nigerian novelist, short story writer, poet, and essayist)—One of Africa's most important contemporary writers, Achebe chronicles the cultural and psychological effects of European colonization on the Ibo, a native Nigerian tribe. His entry will include reviews of his recent novel, *Anthills of the Savannah.*

Anita Brookner (English novelist, nonfiction writer, and critic)—Best known as the author of *Hotel du Lac,* for which she received the Booker-McConnell Prize for fiction, Brookner writes novels that focus upon well-educated, affluent women whose lives are often disrupted by unfaithful husbands and lovers. Recent works to be covered in her entry include *Family and Friends* and *The Misalliance.*

Noël Coward (English dramatist, lyricist, novelist, short story writer, scriptwriter, and autobiographer)—A prolific and versatile playwright, Coward is best remembered for whimsical social comedies that display his talent for creating imaginative plots and witty, acerbic dialogue. Recent revivals of such Coward works as *Private Lives, Blithe Spirit,* and *Design for Living* have renewed interest in his work.

Kenneth Fearing (American poet, novelist, and editor)— Best known for the thriller novel *The Big Clock,* from which the recent film *No Way Out* was adapted, Fearing also distinguished himself during the Depression era as a poet whose verse attacked the dehumanizing effects of a capitalistic industrialized society.

Nadine Gordimer (South African novelist, short story writer, critic, and editor)—Gordimer is respected for examining the effects of the South African apartheid system on both ruling whites and oppressed blacks. Criticism in Gordimer's entry will focus upon her recent novel, *A Sport of Nature.*

Katherine Govier (Canadian novelist, short story writer, and journalist)—In her fiction, Govier often depicts female characters who must confront elements of their past in order to live contentedly in the present. Govier's interest in history is reflected in her recent novel, *Between Man,* which intertwines the stories of a contemporary history professor and an Indian woman who died mysteriously in the 1880s.

Patrick Hamilton (English dramatist, novelist, and scriptwriter)—Best known for his psychological plays *Rope* and *Angel Street,* Hamilton also wrote several novels during the 1930s and 1940s set in and around actual English pubs that portray the disordered lives of criminals, outcasts, and misfits.

Lisel Mueller (German-born American poet and critic)—Using such traditional techniques as metaphor, simile, and personification, Mueller concentrates in her verse on discovering the extraordinary aspects of ordinary objects and events. Works to be covered in her entry include *The Private Life* and *Second Language.*

Tom Wolfe (American essayist, journalist, editor, critic, and novelist)—Regarded as one of the most original stylists in contemporary literature, Wolfe figured prominently in the development of New Journalism, a form of expository writing that blends reporting with such techniques of fiction as stream of consciousness, extended dialogue, shifting points of view, and detailed scenarios. This entry will focus upon Wolfe's recent first novel, *The Bonfire of the Vanities.*

Yevgeny Yevtushenko (Russian poet and novelist)—Among the most outspoken and controversial poets to emerge in the Soviet Union since the death of Stalin, Yevtushenko has written two recent novels, *Wild Berries,* and *Ardabiola,* in which he expands on the personal themes of his poetry.

Lee K. Abbott, Jr.

19??-

American short story writer.

Abbott's fiction is characterized by energetic prose infused with hyperbole, verbal pyrotechnics, humor, and wordplay. Set primarily in the Southwest, his stories typically feature small-town men who engage the reader with their absurd, often exaggerated tales. Abbott has been compared to such writers as Barry Hannah and Harry Crews for his ribald humor and manic, unpredictable prose. Stephen Corey stated: "All of [his] word-mongering is in service of Abbott's deep ambition to make some approach, through the rich yet limited resources of speech, toward the complexities and difficulties of human thought, love, and communication."

In his stories, Abbott frequently highlights the outrageous excesses of characters who yearn to transcend feelings of emptiness and find meaning and purpose in their lives. The works in his first collection, *The Heart Never Fits Its Wanting* (1980), center on vulnerable men who have been rejected by uncaring women but persist in trying to find a suitable mate. In his next volume, *Love Is the Crooked Thing* (1986), Abbott underscores the fragility of life through stories concerning such topics as death, substance abuse, and the Vietnam War. In *Strangers in Paradise* (1986), Abbott probes familial relationships, loss, and the effects of war by focusing on representative conflicts faced by characters who grew up in the American Southwest.

Photograph by Cynthia Farah. Courtesy of Lee K. Abbott, Jr.

SUSAN QUIST

Abbott writes some fulsome and fellatious prose, the kind that simply melts in your mouth, knocks your teeth down your throat. . . .

From the first word [in *The Heart Never Fits Its Wanting*] ("Friends"), you know you have entered the fabulous realm of Oral Roberts. And Pecos Bill and P. T. Barnum and the used car salesman and Vachel Lindsay and Muhammed Ali and Huckleberry Finn. The evangelist, the cowboy, the showman, the conman, the vagabond poet, the athlete, the bad-boy-who-will-not-growup—they're all here, more or less, and ruefully, in a contemporary, tongue-in-chic facsimile of the Tall Tale style, which is apropos to the content: i.e., the ragged individualist pursuing the American dream. Which, though not well, appears to be alive and kicking the hell out of any guy who dares to come near.

There is a lot of violence, mostly confined (thank you, Jesus) to the verbal attack. Here, for example, is Scooter E. Watts, "creepy, brilliant, a loser, weak and consumptive, his guts a quaking moil and true image of Modern Times." Who has "stuffed his clothes in a ditty bag and, hitching, lit out, heading south." . . .

Seeking his in a place called Goree, Texas, "a place of crude but serious beliefs," Scooter spies his battlefield—a golf course viewed through a barbed wire fence. Having landed here as improbably as the golf balls he knocks into the appropriate holes in his roundabout way, Scooter proceeds to make a killing in gophers, club ladies, and longshots, spending most of his winnings on "clothes and gizmos," purchased at Neiman-Marcus with the comment that he doesn't know what it is, "but products gratify my inner self." As opposed to the poetic desserts he finally reaps.

These are delivered by a couple of karmic executioners who move through these stories like those hitchhikers you pass at sundown, only to see them finishing up their breakfast at the Hojo's just as you arrive, forty-five minutes behind them, and you're waiting for their table, but they're in no hurry to leave as they know whatever they do, they will always arrive forty-five minutes ahead of folks like you. . . .

[Another character, Rae Nell Tipton], is a holy terror. Variously costumed in leather and chains, toreador pants, an ecru velveteen jumpsuit, spike heels, black short-shorts and a Spanish hairdo, a Peek-A-Boo bra from Frederick's of Hollywood, and nothing at all, Rae Nell is more than America's answer to Helen of Troy. A "140 pounds of flatland farmgirl," Rae Nell rises from this literary landscape like the Statue of Liberty, on the move and the make, leaving a trail of body parts and moral remains in her wake, the kind of woman men fight, kill, die and lie for, as she enjoys and encourages this form of courtship, loving the winner. But not as much as she loves the fight.

"I'm a writer," she says. "I'm doing research and absorbing experience . . . I specialize in grief and overcoming . . . I want thrills and vanquishing."

Like the men who woo her, Rae Nell is, in her way, hellbound for disappointment as she simply cannot be vanquished, for she thrives on the effort to do it and grows stronger with every attempt. Whatever goes down, she comes out on top and cannot stop herself, nor does she try or want to, as it is not vanquishing she wants but a string of broken hearts, or heads—like Kali, the Indian goddess whose pleasure it is to dance upon Shiva's belly. And, like Shiva, these daredevils Rae Nell teams up with are only too pleased to lie down and take it as she is so agreeable, "making pleasant doggie noises."

The first in her series of escorts is a gentleman by the name of Fleece Dee Monroe and he is the one who delivers the message to Scooter E. Watts, out there on the golf course, as his golfbag itself speaks of medieval hoodoo, being "a cumbersome and infernal item, full of pockets and zippers and chains and three compartments with heavy locks on them. 'This thing's imported,'" Fleece advises his hapless opponent."'I got stuff in here that works without reason or purpose.'"

Which might just as well be said in regards to these stories, I do believe. Or, as Billy Jack Eddy, the famous country and western singer, says of one of the hits Rae Nell has lovingly penned for him, it has "raunch and double meanings." Enough, one suspects, to engorge many a doctoral candidate and book reviewer. Even one such as I, who am rarely tempted to learned endeavor, am moved to speculate.

For example, there is something about Fleece and Rae Nell that reminds one of Jason and Medea, although this one is too lazy and ignorant to pursue it, assuming that some of the rest of you will.

And what about this irritating title? "The Heart Never FITS Its Wanting." Somehow, the word FITS does not. And so it does, by some perverse logic, as it sets your teeth on edge, the better to gnash them, my dear. . . .

Naturally, the title also raises some questions regarding phallic inadequacy, which herein appears unaVOIDable, given the nature of it as personified by Rae Nell, who explains, "I hear the call of bigger things."

It also may remind one of the old saw, "his eyes are bigger than his belly." As that is the case, in every case, this brings us to a minor beef, or bellyache: i.e., whilst reading these stories, one may occasionally feel that one has bitten off more than one can chew, as they are so rich and heavily spiced. I mean to tell you every paragraph is loaded with wit and internal rhymes more complex than poetry dares in these Modern Times, and literate and hip innuendo, and references to military combat, and commando imagery, and so forth, and ALL of this demands attention. So that after awhile one may feel a touch of indigestion. But then it does occur to one that this whopping compression of sensual stimuli may be part of some devious scheme and underlying theme: i.e., American greed. Not just in regards to products that gratify the inner self, but in regards to our quote lust for life unquote.

As Rae Nell so aptly puts it, "Quote I have a fat man's appetite for truth unquote."

While there is much here to ruminate, you do not have to, as these stories can be swallowed whole and absorbed directly into the bloodstream, where they will warm to your cellular memories of your wasted youth and loonies you have known and loved and lost. But mostly, these stories will rekindle your love affair with the English language and for that reason alone should be read, as they are of a High Moral Order. Besides which, they're fun, even if they do have a serious intent, it is so well disguised you need not dwell upon it as you will do that when you least expect it. . . .

Susan Quist, in a review of "The Heart Never Fits Its Wanting," in The American Book Review, *Vol. 3, No. 3, March-April, 1981, p. 9.*

WILLIAM MARLING

The pure products of America only go crazy in our literature, and then because a veiled narrator is stalking a Rip Van Winkle, a Quentin Compson, or an Elsie and hoping for a heart-shot on the nation's tawdriness. In fact, the pure products are still out there, tolerably happy, annoyingly able to quench their miseries in 3.2 beer and softball.

[In *The Heart Never Fits Its Wanting*] Lee Abbott has surveyed their landscape, a dusty stretch from Goree and Olney and Brownfield in Texas on through Oaks, Oklahoma, and out into Arkansas. It is a land "quote counterarticulate, mythopathic and wanton unquote, a meager skyline of grain silos, truck dealerships, saloons and an El Dorado of shit-kicker storefronts." The residents are mythopathic too, if Abbott's names mean anything: Billy Jack Eddy, Scooter E. Watts, Lamar Thibodeaux, Dallas Tanksley, Sgt. Donnie T. Bobo, Fast Eddie Morris, and Rae Nell Tipton. The characters in these ten stories take their own measures before we can confuse them with heroes. In their confessions of brokenheartedness, lust, and woefulness, they set themselves so far below us and are yet so hyperbolic in expression, that a tension of condescension results. "You can measure my need," cries Fast Eddie Morris; he has learned the "secret lingo for Need, and Interior Hurt and The Special Freeing Presence of a Woman." Language is our yardstick on him.

But it is easy, especially on first reading, to lose sight of the connection between the language and the emotion, for Abbott is a dazzling stylist. He works irony, hyperbole, epithet, and anticlimax into sentences that achieve speed by elision, by fragment, that sometimes begin and end with a participle. He uses truisms, aphorisms, and romantic sentiments—the favored American forms of wisdom—to whittle emotion down to size; he is particularly effective when he writes about his alter ego Rae Nell. . . . At once a satire on popular writing and a warning by Abbott to himself, Rae Nell expresses with broken brain the truth about us:

> "I hear the call of bigger things," she was saying. "I don't know tender nor sweet nor innocence. I know fate and government secrets and little beatings in the chest. Hard is what I am, always was, always will be." She was quoting from one of her stories, purely autobiographical. "Hard like mysteries, and deep too. Deep as any insight. Deeper! Quote I have a fat man's appetite for truth unquote."

As in the work of Donald Barthelme, literary pyrotechnics conceal a concern with love: how can you revivify it except by holding it up, slashing it, burlesqueing it? . . . Abbott uses the first person predominantly; his narrators are all hard-luck kids, abject, love-struck and vulnerable. Their problems are heart problems—unrequited love, separation, jealousy—that they tackle with a directness (which Abbott's prose conceals) and a faith in luck that substitutes for Providence. (pp. 335-36)

What changes the lives of Abbott's characters is love; it breaks their luck and creates an empathy that lets them move around behind the hyperbolic language they speak. Their vulnerability becomes an emotional sail, to be filled with the breath of tall tales.

So much happens with this language that we forget the structure of Abbott's stories and only on reflection notice that many of them lack narrative necessity. He has difficulty closing a piece at the pitch he sustains for the first three-quarters of it; in fact, he seems loath to part with his characters, and most of his stories simply linger to an end. His plots need to rise above his art more, and since his themes touch the matter of the human heart, his resolutions demand a sense of *consequence*.

If these stories are also concentrated—reading them is rather like eating a box of chocolates—and sometimes unframed, there is also a sense right to the end of impressive craft, of serious intent. Scooter E. Watts seems to speak for Abbott when he says "that if there weren't meaning or purpose or reason in this good life, there had to be something—sum, quotient, salty residue. 'There's paste or ash or goo,' he said. 'Me, I'm gonna find it, shake its muscular hand.'" (pp. 336-37)

William Marling "Heart Problems of Hard-Luck Kids," in Southwest Review, *Vol. 66, No. 3, Summer, 1981, pp. 335-37.*

ELLEN FRIEDMAN

The voice of Abbott's ten stories [in *The Heart Never Fits Its Wanting*] is manic, garrulous, at moments hysterical, and always just barely sane. One reads these stories to listen to this engaging voice which strings together ideas and physical and abstract images with a calculated indiscrimination. Adding to the sense of randomness is Abbott's obsessive use of the conjunction "and." Its repeated use in linking ideas has the effect of defying our reasonable expectation that prose consist not only of words but also that it express the logical relationships between them. Abbott's language is evocative and suggestive, stubbornly resisting being tied to a specific meaning. In control, this experiment in voice allows true and illuminating portraits, as in this description of a golfer from the story, **"Near the Heart Place of Grue"**: "Lamar Thibodeux was a B card pro, slump-shouldered and pot-bellied, his work a study in secret momentums and human will."

At times, however, the voice is incapable of the right note, and there is a passage of frustrating opacity as in this description taken from the same passage as above. The narrator says, "In front of him toiled a foursome of men, the most anguished of whom had a Puritan swing, all kneecaps and elbows, protobad and reactionary, his follow-through as novel as war, his weak Vardon grip a violation of things beautiful."

Often enough, though, Abbott's governing voice imbues his cartoon-like characters with depth and embroiders his tales with a soulful yearning. And although the voice is not equally compelling in these ten Southwestern tales through which the same handful of characters confront or avoid or desire one another, it succeeds brilliantly in the title story, **"The Heart Never Fits Its Wanting."** The story's narrator, an air force man and ex-baseball player, is grieving over the loss of his wife, Rae Nell, a writer, who has left him for the fourth time. After recounting their bizarre relationship in terms of his longing and her cruel abandonments, the narrator concludes sorrowfully and yet with characteristic wit: "So here I am, frazzled and a shame to my uniform, knowing I'm doomed and wanting my Rae Nell and eager to get back in her stories again." (pp. 93-4)

Ellen Friedman, "High Pressure Fiction," in The Ontario Review, *No. 15, Fall-Winter, 1981-82, pp. 93-100.*

WILLIAM KOON

[The stories in *The Heart Never Fits Its Wanting*] identify Lee Abbott, who teaches at Case Western Reserve, as one of America's really promising young writers, as one of the few new writers who really has a striking voice. The comparisons are going to be with Hunter Thompson, Harry Crews, and Barry Hannah because Abbott's prose has their same wacky energy and unpredictable craziness. Take the opening of the first story in *The Heart Never Fits:*

> Friends, at thirty-four, on the edge of triple ruin, his crazed and minutely crenate brain steaming with waste, Scooter E. Watts was a bona fide numero furtivo—creepy, brilliant, a loser, weak and consumptive, his guts a quaking moil and true image of Modern Times.
>
> (p. 98)

This style is the right vehicle for Abbott's strange world and his stranger characters. Scooter is a wanderer, a man whose dreams get wiped out on a regular basis, one who plays golf at night, hugging himself when he hits a ball well, firing his machine pistol at gophers when he mis-hits. He goes back on the road again after losing the big match to a character who wears burlap on the golf course and rubs his driver against Rae Nell's chest before teeing off. Angry women in their underwear attack minor league baseball players with shotguns, on the playing field. Army privates in Viet Nam wear Bermuda shorts, golf hats, and alligator shirts into combat. The same privates try to lure the Viet Cong out of their caves by offering them Otis Redding records. The senior trip for a high school class is to a whore house in Juarez.

The remarkable thing about all this is that Abbott's characters come out of his wild and disjointed world looking strangely human. Their peculiar situations seem to emphasize their humanity. Love is their primary strength and/or weakness. And it stands out distinctly as necessity in Abbott's absurd world. Pfc. Donnie Bobo, in his Bermudas, may be trying to do away with the enemy, but he would much rather love one of their women. And Tump, who rides with Black Jack Pershing, ends up with a cozy chat with Pancho Villa—much better than fighting.

The blends, I think, are good ones—a tough world and some interesting characters trying to work their way through it on their most basic emotions, a bright young writer with something to say and a startling way of saying it. We should watch for much more from Lee Abbott. (p. 99)

William Koon, in a review of "The Heart Never Fits Its Wanting," in Studies in Short Fiction, *Vol. 19, No. 1, Winter, 1982, pp. 98-9.*

HILARY MASTERS

The people that rip and tear through the stories of Lee K. Abbott, Jr. (*The Heart Never Fits Its Wanting*) also seem compelled to suffer in domains as restricted as the minor-league ball-parks that field some of his characters. Abbott has genuine affection for his people and where violence occurs it is organic and not laid on, but strangely enough, his remarkable gift of language seems to imprison the people in these stories so they never rise above the sentimental level of the country-and-western songs that throb in the background.

Read singly, many of the stories give off a guileless power, but read in one sitting, as a collection, they begin to sound very monotonous, rather like driving through Abbott's Southwest, the car radio fixed on the same funny-sad songs about women deserting men at the K-Mart. The language, at first illuminating and delightful, begins to get tiresome, long-winded—like that of a joke meant to delay an overfamiliar punchline. . . . [Abbott's] voice intrudes on his characters' lives and limits their possibilities, keeps them at a minimum, to serve the purpose of his rhetoric. Almost all of [the stories] are told in the first person, but whether the *I* is a small-town ball player, a third-rate country-western singer or an oil-rigger, it is all the same voice: the good-ole-boy persona of Lee K. Abbott, Jr.

If the men are interchangeable, the women in these stories are fiercely individual, but with a shared characteristic. They always seem to be "leaving" (some attention might be paid to the *heavy* significance put on that soft word by our pop culture), and they pursue the men in the tales with a single-minded devotion only equalled by the female praying mantis. The sexual act smacks of cannibalism and the males surrender to it in flights of little boy dirty talk as if to mask their vulnerability to these Southwestern *succubi*. It is an amusing view, on paper anyway, and in one case a lover returns more and more crippled from each rendezvous—eventually requiring hospitalization. This is a tale told since Boccaccio, and Mr. Abbott gives it no new dimensions, simply setting it to the chords of a ten-string guitar, so the story becomes, like the collection, a kind of bluegrass camp.

However, these stories are to be recommended. The voice is young and there's every hope that the future will bring longer, more mature works in which the characters will be allowed to stand at the plate on their own without the "ostentatious and contrived" pose Abbott gives to a minor-league hitter in his current line-up. (pp. 127-28)

> Hilary Masters, "Some New Totalitarians, and Other Views," in The Ohio Review, No. 27, 1982, pp. 122-31.

KIRKUS REVIEWS

[*Love Is the Crooked Thing* contains] stories of verbal flash and pyrotechnic drive but with less satisfying results beneath the surface. . . .

Fearless and omnivorous in their stylistic reach, these stories too often seem to be conceived more of energy and dash than of durable substance. . . . Striving for a Robert Coover-esque intensity of satire, Abbott too often fails to rise above the flashing surface of his own prose, and at other times falls into an unexplored banality that poses as thoughtfulness. **"We Get Smashed and Our Endings Are Swift"** is the story of two soldiers trained as elite assassins; the horror-descriptions, though, carry the story along as an end in themselves, replacing what ought to reveal itself of the satirist's higher reach: "Oh, I did love the murder: the life-affirming 'Aaaarrrggghhh!' the dying made when they spied the vast What-Not opening to greet them." What is the alternative to such madness-violence? **"Stand in a Row and Learn,"** another army story, suggests only a dewy-eyed ignorance-as-bliss: the narrator's apotheosis takes him to "that place, free of threat and worry, where, in the company of pride and ignorance, we could live handsome and free forever."

Highly ambitious in a number of literary ways, these are stories of undeniable flash and sweep constructed on a foundation of the too-often jejune. . . . In sum: less at the core than meets the eye.

> A review of "Love Is the Crooked Thing," in Kirkus Reviews, Vol. LIV, No. 2, January 15, 1986, p. 64.

AMY HEMPEL

The implicit code behind Lee K. Abbott's fiction seems to be: if you haven't gone *too* far, you haven't gone far enough. Or as a California comic put it back in the 1970's, "There is a light within you—burn it out!"

Not that the lights in the lives of [the eleven stories contained in *Love Is the Crooked Thing*] burn so brightly to begin with. Living in the author's native Southwest—a landscape of dry arroyos, of "trees and buttes and colors from Mister Disney"—Mr. Abbott's characters include a local rocker known as Dr. Filth, a coked-out college professor, a "sissy" outlaw, and assorted "dipsticks" and would-be smoothies.

These are people who "live apart from grace"; that is how Mr. Abbott put it in his earlier collection, *The Heart Never Fits Its Wanting*. The first book showed the author to be something of a linguistic hellion in the manner of such hard-barked wordslingers as Barry Hannah and Thomas McGuane. . . .

Here, as before, Mr. Abbott's stylized hyperbolic prose and loopy humor steal the show. The "bifurcated and multifarious" lectures of the college professor who falls in love with cocaine in **"The Eldest of Things"** give way to his classroom declaration that "he had vaulted across the decades, from gamete to scholar, without benefit of the swerve and downwardness of adolescence." He looks forward to turning on one of his female students with what his drug dealer has promised will be "a mixture likened to the tears of a lost people." . . .

"The Purpose of This Creature Man" gives us the patchy career of a group of 1940's Oklahoma outlaws headed up by a desperado chiropractor named—what else?—Doc. (Reference is made to Doc's autobiography, *Hands Up!*) "I want the massive, love-loose and wicked," Doc says, interviewing prospective no-accounts for a new gang. Accepted are the narrator, a poet who is in it for "seasoning" and the Verdigris Kid, who calls out to his gang as a robbery is foiled, "Darlings, we have company." The gang does time and then regroups. The poet, now minus one ear, says, "I have fled poetry. . . . I am now an essayist. Let's ride." And they do, with admirable self-parody, into the final chapter of Doc's autobiography.

If that last quote sounds more than a little like Barry Hannah, there are plenty of other noises of that kind throughout this collection. And a Vietnam story, **"We Get Smashed and Our Endings Are Swift,"** is territory covered better 11 years ago in Mr. Hannah's story "Midnight and I'm Not Famous Yet."

Mr. Abbott's enthusiastic wordplay is a great deal of fun, as in the following alliterative riff when a soldier puts the war behind him and says goodbye to "that sound the muscles make in the more hormonal moments of menace." But there are times when his craving for the new earns him only obfuscation, times when speech proceeds on the broken leg of non sequitur.

When Mr. Abbott stows the be-bop speed rap for a little peace and quiet, he writes quietly powerful stories like **"Having the Human Thing of Joy"** and **"The Final Proof of Fate and Circumstance."** . . .

"The Final Proof of Fate and Circumstance" is a father-son love story having to do with getting to "that place, made habitable by age and self-absorption and fatigue, that says much about those heretofore pantywaist emotions like pity and fear." The father tells his son an old and terrible story (about an accident in which he killed a man) as a prelude to a *new* and terrible tale, one whose moral, the son later tells his wife, is "Everything is fragile." This reduction is and is not the whole story, but *this* story closes the book in a moving way.

It's a fact that Mr. Abbott's characters mostly sound alike— an outlaw in the '40s and a judge in the '80s, American women and Vietcong all use the same wiggy argot. But it's language coded for laughs, done up with tremendous energy. Mr. Abbott is right when he says, through his outlaw Doc, "Words redeem and give the heart something to beat for."

Amy Hempel, "Linguistic Whiz-Bangs," in The New York Times Book Review, *March 16, 1986, p. 10*

SUSAN WOOD

"Every time Garland told the story . . . he gave it a new title, his favorites being those with sweep and miracle." So begins the first story in Lee Abbott's impressive collection, *Love Is the Crooked Thing*. Indeed, Abbott himself favors titles with sweep and miracle (**"The Purpose of This Creature Man," "The Final Proof of Fate and Circumstance"**) every time he tells *the* story, the one story that all 11 of his stories tell. It could, in fact, be summed up in two of Abbott's titles: that inevitably **"We Get Smashed and Our Endings Are Swift"** makes **"Having the Human Thing of Joy"** all the more precious and imperative.

But the "discrete and illuminated landscape of wanting love and having it" is not always easy to find, and for Abbott's characters the way there is frequently hazardous, almost always touching and often funny, whether it takes them to Vietnam, Cleveland, Ohio, or Deming, New Mexico. What Abbott's characters—these ordinary Burls and Doyles and Dwights and Lamars—must learn is the ordinary lesson, extraordinary for each of us in its discovery, that, as one of them says, "Everything is fragile."

Such knowledge comes in various shapes of loss. For Pfc. Garland H. Steeples [in **"When Our Dream World Finds Us, and These Hard Times Are Gone"**], it comes in the form of a young Vietnamese woman met, and lost, in the Greyhound bus station in Deming, where she is briefly stopped over on her way to becoming a rock and roll star after "working for Jesus." . . . For Garland it is love, the kind in which his heart "just flops over," and the story of this brief encounter becomes "a thing he told maybe a thousand times in 1968," in Vietnam, a legend that survives long after Garland ships out to be repeated again and again, either "embellished or picked clean," by everybody from Edward Landsdale himself to O. T. Wil-

liams, "a Roy Acuff look-alike from Houston." Eventually, the story makes it back home to "the World," to be told for the last time by a Vietnam vet named Onan Motley in a moment of passion "which may have been the high point of an entire life" in which he feels "for an instant or two the shining presence of Garland himself."

Often, the shape of knowledge is death, or its prospect. . . . For Lamar Hoyt, in **"The Human Thing of Joy,"** the knowledge comes in a snapshot he finds among his mother's belongings after her death, a snapshot of his mother as a young, beautiful, and very naked woman, knowledge that he only really understands years later when he discovers that his wife has been unfaithful:

> I have seen it written in a story-book [my son] Buddy has that life is a train ride, with many stations and much clickety-clack—which, though it is only metaphor, may be true; but the ride is not straight because every now and then— as between one event and another—it is revealed, so the book says, that quote you are making a curve and a light is thrown back showing a mountain of meaning rising behind you on the way you've come unquote. . . .

Not all of these stories work equally well. In some of them the voice is so oracular, so extravagant that one feels bludgeoned and the voices begin to sound exactly alike. This is particularly true when Abbott moves out of his familiar world. . . .

The best of them, though, are rife with the miracle and tragedy of life. My favorites are those which feature Lamar T. Hoyt, the golf-playing Chevrolet dealer from Deming, or some variation of this small-town Everyman (sometimes called Dwight, Doyle or Tyler), and given Abbott's recent stories in *The Atlantic*, this seems to be the direction his work is taking. Here is Lamar, recently divorced and about to go out on the town for the first time:

> I stood in front of the mirror for an hour perhaps, studying myself as I have seen others look at my automobiles they can't afford. I said to myself such hopeful phrases as "You look good, Lamar, you really do," and splashed myself with a modern fragrance my son Buddy sent for Xmas. I smelled like a jungle, I thought, which was maybe right for this world.

Lee Abbott is right for this world all right, with all its sorrows and joys, and we can be glad for these stories which remind us that, like Garland Steeples' dreamgirl, we must "Take up the light and shake self's tailfeathers," stories that offer us "a moral which was complex and finicky and a thing as fundamental as shelter, a moral, you know, which resisted all words save those which trafficked in fortune and love."

Susan Wood, "The Illuminated Landscape of Love," in Book World—The Washington Post, *May 11, 1986, p. 9.*

W. C. HAMLIN

[*Love Is the Crooked Thing*] will not be received without reservation by any number of traditionalists, principally because of what appears—at least in some of the stories—to be quaint little subplots devoted primarily to the manipulation of language. . . . That is the bad news. The good news is that Abbott in his 11 tales does indeed take a look at love through a fractured lens in a hazy world; and if love sometimes comes a cropper, it does, nevertheless, keep coming, as it must. This in itself is comforting amid persistent confusion and chaos, and it is good to know that Abbott has channeled his considerable talent and energy into mining the only lode in the universe rich enough for everyone.

> *W. C. Hamlin, in a review of "Love Is the Crooked Thing," in* Choice, *Vol. 23, Nos. 11-12, July-August, 1986, p. 1671.*

THE VIRGINIA QUARTERLY REVIEW

[Abbott's stories in *Love Is the Crooked Thing*] grab a reader and take him along for a big ride and a heartfelt lesson. His characters move, act, and speak often "supported only by a wish and a marvel, and a near miss with love," and they are compelling even in their most foolish posturing. And whether he is writing about soldiers in Vietnam, lovers, rock stars or a gang of outrageously charming bank robbers, Abbott's linguistic power is impressive. His sentences seem to flower and bloom with sheer exuberance, releasing words and intentions into a rich space above logic, a space wrought by pure, romping imagination. But make no mistake. Abbott is more than a word wizard, more than a fired-up poet exploding phrase and rhyme. One would be wrong to take Mr. Abbott and his fiction as anything less than fresh and innovative.

> *A review of "Love Is the Crooked Thing," in* The Virginia Quarterly Review, *Vol. 62, No. 4, Autumn, 1986, p. 125.*

KIRKUS REVIEWS

Abbott's third book of stories [*Strangers in Paradise*] . . . shows him still working eagerly and rambunctiously for vivid effects, but mainly on the surface of things.

"The End of Grief" is an affecting story of a man haunted by his brother's death in the Bataan Death March, but in the pieces that follow, a hyped-up boyishness of tone serves often to undercut the very substance and profundities that Abbott seems to insist repeatedly are there. . . . **"X"** begins as the story of a father's terrible and comic rages, then loses force as it falls in love with its own voice and degenerates into the tropes of the tall tale before succumbing still later to a wash of father-son sentimentality. A vast and threatening world-doom is said to crouch in the wings in these stories ("we are all central, I believe, to events which are leading us . . . to the dry paradise that is the end of things," says one narrator), but Abbott's ambitious comedy tends less to recognize the threat than to diminish and simplify responses to it. **"The World Is Almost Rotten,"** about a lifelong golf rivalry, showcases the author's magical and inventive excessiveness with words and image, yet falls prey by end to a merely breezy style and a comic-book hyperbole; war in general (**"Youth on Mars"**) and Vietnam in particular (**"Category Z"**; **"Rolling Thunder"**; **"Where Is Garland Steeples Now?"**) come on stage, but one feels even there that the words are getting in the way of the subject—pushing, nudging, inflating. A blithe and post-hippie contentedness, it seems, is the true foundation for the whole here holding the fiction at the ground-level of the sentimental. . . .

Gifted in style, and with high claims for the deep probe, but best for those who really want only to close their eyes and listen to the music.

> *A review of "Strangers in Paradise," in* Kirkus Reviews, *Vol. LIV, No. 24, December 15, 1986, p. 1810.*

PUBLISHERS WEEKLY

The same characters keep turning up in the 14 stories in [*Strangers in Paradise*]. They're the men of Deming, N.M.—car salesmen, World War II veterans, teachers and bank officers. Golf at the Mimbres Valley Country Club is central to their lives, as is liquor, the relationship of fathers and sons, and an exuberant, lush style of speech. Sensitive to the humor and dark disappointments at the heart of these lives, Abbott endows their basic ordinariness with epic, often hilariously comic, qualities. . . . While [Abbott's] imagination is extravagant and his ear for the ebullient and generous speech of his characters true, they often speak in the same voice, diminishing each story's individual punch. Abbott writes in the short-story form . . . , but, for this volume, the novel genre might have been more appropriate.

> *A review of "Strangers in Paradise," in* Publishers Weekly, *Vol. 230, No. 25, December 19, 1986, p. 46.*

WILLIAM FERGUSON

[In *Strangers in Paradise*, plots] tend to overlap, a peculiarity that often becomes a virtue; it is as if several fields of force were being directed at a single invisible core of meaning, in a prose at once exuberant and inventive.

Speech comes easily to Mr. Abbott's characters, whether they are cursing under fire at Khe Sanh or speaking in tongues in the locker room of a country club. Communication, by contrast, proves supremely difficult. One of the most successful stories, **"The End of Grief,"** is about how the shocks of war can send incoherence ringing down whole decades. . . .

Strategies of discourse are always suggestive, often desperately sad, as in the bittersweet story about a disturbed soldier in Vietnam who chooses a stray dog as his confidant; under fire, "faced with the impossible choice between life and love," he finds it necessary to kill the animal to protect his hiding place. Back in America, as a peripatetic bandit, he invariably includes the "Vietnam dog story" in his holdup notes, and soon petty bureaucrats across the land—in an image that should please aspiring writers everywhere—are being forced to read imaginative prose at gunpoint.

"Living Alone in Iota" is perhaps the least successful of the 14 stories. Reese, the hapless antihero, has lost his girlfriend; in describing his buffoonish reaction, the author unfortunately retreats into writerly self-parodies (Reese's face is "a moil of desire and grue"). The humor is so unrelentingly Olympian that it begins to feel unnerving and hubristic.

Echoing at times **"The End of Grief,"** **"X"** investigates the darker side of family relationships. The narrator attempts to understand a lunatic childhood experience in which his father, unhappy over a game of golf, destroyed an entire locker room at the local country club. For the son this bizarre episode represents the unknowable X of the human soul; in a truly fearful capitulation, he concludes that he and his dad are the same: "two creatures made blind by the same light." Whatever else Mr. Abbott's X may be, it surely equals a fiction of craft and pathos.

William Ferguson, "Havoc at the 19th Hole," in The New York Times Book Review, February 8, 1987, p. 12.

MARCIA TAGER

Like the American Southwest that is their setting, [the stories in *Strangers in Paradise*] are scorched and crude and sometimes poignantly beautiful. A main character, variously named, threads through many of them. He has grown up in New Mexico and returned there to live, and his spiritual deformity perhaps reflects the deformity of our culture. . . . In some of the stories Abbott becomes both maudlin and macho and even his black humor doesn't save his prose from sounding like a country-western lyric in which everyone is betrayed by faithless love. But in the best of these stories Abbott is clear-eyed, compassionate, funny, and lyrical.

Marcia Tager, in a review of "Strangers in Paradise," in Library Journal, Vol. 112, No. 3, February 15, 1987, p. 159.

STEPHEN COREY

In **"The Eldest of Things,"** fifth of eleven stories in this distinctive collection [*Love Is the Crooked Thing*], we hear of an automobile "so sweetly tuned it seemed capable of speech—a thunder as throaty and pure . . . as oratory itself." Few readers could get this far into *Love Is the Crooked Thing* without realizing how this odd and rhythmic description also refers obliquely to the prose style of its author. Lee K. Abbott is a high-powered lover of language—its sounds and ambiguities, its syntax and silliness—and all his main characters are fellow *amateurs*.

Some of Abbott's word-merchants are registered loonies like Bobby Stoops, the former rock musician attempting a middle-aged comeback in **"The Unfinished Business of Childhood"**: "Fierce wars and faithful loves shall moralize my songs. . . . I suspect I will be vast, and a mighty turmoil to the ignorant many." Others are somewhat saner types from unusual professions, like the turn-of-the-century outlaw, Doc Leroy Toolchin, in **"The Purpose of This Creature Man."** . . . Still others are ordinary citizens inspired, whether by life or Abbott's fancy, to make active *use* of language. . . . (p. 442)

All of this wordmongering is in service of Abbott's deep ambition to make some approach, through the rich yet limited resources of speech, toward the complexities and difficulties of human thought, love, and communication. Abbott refuses to join the swelling army of contemporary fiction writers who propound this or that variety of bastardized and too-often-lame Hemingwayism. He prefers instead titles with "sweep and

miracle"; stories "that featured comedy in large doses and not a little horridness"; stories "about mystery, about the strange union of innocence and loss, which sometimes stands for wisdom." Employing a lush and often wild diction, he is unwilling to settle for Wordsworth's "real language of men in a state of vivid sensation," but seems rather to be trying to invent the languages people might speak if their vocabularies and vocal cords could match their feelings.

The *love* in the book's title manifests itself—sometimes curiously or even perversely—in every story, but it is deepest and clearest (as is Abbott's prose) in the half-dozen tales about families and lovers. In **"When Our Dream World Finds Us, and These Hard Times Are Gone,"** a legendary story is born from a young man's constant retelling of his brief encounter with a "dream girl" in a New Mexico bus depot. His endlessly reworked fantasy carries him through the Vietnam war—an undercurrent present throughout this book—and later serves to comfort others who pass it along to their own loved ones. . . . (pp. 442-43)

[Abbott's] stories are concerned with the painful adjustments we must make for any relationship to endure. In **"The Final Proof of Fate and Circumstance,"** a father reveals to his grown son a whole prior existence involving a first wife and her early death. The father makes himself vulnerable to the son, who then recognizes that every human life is "a scene of hope followed by another of misfortune and doom." And vulnerability is at the center of **"Having the Human Thing of Joy"**—arguably the finest story in the collection—where both the dead and the living are put at risk: the narrator discovers things about his deceased parents and then about his wife, intimate secrets with the potential to crush his images of all three. But with wrenching and gentle selflessness, he accepts their "common, ancient desires" and learns to love them yet again—and more than ever.

Like the poets, psychotherapists, and stand-up comics he resembles, Abbott is not equally successful with all of his lines. His machine of words sometimes runs out of control, driving his prose toward self-parody; and even his best stories should be absorbed one at a time, because some of his narrators can come to sound too much alike. At his strongest he makes us forget any samenesses, but occasionally—most noticeably in **"The Eldest of Things,"** the tale of a drugged-up and dragged-out professor—Abbott seems to be striving for special effects instead of using his brilliant, singular style to lead us to the startling insights of his finest work. (p. 443)

Stephen Corey, in a review of "Love Is the Crooked Thing," in The Georgia Review, Vol. XLI, No. 2, Summer, 1987, pp. 442-43.

George (Granville) Barker

1913-

English poet, novelist, dramatist, critic, editor, and author of children's books.

In his poetry, Barker blends assonance, alliteration, and internal rhyme to convey the physical and spiritual aspects of human life. While much of his early writing demonstrates a social awareness in the manner of such prominent poets of the 1930s as W. H. Auden, Louis MacNeice, and Stephen Spender, Barker's subsequent work is generally considered to parallel Dylan Thomas's neo-Romantic verse in his exploration of metaphysical themes and his rejection of social and political concerns. These later poems exhibit a more direct confrontation of such issues as the existence of God, the nature of religious faith, and human mortality and sexuality. Barker's ability to evolve different styles throughout his career and the moral concepts that unify his work prompted David Gascoyne to comment: "I recognize and salute in George Barker a poet whose work has never ceased to develop, who has been almost uninterruptedly prolific, whose themes have been basic and perennial, and who has remained faithful to his exceptional gift, enriching our langauge and literature."

Barker received no formal education after the age of fourteen. When he was twenty, he published his first collection of verse, *Thirty Preliminary Poems* (1933). Many of these pieces were later republished in *Poems* (1935) and evidence in their elegiac subject matter Barker's preoccupation with death. While these poems were often commended for Barker's inventive use of images, aural techniques, and language, many critics found such elements verbally extravagant at the expense of clarity, a contention leveled against much of his work. However, these verses earned the respect of T. S. Eliot, who was largely responsible for the publication of *Poems,* and William Butler Yeats, who concluded *The Oxford Book of Modern Verse* with four of Barker's pieces. Barker's most celebrated works of the 1930s are *Calamiterror* (1937) and *Elegy on Spain* (1939). The ten cantos of *Calamiterror* present images drawn from bucolic and industrial landscapes to document both the beautiful and the unpleasant characteristics of the world. The title poem of *Elegy on Spain,* which is also included in *Lament and Triumph* (1940), is admired for the nondogmatic contrast Barker provides to the Marxist poems on the Spanish Civil War written by Auden and Spender.

Barker's next collections of new poems, *Sacred and Secular Elegies* (1943), *Eros in Dogma* (1944), and *Love Poems* (1947), mark a gradual change in his verse style. Less syntactically complex, these works feature numerous Biblical allusions, greater erotic content, and references to World War II as well as a more objective point of view. The prophetic tone and Manichean qualities of these volumes, which have elicited critical comparisons to the Romantic writings of William Blake and Lord Byron, prompted Martha Fodaski to note: "In revealing the meaning of the hell and death of the modern world, Barker asserts the value of their opposites and makes poetry of the dualities. At their worst, the middle [period] poems are full of empty rhetoric; at their best, they represent the artistic reconciliation of interpenetrating opposites and a prophecy of better things to come."

Photograph by Mark Gerson

In his later verse, Barker continues to explore themes related to death and love and to document the search for faith in an increasingly complex world. *News of the World* (1950), *The True Confession of George Barker* (1950; expanded, 1964), and *A Vision of Beasts and Gods* (1954) are characterized by Barker's experimentation with different styles and evidence his reading of such poets as Charles Baudelaire, Gerard Manley Hopkins, and William Butler Yeats. In *The True Confession of George Barker,* for example, he adopts the poetic form of François Villon's "The Testament" and Baudelaire's *The Flowers of Evil,* creating a work that was labeled by many critics as sacrilegious and obscene. Similarly, the rhymed quatrains of *The Golden Chains* (1968) display a stylistic resemblance to the poems of A. E. Housman. *Poems of Places and People* (1971), *In Memory of David Archer* (1973), *Villa Stellar* (1978), and *Anno Domini* (1984) include discussions of sex and mortality. *Selected Poems* (1941), *Collected Poems, 1930-1955* (1957), *Collected Poems, 1930-1965* (1965), and *Collected Poems* (1987) provide selections from various stages of Barker's career. Barker's characteristic thematic concerns also pervade his novels *Alanna Autumnal* (1933), *Janus* (1935), and *The Dead Seagull* (1950), as well as his numerous dramatic pieces.

(See also *CLC,* Vol. 8; *Contemporary Authors,* Vols. 9-12, rev. ed.; *Contemporary Authors New Revision Series,* Vol. 7; and *Dictionary of Literary Biography,* Vol. 20.)

HUGH GORDON PORTEUS

The failure of uneducated and sophisticated prodigies to comprehend *Ulysses,* and all that Joyce implies, may continue to produce prose of the kind, but rarely of the quality to be found in *Alanna Autumnal.* This is an infuriating book: pretentious, viciously romantic and 'finished'—simply because it compels judgment by the severest possible standards. The author tells us more than once he is 'a poet' (he is), and that he 'lacks guts' (he does). But Mr. Barker seems to me to have, not only almost all the faults that yield to treatment, but also almost all the qualities that really matter, and that an academic training might easily unfit one to recognize. Mr. Barker's vision is innocent enough: also uncommonly sensitive and strong: also bogged by precocities and preciosities. His malady is an ingrowing soul; his virtue, that he has diagnosed it. His prescription is—Excess: he will rage himself out. [*Alanna Autumnal* and *Thirty Preliminary Poems*], more particularly the *Poems,* record the shedding of his worst verbal excesses. . . . Mr. Barker's work, even at its most verbose, is curiously compact. It has what Eliot has often described as 'intensity'; it has something else that might be described as 'substance,' and which I should define as a physical (almost tactile, as opposed to cerebral) apprehension of the word. There is nothing one could tell Mr. Barker, about his work, that he does not know painfully well. It may be hoped that when he has finished sweating out his latinisms he will 'donate' (a favourite word) some of his attention to his worst vice—exploitation of his own pathos. He deserves watching by those who are least likely to be aware of him:—*e.g.* those who press, as well as those who would suppress, the work of Mr. Bottrall. Mr. Barker's fame has been broadcast, and I know of no writer of his age who deserves so much to be saved from the demoralization of early winnings. Both of these books may be called—without offence—bad books. (pp. 83-4)

> *Hugh Gordon Porteus, in a review of "Alanna Autumnal" and "Thirty Preliminary Poems," in* Scrutiny, *Vol. III, No. 1, June, 1934, pp. 83-4.*

EDWIN MUIR

Those who have read Mr. Barker's first small collection of poems must be struck by the great advance he has made in [*Poems*]. It is an advance most obviously in the power of expression. In his first poems Mr. Barker often used words as if they meant something to him which they did not mean in general use; that was a sign of original perception; but very often he did not succeed in conveying to the reader the particular sense of these words as he clearly felt it. He does so in this volume to an incomparably greater degree, though his gift for the original use of language and imagery still considerably exceeds his technique for dealing with it. But it is excess not lack that makes some of the poetry in this volume as imperfect as it is. There are three or four perfect poems, the most formally beautiful being the fine sonnet beginning **"This destination not to be found in a star,'** and **"I am that face about which fire fell,"** with its succession of lovely images. . . . All the images in this poem evoke a sense of disembodied space and colour, and the movement of the verse has a corresponding lightness, as if the air through which it passes were quite without weight or density.

This power to use words so that they create new objects of the imagination is one of the rarest qualities of poetry; Mr. Barker does not show it so perfectly in any of the other poems as in

["**I am that face about which fire fell**"]; but there are flashes of it or whole spells of it in all but five or six. They are to be found particularly in the longer poems, all of them concerned with death: **"The Amazons," "Luctus in Morte Infantis," "Dædalus"** and **"Elegy anticipating Death,"** the last a very beautiful but uneven poem. There is too much dross in this poetry still, but at its highest level it is quite pure and new-minted, and at no level at all could it be called minor poetry.

> *Edwin Muir, "The Poetry of George Barker," in* The London Mercury, *Vol. XXXII, No. 188, June, 1935, p. 187.*

RAYNER HEPPENSTALL

Mr. Barker is already a poet. His reserves of power—awaiting more definite direction—seem to be very great. And there is more call, [in *Poems*], to list his tics and probe his mendable infirmities than to stretch out praise.

Note first, then, that the air is always full, for Mr. Barker, of beating wings; or else of dim faces. In poem after poem, a spectral Other Self appears: as Wraith-Friend, as Chimera, or as an unnamed spectre. In many poems, some cosmic upheaval is envisaged, as the falling of the stars; in several, the poet's own death, with pleased engrossment in the physiological processes involved. Gold is the colour which dominates Mr. Barker's scenic designs. His one definite Persona is Daedalus. . . . And the moral endeavour is imaged as not stooping over stones, but beating down, with hands, impeding walls, beyond which The Light is.

Mr. Barker's vision, in fact, is a private vision: focused by adolescent concerns which are also eccentric, expressed in symbols which seem to ask for psychologer's rather than critic's comment, and casting up, altogether, a modern reflection of The Light That Never Was. At the same time, Mr. Barker has self-awareness enough (which is opposite to self-engrossment) to make **"Narcissus"** the title of three of his poems. His directly erotic verse is whole and handsome. . . . And eccentricities in Mr. Barker's process have apparently affected the imagery, movement and dramatic tension of his poems; but not so far as to make them inaccessible, as experience, to a reader. When Mr. Barker's poems are inaccessible (which is to say, obscure), the fault is not with his vision, which he has unquestionably striven to communicate, but with his poetical apparatus: as it would be in the case of a poet—Communist or Catholic, perhaps—of declared public vision.

Mr. Barker's language, for instance, is goaded into redundancies and tautologies: sometimes by pure failure to see the language historically, but more often by the straining and piling up of words because they are felt to be not sufficiently expressive (which really means that the notion they were required to express is not sufficiently matured and precise). . . . Though it has to be said that Mr. Barker seldom uses clichés, even the new range of (New Country) poetical clichés: that, indeed, his use of language, while limited and often unsure (and while—with 'I am that land. . .'—he has got a whole poem from Mr. Spender, at Mr. Spender's worst), is his own, as his concernment and his imagery are.

And so is his ear. It is worth remark, in the first place, that Mr. Barker has an ear: it is an organ whose functions have fallen into general poetical disuse, replaced by many kinds of visual appeal. And Mr. Barker's speech is lyrical: that is to say, not necessarily excluding Narrative, Drama (which covers

Satire) and Description, but brief, most often, and concerned with single situations, uncharacterized, issuing rather from the stomach than the head, scored for the larynx rather than the eye. It invites the application, therefore, of a Cantabile criterion; and, judged so, Mr. Barker is a pleasant and efficient lyrist (given the drag of the linguistic situation in which he writes); but an uneasy one. . . . And to be able to write so, in the case of a poet whose ear is at all sensitive, normally, as Mr. Barker's plainly is, implies a strange unease about words, not inefficiency or carelessness: a nervous affection of the throat muscles, a kind of Verbal Sadism, or the same twitching of the faculties, perhaps, as produces one kind of tautologies. (pp. 677-80)

Rayner Heppenstall, in a review of "Poems," in The Criterion, *Vol. XIV, No. LVII, July, 1935, pp. 677-80.*

MICHAEL ROBERTS

The ten cantos of [*Calamiterror*] present a mood and vision, not a story or an argument. The poet looks at the ugliness and guilt in the outer world until the vision becomes a general horror; in the song of birds he hears the cry of pain; he sees privation and suffering in root and flower; and he feels the ugliness and guilt within himself. Within the poem there are repetitions, variations, and developments, but the mood persists through a kaleidoscopic change of images, and the unity of the poem comes from this persistence, not from an imaginative relation of the separate cantos. Images of birds and trees, crystal and water, factories and wounds, follow one another in lyrical profusion; and sometimes the combinations of images are striking and beautiful apart from any consideration of their meaning in the outer world. The melodious but almost meaningless latinisms which Mr. Barker once used have almost disappeared; he now insists on sensuous value as well as music in his words, and he has added to his vocabulary words and phrases that are reminiscent of Stephen Spender, Dylan Thomas, and Frederic Prokosch.

The vision is that of the man who sees the world and stands aside; the mood is one of grief for the ugliness and beauty of the world that is seen and understood; it is not the bitterness and love of the man whose heart aches for his own people and rejoices with them. The people seen in these cantos appear as figures seen or imagined, not as human characters. . . . In these cantos the world is an image of the self, and people are at most simulacra of the self; but continually there is a sense of something lacking, a longing for the reality behind the image that is seen. . . . [*Calamiterror*] is the poetry of the Romantic who is haunted by realities that he can neither disregard nor welcome: "I see England with the underground mines run bleeding along her like wounds." The attitude is the product of a keen eye and a thoughtful mind, but it is wholly contemplative and inactive. "Sin is not to act," says Mr. Barker, protesting against this implicit weakness; and when he speaks of "The contributing and constituting things" of the cosmos, "which contemplated too close make a chaos," he is describing a fundamental limitation of all thought and observation, and this limitation is sometimes exemplified in *Calamiterror*. (pp. 198-99)

Michael Roberts, "Mr. George Barker," in The London Mercury, *Vol. XXXVI, No. 212, June, 1937, pp. 198-99.*

AUDREY BEECHAM

Lament and Triumph represents George Barker's seventh published work; his fifth book of poems. Both in technique and in the maturing of his thought and emotional reactions, the development has been extraordinarily rapid. And for this reason the progress he has made, since the first book of poems appeared in 1933, is worthy of a detailed consideration. Mr. Barker has always been an interesting poet; but his earlier work was often difficult to read and sometimes even distasteful. Words seemed to be forced into their context, images rammed together with an incongruity which may have been intentional, but which produced only a jarring irritation in the reader. . . .

With the early poems, the reader was often bogged by a perplexing syntax which, although it aimed at conciseness or a deliberate ambiguity, would slow up the reading of a poem or bring it to a complete standstill. (p. 273)

But these were hopeful vices. For they showed that Mr. Barker was determined to forge a technique of his own, and would not be content to lapse into one of the accepted forms of his contemporaries, which to the modern poet is a danger greater than that of lapsing into the traditional form of a predecessor. Mr. Barker has now adopted a syntax and system of punctuation which is more conventional, but still unmistakably his own. Its chief virtue lies in its unobtrusiveness: that is to say, it is flexible to the requirements of his poetry, without being unintelligible. By grinding down sentences in the past, he has learnt how to combine the greatest possible economy with the maximum of effect; and from a previous, perhaps exaggerated, concentration on sound values he has learnt to master the subtleties of assonance and half-rhyme. This last achievement is one of the most important technical aspects of his work. For the tendency, among modern poets during the last few years, has been to disregard the sound of words and to concentrate solely on the images and thoughts these recreate.

There is still, however, room for improvement. Sometimes, even in Mr. Barker's best poems, we come across an inexplicable lapse; and the jarring awkwardness of one phrase may ruin, with its effect of bathos, a whole stanza. Nor is the punctuation always successful. (p. 274)

One striking change to be noted in *Lament and Triumph,* is the disappearance of the death theme which dominated all this poet's earlier work, particularly the prose works: *Alanna Autumnal* (1933) and *Janus* (1935). Occasionally it crops up again in his premonitions of destruction; and in the poem, "**O Who will Speak from a Womb or a Cloud?**" there is expressed a yearning for the knowledge and experience death will bring. But apart from rare instances, the obsession would appear to have exorcised itself from his work; or to have gone, at least, into temporary abeyance. (p. 275)

[In *Lament and Triumph*] there is far greater sureness of touch; and *Vision of England '38,* one of the best long poems which Mr. Barker has yet written, concludes with optimism and strength. . . . (p. 276)

Whether the world to-day gives reason for increased optimism is not the point. Mr. Barker has never identified himself with political action, and would not therefore be likely to suffer a setback on account of a temporary defeat of progressive forces all over the world. He watches, with the mind of an artist, events which to a politician may have a very different significance. And because he is content to remain first and foremost a poet, rather than a politician, his "**Elegy on Spain**" is one of the most successful poems dealing with a political subject which have appeared during the last decade. (p. 277)

In **"Vision of England '38,"** he sees nature sharing with man the price which must be paid for destructive impulses. Thus the giant cruisers in Weymouth Bay

> . . . .floated in blood and blossoms,
> The blood of the bathers, the blossoms of the boughs
> That made the boats: under the dreadnought bosoms
> Crushed and bruised under the huge boughs.

This is more than pathetic fallacy; it is a sort of unstated pantheism which revolts against the normal and scientific methods of classification, and sees a fundamental unity between the apparently divergent parts. Humanity, animals, plants, and even ghosts are made to share a common experience. (p. 280)

Reference must be made to one quite exceptional quality in Mr. Barker's work. There are moments when he can achieve a moving simplicity, which has much in common with some of his French contemporaries such as Jules Supervielle and Pierre Jean Jouve, and which gives his poetry values quite distinct from those enumerated above. . . .

In conclusion it may be said that this book represents an astonishing achievement in progress; and that it may well mark a milestone, not only in Mr. Barker's own work, but in the whole movement of modern poetry itself. (p. 281)

> *Audrey Beecham, "George Barker," in* Life and Letters To-Day, *London, Vol. 25, No. 34, June, 1940, pp. 273-83.*

THE DURHAM UNIVERSITY JOURNAL

Those who think poetry should be not only a criticism of life but an exploration of the contemporary scene and a mirror of its problems (and this myopic view is prevalent) will turn with interest to [*Lament and Triumph* by George Barker and *Another Time* by W. H. Auden]. Whether they will find comfort and sustenance in them is doubtful. Whether their contents will be anything but curiosities five years hence is more doubtful still.

Mr. Barker has the better chance of being a poet. Certain pieces in [*Lament and Triumph*], but more particularly scattered lines and images, show that he has an authentic gift. There is excitement in reading him. But at present he has far too great a facility in spinning his own entrails into a private pattern.

> Here as I stand in the garbage of a world,
> The broken pillars and arches on my shoulder,
> Chaos of spiritual collapse tossed and whirled
> Like rags and leaves around me, I shudder.

One has so often read about these prose waste-lands before. Even if the grandiose romantic attitude be granted (and Mr. Barker is persistently romantic—no bad thing—grandiose and turgid) there is no excuse for such slipshod writing. Occasional lines show the sober influence of Langland (Found only the sorrow that I had missed my marvel), but the main influence is, unfortunately, that of Blake at his more confusing, and the most ambitious poem, **"Vision of England, '38,"** is, part of Section III excepted, very bad Blake indeed. There is an **"Elegy on Spain"** (why is it always Spain?), a rigmarole of extreme dissipation in five and a half pages, which might have said clearly that the blood of victims is the seed of liberty. When the gods give Mr. Barker economy of word, a self-critical eye,

a sense of humour, and the courage to cut out all images he cannot make significant, he will write a good book. (pp. 72-3)

> *A review of "Lament and Triumph," in* The Durham University Journal, *Vol. XXXIII, No. 1, December, 1940, pp. 72-3.*

FRANCIS SCARFE

[*The essay excerpted below was written in December, 1940.*]

When art critics were first confronted with the sensual paintings of Van Gogh, they could do little but complain of his drawing and perspective. Van Gogh is all sensation, and one has to accept his *'pure painting'* and refrain from asking for the accuracy of an Old Master. After such acceptance, one might even realize that some profound attitude to life is expressed in that lavish brushwork.

With regard to painting, the public has learnt that lesson, but it has not yet realized that a poetry can also be written which is predominantly sensational, the emotions existing raw and natural, almost in a pure state. That is why George Barker, for instance, though he has produced several books and been applauded in a narrow circle, does not seem to have penetrated to the general public. It must be admitted, however, that though his work has the freshness, the spontaneity and purity of a Van Gogh, he is also what the painter was not, an intellectual. And it is only when reason too strictly controls his emotional vision that his poems fail. He is, perhaps, a self-conscious Van Gogh.

At first reading, Barker annoys, for, like most poets of any worth, his faults are as glaring as his qualities. In the early poems there were innumerable miltonic latinisms and barbarisms, while he was so unsophisticated as to use such quaint words as 'hark' to set one's teeth on edge. At moments one was tempted to call him a pedant, though in reality he was incredibly naïve.

There is little need to dwell on Barker's earliest poems, especially since the best of the **Thirty Preliminary Poems** (1933) were later reprinted in the **Poems** of 1935. (pp. 118-19)

Feeling and sensation are distorted by abstractions and crude phrasing in these poems, which, though they contain the basic imagery and themes of Barker, serve largely as an outcry against adolescence and a breaking of inhibitions which are occasionally distressing to observe. The most important thing about this book is the fact that, at that date, a young poet could be so self-contained as to ignore the stifling but necessary influences of the Eliot and Auden generations. (p. 119)

[By 1934, Barker had] reached a phase when he was playing heavily with language, writing lines like 'Could vagrant self detect correct direction' and passages like

> A creation insulate
> From the corrosive breath
> Of death; prohibiting the
>
> Collision of internecine states
> As two elements conflagrate
> End in ashes, we emulate.

Pedantic, but also evidence of a certain word-curiosity which was to bear fruit. These are about the worst lines in his **Poems** (1935). In most of these poems he was laying on words as Van Gogh laid on paint, in thick explosive masses. Any word would serve his purpose, down to miltonisms such as 'rondure' and 'preparant', and he would re-echo such gloomy puns as 'and him I mourn from morn to morning'. Such things as these allowed the sadism of the critics full scope. Only most of them forgot to say why the poems were worth reading. Not, I think, for the elegant exercise, **"The Amazons"**; nor for **"Daedalus"**, though it has some attractive passages; nor **"Luctus in Morte Infantis"**; nor **"Wraith Friend"**, **"Venerable All Hills"** or **"Fistral Bay"**. But because of the mature concluding lines of **"The Amazons"**, the moving last eight lines of **"Luctus"**, the last ten lines which redeem the whole of **"Wraith Friend"**. These poems, peacocks whose beauty is all in their tail, reveal Barker's strength and weakness: a certain slowness of concentration, a lack of self-confidence perhaps, in the first stages of a poem, with a gathering strength and full flowering towards the end.

The bulk of the 1935 poems are of high quality, especially the **"Narcissus"** poems and a dozen others which are concerned with the main problem obsessing Barker: the nature of identity, that is, the same problem as obsessed Valéry in "La Jeune Parque" and "Le Cimetière Marin". (pp. 120-21)

The paradox of many of Barker's poems is that, though individual lines are often lax, the general effect is strong and he has a great power of concentration on subject. **"I too will end"** is a good instance of this: although the images of flowers, electricity and architecture seem incompatible, they are reconciled by the sweeping treatment. As a final instance, **"Lax though the longing may wear"** shows a good sense of formal pattern, an intricate network of imagery borne on a sound sustaining rhythm.... Here two or three simple themes are inextricably woven together, as similar themes in Mallarmé, not through any mysterious 'alchemy', as the Symbolists would say, but by a spontaneous development. Such a poem, oblique though it is, conveying an instantaneous complexity of feelings, should need no explanation, since, though it is compact, it is not difficult. It illustrates another quality of Barker's best work, a passionate gentleness of image and rhythm, relieved at times by the darker side of a nature which over-insists, as in 'circumscribes shows exhibits'. It is to Barker's credit that in 1935 as in 1933 his qualities, like his faults, were very much his own. (pp. 123-24)

Calamiterror at once roused the admiration of the critics, in spite of certain obvious defects. There is a great deal of repetition, especially in the first half of the book, where a long series of questions are followed by sequences of answers, all asking and answering almost the same things. The imagery itself is limited and repetitive, while the stanza soon becomes monotonous until the line fills out towards the end of the poem. These defects are inherent in the method, which pertains less to poetry than to music and painting. It is what one might call a symphonic poem, the theme being constantly restated and elements of it developed and embroidered until the poem becomes an intricate network of tied imagery. Or at times one has the impression of the poet exploiting every implication of his imagery, as a painter making a picture out of a variation on one colour. Most of the book is well out of the main current of English poetry in the 'thirties, being in method closer to the technique of the Symbolists or to certain aspects of Eliot.

It would be impossible to summarize the 'argument' of such a poem, for its power is not in the argument but in its rich interplay of feeling and image. It can be read as a sort of imaginative autobiography, a struggle from darkness to the light, a development from self-interested pessimism and suicide-impulse to the equation of himself with (as in one of his later poems) 'the mass of man'. At some points one is torn

between comparing Barker with Blake or with Dylan Thomas.... The comparison with Thomas would be false, because, though they are equally 'sensational' poets, Barker is more selective and his vocabulary and texture are more refined. Sometimes, however, he resembles Thomas closely, in such lines as

> My winter woman of margarine and tears,

or:

> I tear my guts out on the platform
> Or rummage in my stomach with bloody hands.

The first few parts of the poem deal largely with the birth-death theme, but in Book V it emerges from principles to facts ('By the Babylonian stream I meant Ealing'); then, after some strange visions of Milton and Blake, after which the poet suddenly becomes apocalyptic and beholds the chaos of the modern world, the subject develops into an intense personal struggle. Book VI, the crisis, contains the best verse description of the 'between two wars' period that has been written, showing the individual caught in a loop of circumstance, and explaining, three years before the invasion of Poland, why poets can no longer exist in Europe. The book then works towards an immense deliverance, a delivery, as it were, from the womb of self into a universal sympathy, in a rising feeling and rhythm for which Barker's peculiar experiments as a poet had already prepared him.... (pp. 125-27)

Calamiterror, with all its faults, is perhaps the most successful long poem of the 'thirties. Its complicated technique and development show that the direct manner favoured then by poets was not necessarily the most modern or the best. At the same time, Barker's development in the poem, from depth to breadth, from personal to public feeling, from overlaid imagery to a startling clarity of language, assured him some future as a poet and a high place among the poets of his own generation. The 'thirties produced a large body of political poetry, much of it infused with a broad imaginative vision and a grasp of human problems. Of all the poems bearing on the Spanish war, Barker's poem will stand with the highest, next to Auden's "Spain" and not below it. (pp. 127-28)

> *Francis Scarfe, "George Barker: A Pure Poet," in his Auden and After: The Liberation of Poetry, 1930-1941, George Routledge & Sons Ltd., 1942, pp. 118-30.*

HARVEY BREIT

When Blake writes

> Who will exchange the new born babe
> For the dog at the wint'ry door?

no answer is necessary. It is only necessary to understand that an answer is implicit. For in asking such a question the poet has come to a conclusion, has arrived at a way of perceiving, of a way of living even—and there will be no respite, just as there couldn't be in a head like Dostoievsky's when he found the question: would you murder an innocent child if that could save the world? Then the world becomes a great drama and living is a condition of continuous tension. The view is moral, is of a moral order where all things are interrelated, interdependent, interpenetrated; it is a vision which oversees all things and oversees nothing. The poetry would be related to the metaphysical poetry which attempted to bring under a single sway all those divergent and oppositional things, and it is entirely possible that good poetry cannot be written without that kind of perceptiveness, whether religious or scientific, whether sensuous or intellectual.

Such a morality and such a sense of tension is in Barker's [*Selected Poems*] and this, together with extraordinary poetic gifts, gives his verse a significance rarely encountered, and to such an extent that it is tantamount to raising our hopes for poetry. Nevertheless there is a good deal of imperfection in Barker and to locate it is, at the same time, to point out the source of its brilliancy, its weight, its excitement. For it will come as no surprise that the poet descends from Hopkins—and that is quite right, as selection and as necessity. In an attempt to apprehend the noble in the small, the future in the past, the mobile in the fixed, and to apprehend it with immediacy and livingness, it is right for the poet to employ those explosions of sounds and images. Yet he is very different from Hopkins, and he is different from Dylan Thomas as well. The heavy-weighted surfaces and magnetic depths, the syntactic weights, in Hopkins and in Thomas, are not so exactly fused in Barker. . . . But Barker is essentially intelligent and intelligible: his work permits proportion as a part of criteria; when he writes

> Rotten in the home of the bone with a worm:
> But though no more than a spot of rot. . . .

he is subjected to criticism that Hopkins and Thomas cannot be subjected to without a certain secondariness.

Again, there are poems in which the poet brings to an idea a fusillade of sound and image over and over, from different fronts as it were, and creates a repetitious dullness. The true relevance of Barker, however, is not in an overwrought line or in successful or unsuccessful poems: it is that every single poem contains a suspension, an intensity and drama, a discovery, a vitality; it is as though every single poem were a new kind of bomber that ranged for thousands of miles and was able to drop tons of explosives all along the route. In one way, it is as exciting as that.

And, too, Barker seems aware of his influences; consequently, he has gotten rid of, in the last poems, the excessiveness, the over-zealousness, that diminished rather than affirmed the natural tension in the work. And a new dignity occurs; in the intense quiet of these later poems one gets to feel more the vision of tragedy, or the steady perception of life as tragic which the earlier, more turgid, poems blurred over. (pp. 159-61)

There are dangers. In so fine and full a talent there is the danger of easy improvisation, of taking a theme and letting your talents go to work on it. In his *First American Ode* Barker indulges himself by calling off the inevitable symbols: Poe and gin, Herman Melville (which ought to have been resisted), Monroe Doctrine, Jefferson, Hearst, athlete, financier, Lincoln, Packard Sedan, Santa Anita, Sandburg, Rockefeller, Roosevelt, and alas, Walt. One wished he hadn't accepted the gambit. There are other mistakes. But they are peripheral: the strong and poignant drama in the poet, his view of the world of objects and ideas as alive and tense, his natural resourcefulness, his full talent inside the materials of poetry, swallow up the errors (they are hardly shortcomings) so that the total effect is unified, complete, exhilarating and enlivening. The kind of moral "activity" in Barker commits him to variety; the methods employed, the language used, holds it all in, frames it, draws the diverse together.

> Who will exchange the new born babe
> For the dog at the wint'ry door?

Barker might have invented this. At any rate, he has grasped the tragic inside it and has made a poetry of tragedy out of it. (pp. 161-62)

> *Harvey Breit, "View of the World," in* Poetry, *Vol. LIX, No. 3, December, 1941, pp. 159-62.*

CLEMENT GREENBERG

What prejudices one—perhaps too much—in favor of George Barker's [*Selected Poems*] is its evocations of the past of English poetry. It is not a question of imitation and influence in any conventional way. Barker owns this past congenitally, has it in his bones as well as his lamp, and proves it by putting the historical conventions and manners of English poetry successfully into the thick of the most recent contexts. Among the traditions he taps is first of all that pre-Elizabethan, populist, underground, almost folkish tradition, most of whose poets were plebeians, which runs from late Anglo-Saxon verse through ballads, morality plays, Piers Plowman, through comparatively little of Chaucer but more of Lydgate, through Skelton and many anonymous poets to Blake and Ebenezer Jones. Even the particular way in which Barker lacks humor agrees with this tradition. Like Langland and Blake, he invents visions, stages allegories, sees wildly, and denounces apocalyptically. He draws also on early Elizabethan dramatic verse with its closed, ringing, metallic line, and on the kind of declamatory verse found in eighteenth-century poetry such as Young's. Barker writes genuine pseudo-Pindaric odes and is an *enthusiastick* poet, stagey and full of violence and rant. His verse is loose-jointed, gallops like the old fourteener, and his eyeball is always rolling. As a modern poet he can be located halfway between Auden and Dylan Thomas, without being tributary to either. He is fond of the same poetic past as Auden, capitalizes on similar conventions and devices, allegorizes abstractions in the same somewhat Rilkean way, versifies loosely, and is moved to write by the state of the world. But the actual complexion of his verse resembles more that of Thomas's: passionate, irrational, full of quasi-surrealist images, the lines heavy with stresses, alliterations, internal rhymes, and long vowels. It is not, however, so closely textured, and its syntax and sense are more obvious. Barker is more extroverted, more conscious of himself in relation to the external.

A fault Barker shares perhaps with Thomas and a good many other of the new English poets is an inability to modulate, to distribute the emphasis so that a poem will move dramatically and take on shape. In Barker's case there is an impression of an unwearying stridency, unrelieved and unshaded. He is capable of other states of feeling than the impassioned, he can be pathetic and elegiac; read closely, his work has sufficient variety from one poem to the other—in quality, alas, as well as tone. But it is within the single poem that he has a tendency to be monotonous; once having set his pitch he has difficulty in changing it. This makes Barker hard to read, and it also prevents him from delivering himself as honestly as he might like to. Having begun a poem on the level of the sublime, to descend is perilous; hence the posturing, the padding and the bombast. The themes Barker is attracted to are an added liability. He has as little intellectual energy as [Marianne Moore]—his greater resonance is owed to the tradition that backs him up and guides his voice—but his poetry's main argument, namely, the plight of the times, will not allow him to avoid that limitation so well. More than violence of feeling is needed to make poetry here. The fustian is to cover up intellectual impotence: "Spain and Abyssinia lift bloodshot eyes as I go by"; "I sip at suicide in bedrooms or dare pessimistic stars''; ''Stood did my bull in the pool of his passion.'' Nor is Barker above Audenesque patter: the whale hides its head from war ''Among the myths and the ideas/Of Atlantis''; there is a ''sexual sky.'' His public poems can be much, much better than this, but generally his poetry is more substantially satisfactory when the self-dramatization takes place on a smaller stage, where the emotions rise from a more personal argument. An authenticity is missing from the odes and elegies which recommends Barker's earlier poems, strained as they are. Fortunately, it returns in the last poems of the book, the Supplementary Personal Sonnets—in my opinion the most perfect things Barker has yet done.

However, one could wish that instead of modifying his ambition Barker would try the more difficult task of developing his powers to equal it. I am tired of small poetry. Poetry is an art equipped to treat everything and to transform everything to itself. . . . Barker's pretensions—and the fact that he does not fall short of them too ridiculously—are at least a reminder of what poetry once could do, of what vast thirsts it once could satisfy. (pp. 617-18)

Clement Greenberg, ''Two Poets,'' in The Nation, *New York, Vol. 153, No. 24, December 13, 1941, pp. 616-18.*

DAVID DAICHES

Mr. Barker's poems [in *Sacred and Secular Elegies*] are very necessary: the note of compulsion is loud in them; they have a fierce and breath-taking originality which compels attention even before it arouses understanding. For the immediate and adequate expression of Mr. Barker's visions and insights mere language seems sometimes insufficient; sometimes we have the feeling that some further medium is necessary to pull the poem together, to integrate the parts and throw each into its proper perspective. Not that the poems lack architectonics: they are constructed with a kind of brilliant abandon, but with no trace whatever of slovenliness. There is an ardor, a spontaneity, a passion (to use an unfashionable word) in these elegies that refreshes the parched reader of modern poetry like rain: the images and ideas are seized hold of with zeal and slapped and thrown into the context they create, so that whole stanzas glow with bright meaning even if the meaning itself occasionally escapes when we proceed to come to grips with the poem. The meaning, however, rarely finally escapes: it remains to lurk beneath the images, never so completely visible as to take away the sense of mystery from the poem, never so invisible as to make the poem merely obscure or irritating—

> Images under them pinned in a cage of shadows
> Struggling to catch the eye.

There is a suggestion of Dylan Thomas in these poems, but the eloquence is essentially original. (pp. 37-8)

It is not always successful: the dedicatory sonnet reads like notes for a poem rather than the completed product, and in other poems whole stanzas sometimes fail to contribute the potential of their imagery to the cumulative effect of the whole. The fault here seems to be a too impatient striding from image to image, or a sudden, unprepared for, change of mood that leaves the poem suddenly stalled, as it were. But at his best Barker's elegies (his most successful poetry so far) have a life and power all too rare in modern poetry. The sacred elegies are better than the secular, and also read better as a related

sequence. The final climax is a worthy conclusion to this unusual volume. These poems have demonstrable faults of organization and a certain unnecessary breathlessness in the sequence of imagery: but they are exciting, and they are poetry, and the critic comes to the last line of the book with his pulse beating faster. (pp. 38-9)

David Daiches, ''The Craftsman and the Poet,'' in Poetry, *Vol. LXIV, No. 1, April, 1944, pp. 35-9.*

LOUIS L. MARTZ

George Barker's new book resembles Auden's [*The Age of Anxiety*] in its style, and also in the strong religious feeling that runs through these *Love Poems,* culminating in the explicitly religious poetry of **''The Five Faces of Pity''** and **''Turn, Turn your Face Away.''** The volume shows that Barker's style has undergone a considerable change since the *Selected Poems* in 1941 introduced his work to America. That volume was wild with clustered images and rank with experiments in metrics and tone color. Barker had not yet, at the age of twenty-eight, developed the control and economy essential to a satisfying achievement. His second American book, *Sacred and Secular Elegies* (1943), showed a notable development in discipline and contained a number of rich poems under firm control. The latest volume goes much further in this direction. In most of these new poems he has given up the long, undulating, loping line, based on five accents, which dominated his volumes of 1940, 1941, and 1943; and he has turned instead to the problem of playing variations on many traditional stanza forms, among them the simple ballad stanza. Readers who remember lines like these from the 1941 volume,

> Who was a sleeping Venus is a demon who
> Clutches my vision down from evergreen heaven
> Strips O the seven marvellous veils from even
> You and reveals the agnostic genetic machine,

will be agreeably surprised to find lines like these in the new poems:

> And in your hand, with tears for water,
>   Proving what I cannot prove,
> The myrtle springs up out of the stigmata
>   As martyrs spring from Love.

As these lines suggest, Barker has not given up his arresting imagery, nor has he lost his interest in all manner of sound effects; but the stanza shows remarkable economy and precision. The impact of the more successful poems here resides in the cumulative effect of a muted, conversational ground-tone, flecked with many dislocations of syntax, and sprinkled with strong images. These materials are molded into flexible stanzas and held together, though often slightly askew, by skilful half-rhymes, assonances, inner rhymes. I do not mean to imply that the whole volume is successful; far from it. There are places where the wry style tears the poems apart, where simplicity gives way to unguarded sentimentality, and where strong images stand out too boldly from a spare context. Barker remains one of the most uneven poets who ever wrote, but his occasional successes keep him near the front of the newer poets. (pp. 335-36)

Louis L. Martz, ''Recent Poetry,'' in The Yale Review, *Vol. XXXVII, No. 2, Winter, 1948, pp. 333-36.*

F. C. GOLFFING

There seems to be considerable disagreement among critics regarding the virtues of George Barker's poetry. The majority, without bothering to qualify their verdict, treat him as a minor adjunct to the Auden-Spender-Day Lewis triumvirate; others as an interesting freak who altogether defies placement; others yet—I daresay a tiny minority—see in him a poet of superb and very personal gifts but of startling unevenness of execution. There is no denying that Barker is harder to place than either Auden or Dylan Thomas, for a number of reasons. His poetic antecedents are not only more various but also more obscure; the tenor of his verse is strangely and unfashionably affirmative (the affirmations being forthright, anagogic and prophetic rather than paradoxical in the manner of Kierkegaard); and his writing abounds in dazzling and unclassifiable conceits that make Gongora or Crashaw look prim by comparison. Though, as Clement Greenberg has remarked, Barker ''owns the past of English poetry congenitally'' [see excerpt above], he does not quite belong in the mainstream; though clearly not a sectarian in matters of technique—of the order of, say, W. C. Williams or Marianne Moore—he is nevertheless sufficiently heterodox to pass for a heretic.

Barker's main heresies are his frequent abuse of hyperbole and pathetic fallacy, and there are several minor ones besides. He has been severely trounced on many of these scores, even by critics who are ordinarily charitable and mild-mannered. Rolfe Humphries speaks of Barker's language as ''pretentious, emulous, nervous, excited, compulsive—*vain.* Where does it get you?'' Yes, where does it get you? The answer is, Certainly not to quiet excellence; possibly nowhere; possibly to grandeur. Eliot's well-known remark about Hardy: ''At times his style touches sublimity without ever having passed through the stage of being good'' seems to apply even more accurately to Barker. True, it resolves nothing; it simply states a paradox; besides, Eliot intended it to be a stricture. But is occasional sublimity really so contemptible a thing? I am inclined to think that it is a triumph within the reach of very few writers and that it should be acknowledged no matter by what questionable leaps or short-cuts the poet has managed to attain it. (pp. 34-6)

George Barker belongs clearly in the same category as Ronsard and Victor Hugo—I can imagine much worse company—because of his fundamental dependence on eloquence. His virtues are those of the rhetorician or, to avoid certain pejorative connotations attaching to that term, those of the enthusiastic devotee of language *qua* language. The intellectual substratum of his verse is either thin or confused; the sentiment often exquisite but never sharply focused. His individual tropes and symbols do not bear close examination; they would be ludicrous were it not for the magnificent rhetoric that carries them along and, finally, welds them together. But the fact remains that again and again Barker manages to weld his linguistic oddities or incongruities into complete wholes and that in each successful instance the result is not only a *rapture* but sheer verbal magic. . . . (pp. 36-7)

George Barker has been a victim of one of the current fashions in criticism: that of judging a poet not by his best but by his worst work. Try Wordsworth or Tennyson—let alone Swinburne or Hart Crane—by that standard and you will arrive at an equally preposterous estimate. But critics nowadays are prone to detect absurdity everywhere except in their own procedures. (pp. 37-8)

F. C. Golffing, ''Mr. Barker and His Critics,'' in Poetry, *Vol. LXXII, No. 1, April, 1948, pp. 34-8.*

ROY FULLER

When considering the Romantic Reaction of the thirties it is sometimes forgotten how close were its leaders—Dylan Thomas and George Barker—to the poetry against which they were supposed to be in revolt. They were old enough, too, to share the ideological aims and political experiences of the decade—a fact which came out much more clearly in the work of Barker than of Thomas. Their earliest poems can be thought of as the outpourings of talented and original adolescents in love with themselves and with words; and their subsequent achievement is perhaps measured best by the degree to which they managed to bring the outside world into their poetry, though some of their admirers have been content with the original verbal dazzle, as in our time painters have been persuaded by their public to go no further than a scrawling childlike vision.

George Barker, by one of those almost-deliberate accidents our epoch imposes on the individual, like Dylan Thomas, missed serving in the armed forces or as an objector. In the declarations of allegiance which were often drawn from writers in the thirties he always, I think, made a point of saying that he was uncommitted politically, but a good deal of his poetry after his first two books constituted fairly direct social comment—witness his **''Elegy on Spain.''** Such poetry was, I believe, as a rule his best. In Barker, in fact, one sees a poet not materially different in essence (perhaps, like Thomas, more in background and education than anything else) from the Auden-Day Lewis-Spender school of the thirties, whose poetic attitude has been determined by the fortuitous or planned distance between the poet and the great issues and events of the age. His limitations arise, in my view, from the attempts he has made to justify the poet as an isolated and sacred word-machine—attempts which arose in the first place from his native and extraordinary verbal fertility and were carried past the point of logic and utility by his failure to find adequate experience and ideology as his youth passed.

In all Barker's books (as, in a lesser degree, in those of Thomas) one finds an amount of near-incomprehensible, often awkward verse of extreme violence. In Barker atrocious puns and meaningless figures of speech abound. It seems to me that such poetry has little value and no power of survival, and that it springs from a wilful retention by the poet of theoretical ideas which run counter not only to the demands of his times but also of his own true nature. Poetry, Barker once said, is 'calling things felicitous names', but such a definition leaves out too much to last a poet all his life.

There is much Barkerian incoherence in *A Vision of Beasts and Gods,* but also much brilliance. The fact that this latest collection does seem to strike a balance between the rational and irrational styles, and is less copious than his others, makes it a critical one in the author's development. It starts with a long poem, **''Goodman Jacksin and the Angel'',** which rather bears the stamp of the long poem obligatory at the start of a collection of lyrics, and ends with a group of poems in the incoherent manner, called **''Justice at Midnight''.** This leaves rather less than twenty short or shortish poems, mostly of an occasional nature, the best of which are in all ways excellent. It is not chance which has made Barker's occasional poems so often successful: the verbal torrent is given strong channels of purpose, and his range of vocabulary enviably transfigures what could easily be a routine exercise. . . . (pp. 85-6)

Thomas and Barker, extremely intelligent men, too often distrust intelligence, and by their overvaluing the first exciting incoherence of inspiration have encouraged a poetry from others which lacks their own highest qualities. It is interesting that they both evolved a technique of reading their own verse which masked its drawbacks. Thomas's trumpet tones made his hearers imagine that some innate virtue resided in nice words. Barker quietly throws away his poems clause by clause, and objections to the preposterous rhetoric and careless rhythms of the worst are momentarily allayed.

It would be unjust to end a review of *A Vision of Beasts and Gods* on this note. As will have been seen, I am not prepared, like some, to accept Barker's extravagances tolerantly and with masked superiority—as the extravagances of a drunk are sometimes accepted. I prefer Barker sober, and this is probably his most sober book. Certainly it contains four or five poems as good as could be written by any living English poet. (p. 88)

> *Roy Fuller, in a review of "A Vision of Beasts and Gods," in* London Magazine, *Vol. 1, No. 9, October, 1954, pp. 85-6, 88.*

ANTHONY CRONIN

The poetry of George Barker has to some extent suffered in critical estimation, both at a time (say ten years ago) when his use of language was fashionable because of a superficial resemblance to that of Dylan Thomas, and at the moment when it may fairly be said to be unfashionable, when rhetoric of another kind is in vogue, through critical attention being concentrated almost entirely on language alone; and it is my purpose here to deal with Barker's work as poetry which manifests a recognizable moral vision of the world in which we live; a vision which I believe to be serious, coherently and systematically expressed, true and contemporary, and since it is true and contemporary, inevitably tragic.

He has published to date nine books of verse, including the long autobiographical poem, *The True Confession of George Barker,* separately published in pamphlet form and later the subject of some curious literary criticism in the House of Lords. He is a religious poet (Barker is in fact a Catholic, but I mean more and perhaps also less than that) and he may like other religious poets be said, almost without exaggeration, to have only one theme. It is that because we live, we live in error. His poems are thus full of divisions and antitheses (they are also, as if to prove their point, full of what might be regarded as mistakes both of taste and language) and they are concerned primarily with choice and the consequences of choice: that is to say they are both moral and masculine. Like other religious poets, like Traherne for example, his experience is at the same time that of exile and home-coming. Barker sees the world as a place of exile and abandonment. . . . In this world of abandonment, love is both the proof of salvation and the proof of loss, for its necessary consequence is betrayal, and when Barker speaks of love his metaphors are metaphors of violence, in fact of murder: the kiss, the knife and the crucifix are seen as one. Critics have spoken of his pre-occupation with guilt, but in fact if Barker's poetry were only or even primarily an expression of guilt it would be what in fact it is not: feminine and acquiescent. What gives it its stature is that, having experienced the guilt as a necessary consequence not only of error but of all action, he has been forced to search for a further illumination, and in his later verse that illumination is actually found, and is found to depend not on any theological or philosophical basis, but to be in fact poetic: I mean that the reconciliation here found and expressed is a perfect example of

poetic apprehension, in the same way (I speak analogically only) as Edgar's "Ripeness is all".

The True Confession, published in 1950, is in many ways Barker's most interesting poem. It is direct autobiography, it reads impatiently, as if its author had determined not to be baulked of the truth by the temptation to rehearse attitudes or poeticisms, it is in fact deliberately rough and unrehearsed and it ought therefore to command the respect of those who feel that it is too late in the day for any sort of elaborate contrivance to be tolerable. It contains passages where Barker achieves by direct statement a clear apprehension of the dichotomy I have described. . . . Barker's task as a poet has always been the properly poetic one of discovering what he has called 'the assent at the source of life'. It is doubtful if poetry has any other function and of course even a poet like Housman, who seems at first sight to be expressing a vision of despair and not of assent, is in fact effecting a reconcilation by the imposition of a poetic order on experience. . . . In an earlier collection, *Lament and Triumph,* there are poems, such as the much-quoted **"Resolution of Dependence"** which express in a moving way a primary assent to life and the purposes of living. . . . But from *Eros in Dogma,* published in 1944, up to his last book Barker's work has shown an increasing daring in the confrontation of moral issues, the negative echoes of our choices and failures to choose, and at times astonishing insight into the terrible isolation of the individual from his acts.

Most of the guilt with which the poems are concerned is connected with the sexual relationship, the act of love and its consequences, the betrayals and the responsibility of generation. Yet it is not the act of love itself that is seen as an illumination, and the tedious researches of certain trans-Atlantic novelists and a good deal of post-Lawrence writing into the subjective emotions of sex have nothing in common with Barker's themes. Quite simply, and inevitably, his poems spring out of a proper poetic reverence for the miracle of life itself and the dichotomy resulting from passion or need on the one hand and . . . reverence and responsibility on the other. . . . Guilty, self-deriding, certain of little except the fact of suffering, the voice that speaks in these poems is a truly contemporary one. Yet it is also the voice of a poet; and, since it is the virtue, it is also the mark of the poet to insist that suffering is not in fact intolerable. Since poetry is the active examination of human suffering it continues because suffering is found on examination to be tolerable; unlike most human activities it is not an escape from suffering or a distraction. Therefore it is a continual gamble, for of course the poet can never know that he will find that life answers in the affirmative: if he did there would be no need to question it. So, in these poems it is the insights and illuminations which return this answer that are the most impressive as poetry. . . . (pp. 45-50)

In asserting that Barker's moral vision is consistent and that his poems have arrived recently at a point of affirmation and consent deeper than the primary one which a poet in any case makes I do not wish to imply that they have a causative, logical order, like chapters in a book of philosophy. He has written poems on all sorts of subjects: political poems which are true expressions of emotion about politics, occasional poems of commiseration or celebration to his friends (some of these are very beautiful) straightforward love poems and records of occasions which can be made to demonstrate nothing more than the existence of a poet in the world of events and objects and personal loyalties. At their slightest, and even at their worst (he has written many poems which to me at least are total failures of communication) they possess the quality which Coleridge once asserted was the primary poetic one: geniality of soul, a quality which in the sense that Coleridge understood it (it has nothing to do with heartiness) is notably lacking in much of the verse of 1956.

He has also written much unavailing rhetoric (apparently out of a belief that words are a sort of dynamo which when set racing fast enough will not only generate enough energy to keep themselves going, but produce the X quantity which is poetry as well). He is unlikely to appeal to the school of contemporary criticism which, though not remarkably successful poetically itself, apparently values poets of the last two or three decades solely in terms of their desirability as models. He is not, as much of the bad verse of the forties amply demonstrated, a desirable model at all. But rhetoric, as Yeats discovered when about the same age that Barker is now, is a two-edged weapon: like a lamp or a ring in a fairy story it has its dangers as well as its obscure powers. No poet is likely to have a greater capacity for survival as a poet than the one who turns rhetoric into the obedient instrument of his vision of the seriousness of human actions, a vision of moral laws and consequences. If, as Yeats did, Barker succeeds in combining this realization with a growing ability to master the simplicities which underlie all confusions, his poetry, like that of the later Yeats, will continue to triumph precisely because of the tensions which threaten to pull it apart. So far he has achieved a compassionate statement which is not dependent on formal belief or faith but is truly poetic because it arises, as Rilke said all poetic compassion did, out of the self, even out of self-pity, while being aware of the objective reality of the suffering of others. To seek and find the nature of poetic compassion is the major task and the major achievement of contemporary poetry. (pp. 51-2)

> *Anthony Cronin, "Poetry and Ideas: George Barker," in* London Magazine, *Vol. 3, No. 9, September, 1956, pp. 44-52.*

THOM GUNN

[George Barker's *Collected Poems, 1930-1955*] starts appallingly: the first poem is not only the worst in the book but one of the worst I have ever seen in print, and the thirty-page *Calamiterror* is a classic of its kind, a compendium of the worst faults of the Thirties and of those of the Forties to which they led. There is a jumble of bowels, blood and bones, and a great many other objects of which it is difficult to discover the probably symbolic justification. Any rhetorical trick is considered fair play; purposeless inversion, absence of expected pronouns and articles, and a horrible form of Hopkinsese involving much deformation of words, bad puns and a ceaseless jingle of internal rhymes. Worst of all, there is a total absence of logical meaning. There is always a theme, it is true (usually that of orgasm), around which is loosely grouped a collection of phrases which offer only suggestions of meaning and approximations of sensation. At best the first half of the *Collected Poems* consists of hysterical confusion with occasional flashes of disconnected eloquence, an eloquence of which Barker himself appeared unable to take a full and calculated advantage.

But from the start of his third book *News of the World* a certain technical discipline becomes increasingly if slowly evident. At first it is only a suspicion of control; but the rhetoric becomes more appropriate and lasts for longer passages.

He has always been an outright Romantic, believing in the superiority of the unconscious forces. The Romantic can adopt one of two strategies: he can acclaim violence and impulse in violent and impulsive writing, or he can acclaim them from the greater distance of clear and premeditated writing. Mr. Barker has moved, and is still moving, from the first to the second of these strategies. His early poetry showed, among other influences, that of Blake's 'Prophetic Books'; the predominant influence now (even more than that of Yeats) is of Blake's short poems. . . .

Even now he is capable of spoiling a good poem (as in the awkward and meaningless ending of **"Letter to a Young Poet"**), and the control could still be applied to greater effect. But the blood and bowels stream less frequently, the structure of the poetry has become tighter, the movement more regular. He has learnt that it is only by the control of energy that energy can ever be defined—or conveyed.

> *Thom Gunn, "Energy Control," in* The Spectator, *Vol. 199, No. 6736, August 2, 1957, p. 167.*

ANTHONY CRONIN

The publication of George Barker's [*Collected Poems, 1930-1955*] enables us to judge his achievement more confidently than reading through the various individual volumes did. We can see, too, how remarkably his work has gained in lucidity, psychological insight and concreteness since the early forties, now that all of it except *The True Confession* has been gathered into one volume. The later poems here are among the most exciting the last twenty years have produced: the early ones seem often to be a rite performed by a young man for his muse, a private mystery, evidently reverent and passionate but not particularly communicative. The gain is partly the result of an abandonment of certain characteristics which were much admired in their day. The threnodic melodies are not heard nowadays: Mr Barker is no longer attempting to conduct the waves.

'I always shake the tree,' Cocteau reports Chaplin to have said to him. Mr Barker has shaken a lot out of his poems. The later ones are barer and tougher and the passionate element, the true conviction, is more apparent now that the words have ceased to destroy each other by violence. It seems to me that the *Sacred Elegies*, which occur about the middle of this book, are the dividing line. This of course is not to belittle his earlier achievement: if I am right, it means that he became an important poet at about the age it is customary to begin to appear fugitively today. The point is really only worth insisting on because his very early work was so well known that it possibly hampers or confuses judgement of what he is doing now.

Yet, with so much in the same book it is impossible not to become conscious of the faults that, though purged, to some extent remain. The chief one is a fondness for abstraction of imagery: the images are often made up as illustrations of the theme; they convey little visually and they are crowded together in such a way that the little is lost:

> Bend your arm
> Under my generation of heads. The seas enfold
> My sleepless eye and save it weeping
> For the dishonoured star.

There is too much allegory. A little later in the poem just quoted occurs the line:

> I see
> The wringing of the hands of all the world.

This is typical of what I think is a tendency to say something in an inflated way by means of a large, semi-abstract image when a simpler way of saying it would suffice. To read through the poems one after another is to become conscious, too, of a certain overfrequent use of adjectives which do not succeed in conveying a visual image and only a very tenuous mental concept, such as 'the house-proud sun' and 'the green-eyed world'.

These are, however, the faults of an imagination which is perhaps too febrile. If the words seem sometimes too large the emotion is unmistakably there—Barker is not playing a game with words. And he is capable, too, of a splendid simplicity which is the result of a resolution rather than an avoidance of experience.... The best of these verses can stand comparison with the best poetry of our time, with Yeats and Auden. They arise from experience explored with great honesty; from a knowledge of the division of real and ideal, wish and deed, love and understanding. The poet is true to his vision of the facts and to his moral vision. More than any contemporary poems I know, they contain the knowledge that we walk in isolation not only from what we love but from the self which loves it. If there is an inflation of language at times there is never an inflation or falsification of experience. George Barker's poems will not be enjoyed by those who evade the possibility of tragedy, of the irrevocable in human actions, of the treacheries that separate us from each other. They seem to me to be, at their best, among the most honest and agonizing, and therefore reconciling, consolatory and elating poems written in English in this century. (pp. 85, 87, 89)

> *Anthony Cronin, in a review of "Collected Poems,"* in London Magazine, *Vol. 5, No. 5, May, 1958, pp. 85, 87, 89, 91.*

ANTHONY THWAITE

Rhetoric, pessimism, violence, an over-ripe vocabulary and a self-indulgent diabolism—these have been the marks of a Barker poem from the beginning. The attitudes have been consistent: that all good poets are *poètes manqués*, that man is a doomed sexual animal, that calamity is our condition. His sense of organization, of weighing a poem's shape against its statement, has never quite matched his technical skill; and his fondness for incidental effects (the clanging pun, the gross word in a chaste context, the monumental word which brings the structure crashing down) has often ruined an otherwise successful poem.

All this has been noticed before. But what began to be apparent in parts of *The True Confession* and in *A Vision of Beasts and Gods* becomes clearer still in *The View From a Blind I*: that Barker has learned that plainness and astringency can succeed where a more sonorous and showy rhetoric fails. There is no diminution of his force or his message, but he has reached a point where he seems able to judge more accurately how much noise per square foot a line or a poem can bear. Who could have imagined, even ten years ago, that Barker could manage the difficult irony of **"Roman Poem III"** (A Sparrow's Feather)? (p. 94)

But it would be wrong to give the idea that the strengths of these new poems are merely negatives ones. There is positive variety. **"The Ballad of Yucca Flats"** is by far the best of all the ballad-type poems Barker has attempted. This story of four horsemen (the fourth of them being the Angel of Death) is one of the very few good poems to have come from the idea of nuclear war.... The images here are made to work, they are

not just verbal gestures in a void. Elsewhere, Barker shows considerable skill as a satirist, in **"Circular from America"**, **"Nine Beatitudes to Denver"** and, nearer home and even sharper, **"Scottish Bards and an English Reviewer"**.... Of course there are failures in the book, and crashing ones: the poem to Francis Bacon, for example, is weighed down with turgid rubbish. But it was Barker himself who wrote: 'I believe that if you have got to make mistakes you might as well make great mistakes, because these will at least show other people what not to do.' Dangerous doctrine for some, but Barker can get away with it. He remains, at worst, one of the great showmen of contemporary poetry; and in *The View From a Blind I* he is at his best. (pp. 94-5)

> *Anthony Thwaite, in a review of "The View from a Blind I," in* London Magazine, *n.s. Vol. 2, No. 2, May, 1962, pp. 93-5.*

IAN HAMILTON

There were signs in George Barker's last book, *The View from a Blind I,* that the long, hectic fever had passed and that he was at last settling down to an exhausted, mildly ironical middle age; random flashes of the old extravagance were still in evidence and there was a routine sprinkling of puns, but none of all this seemed in earnest any more. Nor, though, did his new manner. Being loftily scornful about the beats was not a role to wring much zest from this arch-prophet of the Dionysian, and the casual chatty note did not come at all naturally; attempts at faintly wearied sophistication just didn't have that fractionally managed tact and poise which Auden, say, takes so marvellously in his stride, and the intended flow of easy conversation rarely got beyond the merely bare and prosy. Though the book as a whole was probably more consistently intelligible than any of his others it was also a good deal duller, and false to his real gifts.

Quite what these real gifts are is still something of a mystery, since his successes have all been momentary and of rather different kinds; it is clear, though, that they are most usually displayed when he is least self-consciously trying to be sensible. At his most shrieking and inane, Barker always seemed able to hit off something fine and surprising; one tended to stick with him through the hot growths of sex disgust and religious frenzy on the offchance of a happy accident. A fairly dutiful journey, most of the time, but now and then rewarded. The high-pitched boasting monotone might suddenly falter into a specific nervous tenderness, or it might swell into a legitimate, earned grandeur; out of his profusion of grotesque images there might be one that had real depth and resonance. His theory that to get at the unknown poetry *must* distort appearances, since what is unknown cannot by definition be bodied forth by what is known, was obviously suicidal—doomed to produce a language and a landscape that could flaunt their distance from the 'natural'—but it gave him the licence he appeared to need, licence to take off and see what happened. Barker's work is amazingly uneven, but it is hard not to see this as a necessary price for those few distinguished lines and stanzas that still oblige us to take him seriously. (pp. 85-6)

[*Dreams of a Summer Night*] continues where *The View from a Blind I* left off; if anything, since its subject is one which in the past has fired Barker to his most remote rhetorical extremes—it is more determinedly withheld and clear-headed. The subject is death, both the poet's own anticipated death, the sense he has of being haunted all the time by dead experience and the deaths of certain friends whose memories continue to inhabit him, 'those who sleep in a strange cloud beside us'. (p. 86)

Friends, scenes, situations from the past, these swarm into nearly every poem; isolated moments of response or commitment to the living are invariably blurred by some nagging ghost, some black diffusing intimation. There is little panic, very little really personal recoil; an uneasy resignation, a tendency to morose speculation, an enervated clinging to the old muddle of classical and Christian imagery, but no final sense of a whole functioning personality. When anything concretely his own gets into the poems, Barker retreats from it into the mythological, the vaguely symbolic or the abstract, or he just lets it leak away through one of his porous evocatives—dream, golden and holy are the favourites in this book. In one of the better poems, Part V of the long title sequence, there is a good instance of this; the poem opens with a picnic on a Welsh hill, with the poet eating an apple and looking out across the countryside below; there is some neat description and a pleasant sense of a moment lazily enjoyed. A cemetery is spotted, though, and instead of it merely taking its place as part of what is seen (and by doing so *suggest* the obvious) it is glumly pounced on. . . . (pp. 86-7)

The moment is not only destroyed but is made to seem set up. There is a certain sloppiness of feeling, a too facile *in memoriam* kind of sadness running somewhere underneath these lines, and it is typical of Barker's new manner; we know what he is talking about, most of the time, but we are no longer sure that he cares about it. (p. 87)

> *Ian Hamilton, in a review of "Dreams of a Summer Night," in* London Magazine, *n.s. Vol. 6, No. 3, June, 1966, pp. 85-7.*

BRIAN JONES

The Golden Chains contains 104 poems, all consisting of two rhymed quatrains. The form gives a spurious sense of concentration. In fact, the tight little stanzas are flabbily used, and almost without exception the poems are immensely unapproachable. Much as I sympathize with the mysterious, bardic, incantatory nature of poetry which his work seems to bear witness to, Barker's world is an entirely linguistic construction, and I cannot make the effort to enter a world where only words are real. And such pompous words at that. And there is an almost tragic irony in the fact that a poet who has such a lust for words, who manages them with such gusto, should create so little which is remembered. He loves words, but he doesn't stabilize them. It is this lack of precision which contributes to the monotony of tone to be found in these poems. The only relief from chant is bluster.

> *Brian Jones, in a review of "The Golden Chains," in* London Magazine, *n.s. Vol. 8, No. 2, May, 1968, p. 76.*

DOUGLAS DUNN

For forty years George Barker has been a big bundle of joy on the British poetry scene, his fecund rhetoric and flamboyant imagery sprouting out all over in a consistently productive career. His reputation is established, and has certainly been worked for with dedication. Barker's high-flying kind of verse is now generally unpopular, although if Jeff Nuttall is anything to go by, it may still have its readers in that quarter. There is

much in Barker's [*Poems of Places and People*] which I dislike. The flatulent tautology:

> No matter how
> brief or how small the
> firefly spark or the
> sparkling firefly, still
> we burn also, Carthage, we
> burn too.

The inane questioning:

> What is the meaning of
> the sea or the duty of the
> west wind or the responsi-
> bility of the flowering
> chestnut tree in summer?

Barker offers answers equally unconvincing, and no doubt this will please admirers of Barker's hot-footed to heaven utterance. One line of Barker's work which I endorse asserts itself in **"Drumtochty Castle School,"** a mellow poem of the writer in later years among school-children, and **"In Memory of Robert Macbryde"** is also a controlled poem of age, affectionate and assured. Generally speaking, though, holy George Barker is once again on fire, after his other latter-day collections had seemed to indicate that the rampant visionary had at last been tamed. (p. 72)

> *Douglas Dunn, "Damaged Instruments," in* Encounter, *Vol. XXXVII, No. 2, August, 1971, pp. 68-74.*

ALFRED CORN

[We] generally view the indeterminate, anarchic aspects of art as a manifestation and as a sustainer of vitality.

Confronted with actual instances, however, our commitment to the anarchic in poetry may weaken. My feelings about the poetry of George Barker divide on just this issue. On one side, a tonic satisfaction from contemplating the grand original, all-or-nothing poet he has tried to be—often, we may guess, at the expense of his own personal happiness. On the other, actual readings of the poems, where words in sequence, and not biographies or poetic manifestoes, are what must be responded to. Barker writes *extreme* poems; as though bad taste carried as far as possible might be a form of the Sublime.

The jacket to *Villa Stellar* has this note about the book by its author: "It has two purposes. The first to record biographical instances and the second to record the frames of mind in which these incidents and instances were recollected. I have tried to describe the changing colours of the memory, as the dolphin might, if it could, try to describe the altering colours of its skin as it dies." This comment didn't quite stop me from opening the book, where is to be found an opening dedicatory poem, **"Written at the Waterfall of Vyrnwy,"** and a sequence of untitled lyrics numbered I to LVIII, each less than a page long. The sequence is set in Italy—Rome, Lake Albano, Lerici, Apulia, and (perhaps only in reverie) the source of the Clitumnus, familiar to readers of Vergilian pastoral. About half of the poems are meditations, the rest, at least minimally, narratives. Three other characters figure in the sequence (apart from the narrator): a "Contessa," a painter called Kingsmill, and a woman (possibly Scottish) called Elizabeth Roberta Cameron. The exact relationships among the four are never defined, but to call them friends will do.

The poetic meditations (Barker's "frames of mind") are devoted to the great subjects—eros, death, art, the past, drink, suffering, madness—that have obsessed Barker since the publication of his first book, in 1933. . . . It is in the climate of British 1940s Romanticism that Barker seems least anomalous. If we can reconstruct the temper of the years of the long Yeatsian afterglow, when Dylan Thomas was at his peak, and when Alex Comfort and Anne Ridler were publishing steadily, then Barker's poetry will seem very plausible.

Still, when section XXII of *Villa Stellar* asks the question,

> Can the heart ever return to the house of its origin
>   where
> a window looked out onto that prospect of fields and
>   flowers, always
> it seemed patterned in the harlequin tints of
> early childhood? And where a conjuring stream trans-
> formed a dead dog into Hermes with wings and stars?

the answer must clearly be, "No." Nor will many disagree with the Contessa when, in section XLIX, she says: "I am sick of the bouquets / of broken mirrors and barbed wire and rubber bladders containing / specimens of someone else's intellectual urine / mitigated, if one is lucky, by only the faintest odour / of a self abjuring its pity. I am quite sick of / the honesty that insists upon gurgitating into my lap / simply because I am sitting here."

This is Barker at his most masochistic—a lover's quarrel with the self, no doubt. But, titters aside, fairness demands that these poems be given their due; the Contessa (or Barker) has not really described his poems, or not all of them. Barker has also written novels; and some of the most persuasive sections in *Villa Stellar* resemble bite-sized short stories—funny, in the manner of V. S. Pritchett, grotesque, like Iris Murdoch. (pp. 125-27)

One of the strategies of the book is constantly to vary the tone, the substance, the metric format, as a way to keep the reader engaged. Almost all of the poems use meter, but the long lines are subtly varied; and some periodic forms, with rhymes, are brought in occasionally, even one irregular sonnet. There is never any doubt that, in addition to telegrams from the unconscious, the poem is informed by conscious art.

Barker can write striking and perhaps memorable phrases. He speaks, for example, of "the first livid gleam / of the cut-glass moon as she enters, the dying Diana, / when the wine bottle shines with its mirage of instant solutions. . . ." He demonstrates that rare ability to *image* concepts, to find objective correlatives for thought: "Love is the fact of its object. Without it nothing can enter / the sanctum sanctorum of our subjective perceptions / like the hole in the dome of the Pantheon for the god to descend through." He describes moral codes as "wholly artificial systems we have constructed to protect ourselves," and says they "function / like St Paul's dark glasses, to prevent our being blinded." This metaphoric mode is much more successful than the bald (though geographically pinpointed) metaphysical speculation some of the poems toss off, as when he speaks of "the perception of forfeited paradise, which, once we have left it, / once we have lost it, looks like dirty old newsprint. I have / left in cloudy Umbrian mountains the knowledge that / what we once found is the vision that we lost / only because we found it." A poet beset by so many paradoxes as this might consider some of them well lost, as they seriously mar what is on the whole a book well worth reading. For, despite his grotesquerie and occasional absurd-

ity—because of them, perhaps—he does say unprecedented things. It seems rather futile for critics to make reprimands, yet they consider it their prerogative. At age 67 (and after so many books) Barker is surely aware that they are incorrigible; which need not prevent him from continuing to write as he pleases. (pp. 127-28)

> *Alfred Corn, "Melancholy Pastorals," in* Parnassus:
> Poetry in Review, *Vol. 8, No. 2, 1980, pp. 125-36.*

ROBERT FRASER

In 1933 Barker was asked by the editors of the Prometheans' journal *The Twentieth Century* to review a new critical study of [William Blake's] work by John Middleton Murry, whom he had met before. Blake was already coursing through Barker's bloodstream: less initially the political Blake than the author of "The Mental Traveller" and the Prophetic Books, the fabricator of personal myth. Barker's *Poems* (1935), the first volume accepted by T. S. Eliot at [Faber and Faber], abounds in myths of its own, including appropriately three versions of Narcissus, and, more potently, the spectral landscape of **"The Amazons"**, who, 'ironically echoing down the colonnade of seven columnar decades', voice an invitation to self-destruction which is nevertheless timeless. . . . It is hard to think of any other poetry of its period which appeals so powerfully to both eye and mythic imagination, while calling attention, in 'whispering sibilant fields', to its own aural content. Here already are the love of the visual which sent the young Barker through the National Gallery in search of the canvases of Rossetti, the quest for fanciful domains which the private imagination might invade and conquer, and the attentive ear which was gradually training itself out of a habit of latinate rotundity and into a subservience to the inflections of English prose.

The political unrest of the times attracted Barker's reluctant attention. Ideologically he had little in common with Auden and his group, possessing, as Yeats noted, 'less of their social passion, their sense of suffering'. Yet unemployment and the Spanish War had to be taken into account. . . . In **"Elegy on Spain"** he encouraged the rekindling of a national spirit without, however, paying tribute to either combatant. The poetry of **"Lament and Triumph,"** his third collection, enacts an accommodation with the pressures of history while leaving the artistic conscience room to grow. It is a nice balance, never more memorably expressed than in the celebrated **"Resolution of Dependence"** where time places its demands in the person of William Wordsworth 'with a watch in his hand'. As the clock, which Rupert Brooke had left at ten to three, strikes an inclement hour, Wordsworth and Barker agree a contract with the forces of historical conditioning whose two principal signatories paradoxically join hands in evasion of all chronological limitation. 'The past's absolution is the present's resolution. / The equation in the interdependence of parts', concludes Barker who, lover of old cars and all 'mechanical paraphernalia', loves them most when they break down.

The war brought some change in Barker's personal circumstances without diminishing his fluency. . . . His correspondence of the date and the set of Pacific Sonnets (collected in *Eros in Dogma*) reveal a mind deeply disturbed by separation from Europe and exile in a land for which he had little understanding or sympathy. (pp. 41-2)

The public disruption of those years impinged on his writing only insofar as it helped to raise certain age-old questions. As the presence of Evil loomed large in the political firmament, Barker was driven to seek for an explanation in his mother's Catholicism, buried since his late 'teens. The theme was unfamiliar, yet the reflex entirely typical of him: faced by a crisis of temporal conditioning he devises an answer couched in the language of the eternal. Barker is not, and has not been since boyhood, a member of a parish community; yet only in the works of the great Roman Catholic theologians could he discover a conception of human destiny large enough to do justice to the contemporary holocaust. Attendance at the Mass may have been beyond him, as was the composition of true sacred verse, but in the *Sacred and Secular Elegies,* published in America, he made a discovery. If a conventional religious acceptance was too difficult, the example of Baudelaire, shrewdly diagnosed by Eliot, showed him another way: at least he could blaspheme. It was thus that the unmistakable Barkerian scurrility, that mixture of irreverence and wonder, made its entrance into his work, fusing later with the voices of Villon and Byron to create the complex tone of *The True Confession* (1950).

The work of the late 1940s and early 1950s enfolds the seed of a single mystery. The Fathers of the Oratory had shown the adolescent Barker a passage from Newman's *Apologia* which he found hard to explain: '*if* there is a God, *since* there is a God, the human race is implicated in some terrible aboriginal calamity'. Now Adolf Hitler had unveiled the calamity, and Barker is able to offer the Fathers an answer in the form of that personal myth which he has always been seeking. The poet is a scapegrace: driven by a daemon he can scarcely control he violates all that he holds most dear, but, in so doing, leaves ineradicable traces of his devotion. The daemon is partly his own creative mania, his muse, and partly the irresistible force of his sexuality which lays waste everything in its wake. It is thus that, in his myth of private martyrdom, the Fall from Grace comes to correspond to the dawning of the sexual urge, and sin to coincide with sexual violence.

Though the *True Confessions* and *The Dead Seagull* have both been read as autobiographical, in both the few facts which survive are so transmuted by the processes of the imagination as to be unrecognizable. The thematic interest lies elsewhere, in a vision of Pascalian terror unredeemed by orthodox hope. If human nature is, as Augustine and Newman both claimed, helpless without the intervention of the Deity, wherever is it without him? Pascal had looked into the emptiness of those silent spaces and found God. Barker looked again and saw the silent spaces. (p. 42)

In the early 1930s Barker's interest in the elegiac genre was fed by a mouthing of the great Virgilian originals. In the heavily latinate **"Elegiac Stanzas"** with which *Thirty Preliminary Poems* begin, death features as 'Erasure of our pain/Cessation of unease, whose cancellation/Of decayed disgraces, perhaps gain/A less agitant more absolute location.' In the same period there is a distrust of formality which seeks to give itself elbow-room by imitating the rhythms of conversation. In such poems as **"Allegory of the Adolescent and the Adult"**, this freedom combines with an allegorical technique to suggest the metrical versatility of Middle English verse, which Barker saw as the foundation of Hopkins's revival of Sprung Rhythm. . . . In the pre-war verse these two tendencies jostle shoulders, until in the *Sacred and Secular Elegies* they collide:

> But the principle of evil is not autonomous.
> Like the Liberty Horse with a plume at the circus
> Under the whipmaster it steps proud in its circles.
> When I let slip one instant the whip of the will
> All hell's scot free with fire at the nostril.

Here the verse unit, made 'slightly longer than the classical English line' to ape Roman grandeur, but released from the metrical stringency of strict elegiacs, fails to live up to its promise. Overburdened with meaning and image it strains and then goes slack in the middle.

One solution was for Barker to tighten his metre and clarify his vocabulary. In the verse of *News of the World* (1950) he recalls another late medieval legacy, and achieves lyrical purity by following Auden to sit beside the open fire of the ballad. The fastidious ear which earlier lingered over heaped assonances now satisfies itself with the luminous contours of song. At the same time a revived love of Housman leads to an experimentation with miniature forms which eventually gives rise to the little interlocked brilliances of *The Golden Chains* (1968).

One problem thus solved, however, another presents itself. The metre both of the ballad and of Housman's lyrics is predictable, and the regularity of drubbing fingers attracts Barker no more than does the steady procession of events. Barker's ear is quantitative rather than qualitative: he is more interested in rhythm than in accent. Thus, in the 1960s and 1970s two motivations of the younger Barker—a desire to elude the minimalizations of topicality and a distaste for classical prosody—combine to produce the conversational and socially evasive verse of *Dreams of a Summer Night* (1966) and *In Memory of David Archer* (1973). To some readers it seemed as if the conversationalist had taken over from the poet, reducing verbal melody to fluent chatter. This, however, was to hear the effect while missing the point. The verse of these books represents an attempt to develop a working rhythm that is natural without being casual, flexible without being flat, and—in so doing—to weave a counterpoint between patterns which the ear detects and those which it simply expects.

In Barker's work language and metre are for ever returning to the caves of their origin. His view of the English prosodic tradition is of a spiral through which the word refines itself to an extreme of preciosity and then twists violently back to a new kind of simplicity. In the history of these islands there have been several such moments, less reverses or revolutions than revaluations from an older perspective: the mediaeval alliterative revival, the Romantic revival, the re-emergence of sprung rhythm in Hopkins, the verbal democracy of Auden. It was during the last of these phases, when the hothouse of modernism was flung open to breezes from the Yorkshire moors, that Barker began as a poet. Yet, if the 1930s saw him on his way, the pieties of the period retain little hold. What has survived is the courage of one for whom the struggle against social and linguistic complacency had endlessly to be renewed with weapons which wear themselves out in use, to be replaced by others which are sharper, even if initially cruder. In *Anno Domini,* the impulse is stronger than ever, shaping new tools out of the material of the mediaeval line and caesura. It is a fitting thrust for the youngest septuagenarian in Europe. (pp. 42-3)

Robert Fraser, "The One That Got Away," in PN Review 31, *Vol. 9, No. 5, 1983, pp. 41-3.*

SEBASTIAN BARKER

George Barker's output may be catalogued under ten main obsessions, only the first three of which I shall touch on here: Love or God, Faith, Women, Money, The Trade of Poet, Self-Image, the Stars, Time, Imagery, and Symbolism. The most interesting thing about this list is what is missing from it: people. And though, as in the mainstream of modern poetry—

Eliot, Pound, Auden, Larkin—human beings occasionally make their entrances, it is far more normal to see an attitude to a person rather than a person. A woman, for example, may be seen as a woman, rather than as a person. People are depersonalised or caricatured, as for example Larkin's 'Jan van Hogspouw' in "The Card-Players". The immediate upshot of George Barker's main interests, which are very much in the mainstream, is that they are all abstractions. In general terms, this point is considerably more glaring than the almost total oversight about things scientific. But this, too, can be understood. In fact, in George Barker's latest work science is very much in evidence. (p. 54)

From my list, which merely reflects his most pronounced and recurrent preoccupations in some sort of statistical order, it is evident that George Barker inherited an over-riding concern about the nature of God and a concern, too, about the nature of faith. One of his great allies in his struggle with these abstractions was his sexuality. He refused to give this up, believing, I suspect, that God couldn't possibly be such a prig as to deprive him of it. I see his preoccupation with the abstractions of God and faith rather as I see the life of a man who spends his time working out the molecular structure of insulin. To ridicule a poet for his concern over abstractions to the exclusion of any interest in people is the equivalent of missing the point about what insulin is for and a failure to understand the nature of artistic or scientific succession.

The price that must be paid for such concentrated attention to the origins of mental and physical material is the 'extraordinary egotism' which William James noticed in the recipients of profound religious experience. George Barker writes, 'I have been more unabatingly and voraciously consumed in love than at this moment my mind—and body—feels powerful enough to bear' (*Alanna Autumnal*, p. 4). This remark is typical of many in his early work. We feel at once in the presence of an ego almost exploding with a sense of what lies outside itself. Because *Alanna Autumnal* is about incest with his sister, this is perhaps not surprising. But having said that, no reader can fail to sense the incandescent nature of his original experiences, in whatever area these may have been, nor his fearlessness in writing about them. In fact, *Alanna Autumnal*, published when the poet was twenty in 1933, reveals a writer setting off in life in a deliberately outrageous pose. Those who make a hobby out of following such careers must have been licking their lips for the inevitable pratfall. But it never came. With the publication of *Anno Domini* nearly fifty years later the observer must be convinced that George Barker has reached his destination, the outrageous poses retrimmed as wit, his sexuality intact, and his sense of the miraculous undimmed.

It is an astonishing fact, nonetheless, that there is more writing about another person, and that his sister, in *Alanna Autumnal* (a seminal work) than in all the rest of his writings. 'Elizabeth Roberts Cameron' is described with considerable skill and even greater delicacy in *Villa Stellar* (for instance, no. XIII) but this is very much the exception in his work as a whole, as is his sonnet **"To My Mother"**. The 'extraordinary egotism' essential to anyone who would pursue the object and the grounds of faith seems incompatible in him, and many other modern poets, with a Chaucerian or Shakespearean interest in human characters. And yet, and yet—the whole of his work, the whole of modern poetry, is haunted by the human image, whether by its presence or its absence.

We get, it's true, a masterpiece of self-portraiture, *The True Confession of George Barker*. But this, though brilliantly witty, and possessing as it does a backbone of autobiographical information, together with sketches of the human beings who must go with this, focusses less on himself, his parents, his contemporaries—and a series of remarkably shadowy women—than on his metaphysics. So of course, when the poem was finished—and the first half, published in 1950, was not joined by the second half until 1965—the poet was still in the awkward position of having to choose between silence and further development. His subsequent books, most notably *Dreams of a Summer Night* and *At Thurgarton Church,* show a deepening of interest beyond the joco-serious affirmations of *The True Confession* towards the wholehearted compassionate commitment—which is not any less witty—of *Anno Domini.*

George Barker's great achievement in *Anno Domini* (which is spoken more or less entirely to God) is that through compassion, made almost weightless by wit, he is able, towards the end of his life's work, to suggest a human shambles which seems a little more divine and a divine shambles which seems a little more human. The reason I call this his great achievement is because by excluding human characters from his work he was, like so many others, pressure-cooking himself with the God of the twentieth century. To make this monster less of a monster, and perhaps even to suggest something of the original if hidden human nature within it, might seem to some a hopeless, or worse, an ignoble occupation. But whatever anyone may say, to conceive of God and make this conception visible is a basic human achievement.

The God that he has made turns out to be an intriguing fellow. He is the Compassionate God of the Old and New Testaments made experienced enough in self-knowledge to contemplate good and evil, and witty enough in common knowledge to contemplate the oddities of cosmology and sub-atomic physics. It's worth pointing out that George Barker leaves the mystery of evil in the mind of this God. (pp. 54-5)

Within this serious framework, compassion and wit make delightful and satisfying combination in a deity. Add to this a wonderful freedom from hobby-horsing and butterfly-chasing and we have a picture of a life's work ruled over by a fascinating Power, who evades none of the home-truths about sex or the palpability of evil. We seem to be listening to a poet talking to a God who is not only listening but silently taking part in the monologue. As with any writer, George Barker's God is invoked by the language in which he is addressed. . . .

The Chaplinesque twirling of walking-sticks on the high wire, especially the sustained lunacy and totally impersonal inspiration of the lines on man as a robotical 'shambling machine', might seem astonishing in a seventy-year-old. But something which had been implicit but never explicit in his work till the publication of *Anno Domini* has suddenly found its outlet. He has discovered that his God is human and might actually want to listen to him and might actually enjoy doing so. His metaphysical *angst* has gone. I can think of no other living English poet in danger of this victorious surrender. It is fully implied but never fully elaborated in, say, the poems of David Gascoyne or Elizabeth Jennings.

There is absolutely nothing laboured about his conclusions. Every experience is paid for at source. It is a poem inconceivable from the pen of Chaucer or Shakespeare or even William Blake. For what he has done is to take wit—the dance of the intellect—right into the very fabric of what Blake called The Human Imagination. Blake's imaginative wit, by comparison, is awesome, terrible, and silent. (p. 55)

George Barker's life's work has been about his conscience struggling with his time—a time like no other in its revelations of evil. He writes, 'the human purpose is to hide the glass horse / Of our doubt until the pity / Of heaven opens up a city / Of absolute belief to us' (*The True Confession,* I, 5). He has always been a man who believes in the existence of God. The only trouble was he could never believe in the existence of any of the Gods he could believe in. His approach, therefore, has been the *via negativa.* (p. 56)

Sebastian Barker, ''Bringing God Down to Earth,'' in PN Review 31, *Vol. 9, No. 5, 1983, pp. 54-6.*

DAVID GASCOYNE

In *Homage to George Barker,* the essay which in my opinion displays the most percipient understanding of Barker is that by Patrick Swift [see *CLC,* Vol. 8]. Swift links Barker unequivocally with European rather than insular tradition; St Augustine and Kierkegaard, for instance, are referred to, as are Baudelaire and Pierre Jean Jouve. Swift did not, as he might well have done, refer to another Christian apologist, Pascal, to whom—on account of the latter's leaning to Jansenism—Pierre Jean Jouve was (as Jean Starobinski suggested) probably closer than most orthodoxly Catholic French poets. Like Barker, Jouve was in any case *non-pratiquant.* But I have no desire to add here a redundant gloss on a comprehensive essay that is indispensible to any reader determined to get to the roots of Barker's poetry at its best. Barker has undoubtedly shared many of the sternest convictions of T. S. Eliot, once his mentor and the poet about whom he has written with as sympathetic an understanding as anyone of our generation. In the *True Confession,* George seemed to be out to demonstrate with gusto that for him the self was indeed hateful.

I agree with Paddy Swift that it is necessary to recognise the fundamentally Catholic outlook in Barker's most significant work. George will always appear to me as an almost archetypal Lapsed Catholic. If he suffers complexes, then one of them must surely be involved with the kind of guilt that is commonly associated with being such a one. This also means, I think, that he is intimately familiar with what was once known as the Agenbite of Inwit. The Irishness inherited from his mother is another factor that ought not to be ignored. Added to this, I should guess him to have been at least intermittently haunted by an unusually repellent vision of the Beast with Two Backs. But I only refer to these afflictions, if such indeed they be, in order the more to stress the triumphant assurance of his septuagenarian emergence. . . .

I recognise and salute in George Barker a poet whose work has never ceased to develop, who has been almost uninterruptedly prolific, whose themes have been basic and perennial, and who has remained faithful to his exceptional gift, enriching our language and literature to an extent that remains to be estimated. It would be a simple pleasure to enumerate those of his poems I most admire, or to compile a miniature anthology of my favourite lines; but such is the unified diversity of Barker's published poetry that every reader could do as much and in each case produce a different result. I would rather end by paying homage to the unique combination to be found in his work of a plangent music reminiscent of Dowland's with a remarkable range of imagery concise *concetti* and fierce *fioretti,* resplendent, ominous, or both at once, forged out of an intense personal experience of our particularly 'hard times'. If one believes that this century has represented one unprece-

dentedly critical Occasion, then Karl Miller was right when ten years ago he drew attention to the apparent predominance of 'the occasional' in Barker's work. . . .

There are many current definitions of poetry's purpose; but if one happens to believe that it is to bear witness to the inescapable nature of man's present predicament, while at the same time transfiguring the testimony by giving it utterance that can encourage such endurance as that defined by Barker in [''**Elegy on Spain**''], then his poetry may be regarded as a vindication of the type of poetic enterprise that too often today tends to be regarded as portentously 'apocalyptic'. What it offers us, in fact, is authentic 'News of the World'. (p. 60)

David Gascoyne, ''George Barker at Seventy,'' in PN Review 31, *Vol. 9, No. 5, 1983, pp. 59-60.*

JONATHAN BARKER

For all his formal mastery of English prosody, his love of the elegy and rhetoric, Barker's poems never seem to prefer art to life. The unsuspecting reader approaches the poems expecting artifice and is instead pushed straight back into the paradoxes of human life. Perhaps the technique is near to the prose of Thomas De Quincey, another writer accepting the darker side of man who still touches a raw nerve in us today. The titles of Barker's poems (''**The True Confession of George Barker**'', ''**Calamiterror**'', ''**News of the World**'') at times have a similar calculated shock value to that found in De Quincey's titles (''Murder Considered as One of the Fine Arts'', ''A Vision of Sudden Death'', *The Confessions of an English Opium-Eater*). Titles which owe something to the techniques of journalism and are at once humorous and serious.

George Barker is a writer of secular and sacred elegies (he published a sequence with this title in 1944). His main theme is the tension between the demands of love of God and love of the sensual worlds. Many of his most memorable poems are elegies for dead friends, often painters and poets, a continuity evident in the *Collected Poems.* . . . Given that death so dominates the book it is worth noting that Barker does not express outrage at it as tragic; rather, friends are mourned and celebrated with a vivid sense of their uniqueness. In writing on death Barker celebrates life, an ability shared with the Irish poet Patrick Kavanagh who wrote ''There is only one Muse, the Comic Muse. In Tragedy there is always something of a lie. Great poetry is always comic in the profound sense. Comedy is abundance of life.'' I take Barker to be, in these terms, a comic rather than a tragic writer. He *accepts* life and its paradoxes. . . . (pp. 71-2)

Barker's formal prosodic range is considerable, a talent which makes reading through his *Collected Poems* an education in metre and a varied and enjoyable experience. This ties in with his liking for the elegy in which a natural sense of occasion is matched by a formal stanza pattern. Barker's formal ambitiousness can perhaps be best experienced through a look at some of his longer poems which contain much of his best writing. The much maligned early ''**Calamiterror**'' has at times an overstated rhetoricalness, but just beneath that surface we can find instances of a predominant muscular plain side reminiscent of early Auden. . . . ''**Calamiterror**'' is more interesting than successful, but it enabled Barker to develop the quite different public voice of ''**The True Confession of George Barker**''. The first book of this is Barker's best poem, yet it was excluded from the 1957 *Collected Poems* at the request of Faber & Faber, an error rectified by the inclusion of both books in this edition. The poem is written in the stanza of Francois Villon's ''The Testament'', which enables Barker to find a persona part true, part fiction. The strict stanza form focuses Barker's talents, holds his rhetorical tendency in check and forces him to speak through the form as a frame the rhymes of which are a test of his invention. Byron's best poem ''Don Juan'' works in a similar way, mixing the high and low styles, the courtly formal tone and demotic speech, the battle between the spirit and emotions within the central protagonist. Both poems succeed by setting up a formal pattern of tone and departing from it for specific local effect. Both authors are men with as wide experience of life as of learning, but possibly happier in the company of men of the world than cloistered thinkers. The verse form of both poems reads fast no matter how the reader tries to slow it down, moving back and forth between ideal, even divine, love and sexual. . . . One point which has continually confounded Barker's critics is his ability in the space of a single poem to be first serious on large and sober themes such as death, love, God, etc., and then immediately mischievously humorous and irreverent too. He is equally intensely serious *and* humorous, one minute calling Villon ''frog'', ''dirty dog, / As one barker to another'' and the next switching tone to that of a fine love lyric. . . . Book One quite overshadows Book Two published fourteen years later in 1964, which to my mind is a more subdued performance altogether, not seeking to exploit the tensions developed in Book One.

But earlier in 1954 Barker had already published another long poem **''Goodman Jacksin and the Angel''** in which a tightly controlled stanza again caught that balance between the formal and demotic tones. The poem is a mock-bucolic dialogue of alternate dramatic speeches (reminiscent perhaps of the situation of Louis MacNeice's ''Eclogue by a Five-barred Gate'') between an Angel and Jacksin, an everyman figure plucked from a Medieval morality play. The language is ratiocinative and unforgettable, at once formal and conversational. . . . My look at the longer poems should not deflect us from noticing Barker's lyric poems which range from intellectual argufying to love lyrics proper. **''Summer Song I''** has attracted censure and praise for its flamboyance, to me it has always worked. . . .

There are also the lyrics within **''The True Confession of George Barker''**, the songs from the verse play *The Seraphina,* or *The Golden Chains,* a book length sequence of 104 interrelated eight line poems playing subtle variations on ballad metre. Some of Barker's best lyric writing is to be found in his books of the 1970s, such as **''Morning in Norfolk''** or the second of **''III Poems Written in Surrey''** from *Poems of Places and People.* . . . *In Memory of David Archer* and *Villa Stellar* are written in an altogether freer verse style, breaking the dominant hold of metre in his work. . . . *Dialogues, etc.,* which appeared between these two books, contains the ballad sequence **''Dialogues of Gog and Magog''** which in its rhythmic tautness provides us with the antithesis of Barker's high rhetorical style. . . . So Barker has a range of styles. But it is a mistake to see the rhetorical high style as replaced altogether in the more recent books with a more direct plain approach to language. **''Anno Domini''**, the most recent of the long public poems, has a cyclic structure ending on the opening phrase ''—at a time of bankers / to exercise a little charity'', and returns us to the rhetoric of **''Calamiterror''.** . . . The public generalisations remind us of the early poems of W. H. Auden. I see the two poets as having more things in common than is generally thought: a public sense of moral responsibility towards society, a religious vision, a very wide technical range, a delightfully individual intellectual eclecticism; but most of all, we find in their work the sense of a serious intelligence confronting reality. *The Collected Poems,* then, is a monumental volume providing evidence of Barker's strengths and weaknesses in its 800 plus pages. Even Barker's staunchest admirers do not dispute the unevenness of his writing, but he is also one of those few English poets who need to be read entire for the full range and comprehensiveness of his vision to be properly appreciated. (pp. 73-8)

[George Barker] remains a major figure for me, one of the few living poets in our language whose best work really matters and is sure to endure. This *Collected Poems* makes the proper evaluation of his work possible at last. (p. 79)

Jonathan Barker, ''One Barker to Another,'' in
Agenda, *Vol. 25, No. 2, Summer, 1987, pp. 71-9.*

Mary (Ethel) Barnard

1909-

American poet, nonfiction writer, translator, short story writer, and editor.

Barnard blends elements from Greek history, language, and myth with evocations of her native Pacific Northwest and a feminine perspective to create poems that are admired for their terse style and austere themes. Barnard's first efforts are collected in *Five Young American Poets,* a 1940 anthology that also includes poetry by Randall Jarrell and John Berryman. Much of Barnard's early verse, as well as the volume *A Few Poems* (1952) and several pieces published in various literary magazines, are reprinted in her *Collected Poems* (1979). The conversational tone and scholarly content of *Collected Poems* prompted Sandra McPherson to note: "Fresh seeing, a fidelity to the image, selflessness, wit (and bite, when required), warmth, and intelligence are some of [Barnard's] writing's virtues."

Barnard's recent work, *Time and the White Tigress* (1986), is informed by her anthropological study, *The Mythmakers* (1966). An extended lyric featuring many historical and astronomical references, *Time and the White Tigress* contains ten sections that explore the recording of time and postulate that knowledge is predicated on humanity's ability to formulate scientific theories through the fabrication of myths. Barnard has also received substantial critical acclaim for her translations of the work of the Greek poet Sappho.

(See also *Contemporary Authors,* Vols. 21-22 and *Contemporary Authors Permanent Series, Vol. 2.*)

© *Mary Randlett 1983. Courtesy of Mary Barnard.*

BABETTE DEUTSCH

Miss Barnard hails from Vancouver, Wash., and her poetry [in *Five Young American Poets*] is alive with imagery dictated by her intimate acquaintance with the Northwest coast. This helps to make for an individuality that is less noticeable in the verse of those from more familiar regions. It also accounts for faint echoes of Jeffers in her work, though her early tutor was Pound, and more than one piece exhibits a feminine wit that she could have learned from neither. Hers is the most mature work in the volume, having a lyricism, a clarity, a discernment and a variety not found to the same degree in the verse of her companions. Not all of her poems attain the same distinction, and a few have obvious flaws, but such poems as **"Prometheus Loved Us," "Playroom," "Lethe," "The Rapids," "Provincial," "Fable From the Cayoosh Country"** testify to the freshness of vision and the craftsmanship which she demands of poetry.

Babette Deutsch, "The Younger Generation," in New York Herald Tribune Books, *January 12, 1941, p. 13.*

JANE VAN CLEVE

The Collected Poems is a good mirror of [Mary Barnard's] creative process as I have observed it. First, I think she has a great ability to get inside her subject matter and to invest a poem with "voice." In my opinion, this empathy distinguishes her *Sappho* translation, which has a bite, a worldliness and a humanness at once timeless and contemporary.

Mary is also attracted to a good yarn. Particularly in the *Collected Poems* one sees stories of enchantment and metamorphoses, two ingredients that occur frequently in myth. I can't read a poem like **"The Fitting,"** for example, without feeling the young woman in the hands of her dressmakers is submitting to a much darker tailoring, left ominously unresolved and dangerous. In the poem, **"Ondine,"** Mary has dramatized the mysterious terror of a speaker who has unwittingly stolen from one element to feed another.

Even in her **"Northwest"** poems, where Mary is neither romantic nor heroic in her treatment of landscape, she manages to convey a sense of hidden story in the planks underfoot, the railroad trestle in disuse, or the doorsill buried in "a steep orchard." These poems impress me as both a reader and a writer. . . . As a reader, I'm moved by these poems which trigger in me an intense feeling of recognition.

As a writer, I'm impressed because Mary accomplishes this sense of immediacy by language that can seem generalized, even abstract, like Chinese calligraphy or brushwork. Then, I marvel that this ''aesthetic distance'' can bring the reader up close to an experience. I talked to Mary about this paradox. While she doesn't explain her poetry—ever—, she has acknowledged that she writes about her rivers and meadows in a way that allows readers to see their own rivers and meadows. For this reason, she usually avoids place names or autobiographical information that would limit poems to a specified context. (pp. 109-10)

Finally, I know my friend to be artful, but not artificial. While some writers will count heavily on the exotic image or the loaded adjective, Mary avoids tricks whereby she might manipulate the reader. Particularly she avoids the 'unnecessary.' On one level, her work can seem 'elite,' demanding an intelligence and sensibility from the reader that precludes any compromise of good writing. But on another level I've found her to be democratic. Mary doesn't pepper a text with esoteric references or complex literary allusions. She may use a highly distilled imagery, but this distillation intensifies her communication rather than stymies the reader. Nor is her footing in a poem larger-than-life. I have always been impressed by the presence of a strong personal voice in full charge of a shared experience or insight.

Because this voice is so individualistic, I think Mary's poetry transcends fashions in either the literary establishment or the literary avant-garde. During the Sixties, when other poets were writing political poems, Mary was writing poems like **"The Pleiades,"** which rescues what is beautiful, ageless, and lyrical. This poem is much closer to a piece of music than an editorial. By the same token, during the Seventies, when the women's liberation movement forced a new self-consciousness in female writers, Mary was nursing a parent, looking Death right in the face, and writing terribly honest, unarmored poems like **"Now."** (p. 111)

I consider the appearance of her *Collected Poems* an important literary event because it brings Mary's full voice into play. Readers will be impressed by the originality and the risk-taking Mary reveals in her disciplined but highly dramatic way with language. (p. 112)

> Jane Van Cleve, *"A Personal View of Mary Barnard,"* in Northwest Review, *Vol. XVIII, No. 3, 1980, pp. 105-13.*

JOAN SWIFT

Mary Barnard's *Collected Poems* brings together for the first time highly imagistic and frequently metaphorical work written over the past five decades, including most of the poems in her first collection, *Cool Country* from *Five Young American Poets* (1940), all of the poems in *A Few Poems* (1952), and new uncollected work. (p. 114)

Readers new to Barnard's work—and there must be many— don't know the chronology of the poems. The poet has mixed them all regardless of the time of their composition. I have ambivalent feelings about this arrangement, wanting to know, for instance, the dates of the various poems without having to refer back to earlier publications. On the other hand, ordering the poems without concern for when they appeared in the world gives the book a unity and contour it would not otherwise have had. Each of the seven tailored sections begins with something

young or regained and ends with the lost, with old age and death. And like a single thread through the fabric of the book runs the sense of separation.

The first section opens with two poems so contemporary in subject matter, they might have been written yesterday, although they were first published in 1940. They speak of the kind of separation from the world of achievement women feel because of their gender. In **"Playroom"** the women are children, little girls who sing sadly of ''windows'' and ''lovers.'' They wear their inherited female roles like ''handed-down garments / hanging loosely on small bodies,'' roles which don't really belong to them. **"The Fitting"** shows us a woman being fitted for a gown, the seamstresses binding her tightly, outlining her form, confining her. They could be our mothers, our aunts. ''All women/ these women,'' the poem says. They ''define her body with tape measures,'' breathe ''distortion upon the mirror's reflection.'' The woman being fitted hears the ''knocking of hammers'' outside, most likely wielded by men, ''but her hands will make nothing.'' She is locked in the form for which women—her own kind—are preparing her.

The feminine persona appears in many of the poems later in the book, not only by actual name (**"Persephone,"** **"Cassandra,"** **"Ondine"**), but frequently referred to enigmatically as ''she'' or ''her.'' In **"Inheritance"** she speaks of women who are her own ancestors, cites them by name (Mary Marshall, Mary Noel, Polly Conner, Susan Carroll) and praises them not for any tangible gifts they may have left her but for the pride of womanhood which is hers through them.

But women and their various roles aren't Barnard's primary preoccupation. I find myself, like others before me, delighting in the vivid pictures of the Northwest landscape which she draws with words and in the emotions they evoke. For Mary Barnard is first a poet of the Northwest. (pp. 114-15)

When *Cool Country* appeared, Mary Barnard was in the company of Randall Jarrell and John Berryman, two of the remaining four poets in *Five Young American Poets*. She had already, before she was thirty, won honors for work marked by striking imagery and a style which, although conversational in tone, remained quietly elegant. The *Collected Poems* is evidence that her gifts were durable.

Barnard writes with her eye up close to her object. Even in **"Planks,"** where she can't see—she's taking a walk in deep dusk and it's ''hard . . . to balance in the pit of evening,'' she stays in touch by using her feet, for

> The moment is completed neither
> by fragrance of wild lilac, nor by
> the presence of the darkening river,
> but by the feel of wood underfoot
> and the sound of stepping upon thick planks.

But she also keeps her distance. Barnard apprehends all of nature with a sharp intellect. Paradoxically, though, the mind, even language itself, puts up a barrier separating man from the natural world. (p. 116)

Other separations weave through *Collected Poems.* Isolated from other poets by the distance between her and the east coast where most of them lived, Barnard worked alone almost like a pioneer in a land without tradition or history (**"Provincial I,"** **"Provincial II"**), although a correspondence with Ezra Pound, begun early and continuing until his death, provided important encouragement. (p. 117)

Even in the East, where she spent a number of years both as Curator of the Poetry Collection at the University of Buffalo and as a researcher for Carl Van Doren, the landscape of her native Pacific Northwest in its immensity looms in her poems. Its images separated her from poets whose work was more urban. In **"Encounter In Buffalo"** she finds the countryside "flat, expressionless as the face of a stranger." The railroad embankment is the highest point on the horizon, the freight train itself the only familiar object. (pp. 117-18)

Throughout the book are poems owing their inspiration to Barnard's extensive studies in Greek. Instigated by Pound, these studies resulted in her highly regarded translation of Sappho as well as *The Mythmakers,* a book in which she holds the origins of myths up to a different light. Strong poems such as **"Odysseus Speaking," "Lethe," "Prometheus Loved Us,"** and **"Persephone"** all grew out of her lifelong work in Greek. But for me Barnard is least interesting when she is epigrammatic, as she is in a handful of poems in the middle of the book. Although into at least one she stitches the thread of separation again. In **"Static,"** she is barred from the original beauty of Sappho's poems by a wall of language she must break through:

> whiskered mumble-
> ment of grammarians:
>
> Greek pterodactyls
> and Victorian dodos.
>
> (p. 118)

What I seem to be saying is that Barnard is best writing in a longer line. But seeing this statement so brazenly on the page reminds me that **"Later: Four Fragments,"** a wonderful poem about ageing, is written in very short lines. The fact of the matter is that Mary Barnard is incapable of writing in language unpleasing to the ear, no matter what the line length. In **"A Note On Poetry,"** which served as a foreword to *Cool Country,* she said, "Poets, in their particular field, work with words— not only the meanings of words, but the sounds of words, and this to me is extremely important." Even her earliest published poems were written in conversational cadences rather than meter. And her ear is well nigh faultless. . . . (pp. 118-19)

Joan Swift, "Separations," in Northwest Review, *Vol. XVIII, No. 3, 1980, pp. 114-19.*

SANDRA McPHERSON

Readers looking to discover a new body of fine poetry by an author previously unknown to them may be looking for the *Collected Poems* of Mary Barnard, the translator of Sappho and author of the study *The Mythmakers.* Barnard published her first poem in 1935; as a young woman she was coached by Pound (**"Two Visits"** describes her 1961 and 1964 impressions of him); later she was praised by Williams.

Fresh seeing, a fidelity to the image, selflessness, wit (and bite, when required), warmth, and intelligence are some of her writing's virtues, recalling Williams and Elizabeth Bishop. Yet there is no mistaking Barnard's own sound. She combines the earthiness and isolation of a Pacific Northwest upbringing (her father managed a sawmill) with intellectual excitement derived from her immersion in the classics and her research on myths. . . . A poem on a mountain stands opposite one on Persephone, for this way Barnard can explore both the heights and the underground and can acknowledge a "homesickness" for the "scars of the surface: / furrows, quarries, split wood." Her solitude

and immediacy remind me of the paintings and prose of the Canadian artist, Emily Carr.

Of poetry Barnard says, "To me its most endearing / quality is its unsuitableness." That must be what makes writing so delicious, the nerve to redefine the surf as a wall of falling water for the sea's "defence" or the indulgence of a playful and precise observation. . . . Whether she is writing about an axe or an intimidating visit from an ondine, Barnard's power of attention accomplishes an empathy that twists in us. This captivating volume, beautifully designed and printed, is of literary significance. In 1952 Williams said of a group of her poems, "I am sure they will be remembered. They have a profundity of feeling which reaches the heart." If Barnard's poems are not already in our memories, we are now privileged to have the collection that will put them there. (pp. 249-50)

Sandra McPherson, in a review of "Collected Poems," in The Antioch Review, *Vol. 38, No. 2, Spring, 1980, pp. 249-50.*

VALERIE TRUEBLOOD

In 1940 a book came out that must still bring a dazed parental smile to the faces at New Directions, *Five Young American Poets.* Two of the five were Randall Jarrell and John Berryman, enough editorial prescience for any book, but there was more: Mary Barnard's collection *Cool Country* opened the volume. . . . Her enchanting story **"A Character Must Have a Name"** appeared in the *Yale Review* in 1947; for thirty years a poem or a story of hers could be seen occasionally but she seemed to have become one of those who write something uncategorizable, something people will know exists, perhaps appreciate, but not *want* the way they want a Black Mountain poet or a copy of Laforgue. Writers of this kind are lightly noticed, especially when their output is small or irregular, even when they number Pound and Williams among their admirers.

In 1958 she published *Sappho, A New Translation,* a book I remember coming upon a few years later with delight, and in 1966 her cool-headed *The Mythmakers,* an inquiry into the origin of myth. In it she scrutinized the ideas of the mythologists she called "rhapsodic," who must have found this immensely learned and comical and logical book a torment, and the myths over which not just mythologists but whole suburbs were becoming rhapsodic at that time. From her study she emerged happily acknowledging no time in history or before when anyone, shaman or Greek poet, believed unbelievable things. An example of her touch was the coinage "theo-botany" for the study of plants used in ritual, now called ethnopsychopharmacology I hear.

At last we have her *Collected Poems,* a book of seventy poems of which twenty-nine appeared in the 1940 volume (alas she left out **"Hot Broth"** and **"Chanson Pathetique,"** two of the most personal, and the latter the funniest, of the early poems). These are unaltered and the first striking thing about them is that they anticipate so much of the development of American poetry through the last four decades, sounding truer to the ear of the 80's than the early work of any of the other *Five.* Her gift came to her full-grown it seems. Although a few of the poems depart from her rather terse form and her liking for gradations rather than leaps, the poems are markedly consistent in tone, psychologically poised, untroubled by the urge to experiment. (p. 10)

She loves the wet, austere, green Northwest with its "Mist blown between promontories / . . . / making the grass deep and sweet in all seasons / and the forest heavy," and the rest of the country too but less intimately—seeing it usually from a train, or in the person of a train, such as the freight "knuckling a red sun under its wheels": "With a look deep as the continent, with the casual greeting of those who will meet again, it bestrides the viaduct."

Rain, streams, rivers, pools fill the poems:

> The water whispers in a quick
> flow from under a boulder
> to moisten the thick-standing mint . . .

"Thick-standing mint": this clean, stirring language is everywhere in Barnard's work. It is like Sappho, like Li Po . . . but it is purely, oddly hers: "Bring only flowers / into the invalid's chamber. / Let no squirrel intrude / . . . / Bring humorless flowers," and "My townspeople, my acquaintance, may I / lower you under this river / nose to nose with the salmon?" Who else is writing with this pensive comedy? She reminds me of Doughty (as prose writer) because of her strange combination of weight and lightness—she has his slightly ornery, lonely recalcitrance, and of Henry Green, the writer of a prose like heavy water, the most emotion in the least space. But she is more fully a poet than anybody I've read lately, all of her energies bent on the short, clear, burdened, most hardworking and most effortless-seeming form. A poem of hers is like a pack burro walking on small hooves, carrying a household.

She has a certain criticalness, or acerbity. At the same time she is pathetic in a tearless way, speaking of "handed-down garments" on "small bodies," or a trestle "fallen into disuse." She is at home with a vocabulary of pathos banished by the Imagists before she ever began: "harvest," "darkening kitchens," "lowland pastures," "forever" are words we aren't used to. It is a complex matter because in the thirties when many of these poems were written there was less sentiment in "pasture," "thicket," "covert," "merry." But whatever the conditions of its origin, under her severe restraints this language is not only fresh for a new generation but it sounds downright newfangled. . . .

Barnard's [work] is irenics, the language of peace. Sandra McPherson noted a "rebelliousness in fine-point" [see excerpt above] in these poems and it is true they are never complacent. But Wilde said that "the note of the perfect personality is not rebellion, but peace," and that in utopia the personality "will never argue or dispute. It will not prove things. It will know everything." When I read Mary Barnard's poems I think, "Dispute would be squalid. Proof would be redundant. Here's the world and this is how the eye of knowledge regards it." Her *Collected Poems* are an event in publishing. (p. 11)

> *Valerie Trueblood, in a review of "Collected Poems,"*
> *in* The American Poetry Review, *Vol. 9, No. 6, November-December, 1980, pp. 10-11.*

ROLAND FLINT

Mary Barnard's previous writing, which W. S. Merwin has called "one of the inadequately acknowledged treasures of our time," includes poems, essays and translations, seven books in all. In her new book [*Time and the White Tigress*], Barnard explores the ways people throughout history have made and used myths to describe and understand the passage of time. At its center the poem is astronomical, a meditation on how the moon, stars and the sun, in their relation to time, have been variously understood in different cultures.

Though the author describes this "not as a work of scholarship, but as a work of imagination," it displays considerable learning, and what appears to be an easy familiarity with astronomical scholarship, historical and modern. It is likable as an audaciously strange work, most successful when most figurative and lyrical. The poem is divided into 10 "fyttes," or divisions. . . . (p. 8)

[*Time and the White Tigress*] more often goes right than wrong, as Barnard's flexible five-beat line and rigorous, plain language keep the poem remarkably fresh and alive, no matter how complicated the material.

One must add, though, that the 13 pages of explanatory notes and illustrative drawings point up a problem: In its treatment of the subject, the poem may be too embroidered (or elementary) for astronomers and too dependent on information in and outside the text for the nonspecialist.

To readers like Merwin, already devoted to Mary Barnard, for her previous poems and essays and for her splendid translations of Sappho, this volume (winner of the Western States Book Award for Poetry) will be an interesting new departure by a talent known for diversity, range and large, general powers. (p. 9)

> *Roland Flint, "Intimations of the Infinite," in* Book World—The Washington Post, *August 31, 1986, pp. 8-9.*

ROBERT McDOWELL

[Mary Barnard's *Time and the White Tigress*], nearly nine hundred lines, is divided into ten *fyttes* (from the German *fitze*, a skein of yarn), or cantos, and explores the ageless stories Man has invented to explain his dubious relationship with Time and the Heavens.

"Why should we cease to make myths?" Barnard asks more than once. Her answer is to retell, from our contemporary, clinical viewpoint, the astronomical speculations of Dante, Mohammed, the Mayas, Greeks, Romans, Celts, Pliny, and Yeats. As she explains in her notes following the poem, these excerpts concerning "the ancient sky-watchers" are exceptions to her method, which is to limit herself "to descriptions of phenomena visible to the naked eye." Thus the history of Man becomes the history of our endless efforts to reduce celestial progressions to miniatures.

> Nothing persists in the face of time and its flux
> like the cultural off-shoots of time—calendar customs.

Our history becomes the history of counting.

This is a didactic book, but its lecture is delightful. Interweaving the stuff of myth ("Here is the calendar-priest with his stake and his string") with the stuff of science ("Eclipses . . . occur on the lunar nodes"), Barnard infuses this popular, though often debased, discussion with a considered sense of history. This is the difficult seal the discriminating reader must discover and decode before making a commitment to such a book. Its impression is nowhere more evident than in the restraint Barnard exercises when breaking her myths and tales with the periodic passages of observed natural phenomena. These prosaic intervals do not weigh the poem down; merely functional, they perform their function then disappear, bridging us into the next mythic progression.

In bestowing the 1986 Western States Book Award on *Time and the White Tigress,* the jury panel noted its example "of a time-honored but recently little-practiced genre, the essay-in-verse." This somewhat misrepresents the book, but I will not long digress here to prove it. The essay-in-verse is still the dominant American poem, though the New Formalism, and the resurgence of narrative, especially, have significantly eroded its sea wall. The typical lyric poet who is driven to try something new almost always ends by writing meditations or essays-in-verse. As the lyric wanes, so will the essay-in-verse, and that is our current condition.

Our awareness of the unfortunate progression of singing to explaining has long been with us. Recently, some have discovered storytelling as a fecund alternative. Mary Barnard, who has lived long enough never to have forgotten it, yokes her lyric and didactic flourishes to the engine of myths and tales that drives the book. Would that more practitioners of the essay-in-verse could do the same. "Why should we cease to make myths?" They help us pass the time, and they make us feel more alive:

> we all know about Stonehenge, and mainly
> we know we know nothing; and having said that,
> we all leap in and start guessing. Why not?

Why not, indeed. (pp. 678-79)

> *Robert McDowell, "New Schools & Late Discoveries," in* The Hudson Review, *Vol. XXXIX, No. 4, Winter, 1987, pp. 673-89.*

EMILY GROSHOLZ

Mary Barnard published a volume of essays on early astronomical systems (*The Mythmakers*) 20 years before distilling her research in the poems of *Time and the White Tigress.* . . .

The 10 sections of Ms. Barnard's book treat common themes in astronomical systems of the north temperate zone—Babylonian and Egyptian, Greek and Roman, Chinese, Mayan and Islamic. The 60 pages of poems, with handsome linocuts by Anita Bigelow, are supplemented by almost 20 pages of notes. The notes are a useful ornament, not an intrusion. They explain that people have seen the "sphere of the fixed stars" divided by great circles—in which the Earth and the celestial bodies, including the visible Milky Way, all move and which have been used to explain the seasons and the changing position of sunrise on the horizon; that, for settled tribes, reliably indicates solstice and equinox. In a sky thus ordered, constellations precipitate like crystals—the Great Bear, which never sets around the fixed point of the North Pole; the zodiac, which populates the ecliptic plane, spinning backward through its houses.

Ms. Barnard also provides a great deal of information in her poems, but her explanations of how customs and calendars, mythology and mathematics, arise in relation to stargazing are not in the least prosaic. On every page her habitual iambic pentameter, slightly roughened for variety's sake, builds to passages of great lyrical purity. . . .

Human ritual behavior is the heart of our sociability, in which we affirm our loves, limit our capacity for destruction and re-create the forms of common life. Ms. Barnard reveals how thoroughly ritual has always depended on astronomical ar-rangements of the world. . . . Her depiction of archaic astronomy as the orderly matrix of ritual is passionately compelling.

Yet she never lets us forget how arcane and impersonal a study astronomy is. Our ancestors were not studying false objects, gods and goddesses, the stars, or really any objects at all. They were discovering and inventing systemic patterns, orientations and rangings that cannot be seen but only inferred. . . . The principles of order brought to life in Ms. Barnard's book are at once highly abstract and of the greatest human import, and this must account for the warmth and drama of her wholly impersonal style. (p. 22)

> *Emily Grosholz, "The Importance of Being Learned," in* The New York Times Book Review, *January 4, 1987, pp. 22, 24.*

SANDRA M. GILBERT

[Mary Barnard's] *Time and the White Tigress,* winner of the 1986 Western States Book Award for Poetry, is no less than an attempt to reconstruct the origins of the very idea of time. Best known for her splendid translations of Sappho (1958), Barnard is also the author of many volumes of poetry as well as a prose work, *The Mythmakers* (1966), on which the ten "fyttes" or cantos of *Time and the White Tigress* are based. But although Barnard has carefully annotated her verse history of time-keeping with references to *The Mythmakers* as well as to ancient star charts and other sources, the work seems to me—luckily for readers (like myself) who are untaught in astronomy—to stand quite well on its own.

Discursive, meditative, often deliberately prosaic, *Time and the White Tigress* is an extraordinary book: a kind of plain-spoken scripture, it is not only a chronology of the chronological but also an analysis of the logic that abstracts principles of change from the changing skies. Ranging from culture to culture, Barnard . . . notes that her sky-watchers' first observation is of the heavenly Twins, the constellation of brothers who break "the year into halves" and whose "legends are beyond counting." From this primordial division, she shows, time, with inexorable logic, falls into quarters, into seasons, into calendars, festivals, eclipses, day-labors, night-watches, millennia: history unfolds, can be marked, named, dated.

In many ways, Barnard's revisionary account of origins recalls comparable modernist efforts—D. H. Lawrence's *Apocalypse,* for instance, or H. D.'s *Trilogy,* both of which seek to reconstitute the past by recovering what Lawrence called "the pagan manner of thought" and what H. D. defined as "ancient wisdom." In addition, Barnard's speculations about time resemble T. S. Eliot's meditations in *Four Quartets*—the passage in "Burnt Norton," for example, on "the still point of the turning world.". . . Yet because Barnard is for the most part far less lyrical than Lawrence, H. D., or Eliot, her text makes a curious effect: its tough understatement, its almost willful flatness, gives it an uncanny authority, what I suppose philosophers might call a special "truth status." As we read we feel not, "This is how it *might* have happened" (as we feel when reading Lawrence or H. D.), but, "Yes, this is how it *did* happen."

At the same time, however, Barnard's work seems to be rooted in a mythology that is at least quasi-feminist. Her **"Ninth Fytte: La Donna"** draws on Robert Graves's *The White Goddess* to eulogize the lady of heaven, the moon who is "for the most part" a woman, and her book is specifically dedicated to female sky-watchers, "to the memory of three women astronomers, Maria Mitchell, Maud W. Makemson, Jessie M. Short."

Barnard's reimagining of genesis, moreover, self-consciously elaborates a matriarchal supreme fiction:

> We are following here the spoor
> of a White Tigress who prowled
> Time's hinterlands once
> in the age of Dragons.
> Her teats, dripping a moon-milk,
> suckled the Twins. The savor,
> still on our tongues, is fading.
>
> Here, a pug-mark in the path.
> There, bent grass where she crouched.
> From this I construct a tigress?
>
> A mythical one?
> Perhaps. Why
> should we cease to make myths?

If myths have the coherence and clarity of Barnard's fine verse-essay, why indeed should we cease to make them? Through such visions the pre-history of history begins to become intelligible. (pp. 109-11)

> *Sandra M. Gilbert, in a review of "Time and the White Tigress," in* Poetry, *Vol. CL, No. 2, May, 1987, pp. 109-11.*

Jorge Luis Borges

1899-1986

(Also wrote with Adolfo Bioy Casares under joint pseudonyms of B. Lynch Davis, H[onorio] Bustos Domecq, and B. Suarez Lynch) Argentinian short story writer, essayist, poet, translator, critic, biographer, travel writer, novelist, and scriptwriter.

Considered among the foremost literary figures writing in Spanish, Borges is best known for his esoteric short stories in which he blended fantasy and realism to address complex philosophical problems. Involving such thematic motifs as time, infinity, identity, and memory, Borges's stories combine elements of fiction and personal essay in hybrid forms that resist classification. His prose works were commended by André Maurois for "their wonderful intelligence, their wealth of invention, and their tight, almost mathematical, style." Making minimal use of plot and characterization, Borges employed paradox and oxymoron to combine such seemingly contradictory concepts as universality and particularity, illusion and reality. Occasionally faulted by critics for his refusal to address social and political issues, Borges maintained: "I have no message. I am neither a thinker nor a moralist, but simply a man of letters who turns his own perplexities and that respected system of perplexities we call philosophy into the forms of literature."

The son of a lawyer, educator, translator, and writer who encouraged the natural talents of his children, Borges acquainted himself with a wide range of world literature, particularly British and American classics, at an early age. When the Borges family became stranded in Switzerland in 1914 by the advent of World War I, Borges enrolled at the Collège de Genève and received his degree in 1918. The following year, Borges traveled to Spain, where he published critical reviews, essays, and poetry and associated with the Ultraístas, an avant-garde literary group whose works appeared in the journal *Ultra*. Although widely considered a Spanish variant of German expressionism, Ultraísm also drew from such movements as Dadaism and Imagism. Rejecting the traditional rhymed verse and baroque ornamentalism common to nineteenth-century Spanish poetry, the Ultraístas championed metaphor as a predominant mode of expression and strove in their poetry to transcend boundaries of time and space.

Borges returned to Buenos Aires in 1921 and helped launch several noted Argentinian publications, including the literary magazine *Prisma* and the journal *Proa*. In his first collection of poetry, *Fervor de Buenos Aires* (1923; revised, 1969), Borges utilized Ultraíst concepts to portray colorful individuals and events in Buenos Aires. His next volume, *Luna de enfrente* (1925), contains confessional and love poetry as well as pieces that anticipate his later concern with such topics as time and memory. *Cuaderno San Martín* (1929) consists largely of tributes to deceased poets, among them Francisco López Merino, Borges's friend and associate, who committed suicide.

Borges was also an acclaimed editor and essayist throughout his career. His essays, like his fiction, often combine elements from several genres and are considered nearly indistinguishable in form from his later short stories. Borges's best-regarded

© Lutfi Özkök

volumes of early essays include *Inquisiciónes* (1925), *El tamaño de mi esperanza* (1927), and *El idioma de los argentinos* (1928). Borges won praise for "The Language of the Argentines," the title essay of the third collection, in which he urges writers to reject the artificial stylization common to Latin American letters at the turn of the century. *Discusión* (1932), a collection of film reviews and articles on metaphysical and aesthetic topics, includes the noted essay "Narrative Art and Magic," in which Borges defends the capacity of fantasy literature to address realistic concerns. *Historia de la eternidad* (1936), a volume exploring humanity's concepts of eternity from ancient times to the present, includes "The Approach to al-Mu'tasim," Borges's review of an imaginary detective novel. By critiquing a nonexistent work, Borges proposes that content exists in the reader's imagination and, according to John Sturrock, "that the 'real' aspect of books, their physical presence, does not matter."

Borges's early short stories evolve in style and subject from his essays and are often interpreted as parables illustrating the potentialities and limitations of creative art. His first published story, "Pierre Menard, Author of the Quixote," depicts a modern writer who independently composes portions of a text corresponding precisely to Miguel de Cervantes's *Don Quixote*. According to Katherine Singer Kovács, the contemporary author has created "a new and more profound work, one of particular relevance to his own historical period and life." Borges's first short story collection, *Historia universal de la infamia* (1935; *A Universal History of Infamy*), purports to present a fictional felon's encyclopedia of criminals drawn from history. The translated edition includes "The South," a semi-autobiographical story in which a refined, troubled librarian, desiring the chivalric life of the Argentinian gaucho, becomes involved in a fatal knife fight which may exist only in his imagination. The title piece of *El jardín de senderos que se bifurcan* (1941; *The Garden of Forking Paths*), which Borges described as "a detective story," links two apparently unrelated crimes, one committed in the present, the other in the past. Max Byrd observed that "both crimes blend in a single moment; the solution of one simultaneously resolves the other." This collection also includes Borges's acclaimed story "The Library of Babel," in which a symmetrically arranged library, representing humanity's rational view of the universe, is revealed to contain illegible books.

Borges first attracted attention in the United States and Europe in 1961, when he shared the Prix Formentor, an international editors' prize, with dramatist Samuel Beckett. *Ficciónes, 1935-1944* (1944; *Ficciones*), together with *Labyrinths: Selected Stories and Other Writings* (1962), an English-language anthology of Borges's early stories, introduced his fiction to British and North American readers. *Ficciones*, generally regarded as Borges's most significant collection, contains his widely analyzed tale "Tlön, Uqbar, Orbis Tertius." This story combines fiction with such elements of the essay as footnotes and a postscript to relate the efforts of a group of men to create an invented world free of linear concepts of space and time. As their ideas cohere, reality intrudes, and objects from their imaginary realm begin to appear. The conflict between illusion and reality is again explored in "The Circular Ruins." The narrator of this story dreams that he has created a son but ultimately realizes "in terror, in humiliation, . . . that he, too, was an appearance, that someone else was dreaming him."

The enlarged English edition of *El aleph* (1949), entitled *The Aleph and Other Stories, 1933-1969* (1970), consists of stories and essays from various periods in Borges's career. This work is the first of several acclaimed collaborations between Borges and translator Norman Thomas di Giovanni aimed at producing creative translations that read as though the original pieces were written in English. The "aleph" of the title story is a stone representing the equivalent of all visual images of the universe, containing all points of space, and indicative of humanity's limitless but not entirely lucid perspectives and possibilities. The aleph's opposite, described in "The Zahir," is a magical coin universally representative of every particular coin, real or imagined. According to Diana Armas Wilson, the zahir differs from the universal aleph in that it signifies "a local and particular perspective that a man uses to order reality—any belief, scheme, or dogma that saves him from chaos." Borges's concern with the simultaneity of such opposites as universality and particularity is again evident in the title story of his next collection, *La muerte y la brújula* (1951; *Death and the Compass*). In this work, a detective relies on the extreme rationalism associated with his profession to track down a criminal. He is unaware, however, that the fugitive, true to his role as an illogical, antithetical double, has planned his own death from the beginning. Carter Wheelock observed that "although the victory of one is necessary, it is nevertheless deplorable because the victor is only a perspective, a partial image of reality."

In 1946, after Juan Domingo Perón became dictator of Argentina, Borges was demoted from assistant librarian to poultry inspector for having signed a manifesto denouncing Perón. Following the fall of Perón in 1955, Borges was named director of the National Library of Argentina and was elected to the Argentinian Academy of Letters; in 1956, he received his country's national prize for literature. When his eyesight declined in the late 1950s due to a hereditary disease, Borges limited his literary output to poetry, lectures, and translations. Keith Botsford deemed Borges's later poems "among the most skillful and immaculate in Spanish. Strict in their rules and sober in their imagery, gentle in tone, recollected in tranquility, they are elegiac, formal, symmetrical." *El hacedor* (1960; *Dreamtigers*), a collection of brief poems, quotations, and parables, uses the tiger as an ambivalent symbol of unnatural evil and natural change. In the title poem of *Elogio de la sombra* (1969; *In Praise of Darkness*), Borges proposes the paradoxical notion that old age and blindness may signify deep happiness because of the imminence of death. Dualities involving physical blindness and spiritual sight also pervade *El oro de los tigres* (1972; *The Gold of the Tigers: Selected Later Poems*).

Borges returned to writing fiction in the 1970s, preferring a straightforward, realistic approach to the elaborate fantasies and literary games of his earliest work. Edward G. Warner described the stories in *El informe de Brodie* (1970; *Doctor Brodie's Report*) as "mostly plain, unadorned tales—some harsh, some tender—of love, hate, and the inevitability of death." *El libro de arena* (1975; *The Book of Sand*), although similar in style, returns to the fantastical themes of Borges's early fiction. This volume includes "The Congress," a long story in which a world congress attempts to incorporate all of humanity's views and ideologies by securing thousands of books. Realizing the arbitrary and conjectural nature of their task, the congress eventually recognizes the need to reject limited, predominating world views and destroys the books, concluding that "every few centuries, the library of Alexandria must be burned down."

Beginning in the 1940s, Borges collaborated under various pseudonyms with his close friend, Adolfo Bioy Casares. The authors completed, among other works, *Seis problemas para don Isidro Parodi* (1942; *Six Problems for Don Isidro Parodi*) and *Cronicas de Bustos Domecq* (1967; *Chronicles of Bustos Domecq*), collections of interrelated short stories parodying Argentinian social figures and customs. Borges's best-regarded later essays, many on literary topics, are included in *Otras inquisiciónes, 1937-1952* (1952; *Other Inquisitions, 1937-1952*), while *Antología personal* (1961; *A Personal Anthology*) and *Borges: A Reader* (1981) showcase selected parables, poems, and essays from throughout his career. *Atlas* (1984) contains Borges's late poems and impressions of his travels in Europe. Borges's last published work, *Seven Nights* (1986), collects his lectures on such topics as Buddhism, the Kabbalah, and blindness.

(See also *CLC*, Vols. 1, 2, 3, 4, 6, 8, 9, 10, 13, 19, 44; *Contemporary Authors*, Vols. 21-24, rev. ed.; *Contemporary Authors New Revision Series*, Vol. 19; and *Dictionary of Literary Biography Yearbook: 1986.*)

THOMAS LASK

The difficulty in dealing with Borges's writings in a review is to convey the style, which is at once characteristic and unmistakable and yet one that avoids easy definition or facile analysis. The elements are not hard to list: magic, fantasy, bookish learning, poetic touches, naturalistic details, intellectual gamesmanship and an irony that toys with all of them. The ingredients are not isolated for study, however. They blend and mingle to make their own composition. . . . Since Borges is a learned man, his [pieces in *The Aleph and Other Stories, 1933-1969*] are packed with references to books and authors and out-of-the-way learning. . . .

But this is not mere cleverness. He has a higher purpose: to entice the hearer to come along with him. Borges is always the storyteller, the fabulist, the magician we remember from our childhood, who stirs some primal urge that lies deep in our consciousness. . . .

Fact and fancy, the real and the imagined, live in easy conjunction. In the title story **"The Aleph,"** a science-fiction machine is placed in the most tawdry and ramshackle of houses, wretched verses are concocted by a would-be poet who analyzes his work with a New Critical gravity better due the Divine Comedy; the story concludes with a brief disquisition on the word "Aleph" as the first letter of the Hebrew alphabet, its place in the Kabbala and its use as symbol in Cantor's mathematics "of transfinite numbers, of which any part is greater than the whole." The reference to Cantor may sound technical, yet the definition has its place in the story. It may not seem as if all the parts go together, but Borges's imagination imposes an order where none exists.

Nothing illustrates his playful ways better than **"Death and the Compass,"** which is, if we can use the term, a metaphysical whodunit. There are real murders, three ultimately, and a couple of real detectives, but the clues, the reasoning and the solution could only have come out of a medieval, occult tome or from a recondite volume in Faust's library.

Somewhere in Borges's experience, the knife-wielding gaucho, the street-corner brawler must have made a weighty impression on him, for they turn up again and again in these stories. . . . They are as much slaves as masters of their codes and courage. In **"The Meeting,"** two men with no reputation as knife fighters stumble into a brawl and find themselves fighting with a skill and adroitness beyond their competence. The knives, it turns out, are older than they are, and some of their past has rubbed off into the metal. . . .

Some of the selections [in *The Aleph and Other Stories*] are only a page or two and appear more as rumination than a fiction, though the author might argue that there is no difference. A few of the stories have appeared in English before in other translations. The new versions are fluent and without taint of foreignisms, though **"The Streetcorner Man"** sounds stagy. There are, however, any number of felicities. Mr. Borges has also supplied a biographical essay that touches on the shaping forces of his career, on his life-long allegiance to books and to the literatures of other cultures, his fascination with foreign languages, including Anglo-Saxon, his education and travels in Europe, his early literary successes and his slowly maturing style. Balanced, ironic, yet without artificial modesty, his memoir leads naturally to the man we find in the fiction.

Thomas Lask, "The Storyteller and Magician," in The New York Times, November 16, 1970, p. 33.

GEOFFREY H. HARTMAN

[*The Aleph and Other Stories*] is devoted mainly to [Borges's] stories, and has a wide chronological range, taking us from 1933 to 1969. But it remains an incomplete gathering, since rights to retranslate some of the most famous pieces (such as "Tlön, Uqbar, Orbis Tertius") could not be obtained. It is irritating to have Borges divided this way by competing anthologies, but it may be a kind of justice since he is, in fact, a scattered Orpheus whose prose-parts lament a fading power. The inventor of the Aleph, a miniaturized replica of all visionary experience, knows that human kind cannot bear much fantasy. The present volume, with its charming **"Autobiographical Essay"** and its chatty comments on the stories, is well adapted to readers who wish to be reminded of great art rather than to experience it. With Borges they can flee from too vivid an enchantment into a little wilderness.

There is an art which, like the sounds of a clavichord, provides a perfect setting for thought and conversation. The art of Borges is generally like that: cool, well-tempered, with a consciously easy pace. . . . Lönnrot, the trapped detective in **"Death and the Compass,"** quietly offers his killer a mystico-mathematical reflection before being shot. What is most human—the "irrelevant texture" of ordinary life—escapes from a ruthless plot by running into such asides. Each story, however, continues to demand its victim despite the intricate delay, the charm of detail.

The humanizing asides are felt even more in the stories about the gauchos of Argentina. Here Borges, a reporter of traditions, weaves his thoughts directly into the narrative. In his unusual blend of ballad bloodiness and familiar essay there is sometimes as much reflection as plot: the brutal knife-fight in **"The Challenge,"** little more than a paragraph long, is swathed in asides. Its naked brevity is relaxed by the narrator's comment on the courage of the gauchos, their exact way of duelling, a canto from the *Inferno, Moby Dick,* and so on. While time comes to a point which is also a knife's point, the story swerves, a mental picaresque, from the pure moment of encounter.

No Borges story is without this pointed moment, this condensation of time; yet it tends to be undercut by a mock-realistic setting or a whimsical narrator. So the microcosmic Aleph is found in the cluttered cellar of a second-rate poet, the unsavory Carlos Argentino Daneri. The only way that Borges can conduct his narrative is, like so many symbolists before him, by viewing ordinary life as a needful distraction from some symbolic purity. His humorous realism—names, dates and nature-motifs formulaically introduced—is a pseudo-realism. Even the gaucho stories, for all their local color, are fantasies—knives *are* magical in them, and the knife-fighter's sense of invulnerability is like the eternity-experience recorded in so many of the "fantastic" stories.

The fatality of form, the humanity of the aside—these are the most obvious pleasures given by Borges. There is, in addition, a wealth of small invention, perfect handling of gradual disclosures, and an elegance that makes life appear sloppy. Mixing, with charming ruthlessness, fantasy and fact, Borges reverses that "decay of lying" which Oscar Wilde (one of his favorite authors) had already deplored.

Beyond all this we feel for the narrator, for *his* quest. He is clearly a man trying to get into his own stories, that is, wishing to discover himself rather than an image. Like the fire-priest in **"The Circular Ruins"** Borges sets out to dream a real man but seems unable to dream of more than an intruder. Thus in a great many stories a stranger or interloper comes onto the scene and is given a predetermined lease on life before being eliminated. This figure, whether person or magical agent, never effects a lasting change: having played out its role, or lived its bit of dream, it is "sacrificed.". . .

Surely, Borges himself, as artist, is that intruder. He comes to art belated—deeply conscious of traditions that both anticipate him and will survive his bluff. He is their victim, a dreamer who finds he is dreamt by a larger than personal symbolism—the formal world of legend and archetype with which he must merge. (p. 5)

This living sacrifice of person to myth, of the individual to magic instrument, haunts Borges and is a source of his peculiar pathos. "I live," he says in **"Borges and Myself,"** "I let myself live so that Borges can weave his tales and poems, and those tales and poems are my justification." We are not far, after all, from Mallarmé's remark that the world was meant to become a book. The symbols that purify us also trap us in the end. Symbolism may be nothing more than the religion of over-cultured men; and Borges—curious bibliophile, ardent comparatist—its perfected priest. (p. 43)

> Geoffrey H. Hartman, "No Story without Its Pointed Moment," in The New York Times Book Review, December 13, 1970, pp. 5, 43.

V. S. PRITCHETT

[Borges's] essays and stories [in *The Aleph and Other Stories, 1933-1969*] are experiments, especially in approach. He is outside his subjects yet succeeds, at a certain point, in smuggling himself in, almost posing as a man trying to be an artist and doubtful of whether life permits that. He is interested in the part of our lives which is a collection of metaphysical and intellectual fictions. To avoid archness or whimsicality is difficult for a writer of this kind; he is on the edge of the hoax and the footnote, which can be tedious, especially in the hands of a scholar. (This can be argued against him.)

But, in the main, his imagination is piercing, and his best coups unnerve. He is very much a bookish Don Quixote who has been down in Montesino's cave: the imagination is not to be meddled with; it has its tragic dignity. In **"The Circular Ruins,"** the narrator dreams that he makes a man who can walk on fire; in the end "he understood he too was an appearance, that someone else was dreaming him." His genius lies in insight. The story is an allegory of life creating itself. . . .

It is impossible to avoid spattering a review of *The Aleph and Other Stories* with literary names. Kafka above all, Poe, Baudelaire, Cervantes have occurred, rightly, to most critics. I have two of my own: Calderon of *La Vida es Sueño* and—when one turns to his manner of address—Mérimée. The latter may sound unlikely—I shall go into that later on. This general name-dropping, usually a sign of critical bewilderment, is justified by Borges's own words: "I have always come to life after coming to books.". . .

[Borges was originally] given to highly imaged prose which had something in common with Tlön, his imaginary language; but gradually his manner has become laconic, plain and hard. Things and facts have to carry extra meaning, and are even given a will ("A stone wants to be a stone"). He has kept to short stories because he wants the intensity and discipline of form; they begin drily and bluntly, then proceed to trap us in a mosaic, and at last burst into short flashes of vision, and in that vision we are to see an instant contain the whole of a life, even the history of the universe. (p. 10)

Borges manages to be in and out of his stories with perfect tact. In one or two, like the superb **"Intruder"** or **"The Dead Man,"** and in the gaucho stories, he is outside, brutally direct. . . . The situations have a singeing irony, but not for irony's sake; they contain uneasy psychological perceptions. In **"The Dead Man,"** a young tough is allowed, to his own surprise, to get the better of his gang leader, even to rise to the height of supplanting him and getting his woman. The gang obey the newcomer and love him—but why? Because he is the winner? Because they are cowards? Or reckless? No, because they have understood that all the time he is as good as dead. He must be loved for his moment. The leader will choose *when* to kill him, and does so. The gaucho stories, mainly of meaningless violence, duels without provocation, are to show that the gaucho

> . . . without realizing it, forged a religion—the hard and blind religion of courage—and that this faith (like all others) has its ethic, its mythology, and its martyrs . . . they rediscovered in their own way the age-old cult of the gods of iron . . . no mere form of vanity but rather an awareness that God may be found in any man.

These remarks come from one of his essaylike passages, for he often makes little distinction between the essay and the tale. And this brings me to my comparison with Mérimée. There are one or two personal similarities—though great differences too—the Anglophile touch, the background of erudition, the linguistic, historical, and archaeological and mystical interest. Mérimée was very much "in life" but a wound to sensibility gave him coolness and detachment. He was caught in the impossible situation of reconciling civilization with the primitive, reality with the unbelievable.

In just two of his tales, "Lokis" and "Vénus d'Ille," he is concerned with the unconscious. It is true that the cold and formal Mérimée toys with his metaphysical anxieties and usually has no deeper interest in human nature than its customs. This was partly defensive. He was irreligious and would have been incapable of seeing man in the act of creating God or himself, as Borges has. But there is a common love of hoaxing pedantry and the common approach of the misleading, yet documented essay to the tale in hand. Both writers are elaborate pretenders: the terrible story of "Lokis" affects to arise out of a serious study of the Lithuanian language! Both writers know that to describe the violent or the fantastic, one must begin by playing down and even by appearing brief and perfunctory. And, though with very different intentions, both writers have the art of enhancing the effects of the unbearable, the sinister, and the ineluctable, by presenting it in the elaborate terms of "the record."

The difference is that for Mérimée the record is closed and final: *Colomba* is the last word on the vendetta versus civilization; for Borges, the record is open and continuous, memory feeding on memory, life is a corridor of reflecting mirrors. We are all shadows of a dream. For Mérimée truth lay in documentation; in Borges, we find the balance between life and literature redressed. It has been easy to forget, in our time, that literature has roots in literature, perhaps its most nourishing ones. How flat *Don Quixote* would have been as topical realism. (pp. 10, 12)

> *V. S. Pritchett, "Don Borges," in* The New York Review of Books, *Vol. XVI, No. 1, January 28, 1971, pp. 10, 12.*

RONALD CHRIST

Dutton has issued [*The Aleph and Other Stories, 1933-1969*], the second volume in its projected series of Borges' writings; and, as they appear, these books will inevitably have a settling and solidifying effect on the prestige of Borges among English-speaking readers: these books will give weight and substance to the echo of his genius.

Not because of their bulk alone, though, but because these books come to us with an authority and a grace begotten of one of the most extraordinary literary collaborations of our time.... [Working] in daily sessions, in close collaboration with his personally chosen translator, Norman Thomas di Giovanni, in the familiar atmosphere of his native Buenos Aires, Borges is re-creating his own work in English. In other words, the books in this series are not merely translations but original texts, different from the previous Spanish ones, but fully their equal in sanction, dignity and intention; these books are the product, for the most part, not of the double Borges we know from his famous autobiographical piece, **"Borges y yo"** but the achievement of three minds: the Borges who wrote the Spanish text in the past, the Borges, fully conversant with English and in love with its "verbal music," who collaborates in the re-thinking of "every sentence in English words," and the di Giovanni, nominal translator, who ... cooperated in making "these stories read as though they had been written in English." This method, as the co-workers say, may be new, and if the description sounds like something from Borges' fiction, that's good, because the scheme he has discovered for rendering his work into English is thoroughly Borgesian, even down to the preface to this present volume which he and di Giovanni conclude with both their initials but commence with a sentence insinuated around shifting pronouns: "Since *my* fame rests on *my* short stories, it is only natural that *we* should want to include a selection of them among the several volumes of *my* writings *we* are translating...." (Emphasis added.) The aesthetic, psychological and critical implications of those pronouns are dizzying, and, of course playful: pure Borges; and they do compress a persistent theme in the man's work—meaninglessness of self—as they support his statement in the charming **"Autobiographical Essay"** (written directly in English with di Giovanni) that collaboration requires "a joint abandoning of the ego, of vanity, and maybe of common politeness."

The occasion of this volume, then—this review too—and its "chief justification," as the preface knowingly states, "is the translation itself": after all, the main stories in [*The Aleph and Other Stories*] have long been available in other translations, and this translation is definitive, superseding all others, which in the future can only exist as more or less perceptive commentaries on it. The simple ease, the quiet truth of this prose as it embodies intuitions and perceptions both subtle and inevitable will win new readers to Borges immediately and recall old ones. Among the latter, of course, there will be some who demur: **"Borges and Myself"** is now preferred to the better known **"Borges and I"** and the much annotated "unanimous night" from **"The Circular Ruins"** is replaced by "encompassing night," perhaps in keeping with the principle of Borges' later style which prohibits any word from erupting out of the context. But readers, old or new, who take time to compare specific passages, the opening sentence from **"Borges and Myself,"** for example ("It's to the other man, to Borges, that things happen"), with other translations ("The other one, the one called Borges, is the one things happen to"...) will find that the present version is far better English and much more suitable to the deceptively unassuming, patiently lucid, untir-

ingly calm and gentle tone which *is* Borges—the Borges you hear in your head long after the "methodically strange" stories have become familiar. (pp. 282-83)

On the other hand, the ultimate occasion of this collection is not the translation at all but the reintroduction into English of nine important narratives and the introduction of eleven lesser works, along with fascinating commentaries and an autobiographical sketch by the man who is certainly the most important writer of short fiction today. On this pretext alone the volume stands justified.... [*The Aleph and Other Stories*] serves both as a confirmation of Borges' special genius—evidenced in the first and title story ["**The Aleph**"] about a point in space (underneath a flight of cellar stairs in Buenos Aires) that contains all other points in space—and a brief history of his development—embodied in the succeeding stories. These are arranged in chronological order: the stagey **"Streetcorner Man,"** written in 1933 and telling about the virtually motiveless knifing of a hoodlum in the slums of Buenos Aires; **"The Approach to al-Mu'tasim,"** published in 1935 as a review of a nonexistent detective novel but so true in its fiction that it caused one friend of Borges to order the fake book from England; on to the metaphysical stories of "patterns in time and space" from his great period in the '40s and early '50s; and finally a spare narration called **"Rosendo's Tale,"** published in 1969 as the retelling of **"Streetcorner Man"** from an opposing point of view. The full cycle of Borges' narrative art is exhibited.... [In] furnishing those early and late tales which have never appeared in English in book form before—in furnishing *all* these stories in a translation of such quality and sovereignty—*The Aleph and Other Stories* offers a perspective for the stories on which Borges knows his fame rests, and is accordingly the most useful introduction in English to Borges' fiction. (pp. 283-84)

Ronald Christ, "Borges Translated," in The Nation, *New York, Vol. 212, No. 9, March 1, 1971, pp. 282-84.*

PETER WITONSKI

In recent years the books of Jorge Amado, García Márquez, Pablo Neruda, Julio Cortázar, and, above all, Don Jorge Louis Borges have been published [in the United States].

Unfortunately, the South American works to which all the international kudos have gone have been the products of writers belonging to the primitive Left, writers of books suffused with an eloquent but tedious hatred of the Yanqui gringo....

But there is one notable exception, one writer who refuses to follow the leftist line of his brothers and even revels in his love of America and his passionate hatred of the Left. Most interestingly, this is the writer most highly regarded by his peers throughout Latin America for his genius as a poet, storyteller, and critic—Jorge Luis Borges of Argentina. Borges is also the most widely read South American writer in America—and the rest of the world for that matter. His poems and *ficciones* [in *A Universal History of Infamy*] have been brilliantly translated into English by Borges himself....

Borges cannot be pigeonholed.... [His] literary work defies easy categorization. In literature as in politics, Borges is his own man. The Franco-Iberian influence, which dominates the work of most other South American writers (who have looked to France and Spain for spiritual food), is nowhere to be found in his work. Unlike other Argentinians of his class and generation, his first love was English literature. As a child he learned English from his English grandmother, and precociously devoured the many English books in his father's library. The writers he seems most to enjoy citing are English writers, from the anonymous Anglo-Saxon author of *Beowulf* . . . to Tennyson, Andrew Lang, Walt Whitman, and G. K. Chesterton. In truth, of course, he is the universal bookman. (p. 272)

Borges' grasp of world literature is one of the fundamental elements of his art, but he is no mere literary cosmopolite, divorced from the culture of his native Argentina. On the contrary, he is profoundly Argentinian, and his many references to the literature and culture of his native land may be missed by the reader unfamiliar with Argentina. Borges the bookman is drawn to the literature of the world, which he enjoys citing with mock-pedantry; but Borges the man is drawn to what he has called "the implacable pampas" of Argentina. The so-called "gaucho poetry" that is personified in José Hernández' epic *Martin Fierro*—perhaps the most Argentinian of all Argentinian literary works—continues to inspire Borges as it does no other contemporary Argentinian writer. His many references to the knife-play and philosophy of the gaucho serve to emphasize this point.

In his autobiographical story, **"The South,"** a bookish librarian leaves his post shortly after spending some time in a sanitarium, to recover his roots at his family's ranch in the pampas, only to find himself caught up in a dagger fight with a gaucho. (pp. 272, 274)

It was while convalescing from the severe illness reflected in **"The South"** that Borges began writing the short *ficciones* that make up *A Universal History of Infamy,* originally published in 1935. The collection marked the beginning of Borges' unique method of storytelling. These *ficciones* are not typical short stories. They are often based on real events, and vary in length from one or two paragraphs to a few pages. As his eyesight began to fail, the *ficciones* became shorter and shorter, and in them Borges has tried to compress whole novels, vast ranges of emotion and experience.

In *A Universal History of Infamy* we have a collection of Borges' favorite character types, the punks and toughs of this world, whose meaningless lives derive some meaning from their deaths. In **"The Street-Corner Man,"** the center-piece of the work, we are told the story of a young hoodlum known as The Butcher, who, on the night of his greatest achievement, having established himself as the toughest knifeman in Vila Santa Rita, is knifed to death, stripped of every cent and trinket he possessed, and tossed out a window. *A Universal History of Infamy* is Borges at his best, and I can think of no more diverting reading than that. (p. 274)

> *Peter Witonski, "Borges of the Pampas," in* National Review, *New York, Vol. XXV, No. 9, March 2, 1973, pp. 272, 274.*

ROBERT NYE

[Borges's] subject is fiction itself. The starting point for each story in *A Universal History of Infamy,* for example, is another story. The first piece, **"The Dread Redeemer Lazarus Morrell,"** about a man who frees slaves and then sells them in the American South, derives from something he found in Mark Twain's *Life on the Mississippi.* The second, **"Tom Castro, the Implausible Imposter,"** is built upon materials discovered under the subject of the Tichborne Claimant in the eleventh edition of the *Encyclopaedia Britannica.* Other stories come out of his reading in histories of Persia and piracy, a biography of Billy the Kid, a study of the gangs of New York, a collection of ancient Japanese folktales, and so on.

The intricacy of his imagination is such that his work always hints at offering little less than an alternative reality: a world of fiction running parallel to the real world, standing in relation to it much as a mirror might stand if it had the power to improve and make sense of the chaos of images looking into it. Man, in Borges's rendering, is this chaos of images. His best work is usually about such parallels, such mirrors, and the biggest question posed by it is whether we make them or they make us.

You can see why he appeals mostly to his fellow writers. *A Universal History of Infamy* . . . will not add greatly even to that reputation, and it's interesting to note that Borges himself does not think highly of it. "All the stories in that book were kind of jokes or fakes," he declared in a recent interview with Richard Burgin. "The irresponsible game of a shy young man who dared not write stories and so amused himself by falsifying and distorting (without any aesthetic justification whatever) the tales of others," he says in the preface to the new edition.

The things are certainly very flimsy, and overwritten in a breathy adjectival prose that reminds me of Oscar Wilde at his worst. One straightforward story, **"Streetcorner Man,"** about hoodlums, stands out as a complete failure. A final section, **"Etcetera,"** is more typical of what is worthwhile in Borges. This consists of very short tales of magic, parables in which human villainy is thwarted by something beyond.

> *Robert Nye, "Intricate Imagination," in* The Guardian, *Vol. 109, No. 5, August 4, 1973, p. 22.*

J. D. O'HARA

The highly underrated Honorio Bustos Domecq is the author of *Six Problems for don Isidro Parodi* (1942) and is kissing kin to B. Suarez Lynch, with whom he shares a love of the criminal world. Both have another bond: each is a pseudonym employed by Jorge Luis Borges and his lesser known friend and fellow Argentine, novelist Adolfo Bioy-Casares. For many decades now the two men . . . have allowed Bustos Domecq, a quondam reporter for the Buenos Aires Evening News, to bumble his cliche-littered way into the fine arts on occasion; these [*Chronicles of Bustos Domecq*] report the results. . . .

Bustos grapples vigorously with several journalistic styles. His idioms approach accuracy; his allusions are often felicitous; and his sophisticated references have a disarming air of authority. But he is prone to—he is laid prone by—an exuberant style more common to the hot-blooded south than to our chaste north: "Perfectly structured and steered by an expert helmsman, the brotherhood movement would constitute the bedrock of resistance against the lava-like torrent of anarchy."

On this level the *Chronicles* . . . evoke for us northerners a Perelman among art critics, and they are worth reading for the giggles alone. But Bioy-Casares and Borges share a skeptical interest in literacy and aesthetic matters, an interest elaborately amused and deeply suspicious of all reasoning about the arts. . . . As a result, their fall-guy Bustos encounters artists and art forms comic in themselves, and meaningfully so. One would like to shovel in heaps of instances. One cannot.

The instance already notorious among us is that in which Bustos reports the decision of the World Congress of Historians that "History is an act of faith." The Congress supported this position, you will recall (the story was picked up by the *New York Times*), with such evidence as the seven birthplaces of Homer, the dual nationality of Columbus, and the winning of the battle of Jutland by both sides. This revelation of history as chauvinism caused a flurry of unamused dismay among historians [in the United States], in part because they believed the report and in part because, as laymen have recognized for years, history *is* an act of faith, a belief in things not seen. That the American Revolution was opposed less by the British than by the apathy and hostility of the Americans and that ten Frenchmen joined the Gestapo for every one who joined the Resistance—these may be facts, but they are unlikely ever to be history. The historian is detached, perhaps, but not demented.

This unsettling comedy of skepticism beneath the joking surface pervades many of the pieces on the other arts. Ramon Bonavena sets out to write "a novel of the land, straightforward, with deeply human characters and the usual protest against absentee landowners. . . . I meant to give open-minded testimony about a limited sector of local society." But the limits of his knowledge and the fear of libel persuade him to settle for six volumes describing the north-northeast corner of his writing desk. His fellow among literary critics, Hilario Lambkin Formento, "excluded from his comments all praise and all censure," limiting himself to a closely accurate description of the text. His greatest work is a three-volume criticism of Dante's *Commedia*, in the form of a scrupulously accurate reproduction of the poem. Similarly the poet Hector Urbas wins a poetry contest on the topic "the rose" by submitting a rose. And there are many more. To the casual reader, these may seem simply jokes or, at most, parodies of present artistic notions. But the aesthetic postulates they embody—and their opposites, also embodied—go far toward covering the field; and their slapstick and skeptical presentation will not only amuse you but will open to you a new field of comedy whenever you read reviews of a certain kind.

> J. D. O'Hara, "A Much Needed Void," in Book World-The Washington Post, *April 25, 1976, p. G9.*

PETER HEINEGG

Without the magical name of "Borges" to recommend them, how many of these sketches in this little volume [*Chronicles of Bustos Domecq*] would ever have been translated or reprinted? Surely fewer than half. But, so be it: Borges has earned his celebrity, and readers familiar with his best work (*Ficciones,* say [published in Great Britain as *Fictions*]) will hardly begrudge him a small failure like this. Of course, some of the discredit has to go to the book's coauthor, Borges's old friend, Bioy Casares.

A press release from [the publishers] calls the *Chronicles* a "thoroughly diverting spoof of the critical essay," but Borges and Bioy Casares characterize their book more aptly with the first of their lead quotations: "Every absurdity has now a champion" (Goldsmith). The authors impersonate a fatuous pedant, Honorio Bustos Domecq, who in turn champions a score of absurd movements and demented artists, zanies of a nonexistent avant-garde, with names like Ishmael Querido and Hilario Lambkin Formento. Domecq proclaims the achievements of . . . Federico Juan Carlos Loomis, who labors for years over a

handful of novels, each consisting of a single noun; of Eduardo S. Bradford, who begins a "sartorial revolution" by painting a suit of clothes on his naked body; etc., etc.

Some of these pieces are amusing enough. I liked the opener, **"Homage to Cesar Paladion,"** about the modest plagiarist of a series of classics ranging from the *Georgics* to *The Hound of the Baskervilles*. But much of the rest of the book, especially the latter half, falls flat. The problem with the *Chronicles* is that they fail to live up to their second lead quotation: "Every dream is a prophecy, every jest is an earnest in the womb of Time" (Father Keegan). Even when the jokes come off, they're one-dimensional; they miss that deeper, more suggestive level of "serious" comedy. A case in point is the Paladion section, obviously derived from Borges's earlier **"Pierre Menard, Author of the *Quixote*."** Paladion strikes us as a simple caricature, whereas Menard, the 20th-century academician who manages to write a few chapters of *Don Quixote* independently of Cervantes, seems comically haunting. Borges insists—and convinces us!—that Menard's "modern" text is infinitely richer and more complex than the identical 17th-century version. This sort of fun, unfortunately, lies beyond the reach of the pale composite H. Bustos Domecq.

> Peter Heinegg, in a review of "Chronicles of Bustos Domecq," in America, *Vol. 134, No. 21, May 29, 1976, p. 482.*

ANATOLE BROYARD

Borges reminds me of medieval man, who saw structures, hierarchies everywhere and erected cathedrals to mystery. His work is like those 15th-century paintings of heaven in which a dozen dead people float in featureless space. In his better stories Borges is rather like the great Spanish architect Gaudi, who began what was to have been the world's largest cathedral but never got beyond the facade. . . .

The Book of Sand is a collection of 13 new stories by Borges. In an author's note he says: "If of all my stories I had to save one, I would probably save **"The Congress,"** which at the same time is the most autobiographical (the one richest in memories) and the most imaginative." He also expresses himself as pleased with several of the other pieces, and this is as it should be. A serious author always writes as well as he can and his most recent work is nearest to his altered heart.

But even Borges's strongest advocates may hesitate to compare **"The Congress"** with his earlier stories on the same theme. The Congress is intended to be "mankind's spokesman," or "an assembly to represent all men." As in other Borges works, books are the means employed to effect the necessary synthesis. The Congress first buys reference books, then classics, then everything that is printed, on the assumption that the printed word is the most reliable record of our collective aspiration. Here again, we run up against Borges's bibliomania, his scholar's parochialism. At last, realizing the hopelessness of the task, the Congress burns the books.

In the preface to his latest collection of poems [*The Gold of the Tigers: Selected Later Poems*], Borges says that, in writing a story or poem, "I begin with a glimpse of a form . . . I see the end and I see the beginning, but not what is in between. That is gradually revealed to me, when the stars or chance are propitious." In the case of **"The Congress,"** the stars or chance have not been propitious, for there is very little in between the beginning and the end. It is one of Borges's compulsions to try to squeeze the totality of our experience into an all-embracing metaphor. In earlier stories, he has managed to suggest, in despairing and receding vistas, our vain hope for a comprehensible universe, but here in "The Congress" there is only the collapse of climax into anticlimax.

After a coyly circulocutory opening, "There Are More Things" arrives at a brilliant, typically Borgesian evocation of the uncanny: an empty house whose grotesquely unfamiliar furniture defies every attempt to infer the form or nature of its inhabitant. "The Sect of the Thirty" is another of those exercises in which a philosophically minded author amuses himself by postulating a heretical religious sect whose only novelty lies in its improbability. "The Night of the Gifts" inflates an adolescent escapade into a grandiose puberty rite. After a boy sleeps with a prostitute and then sees a man murdered outside the brothel, Borges asks us to accept this exalted conclusion: "In the bare space of a few hours I had known love and I had looked on death."

There is a story about a people whose poetry consists of a single word, and there are a few other pieces which it would be more compassionate to pass over. . . . ["The Book of Sand"] is another cosmic crossword puzzle, something about a book that has "neither beginning nor end," which is "infinite" for no better reason than that its pages are numbered at random and none can be said to be either first or last.

In his acute, encyclopedic and amazingly witty *Guide to Modern World Literature*, Martin Seymour-Smith remarks that "Borges seeks to overthrow the reader's confidence in external reality." I wonder why Borges should bother, for this would seem to be a gratuitous activity. As A. S. Eddington observed, "To be or not to be is a primitive form of thinking." Eddington would transcend this naive dichotomy with what he calls a "structural" concept of existence, and, in fact, the American short story has been moving in this direction for some time. At his best, Borges creates, or at least evokes, such a structure. If he is not at his best here in *The Book of Sand*, we can still say of Borges, who is now in his 70's and nearly blind, that he is nonetheless trying to see, to reach, as far as he can, and that is the most that any writer can do.

> *Anatole Broyard, "Metafiction," in* The New York Times Book Review, *October 16, 1977, p. 14.*

J. D. O'HARA

The Argentine man of letters Jorge Luis Borges first became known to Europeans and *norteamericanos* as a writer of short prose fictions hovering over some borderline between story and essay and dealing with fantastic happenings or situations. . . . Sensible readers enjoyed these stories all the more as they recognized their foundations in philosophy, logic, and theology and appreciated the knowledgeable and witty skepticism of their learned author.

But recognition of Borges came belatedly, and by then he had outgrown many of these early interests. He has retained his predilection for idealism, but he has become more and more interested in working out and reworking those archetypal situations, characters, and plots that recur down through the centuries. . . . A witty and deeply skeptical man, he accepts humorlessly the idea that a work of literature takes its value from its representation of general themes—love, death, the double, etc. Complex and even contradictory himself, he returns again and again to the cartoon stereotypes of older fiction: the dour

Scot, the tightlipped Englishman, the philosophic explorer, the gaucho as noble savage. . . .

In the 13 stories collected [in *The Book of Sand*], as in his recent collection *Dr. Brodie's Report,* Borges contrives more restatements and variations of central literary themes. (In an Afterword he identifies a few of them: the double, love, heresy. . .) As one might expect, some of these tales are recognizable relatives of earlier Borges stories. "The Book of Sand" describes an endless, infinitely growing book, the library of Babel between two covers; "The Sect of the Thirty" adds a fourth heresy to the "Three Versions of Judas"; and "There Are More Things"—which Borges belittles as a deliberate imitation of H. P. Lovecraft—returns to the minotaur of "The House of Asterion." And the story of which Borges thinks most highly, "The Congress," evokes like many previous stories the idea that the study of the whole world is our joint business.

That is a position Borges characteristically takes, urging us to look beyond ourselves, to recognize our identity with the rest of the human race, past and present, and to lose egocentricity in speculation about the insoluble mysteries of existence. Since he is thoroughly paradoxical, it is not surprising to find that the finest story in this collection is essentially personal and even autobiographical. In "The Other," the elderly Borges, seated on the Cambridge bank of the Charles river, meets his younger self, who is seated in Geneva on the bank of the Rhone. The story never descends to mere autobiography or mere gimmickry, and in its sadly witty development of the two men's mutual incomprehension and indifference even the most skeptical reader can sense a beautifully embodied general truth.

When Borges tells us archetypal tales of self-righteous New Englanders and boastful Norsemen or of primal encounters with the essence of love and death, we—swarmed about by life's pluralistic variety—may find ourselves too far from Plato to believe him. But in a story like "The Other" he deals with materials that all of us, if we live long enough, can verify for ourselves—truths of impression, not of archetypal event; and at such times his intelligence and his well-honed artistic skills work wonders.

> *J. D. O'Hara, "Borges' Book of Dreams," in* Book World—The Washington Post, *October 23, 1977, p. E8.*

DIANA ARMAS WILSON

In an "Author's Note" to [*The Book of Sand*], Borges is careful to promise his readers only a "few variations on favorite themes." When, in addition, he apologizes for the "irreparable monotony" of his production, we are reminded of those feigned little disclaimers so dear to Borgesian narrators. But Borges is not feigning here. One of the more long-standing of those "favorite themes," literary pantheism, appears as a constant in *The Book of Sand*. All readers are familiar with Borges's use of pantheistic formulas, those repetitive schemes that, as Ana Maria Barrenechea suggests in *Borges the Labyrinth Maker* (1965) may be reduced to one approach: "the fusion of oneness and plurality" [see *CLC*, Vol. 1]. These pantheistic expressions generally tend to disguise reality, to act as dissolvents of personality. The opening tale in *The Book of Sand,* "The Other," strategically evokes Borges's old addiction for the literary possibilities of pantheism. In 1969, on a bench in Cambridge facing the Charles River, Borges meets up with his younger self, with an "alter ego" who may be "dreaming him." There follows an entertaining exchange, the two Borgeses talking mostly about literature. In a scenario formally reminiscent of Cacciaguida's prophesying to his descendent Dante, the elder Borges foretells the achievements of his younger self. . . . (p. 138)

Although there are no other encounters between plural egos in *The Book of Sand*, there is hardly a tale among the thirteen that does not muster, close to its finale, some kind of pantheistic utterance. Personalities are everywhere being merged, lost, or forgotten. The lovers in **"Ulrike"** identify with Sigurd and Brynhild to the extent that, at different times in the tale, they hear wolves howling in modern-day England. The believers in **"The Sect of the Thirty,"** upon coming of a certain age, "have themselves mocked and crucified on the summit of a hill.". . . In **"Utopia of a Tired Man,"** which Borges calls "the most honest and melancholy piece in the collection," a man of the future explains his need to live "sub specie aeternitaties": "In our schools we are taught doubt and the art of forgetting—above all, forgetting of what is personal and local." The Borgesian theme of self-recognition, in short, always points to loss of self—often, indeed, to the recognition that one *is* the other. For Borges, a man's personal identity, with all its splendors or eccentricities, is but a transitory aspect of generic Being. Even in **"The Bribe,"** a straight-forward tale about what Borges calls "the ethical obsession of Americans," two clearly polar personalities are wrenched into an unforeseen unity when an Icelandic professor at the University of Texas publicly criticizes the teaching methods of a colleague from New England, with the specific aim of gaining his vote. The Icelander counts on "the curious American passion for impartiality" and is rewarded. Viking and Puritan seem worlds apart until the reconciling *dénouement*: "Still," concludes the duped American professor, "we aren't so different. One sin is common to us both—vanity. You pay me this visit to boast of your clever stratagem; I backed you to boast that I am an upright man."

Unifying two men by equating each of them with a Platonic reality is an old Borgesian trick. What is new in this volume is a long story about a similar enterprise on a grandiose scale—**"The Congress."** In 1971, just prior to the first publication of this tale in Spanish, Borges announced that it had been haunting him for some thirty or forty years: "The story is about a mystical experience I never had, but maybe before I die I'll be allowed to have it." His evaluation of **"The Congress,"** within this same announcement, was high: "It may be, for all I know, my best story or my justification as a story-teller.". . . The tale is about a Uruguayan rancher, don Alejandro Glencoe, who decides to found a Congress of the World that would represent all men of all nations. The efforts of the Congress are likened to "fixing the exact number of platonic types—a puzzle that had taxed the imagination of thinkers for centuries." Seeking for a language appropriate to their enterprise, the Congress sends delegates to Europe to gather information. . . . On the home front, the congressional library begins to grow under the dictum of the Younger Pliny, "According to whom there is no book so bad that it does not contain some good." The Congress begins to buy books insanely. . . . The justification for all this folly is that "everything gives witness." Four years later, thanks to don Alejandro's mystical volte-face, they burn all the books in a patio in Buenos Aires. "Our Congress," don Alejandro explains to the members, "cannot be a group of charlatans":

> The Congress of the World began with the first moment of the world and it will go on when we are dust. There's no place on earth where

it does not exist. The Congress is the books we've burned. The Congress is Job on the ash heap and Christ on the Cross. The Congress is that worthless boy who squanders my substance on whores.

Once again in Borges, the moment of revelation points to the fusion of oneness with plurality.

Although Anatole Broyard noted in his *New York Times* book review [see excerpt above] . . . that "there is very little between the beginning and the end" of **"The Congress,"** I am inclined to agree with Carter Wheelock's suggestion [see *CLC*, Vol. 2] that the story's "failure" may be owing "precisely to its accomplishment." Wheelock ventured the idea, back in 1972, that **"The Congress"** was "not intended to be read but to be studied." What even a minimal study shows is that the Aleph-Zahir conflict symbolically dramatized in Borges's older fiction provides the very scaffolding of **"The Congress."** The Aleph and Zahir—the names of two of Borges's earlier stories—represent, in his fictional world view, two avenues to reality. An Aleph is *not* "another Zahir," as Harss and Dohmann define it in their otherwise excellent essay on Borges in *Into the Mainstream* (1966) [see *CLC*, Vol. 2]; as the universal, transcending vision of mysticism, the Aleph is at the other pole of reality from any Zahir—as "A" is from "Z." Alephic vision, as all readers of Borges recall, is granted to the narrator of **"El Aleph,"** who watches the universe unfolding on the nineteenth stair of a Buenos Aires cellar. Far from such intuitions of eternity, a Zahir is a local and particular perspective that a man uses to order reality—any belief, scheme, or dogma that saves him from chaos. As a meaningful perspective, a Zahir is a poor but necessary substitute for the impossible Aleph. But a Zahir may easily change into an obsession over a given facet of reality: the twenty-*centavo* coin, for instance, that nearly maddens the protagonist of **"El Zahir."** As Borges elaborates in **"The Congress"** on "the zeal that inflamed " its members in setting up their worldwide organization, the reader begins to descry the outlines of yet another magnificent Borgesian obsession. The dedicated Congress does not, as yet, share the conviction expressed by Borges in *Other Inquisitions* (1964) that "there is no classification of the universe that is not arbitrary and conjectural." This insight is reserved for don Alejandro's sudden revelation, coming upon him after a four-year planning period of "a precision that was almost magical." When the Congress finally recognizes that their plan "really and secretly existed"—that it *was* both the world and themselves—they exchange, during the course of a long and joyous night, order for chaos, perspectivism for intuition. What reviewer Broyard sees as "the collapse of climax into anticlimax" may be more accurately read, I think, as the joyous liberation of a congress of zealots from all their structured certitudes: "Every few centuries," one of their enlightened members concludes, "the Library of Alexandria must be burned down."

True to Borges's prefatory promise, **"The Congress"** is essentially a variation on yet another of his favorite themes: the restoration of a cherished chaos—periodically threatened by limited and obsessive world-views—through a decisive act. Echoes of man's attempts to order a chaotic universe are found everywhere in the Borges canon: in and out of dreams, in and through labyrinths, behind mirrors, and at the core of all rivalries. One might say that Borges himself is imaginatively obsessed with human obsessions to simplify reality. **"The Congress,"** then, as the longest and finest of the thirteen tales in this new collection, functions as a gloss on Borges's recurrent tales about this mania. All fixations, even all rigid interpretations, destroy the possibility of vital conjecture—blot out that chaotic universality that is Borges's most cherished intuition. One could say that don Alejandro Glencoe orders the book-burning in order to save the Congress from what Borges most despises—the limited and obsessive world-view of a Zahir. Seen from this angle, it is not too difficult to understand why Borges should look to **"The Congress"** to be his "justification as a story-teller."

Some readers may find the "irreparable monotony" of [*The Book of Sand*] redeemed by the surprising attention it pays to romantic love. Nearly a decade has passed since Harold Bloom [see *CLC*, Vol. 6] complained that Borges, "despite the illusive cunning of his labyrinths," lacked "the extravagance of the romancer."... Borges's sexless tales of the fifties probably invited, from even his strongest advocates, some variant, certainly a gentler and less clinical one, of the charges proffered by Bloom. Even Borges himself had forthrightly accounted for the "very little sex" in his tales: "the answer is obvious. I have been worried all my life by falling in love, sex, and that kind of thing." At least half of the thirteen stories in *The Book of Sand* imply some confrontation with that life-long worry. Some tales simply allude to carnal love, others expand the theme. The tale **"Ulrike"** is exclusively about love—the one-day love affair between a Colombian professor and a Norwegian feminist. Even **"The Congress,"** although basically a tale about a group of bibliomaniacs, alternates their scholarly with their sensual concerns. One must conclude that the Borges of *The Book of Sand,* now close to eighty and writing what he calls "blind man's exercises," has liberated himself, to a remarkable degree, from that so-called "dread of family romance."

He has also freed himself from the baroque and elaborate writing that distinguishes his earlier collections. The tales in *The Book of Sand* have clearly received some legacy from the "straightforward storytelling" that Borges attempted in *Dr. Brodie's Report* (1972): they are far more accessible than the earlier fiction, with its arcane erudition and pervasive sophistries, yet they are as philosophic and as bookish as any of the tales in *El Aleph*. Among the thirteen tales in *The Book of Sand* there is perhaps only one failure: an irksome, almost silly, tale called **"There Are More Things"** that aims to parody an unconscious parodist of Edgar Allan Poe. It is no accident, I think, that Borges has expressed a predilection for the two tales in *The Book of Sand* in which men have become prisoners of their books. The book-burning in **"The Congress"** is the prerequisite to an ecstatic communal deliverance. In **"The Book of Sand,"** the tale that gives the collection its title, a book that is variously called "monstrous," "impossible," "nightmarish," and "obscene" must be deliberately "lost" on a musty basement shelf of the Argentine National Library. In either case, the implication is clear: as possible agents of dogma—of any blinding certitude—books must be periodically destroyed for our soul's health. No matter how infinite its pages, no book can provide us a map of the labyrinth. (pp. 138-42)

> *Diana Armas Wilson, "Latest Fiction by Borges,"* in The Denver Quarterly, *Vol. 13, No. 2, Summer, 1978, pp. 138-42.*

RICHARD O'MARA

You could range back and forth for years through the literature of Jorge Luis Borges in search of the point. That's not a den-

igration. Borges is a universe whose center is everywhere. There is no single leitmotif, no preoccupation that excludes all others. In short, there is no one part upon which all others depend, no secret lessons, no hidden meanings. The same does not apply to the Borges metaphysical essays: they are impenetrable. If Borges endures, it will be as a story teller.

Borges's production is slender and slow forthcoming. To use the sort of metaphor he would probably dislike, there is a fine inner quality, the strength of good construction. André Maurois speaks of the Borges stories, of ". . . their wonderful intelligence, their wealth of invention, and their tight almost mathematical style." This is literature's Mozart, the Bach of belles lettres. Control and clarity are the words that describe his work most precisely. It was Maurois who declared Borges heir to Franz Kafka, a title in some dispute, but with the Frenchman's caveat that Borges would have made *The Castle* into a ten-page story "both out of lofty laziness and out of concern for perfection."

The paradox is not unknown. The languid and obsessive responses are often found in the same person. Borges must be lazy; the evidence for it is his dearth of production. He has also, it is clear, the bloodshot zeal of the perfectionist. He is an incessant polisher. He will allow only the central element of a story to stand, that part that resists the lapidary grinding of his intellect. (pp. 552-53)

Jorge Luis Borges is nearing the end of his life. It is at least possible that before he dies, or shortly thereafter, he will be awarded the Nobel Prize for literature. Borges is surprisingly well received in the English speaking world. It is, I suspect, the anticipation of bestowal that accounts for much of his popularity among American and English readers. I also suspect it is not a genuine popularity. Borges appeals to the quintessential snob. He is slightly exotic, obscure enough that most English-speaking people have never heard of him, and for that reason he offers a certain cachet. And because his output is so slim, he can be taken in small bites, though he is not necessarily easily digested. (p. 554)

Again, this is not a denigration of the writer. Rather it reflects a suspicion of his admirers. Borges is declared a universal writer, probably because of his vast and surprising erudition, his love of the fog-shrouded northern myths and sagas, of Irish poetry, G. K. Chesterton, Swift, Poe, and H. G. Wells. This seems to be a kind of homage that the master of the Spanish language pays to the English-speaking peoples. It may not be that, actually, but at least that's how they take it. Thus his English and American readers accept him, honor him even, for what he has in common with them, not for what he can teach them—about the unique culture that thrives in the region of the River Plate, about the Argentine and Uruguayan pampa and the unpolished men who ride there, and especially of the great lighted hive of Buenos Aires. There is a certain insularity evident among many of Borges's readers, the arrogance of ignorance. Borges, admired for the wrong reasons, is, in a sense, scorned. (pp. 554-55)

[Yet] Borges is a national or regional writer after all. He has none of the exuberance, energy, or hot blood of his great contemporaries in Latin America—the novelists Jorge Amado of Brazil or Gabriel Garcia Marquez of Colombia, nor the explosive poeticism of Pablo Neruda, none of the music of Octavio Paz or Cesar Vallejo. What Borges has is a clear grasp of the mystery of Argentina, a general notion of what animates its people. He is closer to Juan Carlos Onetti and Mario Benedetti, the Uruguayans. Borges does not stand apart altogether; he is firmly in the tradition of the River Plate writers—Onetti, Benedetti, Julio Cortazar, and Bioy Casares, Borges's famous collaborator in the writing of fantastic fiction.

And unlike the many writers outside the River Plate area, with its eternal and unsurprising landscape—those such as Amado, Garcia Marquez, and the Cuban Alejo Carpentier, who set their work within elaborate exotic backgrounds—the River Plate writers tend to be more brooding, internal, solipsistic. (pp. 555-56)

Of all the stories in *The Book of Sand,* **"Ulrike"** is the most romantic. It's about as romantic as a thoroughly cerebral man, as Borges is, can get. It is a haunting story which affirms the power of sentiment against the knife of the intellect. Many men, no doubt, have lived similar experiences with beautiful, unexpected women while travelling. And many have carried with them the warmth that it gave them for long after. To most, of course, it is recalled as a sexual encounter. To some a moment of love. Borges, out of character perhaps, is closer to the latter here.

Perhaps more than any other, **"The Other"** demonstrates the broad scope of Borges's imagination. We can all evoke images of ourselves as we were, and as we are, and we are usually wrong in both estimations. But there are a few who are able to divide the same self into two distinct beings, as Borges does here, a younger and older self, and demonstrate the contrasts that have developed through the years as well as the elements of the personality that have resisted change. (pp. 556-57)

By Borges's own judgement, one of the more complete works of his career is **"The Congress,"** and it is included in *The Book of Sand.* . . . It is long for a Borges story, 23 pages. It sets forth the kind of contrast that may help us understand Borges in both suits, as the universalist and the regionalist.

The congress in question is the Congress of the World. The story is about an assemblage of River Plate intellectuals of varying nationalities and races who gather periodically in Buenos Aires to prepare for an eventual international congress that will be held in neighboring Uruguay—a conference of humanity, an immense gathering at which the representatives of all men will be invited to articulate the needs and desires of their fellows. . . .

The whole enterprise, of course, is preposterous on its face, and rendered even more preposterous by its location, out there on the frontier regions of the West. But there have been other preposterous, universalist enterprises before. (Esperanto, to name one.) And perhaps it is the very isolation and distance from the centers of Western culture that encourage those who live there in their efforts to draw us all in together. Perhaps their behavior is quite appropriate. Anyway, here is Borges, in this absurd setting; and, as expected, the society dissolves and disintegrates under the vast ambition of its own purposes. (p. 557)

The contrast between the civilizing intent of the congress, the purpose which brought them to the estancia . . . and the rustic circumstances of their actual lives on the estancia is most telling. The theme of the civilized city as opposed to barbaric countryside has activated writers since Domingo Sarmiento's *Facundo* defined Argentina's history by it. Even today, artistically, literarily, even commercially, Argentina is two countries—the city of Buenos Aires and the rest of the nation.

It is well known that Borges is a devotee of detective fiction, a lover of Poe and H. P. Lovecraft. Within *The Book of Sand*

there is a short piece titled, **"There are More Things"**; it is dedicated to Lovecraft. It is a horror story, in the Lovecraftian style of *The Case of Charles Dexter Ward* yet with none of the explicitness of that work. But Borges, in imitating Lovecraft, in some ways exceeds him in evoking a sense of horror by suggestion. In the end I was left puzzled as to Borges's intentions: Was it so much a tribute or was it the master writer performing an exercise, and in executing it outdoing the object of the homage? Was it a small arrogance?

Of the other stories much might be said. There are intriguing examples of Borges's well-known pseudo-scholarship, as in **"The Sect of the Thirty,"** of his preoccupation with regal myth and Icelandic and Arthurian legend, as in **"The Mirror and the Mask."**

The most perfect story, from my entirely personal point of view, is **"Avelino Arredondo,"** the tale of the Uruguayan assassin. It is writing of great power and authority. It reveals to us once again that there is no divergence between the internal and the external life, or at least that they are inextricably joined, that what is incubated in the first is ultimately played out in the second.

In **"The Book of Sand,"** the last story in the collection, Borges again returns to the theme of timelessness. Contributing greatly to Borges's power as a writer is his sure sense of the concrete. Writing even of the most ineffable things, he relates his meaning by using the most mundane objects. The most mundane object in Borges's world is the book. His life is constructed for the most part of books—his own, those in the library left him by his father. And so, when Borges reaches to grasp the ethereal, he reaches for the book—the strange book bartered from the mysterious gringo from the Orkneys, the book with no page numbers, with no beginning, no end, that ever changes, a river of mystery, with a weak and meagre flow, like the streams that trickle through the dry Patagonian arroyos that are never exhausted. The metaphor stands begging: Borges is the stream of weak and meagre flow, the river of mystery which cannot be exhausted. (pp. 558-59)

Richard O'Mara, "Literature's Mozart," in The Virginia Quarterly Review, *Vol. 54, No. 3, Summer, 1978, pp. 552-59.*

DONALD A. YATES

In less than a year Borges and [Adolfo Bioy-Casares] had composed [*Six Problems for Don Isidro Parodi*], six tales about Parodi, the taciturn barber from the south side of Buenos Aires who, owing to a set of unfortunate circumstances, had been convicted of a murder he did not commit. Parodi's clients were a colorful lot. The authors characterized them with loving care, producing a gallery of pompous, posturing, vain, or pathetic Argentine social stereotypes, as absurd in their language as in their pretensions.

Since their irreverent and free-wheeling collaboration had surprisingly given birth to a "third" author, whose broadly satirical style resembled neither that of Borges nor Bioy, they lifted two names from their respective family trees and christened him H. Bustos Domecq. The first of the stories, **"The Twelve Figures of the World,"** appeared in 1942 in Victoria Ocampo's literary magazine *Sur.* Borges and Bioy were prepared to publish the entire series there, but when word got out that Bustos Domecq was a pseudonym of *two* writers, their publication was suspended. Borges has pointed out that, since there was no "author" behind the stories, people refused to take them seriously. *Sur* was a dignified cultural organ; Victoria was not amused. Bioy ended up publishing the *Six Problems* in 1942 at his own expense. No one took much notice.

Now, some 40 years later, we have the book in English translation. Its publication has surely been a calculated risk, for the satire—inspired by a distant society at a moment now distant in time—takes precedence over the straightforward presentation of a mystery and its solution. Crime buffs may well be put off. There is also another drawback involved.... It is the extravagant language of the tales, specifically, the speech put into the mouths of the visitors to Parodi's cell. In the first few stories, there is sufficient broad, surface humor to sustain the reader's interest. But as the series progresses, the conceptual parody thins out and the verbal games take over. (p. 9)

As one might expect, the earlier stories are the most entertaining. The first, **"The Twelve Figures of the World,"** is a gem. It is an ingenious formal puzzle; and the foppish journalist, Achilles Molinari, is perhaps the most amusing of the Bustos creations. In the second, **"The Nights of Goliadkin,"** the pedantic Gervasio Montenegro, pointedly invested with membership in the Argentine Academy of Letters, narrates his problem to Parodi with a certain ingenuous charm. The detective's solution is typically curt, sarcastic and arbitrary; because he is a no-nonsense fellow himself, Parodi finds it hard to suffer a fool gracefully.

The following two stories, **"The God of the Bulls"** and **"Free Will and the Commendatore,"** deal with dark doings among members of Argentine monied society. At the heart of the second of these pieces is a brilliant plot idea: the vengeful parent who lavishes success and happiness on his son and then, after adolescence, releases him to a deadly outside world. Justice isn't done to the idea here, but years later each author would return to it independently and with great effectiveness in his own stories.

The final tales, **"Tadeo Limardo's Victim"** and **"Tai An's Long Search,"** seem the most farfetched in plotting and execution. The authors in all likelihood saw this, for at this point they ended the series. But Bustos Domecq would be heard from later on.

The best of the Bustos Domecq style has survived in *The Chronicles of Bustos Domecq,* a delightful series of tongue-in-cheek critical pieces.... The humor of concept and exaggeration is fully under control in these pages. What was most impenetrable in the *Six Problems,* its ciphered linguistic burden, survived only to perish in a novelette entitled *A Model for Death,* published in 1946. Bioy must have seen that the intensely private nature of the jokes would limit its audience....

The publishers of *Six Problems for Don Isidro Parodi* suggest it is "an essential key to understanding Borges' development as a writer." I think there is a deeper truth. The stories were written in 1941 and 1942. Bioy, who had published in the 1930s a series of awkward, tasteless novels and stories, had finally brought out in 1940 a superb novel, *The Invention of Morel.* By 1940, after two decades of agonizing search for an appropriate medium and style, Borges had overcome some keenly embarrassing failures and had just begun to write the first of his celebrated "Ficciones." At last, the two writers must have felt, they were on their way. Thus, in the Bustos Domecq narratives they not only skewered a number of inviting targets from among Argentine social types and modes of speech:

With the disconcerting language of the Parodi stories they were possibly also joyfully exorcising some private ghosts. (p. 11)

> Donald A. Yates, *"The Detective in the Little Gray Cell,"* in Book World—The Washington Post, *April 19, 1981, pp. 9, 11.*

V. S. PRITCHETT

This sportive diversion [*Six Problems for Don Isidro Parodi*] looks like a "cure" for a writer who was feeling his way toward a durable and serious manner.

It is strange now to imagine a writer as distinctive as Borges working with anyone, yet the collaboration [with Adolfo Bioy Casares] excited him. The result was indeed bizarre, and something like a boisterous lark or bout of wrestling with his friend. They were united by a pseudonym, H. Bustos Domecq—combining names of their great-grandfathers—and one can see how the lark was one of those holidays or accidents that stir a writer's latent powers. Part of Borges' intention was to create an Argentine literature for the Argentines, by satirizing the habits of a new society. (p. 137)

Their wild spoofing, punning, and parodying made [the authors] shout with laughter as they wrote, but no one laughed in Buenos Aires. [*Six Problems for Don Isidro Parodi*] was thought to be a bore.... The book certainly flopped. The earliest readers in a very self-satisfied establishment did not grasp that it parodied traditional Argentine illusions and the effects of the exposure of a new-rich society to the ideological turmoil of Europe in the thirties and forties. Alfonso Reyes, the Mexican critic, was one of the few who saw the hidden point of the tales. As for the classicism of Borges, one can now see many signs of the metaphysical writer who would soon after write masterpieces like **"El Aleph"** and **"Tlön, Uqbar, Orbis Tertius."** Many passages bring to mind the mingling strains of Poe, Chesterton, and the philosopher Berkeley, and suggest the strengthening hand of the Borges we know. Mere "mysteries" have no philosophical overtones. We cannot guess who had the ingenious idea of choosing for the infallible detective Don Isidro a man serving a twenty-one-year sentence for a murder committed by someone else.... Don Isidro is a sort of non-perambulatory Father Brown who does his psychological sums in his head. The authors even go to the impertinent length of introducing a criminal adroit enough to disguise himself as Chesterton's famous priest. Don Isidro soon sees through that.

Each tale begins with a misleading situation, which becomes sometimes so crammed with clues that the plot is hard to follow until we reach the acute, if improbable, solution. Part of the fun lies in the pompous introduction to the tales by a ponderous Academician, who also turns up occasionally as a character in the book. He is one of those Argentines of the period who scattered French clichés through their talk.... The real strength of the authors lies in their power of gaudy caricature—and chiefly in the torrent of affected vernacular or self-dramatizing disclaimer which the visitors to Don Isidro pour out. (pp. 137-38)

Where we begin to detect the later Borges is in the serious concern for intellectual enigma, in the view of fiction as a game dignified by fateful, ancient overtones, and, of course, in the faked bibliographical footnotes with which, as a prisoner of his municipal library, he made the hours more bearable. If we take the case of Limardo, in his sleazy hotel, there is first the fact that he is a stranger who is despised. Suddenly, in an astonishingly dramatic scene, he preaches the sacredness of marriage vows to the astounded crooks. Why? Has he come to kill the lover of his faithless wife? How can such a coward, so easily put upon, bring himself to such an act? The excellence of this tale lies in its exposure of the minds of the evasive, watchful crooks, who are comically watching one another and diddling one another as they do so. Don Isidro sees that Limardo had come not to kill but to provoke his own death:

> It was true that he had brought a gun to kill someone, but that someone was himself. He had come a long way. For months and months, he had begged for abuse and insult in order to strengthen his nerve to kill himself, because death was what he longed for. I also think that before he died he wanted to see his wife.

That last sentence is devastating, for the reader has already seen that it is the wife who kills Limardo in defending, as she supposes, her lover. That extra turn of the psychological screw is surely pure Borges.

So also is the elaborate case of Ricardo in **"Free Will and the Commendatore."** This brainless polo-playing young dandy, a boasting womanizer, is the son of an Italian immigrant who has risen to great wealth and has assumed the rank. Don Isidro broods in his cell: the old Commendatore has known for years that Ricardo is really a bastard, the son of his faithless wife by another man. The father's vengeance lies in destroying the young man by covertly encouraging his vices, secretly buying mistresses for him—creating, in fact, a man who is a deceived fraud. . . . Don Isidro ends the tale on a Borgesian note of ambiguity:

> The realization that his whole life was a farce both bewildered and humiliated Ricardo. It was as if suddenly you were told you were someone else. . . . He never said a thing against the Commendatore, whom he still loved. But he left a farewell letter that his father was sure to understand. That letter said, "Now everything has changed and will go on changing. . . . No other father in the world has done what my father has."

I think Father Brown-Borges wrote that suicide note.

The collaborators continued their parodying fit for a few years, until they found themselves getting wilder and more baroque, and then gave up. But they had exploited the fantasy life of the Buenos Aires of their time. Almost at once, the real Borges saw what he wanted to be: a "classicist" in metaphysical fable and conundrum. Their meanings go far beyond the dramas of his own city. (pp. 139-40)

V. S. Pritchett, "Borges," in The New Yorker, *Vol. LVII, No. 14, May 25, 1981, pp. 137-40.*

JOHN SPURLING

[*Six Problems for Don Isidro Parodi*] contains precious little evidence of Bioy's taste for quietness and restraint, unless it is in the character of Parodi himself, an ex-barber serving a long prison sentence for a murder he didn't commit and forced to listen to the elaborate Browningesque monologues of a series of excitable visitors to his cell. Parodi is the *ne plus ultra* of the intellectual sleuth, his actions more or less confined to brewing himself a cup of *maté* and reading newspapers, his

characteristics to being "sententious and fat", with a shaved head and "unusually wise eyes", and his speech to occasional questions along the way and a brisk unravelling of the mystery at the end of each story. Whether or not these unravellings or gists of what actually happened reflect Bioy's influence on Borges, they now read as the most Borgesian parts of the book, comparable in method, though not in resonance, to the stories in *The Garden of Forking Paths*. . . . As Borges wrote in his prologue to *The Garden of Forking Paths*, "the composition of vast books is a laborious and impoverishing extravagance. . . A better course of procedure is to pretend that these books already exist, and then to offer a résumé, a commentary". But in *Six Problems* Parodi's slim résumés are preceded by the prolix explanations of those involved in the crime and it is the predominance of these other voices, these extra, deliberately ridiculous and unreliable narrators, which make the book both laborious and extravagant.

The original idea for *Six Problems* seems to have been Bioy's. At any rate Borges has him propounding it at the beginning of **"Tlön, Uqbar, Orbis Tertius":**

> Bioy Casares had dined with me that night and talked to us at length about a great scheme for writing a novel in the first person, using a narrator who omitted or corrupted what happened and who ran into various contradictions, so that only a handful of readers, a very small handful, would be able to decipher the horrible or banal reality behind the novel.

With the addition of the prison-cell detective to stand in for the small handful of alert readers, the formula is complete and must have looked promising, given that either of the collaborators had a gift for dramatic monologue. On the evidence of this book, neither had, and although Bioy may have made better attempts elsewhere (I have not read his solo works), Borges has steered clear of characterization altogether. His characters do not aspire to be individuals with a sense of interior life but types. . . .

The monologuists in *Six Problems* are types—the leading actor, the man of letters, the society lady, the small-time crook, etc—with a satirical dimension. They are meant, as well as unwittingly corrupting the truth of what has happened, to point up certain absurdities in pre-war Argentinian society. It is hard for an English reader forty years later to assess their accuracy, but they come across as overdone, absurd at two removes, as if the authors had satirized conventional Aunt Sallies instead of the actual people around them. . . .

The book's dust-jacket claims that "these stories are an essential key to understanding Borges' development as a writer". That is certainly true. They belong to his most fertile period, when the provincial poet and man of letters was evolving into one of the most original and entertaining storytellers of our time and they help to define the nature as well as the limitations of his talent. But they are strictly for a very small handful of readers, the Borges freaks. As detective stories they are too far-fetched, as satire too clumsy, and as literature too trivial.

John Spurling, "The Prison-Cell Detective," in The Times Literary Supplement, *No. 4080, June 12, 1981, p. 672.*

WILLIAM BOYD

Any fresh addition to the canon of Borges's works in English is a welcome one. All the more so in this instance since the unavailability of [*Six Problems for Don Isidro Parodi*] has been a tantalising frustration. The mystery or murder story, with its heavy reliance on falsehood or mayhem, is in many ways an ideal vehicle and model for the modernist writer, concerned as he is with exposing the artifice and illusion involved in the writing of fiction. Given the superb skill, the haunting intellectual paradoxes and challenges of Borges's celebrated fictions, what magic would he bring to the conventions of the detective story?

The answer, I'm afraid, is not very much. The blurb's promise that these stories "are an essential key to understanding Borges's development as a writer" smacks of wishful thinking (the blurb also wrongly describes Parodi as a banker). Borges and his collaborator, one feels, were not so much interested in setting up and solving intricate puzzles as satirising contemporary Argentinian life and letters. The murders and thefts described are similarly uninventive. But the narrators who visit Parodi in his cell are flamboyant and extravagant literary poseurs who converse in a variety of carefully stylised voices—from windbag promposity, cranky avant-garde to street-corner demotic. It's inevitable that much of the pleasure once derived from this is now lost, both through translation and through an unfamiliarity with the ins and outs of Latin American literature.

If the *Six Problems* are disappointing detective stories, they do provide—for students of Borges's work—some literary consolations. Parodi is another classic Borgesian artist figure, isolated and self-reliant, to whom the contingencies and inchoate facts of the world are brought. These he synthesises and analyses to construct an ideal narrative, which not only "explains" the bizarre happenings in life but also enshrines them in a logical and pleasing artistic truth.

William Boyd, "*A Little of What You Fancy,*" *in* The Sunday Times, *London, June 14, 1981, p. 42.*

NICHOLAS SHAKESPEARE

In his best work, Borges' characters are usually condemned to death. Their minds are concentrated wonderfully as a result and the metaphysical problems they grapple with become more than intellectual jokes. The trouble with *Six Problems for Don Isidro Parodi* . . . is that everyone survives. . . .

During an essay on **"The Argentine Writer and Tradition"** Borges later writes of "books now happily forgotten" when he tried "to copy down the flavour, the essence of the outlying suburbs of Buenos Aires". By doing so he was made aware that to be an Argentine was to be European. Parodi himself is a victim of this. He is a prisoner in the colonial city that existed before 1947 when Peron took over the railways built, financed and run by the British. A hybrid caricature drawn from Poe, Conan Doyle and Chesterton, he casts no shadow: partly because he receives every visitor with reluctance, whether it be the slick-haired rake or the courteous Chinese, and mostly because they submerge both him and their stories with irrelevant and chokingly verbose tittle-tattle. It is difficult to find anything South American twitching under the tweeds of the monocled actor, Gervasio Montenegro, who laces his narrative with French *bon mots* and refers to a knife wound as the lipstick left by "death's haughty kiss."

Six Problems for Don Isidro Parodi is a book about the mysteries of the dictionary rather than detection. In using the methods of scholarship to solve crime, Parodi is an interesting key to understanding Borges' later development as a writer. There is

much that looks forward to *Labyrinths* and *Fictions* in the intricate conceits, the conscious display of learning and the creation of a fictional world complete with footnotes. Only the characters' awareness of their "ponderous metaphors" and "tiring extravagance" makes one suspect that Borges knows he is better left alone.

Nicholas Shakespeare, "*The Barber of Buenos Aires,*" *in* The Times Educational Supplement, *No. 3400, August 28, 1981, p. 18.*

JAMES ATLAS

A compendious anthology of writings both familiar and unpublished, prose and poetry, early and late, [*Borges: A Reader*] reveals as no other collection of Borges ever has the obsessively literary nature of his enterprise. Crammed with philosophical discourses, bibliographical scholarship, philological research, eccentric folklore, real and spurious erudition, gnomic theories of time, this archive of recondite lore confirms Borges's claim that his life has been "dedicated less to living than to reading." (p. 1)

Perhaps it is this bibliophilic zeal that accounts for the strange unreality of Borges's work. Apart from his gaucho stories, where the knife fights of tough Argentine cowboys out on the pampas are so memorably rendered, Borges dwells in a realm of occult prophecies, apparitions, fantastic episodes: the wizard who could conjure up visions out of a bowl of ink, the stranger encountered on a bench who turns out to be the author as a young man. . . . For Borges, who has been nearly blind since youth, the uncertain border between appearance and reality, the relativity of time, the suspicion that we are living in a dream are more than literary tropes: They are the crucial experiences of a life lived wholly in the imagination. "The world we pretend is real when we read" is the world Borges inhabits.

Borges is a great classifier, a taxonomist of what is known and what might be known. "The only exact knowledge there is," declared Anatole France, "is the knowledge of the date of publication and the format of books." It is this conviction that impels Borges to speculate, in **"The Total Library,"** about a library that would contain everything. . . . (pp. 1, 42)

Not even such an ideal library, though, could hope to be exhaustive, for our sense of any work of art is fluid; it alters over time, becoming a new, unclassifiable work. In his famous story **"Pierre Menard, Author of the Quixote,"** Borges invents a writer whose ambition was to compose a "contemporary Don Quixote"—not merely to copy the original, but "to produce pages which would coincide, word for word and line for line, with those of Miguel de Cervantes." Comparing identical passages from the two works, Borges argues that where Cervantes's language was simply the rhetoric of his day, Menard's was a daring interpretation of history. "The text of Cervantes and that of Menard are verbally identical," Borges concedes, "but the second is almost infinitely richer." Why? Because Menard's is in essence an original work, imbued with a contemporary idiom and style.

What Borges proposes here is a satirical illustration of T. S. Eliot's celebrated idea, advanced in "Tradition and the Individual Talent," that every new work of art modifies our appreciation of existing works of art. "A great writer creates his precursors," Borges declares in his essay on Hawthorne. "He creates and somehow justifies them." And in **"Kafka and His Precursors,"** Borges claims to have found in Aristotle, Browning, the French novelist Léon Bloy and a 9th century Chinese writer named Han Yu "prefigurations" of Kafka. Literature for Borges is a collection of imaginative archetypes reproduced by each successive generation; there is no such thing as originality.

These elaborate theoretical ploys can become tiresome; there is always a danger of coyness in Borges, a whimsical elusiveness that verges on preciosity. When his parodies of scholarship succeed, it is because they mime the plausible. . . . But too often his fanciful scholarship is simply cute: the discovery of a lost civilization populated by transparent tigers; the glosses on obscure cabalistic scholars. There is something forced about Borges's fantasies of the supernatural; they seem contrived, belabored, arch.

Borges's great accomplishment, it seems to me, isn't in his stories but in his literary criticism. Time and again, he manages to distill in just a page or two the substance of a writer's character and work. "The mere happy vagabond proposed by the verses of 'Leaves of Grass' would have been incapable of writing them," he observes of Whitman; Henry James is "sad and labyrinthine," Kafka "almost professionally unreal.". . . And his essay on Hawthorne is one of the most evocative literary portraits I have ever read. Drawing upon the novelist's tales and journals, Borges elicits Hawthorne's loneliness and grim estrangement from the world with the sort of intuitive sympathy no critic since Lionel Trilling has achieved. . . . [What] comes through in this essay is the nearly unbearable somberness that pervades Hawthorne, his fiercely moral effort "to make art a function of the conscience." (pp. 42-3)

Many of the essays included in *Borges: A Reader* have never appeared before in English, and one of the book's virtues is its generous selection from the author's early work. This is more than the random assemblage of marginalia such anthologies often are; it collects for an American audience pieces that enhance and enlarge our sense of Borges's accomplishment. The political essays are especially notable, for they demonstrate a defiant opposition to Argentina's succession of fascist governments and thus temper the impression of unworldliness that clings to Borges. **"Our Inadequacies"** is a compilation of "the Argentine citizen's most apparent defects" that expresses open contempt for the generals who put an end to democracy there in the 1930's; and **"Portrait of the Germanophile,"** published in the midst of World War II, is a vehement denunciation of those Argentines who sympathized with the Nazis: "The Hitlerist is always a spiteful man, and a secret and sometimes public admirer of vicious cleverness and cruelty.". . .

"I'm lazy," Borges confided to Paul Theroux. "A few pages and I'm finished." A just self-estimate, perhaps; his range is narrow, his genius circumscribed by excessive bookishness and an apparent inability to create vivid characters or sustain a narrative. Still, what he has Emerson say in one of the sonnets collected here could be said of Borges himself: "I have read the essential books and written others which oblivion will not efface." (p. 43)

James Atlas, "A Man of His Words," in The New York Times Book Review, *October 25, 1981, pp. 1, 42-3.*

THOMAS M. DISCH

Borges's stature is sufficiently secure that the publication of his apprentice work and other ephemerae can do no harm to

his reputation, and *Borges: A Reader* is by no means exclusively comprised of such materials. It reprints many of his most noted stories and conundrums: **"Pierre Menard, Author of the Quixote," "Tlön, Uqbar, Orbis Tertius," "Theme of the Traitor and the Hero," "The Aleph,"** as well as a number of good poems and numerous essays of sometimes quirky ingenuity though, too often, of little substance. Even at their best, as in his piece on Hawthorne, Borges's essays can seem shambling and lacking in surprise. He is prone to digress and to synopsize at undue length. He spends as many words retelling Hawthorne's "Wakefield" as he would in writing a story of his own, and even then the point of the tale seems to elude him. But most of the previously uncollected work that fills out *Borges: A Reader* is far from his best and some is little more than newspaper filler, as in . . . the page-long **"Virginia Woolf: A Capsule Biography."**. . .

[There] is no conceivable reason short of idolatry for reprinting these refugees from the College Outline Series for American readers in 1981—not, especially, at the expense of omitting so many of his most accomplished and representative tales, masterpieces such as **"Death and the Compass," "The Library of Babel," "The Garden of the Forking Paths," "The Approach to Al-Mu'tasim,"** and **"Funes the Memorious."** Readers who want to put themselves to the trouble of examining Borges's juvenilia should not have to buy yet another reprinting of his classic stories, and readers making their first acquaintance with his work should not be fobbed off with ephemerae. It would not be quite so galling if one could believe the new anthology represented a weighted assessment of the merits of its contents rather than a mere submission to the brute facts of copyright availability.

Having said that, it must be added that *Borges: A Reader* will offer many pleasant surprises to readers like myself who have admired his work without having been completist in their admiration: There is a large midrange between his best and least accomplishment from which the editors have gleaned a selection that tends to focus attention on the second element of the pairing of **"Borges and I."** In that succinctest of self-portraits Borges complained of having to live in the shadow of his own accomplishment and reputation. . . . (p. 4)

[The] Borges of the Nobel Prize short-lists who sits on the right hand of Edgar Allan Poe—that Borges did not write something approaching a quarter of the contents of *Borges: A Reader*. It was rather the all-too-human other Borges—the "I" of **"Borges and I"**—who wrote and rewrote those obsessive and unpersuasive tales of gauchos imagined for the single-minded purpose of being knifed (which is, in Borges, a consummation devoutly to be wished); who wrote, in collaboration with his brother-in-law, the ineffective satire against Peron that so dismally fails to capture . . . the sound of living speech:

> Take it easy, Nelly, now that the switchman's finished eatin' you with his peepers and he's takin' off on the dray, like a big jerk, let your little ol' Donald Duck give you another pinch on the cheek. . . .

Did Christian, pagan, or man ever speak like that? Certainly it could not have been written by Borges. Nor could Borges have written the **"History of the Tango,"** which makes inflated claims for the vanished lyrics of forgotten songs. The author of this essay (and of the gaucho stories) wants desperately to have a focus for a nationalistic pride that cannot, in the political circumstances of Argentina, find a political expression. And so (as it was in America in the '60s) popular music becomes the last refuge of a displaced patriotism. The effect, from a hemisphere's distance, is a bit comic—as though Edmund Wilson were to have gone into ecstacies over the genius of Elvis Presley. (pp. 4, 12)

Thomas M. Disch, "A Mixed Bag of Borges," in Book World—The Washington Post, December 27, 1981, pp. 4, 12.

JOHN UPDIKE

[*The essay from which this excerpt is taken was originally published in a slightly different form in* The New Yorker, *May 24, 1982.*]

Will the traffic in Jorge Luis Borges, once a mere trickle along a few side streets of Buenos Aires and now a thundering jam in the literary capitals of the Western world, bear the addition of *Borges: A Reader*? This volume's dust jacket claims that the mighty Argentine fantasist "has come into English in haphazard fashion, so that the growing numbers of his readers have had to track him down through a confusion of incomplete collections, to piece him together from a set of displaced parts." That this additional incomplete collection, pieced together of poetry, fiction, criticism, journalism, and typically fragmentary Borgesian self-revelations, clears the matter up seems to me moot. Its chronological arrangement, its inclusion of a number of early writings hitherto not translated into English, its biographical and bibliographical summaries, and the individual comments by Mr. Monegal on each of the one hundred eighteen items in the anthology are all special and valuable. But as a selection *Borges: A Reader* lacks the direct authority of the *Personal Anthology* chosen by Borges . . . in 1967. As an introduction to Borges's work, it lacks the stunning directness and purity of *Ficciones;* a reader unacquainted with this writer would do better to begin with that collection, whose publication in English, in 1962, put Borges on our cultural map, or with the more extensive and partly duplicative *The Labyrinths,* brought out . . . in that same year. Even the bilingual *Selected Poems 1923-1967* . . . would serve as a smoother entrée into the master's universe. Borges has been an all-round literary performer—poet , translator, lecturer, anthologist, parodist, editor, librarian—but his short fiction (there is no long fiction) constitutes his ticket to fame and immortality, and *Borges: A Reader* omits such gems of the slender canon as **"The Library of Babel," "The Garden of Forking Paths,"** and **"Funes, the Memorious."** The editors' introduction admits that "the aficionado will notice some of the omissions" but pleads permissions difficulties. They offer instead, along with little classics like **"Tlön, Uqbar, Orbis Tertius," "The Circular Ruins,"** and **"The South,"** a number of early and lesser pieces, some of them uncollected by Borges in Spanish. The chronological arrangement, which for many an author might show a shape of development, in Borges's case confirms our impression that few major writers granted long life have proved so loyal to their initial obsessions and demonstrated so little fear of repeating themselves. "I am decidedly monotonous," he himself has written.

If the book with all its other scholarly apparatus had included an index, we might better trace the remarkable recurrence of topics and allusions. The exact same ninety-word quotation from Chesterton, with the identical ellipsis, is cited three times—on pages 143, 219, and 231. . . . The very first item in *Borges: A Reader* is a poem, from 1923, that fuses dawn in Buenos Aires with a haunting sense of insubstantiality—"that tremendous conjecture / of Schopenhauer and Berkeley / which declares the world / an activity of the mind"—to achieve a tone echoed in the very last lines of the book: "and to think that night would not exist / without those tenuous instruments, the eyes." Dreams, labyrinths, mirrors, multiplications approaching infinity, a plurality of inefficient and even malevolent gods, the dizzying paradox and negation of Berkeleyan idealism, Zeno's second paradox, Nietzsche's eternal return, the hidden individual destiny, the hard fate of gaucho knife fighters and Anglo-Saxon warriors . . .—Borges early claimed these themes and has never let go of them.

The favorite English authors of his childhood were Stevenson, Wells, and Lewis Carroll, and he has never let go of them, either, throughout a lifetime of reading. His praise of Wilde and Shaw is heartfelt; his homage to Joyce and James rather grudging. His own fiction, though not altogether fantastical (there is a quality of endless afternoons, of tinted drabness, which he can always achieve in a phrase or two, and which transports our imaginations to a real locale), evinces little impulse toward the baring of reality and the exposure of sentimentality in the heroic modernist manner of, say, Hemingway. . . . Whereas the multilingual erudition of Eliot and Pound was part of a worldwide search for an authenticity that would help make the native language and tradition new, Borges's erudition, with its quizzical touchstones of quotation and its recondite medieval and Oriental references, is a parody of erudition wherein the researched and the fabricated lie side by side ironically—a vast but claustrophobically closed system that implies there is no newness under the sun. . . . In an essay, **"On Chesterton,"** not reprinted here but published in *Other Inquisitions* (1964), Borges says, "Something in the makeup of his personality leaned toward the nightmarish, something secret, and blind, and central." Those last three adjectives give us the Borgesian essence, that terrible central blankness around which his invocations of "atrocity," "mysterious monotony," and "masked heresiarchs" revolve like chronic planets around a dead sun.

Borges: A Reader lacks just that elegance of the minimal which Borges's work and the books in which it is usually bound invariably possess. The page is too big and the type too small; the clutter of editorial addenda, with their portentous abbreviations . . . , cumbersomely enwraps Borges's own nice pedantries; the effect of reading the selection straight through is of a long bumpy ride in a closed carriage. For this systematic peruser, at least, the claustral, confused feelings dampened even his pleasure in those miniature masterpieces he had read with delight elsewhere, in volumes less farraginous. The chief value of this collection lies in the twenty-eight hitherto untranslated pieces; though they do not enhance Borges's reputation, they do enhance our sense of him as an Argentine, especially as a rather pugnacious young intellectual dandy seeking to reconcile his precocious, cosmopolitan awareness with a blood loyalty to the drab and often brutal backwater where he was born. (pp. 778-81)

The early pages of *Borges: A Reader* contain poems—some of them among his most popular—that show him taking deliberate possession of the scenery and history of Buenos Aires; the act of repossession, by a mind that has wandered far, characterizes his literary production ever after, and gives it its air of haunting dislocation, of surreal specificity and abysmal formlessness, of nostalgia for the circumambient. His first essay reprinted in *Borges: A Reader* tabulates the sometimes poetic inscriptions on old horse-drawn wagons. Its original title, **"Séneca en las Orillas"** ("Seneca in the Slums"), was dropped, as perhaps too telling. Other, later essays examine, with the lofty tenderness of a visitor from an ancient civilization, such local phenomena as the tango and the card game called *truco.* The tango, like the knife fights that so persistently flash through his work, manifests for him a popular, timeless religion—"the hard, blind religion of courage, of being ready to kill and to die."

As a young man of letters in Buenos Aires, in the long years while his unique and elaborately pseudo-factual "fictions" were incubating, Borges was a dashing critic, dismissing Argentine barbarism (**"Our Inadequacies,"** 1931) and accepted aesthetic theory (**"Narrative Art and Magic,"** 1931; **"Prologue to *The Invention of Morel,*"** 1940) with adamant aplomb. . . . He gave the readers of *El Hogar,* an illustrated weekly, whose book section he edited, capsule biographies and trenchant reviews of, among many, Oswald Spengler, Virginia Woolf, and William Faulkner ("That William Faulkner is the leading novelist of our time is a conceivable affirmation"). For Victoria Ocampo's periodical *Sur,* Borges did movie reviews, and the few that are printed here show an Olympian mind robustly engaged with a popular art—an art, like his own, of shadows. . . . Of Orson Welles's masterpiece, he said, *"Citizen Kane* will last as certain films of Griffith or Pudovkin 'last'; nobody denies their worth, but nobody goes back to see them. They suffer from gigantism, from pedantry, from tedium." Such an objection, on an immediate aesthetic instance, to a well-made piece of cinematic magic reveals more of the artist's mind, perhaps, than his rather hermetic formal theories. One might wish that [*Borges: A Reader*] consisted entirely of such fresh and surprising matter, and that an author whose oeuvre already savors of stringent selection and encyclopedic compression had been spared the ungainly compliment of a superfluous recycling. (pp. 782-84)

> *John Updike, "Borges Warmed Over," in his* Hugging the Shore: Essays and Criticism, *Alfred A. Knopf, Inc., 1983, pp. 778-84.*

KELLY CHERRY

[In the lectures which make up *Seven Nights*], the idea of a literary odyssey recurs. Borges quotes from the *Odyssey:* "The gods weave misfortunes for men, so that the generations to come will have something to sing about." The citation crops up in passing; it is a kind of detour—except that, for Borges, the shortest distance between any two points is always what a less *observant* writer might dismiss as a detour. He proceeds by allusion and association, and so, in discussing Dante's *Divine Comedy,* he refers to Homer's *Odyssey* and to the oral nature of poetry, and how poetry, which is song, is also a singing-about, so that the next step is to write that "we are made for art, we are made for memory, we are made for poetry, or perhaps we are made for oblivion. But something remains, and that something is history or poetry, which are not essentially different." This complex of ideas, and the movement among them, unifies these seven lectures. The talks are titled **"The Divine Comedy," "Nightmares," "The Thousand and One Nights," "Buddhism," "Poetry," "The Kabbalah,"** and **"Blindness,"** but the titles should be taken as emblems, not as signs or limits; each talk—shall we say—remembers the world. Reading them will take you everywhere.

Much ado has been made of late about criticism as a creative literature. To think that criticism has ever been anything else reveals, I think, a funny academic gullibility, as if Aristotle, to take an instance, had not been making up the rules of the game as he went along. Borges has always seen—or never forgotten—that what is important about literature is how it makes you feel. "Personally," he notes, "I am a hedonistic reader; I have never read a book merely because it was ancient. I read books for the aesthetic emotions they offer me, and I ignore the commentaries and criticism." (p. 134)

These lectures are not criticism or commentary, though they are more learned than most of either ever is; rather, they are pure enchantment. . . . The enchantment is a property of [Borges's] astonishing, non-manipulative honesty, a candor so guileless that it is magical; thereby, fiction becomes truth, and nonfiction—even lectures—as beautiful as any story. Because he received as if it were something to sing about the particular misfortune the gods gave him—his blindness ("If a blind man thinks this way, he is saved. Blindness is a gift")—his work bears the hallmark of grace, which is the transformation of whatever is temporal and transient into something that is eternal. Enchantment like this returns us, finally, to the beginning—of our lives, the world, our adventure in creation. "All things go off, leaving us," he writes near the end—except that the right words, like these, bring everything back. (pp. 134, 136)

> *Kelly Cherry, in a review of "Seven Nights," in* Parabola, *Vol. X, No. 1, February, 1985, pp. 132, 134, 136.*

JOHN UPDIKE

[The lectures in *Seven Nights*] make an enchanting small book, more loose and open in texture, more affectionate and frank in tone than the gnomic written criticism collected in *Other Inquisitions* and in [*Borges: A Reader*]. . . . The seven topics will not be strangers to those readers who have already trod the narrow, circling paths of the Borgesian universe: in literature, **"The Divine Comedy"** and **"The Thousand and One Nights;"** in religion, **"The Kabbalah"** and **"Buddhism;"** and, in his most personal vein, **"Nightmares," "Poetry,"** and **"Blindness."** (p. 120)

His own mind has become, in his blindness, a library, whose volumes he consults with a charming freedom of association, returning always to the allied sensations of enchantment— "Without enchantment, the rest is useless"—and of horror, of what [Alastair Reid in his introduction] spells out as *"asombro* or *sagrada horror,* 'holy dread.'" Captured within the friendly vessel of Borges' discursive voice ("talking not to all of you, but rather with each of you"), the genie of dread is less alarming than in the abruptly dizzying spaces of the poetry and fiction. . . . Listening, via the printed word, to these relaxed and yet highly explicit discourses, one realizes that never again will there be a mind and memory stocked just this way, with such benign and extensive curiosity, such patient and expectant attention to ancient texts. Bent upon conveying treasure, Borges reveals himself as a treasure. (pp. 120-21)

> *John Updike, "Memory Palaces," in* The New Yorker, *Vol. LXI, No. 17, June 17, 1985, pp. 120-24.*

ELLEN STEESE

Jorge Luis Borges's *Atlas* is a slim scrapbook of poems, dreams, and brief travel impressions. Mr. Borges describes it himself as "prudently chaotic."

He takes in Germany, Greece, Italy, Istanbul, Switzerland—places we all can go. But if some people feel that the wonder has gone out of travel, Borges hands it back to us. For these don't seem to be places we know. Even when he is not telling fables, his comments have a mysterious ring.

Borges is blind, but he is a man who sees with his fingers and with his heart. He gives us a loving picture of the beauty and importance of everyday things. So he sees more than we do.

> Ellen Steese, "Borges Puts the Wonder Back in Travel," in The Christian Science Monitor, *January 10, 1986, p. 26.*

JACK BYRNE

In the prologue to Jorge Luis Borges's *Atlas,* Borges tells us that "As regards this book—which is certainly not, by the by, an atlas...," his travels "have suggested many photographs and many pages of text" which "could be interwoven into a prudently chaotic book.... It does not consist of a series of texts illustrated by photographs or a series of photographs explained by texts. Each section embodies a union of words and images."

And there we have the quintessential Borges, the weaver of dreams and reality, of fictions and the world of facts, labyrinths of the mind and the world of myth.... In *Atlas* he travels in time and he travels in the mind. With his Ariadne, María Kodama, his collaborator and traveling companion, Borges masters the geographical labyrinth of the blind traveler who can never really see what his companion sees. His "prudently chaotic book" creates an atlas of sorts out of the diversity of places, photos, prose, verse, dreams and what the publisher calls an unconventional masterpiece, a "literary scrapbook. Part journal, part fantasy, part 'found object,' *Atlas* proves again that art need not be only a representation of reality, but an integral part of it."

Even the contents verify the length and breadth of his travels, both geographically and intellectually, in his quest of the unknown. In each of his forty-four entries, he presents a picture and a Borgesian comment. **"The Gallic Goddess"** has a photo of a burnt-wood goddess of Diana or Minerva which was "already here," when Caesar arrived.... Other selections take up Istanbul, Bollini's Alley in Buenos Aires, the Temple of Poseidon, a voyage in a balloon in the Napa Valley, Germany, Athens, Geneva, Chile, a brioche, art for city plazas, the theater of Epidaurus, Lugano, tigers, Robert Graves, Reykjavik, the Latin Quarter, Mallorca, the Rhone and the Arve, Madrid, the Sahara, the River Plate, and others. And, of course, there is the labyrinth of Crete, without which there would not have been a proper Borgesian signature, as necessary as the approving stamps of Dedalus and Joyce. (pp. 151-52)

> Jack Byrne, in a review of "Atlas," in The Review of Contemporary Fiction, *Vol. 6, No. 2, Summer, 1986, pp. 151-52.*

NICHOLAS RANKIN

Atlas is a delightful book. There is plenty in this slim volume to justify its price because Borges, like Beckett, manages to say much in few words. Among the five poems, five dreams, many literary and philosophical ruminations, is a memorable tribute to Robert Graves in his last days, "beyond time and free of its dates and numbers".

Borges tells us of meeting a tiger, going up in a balloon over Robert Louis Stevenson's Napa Valley, and discreetly "modifying the Sahara" with a handful of sand. In the Hotel Esja, Reykjavik, Borges gropes round his new room and encounters a pillar. He explores and embraces the white cylinder; sudden happiness comes as he remembers discovering the pure forms of Euclidean geometry in childhood....

Borges reminds us that cities are made of memory and reading, but he also knows the fragility of civilization. In the final fable of *Atlas,* set in Japan, the gods weigh up mankind's inventions. There is "an invisible weapon which could put an end to history", but there is also something "which fits in the space encompassed by seventeen syllables." Borges's faith lies in the infinite potential for meaning of the perfected haiku, not the grandiose chaos of the destroyed atom.

> Nicholas Rankin, "Multum in Parvo," in The Times Literary Supplement, *No. 4342, June 20, 1986, p. 647.*

ANTHONY KERRIGAN

[In one of his lectures in *Seven Nights*], Borges takes us on an intellectual stroll through **"The Kabbalah."** In it he considers the necessity of evil, and its justification, theodicy. The existence of evil is resolved, he finds, in a similar fashion by Gnostics and Kabbalists, both of whom postulated an imperfect God of creation who is not the final God. This distant descendant of God is their heresy.

He cites the Two Libraries of Leibnitz: one containing 1,000 copies of only one *perfect* book, the *Aeneid;* the other boasting only one copy of this perfect book. The 999 imperfect books of the second make it superior. Evil is in the variety, but variety is necessary for the world.

And the varieties of evil, too, are endless. One of them is mundane—most are mundane—and this one is the studiousness with which the Swedish Academy has favored the friends of chaos—and even of the premier Swedish invention, Nobel's dynamite—with the Nobel Prize for Literature, most particularly in the Spanish language in which Borges writes.... [Borges] has rejected the fashionable sociopolitical *Zeitgeist* in his pronouncements, or more precisely, in his quips and attitude, ranging from his support of "imperialist" Israel to his everlasting detestation in his own country of populist Peronism and its allies in the Communist Party. He will doubtless stand up to the erosions of time where the author of not one but two *Odes to Stalin,* Nobel Laureate Neruda, will not. (p. 15)

In treating the Koran as a "magical book" ..., the Argentinian ventures the paradox that this book is "older than the language in which it exists," Arabic, and cannot be studied historically or philologically; it is older than the Arabs; and yet it is not the work of God. It is "an attribute of God, like His rage or His justice." There is a mother of the book, a celestial archetype. "It is in heaven and is worshipped by the angels."

How could the dynamiters in Stockholm appreciate such speculations?

On one of the Seven Nights, Borges discusses **"Poetry."** He gives his credentials as a professor of English, and thus claims his right to outface the pedants—and outrage the pedagogues. Disregard the bibliographies, he tells his students, read the texts. "After all, Shakespeare knew nothing of Shakespearean criticism."

For Borges, literary criticism is merely a branch of imaginative literature (as Alastair Reid reminds us in his introduction). And Borges announces: "There are people who barely feel poetry and they are generally dedicated to teaching it." He attacks abstract thinking and theorizing about poetry, and examines, on the spot, Quevedo's great sonnet dedicated to the memory of the Duke of Osuna.

> Faltar pudo su patria al grande Osuna,
> pero no a su defensa sus hazanas;
> dieronle muerte y carcel las Espanas,
> de quien el hizo esclava la Fortuna.

> His country might fail the great Osuna,
> but he in her defense did not;
> Spain's reward for him was prison, death,
> from her for whom he'd made a slave of Fate.

Unlike the Spanish, my English is unrhymed, but is a simulacrum. The book's translator, Eliot Weinberger (known for his work with Octavio Paz), can handle the prose and doesn't try for rhyme either—but he has the verse wrong. We give it next as an example of how not to proceed (why don't nonbilingual translators *all* submit their work to bilingual scrutiny?):

> The great Osuna might lack his homeland,
> but not the deeds in its defense;
> Spain brought death and jail
> to him whom Fortune made a slave.

To speak abstractly of poetry, writes Borges, "is a form of ennui or loafing." Best to look straight at the text, and he ends—and summarizes—his essay with a beautiful line by Angelus Silesius, the German mystic:

> La rosa sin porque florece porque florece.

itself a translation (by Borges?) of the German original

> Die Rose is ohne warum; sie bluhet weil sie bluhet.

> "[The rose has no why, it flowers because it flowers.]"
> [Weinberger]

Might it not be better to say?:

> The rose, without a why, flowers because it flowers.

Among the other Seven Nights, one [**"The Divine Comedy"**] is devoted to the *Divine Comedy,* during which Night he hails Dante for his "great discovery: the possibility of a dialogue" with the souls of the dead and, as corollary, his recognition of the Other, the third speaker, who in Borges is simply El Otro, and in Dante is the Divinity. Another Night is devoted to **"Buddhism,"** as seen through the eyes of an Argentine European. Still another Night [**"Nightmares"**] is rich with allusions to the *flavor* (among other aspects) of nightmare, and concludes by asking "What if nightmares were strictly supernatural? What if nightmares were cries from Hell? What if nightmares literally took place in hell? Everything is so strange that even this is possible."

No wonder the frozen Swedes never gave him a Nobel Prize. (pp. 16-17)

Anthony Kerrigan, "The World's Leading Non-Nobel Laureate," in The University Bookman, *Vol. XXVII, No. 2, Winter, 1987, pp. 15-21.*

George Mackay Brown

1921-

Scottish poet, novelist, short story writer, essayist, dramatist, scriptwriter, journalist, librettist, and author of children's books.

One of Scotland's foremost contemporary authors, Brown incorporates in his writings elements from Norse sagas, Scottish ballads, medieval legends and myths, and Roman Catholic ritual. He commonly employs simple language and syntax and explores themes that focus on history, religion, mysticism, and the people and life of his native Orkney Islands. Deeply committed to the values inherent in the elemental existence of Orkney's farmers and fishermen, Brown extols the virtues that can be gained through hardship and emphasizes the damaging effects of the forces of progress on Orkney society. While Brown's antiquated prose style and his preoccupation with Orkney have been faulted for failing to engage contemporary realities, most critics compliment his intimate portrayal of a specific locality and his fundamental insight into the common concerns of human existence.

Born in the seaport town of Stromness on the island of Orkney, Brown began publishing his work at the suggestion of Scottish poet and fellow Orcadian Edwin Muir. In his introduction to Brown's initial collection of verse, *The Storm and Other Poems* (1954), Muir stated: "[Brown writes] beautiful and original poems, with a strangeness and magic rare anywhere in literature today." Using metrical unrhymed verse and images of arrested action that critics have compared to Muir's poetry, Brown introduces in this volume his contemplation of Orkney and his concerns with religious symbolism and myth. In his next volume, *Loaves and Fishes* (1959), which was praised for its mature themes and outlook, Brown displays his interest in Icelandic legend, Christianity, martyrdom, and Orcadian history. The pieces in *The Year of the Whale* (1965) employ evocative symbolism and are endowed with a vivid sense of character and place. Combining secular and religious themes, local and epic subjects, these poems range in setting from Orkney during the Viking era to the United States during the presidency of John F. Kennedy. Brown's conversion to Roman Catholicism in 1961 emerges in this volume through his use of litanies and his preoccupation with birth, love, death, resurrection, and religious ceremony.

Fishermen with Ploughs: A Poem Cycle (1971), a sequence of loosely connected lyrics and sections of prose, is often considered Brown's most impressive poetic achievement. Extending his stylistic forms to include triadic runes and incantations and utilizing poetic structures derived from the months of the year, the days of the week, and the Roman Catholic stations of the cross, Brown depicts Orkney life from its first settlements in the ninth century through its present depopulation and imagines future resettlement following a nuclear holocaust. Replete with apocalyptic despair and disillusionment, these poems solidify Brown's position against materialistic progress and exemplify a central idea in his philosophy: "It could happen that the atom-and-planet horror at the heart of our civilisation will scatter people again to the quite beautiful fertile places of the world." *Winterfold* (1976) contains a series of rune-like variations on the stations of the cross and "affirms [Brown's] belief that the journey of Christ parallels the fruitful

Photograph by Gunnie Moberg

journey of all things that follow nature to death, and resurrection in harvest," in the words of Dennis O'Driscoll. This volume has been interpreted as an optimistic postscript to the dark vision prevalent in *Fishermen with Ploughs*. *Voyages* (1984) continues Brown's interest in history, Norse medievalism, and the Orkneys. *Poems New and Selected* (1971) and *Selected Poems* (1977) are representative collections of Brown's verse.

Brown's first collection of short fiction, *A Calendar of Love and Other Stories* (1967), ranges in form from episodic fragments and sketches to heroic sagas. These stories explore a variety of subjects and themes, including the sixteenth-century trial of an alleged witch and a comic account of a traveling Indian shirt salesman. Setting these tales in a time frame extending from the Viking era to the present and generally employing a spare linguistic style influenced by the language of the Old Testament and Nordic folktales, Brown evokes the remoteness of life on the Orkney Islands and, according to James R. Frakes, "[matches] the primitive emotions of his characters [by straining] . . . towards a runic style, manipulating refrains and incremental repetition, folk rhythms and local idiom." In *A Time to Keep* (1969), Brown creates stark, somber tales of life in the Orkneys, featuring authentic depictions of Viking raids and tinkers' weddings and exploring such concerns as love, courage, loss, and honor. *Hawkfall and Other Stories* (1974) is a series of five related pieces depicting the experiences of a single Orkney family from the Bronze Age to the present. Despite experimentation with various styles and occasional humor, *Hawkfall* is centrally concerned with the mysteries of death and is commonly considered one of Brown's darkest works. In the stories contained in *The Sun's Net* (1976), Brown continues to contrast past and present, dream and reality, and life and death while examining the mystery of creation by presenting the notion that each birth is a reenactment of the Nativity. *Andrina and Other Stories* (1982) and *The Golden Bird: Two Orkney Stories* (1987) maintain Brown's interest in history, the supernatural, legends, myths, and the Orkneys.

Brown's first novel, *Greenvoe* (1972), describes the gradual decimation of a mythical Orkney fishing village after the construction of a secret military establishment on the island. By detailing the events of the five days preceding its final demise, Brown suggests that the banal existence of its inhabitants inadvertently contributed to the destruction of the village. Despite its bleak theme, *Greenvoe* concludes with an ambiguous but uplifting promise of resurrection. In *Magnus* (1973), Brown combines the starkness of Norse saga with the ornamentalism of the Roman Catholic mass. The story of the martyrdom and sanctification of twelfth-century Earl Magnus of Orkney, who was killed by his cousin and rival for supreme control of the Orkneys, *Magnus* extends Brown's fascination with the Christian theme of redemption. Brown's third novel, *Time in a Red Coat* (1984), is a fable that chronicles the experiences of a young Eastern princess as she journeys through distant countries and flees the devastation of her homeland by marauders. An innocent figure, the princess begins her travels with a white coat that gradually turns red due to the human folly and injustice she encounters.

An eminent chronicler of Orkney life and geography, Brown has published numerous collections of essays, including *An Orkney Tapestry* (1969), which Seamus Heaney described as "a spectrum of lore, legend and literature, a highly coloured reaction as Orkney breaks open in the prisms of a poet's mind and memory." In *Portrait of Orkney* (1981), Brown intertwines contemporary descriptions and facts with history, legend, and anecdote. Brown's works for the stage include *A Spell for Green Corn* (1970), which is concerned with symbolism, ritual, and the supernatural, and *The Loom of Light* (1972), an adaptation of his second novel, *Magnus*. He has also written radio and television plays and published several children's books, including *The Two Fiddlers: Tales from Orkney* (1974) and *Pictures in a Cave* (1977), and a biographical work, *Edwin Muir: A Brief Memoir* (1975).

(See also *CLC*, Vol. 5; *Contemporary Authors*, Vols. 21-24, rev. ed.; *Contemporary Authors New Revision Series*, Vol. 12; *Contemporary Authors Autobiography Series*, Vol. 6; *Something about the Author*, Vol. 35; and *Dictionary of Literary Biography*, Vols. 14, 27.)

ROY FULLER

Much of [*Loaves and Fishes*] is about drowning and the sea, and the people and scenes of the Isles, but its last section is mainly legendary and Christian, though still using the properties of the earlier part. There are many lines which show the author's sharp sense of character and place; and also his talent for using evocative words without turgidity or windiness:

These were the sounds that dinned upon his ear—
The spider's fatal purring, and the grey
Trumpeting of old mammoths locked in ice.

The poem which begins thus, called **"Dream of Winter,"** continues with further powerful and symbolical passages (e.g. 'A penitential wail / For the blue lobster and the yellow cornstalk / And the hooded victim') and ends:

Spring on the hill
With lamb and tractor, lovers and burning heather.
Byres stood open. The wind's blue fingers laid
A migrant on the rock.

This last is beautifully done, but it seems to belong to another poem altogether and, as in so many of these pieces, the parts fail to combine, and the moral, the myth, disintegrates. Only in some specifically Christian instances does one feel that language and purpose have been properly married, and here too great burden is laid on religion to convince the unbeliever. (pp. 77, 79)

Roy Fuller, in a review of "Loaves and Fishes," in London Magazine, Vol. 6, No. 12, December, 1959, pp. 77-79.

HILARY CORKE

George Mackay Brown's collection of stories, *A Calendar of Love*, looks like one of the few really solid achievements of the year. Stories? Poem-narratives in prose, rather. But *not* poetical prose in the commonly accepted mode of awash-with-rich-lush. These tales, or evocations, all set in the Orkneys, make their points with a spare beautiful accuracy that echoes the emotive landscape of those islands, linear not fuzzy, exact forms of cliff, hill-heave, peat-hag skyline, sudden surprising golden sands, the halcyon or leaden or orphic sea, and never a tree except for rare hull-down outbursts in sheltering clefts; and a strange boreal light over all. Subjects of all times, all sorts. The sixteenth-century trial of an innocent 'witch', presented in best documentary style of the period, terrible in the distancing of the plain pious blind language from the actual spiritual and physical horrors that are being hopefully committed in the name of a god. A lightweight comic account of a traveling Indian shirt-salesman's round of one of the smaller islands. Nothing from cover to cover of all that knowingness, ignorance, and misplaced seriousness or giggling superiority that makes one sick if one picks up almost any current print, and sicker still at the difficulty with which one puts it down. After all that, to enter the Mackay Brown world is like finding oneself at last on a moorland after months in cities or home counties; one is almost deafened by the wonderful silence.

Hilary Corke, in a review of "A Calendar of Love," in The Times Literary Supplement, No. 3400, April 27, 1967, p. 565.

JAMES R. FRAKES

All of the pieces in *A Calendar of Love* are set in the Orkneys: their backgrounds range from the Viking days to the present, their essences from the lyric to the saga. Many are sketches— deft, graphic, incisive, but still sketches. To match the primitive emotions of his characters, Mr. Brown strains towards a runic style, manipulating refrains and incremental repetition, folk rhythms and local idiom. Full of crafty tinkers, lobster creels, kirkyards and hayforks, these stories exploit local color instead of extending it into a more universal art. Despite two stories that are rich and imaginative ("**A Calendar of Love**" and "**Five Green Waves**"), there is more geography than humanity in *A Calendar of Love*. Too many aprons are raised to too many girls' faces. (p. 42)

James R. Frakes, "Promise and Fulfillment," in The New York Times Book Review, *April 28, 1968, pp. 42-3.*

SEAMUS HEANEY

Mr Mackay Brown's imagination is heraldic and formal; it is stirred by legends of Viking warrior and Christian saint; it solemnises the necessary labour of life into a seasonal liturgy; it consecrates the visible survivals of history, and ruins of time, into altars that are decked with the writings themselves. I have never seen his poetry sufficiently praised—and there are the makings of a sizable new collection of poems stitched into [*An Orkney Tapestry*]: it is the work of a man who seems not so much a manipulator of experience as the medium for a whole way of life. The voice may be tuned to the verse conventions of the 20th century but it utters with the excited plain confidence of the ballad. I can imagine some critics finding him eccentric, even exotic; his litanies of names and actions, his prayers and spells may be 'outside the mainstream of contemporary poetry' but they have a deep clear source of their own. . . . If his poetry is regarded as the peak of his work, this book about Orkney represents the geology that projects and sustains it. It is not at all a 'travel book' but a spectrum of lore, legend and literature, a highly coloured reaction as Orkney breaks open in the prisms of a poet's mind and memory. There are two short plays, poems, translations of some smarting imagist verses by the Icelandic sailors who made a pilgrimage to Jerusalem in the 12th century. . . . There is social history compressed into imagery, imagery expanded into elegiac reverie; there are ballads and folklore. The whole thing is a kind of loosely organised poem although there isn't a loosely written sentence in the book. The style is what holds the essays together, plain and carefully locked as a dry-stone wall.

Mr Mackay Brown might be regarded as Barnes to Edwin Muir's Hardy. Both pairs of writers create a country of the mind that is related to a real but passing way of life. Hardy and Muir are more distanced, Barnes and Mackay Brown are more intimately, more umbilically linked to the community. The latter also share an antiquarian passion and give scholarship the kiss of life with a stanza. *An Orkney Tapestry* records, preserves, stretches its own rich myth round the myth-hoard. (p. 254)

Seamus Heaney, "Celtic Fringe, Viking Fringe," in The Listener, *Vol. LXXXII, No. 2108, August 21, 1969, pp. 254-55.*

JO GRIMOND

George Mackay Brown is a portent. No one else writes like [him or has his] . . . feeling for language. No one else stands out against the gravel background of modern literature with forms and colours like those he has taken from Orkney and made his own [in *An Orkney Tapestry*]. He refreshes us in the desert of mass production. He could hardly be less fashionable. Sometimes you feel that he is going to slip into sentimentality,

preciousness, or antiquarian folklore. But this fear confirms his genius. For it is an element in genius that it can go so near these pitfalls without toppling over—the best of Renoir's pictures verge on the pretty.

Again you may feel a twinge of suspicion that some of his somewhat stylised accounts of simple life now lost, could only be written by someone who has led a comfortable, middle-class existence. Much as I admire him, I am aware that his comparative well-being vitiates some of Belloc's rhetoric on the glories of hardship and battle. But this is certainly not true of Mr Brown who has suffered from illness and has never had much in the way of acclaim or reward. His is an innate talent: as true as that of Yeats. A talent which would have welled up wherever Mr Brown lived. But a talent which, while it has obviously fed on wide reading, on religion, on the influence of individuals like Edwin Muir, has been fashioned by Orkney and is used on Orkney material.

It is worthwhile then sparing a moment to consider Orkney. Neither in appearance nor tradition is Orkney Celtic. It can be a green country on blue sea—as you can imagine from the dust-cover of this book. Its land is rolling, not jagged. Its soil is good. Mr. Brown tells us that the people of Orkney (there are only 18,000 of them) are intelligent and he quotes a long list of professors to prove it. . . . Orkney, for all the apparent gentleness of its sandstone, has a fine, hard skeleton beneath. . . . It is this which imposes form on the colour and romance which too often in Celtic art run to the heavy, the shapeless or the rhetorical. . . .

Mr Mackay Brown's imagination uses images taken from landscape, heraldry, artifacts. Though intensely sensitive to individuals and man's condition, strangely enough, though the book is largely about Earls and rulers, crofters and fishermen, the human being is not the first vehicle for his imagination. He is someone, I believe, who is more likely to describe a figure of eight as an hour-glass than a barmaid. And this, I think, is another Orkney characteristic. . . . [On] the whole the figures in Orkney art are subordinate to landscape or the genius of the place. In addition, Mr Brown's imagination owes something to mysticism as well as to the earth. In the foreword he claims 'This book takes its stand with the poets'. It is a bold but justified claim. There are not so many poets and some have only a little poetry in them. We should be thankful for Mr Brown and grateful to Orkney that has fed him.

Jo Grimond, "Genius of Place," in The Spectator, *Vol. 223, No. 7365, August 23, 1969, p. 224.*

JAMES R. FRAKES

[Incisive] and moving are the Orkney Islands stories [in *A Time to Keep*] by George Mackay Brown, whose earlier book, *A Calendar of Love,* I fear I slighted and even maligned [see excerpt above]. What a rare privilege to be able to apologize publicly for my glib misreading of his work as an exploitation of exotic local-color. I should have seen that this regionalist, like Faulkner, has discovered his own little postage stamp of native soil and transformed it into dancing-ground.

These stripped and stark stories sing in their chains with more clarity and grace than our anguish normally permits: tortured friezes like "**Celia,**" "**A Time to Keep**" and "**The Story Teller**"; the perfect vignettes of the tinkers' wedding in "**The Whaler's Return**" and the Viking raid in "**Tartan**"; the fictional fleshing, in "**The Eye of the Hurricane,**" of such big, empty abstractions as love, courage, loss, honor. Granted, Brown's is a very special world, apparently closed but in reality so open it screams its vulnerability. This man works with a compassionate scalpel, rendering the elements once more elemental. And absolutely beautiful.

> *James R. Frakes, in a review of "A Time to Keep,"*
> *in* The New York Times Book Review, *July 19,*
> *1970, p. 31.*

ANNE CLUYSENAAR

Writing in Orkney, Mackay Brown uses not only the methods of ancient bardic poetry but also the counters. We get not only triadic runes and descriptions which avoid the synthesising word or phrase—so that dawn, for example, is described in terms of its effects on the landscape, in a fashion verging on the riddle—but also the old themes and world-view, the old point of reference, an absence of 'felt life' which, despite the great imitative skill of the verse and the prose, is deeply disturbing in a poet personally and poetically committed to a way of life which is threatened by such real social and political forces. It might be said, no doubt, that the avoidance of individualization in favour of types is a crucial part of Mackay Brown's message, a sign of his interest in the persistence across generations of certain basic life-dominating human qualities. However I found the dramatization of some of his stories on TV much more effective than even the best work contained in [*Fishermen with Ploughs* and *Poems New and Selected*], and I think that this is because the camera supplied a lack in the writing, making the sea, the rock, the human face *present*, as the hieratic style alone is unable to do. The poem cycle *Fishermen with Ploughs* adds fuel to a doubt which the style and subject matter of the [*Poems New and Selected*] had already suggested with its lament for John F. Kennedy—which fails to come to grips with Kennedy's real role in politics. . . . At the end of *Fishermen with Ploughs,* a small group of men and women escaping from the *black pentacostal fire* of an atomic explosion arrives by boat in Orkney. They carry with them a bag of grain, their one hope of starting society again at the agricultural stage of development. The grain turns out to be blasted by fire, and the community has to face a descent to even earlier means of survival. But this story is told, it seems, less as a warning than as a framework for the illustration of certain qualities needed for survival. These qualities seem to be summed up by the notion of ruthless male egoism, to which the sexual submissiveness of women forms a natural support. The Skipper, who takes over command, takes over too the dominant position in the valley, steals other men's wives and asserts his physical force to humiliate other men, especially the loving and youthful ecologist, John. Irony? If so, it misfires. The woman who once lived with John comes to him when he has been tied to the Skipper's gable-end and flogged. She is now the Skipper's woman. This is her monologue:

> *Someone must suffer,* I said, *I couldn't help what I did. You stood between me and the sun.* With the nail of my forefinger I loosened slowly a thick dark medal that soldered his rag of shirt to his shoulders then tore it off. A circle of new blood oozed and darkened and welled. I broke the red disk between my fingers. The sunken head rose up like a bird. The scavenger turned cold eyes on me. He shrieked, a gull in the first light.

John's initiation is now complete. The unpleasantness seems here to be more than an outcome of the woman's temperament. In her cruelty and weakness she also serves as an apparently necessary catalyst, perhaps because she responds so deeply to the *sun* of the Skipper's power? Again, after the final disaster to the grain occurs, the Skipper *opens his hands over us in a kind of benediction*. Intelligence and love are, apparently, no match for him. Neither is learning: the choice of the most relevant form of learning, ecology, is clearly significant, as is the fact that the man who possesses it is the weakest member of the group and eventually the outcast. If I have got Mackay Brown's message wrong, why does he load the dice so heavily? The lack of intimate individual realization in style and content seems to reflect, at the very least, a crudity of social perception. (pp. 74-5)

> *Anne Cluysenaar, in a review of "Fishermen with Ploughs" and "Poems New and Selected," in* Stand Magazine, *Vol. 13, No. 1, 1972, pp. 72-5.*

NEIL ROBERTS

Although the occasion for this review is George Mackay Brown's novel *Greenvoe,* I shall be discussing mainly the short stories in the volume *A Time to Keep* (1969) and the play *A Spell for Green Corn* (1970). The subject and inspiration of the novel is close to that of the stories—the life of the people of Orkney, its historical continuity and the forces that threaten it—but I find *Greenvoe* disappointing. In his best work, in touching the lives of his people, he shows the supple, unforcing, pure responsiveness of the true novelist; he does not put his character on stilts, trivialise or otherwise distort them, for some end of his own. Despite the evident attraction for him of their way of life, his novelist's instinct for reality is stronger than any urge to idealise. In the greater part of *Greenvoe*, his first novel, this instinct seems to have deserted him. Not that he idealises, but his characters have too much the air of exhibits. (p. 181)

Mr Brown is a man of many styles and he is not afraid of pastiche. But in most of his stories he has a simple, vivid narrative manner which is quite free from literariness. I also want to try to describe what I can best call the shapeliness or rhythm of his stories. I don't mean by this any merely formal literary quality, but the sense that the stories convey of the shape and rhythm of a life. This is important because for the most part Mr. Brown practises a fairly rigorous externality. He does not explain or analyse his characters (mostly fishermen and crofters) but presents a series of events more or less as in a ballad. (p. 182)

A third important quality to be found in all Mr Brown's work, which is partly an aspect of the two I have already referred to, is a marked and beautiful ceremoniousness of language: both his own, and that of his people. And this brings me to the important question of his *subjects*, in the broader sense. First, at the crudest level of opinion; the effect that might be made on a reader not captivated by Mr. Brown's art. He is strongly attached to the pagan, Catholic and agricultural pasts of his native islands. He dislikes Puritanism, machines, bureacracy and State charity. At the level of crude prejudice-swapping, I suppose I share most of these attitudes but there is of course nothing new about them, and once the list is launched there is a certain deadly predictability about the items. So no matter what the reader's cast of mind the subjects, at that level, are unlikely to be enticing. So let me switch the emphasis from Mr Brown's opinions to his interests. He is interested in art, religion and ritual, their relations to each other and to the agricultural basis of civilisation. He is interested in the relation of pagan to Christian religion, and of the Word of Christ to the word of the poet.

> The word was imprisoned between black boards, and chained and padlocked, in the pulpit of the kirk—impossible for it to get free among the ploughs and the nets, that season of famine. Therefore the lesser word, the fiddle, the poem, the rune, must work the miracle of bread.

> Art must be of *use*—a coercive rhyme, to strand a whale on the rock, a scratch on stone to make the corn grow. What are all these fiddles and statues and books for?

These extracts are from "Storm Kolson's Notebook", printed as an appendix to *A Spell for Green Corn,* and supposedly written by the fiddler who is the central figure in the play. These considerations are in fact more necessary in talking about the play than about the stories. The stories are so achieved, and at the same time so buried in the lives of their people, that they do not demand a response at this abstract level. The play, which is supernaturalistic and symbolic, does. I think it is the most interesting thing that Mackay Brown has done, and his achievement and potential seem to me much larger than when I had only read the stories. (pp. 183-84)

To illustrate the shapeliness and rhythm of the stories, I shall take my favourite, **"The Whaler's Return."** Andrew Flaws has arrived at Hoy from a whaling trip with seven sovereigns. The period is uncertain, but it is evidently a lot of money. 'With this money I'm going to rent the croft of Breck and marry Peterina. I'll stay at home from now on. I'll work the three fields and maybe go on the lobsters when it's weather. I'll never see a whale or an iceberg again'. It is a sixteen-mile walk to Peterina's home, and before he starts he is lured first into one pub and then another. At the second the attraction is a pretty barmaid. 'He thought it might be the last chance he would ever have to speak to a pretty girl. Peterina was good and hard-working, but rather ugly'. He spends a lot of money, but is pleased to get out of Hamnavoe (Stromness), having visited only two of its forty drinking-places. However, when he stops to eat he is tempted to drink again, and also has to pay for the funeral of Peterina's father. Then he is literally dragged into another pub on the road by the landlord. He is thus very drunk when he stumbles on a tinker wedding. . . . Although the wedding is a fantastic affair, and culminates in wild drinking and dancing, the central ritual is serious and dignified, and illustrates the quality of ceremoniousness that I have mentioned. . . . Flaws is discovered by the tinkers and beaten. When he comes to himself it is morning, and he has only two sovereigns left—which is, however, enough to rent the croft. . . . Flaws has passed into this quiet, sober life—his future—through a violent, irresponsible and fantastic journey, and yet the culmination of the fantasy, the tinkers' wedding, was in reality a preparation of [the participants] also for just such a life of sober responsibility.

I can be much less certain in what I say about *A Spell for Green Corn.* The story is somewhat complicated and obscure, so I cannot even give that. The play is spread over three periods: the pre-Reformation age, the age of Puritanism, and the Machine Age. These three ages also recur in one of the best of the stories, which consists of three sermons, one from each age. The main action takes place in the seventeenth century,

and concerns the seduction of a girl, Sigrid, by Storm Kolson, his disappearance and her condemnation for witchcraft. At the same time the harvest is in danger, and is saved by a ritual bonfire, dance, and the recitation of spells. One section is entitled "The Wrong Word" which (with the reference to the Word being locked between black boards, quoted earlier) seems to be a reference to Protestantism. The strongest positive forces represented in the play, however, are not those of Catholic Christianity but dance, music, poetry, sexual love and ritual. There are several references to the withershin dance of evil and when Storm Kolson reappears at Sigrid's execution he does not try to save her but says, 'Sigrid, if only they burn you with ceremony. There dance is everything'. The stress on ceremony is reinforced by the fact that the whole play is a superbly sustained example of ceremonious language, which is sometimes deliberate pastiche, but mostly a formal and dignified version of modern English. Throughout the execution scene Sigrid speaks entirely in phrases from the Song of Solomon, but they are no more incongruous than the Biblical quotations in *The Pilgrim's Progress.* (pp. 184-87)

Greenvoe, as I have said, is disappointing. It describes the destruction of a village by progress in the form of a secret military establishment. Most of the novel is devoted to an evocation of the life of the village, but despite the greater scope offered by the novel form Mr Brown rarely achieves the rhythm that is to be found in all the stories of *A Time to Keep* (the earlier collection *A Calendar of Love* is, I think, much inferior). The sections are very short, and I am afraid that the externality reminds me uncomfortably often of *Under Milk Wood* rather than of ballads. When he takes us into the consciousness of a character, in an extended analysis of the minister's mother's diseased conscience, the result is tedious. It is also the only prose work of Mr Brown's in which I am conscious of overwriting. There are exceptions and isolated triumphs, the most notable being the religious fisherman, Samuel Whaness and his wife. Again the triumph is one of formal, ceremonious language, and despite the dislike of Puritanism that I have referred to the lives of these severe Protestants are treated with a lovely reverence. There is also a superb passage of Bunyanesque pastiche in which Samuel thinks he is drowning.

But the reader who takes my hint about the other works, and agrees with my estimate of them, will read *Greenvoe* anyway.

I have left myself space to say even less than I had intended about the verse. *A Spell for Green Corn* contains two of the best literary ballads I have read; otherwise I can only say that the poems I like best (particularly **"A Child's Calendar"** and **"The Statue in the Hills"**) have a strongly liturgical note. *Fishermen with Ploughs* contains a remarkable prose section in which a group of people flees to the Orkneys after a nuclear war. The group rapidly regresses beyond the assumptions of civilisation and Christianity, and becomes subject to the brutal and egoistic but capable Skipper who has led them there: the originator of a ruling caste. In this there is no theological gloating over original sin, but a calm statement of necessity. There is in fact very little energy of rejection in all Mr Brown's work. This makes it agreeable to read, but also means that there is not much engagement with the contemporary realities that he dislikes. The destructive progress in *Greenvoe* is observed from without, as a menace, not as a human phenomenon (though I must set to his credit a fine specimen of enlightened cant: 'Ours is a compassionate as well as a questing age'.) But this limitation must not be supposed to suggest that there is anything pastoral or nostalgic in his work. The lives he presents are on the whole prosaic and ugly. He would perhaps want to claim that they are human, rooted and ceremonious. The fact that there is enough meanness and ugliness to challenge these claims is partly what makes his best work so compelling. (pp. 188-89)

Neil Roberts, "George Mackay Brown," in The Cambridge Quarterly, *Vol. VI, No. 2, 1973, pp. 181-89.*

THE TIMES LITERARY SUPPLEMENT

George Mackay Brown was converted to Rome in 1961. It is perhaps impertinent to speculate on the private life of a contemporary writer, yet Mackay Brown's Catholicism, in the Marian and Latinate version that he favours, bulks so hugely in his writings that some speculation is unavoidable. . . .

That there are parallels to be drawn between his life and his work he himself has already indicated: the spareness of his prose style, for instance, seems clearly intended to mirror the leanness of Orkney existence. Similarly, his dislike of the modern world—hatred would hardly be too strong a description—must have been one of the factors that led him to avail himself of two thousand years of Church tradition and to incorporate both ailment and cure so strongly in all he writes. There is, again, his geographical isolation to be considered. He was born in Orkney and has not too willingly left, and one could scarcely go farther away in space and time and remain in twentieth-century Britain. It adds up to a writer very much of a piece, with clear-cut strengths and weaknesses, who inhabits—almost literally—a black and white world and who portrays that world in like terms and like manner.

But this unity, undeniable and capable of generating considerable power, is bought at a price. Orkney today is no longer the idyllic place looked back on by Edwin Muir. The impingement on it of progress, one of Mackay Brown's main themes in this new collection of short stories [*Hawkfall*] as elsewhere, drives him either far back in history, in search of life uncontaminated by materialism, or to simplistic divisions between good and evil and blatant manipulations of character to accord with those divisions. The eponymous hero of **"Master Halcrow, Priest"**, with his lovable little sins of too much fishing and beer-drinking, who is pitted—unsuccessfully, of course—against a flock of grim black Calvinists, is an earlier and unattractive example of this. The dividing continues here with the scarcely less insultingly loaded **"The Tarn and the Rosary"**.

The strong sense of continuity, too, that Mackay Brown gets from his shuttling back and forth across the centuries, from his frequent use of the same locations, and descendants of the initial protagonists, in successive sections of the same story, has its corollary in the loss of freedom entailed. The characters in [**"Hawkfall"**], for example, never break loose. They are strangled in pattern. Indeed, they have been subordinated almost out of existence.

One might even say that the spare directness of the writing, with its ballad-like stylizations and repetitions, and the stories themselves, so heavy with history and symbol and myth, are in fact at odds with the characters. These unfortunate people are made to suffer an appalling spiritual and intellectual poverty. They ping-pong helplessly between sea and sheets, between pub and plough, the men endlessly drunk, the women endlessly betrayed, and their thoughts are no less limited. Even

the few who pretend to culture hardly have any. Reading about them in such a prose is a little like finding Neanderthals in a medieval tapestry.

Hawkfall, in short, is very much the Mackay Brown mixture as before. It is fair to add that the earlier staccato simplicities of sentence construction have dwindled, with a resultant gain in flexibility of prose. There is, too, an occasional welcome deployment of humour.

"Between Sea and Sheets," in The Times Literary Supplement, *No. 3786, September 27, 1974, p. 1033.*

JOHN MELLORS

Despite the slayings with axes and brawls in alehouses, George Mackay Brown's *Hawkfall* is short on punch. Tales, yarns, legends, extracts from diaries and snippets from sagas add up to a poetic chronicle of a remote and vanishing life in the Orkney Islands, a part of Britain we think of as Scottish but which once belonged to Norway, and where men are called Olafson and Jansen and Garth. Some of the stories are slight, archaeological fragments rather than complete pieces, but cumulatively they give you the feeling that you have lived in those northern crofts and halls, enduring through many centuries the hardships of historical and climatic circumstance. *Et in Orcadia ego* . . . **"Tithonus,"** for example, is an elegiac account of the decline of a community from the 1920s, when at least the village was still enriched by birth, to the 1970s, when the young have all gone to work in Coventry or Bathgate or Australia and 'there is only one dancer in the island now and he carries the hour-glass and the spade and the scythe.'

The Two Fiddlers, sympathetically illustrated . . . , is a collection of Orkneys stories by the same author for 'young readers'. How young? At a guess I think I would have enjoyed them most when I was 10 or 11. They are fables and fairy stories about battles and princesses and men who change into seals, and, appropriately enough for a young readership, George Mackay Brown is concerned more with action and plot than with description and comment. Nevertheless, his writing remains sharp and stylish; invading Scots are frightened and 'fate-pierced', and when the Orkneymen strike, 'the air blossomed with stones.' (p. 62)

John Mellors, "Real Dazzlers," in The Listener, *Vol. 93, No. 2388, January 9, 1975, pp. 61-2.*

JULIA O'FAOLAIN

George Mackay Brown is a writer in love with the past and with the Orkney Islands where he finds it still precariously lingering. Three tales from [*The Sun's Net*], **"Soldier from the Wars Returning"**, **"The Book of Black Arts"** and **"The Pirate's Ghost"**, would fit perfectly in a collection of hearthside ghost stories of the sort brought out by folklore commissions—only that Mackay Brown's are better written than most. Cleaving to a collective tradition which rests on the work of old oral tale-tellers, his stories make no concession to contemporary taste. Contemporary taste is something which appeals little to Mackay Brown. It draws a crusty rancour from him and some rhetoric, as when he notes the menace exerted on Njalsay Island by the town which lures its dwindling population away from 'the dark earth-rhythms' with its promise of 'a more refined and empty mode of social intercourse'. . . .

In the first story, a doctor remarks that there has not been a birth since he came to Njalsay. Only deaths. 'It seemed like a foreshadowing of the day when the only people in the island were the dead in the churchyard.' By the story's end the doctor has had a vision of a Christmas nativity but, as it is only a vision and happens in a deserted croft called Wanhope, the message is bleak.

Since this author will not follow his absconding characters to the mainland he is left with a shrinking terrain: emptying islands, dream and nostalgia for an idealised past. A story set in the future imagines this past returning: 'Finally, after much suffering, the earth fled from cities and machines . . . A simpler species rose out of the ruins, no less intelligent but with their faces set against science and the ruthless exploitation of the earth and its resources. "Progress" was a word they uttered like a curse.' There is an empty ring to the writing here. The author is pushing his opinions on the reader and falls into slippiness. 'The earth fled . . .' is nonsense.

He is at his best when happily immersed in rural comedy or ghost stories or romancing about a fanciful past. His language then is rich and archaic, his colours high, his pace speedy. I think it is his ability to shift and change rhythm—the art of the cutting room—which permits him to get away with the most outrageously florid metaphors without slowing down his story. '. . . in dream-parlance', he can write, 'they put upon me lustre of water, and afterwards dried me, and then they brought white linen garments . . . and put these immaculate dream garments upon me.' On the opposite page he has the sun shine 'out of the sky in aureate splendour, among quiet heraldries of cloud'. This is flamboyant. It is self-conscious. It is not geared at all to modern sensibility—at any rate not to mine—and yet, thanks to his humour, his convincing dialogue and the action which cuts quickly in and out among the shoals of 'dream-parlance', Mackay Brown managed in the end to make me feel that, yes, all this embellishment is acceptable and even adds a curious, hallucinative enchantment to his narrative. (p. 60)

> *Julia O'Faolain, "New Stories," in* The New Review, *Vol. III, No. 27, June, 1976, pp. 58-60.*

JANE MILLER

[The stories in *The Sun's Net*] are a poet's stories, in which images of contrast—between past and present, dream and daylight, the preoccupations of the living and the insights death might afford—are made real. The first story is set in the present on a "dying" island, where the individual's isolation is matched by the community's, and the doctor, the schoolmaster and the minister separately and secretly record a sense of failing the people they have chosen to live among. The failure is characteristic of the times, and catching. Most of the stories are about the past, and fishermen and pirates, blacksmiths and soldiers and farmers occupy a world neither reduced nor beautified by nostalgia but solidly understood with its names and places and particular people. Ghosts and magic and dreams are believed in, not because of a simple credulousness but because in a thoroughly known world mysteries are the more in need of explanation. The villages are studded with bad eggs and torn apart by dissension, yet individuals are able to choose how to live. Sheep stealing merits death, fornication just a sermon, but transgressors of both kinds know the penalties and accept their logic.

In some of the stories the dead hear what the living are saying about them and are able to rewrite their lives. This has an important meaning for Mr Brown, for if "time is a slow banked smoulder to the living" it is "an august merciless ordering of flames" to the dead. Mr Brown's loved Orkneys are dying, and he has set himself to create in their death throes the "slow banked smoulder" of their past. Changes of mood and fortune in particular lives which are felt by whole communities are what he is best at: a young fisherman jauntily carries three silvery haddock up the hill to the rich farmer's daughter he has decided, against advice, to marry after one evening's flirtation. His haddock are devoured like his optimism, for the girl has already left to make a good Edinburgh marriage. The two stories about John Gow, the eighteenth-century mutineer and pirate, are as good as Melville, making wonderfully tangible the distrust and violence which transform a ship during the night in the middle of the ocean, the atmosphere spreading from John Gow himself, an embodiment of treachery with a gift for inspiring quite exceptional trust and love. A young soldier returns from battle, not knowing that he is dead, nor whether or not his side was defeated, for "in the flushed heart of battle no soldier can know how the dice are falling".

> *Jane Miller, "Battle Stations," in* The Times Literary Supplement, *No. 3883, August 13, 1976, p. 1018.*

DENNIS O'DRISCOLL

George Mackay Brown, one of the finest poets writing in English, was born, like Edwin Muir, on Orkney, where most of his 57 years have been spent. Orkney has only been a part of Scotland since the 15th century, having for several centuries before been in Viking hands. George Mackay Brown's mind moves easily across the borders of time and evinces some of the obsession with time that he has identified as a notable Orcadian characteristic. For him the past is one of the most precise measurements of the present and a far more effective one than "number, statistic and graph" that calculate only the material gains associated with "progress" and the factitious stars it gives people to steer their lives by. The decline of ceremony is not compensated for by the arrival of the motorcar; newspapers are a poor substitute for the gossip of old women in which the Greek chorus had its roots; and the fiddle hanging "like a dry chrysalis" on a crofter's wall made purer music than the gramophones which rendered it silent.

But for all that *apparent* romanticism, George Mackay Brown's Orkney cannot, like Yeats' Inisfree, be seen as a retreat from the mainland and its greasy tills, smoke polluting the lens of the imagination, colourless language. Holding its fabric up to the light of rite and history, Mackay Brown is aware that it is a flawed one, stained with the defects that mark people everywhere and under the eroding influence of the world beyond. If Orkney is not his panacea, neither is his disease the "islomania" which afflicts Lawrence Durrell. Instead of the "indescribable intoxication", while on Mediterranean islands, that Durrell gladly suffers, the Orcadian may experience instead the "morbus orcandesis"—"a darkening of the mind . . . induced in sensitive people by the long overhand of winter; the howl and sob of the wind over moors that goes on sometimes for days on end; the perpetual rain that makes tilth and pasture one indiscriminate bog; the unending gnaw of the sea at the crags."

It is hardly surprising that the rhythms of the sea and destructive whine of a storm should be suggested by Mackay Brown's earliest work, and the grafting of the influence of Gerard Manley Hopkins on to an already brittle dialect could lead to something like verbal overkill. . . .

The ten seasick stanzas of . . . **"The Storm"** make an interesting contrast with a recent, and uncollected, poem from a sequence entitled **"Poems from a Small Island"**. Here the indirect, kenning-like approach suggests in a brief sweep of the pen both the storm and the calm after the storm:

> Bruised fish
> In the oatfield—at the shore
> A dove, feet-up.

One of the notable successes of his first full collection *Loaves and Fishes* (1959) was **"The Stranger"**—a typical poem in the way it bridges the quotidian and sacred with a figure who is both human and divine, and with the introduction of bread and ale which are seen both as the fruits of the peasant's labour and the embodiment of his God on the church altar. . . .

By *The Year of the Whale* (1965) Mackay Brown had found a fully distinctive voice and one which has hardly changed in the collections published since then. The influences he has himself identified in his work, "Norse sagas, Scottish ballads and the ceremonies of the Catholic church" are all obvious in this second collection. The fertility celebrated in **"The Stranger"** is extended in **"Country Girl"** to include the "seven circles" of fertility within which she moves and which may be shadows of the great stone circle of Brogar built by the first Orkneymen. . . .

Love, too, is a way of combining the sacred and the worldly, the local and the epic. . . . George Mackay Brown's ability to write poetry "cut from here and there in one weave of time" was consolidated in *The Year of the Whale* in which, with no straining of language or sensibility, he moved between Viking Orkney and John F. Kennedy's America. Perhaps the best poem in the collection, **"The Condemned Well"**, remembers the different thirsts quenched by the well of its title: the horse with "square barbarous teeth, black curling lips", the bee taking his "tiny ration" and Linky the tailor who "stitched that silk through his rum." But in the name of progress, that "rootless, utilitarian faith without beauty or mystery", tomorrow is to be "the day of the long lead pipe." When the long lead pipe of mineral speculators, in Mackay Brown's novel *Greenvoe* (1972), ruthlessly destroys an island we feel that the rituals and lore of the people who ploughed its soil and sailed its waters have also been destroyed. In a few months the priceless accumulations of thousands of years are wiped out and the fertile pulse of seasons that beat, like a heart, to sustain the islanders, is stilled.

That George Mackay Brown would make a superb prose writer was obvious from poems like **"The Abbot"** and **"Hamnavoe Market"** in which each stanza of the poem is built, often with great humour and irony, around a separate person, and in 1967 *A Calendar of Love*, the first of the four collections of short stories and two novels he has so far published appeared. While characterisation has remained important in his approach to writing poetry, the next collections also contained examples of his distinctive and essentially poetical runes, incantations and litanies. For example in **"The Statue in the Hills"**, from *Fishermen with Ploughs* (1971), each group in the community recites a litany which, based on intimate images from their own lives, makes a forceful prayer. . . .

One poem in *Fishermen with Ploughs* which resembled the title story of his first prose collection ["**A Calendar of Love**"] was **"A Child's Calendar"**, in which the island is described through a child's eyes month by month. Days of the week and Stations of the Cross have been similarly used by Mackay Brown to give a simple, secure, natural architecture to his poems and one that blends well with their landscape. . . .

Besides Ikey the tinker, who cunningly crosses the reader's path in the previous collection, we also meet laird and scarecrow who, at each end of the social scale, have important roles on the island. But while the laird was a temporal lord, the crucified scarecrow who wore his cast-off clothes was a great king. . . .

By the nineteenth century the laird, too, had known poverty in his huge house, his power having declined and the houses on the island having emptied. . . .

The medieval *Orkneyinga Saga* with its haunting account of Saint Magnus and the dramatic story of the rise of Rognvald, whose subsequent deeds included a visit to the Holy Land, provides a further rock of history on which an Orcadian identity can securely rest. The saga, and events of which we are given only a tantalising glimpse in its chapters, are given flesh in both prose and poetry by George Mackay Brown. The Icelandic court poet Arnor is imagined out of the saga and into the poem **"The Five Voyages of Arnor"** (published in *Poems New and Selected* [1971]), a poem in which the harsh Northern names are savoured:

> Rolf rode him down
> In Tingvoe, after the council, and rode on
> Through villages, red-hooved, to the sea
> Far from Inga his sister
> And the lawless cry in the cradle, Inga's and Sweyn's,
> And the farm at Rangower. . . .

It is only because this captures so accurately the flavour of skaldic verse that it sounds less conventionally "poetical" to our ears, and it is difficult to disagree with Peter Porter's testament that the poet has "performed near-miracles in making the skaldic past of the Orkneys a matter for truth and reality in the middle of the twentieth century." The miracle is not merely that of re-creating the language of the past but giving a detached, vivid, challenging and convincing picture of the past seen through the long-range telescope of a medieval prince's eye or the secret letters of a Jerusalem inn-keeper. **"The Masque of Princes"** and the title-sequence ["**Winterfold**"] of his most recent collection *Winterfold* (1976) are particularly successful in this regard. As in his short-story **"A Winter's Tale"**, it is the birth of Christ that brings out the best from Mackay Brown's imagination. . . .

Another ancient device, and one which makes use of Mackay Brown's talent for the understated and brief, is the rune. Runes, like benign flashlights, can, as he puts it himself, "shed a mystery and excitement over the commonest things." The poem **"Runes from the Island of Horses"** includes:

> *Winter*
> Three winter brightnesses—
> Bridesheet, boy in snow,
> Kirkyard spade.
>
> *Entrances*
> Between thief and hoard
> Three narrow doors—
> Furrow, maidenhead, grave.

The new collection, *Winterfold*, which further extends Mackay Brown's range, ends with a series of rune-like variations on the Stations of the Cross which, although over-ambitious and not uniformly successful, affirms his belief that the journey of Christ parallels the fruitful journey of all things that follow nature to death, and resurrection in harvest. But even the Orcadian is losing touch with the natural, with what land and sea tell him: "The sky is scored with television aerials. The old stories have vanished with the horses and the tinkers; instead of the yarn at the pierhead or the pub, you are increasingly troubled with bores who insist on telling you what they think about Viet Nam or the bank-rate or heart-transplants. . . .''

It is not a reaction against knowledge but a reaction against secondhand TV-acquired opinions that Mackay Brown expresses. Thought has become as debased and standardised as the language which could once categorise rain as "a driv, a rug, a murr, a hagger, a dagg, a rav, a hellyiefer" but now say simply "it rains". For George Mackay Brown, believing that decay of language is "a symptom of a more serious disease", poetry holds, like a Norse broch, the archetypal maps that might some day force technology into retreat. Reading all of his work, prose and poetry, one is overwhelmed by the richness of his finds as layer on layer of the past are unrolled like carpets from the "House of History". The questions he raises are relevant to people everywhere who, by the very fact of eating, are bound to the soil. His work implies and exemplifies the doctrine that only fundamental change will take the superficiality out of modern life and "reconcile the warring peoples of the world."

And although the oil platform troubles its waters now and the farmer is as intimate with American TV serials as with clay, people may again, George Mackay Brown suggests, turn to places like Orkney where hardships were embellished and given meaning by myth, ceremony and the company of "characters": "It could happen that the atom-and-planet horror at the heart of our civilisation will scatter people again to the quiet beautiful fertile places of the world." (pp. 49-54)

Dennis O'Driscoll, "Poems from a Small Island,"
in Poetry Australia, *No. 68, October, 1978, pp. 49-54.*

FRANCIS RUSSELL HART

The most original novel to come recently from northern Scotland is George Mackay Brown's *Magnus* (1973).

Magnus derives from saga, saint's life, religious pageant; it is homily and ritual recitation, morality play played out on a sacramental earth beneath a cosmic sky. It celebrates the mystery of a martyrdom and, as the narrator says, "to celebrate the mystery properly the story-teller must give way to a ritual voice." The ritual voice expands and alternates to include everything from a modern slang journalese to religious meditation, from a jeweled formulaic style to stark, sagalike matter-of-fact or evocative romantic symbol. . . . But everywhere is the controlling idea of the sacramental reality of the mass. . . .

The sacramental aesthetic of the mass fused with the luminous starkness of Norse saga: such is the style of *Magnus,* and in such a linguistic world, historical and domestic realism have little place.

The historical matter is the life and death of the Orkney Saint Magnus Martyr, Magnus Erlendson, twelfth-century earl, and his cousin-rival Earl Hakon Paulson. Their wars for supremacy spread ruin through the Orkneys, until finally a peace confer-

ence is arranged, and Paulson cheats and murders Magnus. Paulson begins a long and constructive solitary rule, Magnus is canonized, and the implication is that the sacrifice of Magnus provided a necessary cleansing, a miraculous healing. The implication is somewhat confused when the narrative of Magnus's murder is translated into an unnamed Nazi concentration camp and identified with the butchery of a Lutheran pastor. But the suggestion is that time and place are all one, and the conflict between the earls is the eternal conflict between the unworldly saint and the practical man of action. Historical character is barely sketched. The local reality of the harsh lies of the peasants and the tinkers is suggested with genuine compassion, but their dominant role as universal human chorus overrides cultural representativeness.

In *Greenvoe* (1972), Brown's first novel, locality, mystery, and ritual are, I think, more effectively fused; here, too, Brown's extraordinary talents as short story writer are impressively adapted to the more complex form. In the fictional Orkney fishing village of Greenvoe on the island of Hellya, Brown portrays the wide diversity of a Scottish culture and the blighted wholeness of its history, suggesting at the same time the hidden persistence of its archaic life in ritual. It is a pattern we have seen before in Gibbon and Gunn, with the further elaboration, seen in *Magnus,* of a rich stylistic orchestration. The two books on the shelf of the young ferryman Westray suggest the range: *The Orkneyinga Saga* and *On Love Carnal and Divine: Seventeenth Century Sermons;* echoes from Brown's study of Hopkins and Dylan Thomas are also heard. Within the orchestration each character and domestic grouping carry their own cultural idioms and narrative modes.

The chief characters include three fishermen: one a figure of Old Testament piety and presbyterian cant (Samuel Whaness); one a radical atheist and local historian (the Skarf); one a lazy drunk (Bert Kerston)—all plausible and at times heroic, all free of caricature. Also included are a retired world sailor, Ben Budge, and his devoted sister; the promiscuous spinster Alice Voar and her numerous children by different fathers; the virginal schoolmarm from Edinburgh's Morningside, Margaret Inverary; the "norse god" ferryman and casanova Ivan Westray; the local dimwit Timmy Folster with his burnt-out house and his methylated spirits; the hotel proprietor and his illegal whisky; the laird Colonel Fortin-Bell, his horsy niece, and his Lawrence-obsessed granddaughter; the Indian pedlar (and part-time narrator); and of course the weak but kindly, secretly alcoholic minister, Simon McKee, and his guilt-ridden Edinburgh mother. As the list suggests, there are many little plots here, and one extensive plot—the pathetic story of McKee and his mother (Scottish bourgeois tragedy of the manse). All have their own suspenses and resolutions, deaths, exiles, and reconciliations. All develop in close juxtaposition. The cumulative effect is of a parochial history with wide cultural representativeness.

Yet in a sense, all these lives are thwarted or decadent, and all are set against the two opposing forces of history and prehistory in whose timeless conflict they are caught. Bureaucratic Man has arrived secretly on the island, and the island is doomed to make way for Operation Black Star, a mysterious defense project. The bureaucrat's index cards, "brief cryptic biographies," reject the islanders as insignificant; and shortly they are followed up by the bureaucrat's bulldozers. But the bureaucrat's "history" is a temporary invasion. The hidden prehistoric life of seasonal ritual, having punctuated the book with its ceremonies in the barn at the Bu, returns at the end to the now derelict island. Having scaled the cliff and eluded the fence encircling the island, the children of the exiles hold their harvest ritual in a ruined broch—''this navel had attached many generations of Hellyamen to the nourishing earth''—and bring the word of ''resurrection,'' light and blessing to the ''kingdom of winter,'' ''however long it endures, that kingdom, a night or a season or a thousand ages.''

What is this resurrection that is promised? Is it purely transcendental, or is it cultural? These are the real children of Hellya, and they have returned to their real place; the fence cannot keep them out. The potent Highland myth of the Clearances has been reenacted on a Cold War stage, with the bulldozers of the bureaucrat. The latest betrayers are gone, and with them the doomed dregs of a community, and the effect, as in *Magnus,* is of cleansing.... The exiles have survived. In the archaic remnants of their island is the power to believe that life will return. Time will outlast history; for ''time is not a conflagration; it is a slow grave sequence of grassblade, fish, apple, star, snowflake.'' (pp. 394-97)

> *Francis Russell Hart, ''Jane Duncan and George Mackay Brown,'' in his* The Scottish Novel: From Smollett to Spark, *Cambridge, Mass.: Harvard University Press, 1978, pp. 385-97.*

MARGARET GARDINER

George Mackay Brown describes the ''Orkney mind'' as ''an intermeshing of the practical and the imaginative'' and this could well be a description of his own writing in his *Portrait of Orkney.* Every now and then he abandons the measured language of his prose-pace to break into a little dance, a snatch of poetry—the past, legend and myth, bubbling up to the surface of the present.

The book is divided into sections with orderly headings—People, Land, Sea, Religion, Culture and so on. But since this is neither a guide book with illustrations—its size and shape would preclude that—nor a picture book with commentary, a pleasant anarchy confuses these categories. Contemporary descriptions and facts are intertwined with history, history with legend and legend with anecdote and speculation. This weave—images of weaving, spinning, web and tapestry constantly recur—is surely apt in a portrait of islands whose people, living in a modern world, are nevertheless unusually aware of their past. The evidences are all about them and are part of their everyday lives—standing stones, brochs, cairns and the citadel-like clusters of farm buildings. And weaving is a natural image for an Orcadian: indeed, until quite recently hand weaving would often occupy farmers during the dark winters and today, in summer, fishermen can be seen sitting outside their houses, skilfully knotting their nets.

Although George Mackay Brown writes admiringly of Orkney farmers with their ''miracles of understatement'', he himself—at least on paper—fizzes with enthusiasms. He delights in lists: they clatter merrily down upon the pages—lists of place names, of family names, of sea stories, of the subjects about which Orcadians have written, of Orkney artists, of the people attending the Dounby Show.

It is in the section called ''Lore'' that George Mackay Brown's writing excels: he communicates his love of these folk tales with rare skill. In the charming final section, ''A Nature Anthology'', he also shows his relish of earlier writings about Orkney—extracts from the sixteenth, seventeenth and nineteenth centuries, ranging from reports of monsters and other wonders to careful descriptions of the flora and fauna of the islands.

> *Margaret Gardiner, ''Insular Images,'' in* The Times Literary Supplement, *No. 4071, April 10, 1981, p. 396.*

DOUGLAS DUNN

Much of *Andrina* is concerned with the past, whether that of history or of legends and tales. **''A Winter Legend''**, for example, is a fiery tale on the theme of time and human age. The fact that we can tell what it is about gives the story an uncanny sense of having been handed down through many generations without parts of it having been lost or corrupted in the process of re-telling. Only a poet of Brown's imaginative, historical, religious and place-loyal disposition could have written something that on the face of it seems incorrigibly old-fashioned, but which in the reading convinces with its contemporary language. Much the same could be said of **''An Epiphany Tale''**. A boy who is deaf, dumb and blind is gifted by three strangers, one after the other, with brief moments of the senses he was born without. Whatever the religious significance of this short, brilliantly composed story, it is deeply affecting for the strange beauty of life it conveys, whether of sound, smell or touch.

''The Chamber of Poetry'' and **''Poets''** are, as their titles suggest, more literary pieces, and less convincing. They are almost manifestos on the nature of poets and poetry. In the first, a room in an inn is occupied first by Li Po, later by a lad from the village who has been used to sitting in the pub reading over his beer. This young man is called Terence, the poet in Housman's *A Shropshire Lad*, and that gives some idea of Brown's whimsy here. Later, the innkeeper has a look at the list of guests the room has received. Indeed, yes: a very impressive list.

If the room at that timeless, placeless inn suggests an idea of poetry as a secret, scorned, hidden art, then that is in keeping with the three stories of **''Poets''**, beginning with a Chinese satirist, and ending with a young hopeful whose poem in something called *Diggins—A New Verse Quarterly* changes his status in the community. It is interesting that Brown should hold and dramatize a belief in poets and poetry which many readers will find unreal or sentimental, and that unreality may even be a source of his strength. There is certainly something defiant, grand and lonely about his depiction of poets as solitaries possessed of an asocial dedication; if true, it might have been dramatized with deeper psychological veracity than the conventions of Brown's manner allow, given as it is to folkish brevity and quick, ballad-like explanations (or no explanations). For all the beauty of his crisp, lucid phrasing, it is seldom of the sort likely to lead him into the minds of his characters, while his characters are seldom of the sort ever to invite a fuller embodiment of their mental processes.

''Magi'' offers three accounts of the three kings who brought gifts to Christ in the stable, and where they came from. They are stories about destiny, told with wonderful skill—the third especially, set in the far north of the Eskimos. I can think of no one who writes better than Brown about cold, ice, and weather in general. Again, though, the Eskimo boy whose destiny lies elsewhere than as chief of his tribe, and who spurns the cruel practicalities of hunting and leadership for carving on walrus ivory, is like Brown's poets—men and women who turn their backs on what the community alleges to be their responsibilities.

"King and Shepherd" and **"The Feast at Paplay"** are historical tales, the first showing how a precursor of Genghis Khan decided to turn back for home after an encounter with a shepherd reminds him of his humanity and his own flocks of sheep, the second taking its cue from an episode of the *Orkneyinga Saga*. Brown excels here in his evocative, deft picturing of time and place, with no mention of the actual date or setting. At the same time there is a greater psychological truth in the writing: the characters seem more like people than the figments of a story; the result, perhaps, of the dramatic irony over which the story is cunningly folded.

The title story **"Andrina"** was made into a film for television. . . . Like much of Brown's work it relies for its *frisson* on faith in the supernatural, on how fate follows a wanderer to that moment of truth which explains a life. It is a ghost story in which the crudeness of much writing in that genre has been avoided. Enough of the conventions remain for the credibility of **"Andrina"** to be smudged—although the truth of what it says is beyond doubt. The manner in which the story is conceived, and then told, seems curiously if beautifully out of date, almost as if old ways of writing stories stumble in Brown's work against more recent expectations. In writing so controlled, however, by a poet perfectly at ease with his imagination and a language natural to it, the effect of that apparent collision of old and new can only be fruitful and challenging, as well as, in this case, profoundly enjoyable.

> Douglas Dunn, *"The Supernatural Frisson,"* in The Times Literary Supplement, *No. 4174, April 1, 1983, p. 324.*

DOUGLAS DUNN

Voyages begins with a sequence of twenty-seven short poems—**"Seal Island Anthology"**—in which Edgar Lee Masters's township poetry is acknowledged in the title. Lyric footnotes—short narratives as human asterisks—cumulate in the sequence into a warm proof of Brown's ability to delineate the griefs and merriments of a community. A way of life is depicted through its lyric nodes: a minister, a widower, a croft wife, a drunkard, a returned emigrant from America, a boy dreaming in a classroom, and so on. By now it is familiar territory to Brown's admirers, many of whom, I suspect, revel in his elegiac note, particularly in those passages where an obvious commitment to Orcadian life as an exemplary standard adds an extra dimension of celebration. There is not much danger of Brown's recording of Orkney life becoming sentimental, but it is vulnerable to being read with sentimentality, and used as unearned consolation.

Other short poems in the book are at least as good as **"Seal Island Anthology"**: particularly **"Bird in the Lighted Hall"** and **"Hamnavoe Market."** His historical set-pieces are well drawn, too, although Norse medievalism is an interest which many readers will prefer in small doses.

Whether as story-teller, elegist or memorialist of his place and its cultural affiliations and religious feelings, Brown's backwater convictions are marginal and hardly to be sustained outside the community that supports them. His beautiful elegy, **"William and Mareon Clark"**, while vividly celebrating the founding of a tavern in 1596, and mourning its subsequent demise, may be representative of the feeling and lament of his

work as a whole. . . . It is an elegy in which the poem becomes the only monument to the past persons it commemorates. Brown's work gives the impression of trying to make an Orkney of words, a way of life recorded as a reminder for the future, perhaps a possible inheritance. Old fashioned carved simplicities, like its Christianity, are part of its incorrigible elegiac energy, as well as its attractiveness and decency. He is the least cynical of poets.

> Douglas Dunn, *"Inscriptions and Snapshots,"* in The Times Literary Supplement, *No. 4216, January 20, 1984, p. 54.*

DAVID PROFUMO

"Time" has been a constant fascination [of Mackay Brown], and he is notoriously sceptical about modern notions of progress; his fiction delves into the past, unravelling linear concepts of time and seeking to relate isolated episodes to archetypes. "Time is not a conflagration; it is a slow grave sequence of grassblade, fish, apple, star, snowflake", he wrote in *Greenvoe* (1972), his first novel, and in the long title story from his collection *Hawkfall* (1974) a fisherman experiences exactly this sense of time as he is reborn through the centuries. His latest book *Time in a Red Coat* develops the idea.

It is a fable that begins with a birth. Deep in the past, in an Eastern country violated by Mongol hordes, a princess is born under the eyes of two guardians who bequeath to her an ivory flute and a bag of coins. Barely ageing from the time she reaches maturity until the very end of the saga, this mysterious dark maiden treks through centuries of history on the trail of the Dragon war, passing through many places (Hungary, Russia, Spain) blistered by its violent fire. The strange, thaumaturgic activities of this wandering girl take their toll on her purity, however, and the white coat in which she starts her long journey is gradually besmirched and singed, so that by the time her goal is reached the stigmata of human folly have turned it red.

Like D. H. Lawrence in his stories, Mackay Brown has a penchant for ritualistic action which, when it is successful, can be at once stylized and affecting. *Time in a Red Coat* is composed of recurrent figures and shapes (spiritual symbols, elemental motifs) which remove the need for extensive historical realism. But although Brown conjures his themes—the power of honesty, the meaning of suffering, fertility as miracle—in a way that is often moving, certain episodes have their dynamism reduced by his attachment to the ceremonial. "Ceremony makes everything bearable and beautiful for us", he wrote in his story **"The Tarn and the Rosary"**, and so indeed it may, but in literature it can merely slow things up. Generally, Brown escapes being laborious, but sometimes this novel seems to march on the spot.

Sustaining the myth while staving off the fairy-tale is necessary in this type of rarefied fiction. Seeking to revitalize the archetypes of folk narrative—the journey, the final battle, the magician—Brown's tale runs the risk of dishing up Tolkien rather than T. S. Eliot: it is just plausible that there are dwarves in the mountain, but when we hear "It is she of the black blown hair who comes to the table of the young men to collect their empty mugs" the business begins to smack of sword and sorcery. There may be only occasional lapses of this kind, and only a few plunges into mawkishness, but they are failures of touch in a book so ambitiously conceived.

Brown's strongly metaphoric language is the backbone of his fiction, and one is constantly impressed by the way he runs together the textures of poetry and prose. In numerous local instances the writing has a distinctive shine, and for these the novel is memorable. The flaws of *Time in a Red Coat* are inherent in its scale: Brown is consistently better as a poet and a writer of short stories, and perhaps at the heart of this novel there is a collection of short stories uneasily run together. There is a distracting effect, too, in the sporadic authorial interpolations which, like the odd anachronistic detail, are presumably designed to dismantle the sense of narrative time. They do so, but with little subtlety. The book's crowning chapter boldly achieves the same aim through a surrealistic survey of martial events past, present and future, that collapses most conventions and is the novel's imaginative *tour de force*.

Clarity of image and a lively ear for speech being his principal talents as a stylist, Brown has much to recommend him as a playwright. His material and his language are nicely interchangeable, too, his poems being unusually close to speech and his stage-directions often unperformably poetic ("the burn is supple with trout"). With the contents of *Three Plays* we are back on familiar, Orcadian territory, but there are connections with the concerns and procedures of the novels. In fact, *The Loom of Light,* which treats the martyrdom of Magnus Erlendson, a ruler of twelfth-century Orkney, was effectively the *ur*-version of his second novel, *Magnus* (1973), and is a fine example of Brown's confident inventiveness as regards unity of time in the drama, the action vaulting blithely forward by years between scenes, crossed by wider correspondences that bind them together. The alliterative language of the "Chorus" here recalls *Murder in the Cathedral,* and there is a similar robust sense of the older dramatic tradition behind it.

Overturning temporal conventions is fundamental to *The Well,* a fertility play that shows Brown's fondness for multiple viewpoint. Here, successive generations circulate around an island well, the traditional values and ceremonies it embodies being replaced in the end by the modern "advance" of a mains system. Its arrival prompts the Keeper of the Well to a hymn against progress. The third play in the volume, *The Voyage of Saint Brandon,* a radio piece, is a symbolic religious drama with a tough poetic quality: there are few people writing plays of this type at the moment, and it is a distinctive achievement. There is something of the Townley plays here, but there is also a marked resemblance to Yeats—an independence of tone which is the result of a skilled writer flensing the language down to its bones.

> David Profumo, "She of the Black Blown Hair," in The Times Literary Supplement, No. 4237, June 15, 1984, p. 676.

A. D. NUTTALL

Mr. Brown writes beautifully—too beautifully—in poetic prose. It is not so much that this "fairy way of writing" trembles on the edge of the absurd as that its effects are somehow too easy. Profound movements of human sympathy are mysteriously neutralized [in *Andrina and Other Stories*] (in much the same way professional magicians neutralize the supernatural). Mr. Brown is certainly skillful. Describing the repeated, disastrous plunging movement of a whale, he writes simply, "It sundered the ocean where it fell, and fell, and fell"; at the same time, more complex sonorities are at his command: "The ambassadors of the sea, the breaking waves, seemed to kneel to the

king and promise all." Yet the overall effect is of a mode of discourse at once insulated and insulating. Unesthetic elements are filtered out, and all the ancient strength of the sagas seems to be replaced by a certain inward weakness, as they are made the vehicle of an expertly protected nostalgia.

But the stories themselves are better than the style in which they are written. The rhythms of the sentences lead one to expect the patterned conclusiveness of fairy tales. Instead, one receives moments from stories whose endings can only be guessed. A deaf, dumb, blind child is visited by three enigmatic strangers and, for a brief space of pure happiness, hears, sees and cries out. And that is all. No ancient teller of tales could have broken off there, though ancient anecdotes were sometimes like this. "Marvelous Things Heard," once spuriously attributed to Aristotle, speaks of one Demaratus who, unlike the boy in our story, became dumb for 10 days and afterward remembered that time as the happiest he had ever known. The Greek tale is less lyrical, altogether odder and, one must admit, sticks in the mind as Mr. Brown's does not. Similarly Mr. Brown's six pages about Genghis Khan's great-grandfather, who is turned back from his marauding path by a chance encounter with a shepherd, do not make an ordered story but could have been the matter, say, of an allusion in Dante. The story of the princess in the tower becomes, as one reads, the story of one who is herself turning into (mere) story—not just modern, this, but modernist.

Only "**Andrina**" (about an old sailor visited by the kindly ghost of his daughter) and "**The Battle in the Hills**" (about a real encounter in 1529 between the Orkneymen and the soldiers of James V of Scotland) are tales in the old manner. The first falls into sentimentality but the second has a particularly wonderful twist to it. So—all in all—a good book, creepy, touching, original, even at times humorously self-aware.

> A. D. Nuttall, "World's Loneliest Literature," in The New York Times Book Review, September 9, 1984, p. 32.

PATRICIA CRAIG

George Mackay Brown's Orkney is an unfamiliar, off-shore locality in which everything seems a little richer through being both concentrated and chancy. How long can its distinctive character survive? It was endangered as long ago as the last quarter of the 19th century, the period in which *The Golden Bird* is set. 'What is it, this "getting on"?' demands a sarcastic schoolmaster, one of Brown's crop of characters. 'Getting on', perhaps, entails exchanging an ancestral routine for some newfangled practice: being a servant in a banker's household instead of a croft wife, perching on a clerk's stool rather than fishing the North Sea. Better, says the schoolmaster, that his pupils should stick to those homely activities sanctioned by the pastoral poets of antique times; his audience hasn't the least idea what he is on about. 'Please, sir, you've broke your glasses!' says one of them, bringing him down to earth.

It isn't the first time John Fiord has been brought down to earth, if rumour is to be believed. 'Eagle John' was his childhood nickname, after the bird that stole him from behind a stook in a cornfield, bore him off to its eyrie and then lost him to the infuriated mother, who climbed the crag to retrieve her child. To Fiord, a crofter's son, there is no difference between that eagle's nest and a mare's nest. His job is to knock such nonsense out of the children's heads. 'Eagles, seals, mermaids, trows': these picturesque figments, as he sees it, have a stupefying effect. The islanders, he thinks, should steer a middle course between darkness and ignorance, on the one hand, and a bogus progressiveness, on the other. Having repudiated both of these, they may acquire a certain soundness of outlook. There is, however, something a little arid about the schoolmaster's prescription for fulfillment.

In Brown's sea valley, small events take on an epic significance, like the feud between 'the crofts of Gorse and Feaquoy' with which the story begins. Two acrimonious women destroy the friendship between their husbands, and open the way for a kind of vitiation, which is paralleled by the suggested disordering of the community, the breaking of certain continuities. Hearth-fires peter out that had been kept alight for more than a hundred years. Crofter children start looking to the town or even the mainland for their employment. It's the usual story of restlessness overtaking the young. 'There were more deaths than births in the valley.'

Between the time of the old schoolmaster McFarlane and that of John Fiord, a young woman, a Miss Strachan, comes to teach the children of the valley and outrages the laird by speaking out against blood sports and advocating socialism and sea-bathing. A New Woman indeed. When Miss Strachan leaves, she takes with her a gormless islander to be her husband. 'The Lord help her, poor lass,' says his mother.

The second of Brown's Orkney stories is **"The Life and Death of John Voe"**, in which episodes from the hero's past and present are juxtaposed. John Voe is a one-time whaler who returns to the Orkneys while a Lamas fair is in progress at Hamnavoe: an animated occasion. Drink then gets him in its grip, before marriage to an admirable woman makes a man of him. George Mackay Brown goes in for the decorative incident and the one- or two-line paragraph; it ought to sound portentous, but in the hands of this expert storyteller, it doesn't. It simply adds a forceful outline to the tales. 'The Golden Bird': this is both the eagle of John Fiord's apocryphal misadventure, standing for the wealth of lore appertaining to the island, and the name of a fishing-boat, a marvel of modern workmanship with an oil-fired engine, that comes to a bad end. If there's a moral here, it's that the wonders of the present should not be accepted uncritically.

Patricia Craig, "Getting On," in London Review of Books, *Vol. 9, No. 16, September 17, 1987, p. 18.*

Susan Cheever

1943-

American novelist, memoirist, and journalist.

An author whose novels explore the contemporary female psyche, Cheever garnered significant critical attention for *Home before Dark: A Biographical Memoir of John Cheever by His Daughter* (1984). In this book, Cheever draws from private journals and personal remembrances to record the triumphs and hardships of her father, the celebrated novelist and short story writer John Cheever. She displays candor and emotional detachment in discussing her father's drug and alcohol addiction, his struggle to come to terms with his homosexuality, and his death from cancer. Critics hailed the book as an intimate and illuminating portrait of a prominent American author, and Anthony Burgess declared that *Home before Dark* is "stylistically worthy of its subject, scrupulous as to facts, and objective where objectivity must have been difficult."

In her fiction, Cheever focuses upon affluent women searching for love and self-worth. In *Looking for Work* (1979), her first novel, a wealthy woman attempts to overcome the emotional burdens of a faltering marriage through new relationships and a professional career. Some reviewers found Cheever's characterizations one-dimensional, a complaint frequently directed at her fiction. Others, however, commended her attention to detail and accurate rendering of dialogue. In *A Handsome Man* (1981), Cheever examines the life of thirty-two-year-old divorcée Hannah Bart, who seeks fulfillment in an affair with Sam Noble, a much older man. When the two travel to Ireland in an attempt to mend Sam's damaged relationship with his son Travis, Hannah is forced to contend for Sam's love and attention. Although critics generally applauded Cheever's descriptive skills, several noted an inability to fully develop her thematic concerns. Cheever's next novel, *The Cage* (1982), studies the stagnating marriage of an affluent couple who have nearly exhausted their family inheritances. Some reviewers considered this book an attempt to explore the suburban malaise with which her father's fiction is concerned. *Doctors and Women* (1987), Cheever's recent novel, depicts the disillusionment of a married woman who is suddenly attracted to her mother's physician.

(See also *CLC*, Vol. 18; *Contemporary Authors*, Vol. 103; and *Dictionary of Literary Biography Yearbook: 1982*.)

JOAN SHAFFER

A Handsome Man should not have been a novel; it would have worked better as a short story, a vignette, or even an excursus within a vignette. Cheever's writing is adequate but, except for brief passages where she captures a mood or a thought with telling precision, the book is exceedingly dull. Nothing happens. It is like a faded color photograph: a brief moment of reality is accurately reproduced, but there is no movement or excitement.

© Jerry Bauer

The handsome man of the title is Sam Noble, a 50-year-old divorced president of a New York publishing firm, who is romancing 32-year-old Hannah Bart, a publicity agent for another New York publisher. She learns Sam has a teenage son, Travis, whom he has not seen for years. Hannah wants Sam to attempt a reconciliation with Travis, a high school dropout and drifter, and Sam, though at first resistant, agrees to have his son meet him in Ireland and asks Hannah to join them there. The book relates what happens during the visit to Ireland, which is very little—several pleasant car rides; numerous meals, both good and bad; and more detailed descriptions of fly-fishing than I hope ever to read again. . . .

Hannah and Travis vie for Sam's attention throughout the book—and throughout all those drives, meals, and fly-fishing excursions—until the end when all three leave Ireland, Sam and Hannah to become engaged, and Travis to return to his mother's home.

What little action Cheever does allow occurs just before the departure from Ireland. The incident, however, requires the willing suspension of disbelief: Travis and Hannah, still not getting along, have a remarkably brief assignation—taking no more than a minute to read and, as described, less time to accomplish. . . .

Cheever appends an epilogue, which I still don't understand: it tells us in detail how Travis trained for and ran in the Boston marathon. It made me yearn for the fly-casting.

> Joan Shaffer, in a review of "A Handsome Man," in The New Republic, Vol. 184, No. 20, May 16, 1981, p. 40.

MARGARET MARY MEEHAN

Susan Cheever's *A Handsome Man* is a decided improvement over her first book, *Looking For Work,* yet it remains essentially unengrossing and unimportant. Although she has clearly worked on her writing, problems with cliché, overuse of italics, and the repetition of hollow adjectives indicate a lack of power and confidence in her prose. This is further undermined by the frequent interspersal of short, nonsentences within her paragraphs.

The book has a more complicated storyline than *Looking For Work* and is somewhat less self-absorbed and self-pitying. Most of the novel is told from the point of view of Hannah Bart, a 32 year old divorced woman who constantly refers to herself as a girl. The point of view, however, frequently and inexplicably shifts to other characters within the book. (pp. 163-64)

Cheever makes a serious attempt to deal with the emotional conflicts that are part of many lives, yet her presentation is petty and uninteresting. Many of the basic problems that *Looking For Work* suffered from remain: Hannah Bart is dazzled by the upperclass, by where they shop and eat, where they vacation—often this awe is expressed in an absurd listing of the names of stores, designers, or restaurants. The denouement of the book is from Travis's point of view—the first time in the book—and is unsatisfactory and inconsistent.

Ideologically the book bothered me a great deal. Despite the fact that Hannah is ostensibly an independent woman with a job and an apartment she is extremely male-dependent. She is jealous of Sam's son; she constantly wants Sam to "take care" of her, control her; she has little confidence in herself for all the wrong reasons. Generally, she's sexist and I'm tired of reading that kind of literature. She's a snob and I'm equally tired of that. Furthermore, Cheever's writing and fictional imagination still need a good deal of work. (p. 164)

> Margaret Mary Meehan, in a review of "A Handsome Man," in Best Sellers, Vol. 41, No. 5, August, 1981, pp. 163-64.

JUDITH CHERNAIK

A Handsome Man is meant as a study in the forms of selfishness afflicting lovers, father and son, the young and the not-so-young (Hannah is thirty-ish, Sam fifty-ish). Susan Cheever would probably see herself as a writer in the Fitzgerald tradition ("The rich are their own nation", her heroine discovers). Her prose is clean and transparent, her tone ironic. Author and characters share an obsession with money and the things money can buy, and are irresistibly attracted by the glamour of a world which really seems to have nothing at all to recommend it. Branching out from the Fitzgerald tradition, Susan Cheever is mildly feminist in her evenhanded treatment of personal vanity (the right and wrong clothes play a large part in the heroine's consciousness), and in her reversal of sexual sterotypes, both in bed and, symbolically, in the natural world, as in the account of the heroine's struggle with a large trout. She is good at

capturing the sharp surface impressions of an American touring Ireland for the first time, especially in her account of the food, in which both heroine and author take a keen satiric interest. . . .

But the novel is marred by a pervading slickness, a tendency to slip into woman's-magazine banality. "Why are you attracted to men with these difficulties?" "Have you thought that you might be afraid of commitment?" Such are the questions that agitate the hapless Hannah. Indeed, though we are told that Hannah, an avid reader of Hardy and Conrad, Yeats and Eliot, is exceptionally bright, there is not much evidence of this either in her conversation or her inner thoughts. Even more damaging is the utter vacuity of the "handsome man" of the title, who is distinguished from less handsome men chiefly by an infuriating habit of addressing his girlfriend as "sweetie" or "kiddo" (echoing Bogart, possibly), and who occasionally produces lines of mind-boggling archness: "Wait until I get those tiny limbs of yours upstairs."

> Judith Chernaik, "Trout-fishing in Ireland," in The Times Literary Supplement, No. 4092, September 4, 1981, p. 1001.

RICHARD EDER

Is it fair to talk about Cheever country in connection with *The Cage,* the third novel by Susan Cheever? She is, of course, the daughter of the late John Cheever, whose stories managed to insert the American suburbs, by means of the ghosts he found in them, into the continuing memory of Western culture. It wouldn't seem fair except that Susan Cheever has chosen deliberately, with some courage and less prudence, to start in her father's territory and walk her own wilder track out of it.

Up to the three-quarters mark, *The Cage* is an approximately realistic story about the gritted-teeth suburban marriage of two WASPs of comfortable background and shrinking circumstances. . . .

But the brightness is falling from their air. The old money has dwindled into a limited trust fund and a decent salary. William Bristol's plush job as a writer on a national news magazine—his father-in-law got it for him—shows signs of fraying. Julia Bristol's good looks are slipping and so are her nerves. (p. 1)

The WASPs have shrunk down to their stingers. The feeling between them, perhaps not much more than the shared glow of their privileged childhood, has dwindled to a barely controlled series of tense accommodations. She is sharp and anxious; he is foggy and distracted. What they have lost is not so much the money of the previous generation as its sense of life, its vitality.

Until all this is swept away in an ending that turns it from portrait to fable, Susan Cheever hits every Cheeverlandmark. Martinis, commuter trains, civilized office tensions, squabbles with secretaries or wives that contaminate the day, wistful thoughts of a blonde seen across the street, the acedia of the expensive suburban house—a chrome space-capsule going nowhere. (pp. 1, 7)

But it is no affectionate re-exploration. It is done with a cold insistence; not parody, exactly, but deliberate exaggeration. Details are piled as relentlessly as clods thrown upon a coffin, as if to declare that the blend of affectionate regret and gaunt prophecy with which John Cheever treated his fabled suburbia is a dead view, that only gauntness remains.

The point prepares itself throughout the novel, and becomes explicit when the novel turns to fable. The Bristols go to their summer retreat, the grand, decaying New Hampshire house built by Julia's father in lavish and celebratory style, complete with a menagerie. It is a dead past, the tombstone of the gracious illusion that has kept the Bristols going and that now, literally, entombs them.

In theory the violent ending, with primitive savagery invading the attenuated suburban vacuum, justifies the flatness of the rest of the book. John Cheever wrote of sickness and demons but they inhabited a golden world. The fable coexisted with its flesh-and-blood characters; their martinis may have contained the waters of Lethe but they tasted good; their love affairs may have taken place in the foreknowledge of retribution but they were sweet.

Susan Cheever's fable is all moral and no story. The grapes that tempt her fox are savorless. The Bristols, with their injured sensibilities—they are offended by women in curlers and sightseers eating doughnuts—are vehicles to deplore by, two literary lorgnettes. True, it is precisely this sensibility of two dead souls that Susan Cheever will eventually get in her licks at, but meanwhile it's all we have for company through most of the book. There is no virtue, no courage, no human charm to set against it.

Susan Cheeverland is blasted territory, inhabited by shadows. Its seasons are foreshortened: Flowers come frostbitten from the start. *The Cage* is a bill for a meal that was never cooked, served or eaten. (p. 7)

> *Richard Eder, in a review of "The Cage," in Los Angeles Times Book Review, October 3, 1982, pp. 1, 7.*

SHEILA BALLANTYNE

One of the problems with *The Cage*—which seems not so much a novel as an extended story or even a television script (and as either would have had more impact)—is that it is mostly surface, embroidered with glittery and often repetitive detail. Whole sections are fleshed out with accounts of Billy's and Julia's interminable trajectories between home and office, suburb and city, city and country retreat; a good portion of the book takes place on turnpikes and highways. For a reader to care about either member of this doomed couple, something deeper in them has to be struck, and this Miss Cheever has failed to do.

The closest the author comes to finding an image with any emotional resonance is in describing an old sofa in the guest room of their house—a piece of furniture Julia's father once sat on, with her on his lap, when she was a child. This couch, in Miss Cheever's hands, becomes more than an object or symbol—becomes almost and for a brief time a character. When on the decorator's orders it is hacked to pieces with hammers and knives by Julia and Billy in order to remove it and make way for a "modern" piece, one hurts for it in a way one never could for its owners. (p. 28)

> *Sheila Ballantyne, "Married and Abandoned," in The New York Times Book Review, October 3, 1982, pp. 9, 28.*

BILL GREENWELL

Susan Cheever's third novel *The Cage* is, until its late and agile twist, deceptively uneventful. Much as her first novel *Looking*

for Work did, it chugs along, tugging in its wake the reader, who is surprised to find it so engrossing. Almost idly, it describes a marriage that has lost its gloss; but the writing is so sprightly that humdrum events become entirely absorbing.

This ordinariness is at the novel's heart. . . . What Cheever achieves with startling clarity is a surface naturalism, with a powerful eye for telling, insignificant detail and a feeling for the petty emotions of jealousy and depression. Neither [Billy nor Julia] is attractive, sympathy out of the reader's question; it is the quality of the prose, only occasionally self-conscious, that is irresistible.

Only when the desultory routine of Billy and Julia's relationship is shifted a little by moving into the mouldering mansion, the focal point of Julia's memories, does the novel bite back. Their daughter sends a letter; she won't be with them this summer; she is getting married. The same post brings a boring business letter for Billy, with an ambiguously scribbled message from his secretary. Julia intercepts both; then, on a casually vicious whim, she retaliates by locking Billy in the cage, which he is repairing as an aimless kind of therapy. The moment is thoroughly frightening, making the suppressed tension tangible; the novel's conclusion is masterly. As the final pages turn, the reader recalls a succession of brilliant images, sewn into the subtext, by which we have been prepared for the ending. Cheever is exceptionally talented, this novel superbly compulsive.

> *Bill Greenwell, "Deceptive Calm," in New Statesman, Vol. 105, No. 2707, February 4, 1983, p. 26.*

BRIGITTE WEEKS

Home Before Dark is much more than Susan Cheever's memoir of her famous author father: it is a portrait of the artist as a young man, a middle-aged man, an old man, a sick man. It is, in fact, one of the most moving and intimate books I have read in years. . . .

Her exercise in family archaeology inevitably uncarths pain, beginning with the disintegration of John Cheever's childhood: his father's business failure, his mother's efforts to support the family with a gift shop, the drinking, the divorce, the sale of the family home, above all the lack of affection for an unwanted last child. Psychiatrists were energetic in their efforts to persuade an older, troubled John Cheever, that all his problems stemmed from his relationship with his parents, but Susan, with a perspicacity not shared by the professionals, points out: "He had spent his life escaping the past; he wasn't about to return to it voluntarily." . . .

His daughter brings alive the years before her arrival as skillfully as she does the period of her own growing up. Her narrative, however, is not strictly chronological but laced with insights from later years or flashbacks to earlier times, a method held together by a sense of peace and the knowledge that all struggles are concluded. She retells both the legends and the reality and it is hard to care which is which. (p. 1)

Home Before Dark is no *Daddy Dearest*, a child's settling of scores. The wonder of this book is the astonishing combination of dispassion and compassion with which Susan Cheever portrays her father. She recalls affectionately just how he looked: "He had a Yankee face, with bright blue eyes, puffy eyelids, and narrow lips, but his smile was so complete and friendly that it changed his whole expression." Assembling her portrait, Susan uncovers the personality of her father layer by layer—

although her mother remains a somewhat shadowy figure. Having written this book in part to assuage the pain of John Cheever's death, she realizes, "I know my father better than I ever did while he was alive."

She takes the good times with the bad, the rewards enjoyed and the prices paid. . . .

The clouds began to gather in the 1960s, just as John Cheever became firmly established as a master of the short story and a successful novelist. But appearances no longer matched reality. They masked a middle-aged man losing himself and his talents to alcohol. . . . His marriage, always in peril, seemed to be disintegrating. The children were caught in the crossfire. . . .

Writing about one's own father fighting alcoholism, regaining fame, becoming "his own number one groupie" and finding young lovers of both sexes is an almost impossible task, but Susan Cheever does it—with restraint and understanding. . . . She keeps herself in the background most of the time so that when she *is* on stage the reader has no feeling of exploitation or voyeurism. . . .

Strangely, it doesn't really matter that the subject of this book is one of the great literary names of our times. He could be a politician or a painter or a financier. There will be other books about John Cheever—doctoral theses, literary biographies, lovers' recollections—but there will never be another book about John Cheever like this one. No one will love him quite as Susan Cheever does. No one will fear him and fight with him as his daughter has. "How could I love him?" she asks as he lay dying. With this book John Cheever's daughter answers her own question. For better, for worse, she loved him. (p. 14)

> Brigitte Weeks, "Portrait of the Artist as a Family Man," in Book World—The Washington Post, October 7, 1984, pp. 1, 14.

GEORGE SIM JOHNSTON

Admirers of Cheever's work may be permitted a double standard in approaching Susan Cheever's disclosures about her father [in **Home Before Dark**]. Revelations about a writer one admires *are* fascinating. Cheever, moreover, seems to have been an accessory to his own exposure. He did not light a literary bonfire when he knew he was dying. Nor did he secrete his intimate journals, from which most of his daughter's book derives, in an academic time capsule. Instead, he put them in order, showed them around, and left them with no stipulations. In these volumes, he recorded much that is unseemly—his bouts with drugs, alcoholism, literary groupies, and, near the end, homosexuality. He recorded much else, as well, in prose which is as good as any he wrote. I would give my word processor to be able to read all twelve volumes. But while I may be intrigued by the material Miss Cheever is retailing, I do not think she should be admired for taking it public. At least two reviewers have called her "courageous." Who would want such courage in his family? Her remark to the *New York Times* that "we could not suppress it, he was a public figure," is disingenuous. Flaubert's family sat on his literary remains for years. One admires them for it, while one is also grateful that they eventually let go. The best treatment of this ambivalent situation is Henry James's *The Aspern Papers*. James (who himself lit one of the great bonfires in literary history) comes out against the "publishing scoundrel" who, for the sake of posterity, tries to wrest a bushel of love letters from the aging mistress of a great poet.

After slapping Miss Cheever on the wrist for writing this book, I must say that she has produced a fine work. It is far better written and more adroitly conceived than her novels. The writing is expertly pitched in the key of her father's middle period, and she follows the haphazard, anecdotal strategy of Andrew Field's superb *Nabokov: A Life in Part* with great success. I think this small book will prove superior to any official biography, which will undoubtedly be the size of a cigar humidor and tell us how often Cheever cut his toenails. The book rings true; we seem to be getting the atmosphere of the man without excessive biographical luggage. And the revelations about boozing and sleeping around which have received so much attention are actually a small part of the book. **Home Before Dark** may prove profitable, and may keep alive a career that was not exactly lighting up the literary firmament, but it is not exploitative. And in his daughter's defense it must be said that John Cheever never hesitated in his own work to make the family skeletons dance for the public. (pp. 40-1)

> George Sim Johnston, in a review of "Home Before Dark," in The American Spectator, Vol. 18, No. 2, February, 1985, pp. 40-1.

BRUCE BAWER

[Because of disclosures of alcoholism and homosexuality, **Home before Dark**] provoked controversy when it appeared in America last year. The critics formed two neat ranks. One faction maintained that Miss Cheever had written a loving, heartfelt tribute to her late father; the words 'sensitive' and 'honest' were frequently invoked. The other faction felt that the book was an act of spite: Miss Cheever had exploited her father, had made unfair use of his private journals, had produced a tasteless, sensationalistic book. The latter group of critics have a point. Cheever is so recently deceased—1982—that his daughter's rush to print does seem indecorous, her eagerness to advertise his painful secrets unsettling. And yet the book is no *Daddy Dearest*. It does not hurt Cheever. On the contrary, Cheever comes off as a rather sympathetic character. His personal torments give a human dimension to a man whom many considered something of a cold fish, a snob. The main problem with **Home before Dark,** in fact, is that it doesn't give him quite as much human dimension as one might have expected.

What causes this disappointment to rankle is that there was clearly an abundance of promising material at Miss Cheever's disposal. Some of it, to be sure, has found its way into **Home before Dark**. Miss Cheever's inside stories about the *New Yorker*, like all inside stories about that most peculiar of publications, are fascinating. . . .

The glimpses of Cheever's mind that such anecdotes give us are, in the last analysis, frustrating. They're just not enough. Miss Cheever brings to mind one of those nervously self-conscious film directors who, desperate to avoid being taken for mere storytellers, make a habit of cutting away just when a sequence begins to get interesting or enlightening. The deliberately disordered, patchwork-of-memories structure of **Home before Dark**—unobjectionable in itself—makes it easier for Miss Cheever to carry off this systematic superficiality. So does the style. Miss Cheever has the *New Yorker* in her blood, and she has chosen, in **Home before Dark,** to write in a plain, impersonal manner, rich with maddeningly irrelevant detail, that is almost a parody of *New Yorker* style. The last thing this story needs is a plain, impersonal manner. Nor does it need so many pointless particulars—Miss Cheever gives us, for instance, enough addresses to fill a small-town telephone book. (p. 18)

Bruce Bawer, "Fairyland," in London Review of Books, *Vol. 7, No. 8, May 2, 1985, pp. 17-18.*

DONALD REVELL

Biography, since Boswell, has thrived as an extraordinarily various genre, admitting of the widest possible range of authorial perspectives, intentions, and limitations. *Home before Dark* fashions a loving variousness of its own to offer the reader an experience of John Cheever as strangely rich and finally affirmative as the body of his work.

The book appears to find its narrative form by inverting a phrase ("in the midst of life we are in death") from the Anglican service for the dead, as it is in the midst of Cheever's long, ultimately unsuccessful struggle with cancer that his daughter begins the search for his life. Every aspect of the book is involved with search and struggle. Susan Cheever struggles with her father's diffidence, with his habit of fictionalizing his life to himself and his family, as she seeks to understand the often painful ambiguities of her relationship to him. In so doing, she discovers a man whose entire life was a struggle against insecurity and guilt, self-doubt and self-deception. She finds in her father a restless, sometimes anguished seeker after artistic accomplishment, after security and status, and, most of all, after the freedom to live and to be loved without shame.

Home before Dark does much to change the image of John Cheever, the author who, as he appeared on several segments of *The Dick Cavett Show*—modest but self-assured, subtly Anglicized—seemed the inheritor of that peaceable kingdom *The New Yorker* advertises week after week. Infidelity, alcoholism, and homosexuality are all seen to disturb much more than the surface of his life. But the book is not lurid. It is not a chronicle of excess as some recent works about the confessional poets of the nineteen-fifties have been. It does its subject a service by revealing his struggles to have been more than suburban, his hard-won world view something nobler than the "childlike wonder" some of his critics thought it to be. (pp. 419-20)

[In *Home before Dark*, Susan Cheever offers] her readers the opportunity to love John Cheever as he always hoped to be loved—for both his works and weaknesses, with complete knowledge and complete forgiveness. (p. 420)

Donald Revell, in a review of "Home before Dark," in Modern Fiction Studies, *Vol. 31, No. 2, Summer, 1985, pp. 419-20.*

MADELEINE BLAIS

Doctors & Women, Susan Cheever's fourth novel and fifth book, takes on as its territory some of the same themes and places that obsessed her father, the novelist John Cheever: marriage, modern times and Manhattan.

Kate, a journalist, earns just enough money, according to her husband David, "to put the couple in a higher income bracket." That's one of those snide sayings that infect some marriages, subtle denigration that can erode the union just as powerfully as an affair.

Kate and David have known each other since childhood and their marriage suffers from a sense of having inherited not only David's parents' heavy dark furniture but also each other.…

Except for occasional stabs of longing for offspring, Kate and David lead generally untroubled existences—wan, unexamined Episcopalian lives.

But the complacency is challenged when Kate's mother becomes ill with cancer. Her father has died recently, and the threat of another loss fills her with that peculiar and often unhailed emptiness that comes when a grown child is suddenly orphaned.

She finds herself attracted to the doctor who is helping her mother, who has one of those zealously masculine TV idol names: Macklin Riley.…

Invigorated by decay and injury, he is most attracted not to Kate so much as her hurt leg, which was almost lost in a car accident when she was young while her father—probably drunk—was driving. Kate seems to be the victim of the fantasy that having been injured by one man perhaps she can be saved by another.…

The novel has an interesting medical verisimilitude, lots of doctor's jokes and tons—perhaps too much—of that veiled incantatory doctor's language in which the body's grimiest physical truths get converted into sanitized and polysyllabic codes.

It is odd to think that a writer who would take such care in that area would be guilty of some rather strange lapses from grace in other areas, most notably when downtown on a clear day is described as being "like a postcard."

As a writer, Cheever labors under two formidable shadows. The first belongs to her father, that wry and aching chronicler of suburban malaise, and the second is her own, as established by the publication of her memoir of her father, *Home Before Dark,* a flawless work that became an instant classic in its genre. Fans of that book were hoping that her next novel would be similarily brilliant. It isn't, but the displeasure of having to say that is softened, somewhat, by the pleasure in hoping that her next novel will provide that breakthrough.

Madeleine Blais, "Heart Attacks: Susan Cheever's Story of Love, Death, and a Doctor," in Chicago Tribune—Books, *May 3, 1987, p. 3.*

DIANE MANUEL

Kate Loomis, the plaintive young protagonist of *Doctors & Women,* has potential as a character of the establishment '80s. Comfortably married to a childhood playmate, she lives in a fashionable co-op on Manhattan's Upper East Side and rents a garret room of her own where she does her artsy writing.

But underneath the grown-up bangles and glitz is a petulant little girl who makes no effort to see beyond her own well-powdered nose. As she searches for the cause of her current ennui, she attributes it first to her father's death two years earlier, and then to her mother's recently diagnosed illness. Thus begins a story that takes a long time to arrive at an unconvincing ending. Readers who enjoyed Susan Cheever's previous book—a much acclaimed and captivating memoir of her father, writer John Cheever—aren't likely to feel the same way about this novel. Where *Home Before Dark* was remarkable for its vitality, humor, and grace, *Doctors & Women* has an air of uncertainty that prevents the reader from becoming involved with its cast of characters—two self-centered women unhappy in their marriages, two mothers suffering from the same illness, and two doctors arriving at similar conclusions about the medical profession by different routes. They start the book complaining about their lot in life, and at the end of it they have merely adjusted to circumstances, rather than taking control and rising above their difficulties. Although Cheever does raise some timely issues about medical ethics, she backs away from drawing any conclusions.

Diane Manuel, "Fiction: Novel and Short Stories Explore Contemporary Themes," in The Christian Science Monitor, *June 15, 1987, p. 24.*

SUSAN KENNEY

[*Doctors & Women* is] a book about the complex attitudes displayed by doctors and women in various situations involving each other. But the women are always in subordinate positions—nurses, patients, sex objects—and the contrasts are simply too schematic: good doctor-bad doctor, well-behaved girl-naughty girl, dying patient-recovering patient. There are no women doctors in *Doctors & Women;* they wouldn't fit the scheme.

Some of the best and most moving writing is contained in the sections about hospital life and procedure. It is clear that Ms. Cheever has not only done her research, but also been there; her accounts of medical procedure and hospital ambiance are authentic right down to the contents of IV bags and bulletin boards. Written in graceful prose, these scenes have the power and authority we associate with the best nonfiction. (This is not surprising considering the acclaim she received for *Home Before Dark,* a memoir of her father, John Cheever.

The dexterity of the hospital scenes makes the love interest seem both tacked on and tacky; even the style and grammar suffer, with comma faults galore. . . .

Riley and Kate together are irresponsible, inexplicably motivated and ultimately unlikable characters, while Mallory and Ann are too saintly for words. Mallory is a cardboard paste-up doctor, making such trite observations as "Dan Connors had a terminal disease in its advanced stages, but right now, he was more alive than most people ever were." With lines like that, it's hard to take even the hospital passages seriously. Perhaps it would have been more interesting if Ms. Cheever had seen fit to sic hot-under-the-collar Kate on stiff-necked, upright Mallory, just to muss him up a little bit. Or better yet, combine the stereotypes of Kate and Ann, Mack and Peter into characters who could grapple with the complex human issues raised in the best parts of this book.

Susan Kenney, "Looking for Dr. Right," in The New York Times Book Review, *June 28, 1987, p. 16.*

(Dame) Agatha (Mary Clarissa) Christie
1890-1976

(Also wrote as Agatha Christie Mallowan and under pseudonym of Mary Westmacott) English novelist, dramatist, short story writer, autobiographer, poet, travel writer, scriptwriter, and author of children's books.

Christie is one of the most widely-read authors of the twentieth century. Her immensely popular mystery novels and plays have been translated into more than one hundred languages, and their cumulative sales rival those of the Bible and the works of William Shakespeare. Throughout her prolific literary career, Christie adhered to the conventions of the classic British detective story, offering the reader a cryptic murder mystery and a surprising yet logical solution to the crime. Frequently set in the English countryside, her novels usually focus on a group of upper middle-class British suspects and on a detective who reveals the murderer during a final gathering of the characters. Although many reviewers have faulted Christie for one-dimensional characterizations and for what Edmund Wilson described as the "mawkishness and banality" of her prose, she has won critical accolades for her skillfully deceptive plots. Julian Symons asserted: "The very best Christies are like a magician's tricks, not only in the breathtaking sleights of phrase that deceive us but also in the way that, looking back afterward, we find the tricks to have been handled so that our deceit is partly self-induced."

Many of Christie's mystery novels, particularly those considered classics of her canon, feature Hercule Poirot, a former member of the Belgian police force who was introduced in Christie's first book, *The Mysterious Affair at Styles* (1920). Poirot became one of detective fiction's most famous sleuths by relying primarily on reason and method, shunning the more physical and laborious tactics of Sherlock Holmes and similar investigators. Although *The Mysterious Affair at Styles* is considered an apprentice work which Christie wrote to appease her sister, who believed that she could not master the rigid conventions of the mystery novel, the book is often cited as one of Christie's finest achievements and continues to be among her most popular books.

Christie published several more detective novels during the early 1920s and gained widespread notoriety with *The Murder of Roger Ackroyd* (1926). In this Poirot book, Christie exposes the narrator as the murderer, a revelation that ignited a heated debate among devotees of the mystery novel. While many objected to what they considered a "trick ending," other critics and writers, including Dorothy L. Sayers, defended Christie by arguing that the reader must suspect all of the characters. Despite this controversy, *The Murder of Roger Ackroyd* remains one of Christie's most popular books and was the first in a series of successes that earned her a large, loyal readership. William Rose Benét regarded the novel as "a tale so ingeniously constructed, so dexterously plotted as to warrant our complete admiration." During her career, Christie published more than thirty detective novels featuring Hercule Poirot, among them *Murder on the Orient Express* (1934; published in the United States as *Murder in the Calais Coach*), *The ABC Murders* (1936), *Cards on the Table* (1936), *Death on the Nile*

(1937), *Five Little Pigs* (1943; published in the United States as *Murder in Retrospect*), and *Curtain* (1975).

Christie is also well known for her mystery novels involving the investigations of Miss Jane Marple, a genteel, elderly spinster who resides in a rural English village. Unlike Poirot, Miss Marple uses intuition to solve crimes, often uncovering clues through village gossip. Many critics regard *4:50 from Paddington* (1957; published in the United States as *What Mrs. McGillicuddy Saw!*) as the most entertaining Miss Marple mystery. In this book, Miss Marple inquires into a woman's claim that she viewed a murder inside a passing train. Other Miss Marple novels of note are *The Murder in the Vicarage* (1930), in which she first appears, *The Body in the Library* (1942), *A Murder Is Announced* (1950), *The Mirror Crack'd from Side to Side* (1962; published in the United States as *The Mirror Crack'd*), and *Sleeping Murder* (1976). Christie also achieved popular success with several novels featuring Tommy and Tuppence Beresford, an adventuresome couple for whom good fortune is more important than skill in solving crimes. The Beresfords appear in such works as *The Secret Adversary* (1922), *Partners in Crime* (1929), *N or M?* (1941), and *By the Pricking of My Thumbs* (1968).

In addition to her novels and short stories, Christie wrote several successful dramas within the mystery genre. Many of these plays are adaptations from her prose works and are characterized by entertaining plots featuring surprise endings. *The Mousetrap* (1952) has the distinction of being the longest-running play in British theater history, and *Witness for the Prosecution* (1953) received the New York Drama Critics Circle Award for best foreign play. Other popular Christie plays include *Ten Little Niggers* (1943; also produced as *Ten Little Indians* and *And Then There Were None*), *Appointment with Death* (1945), *Spider's Web* (1954), and *The Unexpected Guest* (1958). During her career, Christie also published several romance novels under the pseudonym Mary Westmacott; a collection of her poetry, *Poems* (1973); and two autobiographical works, *Come, Tell Me How You Live* (1946) and *An Autobiography* (1977).

(See also *CLC*, Vols. 1, 6, 8, 12, 39; *Contemporary Authors*, Vols. 17-20, rev. ed., Vols. 61-64 [obituary]; *Contemporary Authors New Revision Series*, Vol. 10; *Something about the Author*, Vol. 36; and *Dictionary of Literary Biography*, Vol. 13.)

MARGARET BOE BIRNS

Agatha Christie's reticence about herself and her private life were legendary in her lifetime, and unlike many other authors, her novels were not vehicles for self-exploration and revelation. Some critics have found some strong feelings and even confessions in the novels she wrote as Mary Westmacott, but in her memorable mystery novels, she is like James Joyce's ideal artist—disinterested, uninvolved, paring her fingernails as her plots play themselves out. This lack of personal revelation can be attributed to the demands of the whodunit form. Certainly Christie's whodunits seem to have a music box's enduring minor pleasure and a music box's incapacity for strong personal statement.

Nevertheless, one can find Agatha Christie in her novels. Personal themes do emerge, particularly in her novel *The Hollow* [published in the United States as *Murder After Hours*], which can be read not only as a well-crafted mystery but as a therapeutic working-through of issues in Christie's own life. In *The Hollow* we can find several self-portraits of Agatha Christie, the woman and the artist.

Briefly, the plot of *The Hollow* is as follows: Lady Angkatell and her husband are entertaining guests for the weekend at their country house, called The Hollow. Guests include an illustrious doctor, John Cristow and his retiring wife Gerda, and three relations of Lady Angkatell—Midge Harvey, a spunky working girl, Henrietta Savernake, an artist, and Edward Angkatell, a lonely man of means. At The Hollow, John chances to renew acquaintance with an old flame, Veronica Craye, now a glamorous actress vacationing nearby. Soon afterward, John is found dead, shot apparently by a jealous Gerda. Evidence seems to indicate, however, that John could as easily have been killed by Lady Angkatell, Henrietta, Veronica or Edward, who all had reason to wish to see John dead. Christie has here employed the mechanism known as the "double bluff," however, and it is eventually revealed that the original suspect, Gerda, is in fact the culprit.

It has surely struck some readers that the last name of Gerda and John Cristow echoes that of Christie. Further, the germanic awfulness of the name Gerda parallels that of Agatha, and as the novel unfolds, it is clear that we are meant to see in Gerda Cristow one of Christie's half-hidden self-portraits, albeit not a very flattering one.

Christie has written into the Cristow marriage all the conflicts she felt in her first marriage to Archibald Christie. As was Agatha Christie, Gerda Cristow is unhappily married to a man who takes her for granted, if at all; she is also threatened, as Christie was, by her husband's interest in another woman. In Christie's novel, the charming but egocentric John Cristow finds himself vamped by a glamorous film star, for whom the retiring, relentlessly dowdy Gerda is no match. It is of course no secret at this point that Christie's highly publicized bout of amnesia (recently the subject of a major motion picture) was triggered by her husband's love affair with another woman. The fact that Agatha Christie registered at a Yorkshire hotel under the name of her husband's mistress is one indication of her feelings of inadequacy—feelings she also projected into the character of Gerda, who cannot begin to compete with the woman imaged as the flashy Veronica Craye in *The Hollow*. In fact, Agatha Christie's celebrated amnesia is not too far from the psychological process that led her to create alternate realities in her fiction. It is as if, during her amnesiac period, she walked into one of her own daydreams, and then found she couldn't get back out. During her amnesiac state, Christie fulfilled a wish to be like her husband's mistress, solving paleologically the crisis in her marital life. In *The Hollow*, Christie fulfilled another wish—to kill her husband for having betrayed her. For Gerda, convinced her husband is going to leave her for Veronica Craye, cleverly, desperately contrives to murder John.

The novel is, however, less centered on the actual murder of John Cristow than on the neurotic character of the murderer. In fact, the plot of *The Hollow* and the solution of the mystery seem to grow out of the character of Gerda—a novelistic treatment of crime Christie has—rather unfairly—been accused of evading. It is Gerda's neurotic adoration of John Cristow, her self-effacing blind love, that leads her to her irrational, irremediable crime. In Christie's picture of Gerda we clearly have a very self-castigating analysis of her own failures in her first marriage. (pp. 31-2)

By the end of the book, Christie has dispatched the Cristows; and as the marriage crumbles and as the Cristows meet their (psychologically) timely deaths, Christie puts together a more desirable romance in the form of a counterplot involving two characters who also function as "suspects" in that layer of plotting that contains the novel's murder mystery. Midge Harvey and Edward Angkatell function as suspects in Christie's clever puzzle, but their relationship with each other also stands as a counterplot to the story of the Cristow marriage. Their relationship waxes as the Cristows' wanes, rises as the Cristows' falls, and in the final pages we are presented with a conventional "happy ending" in the prospective marriage of the spunky, self-sufficient Midge and the sensitive, protective Edward. Midge is all that Gerda is not, Edward all that was lacking in John, and in this aspect of her plot Christie has fulfilled a wish for a marriage free from crippling neurosis and selfishness.

But while there is a strong and emotionally satisfying element of wish fulfillment in the pairing of Midge and Edward, it is another character in the novel who more accurately portrays an offbeat component of Christie's own identity—her creative self. It is in the character of Henrietta Savernake (yet another 'suspect') that we can find Christie's personal portrait of herself as an artist. While Midge and Gerda are constellated as opposites, there is a curious twinning of Gerda and Henrietta. There is a decided emotional closeness between Henrietta and Gerda. Also unlike Midge, Gerda and Henrietta are both rather unpopular teutonic names, and, also unlike Midge, both Gerda and Henrietta are in love with John Cristow. Henrietta seems to instinctively understand Gerda and the nature of her love for John; it is in fact Henrietta's sculpture of Gerda that both reveals the imbalance of Gerda's make-up for the purposes of the mystery plot, and expresses, possibly universalizes, the pathos of Gerda's situation. Henrietta captures Gerda in stone as Christie has captured her in words, giving her suffering both a personal and archetypal aspect. . . . Henrietta rescues herself through her art, transcends the loss of John by affirming her devotion to another source of gratification. While Gerda has not only invested her erotic but also her religious feelings in her husband John, Henrietta's religion is her art, which seems at least in this case to be a more reliable object of worship. At the end of *The Hollow* Henrietta finds in her work a healing therapy, and there is no doubt that Agatha Christie found her work a similar tonic. (pp. 32-3)

[There] is yet another side of Agatha Christie represented in *The Hollow* that cannot go unmentioned. This is the feathery Lady Angkatell. It is Lady Angkatell who incarnates Agatha Christie's music box virtues. She is light, inconsequential, charming, frivolous and very feminine. She is the archetypal flibbertigibbet, a character designed to amuse as well as function within the whodunit formula as yet another 'suspect.' . . . In *The Hollow,* the character of Lady Angkatell provides a good deal of Christie's characteristic comic sparkle, but at the same time her willingness to carry out her own plan to murder John Cristow shows that she can be very clever and utterly ruthless when she wants to be. Christie's own success as a mystery novelist can be attributed in part to that selfsame ruthlessness. She had no compunction about selecting the most traditionally taboo of characters as her murderer, startling us with a rogues' gallery including a fetching young mother, a charming little girl, a helpful policeman and even the great Hercule Poirot himself, not to mention her even more bizarre murderers, such as the man we would all swear was shot to death pages ago, or the entire staff and resident family of an aristocratic country house, packed like sardines into one railway car on the Orient Express. Like the character of Lady Angkatell, Christie's whodunits offer amusement, but beneath the artful play is much cool calculation, and, at least in *The Hollow,* hidden depths where lurk a revealing series of self-portraits. (pp. 33-4)

Margaret Boe Birns, "Agatha Christie's Portrait of the Artist," in Clues: A Journal of Detection, *Vol. 1, No. 2, Fall-Winter, 1980, pp. 31-4.*

ROBERT BARNARD

In the course of her more than five decades as a professional and prolific writer of detective fiction Agatha Christie acquired for her armory a variety of "strategies of deception," means of deceiving the reader which she experimented with, developed and perfected over the years. (p. 63)

The most popular of these strategies, which turns up time and time again in various forms, is a development of the *Roger Ackroyd* trick. . . . In *Roger Ackroyd* we exclude a character from our suspicions because we see the action through his eyes; in this strategy we exclude him because we are placed in a position of sympathy with him from the beginning. What we have here is not a pattern of narrator as murderer, but one of assumed victim as murderer, or pursuer as murderer. In these books the *donnée* of the story is the pursuit of an unidentified criminal by someone who seems to be the object of a series of murder attempts (*Peril at End House*), who seems to be the victim of some sort of conspiracy (*One, Two, Buckle My Shoe . . .* and *By the Pricking of My Thumbs,* for example), or who is sure there has been committed an undetected murder (*Three Act Tragedy . . .*). It is at the beginning of a book (when he is merely "getting into the story," collecting the necessary data) that the reader is least wary: because the whole investigation starts off from this *donnée* the initiator is exempt from suspicion, he is allied with Poirot or whomever in the search for truth. We are fooled because Christie has worked her favorite piece of legerdemain—she has persuaded us right from the beginning to see the situation the wrong way up. (pp. 63-4)

This particular deception works best with the sort of elbow room that the *novel* gives: when Christie tries it (several times) in the short stories that make up *Poirot Investigates* it is ineffective because the restricted length does not permit any real reader-identification with the supposed victim or pursuer. On the other hand the initiators of the pursuit in *Peril at End House, Three Act Tragedy, Endless Night* and *A Murder Is Announced* are significantly superior to the norm in Christie characterization: either they are marked by strongly individual personalities or else they engage the sympathy of the reader by the pathos and interest of their situation, and thus he is happy to associate them with the principal sleuth in the crusade for truth and justice. When the solution comes around, however, the reader is reminded how frequently the negative potentialities of these characters have been placed before him.

This particular strategy is allied to another favorite one whereby the actual investigator (*Curtain,* "Three Blind Mice") or the sidekick Watson figure as recommended by Agatha Christie's brother-in-law (*Hercule Poirot's Christmas . . . , They Came to Baghdad*) is finally unmasked as the villain. What Christie relies on here, of course, is the familiar tendency of the British detective story (as opposed to the American) to give unequivocal support to the established forces of law and order. (pp. 64-5)

In this strategy Christie deceives the reader by using the traditional attitudes inherent in the detective-story convention, but she also harks back, probably quite consciously, to the very origins of crime fiction. Jerry Palmer (in *Thrillers*) draws attention to the well-known ambiguity in the popular attitude to crime, its unpredictable tendency to elevate the criminal to heroic status and anathematize his pursuer. Inevitably this blurring around the moral edges finds its way into writings about crime in the eighteenth and early nineteenth centuries. . . . Christie was taking an attitude already well established in crime literature, and adapting it to the particular needs of the puzzle-type detective story.

Many of Christie's other strategies of deception also involve the use and twisting of well-worn literary material, of cliché situations and stereotyped characters from popular fiction, where she can predict the reader's response and use it against him. One such strategy . . . uses that perennial literary standby, the eternal triangle. In its most usual form in Christie we are likely to be presented as a starting point with a marriage that is threatened from outside by an alluring and sexually unscrupulous type, usually a woman. The husband is attracted, and the reader's sympathy is inevitably drawn toward the innocent party (the wife) and away from the husband and the marriage-breaker. There is of course a special interest in the recurrence of this pattern because of its relevance to the breakup of Agatha Christie's own marriage. Yet, true to her habits of self-concealment, any easy sympathy the reader may feel for the injured wife almost always turns out to be a snare, and the pattern never remains in its pristine, morally unambiguous shape. The triangle is the basis of at least three of the novels of the classic period (*Death on the Nile, Evil under the Sun* and *Five Little Pigs* . . .) and several short stories, most notably "**Triangle at Rhodes**" and "**The Bloodstained Pavement**." In every case Christie relies on a standardized literary situation, and she pulls off her deception because we can see no further than the cliché. In the denouement to the plot we tend to find that it is the marriage, or the earliest love relationship, that is the enduring one (in either a positive or a negative way), and that it is the intruder who is deceived, to be pitied, and frequently the victim. Notice how *Death on the Nile* and *Evil under the Sun* have virtually identical plots: the stable initial relationships (Simon Doyle-Jacqueline de Belfort in the one, the Redfern marriage in the other) are apparently threatened by a desirable outsider (Linnet Ridgeway with her money, Arlena Marshall with her looks). In both cases the murder is a conspiracy of the original couple against the outsider.

In these stories the triangle is an open one, clear from the beginning; in other books the same material is used but the triangle is concealed, certain basic information being withheld from the reader. Significantly these tend to be late books, for toward the end of her life Christie became less concerned with the 'twenties imperative of playing fair. Thus, in *A Caribbean Mystery* the liaison between Tim Kendal and Esther Walters is kept from us, and so in *Endless Night* is that between the narrator and Greta. But it was obviously a pattern that fascinated Christie, and the interested reader can trace the way she worked out all sorts of variations on it in such novels as *Elephants Can Remember, Towards Zero*, and *Sad Cypress*.

It was not only when she was dealing with the eternal triangle that Christie showed her skill in taking formulas from popular literature (which after all was what she was writing, with the difference that she was out to deceive) where she could rely on a certain response to certain stimuli, and using that response as a way of leading the reader up an enticingly familiar garden path. . . . [This skill is at work] in *One, Two, Buckle My Shoe* . . .: faced with the setup of an international conspiracy to murder a conservative banker on whom the stability of Britain depends, the reader reacts in a predictable way which ensures he averts his eyes from the suspiciousness of the banker himself. (pp. 65-8)

In characterization, too, Christie often creates a pure stereotype, hoping that the reader will discount a figure so obviously drawn from stock—a piece from her standard repertory of cardboard figures, and given one of her standard names (Caroline for elderly inquisitive spinsters, prissy trisyllabic names for lawyers, and so on). One such piece of cardboard is Major Burnaby in *The Sittaford Mystery* . . .—bluff, down-to-earth, a bit of a bore in men's company, a bit uneasy in women's. We discount him, partly because we have seen so many other such figures on the outskirts of Christie stories, partly because the discovery of the body is apparently done from his point of view (though actually Christie keeps well away from his thoughts at this moment, and uses an *Ackroyd* trick, ignoring his activities for a significant length of time). Similarly Christie banks on a certain reader-response to other stock characters—American lady-tourists are merely funny, children are innocent, old ladies are frail and nice—in every case the stock response being used as a means of diverting suspicion from where suspicion is due.

One of the main weapons in Christie's armory of deception is her supreme skill in diverting the reader's attention from the matter of real importance by focusing his attention on some irrelevancy elsewhere. The words "conjuring trick" occur over and over again in reviews of her books, and this is of course the essence of the conjuror's art. This skill is of great importance when clues are being placed, as we shall see, but it can also be seen at work in major matters of plotting as well. For example, there are many books in which the reader is sent off after a false scent by being persuaded to give his attention to the wrong murder, or to an attempted murder that is in reality no more than a smoke screen. (pp. 68-9)

This ploy has been seen in several of the books we have already looked at, most notably *Peril at End House* and *One, Two, Buckle My Shoe*. There are many more: in *Three Act Tragedy* . . . we have our attention focused on the murder of the Reverend Stephen Babbington; in *A Murder Is Announced* on the theatrically set up "shooting" of Lettie Blacklock; in *By the Pricking of My Thumbs* on the supposed threat to the aged Mrs. Lancaster. These are the starting points of the stories. Only they turn out to be the wrong starting points. This technique is seen at its most elaborate in *The ABC Murders* (which is the "real" murder, which are part of the smokescreen?), and at its most beguiling in *After the Funeral* [published in the United States as *Funerals Are Fatal*]. Here the story is set on its way by the tactless remark at the funeral of Richard Abernethy: "But he *was* murdered, wasn't he?" and by the death immediately afterward of Cora Lansquenet, the person who said it. This establishes in the reader's mind a cause-and-effect sequence, with the *initial* death—Abernethy's—as apparently the more important one. Whereas in fact Richard Abernethy is one of the few people in any of Christie's novels to die from natural causes, and the important death is in fact that of Cora Lansquenet.

In analyzing the use of these and all the rest of her stratagems of deception, the question is bound to arise of Agatha Christie's relationship with her reader—always a ticklish problem, as witness the case of Dorothy L. Sayers, whose rather superior manner and aggressively conservative stance chimed in perfectly with her readers' demands in the 'twenties and 'thirties but tend to put readers off today. It would certainly have been easy for Agatha Christie to alienate her audience by the relentless trickiness of her mind. But this never seems to happen, and it may be that her popularity so far outstrips that of her rivals—better writers, more vivid characterizers, nearly as ingenious plotters—because she creates an entirely satisfactory relationship, based on what one might call trustful mistrust. This is attested to by the frequency with which one hears her readers say that she "always plays fair." Where the plots of her competitors depended on detailed knowledge of railway timetables, minutiae of forensic science, a grasp of engineering that could invent yet more fantastic ways of killing men in a locked room—in a word, specialist knowledge of one kind or another—she demanded from her reader only a noticing eye and ear, and a lively grasp of the facts of everyday life around him. Though one has doubts about the use of the word *cozy* to describe her books, certainly it is true to say that the means she uses to unmask her villains are "homely" in the English sense—that is, they are commonplace things one meets with every day. In *Death in the Clouds* . . . she plays around satirically with darts tipped with the poison of the South American Indians, but the real clues are things like an empty matchbox, an extra coffeespoon in a saucer. Thus, though her stories are intellectual puzzles of a certain rarefied kind, she manages to "earth" them by her constant use of commonplace objects from the life around us. The reader feels that the clues relate to his experience, and therefore *ought* to tell him the truth: he blames his own imperceptiveness when the time for the solution comes round, not the author for a showy display of esoteric knowledge. (pp. 69-71)

[Christie's placing of her] clues is miraculously sure, again ensuring that warm readership trust which built her up a devoted following which (unlike Sayers's) still seems strong in the younger generation today. There was the vital piece of information placed before us, we tend to say at the end of a Christie, but we ignored it because of the *way* it was placed. One much-quoted example is the butler and the calendar in *Hercule Poirot's Christmas.* An even better example, because it illustrates how well Christie understood the working of her readers' minds, occurs in *The Sittaford Mystery.* . . . The opening chapters, up to the discovery of Captain Trevelyan's body, occur on the fringes of a Dartmoor deep in snow, with a new blizzard threatening (one of very few examples in Christie of a precise geographical placing). In the first chapter we are told that Major Burnaby and Captain Trevelyan used to go to Switzerland together for the winter sports. Shortly after the finding of the body we are told that there are two pairs of skis in the cupboard of Captain Trevelyan's dining room. But Christie knows her readers: to the English—particularly at the time she wrote—skiing was an upper-class holiday sport. Even today it is still very much a *sport.* It means dazzling dashes down the Swiss Alps. It has nothing to do with covering long distances fast over snow. The English reader will not make the connection between snow and skis (as a Norwegian would immediately) which would enable him to solve the crime.

Inevitably there are some few examples of miscalculation. The clue of the initial brooch seen in the mirror in *Dumb Witness* . . . is one such: the reader certainly ought to see the significance of this—quite apart from the objection made (when the book was published) by the *Times,* arbiter in such matters, that ladies really do not go wandering around houses at night with brooches pinned to their dressing gowns. *Dumb Witness* . . . is in fact the only classic Christie that ought to make the reader feel stupid if he fails to solve it. Elsewhere her touch with the deceptive potential of the objects and smells of everyday life is unerring: if Sherlock Holmes understands the significance of the dog *not* barking in the night, Agatha Christie understands the significance of a room *not* smelling of tobacco in the morning. One of her major strategies of deception springs from her ability to see and use the sinister possibilities behind things that the ordinary reader sees and handles every day of his life. That is part of the comfortable feeling he has when opening a Christie—that murder is being brought, deliciously, home to him. (pp. 71-3)

> *Robert Barnard, "Strategies of Deception," in his* A Talent to Deceive: An Appreciation of Agatha Christie, *Dodd, Mead & Company, 1980, pp. 63-73.*

MARTY S. KNEPPER

To a greater or lesser degree, detective fiction writers Dorothy L. Sayers, Josephine Tey, P. D. James, Amanda Cross, and Anna Katherine Green can be considered feminist writers. But what about the "Mistress of Mystery," Agatha Christie, whose books, written between the years 1920 and 1973, have sold over five hundred million copies and have been translated into dozens of languages? Is Christie a feminist or anti-feminist writer, or do her works fall somewhere in between, in some middle ground? (p. 398)

[Recognizing] that any assessment of a writer's sexual politics will be subjective, it is nevertheless possible to legitimately argue that a writer is more or less feminist or more or less anti-feminist, especially if the crucial terms are clearly defined and if the author's works are analyzed closely. In the case of Agatha Christie, an examination of her sixty-six detective novels reveals that although there are anti-feminist elements in her writings, Christie obviously respects women and has feminist sympathies. (pp. 398-99)

In what respect are Christie's detective novels anti-feminist? Critics Margot Peters and Agate Nesaule Krouse—who, in an article entitled "Women and Crime: Sexism in Allingham, Sayers, and Christie," detect sexism in Christie's writings, while conceding that she is less anti-feminist than Allingham and Sayers—argue that Christie's female characters reflect her prejudice against women [see *CLC,* Vol. 12]. . . . Although, Peters and Krouse admit, Christie does portray women making it on their own in society through their brains, skills, and energies, too many of these women, they claim, are shown to be deadly and destructive. Peters and Krouse point out, furthermore, that in contrast to Hercule Poirot, who uses reason, knowledge, and method to conduct his investigations, Miss Marple relies on intuition and nosiness, and Ariadne Oliver usually fails to uncover the truth because of her untidy mind.

While the arguments of Peters and Krouse are inadequately supported in the article and much too overstated (Christie does *not* make all her independent, competent women characters either deadly and destructive or skinny and sexless), there is truth to their claims that Christie's books display sexism. Certainly some of her most popular detective novels (*The Murder of Roger Ackroyd, And Then There Were None, The A.B.C. Murders, Murder on the Orient Express*) present women in totally stereotypical ways: as empty-headed ingenues, for example, or as gossipy old ladies. Other less famous novels are just as anti-feminist. In *Evil Under the Sun,* for example, dress designer Rosamund Darnley gladly gives up her successful business enterprise when the man she loves proposes and insists she live in the country and devote herself full-time to marriage and stepmotherhood. Lynn Marchmont, in *There Is a Tide,* is only really attracted to her dull fiancé, Rowley Cloade, after he tries to kill her. The main character in *Sad Cypress,* Elinor Carlisle, is a truly romantic heroine, sentimental and helpless: She is obsessed with love for her cousin Roddy, and when she is accused of murdering Roddy's new girlfriend, Elinor, a classic damsel in distress, she must be saved by Dr. Lord and Hercule Poirot. (pp. 399-401)

Christie, it is clear, often uses sexist stereotypes of women, sometimes shows women as inferior to and dependent on men, occasionally idealizes self-abnegating women and monsterizes strong women, and frequently implies that woman's true vocation is marriage and motherhood. Yet Christie should not be so easily dismissed as an anti-feminist writer. Perhaps because readers and critics usually concentrate on Christie's major works, they fail, like Peters and Krouse, to consider carefully some of Christie's lesser-known works, such as *The Secret Adversary, Murder After Hours, A Murder Is Announced, The Moving Finger,* and *Cat Among the Pigeons,* all of which illustrate that Christie is capable of presenting a wide range of female characters that go beyond anti-feminist stereotypes, creating some very admirable female heroes, and exploring many problems women face as a result of the sexism that pervades our society. (p. 401)

[Christie] shows women who are happy and competent (sometimes super-competent) in [numerous] fields of endeavor, many of them non-traditional fields for women: archeology (Angela Warren, *Murder in Retrospect*); medicine (Sarah King, *Appointment with Death*); science (Madame Oliver, *The Big Four*); high finance (Letitia Blacklock, *A Murder is Announced*, and Anna Schelle, *They Came to Baghdad*); sculpture (Henrietta Savernake, *Murder After Hours*); nursing (Amy Leatheran, *Murder in Mesopotamia*); politics (Lady Westholme, M.P., *Appointment with Death*); business management (Katherine Martindale, *The Clocks*); espionage (Mrs. Upjohn, *Cat Among the Pigeons*); acrobatics (Dulcie Duveen, *Murder on the Links*); school administration (Honoria Bulstrode, *Cat Among the Pigeons*); acting (Ginevra Boynton), *Appointment with Death*); and writing (Ariadne Oliver). Of these fourteen examples of competent women in Christie's novels (and there are many more), only three are criminals and none fits the . . . skinny and sexless category.

Christie also presents, in a positive way, a category of women who are generally ignored or ridiculed in literature because their lives are independent of men's lives: the single women. Besides unmarried older women such as Jane Marple, this category also includes lesbians (for example, Hinch and Murgatroyd in *A Murder Is Announced* and Clotilde Bradbury-Scott in *Nemesis*), feminists (Cecilia Williams in *Murder in Retrospect,* for instance), children (Geraldine in *The Clocks,* Josephine in *Crooked House,* Joyce and Miranda in *Hallowe'en,* Julia and Jeniffer in *Cat Among the Pigeons*), and handicapped women (such as Millicent Pebmarsh in *The Clocks*).

Christie's women, furthermore, often defy sexist "traditional wisdom" about the female sex. For instance, young women married to older men are supposed to be mercenary and adulterous, but Christie's Griselda Clement (in *The Murder at the Vicarage*) is totally devoted to her scholarly older husband, a poor vicar. Women, it is also commonly believed, prefer to use their brains to ensnare a mate or run a household rather than to contemplate philosophy and politics. Yet beautiful young Renisenb (in *Death Comes As the End*) is interested in learning about life and death and the politics of ancient Egypt. Another popular idea is that there is something unnatural and unhealthy in a close relationship between a mother and her grown son. From Freud in his writings on the Oedipus Complex to Roth in *Portnoy's Complaint,* modern writers have harshly criticized the overprotective mother. In *Death on the Nile,* however, the characters of Mrs. Allerton and Tim Allerton contradict this idea: This mother and son respect and enjoy each other; they are not devouring, smothering mother and pathetically dependent son, though they have a very close relationship.

Besides writing about all types of female characters, many unstereotypical, Christie also creates some appealing female heroes with whom women readers can identify. This is significant because one of the great weaknesses of literature over the centuries is the paucity of heroic women characters: women who display qualities such as intelligence, imagination, bravery, independence, knowledge, vision, fortitude, determination; women who triumph; women who are not ridiculed, condemned as evil, or killed off by their authors. (pp. 401-02)

The best example of Christie's female heroes . . . is Tuppence Cowley, who appears first in *The Secret Adversary.* Tuppence is much like the other female heroes in the Christie detective

novels, but her character is drawn in much more detail. She is a very entertaining and engaging feminist character.

Tuppence, inappropriately christened "Prudence," grew up as the black sheep in an archdeacon's family, her short skirts and smoking a worry to her Victorian father. Escaping her family at an early age, Tuppence went to work in an army hospital during World War I, where she was assigned the glamourless tasks of washing dishes and sweeping, later leaving for the more congenial war work of driving first a van and a lorry and later a general's car.

Tuppence is not a typical romantic heroine. She is not beautiful, she eats voraciously at every opportunity, she speaks in slangy phrases (many of which, she fears, would shock her poor father), she is unsentimental and practical and businesslike, she resents any suggestion that she needs taking care of, and she insists on paying her own way when she goes places with her old friend Tommy Beresford. Tuppence is, in short, the New Woman of the 1920s.

In an effort to fight poverty, Tuppence joins forces with Tommy, a likeable chap more down-to-earth and plodding than imaginative and quick-witted Tuppence, and they form The Young Adventurers, Ltd. Naturally, they get involved in adventures, and these adventures lead finally to their recovering secret papers that will save Britain and to their exposing a respected solicitor as a criminal mastermind.

The Young Adventurers, Ltd. proves to be, in fact as well as in theory, an equal partnership. Tuppence is no Nora Charles to Tommy's Nick; she is a clever detective and displays brains, courage, and daring. At one point she wrests a gun away from a criminal determined to exterminate her.

The personal relationship that develops between Tuppence and Tommy also proves to be an equal partnership, more so than the relationship between Peter Wimsey and Harriet Vane in the Dorothy Sayers novels. Whereas Peter Wimsey outranks Harriet Vane in wealth, class, intelligence, charm, and detective ability, Tommy and Tuppence are equally poor and respectable and equally skilled at detection, though each has his or her own special strengths. (pp. 402-03)

Few detective writers have created the female heroes Christie has, all of them more or less like Tuppence. It is true that these women almost always marry at the end of their adventuring, but during the course of the stories, these women, like less affluent, less perfect, more human Nancy Drews, prove themselves to be, as heroes, every bit the equal of any man in the stories.

As well as in the diversity of her women characters and in her delightful female heroes, Christie's feminist sympathies are revealed in the way she points out problems women face living in a patriarchy, problems that have not changed much over the centuries. One such problem is the economic oppression of women, as much a reality today as ever. (pp. 403-04)

Because of the economic reality that there are not, in our society, enough high-paying, stimulating jobs for everyone and that someone has to keep households functioning and do the unfulfilling, routine jobs, a sexist attitude toward women and work has developed in our society: specifically, women should not pursue careers in business management, government, in the prestigious, powerful professions; rather, they should work in the home or in the "womanly" (i.e., low-paying, powerless) occupations. This attitude may be changing some, but women with "unwomanly" career ambitions still encounter plenty of problems with occupational discrimination, a fact Christie acknowledges in some of her detective novels. . . . The character Henrietta Savernake, a sculptor in Christie's **Murder After Hours,** has a common conflict many contemporary career women must resolve: She is torn between love for a man, who wants all her attention, and love for a profession, which demands all her energies. Christie also shows in her novels that many of the common "careers" for women in the earlier twentieth century (such as being a maid or a typist or a governess) were as depressing to the soul as they were unrewarding to the pocketbook. . . . Yet Christie sometimes emphasizes the positive rather than the negative by showing clever, enterprising young women, such as Lucy Eylesbarrow in **What Mrs. McGillicuddy Saw,** triumphing over economic adversity.

Women's chief functions in earlier patriarchal societies was to marry and have legitimate children to whom, if male, property could be bequeathed. Even today, there is a terrific social pressure on women to marry, have children, and be sexually monogamous wives. It is ironic that although Christie, a romantic, almost always marries off at least one couple at the end of each novel and implies that they will, no matter how mismatched, live happily ever after, Christie, also a realist, presents relatively few happy marriages in her novels (Tommy and Tuppence are exceptions). (p. 404)

Christie also reveals to her readers the problems women have who get pregnant out of wedlock because society, even in the twentieth century, ostracizes the illegitimate child and the unmarried mother and because it is difficult to earn a living and raise a child at the same time. Eileen Rich, a teacher in **Cat Among the Pigeons,** for example, takes a sabbatical and has her illegitimate baby in secret in a foreign country for fear of losing her job. Millicent Pebmarsh in **The Clocks** gives up her baby rather than face the trials of raising a child as a single woman. In **By the Pricking of My Thumbs,** Tuppence tracks down a pathetic and pathological child murderer who, many years ago, killed her own baby because she didn't feel she could raise the child herself.

Another problem women face in our society is the pressure to make themselves beautiful sex objects to allure men. Because beauty is often the measure of a woman's value (consider, for example, beauty pageants and magazine advertising), plain women often suffer tremendous feelings of self-hatred, jealousy, and rejection. Christie presents sympathetically in her novels the unbeautiful women, the changelings, women such as Mildred Strete in **Murder with Mirrors** and Josephine Leonides in **Crooked House.** She shows how plainness or physical anomalousness can lead women to feel hatred of the men who reject them and jealousy of more beautiful women (Henet in **Death Comes As the End**), how it can lead a woman longing for love to be taken in by a scoundrel with a smooth line (Gladys Martin in **A Pocket Full of Rye,** Kirsten Lindstrom in **Ordeal by Innocence**), or how it can make a woman feel life owes her some recompense for her physical shortcomings (Charlotte Blacklock in **A Murder Is Announced**). But Christie recognizes that the problem of beauty is not all one-sided. She also shows women who have dedicated themselves to achieving their own physical perfection caught in the beauty trap: Linda Marshall, a gorgeous woman in **Evil Under the Sun,** can attract any man's attention, but she has never been able to hold a man's interest because her positive qualities are only skin deep.

Christie's depiction of the various problems women face in their lives reveals her astuteness as a psychologist and an observer of human nature and her awareness of how society discriminates against women. While Christie is, by no means, a radical feminist (her novels are not a sustained critique of the institutions and ideas that bolster male dominance), she does display feminist attitudes in those of her novels which show problems women have living in a patriarchal society. (pp. 405-06)

When all her sixty-six detective novels and hundreds of women characters are considered, should Christie, finally, be characterized as a feminist or anti-feminist writer? As Peters and Krouse point out in their essay, Christie's writings do display sexism, mainly in the form of anti-feminist stereotyping. Disorganized, intuitive, imaginative Ariadne Oliver does not compare as a detective to orderly, competent, knowledgeable Hercule Poirot. Christie's more famous novels, especially the ones written in the 1930s, perpetrate a number of anti-feminist ideas about women. Yet it is distorting the case for Peters and Krouse to dismiss Christie's women characters as "a depressing cast of thousands." In many of her lesser-known novels (written mainly in the 1920s, 1940s, late 1950s, and early 1960s) Christie creates very positive women characters who are competent in many fields (including the detection of crime), who are psychologically complex, who are heroic in stature, who are not inferior to nor dependent on men, women such as Tuppence Cowley, Lucy Eylesbarrow, and Honoria Bulstrode. In these novels Christie also explores, with compassion and sympathy and from a woman's point of view, various problems women in sexist society must cope with, problems ranging from poverty and job discrimination to social pressure to be attractive. The only fair conclusion seems to be that Christie, while not an avowed feminist, let her admiration for strong women, her sympathy for victimized women, and her recognition of society's discrimination against women emerge in the novels written during the decades of the twentieth century more receptive to feminist ideas (such as the 1920s and World War II years), while Christie, always concerned with selling her novels to mass audiences, relied more on traditional (sexist) stereotypes and ideas about women in the more conservative and anti-feminist decades (such as the 1930s). (p. 406)

Marty S. Knepper, "Agatha Christie—Feminist," in The Armchair Detective, *Vol. 16, No. 4, Winter, 1983, pp. 398-406.*

ELIOT A. SINGER

In calling attention to a shared enigmatic quality, the analogy *whodunit* to *riddle* is such a commonplace that it is almost more a synonym than a cliche. Yet analogy is never a substitute for analysis, and the very obviousness of this equation has seemed to mask the extent to which the riddle can provide real clues to the structure of the whodunit. Many traditional speech genres present distillations of fundamental literary devices. In more complex literary constructions, even in a popular culture form like the mystery, the combination of such devices often covers up the simplicity of the devices themselves. Thus, by carefully considering the construction of folkloric forms, it often becomes possible to uncover devices that are essential to literature but concealed in it. This essay suggests that by taking seriously the notion of the whodunit as riddle, that is by applying those devices utilized in riddling strategies to this type of mystery, it becomes both possible and necessary to reconsider the basic nature of whodunit construction. (pp. 157-58)

The dominant conception among both critics and other readers is that reading a whodunit is an almost pure hermeneutic exercise in which bits of conflicting information are given the reader to enable him or her to arrive at a solution through systematic analysis. . . . The reader and the story detective then, are expected to follow the same hermeneutic procedure, sorting through true and false clues and eschewing "red herrings" in order to discover a coherent pattern.

Riddle scholars often refer to solutions as being "arbitrary," and as any experienced reader can attest, in reading a whodunit, it is almost always possible to conceive of several rational solutions that account for at least the most crucial disparate clues. Most whodunits suggest numerous incorrect solutions in the course of the telling, and while these are rejected because of incongruous elements, it takes little imagination to by-pass these incongruities. . . . [Whodunits] whose murderers are arbitrary choices no better than the reader's suspects do not provide satisfactory reading experiences, and their authors cannot expect to achieve consistent popularity unless, like Dorothy Sayers or Peter Dickinson, their writing is satisfying for reasons other than the mystery.

Of all the authors of the true whodunit, Agatha Christie, as is evidenced by her popularity in volume and over time, has had the greatest success in satisfying her readership. The key to this success lies in the non-arbitrariness of most of her solutions. Contrary to the common practice of whodunit writers, which, as [Howard] Haycraft points out, goes back to Poe, Agatha Christie's murderers are not *"the least likely."* Nor are they taken at random from the list of suspects. Rather, more often than not, they are *the most likely*—husbands, wives, lovers, relatives, or others with clear cut motives of gain or vengeance—that is, murderers much like those in real life. (pp. 158-59)

Given the straightforwardness of her murders, why then are Agatha Christie's whodunits so difficult to solve? The answer lies in the reader's mistaken presumption that the mystery is complex and that the texts are hermeneutically structured to enable a reader to imitate the detective or alter-ego in sorting through clues to discover a pattern. Agatha Christie's hermeneutic, however, is a negating one, one that takes a relatively simple murder and through the reading process controverts the reader's reason. To quote . . . that source of wisdom, Miss Marple, "The greatest thing in these cases is to keep an absolutely open mind." What Dame Agatha consciously and insidiously does is *close the reader's mind*. The clues themselves, then, become insignificant, and the solution lies not in untangling their pattern, but in discovering the mechanism by which the reader's mind is closed.

A riddle is enigmatic because there is an obstruction between the image it presents and the referent the riddlee is supposed to guess. In riddling scholarship this obstruction, following [Robert] Petsch, is usually called *the block element*. Roger Abrahams has elaborated upon this concept by delineating four different, though not always distinct, block elements (or riddling strategies): *too little information, too much information, contradiction,* and *false gestalt.* A close examination of the construction of Agatha Christie's whodunits shows that, at one time or another, she makes use of each of these block elements to detour the reader from the solution.

While most Agatha Christie mysteries utilize a multiplicity of riddling strategies, it is usually possible to single out one block element as dominant. The 1939 Hercule Poirot novel, *Sad Cypress*, for instance, is unsolvable because there is *too little information*. In this story a poisoning takes place in the presence of two women, one of whom, as the reader learns at the

outset, is on trial for murder, and hence may be presumed innocent. . . . The other woman, Nurse Hopkins, not only has the opportunity to commit the murder, but having "misplaced" the precise poison used, has the means as well. Moreover, she is seen urging the murdered girl to make a will leaving everything (which turns out to be a considerable legacy not a pittance) to her aunt in Australia. The block occurs because Nurse Hopkins has no apparent motive. There is too little information to connect Nurse Hopkins to the inheritance since the only hint the reader receives is an aside that the unseen aunt is a nurse. The crucial fact, that Nurse Hopkins and the Australian aunt are one and the same, is revealed only in a Perry Mason style ending.

For a satisfying reading experience, as [S. S.] Van Dine insists, "The reader must have an equal opportunity with the detective for solving the mystery. All clues must be plainly stated and described." And since a reader cannot reason out a solution for which there is too little information, but can only guess at it, this mystery riddling strategy is the least fair. It is one, however, to which Christie rarely resorts, and in *Sad Cypress* even the slightest hint would make it trivial to arrive at the solution. (pp. 160-61)

A more reasonable block element is the opposite one, *too much information*. There is a sense in which all "red herrings" are too much information, extraneous facts that lead the reader astray. . . . [Christie] uses many "red herrings"—the embezzling lawyer in *Death on the Nile*, or the imposter archaeologist in *Murder at the Vicarage* are examples—but they are usually introduced late in the text, and are easily identifiable by the attentive reader. Sometimes, however, too much information becomes the dominant strategy for misleading the reader. In *Funerals Are Fatal*, for example, Aunt Cora, who is known for her tendency to state awkward and embarrassing truths, blurts out at her brother's funeral, "But he was murdered wasn't he?" When she in turn is murdered, the police and reader alike assume that her death is a result of knowledge about that of her brother. This awkward "truth," however, turns out to be extraneous information; the brother, in fact, had died an innocent death, and the murderer of Aunt Cora is the only person it could be, her companion and legatee, Miss Gilchrist, who had impersonated the victim in order to produce the misdirecting clue. (pp. 161-62)

Perhaps even more basic to the whodunit than the "red herring" is the block element *contradiction*. Locked rooms, iron clad alibis, falsified times of death, letters from the already dead, and other contradictory clues of time, place, and manner usually must be explained away before a murder can be deciphered. But such empirical contradictions, favorites of writers as diverse as Poe, Conan Doyle, and John Dickson Carr, should not bother the experienced reader, and are usually only used by Christie as secondary devices. (p. 162)

More subtle are contradictions in character, murderous stratagems that seem implausible because they require more physical strength or more intelligence than a given character would seem to possess. In *The Hollow*, for instance, the philandering murdered husband's wife is found standing over the body with a gun in her hand, but is easily cleared since this gun turns out not to be the murder weapon. The contradiction occurs because to throw initial suspicion on oneself in order to be eliminated as a suspect is a stratagem that requires more imagination and intelligence than the wife, "poor Gerda," who is consistently portrayed as a simpleton, would seem to possess. But she is not so simple as all that, as the attentive reader should remember from when early in the book she muses, "It was amusing to know more than they thought you knew. To be able to do a thing, but not let anyone know that you could do it." (p. 163)

[Viktor] Sklovskij, in an early Russian formalist study, has pointed to the false gestalt as a general analogy for the who-dunit. "These mysteries at first present false solutions . . . ," he writes, as in the Russian folk riddle, "'It hangs dangling. Everybody grabs for it.' The solution: 'A towel.'" This analogy is, however, a little broad, and the notion of false gestalt is better limited to those texts that allow not only for alternative solutions, but for general misconceptions. (It should be noted that, while for the riddle false gestalt involves instantaneous recognition of a solution, usually an obscene one, which turns out to be false, for the whodunit this block element is not distinct but is a result of too much information or of a contradiction that leads the reader into forming a false picture of the whole circumstances of the murder, not just of its details.) One such false gestalt occurs in **The Body in the Library** where the reader assumes that the body is who it is supposed to be. This gestalt is reconstituted only when the witness who identifies the body is shown to be an accomplice. Another false gestalt that Christie induces is a misconception as to victim. In **Peril at End House** the reader assumes that, unlike Hastings who tends to jump to conclusions, Poirot is infallible, and therefore, he or she follows the detective in believing that quiet Maggie Buckley has been mistakenly done in instead of her lively cousin, Nick, whose potential assassination Poirot has cleverly deduced. (p. 164)

Most scholars accept any of these four block elements as legitimate riddling devices appropriate to the "true riddle." Much less accepted are those riddles that play with the riddle form itself, what are usually called, somewhat disdainfully, *"riddle parodies."* In riddle parodies what prevents the riddlee from guessing the answer is certain assumptions about the nature of riddling. These may be termed *generic blockers*. All genres set up certain norms and expectations—in riddling, that the question is an enigmatic one, and that the information provided is valid—which help inform the listener's or reader's interpretation. The generic norms and expectations for the riddle and the whodunit are quite different, so while the four basic block elements for the riddle are directly applicable to the whodunit, this is not the case for generic blockers. One can certainly conceive of mysteries that use the riddle parody device of having no enigma to confuse the reader, in which . . . misleading information is given not by a character (in such cases the strategy is simply *too much information* or *false gestalt*) but by the author, or in which, as in many "neck-riddles," the solution is wholly idiosyncratic (carrying "too little information" to the extreme). Such mysteries would, however, involve radical transformations in form, changes in the generic dominant of the sort I have elsewhere termed "breaking genre." . . . But the whodunit as a more complex form also has a multitude of less fundamental norms and expectations not present in the riddle, and these may be used to create generic blockers without calling into question the very nature of the form. (pp. 165-66)

It is absolutely essential to the whodunit that there be an apparent crime (usually a murder), that someone seek to solve that crime, and that the reader not learn of the solution until the final epiphany. All other conventions, while presenting a certain aesthetic and insisting upon fairness to the reader, are merely expectations.

Agatha Christie's genius lies most of all in her ability to prey upon the reader's tendency to confuse expectations with norms to invent *generic blockers* for her mysteries. For this skill, she was reviled by some of her contemporaries: Van Dine dismissed one of her devices as "bald trickery, on the par with offering some one a bright penny for a five-dollar gold piece," and [Raymond] Chandler said that another was "guaranteed to knock the keenest mind for a loop. Only a half wit could guess it. But, as Dorothy Sayers argued, "I fancy . . . this opinion merely represents a natural resentment at having been ingeniously bamboozled. All the necessary data are given. The reader ought to be able to guess the criminal, if he is sharp enough, and nobody can ask for more than this. It is, after all, the reader's job to keep his wits about him, and, like the perfect detective, to suspect *everybody*." Certainly readers do not seem to feel cheated by Agatha Christie's whodunits with generic blockers, which include some of her most famous and best-selling works. (pp. 166-67)

As [I. I.] Revzin has pointed out, the solutions to whodunits involve the equation of other dramatis personae with the murderer, but what he fails to note is that certain dramatis personae, the conventional roles of Holmes, Watson, and Lestrade, are expected to be immune from this equation. Christie has systematically broken this expectation. Her most famous case is, of course, **The Murder of Roger Ackroyd**. Here the murderer, again the most obvious, is Dr. Sheppard, who, unfortunately for the reader, is also the narrator. Christie is eminently fair, here, in that she makes it clear that the role of narrator is of Dr. Sheppard's own choosing, that he is not a particular friend of Hercule Poirot. But the generic block is so powerful that this mystery is almost impossible for any reader to solve. In **A Holiday for Murder,** it is the investigating policeman, Superintendent Sugden, who commits the murder. Again the narrative discourse provides ample clues—Sugden is introduced before the murder takes place, coincidentally arrives on the scene as the body is being discovered, and is around altogether too much for someone in the Lestrade role—but the generic block prevents him from being suspected. In **Curtain** even Poirot becomes a murderer. (pp. 167-68)

Christie also systematically breaks other generic expectations. In several books she uses Van Dine's *only one culprit* rule as a generic blocker. In **Death on the Nile,** for instance, three murders are committed, and everyone has an inviolate alibi for at least one of them. The solution would be obvious in real life: the primary victim's husband, Simon Doyle, and his apparently estranged lover, Jacqueline de Bellefort, are conspirators attempting to inherit a rich wife's wealth. But whodunit conventions so frown upon accomplices that Christie's use of them is surprising and effective. **Murder on the Calais Coach** (better known as **Murder on the Orient Express**) takes this generic blocker even further. The wounds on the body seem to have been made by a dozen different people, and all of the passengers on the train have fabricated their identities to cover up connections to the victim. As in so many whodunits, everyone looks guilty. What makes this novel so original and unsolvable is that everyone *is* guilty.

Another generic blocker is the expectation that *characters who are suspected* by the police are automatically innocent. In Christie's first novel, **The Mysterious Affair at Styles,** the victim's husband Alfred Inglethorp is under the heavy suspicion of the police until Poirot, with great show and effort, uncovers an alibi, which because of its scandalous nature, the suspect is apparently unwilling to use. Since, conventionally, the detective and not the police must be correct, the reader is induced to check the husband off the list of real suspects. But by using a readily discoverable alibi to clear the husband earlier rather than later in the text, Poirot is then free to demonstrate an alternative solution with Inglethorp as the murderer. (pp. 168-69)

Probably the most basic whodunit expectation is that *the murder must be committed by the murderer.* But in **Curtain,** as is appropriate for Christie's terminal Poirot mystery, even this expectation is broken. Stephen Norton does not murder anyone; yet as a catalyst he is *the murderer.* (p. 169)

Most texts withhold key bits of information necessary to their interpretation. . . . But it is in the whodunit that what Barthes calls the *"hermeneutic code"* becomes dominant; the pleasure of the text lies principally in its enigma, and in "the expectation and desire for its solution."

Nevertheless, while all whodunits may be dominated by the hermeneutic code, not all entail the same hermeneutic process. . . . The conventional wisdom is that the whodunit reader, like the detective, starts with a blank slate, and then receives a series of clues, each of which must be deciphered and properly arranged on the slate until a complete pattern can be formed. The process of pattern formation is gradual, and the reading, like the playing of the board game *Clue,* is progressive; presumably, the further along the narrative and the more clues available, the more complete the pattern.

Such a progressive hermeneutic structure most resembles a puzzle, and the author an encoding cryptographer. But, as [Julian] Symons argues, "The deception in . . . Christie stories is much more like the conjurer's sleight of hand. She shows us the ace of spades face up. Then she turns it over, but we still know where it is, so how has it been transformed into the five of diamonds?" Or more accurately, we assume that the card will no longer be the ace of spades, and yet it is. Following a progressive series of Agatha Christie's clues only leads to total confusion: the significance of each is very obscure, and it is impossible to decide which signifiers may, in fact, have empty signifieds. The reader is no nearer the solution and indeed is often further from it, just before the epiphany than at the beginning of the book; the only characters who have really been eliminated as suspects are the dead, and even these not absolutely. (My own experience has been that I have been most successful in guessing the murderer before the first murder occurs, or by choosing from a list of the "cast of characters" before even starting to read.) When it comes, the revelation is sudden and surprising. And it is not built up to by a series of clues; it is systematically obstructed.

When most critics use the terms "puzzle" and "riddle" interchangeably as synonyms for the whodunit, they are missing a crucial structural difference. Puzzles are really solved through the accumulation of clues. Riddles can almost never be solved deductively; the key to their hermeneutic structure is the block element. It is the block element that Agatha Christie has elevated to the prominent hermeneutic device for the whodunit. While she is not the only mystery writer who structures her plots around the block element (nor is it invariably present in her books), she certainly has made the most systematic and best use of it. One text or another of hers has incorporated all of the available kinds of blockers, and even when she has repeated herself, as is inevitable given the paucity of riddling strategies and her prolific output, there is a sufficient freshness to minimize the sense of *déjà-vu.* And by fooling the reader into overlooking the most obvious suspects, rather than by

selecting some clues and ignoring others in choosing an arbitrary murderer, Agatha Christie, almost uniquely, has consistently been able to produce whodunits whose final solutions are the most reasonable and, therefore, the most satisfying. (pp. 169-71)

Eliot A. Singer, "The Whodunit as Riddle: Block Elements in Agatha Christie," in Western Folklore, *Vol. XLIII, No. 3, July, 1984, pp. 157-71.*

MARY S. WAGONER

How important a writer was Agatha Christie? By quantitative measures—sales of books and box office demand for her plays, she may prove the best-selling writer in English in the twentieth century. Her books have outsold any other writer's, and *The Mousetrap* and *Witness for the Prosecution* have become transatlantic institutions. Agatha Christie has found a prodigious reading and play-going audience.

Measuring Agatha Christie qualitatively is more difficult. Despite her popular success, some of her writing is clearly trivial and some, after only half a century, seems extremely dated. No one, for instance, could take Christie seriously as a poet, and not all her prose merits close attention. Her romance thrillers seem either excessively arch or simply silly today, and her spy thrillers tend to be either preachy or absurd. (p. 141)

Though uneven, her straight Mary Westmacott novels would seem to have a better chance of survival than her thrillers. *Absent in the Spring* and *Unfinished Portrait,* in particular, combine interesting narrative techniques and compelling story threads to produce firmly disciplined narratives. These novels merit larger audiences than either has in fact enjoyed. The other Westmacott novels, which mix occultism and frequently glib psychologizing, are less impressive.

The two Christie autobiographical books, *Come, Tell Me How You Live* and *An Autobiography,* are enormously attractive works. Both display the writer's narrative skill; both exhibit her singular personal charm. Yet Agatha Christie's reputation never depended on these efforts.

The Christie achievement must be measured by her whodunits. She dominated twentieth-century classic British detective fiction in all three of its forms: the short story, the novel, the play. As a mystery writer, she outproduced her rivals, even as she maintained an extraordinary level of workmanship for over half a century.

Her detective fiction is outstanding, both for the variety she achieved within the form's rigorous rules for plot development, and for her invention of entertaining, if stylized, characters. Such fiction allows only one basic kind of resolution. The detective must discover who committed the crime and must explain away the puzzlement and misunderstanding the criminal managed to generate. With a Christie whodunit, a reader confidently anticipates an ending that will satisfy expectations, but he can count on being surprised by the manipulation of details that lead to that ending.

Agatha Christie's remarkable success in creating many plots of this type clearly depended on her ingenuity with mutations and permutations of basic patterns. . . . [She] constantly reused situations, characters, clusters of characters, and settings. But she made her tales seem fresh by varying at least one basic narrative element from work to work. . . . No other writer of this century has so fully understood the craft of combining and recombining, to give readers a familiar, yet new, imaginative experience.

In short, she perfected the art of plotting, while her "serious" contemporaries shied away from plot as an oversimplification of the complexities of experience.

Further, as other twentieth-century writers began to avoid highly typed, externalized characters, Agatha Christie polished the art of creating them. . . . Christie specialized in creating figures readily identifiable by their manners and their social or personal quirks, figures belonging to the grand tradition of eighteenth- and nineteenth-century British fiction, the tradition of Fielding, Smollett, Austen, and Dickens. Christie peopled her mystery tales with figures whose manners, dress, and speech invited readers to label them according to their social identities and personal quirks. These characters rarely, perhaps never, reveal new dimensions of human nature. Instead they suggest that an understanding of individuals, whatever social microcosms they occupy, is merely a matter of recognizing what types of people they are.

This comedy-of-manners approach to characterization in Agatha Christie's mystery tales sets up a comedy-of-manners approach to social history, one that focuses on little details of life-style. . . . [With] her specificity about manners, Christie entices willing suspension of disbelief in the kinds of characters and the kinds of situations she invents. She also recorded a time and a place convincingly. Conceivably, future generations may use her works as a source of social history, as twentieth-century social historians now use the writings of Smollett and Trollope.

Finally, the fact that the distinguishing techniques of Agatha Christie's whodunits are out of step with current practices may, paradoxically, represent the most significant aspect of her career. The extraordinary popularity of her works suggests that there are still readers drawn to plot and to typed characters, as well as to the recording of social history. Her works demonstrate the fact that the traditional elements of fiction have vitality in them yet. Because she imbued her mystery making with this vitality, Agatha Christie, who modestly saw herself as a literary sausage maker, may claim a more important place in literary history than she seemed ever to expect. In her subgenera, she kept alive elements of the grand tradition in British novel writing. (pp. 141-43)

Mary S. Wagoner, in her Agatha Christie, *Twayne Publishers, 1986, 162 p.*

Edwin (Orr) Denby

1903-1983

American poet, critic, novelist, dramatist, librettist, translator, choreographer, and editor.

One of the most distinguished and influential American dance critics of the twentieth century, Denby was also an admired poet whose detailed observations of modern urban life, particularly that of New York City, provide insight into the nature of human existence and frequently evoke the history of a specific locality. Written predominantly in modified Shakespearean sonnet form and incorporating experiments with rhyme, rhythm, syntax, and subject matter, Denby's verse commonly employs simple, idiomatic language, sharp physical imagery, and sensuous metaphors. Noting affinities between Denby's writing and nineteenth-century Romantic poetry, Frank O'Hara observed: "With similar delicacy and opacity, and with a great deal more economy, [Denby] fixes the shifting moods, the sympathetic grasp of meaning in what the vulgar see only as picturesque, the pervading melancholy which overcomes the poet when he unites with the inanimate."

The son of a United States diplomat, Denby was born in Tientsin, China, and lived in various European and American locales before settling in New York City in 1935. As a denizen of New York's artistic community for several decades, Denby cultivated a circle of friends that included such modern luminaries as poets John Ashbery and Frank O'Hara, painters Willem and Elaine de Kooning, composer Aaron Copland, choreographer Merce Cunningham, and graphic artist Andy Warhol. At Copland's suggestion, Denby published his first article on dance in 1936. During the same year, he began to contribute a regular dance review column to the periodical *Modern Music,* initiating his distinguished career as a critic. Lois Draegin asserted: "Denby's writing on dance had as its antecedents the work of poet-critics like Valéry, Mallarmé, and Gautier. He wrote prose that was poetically evocative, clear, simply put." Denby's dance criticism first appeared in book form in the collection *Looking at the Dance* (1949), which esteemed dance critic Arlene Croce praised as possibly "the most universally admired book of dance criticism in American publishing history." Denby's later dance pieces are included in *Dancers, Buildings, and People in the Streets* (1965) and *Dance Writings* (1987).

Denby's verse first appeared nationally in *Poetry* magazine in 1926. The poems contained in his initial collection, *In Public, In Private* (1948), feature compressed, irregular rhythms, dense syntax, and subtle shifts in tone. While Denby often utilizes New York City as his setting in these pieces, his subject matter ranges widely, prompting Ron Padgett to comment: "From the variousness of this book emerges the figure of a solitary, meditative man struggling to keep himself together and to see if he fits into the scheme of things." Following several years of travel throughout Europe, Denby published his second volume of verse *Mediterranean Cities* (1956), an informal sequence of sonnets combining an individual sensibility with evocations of the character, mythology, and history of many of Europe's ancient cities. These poems expand upon several themes introduced in Denby's first volume, particularly humanity's relationship to its environment. The chapbook *Snoring in New*

York (1974) features the long poem "Snoring in New York—An Elegy," as well as Denby's final sonnets, which were written in the late 1950s and early 1960s. Ron Padgett stated: "In these later sonnets . . . the rhyme has become looser, stanza breaks done away with, formality of tone left behind." Again focusing on life in New York City, Denby explores such themes as the acceptance of self, the elemental power of place, the inherent beauty of the material world, and the phenomenon of consciousness. Unlike his highly respected dance criticism, Denby's poetry received scant critical attention until the publication of *Collected Poems* (1975). In his review of this book, Hayden Carruth remarked on Denby's status as a "fugitive" poet and stated that his work has "the enduring voice of poetry, the essential voice which carries on in spite of everything that fashion and literary politics can do to silence it." *The Complete Poems* (1986) includes all of *Collected Poems,* with some works slightly revised by Denby, and also collects several untitled pieces previously unavailable in book form.

Although Denby wrote little during the last twenty years of his life, he continued to publish many of his early works. The first draft of his only novel, *Mrs. W's Last Sandwich* (1972; republished as *Scream in a Cave*), was written in the early 1930s, while *Four Plays by Edwin Denby* (1981) is a book of short dialogue pieces written for an early Andy Warhol film that was never produced. Denby also published several opera and ballet librettos, including *The Second Hurricane* (1957), with music by Aaron Copland, as well as adaptations and translations of various literary works.

(See also *Contemporary Authors,* Vol. 110 [obituary].)

HUBERT CREEKMORE

Edwin Denby, former dance critic of *The New York Herald Tribune* has collected his poems—sonnets, lyrics, songs and verses to accompany photographs by Rudolph Burckhardt—into this first volume [*In Public, In Private*]. For the most part they are impressions of the New York scene, rather diffused in impact because subjectively organized as to images and tropes; but often they create a witty or revealing series of comments.

The quality of revelation rarely extends to an entire poem, and the subjective (and obscure) organization prevails. One suspects what a whole poem is meant to convey, but must strain to fuse the tone and theme of all the parts. Lines seem to be distended for rhyme or meter. For instance, from **"Standing on the Streetcorner"**:

> Rock underneath New York though
> Is not a subject for which people do care.
> But men married in New York or else women
> Dominate the pavement from where they stand . . .

In the first two lines, "though" and "do" are examples of distension for rhyme and meter. In the last two, the sequitur completely escapes me; this sort of construction accounts for some mildly surrealist effects in other poems.

"City Without Smoke," perhaps the most unified of the poems, describes the effect of a perfectly clear sky in New York on the people to whom

> the smudgy film of smoke
> Is reassuring like an office, it's sociable
> Like money, it gives the sky a furnished look
> That makes disaster domestic, less horrible.

If only the last two words, anti-climactic and necessary for rhyme, had been left off! The sonnet sequence, **"Dishonor,"** though made up of many truly astonishing images, violent language, and a serious personal theme, does not seem to be integrated in all its parts. If the theme, elusively suggested, is what I take it to be (and will not describe here—that is, what *sort* of dishonor), then some of the sonnets appear to be extraneous. It pursues an uncomfortable confession through twenty-one poems, many of them good, others surreal and grotesque; and one regrets that scattered imprecise expressions, chatty phrases and colloquialisms weaken the sequence.

Mr. Denby has a flair for finishing off his poems with a meaningful couplet, for combining the traditional epigram with the lyric, and for ironic effects, which should result, with more focus and unification and smoothness, in unusually interesting commentaries on city life.

> Hubert Creekmore, "Flaws in the Poetry," in The
> New York Times Book Review, *August 15, 1948,
> p. 18.*

STARK YOUNG

[In *Looking at the Dance*] Mr. Denby presents a collection of his articles that have appeared in *Modern Music, Dance Index, The Kenyon Review* and other periodicals and of his reviews from the *New York Herald Tribune,* on which he has served as dance critic. The range of this volume is so notable that I can give only a hint of it here. It covers technical points, ballets in recent repertory, dancers in performance, recent seasons and many ballets from the past, ballet music and decoration, ballet in books, prints, photographs and films, modern dancers, dancers in exotic styles and dancing in shows. The mere listing of all this can, of course, give nothing short of a sketch of the basic content, so thorough in its intuition, so right in its expression. *Looking at the Dance* represents some of the most distinguished, luminous, tactful and penetrating criticism in any field of the arts that we have ever had in this country. . . .

The great virtue of *Looking at the Dance* is the splendor and light and edge of the thought, the glow of the interpretation, the easy culture and delight of its very approach to the art involved and often, too, of the writing itself. The great rarity in this criticism of Mr. Denby's is that it is written from inside the art. Very few critics of any art, especially the visual arts, are really writing about that art; they are writing of something else—any painter knows that most writing about painting is not about painting, and any passable actor, reading a criticism, knows at a glance whether or not the critic speaks his language. This inmost perception, as it were, is so marked in these Denby pages about the dance that the impression is many times repeated of a kind of brilliant clarity, close to the subject and at the same time free of it. . . .

"If clarity in excitement is one of the classic tenets, the other is human naturalness of expression."

The sense of serenity that Markova creates "is as touching as that of a Mozart melody."

"Franklin . . . with his happy flow of dance vitality and his wonderful generosity as a partner."

Martha Graham "seems to watch over her integrity with too jealous an eye." He speaks, too, of "a mysterious elegance that never leaves her." Amaya has "sometimes a wonderful kind of rippling of her body, more like a young cat's than a girl's."

Those are only a few of the phrases and passages I might quote. But quoting bits as I have been doing may be a bad scheme after all; it may give the effect of forced writing, which is far from true with Mr. Denby; his taste never fails him.

> Stark Young, 'A Critic Recaptures the Dance," in
> New York Herald Tribune Weekly Book Review,
> May 29, 1949, p. 4.*

FRANK O'HARA

[*The essay from which this excerpt is taken was originally published in* Poetry, *February, 1957.*]

I have recently been rereading Mr. Denby's first book, *In Public, In Private*, a kind of "Poet in New York" with its acute and painful sensibility, its vigorous ups and downs and stubborn tone. Since its appearance in 1948, it seems an increasingly important book for the risks it takes in successfully establishing a specifically American spoken diction which has a classical firmness and clarity under his hand. He contributed then a number of our very few fine sonnets and the remarkable city-poem, **"Elegy—The Streets,"** along with other, less perfect, but true, vital poems.

Mediterranean Cities is a handsome publication, printed in Italy and adorned with photographs by Rudolph Burckhardt, the gifted artist and film-maker. The new poems are sonnets on places and, as in Proust, the artist's feelings become the sensibility of the places; *Mediterranean Cities* follows a Proustian progression of sensation, reflection, awareness, spontaneous memory and apotheosis, a progression which proceeds from the signal absorption in locale ("place names") and its accidental characteristics to the emergence of the poet's being from his feelings in "the place." The poet himself eventually is the place.

While the interior of the sequence, the book as a whole, is related to Proust's method in my mind, another reference suggests itself. Unlike the many poems-about-Europe-by-Americans we have had recently, the "Fulbright poems" as someone recently described them, Mr. Denby's sonnets are in the great tradition of the Romantics, and particularly Shelley. With similar delicacy and opacity, and with a great deal more economy, he fixes the shifting moods, the sympathetic grasp of meaning in what the vulgar see only as picturesque, the pervading melancholy which overcomes the poet when he unites with the inanimate; this all reminds one of the English Romantic poets on the Continent, and is reinforced by a cultural maturity like that of the Romantics (whatever one may think of their emotional status) which has seldom been achieved by an American poet in specific relation to the European past and his own present. But, being the work of a modern poet, Mr. Denby's sonnets do not rise up to end in a burst of passionate identification, they light up from within with a kind of Mallarméan lucidity. They are obscure poems, eminently worth understanding, and I find these references helpful, though they may seem to leap about. One of Mallarmé's favorite poems, after all, was by Shelley.

Unless I am very much mistaken, the sequence of the poems (it is not called a sonnet sequence) is very important, and concerns itself with evaluations of art and life, historical and personal, in a serious lyrical manner which, being itself art, is also graceful. Sometimes the poet is isolated before the subject, the self evaluating the subject in traditional fashion.... (pp. 179-80)

This, for the reader, is a sort of landscape-with-poet, and presently we find the picture changing: it is the poet-in-landscape; not the physical prospect, but the past of the place has begun to absorb him.... And this becomes not merely being in a foreign place, a stranger to its myriad times, but also to one's own history.... In a climactic moment the poet finds in himself the living sentence of a culture which may be dying, but is slow to die, is living for his sake, the ambiguous nature of temporality made clear by the timeless exertion of consciousness.... (pp. 180-81)

It seems to me that Mr. Denby in these sonnets has created something modern and intrinsic, sensitive and strong. (p. 181)

> Frank O'Hara, "The Poetry of Edwin Denby," in Edwin Denby: The Complete Poems, *edited by Ron Padgett, Random House, 1986, pp. 179-81.*

SELMA JEANNE COHEN

Were it not for Edwin Denby one might be tempted to say the area of intelligent, civilized, poetic writing on dance belonged exclusively to France. Denby seems to descend, in a logically French manner, from Gautier, Mallarmé, and Valéry. Like all three of them, he is a poet; like Gautier, he has also been a practicing critic; like all three, his writing reveals an acutely sensitive perception, expressing itself in language that unfolds as beautifully as the adagio line of a great ballerina. Among English-speaking dance writers, he is unique.

As revealed in [*Dancers, Buildings and People in the Streets*], Denby's mode of thinking resembles that of his French forebears, particularly that of the theorists, Mallarmé and Valéry. Though he evades their mystical overtones, he too sees dance as creating a world apart from the real world, "seeing art is seeing an ordered and imaginary world, subjective and concentrated.... Art is ... more mysterious and nonsensical than daily life. But what a pleasure it can be." (p. 229)

The rhythm of dance, Denby notes, is not only a matter of time. Dance also has a space rhythm, the rhythm of visual shapes. Dance movements were invented "for the lively display of sculptural shapes"; they suit "the kind of common sense dancing has, but not any other kind."

From this point of view, style is "content" enough for a ballet. Not that Denby necessarily objects to dramatic ballets, though he objects to the overly literal manner in which many of them have been conceived. His taste may be too rarefied for some, but he would be the first to concede that the question is one of taste, not of truth. What he has given us here is a record of his individual sensibility. He is not vehement; he does not demand allegiance.

Happily, the essays in *Dancers, Buildings and People in the Streets* not only enunciate concepts but apply them. Felicities of phrase and of observation abound in the reviews of particular ballets and particular performers. They might add up to nothing. Instead, they add up to a clarity of point of view that serves to sharpen the perceptions of the observer, to illuminate the art for its audience. (pp. 229-30)

> *Selma Jeanne Cohen, in a review of "Dancers, Buildings and People in the Streets," in* The Journal of Aesthetics and Art Criticism, *Vol. XXV, No. 2, Winter, 1966, pp. 229-30.*

BILL ZAVATSKY

Edwin Denby, known widely as one of America's most distinguished writers on the dance, has throughout his 73 years sought little attention for his poetry. Perhaps Denby distrusted his obsession with the sonnet (which most of the poems in his *Collected Poems* are). Nevertheless, I am grateful that [his publisher] has been able to pry loose Denby's delightful work and give it to us entire.

If the range is narrow, Denby emerges here as a singer of the city with an original eye for detail. Not just any city, but "my city," as he affectionately calls New York. *Mediterranean Cities* (1956), his second book, finds the poet in the Aegean, where "young priests smoke at the basin, by blurred sea-gods" (**"Trastevere"**) and where one can see "the gondola's floated gloze / Lapping along the marble" (**"Venice"**), or catch one's breath at the "Holy placidity of lilylike throats" (**"Ravenna"**). But "the mute wide-angle look, to Europe alien" of the wandering American always finds its *point de repère* in Manhattan.

Denby's city is everywhere with him, and his observations of it and its denizens are temperate, often loving. In New York

"You use a worn-down cafeteria fork," hop a subway "For a nickel extending peculiar space," or gaze northward ("from 23rd") down "the vast avenue—a catastrophic perspective pinned to air." Such is the delightful anthology of city minutiae to be sampled in Denby's verse. His city folk even find that "the smudgy film of smoke" in the sky "Is reassuring like an office." And in a poem probably unwritable these days, he celebrates "The sidewalk cracks, gumspots, the water, the bits of refuse" that "reach out and bloom under arclight" and beneath stars "open to bums / Who lie poisoned in vast delivery portals."

Though he invokes "commuter Walt," Denby's is an eye at remove. His poetry discloses little of the human interaction to be found in Charles Reznikoff's marvelous city poems, but rather like a camera forces us into lines of unusual perspective, perspectives like those achieved by his photographer-friend Rudy Burckhardt (for whose pictures he has written accompanying texts), where "In a split second a girl is forever pretty."

Amidst these geometries the solitary figure of the poet, surprised by his own "white face hung in the air before the government marble" of a post office, walking the streets, retiring to his loft alone, baffled by babies and cheered by the company of young friends who "sweetly sink" his "joke on death," weeping over the death of the "Cat-heart that knew me," and dodging traffic: "What a pleasure, I wasn't killed." Despite his hesitations, Denby's **Collected Poems** is an important Baedeker by a sharp-eyed man who has noted down, out of love, what most of us rush right past. (pp. 35-6)

> *Bill Zavatsky, in a review of "Collected Poems," in*
> The New York Times Book Review, *October 17,*
> *1976, pp. 32, 34-6.*

JONATHAN GALASSI

Edwin Denby . . . is a poet whose tendency is always to break out of whatever form he appropriates, though he does depend on regular structures as something to work against. Denby has written a large number of sonnets—as well as some longer poems in stanzas—but they are unlike any others known to this writer: their rhythm is contorted, their rhyme often offhand or overly simple, their diction both informal and truncated. Phrases and trains of thought run headlong into each other in Denby's lines, and the first reaction to his work [in **Collected Poems**] is sometimes uneasiness: one feels in the presence of an uncompromising, eccentric sensibility, a strong esthetic-*cum*-moral impulse which is continually being upset and rerouted as it confronts the corruptions of experience.

Anyone who has read Denby's renowned ballet criticism knows he can be a stunningly fluid writer when he wants to; the same sincerity and openness to experience are characteristic of the prose as of the poetry. But though Denby can produce an absolutely incredible epithet like **"Pear-brown Rome"**, his poems usually choose to be jagged and awkward, because he sees the world that way. One of his most frequent subjects is his home, New York, which for him, as for many contemporary artists, stands as the quintessential metaphor for modern human relations. The city's turbulence, heterogeneity, and barely controlled erotic electricity come through powerful and breathing. . . . (p. 166)

But although Denby is talented at bringing the places he observes to life—not only New York, but the ancient cities of the Mediterranean attract him in their small details, the lively

messiness of their being-in-the-present—the scenes are never evoked for their own sake: they excite moral observations in Denby, for whom the complexities and necessities of human interactions are the primary theme. The world he describes with such honesty is not honest; its inhabitants are constantly confronted by endemic and/or self-created impediments to a more tolerable way of life ("I'd like the room mine, myself me / But as facts go, neither's likely"). The dispiriting stand-off between desire and imagination—embodied as art—and the poverty of the possible is the continual predicament which dominates these poems. Still, Denby is obviously attracted to the world as it is, in all its imperfection, and his generous spirit finds much to enjoy; time and again he returns to art, which he obviously sees as a life-affirming reflection of life, a redeeming human activity:

> For with regret I leave the lovely world men made
> Despite their bad character, their art is mild

This is a living, breathing, unusually valuable book by a poet who should be better known. (pp. 166-67)

> *Jonathan Galassi, "Determined Forms," in* Poetry,
> *Vol. CXXXIX, No. 3, December, 1976, pp. 164-70.*

DAVID LEVITEN

[The **Collected Poems**] of Edwin Denby, the dance critic and amateur, i.e. lover, of poetry, is [rich]. This quotation from his prose, in describing his pet's reaction, suggests the sensuous quality of his own poetry: "My kittens would purr in unison and watch me, bright-eyed, while I read them Shakespeare's *Sonnets*, clearly pleased by the compliment and the sounds they had heard."

In **Public and Private** (1948), some of the volume is apprenticework, but a few poems are fully achieved, among them **"Groups and Series,"** a kind of fusion of the *Sonnets'* quality with metaphysical wit and the delicacy of Pope. In these early sonnets he has not yet gained the sensuous fluidity that will triumph in **Mediterranean Cities** (1956). The scattered internal rhymes—"street," "meet," "eat"—jar, rather than ease the lines on. However, in the **"Poems Written to Accompany Photographs by Rudy Burckhardt"** they do work, along with the doggerel yet epigrammatic wit, since they suit the subject, the topography of Greater New York. If only we had the original photographs!

A last few words about the early poems, namely the **"Songs from Libretti."** In these the cultivated poet is trying to sound like a common man or woman—and with uncertain results. So a shopgirl in love, with grammatical rigor, pronounces "It is I" or, again in the character of a lovelorn girl, appeals to "Miltie" at the very time when Berle, "Uncle Miltie," was grinning for giggles on T. V. I'm afraid this dance critic knows more about Coppelia than about Gracie Allen! . . . Truly, it is with a sigh of relief that, with Denby's early verses behind us, we leave the States and—enjoy! enjoy!—the Mediterranean this Momma Tiresias brings, from a score of years back, like chicken soup to our scrawny American lines. And, as a bonus, an appendix reprints Frank O'Hara's review from *Poetry*, 1957 as a guide [see excerpt above]. (Unfortunately, as in the earlier sonnets, Burckhardt's photographs are not reproduced, so that the sequence, with its unvarying Shakespearean form, becomes a bit monotonous.)

"The poet himself eventually is the place," O'Hara comments; and this does seem central, e.g., in **"Mycenae."** . . . Here the poet begins with Clytemnestra and heroic tragedy (''slow slopes unrolled'') in Miltonic majesty; introducing his friend with him in Agamemnon's tomb suggests affection in the context of death, and ends in present-day Greece with ''oleanders/Blooming white''—an internal rhyme with the end-rhymes ''height'' and ''light'' till the sonnet trails off in an imperfectly rhyming couplet chiming a twilit progress. So here Denby achieves a kind of flickering union of Romantic richness of association with, in conclusion, a hint of classical generalization. And in **''Syracuse,''** his infinite riches in a little room, beginning with the Cold War context of the fifties—''Are you Russians, the boy said seeing us strange''—proceeds to a ''Baroque and Byzantine slum,'' to the elegiac climax and the last line of the octave as the sonnet's climax—''Where once they fought in moonlight and Athens fell.'' . . . And with this I complete our tour, though this short-breathed reviewer could use up all of *Parnassus,* like Pope pointing out ''beauties.''

''Snoring in New York'' and **''Later Sonnets''** are thinner stuff. The meter dwindles to a four-beat line in the sonnets and the substance, correspondingly. Denby lacks the hysterical élan of his younger Manhattan friends. His heart seems back in the Old World and his attempts at verse jottings punctuated by dashes all too often suggest a pale transcription of Ginsberg's camera of the mind without the freedom of the prose poem. . . . Nevertheless, there are lovely lines and passages in many of these poems and certainly **''City Seasons,''** a suite of four New York nature poems, each in four-line, five-beat couplet stanzas, is a slight but graceful success.

Some Major Publisher should publish a *Selected Poems.* It would contribute to our cultural health as Denby's dance criticism has already done so generously. (pp. 274-76)

> David Leviten, ''The Starving Epistemologist and the Sound-Ripe Sonneteer,'' in Parnassus: Poetry in Review, *Vol. 5, No. 2, Spring-Summer, 1977, pp. 270-77.*

GEORGE DICKERSON

What is most remarkable about Denby's poetry [in *The Complete Poems*] is that, in an age when so many writers are absorbed in personal angst, his feelings are often secondary. He is more intent on capturing the essence of things and drawing from them an appreciation of the quality of life around him—this although he seemed to write for his own private needs and was for the most part either shy or indifferent about publishing his poetry. When he does talk about his feelings, he can be harshly self-critical, as in **''A Sonnet Sequence: Dishonor,''** or, as in a later poem, **''Snoring in New York—An Elegy,''** dispassionately objective:

> a single retired man
> White-haired, ferrety, feminine, religious
> I look like a priest, a detective, a con
> Nervously I step among the city crowd
>
> My private life of no interest and allowed.

Indeed, Denby is a reticent, lonely prowler in the cityscape. There he observes mundane things—a naked light bulb in a rented room, the way men carry their shoulders, the bustling city streets, the air between the buildings, the aimless talk of weather—and builds from them his pithy, compassionate insights into the nature of man and man's place in the landscape. In the sonnet **''City Without Smoke,''** for example, he turns

a rare smogless day into a commentary on how urban man has become uncomfortable with nature. . . .

He can be quite critical of the human race, of people who cherish overkill, of arrogant, boastful Americanism or of just plain rudeness. . . . But when he views the sometimes grotesque urban comedy, he does not place himself above it. . . .

In his immaculately groomed sonnets and elegies, the simplicity of his language, the careful observation of everyday objects and the actions of the common man, and the lyrical vision of nature or of city buildings combine to make Denby a descendant of Walt Whitman and Hart Crane. Like Hart Crane in ''To Brooklyn Bridge,'' Denby invests a city structure with a mythic grandeur. . . .

However, at times Denby explores with broken rhymes or rhymeless lines and explosive, jazzed-up rhythms that call to mind the abstract expressionist paintings of his friends Franz Kline and Willem de Kooning. . . . At other times, he has an uncanny ear for the poetry inherent in human speech. . . . (p. 28)

Denby's poetry, however, attains its richest and most complex achievement in a cycle of sonnets called *Mediterranean Cities.* These poems range in subject from the decay of Venice and the opulence of Ravenna to bucolic Segesta and the monumental Parthenon. Denby combines vivid, evocatory descriptions of place with historical or mythological references and aphoristic similes or metaphors as he draws the character, both past and present, of each locale.

These sonnets are masterly in their compression. In the four opening lines of **''Florence,''** for example, Denby alludes to the poisonous habits of the Medicis, recalls Dante's presence there and refers to the sculptures of Michelangelo and other Florentine ''magicians'' of art, all while picturing the River Arno's presence among glum streets. . . . (pp. 28, 30)

Denby captures the essence or character of a place with similes that exemplify his profound powers of observation. In **''Via Appia''** he notes ''the solitude has the face of an actor who / Sits in his wrapper and hears silence return,'' and he calls the Villa Adriana as ''embarrassing as a rich man without admirers / Peculiar like a middle-aged man undressed.''

In this cycle of poems, Denby is also expanding on themes that run through much of his work—man's relationship to an indifferent or alien landscape and man's relationship to history. But as he notes elsewhere with typical wryness, ''The small survivor has a difficult task / Answering the questions great historians ask.'' And if the task is not only difficult but probably hopeless, Denby undertakes it with a gentle wit and mature grace that make reading his poetry a delight. (p. 30)

> George Dickerson, ''Essences and Sentiments,'' in The New York Times Book Review, *November 2, 1986, pp. 28, 30.*

LINCOLN KIRSTEIN

[*The essay from which this excerpt is taken was published in a slightly different form in* The New York Review of Books, *September 29, 1983.*]

Edwin was a great dance critic primarily because he was a fine poet. His poems, while collected and well presented in 1975 [in *Collected Poems*], through the enthusiasm of close friends, are available today for readers who prize good verse as much as good dancing. He is not anthologized. Modern literature courses don't take much account of him, nor is he treated as an important lyricist by many beyond a band of admirers, too often discounted as a coterie. But some poets, now far more fully published, appreciate such poetry; this was the only fame he liked. He accepted the nomination of journalist, but craft and insight lifted him to the level of professional artist. (p. 183)

It is hardly by chance that the most thorough writers concerned with dance were prime poets—Théophile Gautier, Stéphane Mallarmé, Paul Valéry. Other verse makers who observed dancing with some attention, but are rarely read for it, are Federico García Lorca and Hart Crane. It is to these master choreographers of words that Denby is most akin.

When his verse is read with the care it deserves and commands, he may be recognized as the clearest lyric voice of Manhattan since Crane's epopoeia of the Brooklyn Bridge. He shares Crane's quirkiness in implosive short circuits of dense, awkwardly precise rhetoric, odd broken rhymes, reckless rhythm, sharpness of physical imagery and incandescent metaphor. There is a sense of place, of American loneliness similar to that in some of Edward Hopper's paintings. Crane was a hysteric, his hysteria increasing tragically from self-inflamed euphoria. Compulsive self-indulgence did him in early on. Denby was a survivor, who put an end to himself only when old, when he could no longer manage his body. This he accomplished, with much good work behind him, large in instruction and influence. He endured unspoken pain and took a stoic exit, disdaining to burden further his friends or himself. This is a matter more for celebration than for sadness.

His poetry concerns cities in history, past and present, European and American, detailed with domestic intimacy, an experienced tourist's familiarity. Rudy Burckhardt, his lifelong friend and illuminator, provided a visual gloss on specific sites. Controlled accident in snapshots is always present in Edwin's imagery. He had a "photographic" eye and a powerful visual memory. The atmosphere, societies, and qualities of many cities, Mediterranean and American, form an album of superpostcards, more real than any nostalgic material souvenir. (pp. 183-84)

García Lorca, in exile at Columbia University, was miserable in Manhattan. Nevertheless, out of misery, he composed his memorable portrait of Walt Whitman, another psalmist of cities. Whitman's voice resounds in García Lorca, Crane, and Denby, not only for their "love of comrades" and "sleepers," but in their substantial miniatures of cityscapes, their crowds, corner bars, shops which frame fierce and tender lives. There is a short-breathed sonnet by Denby, **"On the Home Front—1942,"** encapsulating a moment in our national story, as every famous wartime photograph does, and its final couplet makes a generalization which is also the portrait of its poet:

> The small survivor has a difficult task
> Answering the questions great historians ask.
>
> (p. 185)

Lincoln Kirstein, "On Edwin Denby," in Edwin Denby: The Complete Poems, *edited by Ron Padgett, Random House, 1986, pp. 183-86.*

DAVID SHAPIRO

Edwin Denby's **Complete Poems** brings before the public . . . a poet who has avoided the canons and anthologies and deserves a permanent place. . . . From 1935 on, he was a denizen of New York, worked with Orson Welles, Paul Bowles, and Vir-

gil Thompson, among others, and became a pioneer dance reviewer. (p. 41)

Denby's work first became known to me through the strange little magazine *Locus Solus,* where I saw the curiously jointed sonnets of his **Mediterranean Cities.** It was years later that I became aware that these sonnets, conspiring with the photographs of that accurate, masterful urbanist Rudy Burkhardt, had emerged as what Fairfield Porter called one of the most beautiful of contemporary collaborations. Denby's dance criticism, and some essays on life in the Thirties among artists, are a model of an empirical yet passionate criticism. His poetry, praised by O'Hara [see excerpt above] and some of the younger poets, also seemed to constitute a kind of dry rebuke to expressionist cadenzas. Denby made a quietistic poetry of the subways that Lincoln Kirstein compares favorably to Crane [see excerpt above]. What sometimes is more appealing than most urban affirmations is Denby's understated minor key, in which cats, libidinous and melancholy bachelors, buildings, and historical traditions all mingle within some learned forms to create a jagged anti-theatrical pose and poise.

If one looks at the sonnets, the form he evidently most admired and mastered severely, though he was capable of extended work in a variety of song-like modes, one realizes that he had the poetic equivalent of de Kooning's Dutch academic training. As a matter of fact, it is perhaps only slightly hilarious that such "academic" underpinnings helped make Denby a fatherfigure among Lower East Side Poets, who almost all foreswore the sterner reaches of scholasticism. Denby was the perfect anti-father figure because he used all his learning so gracefully. He avoided the pedantries of many others dedicated to elegance of form. His sonnets could become as crumpled as paper bags and as rigid as some synthetic fibers. He used the sonnet both as a parodistic resource and created a homage to the sonnet within each belated object of his craft, much as his beloved Balanchine took a lasting pride in pulling apart the conventions of classic ballet. Both Balanchine and Denby were masters of activating classic space with fresh gestures.

I had some contact with this dry and witty intelligence and can testify that his presence, sudden on the subway and magisterial if modest at the dance auditorium, was always an occasion for intense conversation. During a Utopian moment in my own conversion to a Tolstoyan pacifism, he made some lacerating comments concerning man's evil nature. I find his poetry filled with a very sophisticated sense of psychology and a refusal to become the dupe of competing systems. Dance didn't make him a hedonist but kept him an observer of all bodies and places. Criticism informs his poetry, as does psychoanalysis: he is one of the few poets to have written a sonnet on genitals, and it is subtle. Abstract expressionism influenced him, as did the "Pop" art of his many painter-friends, but his own poetry is a curious blend of the representational and the joyfully antimimetic.

On the one hand, many of the poems are bitter-sweet meditations on the power of New York, but the city never overwhelms the quiet bachelor with his obsessive love for cats. Affection in Denby is specific and overwhelmingly direct, for the cold streets of New York and for grey cats, for his friend's young son and for his friends, for Walt Whitman and for his legitimate disciple, Frank O'Hara. The Depression gives him some of his gloomiest and fractured moments of public torpor, but in the Sixties his sonnets are choppy and sophisticated meditations on old age and random joys in city life. Elegant always and disdainful of art without finesse, he ends by underlining the seductive sense of language itself: "Complicities of New York speech / Embrace me as I fall asleep." He is never as acoherent as Ashbery, but many of the late sonnets have a bizarre short-hand style that resembles Chinese poetry in literal translation. He usually makes vigilance itself his theme, as could be expected from a man whose professional responsibilities were those of the eye: "Munificence I eye fearfully / Forest disorder dear to Rudy." Unlike Auden, he doesn't permit his urbane knowingness to diminish to dogma or pedantry. His "grotesque dancer" side seems to have kept him permanently alive to the devilish stupidity of things and the wonder of bright bodies in space. His poetry is a kind of eccentric dancing, and one could make an interesting study of how often he situates people and buildings as a theatrically activated series of presences. It's as if Hart Crane had followed the mincing tones of his "Chaplinesque" rather than a more pantheistic mood. In Denby, precision and energetic flair replace Romantic atmospherics. He is the Balanchine of poetry, to state it baldly.

If one permits me my seemingly impressionistic analogues, I would continue to say that Denby's poems, particularly the sonnet-sequences, are cinematic, and the poet learned by making film-scripts and doing a little brilliant acting in films. Beyond certain formal characteristics, however, Denby's greatest strength lies in his ethos of the personal and the particular, as in a postcard poem brilliantly filled with the names of every possible friend. This homage to proper names is an anti-confessional homage to the promiscuity of language itself. I think one of the ways to praise Denby adequately is to remember that the sonnet form is fabulously difficult to "deconstruct," in the fashionable phrase, and that Denby is one of the very few American practitioners not to succumb to its Medusa-like terrors. He dismantles the usual sense of syllogistic charm in the Shakespearean mode and creates a personal and even diaristic use of the form that keeps it song-like but makes it also more cruelly continuous, prosier, and closer to urban reportage.

The tour Denby gives us of his New York and his Vermont, this non-narrative movie of tender tentatives, is one where collaboration is affirmed as the truest mode of poetry. The meaning of the city for Denby becomes clear as a fruitfully chaotic place where margins criticize the very idea of the center. Denby's poems are memorable—Elaine de Kooning startled many by her poignant recitation of them by heart at his memorial—paradoxically because of their multiplicity. Denby's poems resist the falser, the easier coherences; they provide the solace of truly shattered and shattering perspectives. (pp. 41-4)

David Shapiro, in a review of "The Complete Poems,"
in Poetry, *Vol. CL, No. 1, April, 1987, pp. 41-44.*

Ariel Dorfman

1942-

Chilean-born nonfiction writer, novelist, essayist, journalist, short story writer, and poet.

In his writings, Dorfman examines such topics as exile, life under authoritarian rule, and the influence of popular forms of literature on social and political values. After having established a reputation in South America as a journalist and essayist on popular culture, Dorfman left Chile in 1973 following the military coup of Augusto Pinochet. Since then, he has focused in his work on the plight of the oppressed in his homeland while living in exile in Argentina, France, Holland, and the United States. Pat Aufderheide commented: "Like many Third World writers, Dorfman denies the neat division between art and politics; more impressive, he also refuses to collapse the two categories into one."

Dorfman first attracted attention in the English-speaking world with *Para leer al pato Donald* (1973; *How to Read Donald Duck*), a nonfiction work on which he collaborated with Armand Mattelart. In this book, the authors suggest that the seemingly innocuous Walt Disney cartoon featuring Donald Duck subliminally imparts capitalist values. Dorfman further examines popular culture in *The Empire's Old Clothes* (1983). In this volume of essays, he concludes that such forms of popular literature as comic books, picture novels, children's stories, and the magazine *Reader's Digest* instill false confidence in capitalism and encourage passivity. Although some critics faulted Dorfman for failing to place his analyses within a firm social context, others praised his insights on a rarely studied topic.

Although he is perhaps best known for his nonfiction, Dorfman's recent novels have garnered critical respect. *Widows* (1983) centers on the struggle between an autocratic government and thirty-seven women who suspect that their missing husbands were abducted and killed by the authorities. While Dorfman set his novel in occupied Greece during the 1940s to avoid censorship in Chile, critics noted parallels in the story to recent events in Latin America. They lauded Dorfman's sensitive portrait of the wives and his poignant depiction of young men pressured to execute the commands of a repressive regime. Dorfman's next novel, *La ultima cancion de Manuel Sendero* (1984; *The Last Song of Manuel Sendero*), revolves around the fantastical premise of fetuses refusing to be born until their native totalitarian government eliminates social and economic repression. The fetuses debate the political implications of leaving their wombs to become part of an oppressive nation; eventually, all are born except the book's narrator, the son of Manuel Sendero, who remains in a state of gestation. Dorfman interweaves this story with the tale of two Chilean exiles who refuse to return to their homeland. Although some critics maintained that the novel's style and narrative were overwrought, many hailed its original approach to the subject of rebellion against totalitarian rule as well as Dorfman's intricate use of magic realist techniques to underscore his themes. Paul Stuewe described this work as "a panoramic portrait of a culture fatally divided against itself." Dorfman has also written a volume of poetry, *Missing* (1982), and two novels about

© Jerry Bauer

Chilean life in the 1970s, *Moros en la costa* (1973; *The Coast Is Not Clear*) and *Chilex and Company: A New Guide* (1978).

THE TIMES LITERARY SUPPLEMENT

As Walt Disney's inquisitors, [Ariel Dorfman and Armand Mattelart] frankly admit that they are not the first to be aware of him as a propagandist of imperialism and the American way of life. Still, most of their time [in *Para leer al pato Donald*] is taken simply developing that thesis, with quotations and cartoon clips which (predictably perhaps) can prove more compulsive reading than the prose they are embedded in.

Ariel Dorfman and Armand Mattelart are writing out of Allende's Chile, with more than adequate reason to be daunted by their enemies' enormity within and without, and by their own political precariousness. Their instructions on how to read Donald Duck, on how to find him disenchanting enough to get expelled from your colonial Disneyland club, have an earnest vivacity and a hint of apocalypse. And their insights into the loveless genealogy, the impoverished innocence, the social alienation, the money fetishism, the metropolitan exploitativeness, the presumptuous universality, and so on, of Disney's main characters can excite considerable sympathy for the critics' own morality. . . .

[Any] neo-Marxist devoting so much time to this particular brand of American consumer goods should, ideally, pay more attention to the varying qualities, functions and contexts of humour itself, Marx's and Disney's senses of it differing as they do.

> *"Capitalist Duck," in* The Times Literary Supplement, *No. 3703, February 23, 1973, p. 220.*

STANLEY REYNOLDS

Is Donald Duck a capitalistic plot? Well, isn't everything? Except, of course, when it is tarnished with Moscow gold. Dorfman and Mattelart, two Chilean Marxists, . . . won quite a lot of notice, mostly comical, when they first published *How To Read Donald Duck* in the Chile of the late Dr Allende. When the capitalistic-imperialist press heard that Donald Duck comics had been banned in the brave new Chile, it smiled and said, well, it only goes to show what kind of nutters those leftwing nutters are down there.

But hold on a moment. One of the big heroes of Donald Duck comics is Donald's wealthy uncle Scrooge McDuck and Scrooge McDuck is always manipulating things and rushing off to Latin America and with his money, and his nephew Donald's help, foiling revolutions. And didn't ITT . . .? Well, yes, it did. A page right out of Scrooge McDuck, without of course the whimsy. . . .

Latin America is one of the favourite locales for these adventures and although Latin America is presented as a romantic tourist land, peopled by stereotypical Latins and primitive Indians, Donald Duck comics are very popular—Dorfman and Mattelart grew up reading them. Their book, a best-seller in the Chile of Allende, is a serious piece of sociology, but it is written in a jazzy and light-hearted style; no heavy Marxist polemic this. (p. 432)

Donald is capitalistic propaganda. It is consumer rather than producer orientated. It assumes that the American way of life—capitalistic and consumer orientated—is true democracy. It romanticises Latin America and it ignores the class struggle by ignoring the working class—you never see anyone working in Donald Duck comics except selling something. It is also anti-Women's Lib; no one seems to have a mother (or a father come to that) in the world of Donald and Mickey. But wouldn't Donald Duck comics be most curious indeed if they told it like it is in Latin America?

An adult reading *How To Read Donald Duck* finds himself nodding in agreement. Certainly it must be most insulting to be living in Latin America and have yourself presented as a romantic stereotype (something the English have never had to bear). (pp. 432-33)

Anyone who has never read Donald Duck comics would be surprised at the amount of philosophy in them. Donald and the other characters are forever making home-spun or humorous philosophical remarks. The influence, I think, must be Aesop's Fables, but they are usually about money or the lack of it. Well, I suppose such constant harping on money must anger the Marxist authors and yet there is a lot of meat in one of these comics when you compare them, for example, to the wild nonsense of the English comic of today—to the *Dandy* or the

Beano. The Donald Duck comics, with their preoccupation with history, travel, and current events, are quite sophisticated. It is just this aspect, of course, which makes Dorfman and Mattelart see red or whatever colour Marxists see. They are not the only ones who are reading too much into a small thing. The distributors of *How To Read Donald Duck* have just issued a bulletin. "As a result of arbitrary action by the US Government, acting to protect Walt Disney's interests, it is regretted that, for the moment, the publisher cannot supply *How To Read Donald Duck* to persons who ordered copies in the United States." (p. 433)

> Stanley Reynolds, *"Teach Yourself Quacking," in* Punch, *Vol. 269, No. 7043, September 10, 1975, pp. 432-33.*

ANDREW HACKER

In each successive stage of history, Friedrich Engels wrote, "the most powerful, economically dominant class . . . acquires new means of holding down and exploiting the oppressed class." Religion has served this end, as has purblind patriotism. In our time there have emerged "more highly developed instruments"—also Engels's phrase—to cloud the public's mind with illusions and delusions. So runs Ariel Dorfman's thesis [in *The Empire's Old Clothes*], and he has chosen three of these instruments for detailed scrutiny: Babar the Elephant, the Lone Ranger and *Reader's Digest*.

Mr. Dorfman proposes to demonstrate how our consciousness is shaped. He does so by examining a set of children's books, the adventures of a hero for preadolescents and the workings of the world's most widely read adult magazine. A further feature of *The Empire's Old Clothes* is that the author is a Chilean exile, offering us a picture of ourselves as seen by an outsider. Mr. Dorfman was a professor of journalism and literature in Chile until Salvador Allende fell. . . . (p. 15)

The [Babar] books concern an African elephant who is orphaned when his mother is shot by a "wicked hunter." After his mother is killed, Babar wends his way to Paris, where he is adopted by a wealthy woman. Under her tutelage he is soon sleeping in a bed, bathing in a tub and even driving a car. He also learns how to read and write and how to dress in elegant style. His education over, Babar returns to Africa, where the other elephants, awed by his accomplishments, crown him their king.

For Mr. Dorfman, Babar's story is a lesson in colonialism with racist overtones. "The child," he writes, "has come into contact with an implicit history that justifies and rationalizes the motives behind an international situation in which some countries have everything and other countries almost nothing." As soon as Babar becomes "civilized," he returns (in reality, is sent back) to prepare the natives for the new imperialist hegemony. In this parable, white overlords never appear. Babar does their work for them, adding a liberal veneer by showing that *some* savages can learn Western ways. "Babar's history," Mr. Dorfman tells us, "is none other than the fulfillment of the dominant countries' colonial dream"—domination without tears.

The Lone Ranger, Mr. Dorfman says, reaches older children with action-filled homilies set closer to home. In a typical adventure, the masked rider and his Indian companion (always a few yards behind) defend honest settlers from land barons and their hired thugs. The subtlety here is in casting greed as the villain, acknowledging that excesses exist. But the system is self-correcting, with the Lone Ranger representing capitalist morality. (pp. 15, 28)

Mr. Dorfman explicates these episodes and stories at academic length. He even deciphers the racial and sexual symbolism of Zephyr the monkey and Silver the stallion. For authority, he cites such authors as György Lukács, Antonio Gramsci and Frantz Fanon, blending in the psychoanalytic leaven found in much Marxist writing. Of course, childhood eventually ends (although "infantilization" does not), so capitalist society must fashion new forms of fantasy for adults. For Mr. Dorfman, *Reader's Digest* clearly fills this bill. . . .

In tone and message, the magazine congratulates its readers on what fine folk they are: independent, self-reliant, eager for improvement. Out there, it implies, are others who gripe about the system and look for a free ride; *Digest* people do their bit to make the world work. Mr. Dorfman calls this attitude "feverish individualism," an ideology for solid citizens.

According to *The Empire's Old Clothes*, the *Digest*'s politics transcend its conservative stance on unions, welfare programs and the Communist threat. By emphasizing the human element, the magazine deflects attention away from the injustices capitalism creates. Typically, a problem "is placed before our eyes so we can see how, in some model place together with the inspiration of some exemplary citizen, that problem has found a path toward solution." Thus in an article on pollution, we learn of a young Californian who advocates tree planting as a way to combat smog. Or we read about a retired sea captain who reforms young delinquents by teaching them how to sail. All this benevolence blinds the *Digest* reader to the system's contradictions.

Even on its own Marxist terms, Mr. Dorfman's critique takes too effortless a route. He sticks to textual analysis, with no attempt to set his interpretations in a social context. But the *Digest* addresses itself to a specific segment of the population—largely lower middle class Americans who have done sufficiently well to be willing to identify with the established order. Parsing magazine articles, however, does not tell us how the American economy came to foster the creation of such a group of people or why its members take so uncritical a view of the system. (Interestingly, the upper middle class tends to be far less accepting of it.) This is not to say that Mr. Dorfman should have written a sociological survey. Still, insofar as he is claiming that the *Digest* and Babar and the Lone Ranger have succeeded in winning the hearts and minds of Americans, he is obliged to relate his subjects to their intended audiences.

In this connection, I am not persuaded that either the educated elephant or the masked rider has made that much of an impression. (The Lone Ranger has long been displaced as an American broadcasting staple.) If there is anything that shapes and expresses the current consciousness of young people, it is the music that looms so large in their lives from a very early age. When we examine rock or its sundry variations, we find that the music's message is implicitly subversive, invoking a dissociation from adult society. Even those young people who seek careers and success are less loyal to the system than appearances suggest. This is not to say that they think in revolutionary terms, simply that there is a lot of disaffection out there. A Marxist analysis might view these young people as constituting a class without an economic role apart from consumption. This would explain their political alienation and their search for sensual gratification. But there are no such hints in

The Empire's Old Clothes; Mr. Dorfman shows little curiosity about young people or their intellects. As it happens, since the 1960's America has witnessed a ferment among the young that Mr. Dorfman would probably applaud. Unfortunately, his view of popular culture is so single-minded that he cannot see it. (p. 28) .

Andrew Hacker, "Who Was That Masked Capitalist?," in The New York Times Book Review, *May 8, 1983, pp. 15, 28.*

DENNIS DRABELLE

The story [of *Widows*] is classically simple. A quisling government rules Greece, and its soldiers are out pacifying the countryside. Most of the men from one village have been missing for a year or more, and a newly arrived captain hopes the time has come to forget this unpleasantness. But dead male bodies keep fetching up on the banks of the local river—probably the handiwork of upstream thugs who are still wedded to outmoded terrorist policies—and forgetting is out of the question.

Already an embarrassment to the captain as the novel opens, the corpses become challenges to his authority after local women start identifying them, demanding the right to bury them, taking up riverside vigils when he refuses. Two women both claim the same unrecognizable body, and the villagers parlay the dispute into a righteous conspiracy: 37 women file rival petitions to bury the dead man. Because a German colonel is on the way for an inspection, the captain must resolve the conflict rapidly. His moves and the villagers' countermoves propel the book to a grim conclusion. . . .

Dorfman writes with a piercing intensity, scrutinizing the scene and its inhabitants like the old woman whose failure to blink unnerves the captain. . . .

And the novel draws much of its considerable power from Dorfman's ability to depict his villains from the inside. An orderly to the captain is not the fascist lackey he might have been in more impassioned hands but just a peasant who has spent his life mooning over the local millionaire's lush estate. . . . What *Widows* may have lost in immediacy, [by being set in Nazi-occupied Greece instead of present day Chile], Dorfman has more than compensated for with his empathy and craft.

The Empire's Old Clothes is a handful of essays on what Dorfman calls subliterature: children's and comic books, photo novels, and magazines like *Reader's Digest*. His thesis is that subliterature not only eschews controversy and spoon-feeds artificial optimism but also drums into its readers the superiority of the capitalist high-tech lifestyle to any other kind. . . .

That subliterature upholds the status quo is not a startling insight; one would hardly expect comics and McMags like *Reader's Digest* to foment unrest or soar above received wisdom. But it hadn't dawned on me how insulting some of our cartoons must appear to a keen Third-World eye.

Dorfman helps the reader analyze selected subliterary characters in new ways. He interprets the Lone Ranger and similar outsider-heroes as ombudsmen through whom the common man can "gain access to the workings of the State." And he offers an interesting account of how the Chilean comic-strip *Mampato* once broke with its genre by reflecting the turmoil of national politics. In 1973 the cartoonist sided with the country's plutocrats, and young Mampato's adventures that year amounted to a minor stratagem in the campaign to bring down Allende.

Dorfman also succeeds in pinpointing what is debilitating about Loony Tunes and Fantasyland—that their visions do not percolate upward from ordinary people's collective dreams but gravitate downward from entrepreneurs' strategy sessions. So whereas the best folk tales can give catharsis, Disney's bowdlerized rehashes tend to inflict narcosis.

But Dorfman is insufficiently afraid of repeating himself, and after a while there is something askew in applying references like Gramsci, Rank, and Barthes and terms like "autochthonous" to Huey, Dewey, and Louie. The real rub may be the uncertain identity of Dorfman's audience. Neither kids nor devotees of *Reader's Digest* are likely to plow through it, and hyperliterate U.S. adults will probably agree or disagree with it simply according to their political lights.

Yet in the fairy tale that gave Dorfman his title, it was enough for the child to call out the truth. As a recent exile, Dorfman speaks with a child's freshness when he warns that our subliterature is by no means the apolitical entertainment it purports to be.

> *Dennis Drabelle, "Chile, Cartoons and Commitment," in* Book World—The Washington Post, *June 12, 1983, pp. 6-7.*

CAROLYN SEE

Widows is a novel done at great remove. Dorfman first wrote it, he tells us in an introduction, in the hope that it would be published in his own country, and so went through an elaborate preliminary "setup." He placed his novel in Greece, with a phony translator, taking great pains to make the language sound un-Spanish, so that it couldn't be traced. Then the publishing companies in his own country turned the novel down. Dorfman was faced with a choice: Should he rewrite—locate the novel in his own country?

> I liked the novel as it was. By forcing myself to choose my words with caution, by forcing myself to witness such a traumatic and immediate experience from a distance . . . it seemed to me I had managed to make the plight of the missing people into something more universal. It is our misfortune that is happening today in my own Chile, in El Salvador, in South Africa, in the Philippines.

The plight of the people, the missing, the "disappeared," is exactly what Dorfman is talking about—those unfortunates who are abducted and never heard from again, leaving only their families to mourn them. The "Greek" landscape Dorfman creates here is squalid, obscure, in the middle of nowhere—a stubborn village that refuses to knuckle under to a set of almost equally oppressed military men who have been sent out to quell domestic instability. The setting here is so familiar, and yet so mixed. The 37 black-clad widows who claim each waterlogged and mutilated corpse that floats down the river, insisting that those unrecognizable features *must* be the loved contours of their father, their son, their brother—those ladies are Greek in truth, and come from Greek tragedy. But the military men are straight out of Koestler. They have the same hidden maimed yearnings, and the one requisite "beast" that *no one* understands, not even his colleagues in crime. But no wonder characters and metaphors are mixed. Men have been

killing men and male children for a long time—since long before Herod did in all those boys under two, and certainly after.

The story premise here—that the 37 widows can shame and utterly baffle the regiment simply by "standing up for what is right" in winged wisdom—embodies an even sadder set of wishful thinking than the one about the pen being stronger than the sword. Women know what is *right*, Dorfman suggests. Women, even though they aren't "strong," can save men from their crimes. By putting their emotional money on the good guys, they can shame the bad guys into submission. (pp. 1, 9)

Dorfman appears to see only "right and wrong"; he cares little for the humans under their costumes. (p. 9)

> *Carolyn See, "Oppression on the Line," in* Los Angeles Times Book Review, *June 12, 1983, pp. 1, 9.*

ALAN CHEUSE

The plot [of *Widows*] resounds with the moral thunder of classic drama, specifically that of *Antigone* and *The Trojan Women*. Mr. Dorfman's Antigone is a peasant grandmother rather than an aristocratic young woman. Sofia Angelos's struggle against the reigning military authorities in a country resembling the homeland of Sophocles and Euripides deserves to be compared with the oldest agons we know. First, her ancient father has been carried off by the secret police, then her husband and sons disappear. When a faceless, mutilated corpse of a man washes up on the river bank outside her village, Sofia struggles with the local commandant for the right to bury it as her kin. After much torment, she wins her battle only to engage the authorities again when a new corpse appears on the shore. Interestingly, we see all of this action from the viewpoints of various children, the confused but doggedly determined army officers and judges and civilian flunkies.

Despite the fact that Mr. Dorfman has transported his novel from his native Chile to other places and times, it gains . . . emotional amplitude and political resonance precisely because of the sharply observed details of the bereaved, who suffer no less painfully from the abuses of mortal rulers than they would have from the cruelties of vengeful or indifferent gods. The self-conscious apparatus of *Widows* soon drops away, and the reader, deeply touched, moves as if in a dream of outrage among its tombs of love. (pp. 10, 26)

> *Alan Cheuse, "The 'Disappeared' and the Jettisoned," in* The New York Times Book Review, *July 24, 1983, pp. 10, 26.*

SIMON NORTH

You might think a political analysis of *Babar the Elephant* promises to be . . . boring—a product of the academic tradition that takes too literally Blake's maxim about finding a world in a grain of sand. However, Ariel Dorfman's exposition of popular literature, not just Babar but *The Lone Ranger*, Donald Duck and *Reader's Digest*, is nothing of the sort. Not only is [*The Empire's Old Clothes*] wittily and entertainingly written; it is also extremely interesting.

Dorfman quickly dispels the notion, if the reader harbours it, that children's literature is all harmless fun and that politics can't possibly be a part of its innocent universe. Of course, the idea that it can't is naive, or even arrogant, for just as the coded expression of a world view can be sought by anthropologists in the language and rituals of 'undeveloped' countries, so it can be found within aspects of our own culture. In this way Dorfman contributes to the same development of self-awareness as the feminist exploration of language, which has made visible the previously invisible male orientation of the way we speak and write—a development which potentially liberates us from those semi-conscious tyrannies of thought that trip up and inhibit conscious effort towards personal and social change.

The author is an exiled Chilean socialist living (ironically) in the USA. He sees the huge export of American popular literature to countries like his own as a form of colonisation. This is the perspective from which he introduces the book. Three essays then follow, in which Babar and Donald Duck, *The Lone Ranger* and *Reader's Digest* are scrutinised. By exploring the texts, plots and evolution of the comics, he holds a mirror up to the moral, economic and geographical assumptions of the society that has produced them. (p. 25)

In the last essay Dorfman relates how a comic-strip story allegorised the downfall of Allende, as it occurred, in the defeat of a monster-tyrant called Ferjus. The example demonstrates that, as well as the unconscious infusions, conscious and historical forces are also at work in children's literature. . . .

Dorfman is against dogma and for imagination. Nowhere in the book does he ridicule or condemn those who read the stuff he analyses with such mischievous acuity; but he recognises the importance of undermining its power with imaginative alternatives and criticism. Generalised feelings of resistance against the reactionary doctrines of our culture need to be particularised if they are not to lead simply to a condition of impotent aggression. It is to this process of particularising that Dorfman contributes.

Energised by his passion and unrelenting insight, you look up from the book feeling better able to understand the insidious ubiquity of the status quo, its intimate processes and methods, its neighbourly disguises and indoctrinations. (p. 26)

> *Simon North, "Hidden Dogma," in* New Statesman, *Vol. 106, No. 2739, September 16, 1983, pp. 25-6.*

LEWIS HYDE

In *The Empire's Old Clothes* Ariel Dorfman has sought to make sense of . . . apparent ephemeras of popular culture, mass market children's literature in particular. Why are there uncles but no mothers and fathers in Donald Duck stories? Why is Babar the elephant so interested in elevators? Why does the *Reader's Digest* unfailingly personify distant lands ("China Goes Shopping")? (p. 250)

[Dorfman's] interest in "industrialized works of fiction" goes back to the days when he was a professor of journalism and literature in Chile during the Allende period. Several ideas motivate his argument: that mass-produced fictions teach us "how not to rebel," that they colonize their readers and, because "the world of children . . . constitutes the axis of all processes of domination," that children's literature and "infantilized" adult literature "form the basis for the entire process of cultural domination."

Unfortunately, Dorfman's discussion of the Lone Ranger is the best moment in this frustrating group of essays. As the faint trumpets of his style reveal, he has issued himself stern marching orders. They sometimes lead him to interesting readings,

but more often they lead him to arbitrary and silly conclusions. He notices, for example, that in Disney's comics the adults (the adult ducks, that is) tend to be foolish, while the children are wise and capable. But shall we then say, "in seeing adults stripped of the mask of superiority, these fables allow their young readers a valuable respite from powerlessness," or shall we say, "once the child identifies with other children who are really adults he participates in his own self-domination"? I made up the first sentence; the second is Dorfman's. Arbitrary and silly.

Dorfman repeatedly calls on fables to be something that is not in their nature. Above all, he wishes they revealed a fuller sense of contemporary history. Isn't it true that the Babar stories leave out the racism that has marked Europe's relationship to Africa? Hasn't the development Babar brings his people historically led to ecological disaster? Isn't it the case that Walt Disney never offered "an authentic critique on the origin of [Scrooge] McDuck's wealth"? That all those things are true does not amount to a critique of the works in question. My cat has never washed the dishes, but that is not a good critique of my cat.

As I read this book, I longed for Dorfman to enliven the argument by bringing in something that didn't fit his assumptions. Why not look at some recent socialist fictions? (In the Chinese fiction-for-the-masses that I have read, the state is so busy it makes the Lone Ranger seem positively withered away.) Why not compare "industrialized fictions" to pre-industrial fairy tales? Having told us how the Lone Ranger's altruism wins his horse's loyalty, Dorfman sternly concludes that this "steed emerged from nature in order to advance the cause of justice and never to destroy private property." Yes, yes. But stories of helpful animals responding to human virtue predate such talk by thousands of years. Silver is probably not of the same genus as the silver horses in the Brothers Grimm, but to differentiate them requires a taxonomist more skilled than Dorfman.

The main thing missing from this book, though, is a sense of who reads the tales and why. No mythology can colonize the imagination unless it has some appeal, but no feeling for the attractiveness of these works appears in Dorfman's essays. Babar and the *Reader's Digest* I have never cared for, but I used to love Scrooge McDuck, partly for the kick of fantasizing about unlimited wealth and partly to watch the playing out of the utopian joke that fantasy contains (and which even children intuitively understand): What would happen to cash if you were freed from the assumption of scarcity? When Dorfman points out that "laborers, workers, and peasants . . . are inaudible in the world of Disney," or that Huey, Dewey and Louie never get sick, we have to admit his point, but we do not sense he has any sympathy for the entranced child-reader. That reader has been squeezed out by politics. That I share much of the politics in question only made *The Empire's Old Clothes* more of a disappointment. (pp. 250, 252)

> *Lewis Hyde, "Ducks of the World, Arise!," in* The Nation, *New York, Vol. 237, No. 8, September 24, 1983, pp. 250, 252.*

NICHOLAS RANKIN

In modern Spanish, the verb *desaparecer*, "to disappear", has become transitive. People do not just disappear in South America: unidentified men in unmarked cars "disappear" them. Such abductions of citizens by (para-)military forces is not confined to the Southern Cone of the continent, although after the military takeovers of the last decade (Chile, 1973: Argentina, 1976) it was there that the phenomenon gained prominence. Amnesty International reports at least 4,650 documented cases still outstanding. *Widows* is a novel about those missing persons: *los desaparecidos.* . . . [Dorfman's original intent in *Widows*] was to publish the book under a pseudonym in Scandinavia, and have it "re-translated" into Spanish to circulate in his homeland. The book purports to be written by a Dane in 1941-42, and is set in occupied Greece. But he avoids the realist clutter of local detail, and has contrived a tragedy of universal application. . . .

The central tensions of the book spring from a formalized opposition of the sexes. "War is men's business", says the Captain. "A woman's place is in the house. Or in bed." Also, "For the nation's army, there is nothing more sacred than woman and nothing greater than motherhood. It is in defence of that woman and of the values of the home . . . that we have always acted." Even in resistance, the women are passive, "simply waiting . . . for them, the soldiers, to decide what they were going to do, how they were going to do it, when." But when a patriarchal society has its men taken away, the women are finally impelled to find a tentative strength in each other. . . .

The characters are not vividly particularized. They are human archetypes, and the "Greek" women function as a chorus to the actions of the men. The narrative technique is more complex, with shuffled time-sequences and modernist devices like stream of consciousness sentences without capitals; in Chapter 6 we are faced by a "missing" section x. The Captain's thoughts and deeds are narrated omnisciently, not without sympathy, but always in the third person, whereas the hostage boy veers between "I", "you" and "he", and his twin sister speaks as "I","she", and frequently as "we". . . .

By taking on this subject Dorfman runs all the risks of the political novel: rhetoric, didacticism, rant. But the literary man has the edge on the political animal. *Widows* is a carefully understated work that achieves its best effects by distancing itself from the author's historical situation and by exercising a powerful restraint.

> *Nicholas Rankin, "Habeas Corpus," in* The Times Literary Supplement, *No. 4210, December 9, 1983, p. 1372.*

EARL SHORRIS

[Ariel Dorfman] has written a novel [*The Last Song of Manuel Sendero*] in which the sorrows of exile and disappearance are told with jokes, puzzles and extravagances to enable the reader to feel once more a human response to modern evil.

Like many novels trying to deal with phenomena that seem like madness to the rational mind, *The Last Song of Manuel Sendero* relies on one overarching joke on reality: "Who could have believed that a year and a half after the child had been conceived . . . the kid had still not made its appearance into this world, was still waiting there, inside, refusing to come out?" Yes, in Mr. Dorfman's novel the fetuses have revolted, refusing to be born until the grown-ups end political and economic oppression and permit people their human rights. Among their demands: "Instead of freedom of prices, freedom of food must be declared," the stock of big weapons destroyed, and "everybody has to take off his clothes." All this to prove the

sincerity of the Government's declaration of its "own immediate dissolution."

In the hands of a political satirist, the revolt of the fetuses might have been good for a paragraph or two, a chapter at most, but Mr. Dorfman's unborn are well-rounded fetuses, capable of fear and ambition—hopeful, analytical, political, anxious and decent. And two of them are in love. Through their interuterine network the fetuses discuss the major question raised by their revolt, which is whether the world can be changed from without (that is, by their remaining unborn) or only from within (by their being born and participating in the political life of the society).

The desire for light and breath cannot be overcome, however, and the rebellion begins to fail as the fetuses choose to be born, descending in the elevator that traverses the path from conception to life to death. One after another, they are born and lose the wisdom of the womb. At last, only the lovers, the son of Manuel Sendero and the sweet Pamela, are left in utero, talking over the question of being born, observing what has happened to those who preceded them. When Pamela is born, the revolt ends, for the son of Manuel Sendero loves her too much to remain in another state of being.

If that were the whole story, a simple displacement, tragic and straightforwardly imagined, like Mr. Dorfman's first novel, *Widows,* it would be interesting, an important step forward from the relentlessly dour moralizing of that first effort, but insufficient, thin. *The Last Song of Manuel Sendero* is anything but thin. It refracts the life of Ariel Dorfman and his country into a dozen mirrors scattered across thousands of years. The son of Manuel Sendero is both the teller and the tale, born and unborn, fetus and grandfather. His is but one incarnation of the ethical dilemma of the exile: to punish by withholding one's love and participation or to return. It is, as the novel implies, the central question for all who have become estranged, for fetuses and singers and cartoonists and patriarchs and even for messiahs of all kinds.

The problems of exile and return are confronted here most directly by two cartoonists, David and Felipe, whose realistic story weaves in and out of the tale of the fetuses. The young men plan to produce a magazine in Mexico for Latin American exiles and intellectuals. It will feature a cartoon strip about Carl Barks or Marx or Sparks, an octogenarian from the state of Washington who travels to the land of Chilex with his aged wife, Sarah. Will Sarah give birth to a child in the country that just might be the analogue of the place where the fetuses are in revolt?

As the comic strip is written, the writers argue the merits of returning to Chile. The Government has told David he may come home on the condition that he give an interview to the newspapers, telling of the difficulties of life in exile. Curiously, it is not Felipe, the native Chilean, who is drawn back to his homeland, but David Wiseman, a Jew whose parents brought him out of Nazi Germany to Chile when he was 2 years old. One diaspora illuminates another.

The story within the cartoon proceeds, the lives of the exiles complicate—there are children, David has a *gringa* wife, and there are memories of the beginning and the end of the Allende years. Carl Sparks and Sarah become another refraction of the fetuses and are in turn refracted into their biblical analogues. Ishmael and Joseph are exiles; among the fetuses who refuse to be born are a set of twins; David and Felipe, whose arguments may be the contentions within a single mind, are really deciding whether to be born.

And all the while there is the question of the last song of Manuel Sendero. Who is this man, this singer?. . .

Should we connect Manuel Sendero to Victor Jara, the enormously popular singer of the Allende period who was killed after Gen. Augusto Pinochet came to power? Who is David Wiseman and how is he different from Ariel Dorfman, who produced cartoons and popular radio and television programs during the Allende years, who cares so much about the meaning of popular culture he has not only investigated Donald Duck but also written a book, *The Empire's Old Clothes,* analyzing Babar the Elephant and the Lone Ranger?

This Manuel Sendero, whose child refuses to be born, is mute now. Some say they heard him sing his last song and others say there never was such a song in Chile. And how is it that such an utterly preposterous complex of stories, burdened by too many echoes of the Latin American magic realists and their Yanqui cousin Thomas Pynchon, engages the reader so that David Wiseman's decision becomes important and Manuel Sendero's song achieves meaning?

To agree with the politics of a novel is the beginning of affection, and I agree with this writer, who is one of those gentle leftists for whom no murder can be excused. After this moral connection has been made, after the complications of plot and puzzle have done their work, the richness of the invention breaks through the gate of reality, and the reader touches congruently the soulful imagination of Ariel Dorfman.

> Earl Shorris, "Gestation with a Vengeance," in The New York Times Book Review, *February 15, 1987, p. 9.*

PAT AUFDERHEIDE

[*The Last Song of Manuel Sendero*] by Ariel Dorfman consolidates his reputation as a writer who wrests art from a reality that seems to defy it. Like many Third World writers, Dorfman denies the neat division between art and politics; more impressive, he also refuses to collapse the two categories into one. . . .

The Last Song of Manuel Sendero, re-written since its first publication in Spanish several years ago, is a sprawling, frustrating, challenging novel. It's as imperious and stubborn as its central metaphor: a rebellion of fetuses, who refuse to be born until they can be guaranteed a world worthy of them. The themes are drawn from the increasingly common reality of political and artistic exile. . . .

At a recent conference on Third World culture at Duke University, Dorfman explained with agonizing succinctness the central problem of exile: "Reality is always somewhere else." He went on to say that many exiles discovered on the road the distance between them and the majority of Chileans, even when they had been at home. Both problems inform the delirious dreaming of *Manuel Sendero,* in which a world is struggling to be born. You might call the novel's style "magical proto-realism." Dorfman's central job is to discover the ambiguity, despair, and megalomaniac sense of possibility in a time of political paralysis. He makes language not only into an instrument but a player in that story.

The voices of the novel swirl and collide with each other, in three general spheres: the ether of the unborn; the cramped quarters of Chilean exiles in Paris; and the fantasy world of a comic book which the exiles are working on. In each sphere, the characters overtake the author with unruly gusto, dislocating the reader and recreating the passion and pain of an irrepressible will to liberation.

Easiest to grasp, and bleakest, is the world of-life of two Chilean exiles, militant Felipe and gentler David, who rehash the politics of the Allende years and battle over the feeble efforts of their constrained present. Should they boycott Chilean wine? If so, for how long? How to weigh the strength of invisible protest against the nostalgic solace of that glass of wine from home? How should they structure the comic book they're writing, which they hope will expose the Disney-fascism of international pop culture and create mythic heroes and villains from the debacle of Chile today?

Pettiness, squalor, vindictiveness and humiliation surface in these talks, as do powerful memories. . . .

In the comic book, their homeland becomes "Chilex," where generals solemnly receive an aged Disney artist. They recruit him for a propaganda campaign; he and his barren wife Sarah gradually uncover the ugly reality behind it. Chilex is doing a brisk business in rejuvenating foreigners, having figured out how to leech the lifeblood out of Chilean families. The saga of these naive cartoon characters becomes a second major arena for the novel, in which their self-protective ignorance is destroyed.

Enveloping both plot lines, and sometimes aggressively pushing them off the page, is the mythic, timeless world of the fetuses. They are led by the unborn son of Manuel Sendero, a mute average-Joe whose pregnant wife Doralisa has sunk into a perpetual sleep. Manuel's son is organizing all of the fetuses for a strike, and attempting to orchestrate the actions of his family to prepare conditions for eventual birth. The drama of two organizing efforts, and the sallying forth of new babies, is told by a chorus of fetal voices, future generations who team up with the long-dead to protest the conditions of living itself. . . .

Questions remain open throughout the novel. Sometimes resolved only to be opened again. Everyone is trying to turn chaotic experience and profound desire into coherency and mythic glory. But there is no resolution, no definitive entry into history from this limbo of exile, fetus-hood, political stalemate.

You can watch Dorfman resisting the temptation to force a resolution, plunging back into the turmoil of feeling in situations where something is struggling to be born at the same time as people are struggling not to die. The novel communicates the intensity of that situation not by psychologizing realism but by an imaginative bombardment of the reader's expectations. The proliferating metaphors and imaginative spirals are boldly simplistic, and also wildly energetic and provocative. . . .

"This book is about frontiers and how to pass through them without being destroyed," Dorfman tells the reader at the outset. However, *The Last Song of Manuel Sendero* (whose last name means "Pathway") is not a road map. The vision it provides surely must unnerve many dedicated and earnest political activists, especially those who take their comfort from dogmatism. It may be too murky even to see, for many of those who have no experience living in such territory or who are committed to willful innocence about it.

But in itself, this huge novel is an experiment in ways to survive life at the frontier. Every page, every insistent act of imagination is an act of resistance against the death-in-life of political oppression and the life-on-hold of exile.

Pat Aufderheide, in a review of "The Last Song of Manuel Sendero," in Boston Review, *Vol. XII, No. 2, April, 1987, p. 26.*

GEOFFREY STOKES

Though he initially made his mark with studies of mass culture (*How to Read Donald Duck*) and his journalism, Dorfman's novels have recently received considerable attention. *Widows,* a slim, "realistic" volume set in a Greece that has a more than passing resemblance to Chile, was particularly highly praised, but it hardly prepared readers for the magic-realist sprawl of *The Last Song of Manuel Sendero.*

This is, one should say right off the bat, a novel that deliberately bites off more than it (or, perhaps, we) can chew. Its 450 pages include two separate revolutions of the unborn (who act by refusing to emerge), a realistic dialogue between two exiles, a political comic book (set in a country called Chilex) one of them has just written, the imagined off-page lives of its invented characters (one of whom is, or is based on, the Disney writer Carl Barks), and scholarly comments (from course notes for Prehistoric Amerspanish III, given some 30,000 years from now) on the handful of fragments from the "realistic" story— *and* its embedded comic-book narrative—that have by chance survived. Got the picture?. . .

Dorfman's novel has the advantage of plot, circumstance, drama, and intimate emotions; it may, however, have too much of a good thing, for it constantly threatens to drown itself in circumstance. (p. 10)

Dorfman's imagination has considerable political force; though Pynchon, for instance, has written about fetuses, his inventions didn't organize a strike. There is convincing passion, too, in the interwoven love stories doomed to unhappy endings by the counterrevolution. And, as in the story the unborn son of Manuel Sendero tells his beloved Pamela, horror as well. It begins in a neighborhood known as "The Messengers":

> Back then, kids, post offices were more like reading centers than places to expedite correspondence. Just the way you buy stamps now, back then everybody had to wait for his words to be read and approved before he could mail them. Words became coded, perverted, sterile; they beat around the bush in order to make contact. Tremendous contraband operations. Nothing could be said just like that. And if they caught you, punishment was immediate. . . .

This passage folds in with dozens of others about the corruption of language: the self-defeating codes adopted by the revolutionaries driven underground after the military coup, the gradual deafness of Carl Barks, the unctuous, ubiquitous voice of the junta, The Caballero. Though Dorfman's plot is not easy to follow, there are few loose ends; everything fits.

Which is, finally, a problem. At the end, the book's chief attractions are intellectual. It is convincing, to be sure, but like a crossword puzzle, it engages our minds more than our hearts. The fault, ironically, lies in Dorfman's language. In *Widows,* a much, much shorter book, the occasional clunkiness of the

prose was excused by the conceit that it was a double translation. The language in *Sendero* is more ambitious, and it can't quite bear the weight of the towering structure Dorfman attempts to build on it.

The language matters so much because novelists, unlike journalists, have to elicit the famous "willing suspension of disbelief" from their readers. In "magic realism," the problem is heightened, and every time we trip over a repetitive phrase or get mired in a digressive slough, we are jarred out of our necessary faith. When this happens as often as it does in *Sendero,* our response to the novel becomes pinched. There remains enough strength in Dorfman's book to compel an intellectual assent, but not, alas, an emotional one. In a certain sense, *Sendero*'s truths are the truths that journalism could tell. (p. 11)

Geoffrey Stokes, "Truth Under the Gun," in VLS, *No. 54, April, 1987, pp. 9-11.*

PAUL WEST

To call *The Last Song of Manuel Sendero* a tour de force would be like calling *Finnegans Wake* an obituary notice. The conception is brilliant: a revolt of fetuses who, aghast at the political mayhem in their unnamed country-to-be, refuse to be born. The son of Manuel Sendero begins the revolt, and the rest follow, putting the future on hold. No more children, no more victims, no more tyrants, no more parents, and in the end no more country either.

Nonetheless, the fetus who says I will not serve has volunteered to become, if not a solipsist, at least an underground person, an intrauterine scold, aware perhaps but also impotent, confronting human problems with almost theological obtuseness. Arguing among themselves, the fetuses begin to think they should get out into the world after all and do something about the mess.

Needless to say, once out they conform, lose the Wordsworthian gleam, and at last the son of Manuel Sendero is left alone, in perpetual gestation. It matters little if the reader concludes that the birth never happens: the whole world, past and future, seeps into the womb, as does the seductive presence of Manuel's beloved Pamela. Clearly one has to revise all notions of the womb as a stamping ground, a waiting room, and let these almost 500 pages radiate and flow, surpassing place and time, locus and track, doer and done to. It would be hard to think of a novel more destructive of old dualisms and dichotomies than this, always reminding the reader that it's made of words.

Dorfman's special skill is to make the basic metaphor so structural he needn't insist on it in the texture. We do not easily forget that the country he is writing about is a Catholic one and that brand-new casuistries beset it, not the least of them being: Between contraception and abortion, where does indefinitely and deliberately prolonged gestation fit? If wholly fictional, can it have sociological import at all? And so on. The whole novel is fraught with wonderment, at its subtlest in the long passages of fetal extravaganza, at its most explicit in the sprightly dialogues of David and Felipe, displaced Chileans who argue their way through Mexico and Europe, homesick for what they can't abide.

The writing is just as vivid as the characters, sometimes even more so. We read about a baby within "the savory rumba walls of his mother" and "the misty keyhole of the umbilical cord." Manuel Sendero's song "wasn't exactly a sound, but rather an exaltation of a different light, as if the touch of a blind man could make itself heard," certainly something less dynamic than the "soft stampede of antelopes in her underbelly" evoked elsewhere. . . .

Ariel Dorfman's slight and sometimes homely distortions do more for his novel than a whole host of force-fed hyperboles would. It isn't so much a novel as a compulsive recitative full of voices who overhear other voices in other wombs. Another way of doing the book would have been to expand the basic conceit, rather than distracting us from it with the more hum-drum David and Felipe stuff, but Dorfman goes his own way with burly finesse.

Paul West, "Ariel Dorfman's Fantasy of Political Resistance," in Book World—The Washington Post, *April 5, 1987, p. 5.*

JUDITH FREEMAN

For years following his partisan activities in Republican Spain and subsequent return to Chile, the poet Pablo Neruda was preoccupied with his heritage: his Spanish roots, the Indians of Chile, the Spanish conquest, indeed the whole of Latin America and its exploitation, including Central America, which he once referred to as "the delectable waist of America."

Ariel Dorfman's novel **The Last Song of Manuel Sendero** is a continuation of the concerns, the lament, really, of his coun-tryman Neruda. The lament is a song of exile, sung by one who has lost his home, whether literally through expulsion by an intolerant regime, or by witnessing the destruction of a spiritual base. . . .

In **The Last Song of Manuel Sendero,** a revolution has broken out in Chile. The babies have rebelled and are refusing to be born until their conditions are met and the world becomes a more humane place. Among their demands: Freedom of food must be declared, weapons eliminated—the big arms, the ones that eat up the budget—and "Everybody has to take off his clothes," for reasons the fetuses think are self-evident. The unborn babies are capable of communicating with each other.

They send encouragement through their interuterine network, even fall in love and debate whether they can be more effective in fighting oppression by continuing their strike or by descend-ing the birth canal and working in the world. Finally, seeking light and air and the experience of the world, they are all born except Manuel Sendero, who, lodged in his amniotic bubble, continues to muse over the primary question: Can we struggle best from within? Or without? Shall we go in and try again?

The revolt of the fetuses forms only one part of the book. Intertwined are the "dialogues" of two Chilean cartoonists, David and Felipe, one an exile, the other a political prisoner now released. They're in Mexico collaborating on a cartoon strip whose main character is Carl Barks or Marx or Sparks and his octogenarian wife, Sarah, who, like her biblical coun-terpart, longs for a baby. . . . Drawing on incredibly complex sources and a complex orchestration of voices, **The Last Song of Manuel Sendero** almost sinks beneath its load.

Almost. What saves the book is that finally, notwithstanding a certain frustration with the looping, refracted, run-on, dream-like and fantastic prose, which makes it difficult at times to even distinguish who is speaking (the son of Manuel Sendero? The grandson? Manuel himself?), there emerge the voices of the exile (David) and of the man of conscience (Felipe), so honest and beseeching that they finally sound the siren song, and we are drawn further and further into the magic webbing of the layered stories. Make no mistake, this is a demanding book, but for those who make the effort it requires, the result is a ride on a parabolic roller coaster of timely and humanitarian thought.

The tale of Manuel Sendero is cautionary. "Your poor readers should realize," someone in the book says, "that what hap-pened to us can happen to them, too. They can lose their country, not know how to get it back, search for it forever. One's country can be stolen in the blink of an eye."

Judith Freeman, in a review of, "The Last Song of Manuel Sendero," in Los Angeles Times Book Re-view, *April 5, 1987, p. 1.*

(Florence Onye) Buchi Emecheta
1944-

Nigerian-born novelist, autobiographer, scriptwriter, and author of children's books.

A Nigerian-born author who has resided in England since 1962, Emecheta is best known for her novels which address the difficulties of modern African women who are forced into traditional subservient roles. Praised for her convincing characterizations, thorough presentation of social themes, and vivid sense of place, Emecheta exposes such African customs as polygamy, servitude, and arranged marriages as practices which curtail the power and individuality of women. Emecheta's heroines often challenge their restrictive lives and aspire to economic and social independence. Although some critics categorize her works as feminist literature, Emecheta rejects the label, stating, "I have not committed myself to the cause of African women only. I write about Africa as a whole."

Emecheta's first two novels, *In the Ditch* (1972) and *Second-Class Citizen* (1975), are loosely based on her own experiences as a single parent and are regarded as her most accomplished works. Both books revolve around a young Nigerian woman named Adah and her search for a better life. In the first book, Emecheta depicts Adah's struggle to raise five small children while living off of welfare payments, attending college, and attempting to complete her first novel. The second book recounts Adah's emigration to England and her marriage to a domineering man who attempts to thwart her educational and professional aspirations. Their marriage dissolves as Adah, influenced by the women's liberation movement, begins to assert her individuality. Critics lauded Emecheta for her straightforward prose and amusing yet poignant evocation of her heroine's tribulations. Rosemary Bray commented: "Both books are simply told, bearing the mark of painful authenticity even before you know they're autobiographical. [Emecheta] wrote them to rid herself of rage at a society and a man who could not accept her independent spirit."

Emecheta's next three novels dramatize the problems African women encounter in a traditional, male-oriented society. *The Bride Price* (1976) centers on a young woman who defies tribal custom by marrying a man outside her social class. After her husband fails to pay her dowry, or bride price, she dies in childbirth, as prophesied by tribal myth. *The Slave Girl* (1977), which accuses the patriarchal social system of treating females as commodities, focuses upon the coming-of-age of an orphan girl whose older brother sells her to a distant relative. In *The Joys of Motherhood* (1979), Emecheta condemns the practice of polygamy, the stigma of barrenness, and the pressures placed on African women to produce male children. The central characters are two women who are married to the same man and compete to bear the most children for him. Both women are ultimately doomed in this relationship: one is discovered to be sterile, and the other is reduced to servitude after bearing several children in rapid succession. Katherine Frank stated that these three novels, along with *In the Ditch* and *Second-Class Citizen*, "compose the most exhaustive and moving portrayal extant of the African woman, an unparalleled portrayal in African fiction and with few equals in other literatures as well."

Although praised for its versatility, Emecheta's later fiction has met with less enthusiasm from reviewers. *Destination Biafra* (1982) is a dense historical novel set during the Nigerian civil war. *Double Yoke* (1983) examines the conflict between tradition and modernity in a lighthearted tale of sexual politics at a Nigerian university. In the futuristic fantasy *The Rape of Shavi* (1984), Emecheta comments upon the impact of westernization on the inhabitants of a mythical African kingdom. *Head above Water* (1986) is a nonfiction work detailing Emecheta's childhood in a small Nigerian village, her career as a social worker in London, and the problems she encountered in securing a publisher for her writings.

Emecheta has published several books for children and young adults, including *Titch the Cat* (1979), *The Wrestling Match* (1982), and *The Moonlight Bride* (1983). She has also written two screenplays, *A Kind of Marriage* and *The Juju Landlord,* for British television.

(See also *CLC*, Vol. 14 and *Contemporary Authors*, Vols. 81-84.)

ROSEMARY BRAY

Mother Africa has never been more in vogue. Of course, the search for African heritage is not new. But ever since the first sisters and brothers exchanged names like LaToya and Andre for Rashida and Malik, post-'60s Afro-Americans have been in hot pursuit of their African roots. And with good reason: people who don't know where they've been find it hard to decide where they're going.

Yet this romance with the homeland has been highly selective. Like a timeworn lover remembering the good and ignoring the bad, we have filtered from our knowledge about African life those facts with which we cannot or will not cope. The reality of the lot of African women is one such massive oversight. Poetry about Nefertiti and Queens of Nubia notwithstanding, life for women on the African continent ain't been no crystal stair. . . .

Like all stories that are worth remembering—now that our oral tradition has fallen by the wayside—they ought to be written down. Somebody ought to remind us that wherever in this world black people fight to be free, black women still wait for their freedom (like the girls and women of Zimbabwe, who spent years in the bush as guerilla fighters and returned home as outcasts when the war was over, unable even to vote). Somebody ought to tell the stories of African women who were gentle, who could not or would not fight, and for whom gentleness meant defeat and death. Somebody ought to say something good about African women's intense concentration on the survival of the "tribe"—the family—and their willingness to break with tradition to insure its survival. And somebody ought to write about the African women who were never satisfied—with their lives, with their roles, with their society—and who risked everything to change things. In short, somebody ought to tell the truth about African women, and in the telling illuminate some forgotten truths about Afro-American women. And somebody is—Buchi Emecheta. . . .

The women of Emecheta's novels want a revision of the world order, though they would never express it in those terms. Her characters have no love for Western "civilization" and its resultant discontents, but they are wise enough, rebellious enough, to see that in traditional African culture, women get the short end of the stick. Emecheta's women know, too, that between the rock of African traditions and the hard place of encroaching Western values, it is the women who will be caught. No matter what they plan or dream of, these African women must at every turn confront their true value in the tribe. They are the property of men, the vessels of children (preferably sons), and all that is done or provided for them is toward that end. . . .

But transitional women like Aku-nna [in *The Bride Price*] often resist their fate, even when the price is death. Aku-nna marries the man of her choice, against the wishes of her family, and her bride price is not paid—for which tribal law promises death in childbirth. Death indeed comes to Aku-nna, as she gives birth to a daughter, Joy—a child born far away from the crushing weight of village tradition, but separated, too, from her roots.

Like Aku-nna (and Joy, though the book ends as her life begins), Buchi Emecheta's African women are faced with the painful choice common to black women in transition, whatever their homeland: do you choose subjugation to masculine privilege and retain the security and support of your traditional culture? Or do you break out, reject society's notion of wom-

anhood and, in the rush toward self-definition, find yourself cut off from your source, from what Toni Morrison calls the "ancient properties"? In her art as well as in her life, Buchi Emecheta offers another alternative. . . .

Even as a girl, Buchi broke with tradition. At the age of eight, though she was expected by her family to remain at home and work, she insisted upon going to school. Her family chose her a husband by her 11th birthday; she refused to marry him until she finished school at 16. Not long after their marriage, Buchi's husband went to London to study; in 1962, she and their two children joined him. The culture shock of London was great, but even more distressing was her husband's physical abuse and his constant resistance to her attempts at independence. The breaking point for Emecheta came when her husband burned her first manuscripts. Pregnant with her fifth child, she left him and scrubbed floors while working toward a degree in sociology.

Her first works, *In the Ditch* and *Second-Class Citizen*, are a record of her experiences on the dole, and her life in London until she left her husband. Both books are simply told, bearing the mark of painful authenticity even before you know they're autobiographical. [Emecheta] wrote them to rid herself of rage at a society and a man who could not accept her independent spirit. . . .

Emecheta's later books, *The Slave Girl*, *The Bride Price*, and *The Joys of Motherhood*, are firmly rooted in Ibo culture and tradition; all three pose a challenge to African attitudes toward women. In *The Slave Girl*, the heroine Ojebeta realizes the fact of her lifelong slavery: first sold by her brother to another village, then turned over to her husband and her uncle, but ultimately controlled by the patriarchal African society. In *The Bride Price*, Emecheta explores the pressures on women to submit to ownership. And in *The Joys of Motherhood*, Nnu-Ego, a woman who has endured shame and hardship in order to be a perfect mother, is rewarded with abandonment and death.

But Emecheta's women do not simply lie down and die. Always there is resistance, a challenge to fate, a need to renegotiate the terms of the uneasy peace that exists between them and accepted traditions. . . . Yet there are some traditions Buchi Emecheta would like to recapture. It is a sore point with her that, once Nigerians discovered that Westerners would pay to hear the stories of her people, what was once seen as the job of women became the exclusive province of men. (p. 13)

Emecheta faces much the same task that modern Afro-American women writers face as they attempt to compensate for more than a century of misogyny in Afro-American literature. It is hard for black women who write on either side of the ocean to feel as though they are heard at all. But there are some women who will willingly work for an ideal. The heroine of Emecheta's new novel, *Destination Biafra*, is one of these women. Debbie Ogedemgbe is a well-educated young Nigerian who joins the army to defend her nation. As the story progresses, she learns that her white English lover, Captain Alan Grey, betrayed Nigerian by helping the outgoing white government manipulate a crucial election.

At the end of the novel, after enduring beatings, rapes, and other humiliations, Debbie is offered safe passage to England by Captain Grey. He even offers to marry her, and reminds her that her male comrades have betrayed the nation and left rather than be killed. But Emecheta places Debbie firmly in the continuum of black women's history as she rejects Grey's offer: "I am not . . . a black white man. I am a woman and a woman of Africa. I am a daughter of Nigeria, and if she is in shame, I shall stay and mourn with her in shame."

It is that sense of clear identity that draws me to Buchi Emecheta's work—her ability to understand that black women have two battles to fight, that we cannot divide our own beings, our own histories, no matter who asks it of us. She is telling a central truth—that we are all women of Africa, and that we can find our way home. (p. 14)

Rosemary Bray, "Nefertiti's New Clothes," in VLS, *No. 8, June, 1982, pp. 13-14.*

ROBERT L. BERNER

In a foreword Emecheta tells us that her publisher was forced by high production costs to reduce the original manuscript of *Destination Biafra* by half. This may account for what often seems a rather elliptical narrative and for the frequently clumsy prose which too often blunts the novel's satiric edge. . . .

Emecheta's story is the history of Nigeria from the eve of independence to the collapse of the Biafran secessionist movement, but the foreword makes clear that her intention was to produce a work with a "message." Unfortunately a point of view is difficult to discover in the novel, and the "message" remains unclear. The foreword ends with the hope that "we Nigerians . . . will never again allow ourselves to be so used." How she believes they were "used" is suggested by the speeches of various characters who condemn Britain for providing the arms by which the Nigerian government defeated Biafra. One of these characters is the protagonist, who presumably speaks for the author; but the Biafran leader who condemns Britain for simultaneously arranging shipments of arms to Lagos and Red Cross supplies to Biafra is the same one who tries to use Red Cross planes to bring arms into Biafra.

In other words, Emecheta clearly shows that the abominable atrocities committed against civilians are less the fault of Britain than of hopelessly corrupt and incompetent Nigerian leaders. . . .

Ignoring the clumsiness of the writing and the lack of a perspective from which the "message" could be read, it should be added that *Destination Biafra* has a certain value for its presentation of a classic example of African nationalism gone wrong. A colony achieves independence under the rule of leaders like the one who says, "The Europeans who ruled us . . . did it, now it's our turn." Corrupt government causes a military coup which only exacerbates the tribal antagonisms it was designed to end. Tribal antagonisms lead to civil war and genocide, the common people pay the heaviest price for the moral imbecility of the politicians, and the worst atrocities are justified by anti-colonial platitudes. Whatever her intended "message," that is Emecheta's story; even though it possesses little literary value, it is still a useful outline of a process which has occurred altogether too frequently in modern Africa.

Robert L. Berner, in a review of "Destination Biafra," in World Literature Today, *Vol. 57, No. 1, Winter, 1983, p. 160.*

LINDA BARRETT OSBORNE

In an earlier book by Nigerian novelist Buchi Emecheta, the protagonist, confronted with her husband's disapproval, "prayed that the two of them would be strong enough to accept civil-

isation into their relationship." Now in Emecheta's eighth novel, *Double Yoke,* Ete Kamba and Nko, two students at the University of Calabar in Nigeria, wrestle with the same conflict created by the tension between tradition and modernity and its effects on identity, love, and marriage.

Emecheta, the most prolific and probably the best known woman writer from tropical Africa, has been living in England since 1962. Her first documentary novels, *In the Ditch* (1972) and *Second Class Citizen* (1974), were autobiographical, describing her struggle against poor living conditions and a failing marriage in London, and her experiences with the British welfare system as she raised her five children alone and studied for a degree in sociology. *Double Yoke* embodies the same energetic, candid, and ubiquitous voice of these earlier works, but it lacks their touching immediacy. Like the themes it considers, it is a mixture, the simple narrative laced with ethnographic and sociological details as well as comment on the foibles and potentials of a rapidly changing society. Even as it is propelled by the natural vitality of Emecheta's writing, it is limited by structural problems.

The story follows the quarrel-filled courtship of Ete and Nko as they try to come to terms with their different perceptions of love and marriage. They are both from small villages and both ambitious, but he is the more traditional of the two. When he first meets Nko as a teenager, he thinks,

> he would like her to be younger than he was and to be in a lower grade at school . . . ; after seeing the way his parents lived, he would like to live like that. Not as poor, perhaps, but with a woman who would be like his mother, but with this difference; she must be well educated. A very quiet and submissive woman, a good cook, a good listener, a good worker, a good mother with a good education to match. But her education must be a little less than his own, otherwise they would start talking on the same level.

Nko, however, will not accept this inequality. She wants an education and a husband as well, but not one who will govern her behavior. She refuses to reassure him that she was a virgin when they first made love, a question which drives him to seek advice from the Reverend Professor Ikot, a spiritual and educational leader. Ikot in turn appoints himself Nko's advisor and offers her the choice of sleeping with him or losing her degree. Nko, feeling men have forced her into this position, decides to use "bottom power" to get what she wants. The results are mixed and painful, but in the end Miss Buleweo, Ete's creative writing teacher, helps him to understand his feelings and accept his responsibility as a modern African man who is able to love his woman regardless of her ability to fit traditional molds.

The novel's perspective is strongly feminist, a mature feminism sensitive to the struggle of both men and women to free themselves from double standards and hypocrisy. An older woman student pinpoints the dilemma of Nko and her friends:

> **Here feminism means everything the society says is bad in women. Independence, outspokenness, immorality, all the ills you can think of. So even the educated ones who are classically feminist and liberated in their attitudes and behavior, will come round and say to you, "but I am gentle and not the pushful type."**

While such problems are true for most women, the world Emecheta describes is specifically Nigerian and considerably different from the pre-independence Africa of earlier novelists such as Chinua Achebe. Elements of village life remain, but here the local celebration depicted is a thanksgiving service and party for a young woman who has passed her hair-dressing exams. Lengthy passages discuss the unreliability of electrical power, the difficulty of crossing auto-clogged roads through a major market, or the educated Nigerian's penchant for titles. . . . Not only are the details different, but in a more basic sense so are the values. Characters like Ete and Nko don't question modernity so much as wonder how to incorporate it into their own lives.

Although *Double Yoke* gives us a view of this new Nigeria, it seems to be a view of the surface. One feels the pain of Ete and Nko, but not the underlying complexity of their experience or its deep connections to the communal experience of their country. The sociological passages too often intrude on the narrative, rather than make these connections. Emecheta can write with grace, insight, and humor, but she also uses stock descriptions and awkward language, and the ending is abrupt, leaving several incidents of consequence undeveloped or unresolved. In the end, *Double Yoke* is engaging but uneven, its simplicity of language, structure and characterization not always a mark of clarity but a mark of a turning unexplored. (pp. 4, 14)

> Linda Barrett Osborne, "Growing Pains in the New Nigeria," in Book World—The Washington Post, September 25, 1983, pp. 4, 14.

ROY KERRIDGE

Like Doris Lessing, Buchi Emecheta writes well about the Africa she knows, and describes vividly her first impressions of England, a country she can never quite understand. In their early semi-autobiographical novels, Lessing becomes Martha Quest and Emecheta writes of herself as Adah. Now with *The Rape of Shavi*, it looks as though Emecheta is going to follow Lessing into decline by way of futuristic fantasy.

Shavi is an imaginary country set on the fringe of the Sahara Desert, possibly to the north of Nigeria. . . . To this land, where white men are quite unknown, comes an unlikely hotch-potch of hippie-type Europeans who are fleeing an unspecified nuclear catastrophe. Most of the plot follows that of the standard adventure story, marred by a moralistic tone. A plane crashes among strange tribespeople, white aviators are made welcome by the local king, they find precious stones, repair their plane and escape just as they are going to be forcibly married to native girls. The king's son and heir stows away and has adventures of his own in England.

Writing quickly and carelessly, as if in a bad temper throughout, Emecheta succeeds in spoiling this classic yarn. The white intruders have names like Ista, Ronje and Dorf, to emphasize their international rootlessness, compared with the well-balanced Shavians of Africa. The only character in the book who almost comes to life is the scientist Flip, who emerges as a big roly-poly bear of a man, very hairy and given to jogging. The people of Shavi, most of whom are doomed to an early death from syphilis contracted from Ronje, find the white men repulsive. They compare them to orang-utans, which is clever of them as these apes live in far-off Borneo. However, it later transpires that the utans, whose name means "Man of the Woods" in Malayan, also thrive among the sands of Shavi.

Shavians speak in tribal "prithee-English" so that when they refer to the newcomers as "immigrants" with a unique "culture", it comes as a surprise. A witchdoctor talks like Enoch Powell prophesying rivers of blood, but this analogy is not pursued. In their escape from war, the crew reached Africa in a minute and a half, and then spent days wondering what continent they were on. What kind of top scientist is Flip?

This and other questions go unanswered. Finally, when the crew reach England once more, leaving the Shavians corrupt, unsettled and ruined, they find that nothing atomic has happened in their absence after all; Prince Asogba, the stowaway, is seized by a policeman and dragged straight to Pentonville as an illegal immigrant. There he learns "black military" from West Indians. Filled with bitter hatred, he returns to Shavi and completes the ruin of his people. Here the story ends—compared with Doris Lessing's epics it is mercifully short.

> Roy Kerridge, "More White Mischief," in The Times Literary Supplement, No. 4218, February 3, 1984, p. 116.

JOHN UPDIKE

[Buchi Emecheta] is Nigeria's best-known female writer. Indeed, few writers of her sex—Ama Ata Aidoo, of Ghana, is the other name that comes to mind—have arisen in any part of tropical Africa. There will surely be more; there is much to say. Miss Emecheta's novels, as their very titles indicate—*The Slave Girl, The Bride Price, The Joys of Motherhood*—concern themselves with the situation of women in a society where their role, though crucial, was firmly subordinate and where the forces of potential liberation have arrived with bewildering speed. The heroine of her new novel, *Double Yoke,* is an Efik girl, Nko, who must pursue her education at the cost of losing her boyfriend and sexually submitting to an instructor. (pp. 124-25)

[The novel] takes place in the early eighties, but for all its topicality, and along with the professional finesse that helped make it a modest best-seller in England, it retains certain traces of the oral mode. Like *Forest of a Thousand Daemons*, the book sets up a narrative frame; who is telling the tale, and why, is not taken for granted, and the narrator is not the disembodied third person who relays so much Western fiction to us, as if prose were a camera. A "new lecturer" at the University of Calabar, Miss Bulewao, is introduced with a jaunty touch of self-caricature, and sets her all-male writing class an assignment—"an imaginary story of how you would like your ideal Nigeria to be." One of her students, Ete Kamba, mulling over this tall order, remembers that Miss Bulewao also said "that oneself was always a very good topic to start writing about" and decides to write about what is uppermost in his mind: "He was going to tell the world how it all had been, between him and his Nko, until Professor Ikot came into their lives." The chapters that follow have the form of a flashback, taking Ete Kamba and Nko back to their first meeting, at the thanksgiving celebration for a local girl's passing her examination in hairdressing. . . . As the story of their involvement and of hers with Professor Ikot unfolds, the tale slips more and more into Nko's mind, and away from the talk in the male dormitories—handled creditably but without much zest—to more animated interchanges within the female rooms. Yet it all stays somehow contained within Ete Kamba's flashback, which is delivered in the form of an essay to Miss Bulewao; she asks all the right questions and urges the difficulty toward a solution as happy, given the double-yoked condition of the educated African woman, as it can be. The scribe enabled Akara-ogun to relate his pilgrim's progress to the world; the act of writing still has a power of magical release in the University of Calabar. (pp. 125-26)

The fellowship of women, wherein confession and counsel can be given, is the home base of *Double Yoke,* as it was for *The Joys of Motherhood,* whose heroine Nnu Ego, after a lifetime given to serving her patriarchal society with childbearing, realizes that "she would have been better off had she had time to cultivate those women who had offered her hands of friendship." The female students at Calabar—some of them middle-aged—have mothers who had gone into "fattening rooms" to become suitably plump brides; now they gossip about anorexia nervosa. The sense of relief, of escape from misunderstanding and harm, that accompanies Miss Emecheta's scenes of women together is like fresh air after prison. In the crucial scene of Nko's submission to Professor Ikot, the author in her distaste can scarcely bear to describe the event. . . . That marvellous "He thundered and pushed her around and promised heaven and earth" would deflate even Don Juan. However, absolute feminist fury—the wish to do away with men altogether and make a female utopia—is never expressed by Miss Emecheta or her characters, and the phrase "double yoke" is extended to describe not just Nko's plight . . . but that of Ete Kamba and his fellow young Nigerian males. At the end, Miss Bulewao tells her class that "many of you are bearing your double burdens or yokes or whatever heroically," and spells out "the community burden . . . and yet the burden of individualism." In a Third World country like Nigeria, sexual harassment is even more serious than in the West. Female virginity has a higher value, and so does education. The drop out of the educated élite back into the villages is precipitous; the options to "the system" are few, and the rungs on the ladder of success are rigidly set. Nko, Professor Ikot tells Ete Kamba, is "made for the Commissioner or the Professorial class, you know those on salary level sixteen and over. You'll be lucky to get level seven when you finish here." Monsters and peril still rule in the new Africa, though they take the form of lascivious professors and loss of status. Miss Emecheta does not have to manufacture suspense and seriousness; issues of survival lie inherent in her material, and give her tales weight even when, as in this case, they are relatively light and occasional. Africans still have something exciting to tell each other, which is that the path of safety is narrow. (pp. 126, 129)

John Updike, "Three Tales from Nigeria," in The New Yorker, Vol. LX, No. 10, April 23, 1984, pp. 119-26, 129.

MICHIKO KAKUTANI

When we first get a glimpse of Shavi, Buchi Emecheta's mythical African kingdom [in *The Rape of Shavi*], it looks like an idealized community of noble savages, photographed in living color for National Geographic. Under the benevolent rule of fat, laconic King Patayon, Shavi's people live happily by the shores of the Ogene lakes, tending their cows and date palms. Almost everyone is tall and handsome and content. There is no discord here, no killing. . . . For centuries, in fact, Shavi has been at peace—that is, until one day, a bright, birdlike object tumbles out of the sky. The object, the Shavians soon discover, is not a gift from the gods, but an airplane filled with Europeans trying to flee the coming nuclear holocaust.

In many respects, this setup will remind the reader of Jamie Uys's movie *The Gods Must Be Crazy* in which a Coke bottle, dropped from a plane, disrupts a tranquil African community by introducing the alien Western concepts of ownership and envy. But if Miss Emecheta, like Mr. Uys, is interested in the collision of cultures, her narrative approach turns out to be very different. Though *The Rape of Shavi* has its humorous moments (or moments that are presumably meant to be funny), it is less a comedy than an allegorical tale, filled with ponderous morals about the evils of imperialism and tired aphorisms about nature and civilization.

As befits such an old-fashioned fable, *The Rape of Shavi* features assorted biblical references (the name of the plane that the Europeans have used to flee is the "Newark") and characters who are not fully dressed individuals, but broadly-drawn representative figures. Unfortunately, Miss Emecheta . . . fails to use her considerable charms as a storyteller to endow these creatures with even the slightest hint of real personality, and they quickly degenerate into lumpish cartoon sketches.

Among the white people who crash-land in Shavi are Flip, the requisite liberal, who is forever babbling away about the innocence and charm of the natives, and his alter-ego, Ronje, an arrogant neo-colonial, who believes that "when a white man lands in a place like this, he is always superior. He makes the native his servant, not the other way round." Besides the henpecked king, the Shavian contingent includes Asogba, his arrogant, ambitious son, who is eager to embrace the ways of the West, and his nubile fiancée, who is innocent about everything modern.

One of the few things that the white and black characters in this novel have in common is a truly amazing dimness: one of the European refugees keeps wondering "how could the people of Shavi be that important if no one had ever heard of them," and it takes the Shavians days to figure out that the pale-skinned creatures from the plane are actually human beings. For Miss Emecheta, these racial blind-spots provide an excuse for lots of predictable scenes about the problems of coping with an alien culture—scenes, familiar to us now, from old Tarzan movies and even television shows like "Gilligan's Island." The whites, for instance, worry that the Shavians will either eat them or sacrifice them to their gods; and when those fears are allayed, they begin worrying about how to cope without such Western niceties as birth-control pills.

In the hands of an Evelyn Waugh or a William Boyd, such situations might make for funny and effective satire, but Miss Emecheta is so self-conscious about getting her messages across that she brings every promising sequence slamming to a halt with didactic little announcements. Instead of dramatizing her characters' feelings, she sticks trite homilies in their mouths— "The fact that their culture's different doesn't make us more human than they are," observes one of the more sympathetic white characters—and when it's difficult to saddle one of them with a heavy pronouncement, the author simply spells out the moral herself. . . .

In such works as *A Bend in the River,* V. S. Naipaul addressed this same theme of "black men assuming the lies of white men," and his skepticism of ideology, combined with his fierce, dispassionate prose, invested it with disturbing, emotional power. Miss Emecheta's interpretation, in contrast, is so pat, so superficial, that the reader is barely moved to shrug.

Michiko Kakutani, "Africa Despoiled," in The New York Times, February 23, 1985, p. 16.

PAUL BAILEY

[Buchi Emecheta's autobiography, *Head Above Water*], is certainly long enough, and could have benefited from judicious pruning. It told me more than I wanted to know about Ms Emecheta's fiction, which runs to some 14 volumes. She calls her novels her children, and refers to them in terms of maternal pride. I found myself embarrassed by such excessive devotion.

Yet there is a great deal to praise in this slapdash memoir. Buchi Emecheta recreates the Nigeria of her childhood with a vivid immediacy. The story of Lorlu and his friend Burma, who kidnapped husbands in order to vanquish Hitler, is beguilingly told: many years passed before she discovered that Lorlu was in fact Lord Louis Mountbatten, and that Burma was a country, not a monster. And the chapter dealing with her time at the Methodist Girls High School in Lagos, where the forbidding Miss Humble taught English Literature, beautifully evokes the spirit of moral uplift the missionaries brought to their pagan charges. Ms Emecheta is herself a Christian, and her faith has its origins in the education she received from the ladies who taught her in the immediate post-war years. . . .

Writing of such patent sincerity as Buchi Emecheta's presents the reader—this reader, anyway—with unusual difficulties. The open-heartedness is disarming, true, but the constant appeals to one's affection and admiration caused me to arm myself to the teeth. Still, to expect caution and reticence from her is to ask for a wholly different writer. She is her own woman, and she wouldn't have it otherwise.

> Paul Bailey, "Out of Africa," in The Observer, December 28, 1986, p. 20.

VAL WILMER

[Autobiographies] are not easy, as the author of the acclaimed *The Bride Price, The Slave Girl* and *Joys of Motherhood* acknowledges. Once you get past the early part, honesty can be problematic. Her first two novels, *In the Ditch* and *Second Class Citizen*, were thinly veiled autobiography, but [in *Head Above Water*], without the pretence of fiction, she finds herself on stonier ground. Sometimes she treads carefully, sometimes she stumbles.

It must have been a relief, though, to admit that she was the 'Adah' of her earlier books: arriving in gloomy, hostile England to have her hopes dashed within hours; then to have her expectations of her husband damaged beyond redemption. (p. 30)

The realities of Black life here continued to shock her. She came from a background where education ensured respect and a future. Working with disaffected Black youth in Paddington, she soon realised that though she might have 'made it' educationally, she had done so at the expense of those failed by the education system. She recognized herself as having joined the Black middle-class, the buffer-zone created by whites to keep the 'sufferers' at a distance.

Her frankness about social issues has enraged some Black people in the past and there will be those who will dispute the advisability of her echoing the attitudes of certain 'popular' sociologists when it comes to young Blacks and crime. But she is nothing if not courageous. She admits when she was wrong, describes each learning process undergone. As her story unfolds, it becomes apparent that her Sociology training has a good deal to answer for in shaping her analysis.

Head Above Water, self-published after difficulties with earlier titles, suffers from careless editing. Nevertheless, the story of her progress, sometimes blind and battered, as she drags herself out of 'the ditch', is educational material for those white feminists and others on the 'Black reality' bandwagon who cannot imagine hard times existing outside America's ghettoes and the Black Belt South.

Buchi admits she is not one of the world's greatest writers and, for sure, she is no Alice Walker or Virginia Woolf. But . . . it is in the African story-telling tradition that her work should be seen. Libations of whisky were poured over *Second Class Citizen* when it was published, kolanut broken in celebration by Ibusa friends. She has suffered their criticism as she pursued her personal freedom, but is still a child of her people. (pp. 30-1)

Just as the earlier narratives of Africans-in-England, by Ignatius Sancho and Olaudah Equiano, were eagerly devoured in the 18th century, so Black books continue to find a growing readership. Many white readers are thirsty for a picture of any Black experience as an antidote to centuries of anthropological study. Equally, they are curious to read what Africans and those of African descent have to say about what Langston Hughes called 'The Ways of White Folks'—however bitter the pill may be to swallow. The publisher who told Buchi, 'Africa is out now, Australia is in,' will have little effect on curiosity of that kind. (p. 31)

> Val Wilmer, "Not Drowning," in New Statesman, Vol. 113, No. 2915, February 6, 1987, pp. 30-1.

ANNA GRIMSHAW

Head Above Water may have been made redundant by [Emecheta's] novels. It is curiously empty and lacks the detail and sensitivity of Emecheta's earlier work. In it there are many indications that in her eagerness to get on, she has cut herself off from the milieux which so stimulated and developed her creative talent. This is particularly evident in the only section of the book which compels interest: Emecheta's encounter with black youth in the Harrow Road area. . . . Her description in *Head Above Water* of The Seventies youth club and the Dashiki self-help project, where she worked for a period, is a damning indictment of black middle-class attempts to control rebellious black adolescents. Her writing on black youth fails to convey the camaraderie between the women of Pussy Cat Mansions which permeated *In The Ditch*. Her perspective has changed: she is no longer part of a community, but appointed to be in charge of it. Her position parallels that of Carol, the social worker at Pussy Cat, who behaved with an uncertain mixture of sympathy, patronizingness and control. Emecheta, however, does not make the connection.

Head Above Water documents Buchi Emecheta's struggle to escape the marginality of being black, female and poor in Britain. Unfortunately, she has written much more interestingly about this in her novels. She has certainly arrived, but this book suggests that her success may have been achieved at the cost of losing her creative sources. It is not clear in which direction her literary talents can now develop, but readers should return to her novels to savour the richness of her past.

> Anna Grimshaw, "Out of the Ditch," in The Times Literary Supplement, No. 4378, February 27, 1987, p. 204.

Loren D. Estleman

1952-

American novelist and short story writer.

Estleman has attracted a devoted readership for his novels written in the "hard-boiled" detective tradition established by such authors as Dashiell Hammett and Raymond Chandler. In his books, Estleman employs a taut, energetic prose style to delve into the seedy world of urban crime. Although sometimes faulted for overly complex, implausible plots, Estleman is generally praised for his colorful characterizations and spirited dialogue. Newgate Callendar considers Estleman "among the top echelon of American private-eye specialists."

Many of Estleman's novels are set in Detroit and feature private investigator Amos Walker, a cynical, unsentimental Vietnam veteran who recalls both Chandler's Philip Marlowe and Hammett's Sam Spade. Walker first appears in *Motor City Blue* (1980), in which an organized crime figure hires him to locate a missing girl. The second novel in the series, *Angel Eyes* (1981), centers on Walker's search for a nightclub singer who has disappeared. This book prompted Jean M. White to write: "Estleman knows the seamy underworld of Detroit's mean streets. He has a nice touch for its characters and language. His knife-sharp prose matches the hurtling pace of the action." In *The Midnight Man* (1982), Walker seeks revenge for the near-fatal shooting of a friend in the Detroit police department, and in *The Glass Highway* (1983), he becomes entangled in the city's drug trafficking wars. Other Walker novels include *Sugartown* (1984), in which he attempts to locate a man who has been missing for nineteen years, and *Lady Yesterday* (1987), which recounts Walker's battle with a mob from Colombia.

In *Kill Zone* (1984), Estleman introduces Peter Macklin, a former mobster who works out of Detroit as a freelance assassin. This novel chronicles Macklin's efforts to rescue the hostages of a hijacked Detroit River tour boat. One reviewer remarked that *Kill Zone* has "enough action and colorful characters for three ordinary thrillers." In *Roses Are Dead* (1985), Macklin must discover who has put out a contract on his life, and in *Any Man's Death* (1986), he is assigned to protect a television evangelist from the murder attempts of Macklin's own son. In addition to his detective fiction, Estleman has also created two pastiches of Arthur Conan Doyle's Sherlock Holmes stories, *Sherlock Holmes vs. Dracula; or, The Adventure of the Sanguinary Count by John H. Watson* (1978) and *Dr. Jekyll and Mr. Holmes* (1979). He has also written several novels in the western genre, including *The Hider* (1978), *Stamping Ground* (1980), *Murdock's Law* (1982), and *The Stranglers* (1984).

(See also *Contemporary Authors*, Vols. 85-88.)

BOOKLIST

One more of Sherlock Holmes' astounding cases comes to light [in *Sherlock Holmes vs. Dracula*] as Estleman unearths yet another of Dr. Watson's lost accounts of detective deduction. Filling in the lapses of Bram Stoker's *Dracula,* Watson tells

Photograph by Sally Powers. Courtesy of Loren D. Estleman.

how Holmes was called in to seek out and pursue the Transylvanian vampire when the fiend took to England in search of fresh blood. Estleman creates a decent evocation of the Conan Doyle style in this sprightly pastiche.

> *A review of "Sherlock Holmes vs. Dracula," in* Booklist, *Vol. 75, No. 2, September 15, 1978, p. 154.*

R. F. GRADY, S.J.

[In *Sherlock Holmes vs. Dracula*], Sherlock Holmes and Count Dracula are united, and again the redoubtable Doctor Watson is supposed to be writing the account. The good Doctor is supposed to have died in 1940; at any rate, Mr. Estleman pretends to be editing an account written by Doctor Watson, from a manuscript found in a box deeded to a remote nephew in Canada. It is all of a piece with the original Conan Doyle stories, which should be recommendation enough for any (if there are any left) enthusiasts for more Sherlock Holmes tales or "adventures." The long-toothed Vampire is supposed in this tale to have descended upon England with the threat of turning all he kills into vampires such as he. . . . [The] end is predictable and to this reviewer, unsatisfactory. But the imitation of Watson's late-Victorian prose is admirably done.

R. F. Grady, S.J., in a review of "Sherlock Holmes vs. Dracula," in Best Sellers, *Vol. 38, No. 9, December, 1978, p. 283.*

KIRKUS REVIEWS

[In *Dr. Jekyll and Mr. Holmes*], Holmes and Watson are asked by an acquaintance of Dr. Jekyll's to investigate the unexplainable connection between posh Jekyll and this horrible low-life gnome Mr. Hyde—who is the culprit in various London crimes. So they follow Hyde around (Holmes often in disguise), research Jekyll's past (to Edinburgh and back), gain assistance from Holmes' brother Mycroft, and finally reach the laboratory showdown with poor Dr. Jekyll. Unfortunately, though Estleman does a better, deadpan job of recreating Conan Doyle's Watson style than many, he forgets that, without mystery, there is no Holmes—and here, we know all along what Sherlock is trying to deduce.

A review of "Dr. Jekyll and Mr. Holmes," in Kirkus Reviews, *Vol. XLVII, No. 18, September 15, 1979, p. 1091.*

NEWGATE CALLENDAR

[Will] Sherlock Holmes pastiches ever cease? Nicholas Meyer has done a great deal of damage with his *Seven Per Cent Solution.* Ever since the success of that book, Holmes stories in "newly discovered" Watson manuscripts have been clogging the presses, and most of them are atrocious. The latest in the unlovely series is *Dr. Jekyll and Mr. Holmes* by Loren D. Estleman, and at least one thing can be said in its favor. Mr. Estleman has the Doyle idiom down more securely than most of the imitators. Otherwise it is a pretty lifeless piece of work. It ends with Holmes and Watson telling the story of the case to a writer named Robert Louis Stevenson. (pp. 22, 24)

Newgate Callendar, in a review of "Dr. Jekyll and Mr. Holmes," in The New York Times Book Review, *November 11, 1979, pp. 22, 24.*

JEAN M. WHITE

In Loren D. Estleman's *Motor City Blue,* private-eye Amos Walker's city is Detroit with its sleazy alleys in the shadow of the new Renaissance Center. Walker is hired by an aging mobster to find his ward, who disappeared from a fashionable girls' finishing school. The only lead is a nude photograph of the girl. It takes Walker to brothels, porno shops, a whorehouse madam, and a helpful prostitute drug addict. It turns out that the missing girl also is linked to the murder of Walker's old army buddy, who filmed the execution of a black labor leader by a local Ku Klux Klan.

Walker and Detroit could turn into a winning combination. But Estleman has lapses of florid overwriting that border on parody of the hard boiled style: "a complexion like 12-year-old Scotch going down" and "the air was as bitter as a stiffed hooker."

Jean M. White, in a review of "Motor City Blue," in Book World—The Washington Post, *September 21, 1980, p. 14.*

PHILIP S. COONLEY

Perhaps [*Dr. Jekyll and Mr. Holmes*] really was written by Watson himself. Yet as those who have already raced through the complete works of Sherlock Holmes well know, there is such a longing for more Sherlock Holmes that one could easily embrace a forgery. But why would a forger draw full attention to the storytelling *per se,* choosing a tale whose basic outlines are already well known? Why not concoct an entirely new tale of mystery? Then the reader might so focus on the case itself, that small lapses in the authenticity of style, character, and description, and nuance of deductive reasoning might be missed.... Shrewder Sherlockians than I must look into this case. They'll certainly enjoy it.

Philip S. Coonley, in a review of "Dr. Jekyll and Mr. Holmes," in Kliatt Young Adult Paperback Book Guide, *Vol. XV, No. 1, January, 1981, p. 10.*

JEAN M. WHITE

Amos Walker, who made his debut in Loren D. Estleman's *Motor City Blue* last year, is as tough and hard-boiled as private eyes come. No dowdy clients for Walker. In *Angel Eyes,* he is hired by a nightclub singer with a strange request—to find her after she has disappeared.

Within hours, Walker has stumbled over his first corpse (more to come) and soon finds himself entangled in a web of his client's past relationships. First, there is the powerful union boss, who once gave her a ring. Then there is the long-missing judge, who disappeared in a plane crash and left a mistress as well as a wife and stepson. The judge may have had shady business deals on the side. It all ends in a shootout that leaves more bodies on center stage than the last scene of a Shakespearean tragedy.

Estleman knows the seamy underworld of Detroit's mean streets. He has a nice touch for its characters and language. His knife-sharp prose matches the hurtling pace of the action. But he should block those outlandish metaphors. *Angel Eyes* is unadorned hardboiled detective fiction. No new ground is broken, but it works quite well within the framework of formula. (pp. 6, 14)

Jean M. White, in a review of "Angel Eyes," in Book World—The Washington Post, *October 18, 1981, pp. 6, 14.*

NEWGATE CALLENDAR

About a year ago Loren D. Estleman delivered himself of a novel featuring Amos Walker, a private eye who works out of Detroit. *Motor City Blue* turned out to be a competent composite—and the word is used advisedly—of the stereotypes of the hard-boiled species. Now comes *Angel Eyes,* and Amos Walker rides again.

Rides again, and talks much the same way. Unfortunately, the author is so determined to evoke the Hammett-Chandler school that he leaves his ear and discrimination aside. Here is a tough, street-wise cop talking to Walker: "... and that suit you're wearing went out with poems that rhyme." Nice. Cute. But would that figure of speech have come out of the mouth of such a character? ...

Tough is tough, but inanity is also inanity. Mr. Estleman can write, but he can also be terribly careless. "Angel Eyes" is hired by a dancer in a sleazy nightclub to trace her if she disappears, which she promptly does. So Walker has to contend with a big-time hood, a labor leader and assorted mayhem before he sorts everything out. (p. 41)

*Newgate Callendar, in a review of "Angel Eyes,"
in* The New York Times Book Review, *November
1, 1981, pp. 41-2.*

ROBIN W. WINKS

It's not clear which void Loren D. Estleman would like to fill,
though with his new exploration of the underside of Detroit,
Angel Eyes, he ought to make most readers temporarily forget
their yearning for another Hammett or Chandler. Detroit's Renaissance Center rises over the action in satiric comment on
the grimy action below: a nightclub dancer disappears, the head
of the United Steelhaulers Union is dragged down, and the
denouement is straight out of *Red Harvest.* Estleman handles
the English language with real imagination, perhaps second
only to Joseph Hansen by now, so that one keeps reading for
the sheer joy of seeing the phrases fall into place.

Robin W. Winks, in a review of "Angel Eyes," in
The New Republic, *Vol. 185, No. 21, November 25,
1981, p. 39.*

KIRKUS REVIEWS

In this third episode for narrator-shamus Amos Walker of Detroit [**The Midnight Man**], Estleman's modest yet steady wit
(in both the downbeat narration and the upbeat dialogue) again
just about compensates for the lackluster plotting. Walker is
working for free this time: he owes cop Van Sturdevant a favor;
so when Sturdevant is crippled in a shoot-out with three black
murderers (two of whom are soon killed by the police), Walker
agrees to go after murderer #3—Alonzo Smith—when Smith
is sprung from custody by a black terrorist group. . . . Minimal
suspense and only the mildest final-twist surprise—but the Detroit milieu remains a plus, and the supporting characters (though
not as colorful as in previous Walkers) supply some of the
liveliness that's missing in the action.

A review of "The Midnight Man," in Kirkus Reviews, *Vol. L, No. 13, July 1, 1982, p. 764.*

NEWGATE CALLENDAR

Amos Walker, who made his debut in Mr. Estleman's **Motor
City Blue** (1980), is a private detective who works out of Detroit. In the latest adventure in which he appears, **The Midnight
Man,** Walker is pitted against three killers from Detroit's underworld. When a cop Walker knows gets shot and becomes
a vegetable, Walker vows to find the assassin. A personal
element is involved: Walker and the cop had been working on
the same case.

A bounty hunter enters the case, and what a character he turns
out to be. Walker gets beaten up an awful lot. At the end there
is something of a surprise and Walker, that man of action,
takes care of it the best way he can—with his gun. All this is
tough, side-of-the-mouth stuff, well written, positively guaranteed to keep you awake.

*Newgate Callendar, in a review of "The Midnight
Man," in* The New York Times Book Review, *August 22, 1982, p. 26.*

KIRKUS REVIEWS

[In **The Glass Highway**], Detroit's narrator-shamus Amos
Walker . . . is hired by local TV-anchorman Sandy Broderick,
to find his missing son Bud: though Broderick has not seen
young Bud in years (divorce, remarriage), he's afraid the kid
is about to be arrested as a druggie—making Dad look bad.
And Walker has no trouble locating the 20-year-old runaway,
who is indeed living in seedy, druggy squalor with an enigmatic
young woman named Paula Royce. End of case? So it seems.
But then Bud is found murdered, Paula begs for Walker's help
in fleeing to Canada (not entirely credibly, he obliges), and
she's later reported dead. . . . So Walker, who suffers imprisonment as well as physical abuse, is eager to figure out just
what's going on: clearly it has *something* to do with a drug-
traffic power struggle . . . and with Paula's dead-end past. As
usual, a little too contrived, with that wearisome drug-angle
yet again—but a couple of the twists are neat, Walker's wry-
rough delivery is in good form, and this may be his best outing
yet: varied, busily peopled, relatively fast.

A review of "The Glass Highway," in Kirkus Reviews, *Vol. LI, No. 14, July 15, 1983, p. 791.*

CONNIE FLETCHER

Sometimes what's lost should not be found. Detroit private
eye Amos Walker learns this [in **The Glass Highway**] on a
disappearance case that leads him eye-brow-high into danger.
Walker is hired to find TV news anchor Sandy Broderick's 20-
year-old son, Bud, who has vanished with a young female dope
addict. Walker successfully locates Bud, but is then enmeshed
within the web of a drug-scene power struggle. Good plotting
and the authentic Detroit atmosphere are somewhat marred here
by Estleman's almost grotesque overuse of hardboiled conventions.

*Connie Fletcher, in a review of "The Glass High-
way," in* Booklist, *Vol. 80, No. 1, September 1,
1983, p. 30.*

NEWGATE CALLENDAR

[**The Glass Highway**] is the fourth in the series featuring Amos
Walker, the Detroit operative. He is hired by a television an-
chorman to find a missing (adult) son. Walker promptly finds
him, but the case does not end there. A girl who is a drug
addict enters the picture, there is a murder, and Walker finds
himself helping the murder suspect. Knighthood is still in flower.

So Walker gets into trouble. The police throw him into the
can. His license is yanked. A mysterious hit man starts moving
around, going bump in the night. There is some very tough
stuff in **The Glass Highway,** with dialogue to match. The usual
alienation symbols are ever-present, including the bleak last
sentence of the book: "I drank liquor and watched the snow
cover the glassy surface stretching on and on into the darkness." *The Glass Highway* is written with Mr. Estleman's usual
competence, and he remains among the top echelon of American private-eye specialists.

*Newgate Callendar, in a review of "The Glass High-
way," in* The New York Times Book Review, *October 23, 1983, p. 38.*

PUBLISHERS WEEKLY

Estleman, creator of the Amos Walker private eye series, introduces Peter Macklin, Detroit hit man, in [*Kill Zone*], a book with enough action and colorful characters for three ordinary thrillers. Eight people calling themselves "Siegfried" hijack a Detroit excursion boat and hold hundreds of passengers hostage, demanding the release of "political" prisoners from Michigan's state prison. A cabinet member's daughter is aboard the booby-trapped boat and the FBI accepts the offer of a jailed Mafia don, Michael Boniface, to help, in his bid for parole. The don says, "Get me Macklin," and Macklin takes the job. . . . Good guys, bad guys and "ordinary" citizens are all distinctively portrayed, and the plot twists and turns are dazzling. Macklin may seem a bit remote and shadowy, but that's not inappropriate in this whiz-bang of a book. (pp. 45-6)

> *A review of "Kill Zone," in* Publishers Weekly, *Vol. 226, No. 2, July 13, 1984, pp. 45-6.*

BILL OTT

In *Sugartown,* Loren Estleman's [fifth] Amos Walker mystery, Detroit becomes more than merely a setting: as the city's neighborhoods fall prey to the wrecker's ball, the dreams and even the very histories of its residents become part of the rubble. From this morass, the tough-talking Walker attempts to find a man missing for 19 years. His investigation leads him to a smuggler of religious icons, a cantankerous Russian novelist, and two beautiful women. Estleman deftly manipulates the familiar ingredients of the hard-boiled mystery, but, finally, it is his use of place as metaphor that elevates his novel beyond the usual Chandleresque journey down our changing but still-mean streets.

> *Bill Ott, in a review of "Sugartown," in* Booklist, *Vol. 81, No. 6, November 15, 1984, p. 401.*

NEWGATE CALLENDAR

In *Kill Zone* by Loren D. Estleman, the author tries to get into the world of professional killers. When a terrorist group in which there is a hired killer—let's call him Killer A—takes over a Detroit riverboat and holds several hundred persons as hostages, Killer B is hired by a secret Government agency to get rid of the terrorists. But the head of the local Mafia engages Killer C to get rid of Killer B. . . .

The premise of the book is dubious. Mr. Estleman has tried to create archetypes of today's hired professional killer. He wants us to admire them. At least, in today's confused world (he is saying), here are people who know exactly what they are doing and are supremely good at it. But the ending is ridiculous, and not even Mr. Estleman's considerable literary skill can hide the falsity of his thesis.

> *Newgate Callendar, in a review of "Kill Zone," in* The New York Times Book Review, *December 2, 1984, p. 62.*

KATHLEEN MAIO

One does not have to live in the gutter to be a tough guy. Loren D. Estleman proves that in *Sugartown.* Amos Walker's new adventure opens with an ironic twist on the classic scene of the beautiful dame entering our hero's office. Martha Evancek is a beauty, of sorts—a very old, physically disabled, yet fiercely proud Polish immigrant—who wants to find her grandson, the sole survivor of a domestic murder/suicide tragedy some nineteen years earlier. . . .

The search forces [Walker] to untangle old crimes as he stumbles over fresh corpses. There are bizzare elements to the plot (e.g., Walker held a drugged captive by a mad collector and his malodorous goon), but these cannot blemish the basic credibility of Estleman's story. Estleman writes so well of the threadworn respectability of working people stranded on the edge of an urban wasteland. His vivid and merciless descriptions of the revitalized Detroit root his complex story in reality.

Walker is all a tough guy p.i. should be with his superhuman talent for the cheap come back line and his sex appeal that works well, but not in lasting relationships. Estleman's Amos Walker series remains one of the best the hard-boiled field has to offer.

> *Kathleen Maio, in a review of "Sugartown," in* Wilson Library Bulletin, *Vol. 59, No. 7, March, 1985, p. 487.*

NEWGATE CALLENDAR

[*Sugartown*] is the fifth in the series featuring Amos Walker from Detroit. Walker is the very model of a Hammett-Chandler descendant. He is a big man, very macho, who talks tough and is tough. He hates hypocrisy, phonies and crooks. He pretends to cynicism but is a teddy bear underneath it all. He is lonely, though women swarm all over him.

In *Sugartown* an old Polish woman hires Walker to look for her grandson, missing for 19 years. He also is hired by a Russian writer exiled from the Soviet Union. The writer needs protection from the K.G.B., or so he claims. Apparently the two cases are unrelated. But they can't be in a traditional private-eye novel of this sort. So one reads on to applaud the legerdemain that will being both cases together. Click! They do come together—with a surprise ending, yet.

All the conventions are observed, and that includes all the usual alienation symbols. But Mr. Estleman writes with a surer touch than most practitioners, and he can turn a neat phrase. Walker is romancing a woman, puts some music on his hi-fi and kisses her. "The needle came to the end of the record meanwhile and the arm swept back and the machine turned itself off with a discreet click, like a bellhop letting himself out of the honeymoon suite." Felicitous touches like this animate *Sugartown* and make it one of the better examples of the tough-guy school.

> *Newgate Callendar, in a review of "Sugartown," in* The New York Times Book Review, *March 24, 1985, p. 29.*

PUBLISHERS WEEKLY

[In *Roses Are Dead,* someone] is trying to kill Detroit-based hitman Peter Macklin . . . and, though he has long ago severed his ties with the mob, Macklin seeks out his old associates to discover who put the contract out on him and why. With sharpshooters and sinister flame-throwing giants on his tail, the erstwhile hired killer has other problems on his hands too: his wife is suing for divorce, and his teenage son wants to follow in his father's former profession. . . . Estleman writes in a gritty, hardboiled style, but the plot is confusing and glutted with a plethora of minor characters who detract from the story's credibility.

A review of "Roses Are Dead," in Publishers Weekly, *Vol. 228, No. 8, August 23, 1985, p. 62.*

PETER L. ROBERTSON

In [*Roses Are Dead,* a] gripping sequel to Estleman's *Kill Zone,* hired killer Peter Macklin's connections with organized crime are severed, but a mysterious contract is out on his life. The first two killers are easily foiled, but an Eastern European assassin with KGB connections proves far more imposing.... Although it suffers from almost comic implausibility, *Roses Are Dead* is a guaranteed page-turner that features an intoxicating rush of brutal events and a fascinating antihero in Macklin. The conclusion leaves Macklin bloody but alive, his wife suing for divorce, and his son poised to follow in his criminal footsteps.

> *Peter L. Robertson, in a review of "Roses Are Dead," in* Booklist, *Vol. 82, No. 1, September 1, 1985, p. 4.*

NEWGATE CALLENDAR

[As] tough and grimy as they come is *Roses Are Dead* by Loren D. Estleman. The hero is Peter Macklin, hit man, who has appeared previously in the Estleman *oeuvre.* Macklin, now freelancing and also engaged in divorce proceedings, discovers a contract has been put out on him....

After a while this silly book makes one think of a Bugs Bunny cartoon in which lethal instruments brought to bear against the rabbit explode in the attackers' faces. There is also something here about the Russians, the Central Intelligence Agency and the F.B.I. Forget about it.

In his series about the private eye Amos Walker, Mr. Estleman has proved himself an expert writer, but *Roses Are Dead* reads as though he tossed it off between sundown Friday and sunrise Monday.

> *Newgate Callendar, in a review of "Roses Are Dead," in* The New York Times Book Review, *November 24, 1985, p. 43.*

BILL OTT

Most hard-boiled detectives walk a thin line between being sensitive cynics and tough-talking prigs; unfortunately, Loren D. Estleman's Amos Walker has fallen over the line in the wrong direction. Appearing in his sixth adventure [*Every Brilliant Eye*], Walker is hired by a Detroit newspaper to find a missing investigative reporter, Barry Stackpole, who has been summoned by the grand jury.... Estleman has developed a solid following through five first-rate Walker novels, but his fans are likely to be disappointed by this subpar effort. The mystery itself is acceptable enough, but Walker is simply not very likable here. His continual grousing about the character flaws in his friends makes him sound more like a whiny suburban housewife than a gruff Detroit shamus. C'mon Amos, loosen up or find some new friends.

> *Bill Ott, in a review of "Every Brilliant Eye," in* Booklist, *Vol. 82, No. 12, February 15, 1986, p. 850.*

NEWGATE CALLENDAR

If *Every Brilliant Eye* by Loren D. Estleman does not end with a whimper, it does wind up in a miasma of disillusion. But Amos Walker, the private eye in this series, does not have many illusions. He does, however, have ideals; he is a perfectionist and moralist living in an imperfect and amoral world. At least he is always true to himself.

In *Every Brilliant Eye* he has to track down a friend who has disappeared. The friend, a newspaper columnist, wrote an explosive piece about civic corruption, and a grand jury wants his notes. First Amendment issues arise. But the author is more interested in what makes people tick. And in Walker's world, what makes them tick is greed or self-interest....

Mr. Estleman's picture of Detroit is equally gloomy. Yet there is a kind of poetry in his snapshots of the underside of a city with which he so clearly has a love-hate relationship. The writing remains expert. Certainly Mr. Estleman is as good as anyone continuing the Hammett-Chandler tradition.

> *Newgate Callendar, in a review of "Every Brilliant Eye," in* The New York Times Book Review, *April 20, 1986, p. 32.*

WES LUKOWSKY

Estleman asks us to root for a hired killer in this grim but satisfying mystery [*Any Man's Death*]. The book marks the third appearance of Peter Macklin, a Detroit hit man, and it's the strongest entry in the series. Estleman, who also writes the Amos Walker private-eye novels, has created a surprisingly credible and evolving protagonist. Rooting for the hit man isn't as difficult this time because Macklin, a former Mob employee working free-lance, has been given a peculiar assignment—keeping a TV evangelist alive. Working the other side of the fence has its problems, as Macklin discovers when he finds himself caught between rival Mob families in a struggle for control of a proposed casino industry in Detroit. Matters become even more complicated when Macklin learns that it is his son who is trying to kill the evangelist. Estleman's more mature, less-Chandleresque style and an exciting climax make *Any Man's Death* a clear winner.

> *Wes Lukowsky, in a review of "Any Man's Death," in* Booklist, *Vol. 83, No. 4, October 15, 1986, p. 326.*

NEWGATE CALLENDAR

If Donald Westlake no longer seems to be writing Parker novels (under the name of Richard Stark), Loren D. Estleman has been trying to pick up the slack, as evidenced by *Any Man's Death.* Parker was a thief and amoral gun for hire, and so is Peter Macklin in this Estleman series. Both authors are of the realistic school. Both have tried to present their central figures as highly trained, efficient, unemotional specialists doing a particular kind of job.

But there is a difference. Mr. Estleman lacks the cold, dispassionate quality that Mr. Westlake brought to Parker. He tries too hard, and there are too many false touches, too many inconsistencies, too much sloppy writing. Mr. Estleman chases clichés unrelentingly....

[As] *Any Man's Death* opens, Macklin has left the mob and is acting as his own agent. But he takes on a mob job anyway and then accepts a contract on a public figure. His life is complicated by the fact that his 17-year-old son has also set himself up in business as a hit man. A lot of double-dealing and double-crossing ensues, as well as a kidnapping, all kinds of fireworks and an ending in which the coldblooded Macklin acts in a peculiarly emotional manner—and pays the price.

> *Newgate Callendar, in a review of "Any Man's Death," in* The New York Times Book Review, *October 26, 1986, p. 47.*

ROBERT A. BAKER

Few would argue that the best fictional private eye in the Greater Detroit area is anyone other than Loren Estleman's ex-Vietnam MP Amos Walker. In [*Every Brilliant Eye*], Amos is visited by a redheaded ex-hooker who has been living with his old war buddy, Barry Stackpole. According to the redhead, Barry has fallen off the wagon again despite Amos's earnest efforts to prevent it. Moreover, Barry, a successful newspaper columnist, has written a book that could blow the lid off a labor-union-organized-crime linkage involving the local police force. Everyone wants either Barry or the book, or both, burned. . . .

Regretfully, this is not the best of the Walker outings. Although the writing is as polished and engaging as ever, the story line lacks the freshness and fast pace of *Motor City Blue* or *Angel Eyes,* and the characters are not as sharply drawn as those in Estleman's Shamus Award-winning *Sugartown*. What little violence there is in *Every Brilliant Eye* is so subdued and off-hand that it almost seems irrelevant. The entire work is very low-key and offers little in the way of Estleman's usual suspense, surprise, or excitement. Yet, if you are an Amos Walker fan, you will not want to miss it. If you have never read him before, you are advised to start with one of Estleman's earlier efforts, say, *The Glass Highway* or *The Midnight Man*. These two show Amos and Estleman at their breathtaking best.

> *Robert A. Baker, in a review of "Every Brilliant Eye," in* The Armchair Detective, *Vol. 20, No. 1, Winter, 1987, p. 88.*

KIRKUS REVIEWS

[In *Lady Yesterday*], Detroit shamus Amos Walker (*Sugartown, Motor City Blue,* etc.) goes looking for a reformed hooker's long-lost father—and finds himself in an unexpected death-duel with Colombian mobsters.

Iris, a beautiful West Indian from Amos's past, has gone straight; she's about to get married and settle down in Jamaica. But before leaving the US for good, she wants Amos to help her find her father: a jazz trombonist named Georgie Favor who never married her Jamaican mother, let alone stayed around to be a real father. So Amos starts talking to old jazz players and buffs, searching for near-great Georgie, last seen washing dishes in a local dive three years ago. Meanwhile, however, Iris becomes the target of strange death-threats; when she stays at a motel, the sleazy night manager turns up murdered; then Amos himself is menaced by a Colombian mob chieftain—who has good reason to want Iris out of the country . . . or dead. And it's only after a bloody battle to protect Iris (with help from the Colombian's mobster-rivals) that a much-battered Amos locates Iris' dad—in a small, satisfying twist.

Estleman's metaphor-laden narration for hard-boiled, dour, philosophical Amos occasionally veers off from seedy elo-

quence into silly pretension. . . . And there's only a smidgin of conventional mystery-detection here. But the various plot-strands are woven together without excess contrivance; the lowdown Detroit backgrounds are, as usual, sketched in with moody conviction; and, flavored with jazz-club nostalgia and world-weary gallantry, this is one of the most satisfying—if least flashy—of the Walker exploits.

> *A review of "Lady Yesterday," in* Kirkus Reviews, *Vol. LV, No. 7, April 1, 1987, p. 515.*

BILL OTT

The seventh entry in Estleman's Amos Walker detective series [*Lady Yesterday*] finds the brow-beaten Detroit PI back in good form after the disappointing *Every Brilliant Eye,* in which the wisecracks were telegraphed two lines in advance and the world-weariness sounded too much like literary whining. This time Walker earns his phlegmatic attitude, and the tough-guy patter has the ring of actual speech. The plot involves ex-prostitute Iris' search for her father, a jazz trombonist from the swing era who has disappeared somewhere on Detroit's mean streets. . . . Readers who share Estleman's dissatisfaction with the plastic 1980's—symbolized by Detroit's Renaissance Center—will jump at the chance to lose themselves in this tribute to an age when the music was sweet and the trench coats didn't cost $300.

> *Bill Ott, in a review of "Lady Yesterday," in* Booklist, *Vol. 83, No. 16, April 15, 1987, p. 1251.*

ALAN RYAN

I've read Loren D. Estleman's Sherlock Holmes books and don't like them. I've also read a couple of his westerns. Those I like. But I haven't read his mysteries, and mystery readers know Estleman best as the creator of Amos Walker, a Detroit private eye. *Lady Yesterday* is the latest.

I admire writers who do good first-person narrative, the way James Lee Burke does. Estleman does it, too, letting Walker tell his own tale in a tough but civilized sort of Motor City voice. I like it from the first line that jerks you into the story: "It was February by the time I caught up with Clara Rainey . . ." And I understand Walker when he talks about work that gets to be "like licking stamps eight hours a day." And . . . I recognize the voice that says, "the kind of beat I am sleep can't cure." I like his habit of personalizing the negative element in his world ("I kept on my hat and coat—no one had offered to take them away.") and his smart-aleck turns of phrase, like this one to a thug who wants to know why he went to police headquarters: "I lost my virginity. I thought someone might have turned it in."

Besides all this great narrative and dialogue, Estleman provides a plot with the basic ingredients of murders old and new, women reformed and otherwise, danger, suspense and plenty of action. All of this is good. I'm caught up in the story, but best of all is the way Estleman writes about jazz, the sound of it, the smoky clubs it lives in and the musicians who play it. A few pages, for example, make an old black musician living in a trailer, his music all behind him, as vivid as if you'd known him yourself. Well done. I like Estleman.

> *Alan Ryan, "Lady Sings the Blues," in* Book World—The Washington Post, *May 17, 1987, p. 6.*

Sheila Fugard
1932-

English-born South African novelist and poet.

The wife of acclaimed dramatist Athol Fugard and an established author in England and South Africa, Fugard has garnered critical attention in the United States for *A Revolutionary Woman* (1985), her first novel to be published in North America. In this work, Fugard utilizes the Gandhian concept of *satyagraha,* or passive resistance, to address her country's social problems. Set in a remote South African town in 1920, Fugard's narrative revolves around Christina Ransome, a British teacher and former disciple of Mohandas Gandhi whose faith in Gandhi's nonviolent philosophy is tested when she offers sanctuary to a half-caste student accused of impregnating a retarded white girl. Christina's idealism and trust in *satyagraha* is shattered when the student rapes her and commits suicide before an angry mob. While some reviewers cited historical and linguistic inconsistencies in her depiction of the era, most praised Fugard's skill at rendering emotion and her unusual approach to her subject matter. Elinor Langer commented: "[It] is perhaps the highest tribute to this strange and original novel to say that it has the power to make one imagine, if only fleetingly, a different outcome to events in South Africa than the one for which it seems to be heading."

Fugard's first novel, *The Castaways* (1972), is a surreal account of a group of eighteenth-century settlers who survived a shipwreck off the South African coast. *Rite of Passage* (1977) details the moral dilemmas of a physician who abandons his practice to undertake an anthropological study of a primitive tribe. Fugard has also written *Threshold* (1975), an eclectic volume of confessional and historical verse.

Photograph by John Smallcombe. Courtesy of Sheila Fugard.

THE TIMES LITERARY SUPPLEMENT

Sheila Fugard's first book [*The Castaways*] is a highly original work that is unlike anything else to come from South Africa. In part a meditation on spiritual and political power, it moves with sure imaginative conviction from 1770 to the present and looks farther into the future than most South African writers dare.

Mrs Fugard has established herself as a leading South African poet in the past three years, but her prose—"poetic" in the best sense—is better than all but her most controlled verse. . . .

Using the hallucinations of her narrator to establish her links with the past of the white castaways in an ever-alien Africa, Mrs Fugard probes the future when her narrator escapes from the hospital and meets on the beach "Captain" Patrick Choma, who has liberated his own Cuba of the mind in his fantasies and waits to be joined in revolutionary struggle by "the bread boys, the petrol attendants, the clerks". Counterpointing the madness of the narrator and Choma is the narrator's guardian angel, the Buddhist, "a person compounded of compassion and atonement". The Buddhist is perhaps the least satisfactory part of the book. It is possible that Mrs Fugard felt this, too,

for he disappears at the end, leaving the narrator to "progress in the knowledge of the void" alone. Perhaps the Buddhist has no place in today's South Africa.

"Alien Shores," in The Times Literary Supplement, *No. 3668, November 10, 1972, p. 1375.*

KAY DICK

[In *The Castaways,* Mrs Fugard] uses the technique of hallucination as a framework to a statement on racial issues. Purporting to be the narrative of a patient in a mental home, this fragmentary and disorientated nightmare is preoccupied with visions of the past, reconstructed from the story of eighteenth century castaways suffering total humiliation at the hands of a black tribe, and the future in the daydreams of a Cuban terrorist (another mental patient), both illuminated by the floating presence of a Zen character thrown in for good measure.

What Mrs Fugard is trying to say is clearly socially acceptable—that all men are brothers. Why she cannot state this with less confusion is less acceptable.

Kay Dick, "Death-Haunted," in Manchester Guardian Weekly, *November 18, 1972, p. 25.*

N. M. HODGE

Sheila Fugard, better known for her prose writings than for her poetry, develops a . . . [wide] range of experience in **Threshold**. . . . One anticipates verse concerned with social protest, but such themes are only developed indirectly. The poetry is inward-turning, but her interior landscapes are detailed, often stark, descriptions of contemporary events which have seared western man, and not merely South Africa.

Her work usually shows a firm control of structure and imagery, and the poetic voice is both confident and clear. There is a freshness and simplicity in the direct statement "My passion bounds about like a great dog" (from **"Autumn"**), but the diction at times is either shop-worn or too artificially 'poetic', even descending into the realm of bad pop-lyrics: "A step that isn't there / Only hanging in the mind". The poetess playing sage and seer sometimes grates, but such irritations are soothed in poems like **"The Seasons"** and especially **"The Cannas"**.

> Mirror
> Debauchery of plants next summer in their prime
>
> And in the seasons' stirring of their
> Malicious yearning
> Release the dark in me

in which the natural imagery is fused with a highly-imaginative response by the poetic voice. One hopes Sheila Fugard will continue to develop her abilities. (p. 108)

> *N. M. Hodge, in a review of "Threshold," in* English Studies in Africa, *Vol. 18, No. 2, September, 1975, pp. 107-08.*

CHARLES R. LARSON

[The] racial implications behind [**The Castaways**'s] basic story are so shrouded in obscurity that the reader can never be certain about a number of events which he suspects are crucial to the novel's immediate focus.

The Castaways is ostensibly concerned with a handful of whites (including women and children) who survived a shipwreck off the coast of South Africa in 1770. . . . Rumors of their existence, including women "at the mercy of the Caffre headmen" reached the colonial office and a number of rescue parties were sent out to search for them. One of the men involved, named Richard Rowntree, reported that he discovered a single, male survivor several years later. . . . Through the journals attributed to Rowntree and others, the reader learns a number of facts relating to the original castaways. The most revealing is Rowntree's comment that the white castaways put up no resistance when the Africans tormented them. It was as if the castaways were animals, cowered by a superior race: "Not one man showed any self-defence against the Caffres."

At times, Sheila Fugard's allegory is almost too simple. There is nothing especially original in suggesting that all whites in Africa are castaways, exiles—the same idea is central to Guinean writer Camara Laye's novel, *The Radiance of the King,* published in 1954—but beyond that her meaning becomes more obscure. The wider framework of her story is concerned with the present time, recorded through the hallucinating mind of a man named Christiaan Jordan, a patient in the Port Berkley Mental Hospital. It is through his eyes that we learn the fragmentary tale of the shipwrecked castaways two hundred years ago. . . . Next to Jordan's attempts to reconcile the past history of the European castaways in South Africa, Ms. Fugard juxtaposes his imaginary encounter with the black revolutionary leader, Choma, a descendant of Mulwena, the savage black warrior chief who fought the castaways two hundred years earlier.

Fugard's hallucinated patient believes that he speaks for all white South Africa: "I'm making a journey into my own life that sometimes reaches back into the past and then stretches ahead into the future." He wonders if it is possible for a white and a black South African to meet and have any kind of lasting human relationship. As he says to Choma, "I am the castaway. You are the terrorist." Yet this is not the way things are at all. In two hundred years, their positions have become reversed. (pp. 43-4)

Though the central issue of **The Castaways** is Christiaan Jordan's attempts to come to grips with his guilt-ridden past, the mirage within his mind permits him to glean no meaning from the patterns of life his white ancestors established in Africa. The fragments of the journals of the castaways from two hundred years before and the diaries kept by the men searching for them are bits and pieces of a past he is incapable of putting together. Jordan fails to understand the white man's place in modern Africa because he has not understood his own past. He lives in a self-willed hallucinated nightmare, expecting succor while in truth he fails to understand that the castaways were really invaders.

Ultimately Sheila Fugard's **The Castaways** must be regarded as a less than satisfactory novel. In spite of the general high quality of the writing itself and a number of impressive lyrical passages (Ms. Fugard also writes poetry), she has pushed her attempt to defy the censors too far. The obscurity has rendered much of her story unintelligible. The novel also owes too much to the works of her husband, playwright Athol Fugard—especially to the powerful love/hate relationship he depicts between white and black half brothers in *The Blood Knot.* But there is an even more disturbing indebtedness to Doris Lessing's *Briefing for a Descent into Hell,* a novel that also depicts an hallucinated patient in a mental hospital, undergoing a sea-journey which links his thoughts to those of his ancestors hundreds of years before. Ms. Fugard has even borrowed a term central to Lessing's novel, "inner space," but never does her work achieve the intellectual complexity of Lessing's masterpiece. **The Castaways** is, I am afraid, the kind of novel we are likely to get from South Africa for a long time to come. Sheila Fugard has talent to spare; it is tragic that her country does not permit her to develop it. (pp. 44-5)

> *Charles R. Larson, "Protest—The South African Way," in* World Literature Written in English, *Vol. 15, No. 1, April, 1976, pp. 42-5.*

EILEEN JULIEN

The message of [**Threshold**] is timely, though its tone is far from polemical. Here Sheila Fugard expresses more intensely ideas first explored in her novel **The Castaways** (1972). History has been iconoclastic: Robben Island, Hiroshima, Auschwitz—these are but a few of the twentieth-century realities which shatter and invalidate traditional "images" of civilization, its art and its faith:

> Poverty strikes us
> Not in the belly
> But in the absence of image
> I see myself
> Drift up from the stagnant pool of water
> Narcissus of the

Hydro dam
No limpid Christ
Of Italianate art
Returns my stare
I do not see him
Wherever I look
And I look everywhere.

Recognition of this modern dilemma is a "threshold." The individual must search anew—without and within—to create meaningful new patterns which will replace the old. For Fugard, one symbol of that search is Zen, "the unknowable made known." To rediscover the profound and lasting truth is to probe oneself and to explore external signs. . . .

These poems vary in focus and expression. Anguish and incomprehension at harsh realities are conveyed through a brusque and jarring style. The poet's successful combination of unlikely, incongruous elements often suggests the randomness, disorder and absurdity of "history." But more frequently the poetry is quiet and reflective as it records a spiritual voyage, an almost sacred search for new meaning.

Sometimes Fugard's thought is elliptical or the symbolism obscure; the poems are then more disconcerting than meaningful. Nevertheless, *Threshold* contains many eloquent and memorable poems. Fugard experiments with syntax and employs a beautiful, eclectic metaphor while retaining prosaic tones. This first collection of verse reveals a promising, sensitive poet.

> *Eileen Julien, in a review of "Threshold," in* World
> Literature Today, *Vol. 51, No. 1, Winter, 1977, p.*
> *147.*

HERMIONE LEE

Sheila Fugard's brief, intense novel [*Rite of Passage*] undermines South African civilisation not from within but, more daringly, from the vantage point of primitivism. A doctor, hounded from his practice because a crippled girl drowned herself after his hypnosis, journeys to the land of the 'Pedi' tribe to investigate the 'rite of passage', the circumcision of the adolescent leading to a violent, amoral 'limbo' period before manhood. He encounters a hysterical white boy who has fled civilisation after a traumatic homosexual experience. Dr James becomes a witchdoctor, makes the boy undergo the tribal rite, cures him, confesses to him in his turn, and dies. The hostility that arises between father and son, doctor and patient, is also the catharsis of each man's sexual guilt.

The power of this mythic tale stems from its well-sustained, bare, lyric, descriptive voice, which gives the oddly compelling effect of a translation: 'How could I describe the splendour? I examined a sunbaked bone, and peeled back bark from a stick.' But the significance is not merely stylistic. Behind the primitive world loom the cities and townships, the world of Athol Fugard's *Sizwe Bansi is Dead* and of [Yvonne Burgess's] *The Strike*. Life there is so stricken that the only cure may be in primitive ritual, in the I-Ching and the reading of the bones. But, once cured, will the boy stay in Sekhukhuneland? 'I had survived the Wilderness, but I wondered if I would survive the city? Could I take back my truth of the *mpatho* hut, the *kgoro* fire-stick and the *phiri* cairn to Cape Town, Johannesburg or London?' It is also the novelist's predicament: and she makes her 'truth' highly convincing.

> *Hermione Lee, "Truth to Tell," in* New Statesman,
> *Vol. 94, No. 2438, December 9, 1977, p. 822.*

DAVID WRIGHT

A Revolutionary Woman is no ordinary novel. It is no extraordinary one either, being cut from well-worn if hard-wearing South African themes: racial prejudice, the colour bar, Afrikaner bigotry, white oppression; hung upon another very old peg, miscegenation; and rounded off with yet another old familiar, the lynching party.

The time is 1920, and the story is told in the first-person present tense by a middle-aged English schoolmistress teaching in a Coloured school somewhere in the Karoo. The narrator has been a friend and disciple of Gandhi, a passionate believer in his policy of passive resistance, but unable to understand the enigma of his marriage to the self-effacing, down-trodden Kasturbai. . . . After Gandhi's departure to India and the death of the narrator's Brahmin lover (who, like Gandhi, contracts a child-marriage, which custom is anathema to her as a woman) she has become intensely involved with one of her Coloured pupils, Ebrahim, whom she sees as a son and inheritor of a new, casteless Africa.

Half-Zulu, half-Italian, Ebrahim dreams of escape to Europe, whereas the narrator thinks he should find his destiny in Africa. In the event the boy seduces a mentally retarded Boer girl, is charged with rape, and takes refuge with the schoolmistress, who finds a liberal Boer lawyer—liberal because educated in Europe?—for the defence. She wants Ebrahim to stand trial and thus "strike a blow for true liberty", although the verdict must inevitably go against him and involve a long prison sentence. However, her Boer neighbours take matters into their own hands and mount a posse to lynch the culprit. The final section of the book is a rhetorical dialogue between the twelve men of the posse, the narrator and the Coloured victim, each justifying his actions and point of view, rather like the chorus of a Greek play or the four knights in *Murder in the Cathedral*. It is here that the emotional validity of this odd book is manifest.

There is little attempt at realism, or even fidelity to the period. . . . The style wavers between the wooden and the inflated. . . .

Yet despite such surface irritations, the novel works; its driving emotional energy forces conviction even though the characters hardly ever seem to coincide with reality. They are types, symbols, larger and less complex than life. Indeed this short book is not a novel at all; it reads more like the prose version, by some literal-minded translator, of an effective original poem.

> *David Wright, "African Absolutes," in* The Times
> Literary Supplement, *No. 4272, February 15, 1985,*
> *p. 179.*

J. M. COETZEE

On August 10 this year, during clashes between Africans and Indians around Durban, South Africa, a mob invaded Phoenix Estate, the communal settlement founded by Gandhi, burning and looting. Among the houses wrecked was the Gandhi family house, which had been maintained as a museum.

Thus perished some of the last physical evidences of the twenty-one years Gandhi spent in South Africa, years during which he led the campaign of the Indian South African community against serfdom and exploitation, in the process forging the doctrine of *Satyagraha* ("truth-force") and the tactics of non-violent resistance. Though the mob probably did not think of itself as performing a symbolic act, we may read the sacking of the Gandhi museum as its verdict on the relevance of nonviolence to the South Africa of the 1980s. . . .

In the life of Christina Ransome, the heroine of Sheila Fugard's third novel, *A Revolutionary Woman,* Gandhi and his wife are not only an inspiration but abiding spiritual presences, more real than the world in which she moves.

The action of the novel takes place in 1920, six years after Gandhi left South Africa for the last time. A lone Englishwoman in a Boer (Afrikaner) community, Christina Ransome teaches at a school for Coloured (mixed-race) children in a small country town. Her particular protégé is an eighteen-year-old youth named Ebrahim, whom, against the opposition of the white townsfolk, she is preparing for an examination that will enable him to escape a life that is stifling him.

Infected with the prejudices of his masters, Ebrahim fantasizes that he is a foundling, that he is "really" white. His dream is to flee South Africa and live the life of a dilettante artist in the Italy or Switzerland he has read about. Christina sometimes supports him in his fantasies, sometimes tries to confront him with reality. Her vacillation is one sign that within her the wise Gandhi (who sometimes fuses with the god Shiva) and Kali, goddess of dark sensualism and destruction, are at war: for Fugard's psychology is based on the archaic principle of the *psychomachia,* the contest of gods (or archetypes) in the soul.

In the contest for control of Ebrahim, Kali gains the upper hand. Sex enters his life, and with shock Christina learns who the woman is: Ebrahim is arrested on a charge of raping a simple-minded white girl of fourteen. He does not deny the facts, but argues that it was love, not rape. Determined to conduct the trial on political lines, Christina engages a liberal lawyer.

But when it emerges that the girl is pregnant, a troop of vigilantes, twelve of the town's leading men, ride out to lynch Ebrahim, who is free on bail. Ebrahim takes refuge in Christina's house. Asserting their right to speak for the Afrikaner *volk* and carry out the *volk's* justice, the vigilantes lay siege to the house. Ebrahim declares his love for Christina, then rapes her, then commits suicide; Christina is left mourning over his dead body.

This synopsis gives, more or less, the sum of the action. In all, the narrative is so schematic, the setting so sketchily realized, the dialogue so stiff, the motivation so perfunctory, that we must conclude Fugard had entirely different ambitions in mind than to write a novel in a psychological-realist mode about a crisis in the life of a woman of passionate ideals in the age of (as she sees it) Gandhi and Lenin, fighting reactionary and death-driven social forces, a field that Nadine Gordimer long ago annexed as her own.

What Fugard's ambition is—and here I must begin to guess, since the novel itself, at the same time so slight and so imperiously grand, gives little guidance—is to approach a tale emblematic of South African history through the Hindu conception of *maya,* the illusoriness of historical event; and yet at the same time to oppose the passive fatalism that goes hand in hand with the notion of history-as-illusion by putting forward the ideal of a classless society as a *transcendence* of history, a plateau on which history ceases to be. What happens on the ground in the town of New Kimberly is therefore barely worth devoting one's creative energies to—in fact, to realize New Kimberly, its people, their words and actions, too fully would

be to attribute to them a reality they do not possess. More real is the plane of the great trans-historical forces—personified in Shiva and Kali—whose eternal contest is played out in the world.

If this is indeed the direction of Fugard's thinking, then we can see why the figure of Gandhi occupies the center of her book: as wise seer he looks beyond or through the illusions of history; as political activist involved in worldly affairs he brings nearer the classless society and the end of history.

Fugard has written a novel, not a book about Gandhi, so it is unfair to ask whether her fictional Gandhi is the true Gandhi. But we can ask how Gandhian a book she has written, to what extent it reflects the spirit of the master. *Satyagraha,* confronting the oppressor with the overwhelming truth of the bodily being of the oppressed, seeks with fundamental magnanimity not only to defeat its adversary but to save him as well, as the history of Gandhi's dealings with the British in India testifies, and as the British, in retrospect, realize and are grateful for. How Gandhian is the opposition of Christina to the Boers?

Here the answer must be inconclusive, for the simple reason that Fugard has not constructed an action in which one can see a clear distinction at work in the world between a personal distaste for violence and a political philosophy of nonviolence. I do not hereby wish to draw into question the sincerity of Christina's beliefs (if one can indeed talk about the sincerity of fictional beings). I am pointing to something simpler: a failure of craft. Christina's resistance to the Boers has no effect on the world in which she lives. Nothing changes in New Kimberly. If the Boer harbingers of death who ride the night in black coats and top hats (top hats?) quail at all, it is not before Christina's truth-force but before the Mauser rifle Ebrahim snatches from one of them. Therefore the fable Fugard has invented does not demonstrate the *force* of truth-force. At best it demonstrates that passive resistance fails against men without conscience, or men locked into a particularly grim black-and-white view of the world. "You are a woman. We are men and know what is best," they tell her at the end of the book, and ride off.

The fable does not even, strictly speaking, show us a conscientious choosing of the way of nonviolence: to Christina and Ebrahim, two against many, the way of violence is hardly available. Christina is Gandhian to her marrow—there is no question of that—but the book does not show in what respect Gandhiism is different from any other heartfelt private belief, like theosophy or vegetarianism, that gives its believers a feeling of being clean in a dirty world. (p. 12)

It is tempting to resort to one of the clichés of the trade and call *A Revolutionary Woman* an "ambitious failure," meaning a book that fails only because it tries to do too much—the implication being that it would have succeeded had it only attempted less. There is certainly a degree of nobility about Fugard's heroine, nobility that derives from what is clearly a deep admiration for Gandhi. But one must be frank: Christina's vision of Gandhi may be noble, but it is also adulatory, sometimes sentimentally so. Furthermore, in a book that, with a great deal of passion, advocates the way of ahimsa (nonviolence) in resistance to tyranny, a book that is bound to be read in the context not only of the 1920s but also of the 1980s, there is a real failure to construct a fable which embodies ahimsa as a living force.

I have left for the last the feature of *A Revolutionary Woman* which I find most inexplicable and which, I fear, will discourage many readers. The book is written in a highly stylized English the like of which I have never seen before. The characteristic of this language—to be technical for a moment—is that syntactic subordination is systematically eschewed in favor of coordination. Linguists have long debated how dissimilar two sentences dare be before joining them with "and" produces a bizarre effect. Is "Nitrogen is a gas and Richard III had scoliosis" an acceptable English sentence? Fugard does not write sentences of quite that order of bizarreness, but she does write long paragraphs whose syntax is based on nothing but the conjunction "and"; and when such paragraphs are strung together relentlessly one after another, the effect is one of stunning tedium.

What we see here may simply be an experiment that failed. But there are many other moments of indifference to detail (anachronisms, for 1920, like "energize," "gell," "supportive," "shoot-out"), implausibility (would librarians at Leyden University really allow undergraduates to handle crumbling Egyptian papyrus?), and muddled thinking (why base an indictment of racism on the questionable argument that intercourse with a fourteen-year-old simpleton is not necessarily rape?). *A Revolutionary Woman* does not read like a book that has been labored over long and lovingly. (p. 13)

> *J. M. Coetzee, "Satyagraha in Durban," in* The New York Review of Books, *Vol. XXXII, No. 16, October 24, 1985, pp. 12-13.*

ELINOR LANGER

Both in its theme and in its language, *A Revolutionary Woman* is a most unusual novel. Not only is Christina Ransome a young Englishwoman teaching in a barren Afrikaans-speaking region of South Africa called the Karroo, but she is also a pacifist. Arriving in South Africa at the time Gandhi was leading the campaign among indentured Indian laborers there (the preface to his later campaign for independence in India itself), she came under his influence and became a *satyagrahi*, a member of his passive resistance movement. Her faith in Gandhi is not uncritical—indeed, one of the many interesting things about the book is Christina's continual reflection on the subject of Gandhi's marriage—but it is deep, and following the death of her Indian lover, and a miscarriage, she takes it with her to the Karroo.

There the story, superficially, becomes familiar. A white woman (we would call her a liberal), a Colored boy, hostile neighbors—you know the rest. When Ebrahim is accused of raping a retarded Boer girl and the hooded "kommando" sets out to deliver him to justice, few American readers will fail to envision the Ku Klux Klan. Yet it is not the drama of lynching that Fugard is after: it is the drama of nonviolence. When Christina recognizes one of the "kommando" she says, "Meener Burger, I need some advice. I want to plant some fruit trees, and I prefer peach. But plum would do. I love the blossoms. What do you advise?"

It is hard to image a more brilliant novelistic rendering of the doctrine of revolutionary nonviolence than this attempt to recall the vigilante to his better nature. In fact, the same could be said of the book as a whole. Constructed like poetry, with recurring rhythms and refrains, it sweeps past the clutter of personality and works directly with its characters' souls. Dialogue is not dialogue in the ordinary sense but in the extraordinary sense—also true—in which barely interacting individuals reveal the depths of their hearts. In a sense the book *is*

what it is showing. Its very language is quiet and calm. Whether it is relevant to the present moment is another question, but it is perhaps the highest tribute to this strange and original novel to say that it has the power to make one imagine, if only fleetingly, a different outcome to events in South Africa than the one for which it seems to be heading. (p. 26)

> *Elinor Langer, "Life under Apartheid: The Possible and the Real," in* Ms., *Vol. XIV, No. 5, November, 1985, pp. 26-7.*

FRANCES A. KOESTLER

[*A Revolutionary Woman*] is a novel about apartheid (the term is never used; perhaps it had not yet been coined in 1920), about sexual power and sexual injustice, about a woman's struggle to define herself and her role. Written in a style reminiscent of the kind of high fever in which one drifts in and out of reality, the novel alternates between ritualized formal dialogue and shimmering imagery. Short declarative sentences set up a rhythmic, dirge-like beat as events march to their inexorable culmination. Scenes are deftly captured in a few sentences. . . .

A Revolutionary Woman is Sheila Fugard's first book to be published in the United States. Wife of the South African playwright Athol Fugard, to whom the book is dedicated, she is the author of two previous novels. If they are invested with anything like the power and poetry of the present work, their publication here should not be delayed.

> *Frances A. Koestler, "Sex and Injustice in South Africa," in* Book World—The Washington Post, *November 24, 1985, p. 8.*

GEORGE KEARNS

Sheila Fugard's *A Revolutionary Woman* is, to risk what may sound an odd contradiction, a quiet, almost poetic work about violence. Fugard seems determined to keep out of her writing any brilliance or cleverness that would distract us from observing the *agon* of South African racism or the troubled history behind it. The setting is a small town in the arid Karoo region in 1920, twenty years after the Boer War, two after the Bolshevik Revolution upon which the English heroine, Christina Ransome, now in her late thirties, places so much hope as a beacon leading to a better future. . . . "This is the twentieth century," she preaches to . . . [one] of the Boer men who dominate the town (their women never appear in the novel), "and socialism is the driving force. The Boers must recognize this, otherwise they will fail, and that would be tragedy." Christina has the thoughts of Ruskin, Tolstoy, Shaw and Gandhi behind her, and her innocence is such that she almost expects the Boers to consider her arguments. They, of course, are totally unprepared to think of themselves as a "ruling class." Rather, they see themselves as oppressed by history, threatened by a foreign liberalism, and upholding a traditional way of life in which "God made the races separate" and has anointed them His surrogates, the "just masters." (pp. 125-26)

For an American, reading *A Revolutionary Woman* is like reading a familiar story translated into a foreign tongue.

Fugard attempts, not without a strain upon Christina's first-person narrative, yet not without power either, to raise the tale from tragedy in the sense of lamentable to tragedy on something like a Euripidean scale. She does this by allowing breaks in

the realistic mode that dominates the novel, so that her characters, especially the Boer men, may come downstage to deliver stylized speeches pleading their history. She recognizes,
too, the tangles of the racist-colonial situation; its resistance
to self-righteous anaysis and simple Enlightenment solutions;
the refusal of the oppressed to adopt the culture, manners and
morals of their white liberators; and the sexual crosscurrents
that complicate the motives of oppressors, liberators and oppressed alike. There is at times some clumsy machinery that
has to come into play for Fugard to dramatize all this through
the voice of Christina, who is characterized as an isolated
"progressive" woman of 1920, working from an eclectic ide-
alist-socialist ideology which doesn't quite accommodate all
of Fugard's thoughts. There is a glossary of Indian, Boer and
South African words, which I seldom needed to refer to, but
ignorance of South African history, of the Boer War and its
aftermath, left me puzzled by some references. (pp. 126-27)

> *George Kearns, "Revolutionary Women and Oth-
> ers," in* The Hudson Review, *Vol. XXXIX, No. 1,
> Spring, 1986, pp. 121-34.*

Ellen Gilchrist

1935-

American short story writer, novelist, poet, and scriptwriter.

Gilchrist is best known for her short stories that chronicle the decline of the Southern aristocracy. Much of her fiction is set in New Orleans, a city which she describes in detail to contrast the idealistic hopes of her upper-class female protagonists with the harsh reality of their lives. Gilchrist's characters sometimes reappear in different works, allowing her to examine various stages of their personal development. Gilchrist is consistently praised for her vivid use of language and dialogue, and critics have particularly noted her ability to capture the dreams and frustrations of adolescence.

Gilchrist wrote poems and stories for various periodicals before publishing her first collection of short fiction, *In the Land of Dreamy Dreams* (1981). This volume garnered widespread acclaim for her bold characterizations and low-key prose style. The central figures in these stories are usually wealthy Southern women who escape the restrictions of their upper-class lives through unorthodox, sometimes destructive behavior. Susan Wood praised *In the Land of Dreamy Dreams* as an "auspicious debut" and declared that the stories are "about the stratagems, both admirable and not so, by which we survive our lives." Gilchrist's next book, the novel *The Annunciation* (1983), received less favorable critical attention. Reviewers generally approved of the book's first section, which describes Amanda McCamey's life in the familiar milieu of aristocratic New Orleans. Most agreed, however, that when Amanda joins an artists' commune in the Ozarks in the second part, the book becomes overly sentimental and relies on outdated psychological jargon. Gilchrist regained critical acceptance with her next collection of short stories, *Victory over Japan* (1984), which received the American Book Award for fiction. Some of the characters from *In the Land of Dreamy Dreams* reappear in this volume, which traces the lives of several eccentric female protagonists. Jonathan Yardley asserted that as a result of various thematic connections and similarities in character among many of the stories, "you feel as though you are reading a novel; at the end you have that satisfied, contented feeling only a good novel can give."

Gilchrist's recent collection, *Drunk with Love* (1986), has further enhanced her reputation as a creator of vibrant short stories. Characters from previous works once again resurface in this volume, but some critics noted new concerns in such stories as "Memphis" and "The Emancipator," which delineate interracial love affairs, and "The Blue-Eyed Buddhist," in which the protagonist ends her life in a grand, self-sacrificing gesture atypical of the standard Gilchrist heroine. Judy Cooke praised *Drunk with Love* as a "collection of stories satisfyingly crafted and complete but so full of drama that any one of them . . . might have been extended into a novel." Gilchrist has also published a volume of poetry, *The Land Surveyor's Daughter* (1979).

(See also *CLC*, Vol. 34 and *Contemporary Authors*, Vols. 113, 116.)

© 1985 Nancy Crampton

SUSAN WOOD

I read all 14 of [the stories in *In the Land of Dreamy Dreams*] in one sitting, and was only sorry to be finished. They are "traditional" stories, full of real people to whom things really happen—set, variously, over the last four decades among the rich of New Orleans, the surviving aristocracy of the Mississippi Delta, and Southerners transplanted—a step or so down in status, it would seem—to southern Indiana. The book's jacket says that the "prime ingredients" are "envy, greed, lust, terror, and self-deceit," and although these are certainly present, there is also humor and self-knowledge and love. It is more accurate to say that *In the Land of Dreamy Dreams* is about the stratagems, both admirable and not so, by which we survive our lives.

Even the least attractive characters become known to us, and therefore human, because Gilchrist's voice is so sure, her tone so right, her details so apt. . . .

Many of the stories in *In the Land of Dreamy Dreams* are peopled with children and adolescents, and it is unusual to find a writer who understands them as well as Gilchrist does. (p. 4)

It would be difficult to pick a favorite from among these stories, though high on the list would be ["**In the Land of Dreamy Dreams**"], a tale of a crisis in conscience among the elite of the New Orleans Lawn Tennis Club. There are few flaws here, though the ending of **"Rich,"** with its suggestion that Helen, Tom Wilson's adopted daughter, is really his own illegitimate child, rings slightly false, and **"Revenge,"** it seems to me, would have been better without the last sentence.

But, on the whole, reading *In the Land of Dreamy Dreams* reminds me that the short story at its best can be the most satisfying of genres. Indeed, the end of **"Perils of the Nile"** could serve as an epigraph for the entire volume. Bebber, a motherless misfit of a boy, finds the ring lost by his only friend, and instead of returning it to her immediately, hides it so he will have an excuse to go to the girl's house in order to see her mother, with whom he is in love. After bathing and dressing in his best clothes, he sets out on his mission: "Bebber walked on down the street, the rays of the setting sun making him a path all the way to her house, a little road to travel, a wide band of luminous and precarious order." *In the Land of Dreamy Dreams* takes us down just such a luminous and precarious path. (p. 13)

Susan Wood, "Louisiana Stories: The Debut of Ellen Gilchrist," in Book World—The Washington Post, March 21, 1982, pp. 4, 13.

BRUCE ALLEN

A vigorous style is . . . on display in the bold tragicomic stories of Ellen Gilchrist's *In the Land of Dreamy Dreams*. These are vividly nasty portraits of adolescents pleasuring themselves with monstrous lies, spoiled Southern belles who get their doting rich daddies to pay for their abortions, lamebrained *nouveaux riches* who can't handle the consequences of their prosperity. Gilchrist keeps an amused ironic distance from her characters: the oddly summary, noncommittal tone (she sounds, at times, like a foulmouthed Flannery O'Connor) adds real force to her aphoristic wisecracks (about the brain-damaged girl who "went through stages of biting other children at the Academy of the Sacred Heart of Jesus"; or the socialite who foresees "the entire culture of the white Christian world . . . besieged by the children of the poor carrying portable radios and boxes of fried chicken").

A few of the shorter stories are really only vignettes, but even these have their moments. . . . I especially liked Gilchrist's portrayal of "the most beautiful woman in the state of Louisiana" accompanied by "a Zen Buddhist carpenter," off in a canoe to rescue her mother during a flood (**"There's a Garden of Eden"**), and the terrifying comedy **"Rich,"** a sequence of catastrophic chain-reactions that might have been imagined by F. Scott Fitzgerald on a night out with Nathanael West. This is Ellen Gilchrist's first book, and she is really a writer to watch. (p. 486)

Bruce Allen, "American Short Fiction Today," in New England Review, Vol. IV, No. 3, Spring, 1982, pp. 478-88.

JIM CRACE

Ellen Gilchrist's witty volume of "Short Fiction", *In the Land of Dreamy Dreams,* does its best to obscure its own considerable merits. With the connivance of its dust-jacket rodomontade, the collection masquerades as a blunt and loving examination of New Orleans and the Mississippi delta. Gilchrist's title is taken (and slightly misquoted) from the refrain to that jerky Southern foxtrot, *Way Down Yonder in New Orleans* ("In the

Land of Dreamy *Scenes*"). Her text—with almost Miltonic confidence in the authority of proper nouns—is obsessively signposted with street names and Louisiana landmarks, from the Huey P. Long Bridge and the Audubon Park to the graceful stucco mansions on Exposition Boulevard and the state tenements of the St Thomas Street project.

Yet it is only the outward apparel (and, to some extent, the narrative drawl) of these engaging moral tales which evokes the South. New Orleans presents itself in clear, painstaking detail, but the broad demotic idiosyncrasies which define any city are neglected. Indeed, those few tales which foray north for their settings, the campus of Seattle University (**"Suicides"**) and the high-rise abortion clinics of Houston (**"1957, a Romance"**) are barely distinguishable in tone and demeanour from the majority set amongst the levees and bayous of the delta.

But *In the Land of Dreamy Dreams* cannot be dismissed as little more than an anecdotal street plan. As the stories accumulate, Gilchrist's true obsession reveals itself. Municipal spirit of place is . . . a minor concern. The self-conscious parading of exact Southern locations is a protective screen beyond which an entirely different territory is explored and mapped. Gilchrist's "Land of Dreamy Dreams" is Adolescence.

Her characters, for the most part, are children subjected to the arbitrary dislocations of family life, and the "cold-eyed, white-armed . . . terrors" of puberty. . . .

These first-person narratives betray a sophisticated, writerly sensibility which at times goes beyond the years and understanding of the speaker. . . . Rhoda, the ten-year-old chronicler of **"Revenge"** (this volume's masterpiece) describes "a full moon . . . caught like a kite in the pecan trees across the river", and a waterside house which "shimmered in the moonlight like a jukebox alive in a meadow".

Occasionally, too, one detects in Gilchrist a loss of nerve with her fragile, modest plots, so that perfectly poised tales are laden (for ironic purposes, perhaps) with the ballast of a final prose sunset. . . .

But if Gilchrist's narrative voices are sometimes less than authentic, and the writing is occasionally inappropriately earnest, the rewards elsewhere for the reader are a sustained display of delicately and rhythmically modulated prose and an unsentimental dissection of raw sentiment. Her stories are perceptive, her manner is both stylish and idiomatic—a rare and potent combination.

Jim Crace, "The Cold-Eyed Terrors," in The Times Literary Supplement, No. 4150, October 15, 1982, p. 1142.

JEANIE THOMPSON AND ANITA MILLER GARNER

Gilchrist's regional success has been explained in much the same way the regional success of writers like Walker Percy, Eudora Welty and, more recently, John Kennedy Toole has been explained: that is, readers in the South cannot resist the descriptions of settings, landscapes, dialects and societies which, love them or not, are easily recognizable as home. Yet, like these writers, Gilchrist writes fiction that is more than regional. Indeed, if it is regional, it is so in the sense that the works of Dostoyevsky and Flaubert are regional, which is to say that it represents not regionalism so much as the successful capturing of a social milieu. Gilchrist captures the flavor and essence of her region without drowning in its idiom. She does not diminish her work by parroting already established Southern voices or depending upon stereotypes of landscapes and character. The view that Gilchrist gives us of the world is a very straight and narrow path of realism, traditional fiction peopled with characters whom life doesn't pass by, characters who lust and kill and manipulate, and most importantly, dream.

The focus of Gilchrist's realism in *In the Land of Dreamy Dreams,* as well as in her novel, *The Annunciation,* is the female psyche, for Gilchrist puts us deeply inside a female point of view in eleven of the fourteen stories as well as in much of the novel. Even in **"Rich," "The President of the Louisiana Live Oak Society,"** and **"Suicides,"** stories in which she employs a more nearly omniscient point of view, her narrators still manage to sound as if they are characters in her stories. . . . The result of an intense focus on the female point of view and a shortage of three-dimensional male characters will undoubtedly result in charges by some of Gilchrist's lack of range. Fortunately, the placement of **"Rich"** as the first story in the collection presents Tom Wilson, perhaps the only fully rounded male character in the book. The glimpses we are given of his coming to terms with a hatred of his difficult daughter Helen, are some of the most poignant and human scenes in the collection. Yet, when we put all the stories together, add up all the views the reader gets of the female mind, the composite suggests that Gilchrist's treatment of women is very traditional and in several areas resembles that of her predecessors.

Like at least two Grandes Dames of Southern fiction, Eudora Welty and Flannery O'Connor, Gilchrist evidences a type of Romantic Calvinism in her view of women. On one hand, she seems delighted with the idea of innate depravity, while on the other she seems convinced that a woman's life is often like an extended downhill sled ride, starting out with much promise for excitement and speed, but troubled by ill-placed obstacles, icy spots, and a fizzle at the end. (pp. 101-02)

In their downhill journey through life, the protagonists of [Gilchrist's] stories run into obstacle after obstacle to mar their gorgeous, effortless journeys. In **"1957, a Romance,"** Rhoda fears another pregnancy and cannot face what she perceives as the ugliness of her body. In [**"In the Land of Dreamy Dreams"**], LaGrande McGruder finds her obstacle in the form of "That goddamn little new-rich Yankee bitch," a crippled, social-climbing Jewish woman who forces LaGrande to cheat if she wants to win in a game of tennis, the only thing important in LaGrande's life other than her integrity and pride at being at least a third-generation member of the New Orleans Lawn Tennis Club. In **"The President of the Louisiana Live Oak Society,"** Lelia McLaurin's life tumbles into chaos as the trappings of the social revolution of the sixties—blacklights, marijuana, and pushers—trickle down into her adolescent son Robert's life and then into her own carefully ordered home. Lelia's buffer from such madness and social unrest is to visit her hairdresser, who shares Lelia's psychiatrist and who creates for Lelia a hairdo that resembles a helmet.

Thus in gathering for the reader a whole cast of female characters in various stages of life, with the character Rhoda appearing by name in four of the stories, Gilchrist achieves a kind of coherence of style and voice that is absent from many first collections of short fiction. She invites us to compare these women with each other and determine whether or not the sum of their experiences adds up to more than just their individual lives. The result is a type of social commentary that pervades the work, full of sadness and futility. By dividing the collection into sections, Gilchrist emphasizes how "place" has affected these females' lives, and how what has been true in the past may exist nowhere other than in dreams in the future. The rural and genteel Mississippi in which Matille and the very young Rhoda summer seems to offer little preparation for the life in which Rhoda finds herself in 1957, in North Carolina with a husband and two small sons and the fear of a third child on the way. Clearly nothing in LaGrande McGruder's life has prepared her for the disruption of a society she has always known, nor for the encroachment of dissolution upon her territory. Similarly, Lelia McLaurin's only plan for escape is a weekend spent with her husband on the Mississippi Gulf Coast, just as they used to do in the old days, driving to Biloxi with a shaker full of martinis.

With the creation of Amanda McCamey, the female protagonist in her new novel, *The Annunciation,* Gilchrist may be reversing the trend set by Rhoda, LeLe, Matille, even LaGrande McGruder and Lelia McLaurin. Amanda is possibly Gilchrist's first female protagonist who may be elevated to the class of *hero.* Although Amanda has in common with her "sisters" a penchant for the downhill slide, a heavy cargo of guilt, and a similar Mississippi Delta/New Orleans background, she redeems herself with an honest attempt to flee "the world of guilt and sorrow," to borrow a phrase from Flannery O'Connor, by literally asserting her will against the forces that would slow her down in her bid for a self-directed, meaningful life.

Amanda is the central force of the novel, most of which is narrated in a close third person through her perceptions, though occasionally Gilchrist, like O'Connor, dips into the consciousnesses of other characters for a balancing effect. Still, it is Amanda's story, her quest to know who she is and how to live her life that is the main theme of the novel.

The Annunciation is divided into three sections: "Cargo," "Exile," and "The Annunciation," the latter being about four times as long as the second, which is twice as long as the first. This structure invites questions: What is Amanda's "cargo"? From what or whom and to where is she exiled? Is "the annunciation" intended as a scriptural parallel? If not, is it used ironically?

Amanda's "cargo" we learn is in part her guilt over a child born out of wedlock and given up for adoption when Amanda is just fourteen. (pp. 104-06)

Growing up in the same small Mississippi county, Issaquena, which figured prominently in at least three of the short stories, Amanda is drawn from an early age to her athletic, darkly handsome first cousin Guy. They seem to be the pride of the stock on Esperanza plantation, and as children they develop an intense loyalty that later blossoms into sexual attraction when they are adolescents. When Guy is eighteen and a football sensation in Rolling Fork, Mississippi, and Amanda a precocious fourteen year old, she seduces Guy. Though she desires him physically, she also feels a spiritual need to keep him near. . . . Amanda becomes pregnant and is sent to a Catholic home for unwed mothers in New Orleans. This is the beginning of "what she must carry with her always. Her cargo." From then on she is irretrievably split from Guy, and, for a good part of her life, from herself. The fact that the baby girl she delivers by Caesarian section is taken from her, remembered as a slick, slippery thing with eyes squeezed shut, haunts her throughout the novel. (p. 106)

Amanda's period of "exile" takes place in New Orleans, the land of dreamy dreams, where she enters Uptown society by marrying Malcolm Ashe, a wealthy Jewish management law-yer. Their childless marriage is further marred by Amanda's alcoholism—a state that existed prior to their union. In the "Exile" chapters, Gilchrist covers some of the same territory traversed in the New Orleans society exposé stories of *In the Land of Dreamy Dreams:* the Junior League women, the po-litically corrupt men, materialism of the rankest sort, "good" schools, worried children, class consciousness, racism, and sterility. Amanda eventually sobers up, awakening to realize that these people either hate each other or themselves. "What am I doing here?", she wonders but, until she stops drinking, she can't find her way out of the maze.

Amanda's ticket out of town is the interest that she develops in language translation while pursuing a degree at Tulane Uni-versity. Chiefly with the support of her black maid, her friend and "ally" Lavertis, Amanda is able to stop drinking and find the encouragement to go to school. (p. 107)

Amanda's exile is both literal and metaphorical. Exiled from her home territory, the family plantation, Esperanza, in Mis-sissippi, she has not yet found her second home, Fayetteville, Arkansas. On a figurative level, she is exiled from herself through her drinking and also in her lack of knowledge as to who she is and what she should do with her life. Childless, without a career, the wife of a rich man, living with guilt over her daughter, Amanda is in despair most of the time. Yet one of the main themes of *The Annunciation* is Amanda's bid for freedom through self-knowledge. During their time alone at their grandmother's funeral, Guy offers to leave his wife and take Amanda some place where they can be happy. Amanda, who is waking up from a dream of happy-endings, refuses his offer, saying, "all I'm really trying to do is find out what I'm good at. So I can be a useful person, so I can have some purpose." When Guy says he can give her anything "that goddamn ingratiating Jew" can give her, she replies that she's not interested in money. "I want something else," she tells Guy. "Something I don't know the name of yet."

Eventually, Amanda gets a chance to name her desire. She becomes involved in translating a manuscript smuggled out of the Vatican and put into the hands of Marshall Jordon, a seventy plus year old translation scholar from the writing program at the University of Arkansas in Fayetteville. Ironically, Amanda will translate a manuscript of poems in middle French by a poet named Helene Renoir, who also had an illegitimate child, was sent away to live with nuns, and who chose to hang herself at age twenty-one. It is Amanda's involvement with this proj-ect, her separation and eventual divorce from Malcolm, and her move to Fayetteville to start a new life as a single, working woman that constitute her deliverance from exile. Thus the stage is set for her "annunciation." (pp. 107-08)

Gilchrist's choice of *The Annunciation* as a title for her novel about a woman who, after giving up one child at age fourteen, gives birth to a son thirty years later on Christmas Eve leads one to question how closely the novelist intends to parallel the biblical annunciation. Perhaps the author is playing with this motif, suggesting a modern version of "miracle." If one goes to what is considered by many to be the loveliest of the four gospels, St. Luke, and reads the disciple's account of Mary's annunciation, some parallels can be seen to Gilchrist's novel. However, a word of warning is in order at the outset: while this approach sheds interesting light on Gilchrist's structure and helps clarify certain details in *The Annunciation,* the main character's hardline stand against organized Christianity, and the Roman Catholic church in particular, makes the possibility

of the author's intention to render a strict biblical reference or allegory highly unlikely. Neither is Gilchrist satirizing Chris-tianity; rather, she takes what she needs to shape her narrative. Still, what she appears to need of the New Testament is quite revealing.

To begin with, Amanda is told of her pregnancy by a masseuse who has looked into her eye and seen "a little configuration." This "unwashed hippie doctor of the hills with his gorgeous tan," is, coincidentally, named Luke. After learning her amaz-ing news, Amanda plays briefly with the idea that Luke is "the angel of the Annunciation." Somewhat comically, she imag-ines that he has almost struck a classical pose of the annun-ciation angel: "His hands were folded at his chest. He might have dropped to one knee." In addition, she notices that she is wearing the Virgin's colors, "blue shorts, white T-shirt," and calls herself "Maria Amanda Luisa, the gray-blue virgin of the middleweights." Luke's words, *"a special case. A very special child,"* ring for her, and she wonders whether her young lover Will is her "Joseph leading the donkey." But Amanda puts her feet back on the earth when she admits that "he is not here. . . . I have not even heard from him and there is no donkey." Amanda, the High Blasphemer, decides that "it's time to think straight," and so for the moment she ends her flirtation with outright scriptural comparisons. (pp. 110-11)

Like the Virgin Mary, Amanda has a close relationship with a female companion, Katie Dunbar. For Mary it is the mother of John, Elisabeth (who also experienced a miracle), and it is in her presence that Mary sings of the angel's visitation and her joy. Though there isn't a strict parallel to this in *The Annunciation,* Amanda is comforted repeatedly by the "ex-perienced" and wise Katie at the potter's home. Finally, one notes that St. Luke refers to Judea as "hill country" and Gil-christ sets her final portion of the book, "The Annunciation," in the hills of northwest Arkansas.

Perhaps a more productive comparison to make, however, is the fact that Mary's news comes to her as a disturbing reve-lation, and Amanda is likewise extremely troubled by her un-expected pregnancy. She is unmarried, forty-four years old, presumably has experienced an early menopause, and is about to embark upon a possibly auspicious career as a translator of middle French and as a writer. The prospect of having a baby and the ensuing duties of motherhood appear to stand directly in her path toward self-determination. Gilchrist deals with a sharply realistic situation: a woman who perhaps must choose between a career and motherhood, options which until this point have both been closed to Amanda. She struggles with the conflict, and even goes to Tulsa for an abortion, but then she changes her mind, gets drunk to celebrate and has to be taken care of by the Good Samaritan Katie. At this point Amanda seems to have reached a low point, but like Mary, she comes to believe that nothing is impossible and so decides to have the child. (pp. 111-12)

As the novel closes, Amanda drifts to sleep shortly after de-livering her son, "dreaming of herself in a white silk suit holding her beautiful daughter in her arms." She at last has the courage to imagine the reunion a happy one, though for-merly she had always dreamt of the meeting in nightmare. Perhaps at this point Amanda goes beyond courage to hubris, as she continues: "My life leading to my lands forever and ever and ever, hallowed be my name, goddammit, my kingdom come, my will be done, amen, so be it, Amanda." In her blasphemy of the Lord's Prayer, Amanda McCamey gropes toward self-respect, forgiveness and love. (p. 113)

Guided often in her life by lust, hunger, greed, and curiosity, Amanda finally, at age forty-four, begins to direct her own life with loving intelligence: "My life on my terms, my daughter, my son." The lyricism of the ending of *The Annunciation* is a hymn to self-determination, from which we can only wonder at the reserves of Amanda McCamey's imagination and strength.

In her two works of fiction to date, Ellen Gilchrist portrays the workings of a complex female psyche through a variety of women of all ages. Rhoda, Matille, Alisha Terrebone, and Amanda McCamey, to name a few, are all mined from the lode of a larger consciousness which Gilchrist is working with amazing confidence. It is encouraging to see that with *The Annunciation* a possibility for redemption appears on the horizon for Gilchrist's anguished but tenacious women. The writer has struck one element that may lead to a greater wealth for her characters: courage to face the truth about themselves. With this discovery, Gilchrist's women may go further in future works to develop a realism that not only entertains but ennobles. (pp. 113-14)

> *Jeanie Thompson and Anita Miller Garner, "The Miracle of Realism: The Bid for Self-Knowledge in the Fiction of Ellen Gilchrist," in* The Southern Quarterly, *Vol. XXII, No. 1, Fall, 1983, pp. 101-14.*

BRIAN MORTON

Ellen Gilchrist goes some way towards reinventing [some of the clichés of "Southern Fiction"]. The stories in her first collection, *In the Land of Dreamy Dreams,* were so strongly reminiscent of Carson McCullers and Flannery O'Connor that occasional references to Vietnam, "American Pie" and Equal Opportunity law came as a shock.

Gilchrist does manage, though, to avoid the overheated moral fervour of "Southern Gothic". Raised on the Mississippi delta, the "land of dreamy dreams", she now lives and writes in New York. This gives her a certain distance from her material, and a self-consciously modern concern with narrative form and with the processes of the literary imagination. Her South is an imagined place, a dreamscape; she is very little concerned with the actual South's landscape or history. Her characters are city people and her subject, almost invariably, is the set of imaginative strategies by which they fend off boredom, inertia, heat and the aimlessness of their lives.

The Annunciation, Gilchrist's first novel, is a highly "literary" book; the experience it describes is almost entirely second-hand, vicarious, mediated by somebody's imagination, filtered through drink, dope and fantasy.

Amanda McCamey is a would-be poet, lured from the hard-drinking whirl of New Orleans to Fayetteville in Arkansas to translate the sonnets of Hélène of Aurillac. Amanda is in the line of Gilchrist's other protagonists, living more in others' imaginations than in their own; they dream of being Zelda Fitzgerald, of being loved by Hemingway's Colonel Cantwell, of having their feet bound and undergoing appalling labours like Pearl S. Buck's heroines, of the kindness of strangers. As a teenager, Amanda has a child by her cousin . . . ; the child is farmed out for adoption. Mother and daughter, both poets, lead parallel lives, masking their emotional and artistic infertility in obsessive tasks, games and self-examinings. The Biblical strain, hinted at in the title and in an epigraph from St

Luke, is an ironical one, buried in mother's and daughter's search for each other.

It is hard to separate Ellen Gilchrist's failures of execution from the emotional failures of her characters. There are too many gestures redolent of the too many books they have read; they are prone to quotation, to aphorism—"It seemed to Amanda that near the smell of whiskey someone was always crying." Gilchrist's pages are marked by uneasy shifts of tense and grammatical mood, and while this reflects something about her southerners and their milieu, it also presents a confused verbal surface.

> *Brian Morton, "Southern Death," in* The Times Literary Supplement, *No. 4227, April 6, 1984, p. 368.*

CHARLES STUBBLEFIELD

Gilchrist is a southern writer in the tradition of Faulkner, O'Connor, and Welty. She knows the New South, its institutions, its mores, and its people as Faulkner, O'Connor, and Welty knew their earlier South. And although [*The Annunciation*] is a contemporary story about a modern woman, and although there are changes on the surface of southern society, little has changed in the way family and the land—the institutions, myths, and traditions which the family and land perpetuate—hang like shadows over the lives of these people. They are all the victims (and the price is a terrible one) of the society they inherit and of the society they blindly support.

Though *The Annunciation* is not a "feminist" novel, it is an ardently pro-woman, pro-human novel. It is a story of the human heart and the way it is twisted and wrenched by the loves that are fostered there. It is the quest of a woman to understand and repudiate the loves that do not sustain and regenerate her, and to understand and develop the personal freedoms that do. The quest begins with four-year-old Amanda McCamey, beside her mother at the wheel of a Packard automobile, arriving at their ancestral home in Issaquena County, Mississippi, her mother crying at the sight of the land of her birth, her eight-year-old cousin Guy, his eyes bright with anticipation, waiting for her at the end of a long hallway. Forty years and three hundred and fifty pages later we leave Amanda scarred but triumphant. (pp. 107-08)

The Annunciation begins in the Mississippi delta country and moves downstream to New Orleans for most of its length. The last movement of Amanda's quest, however, seeks the freedom and relative purity of the mountains around Fayetteville for its climax and denouement. This movement from the social turgidity and decadence of the traditional and formalized society of New Orleans to the freedom and purity of the mountains is reminiscent of Hemingway's *The Sun Also Rises.* Though everything that happens to Amanda in the mountains is not good, it is in the mountains that she finds a society intellectual and liberal rather than conservative and unthinkingly obedient to the social mores of a corrupt past. In the mountains she finally frees herself from the thralldom of her old life. She finds her own voice, and she and Fate and her friends carve out her new freedoms.

Amanda's story is not everyone's story. From the beginning she is a "different" child. Her waywardness as a child, and later her rebelliousness as a woman, are natural, instinctive rather than intellectual. She is as pure in heart and intent as Henry David Thoreau. Though there is much to corrupt her, she remains relatively untouched by corruption around her.

Fourteen and pregnant and virtually without power, she lets her grandmother and the Catholic nuns dictate her course of action. They are motivated to hide the shame and to build an elaborate lie to protect the family name. The lie festers and Amanda is the principal sufferer. She is sickened unto death by the time she discovers, quite by chance, her salvation in translating the poetry of an eighteenth-century nun, whose story somewhat parallels her own. She is saved not by any message embedded in the poetry of the nun, but rather by the demands of the translation and the demands of the professor for whom she is doing the translations, which bring her to an understanding of her own plight. The translations, coupled with her new friendships in Fayetteville, help her, with the considerable assistance of her own irrepressible sense of self-worth, to win through to her freedom.

At this point Annunciation becomes Renunciation. She renounces family, husband, New Orleans, her old life, Guy. She learns, lesson by bitter lesson, to make her own decisions guided by her own heart and mind. She develops the strength to assert her decisions and to carry them through. Some of the scenes in New Orleans when she sets herself athwart the grooved patterns of action and thought are memorable. "She isn't afraid of anything," one character in the novel observes. "I don't think I ever met anyone that fearless."

Gilchrist too is fearless. She creates no easy dilemmas, nor does her story provide any easy answers. While Amanda's story is ultimately anti-family, no one in the family is a monster of evil. Their love for her is genuine, but it is misguided. That is most brilliantly underscored in the incestuous relationship between Amanda and Guy. They love one another as family. The family is close-knit; in such a family incest is only a touch away. Nor does Guy seduce her or force her against her will. The seduction is mutual. The love is natural and free and open between them. The harm comes not in the love, but in the aftermath of it and what is done to Amanda as a result of it. It is no wonder that she is violently anti-Catholic as she grows older and observes and reads of Catholics in history and literature. Nor is it a surprise that ultimately she renounces her father's family, as well as her husband's. New Orleans, its institutions and its people, is shot through with corruption. It is no place for Amanda, nor for any other free person. (pp. 108-09)

Gilchrist has taken on the Church, the institutions of one of the oldest cities in the United States, and those who think that family is the cornerstone of American life. This novel says no to all of these things. It says yes to the liberal mind, to the scholarly habit of thought and work (one of the few positive portraits of the values of the individual life of the mind fostered in colleges and universities) and to individual, personal freedom. It will appeal to those who use their minds as they read; it will be damned by those who don't. But Ellen Gilchrist has added one more significant document to the chronicle of books that celebrate the triumph of the human will and spirit over the forces that would shackle it or pervert it. (p. 109)

Charles Stubblefield, "A Triumph of the Human Will," in Prairie Schooner, *Vol. 58, No. 2, Summer, 1984, pp. 107-09.*

MEG WOLITZER

Drunk With Love, Ellen Gilchrist's new collection of short stories, is filled with strong, occasionally dazzling pieces of fiction, yet somehow the whole does not equal the sum of its parts. This is an odd phenomenon, and while it doesn't take away from the pleasure to be had while reading the book, it does leave the reader feeling slightly dissatisfied upon finishing it.

What's missing here is a thread of commonality running through all the stories. Instead, we have a variety of quirky characters leading all sorts of dissimilar lives. It's as though Gilchrist is showing us her range of knowledge, which is considerable, rather than stopping and dwelling on the elements in her prose that are most successful and moving. It almost seems as though the author isn't sure of where she's strongest, so she's giving us everything she knows.

The reader, for one, has definite opinions as to where Gilchrist's writing really takes off. ["**Drunk With Love**"] is an uneven tale of a few people living in Berkeley, and while it rambles on in what seems an aimless manner, it surprises us with a terrific, surrealistic ending. Nora Jane, who has recently learned she is pregnant with twins, fades from the story at its closing moments to give the spotlight to the twin fetuses themselves, who suddenly come to life and begin to speak. . . .

Gilchrist presents the twins as aliens about to land on Earth, and this sense of her characters as outsiders is a theme that occurs a couple of times in the collection, to great success. She is especially sensitive to the alienation that children and adolescents feel, and to the tenuous hold they often have over their own lives. In this volume, Gilchrist resuscitates several of the characters from her much-praised earlier collection, *Victory Over Japan,* and among them, we find Rhoda, a precocious young girl growing up in the 1940s, entering into a life she does not fully understand, nor can she fully control. Gilchrist gives us a well-rendered account of the feelings Rhoda has upon her family's imminent move. Surprisingly, Rhoda and her mother become collaborators during the melancholy drive to their new home in the story **"The Expansion of the Universe."** . . . (p. 2)

The next story in the collection, **"Adoration,"** takes a leap ahead in years, and we learn that Rhoda is now married and putting her husband through school. It is a tribute to Gilchrist that the reader feels a pang at the gap of time that has passed, and all the facts we don't know about Rhoda during the intervening years. Did her boyfriend die? Did she bear the move to her new home? Actually, we can infer the answers to these questions, and Gilchrist is a subtle enough writer to suggest a good deal about Rhoda without coming out and giving it all away. The author is best, in fact, during those small, oblique moments, which are present in several of these stories, and are curiously absent from others.

"The Emancipator," for instance, is a disappointing tale that almost feels allegorical, about the marriage between a young woman with a social conscience and a sexy Lebanese man whose visa is about to expire. The relationship leads quickly to an obvious end in tragedy, and the reader can see it coming a long way off and does not feel satisfied.

Gilchrist is heavy-handed in this story, as she also is in **"Belize,"** which gives us a vacation of some bored rich people, but doesn't take us anywhere we haven't been before. Gilchrist's prose flags here as well, and the writing feels too laconic, the sentences choppy and flat. . . . Perhaps the flatness of the prose is being used to help us imagine the flatness of the characters' lives, but in this case, the imitative fallacy is at work, and we are simply lulled by what is going on, not enlivened.

Drunk With Love is quieter in tone than much of the author's earlier work and has less of a regional air to it. Gilchrist can be very funny and witty, yet the most powerful stories in this collection are the more somber, delicate ones. When Gilchrist reaches for emphasis, she occasionally ends up telling rather than showing; her characters often speak in capital letters, which is a lazy way to show how angry or upset they feel. One wishes she had spent a little more time on the motivations behind such emphatic words.

Gilchrist has a strong eye for characters, and in *Drunk With Love,* she has created some very distinctive personalities, such as Annalisa Livingston, a woman who writes a church criticism and gossip column called "Our Lady in Your Pew," in the story **"First Manhattans,"** or Anna, a writer having a love affair with a red-haired pediatrician in the story **"Anna, Part I."** The reader suspects, or at least hopes, that these women will return the next time around.

Despite the unevenness, *Drunk With Love* is well worth reading. There is little cohesion among the stories, but most of them contain small gems of prose, and even an epiphany here and there, if the reader is willing to be patient and go slowly through. (pp. 2, 12)

> Meg Wolitzer, in a review of "Drunk With Love," in Los Angeles Times Book Review, *September 14, 1986, pp. 2, 12.*

WENDY LESSER

One's first impression on reading Ellen Gilchrist's stories is of a world alive with numerous distinctive characters. . . .

Like someone taking home movies—but with a clearly focused and artfully held lens—Ms. Gilchrist catches her people at various stages in their lives, introducing them at one point and then revisiting them later. The strength of their personalities, and the fact that they reappear throughout her published work, create a sense that they have a life beyond the page: we need only wait for Ellen Gilchrist to bring that life forth, and if our curiosity isn't satisfied in one book of short stories, we can dig up an earlier volume or wait for the next. These characters, Ms. Gilchrist's technique implies, will be with us till death do us part.

This is rarely true of the marriages in her fiction. . . . Whether set in steamy New Orleans, anonymous New York or flaky Berkeley, her stories repeatedly chronicle the disintegration of relationships. Avarice and alcoholism are common causes; so are depression (especially in the women), an obsession with appearance (diets are a prominent theme) and the women's desire to establish a creative life separate from the men. Not one man in *Drunk With Love,* her latest collection—not one man in her whole body of work, with the possible exception of a youthful Arkansas guitar-player in *The Annunciation*—is good enough for the women he takes up with.

In this collection, that tendency is exaggerated to the point where two of the husbands (a Lebanese immigrant in **"The Emancipator"** and a black man in **"Memphis"**) murder the blond young women who have foolishly married them. This is touchy business for a white Southern writer to deal with, and Ms. Gilchrist does not handle it well. Whereas a writer like Flannery O'Connor could distance herself from Southern racism even as she presented it from within, Ms. Gilchrist seems implicated in her own characters' attitudes. Thus a third interracial relationship, between a black chauffeur and his older

white employer in **"First Manhattans,"** suffers gravely from the disturbing clichés placed in the mind of the black character: "Next thing I know she'll be wanting to get married, Kenny thought. These white women go crazy."

One would like to write off this kind of stereotyping as an aberration, but unfortunately Ms. Gilchrist's work is riddled with it. Her Jews tend to be smart, rotund and money-grubbing; Catholics, she suggests, are always viciously sanctimonious; mountain boys have unrestrainable sex drives; Californians spend their lives in hot tubs; and so on.

In fact, when you look at Ellen Gilchrist's stories closely, the illusion of variety begins to wear off. From a distance, you seem to be glimpsing a wild, well-populated, vastly amusing party, its lights and laughter occasionally discernible through a screen of thick trees. But as you approach the trees and peer through—as you piece together the fragments from her various stories—you notice that there is only a small number of people at the party after all: a weary, neurotic Southern wife, her overworked, insensitive Jewish husband; a cynical female artist or two (one of them a red-haired writer); some faithful black servants; an irresponsible, charming lover; and few others. They may change clothes and appearances at times, but they are basically a tiny group, vainly trying to simulate the enormous gathering they wish they were attending. Next time Ms. Gilchrist should invite some new guests.

> Wendy Lesser, "Home Movies," in The New York Times Book Review, *October 5, 1986, p. 18.*

D. D. GUTTENPLAN

Dear Ellen Gilchrist:

Ever since the first page of *In the Land of Dreamy Dreams* you have been my Favorite Living American Writer. I've read all your books. I want to run away with Nora Jane Whittington, ex-bandit and expectant mother. I know she's only a character, but to marry her off to either of the two jerks she's considering in the title story of *Drunk With Love* would be a big mistake. Promise me you'll at least think about it.

I figure you're a kind of Mississippi magical realist, and can get away with almost anything. Take the beginning of **"The Last Diet"**: "On the twenty-fourth day of August, nineteen hundred and eighty-five, JeanAnne Lori Mayfield, third child and only daughter of Mr. and Mrs. Johnny Wayne Mayfield of Fayetteville, Arkansas, ended her last and final diet by running her navy blue Toyota sedan into a doughnut shop." That sentence has a lot going for it: tradition, rhythm, funny southern names, and a good eye for detail. And though it is raucous, practically redneck, in tone, the story that grows out of it is, in a low-key way, heartbreaking. But the reader doesn't notice this until it's too late to do anything but keep on turning pages.

A writer who can surprise that way is worth sticking by. . . . Even when her new book [*Drunk With Love*] is a little softer-edged than I'd like. So I'm still with you. But I'm worried.

Reading your stories has taught me a lot about how to pay attention—to the baby carriage on the stairs in **"Rich,"** the fur bedspread in **"There's a Garden of Eden,"** the little girl's tent in **"Traceleen at Dawn."** I'm not talking about Chekhov's pistol, hanging on the wall, ready to end the play with a bang. I'm talking about the easy-to-miss details that keep all unhappy families—and happy ones too—from being alike.

So when I read your new story **"The Emancipator,"** I really started to get nervous. Early on the main character, an ex-Peace Corps worker named Mae, asks herself a rhetorical question: "Surely it was there, a simple place where men and women could lie down in joy and rise up in joy." The answer, of course, is, No such luck. Mae marries a Lebanese exchange student; he beats her for not learning how to make Turkish coffee, then he strangles her. The very next story in the book is called **"Memphis."** It begins like this: "Her horror and fascination with his size. His power, his hands, feet, mouth, dick, all that stuff that carried her across the door of that little frame house on T Street and kept her there until her neck snapped."

Like Mae, the woman in **"Memphis"** is white. Her lover is black. Now I am from Memphis, and it's possible I'm over-sensitive, but I think something is going on here.

I'm referring to race. In the past, you always treated relations between whites and blacks as the central and most interesting fact about life in these confederate states. Often your sharp eye—and implacable honesty—made me wince with recognition: "Robert's mother was a liberal. She never called black people niggers or Negroes even when she was mad at them." You even managed to put life into that stock figure of post-plantation fiction, the maid. . . .

So no, I don't believe you are a racist. Even now, even when you've gone and put two stories together, back-to-back, which seem to say: "Cross the line and you're dead. Sleep with a black man and he'll kill you for thanks." At least, no more than any of the rest of us. But I had to think about it quite a while.

I thought about Traceleen and Gus, the teen-aged black dope dealer in **"The President of the Louisiana Live Oak Society."** I wondered why practically all the black characters in your stories are servants—and then I felt like an idiot for wondering. I took a hard look at the narrator's summing up in **"Memphis":** "Black people. We brought them here. Someone did. Not me. We are being punished forever, the bringers and the brought." And I realized that the whole topic made me uncomfortable. Which may well have been your intention.

The funny thing is that much of *Drunk With Love* is pretty lightweight stuff—a few early chapters in the life of Rhoda Manning (a kind of prequel to *Victory Over Japan*), a couple of midlife romances, a story about skin diving. It's almost as if the effort of writing **"Memphis"** and **"The Emancipator"** took all the passion out of you, leaving dreamy bemusement. I hope you get over it. I hope you write more. Soon.

> *D. D. Guttenplan, "Lie Down with Darkness," in* The Village Voice, *Vol. XXXII, No. 4, January 27, 1987, p. 54.*

JOHN MELMOTH

A number of Ellen Gilchrist's new stories [in *Drunk With Love*] require us to accept that things go harder for the rich and pampered than they do for the rest of us, that it is more painful to be loaded but miss out on that final, essential 1 per cent than it is to be used to having nothing in the first place. The fact, for example, that Sally in **"The Blue-Eyed Buddhist"** is dying of kidney failure is supposedly more poignant because she is leaving behind lobster suppers and cruises around the Virgin Islands. Gilchrist's poor little rich girls certainly take it to heart when reality fails to conform to their requirements.

Other stories make the opposite, more prosaic and obvious point that things are never so bad if one is able to cry all the way to the tennis/yacht/bridge/supper club. . . .

Either way, there is no nonsense about money not making any difference. Loot is the primary fact of life for the majority of Gilchrist's characters; it both shapes and inhibits their development. The possession of money may not consort easily with maturity, but there is no denying that it improves the appetite. Gilchrist's women are activated by an insouciant, piratical rapaciousness which blurs the distinction between being drunk with love, drunk with power and just drunk. Rhoda is the paradigmatic case; in **"Adoration"**, the iron willpower of the spoilt brat emerges as an almost mystical determination not to miscarry during her "ecstatic pregnancy". When Mrs Beadle in **"The Young Man"** wants a toy boy she orders one from a mail order catalogue. When he proves beautiful but dull she trades him for a woman with "long legs and a long waist. A singing voice. Piano skills." Her conception of what is due to her *amour propre* is nothing if not precise. . . .

Gilchrist has doubtless discovered by now that being endlessly compared with Carson McCullers and Tennessee Williams can pall. None the less, she is self-consciously a Southern writer, and never more so than when she exploits the vein of steamy gothic that follows the course of the Mississippi. In **"Memphis"**, Katherine Louise ("Baby Kate") challenges her kind's taboos against miscegenation. She is fascinated by her black lover's "size. His power, his hands, feet, mouth, dick, all that stuff." That matters will end tragically is never in doubt; like a modern Desdemona she does little to defend herself. Her aunt acknowledges that Baby's death is what the genre demands: "Anybody in my family could tell a version of this. This is the real story. Of whisky and slaves and bored women and death."

Drunk With Love fixes a talent to provoke in the process of being house-trained; the stories are not as nasty, funny or sexy as their predecessors. Even violent death is not what it was. Baby Kate's lover dispatches her with a good clean break of the spine, whereas in the earlier **"Suicides"** Philip went to work on himself with half the contents of a hardware store—"He bought saws and ice picks and hammers and knives and staplers and drills." The collection creates a sense of *déjà vu*, of things done well because they have been done before. The return appearances of Nora Jane and Rhoda reinforce this sense of familiarity, which compromises Gilchrist's more over-wrought effects.

> *John Melmoth, "Poor Little Rich Belles," in* The Times Literary Supplement, *No. 4379, March 6, 1987, p. 246.*

JUDY COOKE

There's nothing poignant about Ellen Gilchrist's *Drunk With Love*. It's vivid, exhilarating, continually surprising; a collection of stories satisfyingly crafted and complete but so full of drama that any one of them, you feel, might have been extended into a novel. . . .

["*Drunk With Love*"] introduces Freddy Harwood on a bad day. . . . He has to face the fact that his girlfriend, Nora Jane (whose middle name should be Hurricane) is pregnant. What he doesn't know is that he's also about to encounter fire, earthquake, hospitalisation and the results of his girl's amniocentesis. The ending of the story envisages Nora Jane's twins, old Yuppies in the womb, trying to figure out Mom.

> 'She's always changing. Up and down. Up and
>   down.
> Get used to it. We'll be there soon.
> Let's don't think about it.'

Quite an act to follow—but the author continues at this smart pace, page after sparkling page. She is particularly good on the American South, where she lives (although the New York stories are classic; as, indeed, are the small-town ferocities of Rhoda, from Harrisburg, Illinois). **"Traceleen at Dawn"** is set in New Orleans and follows the fortunes of Miss Crystal, Mr Manny and their fire-raising little girl through the narration of a faithful black maid. The sense of place, the psychological subtleties, the vivid characterisation—these are the qualities which have already earned Ellen Gilchrist acclaim. This latest book finds her on top form. (p. 27)

> *Judy Cooke, "Intimate Voices," in* The Listener,
> *Vol. 117, No. 3003, March 19, 1987, pp. 26-7.*

ALISON FELL

Ellen Gilchrist's prose is as taut and spacious as Joan Didion's or Margaret Atwood's and, like them, she turns a wry, ap-praising eye on her own spoilt America. Drunk with consumption as much as *Drunk with Love,* Gilchrist's characters have a terrible time coping with their appetites. 'The body is not on your side in anything,' muses the tragi-comic heroine of **"The Last Diet"** as she arms herself yet again for the good fight, and drying out is Miss Crystal's problem in **"Traceleen at Dawn",** a wicked tale of a Southern belle as narrated by her devoted black maid.

On the pitfalls of women's hunger for love, Gilchrist's tone is more sombre and cautionary. Unfortunately, in **"Memphis"** and **"The Emancipator"**, both stories of mixed marriages, the theme of naivety or masochism in women is quite overshadowed by the brutality of the black husbands. This is tricky territory for a white writer and I, for one, was uneasy with the result. In **"Anna Part 1"**, on the other hand, where a woman writer extricates herself from an affair with a married man and goes staunchly back to work, Gilchrist's pitch is near-perfect. It takes skill to convince us that, in the middle of all this excess, some people do fall seriously—or ludicrously—in love, but this she does, reminding us with a lovely laconic touch that 'In a band of stars a billion light-years long this was not the only important thing going on. But it was one of them.' (p. 29)

> *Alison Fell, "Heaven and Hell," in* New Statesman,
> *Vol. 113, No. 2923, April 3, 1987, pp. 28-9.*

William (W.) Goldman
1931-

(Has also written under pseudonym of Harry Longbaugh)
American novelist, scriptwriter, nonfiction writer, dramatist,
short story writer, author of children's books, and critic.

Best known as the scriptwriter for such successful films as
Butch Cassidy and the Sundance Kid and *All the President's
Men*, Goldman is also recognized as a diverse novelist who
has earned critical praise for his imaginative story lines and
lively, straightforward narrative technique. Lawrence Block
observed: "Lack of tension has never been a problem for William Goldman, who has shown himself capable . . . of writing
virtually every kind of book but a dull one." Goldman's first
published work, *The Temple of Gold* (1957), details the clash
between protagonist Raymond Trevitt's youthful ideals and the
disconcerting realities of adulthood. The book examines two
of Goldman's primary concerns: loss of innocence and the
dichotomy between illusion and reality. Goldman further explores these themes in his next novel, *Your Turn to Curtsy,
My Turn to Bow* (1958), in which Chad Kimberly's self-de-
lusions bring about his mental breakdown. *Soldier in the Rain*
(1960) chronicles the comic and tragic aspects of military life
during the Korean War.

Goldman's first popular success, *Boys and Girls Together* (1964),
concerns six disillusioned youths from the Midwest who flee
their claustrophobic home lives and meet in New York City.
David D. Galloway declared that this novel "spins together
with unflagging vitality and inexhaustible inventiveness the
multiple, frequently contradictory experiences and values which
make up American life." In *The Thing of It Is . . .* (1967) and
its sequel, *Father's Day* (1971), Goldman traces the damaging
effects upon family members of the deterioration of a marriage.
*The Princess Bride: S. Morgenstern's Classic Tale of True
Love and High Adventure; The "Good Parts" Version, Abridged*
(1975) is a comic fantasy that incorporates and lampoons elements of the fairy tale, the medieval adventure story, and the
romance novel. *Tinsel* (1979) exposes the hypocrisy within the
American film industry. In *Control* (1982), Goldman examines
a society in which thought control and reincarnation take place,
and in *The Color of Light* (1984), he presents the story of a
novelist who fails to live up to his initial success.

In several novels, Goldman employs conventions of the psychological suspense thriller. *No Way to Treat a Lady* (1964),
published under the pseudonym of Harry Longbaugh, recounts
a Manhattan detective's efforts to track down a psychopathic
strangler. In *Marathon Man* (1974), a college student is unwittingly drawn into a elaborate ploy to obtain diamonds that
were smuggled into the United States by Nazi war criminals.
Brothers (1986) is a sequel to *Marathon Man* in which the
student's brother, a government agent believed to have been
killed in the first book, is revealed to be involved in a clandestine plot with American intelligence forces. *Magic* (1976)
centers on a schizophrenic ventriloquist whose alter ego, the
wooden puppet Fats, dominates his thoughts and actions, *Heat*
(1985) is written in the tradition of the "hard-boiled" detective
story as practiced by such authors as Raymond Chandler and
Ross Macdonald. Set in Las Vegas, this novel concerns a

© *Jerry Bauer*

private investigator who becomes entangled with the mafia
when he avenges the violent beating of a prostitute.

Goldman's screenplays have earned substantial critical acclaim
and have garnered him Academy Awards for *Butch Cassidy
and the Sundance Kid* and *All the President's Men*. His other
screenplays include *Harper*, *The Hot Rock*, *The Great Waldo
Pepper*, *Marathon Man*, *A Bridge Too Far*, *Magic*, and *The
Princess Bride*. Goldman has also written a book for children,
Wigger (1974), and two nonfiction works, *The Season: A Candid Look at Broadway* (1969) and *Adventures in the Screen
Trade* (1983).

(See also *CLC*, Vol. 1; *Contemporary Authors*, Vols. 9-12,
rev. ed.; and *Dictionary of Literary Biography*, Vol. 44.)

DAVID DEMPSEY

The scapegrace hero who has come to be such a familiar figure
in recent American fiction turns up in this first novel [*The
Temple of Gold*] by William Goldman as one Raymond Euripides Trevitt, a young man who just can't seem to "find the
handle." This is what Zachary ("Zock") Crowe, his best friend,

123

is grasping for too. Between them it becomes a kind of adolescent mystique, a latchstring to the temple of gold.

The handle I'll buy, but the temple of gold I'm not sure of. It is a literary symbol that sits a little too heavily on an unassuming and rollicking kind of story that is better off without Significance. For Mr. Goldman never probes very deeply into his characters—and we have only his word for it that they behave the way they do.

Euripides, so named by a father who teaches Greek literature, is distinguished by an uncommon affinity for disaster. . . . In the Army, his buddy is one Ulysses S. Kelly, a depressed type who blows himself up with a hand grenade, wounding Euripides in the bargain. Zock himself is killed in an automobile smash-up with Euripides at the wheel. Eventually, young Trevitt goes back to college, works on the literary magazine and marries a creature named Terry Clark, who shares her charms with other men.

Where do we go from here? Mr. Goldman is not sure. And *The Temple of Gold* is reeled off at such a fast clip that the reader is not given time to ask. . . . It is a readable novel. There are moments of tenderness, of real humor. It is facile—but it leaves no echoes. Its chief handicap is too much fountain of youth.

> *David Dempsey, "In Search of a 'Handle'," in The New York Times Book Review, November 17, 1957, p. 54.*

HERBERT MITGANG

William Goldman has a lot going for him in *Soldier in the Rain,* a novel about training camp life in a clay-colored Southern locale at the end of the Korean war. He's got the country boy in uniform, big grin and all, once met in Mac Hyman's *No Time for Sergeants.* And he also has a few garrison deceptions that Nat Hiken's "Sergeant Bilko" sustains endlessly but without, unfortunately, a Phil Silvers to carry them off.

The author attempts to go beyond the familiar laugh situations. After two-thirds of the book is devoted to this sort of material, suddenly the reader is asked to switch gears and accept the fact that *Soldier in the Rain* is really a serious work about a troubled youth whose behavior is related to lack of family in the past. It could be that some readers will accept this, for the intent of the author is to draw a poignant character. This reader does not. Sergeant Eustis Clay, the soldier in the rain of the title, is so naïve that he seems to be a city novelist's version of a Tennessee ridge-runner. . . .

The author's strong point is that he does capture the talk and the ways of young people. (He also knows his J. D. Salinger.). . . The reporting of the community and its mores as well as isolated views of military life in a training camp are the work of an able observer. . . .

Yet that is not enough because the garrison life—unlike the combat life—has no built-in drama. In the training camp days of early World War II, Marion Hargrove's *See Here, Private Hargrove,* seemed like the last word in innocent-private-exasperated-sergeant merriment, but it only took a year or so of real war to date and even expose the nonsense. It is one thing to play it for laughs only, manufacturing absurd situations. What the author of *Soldier in the Rain* is asking the reader to do is, in effect, recognize that a Sergeant Bilko had a troubled youth. Who cares? Nat Hiken would never pull a Punchinello switch on a trusting audience.

> *Herbert Mitgang, "Bugles and Belles," in The New York Times Book Review, July 17, 1960, p. 26.*

PHOEBE-LOU ADAMS

[*Soldier in the Rain*] starts out like a standard military farce. Sergeant Eustis Clay, Mr. Goldman's hero, is, from the Army point of view, a canny veteran who contrives to live quite happily at Camp Scott in the last days of the Korean War, conduct a giddy social life, maintain a friendship with the local intelligentsia, do very little work, retain his rank, and accomplish all this with a minimum of annoyance from the authorities. (p. 97)

Almost every episode in *Soldier in the Rain* is funny in itself. . . . But while the chatter is comical and the action often wildly absurd, the book as a whole is sad. Brightness falls from the air, friends get transferred or killed, the base closes, and the little town turns out the neon lights and goes back to sleep. Only the indomitable Eustis is left, and he, although he doesn't know it, is well on the way to becoming a professional re-enlister, a refugee in uniform. . . .

Occasionally Mr. Goldman tries straight sentiment and becomes both saccharine and implausible, but these lapses are too few to spoil the book. About 90 per cent of the time, *Soldier in the Rain* balances neatly on the narrow line between laughter and tears. (p. 98)

> *Phoebe-Lou Adams, "Two Musketeers," in The Atlantic Monthly, Vol. 206, No. 2, August, 1960, pp. 97-8.*

CONRAD KNICKERBOCKER

Men like Herman Wouk, Leon Uris, Harold Robbins, and Irving Stone sit atop a golden world glittering with best-seller lists, in-store promotions, paperback rights, foreign rights, movie rights, maybe even an interview with Jack Paar. Success in this world depends on knowing the game, and the name of the game is deception—the ability to convince the reader that existence is not as it might seem, boring, inexplicable, and dangerous, but full of wonderful probabilities. . . .

The game's rewards are rich; the contenders for championship are many. With his fourth novel, [*Boys and Girls Together*], William Goldman becomes a contender. . . .

The gang in *Boys and Girls Together* is a group of young people with interminable life histories. One is a brilliant, half-crippled Princeton townie who sulks for awhile on that campus; another is a card from St. Louis, who does likewise at Oberlin. (One means to write, the other to break into the theater.) A fat deviant from Cleveland yearns to produce on Broadway. A female Paul Bunyan from the tall timber yearns to be a Broadway actress. A disadvantaged, parent-battered Chicago youth called Rudolph Valentino Miller finds he can act—and so on. All are blocked, in various ways, by heredity, environment, or both. All of them, after endless postponements, move dismally toward New York. Here, through some peculiar catalysis of banality, they get together at a party. One of them jumps off a fire escape, crawls back upstairs and dies amid the warm Scotch and hors d'oeuvres. A comforting climax, as probable, familiar and uncomplicated as all the violences we seek on the television and movie screens to quiet our doubts.

Familiarity is the secret of the game. Playwrights are homosexual, of course, as elderly delicatessen owners are kind and wise. If an aspiring stage director receives his first assignment, he runs skipping through Greenwich Village yelling, "I've got a play!" Sexual conquest must be celebrated by gamboling in the rain. Adulterers speak in three-word sentences, lip to lip. Recognitions shiver—but not the pang of life confronted. Instead, Mr. Goldman pays homage to the thousands of images flickering down the generations in open-air theaters, miniaturized in darkened living rooms, the fire of dreams consumed and truths denied.

Boys and Girls Together extends the Californiazation of the novel. Finely packaged, it works in aerosol fashion. Two ounces of material, pressurized with a harmless gas, produce foam and noise when released. Meanwhile, the void yawns and the game goes on.

> *Conrad Knickerbocker, "Playing the Game," in* The New York Times Book Review, *July 26, 1964, p. 24.*

DAVID D. GALLOWAY

In *Boys and Girls Together* William Goldman has composed (or perhaps 'compiled' is the better word) a singularly American novel. It is a polymorphous book that spins together with unflagging vitality and inexhaustible inventiveness the multiple, frequently contradictory experiences and values which make up American life. The sprawling structure of the novel accommodates a varied host of characters; their several and often interlocking stories are revealed in a dazzlingly versatile language which suggests that, as technician, Goldman belongs to the diverse and distinguished company headed by Cheever, Bellow, Updike and Malamud.

The book chronicles the experiences of six young people (and an almost uncountable chorus of satellite figures) whose lives all begin in that vague Middle West from which Nick Adams and Nick Carraway once emerged; and their lives converge on 'the sidewalks of New York'.... Here, however, one finds boys and boys together as well as boys and girls, the focus is more often the mattresses than the sidewalks of New York, and the movement of the concluding chapters is not so much a 'light fantastic as a *danse macabre*.

The pitfalls of this sort of macrocosmic novel are obvious, and not all of them have been avoided; lacking a constant narrative focus, the book often seems in danger of dissipating itself in a fury of centrifugal energy, and no doubt many readers will feel that its imposing bulk (744 pages) is unjustified. The final section of the novel, which narratively and thematically attempts to fuse the many tales together, never manages to appear greater than the sum of its interesting and diverse parts....

Boys and Girls Together depends for its final shape and cohesion not so much on an annealing conclusion as on the thematic parallels between the six major characters' intense and often frustrated quests for love; here one sees Goldman's masterful gift as story-teller, and if there are too many stories, it is too much of what seems a very good thing indeed. (p. 334)

> *David D. Galloway, "The Light Fantastic," in* The Spectator, *Vol. 214, No. 7133, March 12, 1965, pp. 334-35.*

MARTIN LEVIN

[*The Thing of It Is . . .*] catches the spirit of a young couple whose marriage is foundering on a trip abroad. Rarely does Mr. Goldman get beneath the surface qualities of Amos and Lila McCracken, as they bicker and snarl their way from London to Venice. But he does capture the bottled-up hostility felt in a London taxi; a nightmarish spat in the Whispering Gallery of St. Paul's; the bleakness that is accentuated by the carnival atmosphere of Piazza San Marco. The husband is a successful song writer, unsure of himself, ashamed of being part Jew and of being regarded as a "sissy" from boyhood. His wife is not identified even by such standard characteristics as these, but by a strain of exasperated bitchiness. Their conversation has the ringing authority of dialogues overheard through motel walls. It compels attention—but it does not linger.

> *Martin Levin, in a review of "The Thing of It Is . . .,"* in The New York Times Book Review, *April 19, 1967, p. 41.*

JOHN W. HATTMAN

[*The Thing of It Is . . .*] shows the disintegration of a marriage; yet the thing of it is that the three people involved desperately need one another. Amos McCracken, financially successful songwriter, and his wife Lila realize that their marriage is falling apart. In a last effort to save it, they and their six-year-old daughter Jessica have travelled to London....

The family crack-up is made terribly vivid and disturbing when the fights between Amos and his wife take place in front of the child. In a pathetic gesture, the child begins mock games, imitations and demonstrations of knowledge in an effort to distract her parents from their vicious battles. The parents even use the child as a weapon against each other, Amos trying to prove to Lila that Jessica loves him more than her, Lila responding by trying to make little Jessica see her father as a failure....

The Thing of It Is . . . is dissatisfying in that it leaves all basic questions unanswered. It demonstrates the statement of Amos' analyst that, "It's just goddamned difficult for two people to live together". But it shows no meaningful rewards of love that might make a marriage worth the effort. The language is often vulgar and the sexual passages are graphic, but this seems necessary to present the reality of this warped marriage. The question is whether or not the warped marriage is worth presenting.

> *John W. Hattman, in a review of "The Thing of It Is . . .,"* in Best Sellers, *Vol. 27, No. 3, May 1, 1967, p. 52.*

WILLIAM B. HILL, S.J.

William Goldman is apt to give a reader some bewildering moments but he is not likely to give him dull ones. He races along through narrative and dialogue, managing to be both swift and vivid; and, using all his skills, he manages also, in *Father's Day*, to give a sad, pathetic picture of a lost man.

The title is a good one—not Father's Day in June but the one day that Amos McCracken spends with his daughter, an appealing little six-year-old. There are flashbacks but only brief ones, essential to the narrative.... Amos is a fading song writer and increasingly unable to cope, increasingly exasperated with the world around him, a loser. The day brings out all the affection he has for the child and his wisdom in dealing with her; and if he takes off into fantasy from time to time, puzzling the reader for a moment, it is only because the fantasies explore some of his longings for wholeness, and some of his dreads.

There are a couple of brief and explicit scenes between Amos and his mistress but for the greater part this is the sad, effective portrait of a man bound in an acerbic marriage to a woman who might have been different but is in fact cruel and stupid. (pp. 535-36)

> *William B. Hill, S.J., in a review of "Father's Day,"*
> *in* Best Sellers, *Vol. 30, No. 24, March 15, 1971,*
> *pp. 535-36.*

S. K. OBERBECK

In defense of silliness during these dire times, we recommend William Goldman's charming hoax *The Princess Bride,* a fantasy adventure of knights, beasts, dark vendettas, absurd duels and swooning passions. Goldman says it was written by one "Simon Morgenstern" and first read to him by his father when he had pneumonia as a child. Actually, of course, it's the novelist and Oscar-winning screenwriter . . . concocting a "classic" medieval melodrama that sounds like all the Saturday serials you ever saw feverishly reworked by the Marx Brothers. Goldman's "good parts" version allows him as "editor" to "restore" the juicy grownup stuff that was cut out of the children's version.

His ridiculously swashbuckling fable is nutball funny, a sweet-and-sour delicatessen of Graustark and Klopstock that relates the adventures of the beauteous Buttercup, a Candide-like hero named Westley, the bloodthirsty Prince Humperdinck, the masked Man in Black, Count Rugen, three Marx Brothers zanies and other denizens of the lands of Florin and Guilder. (p. 97)

Buttercup sounds more like a Jewish princess than a medieval maid, and the prince, worried about "overexposure," cozens her into marriage like a movie mogul propositioning a hopeful starlet. "Editor" Goldman explains such anomalies with a simple footnote: "You think a guy named Simon Morgenstern was an Irish Catholic?" Anyway, he deserves a few dollars for the daffy tale he concocts out of Guilder and Florin. (p. 98)

> *S. K. Oberbeck, "Shaggy Dog," in* Newsweek, *Vol.*
> *LXXXII, No. 12, September 17, 1973, pp. 97-8.*

GERALD WALKER

[*The Princess Bride: S. Morgenstern's Classic Tale of True Love and High Adventure* is] a witty, affectionate send-up of the adventure-yarn form, which Goldman (as the screenwriter for *Butch Cassidy and the Sundance Kid*) obviously loves and knows how to manipulate with enormous skill. You could say that it's the novelistic equivalent of Sandy Wilson poking fun, in *The Boy Friend,* at his equally obviously adored twenties musical comedies—except that Goldman goes even further. He has set up the story with an intro telling how as a boy, he loved having his father read him the alleged S. Morgenstern classic, but that when he himself gave the book to *his* 10-year-old son, the kid stopped reading after an early chapter. Goldman goes on to say that he then actually read the book for the first time and found that his father, in reading aloud to him, had simply and wisely skipped or telescoped the boring parts, hence this

"good parts" version "abridged" by Goldman. He keeps breaking up the narrative with red-inked passages, explaining what he's cut here and why. What this introduces is a kind of comedic extension of Brecht's distancing effect, alienation to provoke not an intellectual response, but an *entertained* response. And it works.

> *Gerald Walker, in a review of "The Princess Bride:*
> *S. Morgenstern's Classic Tale of True Love and High*
> *Adventure," in* The New York Times Book Review,
> *December 23, 1973, p. 14.*

GENE LYONS

The Marathon Man of William Goldman's [*Marathon Man*] is a graduate student with two goals: to be a greater runner than Paavo Nurmi, and to write a dissertation exonerating his father, a historian harassed into suicide by Joe McCarthy. Rather he becomes entangled in a plot to avenge two former Nazi war criminals, learning along the way the pleasures of torture and mutilation—from both sides. The entire plot hangs on the secret that "Doc," the student's businessman brother, and United States Government karate hit man "Scylla, the rock, who could kill with either hand," are in fact the same person. Since both are extensively treated in limited third-person narration previous to that revelation, it seems rather unsporting of Goldman to keep it from the reader. No matter, though, for the depth of characterization is such that one would experience an equal jolt upon finding out that Nancy is Sluggo in drag. This sort of nonsense, together with the cinematic layout and almost childishly mawkish style leads one to suspect that this is one of those cases where the screen-play is father to the novel. Part of the promotional package, as it were.

The socially redeeming deep hidden meaning of the book is found in the lines delivered by the erstwhile student as he slowly pumps bullets into the dying fascist: "all this time we should have been giving back pain. That's the real lesson. That's the loser's share, just pain, pure and simple pain and torture, no hotshot lawyers running around trying to see that justice is done." A liberal's *Death Wish.* With pictures it just may go.

> *Gene Lyons, in a review of "Marathon Man," in*
> The New York Times Book Review, *October 27,*
> *1974, p. 51.*

WILLIAM R. EVANS

[*Marathon Man*] is full of surprises. . . . Goldman is a master of swift action, mystery, and suspense. His style is crisp and straightforward, which means our interest is held in spite of many intricate ins and outs in the plot. One method Goldman uses successfully is to introduce the reader early in the book to characters who apparently have nothing to do with the main action of the story. We learn something about them, then they are dropped, then they reappear later in significant positions. Eventually all the pieces of the puzzle fit together and we see that from beginning to end every character and every event means something. The episodes that seemed irrelevant turn out to be meaningful, usually in retrospect.

As in most adventure stories, there are some rather farfetched incidents, but they can be overlooked. The author's sense of invention is so fertile and apt that one or two excesses don't really matter. . . .

Unlike many thrillers, **Marathon Man** has some serious implications. Upon finishing it, the reader finds that the issues of hatred, war, destruction, and revenge focus in the mind. Are these things naturally part of humankind? Are we condemned to go on making the same mistakes, year after year, decade after decade? If such a thing as a timely, relevant, thoughtful novel of suspense exists, this is it.

> *William R. Evans, in a review of "Marathon Man," in* Best Sellers, *Vol. 34, No. 15, November 1, 1974, p. 335.*

SHELDON FRANK

William Goldman is really collapsing as a novelist. His early books were well-crafted, moderately interesting, psychological novels, and he had a distinctive talent for creating characters through dialogue. But in recent years he has tried to graft his natural style onto genre forms. The results, to be kind, have been uneven. Most recently he wrote the highly gimmicky unthrilling thriller **Marathon Man,** and now, in **Magic,** he is dallying with Grand Guignol. The story involves the bizarre psychological disintegration of a young magician. Goldman can still write adequate dialogue, but he sets up his shocking scenes with the subtlety of a pile driver. **Magic** is a gross assault on the reader's senses. (pp. 40-1)

> *Sheldon Frank, in a review of "Magic," in* The New York Times Book Review, *September 12, 1976, pp. 40-1.*

EDWARD F. WARNER

Magic is a fascinating novel about the dark world of a man's mind driven to its inevitable end. (p. 278)

The novel deals with the quest in life of Corky, a struggling magician, who is searching for the fame and fortune he desperately needs in order to find fulfillment. His craving for personal recognition is so overpowering that he is driven to extreme and erratic measures to achieve it. The startling conclusion is a fitting result of the psychological action of the entire novel.

Many times a reader feels forced to certain moods or frames of mind as a result of the use of contrived terror, but Goldman is able to weave a sound, natural narrative and from this produce an even more compelling, and therefore more devastating, horror in the actions of his character.

Aside from a rather fragmented approach at the inception of the novel, a technique which later we find out was necessary, the novel reads extremely easily. (p. 279)

> *Edward F. Warner, in a review of "Magic," in* Best Sellers, *Vol. 36, No. 9, December, 1976, pp. 278-79.*

WALTER CLEMONS

[In **Tinsel**], the talk is incessantly baroque and the deals and double crosses have a convincing ring of insider's expertise. Since his screenplay for **Butch Cassidy and the Sundance Kid**, Goldman has been a phenomenally successful screenwriter, and his most recent books, **Marathon Man** and **Magic**, looked rather thin on the page, as if waiting to be photographed, which of course they immediately were.

Tinsel is much more specific, with a satisfying nuts-and-bolts supply of corroborative detail. It's about the financing and casting of a film about the last hours of Marilyn Monroe. When Raquel Welch refuses to appear nude in the part, the field is opened to three sex symbols in varying degrees of professional eclipse, one of whom, [as the producer] Garvey hopes, may "give us what Swanson gave Wilder in *Sunset Boulevard.*

Goldman has invented three interesting women who don't seem pasted together out of old gossip-column items. This is a distinct novelty in fiction about Hollywood. Their careers are independently plausible, and one of them, Dixie, a TV celebrity who retired to marry a rich dentist, is full-blooded enough to make the book worth reading away from the beach. . . . **Tinsel** is nasty, hard-edged entertainment.

> *Walter Clemons, "Fleshing Out Fantasyland," in* Newsweek, *Vol. XCIV, No. 7, August 13, 1979, p. 73.*

JULIA CAMERON

"Junk" is the genre into which **Tinsel** does not so much fall as leap. I suspect we are meant to mince words about this— "A man who cares more about his craft than his critics" says the jacket copy—but I don't mean to do that: William Goldman writes junk. He writes gloriously good junk sometimes and gloriously bad junk other times, but junk always and I suspect that's why I and a lot of other people have read him so faithfully these many years. . . .

A taste for Goldman, like a taste for junk food, is something that crops up in adolescence and lingers into adulthood where it takes the form of a periodic binge. Not since **Boys and Girls Together** has Goldman given his fans something so unabashedly "bad" to binge on. After his more serious books like **Marathon Man** and **Magic, Tinsel** comes as an enormous relief. . . .

I am afraid that Goldman will be unfairly accused of having written a "T 'n' A" book. This is simply not true. What Goldman has written is something enormously more rarified than that: a "T" book.

Breasts bobble, jiggle, loom, sag, jut, heave and peek from almost every page of **Tinsel**. "You're hurting them!" Goldman introduces one character, not two, a charming woman named Pig. "Poor babies," he finally writes her out. It is the first time I recall an author equating character development and bust development and I must say it struck me as something of a breakthrough. Philip Roth should love this book.

It occurs to me, however, that some people may not be quite so acutely keyed into Goldman's breast motif. Those people may, in fact, fall for the ploy that this book is really about Hollywood and not about breasts. After all, **Tinsel** tells us right on the dust jacket that Goldman is one of the "best-known and most-respected scriptwriters in the country today"—a line that tickled my scriptwriter's heart, comparing favorably, I thought, to being touted as "the best imitation margarine." Scriptwriters by definition are neither "best-known," nor "most-respected," except, perhaps, in Hollywood. I am a scriptwriter and I live in Hollywood and I can assure the reader that this book is really about breasts. There are those who would argue that Hollywood is really about breasts, and it's a good point— in fact, two of them: if Hollywood is really about breasts, then so is this book. . . .

The gap—or should I say the "cleavage"—between Goldman's talent as a writer and his talent as a thinker is brutally exposed in *Tinsel*. As his dialogue frequently proves, Goldman is a man who can write like an angel. As his narrative proves equally, however, many of his ideas could dance on the head of a pin. Scriptwriting plays to Goldman's strengths. (We have *Butch Cassidy and the Sundance Kid* and *All the President's Men* to thank him for.) The novel plays to his weaknesses.

Julia Cameron, "Hollywood Up Front," in Book World—The Washington Post, *August 19, 1979, p. 12.*

RICHARD ANDERSEN

The current of escape, an important theme in American history as well as literature, runs deep through each of Goldman's [first] ten novels. Generally, his protagonists are fleeing a society that encroaches on their desire to lead their own lives, but their flights also include an abandonment of innocence and former values for the discovery of adult realities and the rebirth of new identities. Most of Goldman's escapists are either individuals who no longer believe in the illusions by which they were brought up to live, or else they are impulsively reacting to their own conditioning in the hope of finding something better. They run the gamut from Raymond Trevitt, with his initial trust in the institutions of our society in *The Temple of Gold,* to Corky Withers, whose escape in *Magic* is one of desperation rather than hope. Hopeful or not, the escapes of Goldman's characters are more than just escapes. With the exception of the suicides in *Boys and Girls Together, Soldier in the Rain,* and *Magic* and the daydreams of Peter Bell and Eustis Clay, none of the escapes treated in Goldman's novels is permanent. Although Raymond Trevitt of *The Temple of Gold,* all but one of the characters in *Boys and Girls Together,* the heroes in *The Princess Bride,* and Babe Levy of *Marathon Man* will return to the societies they have left, they will not be the innocent people who originally fled them. Some of them may have achieved a greater degree of maturity for themselves, but most of them suggest no substantial growth. Consequently, what seems to be of most importance to Goldman is not the ends of his characters' escapes but rather the experiences of the escapes and the needs that brought them about.

The illusions men and women live by, which often make human existence more miserable than it need be, provide the core from which all of Goldman's protagonists seek to depart. Ironically, what they escape to is more often than not other illusions. Because of the artificial distinctions society attaches to the illusions it propagates about race, religion, and material gain, rarely are the human needs of society's individual members recognized.

In *The Temple of Gold,* Raymond Trevitt suffers a beating for his well-intentioned overfeeding of his father's fish, rejection by his mother for disturbing a faculty wives' party with the news of his dead dog, the loss of his friendship with a black student of whom his father does not approve, sexual rejection at the hands of Annabelle, who prefers the more prestigious Professor Janes, and failure to attain an editorship he deserves and needs to gain some sense of self-respect. When Raymond's reckless reaction to the forces of an uncompromising, inhuman society inadvertently causes the deaths of his closest friends, he tries to escape the society he knows in Athens, but discovers only frustration and intolerance elsewhere.

In *Your Turn to Curtsy, My Turn to Bow,* Chad Kimberly is driven by his ambition-oriented society into believing that he is Christ. As inhuman in his demands on his disciple as society has been on him, Chad's schizophrenia frightens Peter Bell into a life of escapist daydreaming. Ambition is not the only illusion that drives the protagonists of *Boys and Girls Together* to New York; most of them are escaping from the unbearable circumstances of their home lives. Nevertheless, their hopes for self-improvement are dashed by unsuccessful love affairs, parents who will not release control of them, professional failures, embarrassing social exposures, and suicide. In *Soldier in the Rain,* Eustis Clay, a successful product of the military-economic complex, is more concerned with making easy money and gaining material comforts than about the abuse Jerry Meltzer suffers because of his Jewish heritage or the loss of Maxwell Slaughter through suicide.

Like the illusions fostered by racial and religious prejudice and materialistic ambition, the great American illusions about success also cause unhappiness and frustration. In *The Thing of It Is . . .* and *Father's Day,* the talented and financially successful Amos McCracken spends an enormous amount of money trying to save first his marriage and then his relationship with his daughter. In the end, his guilt-ridden personal failures lead him to create fantasies that enable him to fulfill the images he has of himself but that also pose a serious threat to the safety and well-being of others.

Westley and Buttercup of *The Princess Bride* believe that their love can conquer all, but they discover they also need the help of a muscleman and a wizard swordsman just to escape from the forces that work to control their lives in Florin. (pp. 107-09)

The Princess Bride is the last novel in which Goldman's characters believe they can escape temporarily from society's life-controlling forces. The protagonists of *Marathon Man* and *Magic* have no time to withdraw and ponder their situation. When they attempt to do so, they are quickly pursued by agents of the wasteland makers and must concentrate all their energies on battling both themselves and the powers that strive to control them. Unlike Amos McCracken of *Father's Day* and Kit Gil of *No Way to Treat a Lady,* Babe Levy of *Marathon Man* and Corky Withers of *Magic* cannot retreat to a fabulous land to try and make themselves whole; they already live in a fabulous land, where they are constantly assaulted by its empirical and psychological facts. Forced to encounter a vast confusion of fact and fiction, to deal with pain and death, and to seek power against forces that are difficult to pinpoint and consequently understand, Babe and Corky must stay rooted in a system that attempts to deny their vitality while creating illusions that life is what it should be. What affirmation Goldman's protagonists can achieve in this world seems to be the small but valuable awareness that life is simply better than death.

As a fabulist of thrillers, some of which come close to providing a cinematic experience, Goldman may be considered an accomplished and inventive storyteller, and, in thematic terms, a serious artist. Though his angle of vision has become increasingly more violent and absurd, he has not given way to despair or cynicism, but has managed to deal with his resignation about the human condition without losing his sense of humor or concern for humanity. Whether he will ever be labeled an important novelist depends on how well the books that incorporate this tempered vision survive the test of time. As they are read today, however, Goldman's works provide an unassailable argument against the novel-is-dead critics and effectively contribute to the life span of our literature's most popular and therefore most important genre.

Richard Andersen, in his William Goldman, *Twayne Publishers, 1979, 119 p.*

EVAN HUNTER

In suspense-writing jargon, a "reader cheater" is a story in which facts essential to an intelligent unraveling of the mystery are withheld from the reader. I would hesitate to label William Goldman's [*Control*] an outright reader cheater, but when misdirection comes within a hairsbreadth of deception—well.

Let me say as much as I can without giving away the intricate plot. *Control* has to do with mind control and reincarnation. The premise, as stated midway through, is that we (*and our* global enemies) can control the future by controlling the past. . . .

I confess at once to being a person of subintelligence who did not understand the plot of the film *Bullitt,* one of the few successful movies Mr. Goldman seems *not* to have written. . . . I further confess that I had to read his novel *twice* before I fully understood what was going on. Again, being limited in what I can tactfully reveal of the plot, suffice it to say that part of the story takes place in 1981, another part in 1960 and yet another in 1876. Yet for the first 245 pages of this 305-page book, there is no discernible clue that we are in any time frame but the recent present, an omission that heightens suspense at the cost of clarity. Moreover, the deception is deliberate; Mr. Goldman writes too well for us to assume he lost even momentary control of his book.

His pacing is swift and sure throughout, his dialogue crackling and humorous, his sense of background (New York, in this case) impeccable. He can shift character voice at the drop of a hat, writing adroitly and knowingly about a wide variety of human beings. . . .

One of these days, someone is going to produce a learned treatise on the somewhat wide-screen, ultrasophisticated, slick style of Los Angeles screenwriter-novelists like Mr. Goldman and John Gregory Dunne. Meanwhile, I suppose we should count our blessings. When their obvious talents produce such entertaining novels, perhaps the trip down the garden path is worthwhile. But in this case, oh, how I wish Mr. Goldman had played it a bit more honestly.

Evan Hunter, "How to Change the Past," in The New York Times Book Review, *April 25, 1982, p. 13.*

ELIZABETH WHEELER

William Goldman cheats.

Oh, he's clever about it. In his latest novel, *Control,* you don't realize what he's up to until you've been had—but good. And enjoyed the process. But he cheats—all the same.

For one thing, *Control* is all plot. Often the plot is pretty good—though Goldman is not above the odd red, or in one instance red-headed, herring—but that's all there is. It's Henry James in reverse and, as a result, *Control* fades quickly from memory. There's nothing to mull over without authorial consciousness, without a point of view.

The writer, however, is not the only missing person in the novel. *Control* also lacks characters. Oh, there are plenty of

folks hanging around . . . but they aren't people. They carry nothing of their own histories about them, offer no convictions from their pasts or presents. The plot, in fact, makes dispensing with such burdens a necessity.

The final cheat, in contrast, appears almost gratuitous. *Control* closes with a tricky-wicky ending that would help anyone struggling to define the difference between false and dishonest. It doesn't contradict the facts, which would be false; it merely has nothing to do with them. And if that's not enough weaseling, Goldman gilds the lily with one of those hero-survives-against-all-odds finales that seem mandatory in this post-television era. . . .

Goldman is a skilled and prolific writer. He no doubt knew how much, and how little, he was up to in *Control.* The book is intriguing, engrossing, fascinating. It isn't a good novel, but it's one hell of a reading experience.

Elizabeth Wheeler, "Goldman: When the Cheater Wins," in Los Angeles Times Book Review, *June 6, 1982, p. 10.*

DAVID QUAMMEN

At the end of his new novel, William Goldman notifies us that *The Color of Light* was created during "February 21-Memorial Day, 1983." Having been written at breakneck speed, it is probably best read the same way. That will bring you with merciful dispatch to the engrossing part, which begins about 35 pages before the conclusion.

Chub Fuller is the protagonist, a precocious writer who scores a great success with his first book, a collection of autobiographical stories, and then for 10 years finds himself crushed and defeated by the effort to produce a big novel. *The Color of Light* describes his passage, several times over, from hope to disillusionment and back again. . . .

The first of its three parts covers Chub's undergraduate years at Oberlin. We are shown his breathless desire to be a writer, and two secondary characters of abiding importance are introduced—a beautiful woman and a portly, acerbic friend who has been crippled. The woman is B. J. Peacock, later Chub Fuller's wife and still later a focus of his most painful memories. The friend is Stanley Kitchel, obnoxious and unpredictable and faultlessly loyal to Chub, a good creation who gives life to this book each time he reappears. . . .

The second section recounts [Chub's] loss of purposefulness, his marital travails, his deep love for his stepdaughter and then her accidental death, an implausible event treated with all possible bathos. In the third section, Chub has fallen still lower, living a dreary existence without even the self-delusion that his big novel is still progressing. . . . Then suddenly *The Color of Light* becomes a murder mystery.

This turn of plot provides some intensity and focus, but it comes as too little too late. Until then, the novel has been swerving in so many directions, interrupted so often by the author's insistently clumsy parenthetical asides, hijacked into so many page-filling digressions, that even the prospect of a foul murder to be solved and one final epiphany cannot make the book into a satisfying whole.

And there's another problem—language. At its best, Mr. Goldman's prose is breezy and conversational, lacking any embellishment that could impede the flow of the story. But at its worst and too often, it is flaccid, monotonous, carelessly un-grammatical, clumsy. In a word, hasty. That again.

Some people might argue that the speed at which a work was written is irrelevant—their backhanded implication being that no matter how much more time the author had taken, no matter how much more care, he was incapable of improving it. I'd rather give Mr. Goldman the benefit of the doubt.

David Quammen, *"Living to Find Material,"* in The New York Times Book Review, *April 15, 1984, p. 18.*

ELIZABETH MEHREN

[Far] from lyrical, as the title might suggest, **The Color of Light** is actually leaden. Where it should shine, it shuffles. But let's get specific:

Writers obviously love to write about writers. It's an old trick, a way to publicly disrobe, but to do so behind the scrim of a story. When the device works, the author can blush and say well, yes, as a matter of fact it was (to use the words of Goldman's publicist) "intensely personal"; yes it was an alter ego experience.

In the case of William Goldman and Chub-to-his-friends Fuller, one certainly hopes not. Fuller may be a flawed genius of a writer, a kid who weaves a fine first story, but he is also a bit of a dolt. When he writes (almost never, after early fame and great expectations are secured in the first third of the book), he does so frenetically and, astonishingly, almost letter perfect on the first draft. This is one of the qualities that captivates the (how convenient) book-publishing-scion who becomes his best-best best friend and mentor. . . .

Chub's relationships with women test the definition of naive. They all desert him, whether it's in the Hawaiian surf or out a window in midtown Manhattan. Like made-for-miniseries characters, they are rendered piecemeal and undeveloped, evincing, in most cases, qualities only a man could think of. (Tell me, is there a woman alive so embarrassed about her Caesarean scar that she only makes love in a half slip?)

Then again, many of the male characters are equally skimpy. Of course the creaky male librarian and Chub's major profes-sor, also male, are lovers. Of course his buddy on the police force is black: cop by day, law student by night. Sometimes they are so similar as to become confusing, a problem that also afflicts the book's chronology.

As we (at last) leave him, Chub still has yet to finish his story-within-a-story, *The Dead Pile*. It's a shame, because the prom-ise of that book seems so much greater than **The Color of Light** itself. "Life is material," Chub keeps telling himself, but not all material, obviously, is worth writing about. Even the weak-kneed and hackneyed characters of this book might have man-aged to limp along with a strong story for support. Alas, it's just not there.

Elizabeth Mehren, *"Fuller's Brush with the Lint of Life,"* in Los Angeles Times Book Review, *May 20, 1984, p. 10.*

DAVID MAMET

[The] wonderful thing about William Goldman's novels is this: they create a world in which we would like to live. That world is the world of *Invention*. This stuff is *satisfying*. Here in his new novel, **Heat,** we have a Tale of America. We have The Glider, a hit man from Tahoe who is a double for Fred Astaire; Baby, ruler of the Vegas Combination; Rainbeaux Wylie, am-bitious woman; Cyrus Kinnick, computer millionaire from Bos-ton; Ashley and Darryl Paxton, two media evangelists who've now turned to God.

And we have Shootouts, Punchouts, Rape and Revenge, a Gambling Binge written in the galloping style of Count Vron-sky's steeplechase. We have changes of fortune, identity and sex. We have the American language written with the glorious vitality of the self-taught: "The accent was so heavily British it made you want to break something."

And we have a lovely American Hero in Nick Escalante—contributor of the chapter "Give In to Win" to the book *Our Friend Violence,* a modern paean to the martial arts. Escalante is a Mexican-American, a former military policeman in Saigon. He is currently a private eye who describes himself as a chap-erone. He is an aficionado of airline timetables and travel literature. He longs to earn enough money to escape Las Vegas and set off on five years of uninterrupted travel.

What's the book about? Escalante is suffering through his 5,000th morning in Las Vegas. He wishes, at this auspicious juncture, to be presented with a test. He wants his inertia and impris-onment shattered (who counts time in days but prisoners?). He wants to be forced to confront himself. He wants a new life.

The gods—ever happy to oblige—answer his request with sev-eral tests, the correct response to any of which will be sufficient to transport him out of Vegas. His best friend, Holly, is beaten up and raped by three heavy-hitters. . . .

Holly begs Escalante to obtain revenge, and he enters the lists against the armed thugs who are trying to kill her. . . .

In the best tradiion of earlier heroic models, Escalante accepts *all* the tests offered him—of friendship, of arms, of augury by blackjack. And as the book closes, he is still accepting them. What does this mean? Well, he don't want to leave Vegas. And neither do we at the end of the book. As with many of Mr. Goldman's novels, we wish it to continue forever.

Mr. Goldman is a master storyteller and has done a master's trick. He has made us wish for ourselves the same thing the protagonist wishes for himself. In **Heat** it is this: to live forever in the safe and magic world he has created—the world of Friendly Hookers; of Roxy, the waitress of table 75; of hon-orable gangsters; wealthy benefactors; sneering toughs whose faces soon will be ground in the dirt, and interesting friends who will be true to us till death.

What a wonderful world.

David Mamet, *"Las Vegas, Love It or Leave It,"* in The New York Times Book Review, *May 19, 1985, p. 15.*

MARK SCHORR

Fans of Mike Hammer, the Executioner or the Destroyer will love [**Heat**], featuring larger-than-life bodyguard-adventurer Nick Escalante. In Escalante's own words, "Well, I've been knocked down, blown up, lied to and shot at, so nothing surprises me much anymore except the things people do to each other. I'm not a virgin, except in my heart."

Later, a woman says to the 6-foot, 3-inch "master of edged weapons," "You're not a violent man, then?" and Escalante responds, "I'm just good at it."

So, if you're expecting John Cheever, you better look elsewhere. . . .

Goldman, who gave us the most stomach-churning torture scene in recent years—his *Marathon Man* Nazi dental work was as memorable as a root canal—shows that he has plenty of blood and guts left in his word processor as he picks at the lice on the underbelly of Las Vegas.

There are a few light touches, notable scenes like Escalante seeking solace at the Liberace Museum, or his trip to Los Angeles. Goldman's Los Angeles gives Las Vegas a run for its money when it comes to greed, lust and oddballs.

The novelist-screenwriter is at his witty best when he's commenting on the less violent, bizarre characters, not when he's trying to rival Mickey Spillane.

> *Mark Schorr, in a review of "Heat," in* Los Angeles Times Book Review, *June 2, 1985, p. 9.*

CHRISTOPHER LEHMANN-HAUPT

[It's] almost impossible to figure out what's going on in William Goldman's latest thriller, *Brothers,* whose dustjacket advertises it as a sequel to the author's earlier novel *Marathon Man.* In fact, not until the book's final pages do we understand what is meant when the director of a mysterious organization called the Division tells the protagonist that "the subtext of everything is this: there's going to be a world war, America is going to start it, and counting you, three of us know."

It would be greatly to the story's credit if it succeeded in puzzling us constructively. But Mr. Goldman mainly bewilders us as to his ultimate aims, and seeks to keep us entertained in the meantime with gimmicks. Some of these are clever enough. There is a scientist known as "Arky" Vaughan (after the great Pittsburgh Pirate ballplayer) who has concocted a suicide potion so strong that it induces a boy and girl to stab themselves to death just after the boy has fulfilled his dream of starring in a playground basketball game in Harlem.

There's another scientist named Milo Standish who has come up with a "compliance fluid" that induces a sadistic homophobe to submit to sodomy. There's every sort of exotic violence and outlandish form of revenge. There's even a computer theory that sees a correlation between the popularity of male action dolls and the outbreak of war.

But these gimmicks are often so willfully inventive that one is almost challenged *not* to be entertained by them. It's as if the author's ego were at stake instead of the survival of civilization that the book feebly pretends to be concerned with. . . .

And what does all this have to do with *Marathon Man*? Not much. The protagonist of *Brothers,* known as Scylla, happens to be Hank Levy, the older brother who was killed in the earlier novel, leaving his brother Babe to do all that running away from the Nazi dentist. Well, it seems that Hank didn't die after

all. He came close, but he's been regaining his strength on a remote Caribbean island, waiting for the call to do battle against the Bloodies. Babe and his wife, Melissa, a brilliant phoneticist, do figure vaguely in the plot of *Brothers,* but they're so far from being essential that one has to suspect that Mr. Goldman included them just to remind us of *Marathon Man.*

> *Christopher Lehmann-Haupt, in a review of "Brothers," in* The New York Times, *February 5, 1987, p. C24.*

STEPHEN DOBYNS

Scylla lives! He was last seen, in William Goldman's *Marathon Man,* being dragged off by his enemies after lying (seemingly) dead on the floor of his brother's Manhattan apartment for about four hours, sliced from groin to breastbone by a mad Nazi dentist. What really happened, we learn in this sequel, was that Scylla was patched up and transported to a tiny desert island in the Caribbean, where he has spent the last 10 years toughening himself. And now here he is at 45, stronger than ever, a modern-day Frankenstein's monster, ready to kill again, but for the good guys, of course. . . .

The villains this time are not Nazis or Communists, but Americans. At the highest levels of our Government, the power dealers are divided—between the Bloodies, who want an immediate war with the Russians, and the Godists, who want peace. What keeps the Bloodies from starting a war is the fact that the Soviet Union's military power is more or less equal to our own. We lack the edge. . . .

Readers looking for a more or less realistic spy novel in the manner of John le Carré's will be disappointed with *Brothers.* Those looking for a fanciful but exciting spy novel in the manner of *Marathon Man* will also be disappointed. *Brothers* is implausible, poorly plotted and sadistic, with a great wash of gratuitous violence. Also, there is a lot of chaff.

Indeed, *Brothers* is hardly a novel at all but a comic book without pictures, something along the lines of *Masters of the Universe.* Even the characters have similar names. . . .

Since this is a sequel Mr. Goldman also brings back Scylla's brother Babe, the rather likable fanatic runner and history student in *Marathon Man.* These days he is an associate professor at Columbia and married to his old professor's beautiful daughter. But he serves no purpose here, doesn't further the plot and is brought back only to be emotionally destroyed.

But perhaps it is wrong to enumerate the flaws of this novel because, really, *Brothers* isn't a novel at all but a book about killing. How much fun it is to kill, how amusing, how laughable. Killing—what an easy solution to one's problems. Killing—what a pleasant way to pass the day. There are about two and a half dozen killings even before the reader reaches the final slaughter. But these are the small deaths, the fictional ones. The deaths that bother me most are those of the trees that were cut down to make this book.

> *Stephen Dobyns, "Ma's Perfect Killer," in* The New York Times Book Review, *February 15, 1987, p. 18.*

Julien Gracq
1910-

(Pseudonym of Louis Poirier) French novelist, short story writer, dramatist, critic, translator, and poet.

An internationally respected literary figure, Gracq explores such concepts in his fiction as humanity's search for meaning, the importance of myth in interpreting experience, the supremacy of the imagination, and the dialectics of death and resurrection, salvation and condemnation, and dream and reality. Also concerned with the dynamics of the historical process, Gracq examines continuities between history and geography by emphasizing the effects of locality on events. Characterized by elements of surrealism, Gothic romance, and Celtic myth, his novels evoke an atmosphere of unreality and ambiguity in which characters are removed from the concerns of daily existence. Gracq makes extensive use of metaphor and symbolism and frequently augments his traditionally structured prose with experiments in typography, syntax, and language.

In his first novel, *Au château d'Argol* (1938; *The Castle of Argol*), Gracq relates the macabre story of three characters engaged in a metaphysical adventure at an isolated medieval castle in Brittany. Culminating in the vicious deaths of two of the characters, *The Castle of Argol* examines such themes as the attainment of spiritual regeneration through death, the recovery of lost innocence, and the machinations of dialectic methods derived from the writings of nineteenth-century German philosopher Georg Wilhelm Friedrich Hegel. Based on the notion that the formation of a concept inevitably generates its opposite and that interaction between the two leads to resolution or change, Hegelian dialectics provide Gracq with a model for the forces that have shaped human conflict and development. This philosophical archetype, as well as the quest motif, recurs throughout Gracq's works.

In his second novel, *Un beau ténébreux* (1945; *A Dark Stranger*), Gracq continues to explore many of the themes introduced in his previous book but in a manner more closely related to modern life. Set in a secluded hotel and involving a group of young people on holiday, *A Dark Stranger* focuses on a central character whose search for the meaning of existence drives him to suicide. Christopher Robinson stated: "The tension between the real world and [the protagonist] . . . leads to revelation for the few and destruction for the hero himself, but the destruction remains a higher destiny than that of those who refuse life's possibilities by their acceptance of compromise and convention." In *Le rivage des Syrtes* (1951; *The Opposing Shore*), Gracq develops his theme of a world of dualities through the tale of two countries—one decadent, the other barbaric—engaged in suspended confrontation for three hundred years. By provoking a war with the neighboring state which will completely annihilate his homeland, the protagonist cures his country's spiritual malaise at the price of physical destruction and accomplishes, according to Elisabeth Cardonne-Arlyck, "the suicidal gesture a whole people secretly yearned for." Yet, Cordonne-Arlyck continued, resurrection through death is not Gracq's main subject: "By Mr. Gracq's own account, *The Opposing Shore* can be read as a meditation on what he calls the spirit of history and particularly on the 'apocalyptic cloud' the rise of Hitler spread over the European consciousness. Read

Courtesy of Julien Gracq

in that fashion, the novel casts a rather sinister light on France's complicity in the 1930's with impending disaster." Although he refused the honor, Gracq was awarded the Prix Goncourt for *The Opposing Shore*.

Gracq's last novel, *Un balcon en forêt* (1958; *Balcony in the Forest*), again contrasts the existential world of the multitude with the essential world of the individual and addresses the concept of anticipation. Set in an isolated outpost in the Ardennes during the period before the German offensive there in May 1940, *Balcony in the Forest* evokes the dreamlike existence and spiritual development of the central character. As in Gracq's earlier works, spiritual fulfillment carries consequences. Christopher Robinson observed: "[The protagonist] ignores the imminent reality of the war, and allows himself to be killed (if his final falling asleep *is* death) by the inevitable German attack."

In addition to his novels, Gracq has published *La presqu'île* (1970), a collection of three stories in which the tension between mind and body is portrayed less violently than in his novels. His play, *Le roi pêcheur* (1948), is an interpretation of the Grail legend, and his translation of Heinrich von Kleist's *Penthesilea* attests to Gracq's interest in mythology. Gracq has also published a collection of prose poetry, *Liberté grande*

(1946), and several volumes of critical essays, including *André Breton* (1947) and *La littérature à l'estomac* (1950).

(See also *CLC*, Vol. 11 and *Contemporary Authors*, Vol. 122.)

J. H. MATTHEWS

[Jacques Nathan] implied, in a cautiously phrased rhetorical question, that Gracq's purpose [in writing *Au Château d'Argol*] may have been nothing but a "discreet parody" of the Gothic novel, executed with a virtuosity for which the critic gave full but grudging credit. It is as though Nathan believed that no writer stylistically so gifted could wish seriously to display his talent in a narrative mode which has generally commanded little respect in the twentieth century.

There might appear to be some excuse for considering *Au Château d'Argol* as no more than a literary exercise, devoid of serious intent and valuable only for the opportunity it affords its author to display gifts he has not yet had occasion to use. But an "Avis au lecteur," entirely ignored by Nathan, disposes of this hypothesis. This preface places Gracq's novel, for which *The Mysteries of Udolpho, The Castle of Otranto*, and "The Fall of the House of Usher" are models, in the light in which we may correctly judge its value. Moreover, nothing in what Gracq writes suggests that his purpose is parody: ridicule, as his introduction indicates, will be absent from *Au Château d'Argol*. In fact, far from desiring to modify in any way the characteristic mood of the Gothic novels, Gracq wishes to retain it.... Gracq's aims, therefore, call for some emphasis, as they control the descriptive elements in his narrative and the use made of them. "The always fascinating repertory of crumbling castles, noises, lights, spectres in the night, and dreams," he observes, "enchants us above all because of its complete familiarity, giving to our feeling of uneasiness its indispensable virulence by warning in advance that we are going to quake. It has not seemed possible to leave this out without a most crude fault of taste being committed." (pp. 91-2)

As its author confesses, *Au Château d'Argol* was written to pay homage to the enchantment the Gothic romance had always held for him. His sincerity of purpose ensures his novel's authenticity and saves it from that appearance of mere amusement.... What lends distinction to Gracq's adaptation of the novel of terror is that, for him, Gothic influence coincides with the influence of surrealism, which he is just as prompt to acknowledge. (pp. 92-3)

The directness with which Gracq avails himself of the structure and mood of the Gothic novels does not diminish the significance he wishes to reserve for the narrative he relates. *Au Château d'Argol* provides the occasion to pose a question which, as his *André Breton* explains, is of paramount concern for its author: "With the completion of the exploration of the planet (the exploration of matter has not the same imaginative reverberation)," he affirms, "the era of diffuse and wandering adventure has closed that of the Arthurian romance as well as of Robinson Crusoe.... Hence, a consequence he does not neglect to bring to his readers' attention: "The tragic element of the adventure for a modern reader no longer is born of the oppressive fear of obscure material dangers in conspiracy against the hero, but of the anguished feeling accompanying us each moment of the impossibility that *chance* remain open to him

any longer in a world which from day to day before our eyes has hardened like ice."

We first meet the hero of *Au Château d'Argol,* making his way to the castle he has rented—"in extravagant trust in chance"—without even viewing it. Gracq's Albert, no less than Hebdomeros a representative surrealist figure, is "built to penetrate the most subtle arcana and to embrace its most exciting realities." The true orientation of the tale Gracq tells may be inferred from this observation in his *André Breton*: "The only question, the real question which basically moves readers universally, in the irresistible afterthought that *perhaps* it could be not without solution, is that which the author of 'Rouletabille' has materialized in one of his masterly works: Can one get out of a room hermetically sealed?" In Gracq's view the question, considered in its figurative sense, is eminently well posed. Subconsciously, he believes, the reader raises in his own mind the even more intriguing question: "Can one get out of this room we all live in?" The anguish prompting this question lends vitality to *Au Château d'Argol*, giving special value to the location in which the action is set, to the people who take part, and to the relationship they bear one to another. In a sense this novel consists, therefore, in a confrontation of presences. Man, motivated by that need for knowledge Gracq discovers in Albert, finds himself fortuitously in a castle—and the surrealists have given sufficient proof that they, like the Gothic novelists, regard the castle as a *privileged locale*—against the backcloth of an enigmatic countryside, in which we are made particularly aware of a mysterious forest. But the surrealists, their responsiveness gathering momentum from those who have gone before, *remagnetize* (to adopt a figure of speech which has special meaning in surrealism) the image of the forest. The paintings of Ernst, Matta, and Lam attest its compelling attraction, and *Au Château d'Argol* also offers evidence that in surrealism we witness the reinvention of certain myths to which it has given new life and orientation.

The castle in which Albert, making his instinctive appeal to objective chance, has chosen to live provides the theater where events are acted out. One cannot but notice here that, when discussing the special unity of the surrealist group in *André Breton*, Gracq remarks: "It is rather the idea of a closed and separate *order*, of an exclusive guild, of a phalanstery which tends to be enclosed by some sort of magic wall (the significant idea of 'the castle' lurks in the background), which seems to suggest itself inevitably to Breton from the beginning." With Albert, Herminien, and Heide, Gracq establishes his own group, living in separation from the world, so cut off from society that the isolation of the castle is, in the novel, only one of several factors contributing to a feeling of inescapable remoteness.

The events of the novel follow their ineluctable, inexplicably predestined course outside the limitations of normal time sequence. Albert and his friends seem to live in a timeless vacuum in which day-to-day changes in the weather serve not so much to give a sense of seasonal change as to provide landscape moods, appropriately complementing the action and playing a part in its development. Nature, in this way, both guarantees against outside interruption and clearly delimits the field of action: "The solitude which surrounded the castle closed again, vigilant, about the visitors whose stay seemed very soon destined to take on indefinite duration." The timeless atmosphere on which Gracq insists is by no means reassuring to the people he presents. Herminien, jealous of a growing intimacy between Albert and Heide, finds himself agonizingly aware of the moments they spend together: "The pendulum of the clock had just reminded him, with the poignant familiarity of the first evening, of the torture each second represented for him, until the hour of dinner, an empty and purely fantastic time, the horror of which consisted entirely in its differentiation, perceptible for the first time, from temporal duration, a time from which the flow of any truly vital phenomenon seemed to have withdrawn, since Heide was then beyond his reach."

The personages of *Au Château d'Argol* have not withdrawn to this place of privilege simply to escape. They have done so to experience life more keenly, safe from encroachment by extraneous and irrelevant distractions. Time is both present and absent, and Albert and his companions are sensitive to this fact. . . . (pp. 95-8)

The emotion produced in Albert by this timeless sense of the passage of time is one of disquiet, enhanced by the atmosphere of unreality in which events are enacted. When Albert, Heide, and Herminien swim far out to sea, "in the distance a yellow line, thin and almost unreal, marked the limit of an element they believed they were renouncing completely." All three finally feel the "call of the land," and return, however reluctantly, to shore. Despite their isolation from the rest of mankind, none of them can know a permanent sense of release. Fatality in this narrative is too closely linked with elements unexplained and inexplicable, borrowed from the Gothic novels and functioning beyond rational interpretation. The foreknowledge of fate makes its effect all the more upon Albert, Heide, and Herminien because they do nothing to resist it. On the contrary, they deliberately make themselves available to it (Gracq significantly borrows André Gide's word *disponibilité*). Swimming together, the three of them "estimated with lucidity the unretraceable distance they had already covered," and with "voluptuous rapture" realized that they would not have the strength to return.

In *Au Château d'Argol* there is no turning back. Events take on the accumulated meaning of a search, reminiscent of the one undertaken by the hero of Chirico's *Hebdomeros*.

In this connection, the "Avis au lecteur" carries a revealing mention of Wagner. Gracq blames Nietzsche for too readily imposing a Christian interpretation upon the composer's "poetic testament," and for being responsible, in this way, for leading later critics in the wrong direction; ". . . toward an order of research so patently superficial that the violent discomfort we experience upon still hearing mentioned today 'the master's acquiescence in the Christian mystery of redemption,' while the work of Wagner has always very clearly tended to widen more and more the sphere of its subterranean or, exactly, infernal research, which would be sufficient in itself to let us understand that *Parsifal* signifies something quite different from the ignominy of extreme unction on a corpse that is, moreover, all too clearly recalcitrant." Concerned to examine the problem of salvation and condemnation (which, following Hegel, he refuses to regard as dialectically separable determinations), Gracq sees no objection to his readers' viewing his narrative as "a demoniac—and for this reason perfectly justified—*version* of Parsifal," just as his play *Le Roi pêcheur* (1948) was to prove to be a version of the legend of the Grail. In both texts Gracq excludes even a suggestion of Christian significance in the events he recounts. (pp. 98-9)

The double influence of Wagner and Hegel makes itself felt in *Au Château d'Argol*. And this combined influence may be seen to be closely connected with the surrealist view of existence conveyed in the novel.

Early emphasis is placed on Albert's admiration for one of the surrealists' preferred philosophers, Hegel, "that king of the architecture and science of wholes," the thinker who "has uncrowned all abstract knowledge of its glory." Albert holds dialectics to be "that lever derisively demanded by Archimedes which would move the world." His respect for Hegel, whose writings he takes to the Castle of Argol, is demonstrated in his way of life and outlook, throughout his stay. Of Hegel, Gracq writes: "His magnificent dialectic seems to be a reply from above to Albert's disquiet. Thus, knowledge alone delivered him; essential, living knowledge: in his mind Albert casts a glance over his studious life as a recluse and, with pride, fully justified himself for it." Using to advantage his noteworthy lucidity, Albert sets himself the task of gaining knowledge. Meanwhile, the knowledge he seeks is of a kind that induces him to place special value on the teachings of Hegel. Albert's search, like Hebdomeros', is typically surrealist in nature. Hence, what he really wishes to attain through knowledge is self-knowledge.

Opening Gracq's *André Breton* we read that "the whole of man" consists in being "an ego forever caught up in the magnetic whirlwind of a system of 'egos' and always in some degree 'gravitating'." The meaning of these words becomes plainer a little later when Gracq defines the motivating element in Hegel's thought as that of "polarization," and adds: "It is only by *entrusting* ourselves to the image of two poles repelling one another and simultaneously producing one another that we get past, and get blindly past, the initial link in the Hegelian spiral, its 'moment of departure,' which is the dialectical bipartition into being and nonbeing." (p. 100)

The drama acted out in *Au Château d'Argol* beneath the surface of the Gothic romance is thus of a profound significance, underlined in the following: "Perhaps Hegel would have smiled to see walking by the side of each of them, like a dark and glorious angel, a ghost both of the person's double and of his opposite, and then he would have asked himself about the form to be taken by a necessary *union* which this book above all ends could not have the aim finally to elucidate." Gracq's use of the image of magnetic poles takes on its full value only in connection with this aim. (p. 101)

Gracq gives due stress to the close ties existing between Albert and his friend Herminien who appears, apparently uninvited, at the Castle of Argol in the company of a woman Albert has never met before. Herminien shares the lucidity which is characteristic of Albert and also possesses to an astonishing degree "a singular aptitude for seeing clearly into the most turbid motives of human conduct." Herminien and Albert, therefore, have much in common and are shown to be necessary to one another. In their conversations "each, with complete good faith, tried truthfully to come close to his most secret nature in a sort of dialogued confession in which the mind ceaselessly sought, in order to take its flight, the support of another attentive and comprehensible mind." Herminien's "demonic lucidity" makes possible in Albert a sense of "double sight," as they share "a system of values belonging to themselves alone." At the same time: "So many strange tastes in common, ritualistic perversions of a language of their own which they taught one another . . . had in the end produced between them a dangerous, intoxicating, vibratile atmosphere, which dispersed and was reborn at their contact as if the plates of an electric condenser had been moved apart or brought together."

The result is a potentially explosive relationship in which the presence of Heide is destined to provide the necessary spark.

Heide epitomizes surrealist woman. Like Matilda in Lewis' *The Monk* she is "less a personage than a continual temptation." And Gracq, who cites this phrase of Breton's in his *André Breton*, adds in parentheses "read an *attraction*," thus reminding us of the magnetic quality which he prizes so much. He concludes: "The 'revelation' which Breton places so high is above all a sudden electrical discharge." This is produced in *Au Château d'Argol*, as in *The Monk*, by the proximity of a remarkable heroine.

Albert meets his guests, filled with a premonitory mingling of intoxication and disquiet. "In a second," we are told, "Heide completely filled the room, the castle, and the countryside of Argol with her radiant and absorbing beauty." The enigmatic nature of surrealist woman—so admirably captured in the verse of Breton and Éluard and in the photographs of Man Ray—makes of Heide a perfectly "unknowable" person. She fills the role of intermediary between man and the unknown, "passing back and forth over the magic threshold forbidden to man." It is emphasized that with the arrival of Heide at the Castle of Argol *"Something had changed."* The setting sun sheds on her "the light with which Rembrandt has surrounded his Christ" on the road to Emmaus, and like Hebdomeros at one moment, she even seems to walk on the waters. Gracq makes sure to leave us in no doubt that the function reserved for Heide in the relationship existing between Albert and Herminien is that of "catalyst."

Their first evening together, gazing from the battlements, Albert and Heide feel "the alarming weight of the *event*," while Herminien, left alone, is lost in "absorbing dark thoughts," to which the monotonous ticking of a massive copper clock soon lends "a character of inexorable fatality." At this moment Herminien understands that every individual carries within him "the instinct for his own destruction" just as much as he retains concern for his personal safety. None of the three knows exactly what will result from their meeting, but even Heide experiences a sense of disquiet, "a strange anguish." The inevitable progress of events admits no resistance, however. Heide is "entirely submissive," although, in the act of love, "barricaded behind her immobile beauty." This provokes from both men an "involuntary homage," lying at the source of the jealousy which separates them "like a wall of hostility."

Hostility, like the suffering which accompanies it, is displayed in the reactions of Albert, whose responses are complicated by his friendship for Herminien. A "delicate mechanism, as though polished by long use, a winged machine seemed to him to be set in motion with fateful slowness and to draw him after Herminien with the insistence of a spell toward a *dénouement* unpredictable for him in every respect." The emphasis so often placed upon inexplicable but ineluctable necessity in *Au Château d'Argol* insistently points to the continued presence and direct influence of objective chance. In this sense the presence of Heide must be regarded as fortuitous indeed, but all the more significant for being so. It makes possible the catalysis necessary if Albert and Herminien are to pursue to the ultimate their search for self-knowledge. Hence Heide's curiously passive role, which demands of her no more than that she exist and stand between the friends.

In the purified atmosphere in which his personages are placed, remote from the petty concerns of day-to-day existence, Gracq explores potentialities and examines consequences in complete indifference to the "psychology" of the people he presents. It is not unworthy of notice that his *André Breton* declares, "The only true obscenity of which a literary work is capable consists no doubt in calling attention with the pen to those intestinal zones of 'interior life'." The novelist's purpose is simply to prepare Albert and Herminien—and Heide also—for the full discovery of themselves, in circumstances his preface qualifies as "commonly considered as scabrous." (pp. 102-04)

The "incomparable Event" that is the crux of the action in *Au Château d'Argol* is a sadistic attack upon Heide for which Herminien is responsible. Prepared by no analysis of motives, unannounced and brutal in its impact, this act is described as having taken place "beyond the paltry discriminations of good and evil." Consequently, thanks to "a vengeance of dialectic," Albert recognizes in himself a "fraternal connivance" which even further places Herminien's conduct beyond a form of moral condemnation surrealism refuses to endorse. Herminien's act is an exacerbated assertion of desire in the face of restraints which the surrealists regard as a curtailment of human liberty. Since for Albert as much as for Herminien the pursuit of desire takes its place logically in the search for self-knowledge, both must necessarily learn from the incident. And so must Heide: "Without hate, without anger, mortally crushed, she still felt Herminien's power on her like the salty, fortifying deluge of living sea water in which, without shock or effort, the speed of mysterious waves had borne her along to deposit her in a voyage of no return on the *other shore* of the Ocean, whose solemn and disconcerting expanse she explored in a calm light with the grace of a child's touch and as though returned to her original virginity." Even Heide, then, does not really condemn Herminien's action. She displays instead a disturbing but revealing submissiveness, which foreshadows Marie's in Joyce Mansour's *Les Gisants satisfaits*, written twenty years after *Au Château d'Argol*.

But just as Herminien's act cannot be dismissed as having no beneficial effect upon the actors of this drama, so, in accordance with the dialectical principle, it becomes a source of suffering. Paraphrasing Baudelaire's phrase, "I am the knife and the wound," Gracq demonstrates that each is "the victim and the knife," and emphasizes that it is by Albert, not by Herminien, that his heroine has been "*disincarnated* for ever." In itself Herminien's amoral behavior may solve nothing, but it does allow the three persons involved to become better aware of something which Chirico's Hebdomeros had felt before them: the need for a solution. The "unavowable ties" binding Albert and Herminien now form a "slip-knot" destined in the final scene to strangle them both, while yet "reuniting them." After the death of Heide, who has been buried beneath the gravestone upon which, even before meeting her, Albert had carved her name, Herminien hastens to the spot in the forest where Albert and Heide used to meet. Although he senses that someone is behind him, Herminien, Albert's "lost soul," does not turn around: *Au Château d'Argol* closes as he feels "the icy steel of knife slip between his shoulders like a handful of snow."

While Heide finds regeneration and purification through rape and mutilation, Albert, in the murder of his "other self," carried out with a lucidity which even Herminien recognizes must have its inevitable consequence, recovers lost innocence. As one of the fundamental motivating impulses of surrealism is the urge to return to a paradise lost, Gracq's "Avis au lecteur" concludes appropriately, placing the issue beyond question: "The vigor, convincing in itself, of 'that which is given' as metaphysics so magnificently puts it, in a book as in life, should exclude forever all evasion in silly symbolic phantasmagoria and incite us once and for all to a decisive act of purification." Despite the fact that he places his novel in a timeless world far from our own, guarding its inviolability within the walls of a Gothic castle, the author of *Au Château d'Argol* displays his fidelity to surrealism in a narrative which refuses to reassure or to placate and which, on the contrary, assumes the value of an act of incitement. His novel is therefore an extended restatement of surrealist aims, as these are summarized on the first page of Breton's *Second Manifesto of Surrealism:* "Everything leads us to believe there exists a certain point in the spirit in which life and death, real and imaginary, past and future, communicable and uncommunicable, high and low cease to be perceived contradictorily. Now it would be in vain if anyone were to seek any motive for surrealist activity other than the hope of determining this point." (pp. 104-06)

J. H. Matthews, "Julien Gracq," in his Surrealism
and the Novel, The University of Michigan Press,
1966, pp. 91-106.

ANNIE-CLAUDE DOBBS

Julien Gracq's novels are each characterized by a similar vision of the world and a similar quest. Every protagonist, every one of Gracq's "poets," shuns the visible, anodyne, everyday world of existence and substitutes a hypothetical, invisible, essential world—a world of the dream. From beginning to end, he never ceases wanting to enter the dream, although he is aware of the transgression his desire constitutes. In his novels Gracq endeavors to trace the boundary, be it arbitrary or problematic, which separates his two worlds; but the boundary remains ambiguous, just as the second world is never elucidated. Likewise the observer's feelings are ambiguous, ranging from fascination to indifference, from exaltation to anxiety, or even at times injured innocence when confronted with a universe whose meaning eludes him.

In order to differentiate between the two worlds, real and hypothetical, which are viewed from different angles, the author employs distinct and complementary sets of stylistic devices in each of the four novels considered in this study: *Au Château d'Argol, Un Beau Ténébreux, Le Rivage des Syrtes, Un Balcon en Forêt.* The stylistic distance between one device and another in each set corresponds to the parallax between the two angles of vision and the degree of separation of the two worlds. These sets of devices are different enough to give each novel stylistic originality, yet analogous enough to impart a remarkable unity as well as diversity to the whole of Gracq's work.

For indeed the originality of Gracq's work, as he himself suggests, is to be seen in the contrast between the poverty of content and the richness of form. A small number of themes, always the same, are repeated from one novel to the next, but the narrative manner and the spectrum of stylistic devices are different in each and never duplicated.

One of the most notable aspects of each novel, especially the first, *Au Château d'Argol,* is the deliberate thematic distance between external reality and the world of the book, as well as the meticulous precautions Gracq takes to maintain that distance. Even the title, for the careful reader at least, is an indication that Gracq is substituting suggestiveness for exhaustive narration, conjuring up the idea, as it does, of a fleeting visit rather than a prolonged stay: *Au Château,* not *Le Château.* Indeed, at the end of the novel the mystery of beings

and things remains intact and goes far beyond the written page. The stylistic distance is not only in the title but in the preface which precedes the work and cautions the reader against the esoteric qualities of this story which is not meant to be "read by all."

Beyond the double warning of title and preface, the distance between Argol's world and the everyday world is to be found in the extreme literariness of the work—literariness as much of content as of form. The reader is warned in the beginning by an explicit reference to Balzac and an implicit reference to the gothic novel that he will be confronted by a specialized context in which hyper-romantic settings and themes as well as archetypes will all be easily recognized. To quote one critic, the author's mythology is "encoded within cultural allusion," at the beginning at least. Then little by little a certain dramatic tension arises from the intermingling of the conventional on the one hand and, on the other, the author's innovations and corrections by which he creates his own gothic novel. Progressively the reader's attention is drawn by a small number of stylistic devices, unique to this novel, which underline the distance already existing at the thematic level.

A certain number of idiosyncracies of style, which constitute by their very presence a deviation from the norm, build up the impression that the author is making use of two styles, the one reticent, secretive, convoluted, evasive, the other amplified, hyperbolic, intensive, and that these two styles correspond to two narrative manners: evasion and intensification.

In the first portrait of the novel in which Gracq describes the new owner of Argol, a young aristocrat with a mysterious past, the conjunction "mais" occurs five times within two very short paragraphs, correcting each time what has just been said. The force of the declarative clauses is attenuated by this extraordinary polysyndeton, as if the author were hesitant to proceed and somehow baffled by his character's complexity.... In each case the conjunction marks a reticence of the narrative voice. On the stylistic and thematic levels, this device evokes a closed world, difficult to enter in the concrete as well as the figurative sense: castle and text, from the very beginning, bristle with obstacles.

The author's reticence and secrecy is also apparent in the abnormal recurrence of three key verbs which are used synonymously: instead of the verb "être," he almost invariably substitutes "sembler," "paraître," "apparaître" ("to be, seem, appear"), in describing a world of appearances, thus making it difficult for the reader to distinguish between visible and invisible, real and unreal or even surreal. The repetition of each one of the three or of all three together also indicates that the narrative manner is speculative rather than affirmative.

A final form of stylistic evasion is the frequency of parentheses which purposely complicate the evolution of the sentence, lengthening it, prolonging its suspense, delaying the climax. These syntactical convolutions, less anodyne than their purely typographical character would lead one to believe, contribute to the feeling of uneasiness which pervades the text at all levels.

Added to and opposed to the syntax of evasion, reflecting as it does the speculative nature of the novel, there is a syntax of intensification that describes a world in which, despite the conventions underlying it, beings and things are evidently quite exceptional. Here again the devices are not only stylistic but typographical. This syntax of intensification is based first of all on an abnormally frequent use of superlatives and other forms of hyperbolic vocabulary. Gracq multiplies the epithets which stress, as he says, the "altitude" of places and people, and the adverbs which put happenings into relief: "extrêmement, particulièrement, rigoureusement, surabondamment, indissolublement" ("extremely, particularly, exactly, superabundantly, indissolubly"). The long paragraph which describes the front of the castle is riddled with adjectives which dictate surprise: "rare, frappant, étonnant, inquiétant, surprenant, accablant" ("rare, striking, amazing, disquieting, astonishing, overwhelming"). Like the syntax of evasion, this sort of exaggeration slows the tempo of narration. The pages, ballasted as they are with intensifying adverbs and adjectives, read less rapidly than those of a text where nothing snags or pulls down the reader.

Along with this sort of vocabulary are found analogous instances of syntactical intensification which help in reinforcing the distance. In a stylistically very literary form of writing, the pluperfect subjunctive which should not appear abnormal astonishes the reader, not so much by its frequent occurence as by the liberty with which the author uses it. (pp. 141-44)

In the first chapter—a key chapter because most of the characteristic stylistic devices are introduced, one finds words and groups of words without precise affective connotations, that is, trite or conventional expressions: "l'angoisse du hasard, le recours en grâce insensé à la chance, le caractère presque fatal du visage, hasard, chance, grâce" ("the throes of chance, the mad petition to chance for clemency, the almost fatal character of his countenance"). The style which describes the young lord of the manor is conventional and archaic, as if the writer, by this anachronism of form, wanted to underline the distance of his character from the contemporary everyday world. Still, little by little, surprise yields to habit, irritation to acceptance, for the reader who has deciphered the true nature of Gracq's triteness.

Indeed Gracq's use of the commonplace is neither a symptom of inertia nor the conventional ornament of a conventional world. As Riffaterre has observed, if the cliché is stereotypic, it is far from banal. In the context of the story, it even constitutes boldness of style. In *Au Château d'Argol,* the cliché serves both as "agent of expressivity" and "point of irony." To the extent that it fills out the conventional world to which it belongs, it emphasizes the flagrant divergence between the world pre-existent to the story and the superimposed and complementary world which Gracq is creating. In place of the real world Gracq proposes a world in the process of being created, original despite its clichés.

The syntax of intensification also includes the peculiar typographical layout, which again is indicative of Gracq's precaution in maintaining the distance between book and life. In this universe of the exceptional, where beings and things are immediately transposed in a higher key, words which are used to describe them and to differentiate them are themselves transposed thanks to the author's unusual typography.

Each page is stuffed with italics which tend to baffle, confuse, mislead the reader. Far from being the landmarks on the page they should be, they are often stop signs. Gracq's system of roadsigns is based on surprise: sometimes an italic emphasizes a syntactical anomaly making it doubly striking; sometimes it puts into relief a word of an idiolect; sometimes, on the contrary, the italic is there, quite arbitrary, in striking contrast to the weak meaning, the feeble connotation of the word it underlines, but always slowing the tempo and drawing attention to itself.

In Gracq's first novel, his manner of narration exactly parallels his manner of seeing, his vision; the stylistic effort is tied to an optical effort: he tries to encompass a totality. In this stylistically closed world the two-pronged device—evasion-intensification—expressing, as it were, each time a deviation from the norm, corresponds to a double movement of the eyes—the first carefully focused and somewhat reluctant, the second bold, wide, elevated.

A syntax of uneasiness reflecting an uneasy vision is progressively constituted. It is based on the tension resulting from the interaction of certain opposed stylistic devices which transcribe opposed visual categories: forms—straight, winding; substance—hard, soft; color—bright, faded; perspective—open, closed; the gravitation of the banal around the poetic and vice versa; the strength of certain parentheses and italics and the deliberate vagueness of the key verbs which evoke appearance rather than reality; the presence of slowing elements in a context of expectation. However, because they are equally distributed, the two stylistic devices slowly equalize each other and their impact is cancelled out; the divergence, so evident at the beginning, becomes convergence. At the story's end, tension at the thematic level as well as the stylistic is absorbed in a "solution poétique" inherent in all of Gracq's works.

In *Un Beau Ténébreux,* a novel written much later than *Au Château d'Argol* and which is in an altogether different vein, the author contrasts two different types of humanity and categorizes their physical and linguistic peculiarities which he delimits once and for all but which he will amplify further in later novels. The first group, the common herd, which includes almost all of his characters, is notable for its mediocrity, its lack of curiosity, and its dull desire for comfort and security. The other group, a small, always alert élite, is recognizable by its fanatic, even audacious curiosity, its taste for danger, and its will to be balanced on the limit of the possible. Solitary watchmen, these beings rise above the sleep of the world.

Just as the two types of humanity have completely different perceptions of the world—the one clear, the other blurred—they are viewed and represented by the author in opposite ways. The élite is brought into sharp focus and even magnified while the common herd remains fuzzy and distant. Two opposed sets of stylistic devices are used in the narration and in the speech of the protagonists themselves to convey the two forms of perception.

The two forms of vision as well as the two sets of devices are present in Gracq's description of the beach used as a backdrop to the story, and of the young idle band of tourists vacationing there. When Gérard, one of the élite whose diary is part of the novel, records his personal impressions, and when Gracq corrects or supplements them objectively, their style is the same, notable for the recurrent and monotonous use of a limited number of diminutives. Evidently deliberate, it is a foil which sets off the opposite and complementary device. . . . From his privileged vantage point and with the downward, all-encompassing gaze so characteristic of Gracq's hero, Gérard contemplates the beach which is a metaphor of the author's geography. If hero and reader do not clearly see the beach and its "emmêlement," it is because the eye refuses to validate a world which is lacking in relief and significance. The fuzzy image betrays a desire to ignore. The crowd is there, numerically large, but in reality it is as small as a swarm of insects. Whether full or empty, the world of the beach, blurred to the eye, is also almost inaudible to the ear, resembling the "brouhaha." Hubbub and swarming both represent the general confusion of the everyday world and the inability of the eye and of speech to fix its meaning, if indeed it has a meaning. The babbling of the common herd, its meaningless verbosity, is rendered by a set of clichés which constitute its only means of expression and which reflect its inability to perceive or to say anything of significance. It is a world deprived of vision and of speech. (pp. 145-48)

Opposed to the multitudinous, colorless, and microscopic world symbolized by the beach is Gracq's other world, singular, colorful, and magnified. The profile of his true hero stands out in stark relief. The author replaces entomological images, which all conveyed the larval essence of a world asleep, with metaphors evoking a world of exception and "altitude," where the watchmen are endowed with a prestige that is both royal and divine. Here the metaphors are of the sacred, borrowed from the Bible or legend, celestial or diabolical in nature. Prince, king, or god, the protagonist casts on the world "un regard d'archange ennuyé" which "décolore tout" ("the look of a bored archangel," "alters the complexion of things"). Capable of transfiguration, he has the "geste hiératique d'officiant," the "sacerdoce soudain," inspiring an "état de transe" ("the hieratic gesture of the priest," "the sudden sacerdotal status," "a state of trance") in those he draws on. In all the different games in which the hero stakes his money or his life, games invariably taking place in the most theatrical of settings and revealing Gracq's obsessive preoccupation with the theater, the hero remains a "solutionniste de première force," justifying his role as a "dérangeur," as a "sacrificateur" ("expert player," "troublemaker," "sacrificer"). Worthy emulator of Faust, of Lohengrin, and of Christ, in perpetual temptation and torment, his speech is prophetic and cryptic, often literally transcribed from the New Testament, especially at the end of the story. There the ritual sacrifice accompanying the hero's suicide (the result of a pact which has tied him to his mistress, herself "royale") is, in language and art, obviously propitiatory.

Thus from beginning to end Gracq contrasts two kinds of speech and two styles: one is descriptive of and inherent in the microscopic world of mediocre collectivity, the other, dramatic and parabolic, belongs to the magnified and heroic world of the watchmen and visionaries. Ethics and aesthetics are closely knit: the minimizing style expresses the failure of collective humanity; the maximizing style asserts the validity of the solitary venture. If the distance between the two, patently obvious from the beginning, grows gradually, at the end of the story the maximizing style completely sweeps away the other and becomes the only form of speech and of vision which is significant in Gracq's universe.

Of all Gracq's novels, *Le Rivage des Syrtes* is the most ample, carrying with it cosmic and visionary overtones. The theme of a world of two dimensions, one infinitely small, the other infinitely large, which Gracq had begun in *Un Beau Ténébreux,* is here more fully developed and raised to the scale of two imaginary countries locked in an historic confrontation. The vision given of the drowsing, imprecise territory of the Syrtes, suspended between two wars, is essentially speculative. The author aims, through his stylistic techniques, at imitating the constant motion of an eye going to and fro from the visible to the invisible, from the real to the unreal. The vision is at times divergent—taking in the scattered and the minuscule, at times convergent, producing a series of overpowering close-ups. Divergent and convergent, blurred and sharp images alternate, either in opposition or in combination. Little by little, as the

"poet's" eye focuses and the authority of his own vision strengthens, the blurred is eliminated and an exceptionally well-defined vision becomes dominant at the end of the story.

Here again the optical distance is parallel to stylistic distance: the small and scattered is expressed through precise and prosaic words, the magnified and concentrated through groups of words, poetic and vague, which gravitate around the central theme. Their strange and unexpected associations are the stylistic counterpart of the protagonist's ambiguous quest.

Included in the distant vision are panoramas of large but fuzzy territories peopled with masses of undifferentiated inhabitants whom the "poet" relentlessly tries to outdistance. Inevitably, as in *Un Beau Ténébreux,* the observer is reminded of insects and larvae. Diminutives once again fix the image of a swarming, hive-like, derisory world. The scene as viewed by Aldo, the "Official Observer," from his window at the Admiralty recalls the beach in *Un Beau Ténébreux.* Aldo notices "les pulsations faibles de cette petite cellule de vie assoupie, tremblante à l'extrême bord du désert," "le cheminement des rares allées et venues" ("the faint throbbing of the small and drowsy life cell, quivering at the very edge of the desert," "the plodding of infrequent comings and goings"). His feeling for the frail beings who are unaware of the danger of the "wasteland's far edge" is less that of sympathy than that of indifference or mild impatience.... The concentration of diminutives, the double image both homely and entomological, the subsequent repetition in the page of words and epithets with the same connotation ("petit, minuscule, rare, fourmi, fourmilière, termitière") ("small, minuscule, infrequent, ant, ants' nest, termitary") all suggest a world of aimless good will, but one which is vulnerable and defenseless. (pp. 149-51)

Nevertheless, this world is far from being as static as it would seem at first; early in the novel the author hints at the possibility of movement, of a change from sleep to bad dream, from bad dream to wakefulness, from inertia to animation.

The Admiralty, a fortress which has long been redundant, gradually emerges from its sleep under the slow surge of obscure forces and the initiative of the "poets." Gracq introduces a new series of images to describe its metamorphosis, replacing the minute and the vague by the gigantic and the precise. What was small, blurred, and limp now becomes enormous, well-defined, and hard.... Previously the fortress had been described by diminutives and other terms inappropriate to its putative function. Now the misuse of objects and of language has disappeared. The words which describe the fortress reinstated to the use for which it was intended are appropriate and expected: military, precise, aggressive, just like the building they define.

In contrast to Maremma and Orsenna is the ancient city of Sagra, belonging to Gracq's favored and heroic world with its visible and invisible planes. Reduced to a skeleton of stone, it displays its ruins without nostalgia. In a silent dialogue with the ruins, the "poet" Aldo experiences the ambiguous feeling so characteristic of the dream in Gracq's works: "Je me sentais de connivence avec la pente de ce paysage glissant au dépouillement absolu" ("I felt in collusion with the slope of that landscape sliding toward total divesture").

In place of diminutives, the author uses a vocabulary of compelling force: entomological images are replaced by geological, mineral, sidereal ones and cinematographic jargon, which endow the landscape with an epic dimension. While the eye could encompass the blurred world of the Syrtes, Sagra remains impenetrable; its "gigantomachie déchaînée," its "violence prodigue," its "poussée turgescente" ("unleashed gigantomachy," "unparalleled violence," "turgescent thrust"), stand like a screen between city and observer. The surging piles of stone sustain the unviolated mystery. The contrast between Sagra and Maremma is arresting: these seemingly dead ruins are more alive than the world of the Syrtes which is sleeping under its intact stones. The observer's attention is struck by the contradiction and the paradox of an inert world which is alive on the one hand, and a living world which is inert on the other.

In this story, as in *Un Beau Ténébreux,* Gracq combines both visions in the same description so as to present, with all immediacy possible, the distance separating the "poet's" exorbitant desire and the world that he covets but which is ultimately only hypothetical. . . . The ship which carries both man and dream is a fragile craft "minuscule et dissous"; the world toward which it sails, potential and possible but improbable, symbolized by the rising smoke "flexible et molle" and its "volutes orageuses." The world of everyday humanity, infinitely small and insignificant, objectified by the boat, contrasts with the enormous and encompassing but subtle and intangible world of the dream. (pp. 152-54)

In the world of the infinitely large are to be found the "poets" themselves. They are portrayed in a small number of well-delineated autonomous portraits. In a novel in which slow and rapid tempi alternate (corresponding to themes of inactivity and activity, dispersion and collection), each portrait has a specific function. They punctuate the novel, grouping together themes and images scattered throughout the narration, just as the "poet" himself, a "catalyzer" and a "condenser," regroups, according to Gracq, the forces of the real world.

In all his portraits Gracq multiplies images and comparisons to bring out the extreme complexity of the character portrayed. Yet behind the apparently disparate images, a unity becomes visible. . . . (p. 154)

In *Le Rivage des Syrtes,* the flat, sterile surface of the wasteland is relieved by singular portraits and panoramas (Aldobrandi, Vanessa, the Admiralty, Sagra) which rise above the somnolent world of everyday existence. By virtue of their complexity and mystery, these peaks of Gracq's universe are not easily reducible to their components as is the world above which they rise, the latter always being described through diminutives as monotonous as the reality depicted. At the end of the story, it is the peaks which dominate; the wasteland, with its swarming masses of insect-like inhabitants, is left behind and the "poet's" vision is imposed on the reader. (p. 157)

Un Balcon en Forêt, seemingly a war story, is in fact as much the work of an historian as that of a story-teller. Indeed, the originality of the novel stems from this fact: from beginning to end the war correspondent reporting day to day details gives way to the poet. The title, carrying an indication of Gracq's characteristic double theme, constitutes in itself a first "coefficient of negativity." It sums up the marginal and parabolic nature of the purported war story, stressing the distance which separates, as in all of the author's works, the world of the book from concrete reality. Unquestionably there is a war since repeated echoes of military activity may be faintly heard at the small garrison, the "balcony" of the novel's title, although they are muffled by the surrounding "forest" which, as ambiguous as the war itself, both threatens and protects. But

because it is unseen and imperfectly defined, the war remains a menacing and a disturbing presence.

The narrative voice is at times credulous, at times unbelieving, at times confident, at times uncertain, as it accepts or rejects a reality which is tangible at first but slowly deteriorates, becoming vague, conjectural, a possible prevarication. The author's irony lies in the distance which separates his two visions and his two narrative manners which may be best categorized as ponderous and facetious.

At the beginning of the story, the author describes with all possible gravity the ugliness of the world. The factual and prosaic style corresponds to the drabness of the theme. . . . (p. 158)

However, the mood and the technique which are to characterize *Un Balcon en Forêt* soon become apparent. In order to make the existence of the phony war seem questionable, even improbable, the author underlines the extraordinary deterioration of the military outpost he is describing. Stylistically this deterioration may be sensed in the constant combination of his ponderous and facetious manner. The key image symbolizing the double vision is the command post inhabited by Lieutenant Grange: it is composed, on the one hand, of a blockhouse, a squat and reassuring mass of reinforced concrete, but, on the other hand, the apparently invulnerable refuge is surrounded by a flimsy shack, "pavillon de meulière banlieusard et triste" ("a dingy suburban pavilion"), with a hen-house and a rabbit-hutch beside it, and with empty tin cans and bits of moldy bread scattered around it. Thus in the first description the solid and noble military structure is domesticated and vulgarized. On the visual as well as on the stylistic level the ponderous and the facetious are inseparable and complementary. . . . In *Un Balcon en Forêt,* war is a mere pretext: throughout, the author challenges not only the existence of the war but also that of the world itself.

Little by little the landscape of Gracq's ideal world is superimposed on the banal ugliness of the military outpost. Once again the author contrasts the existential world of the multitude with the essential world of the individual. . . . The differentiation between the existential and the essential is made through a double series of images: the one describing the world as it is: "étroit, englué, terré," the other describing a world which extends out from the concrete one: "ample, sec, géodésique."

Further on in the novel, in the course of portraying one of his ideal landscapes, Gracq defines the chaste delight experienced by a man who finds himself finally alone, isolated, cut off from everything, in a forest which guarantees his exceptional "détachement". . . . As in his previous works, especially *Le Rivage des Syrtes,* Gracq uses cosmic and aquatic images to evoke a world relieved of its human gangue, as poetic and as immaterial as the world of the dream to which it is related.

That this ideal world is more dream-like than real is apparent from a style which contrasts remarkably with the matter-of-fact narration found at the beginning of the story. (pp. 159-60)

The syntactical restriction immediately following the strong statement (complète, cependant), the adverbial oppositions (complètement, pas complètement; de près, de loin), and the final comment on the pleasure derived by the Lieutenant from the general uncertainty, all suggest that the world created by Gracq is a subjective one in which the real and the unreal, the possible and the impossible, the probable and the improbable, may well be synonymous. (p. 161)

To describe the phony war and to show how little it affects either Grange or Mona, Gracq uses language drawn from various kinds of entertainment: parlor games, sports, the drama—the last being the total art form of diversion for Gracq. For the Lieutenant, the military alerts, interjected in the long "divertissement" and the "vacances" ("entertainment," "vacations") (in the etymological sense of these two words) which this phony war constitutes, seem to be "puits du jeu de l'oie" ("a kind of forfeit"); soldiers in rout along the road have the "rictus ralenti, âgé d'un boxeur qui s'accroche aux cordes" ("the corners of their mouths in the slow, tired grin of a boxer hanging from the ropes"); barbed wire barricades, "gros boudins nickelés" ("great nickel-plated rolls"), seem to turn the land surrounding the blockhouse into a "gymkhana pour bambins" ("playground"); the small terrace of the deserted café, similar to a "scène" ("stage setting"), belongs to the décor of the "théâtre de guerre." (pp. 161-62)

Yet generally the facetious manner is of a more prosaic nature and is used to describe the world of collective humanity to which Grange belongs by his military functions, if only intermittently. The Lieutenant and his orderly are present at the exodus of tanks "comme des concierges désoeuvrés à califourchon sur leur chaise basse" ("like concierges straddling their kitchen chairs on summer evenings"). In front of them, "les hommes sur les véhicules passent muets et indifférents, vaguement allérents, vaguement allégoriques, comme les pompiers assis en rang le long de leurs échelles" ("the men on the tanks rode by, mute, indifferent, and almost all allegorical, like firemen sitting in rows along their ladders"). War no longer has its traditional trapping of nobility and gravity; it is homely, facetious:

> On sentait que la guerre au milieu du paysage s'était mise dans ses meubles avec le sans-gène—un peu épuisant—de ces locataires encombrés qui n'en finissent plus de voir arriver leurs malles.

> (One felt that the war had installed its furniture in the landscape with the—exhausting—casualness of those overprovided tenants who never see the end of the trunks they are expecting.)

Everything in it is reassuring, even the bombardments "onctueux et gras, plaisants à l'oreille" ("unctuous and oily, pleasing to the ear"), with bombs that go down with a "plop, cotonneux et mou" ("soft, cottony 'plop'"): the infantile onomatopoeia underlines the impression of pleasure and play which are inseparable from the notion of an entertaining war, a kind of "parenthesis" in the routine of the world.

Gracq's narrative technique is thus characterized by a constant deviation. Beings and things are stripped of their normal functions. This singular vision is based upon a singular use of words: not only do objects and men seem suspicious, but words themselves become suspect. The bewildered observer puts into question the existence of the falsely reassuring world and tries to distinguish reality from appearance.

At the end of the story, however, the divergence between the ponderous and the facetious disappears: a convergence is sketched through the "solution poétique" which, since *Au Château d'Argol,* has distinguished each of Gracq's works. The blowing-up of the block-house, the last concrete expression of a suspect reality, takes place in "la forêt galante de Shakespeare" ("a Shakespeare Arden"), in the "décor d'opéra de la forêt dérisoire" ("the forest's absurd opera decor"). The

final pages are notable for the number and density of both themes and images which refer to pleasure and to solitary exaltation. . . . And as the real world of the multitude yields to the dream world of the solitary individual, the author's half-ponderous half-facetious narrative manner dissolves into one which is completely poetic both in conception and expression.

Gracq's technique, in each of the four novels, is basically the same: in order to stress the distance between the world which he refuses and the world which he proposes, the author uses in each novel two sets of stylistic devices which, although they vary from one novel to the next, correspond in the most rigorous manner. The style that depicts the world of reality is evasive in *Au Château d'Argol,* minimizing in *Un Beau Ténébreux* and *Le Rivage des Syrtes,* ponderous in *Un Balcon en Forêt;* the style that suggests the world of the dream is hyperbolic in *Au Château d'Argol,* magnifying in *Un Beau Ténébreux* and *Le Rivage des Syrtes,* facetious in *Un Balcon en Forêt.* Yet at the end of each story the two styles are fused in a "solution poétique," the only one which can absorb the contradictions inherent in Gracq's vision.

The rich complexity of Gracq's vision and Gracq's universe is reflected by his stylistic richness. To portray the conventional world, worn out and near its end, a world having neither true speech nor sight, Gracq uses worn-out words, stereotypes and clichés. To delineate the vigor and splendor of the new world he is positing, however, Gracq uses an idiosyncratic language of his own invention—difficult images, the sign of an esoteric world not easily entered; anomalies and contrasts, the sign of an unpredictable and surprising world; neologisms, the sign of a world in formation, resolutely new. For an unprecedented vision, the reader is presented with an unprecedented vocabulary.

The tempo is also carefully regulated and adjusted to the ritual of expectation, and the final vision is always delayed since, in this posited world, if the curtain does rise it invariably rises somewhere beyond the written page. Expectation and suspense are reinforced by syntactical factors which slow the tempo and by curious typographical procedures.

What intrigues the reader in Gracq's work is the effectiveness of the various literary devices. In order to convey his vision in its totality—the visible and the invisible, the real and the unreal, Gracq creates a language made up of convention and innovation, in which there is no dogmatic or definite correspondence between words and what words represent. The stylistic devices which have been studied reflect an aesthetic of uneasiness which underlies, in all of Gracq's work (novels, theater, poetry), the theme of the hazardous and mysterious Quest. (pp. 162-64)

> *Annie-Claude Dobbs, "Reality and Dream in Julien Gracq: A Stylistic Study," in* Twentieth Century French Fiction: Essays for Germaine Brée, *edited by George Stambolian, Rutgers University Press, 1975, pp. 141-65.*

CHRISTOPHER ROBINSON

[Julien Gracq] has philosophical affinities with the surrealists and earlier traditions of irrational poetry, affinities confirmed by his critical essays on André Breton, Poe, Lautréamont and Rimbaud. Surrealists have tended, particularly since World War II, to put emphasis on the need for a new mythology to express the gap between human desire and the means available to satisfy it and to embody a potential solution to the problems posed by this permanent conflict. Artaud in *Textes mexicains pour un nouveau mythe* (1953) and Benjamin Péret in *Anthologie des mythes, légendes et contes populaires d'Amérique* (1959) looked to Central and South America for possible sources, but others have seen the anti-rationalist qualities of Celtic myth as equally fruitful. It is not surprising then that Gracq's first two novels, *Au Château d'Argol* (1939) and *Un beau ténébreux* (1945) and the title story of *La Presqu'île* (1970) ["**La Presqu'île**"] are all set in Brittany, the centre of France's Celtic tradition, or that his play *Le Roi pêcheur* (1948) is based on an episode from the Grail legend (to which thematic allusion is also made in *Au Château d'Argol*). This is not to say that Gracq uses pre-existing myths as a special kind of intellectual or emotional vehicle in the way that Giraudoux and Sartre do. He is not using a familiar framework to promote new responses to details. He is developing a new interpretation of existence which has its roots in a particular medieval tradition.

His introduction to *Le Roi pêcheur* is rich in indications of what he considers the function of myth to be. As one might expect from the man who wrote of Kleist's *Penthesilea*, which he translated in 1954, that like all truly symbolic works the play had no precise meaning, he is anxious to preserve the open-endedness of myth. Hence his distaste for the closed circle of fault and retribution inherent in both classical and Christian traditions. In the Arthurian cycle, with its 'elective community' and quests for the suprahuman, he finds a particular resonance. . . . It is particularly the status given to desire, the temptation of absolute love which Tristan represents, the temptation of divinity embodied in Perceval, which Gracq finds significant. He is emphatic that the Christian overtones of Arthurian myth, especially the Grail stories, are an accretion. Their symbolism can express a wider concept of man's search for the meaning of existence than the traditional religious interpretation permits.

Gracq's first novel *Au Château d'Argol* is set in an atmosphere only one remove from the legendary events of *Le Roi pêcheur*. Its hero, Albert, like Perceval, has begun his quest for complete knowledge at the age of fifteen, and is particularly interested in the inner meaning of myths. In his Gothic retreat Albert is visited by Herminien, 'his double and his opposite', and by Heide, a hauntingly beautiful girl who incarnates the temptation of the feminine principle. These characters, according to Gracq's own 'Avis au lecteur', are involved in a demonic version of the Parsifal story, demonic because Herminien represents the evil side of Albert's own nature and because the moral values of the book are deliberately confused. The tension that builds up between Albert and Herminien leads to a vicious attack by the latter on Heide in the forest and thence to Albert's discovery of his own fascination with blood, in the form of Heide's wound. It is in the attempt to free himself from this attraction that he murders Herminien. So that what began as a quest for metaphysical revelation ends in violence. Throughout this narrative a sense of foreboding and fatality are maintained; for example, Albert carves Heide's name on a cross without yet knowing who she is. What is not clear is how far the action represents destruction and failure, how far purification and achievement. As with Perceval's decision not to see the Grail at the end of *Le Roi pêcheur*, the symbolism is deliberately ambiguous.

Un beau ténébreux transposes the same themes a stage closer to the surface of modern life. The remote location this time is a hotel, the isolated group among whom the drama is played out are youngish people on holiday; each of them has a type

role, sometimes clear—Jacques the adolescent, Irene carnal womanhood—sometimes indefinite—Gérard, dreamer endowed with some kind of second sight, Christel elect spirit destined for sorrow. At the core of the novel is the figure of Allan, the '*beau ténébreux*' of the title, who awakens instant fascination or hostility in the other characters. He is a catalyst bringing destruction yet like Perceval a man in motion unlike the static world around him.

The climax of the story is again highly ambiguous, for Allan's search for the meaning of existence (he himself compares it to the Grail quest) leads him to suicide, despite the efforts of Gérard and Christel to deflect him. His death is an act of pride, a desire to achieve god-like status in the eyes of the faithful. Yet at the same time it is an act into which he has been forced. In an interesting image, Gérard, in his forebodings, has prepared us for just this ambiguity. He observes that the part of the Christ story which most appeals to him is the period between the Resurrection and Ascension, when mysterious forces seem at work everywhere, and there is an immediate contrast between the feverish activity of the initiates, aware that their hero is about to go away, and the hostility of the settled part of humanity, 'that taste for merciless man-hunting which awakens in the heart of closed families'. The tension between the real world and a man who, far more than Hugo's Hernani, has the right to say of himself 'I am a force in motion', leads to revelation for the few and destruction for the hero himself, but the destruction remains a higher destiny than that of those who refuse life's possibilities by their acceptance of compromise and convention.

This theme of electing for death is developed further in Gracq's third novel, *Le Rivage des Syrtes* (selected for the Prix Goncourt in 1951, though the author indignantly rejected the award in protest against the whole French prize system). At times one feels uneasily that this novel has moved too far towards the paradox which Giraudoux expresses in *Electre*, for the hero Aldo arouses his fatherland, Orsenna, from the state of torpor in which it has lain for three hundred years by deliberately provoking a war with the neighbouring state of Farghestan which will completely annihilate Orsenna. Like Electre, who is in Giralducian terms also a creature of destiny, Aldo cures spiritual malaise at the price of complete physical destruction. This rather clumsily abstract novel does, however, emphasise a new aspect, anticipation, which is almost the entire subject of *Un Balcon en forêt* (1958). This could hardly be more different from its predecessors in superficial subject, since it is set in the Ardennes during the 'phoney war' period before the German offensive there in May 1940. In fact, however, familiar themes reassert themselves. Grange the central character grows to find spiritual fulfilment in his dream-like communion with the forest where he is stationed in an isolated outpost. A mediator in this fulfilment is Mona, another incarnation of the special power of love. But spiritual fulfilment leads to detachment from physical reality: Grange ignores the imminent reality of the war, and allows himself to be killed (if his final falling asleep *is* death) by the inevitable German attack.

In his last major work, *La Presqu'île*, a collection of three long stories, the tension between mind and body is presented in a much less violent form. "**La route**" and "**Le roi Cophetua**" are stories touched by war in the background, but the long central story ["**La Presqu'île**"] is another study in waiting, set in the Breton countryside. Simon is waiting at the station for Irmgard; the whole of the story is outlined in his passing thought: '. . . she won't come . . . Perhaps it's even better if she doesn't come now'. When she fails to come by the morning train, he decides to spend the rest of the day exploring the peninsula where he had spent his childhood holidays, before returning to the station in the evening. What follows is a long exploration of the form and mood of the Breton landscape intercut with Simon's anxieties. The mythical level is kept to odd images and references, for example, '. . . it was almost like the thickets of thorn bush and the more than usually drab stretches of moorland which lead travellers astray on the very edge of the Castle Perilous'. Gradually Simon realises that meaning and pleasure lie more in expectation than in fulfilment. Irmgard's arrival is an anticlimax:

> . . . he felt that the hollow opening up within him for joy was not filling; all that was left was a neutral rather abstract feeling of security which was doubtless happiness at finding Irmgard again.

The *doubtless* undercuts all. Simon's quest is over; he is condemned to stasis. (pp. 165-69)

> *Christopher Robinson, "Philosophical Dilemmas,"*
> *in his* French Literature in the Twentieth Century,
> *Barnes & Noble, 1980, pp. 132-77.*

ELISABETH CARDONNE-ARLYCK

At last, 35 years after its first publication in French, Julien Gracq's major novel, *Le Rivage des Syrtes,* is available in English. . . .

Syrtis Major was the ancient appellation of the Gulf of Sidra. Long before being named the "Death Zone" by Col. Muammar el-Qaddafi, the gulf was reputed perilous to ships. Virgil called it "inhospitable Syrtis," not only for its strong currents and shifting sands but for its wild shores and the nomadic tribes of the bordering country. In different ways, the French title *Le Rivage des Syrtes* and its English counterpart, *The Opposing Shore,* conjure up this old image of an alien coast, clearly still vivid in the Western imagination.

Yet Mr. Gracq's Syrtis will not be found on any map, ancient or modern. The author uses his extensive classical culture and Proustian sense of names to create a geography of the mind. . . .

Mr. Gracq made his literary debut in 1938 with *The Castle of Argol,* which André Breton heralded as the first truly Surrealist novel. It was, in fact, a departure from a movement Mr. Gracq had never joined. Although he maintained his admiration for Breton and the Surrealist project ("full of *departures* which no arrival will ever belie"), he cut away from them in an idiosyncratic blend of linear storytelling and poetic reliance on language: "The winds and currents, that is to say the hazards that language causes, often determine the itinerary; but no one ever launched out across an unknown sea, unless an imperious ghost, impossible to dismiss, had beckoned to him from the other shore." Referring to his own work, Mr. Gracq never describes the object of narrative desire as reality or truth but as "internal music" or "secret iconography."

His metaphor of the pursuit of a phantom across an unknown sea could also serve as a plot summary of *The Opposing Shore.* Aldo, the narrator and protagonist, belongs to one of the ruling families of Orsenna, an ancient and decadent city that for 300 years has been in a state of suspended war with the barbarian country of Farghestan. Sent as a state observer to Orsenna's dilapidated naval base of Syrtes, Aldo surrenders to his fas-

cination with Farghestan; he crosses the "forbidden line" that divides the "dead sea" by sailing to the city of Rhages on the enemy's shore. There his ship is welcomed with three cannon shots. Having by this irreparable act rekindled the war that will destroy Orsenna, Aldo discovers that he has accomplished the suicidal gesture a whole people secretly yearned for.

Mr. Gracq believes with Nietzsche that "only where there are tombs are there resurrections." But the theme of resurrection through death, which permeates the speeches of Orsenna's prophets of doom, is not the author's central subject. By Mr. Gracq's own account, *The Opposing Shore* can be read as a meditation on what he calls the spirit of history and particularly on the "apocalyptic cloud" the rise of Hitler spread over the European consciousness. Read in that fashion, the novel casts a rather sinister light on France's complicity in the 1930's with impending disaster.

Mr. Gracq is by training a historian and geographer. . . . For him history and geography are one, and the perception of their continuity is essential to his literary sensibility. The dynamic sense of history he shares with André Malraux paradoxically carries with it a renewed ability to find in the very apprehension of an ominous future an acute delight in the physical world, a renewed interest in attending to its changing moods. His stories increasingly reveal a pastoral longing for an "earth swept clean of men"; his vibrant but solitary characters seem more like "human plants" growing from their physical surroundings than psychological or sociological entities.

In presenting this vision, Mr. Gracq's chief stylistic device is a relentless and intoxicating use of metaphor. Impatient with syntactical constraints, he likes to open his sentences to chance encounters. The outcome of his descriptions is palpably unpredictable, an unstable world like the lagoon of Syrtes and the sands of Farghestan, its components (locales, characters, events, moods) constantly shifting in relation to one another, but the narrative is pushed forward by a desire for meaning—for Sense—that proves illusory. This recurrent movement of self-erasure would appear to link Mr. Gracq with Samuel Beckett, Claude Simon or Marguerite Duras. But in his writing it is less a strategy than the result of metaphorical overflow. And the deliberate *mise en scène* of an obsessive pursuit of something "beyond" fills the text with images of desire. Although sexual scenes are sparse, Mr. Gracq's fiction is charged with erotic tension. He conceives of reading and writing in sexual terms, writes of language that "the knowledge of its handling has much to do with the slow and patient skill of the erotic." Literature is "a repertory of *femmes fatales*" and true reading "the naked desire of an elected flesh." . . .

The Opposing Shore is Mr. Gracq's best-known and richest work. It has already been translated into six languages, and its long overdue appearance in English reminds us of one of the more stimulating and original imaginations in contemporary French literature.

> *Elisabeth Cardonne-Arlyck, "The Beckoning Ghost,"*
> *in* The New York Times Book Review, *June 22,*
> *1986, p. 9.*

TOM LeCLAIR

Like Camus' *The Plague,* *The Opposing Shore* may have had, in 1951, dual historical inspiration: the recent German occupation of France and the French occupation of Algeria. But Gracq, years before the Algerian revolt, saw far below the geopolitical machinations his narrator "discovers." One deeper plot is revealed through Aldo's obsession with maps. "The territory is not the map," semanticist Alfred Korzybski kept saying. But Aldo and Orsenna exist unconsciously within their maps—paper plots—of Farghestan; within Orsennian cultural codes that are invisible to Orsennians; and in a language perpetuated without change or life. These are now familiar themes of the "Nouveau Roman" and post-structuralist criticism, but Gracq was subtly applying these ideas in 1951 to a cultural border he prophetically realized would be dangerous.

The novel is, deeper yet, a psycho-sexual anthropology, an inquiry into the white European's relation with his neighbor of color, a racial difference Gracq knew was related to such historical events and figures as the Crusades, the Barbary pirates, and "maddog" Gadhafi. In Gracq's long and wide view, the "Third World" would be a misnomer: North Africa is the Other World, what his narrator pregnantly calls "the other side," the exotic object of European fear and desire that gives the translation its title.

Prophecy comes swathed. Profundity requires abstraction. Anthropology demands distance. For these reasons, *The Opposing Shore* is a ponderous, pondering book. Most of it takes place at night; "somnolent" is a word frequently repeated and an accurate description of the novel. Character, event, and setting are all muffled by Aldo's circuitous, furzy prose. Reading Gracq is like being aware that you are sleeping for hours waiting for a dream, and this is precisely Aldo's "action": waiting, preparing, waiting, and finally making his night-sea journey across the line of sense and safety. . . .

The Opposing Shore is not meant for mall bookstores. That's unfortunate. It's more instructive to fall asleep over this novel than to stay awake for the late news from Libya or Washington. In its occulusions, deferrals, and profound insight, *The Opposing Shore* is what Kafka would have composed had he written *The War* instead of *The Trial*.

Tom LeClair, "Across the Line of Sense and Safety," in Book World—The Washington Post, *Vol. XVI, No. 30, July 27, 1986, p. 9.*

Jorie Graham

1951-

American poet.

Graham writes complex philosophical verse in which she explores relationships between mind and body, flesh and spirit, and imagination and reality. By creating elaborate networks of ideas in lyrical arrangement, Graham attempts, as she states in her poem "The Nature of Evidence," "to catch the world / at pure idea." Several critics have noted the influence of Wallace Stevens on Graham's work, citing her interest in the processes of thought and poetic creation and her emphasis on aesthetics over characterization and personal concerns. Graham's childhood, which was spent in Europe, and her lifelong enthusiasm for art figure in much of her poetry. While critics occasionally fault Graham's verse for obscurity and impersonality, many laud her intellectual range and imaginative use of metaphor.

Graham's acclaimed first collection, *Hybrids of Plants and of Ghosts* (1980), reveals her preoccupation with death and change. In these poems, Graham deftly weaves images, ideas, and emotions while making intricate associations between such activities as writing, sewing, painting, and gardening. In a review of this book, Dave Smith commented: "Most remarkable about Jorie Graham . . . are her sustained control and a music not like anyone's among us; the creation of a voice we seldom mistrust—yet about whom hardly anything personal is revealed." In her second volume, *Erosion* (1983), Graham analyzes relationships between the mental, spiritual, and physical worlds. Many of the poems in this collection reflect her interest in the darker aspects of art, nature, and history. Askold Melnyczuk described *Erosion* as "by turns an argument and a meditation on appearance and reality, and on the self exploring the volatile boundaries between them."

The End of Beauty (1987) marks a change of direction in Graham's work. More ambiguous and indeterminate than that in her earlier books, Graham's verse in this volume also introduces such devices as blank spaces and algebraic variables to question the concept of the poem as a closed unit. Using an oracular tone and highly stylized language, Graham attempts to define the self through the qualities of biblical and mythic figures. Helen Vendler praised the poems in *The End of Beauty* as "the best ones in recent memory."

(See also *Contemporary Authors,* Vol. 111.)

DAVE SMITH

Jorie Graham's *Hybrids Of Plants And Of Ghosts* is not for the inattentive nor the faint-hearted reader. Hers is an intricately shaped poetry that is as given to decorum as to discipline. Though she alludes occasionally to Frost and to a bevy of modern painters, her large ghost is Wallace Stevens and his verbal sleight of hand. Like Stevens, Graham thinks, sees, muses, ruminates, and makes the art of poetry (which unlike her contemporaries she does not often invoke directly) the

Photograph by Layle Silbert

sufficient engine of her faith. But very few poets may be named beside Stevens except to their disadvantage, and Jorie Graham is not Stevens. Nevertheless *Hybrids Of Plants And Of Ghosts* seems to me as promising a first book as any recently published.

Why it should be that younger poets speak less to youth's buoyant folly and joy than to the sober, the ominous, the tragic, I do not know. Death and the paradox of renewing beauty is Graham's constant occupation. In **"Strangers"** she writes that "Indeed the tulips / change tense / too quickly." Her world is entirely implicated by these terse lines: the imagery of the green world that dies; the unknowable paradox of time that contains, as she says elsewhere, "histories / where only present tense survives;" the formal, nearly syllogistic speaker whose emotion is betrayed by that "too quickly." As Graham says in **"The Nature of Evidence"** she would "like to catch the world / at pure idea" and that effort keeps her at what she cannot examine too closely, the endless blooming and withering which the mind may know only as image and sensation but which it is always trying to turn to abstraction. Because she is so relentlessly cerebral and lyrical, Graham does not much help a reader with story, location, or those commonplace and easy ironies by which poems resolve to a "meaning." Instead she speaks often of tracks, shadows, disappearances. She conceives of life as thicket, weir, gardens going to seed, a "nation of turns," and a locked kingdom. She is compelled to definitions

("A man full of words / is a garden of weeds."), epistemological transformations involving words and things, and deft glances into what she calls "a small believable cosmology."

Most remarkable about Jorie Graham, perhaps, are her sustained control and a music not like anyone's among us; the creation of a voice we seldom mistrust—yet one about whom hardly anything personal is revealed. We do not discover where she lives, how many children she has or hasn't, what her father's occupation was, the sort of thing that invites us to know *her* and the thing we think so necessary until we have too much of it. When, in **"Self-Portrait,"** she defines herself, it is as a solitary observer whose "looking is a set of tracks" in fresh snow. Yet she is so detached that she does not contact or change what is seen, and may say of herself, "I want to change for you, / though it would be by trying to stay the same." Her point is Heraclitean; change is constant but in no predictable pattern. This is a particular angst for Graham because it means Death is inexplicable.

Perhaps it only means, however, that Graham is preoccupied with the philosopher's bullet: what is real and what is not? In the end her only answer is the music of the saying, which Stevens knew well enough. That is surely why she so frequently writes of painting, sewing, writing, gardening—those skills and interests which used to be the mark of the 'finished woman'— but it is the music of poetry which informs and drives her writing beyond mere finish, which lifts the order of perception and its object into a passionate clarity. . . . Wherever she begins, the moment leaves Jorie Graham convinced "Something we don't know is complete without us / and continues." The effort to know what that might be, hence what we are, that search for salvation, leads only to the things of this world, and they are dying. This fix is as true now as it was for Matthew Arnold, who is echoed in **"Girl At the Piano"** where Graham writes, "Your sleep beside me is the real, / the loom I can return to when all loosens into speculation." Except it isn't quite true or satisfactory. This accounts for an evanescent sorrow everywhere in these heady poems. Not what she doesn't know but what she knows too well to escape—that is what haunts Jorie Graham so that she must try to metamorphose everything into the poem that is the final stay, the living thing set against the freeze of syntax. (pp. 36-7)

I wish that Graham would notice that she is sometimes slack and redundant, that there are moments of defiant obscurity, and that she needn't be quite so parsimonious with feeling. But this is small complaint for a book with poems as good as **"Hybrids of Plants and of Ghosts," "Cross-Stitch," "Drawing Wildflowers," "Netting," "The Geese,"** and **"Now the Sturdy Wind."** What I want to say is merely this: Jorie Graham will write no book that I will fail to read. (p. 37)

Dave Smith, "Some Recent American Poetry: Come All Ye Fair and Tender Ladies," in The American Poetry Review, *Vol. 11, No. 1, January-February, 1982, pp. 36-46.*

CHARLES BERGER

In a blurb on the back cover [of *Hybrids of Plants and of Ghosts*], Marvin Bell says of Jorie Graham: "From any event she arcs bravely into the farthest reaches of mind." What this means, I think, is that her poems tend to begin with sharp visible detail, then move out and away into realms of speculation. Graham creates an illusion of "reaches" being traversed, if only because her variations on that opening chord

become far more distant and difficult to follow. Just how much conceptual ground gets covered in these rhetorical stretches is another matter. I think she mars most of her poems by extending them too far beyond their centers of fused meaning; her power lies in compression, not expansion. Every poem in *Hybrids of Plants and of Ghosts* contains some haunting epigrammatic kernel, but too few of the meditations branching outward from these moments sustain a clear and convincing intensity. By trying to bring too much inside the poem, Graham only insures that the reader will leave with what she must regard as too little: bright seizable instants of perfect expression. (pp. 36-7)

Graham is a poet who avoids the occasional event. She makes poems out of her own considerable intelligence: "They say the eye is most ours / when shut, that objects give no evidence / that they are seen by us." The last two lines here are separated by a stanza brreak, white space intervening to illustrate what Wallace Stevens called "the dumbfoundering abyss between us and the object." An ascetic poet, Graham chastens the eye's desire to rove, although she allows the mind to wander where it will. This can result, paradoxically, in a dissolution of the striking image into mere talk. . . . (pp. 36-7)

Charles Berger, "Laurels," in Poetry, *Vol. CXL, No. 1, April, 1982, pp. 35-7.*

THOMAS SWISS

Jorie Graham's [*Hybrids of Plants and of Ghosts*] is undoubtedly the finest first book of poems issued in the Princeton Series under the editorship of David Wagoner. What initially strikes the reader on coming to her work is that almost all of the poems are set as arguments; arguments not with the world but with the self *about* the world. Borrowing many of the traditions of prose discourse without succumbing to prose rhythms, Graham uses her powerful and passionate intelligence to persuade the reader to see, as she clearly does, "the world as pure idea."

Graham has taken to heart Stevens's thesis that life consists of propositions about life. Whether the movement of the poem is inductive (**"Mirrors," "Tennessee June," "How Morning Glories Could Bloom at Dusk"**) or loosely deductive as in the haunting first poem **"The Way Things Work,"** Graham is busy testing her ideas. "Flight is an arc to buttress the sky," she writes in one poem; in another, she argues that "there are moments in our lives which, threaded, give us heaven." Abstractions and concrete images are masterfully woven in a way which allows the poems to proceed associatively without ever seeming arbitrary. (p. 345)

Graham's love for words—for their music as often as for their meaning—is twinned with an understanding of the limits of language. She is a cautious writer, hesitant to surrender to language the emotional details of personality. This particular attitude results in a generous self-effacement in the poems. There are no detailed descriptions in the poetry, but Graham is nevertheless attentive to a select group of specifics (colors; the names of flowers, trees; sewing materials) which she explores as illustrations, metaphors. As she writes in the poem **"Strangers,"** "we have no mind / in a world without objects."

Many poems are meditations in which the speaker calls up a memory, real or imagined, in order to dislocate the remembered object or event. . . . In Graham's world, experiences are always "clues" to or "evidence" of principles, whole processes.

In *his* first book, John Ashbery wrote, "Everything has a schedule, if you can find out what it is." Graham, too, is trying to discern the schedule or, in her own words, "the idea that governs"; and while realizing that the task may be impossible, she convincingly finds comfort in believing that by moving from "station to station," "eventually pattern emerges." (pp. 346-47)

Thomas Swiss, "Moving from Station to Station," in Southwest Review, Vol. 67, No. 3, Summer, 1982, pp. 345-49.

WILLIAM LOGAN

[In *Hybrids of Plants and of Ghosts,* Jorie Graham markets transformation]. It is her characteristic trope ("See, / transformation, or our love of it, / draws a pattern we can't see but own"), and to it she allies a rare passion for the abstract. Her insights are profoundly poetical, not logical; but they live on the remembered edge of philosophy. . . . Statements of relation rather than object, her poems occasionally lack specification. Whether this is a necessary order or an evasion may only be determined by the poems which have, as most of them have, a referable world. (p. 222)

Graham is a poet convinced that everything will come out right, that if she works her changes long enough, the solution will pop into place, as on a Rubik's Cube. As might be expected of someone so entranced by relation (and someone so willing to destroy the separating function of title), she is intensely aware of the relative properties of language:

I Was Taught Three

names for the tree facing my window
almost within reach, elastic

with squirrels, memory banks, homes.
Castagno took itself to heart, its pods

like urchins clung to where they landed
claiming every bit of shadow

at the hem. *Chassagne,* on windier days,
nervous in taffeta gowns,

whispering, on the verge of being
anarchic, though well bred.

And then *chestnut,* whipped pale and clean
by all the inner reservoirs

called upon to do their even share of work.

The poem continues, but the girl taught three names for the tree finds the object itself in none of them. Things do not exist in language, but properties may; that is, the girl associates different aspects of the chestnut with its Italian or French or English name. Raised in Italy, educated at the Sorbonne, N.Y.U., and Columbia, Graham experienced in some form the tri-lingual upbringing described by George Steiner in *After Babel.* It may have contributed to her existence in the abstract. Since any particular is subject to the shifting allegiance of language, only the idea of the tree—like the tree itself—is firm, unlike the "human tree / clothed with its nouns."

Graham thinks before she feels. Her poetry is dedicated to the delight of thinking, to the triumph of verbal arrangements. In a poetry that does not seem to require or command emotion, any obscurity may seem due to abstract conceptions, though it may only be a failure to clarify relations between particulars. Having chosen a subject—there seems no necessity in the choice, as long as it can be forced to have poetic resonance ("as if

grown upward / from the meaning of the thing itself")—Graham composes elegant variations upon it. She takes, say, ambergris

Because our skin is the full landscape, an ocean,
we must be unforgettable or not at all.

Squids that are never seen alive surface
to follow the moonlight on the water—anything

that flees so constantly must be desirable.

(**"Ambergris"**)

This may seem like inspired trifling, but it is not erratic. Graham trusts that language which sounds good means well. The first two lines pretend to logical exaction ("Because . . . , we must . . ."), but the terms of identity between skin and ocean are tantalizingly undefined and the terms of choice ("unforgettable or not at all") spuriously conclusive. The assertion is unconvincing, as is the following one ("anything // that flees so constantly must be desirable"). Retreating soldiers, delinquent children, bank robbers (who may be "wanted" but are hardly desirable) seem contrary instances. (pp. 223-24)

Graham is a poet of process more than completion, who must be quoted at length to catch the winding of her thought. Her unit is not the stanza or line but the sentence. Because her enjambment is essentially dramatic, the length of her lines varies enormously, from one syllable to twenty-two. Delicately pointed and weighted, her sentences are intricate and functional, like Ashanti goldweights. At times, however, she seems to put down whatever association, however tortured, occurs to her (examine: "the tree . . . elastic // with . . . memory banks," "whipped . . . clean / by . . . inner reservoirs," "landscape, an ocean"); though kinetically inventive, her poems are often gaseous, whirling that excess energy into vacuum.

Graham's more interested in toying with ideas than in analyzing them. She takes one seriously for a line or two, until there is another to be taken up and discarded. She is never awed or frightened by their implications—her attitude is insouciant, as if every idea were equal, as charming and fascinating as a Fabergé egg. . . . (pp. 225-26)

Because she never takes alarm at what she has said, Graham never finds in ideas what is always there: an absolute questioning of ourselves. Her poems are closest perhaps to Laura Jensen's, verbally as stunning but more intellectual in their grasp of the world. Despite the abstract tendencies described, Graham is very much a poet of the world ("We have no mind // in a world without objects"), the natural world. Half nature, half spirit, *Hybrids of Plants and of Ghosts* is aptly titled—the quote is from Nietzsche. Again and again she returns to the outdoors and (not surprisingly for a poet in love with the transformed) the seasons, drawing her lessons by a sort of modernist naturalism. . . . (p. 226)

Because most of her poems live more in the world than in abstraction, her meanings can be puzzled out. Her obscurity comes from too great a love of rhetoric—the multifarious implications of her best lines must be patiently reduced, pared away often to some humdrum application. (p. 227)

When dealing with personal history, she becomes skittish, unsure what to leave said or silent. Other people rarely figure intimately in her work. This is hardly surprising, since Stevens seems her chief poetic mentor. The abstract has its own safety, as does a nature shorn of people. Because her stance is isolated, the poem most an *ars poetica*, **"Drawing Wildflowers,"** is dedicated to things, not people. . . . (p. 228)

The enchantment of her work is that it can be analyzed without being encompassed. Such poems *may* seem endlessly refreshing because they never actually get anywhere. Because they are not built from one meticulous insight to another (her composition seems intuitive), her poems are full of those repetitions the mind at speed produces to ease its way. Her images, like her strategies, tend toward xerography. . . . In addition to dressing up nature, Graham is preoccupied with metaphors of sewing and weaving. . . . That she finds a high proportion of her metaphors in such a small area of experience (and there is another series of tropes on knots, another on fabric) suggests how narrow a poet Graham can be. Once the reader has identified a few of her strategies, she loses a little of her freshness. Because her meditations so depend on process, on the spinning out of associations, her closures tend to be artificial. The closures are often, in fact, only metaphors of closure. . . . It is probably unconscious, this way of assuring her imagination that something has been completed, though it hasn't ("Something we don't know is complete without us / and continues").

The abstract is the most difficult subject in poetry. Unable by talent or temperament to concentrate her work upon it, Graham produces only coruscating abstractions; the intermittencies that are the very terms of their pleasure are the terms of their limitations. The seasons and landscapes she writes from, or on, are less intriguing than the lesson she draws from them—she has created not an interesting world but an interesting mind. Occasionally, as in **"Ambergris,"** the search for such a world becomes an effective strategy for creating one; or, as in **"In High Waters,"** the furious improvisations themselves become a reason for questioning action. But these are secondary turns, strategies turned on strategies. When her poems are more direct they are minor. For her, the abstract *is* a necessary order; the real world constitutes the evasion (as if the abstract were real and the real mere philosophy).

Graham doesn't yet know how to enforce her ideas, or how to make them demand emotion from the reader, to place him where to read such an idea is to feel an emotion. Perhaps in this kind of poem it is not necessary for her to do so. There have been other poets whose ideas of order have required a poem based—just as, theoretically, life might have been based on silicon instead of carbon—on mental presence, the line-by-line excitement of intellectual rather than emotional energies. Cocooned in their mental world, however, these accomplished and startling poems reveal a life not so much unreachable as uninviting—the reader often seems a superfluity to them. They are the products of a mind working at heat, going on and on partly from instinct, partly from joy. . . . (pp. 228-30)

William Logan, "First Books, Fellow Travelers," in Parnassus: Poetry in Review, *Vol. 11, No. 1, Spring-Summer, 1983, pp. 211-30.*

HELEN VENDLER

Jorie Graham's [*Erosion*] brings the presence of poetry into the largest question of life, the relation of body and spirit, a relation more often considered by theologians and philosophers these days than by poets. Miss Graham's subject is the depth to which the human gaze can penetrate, the opening in reality into which the poet can enter. Under the clothed she seeks out the naked; over the soil, the air; inside the integument, a kernel; through the cover of the grass, the snake; from the bowels of the earth, the disinterred saint. Against writers who press against the opacity and resistance of the material world, she suggests its profundity and penetrability—though there seems to be no stopping place for that penetration.

This is a poetry of delicate and steady transgression in which the spirit searches the flesh and the flesh the spirit, melting and dissolving the boundaries thought to separate them. The nature of the spiritual, as Miss Graham sees it, is to be entirely rooted in the physical, and in consequence her poems have a strong visual and sensuous presence leading to a lofty inner vision—"a puzzle unsolvable till the edges give a bit and soften." It is that softening that allows us to enter these "syllables becoming thought" where "blossoming sustains the linear."

I have been quoting from Miss Graham's excellent first book, *Hybrids of Plants and of Ghosts* (Nietzsche's definition of man). Though the second book is recognizably descended from the first, it takes up far more hazardous subjects, including autopsy, extermination camps, murder and blindness. The serene depth ultimately attained by these poems has been taught to Miss Graham (who grew up in Italy) by the contained tragedy of painting: There are poems here about Masaccio, Signorelli, Piero della Francesca and Klimt. In stationing their figures around a central tragedy or a moment of crisis and yet finding a way to exhibit them in form, paintings are a guide to the poet. . . .

At the heart of these poems, some "contained damage" rests, contained by a damasked surface. The evenness of Miss Graham's line and the gravity of her gaze suggest the length of time that the damage has been considered. (p. 10)

The attempt to find all the stops, to range through the gamut of possibility, makes Miss Graham a poet of landscape and memory as well as a poet of art. She is expert in finding in the natural world, in her own life and in history correspondence for those spiritual motions, impulses, currents, apprehensions and emergings that intangibly make up our inner life. Her poetry, though so fully at home in the mental, the imagined and the speculative, grounds itself nevertheless in that desire that is, as she says, the engine, the wind of the body: "Passion is work / that retrieves us / lost stitches. It makes a pattern of us."

Miss Graham does not avert her glance from the relentlessness of the search of art. In a poem on Signorelli's *Resurrection of the Body*, she reminds us of the painter's use of autopsy to ensure anatomical accuracy, extending even to the autopsy of his dead son. . . . In elaborating her intricate surfaces over damage and grief, Miss Graham continues, with her haunting indwelling musicality, to make the pattern that constructs us as we read it. (pp. 10, 15)

Helen Vendler, "Patterns Made by Passion," in The New York Times Book Review, *July 17, 1983, pp. 10, 15.*

SVEN BIRKERTS

In the sixth book of Virgil's *Aeneid*, Aeneas descends into the underworld to speak with the shade of his father, Anchises. As they stand together by the banks of Lethe, Anchises points to a crowd "to whom fate owes a second body," and the hero cries out in protest:

> But, Father, can it be that any souls
> would ever leave their dwelling here to go
> beneath the sky of earth, and once again
> take on their sluggish bodies? Are they madmen?
> Why this wild longing for the light of earth?
>   [—trans. Allen Mandelbaum]

Two millenia later, in a poem entitled **"At Luca Signorelli's Resurrection of the Body,"** Jorie Graham writes:

> See how they hurry
>   to enter
> their bodies,
>   these spirits.
> Is it better, flesh,
>   that they
> should hurry so?

When Virgil wrote his lines, the commerce between bodies and spirits was popularly assumed. In our time we are apt to regard it as a poetic conceit. But Jorie Graham, pondering Signorelli's fresco, choosing to ponder it, is every bit as serious as her predecessor, and every bit as literal. *Erosion,* her second book, gives passionate voice to that all-but-unmentionable entity, the human soul. . . .

[Stitch-pattern] lines and incremental accelerations are characteristic of Graham's prosody. Pauses and linebreaks are carefully manipulated. The momentum is heady, but expert tacking keeps it under control. She is a difficult poet to quote in snippets; one hesitates to cut short such urgent, delicate breathing.

In the Signorelli poem, as elsewhere throughout the book, Graham reveals her preoccupation with the split between body and mind, flesh and spirit. Like Blake, she indicts excessive rationality, the impulse to break everything down into components and particles. Poem after poem re-states the problem and then summons formidable energies of imagination to close the rift. Images of mending, healing, and stitching abound. What reason has sundered, imagination will make whole. And Graham, with her unusual metaphysics, her belief in higher spiritual orders, has a range of imaginative association that is rare in contemporary poetry. . . .

In **"I Watched A Snake,"** the sinuous movements of a small reptile in the grass yield an imagining worthy of Donne:

> This must be perfect progress where
>   movement appears
> to be a vanishing, a mending
>   of the visible
>
> by the invisible—just as we
>   stitch the earth,
> it seems to me, each time
>   we die, going
> back under, coming back up . . .

This would be a clever conceit and nothing more were it not for the fact that Graham believes her imagery. Her diction is sincere. There is no sense of barrier between poet and poem. And as we entrust ourselves to the language, we experience the interpenetration of matter and spirit on the grandest and also the most microscopic of levels. In the poem **"Erosion,"** running pebbles through her fingers, Graham remarks: "Each time / some molecules rub off / evolving into / the invisible."

But for all of this concern with spirit and matter, Graham is not an overtly religious poet. The poems are religious only *en passant.* She will address Santa Chiara or Saint Francis, but even on these occasions it is more the intensity of their faith that she celebrates and less its Christian meaning. Graham, like Rilke, invokes a spiritual force that defies clear-cut definition. . . .

Graham is not quite as ethereal as I have perhaps made her sound. There is a fibrous resilience in these poems as well. She is very much aware of the world enduring outside the self, and she knows that the mind can never penetrate it deeply enough. Because "there is / no deep enough." . . .

Readers seeking the staple goods of late twentieth-century poetry—flat narration, wry autobiography, exhumed solitudes—will find little satisfaction here. This is an enterprise of a higher order.

Sven Birkerts, in a review of "Erosion," in Boston Review, *Vol. VIII, No. 4, August, 1983, p. 38.*

MARY KINZIE

Erosion is a profane gnostic text, devoted to the cult of victims who have suffered violence and to the painters, poets, and religious and historical forces who have done violence. The poems are often the working-out of a generalized prurience, all their energy directed toward the soothing of an entirely self-evolved itch, the fascination with decay and wounded tissue juxtaposed with beautiful and sleek and unmarred creatures. While Jorie Graham tries to enlist our support by declaring how much she is touched by others' pain, it is she, after all, who decided to focus upon these excruciating moments (a rape, a castration, a murder, an exhumation, the torture of St. Francis, Signorelli's aesthetic autopsy on his son, and so forth). Furthermore, all blame is withheld; responsibility for actions is never demanded; malice is treated as if it were accident; and indeed the connections between one act and another, or between an act and concomitant, pleasant, realistic detail is purely arbitrary. The poet's usual response is a half-shrug of wonderment at how awful the world is, and a satisfied reiteration of exuberant perceptual "sensitivity":

> Far in the woods
> in a faded photograph
> in 1942 the man with his own
> genitalia in his mouth and hundreds of
> slow holes
> a pitchfork has opened
> over his face
> grows beautiful.

Surely this is the wrong rhetoric to use under the circumstances. Even if the prettifying is intended as irony, where is the confident and forcefully invoked convention that tells us of ironical devices to display indignation? In the absence of such a context, the terms *slow, Grows,* and *beautiful* are offensive gushing. They are on a par with the gratuitously sweetened-up natural details that come next: "The ferns and deepwood lilies catch the eye. . . . The feathers of the shade touch every inch of skin."

Perhaps the poet does not know how to write about outrage or morality because the categories of ethical judgment have eroded. The very language of good and evil has been irretrievably coarsened, as a selection of phrases and claims from Graham's poems makes clear. Beauty is said to emerge from hurt, or from hurt held in: "contained damage makes for beauty." Ethical terms are wrenched out of context: wasp nests are "a dark gray freedom." Good and ill are as little distinguishable and their difference as little burdensome as flickering light and shade: "right and wrong like pools of shadow"; "the architecture of grief, its dark and light"; "the light keeps stroking them as if it were love." Various oxymora confuse rather than adumbrate the contrasting terms. . . . Exaggeration undermines some phrases. . .; while shrillness and ineptitude work against others. . . . And finally, that disturbing equation between all available abstract nouns: "that measuring, that love"; "that love. That deep delay"; "How far into the earth can vision go and still be love?" "one lust . . . one long chord of justice."

Most of the assertions from which I have quoted are so fuzzy and ambiguous it is hard to clear them up; but there are some maxims like the following that are simply and outrageously false: "There isn't a price that won't live forever"; "You have to hate one thing and hate it deep and well"; "We are defined by what we will not take into ourselves"—this last, a fairly taxing hypothesis to prove, as it constrains the researcher to list the universe. And when the speaker of a poem on the Viennese painter Gustav Klimt asserts, "I think I would weep for the moral nature of this world," myriad queries arise. Why "would weep" and not "could weep"? Indeed, why not "*do* weep"? Why only "think" she would weep—is certainly impossible even in something so basic? What is "moral nature," when there is no allowance made for the discernment, let alone castigation, of wrong, falsehood, sin, malice, or evil? Would not "the *immoral* nature of this world" better prepare the way for the horrors with which the poet proceeds to decorate this poem? The filmy uncertainties of the verb constructions and the reaching for authority from ethical categories without being able to explore or apply them, are evidence of an undisciplined and unripe apprenticeship. (pp. 44-5)

> *Mary Kinzie, "Pictures from Borges," in* The American Poetry Review, *Vol. 12, No. 6, November-December, 1983, pp. 40-6.*

PETER STITT

Jorie Graham's second book, *Erosion,* is built around a struggle between idea and experience, a struggle mediated by, though not quite settled by, style. . . . For Graham, [the issue of the mind/body problem] seems to resolve itself into a contest between the attractions of Platonism—which prefers a world of ideal forms, of ideas, of timeless perfection—and those of realism—which prefers the physical universe *despite*, or perhaps even because of, its limitations. Probably the best-written poem in *Erosion* is **"Reading Plato,"** the title of which indicates its underlying concern. The poem takes for its central character a fisherman friend of the poet who spends all winter tying flies to be used against trout in the spring. Graham makes it clear that this person has in mind a Platonic notion, the ideal form of the fly, which he is trying to translate into reality. A crucial part of the process is his use of deer hair, "because it's hollow / and floats."

When spring comes, he joins other men on the water to test his workmanship. The poem concludes by pointing out how:

> . . .our knowledge of
> the graceful

> deer skips easily across
> the surface.
> Dismembered, remembered,
> it's finally
> alive. Imagine
> the body

> they were all once
> a part of,
> these men along the lush
> green banks
> trying to slip in
> and pass

> for the natural world.

The first part of this passage emphasizes that an idea ("our knowledge") of a thing ("the graceful / deer") has been translated into physical reality (the fly). The long concluding sentence embodies a remarkable achievement; it begins by referring to the individual hairs which make up the fishing lures, but transforms these through an adroit use of grammar into the individual men, who are then also seen as parts of a previously dismembered whole—the Platonic ideal of humanity.

Graham is obviously strongly attracted by the Platonic vision at the heart of this poem, which, significantly, is placed early in the book. It is after this that the idea of "erosion" comes into play; in the poem [**"Erosion"**], Graham writes:

> . . . Always
> I am trying to feel
> the erosion—my grandfather, stiffening
> on his bed, learning
> to float on time, his mind like bait presented
> to the stream ongoing. . . .

The effort is to give up the comforting myth of a world of timeless perfection, free from mutability and death. By the end of the book, we realize that Graham's true sympathies do lie on the anti-Platonic side of things. In the final poem of the volume, she resoundingly casts her lot with reality. . . . It is the most obvious disadvantage of reality—the fact that it is ruled by time and mortality—that determines its great advantage over the realm of timeless perfection. In this book, "Death" does turn out to be "the mother of beauty," and Jorie Graham ends up in it wishing to move, like Robert Frost, "To Earthward" rather than "towards heaven."

The thinking here is superbly subtle and reveals a mind of considerable intelligence and learning. If there is a problem in Graham's work, it comes not in the area of content but in the area of style. For some reason, in many of these poems she affects an unnatural pose of ignorance. For example, in a poem called **"Love,"** she speaks of "the man // known as Saint / Francis," as though she herself does not know who he is. Over and over, people are presented as having to explain things to this poet, who apparently wants us to think she cannot figure them out for herself. The poem **"Tragedy"** ends: "You win when everything is used and nothing's / changed is how it was explained / to me." The very next poem speaks of ocean waves that come to shore on a calm day; they are "the living echo, / says my book, of some great storm far out at sea." And in the following poem, the wisdom comes not from a book but from a dead ancestor: "You can stay dry / if you can step between the raindrops / mother's mother// said."

How dreary, how irritating, how false all these phrases are. What they result from is an odd lack of self-confidence on the author's part. Most poets writing today are not nearly as smart as Jorie Graham; unfortunately, she seems to feel that she must write like them anyway, as though that were simply the thing to do, like eating your salad with your salad fork. *Erosion* is a wonderful book, challenging, thought-provoking, subtle; but it would have been even better if the writer had written with greater confidence in herself, her own way of saying things. (pp. 898-900)

> Peter Stitt, "A Variegation of Styles: Inductive, Deductive, and Linguistic," in The Georgia Review, Vol. XXXVII, No. 4, Winter, 1983, pp. 894-905.

DAVID ST. JOHN

In her second book of poems, *Erosion,* as in her much-praised first collection, *Hybrids of Plants and Ghosts,* Graham is focused intently upon the relationship of the mind and spirit with the world of the external, the world of flesh and earth. Her method is discursive, but poetically not didactically so, and her impulses, even when considering the nature and implications of works of art, are invariably philosophical. Graham constantly questions the mind's influence upon "the real," and whether that influence is true or imagined, accomplished or desired; she questions the discrepancy between historical time and time as corrupted by memory; she questions how the spirit articulates itself in the world of nature and the world of art.

Graham's poems are often meditations upon themselves in process. The mind's multiple intersections with a subject or an occasion in turn create a moving locus for a poem, and the shifting play of images and ideas is held by what is their discursive authority. She distrusts, and rightly so, any rigid or fixed perspective, and the restless metaphors of her poems often signal the urge toward an abstracted verbal equation. Even at these times, when her "subjects" might seem most remote, the poems refuse the pull of circularity and the impulse to become reductive and enclosing. Instead, she allows her poems an appealing open-endedness, granting them a syntactical but not an intellectual closure. I suppose I'm making these poems seem much less earth-bound and substance-filled than they in fact are; yet, in looking at what are the desires for the abstract and philosophical in her poetry, I think we can see most clearly where Graham's great originality and vision rest. (pp. 371-72)

> David St. John, "Raised Voices in the Choir: A Review of 1983 Poetry Selections," in The Antioch Review, Vol. 42, No. 3, Summer, 1984, pp. 363-74.

SVEN BIRKERTS

The End of Beauty is Graham's third collection. In the four years since her last book, *Erosion,* she has made a decisive turn—away from accessibility and resolution and into a realm of difficult ambiguity. My guess is that she has fallen under the spell of Rilke, for her voice has taken on something of his tone of prophetic intimacy. What's more, Graham has adopted a Rilkean approach to subject. Focusing on a biblical or mythological episode—Adam and Eve, Apollo and Daphne, Demeter and Persephone—she breaks the familiar narrative line into freeze-frame sections to highlight the confusion of contending forces. She is confident enough about her approach to dare to retell Rilke's own retelling of the Orpheus and Eurydice legend.

Graham's tactic of slowing and interrupting narrative sequences affords her an enormous freedom of expression. In less gifted

hands, chaos would quickly result. But she has ways of preserving control. In a poem like "**Self Portrait as the Gesture Between Them,**" which culminates with the plucking of the apple in the Garden of Eden, she relies upon the shaping suspense of the foreseeable—inevitable—moment. Other poems, like "**Pollock and Canvas,**" sustain cohesion through a careful braiding of discrete narrative strains. In that poem, Graham arrests the painter's gesture before his brush ever touches canvas. Into this dimension of pure possibility, Graham intercuts a parallel image-sequence of a fishhook aloft in the suspended moment of the cast and another of God resting after the creation. . . .

The poem is nine pages long and . . . somewhat abstract in its argumentation. Graham ultimately works it around so that the two ideas of freedom are paradoxically inverted: the Creator's stepping back and "letting in chance" reverses the termination of freedom represented by the painter's first stroke. "**Pollock and Canvas**" is not without its passages of turgid opacity—Graham sometimes overreaches and loses her reader—but its ambitiousness, the thrust and parry of images and ideas, is liberating. If it's true that free verse has been languishing, then this work brings the possibility of rejuvenation.

Graham's vision embraces flux and transformation. She discovers in her narrative the critical or pivotal moment; she then slows the action to expose its perilous eventual consequences. "Freedom" and "necessity" are, in Graham's world, crude coordinates; her scenarios are thick with ambiguity. Indeed, the first of all stories, the taking of the fruit, is a paradigm of the blurring between free action and necessary order—here is a case of necessity including a provision for freedom. . . . Graham demands patience and application from her readers. And when she rewards them, it is not with neatly finished artifacts, but with a sense of the hazards and unknowns of poetic thinking. *The End of Beauty* is open and provisional. Its vector reaches off the page into a future alive with possibility.

> Sven Birkerts, in a review of "The End of Beauty," in VLS, No. 56, June, 1987, p. 5.

J. D. McCLATCHY

[Jorie Graham's] first book, *Hybrids of Plants and of Ghosts* (1980), announced a poet of large ambitions and reckless music. She is attracted to ecstatics, saints and artists, and tries to push a poem past its conventional limits, so that it becomes a kind of energized field within which her subjects—herself, really, projected into ceremonial occasions—can be both condensed and exploded. Less bold but more consistent and finished, her second collection, *Erosion* (1983), also strained "to catch the world/at pure idea." Hers was sometimes an awkward or gassy poetry, but haunting and undeniably forceful.

In *The End of Beauty* she pushed herself even farther. Her voice is hieratic. Most of the poems are abstract, stripped of context. The style will strike some as mysterious, others as grandiose. There are passages that sound like a bad translation of Rilke ("moving in and out of these rooms that there be a *there*/for you") and lines mannered beyond belief. A series of obscure self-portraits, in which the self is refracted through attributes of mythological characters, is tediously divided into numbered sections. One has 66 lines cut into 33 parts. Section 14 reads, in its entirety: "taken from her, this freedom." Elsewhere we are given material that has not evolved beyond the notebook stage. . . . The privacy and difficulty of these poems are part of their demanding appeal. But the fussy pretension, muddle passed off as complexity, is not.

It must be said, though, that many of the poems stand out starkly against the flat landscape of much contemporary poetry. And even in those superior poems where her control can be felt and admired, there are choices that astonish. . . .

"**Breakdancing**" compares the pop sidewalk phenomenon to St. Teresa's visions of Christ; the effect is startling and convincing. "**Pollock and Canvas**" directs us to the transcripts of cloud over a pond—nature adjusted to the artist's eye. "**What the End Is For**" blends difficult love and the nuclear threat. In these and other poems, Ms. Graham writes with a metaphysical flair and emotional power. As her poem on Pollock says, here is depth, not just the sensation of depth.

J. D. McClatchy, "Catching the World," in The New York Times Book Review, *July 26, 1987, p. 9.*

HELEN VENDLER

The End of Beauty is the title Jorie Graham has given to her powerful new volume of poems. With this title she situates the book, and herself, at that watershed in creative life when "beauty" can no longer be seen, in any simple sense, as the aim of art. . . .

American writing has never had an easy conscience about being "merely" beautiful. There is a marked moral strenuousness in American poetry from Anne Bradstreet through Robert Lowell. But American poetry has usually passed from the beautiful to the tragic through the strait gate of the ethical. Whitman's ideal brotherhood, Dickinson's select society, Stevens' major man, Eliot's Hindu commands ("Give, sympathize, control"), Berryman's end-man Conscience all represent controls put on aesthetic delectation by the moral sense. I think Graham has found a different way—the way of thought—to pass from the beautiful to the tragic, and *The End of Beauty* offers, in consequence, a new sort of poetry.

When poets shift ground, they shift form, too, and Graham's book turns visibly away from her earlier, self-contained, short, "beautiful" lyrics in *Hybrids of Plants and of Ghosts* (1980) and *Erosion* (1983). *The End of Beauty* investigates not a new control (Wordsworth's phrase about his turn from pleasure to duty) but, rather, a new speculative abundance. Though Graham's long meditations have something in common with John Ashbery's, Ashbery's deliberate geniality even in suffering (on the theory of nothing in excess) is very far from Graham's exultant or sardonic or ecstatic cascades of language. For her, once the end of beauty has been glimpsed everything is up for reëxamination. If not beauty, what? And Graham's answer is not morality but free and far-ranging thought.

Graham's new manner goes to visible extremes. She aims at what Keats called "solitary thinkings; such as dodge conception to the very bourne of heaven," and when she comes to a concept not yet conceivable she leaves a gap in the middle of a sentence:

Like a _____this look between us . . .
  this long thin angel whose body is a stalk, rootfree,
    blossomfree,
  whose body we are making, whose body is a _____

Thought is revealed to be a progress that sometimes goes haltingly, perception by perception. . . .

Thought plays in long arabesques, long lines made to encompass what Graham calls (in a poem about Penelope) "the story and its undoing, the days the kings and the soil they're groundcover for." This manner—its spill and hurry and, equally, its halts and breaks—simulates the psyche as Graham understands it. What the end of beauty provides is the beginning of wonder. If the ideals of shape and closure (provided as much by moral control as by aesthetic finality) are not to be the guide of life and art, then what can be the guide but contemplative thought? Graham trusts, if anything, the roaming cinematography of the mind, which pictures and replays the necessary decisions of life and keeps them perpetually in question.

This poetics leads to poems—the best recent ones in memory— on human self-division. Marriage is one of Graham's recurrent topics: as a type of self-limiting action (this person and no other; this life and no other) it gives a nameable shape to existence, but as circumscription it is struggled against even though it's been chosen. Similarly, human intelligence reaches not only toward investigation (pure science) but also toward consolidation of that hypothesis into material form (technology, the embodiment of inquiry). The wish of the speculative mind to halt its drift and take visible shape leads not only to marriage but to atomic piles and B-52s, which are as much at home in Graham's poetry as are the other decisive shapes (paintings, myths) that human culture has taken. The intrapsychic conflict between drift and shape is, in this book, insoluble and therefore tragic. As in any true tragedy, both sides are in the right.

The sheer freedom invoked by Graham's poetry is liberating. . . . Graham's lines mimic the fertile ruses of the mind— exploratory rush and decisive interruption, interrogatory speech and intermittent silence. The lines ripple and pause, utter and subside. The poems are often long, like sonatas, carrying the musical moment of process through its hurry, its delay, its fears and repentings, its tragedies of fixity, its restlessness and rebellion. Graham, if we compare her with her Romantic predecessors, is nearest to Shelley in her creation of clouds of thought, accumulating and breaking open in a shower of consequences. (p. 74)

In an essay called "**Some Notes on Silence**," explaining why she writes poems of inconclusive, ongoing presentness, Graham contrasts such poems with narratives, reminiscences, and prophecies—poetic forms that are strung on the temporal axis of past, present, and future:

> Narrative sequences . . . believe in the changes
> of history and experience . . . while [poems that
> engage silence] often view the flesh itself . . .
> as the obstacle, and crave stillness, form, law,
> over the formulation of hope which is *cause
> and effect*.

She adds that poems in the past tense are told by a survivor of the experience recounted. Such poems are containers for understood experience rather than a precarious enacting of experience as it is being undergone. "A poem which is an *act* could be the very last act, couldn't it, every time?" she says.

Rushing into temporality, Graham's new verse resembles Action painting in words. Graham used to think that poetry could not have a double protagonist. In *Hybrids of Plants and of Ghosts* she wrote:

> We are able to listen to someone else's story, believe in
> another protagonist, but within,
> his presence would kill us.

But now, in tragic verse, the inner second protagonist is remembered with a vengeance, and many of the new poems are written by a single self playing two opposed mythological parts (Demeter and Persephone, Apollo and Daphne, Orpheus and Eurydice). What is the self, these poems ask, but the gap between two inner personae bound in a single drama? At the beginning of *The End of Beauty,* the figure for that gap is the gesture by which Eve offers the apple to Adam; in a moment, he will take it, bringing paradisal reverie to an end by introducing into life the principle of choice, definition, closure. Though this poem is about a long hesitation before marriage, it can also be read as a poem of self-knowledge by Eve, who decides, like Persephone, for "a new direction, an offshoot, the limb going on elsewhere".... (p. 75)

It is, of course, not sufficient for a poet merely to announce that she is both parties; the double consciousness has to convince. Poems on myth have tended to adopt one side of the story as their own. But Eurydice in Graham's version both does and does not want to resume her body and be loved; Orpheus both wants her back as she is and wants her back on his terms. Eurydice's double wish (to rise up to Orpheus and to sink back to Pluto) and Orpheus' double wish (to raise her as she was and to redefine both her and himself) are voiced in an intricate portrait of the self at many cross-purposes, freeing lyric from its perennial trap in a single voice.

Here Orpheus is the sun, Hades the river bottom, and Eurydice, after thinking she might rise and be reincarnated among the weeds at the surface, decides against embodiment and begins a shadowy return to darkness:

> the weeds cannot hold her
> who is all rancor, all valves now, all destination,
> dizzy with wanting to sink back in,
> thinning terribly in the holy separateness.
> And though he would hold her up, this light all
>   open hands,
> seeking her edges, seeking to make her palpable
>   again,
> curling around her to find crevices by which to
>   carry her up,
> flaws by which to be himself arrested and made,
> made whole, made sharp and limbed, a shape,
> she cannot, the drowning is too kind,
> the silks of the bottom rubbing their vague hands
> over her forehead.

The rhythms of cinematography—this moment, then this moment—direct such incremental writing, and the inevitable present tense of film is assumed as a natural formal principle in this poetry, marking it with the signature of a postmodernist generation.

Like some of her predecessors, Graham is determined to track ongoing mental action even at the risk of diffuseness.... Graham keeps creative energy alive and unpredictable in these poems by sudden changes of focus; her psychic elations and hesitations are Romantic in their volatility but post-Romantic in their skepticism, their self-interruptions, their own stage directions.

She unexpectedly mixes stage-set instructions and demotic American phrases with mythic plot and lyrical description. Her retellings of myth would be reverent (in their inquiry into the psychic reality of such immemorial stories) were they not so irreverent. (On Apollo and Daphne: "The truth is this had been going on for a long time during which/they both wanted it to

last.") Such moments are like brusque interruptions in music, a deliberate going against the grain, where irritability and discord reflect the difficulty of proceeding. One follows these poems as one follows music—not a music like Ashbery's, which eddies back to its beginning, but a music onwardly purposive, obliterating its past. It is the music of will—a hoping or thinking or exploratory will, sometimes jeering, more often frightened, fatally seeing the other side of its own intentions. It follows some invisible line of possibility (curiosity, love) into actuality (suffering, fixity, disappearance). It imagines, in short, what is happening in the restless contemporary flux of thought untethered by a stable culture.

Graham, the daughter of American parents living in Italy, grew up trilingual (through French schooling) and has an unembarrassed range of cultural and linguistic reference, which she does not censor out of her poems. In contrast, for instance, to Adrienne Rich's language (deliberately impoverished in the service of availability to the uneducated), Graham's is opulent. However, it does not assert high culture as an unquestioned value. Graham is one of a generation to whom the whole past appears in an anthropological light: classical and Christian motifs, conventional psychology and Freudian orthodoxy, divorce and marriage are all equally familiar, all equally questionable. To this skeptical generation the iron laws of physics and biology seem the only believable truths, and Graham is drawn to rewrite Shelley's necessitarian "Ode to the West Wind" in her own hymn to Necessity, a memorable poem entitled (from Wyatt) **"Of Forced Sightes and Trusty Ferefulness."** (pp. 75-7)

In enlarging her scope to include the metaphysical questions of necessity, intentionality, human self-definition, and cultural inscription, Graham, like other philosophical poets, reminds us that human beings have, in addition to an erotic, domestic, and ethical life, a life of speculative thought. But Graham's thinking is not only cool and speculative; it has a strong component of the ecstatic (and its dark counterpart, the despairing). The European contemplative saints (St. Francis, St. Clare, St. Teresa) figure in Graham's poems as models not only of spiritual concentration but also of psychic rapture. The rapture of the contemplating mind is not a new topic in poetry, but it tends to be forgotten in our pragmatic America. In the classic narrative of contemplation, early ecstasy is followed by tragic desiccation, after which the contemplative, rescued by joy, rests again among the lilies of fulfilled desire. It is strange to find this European story beginning to unfold once more in a young and mesmerizing American voice; one wants to hear its continuation. (p. 77)

Helen Vendler, "Married to Hurry and Grim Song," in The New Yorker, *Vol. LXIII, No. 23, July 27, 1987, pp. 74-7.*

JESSICA GREENBAUM

Even an admiring poet may feel like a greenhorn on coming to *The End of Beauty.* Both astonishing and bewildering, this third book by one of the most highly regarded young poets in America is often addressed directly to the reader, but is probably rarely accessible to most of us.

Graham's first two books, *Hybrids of Plants and of Ghosts* and *Erosion,* established her as a poet of unconforming, unrestrainable intellect. Her poems, many of which refer to writers and painters, often reflect her European childhood and lifelong involvement with art. They don't touch on the domestic part of life as much as they spiral away from the tangible world, tracing the path of perception into idea and philosophy. . . .

In part, *Erosion* concerns itself with the place of human beings within the animal world. *The End of Beauty* continues to explore the sense human beings make in the scheme of things, but this third book takes as its context our evolution from mythical beginnings. In her new poems, Graham is constantly superimposing the cultural frames of myth on contemporary life. . . .

In many ways, Graham's new poems are radically different not only from her previous ones, but from anything else around. Her formal devices include blanks to be filled in by the reader. . . . These blanks are sometimes accompanied by the algebraic variables x and y. . . . (p. 206)

Creating choices for the reader does at least two things. First, it challenges the notion that a finished poem is a hermetic, untouchable unit. Second, it puts the poem "above" choice, as if finding *le mot juste* is no longer the poet's task. The poem's intelligence is unalterable by small changes; it speaks at a level of abstraction beyond the influence of single words. For this and many other reasons, it is unclear to me what a reader needs to bring to this volume in order to be communicated to by it. But arguments can surely be made for the spell of poetry over the forthright clarity of it, as any admirer of Wallace Stevens or John Ashbery will tell you. Some poets are able to entrance a reader who cannot follow exactly, but who trusts the poet's intelligence enough to watch, to keep listening as the poet makes his or her unpredictable leaps through the vast sky of association. (pp. 206-07)

Much of Graham's work is an exquisite exploration of the process of imagination. Her poems often show a formal allegiance to intellect, beginning in one thought and wending their way into principle and revelation by tapping all the writer's intelligence, not just that immediately surrounding the subject. "Vertigo," which is about intelligence itself, begins:

> Then they came to the very edge of the cliff and looked
>   down.
> Below a real world flowed in its parts, green, green.
> The two elements touched—rock, air.
> She thought of where the mind opened out
> into the sheer drop of its intelligence

Although Graham maintains the metaphor to the end, she spends a good part of the poem asking questions related to it:

> . . . How is it one soul wants to be owned
> by a single other
> in its entirety?—
> What is it sucks one down, offering itself, only itself,
>   for
> ever? She saw the cattle below
> moving in a shape which was exactly their hunger.
> She saw—could they be men?—the plot. She leaned.
>   How does one enter
> a story?

Such poems are like living cross sections of the braiding process of thought, often beginning suddenly and ending with a hyphen, or no punctuation at all. Here too, Graham's form disrupts convention and pushes into the future. Because so much of the poetry we see being published and praised is formulaic, our notion of contemporary poetry often habituates itself to the subtle lure of the familiar. For instance, we are quite prepared for poems in which the speaker is set in one emotional doorway

and takes the length of the poem to walk out another. We are so used to this dramatic path that we almost take it before the poem does, knowing that sooner or later, like any overworked horse, the ordinary poem will break into a run and head for the stable. Sometimes the reader gets there first.

Still, many readers will wonder: are Graham's formal devices a self-conscious attempt on her part to forge a new poetic mechanism, or are they essential to the experience of the poems, or both? Do the blanks and variables serve up a volume of intellectual Mad Libs, or a new dimension of poetic experience? Perhaps the most engaging and magnificent poem in this volume, **"What the End Is For,"** employs none of the devices mentioned above. Using the stanza form she made her signature in *Erosion* (a roughly symmetrical six-to-eight-line stanza with even-numbered lines indented), Graham tells two stories at once. The first is about being shown a fleet of bombers in North Dakota:

> A boy just like you took me out to see them,
>   the five hundred B-52's on alert on the runway,
> fully loaded fully manned pointed in all the directions,
>   running every minute
> of every day.
>   They sound like a sickness of the inner ear,
>
> where the heard foams up into the noise of listening,
>   where the listening arrives without being extinguished.

Graham uses repetition between sentences ("where the heard foams up," "where the listening arrives") so effectively that the reader experiences something analogous to the backstitch in sewing—we go back half a step into what's already been said, then are moved forward, so that our connection to the poem is both fortified and stretched at every turn. That is one part of the poem's spell, part of the way we are engaged with it as a whole, not just with what narrative and logic we grasp. (pp. 207-08)

The End of Beauty, like the poems it contains, is a process, a cross section of the author's evolving, unstoppable intellect; it should not be judged by its star metaphors or most exciting turns. Graham's intuition is the volume's true narrator. Her maturity as a writer is evidenced in the risks she takes and in the set pieces she does not write. She makes no attempt to seduce the reader through cleverness, but only to challenge her own mind and see if we can hang on for the ride. (p. 208)

Jessica Greenbaum, "Evolution," in The Nation, *New York, Vol. 245, No. 6, September 5, 1987, pp. 206-08.*

THOMAS GARDNER

Jorie Graham is a poet who has published three remarkable books since 1980—*Hybrids of Plants and of Ghosts, Erosion,* and *The End of Beauty*. Like many contemporary poets, she locates her work within what she calls "the gap" or "eternal delay" between language and what it refers to—words producing not direct access to experience but, in her words, "the long sleep of resemblance" or "the place where I'm erased." There are, on the contemporary scene, many different ways of working with this disjunctive awareness, but as the following reading suggests, Graham is in the process of developing an approach to the problem notable both for the power of its ambitions and the subtlety of its unfolding. (p. 1)

Graham attempts in [*Hybrids of Plants and of Ghosts*] to push beyond, or entirely dissolve, what she calls the "perfected argument" of language—a gesture which was one of the essential projects of American poetry in the 1960s and early 70s. Turning away from the dead, wintered-over "evidence" of the world's springtime fecundity, she rails in one poem at all such alphabets: "no, it's not enough to understand / it's there because it's gone." It's tangibly there only because it's actually gone—how might one dissolve this iron rule of language? Her first book adopts a fairly simple opposition. We are driven by what she calls two "overlapping" ways of "mapping": seeing as the sun does ("it is what is not animal in us, the best intentions we still have / at the moment of perception: to see it all. / Then we grow hot, tragic and fleshed / with intellect, / dividing") or as the moon does, "blur[ring] the facts, / its shade not keen or rational like that of sunlight / seeking to capture the nature of its subject; / it seeks, rather, to let it go, / to show what it is not." These early poems, predictably, yearn for an existence beyond the sunlight of language. . . . (p. 2)

A number of poems in this first book, however, without being able to act on the insight, express a sense of doubt about such an arrangement. **"Tree Surgeons,"** for example, contrasts an elm in a neighbor's yard being trimmed into a statement of symmetry, precision, and clear meaning ("How evenly it is rid of itself, tree of no nuance, no preference") with an elm in her own yard: "shaggy, / headed some other way." Content at first to slyly deride her neighbor's faith in a world where "each grain / falls into place," preferring instead her own wandering, shapeless growth, Graham ends the poem uneasy with that too simple distinction: "I cannot say why, but they are much too safe from one another." **"The Geese"** works out a similar contrast—this time between the "elegant," goal-oriented "code" of geese following "a most perfect heading" overhead and spiders down below for whom "things will not remain connected, / will not heal." This time, however, instead of choosing the unbraiding lines of spiders over the confident language of geese, she attempts to place herself between those options. . . .

Graham's next two books work out the implications of this self-critical undercurrent, suggesting that rather than the impossible fantasy of refusing language entirely there are other—to my mind, more convincing and original—ways of letting the invisible "nothing" catch you. What she tries to think through in these books is how, by remaining within and exploiting the built-in limitations of language, one might develop a shadow version, a negative, of what can't be presented directly. Rather than yearning for a world not coded by language, Graham attempts in these books to trace the way "silence" or "the invisible" erodes our structures—her assumption being that such "accurate failures" of language might testify to the forces which break apart their attempts at rendering. (p. 3)

Erosion, from its opening poems, declares its willingness to remain within what Graham calls our "mother / tongue, dividing, discarding"—within a language which, like the scirocco wind she hears outside the rooms Keats died in, in the name of "working / the invisible," simply fingers and refingers "every dry leaf of ivy" because it "must go over and over / what it already knows" *and* within a language which, like the softening grapes outside the same window, might yet, in suffering a weakening of its "stark hellenic / forms," find a way "to enter." **"To a Friend Going Blind"** carefully lays out this theory. Addressing a friend whose approaching blindness is a version of our own language-bound separation from

our surroundings, she describes a detour around the "entire inner perimeter" of a walled, medieval town taken because she "couldn't find the shortcut through" to the world beyond the walls, seen occasionally flickering through its cracks and gaps. Next, still not directly touching the issue of blindness, she drifts to an account of another friend teaching her how to cut a dress pattern:

> Saturdays we buy the cloth.
> She takes it in her hands
> like a good idea, feeling
> for texture, grain, the built-in
> limits.

Moving back to the detour and linking the two stories, she describes her wandering within the walls' confines as "a needle floating / on its cloth"—a needle at ease with the separation imposed by the walls, finding them in fact to be central to her quite overpowering experience of the world breaking through its gaps. . . . [Taking] on the conditions of blindness, as with acknowledging the ultimate limitations of one's language, as it forces us to put aside the drive to master the world, also permits us to run our hands along the cracks and gaps explosively patterning all of our attempts to order things. There is never a shortcut through.

For the most part, the poems in this second book are more concerned with explicating than with enacting this theory—often turning to the world outside for emblems of the process: a snake, driven by what she calls its "hunger / for small things—flies, words," describing in the broken pattern of its visible / suddenly invisible progress through the grass the possibility of stitching ourselves to the "sturdier stuff" of the unseen; or men burning a field in late summer, staring in from the borders at a stark harvest "only visible, believable, / [when] caught through / this blinding / yield." There are, however, a number of poems where she begins the more difficult task of modulating the certainty of her own uses of language: forcing the poems to contend with what would threaten their ways of moving, driving them toward failure in order to trace the erosive effects of "what it is that escapes me, what judges me." (pp. 3-4)

All the poems in . . . *The End of Beauty* attempt to locate themselves actively in what Graham calls the "slippage" of language which renders unstable the delicate, wisteria-scented surfaces we call beauty. In fact, the poems seem to work together as a single, self-critical struggle. . . . [These] poems, when read as a whole, take up and dismantle the fundamental ways we organize the world (description, destination, form, pattern, meaning), move on from that acknowledgment of blindness to a celebration of what can be sensed in those newly exposed gaps, and conclude with an attempt to develop new structures that might simultaneously use and undo their patterns. In doing so, as Graham puts it, she is "keeping the gap alive." Though the poems are everywhere riddled by the physical "breaks against smooth sequence in sense" I have quoted her earlier praise of, it is this extended pattern in which the poems turn back on themselves, courting their own destruction by examining their own processes, which strikes me as the book's most significant achievement.

One of the ways this development is charted is by a series of self-portraits which, appearing throughout the book at regular intervals, enable her to acknowledge and exploit the inherited blindness of her position as a language user. Reading her position either explicitly (**"Self-Portrait as Apollo and Daphne"**) or implicitly (**"Orpheus and Eurydice"**) through the history of man's self-reflections, Graham simultaneously plays out and exposes the limitations of that inheritance. That is, she accepts the inheritance testified to by these accounts, reading them as commentary on her current activity. (pp. 6-7)

Finally, the book turns to the question of how to develop a stance that can both use and undo the patterns proposed by language, a poetry contesting itself in order to bring to prominence the gaps where it breaks down. If Daphne is the moment language fails to impose its outline, how might a poet who, she continues to insist, is reflected in both Daphne and Apollo, keep that awareness alive? **"Self-Portrait as Hurry and Delay (Penelope at Her Loom)"** works at the problem. Rather than splitting off language's logocentric and disjunctive drives into two opposed figures, Penelope, unweaving by night what she had done by day, creates "a shapeliness / . . . something that is not something else" and *then* "work[s] her fingers into the secret place, the place of what is coming undone / . . . there, where the pattern softens now, / loosening." . . . I would suggest that the way the acknowledged inheritances of these self-portraits contest the very attempts to describe, master, and interpret [what] they are examples of allows Graham to demonstrate just such a way of enacting and exploiting language's blindness. Like Jackson Pollock, the subject of another poem, who, choosing no longer "to make it end somewhere, / to make it beautiful / . . . hovering, his brush able to cut a figure / on the blank and refusing," Graham uses the self-questioning strategies of these poems to expose their vulnerabilities, these frail structures of language, and point us to what must have eroded them.

Perhaps the strongest of such poems is the book's concluding poem, **"Imperialism"**—a piece which begins with the grandest ambitions of language already splintered: here, the dream of imperialism, that we might through language extend our authority over previously unmapped realms. Picturing that failed dream as the inability of a dust and gravel road to "hold" the shadow that momentarily touches their firm surfaces, Graham opens this meditation with a question raised by that failure. Of

what value, she asks, are such insubstantial marriages? . . . That question—essentially a response to the exposed inadequacies of art, language, bodies—was forced on her the night before during an argument in which the sputtering of a lamp splintered the form of her partner's face into a series of glimpses . . . Just as the bodies of the landscape were unable to hold a passing shadow, so the dissolving body of this face was never able to grasp and hold the dark, unspeakable undercurrent of the night's conversation. Of what use, then, are the shapes and faces we offer? (pp. 8-9)

Graham's answer to the question of the value of our fluttering marriages of bodies and shadow, point-of-view and the darkness, comes, appropriately enough, in an unspoken story—a memory glimpsed, we might say, through the gaps made visible that night by the couple's failure to "clarify and nail it shut." An extraordinary account of being taken as a child to the Ganges, passing through "tens and hundreds of thousands of bodies mostly / wet and partly naked even now pressing to get to / waterfront," and watching the "ash and cartilage" of other bodies being burned on pyres and then shaken over and dissolved into that great river—that story becomes a vision of both the utter irrelevancy of bodies *and* of something "visible / and utterly blank" beyond the world of flesh: . . . Glimpsing, that is, a silence or darkness beyond bodies through an overpowering experience of the erosion of the claims of flesh, Graham, as a child, had a momentary insight into both what is beyond language and a means of reaching it. That, she realizes, is the value of the fragile, easily-broken structures we make. Like a man in the Ganges opening and shutting a white umbrella under the water and thereby offering a vision of the dissolution of bodies ("the dark brown ash-thick riverwater rode / in the delicate tines as he raised it rinsing") so her poems throughout [*The End of Beauty*] strive to testify to the failure of language and to the flickering presence of the silence beyond. (p. 9)

Thomas Gardner, "Accurate Failures: The Work of Jorie Graham," in The Hollins Critic, *Vol. XXIV, No. 4, October, 1987, pp. 1-9.*

Nicolás Guillén

1902-

Cuban poet, journalist, and editor.

Guillén is recognized by many critics as one of Cuba's finest poets and as an important figure in contemporary West Indian literature. Named National Poet of Cuba by Fidel Castro in 1961, Guillén chronicles the turbulent social and political history of his native land. He is also credited as one of the first poets to affirm and celebrate the black Cuban experience. The majority of Guillén's poems are informed by his African and Spanish heritage. He combines the colloquialisms and rhythms of Havana's black districts with the formal structure and language of traditional Spanish verse to address the injustices of imperialism, capitalism, and racism. Robert Márquez characterized Guillén's work as "a poetry which is explicit, deceptively simple in style, militant in its assumptions, one which reaches out to the Third World and looks forward to liberation, then peace."

Guillén's first acclaimed volume of poetry, *Motivos de son* (1930), introduced to a literary audience the *son,* a sensual Afro-Cuban dance rhythm. In this collection, Guillén utilizes the rhythmic patterns of the *son* to evoke the energetic flavor of black life in and around Havana. Although some readers accused him of displaying negative images of black Cubans, Guillén was praised for originality and for blending Afro-Cuban idioms and traditional verse. Guillén expanded his focus in his next volume, *Sóngoro cosongo* (1931), to include poems depicting the lives of all Cubans, with emphasis on the importance of mulatto culture in Cuban history.

Following the demise of the corrupt government headed by Gerardo Machado in 1933 and the increasing industrial and political presence of the United States in Cuba, Guillén began writing poetry with overtly militant implications. In *West Indies, Ltd.* (1934), he decrys the social and economic conditions of the Caribbean poor in somber poems imbued with anxiety and frustration. Guillén attacks imperialism through his recurring description of the region as a vast, profitable factory that is exploited by foreign countries. In 1937, Guillén joined the Communist party. That same year he produced *España: Poema en cuatro angustias y una esperanza,* an extended narrative poem chronicling the Spanish Civil War, and *Cantos para soldados y sones para turistas,* a volume denouncing the escalating military presence in Cuban society. He also employs biting satire in poems which contrast the darkness and squalor of Cuba's ghettos with the garish ambience of downtown tourist establishments.

Guillén spent much of the 1940s and 1950s in exile in Europe and South America during the height of the Fulgencio Batista y Zaldívar regime. His works of this period reflect his opposition to Batista's repressive policies and denounce racial segregation in the United States. The poems in *La paloma de vuelo popular: Elegías* (1959) favor revolution, praising the activities of such political figures as Castro and Che Guevara. Guillén returned to Cuba following Batista's expulsion in 1959, and in 1964 he published *Tengo.* In this volume, Guillén celebrates the triumph of the Cuban revolution and the abolition of racial and economic discrimination. Many of Guillén's poems have

been translated into English and collected in such volumes as *Man-Making Words: Selected Poems of Nicolás Guillén* (1972) and *¡Patria o muerte!: The Great Zoo and Other Poems* (1972).

(See also *Contemporary Authors,* Vol. 116.)

ROBERT MÁRQUEZ

Despite the current vogue among publishers for all forms of neo-African literature and a complimentary flowering of interest in writers from the Third World, Nicolás Guillén's name is still generally unfamiliar to the American reading public. This is unfortunate, for along with Pablo Neruda, César Vallejo, and García Lorca, all already widely translated, Guillén, poet laureate of revolutionary Cuba, represents the very best in Hispanic poetry and is at the same time the undisputed leader of an important trend in contemporary Latin American letters. Guillén is also an open stylist whose manner does not simply anticipate a coterie audience. The publication of this anthology-translation [*¡Patria o Muerte! The Great Zoo and Other Poems*] is therefore timely and particularly satisfying.

Since his first widely acclaimed *Motivos de son* (1930), Guillén, a mulatto, has been regarded as the major exponent of Black poetry in the Spanish-speaking world. But his thematic scope is wide, and although primarily known as a poet of folk rhythms, Black and popular themes, he is also recognized for his humor, for his artistic refinement, for the sensitivity of his love ballads, and for the compassionate poignancy of his political and revolutionary verse. He is not, strictly speaking, a poet of Negritude. Unlike Aimé Césaire and the poets of the French and English Caribbean, his concern with Negro culture and his condemnation of white hypocrisy and injustice do not include a direct repudiation of European (in this case Spanish) cultural traditions. Guillén is more properly the poet of a people and his principle concern has been the creation of a poetry with a distinctively Cuban flavor, one which reflects—and helps consolidate—the Cuban national identity. (pp. 13-14)

Guillén, like the majority of the writers of his generation, began his poetic career in the shadow of Rubén Darío. But it was "the worst Darío," he later confessed, "the Darío of tintypes and enamels, with swans, fountains, abbots, pages, counts, marchionesses, and all those other knick-knacks." . . . [By] 1922 [Guillén] had managed to complete his first small book of poems, a collection whose rather unpoetic title, *Cerebro y corazón* (*Head and Heart*), hinted at the author's tragic ambivalence. It was a derivative work of little poetic distinction which, to the writer's credit, he never published [until 1964, when it appeared as an appendix to the first volume of Angel Augier's biography, *Nicolás Guillén: Notas para un estudio biográfico-crítico*], but which does give us some sense of Guillén's developing technical and rhythmic expertise and of his skeptical and misanthropic outlook at the time. "Lord, Lord, . . . why is humanity so evil?" he pleads in a tone reminiscent of the decadent poets. *Cerebro y corazón* also evinced a tendency to evade reality, an avoidance of the mundane and the popular, and a conception of art that is aristocratic and romantically formalistic. (pp. 15-16)

When Guillén's next book, *Motivos de son,* appeared, it therefore heralded the appearance of a new authenticity and was an immediate and scandalous success. These eight poetic monologues for the first time allowed the Negro to speak for himself and from his own perspective. They were at the same time based on the repetitive rhythms of the *son,* were therefore deeply rooted in the Cuban folk tradition, and spotlighted the daily world of the Black *habanero.* In the prologue to the book, Guillén made it clear that unlike those who came before, he intended to

> incorporate into Cuban literature—not simply as a musical motif but rather as an element of true poetry—what might be called the poem-son . . . My *sones* can be put to music, but that does not mean they were written precisely for that purpose, but rather with the aim of presenting, in what is perhaps the most appropriate form, representative scenes created with two brush strokes . . . ordinary people just as they move around us. Just as they speak, just as they think.

Nevertheless, Guillén's first published book of poems was not entirely unrelated to the work of his predecessors in the *negrista* movement. The total effect of the collection is comic and picturesque. The poet's vision of the world of his creations is a mixture of roguishness and sympathetic amusement. He also focuses on the sensual and frivolous features of that world,

and though he faithfully transmits the nuances and subtleties of popular Black speech, he highlights the entertaining characteristics of its linguistic distortions of the normative language. Yet the book contains an implicit, compassionate, critique of life in Havana's Black slums—a social dimension almost entirely lacking in the earlier *negrista* poetry. The purists considered the book an affront, but their opposition to it—which was not entirely literary—was dismissed and Guillén's reputation as a poet became firmly established.

A year later (1931) he reissued *Motivos de son,* along with a series of eight new poems, under the title *Sóngoro cosongo.* The new poems did not abandon the sensual accents of the earlier work (e.g., "Madrigal" and "The New Woman") but indicated something of a shift in emphasis and perspective. Guillén dropped the comic distortions of speech which gave the first poems their distinctive flavor in favor of a more normative poetic language that relied on onomatopoeia and *jitanjáforas,* [a word of no particular meaning invented by the artist and used for its suggestiveness], to suggest the totemic and rhythmic world of Africa in Cuba, in combination with the *romance* and other meters more typical of the classical Spanish literary tradition. This gave the poet a new freedom, a broader poetic scope, and with it appear the first insinuations of a poetry of social protest. In "Sugarcane," for example, the reader is given a terse glimpse of the anti-imperialist feelings which are to become one of the major preoccupations of Guillén's later poetry. The Negro, moreover, had ceased to be a superficial personality out of popular folklore and had become a character of some depth, part of the national dilemma, an indispensable part of the national heritage. Guillén was moving toward a clearer definition of his role as the poet of a people. He became concerned with the elaboration of a genuinely Cuban poetry, a poetry which would reflect the true history and racial composition of the island. (pp. 18-20)

The publication of *West Indies, Ltd.* (1934), immediately after the revolution which deposed the dictatorship of Machado (1925-1933), marks a significant transition in the development of Guillén's poetry. *Motivos de son* exposed the reader to the anecdotal and purely external; *Sóngoro cosongo* penetrated deeper into the world of the Black but spoke to the whole Cuban nation. With *West Indies, Ltd.,* the poet expands his area of concern to encompass the entire Antillean archipelago. Furthermore, here the elements of social protest come into prominence. . . . [These] strikingly lyrical poems are clear indictments against the abuses and injustices to which the people of the Antilles—and particularly Cubans and Blacks—are collectively subjected under imperialism. The tone is anguished and bitterly elegiac and the mood, though somber, mirrors the frustrations of the incipient revolutionary (see particularly "Riddles" and "Guadeloupe, W.I."). It is the first important step in Guillén's evolution toward Marxism and toward an art of unambiguously militant convictions, although at this stage his protest is a purely visceral indignation, rooted in broadly nationalist and humanitarian ideals with little specific ideological content. "Sabás," however, does offer some indication of the direction in which his thinking will go and of the militancy which will become characteristic of Guillén's verse after 1934.

In 1936 the Spanish Civil War broke out. A year later Guillén, like artists from all over the world sympathetic to the Republican cause, traveled to Spain as one of the Cuban delegates to the antifascist Second International Congress of Writers for the Defense of Culture. In that same year, 1937, he joined the Communist Party and, under the impact of the war, wrote

España, poema en cuatro angustias y una esperanza (*Spain: A Poem in Four Anguishes and a Hope*), a poem of epic proportions in which—as in works on the same theme by César Vallejo and Pablo Neruda—the poet laments the Spanish tragedy. He also published his *Cantos para soldados y sones para turistas* (*Songs for Soldiers and Sones for Tourists*), poems in which the *son*, once limited to the realm of the anecdote and the dance, is turned into an instrument for mocking the American tourist in prerevolutionary Cuba and for denouncing the more salient features of American colonialism on the island. The various *cantos* see the soldier—Cuban or European—as a pawn in the service of imperialism whose role will qualitatively change only with a change in the social structure. The tone of these poems is solemn and accusatory and it is clear that Guillén's allegiance is to the great mass of Cuba's dispossessed— although he also shows a genuine compassion for those victims who, like his soldiers, are unaware of the reality of their own situations. This is as clear in **"Why, Soldier, does it seem to you . . ."** as his anti-fascism is in **"Soldiers in Abyssinia."** (pp. 21-3)

[*El son entero* (*The Entire Son*)] brought together the different elements of theme and style which had by now become representative of the poet's work: the *son*, the "mulatto poem," the atmosphere of pain and accusation. There was also the strict identification with the Negro, wherever he might be, although, as in **"Sweat and the Lash,"** the author had progressed far beyond an interest in the merely picturesque literary motif: "I deny the art that sees in the Negro only a colorful motif and not an intensely human theme," he explained during one of his lectures in 1947. He did not want his readers to forget that, particularly in the United States, the Negro was still being denied his most elemental human rights. He wanted his poems to transmit that reality and, to the degree that it was possible, to incite his public to change it. (p. 23)

El son entero was followed in 1958 by *La paloma de vuelo popular* (*The Dove of Popular Flight*) and *Elegías* (*Elegies*), in which the melancholic undertones of his previous books and the already implicit identification of Cuba with the rest of Latin America were crystallized. These two books (usually published together) also provide the reader with the substance of Guillén's hopes for the future and with his vision of the revolution as the only real possibility for Cuba's—and by extension, Latin America's—liberation. These are simple songs

> of death and life
> with which to greet a future drenched in blood,
> red as the sheets, as the thighs,
> as the bed
> of a woman who's just given birth.

Implicit in Guillén's concept of a "mulatto poetry" was the universalist premise that, after 1934, had led him to see the Negro as part of the great mass of the disinherited. It was now quite evident that for Guillén—as for Frantz Fanon—the "Negro problem" was not a question of Black men living among whites, but of Black men systematically oppressed by a society that was racist, colonialist, and capitalist, but only accidentally white.

In an effort to combat that society—a society symbolized by the international and domestic policies of the United States— more successfully, Guillén began to employ a number of techniques which, although foreshadowed in his earlier poetry, were used with increasing frequency in his later books. He began, for example, to sprinkle his verse with words and phrases from standard American English with an intent that recalls the hidden meanings behind the title of *West Indies, Ltd.* Many of these poems are addressed directly to the racial and political situation in the United States as well as other parts of the world (see **"Puerto Rican Song"**), and, as a result, figures from contemporary politics begin to make their appearance. The specificity with which Guillén indicts individuals like Eisenhower, Nixon, Orville Faubus, and a host of others is contrasted with the use of symbolic and anonymous names—"John Nobody," "John Blade," or simply "John"—to indicate the great mass of ordinary people with whom his sympathies lie. After the success of the Cuban Revolution, the interest in current affairs and Yankee political figures was complemented by the appearance of figures out of Cuba's revolutionary past and present (Antonio Maceo, José Martí, Fidel Castro, Che Guevara), with whom those less palatable individuals were contrasted. In *La paloma de vuelo popular,* the playful humor of Guillén's earliest works turned to irony and a wry sarcasm. In the *Elegías*, on the other hand, a sense of loss was added to the sense of outrage. These were in the main laments on the death of friends and victims or—as in **"My Last Name"**—for an entire history. In addition to the poet's usual stylistic vehicles, a variety of forms and meters were juxtaposed.

With the triumph of the Cuban Revolution, Guillén saw the fulfillment of his hopes and prophecies. He embraced the Revolution wholeheartedly, and its unfolding, along with the personalities who led it, immediately became a major theme of his poetry. . . . The poet was filled with a new serenity, while the expressiveness of his poems reached a peak of revolutionary fervor. All this is manifest in *Tengo* (1964), and is nowhere more evident than in the poem that gives that book its title. Its very simplicity—"I Have"—already reflects the new sense of pride in and comradeship with the Cuban people. The new spirit of exuberance is unmistakable as the poem unfolds and Guillén's collective protagonist, at first surprised and bewildered by the sudden turn of events, is moved to take stock of his new relationship to reality. He concludes that he has finally come into possession of his birthright as a man: "I have, let's see: / I have what was coming to me." (pp. 23-6)

Guillén's celebration of the Cuban Revolution is more implicit in his latest collection of poems, *El gran zoo* (1967). By then the Revolution was an irrevocable fact of history, and from the perspective of that particular reality Guillén's witty little book treats the reader to an ironic interpretation of the contemporary—and particularly the capitalist—world which is now considered part of Cuba's bleak pre-history. Guillén therefore takes his audience on a tour of a symbolic zoo and introduces a mosaic of characters, animal, mineral, and vegetable, which reveal to the reader-tourist a vision of the universe in microcosm. The author's invitation to follow him through this menagerie, is not, however, entirely disinterested: on the one hand, we are invited to tour a zoo and see the "animals" in it; on the other hand, and more significantly, we are given a peculiarly Cuban tour of that zoo. More important than seeing just exactly what is caged is the realization that it is Cuba, and Guillén the guide, who are free and *not* caged and who interpret and reflect upon what *is.*

This is a volume which, in structure and style, is unique in Guillén's work. At the same time that the symbolic device of a zoo serves to create an organic totality, the poet moves away from the modes and forms of his previous works in favor of a stylized and elemental language in which everything is reduced to personification and metaphor. The lines are generally very short, the style clipped; rhyme is infrequent and the meter is inconsistent and at times reminiscent of free verse. The intent is to mimic the impersonal tone of plaques and of official notices and announcements, although alternating notes of pride, concern, amusement, and distaste creep into the comments of our host. The total effect of each of the poems is largely dependent on their interrelationship with each other and, although the great majority could stand alone, there are some which have no particular *raison d'être* except in terms of the book.

Guillén's major preoccupations are still present, although they are more pointedly synthesized: his uncompromising allegiance to Cuba and his rejection of a world ruled by greed and imperialist aggression are present in **"The Caribbean," "The Usurers,"** and **"The Eagles"**; his concern for the total liberation of the Black man is clear in **"Lynch"** and **"KKK"**; implicit in **"Tonton-Macoute"** is the poet's revolutionary vision of a more humane world. (pp. 26-7)

His most recent poems, some of which have been published in various Cuban journals . . . have been collected in a soon-to-be-published volume entitled *La rueda dentada* (*The Serrated Wheel*). It is clear from such poems as **"I Declare Myself an Impure Man," "Problems of Underdevelopment,"** and **"Propositions on the Death of Ana,"** that Guillén intends to continue writing, from a particularly Cuban perspective, a poetry which is explicit, deceptively simple in style, militant in its assumptions, one which reaches out to the Third World and looks forward to liberation, then peace. (p. 28)

> *Robert Márquez, in an introduction to* ¡Patria O Muerte! The Great Zoo and Other Poems *by Nicolás Guillén, edited and translated by Robert Márquez, Monthly Review Press, 1972, pp. 13-29.*

KEITH ELLIS

Guillén's pre-revolutionary work is well known for its social commitment, for its incisive attack initially on what he convincingly showed to be grave injustice within Cuba. His *Motivos de son* of 1930 revealed that injustice resulted from a misperception and undervaluing, due to bias, of the contribution of black Cubans to the life of their country. Thus the eight poems of this little book emphasize the language and preoccupations of this sector of the population and display a musicality based on the rhythms of the *son*, a popular musical form that had originated among the blacks and which was held in disrepute by the middle classes. In poems of *Sóngoro cosongo* of the following year, he emphasizes the view that Cuban culture was really a mulatto culture, a product of the confluence of the Spanish and African cultural streams. Thus Guillén at this early stage of his career made it clear that he was not representing the black sector of Cuban society with the aim of separating it from the mainstream. His preoccupation in *Motivos de son* and in *Sóngoro cosongo* was rather with the whole Cuban society, with having Cuba identify itself correctly and within this context, with having the African contribution to Cuban culture rightfully acknowledged.

The other important aspect of his poetry emerged clearly in the books beginning with *West Indies, Ltd.* (1934) and was continued with emphasis and made definitive in the book of 1937, *Cantos para soldados y sones para turistas*. This aspect had to do with his recognition of the basic reason for the racial discrimination, the poverty, and the underdevelopment that existed in Cuba and in the other territories of the Caribbean. He found imperialism to be at the root of all this and suggested that harmony and fulfilment could not come to these territories until imperialism was vanquished. He came to adopt the view that with the overthrow of imperialism all these evils would be abolished in a Marxist society. He was intimately concerned that this should be achieved in Cuba; but he was also concerned that it should be achieved throughout Latin America and the Caribbean. Serving aptly in the presentation of these views are sharp irony, searing satire, plaintive elegiac accents and accessible language accompanied by a wealth of attractive music. Without understanding these key aspects of Guillén's poetry prior to the Cuban Revolution, one may have difficulty in attempting to understand the course of his poetry since the Revolution.

In the first place it is natural that—once the Revolution could be identified as a Marxist, anti-imperialist revolution, as a force that would bind the Cuban population together through the removal of the barriers of class and of race—Guillén would support such a revolution to the fullest extent. Consequently, in his collection of poems of 1964 entitled *Tengo,* a new element of open joyfulness enters into his poetry. With unbounded enthusiasm he sings of the recovered land, of liberty, of the possibility of singing again, of laughing again, and of the necessity of all Cubans to work together in the process of reconstructing the society. But underlying his joy is a sense of conflict existing in one of two situations: either in the antithesis between the past time and the present or in the necessity of struggling against enemies of the Revolution to safeguard what Cuba had won. Thus, Guillén recalls the hard struggle that the black had against racial discrimination in Cuba in a poem like **"Cualquier tiempo pasado fue peor";** and in the same poem he shows his particular concern about the jeopardy in which the very language of Cuba was put by the penetrating presence of a foreign power with a different language. At the same time he shows sorrow for those who fell in the fight for liberty; he shows solidarity with those who remain exploited in colonial or neo-colonial systems; and he uses harsh satire, the old Guillén satire, against those who would re-open the way to imperialism by their counter-revolutionary action. To represent this vast range of topics and of emotion, Guillén employs a fittingly broad range of metrical forms: the old Spanish 'romance,' the 'décima' (the most widely used metrical form in Cuba), the sonnet, 'letrillas,' 'elegias,' and 'sones.' Such a display was quickly pointed out by Cuban literary critics such as Portuondo as a model for poets, for artists, in revolutionary Cuba. Guillén was discovering modes of expression that suited aptly the post-revolutionary posture of his new poetry.

This inventiveness, this blending of old forms and of revolutionary political content to achieve a new kind of poetry with no barriers between it and the people is what Guillén demonstrates in the book *El gran zoo.* The bestiary, used even by a poet like Pablo Neruda in a traditional sense to give the human character traits of certain animals, is transformed by Guillén in this work. Guillén's animals are the animation of certain political and social concepts and phenomena. So that hunger, for example, comes to be represented as 'an animal, all eyes and teeth.' Guillén had written some poems in his very first collection of poetry entitled *Cerebro y corazón,* in which he dwelt upon the relationship between certain technical, scientific achievements and the animal world, in a poem like **"El aeroplano,"** for example. And now these poems of *El gran zoo* came to remind readers of works of that very early period. (pp. 9-11)

Guillén has continued, in books that have followed *El gran zoo,* to display this widening range in his poetry. In them the emphasis on blackness that he showed in his two important early books of poetry is no longer evident. He sees no need for it within Cuba; and he has explained . . . that if he had continued after the Revolution to dwell on the situation of the blacks in Cuba he would have been isolated and more so when he himself personally believes that the struggle cannot be racist but must be revolutionary, that is, it must be a struggle to abolish the division of society into classes since this division is the source of racism. He believes that the Revolution has dealt a death blow to racism in Cuba. At the same time, however, he remains vigilant against abuses suffered by blacks throughout the world. In a poem on Martin Luther King, published in *La rueda dentada* (1972), for instance, he ridicules a statement by the Russian poet Yevtushenko that King's skin was black but his soul as pure as white snow. The book *La rueda dentada* reveals the wide variety of subjects that can be of interest to a revolutionary poet: work, love, sculpture, painting, etc. And his very latest book, *El diario que a diario,* also of 1972, is an artistically daring mixture of genres of poetry, of political caricature, journalism, advertisement writing, etc., to form a panorama of Cuba's historic evolution from colonial times to the Revolution of 1959.

The writing of socially committed literature is a task that involves more delicacy than is generally recognized. For first, a reader may be unreceptive to the work only because he or she is unsympathetic to the viewpoint advanced. Also, writings about specific social problems can easily be uninteresting to readers who are either too little or too greatly distanced from the problems. The former may tend, because of their familiarity with the problems, to find their literary representation to be trite and superfluous. The latter, conversely, may find it to be remote and trivial. The need in such literature, then, is for mature perception, invested with art. But then there are other difficulties, principally the subtle distracting powers of art that Bertolt Brecht has so often discussed. Aggravating this difficulty is the tendency to see poetry as pseudostatements, as I. A. Richards would have it, as stating only provisionally and not containing concepts in which there can be a real basis for belief. Besides, it is widely recognized that in the literary work the signified is determined by the total literary context, and that to this context contribute elements that resist the writer's control. Thus it is possible that a poem which is intended to be socially committed or which is apparently socially committed may not really be so. (pp. 11-12)

Conscious of all these difficulties, let us examine Nicolás Guillén's **"Prólogo"** from his collection, *La rueda dentada* of 1972. . . . The poem at first glance deals with a wheel, with the functional disability of a defective gearwheel, and suggests in the last stanza the happy fulfilment of the working of a sound wheel. The poem begins with verses that each presents expectation and then frustration. The gearwheel of the first hemistich is shown to be defective in the second. Its expectant beginning of a turn in the third hemistich is shown to be abortive in the fourth. The unproductive consequences of the faulty tooth are developed in the second stanza and are heightened by the use of the anaphorical 'no,' negating verbs with intense assonance in 'a' that indicate action and progress. . . . In the third stanza hyperbolic enumeration is used to indicate the impossibility of any external force making the wheel effective. So the conclusion . . . introduced by 'como se sabe,' comes when that idea has been well established. Its repetitious nature is underlined by the use of adnomination. . . . The reappearance of the second and third verses of the poem to close this stanza and this first part of the poem further emphasizes the inade-

quacy of a gearwheel whose revolutionary capacity is limited to an incomplete revolution. And all the while there is the musicality of the poem, skilfully used to accentuate starting and stopping, the anticlimactic direction of the verses. The marked caesura equally dividing the twelve-syllable dactyllic verses ensure rhythmic accompaniment to the meaning of the verses. (pp. 12-14)

[The] smoothness of movement leads to the final stanza which with its exclamations exhorts the gearwheel to productive action, action that is achievable only when the teeth of the wheel are sound and are working in concert.

It thus becomes clear that [**"Prologo"**] is a parable, an extended metaphor, carrying a message aimed at facilitating the process of reconstruction. The message is that there can be no weak link in the human chain of participants in this process. The primary audience to whom the poem is addressed is of course the Cuban people, but it may have relevance to other situations. The parable is a universal and perennial device for imprinting a message on the minds of its hearers by presenting the message in engagingly simple terms. Guillén enriches this tradition with musicality that is warmly inviting to his public. This poem with its demonstration first of the cause of futile effort and then of the correction that leads to fruitfulness shows Guillén's ability to put poetry at the service of cohesive reconstruction.

For doing this, for fitting poetry to the needs of Cuba at a specific historical moment, Guillén would make no apologies to those readers who are insistent universalists. He would surely say, let them at least assume the attitude that marks the sensitive reader of literature: the 'amplitud' that José Enrique Rodó was happy to possess or the 'negative capability' of which John Keats wrote. Let them above all recognize the right of underdeveloped countries to express in their way their own cultural preoccupations. . . . It is on account of his ability to define and elaborate artistically at different times in its history the legitimate concerns of his nation that Guillén is regarded in that island, by popular acclaim, as Cuba's national poet. His work, perfectly adapted as it is to the needs of the first post-revolutionary society in Spanish America, represents a new stage in the practice of literary Americanism. (pp. 14-15)

Keith Ellis, "Literary Americanism and the Recent Poetry of Nicolás Guillén," in University of Toronto Quarterly, *Vol. XLV, No. 1, Fall, 1975, pp. 1-18.*

LLOYD KING

Nicolás Guillén is Cuba's most honoured poet. There is little doubt that most of his aspirations as a political activist and 'social protest' poet have been realized since the Cuban Revolution. Within Cuba itself his most popular collection of poems is his *Songs for Soldiers and Ballads for Tourists (Cantos para soldados y sones para turistas)* which he originally published in 1937. These poems are anticipatory blueprints of the relationship between the people's militia, formed since the Revolution as part of Cuba's embattled response to U.S. aggression, and the Cuban people. Written at a time when the soldier seemed rather to be the tool and guardian of U.S. interests and the power hunger of Fulgencio Batista, they yet called on the soldier to recognize his links with the ordinary folk who were the victims of exploitation and political gimcrackery, and the need to forge fraternity with the oppressed masses. The *sones para turistas* expressed the repugnance felt by many Cubans towards the insensitive American tourist, and sought to dramatize the resentment and bitterness towards him as an insane but all too visible symbol of the rigorous and painful grip on Cuba's monoculture economy by American imperialist-capitalist interests.

As is well known, the Cuban Revolutionary leadership ran out the tourists and the capitalists and aligned itself with the Cuban Communist Party, of which Guillén had been a member since the thirties. The Revolution also acted swiftly to eliminate a feature of Cuban life against which Guillén had campaigned both in verse and prose, namely racial discrimination; it desegregated the schools and the beaches and provided equal educational opportunity for all. Guillén has expressed his recognition of this reality in a poem **"Tengo"** (**"All is mine"**). . . . (p. 30)

When Guillén wrote **"Tengo"** in the post-revolutionary period, it must have seemed to him that he and other militant Cubans—artists, trade unionists, ordinary folk—had reached the end of a long process of struggle and desperate affirmation during a dark night of dictatorship and violence, to bring in the dawn of a socialist state in the Americas. For Guillén it was a process which had always had to do with the achievement of an integrated national personality, based on a discovery of the common Cubanness of whites and blacks in Cuban society. But equally Guillén realized that this objective could not possibly take shape until external capitalist interests were tamed along with their capacity for disruptive activity. Thus the two constants of his verse were related to internal racial integration and socialist militancy. His verse therefore came to be prophetic of some of the main objectives of the Cuban Revolution itself. (p. 31)

[In 1930], Nicolás Guillén published eight 'negrista' poems in the newspaper *Diario de la Marina* with the general title *Son Motifs* (*Motivos de son*) and in 1931 included them again with others in book form, with the title *Sóngoro Cosongo*. Guillén was immediately recognized as a writer who had his finger on the pulse of folk sensibility. . . . Guillén seemed instinctively to realize the opportunity to blend the scribal and oral traditions and derived the rhythms of his verse from a popular musical form, the 'son', which had been born of the contact between African rhythms and the creole environment, a form which had long been frowned on by polite Cuban society. In one long magical moment Guillén came to prefigure some of the obsessions of future Caribbean writing. (pp. 35-6)

The poems of *Son Motifs* explored a variety of folk urban situations. Two of the poems **"Ay negra, si tu supiera"**, (**"Aye, black lover, if you only knew"**) and **"Búscate plata"** (**"Go and look for bread"**) deal with women abandoning their lovers because they have no money, a situation related to the effects of the Depression. Two others **"Ayer me dijeron negro"** (**"Yesterday I was called nigger"**) and **"Mulata"** refer to the antagonism between mulatto and black. In **"Yesterday I was called nigger"**, Guillén strikes what was to be a recurring note of his verse suggesting to some person who passed for white that he has African/black blood:

> Tan blanco como te bé,
> y tu abuela sé quién é.
> Sácala de la cocina,
> Sácala de la cocina,
> Mamá Iné.
>
> (As white as you look
> I know your grandma (the cook)
> Bring her out of the kitchen
> Bring her out of the kitchen
> Mamma Inés.)

This Caribbean picong uses the sharp-edged social barb to puncture the pride along the colour and class line. The most disturbingly ironic of the poems is **"Negro Bembón"** (**"Thick-lipped Nigger"**). The speaker, Caridad, is presented telling her Negro boyfriend with thick lips not to allow himself to be wounded by the mocking intent of those who call him 'negro bembón', and seeking to turn the epithet into a term of endearment. Hers is in a certain sense a Négritude position, for she urges the man to assume freely a term which the society uses in a 'denigratory' manner:

> Por qué te pones tan bravo
> cuando te dicen negro bembón
> si tienes la boca santa
> negro bembón.
>
> (Why do you get so vexed
> When people call you big-lipped nigger
> Since your mouth is very attractive
> You thick-lipped nigger, you?)

However the poem cannot sustain a Négritude interpretation because in the last two lines we learn that the 'negro bembón' is really living off his mistress's earnings, whatever her line of work may be.

When he widened the collection of poems in *Sóngoro Cosongo*, it was noticeable that many of the poems dealt with the self-contained violence of the low-life of Havana. **"Velorio de Papá Montero"**, (**"Wake for Papa Montero"**) was inspired by a popular 'son' of the time, and evokes with a mix of irony and sadness the death in a drunken brawl of a folk character. **"Chévere"** (sweetman) is a short dense image of concentrated violence, orchestrating the movement of a man's rage till he slices his unfaithful woman to death. (pp. 36-7)

Guillén's ghetto images were not calculated to win the approval of coloureds who were seeking to project an image of respectability, and in an interview with Antonio Fernández de Castro in the newspaper *La semana*, we find him denouncing those who were unwilling to acknowledge the 'son' as a part of their culture. These attitudes of shame and self-contempt were particularly striking, Guillén noted, since the 'son' was popular in Paris and even in Cuba was now accepted in the most exclusive society, and yet many Negroes demonstrated public hostility to this popular art form because it was lower-class and 'incompatible with their spiritual delicacy and their grade of culture'. (pp. 37-8)

One of the most hostile critics of the influence of Afrocuban folk forms on the wider Cuban sensibility was Ràmon Vasconcelos, a Cuban journalist resident in Paris. A self-styled watchdog of Cuban culture, he wrote from Paris to discourage Guillén from the idea that the Cuban 'son' could be used and become popular in the way that the American 'blues' had been, since it was not at all suitable for social commentary or serious purposes. . . . Vasconcelos's attitude was so outrageous that one would have expected a stinging reply, but Guillén's answer was quite mild. He explained that his use of the 'son' was simply in line with the world-wide interest in popular forms, and that the 'son' poems were not in the majority in *Sóngoro Cosongo*. He even went on to lament that it was a pity that to use the speech rhythms of the folk seemed to require heroism.

This moderate reply to Vasconcelos exposes the weakness in Guillén's mulatto position. One senses that he has always been a little afraid of being called a black racist. Thus in an interview with Keith Ellis, published in the *Jamaica Journal* in 1973,

Guillén when asked about his attitude to Négritude, at first dismissed it contemptuously, then went on to admit that the assertion of blackness and of neo-African values was certainly necessary in a colonial situation. But he sees it as above all 'one of the manifestations of the class struggle'. In other words, he felt that 'black assertiveness' in post-revolutionary Cuba was wrong, but even before this he always rejected the use of the term 'Afrocuban'. One need not be a black racist in order to question Guillén's attitude. (pp. 38-9)

It is not a little amazing that Guillén was never tempted to adopt a Négritude position, particularly as even sympathetic white Cuban critics were not persuaded by his claim that Cuba's was mulatto. (p. 39)

In *Sóngoro Cosongo,* Guillén had captured something of the downbeat of ghetto life, a sense of its cynicism and violence, the rhythms of its speech. His next collection of poems, *West Indies Ltd.* (1934) shows that his political awareness had sharpened, for these were the years of the Depression and of the inept and brutal dictatorship of General Machado who finally fell from power in 1933. Behind him, there was already the example of another mulatto poet, Regino Pedroso, who had been converted to Marxism and the Communist Party in the twenties. In one of his better known poems, "Hermano Negro" ("Brother Black"), Pedroso called upon his black brothers to acquire a right consciousness and to recognize that race prejudice was secondary to economic exploitation. They ought to reconsider their role as entertainers for the western world and understand that they were a part of the exploited proletariat. . . . Once Guillén got the message, his folk characters assume the elemental posture of exploited men. The poet's own posture is that of a member of the revolutionary vanguard, sharpening the consciousness of the masses. The movement in tone and perspective anticipates the classical transferral of aggression which Fanon analysed in *The Wretched of the Earth,* whereby that violence which the sub-culture practised against itself, as exemplified in poems such as "Chévere" and "Velorio de Papá Montero", must now be directed outwards against the colonialist exploiter and the bourgeoisie. Such poems as "Caminando" and "Sabás" reflect this new mood and show Guillén undertaking the task of political education. In "Sabás", the poet calls upon Sabás, servile because reduced to penury in the Depression days, to recognize his moral and economic rights and to understand that when the society will not allow him the dignity to survive as a human being, he must be prepared to claim his rights violently if necessary. The irony is both sharp and bitter:

Porqué Sabás la mano abierta?
(Este Sabás es un negro bruto)
Coge tu pan pero no lo pidas;
Coge tu luz, coge tu esperanza cierta
como a un caballo por las bridas.

Why Sabás do you hold out your hand?
(This Sabás is really a foolish nigger)
Take your bread, don't beg for it
Take hold of your senses, take firm hold of your hopes
As of a horse under sure command.

In 1937, Guillén published his *Cantos para soldados y sones para turistas,* and although his earlier collection *West Indies Ltd.* (1934) and later *El son entero* (1943) have a better selection of poems, they were not greeted with as good a press as the *Songs for soldiers.* Guillén's Party colleague Juan Marinello . . . hailed the *Songs for soldiers* as a definitive triumph of the

American melting pot. What strikes one about this claim in relation to the poems is the fact that Guillén here abandoned the Afrocuban stance which is so easily picked up in the other collections. One must therefore conjecture that there was possibly some pressure on the poet to move away from his 'negrista' image, perhaps to come closer to Marti's dictum that 'Cuban was more than black, more than white'. Perhaps also a bland poem like "Balada de los dos abuelos" ("Ballad of the two grandfathers") in which slave-owning conquistador grandfather and enslaved African grandfather are reconciled in the poet's dream, has been played up by some critics for the same kind of reason. There was a lot of truth in Cintio Vitier's judgment on Guillén that 'the new theme is not just a fashion, a subject for literature, but the living heart of his creative activity'. But because he has always been sensitive to the charge of black racism and to the ideological posture of the Party in Cuba, he has also had to react to the association of his name with Négritude.

This is confirmed by a poem "Brindis" ("Cheers!") which he wrote in 1952 but which has never appeared in book form till the recent publication of his *Obra poética.* "Brindis" is addressed to the famous black American singer Josephine Baker who in her day was the toast of Paris and who met with racial discrimination on returning to the United States. In disgust and anger, the poet tells la Baker that she might well have been lynched and he introduces a mood of violence which again anticipates one response of black militants which eventually came to pass. . . . In a few lines, Guillén evokes the long hot summer, the incendiary fury which would take place in ghettos like Watts years later. What is equally interesting, however, is that Josephine Baker had also visited Cuba, and there had also been refused a hotel room by a racist management. But the Cuban incident had drawn from Guillén an article written in sadness rather than in anger. It can be argued, and quite rightly, that Cuba did not have a Ku Klux Klan and that white Cuban racism was milder; but it is also clear that it was felt to be 'politic' to focus on the more extreme brutalities which occurred in the United States. The poet could both deliver a blow against racism and associate it with imperialistic capitalism.

One way in which Guillén tried to hit at the Cuban bourgeoisie was by insisting that most of its members had some concealed African ancestry, for example in the poem "Canción del bongó" ("Bongo song"):

Y hay titulos de Castilla
con parientes en Bondó.

(There are those with patents of nobility from Castille.
Who yet have relatives in Bondó.)

Guillén in such poems was striking an embarrassing note for whereas in Latin countries those who can pass for white are considered white, in the United States a drop of African blood makes a man black. The Cuban bourgeoisie who identified their interests so closely with American capitalists and American standards would therefore not particularly appreciate what the poet was taking pains to advertise.

In 1943, Guillén published *El son entero* with a number of negrista poems, "Sudor y látigo" ("Sweat and the whip"), "Ebano real" ("Royal ebony"), "Son número 6" ("Son No. 6"), "Acana", and even a rather embarrassing poem which calls upon Shango and Ochun to guard Stalin whom 'free men accompany singing, "Una canción a Stalin"'. These poems do not add anything new to his output although they show once again how strongly influenced by the oral tradition Guillén was. A much more interesting later poem is **"El apellido"** (**"The surname"**) in which Guillén again worries about the way in which the African connection is vulnerable to the Hispanic mould, even in such things as names. . . . Finally one must mention a not-too-good poem **"Qué color"** which was provoked by a comment of the Russian poet Yevtushenko on the death of Martin Luther King that his soul was white as snow. Guillén insists rather that Luther King's soul was as black as coal, 'negro como el carbón'. **"Qué color"** shows the way in which Guillén and the Cuban Revolution are solid supporters of men who struggle against oppression and imperialism everywhere. Amílcar Cabral and Angela Davis are very popular in Cuba. Nevertheless, Guillén would never write of a *Cuban* that his soul was black as coal, on the basis that the Revolution has abolished the emotive connotations of colour.

The Marxist attitude to colour, which is Guillén's own attitude, is that it is irrelevant in a socialist state. It counts upon Revolutionary policy of equal opportunity to reverse a variety of instinctive attitudes about race, bred during more than one hundred and fifty years of Cuban history in the context of the white racist attitudes of western civilization. At the primary level of what we accept as the basic human needs and rights, the right to a balanced diet, educational development, etc. no one can disagree with the Cuban perspective. However, at a second level of reference, that of cultural formation and a variety of subtle attitudes, this writer, whose experience is that of the English-speaking Caribbean (where black men have attained the highest offices) and who has seen how readily a Euro-oriented environment can twist and confuse men of African ancestry, must express some reservations about the Cuban Revolution's desire to straighten out the kinks and achieve a determined uniformity in Cuban cultural life. (pp. 40-4)

> Lloyd King, "Nicolás Guillén and Afrocubanismo," in A Celebration of Black and African Writing, *edited by Bruce King and Kolawole Ogungbesan, Ahmadu Bello University Press, 1975, pp. 30-45.*

CONSTANCE SPARROW DE GARCÍA BARRIO

Prior to the beginning of the twentieth century, the image of blacks in Spanish-American literature had been limited to a few prototypes. This repertoire included the black as a physical dynamo, the meek and loyal slave, the sexually stirring mulatto woman, and the brave Afro-Spanish-American soldier fighting in the service of colonial authorities. Blacks themselves, during the colonial period, were rarely in a position to contribute to the making of their own literary image. They found themselves hindered by the lack of means to become literate since their learning to read and write was discouraged. If they managed to gain these skills, societal and governmental restrictions compelled them to write on themes alien to their own situation. (p. 105)

About 1900, a Negro vogue began in Europe. It seemed to provide an external stimulus for the study of blacks in Latin America, and their incorporation in literary works. In the late 1920s and early 1930s, Cuban writers, especially poets, avidly sketched black protagonists, but hardly ventured beyond the caricatures and customs presented in colonial literature. Moreover, for most of these writers, the inclusion of black characters represented no more than a parenthesis in their careers.

The Cuban mulatto poet Nicolás Guillén . . . proves an exception. He is the only major practitioner of Negroid poetry in whom the figure of the black man outlives the vogue of the first third of this century. Furthermore, during his career the poet has created black figures new to Spanish-American literature. These creations dynamically express the intense social concern and heightened political consciousness of the author. (pp. 105-06)

In 1930 Nicolás Guillén published his first collection of Negroid poems, *Motivos de son.* In it, he offers a potpourri of dark island types. While highly chromatic, this presentation of the lower strata of Cuban blacks is quite traditional in its predominant eight-syllable line, and in its reproduction of the peculiarities of the Spanish spoken by these islanders as well:

Por qué te pone tan bravo,	Why do you get so mad,
cuando te dicen negro bembón,	when they call you "Big-Lips,"
si tiene la boca santa,	because your mouth is sweet
negro bembón?	Big-Lips?
Bembón así como ere	Big Lips just as you are
tiene de to	you have everything
Caridad te mantiene,	Caridad supports you
te lo da to.	you have everything.

As significant as the dropping of the final *s* of *pones, tienes,* and *eres,* and the reduction of *todo* to *to* is the theme of identity. The *bembón,* or big-lipped Black, objects to the epithet in spite of its accuracy. The poet contends that the bembón's mouth is large but sweet, and he has no grounds for complaint since he is being supported by his sweetheart Caridad. In another poem, Guillén reproves a mulatto woman who has laughed at his broad nose and called it a *nudo de corbata,* knot of a necktie. He replies that he would prefer his black gal to her any time.

In his next collection, *Sóngoro Cosongo* (1931), Guillén seems to divide his efforts between traditional black characters, and the shaping of new types. **"Rumba"** and **"Secuestro de la mujer de Antonio"** both capture the sexual implications of the rumba danced by a mulata. The knife-wielding *chévere,* prefigured in the *negro curro* of colonial literature, is the subject of **"Velorio de papá montero."** The poem **"Chévere"** provides a briefer statement on the same type. Although *Sóngoro Cosongo* and *Motivos de son* share traditional elements, the former lacks the apparent lightheartedness of the latter. This new sobriety is conveyed in the elimination of dialect, in an ironic address to the question of racial identity, and in a concern over the exploitation of Cuba by the United States. One of the most striking poems in *Sóngoro Cosongo* is **"Caña."** Its terse lines denounce American economic control, its effect on the land where sugar cane is grown, and the anonymous black who cultivates it.

Guillén examines the United States from another vantage point in **"Small Ode to a Cuban Boxer."** He warns the boxer, who is about to travel to New York, that, "The North is wild and crude." The boxer's English is precarious, and his Spanish not much less so, but the poet tellingly suggests that the fighter's fists are what he will need to "speak black Truth." (pp. 106-07)

Three years later, in *West Indies Ltd.* (1934), the poet's attitude has become much more aggressive. Allusions to the clenched fist, later to be the symbol of the Black Power Movement, fill this collection. He asks why the fists of the dock workers haven't been raised in a single decisive gesture:

> Oh strong fist, elemental and hard!
> Who restrains your open gesture?

In "**Ballad of Simón Caraballo,**" a black beggar sings his sorrows, but the lines that spotlight his hands reveal anger and potential violence:

> I
> black Simon Caraballo,
> sleep on a door step now;
> a brick is my pillow
> my bed is on the ground.
>
> . . . . .
>
> . . . . .
>
> I don't know what to do with my arms
> but I'll find something to do
> I,
> black Simon Caraballo,
> have my fists closed,
> have my fists closed,
> and I need to eat!

In describing another black, Sabás, who begs from door to door, the poet poses the question three times: "Why, Sabás, the open hand?" He urges Sabás to demand what he needs, and discard his open-handed attitude. . . . (pp. 107-08)

Guillén chose to invest another poor black character with his most urgent message in 1937, when *Songs for Soldiers and Tunes for Tourists* was published. This figure is distinctive in his immunity to the venality associated with the tourist trade. A musician, he warns the tourists that his song, unlike that of many of his countrymen, will not soothe them like the rum they drink because José Ramón Cantaliso—perhaps the artist's self-portrait—is a singer-of-truths. . . . (p. 108)

The model of the singer-of-truth, whose voice has grown more strident, reappears in "**Son venezolano,**" from *El son entero* (1947). This time he bears the name Juan Bimba, and makes a frontal attack on foreign exploitation of Cuban and Venezuelan products:

> I sing in Cuba and Venezuela,
> a song that comes out of me.
> What bitter oil,
> caramba,
> oh, how bitter this oil,
> caramba,
> that tastes like Cuban sugar!

In *El son entero,* Guillén pours the seething anger of the beggars into a new vessel, that of the rebellious slave. The enslaved black, who has been recovering from a beating, rises to slay his master in "**Sweat and Whip**":

> Then the silent sky,
> and under the sky, the slave
> stained in the blood of the master.

Violent self-assertion would inform some of Guillén's later black figures too. This position is summarized in "**Sports,**" a poem from *La paloma de vuelo popular* (1958). The poem contains a catalogue of black prize fighters from both Americas,

> But above all, I think
> of the Patent-Leather Kid, the great king without a
>   crown
> and of Chocolate, the great crowned king,
> and of Black Bill, with his rubber nerves.

Guillén implies that their victories as individuals are enhanced by the pride they inspire in other blacks. Repeated mention of the Cuban chess grand-master José Raul Capablanca seems to countervail the importance given to physical stamina. Intellectual vigor is also necessary.

During this period, racism in the United States, with its concomitants of segregation in schools and lynching, claimed Guillén's attention. In "**Little Rock**" and "**Elegy to Emmett Till,**" the poet gives voice to his indignation. "**Elegy to Emmett Till**" was written for a fourteen-year-old black who was lynched in Greenwood, Mississippi, in 1955. It minutely describes a "danse macabre" over the mutilated body of the boy. . . . (p. 109)

In 1959, the revolution of Fidel Castro triumphed. One of its goals, the eradication of racial discrimination, was accomplished through the immediate integration of schools and all public facilities. Guillén jubilantly reflects on the changes wrought by the revolution in *Tengo,* written in 1964:

> I have, let's see
> that being a black man
> no one can stop me
> at the door of a bar or of a dance hall
> Nor in the vestibule of a hotel
> scream at me that there's no vacancy.
>
> (p. 110)

Still directing his attention towards the United States, Guillén included a poem in praise of the will and militancy of Angela Davis. Although it appears in *La rueda dentada* (1972), it depicts the heroine as being made of the same elemental stuff that gave strength to the "**New Woman**" of 1931. . . . ["**Qué color,**" a] poem dedicated to Martin Luther King also appears in this volume. It comes as a reply to the Russian poet Evtushenko, who described King as a black man with ". . . a most pure soul like white snow." Guillén, in his violent rejection of this image, ends his poem by saying that King's soul was "black like coal." Guillén was understandably provoked by the use of the words "white snow" to describe a black man who had lived many of the ideals that Guillén saw as essential. For more than forty years, Nicolás Guillén has forcefully treated blacks in his poetry. During that time, one can observe a transition from the presentation of the usual black figures, speaking in a typically distorted manner, poured into the traditional octosyllabic lines, to the naissance of startling new blacks, whose profiles are often etched in free verse.

Guillén seems to begin by making plastic his vision of ideal men and women in "**Arrival**" and "**New Woman.**" Once the ideal has been described, the poet proceeds to grapple with raw reality. Thus emerge the black beggars. Guillén would make of his poems a *maraca* or *güire,* a percussion instrument whose beat would awaken the beggars to a sense of self-worth and the need to fight. He tells them to demand a share of society's goods rather than beg for them. The tone of this poetry grows increasingly tense and combative, and may be summed up in the clenched fist, an image which appears repeatedly.

A third new black figure is the singer-of-truth, José Ramón Cantaliso. Poverty has made him hypersensitive to the economic ills that the tourist trade has brought to Cuba. His song stresses the suffering of poor Cubans, and while the tune does not please the tourist's ear, it cannot be changed by their dollars. Later, the song of Juan Bimba, a character in every way similar to José Ramón Cantaliso, denounces parasitic foreign business interests in the Caribbean.

In much of Guillén's later poetry, there seems to be a conformity between the black figures he has drawn earlier and the concrete men and women whom he makes the subject of his poems. The premium which Guillén places on physical strength and an indomitable spirit is incarnated in Kid Charol, Kid Chocolate, Johnson, and Black Bill, all of whom are boxers. These traits are also seen in Jesús Menéndez, who sought power for the Cuban sugar workers through organization. His mission was parallel to that of Cantaliso, who aimed to jar tourists and islanders out of the old pattern with his song. Angela Davis and Martin Luther King also provide living examples of the militancy and purpose that Guillén has placed in some of his fictional figures.

In assessing Guillén's contribution to Spanish American literature, Cuba's long colonial status must be kept in mind. In 1898, the island was freed from Spanish domination only to immediately become a functional protectorate of the United States. Frantz Fanon, in discussing the shift from colonial mentality to national consciousness [in *The Wretched of the Earth*], states that the change is usually accompanied by a break with past artistic expression. (pp. 111-12)

Although Guillén has forged new types, he has written a variety of other poems of ethnic content as well. On occasion, he has delved into Afro-Spanish folklore and religion. He also wrote a lullaby for a black baby, conspicuous because of its late date of publication, 1958. The question of racial identity is handled in various guises throughout his career. Guillén never loses historical perspective, as **"Noche de negros junto a la catedral"** (1966) reveals. His creation of new figures and the cultivation of other Afro-Spanish themes measure the depth of his commitment. (p. 112)

> Constance Sparrow de García Barrio, "The Image of the Black Man in the Poetry of Nicolás Guillén," in Blacks in Hispanic Literature: Critical Essays, edited by Miriam DeCosta, Kennikat Press, 1977, pp. 105-13.

RICHARD L. JACKSON

[Nicolás Guillén] has lived long enough ... to become the premier black poet writing in Spanish. Guillén's earlier poetry was definitely non-black and largely inconsequential, of interest to contemporary readers only as illustrations of his early expertise and technical domination of traditional Spanish verse forms, particularly those in vogue during and just after the literary reign of Rubén Darío, and as contrast they illustrate, as well, how far he has come in the blackening process he underwent from *Cerebro y corazón* (1922) to *Motivos de son* (1930). Before this metamorphosis, Guillén's literary output in the twenties, with only a very few exceptions, followed European models. Literary historians who want to "de-blacken" him or turn him into a nonblack poet can find ample evidence in these adolescent poems to support their view which, as best expressed by Luis Iñiguez Madrigal, is that Nicolás Guillén is not—nor has he ever been—a black poet in language, style, or theme. Madrigal has another view, namely, that Nicolás Guillén is not even a predominantly social poet, but one who writes primarily on "other" themes. Madrigal can find some evidence in these early poems to support both his views, as Guillén's pre-*Motivos de son* work is dominated by such universal or colorless themes as love, death, nature, religion, and other abstract head and heart ("cerebro y corazón") subjects.

But a turning point came early in Guillén's literary career when he decided to focus his attention on the true black experience in the New World, starting with his native Cuba, where he saw the black as the one most affected by imperialist exploitation and other evils.... Guillén abandoned the white muse he had followed in his youth and infused his literature with a black sensibility which has permeated his work for more than forty years.... The appearance of his *Motivos de son* in 1930, an authentic literary happening, was upsetting, unsettling and controversial, partly because they broke momentarily with traditional Spanish verse expression and partly because they dealt with authentic black characters, but largely because they brought to literature a new and genuine black concern, perspective, and poetic voice, which even some blacks misunderstood.

The *Motivos de son* had a strong impact on black and white Cubans alike. White readers, after getting over the initial shock of seeing authentic blacks in literature, were pleased to see them appear because, on the surface, Guillén in *Motivos de son* seemed to highlight the comic and picturesque side of the black locked into an uneducated happy-go-lucky lower class image. Black readers were quick to react negatively against the *Motivos de son* largely for the same reason. They were not pleased to see the *negro bembón* given center stage in literature nor were they pleased to see what appeared to be the perpetuation of stereotyped images of the black. Both groups, however, soon came to realize that Guillén's *Motivos de son* went far deeper than racial insult and superficial entertainment.... It was soon recognized that the *Motivos de son* incorporated into formal poetic structure distinctive oral forms from the musical heritage of black people, but popular song and dance forms (the *son*) that were familiar to all Cubans. Black and white Cubans came to understand that Nicolás Guillén was using black talk and black rhythms to set escape motifs like wine, women, and song against a harsh background of unemployment, poverty, prejudice, and misery while making, in effect, a subtle plea for black pride and racial identity as well as for more awareness of social inequities, and of the growing presence of the United States in Cuba.

Although many critics prefer to hasten through this black period in the poet's development, moving on to what they think are his less racial stages, we cannot overestimate the importance of Guillén's work in the late twenties and early thirties. In these years Guillén laid the groundwork that gave his later work meaning and direction, rejecting the white aesthetic whether adhered to by whites, mulattoes, or blacks. It is also during this period that he first declared the black to be as Cuban as anyone else. Guillén attacked in particular during this period the black's own propensity to abrogate his rights by forfeiting them to white Cubans who, though not always backed by law, were willing to take advantage. To Guillén the black's own black phobia, that is his own fear of being black and of identifying with his *son*, his *rumba*, and his *bongó*, was the first obstacle to overcome as he sought ways to restore value to a people long denied it. Rejection of the white aesthetic and a plea for black recognition are really the keys, paradoxically, to his theory of *mulatez*, of a mulatto Cuba. In essence this theory represents the elevation of the black to the level already occupied by whites. Guillén's desire to write Cuban poetry, and not black poetry, is really the culmination of that elevation since Cuban poetry after Guillén can never again mean solely white or European poetry. Moreover, Guillén's subsequent rejection of the term Afro-Cuban paradoxically is the most problack statement he could make. To him the term "Cuban" already includes the "Afro," for the term has come of age and been elevated to the highest degree. Without the black, in other words, there would be no theory of *mulatez;* instead, there would only be white poetry in Cuba. Guillén, then, forces the black man into social recognition, and the white Cuban's acceptance of that theory is in effect a compromise.

Guillén's blackening process, his metamorphosis from a white escapist poet to a black poet, represents a rejection of the white aesthetic in general. More specifically, though, his defiant turnabout can be seen as a black reaction to poetic Negrism, which was a local movement staffed by white intellectuals largely in the Caribbean whose interest in things black in the late twenties and early thirties coincided with the black as *nouvelle vogue* in Europe and America. Rather than associate Guillén with poetic Negrism, we should see his dramatic conversion to blackness in the late twenties and early thirties as a reaction against this white literary fad that was sweeping the world, one Guillén himself defined as

> circumstantial tourism which never penetrated deeply into the human tragedy of race, being more like excursions organized for photographing coconut trees, drums and naked Negroes, whilst there existed the seething drama of the flesh and blood Negro bearing the scars of whiplashes, a Negro now fused with the whites to produce an indelible mulatto imprint on the Cuban social scene.

(pp. 80-3)

By drawing directly from the black experience and by giving black reaction to that experience in the *Motivos de son,* Guillén pits the black as speaker from his own environment against the superficial interest in blacks, thus revealing a closeness to the subject, scene, or emotion depicted in each *poema-son* not found in poetic Negrism. It is this closeness, together with Guillén's understanding of his subject, that gives the *Motivos de son* their startling authenticity and Nicolás Guillén the title of authentic black poet.

Guillén lost little time in reaffirming that his conversion to blackness was not a passing fancy. One year later, in *Sóngoro cosongo* (1931), his second volume of black verse, he again set himself apart from the *negrista* craze.... The poems in this volume almost without exception continue to deal with the black experience in Cuba. Just as the semblance of self-mockery and black insult had helped gain respectability among the white *literati* for the *Motivos de son,* so too does his use of the term mulatto (which gives the white a share in blackness) for his black verse, help protect *Sóngoro cosongo* against white backlash.

If anything, the black racial nature of Guillén's poetry intensifies in *Sóngoro cosongo.* The language changes a bit, becoming less colloquial, and the form moves closer to recognizable Spanish verse. The emphasis, though, is the same: black pride, the black experience, and black types continue to dominate his poetry.... But unlike the *Motivos de son* where the black is largely the speaker and singer, in *Sóngoro cosongo* the black, for the most part, is spoken about. The *Motivos de son,* in other words, is closer to black speech and black song (*son*) in poetic form, while *Sóngoro cosongo* is closer in several poems to the Spanish *romance* or ballad form, but with *son* elements. *Sóngoro cosongo* represents growth as Guillén includes variations on the *son* form while enlarging the black world he is introducing by bringing in black folklore, superstitions, even negative types. The black world of the time he represents was not always a pleasant one, but his point is clear: the black has arrived and literature must recognize this fact.

Perhaps the best illustration of this point can be seen in **"Llegada"** (**"The Arrival"**).... In this lead-off statement which ostensibly describes the arrival of the black as slave to the Island, Guillén repeatedly writes as refrain "¡Aquí estamos!" ("Here we are!") as the poem develops into yet another expression of black racial affirmation. **"Pequeña oda a un negro boxeador cubano,"** which Guillén first published in 1929, one year before the *Motivos de son,* has the same turning-point impact. This poem, like **"Mujer nueva"** whose black woman figure "trae la palabra inédita" ("brings new knowledge"), is a strong call for racial pride and black identity. To be sure, **"Pequeña oda a un negro boxeador cubano"** can be read on several levels: (1) as a poem about a black boxer; (2) as a poem where the black boxer acts as symbol for all blacks in struggle; and (3) as a poem about a struggle between nations, more specifically, about impending conflict between Cuba and the United States. But it is the final verse of that poem, where the poet exhorts the black to "hablar en negro de verdad" ("speak in real black talk")—a phrase that certainly refers to more than just black dialect—that underscores the authentic blackening of the poet in this early period. From the black fist of the boxer in **"Pequeña oda a un negro boxeador cubano"** to the black fist of the slave rower in **"Llegada,"** who has now exchanged his oar for a knife..., there is really very little distance. These three poems, **"Pequeña oda a un negro boxeador cubano,"** **"Llegada,"** and **"Mujer nueva,"** and others in *Sóngoro cosongo* are very black indeed even though they do not contain any of the phonetic speech characteristic of his *Motivos de son.*

In 1934 Guillén published *West Indies Ltd.,* a volume widely hailed as his first volume of social (as opposed to racial) protest poetry. But it is in this volume in which Guillén widens his perspective or attack that he, at the same time, deepens the blackening process begun in the late twenties.... It is evident that Nicolás Guillén focuses as well on the dispossessed white, "Dos niños: uno negro, otro blanco... ramos de un mismo árbol de miseria" ("Two children: one black, one white... two branches from the same tree of misery"), to illustrate yet another victim, like the black, of United States imperialism in the Antilles, but it would be a mistake to accept that Guillén's concern for the black in this volume is only a symbolic one. The poet continues to depict specific black figures and black folklore, and he also continues his program of instilling black pride in those blacks like Sabás—in a poem of the same name—who continue to go about with their hands out begging rather than shaking the strong black fist.... Guillén perhaps more insistently than in his two previous volumes of black verse makes himself the focal character in many of the poems as time and again he emphasizes his own black identity. In **"Palabras en el trópico,"** the poet speaks of his "dark body," his "curly hair." In **"Adivinanzas"** "the black" becomes "I." Either he or other blacks like "I, Simón Caraballo the black" in **"Balada de Simón Caraballo"** or "The blacks, working" in **"Guadalupe W.I."** are the stars. Most importantly in **"West Indies Ltd.,"**... it is clear that Guillén's concerns have moved beyond Cuba, but it is equally clear that the poet of black pride admonishing Sabás is the same poetic voice speaking at times in the sarcastic tone of an intelligent observer and at other times through the *son* sung at intervals throughout the poem by Juan el Barbero. This is a point the poet does not want the reader to miss, as he closes this poem with the words, "This was written by Nicolás Guillén, *antillano,* in the year nineteen hundred and thirty-four."

Despite Guillén's ever-widening circle of concerns that he has pursued throughout his long career, he has never left the black man behind or out of his poetry. In one of the few published studies of its kind, Constance Sparrow de García Barrio recently traced Guillén's creation of new black characters through his later poetry that includes poems, for example, on such contemporary black figures as Martin Luther King and Angela Davis [see excerpt above]. In *Tengo* (1964), Guillén, significantly, speaks specifically as a black man in praise of Castro's Cuba where some allege, including Guillén himself, racial identity is no longer important. Throughout his career it has been his insistence on elevating the black that has given his poetry the extra dimension and excitement that makes him a "classic poet" who "has a clear understanding of his art and an absolute control of his technique, as well as something to say." It is this "something to say" that distinguishes his *Motivos de son* and his later poetry from his earlier nonblack work and that sets his verse off from the *negrista* poetry of his white contemporaries. It is also this "something to say" that had a profound effect on Fernando Ortiz, the white Cuban specialist on things black, whose racist research had provided source material and orientation to white *negrista* poets *prior* to Guillén's appearance and domination of the Cuban literary scene in the late twenties and early thirties.

Guillén not only turned himself and *negrista* poetry around but his theory of *mulatez* seems to have been instrumental in turning Ortiz away from a rather clinical examination of the black largely as isolated criminal and slave and more toward the integration of blacks and whites in Cuba, the essence of Ortiz's well-known concept of *cubanidad*, which he developed in the forties.... Before Guillén's conversion to and insistence on blackness in Cuba, Ortiz was known in part for his *Glosario de Afronegrismos* (1923), a collection of African words and words that sound African that, because of their rhythmic quality, proved useful to the *negrista* poets. He was known also for what can be called his "unholy trinity," a series of works on "el hampa afro-cubano": *Los negros brujos* (1906), *Los negros esclavos* (1916), and "Los negros curros," a lecture he gave in 1911 whose title he had planned to give to a third volume in the trilogy.... Before Guillén, in short, Ortiz's emphasis was on the Cuban black, not on the black Cuban or the mulatto Cuban, and on the "Afro" part of the term "Afro-Cuban"—an isolated, negative part at best.

Guillén's decision, then, during the late twenties and early thirties to write as a black about blacks and to blacks, and to whites and mulattoes, too, was an influential one that represented a new departure for himself and for his contemporaries. But what was the immediate impulse that brought him to that new commitment? Literary historians and Nicolás Guillén, too, usually point to a moment in 1930 when the words and rhythm of *negro bembón* came to the poet in a dreamlike trance after which the *Motivos de son* were written, dashed off, as it were, in white hot heat. But what put him in that trance in the first place?... We know that his turning point was inspired in part by his own personal experiences of racism, by his awareness of worsening economic conditions for blacks in Cuba, and by the control of the black literary and cultural image that was being taken over by white intellectuals like Fernando Ortiz and the *negrista* poets. We know also that Guillén had many local black models to emulate, including his father.... But most of all, I believe, the black model or example set by Langston Hughes provided one of the most immediate sparks.

Langston Hughes, the dean of black poets in the United States, was already famous when he made his second trip to Cuba in February 1930. Guillén met Hughes on this trip, showed him

around, and as a journalist published an interview he had with him that he called **"Conversation with Langston Hughes."** ... For a black writer who had already begun to see that the black problem was really a white problem, the black pride and racial flavor of Langston Hughes' verse and manner had to have an impact on any black, certainly on one who writes. I think what moved Guillén deeper into his blackening process was Langston Hughes' physical or somatic appearance. In Guillén's words, Hughes, "looked just like a little Cuban mulatto. One of those dandies who spends all his time organizing little family parties for two dollars a ticket." This description, of course, is negative, but Guillén's appraisal of "this great Black poet," "one of the souls most interested in the black race," is overwhelmingly positive. The impact for Guillén, I believe, comes with the realization that Hughes, a mulatto like himself, could genuinely identify with blacks with a dedication so intense that his only concern "is to study his people, to translate their experience into poetry, to make it known and loved." When Guillén says that Langston Hughes is unique, we have to understand this statement to mean both Hughes' total concern "with everything related to blacks" and the fact that this concern can come from a mulatto. (pp. 83-8)

It is not surprising, then, that Guillén's conversion to blackness becomes complete shortly after Hughes' departure from the Island.... Nor is it surprising to see the *Ltd.* of Hughes' *Scottsboro Ltd.* (1932) reappear in Guillén's title *West Indies Ltd.* (1934), or to see Guillén try the *son*-form, which sometimes has a blues effect, considering Hughes' earlier success with blues and jazz forms in poetry. One also can see the striking similarity between Guillén's black credo in the prologue to his *Sóngoro cosongo* (1932), especially the part where Guillén says that it does not matter if people are not pleased with what he is doing, and Hughes' own well-known declaration of artistic and racial commitment published five years earlier. He wrote in that piece, "If white people are pleased we are glad. If they are not it doesn't matter... If colored people are pleased we are glad. If they are not their displeasure doesn't matter either." Were it not for such credos firmly rooted in black ethnic identity, it is possible that the later revolutionary vision these two poets developed might not have been so intense. (pp. 89-90)

I see a compatibility between Guillén poet of negritude and Guillén poet of revolutionary Cuba. Guillén need not have continued with the black talk of the *Motivos de son* to be considered a poet of negritude.... Nor was it necessary for him to abandon the black man to be considered a universal poet. Although Guillén now rejects the term negritude that he insists on seeing in its strictest sense, there can be little doubt that he was just as much a forerunner of the term in its strictest racial sense as he is now a leading exponent of what I have called elsewhere the negritude of synthesis, which is negritude understood in a broader sense that does not reject "a quest for an antiracist, possibly universal culture, 'the culminating point of the dream of every serious advocate of Negritude,' a universal brotherhood in which the black man will establish solidarity with all mankind." The organization of this section on the Major Period reflects the central role Guillén played in the development of black consciousness and black literature in Latin America in the thirties and forties, when—under his influence—the black as author became just as visible as the black as subject. This period is major because of the high visibility given the black as author through the appearance of works like Pilar Barrios' *Piel negra* (1947) and Virginia Brindis de Salas' *Pregón de Marimorena* (1947) in Uruguay, Juan

Pablo Sojo's *Nochebuena negra* (1943) in Venezuela. Adalberto Ortiz's *Juyungo* (1943) in Ecuador, and Jorge Artel's *Tambores en la noche* (1940) and Arnoldo Palacios' *Las estrellas son negras* (1949) in Colombia. These works and others such as Guillén's *El son entero* (1947) that follow his initiative of the thirties, made the forties especially a fertile decade for black writers in Latin America. (pp. 90-1)

> Richard L. Jackson, "The Turning Point: The Blackening of Nicolás Guillén and the Impact of his 'Motivos de son'," *in his* Black Writers in Latin America, *University of New Mexico Press, 1979, pp. 80-92.*

O. R. DATHORNE

The heaviest concentration of interest in the Black world came not from Englishmen, Frenchmen, or White Americans, but from Whites in the Spanish-speaking New World. The movement, which was a spin-off from the Harlem Renaissance, sought a symbol for Caribbean man. The wars against Spain for independence meant that the European was not acceptable as a figure of unity, but the African was; therefore, the physical product of Africa and Europe—Mulatto and Mulatta—became for these writers the emblem of New World experience.

In many ways, Negrista was a perversion, for in their frenzy to exalt, these poets and novelists distorted the reality of the Black experience. It may be argued that they were themselves unfamiliar with this experience and hence they needed to invent. Whatever the circumstances, Cuba was the central point of an important way of seeing which lasted until the beginning of World War II. It spread throughout Central and South America and was particularly noticeable in Mexico, Brazil, Argentina, the Dominican Republic, and Puerto Rico. Federico García Lorca visited Cuba and wrote two poems in this vein, giving the movement a kind of European stamp of approval. Negrista poems were also written by writers in Columbia, Costa Rica, Chile, Guatemala, Honduras, Nicaragua, Panama, Peru, El Salvador, Uruguay, and Venezuela.

The literature was Mulatto, which these writers perceived as truly Caribbean. The vestiges of Africa were invested with fanciful notions. The Mulatta was sensuous, happy, and dancing. . . . Parrots, snakes, roosters, drums, rum, the sun, dancing, and music permeate this poetry. A list of names might sometimes suffice to give an apparently African note to the poetry.

This does not emerge from a vacuum. The Cubans were showing Europeans such as Picasso and Gide that homemade images could conjure up an African world in the Caribbean. (pp. 175-76)

The poet who managed to effectively combine song, dance, and laughter with the mistaken excesses of mirth and the piety of religion, as well as the true ache of wounded feelings, was Nicolás Guillén. His anthologists say as much: "While it has always been plain to the point of commonplace that Cuba is a lively protean synthesis, so to speak, of the White Spanish thesis and the Black African antithesis, no one before Guillén had affirmed such a bold affirmation of the latter." They find that Guillén's eight *son* poems achieve an insider's view. What, in effect, he repeats in *Motivos de son* is that people are hungry, do not easily identify with their own blackness, and live in moral squalor. He moved away from this to a fiercer, better poetry in which the harsh hammer of Marxism was hurled against the imperialism he saw in Cuba.

Guillén's advantage was that he wrote in *Motivos de son* authoritative monologues that, while utilizing the *son* much as the Negrista poets had, sought to focus on life in the slums of Havana. (pp. 185-86)

As early as 1930, one hears in **"Bucate plate"** of the search for essentials. A woman's voice speaks for her poverty and how she has to eat crackers. She will run off soon if matters do not improve. The world of *Motivos de son* is one of pimps, whores, and poor people, who wistfully desire the appearance of wealth. **"Negro bembón"** is about a small-time pimp who achieves fanciful desires; the irony is that all he seeks and gets is a white suit, two-tone shoes and a life free of the doldrum of work. But, as Guillén reminds us, in the refrain throughout the poem, he is still "Negro bembón" (nigger lips).

Motivos de son was reissued with eight new poems as *Sóngoro cosongo*. The title itself was clearly a *jitanjáfora*, meant to conjure up Africa, although Guillén himself had described this as "Mulatto" poetry. Some of the poetry is remarkably modern; for instance, the Black woman's praise could have been done by Haki R. Madhubuti or Imamu Baraka in the United States.

> Con el circulo ecuatorial
> ceñido a la cintura como a un pequño mundo
> la negra, mujer nueva
> avanza en su ligera bata de serpiente
>
> With the circle of the equator
> tied round her waist like a small world
> the Black woman, the New Woman
> advances in her airy morning serpent gown.

Certainly there is exaggeration; the movement, the serpent, and even the circle, suggesting the procession, are elements from the earlier Negrista poetry of Tallet and Guirao. But there is a different feeling here—of discovery. The stereotyping is no longer part of the poetry, though conceivably it may well be argued that the Black woman is stereotyped. Guillén radiates a freshness. He says in *Sóngoro cosongo* that "the word comes to us humid from the forests," and perhaps this is what is occurring in the poetry. Sometimes he falls back into the Negrista morass, as in **"Canto negro,"** which is full of *a* and *o* sounds, *jitanjáfora*, and drum and dance sounds. "Tamba, tamba, tamba, tamba, tamba del negro que tumba"—the happy Black man is dancing again. Here Guillén stops, for he handles neither the favorite *comparsa* theme nor the violent sweaty lovemaking of dancing Blacks. From these early poems he recognized the absurdity of distortion. (pp. 186-88)

Guillén's sound in his first two volumes is that of a jeer. It is directed at the self, for allowing the dreadful visitation of poverty and American overlordship and for turning the other cheek. Biblical references, absent in later poetry, are found here and there. The poetry is still seeking an authentic voice. One sees the duality in *West Indies Ltd,* epitomized in the well-known **"Balada de los dos abuelos,"** wherein the African past becomes a point of tension. Who is Afro-New World man, the poem asks. Should he harken to the lighter or the darker side? No pat solution is given; the poem recites the dilemma.

Guillén saw the connections in the Black world of the thirties and the manner in which Blacks in Cuba and the United States were related. He was a friend of Langston Hughes and had read his poetry. *West Indies Ltd* expanded his concerns beyond Cuba to the entire Caribbean. He did not join the Communist party until 1937, and it is fair to see *West Indies Ltd* as both a swan song and a new start. In ["**West Indies Ltd**"], several tones may be noted. The West Indies is berated partly as Aimé Césaire does in his *Cahier d'un retour au pays 'natal* (1939), and equally the West Indies is laughed at, as Palés Matos does in "Elegía del Duque de la Mermelada." But it is praised and commended.

Overall the tone is one of irony and bitterness, unlike *Motivos de son*. Here the poet seemingly speaks with his own voice and on behalf of a wider group. The Cuban dictator, Machado, had been deposed in 1933, and the laissez faire conditions that predated his downfall must have struck deeply at Guillén. But it is certainly not a Negrista poem about Cuba; indeed there are no *jitanjáfora* or Negrista jargon, but only one harsh repetition. Instead, familiar images from Guillén's two previous books are given a new significance. The reference to "un oscuro pueblo sonriente" (a smiling dark populace) is meant to be as harsh as it sounds. There are no good points given here for laughing, since life is always tragic.

No dignity is awarded to the laborer—Black, White, Chinese, or Mulatto. The past is shameful, for "bajo el relampagueante traje de dril/andamos todavía con taparrabos" (beneath the dazzling white drill of our clothes we still wear loincloths). The reference here is interesting if only to show how far Guillén had departed from the romantic notions of his Negrista peers. This is the beginning of the criticism of a downgraded people, and he refers to "puertos que hablan un inglés que empieza en *yes* y acaba en *yes*" (ports in which they speak a type of English which begins with yes and ends with yes).

The image of the fist reappears. Previously the Black man had been enjoined to use his fist to shape a new world. Here the fist is helpless, for the Black man does not recognize his own self-worth and is therefore incapable of destroying the negative images of himself.

Sugarcane is the real villain, and it is mentioned implicitly in the poem. In addition to this it takes on a larger dimension. Just as the laborers burn the fields before cutting the cane, so must a revolution erupt in order to get rid of the large landowners. The music of the cha-cha is not the docile sound of Mulattoes dancing. So when he writes, "Cortar cabezas coma cañas / ¡chas, chas, chas, chas!" (Cut down heads like cane / cha, cha, cha, cha!), this is no musical adornment.... And when he adds, "Arder las cañas y cabezas" (Burn both canes and heads), he achieves a violent climax in which images and message are superbly fused in poetry that reveals the depth of his anguish and a reminder of slavery, past and present, in the criticism of a poor people who seem to seek nothing. The child who plays at killing another child is an injunction to act, to do away with weak conformity. The end is superb and triumphant with the reappearance of fire, palms, sugar, coffee, and the American exploitation of the West Indies. Then once again the image of "un puño vengativo" (a vengeful fist) appears, followed by "son de esperanza estalla en tierra y oceano" (the *son* of hope bursting over land and ocean). The year was 1934; Guillén had anticipated the Castro revolution by a quarter of a century.

Guillén's importance underscores the Negrista movement. What he emphasized was surely this: there had been no past models for him or the poets who were his contemporaries. There was folklore and, when not distorted, Mama Inéz, a kind of earth mother who appeared with monotonous regularity, to link the poets more firmly to their roots. The two Black writers in Cuba who had preceded Guillén—Juan Francisco Manzano and Ga-

briel de la Concepción Valdés (or Plácido)—wanted "to 'bleach out' any strains of a darker sensibility." They cannot be faulted for this, since in large measure, they were products of a Spanish mind. The leaders of the Negrista movement—Camín, Guirao, Tallet, Valdés, and Ballagas—saw the Black experience in a fanciful and exotic manner. Guillén's task was to alter their oversweet simplifications and show the complications of blackness, not just for Cuba, but for the entire Caribbean. (pp. 188-91)

> O. R. Dathorne, "Afro-New World Movements: Harlem Renaissance, Negrista, and Négritude," in his Dark Ancestor: The Literature of the Black Man in the Caribbean, *Louisiana State University Press, 1981, pp. 172-209.*

KEITH ELLIS

The reader of twentieth-century 'Western' poetry is normally receptive to an approach to poetry that is quite different from Guillén's. In the English-speaking world, it is usual to encounter readers who consider such poets as T. S. Eliot, W. H. Auden, and Robert Lowell to have registered and defined the nature of modern consciousness. Modern consciousness so defined—and to such definers may be added such Third World poets as Octavio Paz, Jorge Luis Borges, and Derek Walcott—usually has to do with a sense of lostness, of the alienation of the individual in an abusive, confused, disintegrating, absurd society. These contemporary versions of the *poète maudit* tend to make of poetry a means of self-affirmation. In the quest for identity and for nirvanas, society is sweepingly shown to be unsatisfactory, no gesture being made to rectify its specific defects. Thus Lowell as candid spokesman says: 'We are free to say what we want to, and somehow what we want to say is the confusion and sadness and incoherence of the human condition.' Personal systems are constructed based on unique perceptions and reactions supplemented by borrowings from exotic, often nihilistic, religious and philosophical currents, on claims to transcendence and a heavy reliance on irony—irony as a way of life, as characteristic of the 'human condition' rather than irony of the kind found in Guillén's work that is applied to specific social situations from a clear moral perspective. Conceits involving the abstruse reconciling of apparently dissimilar elements are common; and since the search for identity spurs a corresponding search for a supposed primordial purity of the word, hermeticism results and is usually accorded positive value. The contemporary reader, accustomed to the challenge of deciphering such obscure poetry, may well tend to regard as superficial, and react superciliously to, poetry that seems readily intelligible. But an illusion is at play here, for the difficulty present in poems that deal with idiosyncratic poetic visions and systems is in most cases one-dimensional because once the text has been deciphered, the game is over. The reader has had a viewing of a private world where factors such as maturity, cogency, and accountable knowledge are largely irrelevant. By contrast, the long literary tradition formed by the probingly humanist production of such writers as Aeschylus, Dante, Cervantes, and several Spanish-American writers—and to which Guillén has made his contribution in keeping with the scientific advances available to him—is multidimensional. Within this tradition the artistic means are remarkable in themselves, and they possess an altruistic function that is not limited to the promotion of art. They are used to evoke a critical view of a wide range of mankind's vital social experience. The reader is thus faced with the task of appraising artistic means that are bound up with aspects of the comprehensive viewing of society as these aspects are exposed. The reader is obliged to make reference to several areas of knowledge in the process of reading, and depth and maturity of vision become relevant considerations.

In Guillén's case, the reader is required to assess the effects of numerous artistic forms, for one of the attributes of Guillén's poetry is the functioning (with the result of clarity rather than obscurity) of semantic and musical devices that are not exceeded either in abundance or in range by the princes of darkness. Also, his integrative outlook is comprehensive, revealing itself in an attitude that is unfriendly to a disassociated cultural epistemology and in favour of linking the humanities with the sciences, of mobilizing 'sputniks y sonetos' in a unified struggle against backwardness. The reader must, therefore, have a capacity for absorbing material from the various fields with which he deals: from art, economics, history, literature, music, philosophy, politics, science, sociology, and sports. He must also be respectful of his fellow man. In fact, this last quality helps him to understand that the tendency to grasp the meaning of phenomena without the constraints of academic disciplines is widespread among readers and potential readers, and that works in this transdisciplinary vein are apt to be perceived or received naturally as being reflective of life as it is normally lived. Nor does such a reader necessarily defer to the specialist even in matters that in this context of comprehensiveness touch on the specialist's own field. It might be said, for instance, that because of his natural interest in growth, development, and the humanitarian ends of his labour, the ordinary worker is likely to have a better understanding of some essential aspects of economics than even a renowned economist of the monetarist school. Also, at a time when attempts are being made to lend reverence to the expression 'cado loco con su tema' ('to each madman his obsession') and irrationality and Dionysian attitudes are widespread (due to the efforts of such schools of psychiatry as that headed by R. D. Laing), the reader must resist the temptation to see any paradox in the fact that Guillén is a poet of accountable rationality. Where this poetry goes against the grain of the reader's ideological formation, which will usually be the case in the English-speaking world and indeed in most of the Spanish-speaking world as well, he must show at least that 'willing suspension of disbelief' that Coleridge influentially prescribed for the appreciation of literature. But preferably he should read Guillén soberly; for the solid rationality that underlies his creations makes them apprehendable as truth and illustrations of how ever-broadening experience serves to determine consciousness. The steady expansion of consciousness, reflected in the content of successive books, forms an overall pattern that contrasts with the circularity, the trip from infancy toward maturity and back in old age, often found in the works of poets where the 'I' presumes to remove itself from its broad, evolving circumstances.

The opening up of paths to various fields is another aspect of the developmental attitude underlying Guillén's work. His wide span of interests has been channelled, by an ideological outlook that has grown in firmness with time, into a powerful current of poetry. Always a conscientious artist, he mastered early the conventional forms of Hispanic poetry and soon contributed innovations and variations, some of which derived from his discernment of the artistic possibilities of popular Cuban culture. This innovative virtuosity has constantly permitted him to find forms appropriate to expressing, first, advanced insights into the conditions of his country—for Cuba is the trunk of the tree of his poetry—and the universal ramifications of these insights. The lucidity and impeccable gracefulness with which his social perceptions emerge from his poems and the mature coherence of his total work make this Cuban, West Indian, and Spanish-American poet an outstanding international figure who occupies a high and secure place in the history of poetry. (pp. 212-14)

Keith Ellis, in his Cuba's Nicolás Guillén: Poetry and Ideology, *University of Toronto Press, 1983, 251 p.*

Tina Howe

1937-

American dramatist.

Howe's plays feature eccentric characters who interact in such unusual dramatic settings as a museum, restaurant, or beach. Howe, who stated that she views life in "absurdist, antic terms," explained: "I discovered that you could have a lunatic point of view if you transported the audience to some exotic locale, so I set out to find settings never put onstage before and somehow animate them, show that stories could take place there too." Blending humorous dialogue, slapstick, and satire, Howe explores such topics as creativity, art, human relationships, and behavioral peculiarities. Ross Wetzsteon described Howe's work: "The extravagance of her surfaces, the quirky characters and daffy dialogue, interact with the black passions of the interiors to form plays that can best be characterized as poetic farces, as antic elegies."

Museum (1976), Howe's first major play, is set in the contemporary art wing of a municipal museum. Through the remarks and actions of casual observers and patrons who comment upon the exhibits, Howe exposes characteristic pretensions of artists and connoisseurs while commenting upon the impact of modern art. *The Art of Dining* (1979) is set in a gourmet restaurant owned and operated by a married couple. By focusing on the offbeat behavior of the owners and customers, Howe explores human idiosyncrasies and underscores the individual's need for emotional connection with others. Critics were particularly impressed with Howe's slapstick depiction of a socially inept female author who relates her troubled childhood to her publisher.

In *Painting Churches* (1983), one of her most acclaimed works, Howe concentrates on the complexities of human relationships. This play centers on three members of an elite Boston family: a distinguished elderly poet, who shows signs of senility; his wife, who longs for the romance and affluence of their past and who must come to terms with her husband's condition; and their daughter, a young painter, who seeks her parents' approval. Containing humor and pathos, the play addresses such concerns as aging, mortality, and strained familial relationships. *Museum, The Art of Dining,* and *Painting Churches* are collected in *Three Plays by Tina Howe* (1984).

Howe's recent play, *Coastal Disturbances* (1986), is set on a private beach and revolves around a romance between a lifeguard and a vacationing photographer. Their relationship is observed and commented upon by various affluent characters whose complex emotions are revealed through a series of impressionistic vignettes. Moira Hodgson lauded *Coastal Disturbances* as "a charming play, a landscape of the human heart in miniature."

(See also *Contemporary Authors,* Vol. 109.)

CLIVE BARNES

It certainly looks like a play, and often it sounds like a play. It has the feel of a play, and almost the dimensions of a play. But it isn't a play. The play in question is Tina Howe's *Museum.* . . .

Museum is really an extended revue sketch—sometimes bitchily funny, but overextended, shapeless, revelling in cheap laughs at easy targets (the French or homosexuals, for example) and offering no viewpoint. This is one art show that is almost pre-Giotto in its lack of perspective.

Miss Howe . . . does here, however, reveal a shrewd satiric eye. Her caricatures are certainly campily exaggerated, but many of them are rooted either in truth or the popular truisms of prejudice. She is particularly good on the jargon of art talk and art attitudes—possibly she was once bitten on the leg by a hydrophobic art critic wandering around a gallery.

Museum is nothing but a collage of jokes and a fresco of characters. It is set in an art gallery on the last day of an exhibition called "The Broken Silence." In this gallery the silence is broken like a reed. Every crank and weirdo in town comes in to talk—although I must admit I did not notice a transvestite. Miss Howe did miss that one. (p. 344)

A lot of it is very funny—a Japanese photographer who eventually turns out as coming from the Midwest, a suburban couple dutifully wandering round linked by the umbilical cord of one of those tape recorded tours of the exhibit, the phlegm of guards and the hilarity of philistines. And also there is the sense of exposing modern art, like the Emperor's new clothes, for the fraud the author thinks it is.

In many ways—and all of them unfavorably—the work resembles a Jerome Robbins ballet, which I imagine Miss Howe has never even seen. She seems the sort of person more happy reading about art than actually experiencing it. The ballet was *The Concert,* and it is a wonderful phantasmagoria into the behavior, attitudes, emotions and fancies of people at a piano recital.

Now Robbins is a genius and it is unfair to compare a mature work by him with a long sketch by a young playwright. Yet you felt that Robbins loved music, loved Chopin, and even loved the very people he was gently, but hilariously, mocking. Miss Howe seems to hate art and all the people associated with it. And this approach, even disregarding the obvious disparity in their proficiencies at their chosen professions, is what makes all the difference.

Don't mistake me. There are plenty of laughs here, a decent sense of irreverence, and a most amusing puncturing of pretentiousness. All this is fine, but in my submission it does not add up to even a short play, and its satiric material would have found a happier home in some other medium—such as revue, cabaret or even television. (pp. 344-45)

I imagine some people will enjoy *Museum* a lot—responding both to its zaniness as well as its satire. It frankly caught me on the wrong side of my conscience—and even while it amused me, it annoyed me. But never trust a puritan. (p. 345)

> Clive Barnes, ''Art Is Off the Wall in Howe's 'Museum','' in New York Post, *February 2, 1978. Reprinted in* New York Theatre Critics' Reviews, *Vol. XXXIX, No. 5, 1978, pp. 344-45.*

RICHARD EDER

[*Museum*] gives us the pictures' point of view. That is, the three exhibits in the unchanging white gallery remain fixed for the whole time, except for one which may or may not be having a mystical experience. It is the people who flash by and blur.

They come on singly or in pairs. The whole play is, in fact, a series of entrances. Each person or couple stumbles in at some point of personal extremity. Each represents a single mood, a single condition or obsession or quest. And gradually the gallery becomes a parable of humanity, a kind of City of Man.

There is fog in the streets. The play's form is a comedy of absurdities with a serious message. It is serious but it is also extremely diffuse. Whiffs of message seem to emerge but they are ambiguous. Essentially the play is as abstract as the three exhibits onstage.

Each of the three engages different visitors and in different ways. One is a series of three totally white paintings along one wall, by a French painter described as ''a reductionist.'' His mother and father could neither hear nor speak, we are told, and so he discovered expression for himself. At the play's end the old couple appear and observe, mutely, their son's work.

The observation extends to us, the audience. More of the paintings are hung on the stage's ''fourth wall,'' and so the visitors move around studying first canvasses that we see and then the canvasses that we are. We know what a picture feels: The eyes that look at us are clogged with their own fantasies.

Aside from the parents, the blank white paintings attract a voluble and assertive French couple, a rapt schoolgirl, and a matter-of-fact student who, in the best *New Yorker* cartoon style, sits down to sketch them.

Along another wall there is a very different exhibit—a series of soft sculptures of people, all hung from clothesline. Another schoolgirl is drawn to this one: She wants to be laundered and hung up beside them. A basket of clothespins on the floor attracts a whole parade of would-be pilferers.

The third exhibit, on pedestals, is a series of sculptures made out of bird and animal bones. . . .

The visitors do all kinds of things, some very funny. There are two young shoppers with Bergdorf Goodman shopping bags. . . . Quite ignoring the exhibits, they talk about a man. Not the man himself but his clothes, or rather the fabric of his clothes. They are obsessed with fabrics and the grim future when all fabrics will be synthetic.

Their conversation becomes entangled with that of two homosexuals whose own vision of Armageddon is not synthetic fabrics but the rising price of museum admissions. . . .

There are other visitors who do a lot or a little to enliven these tenuous proceedings. . . .

And linking all these disparate visitors there is the Guard, an everyman, a master of ceremonies, a man who is trying to hold off the world's chaos. . . . [He] is refreshingly tangible, as he talks about ''his'' exhibits and tries desperately to protect ''his'' clothespins. He takes everything personally, like the museum guards in Houston who say ''Howdy'' every time somebody wanders into their particular gallery.

At the end, when he is briefly absent, the visitors descend upon the soft sculptures and rip them apart.

Is the play about how civilization destroys artists? Is it about how people use art for their own selfish fantasies? Is it about the selfishness of art, remaining aloof from humanity?

When the guard returns he has an explanation, of sorts. ''They wanted more,'' he says. Maybe so. So do we. . . . [*Museum*] is sometimes interesting and sometimes funny and sometimes expressive. But it never commits itself clearly to what it is expressing, and it never really makes much of an impression.

> Richard Eder, ''Paintings Are 'Museum' Characters,'' in The New York Times, *February 28, 1978, p. 28.*

JOHN BEAUFORT

Museum is as much fun as a Feiffer cartoon of an avant garde event. Playwright Tina Howe has chosen the closing day of a group show at the Municipal Museum of Art for her once-over-lightly satire of contemporary art, its mystique, affectations, and its sometimes mystified devotees. Clearly a veteran of the museum and gallery scene, Miss Howe has observed and eavesdropped with wicked attention to every affectation, delirious gasp, and philistine guffaw expressed by frequenters of these cultural haunts. The carryings on have amazed and amused her, and she shares her reactions in a sharply comic theatrical essay.

Venturing into the gleaming, pleasantly proportioned gallery space . . . are a cross-section of the museum-going public. It includes sophisticates and would-be sophisticates; novices and veterans; three photographers and a copyist; some tourist types with inevitably uncontrollable walkie-talkie cassettes; ardent admirers of the three artists represented; and a trio of matrons whose hysterics over the white-on-white abstracts is exceeded only by their wonder at the real, round-headed clothespins in the laundry basket beneath a papier-mache Construction hanging on a clothesline.

The Construction is part of an exhibition entitled, "The Broken Silence." The constructionist shares the special exhibit in the museum's American contemporary wing with an abstractionist and a sculptor of found objects. When "Prometheus Singed" catches fire, *Museum* really takes off. In the course of her 80-minute dissertation, Miss Howe manages to touch on a catalog of latter-day phenomena from plastics to vandalism, from artistic fads to the fate of the museum itself as an institution. . . .

Miss Howe is a dramatist to watch.

> *John Beaufort, in a review of "Museum," in* The Christian Science Monitor, *March 1, 1978, p. 26.*

EDITH OLIVER

[*Museum*] is an enchanting show—a comedy set in a municipal art museum during the last day of " 'The Broken Silence,' a special exhibit of the Contemporary American Wing." The play is itself a collage of words and characters and action, as various spectators drift in and comment on the art works on view. These include, most spectacularly, a clothesline hung with dressed dummies, with a basket of clothespins beneath it, and some glass display cases containing found objects—mostly feathers and animal skeletons. And, of course, there is no lack of invisible paintings on invisible walls. At the opening, an announcement over a loudspeaker tells us that a picture at the Uffizi Gallery, in Florence, has been shot and destroyed; and, indeed, the whole play has an elusive, valedictory air about art—all art, that is, and maybe even Western civilization, if it comes to that. A girl meditates on the possibility that museums will disappear as structures and people will become the view; a woman comes in, looks at the pictures, starts to cry, and leaves; a number of bewildered people wander through, searching for hooked rugs and quilts. The characters' response to the modernist movement in American art, as here displayed, ranges from the ecstasy of three girls, one of whom actually hugs the dummies on the clothesline, through the wild laughter of a trio of middle-aged women, to the downright savagery of a number of spectators at the end. But Miss Howe's airborne play is anything but dogged or "theme-y" or insistent. It has plenty of wit and humour, and no idea appears to be emphasized over any other. Each successive incident builds and then dissipates, yet the play takes shape and holds firm. (pp. 67-8)

All is clear; the humor, which could so easily have got out of hand, is always in key; and the emotions, big and small, are believable. (p. 68)

> *Edith Oliver, "The Gallery," in* The New Yorker, *Vol. LIV, No. 3, March 6, 1978, pp. 67-8.*

WALTER KERR

In most plays about restaurants the people are real and the props are fake. In Tina Howe's *The Art of Dining,* . . . the props are real and the people are fake.

It's not a fair exchange. The sight of all that luscious food, cooked and uncooked, is only apt to make you hungry, no matter how satisfactory your pre-theater repast may have been. Virtually the first thing on view, as the lights go up on an immaculately appointed kitchen, is an absolutely stunning bass, rippling and gleaming in its dewy freshness as Ellen—who is both proprietress and sole cook—fondles it as though it were a newborn babe. You have a feeling that her intense fondness for the creature is going to preclude her popping it into any oven, even though customers are beginning to straggle into the stain-glass dining room beyond.

She steels herself, though, and into the oven it goes. After all, she can lavish her oohs and ahs, her gurgles and coos, on the eggs she is taking a whisk to as she dashes off a Hollandaise sauce. . . .

Ellen is married to Cal, who has floated a sizable loan to open their new Golden Carousel restaurant, with its antique merry-go-round horses mounted proudly near the windows. Cal has a treacherous dual relationship with the props. He is so dazzlingly efficient at slicing lined-up rows of mushrooms—they fall like dominoes under the lightning-bolt fury of his attack—that his expertise earns him the first, and possibly the solidest, applause of the evening.

On the other hand, he is morally incapable of keeping his fingers out of the foods being prepared. While worrying about his profits, he is eating them. Gone are the grapes that were to have been served with the duck. . . . Having eaten up the fresh fruits, he must finally resort to canned peaches for garnishing; these he downs whole, drinking the juice as a chaser. Ellen gets very mad at him.

The customers scarcely seem to notice they're not quite getting what they ordered. (The Golden Carousel is becoming phenomenally popular, for reasons Miss Howe does not pause to explain.) At one table a husband and wife are preoccupied with offering champagne toasts to themselves, to their children, to the husband's long and curly eyelashes, to the wife's "terrific pair of snowy white thighs." They do not seem to be drunk.

At another, three "girls" of indeterminate age are celebrating the birthday of one by fighting over who ordered what, by announcing themselves "stuffed" after something less than a bite, by settling down to a discussion of the respective qualities of their breasts. They do not seem to be congenial, or interesting.

If the playwright has at least the beginnings of a few comic notions for the couple in the kitchen, she seems to have applied no energy at all to making her diners worth listening to; they are either speaking at cross purposes in lines of equal length, or subsiding into grumpy monosyllables. Automata is what they are. With one most startling and satisfying exception.

Arriving to meet a publisher over dinner, a young, pretty, near-sighted girl, comes within inches of wrecking the restaurant before she has quite been seated; scattering the contents of her purse as though there were chickens to feed, walking into a four-wheeled serving table that immediately takes on a life of its own, permitting herself to be forcibly seated and virtually lifted to her table, she is a menace and at once a delight. . . .

The Art of Dining neither goes anywhere nor says anything in its hour-and-a-half course. It's a one-finger exercise for its author, not so much a play as an eavesdrop.

> Walter Kerr, "Stage: One Star for 'Art of Dining'— Dianne Wiest," in The New York Times, *December 7, 1979, p. C23.*

BRENDAN GILL

[*The Art of Dining* is] a delightful little comedy, about a couple of young people who have just opened a restaurant somewhere in New Jersey and are not very good at running it. An assortment of customers drift in, drink, eat, chat, and undergo a few infinitesimal misadventures, whereupon, to our astonishment but not our dismay, the play is over. . . . Miss Howe at her best . . . [is reflected in her creation] of a sensationally awkward, nearsighted young writer, who, dining with her middle-aged publisher, manages to spill a full plate of soup into her lap and on being furnished with a second plate drowns her lipstick in it. Is it possible that comedy, so long in short supply, is enjoying a revival? To have had *The Art of Dining* . . . at the same time as *The Sorrows of Stephen* may be a benign portent. (pp. 100, 102)

> Brendan Gill, "Surviving" in The New Yorker, *Vol. LV, No. 44, December 17, 1979, pp. 100, 102.*

JOHN SIMON

I liked Tina Howe's last play, **Museum,** in which, by capturing one day in the life of a room in a megalopolitan museum, she managed to convey a good deal—not so much about the art world, though some museum personnel were deliciously lampooned, as about the world in general as it impinges on art, and as art brings out its pretensions and manias. The subject was large enough, and the human vignettes that flitted across the stage—whether artists, museum staff, or visitors of every stripe—constituted a sufficient microcosm for ecumenical satire. Now, however, in *The Art of Dining,* Miss Howe has set her sights too low: a husband-and-wife team of waiter and cook who run a gourmet restaurant in New Jersey, and the seven patrons who, on a freezing winter night, come to thaw out in the warmth of good food and drink. But these nine simply aren't enough to make a revealing cross section of anything, and eating itself (at least as handled by Miss Howe) does not prove an adequate vehicle for incisive comments on the human condition. We have to make do with the non-gourmet fare of a thin gruel of jokes and superficial observations.

A wife who is absorbed in her cookery (sublimation?) and a husband who, while drooling over future profits, absentmindedly gobbles up the irreplaceable ingredients of his wife's culinary marvels (overcompensation for sexual failure?) and sabotages both the quality of the dishes and his wife's morale— there is no diverse or great comic-dramatic potential in this, especially since we are never told what causes the wife's overzealousness at the stove and the husband's esurient depredations. They remain sources of gags and farcical recrimination, and the wife's motive for going on a temporary strike, but they do not illuminate the relationship.

That middle-aged diners have come up with an erotics of eating (pointing to items on each other's menus becomes a form of sexual stimulation) or that a trio of bachelor women celebrating the birthday of one of them should play musical chairs with their dishes (each grabbing another's order and claiming it as

her own) is neither particularly funny nor especially character-revealing and just barely, if at all, believable. Though these two sets of table companions occasionally prove smile-worthy, they never achieve the veracity of roundedness or the vivacity of insight.

The couple at the third table is more interesting. She is an aging, unmarried fiction writer whose collection of short stories, to her own utter bewilderment, the publisher who invited her to dinner will bring out. She has had a troubled childhood and an adulterated adulthood; she cannot eat and is so deep-seatedly maladroit as to wreck or at least gravely imperil every object remotely within her reach. And she keeps jabbering away in pear-shaped paragraphs about her wretched childhood and outlandish mess of a mother—all stories guaranteed to cut off her publisher's appetite, however potent and entrenched. The way in which the authoress undermines her host's gustatory joys is, at times, riotously funny, and the awkwardnesses that pass between the two range from bumptious farce to inchoate pathos.

Nice, but not enough. Every group of diners, like the restaurateurs, goes schematically from banter to vituperation, then, after a minor crisis, to reconciliation through food. In the process, some workaday follies and foibles pertaining to the making and consuming of food, along with a very few others, do get skewered, but there is hardly enough of them for one order of shish kebab. The triviality of it all is not conducive to highly developed performances: Exaggeration, repetitiveness, and coasting along surfaces is all we can expect and almost all we get. (p. 73)

> John Simon, "Undercooked and Begrimed," in New York *Magazine, Vol. 12, No. 50, December 24, 1979, pp. 73-4.*

HAROLD CLURMAN

A tasty dish is offered us in Tina Howe's *The Art of Dining.* . . . It is a sprightly celebration of the culinary craft. . . .

Tina Howe has a special curiosity and a knack of thumbnail cartoons—*New Yorker* fashion—of oddball figures in our metropolitan areas. This penchant for rapid sketches of "way-out" creatures (who are actually types we might observe everywhere around us, if we had the author's quick eye) was already evident in *Museum.* . . . The "marionettes" in that play haunted an art exhibit. *The Art of Dining* focuses to even pleasanter effect on a suburban eatery that aspires to *haute cuisine* status.

The most brilliant snapshot in this gallery is the character of Elizabeth Barrow Colt who, I vow, is as gifted as she is screwy. Our literary culture has greatly benefited by a bevy of such dislocated and ill-adjusted females blessed with a keen sense of everyone in their environment. These women have the ability to set down in writing things pungent or pathetic with unerring accuracy and dispatch. (p. 30)

> Harold Clurman, "Theater," in The Nation, *New York, Vol. 230, No. 1, January 5-12, 1980, pp. 28-30.*

FRANK RICH

Margaret Church, known as Mags, is a young artist about to have her first one-woman show at a 57th Street gallery. Her specialty is painting portraits in an impressionistic style that's been acclaimed as "a weird blend" of Bonnard, Cassatt and Hockney. In Tina Howe's *Painting Churches,* Mags returns to her childhood Beacon Hill home to do just what the play's title promises—to paint a portrait of her elderly Brahmin parents, Gardner and Fanny Church.

The painting, though eventually completed, is never revealed to the audience. What we see instead is a play that provides a portrait of the Churches in the exact, ravishing style of Mags's art. *Painting Churches* . . . is in the dreamiest impressionistic spirit. It remakes reality with delicate, well-chosen brush strokes, finding beauty and truth in the abstract dance of light on a familiar landscape.

Were it rendered in an ordinary, flatly representational manner—the theatrical equivalent of, say, Norman Rockwell—this play's landscape would be unbearably familiar: it's another family drama in which the prodigal child returns home to resolve her relationship with her parents, even as the parents settle scores with each other. The accompanying themes—the indignities of old age and death, the misunderstandings between generations—summon up the dread specter of *On Golden Pond.* It's a high compliment to Miss Howe, the author of *The Art of Dining* and *Museum,* that the old bones of her material rarely peek through her writing's high, lacy gloss.

The play is set at a time of transition for all three characters. As Mags is about to start her career in New York, so her parents are winding one down in Boston: they're packing up their belongings to move permanently to their summer cottage on Cape Cod. Gardner, a revered poet who was once the peer of Pound and Frost, is increasingly "ga-ga" of mind and short of cash. "His last Pulitzer Prize didn't even cover the real-estate taxes on this place," explains Fanny, a grande dame who is angry at her husband for preceding her into senescence.

What makes *Painting Churches* surprising and involving is the playwright's Jamesian use of shifting points of view. In Act I, our sympathies are with the daughter and doddering father. Both seem to be neglected by the domineering, selfish mother, who is more concerned with maintaining her wardrobe and patrician airs than her family's emotional needs. But Miss Howe redeems Fanny in Act II by showing us the full severity of the lonely burden this proud woman now bears, as well as the frailties of her husband and child. "If you want to paint us," she says to her daughter late in the play, "paint us as we really are." In *Painting Churches,* both Mags and the audience are taught the same lesson in perception: whether painting or observing a family portrait, it's essential to see beyond the surface reality.

A few lapses aside, Miss Howe is both subtle and humorful as she deepens our perspective on the Churches. A monologue in which Fanny remembers the sexual thrill of sledding with the young Gardner becomes a fading but vibrant glimpse into a passionate marriage that time has disfigured. When Mags recalls how she once melted crayons on a radiator to get revenge on her parents for punishing her, the speech proves a telling account of how the girl first found her "own materials" and "abilities" as an artist. Yet, once Gardner and Fanny fill in their own selective memories of the same incident, the speech becomes an equally incisive paradigm of the missed connections that have haunted this family for a lifetime. . . .

[The] Churches' living room could well be both Mags's and the author's blank canvas. It's been stripped of most furniture and shrouded with gray canvas in anticipation of the new tenants' paint job. A spring glow hangs in the air; the mural-like Colonial wallpaper has faded into a non-representational impressionistic swirl.

But this composition, like Mags's, can only be finished when Gardner and Fanny finally arrive at their most truly revealing pose. They find it on moving day, when they waltz around the room one last time, emulating the dancers in their favorite, half-remembered Renoir. As they do so, the portrait of the Churches on stage perfectly fits the judgment Gardner has rendered about the daughter's completed portrait a few moments earlier. "The whole thing shimmers," he says, in a line of art criticism that can also serve as an apt description of Miss Howe's lovely play.

Frank Rich, "Theater: Bostonian Life in 'Painting Churches'," in The New York Times, *February 9, 1983, p. C16.*

JOHN SIMON

Painting Churches, by Tina Howe, is as surprising as its title. The Churches being painted turn out to be Gardner and Fanny Church, a Boston Brahmin couple. He is a distinguished poet sliding into dotage; she, his eccentric and giddy, but still fundamentally sane, wife. They have sold their Beacon Hill house and are packing up to move into a small Cotuit cottage. The painter is their reasonably batty daughter, Mags, who is beginning to make it as an artist in New York. She will do one last double portrait in the bare living room—wintry, though outside it is spring—and help with the packing. Before the inevitable "exeunt severally," there is to be some drinking and fighting, and quite a bit of reminiscing and mutual revelation. It is an old story, but, among these blue-bloods and artists, it takes on an odd slant, more wistful and extravagant, that points private truth toward universality.

Miss Howe, with all that authentic background behind her, with wit, sympathy, and a kind of devil-may-care *désinvolture* to spare, shows how curiously brilliance and naivety, politeness and intransigence, magnanimity and cattiness can cohabit in these three beings who exacerbate and sustain one another with their tenuous, inexact yet loving, outreach. In the first half, a comic, even absurdist, abandon prevails, with the emphasis on the trio's dottiness. Then, as Gardner becomes more senile and sweetly pathetic (as well as difficult) by the minute, the women reveal the strength beneath their bizarreness, the endurance under the flutteriness. [Howe] has demonstrated in previous plays her ability to meld the grotesque and the touching; here the fusion glistens with the pride of a successful alloy. Occasional longueurs and exaggerations disappear into the overall iridescence; these gallant, outlandish people are irresistible. (p. 54)

John Simon, "The Miller's Stale," in New York Magazine, *Vol. 16, No. 8, February 21, 1983, pp. 52, 54.*

ROBERT BRUSTEIN

Tina Howe's *Painting Churches* has been warmly received, and I'd like to add a cheer and a half. The playwright is sensitive and civilized. . . . Yet this study of family life in disintegration struck me as mild, dusty, slightly contrived. Presumably the playwright (the daughter of the late radio commentator Quincey Howe) is working out her problems with her parents, but although this promises something resembling the tortured excavations of *A Long Day's Journey,* what we get instead is the dotty charm of *You Can't Take It With You,* the eccentric mannerisms of *Arsenic and Old Lace.* The father and mother are comically absent-minded; the daughter, who has come to paint them, is giddy and hysterical; the early events amuse us with the way Dad wears his overcoat and three scarves inside the house ("Gee, it's hot in here") and tries to talk with his mouth stuffed with saltines.

In the second act, the play turns darker, as we discover that Father suffers from senility and incontinence, and Mother harbors recriminations over her daughter's selfish failure to recognize his condition or share responsibility for it (you may remember [in *Death of a Salesman*] Linda Loman charging Biff and Happy with similar failures in regard to Willy), but by this time it's a little late to instill a somber mood—especially when the playwright is more concerned with getting the parents to accept their daughter than with depicting their bleak future once they move to Cotuit. (p. 24)

> Robert Brustein, "*Squares in the Circle*," *in* The New Republic, *Vol. 188, No. 13, April 4, 1983, pp. 22-4.*

GERALD WEALES

Tina Howe's *Painting Churches* is one of those remarkably theatrical plays which manage to stir up doubts about both genre and contents even while it entertains. It begins in monologue as Fanny Church, a decayed Bostonian. . . , divides her attention between the Lily Daché hat she has just bought for eighty-five cents from a thrift shop and the family silver which she is packing for their departure from the home they can no longer afford. Her husband Gardner is a major American poet, friend of Frost and Pound, a winner of Pulitzer Prizes and presidential medals, and, although he seems saner than Fanny if somewhat preoccupied, he has become gaga, to use her word. Into their partially dismantled world of games and querulous affection comes their daughter, all bounce and would-be amiability, a vision in her Soho glad rags who may be a major American painter in the making. For much of the first act, *Painting Churches* (the title comes from the fact that Mags wishes to do a portrait of her parents while Tina Howe is doing one of all three Churches) has the look of a dotty-family comedy.

Howe has more serious work at hand, however—work that never quite gets done. The play is concerned with both the physical and mental indignities of growing old and the conventional parental-child conflict. . . . [Gardner's] professional decay has its counterpart in the collapse of the once beautiful marriage of the Churches which exists now only in the parody that the two of them play out under the commanding direction of Fanny. Howe . . . wants to suggest that Fanny's icy inanity is a survival pose, her way of sustaining Gardner, jollying him toward the grave that she longs to share. (p. 16)

At the end of the first act, as Mags's babbled demand for recognition brings the broad comedy to a close, the show becomes darker. There are still many laughs . . . but both Fanny and Gardner get angry or pathetic scenes which indicate that growing old is not a joke and the rebellious, loving daughter has her confrontations. Interesting scenes though these are, they seem to grow out of the playwright's skill, not out of the characters. Where the play goes wrong, I think, is in the hilarious scene in which the parents discover how tasty soda crackers are and vie for the box with total concentration while the daughter is trying to tell them that she is about to have her first one-woman show at the Castelli Gallery. The scene is as delicious as the soda crackers, and I and everyone around me laughed noisily; yet I suspect that the scene should be as horrifying as it is funny and the seeds for the later harsher tone planted here.

One other difficulty with the play is that it seems to have lost a generation. It is difficult to see Mags as the daughter of Fanny and Gardner. Granddaughter would be more appropriate. If Gardner published his first book of poetry before Robert Frost's *North to Boston* came out, then the Churches—or he, at least—should be well into their eighties which would square with the lines about incontinence and gaga-ness. Although Mags is teaching at Pratt, she cannot be over thirty, as her description of herself as a young beginner seems to indicate. . . . Biologically, the relation is possible, I suppose, but it strains belief. What's more, both the old Boston/Pound-Frost parental context and the art world that Mags inhabits begin to seem gratuitous. David Hockney is the only name Mags mentions which has a strong immediate reference; the others seem to have been chosen because they are recognizable. When Mags says that as a portrait painter she is "so far out she is in," not only is the line a cliché epigram, but it makes little sense in the current art world. I labor these points for two reasons. For one thing, Howe seems to want *Painting Churches* to deal with change in the social and artistic sense as well as in human terms. If her concern is only the latter, however, these disquieting specific references still intrude, as they would not if the movement from laughter to pathos were completely absorbing.

Painting Churches keeps promising more than it delivers. Still, it is worth seeing because Tina Howe is clearly a talented playwright with an attractively oblique way of seeing, her play is acted with vigor, and the early scenes are triumphantly funny. (p. 17)

> Gerald Weales, "*Howe's Churches: Promises More than It Delivers*," *in* Commonweal, *Vol. CXL, No. 1, January 13, 1984, pp. 16-17.*

CLIVE BARNES

Tina Howe is clearly a playwright of sensibility rather than statement. In *Coastal Disturbances*, . . . she has given us a tender, overwrought, yet recognizably honest short story—in legitimate dramatic form—about love.

Love on a beach. At the end of a hot hazy summer. Love in different guises. Love that is happy, love that is exciting, love that is simply contented.

Nothing much happens. No one dies of a broken heart, is drowned at sea, or even eaten by an inquisitive shark. Feelings are noted and explored.

Holly is a young New York photographer escaping to the Massachusetts beach of her childhood, running from a crazy, New York-style affair: a mixture of chic, charisma, and chemistry called Andre, who owns a gallery.

She meets Leo, an uncomplicated hunk of a lifeguard full of muscles, gentleness and the poetry of living.

Andre—what else?—comes to reclaim her. What to do? Andre makes her feel alive. Leo only makes her feel happy.

Meanwhile, as a mild subplot on the same sandy strip, there are the septuagenarian Adamses bickering about this and that—chiefly about his unending minor infidelities—but, after nine children and a long life, reasonably cheerful.

Two other women and their obstreperous children make up the other pebbles without which no beach could be complete, but the essence of the play is Holly and her summer triangle.

It is a lazy play, but lazy in mood rather than functioning. Howe's description of two types of love in a warm climate are delicately observed, and brilliantly presented.

The contrast between the two men—the playwright adroitly avoids making Andre the shallow poseur that Leo envisages—is beautifully done, and both their major love scenes with Holly are unaffectedly persuasive.

The contrast with the others seems more strained, but a seemingly irrelevant scene with a beached whale produces an outburst from Leo about man and nature which, oddly enough, is conceivably the best thing in a play that never is less than seismographically sensitive. . . .

In *Coastal Disturbances,* Tina Howe has written the kind of play that hardly disturbs, yet has within its flimsy fabric a gem of truth. That is ample enough.

> Clive Barnes, *"A Gem of Truth in Flimsy Fabric,"*
> in New York Post, *November 20, 1986. Reprinted*
> in New York Theatre Critics' Reviews, *Vol. XXXXVII,*
> *No. 16, 1986, p. 129.*

FRANK RICH

[In *Coastal Disturbances*], the weather above is inevitably a metaphor for human frissons below. . . . The people in *Coastal Disturbances,* four generations' worth of vacationers on a private Massachusetts beach, are always welling up with exhilaration or lust or love or anger whenever one least expects. . . . [The] emotional cloudbursts, no less than the meteorological, can take the breath away.

A modern play about love that is, for once, actually about love—as opposed to sexual, social or marital politics—*Coastal Disturbances* usually just lets its disturbances happen. A heretofore chipper divorced woman named Ariel starts to chew out her young son and suddenly loses self-control, flying past boiling point to violent rage. Ariel's old Wellesley roommate, the pregnant Faith, gossips merrily once too often about the beach's "well-endowed" lifeguard, Leo, and finds herself breaking into uncontrollable, sidesplitting laughter. The play's heroine, a photographer named Holly Dancer, tells the lifeguard a phantasmagoric fantasy about an orgiastic all-night party of well-heeled, anthropomorphized dolphins, and, as she does so, Leo can't resist the frantic urge to bury the dream-dizzied Holly in the sand.

These incidents are, respectively, aching, hilarious and erotic. In each of them Ms. Howe takes a specific character's concern—the battle-scarred Ariel's hatred of men, Faith's ecstatic anticipation of motherhood, Holly's and Leo's growing sexual attraction—and distills it into a concentrate of intoxicating feeling. Yet, like Holly, who is seeking a "wider focus" in her photographs and life, the playwright wants to examine love from all the additional points of view she can find.

An older couple, [the Adamses], provide the perspective of age: having survived nine children, decades of marriage and infidelities, they now can see that younger people are "always losing things" that they at last have found. At the other end of the cycle are Ariel's son, Winston, and Faith's adopted daughter, Miranda—kids already parroting both the "kissy" and tragically self-destructive behavior of adults. . . .

Ms. Howe's vignettes are brief and pointedly impressionistic—in the style of the young painter who kept trying to find the right angle on her parents' portrait in *Painting Churches.* In *Coastal Disturbances,* [Mrs. Adams], who could be the Brahmin mother in the previous play, paints tightly composed, realistic beach scapes. "Hold still!," she complains as the scene before her shifts. "Why does everything have to keep moving?" Ms. Howe understands that everything must keep moving, that there is no "right" angle, that love and its responsibilities are something to "figure out as you go along." Not for nothing is [Mrs. Adams] reading Quentin Bell's biography of Virginia Woolf on the beach. Ms. Howe, who shares with Woolf what one character calls "the transforming eye of the artist," sees all her people, the men included, in the funny, sexy and finally forgiving round. . . .

Coastal Disturbances nonetheless subsides in Act II, when Ms. Howe settles for working [Leo] and [Holly] into a conventionally bittersweet summertime triangle, completed by an unexpected visit from Holly's big-city roué and capped by a *Tempest*-flecked reconciliatory ending that is schematic and sentimental. Other characters, especially the contrasting young mothers, leave well before one wants to bid them farewell. But if Ms. Howe is hardly the most able maker of finished plays in our theater, she must be one of the most perceptive and, line by line, most graceful writers. *Coastal Disturbances* is distinctly the creation of a female sensibility, but its beautiful, isolated private beach generously illuminates the intimate landscape that is shared by women and men.

> Frank Rich, *"Stage: From Tina Howe, 'Coastal Dis-*
> *turbances',"* in The New York Times, *November*
> *20, 1986, p. C25.*

JOHN SIMON

To classify Tina Howe's *Coastal Disturbances* as a slice-of-life play would be as niggardly as it is truthful. For although Miss Howe is expert at using public places—a restaurant, museum, or, in this case, beach—for crossroads and cross sections of humanity, she does not stop there. We do not find out merely how various people react to art or food or lolling about on a beach (and swimming and tanning seem to be distinctly secondary here to lolling); we learn about people *in extremis.* Because in Miss Howe's only slightly intensified world, confronting art and dinners out, or shedding some clothes and running about barefoot in the sand, can be quite enough to bring out both the best and the beast in us. And, above all, the real in us—the silly, pathetic, gallantly pretending, fragile truth of us.

The play begins slowly and modestly, slicing away at life manually rather than with some fancy Cuisinart. Exercising in the sand or posing on his perch is Leo the lifeguard, the cynosure of women's fantasies and a sort of latter-day Hal from Inge's *Picnic,* but more truthfully observed. He surveys a bit of sandy, New Englandy beach, sheltered and aseptic, onto which people drag their diversely messy or resignedly understated lives. There is Faith Bigelow, the youngish banker's wife, proud to be pregnant at last after a long wait, and her brattish adopted child, Miranda; there is her friend and houseguest, Ariel Took, just out of an institution after a garish divorce and the discovery she can bear no more children and barely cope with her precocious, uncontrollably high-spirited ten-year-old, Winston. Insecure and emotionally starved, she's always on the edge. More controlledly edgy is Mrs. Adams,

M. J., who, after decades of marriage and children, has not forgiven her husband, Hammie, a retired and irrepressible eye surgeon and lothario, who lends a studiously deaf ear to her genteel carping. She ends up taking out most of her frustration on her quite good beachscapes—watercolors, of course.

Into it all walks gorgeous young Holly Dancer, a kind of holy fool dancing through life, a photographer caught between talent and neurosis, between sex and shrinking from sex, between a disastrous affair with a slippery New York gallery owner (who strings her along about putting her show on and getting his divorce) and a nice, quiet nervous breakdown at the beachside house of a sturdy Massachusetts aunt. Leo is smitten and Holly is tempted, as the other women watch with mixed emotions. But fear not, the developments will not be obvious—or, at least, no more so than in life. And they will be acted out, observed, and commented on with that poetic freshness, slightly crazy honesty, and lovableness bristling with terror that are Tina Howe's very own way of decorating life—not to make it less true, mind you, only more livable.

What makes the play so exhilaratingly and painfully believable is that the author puts a part of herself, or a part of the people she has known and absorbed into herself, into all her characters, so that she has a personal stake in all the little successes and gaffes, miseries and releases from misery, occasional highs and absolute hells with which the beach is awash. Everyone is felt from within; no one is patronized, simplified, rejected. But this wouldn't be enough if she didn't also possess the loupe of loneliness, the magnifying glass a shy but feelingful person holds over everyday events until, under the beams of her scrutinizing, they flare into poetry. Miss Howe's people either speak trivialities—but desperately suffered or acutely enjoyed trivialities—or they launch into bizarre, lyrical monologues, utterly fanciful and ferociously right for them. It all ends as a mosaic whose tesserae are of wildly uneven sizes and do not properly fit; but even the gaps between them sing out and a picture does emerge: lopsided, ludicrous, and heartbreakingly sweet.

The characters speak, pell-mell, to, at, through, or past one another, often in cacophonous simultaneity as active misunderstanding and passive misunderstoodness wistfully overlap. Not only words, actions, too, are non sequiturs—and hardly a one that doesn't beget laughter or honest anxiety. The words tend to be, deliberately and appositely, inadequate to the situations; the happenings, achingly or uproariously, inadequate to the words. On the simplest level, this, after a sliver of glass has been extracted from a child's foot: "How in hell does a piece of broken glass get on *our* beach?" "You're not safe anywhere any more. A friend of mine went to a birthday party in Ipswich and found a razor blade in the chili." What foolish pride, self-absorption, irrelevant madness in that sliver of non-conversation! But it is the lengthier arias that best convey Miss Howe's music bittersweetly mocking or extravagantly aquiver, terrified of succumbing to silence. (p. 148)

Just as Holly wants to switch from nudes to deeper penetration with X-ray photography, Miss Howe has looked deeper into the soul even than in *Painting Churches,* and brought us images that are entertaining, scary, and beautiful. (p. 150)

John Simon, "Written in the Sand," in New York Magazine, Vol. 19, No. 47, December 1, 1986, pp. 148, 150.

ROBERT BRUSTEIN

Set on a North Shore beach, where the same group of sunbathers and their precocious children keep returning through late August to lay their blankets (unaccountably) on the same dune near a lifeguard station, *Coastal Disturbances* is a one-acter elasticized to two hours that finds its climaxes when a whale gets beached or a child steps on a piece of glass. Yes, people also fall in love and feel disappointed with their lives, and I know what Chekhov said about significant events happening under the surface of everyday trivia. But virtually nothing happens under this trivial surface except a lot of chat among neurasthenic vacationing Brahmins about their personal relationships. (Typical example: "I'm just so alive with him. I can't explain.") Howe's overinsistent insight in the play is that people get snippy when their romantic emotions are thwarted, but she failed to make me interested enough in her characters to care *how* they feel. Meanwhile, the work has been structured in a series of aimless episodic scenes marked "Wednesday, 2 in the afternoon" or "Tuesday, near dusk," as if it were a pseudodocumentary action film about tracking down terrorists in Central Europe or drug dealers in L.A. (There's no point whatever in identifying the precise time of day or day of the week if you don't dramatize its relevance to the action of the play.) *Coastal Disturbances* is all very vapid and bloodless, totally lacking in density, and Tina Howe, who is certainly equipped to create wilder adventures than this, should not be encouraged to dissipate her talents in thin-lipped exercises about life among the boring and the bored. (pp. 26-7)

Robert Brustein, "Headline Hunting," in The New Republic, Vol. 196, Nos. 1 & 2, January 5 & 12, 1987, pp. 25-7.

MOIRA HODGSON

Coastal Disturbances, an enchanting new play by Tina Howe, takes place over two weeks toward the end of summer at a private beach on Massachusetts's North Shore. As the characters come down to the seaside, they are captured in a series of vignettes: snatches of conversation; an embrace; a child carrying a revolting pile of seaweed; a mother scolding; an elderly woman painting landscapes; a beached and bleeding whale. It is like flipping through a series of summer snapshots. (p. 25)

In *Coastal Disturbances* Howe lets us glimpse the inner lives of her characters, who are vivid and recognizable; these fleeting impressions are created by short bursts of charged dialogue. Faith, a happily pregnant mother with a rambunctious young daughter, Miranda, laughs a little too hysterically when she gossips about the handsome bronzed lifeguard and suggests that he pads his bathing suit. In another scene, Ariel, divorced mother of a delightful but uncontrollable boy, suddenly flies into an unprovoked rage, screaming at the lifeguard and her son. Her normally cheerful, rather brittle facade is peeled back to reveal the wounded manhater she has become.

A romance develops between Holly, a young photographer, and Leo, the lifeguard. . . . Holly is daffy, scattered, dizzily romantic and, like Diane Keaton in a Woody Allen film, at times so irritating you could strangle her with pleasure. Leo can't make her out, for beneath his gorgeous body and jocular manner he is a simple fellow, vulnerable and naïve. (pp. 25-6)

The play has a remarkable love scene in which Leo buries Holly up to the neck in sand as she rattles on in a fantasy about an orgiastic party given by dolphins. He, only half-listening, tenderly caresses the mound of sand.

Tina Howe is very good at dialogue, whether it is the sort of Pinteresque exchange where neither person is listening to the other, or whether it is a sudden emotional outburst. . . . The weakness comes in the play's routine climax, when the roué with whom Holly has been in love in New York arrives to break up the summer romance. "Innocence eludes me," he tells her, "but you walk with the angels."

Coastal Disturbances is a charming play, a landscape of the human heart in miniature. (p. 26)

> *Moira Hodgson, in a review of "Coastal Disturbances," in* The Nation, *New York, Vol. 244, No. 1, January 10, 1987, pp. 25-6.*

David (John) Hughes

1930-

English novelist, critic, nonfiction writer, editor, travel writer, and scriptwriter.

An author of diverse novels depicting life in twentieth-century England, Hughes often focuses upon troubled protagonists who turn to their pasts for self-knowledge and an understanding of their futures. He employs sensuous language, disjointed time frames, and multiple narrators to advance his thematic concerns. According to Peter Levi, "[Hughes's] books are perfectly organised, highly professional, and thoroughly modern. They are sensitive without being unreadable, and they have plots that . . . offer an oblique vision of the real world." While Hughes has not gained a large popular following, critics have hailed his novels as inventive and penetrating studies of the human condition.

Although Hughes's first three novels were marginally reviewed, critics noted a creative progression with each book. In his first novel, *A Feeling in the Air* (1957; published in the United States as *Man Off Beat*), an advertising executive attempts to reevaluate his life following a mental breakdown. *Sealed with a Loving Kiss* (1959) concerns a former physician who becomes involved with a questionable religious community after losing faith in himself and humanity. *The Horsehair Sofa* (1961) is a farce detailing a couple's attempts to achieve marital bliss. Hughes earned widespread critical attention with his fourth novel, *The Major* (1964). The protagonist of this work, an unstable British army officer who relishes war and killing, returns home from duty in Germany and vents his frustrations on his family. Elizabeth Jennings called *The Major* "a great advance on the rather quiet, and not always assured, earlier novels by Mr. Hughes."

Hughes's next novel, *The Man Who Invented Tomorrow* (1968), is a satire of the television industry. Loosely based on Hughes's experiences as a writer of documentaries for the British Broadcasting Corporation, this book details a program celebrating the centenary of the birth of H. G. Wells. As members of the production staff become immersed in this project, they are influenced by Wells's philosophies and literary themes and acquire new insights into their own lives. In *Memories of Dying* (1976), an elderly man named Hunter, who has committed several crimes during his lifetime, invades the troubled conscience of protagonist Richard Flaxman. As Flaxman relives Hunter's experiences, he gains a better awareness of himself and his world. John Mellors asserted that Hughes's use of multiple time frames and narrators allows this novel to "cast its own spell on the reader and haunt him with its many themes and questions." *A Genoese Fancy* (1979), an initiation novel set in Hughes's native Wimbledon following World War II, centers on the relationship between an orphan and the uncle with whom he lives. In the lighthearted comedy *The Imperial German Dinner Service* (1983), Hughes depicts a man who is obsessed with a Wedgwood dinner service that was commissioned by Kaiser Wilhelm of Germany. This service is revealed to be of more than monetary value to the protagonist, as each dish represents different periods of his life. John Walsh noted: "Few writers could make the collecting of plates an exciting

prospect; fewer still could turn it enjoyably into a convincing metaphor of spiritual fulfillment."

Hughes's ninth novel, *The Pork Butcher* (1984), is a tale of guilt and redemption revolving around Ernst Kestner, a former German soldier dying of cancer who journeys to the French village where he had participated in the slaughter of its inhabitants during World War II. Accompanied by his daughter, Kestner relives his involvement in the atrocity and mourns the death of the woman he loved, a victim of the massacre. Patrick Parrinder described *The Pork Butcher* as "a moral fable, brief, sensational, and hauntingly tense." *But for Bunter* (1985; published in the United States as *The Joke of the Century*) is a comedy focusing upon Archibald Aitken's claims to be the model for Billy Bunter, a popular character in English pulp fiction of the early 1900s. When Patrick Weymouth, a civil servant and amateur historian, contacts Aitken to discuss his claim, Aitken intimates that he had influenced, either directly or indirectly, both world wars and the sinking of the *Titanic*, among other historical events. Sally Emerson deemed this work "a funny, outrageous book written with freshness and pace."

Hughes's nonfiction books include *J. B. Priestley: An Informal Study of His Work* (1958) and *The Road to Stockholm and Lapland* (1964). *The Rosewater Revolution: Notes on a Change of Attitude* (1971) is an experimental work that incorporates autobiographical elements.

(See also *Contemporary Authors,* Vol. 116 and *Dictionary of Literary Biography,* Vol. 14.)

D. R. BENSEN

Gunner, the principal character in David Hughes's **Man Off Beat,** is in the tiny Welsh village of Wender for a rest cure after a nervous breakdown. A reader, particularly an American reader, may feel that this quiet first novel is a rest cure for him—a relief from the stridency, urgency, and violence of much current writing.

There is very little of conclusiveness or assertion in the book. . . . Like Gunner, the reader may wait impatiently for things to start happening; but he should soon be soothed by the book's muted charm and leisurely pace. Gunner's wry but hopeful affair with a widowed hotelkeeper, his encounters with an ecstatic curate—even his dreamlike desecration of a church—carry the story along without ever becoming obtrusively dramatic.

While Mr. Hughes works, so to speak, in shades of gray, a reviewer need not be at all tentative in saying that, within the bounds he has set for himself, he has done commendably well. He conveys admirably a feeling of scene and personality; he has a keen eye for motivation and detail. His untroubled study of a troubled man does not go very deep; but what he chooses to observe he conveys pleasurably and convincingly. More ambitious novelists would have made more of the character and situation, but it is not likely that they would have done as finished a job. (pp. 31-2)

> *D. R. Bensen, "Soothing Sojourn," in* The Saturday Review, *New York, Vol. 41, No. 6, February 8, 1958, pp. 31-2.*

THE TIMES, LONDON

Mr. David Hughes employs a small canvas and writes soberly, but he . . . has an eye for eccentrics. **Sealed with a Loving Kiss** might be called a study in the morose and awkward, but it must not be thought that Mr. Hughes makes either Rex Benbrook or Barbara Hemming uninteresting to the reader. They are lonely, rudderless, and without any particular purpose in life, but Mr. Hughes has cleverly stressed their considerable possibilities, from their meeting in Berner's respectable restaurant until the dénouement in a village high up on the Chilterns. As a background or supporting cast he has produced a little brotherhood of clerics and cranks in Hampshire which Rex joins in his search for an idealistic career. Although Mr. Hughes is not yet experienced enough as a novelist to hit off an odd or grotesque personality with complete success he has a delicate, scrupulous talent which may in time produce an impressive yield.

> *A review of "Sealed with a Loving Kiss," in* The Times, *London, October 1, 1959, p. 13.*

MELVIN J. FRIEDMAN

David Hughes peoples this novel [**Sealed with a Loving Kiss**] with inverted old lechers, disillusioned young men and women— all thoroughly unwholesome types. Rex Benbrook, a doctor turned journalist for a suspicious religious publication, goes through the usual sexual experience that we have come to expect from the protagonists of the new generation of English novelists. He lacks, unfortunately, the wit of a Jim Dixon (*Lucky Jim*), the pathos of a Joe Shaw (*The Contenders*). (pp. 402-03)

David Hughes characterizes Rex Benbrook as "a young fellow, neurotically saddled with the problems of his own generation." He encounters, in less than two hundred pages, a frightening succession of homosexuals, parasites, and lonely women— finally rejecting them all. He has something in common with the picaresque hero who moves from one vaguely sordid adventure to another. We are mildly amused at these unlikely escapades, but never moved or convinced by them. Rex Benbrook, like most of Hughes's other creatures, is too much of a fake to be entirely credible. (p. 403)

> *Melvin J. Friedman, in a review of "Sealed with a Loving Kiss," in* Books Abroad, *Vol. 34, No. 4, Autumn, 1960, pp. 402-03.*

PENELOPE MORTIMER

Pornography, according to Mr. Geoffrey Gorer, is very seldom well (as distinct from effectively) written. I hope Mr David Hughes will understand me—with forgiveness if necessary— if I say that given the paradox of living in a society in which it was no longer necessary, he could write exquisite pornography. The only things that irritated me, on a surface level, about his new novel, were the euphemisms. Since the story of **The Horsehair Sofa** is entirely concerned with sex, this is rather like writing a novel about engineering without mentioning nuts and bolts. No one could say, however, that Mr Hughes doesn't beat about the bush with great elegance.

Marcus Gore, thwarted all his bachelor life by prudish debs, marries a thoroughly nice girl called Priscilla. Even his spirit is not particularly willing: his flesh, tricked for so long, is quite unable to cope. He scurries frantically into ever more complicated fantasies, his wife co-operating in a dogged but unrewarding hope of success. Finally, with an ingenuity that seems by this time a little frayed at the edges, she impersonates a chorus girl for whom he has a slight fancy. It works. Perfectly aware that this is his wife, but liberated at last, he makes love to her. . . .

Mr Hughes tells us he writes from the heart. Whether this book, with its final exhortation to all public schoolboys to 'tune their bodies' before jumping into marriage, its conclusion of beatific confidence in wives who too frequently visit Harrods, is all that the heart contains, I do not know. I believe that this book is intended as satire in the early Andrew Sinclair *genre,* although it is far better written. But I may be wrong. If so, woe. (p. 1442)

> *Penelope Mortimer, "Out of Order," in* Time & Tide, *Vol. 42, No. 35, August 31, 1961, pp. 1442-43.*

ERIC KEOWN

The Horsehair Sofa is an odd little book that starts very amusingly and then slowly peters out. The comedy of a marriage that is blissfully happy everywhere except in bed, it is rich in euphemism and David Hughes gets full marks for exemplary tact. His account of the embarrassments of the first night of a honeymoon in a ghastly hotel may not be recommended reading for Aunt Hester, but it is very funny and as an antidote to the romantic view of marriage refreshing. But this vein is soon worked out, and thereafter Mr. Hughes's invention is strained till it creaks. (p. 404)

> *Eric Keown, in a review of "The Horsehair Sofa," in* Punch, *Vol. CCXLI, No. 6313, September 13, 1961, pp. 403-04.*

ELIZABETH JENNINGS

[*The Major* is] concerned with an obsession. Major Kane returns to routine duty on Salisbury Plain, but is still possessed by thoughts of fighting and violence. He cannot get wartime army life out of his mind, everything he sees is interpreted in terms of it. . . .

But *The Major* is a far more sinister book than merely the study of an army officer who has gone to seed and to senility. Kane is brutal and masochistic; violence, both in a wish for a death and killing and in a desire for the crudest forms of sex, have become deeply rooted within him, and the novel ends with murder and suicide. Ulla, the Swedish *au pair* girl, is the only character who understands the full horror of the situation. . . .
The Major marks a great advance on the rather quiet, and not always assured, earlier novels by Mr Hughes. It is often violent, yes, but the novelist seems to have acquired a full knowledge of the violence he is depicting; one needs to be a mature writer to able to do this, and David Hughes is still a young novelist.

> *Elizabeth Jennings, in a review of "The Major," in* The Listener, *Vol. LXXI, No. 1838, June 18, 1964, p. 1005.*

ELIOT FREMONT-SMITH

The short, tight, single-track novel can carry considerable power by virtue of its concentrated focus; but if the focus wavers, the spell is likely to be broken. The focus of David Hughes's short, tight novel [*The Major*] is on a disgruntled British Army major who seethes with barely controlled violence and hate. Shunted home from Germany, bored with peacetime England, his violence breaks out in ways at once vicious and ludicrous. . . .
But as the major disintegrates, the novel's single track gives way to social tract—against Colonel Blimpism, war-lust, the hypocrisy of the press and other easy devils—and the spell is broken. The major's name, Kane, is suddenly exposed as merely one of many obvious, yet not quite right, symbols; his psychopathic drive toward destruction becomes less a stifling agony than a device on which the author can flex his muscles while pretending not to sermonize. Yet for all this, Mr. Hughes's book is a near-miss (less taut novels have similar faults concealed beneath the lard); his next may be one to watch.

> *Eliot Fremont-Smith, "End Papers," in* The New York Times, *March 31, 1965, p. 37.*

MARY SULLIVAN

If you have grown nostalgic for those television documentaries made of stills of the great man's family, friends and veritable little truckle bed, *The Man Who Invented Tomorrow* may console you for the kind that impose the present and monkey with the past. Armstrong, who is directing a prestige half-hour film on H. G. Wells, has carefully gathered a team he thinks will be entranced with his trendy notions, and is all set to package yesterday's prophet for today's mass audience. Lots of loca-

tion, he thinks (no matter if the wrong ones), girls, backchat from Wells about what we've come to. But somehow Wells refuses to be knocked into that fashionable shape. Hubert Dane, the actor portraying him, is something of a Wells character himself, a bit of a failure, a bit crushed by circumstance, but capable of an obstinate vision. He becomes so immersed in Wells and his works that he feels he has become him. . . . The rest of the team, though vaguer about Wells, are similarly haunted. Wells evades them in the finished film, but he is persistently and discomfortingly present through the quarrelling, bed-leaping and tearing up of scripts that surround its making.

The liveliness of the film's dead subject is at the centre of the book, but David Hughes is not bound to that at the expense of everything else. He is sympathetic to the possibilities in Armstrong's approach to his work, and makes you understand his professional pleasure, even while sabotaging it with the intractable spirit of Wells. It's a clever novel, unpretentious about its delicately lodged theme, and very funny indeed about the inner and outer turmoils of telly-men at work.

> *Mary Sullivan, "Visible Men," in* The Listener, *Vol. LXXIX, No. 2031, February 29, 1968, p. 279.*

R. G. G. PRICE

The Man Who Invented Tomorrow is an odd little fancy about making a television film on H. G. Wells. There is a good deal of booze, sex and TV "shop," though obviously there is a deeper intention which doesn't really come off, partly because of the half-heartedly satirical tone of the off-camera stuff. It all flips by easily enough; but it won't add much to Mr. Hughes's considerable reputation.

> *R. G. G. Price, in a review of "The Man Who Invented Tomorrow," in* Punch, *Vol. CCLIV, No. 6652, March 6, 1968, p. 358.*

JONATHAN RABAN

Most autobiographies switchback from being written too thinly to being hastily patched up with anxious purple passages, in an unhappy combination of gouache and invisible ink. David Hughes has contributed the fatal additive of imagination, and *The Rosewater Revolution* is an ingeniously wrought structure which manages to conflate the properties of both a bad autobiography and a bad novel.

Yet he is on to a good idea. An imaginary self, sometimes 'I', sometimes—rather a cheap touch—'Hyde', goes on a series of weekend trips to Herefordshire, where he visits the battlefields of the Civil War and attends a performance of *Comus*. On these weekends he is accompanied by some living friends and, intermittently, by characters based on three friends who have died. The Civil War comes, more and more, to take place inside his head as he shifts from decent, commonplace, public-school liberalism to a style of implausibly fashionable post-revolutionary consciousness. Weekends in the country, with their usual mishmash of booze and sex and picnics, not infrequently tend to scramble the brains like this; and, fallacies of imitative form aside, *The Rosewater Revolution* reads like just such a weekend. What it doesn't allow for is the fact that Saturday's sunny stroke of genius invariably goes, by Monday, as flat as the leftover tumbler of Alka Seltzer by the bedside. Talk, and life too, may thrive on weekends, but literature, alas, doesn't.

What a fine Saturday ploy it would be, for instance (over a bottle of Niersteiner), to have a novel written in the form of an autobiographical journal, on which the right-hand pages would carry the narrative while the left-hand pages would contain footnotes: biographies of real characters, sources of imaginary ones, useful quotations, epigrams that one couldn't quite fit into the story itself. One could write flatly, just how it was. . . . It would be like a scrapbook, a dramatised slice of continual self-inquiry. You could put *anything* in.

And Hughes does. Much of what he writes is as skimpily anecdotal as an exercise in Esperanto. He has his lunch in Ledbury, and we're told that there was a parking space amongst 'the barricade of cars' outside the pub. Or:

> We drank whisky and talked. The river faded
> away with the sun and the church receded and
> the evening lengthened. We had chicken with
> herbs and a riot of vegetables and red wine.
> John talked in his persuasive way, deceptively
> soft, about photography . . .

These barricades and riots and deceptive softnesses are not so much to do with the revolution written in rosewater as with the embarrassment of the autobiographer as he licks his diary into shape for public consumption. History, and the inside of his own head, liberate him into an alternative prose style which is a long wallow in mud and blood. . . .

The book is, I suppose, closest in tone to Julian Mitchell's *The Undiscovered Country*—another novel which tries to marry autobiography to baroque fantasy, and does it much more successfully. The trouble with Hughes's writing is that it turns into an unconscious parody of whatever style it aspires to. It has the authenticity neither of life nor of art. We are told that there is anguish here, but the anguish looks, in its context of overblown imaginings and under-observed facts, unprepossessingly like whimsy. The great strength—and, ultimately, the weakness—of *The Undiscovered Country* was its cunning, its sly self-watchfulness as it calculated its effects. In renouncing cunning, and going for the full frontal assault, Hughes has endowed actuality with the crude and unlikely proportions of a novelette.

> *Jonathan Raban, "Saturday Book," in New States-*
> *man, Vol. 82, No. 2107, August 6, 1971, p. 185.*

JOHN MELLORS

All good ghost stories pose nagging questions, the stock one being: 'Is the ghost really there, or does it exist only in the mind of the beholder, product of a dream, of hysteria, of actual or imagined memory?' David Hughes leaves it quite open, introducing the 'presence of a man' to his narrator in the most mundane circumstances, in an aircraft flying to Nice. Indeed, it is nearly halfway through *Memories of Dying* before the narrator admits to a 'shudder—as though a touch of the supernatural had crept into the experience without my noticing'.

Flaxman, in his mid-forties, married with two children and 'a reasonably high-powered job', is alone on holiday, when he suddenly feels the presence of 'an apparently dying man' in his mid-seventies, who had 'lived through two wars and killed in both'. Flaxman begins to 'know' Hunter (haunter?); the facts of Hunter's life are 'like memories on the tip of the tongue, shadows at the edge of the mind'. He resents being possessed by another, and decides to turn the tables by pursuing his pursuer. The quest leads him to his own home town and his own past life.

Hughes has a 'take it or leave it' attitude to the mechanics of the 'haunting'. It just happens, without explanation, and the author moves confidently, between one sentence and the next, from the 'I' of the narrator to a third-person account of Hunter's past and present life. This works very well, allowing the novel to cast its own spell on the reader and haunt him with its many themes and questions. Self-knowledge is one object of Flaxman's hunt for Hunter: to confront 'areas of myself which I had missed'. Another is 'to get to the bottom of my century': where has mankind gone wrong?. . . The narrator (author, too?) is angry at missed opportunities, at dying in life, i.e., failing to realise one's true self. Can we, perhaps, through art or some other creative act of will, 'rewrite' our own lives and so, in some sense, change the course of history? *Memories of Dying* ends with the narrator's hope that he can 'take my own horrid century in my arms and shake some sense into it'.

> *John Mellors, "Ghosts," in* The Listener, *Vol. 95,*
> *No. 2462, June 17, 1976, p. 790.*

MICHAEL IRWIN

Memories of Dying could have been written expressly as a counterpart to another novella published this year: Mai Zetterling's *Bird of Passage*. In both books the central character, who is also the narrator, goes abroad to work through a personality crisis. In both books solitude, aimless travel through strange surroundings and an exorbitant intake of coffee and alcohol accelerate a process of disorientation and collapse that proves to be a necessary prelude to recovery. But where Mai Zetterling's heroine begins to resolve her problems by coming to terms with herself, with her own past, David Hughes's hero, the middle-aged Richard Flaxman, has to abandon his own identity and comprehend the past of another man. . . .

Devoid of ideals, affections or interests, he is taking a holiday in France to avert a possible nervous breakdown. On the plane he becomes aware that his mind, like an ill-tuned radio, is picking up alien signals. He is experiencing the thoughts and emotions of a dying man, a stranger. Gradually this invading presence defines itself into an elderly, ex-teacher named Hunter.

As he approaches death Hunter is recalling his past. . . . In a dying attempt to expiate [his] sins he has projected his recollections into the mind of Flaxman, whom he had once spoken to, years before, in a moment of anguish.

Memories of Dying is explicitly, perhaps over-explicitly, allegorical. Hunter, born in 1900, stands for all that has gone wrong in the twentieth century, for the violence that has destroyed or denatured love. . . . In grasping Hunter's story Flaxman is comprehending the past that has shaped him and can at last begin to escape its consequences.

There is more meaning yet, but I hesitate to interpret further. The main pleasure for the reader of the book will lie in tracing pattern and significance for himself. David Hughes plays the Nabokovian game of doubles with some skill and has written a compact, intricate novel. But for me it has two major limitations. First, it is *all* meaning: the novel has so little autonomous fictional life that to elucidate it is almost to explain it away. Second, although the publishers describe the story as "a rich metaphor" it seems rather to be an exercise in personification. Hunter's career has been invented specifically to exemplify our century. Even if we accept that it does so—and

I am by no means persuaded myself—it must surely represent not an explanation but a tautology.

Michael Irwin, "Takeover Bid," in The Times Literary Supplement, No. 3875, June 18, 1976, p. 731.

JOHN NAUGHTON

David Hughes's new novel [*A Genoese Fancy*] conjures up memories of the immediate postwar era in Britain: a time of jam sandwiches, socialist austerity, National Service, nylons and suspender belts. The story revolves around Lionel, a school-leaver suddenly orphaned by a motor accident, and his uncle Norman, a Wimbledon shopkeeper of modest means. Lionel is clever, dreamy and impractical, a great fan of Donne; Norman, in contrast, is a practical man, a staunch Tory who has always matched his aspirations to his own estimate of his capabilities. . . .

The plot, such as it is, is insubstantial and allegorical, being primarily concerned with the contrasting developments taking place in its two heroes. Lionel converges on the 'realities' of life, while his uncle diverges like a premature hippie. The very considerable charm of the book lies in the delicate and ironic touch with which Mr Hughes recounts these goings-on in deepest Wimbledon.

John Naughton, "True Butchery," in The Listener, Vol. 102, No. 2638, November 22, 1979, p. 721.

IAN STEWART

While there is nothing overworked about the air of suburban actuality in David Hughes's new novel [*A Genoese Fancy*] the reader will nevertheless perceive it with dream-like clarity. He will do so by identifying with the lives of a grocer named Norman Pringle and his nephew Lionel, lives which themselves have the absurd unpredictability and terror of a dream.

The story is set mainly in the not-so-chic part of Wimbledon in the late 1940s. Lionel, recently orphaned when his parents' car was in collision with a bus, moves into a tiny room above Norman's shop. Leaving school, he is as confused about his future as Norman is about his new responsibilities. . . . The young man's imprisoning world is confined to thoughts of marrying Diana, his WAAF friend, to keeping his old school friend Marius out of his bed, and being seduced by Marius's aunt. Losing his sense of reality, it seems to him on the parade ground as if he is dying inside his uniform. Mr Hughes excels in his subtle perception into the dilemma of youth confronted by "the huge anonymity of experience, so aimlessly painful . . ."

Lionel is saved by his uncle's inspiration. Norman, who had fought in the First World War and whose brother-in-law (Lionel's father) had worked with the Imperial War Graves Commission, has a vision of the great writers of the past, and of the men who died in the trenches, all marching through Wimbledon willing the world to become a better place as a result of their great thoughts, feelings and sacrifices. . . . Norman, who had always seen the First World War as a responsibility to begin again, has now taken up the challenge which everyone else has ignored. He has sacrificed everything to make the world fit for Lionel to live in and has not done so in vain. The boy agrees to accompany him on a trip to Flanders, and seems likely to drop his objections to going up to Oxford.

A Genoese Fancy is a profoundly truthful and very funny novel about a middle-aged man and his nephew growing up together, and David Hughes displays a masterly touch in capturing the pathos and the farcical absurdity of their experience life.

Ian Stewart, in a review of "A Genoese Fancy," in The Illustrated London News, Vol. 268, No. 6978, January, 1980, p. 64.

JOHN WALSH

David Hughes's past novels have often concerned themselves with individual obsessions (*The Major, Memories of Dying*) and private fantasies (*The Man Who Invented Tomorrow*) working themselves out in well-realised public arenas, in which the protagonist becomes a *contra mundum* hero simply by virtue of his quest.

The same quality of Quixotic self-fulfilment informs his new novel, but with a sharper edge to its plot and a more dynamic narrative line than in his previous books. **The Imperial German Dinner Service** is a headlong flight through European topography and twentieth-century history, in which an embittered, cuckolded, redundant, middle-aged journalist Roland Patcham develops an obsessive desire to collect the scattered pieces of the eponymous crockery (all 1000-odd items of it), which had been a gift to Kaiser Wilhelm commissioned from Wedgwoods before the First World War. The commemorative tableware features, in scenes of breathtaking impressionistic beauty, the England of the day, from a Norman church in Dorset to the clothcapped porters of Covent Garden. It thus constitutes a whacking symbol of Britain's Heritage, the Home Counties *Belle Epoque* and the triumph of Old Ways, before their innocence disappeared in the trenches of the Somme.

To Patcham it represents much more: throughout the novel, clues are scattered as to why he should be so devoted to reclaiming the collection for himself. He finds, for example, that individual pieces discovered along the way carry direct associations with his own history—his schooldays, his marriage, poignant memories of holidays in happier times with his erring wife, Sophie. . . .

David Hughes writes extraordinarily well, dispensing with Tacitean economy a mixture of cool aperçus, hilariously acid throwaway lines of description . . . and offering postcard-length vignettes of the lands through which his hero passes. The story moves along with dizzying speed, allowing the reader to suspend sizeable amounts of disbelief at its coincidental twists and emotional turns.

The dénouement is perhaps tidied up too abruptly for comfort—Roland's search comes to an arbitrary conclusion in Iceland, he is reconciled with his wife, and the Dinner Service goes on public display, leaving its various symbolic associations wholly unreconciled. But the book has such unity of tone and style, takes such a fresh and angry look at the debris of the century, and deploys so many incidental delights, that one is carried unprotestingly through its slim length. Few writers could make the collecting of plates an exciting prospect; fewer still could turn it enjoyably into a convincing metaphor of spiritual fulfilment.

John Walsh, in a review of "The Imperial German Dinner Service," in Books and Bookmen, No. 334, July, 1983, p. 36.

DAVID MONTROSE

The original Grail was a chalice used by Christ at the Last Supper; the grail at the heart of David Hughes's eighth novel [*The Imperial German dinner service*] is a more extensive item of tableware: a Wedgwood dinner service of over a thousand pieces commissioned by the Kaiser shortly before the first World War.... In the aftermath of war, the set was dispersed, "some broken, much lost." The Grail Knight who sets out to re-assemble it is Roland Patcham, an indolent, middle-aged, hard-up, out-of-work journalist married to Sophie, fifteen years his junior, a "spoilt, well-off, beautiful" and busily in-work journalist. Patcham's motives are both pecuniary and romantic. The service is worth at least a hundred thousand pounds; there is also "the mystery." ...

Patcham swiftly acquires a rival, but this merely reinforces his uncharacteristic zeal: it is Courtney Ranston, director of National Arts (libel lawyers' code for the Arts Council), once Patcham's best friend, now Sophie's latest lover. Ostensibly, Ranston is collecting the service for the nation; his real motives are self-aggrandisement and a desire to curry favour with a certain royal personage who is taking an interest....

The Imperial German dinner service is the kind of thriller which attempts to make a statement about the nature of obsession. Unfortunately, Patcham's obsession is stated rather than conveyed. Hughes's tone does not help: aiming, presumably, to be light and sardonic, he sounds merely facetious. Several hardly credible episodes turn on assorted characters—a dealer in militaria from Antwerp, the proprietor of a transvestite bar in Hamburg, the embittered wife of a Swedish manufacturer—being sufficiently impressed by Patcham's ruling passion to hand over items in their ownership without accepting payment. And the ultimate statement that does emerge simply reiterates the standard wisdom that the value of a quest more often derives from the pursuit than the final accomplishment. Nor does the novel impress if considered purely *as* a thriller. Patcham is required to surmount few obstacles; Ranston's men are easily outmanoeuvred, while competition from German interests—of whom there are promising early rumours—never materializes. Thrillers can survive a host of literary deficiencies; they can't survive a deficiency of suspense.

> David Montrose, "Some Broken, Much Lost," in The Times Literary Supplement, *No. 4198, September 16, 1983, p. 1002.*

PETER LEVI

David Hughes is at a... difficult stage of literary career, having written seven novels before [*The Imperial German Dinner Service*], a study of J. B. Priestley, and a social history of England published only in Sweden. They have not brought him great fame, or I suppose fortune.... But he has the qualities you expect. His books are perfectly organised, highly professional and thoroughly modern. They are sensitive without being unreadable, and they have plots that make a pattern, that offer an oblique vision, of the real world. *The Imperial German Dinner Service* is written with a freshness and put together with a skill that must mean David Hughes is still developing. He is a miniature novelist, or at least he has written miniature novels. This one is readable, entertaining, plausible as a fiction, and I think morally true. In this generation minor prose writers are best.

The story is about a quest for the scattered dishes of a Wedgwood dinner service with British scenes, made for the Kaiser in 1914 and rediscovered by the hero....

Publishers are mad on the quest motif in books, and so are readers evidently. In this case it works, and curiously so does the element of personal identification and allegory. In the end, the novel turns out very sweetly to be about love. The language is clipped but the sentiment powerfully simple. The Shakespearean order of nature gets restored, so far as possible in a modern novel: which means not quite.

> Peter Levi, "A Windbag and a Miniaturist," in The Spectator, *Vol. 251, No. 8097, September 17, 1983, p. 22.*

JAMES MELVILLE

David Hughes is a respected and prolific writer, whose last novel *The Imperial German Dinner Service* was widely acclaimed. Blessed with a fertile imagination, he nevertheless prefers to work on a small canvas, and has once more chosen to do so in his new book [*The Pork Butcher*]. The elderly widower and prosperous pork butcher Ernst Kestner has learned that he will probably die of cancer within three months, but he is not particularly cast down by the news. Putting his affairs discreetly in order, he sets out by car from his home in Lubeck ostensibly to visit his married daughter Tina in Paris, but in reality to pursue the forty-year-old ghost of the only person he has ever loved, and whom he, as a young soldier saw die in the massacre of the whole population of her town. The horror he has lived with is that he was himself one of the executioners.

Kestner sets out to revisit the scene with his daughter as an initially unwilling companion and finds a kind of peace in a bizarre climax.... Slight though it is, the book is rich in sensuous narrative and sly characterization—Tina's husband Henri is particularly memorable—and both style and content more than once reminded me of the work of H. E. Bates. *The Pork Butcher* is something less than a novel, but is nevertheless a haunting, absorbing *conte*.

> James Melville, in a review of "The Pork Butcher," in British Book News, *July, 1984, p. 425.*

PATRICK PARRINDER

David Hughes's *The Pork Butcher* is a worthy winner of the W. H. Smith award.... In this, his ninth novel, Hughes has written a moral fable, brief, sensational, and hauntingly tense. The word 'haunting' is used advisedly. Ghost stories, with their Gothic associations of night-shirted wraiths and clanking chains, are held in contempt by most literary people and would doubtless have received the most dampening of acknowledgments from E. M. Forster. It may seem perverse to suggest that *The Pork Butcher,* a novel addressing the most profoundly serious concerns of contemporary history, belongs to this genre. Yet since Ibsen we have known that the persistence, the unseen influence, of events and people belonging to the past is one of the perennial themes of modern writing. That we so readily think of societies as being 'haunted' by their recent history is an indication of the links between collective memory and conscience, and the art of the storyteller. (pp. 15-16)

Ernst Kestner, Hughes's pork butcher, is a German ex-soldier who feels impelled to revisit the scene of a World War Two massacre in occupied France. Kestner is in his sixties and is dying of lung cancer.... Though his daughter has settled in Paris, it is the first time he has re-entered the country where he was formerly stationed.... His determination to plead guilty to a half-forgotten war crime is treated at first as an inconvenience, a display of bad taste. The massacre and pillage of Lascaud-sur-Marn, in which he participated, has been commemorated by turning the ruined village into a shrine, a museum-piece frozen in time, Kestner's return stirs up the ghosts which are lurking unappeased behind the names on plaques and the anonymous relics in glass cases.

An English novelist probing the ancestral relationship of France and Germany puts himself in an awkward position, somewhere between agent-provocateur and bomb-disposal expert. Hughes handles the responsibilities of his undertaking boldly and delicately. His plan requires that, at the climax of the novel, Kestner should confront a figure who can be represented as his Gallic opposite number. This is the reason for Kestner's meeting with the brother of Jeanne, the French girl with whom, in the days before the massacre, he had been intoxicatingly in love. Jeanne's brother, a Resistance fighter, had been absent from the village on the fatal day: now he is a successful politician whose career has risen, phoenix-like, from the ashes of home and family. He and Kestner visit the ruins of Lascaud by moonlight, and the politician swears that in the morning he will have this 'stupid memorial to stupidity' bulldozed to the ground. It is too late, of course. The elaborate civility which characterises the two men's encounter cannot survive their exposure to bloodstained ground and unhoused spirits. The outcome is swift and melodramatic, but everywhere Hughes shows a mastery of controlled melodrama, without a hint of psychological falsity.

Blood-guilt alone, it is clear, would not have driven the 'old pork butcher feeding off the fat of his memories' back to this place. Kestner is a sensual man (his appetites are stressed throughout the novel) and his frenzied love-affair with Jeanne had gone so far that he had agreed to desert from the German Army.... Forty years later he can no longer resist his longing to confess his peculiarly torrid and intimate role in the tragedy. His romanticisation of Jeanne's memory has been undimmed by the years, but to her brother it appears that 'you merely played, as nations do when their spirits rise, the stupidly easy game of destroying each other.' Kestner's urge to revisit France leads to a second bout with the 'icy risks' of self-destruction, as the spirits that rose once rise again.

Most frightening of all, perhaps, is what Hughes's novel has to say about the nature of freedom.... Both Kestner and his French opposite number have known the unholy experience of 'liberation' in the midst of holocaust. A few days or weeks after the massacre, and following some momentary inherited impulse, Kestner entered a church and lay grovelling on the ground, in a 'hopeless tantrum of hope' that he might be forgiven for what he had done. Hughes marvellously exposes the evasions and fantasies, the temporary sentimental appeasements that 20th-century people and nations offer their evil spirits. But he offers no hope of exorcism, unless indeed storytelling can somehow help to lay our ghosts....

Like any fine novel, *The Pork Butcher* is a reminder of the strengths of the novel form itself—the strengths, that is, which it derives from its dependence on fictions and fictional characters. Fictive melodrama directs us away from externals and towards the core of feeling and understanding that can be drawn from events. One of Hughes's earlier novels, *The man who invented tomorrow,* explored the making of a TV documentary

about a famous writer, H. G. Wells. In *The Pork Butcher* it would not have been appropriate to explore the contrast between fiction and documentary explicitly or self-consciously. In fact, it would be absurd to suppose that every novel ought to be a meta-fiction or self-conscious novel. More defensibly, one could recommend that every writer ought to produce at least one such novel. (p. 16)

Patrick Parrinder, "Cover Stories," in London Review of Books, *Vol. 7, No. 6, April 4, 1985, pp. 15-16.*

GREGORY A. SCHIRMER

David Hughes's ninth novel, a small, tightly constructed book, is rooted in the author's preoccupation with the continuing effects of this century's two major wars. Set in present-day Europe, *The Pork Butcher* deftly explores the inescapable burden of the past on the present, and has much to say about the nature of love in our times.

The novel is organized around a long-delayed journey of expiation. Forty years ago, the protagonist, a 64-year-old German butcher named Ernst Kestner, participated in a massacre by German troops of 700 inhabitants of the French village of Lascaud....

A scene of collective horror, Lascaud was also the home of the one woman Kestner ever loved, the young wife of a member of the French Resistance. For 40 empty years, Kestner has lived on the memories of one brief moment of passion, a passion that burned all the more fiercely because it was founded on risk and inflamed by it....

By contrast, the postwar generation—embodied in Kestner's daughter, Tina, unhappily married to a Frenchman and living in Paris—seems capable only of a desultory, disappointed love. Kestner's memories, rendered in a poignantly lyrical prose, are sharply counterpointed by the inert, at times Pinteresque quality of the conversations between him and his daughter as they travel south toward Lascaud....

But Mr. Hughes puts a postmodernist twist on the romantic memories of the father and the deflating realism of the daughter. Kestner is driven to confess his secret privately to Tina and publicly to the major of Lascaud, whose family was destroyed in the massacre. Because the reader hears Kestner's story several times—in Kestner's memory and in his revelations to Tina and the mayor—he is forced to confront the extremely relative nature of fictional and historical truth. "Facts change their nature as readily as people can," the mayor tells Kestner. "There is nothing absolute about either."

Nonetheless, Mr. Hughes clearly insists in *The Pork Butcher* that man's hope for a better future depends in large part on trying to interpret and understand the past. At the end of the novel, after their confrontation with the nightmare of recent European history, private and public, Kestner and Tina are rewarded with a chance to redeem themselves—for Kestner, in the book's dramatic climax, a final opportunity to absolve himself; and for Tina, a love affair that holds at least some promise of the passion that she has lived without for so long.

Gregory A. Schirmer, "A Taste for Risk," in The New York Times Book Review, *May 19, 1985, p. 15.*

SALLY EMERSON

In the most memorable episode in David Hughes's flamboyant new novel *But For Bunter,* the narrator is swept off to luncheon in Boulogne by the hero of it all, Archibald Aitken, the man on whom Billy Bunter was based, or so he claims. Now a wicked, sybaritic old man with a gift for stirring up trouble, he informs the narrator, Patrick Weymouth, that he held a luncheon in 1920 at that very restaurant for those on whom Frank Richards, creator of Greyfriars, based his young heroes. . . .

With great ingenuity and panache David Hughes makes Archibald responsible, directly or indirectly, for much of 20th-century history from the sinking of the *Titanic* to the whole of the Second World War. His portrait of the old man and his rambling house and bizarre companion is quite superb.

The motor power behind this rewriting of history is the relationship between the narrator, his secretary and his divorced wife who sets him off on the trail of the enigmatic but verbose Archibald. Before he was inspired by the search for the truth about Greyfriars Patrick was passionless, treating his affair with his secretary rather as another letter to be dictated. Through their mutual obsession with Bunter, however, he grows up and they grow together.

It is a funny, outrageous book written with freshness and pace by a writer who is beginning to be as well known . . . as he deserves to be.

Sally Emerson, in a review of "But For Bunter," in The Illustrated London News, *Vol. 273, No. 7046, September, 1985, p. 63.*

PATRICIA CRAIG

'But for Bunter the result might have been serious,' says a character in the *Magnet* 'India' series of 1926, giving credit to the fat schoolboy blunderer whose tomfoolery—quite by accident—has saved the day. It's a custom of Bunter's to run headlong into things, with preposterously beneficial results for all concerned. David Hughes, in [*But for Bunter*], takes this trait and turns it on its head: the outcome of Bunter's intervention in certain notable episodes of the 20th century is very serious indeed. By this account, Bunter is personally responsible for the arrest of Crippen and the sinking of the *Titanic*, not to mention the Somme debacle and consequent prolonging of the First World War. . . .

Billy Bunter? 'Bunter,' states Hughes's narrator firmly at the start of the novel, 'was a character in a schoolboy paper called the *Magnet*. He came on the scene in 1908 when he was 14 and vanished from it, having added not a year to his age, when the paper ceased publication in 1940.' (There's a slight error here: Bunter's age is always 15.) A figment of popular culture, in other words, of no more substance than Desperate Dan. Ah, but Hughes imagines the future author of the Greyfriars stories, in or about 1907, doing the rounds of English public schools in search of characters to insert into his projected schoolboy series, and—having exhausted the possibilities of Eton, Harrow and so on—pouncing jubilantly on an outsize figure found attending a rather less venerable establishment. Archibald Aitken. It's Aitken-Bunter who's imposed himself on the 20th century, just as Bunter—a peripheral character to start with—imposed himself on the Companion Papers. . . .

Having invented a striking prototype for an imaginary dumpling, Hughes goes on gleefully to appropriate some public figures for the rest of the *Magnet* cast: for instance, we are asked to suppose that Frank Richards (his real name was Charles Hamilton, but Hughes affects not to know this), scouring Eton with a literary purpose in mind, came face to face with a boy called Anthony Eden and put him down on paper as Harry Wharton. . . . The author of *But for Bunter,* indeed, has a lot of fun selecting later celebrities with whom to equate the jolly boys of Greyfriars, though this is something of a hit-or-miss procedure. . . . The success of this particular game depends on the appropriateness of the linkages effected. For poor Mr Quelch—the formidable form master—Hughes crosses A. E. Housman with Jack the Ripper. It really isn't a suitable concoction. Mauleverer, though, seems a proper boyhood embodiment for the Prince of Wales—and Mrs Simpson is brought in satisfactorily to extend the role at Greyfriars reserved for Marjorie Hazeldene, an especially ripping schoolgirl in everyone's view.

Where in all this, we might ask, is the Bounder of Greyfriars? Another strand in contemporary history might have been adumbrated by means of this particular figure: a delinquent one. Burgess or Blunt would have fitted the bill. But it's clear that Hughes has been chary of apportioning waywardness to anyone other than his hero, Aitken-Bunter, to avoid displacing the classic Owl from the centre of the stage. Some decided liberties are taken with the character of Bunter, not all of them justified by the assertion that Frank Richards got it wrong. That's fine for the purposes of Hughes's novel, but not when it's carried back to the stories themselves. Bunter was never knowingly a mocker or a lord of misrule. He wasn't at 'the head' of any clique—on the contrary, he epitomises the hanger-on. When Hughes mentions Bunter's 'magnificent frailty' we may wonder how this attribute evolved out of such habits, peculiar to the Owl of Greyfriars, as tittering at others' mishaps and getting himself in a jammy state. It's a failing of *But for Bunter* that it resorts too often to hyperbole. . . . But the theme of the novel is inspired and audacious. Even if he doesn't quite pull it off, David Hughes deserves a lot of credit for his attempt to furnish a merry commentary on the infatuation with the English public school and its ethics which persists in certain circles, and the implications of this attitude for society at large. (You could call it another manifestation—a more frivolous one—of Hughes's concern with the 'evasions and fantasies' by which people live, noted by the *LRB* reviewer of *The Pork Butcher* [see excerpt above by Patrick Parrinder].) The mingling of the Greyfriars Remove and various historical moves makes a splendid ploy, but a slightly sharper touch would have been required to get the utmost funniness out of it. (p. 15)

Patricia Craig, "Larks," in London Review of Books, *Vol. 7, No. 16, September 19, 1985, pp. 15-16.*

DAVID SEXTON

"Billy Bunter", George Orwell reluctantly admitted in 1940, "must be one of the best-known figures in English fiction; for the mere number of people who know him he ranks with Sexton Blake, Tarzan, Sherlock Holmes and a handful of characters in Dickens." . . .

[*But for Bunter*] aims to examine, not just profit from, the prominence of Bunter in the English middle-class male psyche.

Patrick Weymouth is a fifty-year-old senior civil servant, working on "where and how and why English culture has taken the wrong turn".... He encounters eighty-nine-year-old Archibald Aitken, an obese rogue who claims to be the original of Billy Bunter. The rest of the book is taken up by the gradual disclosure not only that this is the case, but that Aitken/Bunter has influenced every important event in British history this century, and that many who figure in the latter were also characters from the stories.... Lord Mauleverer was Edward VIII, Harry Wharton was Anthony Eden, Bob Cherry was Montgomery, Johhny Bull was J. B. Priestley, Hurree Jamset Ram Singh was Nehru, Frank Nugent was Oswald Mosley, Fisher T. Fish was T. S. Eliot, and so on.

These identifications were obviously the inspiration of the book, for apart from the gradual revelation of them, it has little plot. Weymouth ends up enormously cheered by the perception that twentieth-century history has been nothing more than a gigantic expansion of the pranks of Greyfriars....

Hughes is a highly competent novelist, and *But for Bunter* is not ill-written. But why did he think he had a good idea here? It seems in no way to follow from his previous novel, the prizewinning *The Pork Butcher*.... A closer look, however, reveals continuities: some of them disconcerting, like the unexpected appearance of words such as "chortle"; the extended descriptions of food, and the theme of an ageing man trying to make sense of the part he has played in the history of his time.

But for Bunter expresses, I suspect, a serious feeling that "the facts of this century simply aren't good enough as they stand". The feeling is reasonable, but the version of history which is substituted is just a club joke. "If only culture were a public school", says Weymouth's minister. In England, alas, for many it is.

David Sexton, "Taking the Grin Out of Greyfriars," in The Times Literary Supplement, *No. 4303, September 20, 1985, p. 1028.*

Josephine Jacobsen

1908-

Canadian-born American poet, short story writer, critic, and essayist.

Jacobsen's poetry is noted for its spare, elegant language and broad range of form and subject matter. She explores such concerns as communication, death, love, spirituality, and primitive modes of thought and behavior in verse often imbued with animal and natural imagery. Although Jacobsen often examines dark and mysterious elements of life, she is regarded as a poet of affirmation who articulates her themes with intelligence and conviction. Critics note that Jacobsen's poetry derives its power from her skillful use of metaphor, irony, and understatement blended with wit and compassion. Joyce Carol Oates echoed the sentiments of many critics when she asserted: "Josephine Jacobsen's characteristically understated poems [attempt] to calibrate, in exquisite, polished and unfailingly intelligent language, the wonders and horrors of the interior landscape."

Jacobsen gained critical attention with the publication of *Let Each Man Remember* (1940). This volume, which features fifteen love sonnets and a section of metaphysical lyric poems, reveals her ability to compose poetry within disciplined forms. *The Human Climate: New Poems* (1953) contains intensely personal verse in which Jacobsen conveys through direct and incisive language her views on the injustices and hypocrisies of the world. Jacobsen's next work, *The Animal Inside* (1966), displays her range of subject and form. This collection contains poems about animals, including a sestina on hummingbirds, as well as meditative pieces probing love and death. Included in this volume is the poem "Painter in Xyochtl," which depicts the ritual murder of an American artist presumed to be the devil by a tribe of Central American Indians. Jacobsen's rendering of this event was praised for offering a sensitive portrait of the primitive mind.

In *The Shade-Seller: New and Selected Poems* (1974), Jacobsen further reveals her interest in primitive natural forces. Claire Hahn commented: "[Jacobsen's] awareness of the wild, harsh beauty of the primitive inevitably invites comparison with D. H. Lawrence. . . . [She] shares with him the authoritative power of expressing an acute perception of other modes of existence than the human." In her next collection, *The Chinese Insomniacs* (1981), Jacobsen examines the role of language in building and maintaining human relationships and community. In many of these poems, she employs a detached tone and minimalist structure to emphasize her themes. Jacobsen's recent collection, *The Sisters: New and Selected Poems* (1987), contains representative poems from her five previous volumes as well as new works.

Jacobsen is also highly respected for her short fiction, which is collected in *A Walk with Raschid and Other Stories* (1978) and *Adios, Mr. Moxley* (1986). Set in such diverse locales as Baltimore, the Caribbean Islands, Mexico, and Morocco, the pieces in these volumes are considered powerful in their examination of loneliness, betrayal, oppression, illness, and dishonesty. Jacobsen's stories often end unresolved, leaving the reader to speculate about the future of her characters. Critics attribute the impact of Jacobsen's short fiction to her skillful

Photograph by Layle Silbert

characterization and evocative prose. Jacobsen has also collaborated with William Mueller on two respected critical studies, *The Testament of Samuel Beckett* (1964) and *Ionesco and Genet: Playwrights of Silence* (1968).

(See also *Contemporary Authors*, Vols. 33-36, rev. ed. and *Contemporary Authors New Revision Series*, Vol. 23.)

AMY BONNER

[*Let Each Man Remember*] opens with a group of fifteen love sonnets, **"Winter Castle,"** celebrating the turns and reaches of passion in "this black heap / Lifting its stones from these forgotten snows." The opening sonnet sets background and atmosphere:

> This rage shall be our sweets of spring. No birds
> Shall sing at these cold casements, and the day
> Will bring no sun to thaw such ice—but words
> That shall be spoken here and in such way
> Not all July as these shall burn so bright
> Within this sorrowful and savage night.

The sequence closes on the same bleak, wintry note: "Forever shall we stand / Hearing the wind along the frozen land." This poet is at home in the sonnet, and some of her sonnets are the best pieces in the book, although they are marred by the frequent use of "ere" (sometimes alternating with "before," according to metrical convenience). Perhaps some of Miss Jacobsen's earlier work has been included among the lyrics in the second section, for there is a marked transitional quality, an unevenness, not only among the poems but among the lines of individual poems. However, though [Jacobsen] does not always quite realize the full intention of her poem, she is clearly well on the way to the goal of discipline defined in her artist's credo, **"Poet, When You Rhyme."** The lyrics in metaphysical vein have yet to attain a certain austerity which we associate with this genre. Among these, **"Immortal Element"** is the most successful. (pp. 288-89)

Amy Bonner, in a review of "Let Each Man Remember," in Poetry, *Vol. LIX, No. 5, February, 1942, pp. 288-89.*

SARA HENDERSON HAY

One encounters so much dehumanized and impersonal poetry these days that it is pleasant and stimulating to meet poems which are intensely personal, even opinionated. Josephine Jacobsen's **The Human Climate** is the work of a poet who is decidedly herself, who speaks her convictions briskly and boldly. The phrase "of course" and the implication "of course" appear frequently in these poems. She feels passionately about the cruelties and the injustices and the hypocrisies of the world, and she is no hesitant partisan of the victims. The emotional impact of her poetry is considerable, and its effectiveness is compounded of her own deep feeling and her skill with her medium. She is never incoherent or diffuse; her idiom is direct, incisive, economical.

Miss Jacobsen's approach, while intensely personal, as I have suggested, is controlled and disciplined. Irony, understatement, the trenchant and telling phrase are the tools she uses to drive home the points she wishes to make. The poem entitled **"For Any Member of the Security Police,"** for example, cloaks its passionate denunciation behind an icy and bitterly satiric inquiry:

> Let us ask you a few questions, without rancor,
> In simple curiosity, putting aside
> Our reactions or the rising of our gorge,
> As a child asks How does it work? . . . . .

The innocence of the child as contrasted with the guilty adult, the helpless, the beaten down, "the odd, the inward-turned, the isolated," those seeking escape from whatever tyranny, engage her attention and her compassion. There is, to be sure, more than a hint of indebtedness to T. S. Eliot in some of these poems, . . . but in the main Miss Jacobsen's work bears no imprint except her own.

Compassion is the keynote, and there are wit and generosity in such counsel as **"Give to the Rich"**. . . .

Sara Henderson Hay, "Personal Poetry," in The Saturday Review, *New York, Vol. 37, No. 3, January 16, 1954, p. 21.*

HENRY RAGO

Josephine Jacobsen at her best can move very gracefully from line to line and carry the whole poem with her, and for a good

while now she has been seen at her best in many places. In her new book [*The Human Climate*], I'd point out **"They Were Showing a Film of Bermuda in Hammond II"** and **"The Storm Cleared Rapidly,"** both from the sequence **"April Asylum,"** as two quite distinguished poems; and her **"Ballad of Henry, Bridegroom,"** with its more special tricks, as a poem equally good. At her second-best, she gives us good Passages—particularly in the sequence **"Variations on Variety"** and in the poems **"Light"** and **"The Birds."** At her third-best, she gives us Moments. I'm grateful for some of these moments, when they are reaches toward the luminous; I'm less grateful for them when they go in the opposite direction and sacrifice the movement of the poem for the slightly garish, suggesting—while remaining above—the chromium-plated image and want-ad syntax which are the conventions of the quasi-modern. "Suggesting" was the careful word; nothing stronger; but for a poet as good as Josephine Jacobsen, the risk of even free association is bad enough. (pp. 173-74)

Henry Rago, in a review of "The Human Climate," in Poetry, *Vol. LXXXIV, No. 3, June, 1954, pp. 173-75.*

WILLIAM JAY SMITH

The scene of Josephine Jacobsen's **The Animal Inside,** a third collection, ranges all the way from Pennsylvania to Haiti. With an eye attracted to small natural detail, she writes of starfish and reindeer; one of her finest poems is a sestina on hummingbirds, **"The Murmurers."** Its key words, "feather," "flower," "wing," "light," "sun," "air," are characteristic of Mrs. Jacobsen's work, which has a lightness and airiness about it. She is sometimes excellent in observing people close up, as in **"Deaf-Mutes at the Ballgame."** But Mrs. Jacobsen is never merely pictorial; she is interested in "the animal inside the animal," the spiritual motivation of reality. Her observant eye and varied interest, reflected in a broad range of skillfully handled stanza forms, makes for a most attractive volume. . . .

William Jay Smith, "Commitment," in The New York Times Book Review, *December 11, 1966, p. 60.*

LAURENCE LIEBERMAN

Josephine Jacobsen is gifted with the power to get outside her own personality and assume the identity of the subject that absorbs her. The more daringly remote her subject—the further it carries her outside herself—the better she writes, and Mrs. Jacobsen has a knack for choosing subjects most tractable to her talents. Even when she deals with deaths in her family [in *The Animal Inside*], she cultivates an odd impersonality. She always chooses far relatives—cousins, uncles—not near ones: deaths she can sink into to the hips, but not over her head and shoulders; deaths which are her own, and not her own, at once. Despite the limited intimacy, there is no loss of intensity. The measured portions of personal involvement allow emotional leeway for her to explore the geography of death with detachment.

Especially moving are the poems which illuminate primitive or mythical styles of thought. **"Painter in Xyochtl"** resuscitates the true story of an American painter murdered by a tribe of Central American Indians. The poet is so successful in suspending civilizing judgments, she is able to suggest total absence of brutality—great humaneness, even—in the chiefs, who exercize restraint before committing the ritual murder of the man they take to be a devil. The poem is Lawrentian in its authoritative grasp, its sensitivity to the primitive mind. (p. 398)

Laurence Lieberman, "Art in Transition," in Poetry, Vol. CIX, No. 6, March, 1967, pp. 395-99.

SAMUEL FRENCH MORSE

Josephine Jacobsen, in *The Animal Inside,* reveals an admirable range of subject and form and is, in some respects, her own best critic: "Not being of a primitive tribe / I speak in metaphor..." she writes, in **"Arrival of My Cousin."** The cumulative effect of her book is of too much metaphor and, despite her mastery of a variety of modes, too little discipline. She finds it difficult to resist putting everything in; for example, one may cite the first stanza of her sestina, **"The Murmurers"**:

They are formidable under any feather
and each name; of fly, of sharp sound, soft sound or
    flower:
oiseau-mouche, zum-zum, beija flor—these on the
    wing.
Their color? Science cries like a lover, of their light:
Heliomaster, Stellula, Chrysolampsis, Sapphira—sun
fire, star fire, torch fire, jewel fire in the air.

It is as if a responsiveness to light, sound, and the unexpected correspondences around us by themselves made poetry. Ultimately, the attraction of *The Animal Inside* depends on the reader's ability to share Mrs. Jacobsen's enthusiasms. (pp. 118-19)

Samuel French Morse, "Poetry 1966," in Contemporary Literature, Vol. 9, No. 1, Winter, 1968, pp. 112-29.

ROSEMARY F. DEEN

The Animal Inside collects nearly seventy poems of Josephine Jacobsen, going back to 1953, and what a pleasure it is to have them. What you notice first is a sureness of language, hard to define but easy enough to recognize in experience. You read to a point where you sense what must come and at the same time know that it exceeds language. But then she always says the right thing. Finally you realize that the source is not fixed, like a cornucopia, but a living principle—a way of seeing. So all good poetry humanizes us by attaching our trust to the possible human enterprise.

This special kind of speech is what much of the poetry is about. It has two qualities: it is close to silence and it is articulated richly. So it loves understatement; there is not one shout in 100 pages. But this "silence" is more than few words; it is the need for speech. Poetry tries to keep speech and the need for speech together because only the emptiness we experience... calls out the most complete satisfaction. "All need is dry. Rain is the metaphor," is how Mrs. Jacobsen puts it. In another poem, water even in abundance—in strawberry gardens or in a volcano's deep core—is "the merest blandest brush with water." But the "days of a desert blind and cracked and white with light and stones, bones, bone stones and limbs of barebone trees" produce water "in the mind, the ear, the bone": "All that land hummed like a wire with absent water." So, like Andersen's mermaid, selling her tongue to be human and articulating swans into men in her extremity, the poet is "mute": "silent... in the terrible silence of speech."

Ordinary silence, of course, is the lack of a listener. The full articulation of Mrs. Jacobsen's poems grows out of their dependence on a listener. The fact that listening is active gives poetry richness by making it "obliquely run"—giving it "angle." Communication, like the "songless" hummingbirds' plumage, requires "three in one—light, angle, eye, to flower into their color." "Interference is the cause of iridescence."

This indirect relationship is frequently expressed by the metaphor *cousin.* The great starfish in its "water's stellar space" is the "cool cousin marine" of a star. We cannot make that relationship more direct without destroying it altogether. Hauled out and stung to death by ants, the starfish warps: "Here is your sting. O death, where is your star?" We speak to our dying cousin only indirectly, "of how the tendrils of vines Curl opposite ways in the opposite hemispheres," but with richer articulation, trusting that indirect relationships extend into death's opposite hemisphere. Like those tendrils, Mrs. Jacobsen's delicate and "silent" poetry makes connections that are all alive and strong. (pp. 416-17)

Rosemary F. Deen, in a review of "The Animal Inside," in Commonweal, Vol. LXXXIX, No. 12, December 20, 1968, pp. 416-17.

CLAIRE HAHN

Josephine Jacobsen's voice is assured and quiet. The surface of her poems [as evidenced in *The Shade Seller: New and Selected Poems*] is calm, deceptively so. She is a brilliant technician capable of fascinating the reader with rhythm and texture, of lulling him to sensuous rest by the purest poetry. Then she abruptly catches him by the throat with the revelation of some terrifying primal truth.

Jacobsen's poetry is not limited or easily categorized, however. The range of her subject matter is wide and her vision often wryly compassionate. The most commonplace object elicits her meditative attention. She actually writes a poem about a dishwasher and makes it a comment on the human predicament. But it is in her incredibly penetrating vision of civilization transparently superimposed on the primitive forces of nature that she is most powerful. **"Bush Christmas Eve"** is a marvelous poem, reminiscent in theme of Blake's "The Tyger." In the poem Jacobsen has her persona remember the mild animals in pictures of the crèche as she looks out at "the green jelly of Hyena's eye" and sees the crocodile grinning at "the oldest coldest jest." The poem concludes with a stunning act of faith:

Welcome. I cannot bless
that green, that grin.
You who imagined them, bless
them by coming.

And since I bless
you coming, why, I praise
and bless what you imagined,
with you between them.
Only come.

Her awareness of the wild, harsh beauty of the primitive inevitably invites comparison with D. H. Lawrence. Jacobsen's **"The Wild Parrots of Bloody Bay," "The Foreign Lands," "Future Green,"** are not Lawrentian footnotes or echoes but she shares with him the authoritative power of expressing an acute perception of other modes of existence than the human.

These are poems informed by wisdom and passion. The title poem of her volume suggests Jacobsen's ideal. She is a "shade seller." In the "candescent sand and a great noise of heat" that is the contemporary world, she speaks the word of her poetry, "heavy / and wide and green." A reader steps gratefully into that shade. It offers respite, a place of perspective. Josephine Jacobsen is an important voice in contemporary American poetry. (pp. 217-18)

Claire Hahn, in a review of "The Shade Seller," in Commonweal, *Vol. CI, No. 8, November 29, 1974, pp. 217-18.*

JAMES MARTIN

In any century or era, there are ideas and images which become temporarily conventional, but beyond these, or possibly within them, there are more basic ideas, bound by neither time nor nationality, which *should* be written about. These basic ideas constitute our myths, our shared experience, and will always pre-occupy the human mind, without the popularity of fad and fashion. Through time, they have proved either too strange or too familiar for final conclusions. *The Shade-Seller,* by Josephine Jacobsen . . . [explores and defends] these pre-occupations.

The Shade-Seller is not only pleasurable to the ear, but almost tense with demands that the reader comprehend, relate. The poems have the inevitability of natural events like the migration of birds or the approach of rain. Carefully made, they seem to break down the world and digest the meanings that are inescapable. Josephine Jacobsen has sifted thoughts cautiously, put down words gently, desiring, above all, to speak sincerely. (p. 113)

Ms. Jacobsen has always been a poet of affirmation and her new book retains the strengths of her earlier work. She celebrates love and language and helps us see that we belong, that our common interests are more important than our individuality. . . . (p. 114)

James Martin, "Questions of Style," in Poetry, *Vol. CXXVI, No. 2, May, 1975, pp. 103-15.*

PUBLISHERS WEEKLY

[The pieces collected in *A Walk with Raschid and Other Stories*] are, as one might expect, remarkable stories, beautifully written. They tell of particular moments of triumph, pain, tragedy, humiliation, pity, of people who are fully human as they make choices, act, realize the potential of their lives. In **"Late Fall,"** Father Consadine confronts the lion and the desert in his own way beneath a hard, blue but darkening Vermont sky as night and leaves fall. **"Nel Bagno"** has Mrs. Glessner trapped ludicrously, her panic and relief moving her across thresholds. In [**"A Walk with Raschid"**], the Gantrys encounter a young Moroccan and find that some gulfs cannot be bridged. Gemlike, lovely stories from Jacobsen. . . .

A review of "A Walk with Raschid and Other Stories," in Publishers Weekly, *Vol. 213, No. 24, June 12, 1978, p. 71.*

CHOICE

[*A Walk with Raschid and Other Stories* is a] first collection of short stories that is first rate. It will surprise none of the ad-

mirers of Josephine Jacobsen, well-known for her poetry, that her prose is perceptive and acute. The stories, conventional in form, emphasize plot and character. They are both moving and disturbing; their impact is powerful. In [**"A Walk with Raschid"**], a particularly fine example of all that the genre is capable of, Jacobsen explores the nuances of love and treachery and their interrelatedness. Once read, it is not soon forgotten.

A review of "A Walk with Raschid and Other Stories," in Choice, *Vol. 15, No. 10, December, 1978, p. 1368.*

JOYCE CAROL OATES

The Chinese Insomniacs is the fifth book of poetry by a writer who has distinguished herself over the past three decades in fiction and criticism as well as poetry. . . . Josephine Jacobsen's characteristically understated poems attempt to calibrate, in exquisite, polished and unfailingly intelligent language, the wonders and horrors of the interior landscape. . . .

The Chinese Insomniacs is Miss Jacobsen's first book since *The Shade Seller: New and Selected Poems* (1974). Like that deftly modulated collection, this book manages to be many things—the record, in verse, of an uncommonly intelligent sensibility confronted with the ironies of daily life; a terse, elliptical, highly civilized meditation upon mortality; a splendidly inventive formalist examination of wildly disparate "forms"—among them a starving Eskimo woman, spiders whose improvised web-spinning suggests an uncanny kinship with the poet, an elderly gentleman cursed by senility, and doomed African animals contemplating their "million bones benevolently whitening." There are poems with titles that are both arch and apologetic—**"Language as an Escape From the Discrete," "Elective Affinities," "Bulletin From the Writer's Colony"**—but the poet's strategy is to look very close, to examine with a jeweller's resolute eye the enigma at the heart of the concrete. (p. 13)

The poems are reminiscent of John Crowe Ransom, Elizabeth Bishop, Emily Dickinson—each a fastidiously imagined, brilliantly pared back, miniature narrative that nearly always yields up a small shock of wonder. Like the beautifully made and frequently alarming stories in *A Walk With Raschid* (1979), the poems display an art that conceals itself without being coy or evasive. Death's intimacy is a constant theme: "Plurality in death / fogs our mind" one poem boldly announces. But the manner is graceful, gracious, unforced, choosing to focus upon the quirkiness of the particular in order to illuminate the abstract. . . .

Like Elizabeth Bishop, Josephine Jacobsen might be considered a poet's poet—meant, in this case, as the highest praise. Both her fiction and poetry give pleasure after countless rereadings; the full worth of her accomplishment has yet to be measured. One might begin with **"Short Views in Africa"** in this volume, or such small, perfect, gemlike stories as **"Breath"** and **"On the Island"** from *A Walk With Raschid.* Here is powerful emotion filtered through an uncommon intelligence. (p. 28)

Joyce Carol Oates, in a review of "The Chinese Insomniacs," in The New York Times Book Review, *April 4, 1982, pp. 13, 28-9.*

ROSEMARY DEEN

Good poems have some of the qualities of objects; solid, less destructible than their creators, recognizable even in the dark. Josephine Jacobsen's poems [as evidenced in *The Chinese Insomniacs*] are like that now. Their big, thematic words haven't tamed them, or blown them apart; the themes have gone into the structure of the poems. Her poems are not *about* love and death, or about herself in the way confessional poems are. So we can't name them with names outside the poems. What we might call *loss,* she sees, by "time's trick," fused with its counterpart, permanence: "the rose and green are set now on the apple's icy bark."

Reading these beautiful poems, we see how the "universal" in poetry is structural rather than thematic, a poet's themes being really promises, suggesting a world we want to inhabit. Josephine Jacobsen's poems construct out of language a "universe," a world complete in its own terms, so that within it all the poems' sentences are "universal," even those that don't assert anything. A word in one poem answers a word in another, apparently very different poem in the same way that the opposed, polar terms of metaphor are in speech together. Poetry like this stands for something important about language: that we *learned* it, that language is potentially the human society inside us.

This intellectual quality of Josephine Jacobsen's poems is what makes them serious and keeps them from the dark. The disappearance of the subject into the poem is one of the things she means by "silence" ("the gardens go into their / naked rose"). "Silence," embraced as it is by quotation marks, sounds highfalutin, but it's a pretty accurate word. "Silence" is anti-heroic, the opposite of *rhetoric,* where rhetoric celebrates the claims of power. (p. 502)

"Silence" in these poems is itself the possession (rather than the assertion) of power, especially of experience for which words are not adequate: "the illiterate body says hush, / in love says hush; says, whatever / word can serve, it is not here." The emblem of such power in Josephine Jacobsen's poetry is the animal. We catch glimpses of a beautiful and terrifying power within us which we can recognize better when we displace it into animals, and even place the animals into the myths of our culture. The cribbage players behind their glass wall window in **"A Motel in Troy New York"** see a "huge swan / . . . looking in: cumulus-cloud body, thunder-cloud dirty neck / that hoists the painted face / coral and black. Inky eyes / peer at our lives." It stands there, "squat on its yellow webs / splayed to hold / scarcely up the heavy / feathered dazzle," then it goes back to the water where it "sets sail / in one pure motion."

> and is received by distance.
> That crucial soiled snake neck
> arched to a white high curve
>
> received by distance
> and the shadowy girl
> across the water.

The child in **"The Leopard-Nurser"** imagined her vocation to "the speechless hurt great leopards / . . . beautiful, fluid and fatal / to all save me, their skilled / and speechless nurse." *Fluid* suggests that animal power is not "regulated," ruled from outside, the way we are by clocks. (pp. 502, 504)

Negative silence, the refusal or inability to speak, is the soul asleep. The real evil in speechlessness is that without language

we are "discrete." Because language stands for what we have learned, it builds a certain relationship: not *eros* ("the illiterate body says hush"), not *agape* (for things may be words, "clear as those hasty sticks / the soldier crossed and held, high / in the rosy smoke for Joan"), but *philia,* the relation Mrs. Jacobsen always calls *cousin.* In the family of man, we are all cousins. So *calling* someone *cousin* means we recognize the relationship, acknowledge an identity. Speech creates the community of those we talk to directly, struggle with in words, whom we don't lie to or ignore. The community need for speech is so deep that the lack of it deforms human enterprise:

> All the terrible silences listen always; and hear
> between breaths a gulf we know is evil.
> It is the silence that built the tower of Babel.

Poetry is one way language is "an escape from the discrete." In its need for the "silence" of speaking indirectly, of pleasure too deep for words expressed in ringings of rime, charged rhythms and leanness of language, and in the way it keeps on trying to speak the unspeakable, it identifies us. In *The Chinese Insomniacs* there is a "companionable" league of those "who had to watch," staying awake across time: Crashaw, Hardy (**"The Travelers"**), Chinese poets in 455 AD and 500 BC, Yeats, Shakespeare, and the poet who watches hunters in the woods outside the writers' colony. . . .

Often our culture seems to be outside us when we study it, but it is inside us when we speak a more than private truth. Josephine Jacobsen's literate universe is a token of possible human life. The learned, skilled, practiced "silence" of poetry speaks the images of companionable human life that may help us to hang on to it. (p. 504)

Rosemary Deen, "The Human Society inside Us," in Commonweal, *Vol. CIX, No. 16, September 24, 1982, pp. 502, 504.*

SANDRA M. GILBERT

[Language] is often Josephine Jacobsen's theme, especially the irreducible strengths and limitations of language's ability to convey the limits of life. Hers, says William Meredith in a blurb on the jacket of *The Chinese Insomniacs* . . . is "a tough generous mind which is continually surprising wonder from its cover in ordinary speech," and [his remark's] . . . emphasis on the secret complexity of "ordinary speech" particularly reflects Jacobsen's own consciousness of the poet's severe obligation in an age when, as she notes in **"Finally,"** nouns cannibalistically "swallow up / their adjectives." Thus her monosyllabic **"The Monosyllable,"** which may well have been written in virtuoso response to a challenge as playful as the one that produced Keats's "On the Grasshopper and Cricket," articulates her *credo* as well as that of many of her contemporaries with admirable, even allegorical succinctness. (p. 161)

On the one hand, this witty and metaphysical verse is a time-haunted poem. Like so many of Jacobsen's other works, it is about the erosions that strip the self to bone, about the way "the thin knives of the clock / shred minute by minute" (**"The Night Watchman"**) and the inexorable advent of the season "when we learn / or do not learn / to say goodbye" (**"It is the Season"**). Indeed, the answer to the riddle implicitly posed by the deadpan title—**"The Monosyllable"**—is no doubt "time," and in particular time as that process which does "not stall" as it shrivels the inessential. On the other hand, however, the strategy of minimalism—a self-conscious deployment of ferociously bare, fiercely unpretentious language and brief brusque lines—is exactly what Jacobsen uses to defend herself against time's diminution of her life. Thus, in an especially exemplary manner she combats the malady of the quotidian with the melody of the quotidian. For though she fears and dislikes linguistic excess, preferring, like most post-modernists, the "Thing made word—blameless uncheating / speech" (**"The Things"**), Jacobsen is also stalked by silence, by the unspeakable loneliness that is the final threat of time. In **"Language as an Escape from the Discrete,"** therefore, she confronts dumbness with dread:

> When the cat puts its furred illiterate
> paw on my page and makes a starfish,
> the space between us drains my marrow
> like a roof's edge.

If impure or excessive language implies duplicity or bombast, the denial of language results in disorder, disease, death:

> All the terrible silences listen always; and hear
> Between breaths a gulf we know is evil.
> It is the silence that built the tower of Babel.

Again, in her collection's title poem, **"The Chinese Insomniacs,"** Jacobsen quietly sets a vision of consciously spare yet deeply ambitious language against the assaults of time, and with the exception of a few slightly mannered line-breaks her own speech is here as unpretentious as the speech of the verse she celebrates. Beginning "It is good to know / the Chinese insomniacs," she affectionately recreates the nighttime sorrows and songs of a male poet and a female poet, one who lived in 495 A.D., one who lived in 500 B.C. Their works, she tells us, are suitably undemanding:

> She says her sleeve is wet
> with tears; he says something difficult
> to forget, like
> music counts the heartbeat,

Indeed, her attitude toward them is one of amiable irony, for after all she has, as her poem confesses, forgotten exactly what it was the Chinese gentleman said that was "difficult / to forget." Yet still, despite the amnesia of history, and the "tough, lean" obliterating monosyllable of time, she insists that

> It is good to have their company
> tonight: a lady, awake
> until birdsong;
> a gentleman who made
> poems later out of frag-
> ments of the dark.

Even at its most unassuming, says Jacobsen, craft will endure and console. The craftsman may be, must be, obliterated, a point she makes most brilliantly in **"Trial Run,"** her anecdote of Noah's Ark, whose carpenters understand at the last moment that "the only part of them to go would be the job." Yet such makers can finally comfort themselves with the recognition that their sacred product rode the flood well enough "so as to argue / some future fortune for a carpenter."

In her colloquial austerity, her simultaneous commitment to art and to understatement, Jacobsen often recalls Elizabeth Bishop, that crucial female traveler who learned, earlier than many of her contemporaries, to nourish her art at "rocky breasts." Poems like **"The Dream Habitués"** and **"Arachne, Astonished,"** for instance, with their idiomatic irony, their chatty delicacy, seem to place Jacobsen directly in the Bishop

line. In the first, noting that it's "Odd we've never met there, / spending all that time. / But then, it's a big country," she offers a satiric vision of dream land, comforting herself in the end with—as so often—a bone-haunted proviso: "And if one wishes, / one can always wake. / Or, so far, I have." In the second, meditating on a spider, she speculates again on the exigencies of art, particularly on the artist's unlimited capacity for struggling within and against limits. The poem's last two stanzas, like the conclusion of **"The Dream Habitués,"** are notably Bishopesque in their casual but conscious rejection of, say, [Dylan] Thomas' intense rhetoric as well as in their invention of an apparently improvisational formalism. In fact, their subject is precisely the process by which the style of this and other Jacobsen poems is created:

> Well, there are situations which ape
> that of weightlessness; without guide-
> lines, demand that thread from the guts take formal
>   shape
> while the cruelly uninflected voice says, "Improvise!"

> O weightless, astonished Arachne, such
> original alterations, situational spinning
> of constructions! You frighten me very much.
> Am I to understand, then, there is no end, none, to
>   beginning?

That the spider is both female (Arachne) and domestic (involved in "situational spinning"), however, also connects Jacobsen with the "household Gods" of dailiness. . . .Despite the literary overtones of its title (or perhaps as a comment on such overtones), for instance, her **"Elective Affinities"** is a *terza rima* celebration of the "curious daily rendezvous" between the newspaper deliverer who calls himself "Your Morning Eagle Boy" and the poet/reader to whom he brings a "diet of silliness and rape, / of murder most detailed." (pp. 162-65)

Finally, and perhaps most dramatically, Jacobsen's **"Food"** sketches a portrait of an archaic cook—"A woman of the more primitive tribes / of Eskimo"—whose essential domesticity functions as the ultimate defense of minimalism against the grandiose claims of supreme fictions. This woman's husband/ master, says Jacobsen, knows that "To trap, to kill, to drive / the dogs' ferocity is heroic to tell: / full-bellied sagas' stuff." Narrating the adventures of his life, he is, we might say, a Thomas or a Stevens, who remembers his childhood as "lamb-white" and dreams of catching tigers in "red weather." As for his wife's work, however:

> By her breath, flesh, her hands, no
> reputation will be made, no
> saga descend. It is only the
>
> next day made possible.

Like Jacobsen herself, who has learned to negotiate in and with monosyllables . . . , the Eskimo wife is a realist who sagaciously renounces sagas of baboons and periwinkles in favor of the white nightgowns which make the next day possible. (p. 165)

Sandra M. Gilbert, "The Melody of the Quotidian," in Parnassus: Poetry in Review, *Vol. 11, No. 1, Spring-Summer, 1983, pp. 147-67.*

NANCY SULLIVAN

To speak of power in connection with poetry is to conjure up images of the poetry Mafia, cultural politics, and various other questionable arenas which by definition seem antithetical to the genre. Josephine Jacobsen's concerns are certainly not with poetry hustling; they are with the intrinsic nature of the poem itself. In a poem called **"The Poem Itself"** she clarifies the issue:

> From the ripe silence it exploded silently.
> When the bright debris subsided
> it was there.
>
> Invisible, inaudible; only
> the inky shapes betrayed it.
> Betrayed, is the word. . . .

Here the pure poem escapes to speak of and for itself. It *is*. Pure energy. In a lecture called "The Instant of Knowing" delivered in Washington in 1973 while Josephine Jacobsen was Poetry Consultant to the Library of Congress, she commented that one must not "veer from the core of the job . . . As I see it, the cause, the purpose, and the end of the position of Consultant in Poetry is poetry itself, as poetry is the poet's own job. . . . The center of everything is the poem. Nothing is important in comparison to that. Anything which in some valid way is not directly connected with that current of energy which is the poem is dispensable."

A poem need not have power as its overt subject in order to concern itself with that issue. The "current of energy which is the poem" conspires with and enhances whatever subject it ignites. This is certainly true in **"The Poem Itself,"** and as additional examples I might have cited any number of poems from *The Animal Inside* such as **"Deaf-Mutes at the Ballgame"** or **"Yellow"** or even earlier poems which reflect her theory of poetry as energy and, therefore, as a vehicle of power. (pp. 2-3)

In one of the "new" poems in *The Shade-Seller, New and Selected Poems* called **"Gentle Reader"** Jacobsen's subject is her response to reading a genuine poet, "A poet, dangerous and steep," as opposed to a versifier or "a hot-shot ethic-monger." Jacobsen recognizes the real thing in an instant, in a blast of light and comprehension. The short poem ends with this stanza:

> O God, it peels me, juices me like a press;
> this poetry drinks me, eats me, gut and marrow
> until I exist in its jester's sorrow,
> until my juices feed a savage sight
> that runs along the lines, bright
> as beasts' eyes. The rubble splays to dust:
> city, book, bed, leaving my ear's lust
> saying like Molly, yes, yes, yes O yes.

Josephine Jacobsen's theory of poetry as energy, as power, is here realized and made incarnate in the brightness of "the beasts' eyes" and "the ear's lust." The poet *knows* that she has encountered the real thing. . . . In this poem, both the articulation of the theory in such radiant language and the theory itself miraculously fuse, and that, says Josephine Jacobsen, is what poetry is all about.

In an intricate poem called **"Language as an Escape From the Discrete"** from Jacobsen's 1981 collection, *The Chinese Insomniacs,* an arc is constructed from the insect world where two wasps mate (or fight) to a cat who puts "its furred illiterate / paw on my page" and who, like the poet, drinks milk and will inevitably experience one breath which will be final. The fourth stanza introduces a human element in the person

of a questioning child, and the arc is completed in stanza five by the adult who

> in love, says hush; says, whatever
> word can serve, it is not here.
> All the terrible silences listen always; and hear
> between breaths a gulf we know is evil.
> It is the silence that built the tower of Babel.

The darker side of the poet's ongoing search for the radiant center is thus energized by this exploration of the frustrating side of the medium of language. The poet gropes and grapples and finally turns the inarticulate into an advantage: all silence is not golden. Babel with all of its ensuing conflicts was inevitable and necessary.

In a more recent poem, **"The Motion,"** not yet collected into a volume of poems, Josephine Jacobsen examines the hush of the moment of change. What is transition? When and how does the geranium's bud burst into full flower? Time and the seasons move forward yet "turn over / without stir or whisper." The energy crouches unseen, a flicker. Note the beautiful closure of **"The Motion."**

> If I could see it happen, I could
> know when all tides tip; low luck
> shifts; and when loss is ready. When
> you are saying goodbye to someone you think
> you'll see next week. And don't ever.

These lines, in their wisdom and scope, are beyond comment as the mysterious, stoppered aspects of natural forces beckon Jacobsen into truth's fathomless mysteries. (pp. 3-4)

Josephine Jacobsen often writes poems one must characterize as "narrative" in that they are animated by some progression or action that culminates in a resolution. The characters in these narrative poems are people we come to care very much about such as Mr. Mahoney in **"Mr. Mahoney"** or Father O'Hare and Mrs. Pondicherry in **"Pondicherry Blues"** or Mrs. Mobey in **"Spread of Mrs. Mobey's Lawn,"** all poems in Josephine Jacobsen's most recent collection *The Chinese Insomniacs.* Another poem in this volume called **"The Fiction Writer"** reveals not only her commitment to the storyteller's art but her ability to evoke its mysteries:

> Last night in a dream
> or vision or barrier broken
> strange people came to me.
> I recognized them.
>
> Some I had made, I thought.
> Still they were strange—fuller, somehow—
> with distinct objects ahead of their steps.

(p. 4)

Josephine Jacobsen's short stories are classic examples of the genre. Something happens in them; people change; development occurs. This is also true in her numerous narrative poems. Jacobsen dislikes stories with tidy endings, the climactic sentence. Her stories are open-ended. . . . Most of Josephine Jacobsen's best stories are concerned with her belief that human beings when given power all too often misuse that power. The themes of these stories, and of many of her poems, are political in the cosmic rather than the literal sense. Sometimes the accoutrements of the powers struggling involve a conflict between blacks and whites in her native Baltimore or on tropical islands where blacks are in the majority rather than in the minority, at least in numbers; sometimes the power struggle revolves around the oppression of the young by the old or vice-versa. Among her newer stories, **"Sunday Morning," "The Squirrels of Summer,"** and **"Protection,"** for example, explore these conflicts. While the settings and situations in the individual stories vary considerably, the theme is a constant.

In one of Josephine Jacobsen's best known stories, **"A Walk With Raschid,"** one finds a classic Jacobsen situation. The setting is exotic: Fez, Morocco. The happiness of the recently married heroine, Tracy Gantry, is threatened by the invisible presence of Oliver, son of her husband James Gantry's previous marriage. This lurking presence is mirrored in the character Raschid, a small ten-year-old Arab boy, a child as dark as Gantry's own son is fair and who is the same age as the absent Oliver Gantry. The tight plot which encircles the story revolves around a walk with Raschid as guide, which never takes place, but in the end provides the impetus for speculation as to the future of all of the characters, and especially about the lasting power of James Gantry's second marriage to Tracy.

James Gantry experiences an instant rapport with Raschid when he arranges for the boy to take him and a somewhat reluctant Tracy on a guided tour of the town on their last day in Fez, instead of their going to visit a film director who is an acquaintance of a restless, aimless couple they've met at the hotel. Tracy is less enthusiastic about the arrangement not merely because she wishes to meet the director but because, as we surmise later, she recognizes James's paternal attraction to the boy Raschid, who reminds him, in a perverse way, of Oliver, who is her chief rival for James's love. Secretly, Tracy pays off Raschid before he can take them anywhere. Reacting to this demeaning bribe, he kicks her. The story is beautifully crafted; at its conclusion we are forced to speculate about the future of the Gantry marriage.

A darker strain becomes more apparent in many of Jacobsen's stories published since the volume *A Walk With Raschid*. In a recent long story with an island setting, which has a peculiar similarity to **"A Walk With Raschid,"** and which is called **"The Mango Community,"** (recently published in *The Ontario Review* and soon to be reprinted in the O'Henry anthology of *Best Stories of 1984*), an unmarried American couple, Jane Megan, a painter, and Henry Sewell, a writer, along with Dan Megan, Jane's fifteen year old son by a previous marriage, are discovered by the reader living on the island of Ste. Cecile where they've come for an indeterminate stay. The surface conflict is both political and racial on this island where one's color determines one's destiny. The Vice-Consul urges the Americans to leave before the growing political tension erupts into a malignant violence. Their next-door neighbors, the Montroses, are native blacks; the Montroses' son, Alexis, and Dan play cricket together and come to symbolize much that is latent in the rest of the story and in the culture. Jane, as mother, is obsessed with the notion that Dan might be shot, arrested, or otherwise hurt. As it turns out, it is Alexis who is "hurt" in a most awful manner: paralyzed for life as the result of the brutality of the local police and thus never again able to aspire to his dream of becoming a professional cricket player, a profession that would buy his way out of the poverty that is the lot of his people on this their native island.

Alexis's accident is partially the result of happenstance and of Henry Sewell's pseudo-liberal political leanings, which tempted young Dan to join him on a political march. Without his parent's knowledge or permission, Alexis also joins them. Jane discovers the tragic result of the march when she returns from what had been a very rejuvenating painting session.

The Montroses respond to the assault on their son with spartan rage. Mr. Montrose snarls at Jane, "You go to hell. . . . Evil, evil, evil. All of you. Go home—if you have one." Jane and Dan do go home. Henry Sewell remains on the island to try to "fix things." The double doors close on the story leaving the essential questions unanswered but exposed and discussed. The questions posed are more interesting than any possible answers might be. Will Jane and Henry meet again, marry, make a good life together with Dan? Have the circumstances over which they had little control made or broken them? The reader is left to speculate on the futures of these three characters as well as the nationals left on Ste. Cecile. All of these fictional people have a life beyond the events in the story, as is true in all of Jacobsen's best stories.

A close examination of the wide spectrum of Josephine Jacobsen's short stories reveals a great variety of characters and situations as well as a diversity of settings, but all of them enlighten the reader through a similar integrity of vision. Her carefully plotted, meticulously written stories reveal a conscious awareness of the dark vein running through human endeavors. There are no "happy endings" in the traditional sense, only pockets of knowledge which will guide their readers towards a more sensitive and informed view of their own responses to them. Jacobsen's stories are harbingers of quiet, sometimes dark, but always reliable wisdom. (pp. 7-8)

Throughout her fortunately long and energetic literary career, Josephine Jacobsen's work has shown persistent and humane power. The clarity of her vision and the competence of her technique, even the selection of central themes, have been consistent in her prose and poetry. These elements are evident in her earliest work. The title poem of her first collection *Let Each Man Remember* (1940) describes various reactions to stress. The cogent metaphor is selected from one recurring trauma of daily living—how people get up to face a new day. It is a situation which is not less terrifying for its commonality.

> It is indisputable that some turn solemn or savage,
> While others have found it serves them best to be glib,
> When they inwardly lean and listen, listen for courage,
> That bitter and curious thing beneath the rib.

In the more than 45 years since writing those lines, Jacobsen has listened well to courage, "That bitter and curious thing beneath the rib." (p. 10)

Nancy Sullivan, "Power as Virtue: The Achievement of Josephine Jacobsen," in The Hollins Critic, *Vol. XXII, No. 2, April, 1985, pp. 1-10.*

STEPHEN GOODWIN

Josephine Jacobsen is best known as poet. *Adios, Mr. Moxley* is her second collection of stories, and it bears the poet's touch. In the most unostentatious way, she turns one striking sentence after another. Here are the opening lines of **"The Mango Community"**: "The vice-consul again looked at his shoes. He appeared to be, not critical but, more annoying, embarrassed."

This deft turn of phrase is also, obviously, a turn of mind. It is present in all 13 of these stories; and if several of them are deliberately small stories, they are quite perfected. The precise moments that Jacobsen has chosen to render, succinctly, feel not only full but brimming.

A number of the stories take illness as their subject; several are set in resorts; a recurring theme is the small criminal impulse—the maid who decides to blackmail her employer so that she can send her gifted son to a private school, the presentable officer who skips out of the hotel without paying his bill. More important, however, Jacobsen is able to create in all of her stories a sense of decorum—a minor virtue, perhaps, but one which gives rise to integrity and courage.

Jacobsen is in her seventies, and she is past pleasing anyone but herself. She is quite certain, at any rate, of what is and is not important, and why. These stories, consequently, have a bracing rigor about them, a keen independence, and the clean ring of truth.

> Stephen Goodwin, "Short Stories: The Art of the Matter," in Book World—The Washington Post, November 30, 1986, p. 4.

ROSEMARY DEEN

At a time decades ago when "religious" poetry was plentiful, [Jacobsen] was recognizable as a Catholic poet, and now in leaner times, there is the same proportion of religious imagery in her poems. She is steady. We get in *The Sisters: New and Selected Poems* what we got in *The Animal Inside* (1967) twenty years ago, very crafty poems, richly-minded. (p. 322)

Josephine Jacobsen, like her contemporaries Auden, Roethke, Elizabeth Bishop, writes "modernist" poems, in which every part builds up a metaphoric or mythic whole. Language and myth in these poems *implicate*: their parts imply each other. As you read it, the poem seems to unfold. The ending articulates the beginning, so endings are subtle and satisfying. A surprise seems to "solve" the poems, but the end was there in the beginning, in, say, the metaphor or word-play latent in the radical of a word.

Here are some examples. The insomniac speaker of one of Mrs. Jacobsen's poems anticipates the release dawn will bring her. When the cock crows, "the dark is crazed like a plate." *Crazed* describes the breaking of dark like pottery glaze, implies the plenty of light you need to see such a fine pattern. Psychologically, *crazed* displaces and lightly disarms the insomniac's state of mind. The speaker of **"Short Views in Africa"** spends the night watching the wild animals through "the blind's / chink," a nice predicament. A *chink* is a good vantage and a good focus, but *blind* rather cancels the advantage. The swimmers in *The Sisters* are trying to stay safe against an "invisible tide." But the poet points out that these tides have "come from over the bones of boys, / of girls gone down. . . ." So when from these waters the swimmers emerge "brilliant with drops," the word *drops* has emerged from "gone *down*," and the swimmers "rise" in an imagined or humanized "resurrection," though that's the reader's word, not the poet's.

Myth-wise, the modern poem is a kind of *palimpsest*, to use Galway Kinnell's word: an inscription written on a parchment over a barely visible mythic text not quite scraped off. For example, **"A Motel in Troy, New York,"** begins with a shadow falling on cribbage players from their motel window.

> A huge swan
> is looking in: cumulus-cloud body,
> thunder-cloud dirty neck
>
> that hoists the painted face
> coral and black. Inky eyes
> peer at our lives.

The swan is very accurately observed. But the more perceptively humans see animals, the more unnervingly alien they appear. The words *inky* and *painted* seem plainly descriptive, but they are terms from human culture. They signify writing or print and art, so they set the animal swan a little more apart from us. What is set apart always begins to feel like the sacred. The swan is ordinary, of course, with its "dirty neck."

> It stands
> squat on its yellow webs
>
> splayed to hold
> scarcely up the heavy
> feathered dazzle.

The ironic finesse of the writing (from *squat* to *feathered dazzle*) is a wonder and a pleasure, and such poems don't have to mean more than their triumphant writing. But the poem isn't over.

The swan breaks its stare and "waddles rocking" to the pond where it "Sets sail" and in its element is transformed "in one pure motion." It grows distant, and as the poem ends, the swan becomes less self-contained than its natural description implied. The swan is

> received by distance
> and the shadowy girl
> across the water.

What girl? says the ordinary reader who is familiar with—has been through—Troy, New York. Then the faint text under the newer ink of this present poem appears. The momentary puzzle of the ending sends us back to reconsider the "cumulus-cloud . . . thunder-cloud," sky-god aspect of the swan. "Set sail" now seems suggestive, if *Troy* makes us think of Agamemnon's expedition.

An early twentieth-century poet would have made the swan incandesce into its myth. Yeats's poem names Leda and Agamemnon, though not Zeus, and enacts a vision of a pagan annunciation. But Mrs. Jacobsen's poem isn't simply understating Yeats or Greek myth. What interests her is the way the *humans* see the swan, and the way the swan turns away from our lives so that we can't receive it, as animal or god. The "shadowy girl" is the Leda or vanishing point of our perception. The poem is a human look at something not human, ending in the irony of the absent girl—for without Leda, the swan can't be Zeus. In Yeats's poem the annunciation depends on the god; in Mrs. Jacobsen's poem the existence of the myth depends on the imagined, human girl.

The poem pulls out a whole tissue of Josephine Jacobsen's thematic images. Two especially are remarkable: the Animals and the Watcher or Watchman. Animals to begin with are partly the "animal inside," *anima*, the sensate flesh and bone, the principle of bodily life or body-soul. Mrs. Jacobsen is clearly an incarnationalist. Partly the animal is the wild in its constant but alien relation to the human: "The wild is a way of breathing; a kind of breath." So the animal or the wild is the mind's longing for metaphor or antithetical images of itself. Hummingbirds, working metaphors like all animals to the imagination, teach the Trinity:

> requiring three in one—light, angle, eye, to flower
> into their color. . . .
> Interference is the cause of iridescence . . .
> its color is structural. . . .

The poem **"Bush"** describes lions leaving a water hole at dawn. There is no mention of their kill, but a few lines later we see that

>   the drum of the zebra's body
>   is lined with red sunrise.

The metaphor skips the "natural" link of the lions and their prey, the zebra, and connects the opened body of the zebra to the rising sun.

Metaphor is the structural equivalent of consciousness and self-consciousness, the Both/Otherness of human perception. The best example is the cave painter of the hunt in the poem **"In the Crevice of Time."** Looking at his painting he sees:

>   not shank or horn or hide
>   but an arrangement of these by him, and he himself
>   there with them, watched by himself inside.

Apart, the painter arranged. At the same time he has painted himself, and so he is present, identifying-with, "there with them." And all of it is "watched by himself inside."

In the dialectic of consciousness, absence evokes presence; deserts more than strawberry gardens hum "like wire with absent water." The natural insomniac can't sleep through the dark, but moral or metaphoric insomnia is the power to stay awake and take in the dark. The refusal to accept "distance" is a mode of conscience. The starved child, nothing but "skin, breathing / wrapped over bones,"—when that child is "overseas"—is not on our own doorstep. When we can ignore it because it is distant, then we "feel distance . . . as a priceless pain-killer / locate and disconnect, reality." So "Distance is our quack-doctor."

The latest version of this doubleness turns up in ["**The Sisters"**]. One sister, "B," like a daylight self, is "better adjusted." The other, "A," is both "sharp-eyed," and "a great sleeper." She is apt to return to "some spot they've already seen" and talk about it when she gets back. As letters, A and B, they suggest writing and language, or one woman divided into her self-sisterness: "Before bed, A looked at herself in the mirror, using B's eyes."

"Identify what you will not renounce" might be one of Josephine Jacobsen's mottos. In her body of poetry crowded with losses, almost no poem without its image of death, she works harder at identifying than lamenting. The watcher is awake because her brain is working. Writing lets us look at ourselves in its mirror, using the writer's eyes. We are grateful we've had Josephine Jacobsen's steady eyes for so long. (pp. 322-23)

Rosemary Deen, "Eyes That Do Not Sleep at Dawn,"
in Commonweal, *Vol. CXIV, No. 10, May 22, 1987,*
pp. 322-23.

LAWRENCE RUNGREN

[As reflected in *The Sisters: New and Selected Poems,* Jacobsen's] is a poetry of careful craft, of a quiet delight in the natural world and a painterly appreciation of light and color. She often employs relationships of distance and circumstance to probe the mystery at the heart of the human condition, whether it be in the finely calibrated closeness of the sisters of the title poem or in the greater division in **"The Presences"**: **"Creatures," "Clouds," "Now."** . . . Including some fine new poems as well as selections from five previous books, this is the work of a writer who deserves to be better known.

Lawrence Rungren, in a review of "The Sisters: New and Selected Poems," in Library Journal, *Vol. 112, No. 10, June 1, 1987, p. 116.*

MARILYN HACKER

The work of Josephine Jacobsen is one of the best-kept secrets of contemporary American literature. She is a coeval of Auden and Roethke, Bishop, Miles and Rukeyser. . . . Unlike those others, she is still alive and writing. She shares with Bishop a passion for travel and a sense of being most at home somewhere radically else; with Miles, moral imperatives expressed through the quotidian, the anecdotal; with the later Auden, an aesthetic informed by faith; with Rukeyser, the theme of human interparticipation, the credo *nihil humanum a me alienum est*; with Roethke (and James Wright), the love for the human creature others would find grotesque, merely pitiable or fatally boring. . . .

Jacobsen is an idiosyncratic, unfashionable and accessible writer, whose work, neither polemical nor hermetic, eschews irony for the clarity of intelligence and ethical engagement. Her season is spring, her setting as often a hospital (for diseases of the body or the mind) as a beach, a hotel room or a church: places of passage, providing occasion for communication/communion, terror, sometimes epiphany. The old, the infirm, the nondescript celibate middle-aged of both genders are often her protagonists, her personae. The young appear at the perilous end of childhood, even in their twenties, with sexual and emotional initiation behind them; moral initiation, at any age, is Jacobsen's more likely focus.

Jacobsen's vision is tragic, and, in both her poetry and fiction, is made manifest most frequently in observations of the quotidian. Comfortable, unexceptional interiorities are shattered by their intersection with others, with events overdetermined by race and class in ways the privileged sometimes deny. The sins of omission, of inattention, capture this writer's imagination, as do their apposite virtues: paying attention to conscience and the world; active *agape,* learned when there is time to change, to learn. In the story **"Protection"** [from *Adios, Mr. Moxley*], a timid retired white man, puzzling the nature of gratuitous malice with which he has been confronted, inadvertently causes the murder of a black youth by the security guard whose racist assumptions he has challenged. In **"The Mango Community,"** a sabbatical-year white family's dabbling in West Indian revolutionary politics leads to the crippling of their child's black best friend, who cannot choose, as they can, to stay or go, to be or not be involved. In a smaller instance of the same moral failure, in **"Season's End,"** the trust of a likable, gifted Hispanic scholarship student is eroded by his teacher's own momentary lapse of trust; the two lose equally in being lost to each other. (p. 644)

There is an element of sexual conservatism in Jacobsen's stories: Unmarried lovers always end up badly, with a fatal flaw to the relationship laid bare (**"The Mango Community," "The Ring of Kerry," "Motion of the Heart"**); the refusal of marriage signals a refusal of commitment, responsibility. The one homosexual character (in **"Motion of the Heart"**) deceives the young woman he would marry to "normalize" himself while urging on her an abortion, which she refuses, along with him, when the truth is (contrivedly) made known. Still, I have read enough stories of a man suppressing, then claiming, his gay identity, thus leaving a shadowy female character for whom no emotions or consequences are imagined, to find Jacobsen's point of view corrective. And the love of the housekeeper, Shauna, for asthmatic, androgynous Mrs. Adair, in **"The Ring of Kerry,"** dwarfs at a glance the conditional connection of the story's heterosexual pair.

This conservatism, too, must be put in the context of Jacobsen's being a Roman Catholic writer, whose active faith informs her work, whose faith's enactment has provided her with subject matter. The mass is the final "instance of communication," celebrated on the Philadelphia docks in a

> cold great warehouse Sunday still,
> up still cold stairs, along
> a dark dim cold thin hall through a
> brown door into a small square
> room with lit
> peaky candles

and in Jacobsen's beloved Grenada by "the black tall priest / his sash embroidered with nutmeg bursting / through its mace," at a service for the healing of the sick in **"The Chosen,"** [a poem contained in her recent volume *The Sisters: New and Collected Poems*]. . . . (pp. 644-45)

The disabled, the retarded, the mentally and the terminally ill are frequent characters in Jacobsen's poetry and fiction. Two of the stories take place in hospitals on the eve of major surgery. But in **"Adios, Mr. Moxley,"** quotidian connections, from passionate love to intense annoyance, fall away in the face of the mortal question, while in **"Vocation"** a woman recognizes and confronts what is, for Jacobsen, the human nadir: the passionless will to cause pain. Jacobsen's hospital is a Flemish painter's parlor; much is revealed on a small canvas. [The title character of the poem **"Mr. Mahoney,"** who roams the halls], is a confused old man stripped to (but not of) his basic humanity by impending death:

> Tranquilized, Mr. Mahoney still eludes.
> At 2 A.M. in my dark 283
> the wide door cracks, and sudden and silently
> Mr. Mahoney's nutty face obtrudes.
>
> It is gently snatched back by someone behind it.
> "That is someone *else's* room. Yours is this way. . . ."

But Jacobsen writes about death and the knowledge of death (whence comes one kind of heroism) in many settings: a cocktail party, a suburban lane, the bank of a dam. . . . In both [**"Mr. Mahoney"** and **"I Took My Cousin to Pettyboy Dam"**], the speaker is present as observer, her own life only intersecting with the drama enacted. But she is not a visitor in Room 283: She knows that she, too, at a less rapid rate of disengagement, is dying.

The title poem of [*The Sisters: New and Collected Poems*] invites comparison by name and subject with several other texts. While gender and the condition of women as a class are not Jacobsen's primary subjects, they are not refused subjects; nor would Jacobsen refuse to be described as a woman poet, not only in the fact of her gender, but in her cross-generational relationship with a tradition.

"The Sisters" is also the title of an *ars poetica* by Amy Lowell, imagining in witty blank verse visits with Sappho, Barrett Browning and Dickinson, meditating on the "queerness" of "women who write poetry" and their/our interdependence. Since Lowell, a duality between or within women (in partic-

ular, between practicality and imagination, the analytic and the synthetic, sense and sensibility) has so often been the subject of women's poems as to constitute a recognizable theme, a genre like the elegy or the epithalamium. In Elinor Wylie's "Little Eclogue," sisters called Solitude and Loneliness, "One like a moth, the other like a mouse," are divided (with authorial irony) by romantic love. Thirty years later, in "In Mind," Denise Levertov contrasted a woman "smelling of / apples or grass" in a "utopian smock," "kind," who "has / no imagination," with a "turbulent moon-ridden girl / or old woman" "who knows strange songs" but "is not kind."

Jacobsen's **"Sisters"** are, at first reading, a less-metaphorical, fleshly pair at a Caribbean resort, rendered in five-line stanzas by an observer more neighborly than omniscient. Sister *B* is "easily pleased"; *A* is "erratic," given to investigations of the unexpected. "The little group of graves by the Old Men's Home" tempts her back:

> to examine the yellow
> and violet cellophane, the rubber pond-lilies
> floating on dust; the whole glittering heap
> of rainbow mound.

After her burst of energy (we do not read these as young sisters) she falls asleep on the beach, while *B* swims. But, the observer makes it clear, these sisters "recoil" at the thought of separation. "Before bed, *A* looked at herself in the mirror, using *B*'s eyes," and, while there is no mention of creator and nurturer, poet and muse, no overt statement that *A* and *B* are more than middle-aged spinsters on holiday, I read a synthesis here that could not yet have been made by Wylie or Levertov. The athletic, good-natured *B*, who exults in sunlight and lobsters, and the mercurial, curious *A*, whose imagination is awakened and exhausted by death, participate in each other willingly and surely as the nouns "solid as objects" complete the abstract "*who, why, go*" in poetry as on the sisters' Scrabble board. Woman and poet are not polar; they describe a whole.

For Jacobsen, the aims of a woman's art are those of an art committed to human survival: She is cool toward any art that is not. In **"Food,"** woman's work is the irreducible basis of human possibility:

> To trap, to kill, to drive
> the dogs' ferocity is heroic to tell:
> full-bellied sagas' stuff.
>
> The clawing for heather, the black curved nails,
> cramped breath for smoke, smoke for breath,
> the witch mask clamped on the bride face
>
> bring nothing but life for the nourished.
>
> . . .
>
> By her breath, flesh, her hands, no
> reputation will be made, no
> saga descend. It is only the
>
> next day made possible.

Josephine Jacobsen's writing makes the next day possible. (pp. 645-46)

Marilyn Hacker, "Mortal Moralities," in The Nation, New York, Vol. 245, No. 18, November 28, 1987, pp. 644-46.

Diane Johnson

1934-

American novelist, biographer, critic, scriptwriter, and short story writer.

Johnson is well known for her sophisticated, witty novels about intelligent yet emotionally insecure women who are dissatisfied with their lives and seek love and fulfillment in unfamiliar surroundings. Johnson's heroines, who are often at odds with manipulative or nonsupportive husbands and lovers, usually perceive their lifestyles as stifling and detrimental to their sense of identity. Although some critics have categorized Johnson's works as feminist literature, Marjorie Ryan holds a dissenting view: "[Diane Johnson is not] a 'feminist writer' in the contemporary sense. She is a contemporary writer with an interest in dehumanization, loss of personal identity, rents in the social fabric; and she sees these conditions as affecting women perhaps even more acutely than men." While sometimes faulted for incomplete characterizations of males, Johnson is consistently praised for insightful and realistic depictions of modern women in crisis.

Johnson's first two novels are comedies about women entangled in unusual relationships. *Fair Game* (1965) revolves around Dabney Wilhelm, a young woman who is romantically pursued by four men. After a series of unsettling incidents in which each admirer attempts to exploit her, Dabney becomes involved with a man whom she believes will encourage her individuality. Karen Fry, the protagonist of *Loving Hands at Home* (1968), marries into a Mormon family with whom she has nothing in common. Inept at housekeeping and motherhood, which are of primary importance to her in-laws, she seeks fulfillment outside her marriage. After leaving her husband, Karen learns that she is equally ill-equipped to cope with a new environment, and she returns home, vowing to leave again once she discovers her purpose in life. Johnson's next novel, *Burning* (1971), is a satire of casual southern California lifestyles. This book, which takes place during a single day, details the misadventures of a couple who unwittingly become involved with their neighbor, an unorthodox psychiatrist. After succumbing to a plethora of hallucinogenic drugs and sexual encounters with the doctor and several of his patients, the pair reveal disturbing secrets about themselves. J. R. Frakes commented: "Mrs. Johnson superintends this asylum with cool disdain and a remarkable neo-classic elegance of phrase, sentence, and chapter. It's comforting to know someone competent is in charge."

In her fourth novel, *The Shadow Knows* (1974), Johnson departs from her earlier fiction by combining elements of the suspense tale and the psychological thriller and employing a first-person narrative to present a disturbing portrait of a troubled woman known only as N. A divorced mother of four children, N. becomes the target of several acts of violence that culminate in rape. In her quest to identify her attacker, N. discovers the malevolence within herself. Although some passages in the novel suggest that N. may be fabricating her story, these incidents, whether real or imagined, lead her toward a new understanding of herself. Jonathan Yardley called *The Shadow Knows* "extraordinarily vivid, intricate and affecting," and Pearl K. Bell asserted that the novel established Johnson as "one of the genuinely arresting voices in American

writing today." *Lying Low* (1978), Johnson's next novel, is set in a rural home in the Sacramento Valley and chronicles four days in the lives of three disparate characters: Theodora, a sixty-year-old woman who has dedicated her life to art and moral order; Marybeth, who is in hiding for crimes committed as a student radical in the 1960s; and Ouida, a Brazilian immigrant who fears deportation. When outside forces threaten to disrupt their already fragile existence, the protagonists begin to reevaluate their lives and make decisions about their futures. Robert Towers called *Lying Low* "a nearly flawless performance—a beautifully constructed, elegantly written book, delicate in its perceptions, powerful in its impact."

Johnson's recent novel, *Persian Nights* (1987), centers on Chloe Fowler, the wife of a renowned American physician, and her experiences in Iran on the eve of the country's 1979 revolution. When her husband is summoned back to the United States for a medical emergency, Chloe befriends a closely-knit group of wealthy Americans and westernized Iranians and becomes romantically involved with an American surgeon. Johnson sharply contrasts the idle lives of the Americans with the escalating political tensions surrounding them. Some critics suggested that Chloe and her companions represent the indifference of American foreign policy toward Iran during this period as well as the inability of westerners to understand Islamic culture. Joyce Johnson maintained that "it is heartening to read a novel with so much texture, intelligence and content—one that also manages to be undidactically 'political'—in a period when the fabric of so much fiction seems as diaphanous and insubstantial as a nylon curtain."

Johnson is also a respected nonfiction writer. *Lesser Lives: The True History of the First Mrs. George Meredith* (1972) is a biography of Mary Ellen Peacock Nicolls Meredith, the daughter of novelist and poet Thomas Love Peacock and the first wife of novelist George Meredith. Contending that Mrs. Meredith has been misrepresented by literary biographers as an adulteress whose transgressions led to her ruin, Johnson portrays her subject as a precursor of contemporary women seeking liberation from a repressive society. While some critics faulted Johnson for taking novelistic liberties with historical facts, Hilton Kramer asserted that she "has succeeded in writing a first-rate book that illuminates not only the 'lesser lives' of the first Mrs. Meredith and her lover but also the larger moral and literary terrain of Victorian society." *Terrorists and Novelists* (1982) is a volume of book reviews and essays that were originally published in such periodicals as the *New York Review of Books* and the *New York Times Book Review*. *Dashiell Hammett: A Life* (1983) is the first biography of Hammett to be written with the permission of Lillian Hellman, his longtime companion and executrix of his literary estate. Although critics noted that Johnson did not unravel the mystery of Hammett's creative decline, they acknowledged that her access to Hammett's private correspondence helped divulge new information about his personal life. Johnson also collaborated with Stanley Kubrick on the screenplay for the film *The Shining*.

(See also *CLC*, Vols. 5, 13; *Contemporary Authors*, Vols. 41-44, rev. ed.; *Contemporary Authors New Revision Series*, Vol. 17; and *Dictionary of Literary Biography Yearbook: 1980*.)

RIVA T. BRESLER

[Diane Johnson's] sophisticated Southern California comedy [*Fair Game*] centers about an attractive young woman of poise and presence, and the four men—all connected with each other in some manner—who are fascinated by her. The men involved are the upright young heir whose mistress she is (now beginning to question her fitness for conventional wifehood); a courtly, middle-aged literary notable—and some will think of Henry Miller—who wants to stimulate her intellectual creativity; a far-out, but not way-out psychiatrist, anxious to see her express herself emotionally; and a nice, sensitive "good guy" who falls in love with her. Their relations with her, purposeful and otherwise, form a slight plot recounted with delight, deftness and a wit expressed in phrase as in incident. Even when skirting the edge of farce, Miss Johnson is reasonable and original, relating fables—and even a gentle moral—with a cool irony that makes one believe she has well enjoyed Jane Austen. (pp. 4360, 4362)

> *Riva T. Bresler, in a review of "Fair Game," in* Library Journal, *Vol. 90, No. 18, October 15, 1965, pp. 4360, 4362.*

MARTIN LEVIN

Momism still lives in [*Loving Hands at Home*], Diane Johnson's farce about a Mormon enclave in Los Angeles. The Frys

are a close-knit group—mother, father, three married sons, 11 children—who gather every Sunday for a family dinner and browbeating session by Mother Fry. Karen, the only non-Mormon and the narrator, is a little nut who fancies herself the only nonconformist in the bunch. . . . But from one Sunday dinner to another, it develops that there are even more paradoxical Frys among the dutiful homemakers. Joan, mother of seven, finds strength through sex with visiting handymen. Patty, the perfect hausfrau, is adjusting with difficulty to her husband's affair with his lady boss. Even Mother Fry, a hilariously caricatured matriarch, reveals unplumbed depths of venom when under the influence of home-cooked mushrooms. . . .

Miss Johnson's characters are as real as Halloween masks, but the idiosyncrasies they are assigned are inventive and amusing.

> *Martin Levin, in a review of "Loving Hands at Home,"* in The New York Times Book Review, *October 27, 1968, p. 68.*

THE NEW YORK TIMES BOOK REVIEW

The marriage of George Meredith and Mary Ellen Peacock, daughter of the poet-novelist Thomas Love Peacock, endured eight years. Everyone who knew them was aware that for at least half that time they were miserable. In 1857 she eloped with the minor painter Henry Wallis. Four years later she died. Meredith hardly spoke of her again. . . . Now, in this curiously titled volume [*Lesser Lives: The True History of the First Mrs. Meredith*], comes Diane Johnson . . . to champion Mary as "a new—a modern—Victorian heroine," a liberated woman, a tragedienne before (or after) her time.

Diane Johnson has had access to some fascinating unpublished material; but her manner of writing about Mrs. Meredith and other "lesser lives" in the mid-Victorian literary world may rouse readers' hackles. Zealous to see justice done her heroine, she twists Meredith into a standard Victorian moralist and worse—proud, selfish, pompous, hypocritical, devious, a monster of cold insensitivity. Because she actually knows so little about Mary's precise movements or states of mind, she has had to shore up her defense with a reiteration of "perhaps," "maybe," "possibly." She is eager to demolish Victorian attitudes in the manner of Lytton Strachey, but she lacks Strachey's knowledge of the period and his literary skill.

> *A review of "Lesser Lives,"* in The New York Times Book Review, *December 31, 1972, p. 19.*

HILTON KRAMER

Biographers of [Thomas Love] Peacock and [George] Meredith have . . . treated Mary Ellen Peacock Nicolls Meredith as one of those minor figures that adorn the chronicles of their more illustrious contemporaries, but she has never before emerged as a subject in her own right. As Diane Johnson observes in [*Lesser Lives*], her biography of this extraordinary woman: "The owner of a lesser life does not much survive a century of time, especially when the life was embarrassing to a major life or two." But Mrs. Johnson has had the inspiration to realize that "a lesser life does not seem lesser to the person who leads one." Suspecting that a significant story lay hidden in this life of a figure usually accorded "a paragraph or a page" in the lives of others, she has succeeded in writing a first-rate book that illuminates not only the "lesser lives" of the first Mrs. Meredith and her lover but also the larger moral and literary terrain of Victorian society, especially in its relation to the gifted women whose fate was so often sealed by the sexual conventions of the period. . . .

It is a marvelous story and a very sad one, and Mrs. Johnson has told it very well. Her book is obviously written under the imperatives of the feminist movement, yet for the most part it escapes the curse of books written with an ideological intent. It never takes a simplistic view of experience, and it uses its spare documentation with a notable intelligence and skill.

In one of the notes to *Lesser Lives*—and it should be said that the notes are an essential part of the book, at times rivaling the main text in readability and interest—Mrs. Johnson calls our attention to the relation of literary biography to the fictional styles that influence it. She has herself adopted a sort of "novelistic" approach to her material, and, without falsifying it, has succeeded in writing a book that is far more compelling than many of the novels written under a similar imperative.

Hilton Kramer, "A Victorian Scandal," in The New York Times, *January 23, 1973, p. 37.*

ANATOLE BROYARD

"Maybe the reason novels exist," Diane Johnson says, "is to disguise human musings." In her case, the same might be said of book reviews, for hers are full of human musings. Quoting E. M. Forster's remark that "Each of us knows from his own experience that there is something beyond the evidence," she goes beyond the evidence of each book discussed in *Terrorists and Novelists* and raises the question of its subject again in her own way. She is not so much interested in rendering a judgment as she is in inquiring into the book's occasion, its reason for being. If she were not so eminently down-to-earth, it would be tempting to say that she supplies each book's philosophical aura. . . .

In [one] of her musings, she says, "Literary biography usually concerns itself with how an artist's life and personality influence his work, and usually fails to engage the problems of how the writer's work affects the growth of his personality." Though this is a brilliant observation, it's delivered casually, like most of her best lines. You never hear her clearing her throat, like so many other literary critics. . . .

It's odd that Miss Johnson, herself a modern novelist and frequent reviewer of current fiction, should be more rewarding in writing of George Sand and Charlotte Bronte than of Don DeLillo and Donald Barthelme, two contemporary authors that she admires. The reader may wonder whether she's less interested in writing by men. When she says, "No other subject, it seems, is regarded so differently by men and women as rape," this statement does seem to suggest some kind of imaginative deficiency either in them or in herself.

Her long piece on C. D. B. Bryan's *Friendly Fire,* though, is very good. The story of the refusal of a mother and father to accept the apology of the United States Army for the "mistake" that caused their son to be killed in Vietnam by our own artillery seems to strike Miss Johnson as heartening evidence that ordinary people can still tell when "the word 'tragedy' is used to abridge complexity." As long as Miss Johnson is writing reviews, nobody is going to get away with abridging complexity, no matter which words they employ.

Anatole Broyard, "Beyond the Evidence," in The New York Times, *October 16, 1982, p. 10.*

BENJAMIN DeMOTT

Remarks aren't literature, Gertrude Stein famously remarked to Ernest Hemingway, and everybody more or less agrees. But *good* remarks—witticisms, epigrams, aphorisms, what you will—are luxuries no smart reader of verse or prose likes doing without. One strength of *Terrorists and Novelists,* a collection of reviews and review-essays by [Diane Johnson]. . .is that it's jammed with good remarks. Miss Johnson observes—reviewing Norman Mailer on Gary Gilmore—that so-called true-life novels "encourage. . .literary ambulance chasing.". . .

A male biographer who skips over an extended stretch of misery in Colette's life rouses her to reflect, drily, that "whereas men like experience in women, they tenderheartedly hate them to have troubles."

What's more, contrary to the impression left when selected glittering snippets are flashed on a reviewer's screen, as above, Miss Johnson is nothing like a show-off. Her wit is unselfadvertising, employed in the service of argument not dazzle: Eagerness to wound, or to be cried up by fools as "devastating," or to adopt queenly social poses, nowhere disfigures her page. Even if the book had lacked rhetorical dexterity, I'd have profited from *Terrorists and Novelists,* the intelligence at work in the majority of the pieces is uncommonly flexible and sound-valued. But, thanks to Miss Johnson's gift for analogy— also her sense of where and when to brace a paragraph with quick, wry, rimshot irony (such as that fine "tenderheartedly" on which, for a second, I struck out, looking)—I was as often delighted as improved. . . .

The prize item in the collection, in my opinion, is the review of Elizabeth Hardwick's novel, *Sleepless Nights.* I recommend it strongly to anyone out there who's fretting about the decline of taste in the contemporary world of letters. Miss Johnson's appreciating self is relaxed and unpedantic; she quotes excellent sentences and tells us, at once lovingly and penetratingly, what kinds of excellence they represent; the effect over all resembled, for me, that of a lively movement in a first-class violin and piano sonata. I was also impressed by the commentary on Mr. Bryan's *Friendly Fire,* which, advancing from formal to moral considerations, shrewdly explores the frustration visited upon audiences by certain blendings of fictional and journalistic modes.

Less satisfactory are the pieces on novelists, largely because of excessive deference to received views. E. L. Doctorow, Joseph Heller, Donald Barthelme and Toni Morrison are handled here as glamour stocks to be duly recertified, not as reputations to be freshly examined. Saul Bellow is predictably roughed up, for reasons having more to do (I thought) with his status as an institutionally overbought laureate than with the defects of *The Dean's December.* And the notice of Mr. Mailer's *The Executioner's Song* seems timid. (p. 12)

But for most of its length *Terrorists and Novelists* is quite unsmutched by timidity. Miss Johnson is never intimidated by sexist cant; she often uses "manly" (as well as "womanly") as a term of praise. Her book has room for truths of the sort that simple heads sometimes abuse as "racist.". . .

The standard of values by which Miss Johnson's key estimates are made is admirably independent of fashion. (Almost invariably she assesses the quality and intensity of an author's responsiveness to other minds; her revelatory contrast is between Henry James, of whom she correctly says that his "understanding of others was perfect," and John Ruskin, whose "vanity and egoism" prevented him from grasping that others actually existed.) Miss Johnson is overfond of the word sly, and here and there—animadverting, for example, on the alleged American need for a frontier—she presents old light as new. But that happens rarely, and, in a critic who's a disciplined skeptic of The Latest, it's easily forgiven. (No European crazies—no theorists, apocalyptics, film maniacs—are saluted here.) The last sentence of Miss Johnson's praise of *Sleepless Nights* says, with likable directness, that "this book brings happiness." The same holds, obviously, for **Terrorists and Novelists**. (p. 34)

> Benjamin DeMott, "Intelligence at Work," in The New York Times Book Review, *October 31, 1982, pp. 12, 34.*

KATHLEEN CHASE

When reading book reviews, I turn to Diane Johnson's contributions with anticipatory pleasure. One cannot go wrong in singling out her reviews, for the style is the woman. The reward lies not only in the enjoyment of her distinctive style but also in the in-depth way she sifts and weighs the books' contents. To have so many of her essays collected in [**Terrorists and Novelists**] is a treat.

Ranging from the autobiography of Maxine Hong Kingston to the travels of Edward Hoagland, from Joan Didion to Saul Bellow, from Doctorow to Barthelme, these essays keep one's interest and imagination on edge. Not only does the author do justice to the books, she delights with her wit, insight and arguments as well as her brilliant metaphors. . . .

[Johnson's reviews] cause us to reflect and to want to read those books we may have missed. It has been difficult to make selections among such a rich assortment of good writing and reporting. The reader will have to savor, sort out and enjoy.

> Kathleen Chase, in a review of "Terrorists and Novelists," in World Literature Today, *Vol. 57, No. 3, Summer, 1983, p. 461.*

CHRISTOPHER LEHMANN-HAUPT

Often enough, the problem with reviewing a successful biography is deciding whether the subject or the author should receive the praise. Should one congratulate the subject for having lived an interesting life or commend the author for having made the life *seem* interesting? In the case of **Dashiell Hammett: A Life**—the first book about Hammett to be authorized by his close friend and executor, Lillian Hellman—it would appear that its author, Diane Johnson, is the one who should be given the credit.

Until now, the enigma of Hammett's life has been such as to confound the efforts of at least two biographers—Richard Layman, whose *Shadow Man: The Life of Dashiell Hammett* was long on detail but short on conclusion, and William F. Nolan, whose *Hammett: A Life at the Edge* was erratic in both respects. Always certain questions remained insufficiently answered. . . .

[The] biggest question of all: why did he stop writing at the peak of his success and never finish another novel after the publication of *The Thin Man?* Was it really, as some have suggested, that he quit because he thought he had made enough money, and had no interest in writing beyond making money? Both Mr. Layman and Mr. Nolan provided tantalizing glimpses

at possible answers, but Hammett's many contradictions remained unreconciled.

How is Diane Johnson's biography different?

There is no denying that being authorized has helped the book enormously. The best new anecdotes and the most revealing new details are present because of Lillian Hellman's cooperation. The myth-making goes on, but within the framework of the myth we can see how Hammett could be, among other unattractive things, a disgustingly sloppy drunk and a compulsive chaser after prostitutes. . . .

What is even more impressive, however, is the spaciousness of Miss Johnson's biography. It is roomy enough to accommodate Hammett's contradictions and tensions, which, she insists, were "typical of his generation and nationality." There is the Hammett that Miss Hellman loved and mythologized in her memoirs, but there is also a Hammett who existed in the eyes of others, as well as within the dungeon of his impenetrable loneliness. . . .

More important still, there is in **Dashiell Hammett** both a psycho-analytic profile of its subject and a dialectical one. Yet neither is insisted upon. One can draw the nutshell conclusion that something in Hammett's upbringing made him so extremely angry—at his father, at authority, at himself—that he never got over it, especially when the achievement of success and riches threatened to remove the barriers that hid the true objects of his fury. Thus he squandered his money and erected his writer's block. . . .

Yet Miss Johnson never tries to exploit such a thimbleful of psychohistory (which in any case is mine, not hers; she only provides the raw material). Never does she cheapen psychology by employing it to undermine Hammett's motives as a political activist. The picture we get here is of an underdog who made a code of honor out of nipping at the ankles of the bullies wielding the clubs. He never forgot where he came from. . . .

None of which is to say that even in Diane Johnson's capable hands, Hammett doesn't remain something of an enigma. . . .

Silence was Hammett's weapon—silence turned against all bullies and lovers, against his readers and himself. At the bottom of that silence was an ocean of anger: that much this biography makes very clear. The mystery that remains—that will probably forever remain—is the true source of that anger.

> Christopher Lehmann-Haupt, in a review of "Dashiell Hammett: A Life," in The New York Times, *October 5, 1983, p. C25.*

JONATHAN YARDLEY

[Dashiell Hammett] was, in the apt phrase of his first biographer, Richard Layman, a "shadow man"; his second, William F. Nolan, described him equally aptly as having lived "a life on the edge." But if these two books suggested that Hammett's life was somehow mysterious and incomplete, perhaps that was because their authors had been denied access to his letters and papers by his companion and executrix, Lillian Hellman. So when it became known that Hellman had at last decided to permit an "authorized and definitive" biography of Hammett, and that she had chosen Diane Johnson for the task, hopes were raised that the mystery of Hammett would be solved; unfortunately, though perhaps unsurprisingly, it turns out that it has not.

This is not for want of trying on the part of Johnson [in *Dashiell Hammett: A Life*] . . . ; she tries so hard that the biography positively aches with the effort of it, until finally it just wears her down. In part, I am sorry to say, this is her own fault: she has chosen an odd narrative strategy, she is given to sudden and unappealing shifts in tone and tense, and she has not resisted the temptation to pad the pages out with documents. But in larger part the fault, or the explanation, lies with Hammett himself: he left, as it turns out, no trace by which to track him; the papers and letters in Hellman's possession, though occasionally interesting, leave the mystery as dense as ever.

Which is to say that Johnson, like every previous Hammett biographer, fails to penetrate through to the inner man; like the others she can give us the who, what, where and when, but the *why* eludes her. . . .

Johnson has not in the end come up with a significantly more fully-fleshed Hammett than did Layman or Nolan. The basic facts remain the same. . . .

During his lifetime he was widely praised as the founder of a new style of detective fiction that elevated the genre into the precincts of literature; he wrote a clipped prose that seemed appropriate to a world in which silence predominated, he depicted the underworld in a realistic and unsentimental manner, and he took on serious themes in a genre to which they had previously been alien. The praise may not have been good for him. He may, Johnson suggests, have recognized it as excessive and misplaced:

> A present of fame, of literary reputation, was like a hot coal in his pocket, reassuring, hand-warming, but if he drew it out to look at it, it turned into cinders. The greater his reputation, the more trivial to him seemed the stories from which it arose, the more incumbent upon him to write differently and better and greater and more, and the more impossible to do any of this. . . .

This is a plausible explanation for Hammett's failure to write anything to speak of except letters following the publication in 1934 of *The Thin Man*, but I am inclined to a simpler and less flattering one: that when Hammett reached a point in his career when he seemed to have no financial reason to keep working, he stopped—and when it became necessary for him to resume, he was too far out of the habit to do so. He does not seem to have been a lazy man, but he was possessed by no discernible ambitions and his clear tendency was simply to go with life's flow; like his contemporary Ring Lardner, to whom in some respects he was strikingly similar, he had little appetite for a literary challenge and preferred, all things considered, play to work.

Diane Johnson seems to recognize these limitations and shortcomings, though she is not insistent about them, and this knowledge may explain the uncharacteristically flat tone of her biography: she appears to be in the position of explicating and defending a position—the high literary reputation of Dashiell Hammett—in which she does not believe. Beneath all her brave words on his behalf, she seems to agree with Hammett that his work, however honorable, isn't worth all the fuss. . . .

There are other problems: Johnson is given from time to time to non sequiturs; she moves back and forth between the past and present tenses with no evident method; she quotes much too much from Hammett's letters, which are less interesting than one might hope, and from various public documents; she attempts to take on the voices of various individuals as she describes their thoughts, which means that when she is inside the heads of his daughters she lapses into something perilously close to baby talk. She does tell us more about his relationships with his wife, his daughters and Hellman than we have previously known; she also paints a poignant portrait of his dogged adherence to personal and political principle during the McCarthy years. But none of this, however diverting, bears on Hammett's work, the deepest sources of which remain as much a mystery as ever.

> Jonathan Yardley, "The Public Face of the Private Eye," in Book World—The Washington Post, October 9, 1983, p. 3.

PEARL K. BELL

There were three Dashiell Hammetts, not one. There was the writer who perfected a new kind of detective story, featuring a tough, amoral sleuth. . . .

There was also Dashiell Hammett the Communist, who in 1951, as one of the trustees of a bail-bond fund for indicted Communist leaders, went to jail rather than reveal the names of the contributors to the fund. (p. 39)

Finally there is Dashiell Hammett, the tragic figure of Lillian Hellman's memoirs. . . . For her he is a hero of our time. In the short introduction to *The Big Knockover*, a collection of Hammett's stories published in 1966, Hellman wrote a moving account of Hammett's life and her life with him. . . . Hellman reprinted this introduction at the end of *An Unfinished Woman*, and one would have assumed there was no more that needed to be said.

In recent years, however, Hellman became caught up in the wars of historical interpretation. She was determined to rewrite the history of the left-liberal intelligentsia of America, to establish her version of the 1950s as the dominant one for future historians. . . . Though Hellman had already presented her version of that period in *Scoundrel Time*, a full-scale biography of Dashiell Hammett, despite the fact that there have been two others, becomes a natural counterpart. To this end, Hellman authorized Diane Johnson to write it.

It would be hard to think of a biography more thoroughly held captive by the authorizing strings than the one Johnson has produced [in *Dashiell Hammett: A Life*]. Hellman's unwavering vigilance casts its shadow on every page. Though Johnson has made abundant use of letters, documents, and personal memories that Hellman did not share with the earlier biographers of Hammett, she has made no effort to find her own point of view, to understand Hammett's life and radicalism with an independent eye and mind. Because she is a political naïf, and lacks the qualifications of an historian or a political analyst which are essential for the study of this life, she has swallowed Lillian Hellman's version of the man and his politics hook, Partyline, and sinker. Such self-effacement is not what one might have expected from Johnson. . . . Because Diane Johnson has undertaken this project against the grain of her own lively intelligence, she has written a bad book.

That she is in over her head is evident from the start in the flaccid prose, the irresolute jumbling of detail, the pointless shifts in tone. For an intelligent critic she is remarkably apathetic about the biographer's crucial task of analyzing and evaluating the work which gave Hammett his high literary reputation. Beyond a few uninspired generalizations in her introductory remarks, she has almost nothing to say about the writer who wrenched detective fiction out of its genteel Holmesian sockets and, drawing upon his own experience as an operative for the Pinkerton Agency, created a unique kind of detective. . . . (pp. 39-40)

So seductive was Hammett's portrayal that this hard-boiled detective soon found his place among the fantasies that feed American popular culture. The novels and the movies they became . . . brought Hammett blazing success, both financial and critical. He had caught to perfection the high-riding, crime-ridden American world of the 1920s, and the rewards were immense.

Yet in the early 1930s, after he published his fifth and last novel, *The Thin Man*—his least characteristic book, one drawn from a public café-society persona that was alien to his own dark nature—his career as a writer came to an end, thirty years before his death in 1961. Johnson has all the facts about the demons that assaulted him, but she seems so timid about interpreting and judging what she records that we end the book with little more understanding of Hammett's tortured personality than we began. (p. 40)

For some thirty years Hammett struggled to write another novel—only the weak, autobiographical fragment, "Tulip," remains from those futile efforts—but everything got in the way: booze, politics, war, and a writer's block that grew bigger all the time. Yet, faced with a wealth of anomaly and paradox that ought to make a biographer wonder and think, the best Johnson can do in summing up Hammett's character is a dubious paradox of her own: "The heroism of his life lay not in his Horatio Alger success, rather it lay in the long years after success, when money and gifts were gone. It is the long blank years that prove the spirit."

Politically, of course, those years were not blank. What Johnson is referring to in this high-minded but fuzzy accolade is Dashiell Hammett the political martyr. And this is where Johnson's abdication of independent judgment becomes most disturbing. That she means to concentrate on the political aspects of Hammett's life is clear from the opening chapter, since she begins not with his family background or his birth, but with his stay in prison. First martyrdom, then childhood.

When Hammett refused to answer questions about the bail-bond fund and received a six-month sentence for contempt of court, he told Hellman: "If it were more than jail, if it were my life, I would give it for what I think democracy is, and I don't let cops or judges tell me what I think democracy is." True, these are stirring Gary Cooperish words, but it is possible to take this declaration of incorruptibility at face value (as Diane Johnson does) only by ignoring Hammett's political history. Just what he thought democracy is turns out to be more problematic than it looks. (p. 41)

Nine days before the Nazi-Soviet pact was announced, Hammett, along with some other members of the Stalinist-controlled League of American Writers, signed a statement denouncing "right-wing forces [who] have encouraged the fantastic falsehood that the U.S.S.R. and the totalitarian states are basically alike." When it turned out to be not so fantastic, Hammett, far from joining the massive defection from the Party, supported its anti-imperialist war stand, and continued to do so until Hitler invaded Russia. In an astonishing footnote to this period, Johnson remarks that Hammett

apparently accepted the Hitler-Stalin pact in accordance with the Party position. People who discussed politics with Hammett remember that . . . he had a notably long view of political events when many of the people he and Hellman knew were precipitated into varying crises of spirit.

This notion of a "long view" attests not to Hammett's superior political wisdom, but to Johnson's political naiveté. As for the Party's about-face after Hitler invaded Russia, wasn't it nice, she sighs, that "people on both sides of the question of [the pact's] morality spoke to each other once again." If she can believe this kiss-and-make-up view of radical quarrels, she can believe anything.

And she does, sketching a more simpleminded black-and-white cartoon of the McCarthy period than Hellman's chronicle of defiance. "It seemed to many people," Johnson writes, "that hypocrisy, villainy and self-serving dishonor were the national afflictions; a war that had been fought against fascism seemed instead to have made the world safe for fascism in the form of persecution by the American government of people living in America." Malicious and destructive as Senator McCarthy and the Communist hunters in the House Un-American Activities Committee undeniably were, they did not succeed—came nowhere close to it at any time—in transforming America into a "fascist" state. Nor has Johnson resisted the urge to sneer at former Communists, lumping those who "regretted" having been in the Party with those who "were afraid of trouble," as though fear and regret were the same. According to Johnson, there was no moral difference between those who, as she puts it, "repented of their errors" and those who "denounced" their former friends. Anyone who called himself an anti-Communist in those days was ready, she declares, "to disclaim history, investigate it, excoriate it and rewrite it." What she does not say is that it was the Communists who were disclaiming and rewriting history. (pp. 41-2)

At no point has Johnson taken the trouble to think about the nature of the Communist regime and the Party that the faithful like Dashiell Hammett were supporting at the time. How did he react, one wants to know, to what was going on in Russia as well as what was going on in the United States? . . . Did Hammett have anything to say in 1956 when Khrushchev began to reveal the enormity of the atrocities committed by Stalin? Or about the Hungarian Revolution, which was initiated by writers—Julius Hay and Tibor Dery—who were also Communists? Did he not know anything about the concentration camps in the Soviet Union? None of these questions are raised by Johnson. Yet they are questions that no responsible biographer of such a man can ignore with impunity. If she could not find any satisfactory answers, if Hammett indeed preferred to remain silent about the mounting revelations of Stalinist horror, surely *that* would be worth mentioning.

What, then, is this authorized biography? It is a political act that seeks to fix an image of a time, and the character of the literary intelligentsia that participated in the politics of that time. In her life of Hammett, Johnson has tried to exemplify Lillian Hellman's mythologizing of history, according to which only such persons as Hammett were the men of honor of the 1950s. Looking at the record of that era, however, who can believe it? How shabby. (p. 42)

Pearl K. Bell, "Red Harvest," in The New Republic, *Vol. 189, No. 19, November 7, 1983, pp. 39-42.*

CHRISTOPHER LEHMANN-HAUPT

Privileged Americans in Iran shortly before the fall of Shah Mohammed Riza Pahlevi. Cultural values colliding at a time of social ferment. An outing to explore and picnic at Shahpur's Cave at Nam-al-Rush, attended by a party of Iranians and Americans who are colleagues at a hospital in Shiraz. One thinks of E. M. Forster's *Passage to India,* of course. So does Diane Johnson in her latest novel, **Persian Nights.**

In this seemingly significant scene, Chloe Fowler, the American protagonist of Ms. Johnson's richly ornamented story, prefers not to descend ''a stairway of wettish rock leading down into invisible blackness,'' which ''looked appalling to her.''

''Perhaps you are thinking of the Marabar caves, and Miss Quested,'' says another member of the party, Dr. Ali Yazdi. ''Remember Miss Quested?''

> Chloe, not thinking of books, said that she didn't know a Miss Quested, and Dr. Yazdi laughed with pleasure at catching her lacking in knowledge of her own literature. *''Passage to India,''* he whispered, leaning intimately toward her ear. ''When Miss Quested, finding herself alone with Dr. Aziz, imagines she has been molested. Or is molested. It is never quite clear.''

This incident—in which Dr. Yazdi has twisted the plot of Forster's novel for his own erotic purposes—is typical of **Persian Nights.** Yazdi's gambit will turn out to have almost no consequence in the events that follow, just as the party's discovery of a battered and dying man in the depths of the caves will not in the long run amount to very much.

But we readers believe at the time that these incidents are going to matter, and the characters do, too. Chloe Fowler will wonder what she has done to invite Dr. Yazdi's assumption of intimacy between them. Other members of the outing will suffer a near-comic nightmare trying to dispose of the body. Both we and they will find it hard to distinguish between what is important and threatening to them and what is not.

This confusion contributes to the exotic atmosphere of the novel, for in a foreign setting it is always hard for strangers to tell what really matters. Moreover, it increases the anxiety produced by events for both the characters and the reader, as well as heightening the sense that time is passing faster than it really is, for when much of little consequence occurs, it serves to slow time down. Finally, the amusing busyness of the story's surface emphasizes the triviality of personal affairs, particularly in contrast to the profound upheavals that Iran is going through.

All these techniques work particularly well with the character of Chloe Fowler, who arrives in Shiraz alone and frightened because her husband, a physician, has been detained at home by a medical emergency. Chloe is a remarkable example of an ordinary person made interesting simply by virtue of the events we witness through her eyes. She is forever berating herself for being unliberated and useless—an amateur among medical professionals with her grant to work with Sassanian pottery shards.

And yet she proves surprisingly resilient and adaptive as she becomes a focal point of the suspicions, jealousies, petty intrigues, and sexual longings of the elite American-Iranian medical community in which she finds herself. We come to identify with her even in her goodhearted meddling, and fear for her when it appears to have brought disaster down on her head. . . .

True, the novel pays a certain price for the almost Victorian ornateness of its technique, which extends to employing chapter titles followed by four-line excerpts from Edward FitzGerald's translation of the *Rubalyat of Omar Khayyam.* A certain strain is produced by the tension between the story's busily meaningless surface plotting and the deeper rumble of the social revolution in the background. Occasionally, the events in the foreground seem merely silly and the sense of the exotic deteriorates into unreality.

But the scenes that are on target draw blood. Perhaps the most powerful is the final one at the airport, when the departing Americans line up hysterically to trade their remaining Iranian money for caviar that the falling regime puts on sale. . . .

If you read in a newspaper a report of that caviar mob scene, you would shake your head with revulsion. But the way that Ms. Johnson develops it, you know that you too would be in that line, cursing and elbowing and worrying that the supply was about to run out, just like the characters that she has drawn with such clear-eyed yet subtle intelligence.

> *Christopher Lehmann-Haupt, in a review of ''Persian Nights,'' in* The New York Times, *March 16, 1987, p. C16.*

JOYCE JOHNSON

[In **Persian Nights** it is] quite apparent that Diane Johnson has set out to write an American version of *A Passage to India.*

Chloe Fowler, however, is significantly different from E. M. Forster's Adela Quested. While the two share curiosity, a spirit of adventure, and a heedless, innocent sense of freedom that leads them into carelessness in foreign places, Adela Quested is ultimately shown to be made of stern moral fiber, a young woman capable of an act of selflessness. Chloe Fowler, much as she tries and puzzles, can never quite get beyond the self. A pretty woman, married to a successful thoracic specialist, she has led a privileged, conventional, vaguely discontented life that has not even been disrupted by her 2½ affairs. When her husband is unexpectedly summoned back to San Francisco as they board a plane in Rome, Chloe must go on to Iran without him. There she will come to discover that she is ''cursed with a nature that could not grasp the tragic and went on with egotism and vanity in spite of her conscious wishes.''

Persian Nights is social comedy deftly played out in the shadows of an historical tragedy. It is set in a country where the nights are perfumed with roses and where packs of wild dogs roam the street, where one Westernized Iranian wife wears pantihose with her tennis costume and another is assaulted by an ink-throwing fanatic as she carries a case of Pepsi to her car. Americans like Chloe Fowler must struggle with the disrepair and bad odors of their charmless accommodations; Iranians must live in fear of being reported to the SAVAK, the shah's secret police. (p. 1)

Iran is Chloe's *trip;* it exists for her consumption, amusement, edification—even her self-actualization. Her husband Jeffrey never does show up, so she is free to indulge in an affair with Hugh Monroe, a handsome surgeon from Rochester, who seems to be involved in some secret mission. Perhaps he is even CIA, but Chloe is enjoying herself too much to get around to asking him. She would be astonished to learn that she herself is thought to be CIA by the justifiably paranoid Iranian director of the hospital. Indeed, by the middle of the novel, everyone around her is deeply, ludicrously suspicious of everyone else. In the midst of this intrigue, Chloe indulges herself further with a brief dalliance with the handsome, exotic Abbas, [an Oxford-educated surgeon]. She is a woman who would like to have emotions, but in truth the ones she has don't run very deep. . . . Chloe realizes at a cocktail party at Azami Hospital that she is free to sleep with every man in the room. But what does that really mean? Although her experiences abroad stretch this woman to her limits, even her quest for experience is only another exercise of privilege.

As Diane Johnson sees it, Chloe Fowler reflects a peculiarly American malaise of the spirit. A certain emptiness, a feeling of never having been tested—as if the outlines of character have been fuzzed over by too much abundance, even too much freedom. Perhaps it is a quest for meaning that drives well-intentioned, self-assured Americans like Chloe overseas to places like Iran, where they attempt to apply the American Way to cultures they cannot comprehend. (pp. 1, 13)

Johnson is such a witty and accomplished novelist that one wishes she had produced a more polished book. There are disconcerting patches of carelessness in *Persian Nights*—particularly in passages that lapse for no good reason into the all-too-fashionable present tense, creating an effect that is more rushed and perfunctory than immediate. The complicated action of the climactic shootout in the ruins of Persepolis where Abbas is killed seems quite clumsily handled. Nonetheless, it is heartening to read a novel with so much texture, intelligence and content—one that also manages to be undidactically "political"—in a period when the fabric of so much fiction seems as diaphanous and insubstantial as a nylon curtain. (p. 13)

> *Joyce Johnson, "A Passage to Iran," in* Book World—The Washington Post, *March 22, 1987, pp. 1, 13.*

JAYNE ANNE PHILLIPS

Diane Johnson is the author of six novels, among them the literary mystery *The Shadow Knows*. That work . . . is a classic in its genre, a textbook on menace and suspicion, on the nature of fear itself. The protagonist, N, a divorced mother studying for an advanced degree, living in a housing project and pursuing an affair with a married lover, discovers who she is by projecting her fears about herself onto the very real threats surrounding her.

In *Persian Nights,* Ms. Johnson deftly urges a similar if less engaged heroine onto a world stage. She focuses not on one perception of events but on several, and investigates the question of moral responsibility against the backdrop of Iran shortly before the 1979 revolution that toppled the Shah. *Persian Nights* is funny, incisive, frightening and eminently skillful. In addition, it displays the Cassandra-like quality of good fiction and dovetails nicely with continuing Iranscam disclosures currently dominating the American press. When we read, at a climactic moment in the novel, "It seems the Americans are gun runners," the word hit home with a sickening thud. Ms. Johnson's novel might be read as a primer by any Westerner unfamiliar with Iran—that is, by anyone who has not lived there for some weeks, unprotected by the artificial host apparatus set up for Government-sanctioned visits.

Chloe Fowler has arrived in Iran alone and exhausted. Her husband, Jeffrey, a thoracic surgeon, has intended to share Western knowledge and expertise with the staff of Azami Hospital in Shiraz, but his partner has had a serious accident. Jeffrey encourages Chloe to go ahead—he will join her later. . . .

Chloe finds herself in Azami Compound—a kind of hospital protectorate, a large group of walled cement dwellings inhabited by foreign doctors and nurses, or by Iranians who live like foreigners. Villa Two, with its linoleum floors, army cots and stench of cat urine, is not what Chloe had expected as quarters for a famous visiting surgeon in exotic Iran.

The visiting American doctors are "restless, divorcing, eager for a vacation." The Fowlers are restless and the Fowlers are divorcing, though Chloe doesn't know it yet. And who is Chloe Fowler? A housewife, mother of two school-age children, who is unfashionably active and happy at home, or thinks she's happy: "She was, she was apt to say, the most unliberated woman she knew, but this statement was a form of vanity." Chloe has been "harmlessly" unfaithful to her husband, but imagines she bears no responsibility for her actions; because she is unimportant to the world, she imagines she is unimportant to herself. She appears to be your basic "docent." But there are indications she is more. From the start, she asks herself important questions: Who are you if you are a wife? "If you were a doctor you were morally neutral . . . because the poor people needed medicine under any regime. But if you were a wife were you more, or less, morally neutral?" . . .

The Americans, alternately fascinated and terrified, apprehend reality in varying degrees. Mysteries abound. Who is stealing chemicals from the hospital labs at night? Are the recent crashes of several American-made F-14's the result of faulty Iranian maintenance or of sabotage? The sight of men with machine guns is common, which "seems ill-advised . . . in view of the Shah's expressed wish to encourage tourism." International corporations, who seem to gather intelligence and protect their interests more effectively than governments, are first to scent the winds of change; the Mitsubishi wives are leaving and the Proctor & Gamble dependents are on alert.

The Americans of Villa Two prepare to leave, but at least one of them is reluctant to go. Chloe pursues her temporary vocation at the university, surprising herself "by having a gift for the painstaking work of fitting shards together," but her life is in pieces that prove impossible to reassemble. In a gesture that is a symbolic denial of her identity, Chloe gives the desperate Noosheen Ardeshir her passport so that Noosheen can leave her husband and travel to her parents in India; Noosheen will mail the passport back, or Chloe will report it lost and get another. It is always Chloe's mistake to suppose she is safer than she really is, yet she knows that safety has been her undoing. She now realizes she has been wrong to stay married to Jeffrey. He has come to realizations of his own and tells Chloe in a letter that he has a lover and wants a divorce. Previously, Chloe has been a traveler; now she is homeless, ambivalent about herself and about [her lover] Hugh. "It had never before in her life occurred to her she might be bad. . . . Was it necessary to decide on your own character? No. Yes! . . . It mattered, in the fabric of the world, whether a person was good or bad."

Ms. Johnson raises similar questions about governments, about motivation and intent behind policies, about the attitudes of one culture toward another. Is Iran a culture made vulnerable to one leader's orthodox fanaticism by the overadherence to Western values of another? Ms. Johnson doesn't ask, but we see the innocent Noosheen Ardeshir return voluntarily from her attempted flight, wearing a chador, animated by scenes of revolution she has witnessed in Teheran.

Chloe and the other Americans finally get on planes and depart. Like any good mystery writer, Ms. Johnson resolves (literally in midair) all questions, revealing the overlapping truths of who did what within this intimate circle. But Ms. Johnson's complicated themes resonate beyond her understandable characters.

It may be said that Chloe Fowler and her Government possess certain qualities in common. American politicians increasingly seem the (traditional) housewives of foreign policy: limited in actual experience, isolated, dimly philanthropic, protected from catastrophe by material wealth and due process of law. America can be said to drift along, uncertain how to proceed as a moral agent in a world that remains almost wholly foreign. Ms. Johnson beautifully represents a deeply personal parallel in the changed perceptions of her characters. These unsuspecting Americans return shaken from their Iranian good deed/vacation. One does not possess human dignity, they have discovered; one attains it via a process of moral choice. One does not possess understanding, but develops it in the risky arena of what is to be understood.

Jayne Anne Phillips, "The Shiraz Quartet," in The New York Times Book Review, *April 5, 1987, p. 8.*

DOROTHY WICKENDEN

Diane Johnson specializes in an artful blend of high anxiety and deadpan humor. She tells stories that are both shocking and droll, filled with mordant observations about the disjunction between people's perceptions of themselves and their world and the unadulterated truth. In *Persian Nights,* as in *Lying Low* (1978), a novel about a former terrorist living under an assumed identity outside Sacramento, Johnson has written a social and political satire. But here she moves far beyond the confines of suburban California, where most of her novels are set, and drops her characters in Shiraz on the virtual eve of the Iranian revolution.

Six months ago Johnson's scenario might have appeared far-fetched. In the wake of the revelations about the Reagan administration's Iranian adventures, it seems almost tame. She portrays a group of Americans who comically stumble into a political morass, the depths of which they repeatedly underestimate and misjudge. Embodying a mixture of American bravado and naïveté, her characters are swept up in a social, religious, and political revolt that dwarfs their ambitions and concerns. *Persian Nights* contains no overt political message. Instead, the Islamic uprising is used both as an exotic backdrop for the story and as a dramatic device with which to parody the parochial traumas of a little band of Americans abroad.

In Johnson's fiction the sinister lurks just beneath the commonplace. As the persecuted heroine puts it in *The Shadow Knows* (1974): "Other people in the world seem to be masked figures wandering dreamily around who will for a flash pull away their masks, wink atrociously at you, grimace, then everyone is muffled up again wearing ordinary smiles." In *Persian Nights* the anticipation of this unmasking is no less unnerving, since the characters must contend with a strange and turbulent culture, as well as with the inherent strangeness and turbulence of the human psyche. The confrontation between Iranian fundamentalism and American optimism takes various startling forms as everyone seems to become infected by the mistrust that is seeping across the country: Iranians suspect various Americans of being CIA agents; Americans can't distinguish between Savak agents and rebels. Friends withhold confidences, and lovers are secretive and duplicitous.

All of this is promising. Johnson's portrait of the Americans is sharply satirical. The context she has chosen for them is the international lecture circuit, which, as David Lodge showed in *Small World,* contains many possibilities for preposterousness. This time the group consists of doctors, most of them acquaintances from previous gatherings, invited to practice for several weeks at the medical school in Shiraz. (pp. 45-6)

These visitors believe that they are tolerant, open-minded people, and they have no trouble imagining a more enlightened future for Iran—and for themselves. In fact, they are benignly patronizing neocolonialists. Safely ensconced in the medical compound, they at first remain untouched by the growing political unrest. . . .

Johnson shows, through stock comic conventions and characters, the collision between two insular cultures. At the same time, she apparently had a more complex novel in mind. She infuses the labyrinthine plot with considerable suspense and two mysteries, which are jointly solved in the final pages of the novel: Hugh engages in a highly secret political mission before joining his companions in Shiraz; and during a sightseeing expedition, Chloe and her companions come across a badly injured man deep in a cave. When he dies, no one can vouch for his nationality, let alone his identity; the police decline to investigate, and the hospital refuses to take the body off their hands. Throughout it all, the novel builds steadily toward the climax at the ruins in Persepolis, where the tourists from Shiraz suddenly find their own lives threatened by American gunrunners and plunderers and Iranian rebels.

The problem with *Persian Nights* is that Chloe, at first amusing as a solipsistic—and intermittently astute—innocent abroad, eventually becomes tedious and predictable. Johnson seems to have been torn between her intention to present Chloe as an appealingly flawed character and her enjoyment at mocking her. Meanwhile, the narrative, which promises to develop from a social comedy into a political drama, degenerates into an elaborate farce. Doubtless this was Johnson's intention: her characters, muddled when it comes to personal politics, reveal an extraordinary ineptitude when they discover the world of bombs and guns and ideological passion. But though Johnson is deft at satirizing privileged Americans, she is clumsy with the Iranians. Because she never takes the novel much beyond Chloe's myopic perspective, the Iranian characters remain flimsy and half-formed. Their function is to provide comic relief, and to move the plot forward by robbing the heroine and her friends of a few cherished illusions.

The novel's two central Iranian figures, Abbas and Noosheen, are the Americans' counterparts—idealistic, impetuous, and foolhardy. Chloe has maintained a stubborn belief in the moral purity of her new friends: Abbas, a handsome, brooding young doctor trying to recover from the recent deaths of his wife and baby, and to reconcile his ambivalent feelings about his comfortable life (his brother is a rebel in exile in Paris); and Noosheen, a spirited student of Victorian poetry chained to an ancient, desiccated husband. . . .

Chloe impulsively concocts a risky plan to help Noosheen leave her husband and flee the country, and then spends a few contrite days worrying about her meddling—only to learn that Noosheen has returned. . . . (p. 46)

The narrative's turning point is provided by Abbas's failed act of heroism at Persepolis, yet like Noosheen's abortive flight, his attempt to save his country's treasures from the plunderers is contrived and implausible. Johnson herself seems unconvinced by the tragedy of his death; she simply needed a culminating event that would break up the colony and send them home with mild regrets about their moral indolence. The prose too becomes sloppy as Johnson wraps up the drama and delivers a few final barbs to her prattling protagonist.... (pp. 46-7)

Persian Nights is an odd combination of ambition and laziness. For all the blending of genres, the buildup of suspense, the well-pitched dialogue, and the facile wit, Johnson fails to fulfill the expectations she raises. Foremost an entertainer and a cynic, she rarely allows her characters a fair measure of power over their lives—just what they always think they're achieving. In her light California comedies, where people idly fiddle with the fates of others, this restriction works quite well. In *Persian Nights,* where the stage and the stakes are considerably larger, the effect is not one of sardonic sophistication, but of painstaking triviality. (p. 47)

Dorothy Wickenden, "Trivial Pursuits," in The New Republic, *Vol. 196, No. 16, April 20, 1987, pp. 45-7.*

ROBERT IRWIN

A few years ago the social world of expats in Istanbul was entertainingly portrayed in Maureen Freely's novel *The Life of the Party.* Diane Johnson's book [*Persian Nights*], however, focuses on Americans who are more transient, less self-sufficient. They mingle with the Iranian doctors and treat them with friendly arrogance. Abbas, Ali Yazdi, Bahramian and Fahramani attend the same parties as the Americans and participate in the innuendoes and affairs. Chloe wonders who is sleeping with whom and who will turn out to be the inevitable Savak agent. The atmosphere of pre-revolutionary Shiraz is evoked with remarkable accuracy....

Up to a certain point *Persian Nights* is a highly literary exploration of sensibilities and of the meeting between East and West. The characters themselves underline the literary nature of this encounter. When Chloe and Ali Yazdi find themselves alone together at the mouth of the Cave of Shapur, Ali Yazdi knowingly refers to Adela Quested and *A Passage to India.* But Diane Johnson tells a story ("oh dear yes") and what the Americans find in the Cave of Shapur bears no resemblance at all to whatever happened in the caves of Marabar. As the days and nights pass, apparently plotless rivulets of conversation and incident will come together in a mighty confluence of action and incident. Trivial nagging questions prove not to be so trivial after all. Betrayal and revelation follow one another in swift succession. Diane Johnson expertly delivers her surprises. All the same, the events which follow an outing by the Americans to a *son et lumière* at Persepolis seem to belong to another and cruder, action-packed novel. Only in the last chapters does Johnson return to form and give us a convincing and subtly written portrayal of the well-meaning but ultimately shallow Chloe joining her rather similar compatriots as they hasten to pull up the roots they had so briefly put down in Shiraz and bolt for the airport.

Persian Nights is not exactly an adventure story, but rather a study of a certain kind of woman and the failure of that woman's heart and commitment when faced by the real prospect of adventure. It is well done. Though the thrillerish plot may be a trifle absurd, the political mysteries are skilfully interwoven and the atmospheric creation of a time and a place on the eve of revolution is wonderfully accomplished.

Robert Irwin, "The Eve of Destruction," in The Times Literary Supplement, *No. 4396, July 3, 1987, p. 714.*

Clarence Major
1936-

American novelist, poet, critic, editor, essayist, and short story writer.

A leading figure in American experimental fiction, Major employs self-reflexive narratives and authorial intrusions to explore the nature of fiction and reality and the relationship between author, reader, and text. Using vivid imagery and disjointed assemblages of fiction, commentary, and allusions to literature and popular culture, Major asserts the primacy of imagination and examines the role of language in creating reality. Major's novels usually focus upon young black men striving to attain self-definition in a disordered and hostile society. Jerome Klinkowitz views Major's fiction as a deviation from the tradition of social realism commonly associated with most black American authors who explore similar subject matter. Klinkowitz noted further: "Major's innovations have made a fully nonrepresentational fiction possible. Such a radical aesthetic makes for an entirely new kind of fiction."

In his first two novels, *All-Night Visitors* (1969) and *NO* (1973), Major develops a fragmented presentation to reflect the chaotic lives of his characters and to focus upon the relationship between language, fiction, and reality. *All-Night Visitors* centers on Eli Bolton, whose bawdy adventures serve as his means for achieving manhood and individuality and for maintaining control over a menacing environment. In *NO,* Major portrays a nightmarish world in which the American South is a metaphorical prison; he implies that the human imagination can recreate reality to overcome oppressive social values and attitudes. In order to represent the confusion besetting his protagonist, Moses Westby, Major blurs Westby's identity, introduces abrupt shifts in time and narrative perspective, intermingles fantasy and reality, and uses typographical oddities and violent incidents. Most critics consider Major's next two novels, *Reflex and Bone Structure* (1975) and *Emergency Exit* (1979), his most accomplished works of fiction. In *Reflex and Bone Structure,* Major subverts the conventions of the detective novel by deliberately leaving the mystery of a murdered couple unsolved and focusing instead on the process of writing. This approach reflects Major's belief that fiction manufactures its own reality. In *Emergency Exit,* Major interweaves a conventional narrative about a love triangle with short digressions consisting of fantasy, anecdotes, dreams, and poems in order to stress the artificial nature of fiction and the subjective quality of truth and reality.

After a hiatus during which he taught, lectured, and traveled, Major published *My Amputations* (1986), a picaresque novel about an ex-convict, Mason Ellis, who kidnaps a noted author, adopts his identity, and undertakes an absurdly humorous lecture tour. Ellis's travels lead him to Africa, where he hopes to find a secret code that will reveal his true self. Ironically, nobody suspects that Ellis is an impostor. Greg Tate commented: "Major proclaims invisibility as the black American writer's private hell," adding that "Major writes with one of black letters' most experimental fictive voices (as well as its most lyrically unhinged), and the pleasures of [*My Amputations*] come more from the fluid sophistication of the text than from its venting of authorial ire." *Such Was the Season* (1987)

Photograph by Pamela Major. Courtesy of Clarence Major.

departs from Major's customary experimental style. Narrated in lyrical black American dialect by Annie Eliza, a Georgia matriarch, this novel focuses on Annie's battle to preserve unity among the troublemaking members of her extended family.

Major's verse exhibits the unconventional forms and heightened awareness of language characteristic of his fiction. According to Fanny Howe, Major's poetry welds "a complex modern diction to a constant historical consciousness." His poetry has been collected in such volumes as *Love Poems of a Black Man* (1965), *The Syncopated Cakewalk* (1974), and *Inside Diameter* (1985). Major's numerous nonfiction works include *Dictionary of Afro-American Slang* (1970) and *The Dark and Feeling: Black American Writers and Their Work* (1974). The latter book reveals the intellectual foundation of his writing and outlines hardships faced by black American novelists. Major has also served as editor and publisher of the *Coercion Review.*

(See also *CLC*, Vols. 3, 19; *Contemporary Authors*, Vols. 21-24, rev. ed.; *Contemporary Authors New Revision Series*, Vol. 13; *Contemporary Authors Autobiography Series*, Vol. 6; and *Dictionary of Literary Biography*, Vol. 33.)

PETER QUARTERMAIN

The storyline of *Emergency Exit,* about the Ingram family ("rich niggers from Inlet, Connecticut") and their friends, lovers, mistresses, consists of a series of more or less self-contained, straightforward narrative fragments interrupted by clusters of one-paragraph "takes" culled from dreams, real or imaginary cures for disease or against witchcraft, incidents in the life of Clarence Major, bits of conversation, news reports, city- and landscapes, and so on. There are also monotone reproductions of paintings, a photograph of Clarence Major and about a dozen cows (the text tells us there were thirty of them), quotations from literary (and other) sources, bits of telegrams, conference programs, bibliographies, phone books—and even, on page 174, a representation of a tennis match ("WA CK OCK"). It's all great fun, and when, about a dozen pages before the end, a whole page asks "Well, dear reader, how do you feel about it?", the sheer energetic gusto of the book has carried us along and we have been, well, entertained. And even, indeed, charmed. All through the book there is the author himself (or so he claims), who takes up more and more of our attention in the second half, until the distinctions between the fictive world of the story line and the (presumably) "real" world of the fragments breaks down completely and Deborah Ingram, "my favorite character in this whole book," says the author, "has become my lover." There are savage little asides about Hollywood, politics, religion; there are juxtapositions of dreams and "reality"; there are comic and/or grotesque fantasies. There are some fine sequences and fragments—notable conversations, for example, between Julie Ingram (the daughter) and her lover/boyfriend Al; descriptive vignettes of people crying, playing, swimming, dreaming; brilliant images drawn (or so it seems) from Hieronymous Bosch. These have somewhat the effect of set-pieces in the novel, and they manage both to remind us that what we are doing is reading a novel and, at the same time, that we are looking at the world. One effect of traditional narrative and novelistic conventions, after all (and especially in self-styled "experimental" writing), is to remind us that the novel does refer to a world "out there" as well as it does to the one "in here." They remind us, that is to say, of the novel as a representation. As we read the book, we find that the two kinds of writing—the story line and the interruptions—become increasingly interdependent, so that what occurs in one generates something in the other. In the story, the town of Inlet has recently passed the Threshold Law, which forbids all women over the age of eighteen from walking through or touching any doorway (they must be carried by men), and we follow the domestic fortunes of the Ingrams against this background. In the fragments, we perceive a wider and wider range of diversity in the world of man and the world of nature, in the external world of matter and the inner world of dream and thought (*and* in the writing), and as the novel gets cumulatively richer the two merge and we cease to question (if we ever did) the accuracy of the representation, and take the world of *Emergency Exit,* which is also the world of Clarence Major, on trust. The book thus teaches us how to read, is its own instruction manual. (pp. 66-8)

The characters in this novel . . . sense strongly that they lack substance, are "unreal". Jim Ingram says he has "no sacraments or creeds," Julie asks "will I ever find the center of myself?", and so on. One might reflect, of course, that they feel like this because they know they are only characters in a book, but such a reflection plays no part in Major's novel. . . . The people in this book, with the possible exception of Deborah Ingram, have no sense of themselves as things, and their sense of their own unreality derives from two sources. One is a trapped sense of being, as Julie puts it, "bound up in the cultural structure he was born into" (thus Al, at one point, "felt like a movie character. Hello movie character"), and the other, related to it, is from an overlay of language, theory, explanation, discourse, of sheer words for the sake of words or thought, which hide the reality underneath, disguise and falsify the thing, the self, by insisting that one think about it rather than touch it. Like the Ford car, the electric light bulb indeed does have a greater place in "the American experience" than has the novel, and Major recognizes that "understanding" is only one way of perceiving the world of things, and that it provides a partial or distorted view at best, since it covers the world in words or filters it through thought. Or through invention. Gertrude Stein's words, "everything is why they went," is an attack on reasons, and early in the novel Barbara, Julie's younger sister, says, "I want a message," Julie "Tells her straight, the message is here always and it's always the same": one experiences things by *being,* and by permitting *them* to be.

Thus the main thrust of the book's dynamic is in the play between the world as thing and the world as not-thing (invention, word), and when Major lets his book act out this interplay by itself, without commentary, then it is a fine and at times passionate celebration of the world of things, of people in that world, and at the same time a plea for language uncluttered by overlays of artifice and thus of falsehood. It is equally an excellent diagnosis of the traps people fall into, the ones they themselves build as well as those others build, out of words, out of desire, out of expectation, and out of hope, and of how they put their trust in women, or in sex, or in violence, or in position, or in myth, as a means of escape (Emergency Exit). But when he insists, as he does at the very beginning of the novel (and, indeed, throughout) that we not only interpret it but interpret it along particular lines, then he insists on an overlay of *meaning* and of expectation which we must cast over our experience of reading the book, whereby we apprehend the things and events in it according to a discursive pattern the main thrust of the book would deny. *Emergency Exit* opens with a prologue, a learned little discourse on symbolic meanings. It begins: "Stop. The doorway of life. Take this cliché with ancient roots as a central motif." Thus it instructs us, orders us, how we are to read—seeing connections, themes, symbols; seeking "understanding", along particular lines. The prologue discusses the origin and symbolic meaning of carrying brides over thresholds ("A respect for blood as the source of life was at the bottom of it"), of the symbolism of blood, menstruation, women, and of the uterus/vagina as threshold. A mythology is proposed, at the center of which is Woman— and it then becomes incumbent upon the reader to see the women in this book in such terms. Lest, however, we miss the point (that in this book we are in the realm of metaphor, and symbol, and this book—you'd better believe!—is *about* something) there are lots of references to thresholds and "superior pussy." Major deliberately uses such sophomoric clownishness and a fair amount of cliché to drive home the fact that we are in the realm of "significance"; and it is here that the book gets tiresome. We learn very early, for example, that James Russell Ingram's mistress is named Rosalyn Carter, that Allen Morris (whose love affair with Julie is chronicled in the narrative), 28 years old, black, is a drug pusher from Harlem. In the eyes of his ex-mistress Gail he is "Allen the revolutionary." Names, characters, events, are clichétic, invoke stock responses—and remind us that this is a story and that "I", Clarence Major, is writing it. It is very much a part of the book's purpose that the author be present, but the means Major has chosen are rather labored, and give the book an occasional air of coy self-consciousness that, irritating as it is, on the one hand suggests that he trusts neither his material nor his reader, and on the other severely undercuts the unusual excellence of the book by dissipating its energy and muddying its perception. Towards the middle of the book Major tells us that for Julie and Al "the world was yet undiscovered." In the long run, that is true of what this book offers—too much is disguised. (pp. 68-70)

Peter Quartermain, "Trusting the Reader," in Chicago Review, *Vol. 32, No. 2, Autumn, 1980, pp. 65-74.*

SARAH E. LAUZEN

Emergency Exit is a celebration: a vibrant assemblage of discrete bits of fantasy, dream, images, definitions, anecdotes, surrealism, and story. In his fourth novel, Clarence Major creates, by a principle of formal diversity, an Open Door Novel, one that accommodates all kinds of brief excursions out of the ordinary frames of consistency, coherence, and genre. This diversity results in neither random hijinks, nor pure structure, but structure in the service of texture.

Emergency Exit is a tease: offering its own heavily symbol- and motif-laden pages as a decoy for the recuperative ability of the modernist reader, it exuberantly resists exegesis. Here is a book that truly "changes as it goes," canceling out hypotheses as it revises and dismisses its own codes and clues. Reading *Emergency Exit* is like reading parts of Wordsworth, a Cheerios box, and *Finnegans Wake* in rapid succession. And not only can mode change sentence to sentence, but subject might also change as details, characters, and themes appear and dissolve without narrative consequence. The book floats on a shimmering surface all the while pretending to be anchored to a strict underlying structure.

Emergency Exit is written in short, discontinuous takes with units ranging from a single sentence to 3- or 4-page clusters. First and most dominant is the narrative—the story of the relationships among the Ingram family and friends in a town called Inlet, Connecticut. This narrative is complicated by the Threshold Law, the major thematic element, and further by a truly miscellaneous museum of techniques that alternate with and infiltrate the narrative sections in an apparently random way. This museum includes a range of rhetorical devices, from dimestore self-consciousness ("He was hot, like a character in deterministic fiction of the 1930s.") to pure non sequiturs ("Rea cut her fingernails on Friday night she "died" instantly she was a virgin."). There are quotations from *Krazy Kat, The Portable Tolstoy,* and *Emergency Situations in Driving....*

From the very first pages of *Emergency Exit,* realism and surrealism combine to create multiple, alternate but coexisting worlds. In the world of *this* book, a walking, talking plant interrupts Al's lakeside brooding; Humphrey Bogart shares a drink with Jim Ingram; Harry Houdini delivers an herbal tea recipe guaranteed to change Rosalyn's life; "Grown men dressed as women in high heels strut about in their tiny rooms to understand what happened...." Inside this synthetic world, the ground rules are always subject to change: women giving birth is just as odd or ordinary as Superior Pussy, Inc., artificial vaginas by mail.

"Gimmick is trying to find a more secure footing in this world"—the gimmicks of plot, character, narration. Due to the *gimmick* of the word fork, Julie is able to fix breakfast, which consists of eating her own words, "I mean bacon and eggs." Major addresses the charge of gimmickry in contemporary fiction with the observation (which ought be a commonplace) that language itself is a gimmick, no one ever escapes gimmicks, there is no a priori....

Emergency Exit is sprinkled with definitions from *A Dictionary of Symbols, Dictionary of American Folklore, Mongolia's Culture and Society,* as well as the Seattle yellow page listings for "door." Spreading threshold/doorway/inlet/vagina connections out on the surface, Major defuses the possible interpretive weight of the assembly, turning it into a mock-symbol. He uses the equivalent of symbol not for its symbolic import, but as a token—one among many—in a formal strategy, one befitting a Revolving Door Novel.

Thresholds/margins/frames. *Emergency Exit* easily accommodates many interpretations, for instance, this: The narrative point of view, situated as it is between subject and reader, encloses that subject within the frame of the imagination. The doorway of life/the threshold of the text. The arbitrary nature of the Threshold Law points to the arbitrary nature of the demand for narrative. Inlet(t)ers respond by pissing on the diamond-studded threshold of City Hall; *Emergency Exit* responds by violating the frame of the text....

Emergency Exit is a book of movement, mood, energy. As Christopher Butler describes Jackson Pollock's paintings: "They do not define representative images, or outline planes, their surface is not sectioned off into separately characterized areas, there are no climatic areas of colour intensity, no field and ground relationships, no focal points to settle on".... Other than the narrative, none of the rhetorical devices is more dominant than another. Even the frequently repeated images and phrases don't resolve into motifs but simply add to the texture of *Emergency Exit.*...

Opaque, oneiric, improvisational, *Emergency Exit* may be a book, as Robert Adams claims of *Ulysses,* that loses as much as it gains from close critical scrutiny. The whole book from the first word ("Stop") to the last ("stop") is a loop, a revolving door whose threshold we cross repeatedly. *Emergency Exit* is an endless performance, despite its promises: "the only way to get out of this show is to keep all the way to the exit...."

Sarah E. Lauzen, "Surface, (Symbol), Loop," in The American Book Review, *Vol. 4, No. 6, September-October, 1982, p. 8.*

JEROME KLINKOWITZ

Major is a leading stylist and innovator in the second wave of American experimentation. His first novel, *All-Night Visitors* (1969), challenged the emerging black culture of the earlier 1960s which had yet to merge its own aesthetics with the revolution going on within the mainstream culture's fiction. Major's second novel *NO* (1973), likewise shows more of his own developing interests (especially in the lyricism of Jean Toomer and Gertrude Stein, innovators of a half-century earlier) than evidence of racial politics. His works of the mid- and late Seventies, *Reflex and Bone Structure* and *Emergency Exit,* employ a wide range of experimental techniques to push fiction beyond a mechanical self-reflexiveness into true literary self-apparency.

Reflex and Bone Structure reveals its own compositional process on every page, yet it still manages to tell a story replete with human fascination. As Tzvetan Todorov has remarked, of all fictive sub-genres it is the detective novel which "tends toward a purely geometric architecture," and it is that form which Major chose for his first experiment with self-apparency. In detective fiction, the subject matter of the plot has been concluded before the novel begins: The crime is an established fact, and now the author and reader must concentrate on its solution. In other words, the novel must compose itself not around the unfolding of a represented story but rather with the more epistemological business of sorting things out—mediating, as it were, between the a priori fact and the reader's appreciation of it. The text, therefore, assumes a reality of its own, as the reader's relationship to the author takes on the deeply realistic qualities of the detective's posture toward the crime. Narrative action is not something reported or even reflected; it is the existence of the book itself.

Yet *Reflex and Bone Structure* is more than a conventional detective novel, for every element of its composition—character, theme, action, and event—expresses the self-apparent nature of its making. Characterization is done through metaphors, emphasizing artifice to the point of allegory. Even events take on this supra-real quality. . . .

Every element within Major's narrative is animated, sometimes by the characters and other times by the narrator himself. . . . Anthropologically speaking, there is no simple reality in this novel, only a plethora of cultural descriptions all competing for persuasive presence. An actress on TV is never just that; there is the role she's playing, the physical conditions of the production within which she works, plus the equally real life she may be living at that very moment in her apartment across town. Television, music, fantasies, and history—all conspire to create a larger reality which Major's writings dutifully embrace. . . . (pp. 203-04)

Within the narrative of the crime's detection (Cora has been murdered), Major treats us to the characters' own projective fantasies. . . . The narrator is prone to these same fantasies as well; indeed, the characters' fiction making is simply a microcosmic example of his own activity in creating this novel. Therefore he marshals these emotions to help construct *Reflex and Bone Structure*. His own feelings for Cora are ravaged by the jealousy he feels when pairing her with the other two males, Canada and Dale. His imagination sometimes runs to violence, picturing his characters in airplane crashes or explosions—as well he might, for he is after all writing the novel and enjoys a God-like power over his creations. Most importantly, he has his own voice in this fiction, convincing to the reader because it reveals his fully human plight in dealing with the emotions at hand. . . . On a more specific level, the narrator identifies problems he is having with his characters. Cora comes easily, for she is his obsession. Canada he respects, partly because this figure can wield the violent impulses which the narrator can only express in writing. But Dale, the necessary third point of this triangle, presents a problem. Throughout . . . this brief novel there are no less than seven references to this dilemma. "I have almost no sense of Dale except I know I don't like him," we are told, and soon the narrator sends him out to North Dakota so he can have some creative rest. "The fact that Dale really has little or no character doesn't help matters," he complains. "I cannot help him if he refuses to focus."

There is even a bit of jealousy here, for "whatever it was about him that attracted Cora shall always remain a mystery to me." There is a temptation to punish this character, to run him through a series of embarrassing episodes, but in the end the narrator admits the key to the problem: "Dale was never meant to make it. He was that side of myself that should be rewritten. Dale was an argument I had with the past." Here once more a temptation of the life-seeking reader—that characters are projections of different facets of the author's own personality—is turned around to become a self-apparent component in the work itself.

Cora is indeed the narrator's obsession, and the male figures—Canada and Dale—have been the respectively positive and negative aspects of his own mania which blossom forth into fiction. The only unconventional aspect of all this has been Major's willingness to let the reader see behind the scenes and to incorporate this perspective into the making of his novel. There are many ways to approach Cora. "Canada tries too hard some times," we're told at the beginning. "He tries to crack into Cora. Burst into Cora. Open Cora with his sledge-hammer. But I weave *around* the stern cathedrals in her holy city, her very pure spirit." A world war can erupt over a person as a sex object, Major recalls, alluding to Troy and subsequent human disasters: *Reflex and Bone Structure* is an attempt to locate this energy within one narrator and show how it can create a novel just as well.

Throughout the novel Major makes integral references to the work at hand. . . . Major's travails as author are much like the fictive-making agonies of his characters within their various jealousies, fantasies, and paranoid reactions; because he establishes the identities among these acts and the correlative reality between his feelings and his characters', *Reflex* becomes a meaningful text for the reader—both as an adventure of its characters and of its author. Having alerted his readers to what's happening, Major can move his perception from character to character as the mood demands, so that ". . . I'm never alone. It is either Canada or Cora and sometimes Dale." At times they can become fictionists as well, as Canada "invents and reinvents the world as he wishes it to be." What is real for a character is just as real for the author, and vice versa; the text of *Reflex and Bone Structure* is essentially one thing, added to the world, rather than a representation of any one part.

At the heart of it all is the narrator's obsession with Cora. . . . The novel becomes his infatuation, his seduction, his recreation of her. . . . Once vitalized, Major can do what Beckett requested of Joyce, that his fictions not be about something but rather be something themselves. . . . Above all, as in a detective novel, the final truth is less important than the process of getting to it in its full implications. (pp. 204-07)

Emergency Exit [Major's next novel] is an even fuller work, just as any novel per se eclipses the effect of a sub-genre in effect. In it Major focuses on every componental level of writing as a thing in itself, creating a virtual catalogue of self-apparent effects in fiction. Superintending the whole is an anthropological device around which the novel's action is based: the institution of a "threshold law" which requires all the women of a modern American town to be carried across doorways, a symbolic act based upon ancient tribal taboos regarding menstruation. "Stop: The doorway of life," Major's novel begins, and then immediately takes "this cliché" and revitalizes the dead metaphor with meaning. As Wittgenstein would suggest, it is all a problem with language, here expressed as a "male attitude toward the female" which because of fundamental confusions between signifier and signified leads to a misconstrued symbology:

> Because women are eternally guilty of sin they had to be lifted and carried across the threshold and they could not *touch* the doorway. Yet they, the givers of life itself, were the *source* of the symbolism and the ritual. They were the doorway of life.

A threshold law, then, is an originally transparent signifier which because of faulty syntax has become an opaque sign, a thing in itself, signifying nothing but its own dead language.

Major parallels his own act of writing with *Emergency Exit*'s theme, using each component in fiction, right down to the very words themselves, as opaque objects before incorporating them in the novel's larger syntax. In this manner words, sentences, paragraphs, vignettes, short stories, and the plot line itself are established as things in themselves before taking on their larger referential duties—and even then the reader's attention will be directed not off the page but back to it, where each word was first introduced as an artifact. (pp. 208-09)

"... in a novel, the only thing you really have is words," Major emphasized in his interview with John O'Brien. "You begin with words and you end with words. The content exists in our minds. I don't think that it has to be a reflection of anything. It is a reality that has been created inside of a book." Therefore his strategy in *Emergency Exit* is to emphasize that every device of human interest (which critics of conventional fiction demand) is first of all a problem in language. His elementary notion of "threshold" is explored by studying every dictionary meaning of the word, from Webster's to dictionaries of symbols and indices of folklore. We are also given other documents reporting the word's effect on the community: the phone book, card files in the library, and arrests on the police blotter for its violation. As for the novel's action, it is established to be first of all linguistic. Individual sentences are written on the page, apparently leading nowhere, so that the reader's attention is to their writerly art. (p. 210)

The plot itself is emphasized as artifice at every turn. As in *Reflex and Bone Structure,* Major makes frequent reference to his act of writing, even "employing gimmicks," and near the end begins an affair with a character whose liaisons have formed an interesting part of the story (and who has certainly been seducing the reader). Characters themselves are described in surreal terms, so that there is little chance to get lost in their verisimilitude.... (p. 211)

To forestall any attempt to receive Major's characters as real, yet to place his inventions within an even more sociologically precise category, he mixes in the self-apparent inventiveness of cartoon figures with the more ordinary actions of his plot.... (pp. 211-12)

On at least a dozen occasions Major refers to some ensuing action as "like a soap opera" or to a person as behaving "like a character in naturalistic fiction." Here again the effect is double, using a type of literary-historical shorthand which contributes to plot and characterization while at the same time noting that it is all arbitrary convention. At times Major can be a theorist as well, such as when his narrator remarks, "He could hear her going and coming. The process of her movements was like Gertrude Stein's fiction. She was in the continuous present"—an indication that aesthetics is just as much about life as it is of art. When someone is introduced as "a

very realistic person," theory and practice coalesce, reminding us that choices in fictional theory are finally indices of personal value.... As all self-apparent fiction ultimately must do, *Emergency Exit* summons the full range of the reader's experience to complete the work, conventions being important not only for what they capsulize in fiction but also for the attitudes they bring from real life. It is all artifice, and knowing that yields a fuller reading. (pp. 212-13)

Emergency Exit, therefore, demonstrates how the familiar materials of novel-making can be used as things in themselves while still providing all the human interest readers demand. Indeed, self-apparent fiction compliments the reader by providing more to do. Major's novel summarizes in form the history of the last half-century of American art, from the building blocks of abstract expressionism through a certain pop iconography (once again, things from real life as themselves) to the experimental techniques of the superrealists. A regard for the material integrity of art's own making has been at the center of these developments, and with *Emergency Exit* Major shows us how they can be natural for fiction as well. In the face of such work, even realism becomes different, self-apparent in a way that it never was before, just as the radically new superrealism in painting grew from the principles of abstract expressionism. In this way the techniques of Major's fiction enrich the mainstream, creating a style of "experimental realism" in which the simple act of vision becomes not just an integral work of art but an interpretation of our cultural act of seeing as well. (pp. 213-14)

> Jerome Klinkowitz, "The Self-Apparent Word: Clarence Major's Innovative Fiction," *in* Studies in Black American Literature: Black American Prose Theory, Vol. 1, *edited by Joe Weixlmann and Chester J. Fontenot, The Penkevill Publishing Company, 1984, pp. 199-214.*

JOE WEIXLMANN

Clarence Major's *Reflex and Bone Structure* is one of the most formally exploratory fictions of the 1970s. More clearly disruptive, even discontinuous, in its narrative flow than [Ishmael Reed's] *Mumbo Jumbo;* more obviously lacking in closure than [Toni Morrison's] *Song of Solomon, Reflex and Bone Structure* undermines the central expectations of the who-done-it. Not only do we never learn, in any meaningful sense, who did, but we get fragmentary, not infrequently conflicting accounts of the details of the murder of Cora and her lover Dale. One of the few metafictions in Afro-American literature, *Reflex and Bone Structure* combines the story of its own processes as a fictional work with tale of Cora and her lovers—who include not only Dale but also Canada and the narrator. Indeed, in certain important ways, Major's account of his novel's processes and construction *supersedes* the story of the book's characters. That Dale, the narrator, and the free-spirited Canada slide in and out of bed with Cora, and otherwise interact with one another, involves the reader at one level, as does the mystery surrounding Dale's and Cora's deaths; but it is the metafictional aspect of *Reflex and Bone Structure* which carries the novel's intellectual weight.

Clues concerning the crime pop up regularly, only to have the narrator inform us that he has made them up. And while we do learn, on the book's last page, that the narrator has, in one sense, caused the characters' deaths—"They step into a house. It explodes. It is a device. I am responsible. I set the device"—, his act is the act of a storyteller *as* storyteller; his device is a literary one. Any "real" explanation for the explosion will have to be found elsewhere.

What Major has set out to investigate in *Reflex and Bone Structure* is nothing less than the nature of reality. Whereas the central premise underlying the so-called "realistic" school of American writing, of which the traditional detective novel, along with the preponderance of black fiction, is so much a part, is that fiction directly mirrors life, *Reflex and Bone Structure* makes explicit what Major's earlier novels *All-Night Visitors* (1969) and *NO* (1973) merely hint at: that fiction cannot, and therefore should not endeavor to, capture life's realities in an undistorted, mirror-image manner. On the contrary, fiction creates its *own* reality, one which has no absolutely direct reference to events outside itself; literature is necessarily bound to the phenomenal world only by its status as an artifact within that world (namely, that thing which we call a book, or a performance) and by virtue of its being an extension of an author whose imaginative act brought the work into existence.

The appearance of what may, here, seem to be philosophical posturing vanishes once one explores the implications of the concept. What is implicit in Major's metafictional insight is a statement of the need to question sternly all received "truths." Major wants his reader to recognize that the concept of literary realism which allowed fictional detectives like Sherlock Holmes to assemble all of the clues in a case and, from them, reason back to one, absolute, objectively verifiable solution to a mystery can, today, be shown to be invalid. Modern physics (not to mention experience) has shown ours to be a multivalent world, in which investigation is more likely to widen the number of possible alternatives than it is to ferret out a single, unassailable answer. (pp. 29-31)

> *Joe Weixlmann, "Culture Clash, Survival, and Trans-Formation: A Study of Some Innovative Afro-American Novels of Detection," in* The Mississippi Quarterly, *Vol. XXXVIII, No. 1, Winter, 1984-85, pp. 21-31.*

RICHARD PERRY

My Amputations is a dense and complex work, as readers familiar with Clarence Major's four previous novels . . . might expect. A book in which the question of identity throbs like an infected tooth, *My Amputations* is a picaresque novel that comes wailing out of the blues tradition: it is ironic, irreverent, sexy, on a first-name basis with the human condition, and defined in part by exaggeration and laughter.

Mason Ellis, the protagonist, is an endearing character who's gone through periods when, were it not for bad luck, he'd have had no luck at all. He is a writer whose muse has deserted him. His first marriage results in five children, for whom he and his wife have difficulty providing. Told by a welfare worker that the father's absence would mean larger checks for the family, the parents agree to split up. . . .

Early in the novel, Mason is in a Kafkaesque predicament. Serving a sentence in Attica for a crime he didn't commit, one day he sees on television an award ceremony during which a writer he is convinced is passing for him—but using an assumed name—accepts a prize meant for Mason.

Upon his release, Mason goes searching for the impostor, accompanied by acquaintances who include a pornographic film actress, an American Indian and a man named Jesus. He finds the impostor, kidnaps him and subjects him to tortures designed to extract a confession. But the man, Clarence McKay, won't break, and Mason, his certainty shaken, is suspended in a frustrating twilight zone—holding a man who he believes has stolen his identity and who won't (or can't) give it back. In a caper worthy of good adventure novels, Mason disposes of the impostor and creates an identity by appropriating the latter's assumed name (and cash award). He also complicates what by now has become his consuming question: who am I, really?

Is Mason suffering from delusions? Is he just another recidivist ex-con? These legitimate questions fade in the face of his obsession with who he is; all that matters for readers, as for him, is *his* question.

Possessing money and acclaim, but tormented by fear that he'll be exposed, Mason goes looking for an answer. His quest, like that of more than one American writer before him, takes him to Europe, where he encounters underworld thugs, neo-Nazis, literary groupies and several Greek citizens fond of antebellum Southern costume parties. Ultimately, Mason arrives in Africa, where he meets a Liberian tribesman who holds an envelope in which, apparently, the secret of Mason's true identity is enclosed.

Mr. Major has said that one of his objectives in writing is to "attempt to break down the artificial distinctions between poetry and fiction." *My Amputations* is distinguished by a rich and imaginative prose poetry of evocative power. Sometimes the effect is spectacular, like the eruption of fireworks against a dark, featureless sky. . . . At other times the language is a distraction that calls attention to itself and delays the unfolding of a story I want very much to continue reading.

One of the most provocative aspects of *My Amputations* is Mr. Major's third-person narrator. Street-smart, versed in the blues, jazz, literature, art, European classical music and philosophy, this narrator is familiar with the cultural signposts of Western civilization. Not only is he hip and learned, he is brash, often injecting himself into the novel by commenting on the action or blurring what small distinctions exist between reality and dream. He strikes me as a voice who knows who he is, an ironic and sometimes disconcerting counterpoint to the tale of a man whose thirst for identity literally threatens his life.

The narrator doesn't reveal the source of his identity, at least not directly, and for good reason. Were we able to isolate him outside the novel, he would probably smile and say that the question of identity is extremely personal and not easily deciphered. Perhaps, sometimes, it is not decipherable at all. But Mr. Major has demonstrated in *My Amputations* that the attempt to do so can prove the stuff of an imaginative and compelling tale.

> *Richard Perry, "Hunting the Thief of Identity," in* The New York Times Book Review, *September 28, 1986, p. 30.*

JEROME KLINKOWITZ

[Major's fiction] has been a closed book since 1977 when he completed the novel *Emergency Exit*. Having nearly a decade elapse without seeing a new work from such a significant novelist is cause for concern, but Major's *My Amputations* . . . draws its substance from just this predicament. Looking at the earlier work, [critic Keith E.] Byerman notes that Major's characters create texts as a strategy of survival; *My Amputations,* however, is a novel which explains a decade's silence, a negative autobiography of a life that didn't happen, and as such it is the perfect fiction for Clarence Major to publish in 1986.

The theme of this novel reflects the approach to literary art which has developed among writers living in Boulder and teaching at the University of Colorado. Although Steve Katz, Robert Steiner, Ronald Sukenick, and Clarence Major are among the most individualistic and certainly most idiosyncratic of American writers, they hold one important belief in common: that fiction isn't about experience, it's more experience itself. . . .

Readers of these works are given more than just an account of characters, settings, and themes. . . . By effacing the distinction between art and life, these writers avoid the biographical fallacy which would lead to a corny and self-indulgent confessionalism—they're not writing "about" anything, much less themselves. But from an honest confrontation with themselves writing, fiction is produced which yields all the requisite products of novelistic art: a rhythm to existence, a generative energy behind it, and a sense of continuous flow which gives some intimation of the texture of life.

Major's *My Amputations* is a triumph of this technique because the author's recent life of fiction has been such a silent affair. No writer since F. Scott Fitzgerald has allowed himself so much time away from novel writing yet done so well with the eventual next book. Fitzgerald, of course, suffered from extenuating circumstances, losing major parts of intervening decades to partying, drying out, and picking up the pieces from his famous crack-up. Major's discipline has been more self-consciously applied: teaching, travelling, and working in other media, from poetry to quasi-documentary writing to paint. Yet *My Amputations* shares with the older novelist's work a sense of having turned conditions supposedly antithetical to art into writing which is artistically successful by anyone's terms.

The first point of success is with the approach to the work itself. In *Emergency Exit* Major saw this phase as an archetypal threshold which characters crossed at the risk of entering a whole new world; only the writer himself could have access to that escape door labelled "emergency exit," and the closer he got to his creations the harder it would be to find the way out. *My Amputations* begins with another door, the door to a closet wherein lurks The Impostor, master of darkness and exitless mystery—the very substance of that life of fiction Clarence Major hasn't lived since late in '77. It turns out that The Impostor has been living the author's public life these past ten years: publishing, doing readings, lecturing abroad, and generally carrying on as critics and readers may have presumed Clarence Major himself had been doing.

For Major's own life of fiction, he places himself in Attica prison for the duration of The Impostor's career, then makes a break to track the man down and assume his proper identity. The breakout is his testament to inspiration—before it "he'd been a blind bat struggling to embrace the sky," but now he soars freely by his own direction. Pursuing The Impostor, he confronts his past and articulates it in the concisely accurate shorthand terms available to writers on a roll: the special quality of evening in the South becomes "dusk. Jean Toomer dusk, Red moon. Half moon. The whole bit," and the doings of some hostile police instill a "Richard Wright-fear." Buddies don't get home late, they get the "Last Bus Blues"; Billy Eckstine, Cab Calloway, and Charlie Parker hit the turntables just in time to set the right mood. When family life is tough, the repair bills come wearing ski masks; from another angle,

when the author and his friend break into The Impostor's apartment, "They moved like charged sentences." In *My Amputations* the alternating metaphors of art for life and life for art are played against each other and accelerated into a style of vision until all distinctions are comfortably erased. With this accomplished, Major's new life of fiction is underway.

The fun begins when the author tracks his nemesis across Europe, trying to recover the literary reputation he lost when "You stole my manuscript, while I was in the joint." There's even a twist behind this, as the author has been reading this book "over and over again till he convinced himself he was the writer and no longer the reader," a play on self-reflexivity which is responsive to the subtleties of literary theory. Just as the allusions to American culture animate each character's action, the author's involvement with his own story deepens this novel's dimensions: "I come here with my life before you," he tells an audience when he can think of nothing else to say, "I am a writer whose muse ran off. I'm just beginning to find myself on my own. I want to speak to you about my new effort to recreate myself. . ." Yet the world offers its own hard resistance, as the author pursues The Impostor from Britain to France and down into Italy, at each point having the situation blow up in his face according to the region's particular brand of terrorism. When the author "comes to the end of his running" in tribal Africa, more is resolved than a simple plot line, though all of the plot's problems are handled too. Major's conclusion simultaneously fulfills his book's cultural, technical, and biographical destinies simply because his writing has labored successfully to identify them all with one another.

Jerome Klinkowitz, "Art as Life," in The American Book Review, *Vol. 8, No. 5, September-October, 1986, p. 12.*

STUART KLAWANS

At the end of this review, I will do the unforgivable and reveal the punch line of Clarence Major's new novel, [*My Amputations*], since that may be the only way to convince you to read the book. Mere description cannot convey the wild humor and audacity to be found here, nor the anxiety and cunning. The virtues of *My Amputations* are all active ones, best summarized, perhaps, as jumpiness. Only a demonstration of them will do. Major . . . has produced as his fifth novel a fantasy of the black writer as con artist, kept on the run over three continents. Part travelogue and part imaginary self-portrait, the book begins with its protagonist huddled in a closet in New York and ends with him in a hut in Liberia, having by that point met the Devil and worse. He has, in fact, met himself. Mason Ellis, the character on the run, is a half-mad ex-convict who imagines himself to be, of all people, Clarence Major—or perhaps Clarence Major, huddling in the closet, fears he's really Mason Ellis.

"The background of such a madman is at least of clinical interest. I strain to find something good to say." Thus the narrator, early in the novel, about Mason. Raised in South Chicago by a stepfather who's the Man of Rules and a mother who's the Woman of Blues, Mason does a tour in the Air Force, reads everything he can lay his hands on and, after his discharge, makes the mistake of going home. . . . In the space of three pages, Mason fathers nine children with two women and then lights out for New York, where the police pick him up on the Lower East Side for looking wrong. The charge sticks, and Mason does his next tour of reading in Attica. There, he becomes convinced that he is not merely the reader but the author of certain books, and that an imposter has stolen his identity and his $50,000-a-year grant from the Magnan-Rockford Foundation. (p. 90)

Released from jail, Mason sets out to collect. With the help of a private eye—who turns into the Claire Quilty of the book—he tracks down the Impostor, who is living on the Lower East Side under the assumed name of Clarence McKay.... Soon Mason has kidnapped CM and is holding him in a closet on West 72d Street.

It is not enough for Mason to capture CM. He must also claim, or perhaps reclaim, his identity. For that, he needs money. In the company of petty crooks, Mason undertakes a series of crimes that might well have been planned by Laurel and Hardy. The narrator, it seems, takes a malicious pleasure in subjecting Mason Ellis to slapstick; perhaps this is the only revenge CM can exact for being represented by such a lowdown ME. Mason is just capable enough to buy a fake passport from the Mob. With that in hand, he diverts $50,000 from the Magnan-Rockford Foundation, signs up with a speakers' bureau and sets off on a lecture tour.

Perhaps the summary I've given so far seems crammed with incident. Forget it. That was merely the setup—an artful setup, granted, but ultimately just so much machinery. *My Amputations* begins in earnest when Mason hits the road, and the riddle of his identity becomes secondary to the puzzle of what the hell is going on in the world. (pp. 90-1)

But what kind of puzzle is it? In Florence, "He looked into the facade of the city: workers in stone had made it a towering monument to something he reluctantly understood. Well, even *he* was beginning to realize the real subject of his story wasn't this damned quest he'd thought he was on." He goes to the Uffizi, kneels on the street before Dante's house, spends hours at the Medici Chapel. In Athens, he appeals to the sculptures in the National Museum. They, too, give no help. It seems that Mason, like poor Claude McKay, has aspirations to the universal.... [Several] esoteric experiments fail as well. He locates oracles, all right, but they tell him things such as, "Father Divine is the supplier and satisfier of every good desire." It later turns out they have been restored by the Magnan-Rockford Foundation.

Magnan-Rockford, like the shadowy detective, keeps turning up in unsettling places. Mason knows he is being followed, but how is he being used? "He refused to believe himself a Pynchon yoyo or an Ellison dancing Sambo paper doll." Yet, before he leaves for the ultimate destination, Africa, he accepts a commission from the head of the speakers' bureau—quite possibly a Magnan-Rockford front. The man gives Mason a sealed envelope addressed to Chief Q. Tee, who can be found near Monrovia. His instructions are to deliver the envelope unopened.

Before Mason goes to his fate, let me ask: Just how universal *is* he? The question seems appropriate for two reasons. First, the earlier parts of the book, with their recollections of Mason's youth, have an urgency that's missing from the rest of the novel. Much of the later travelogue is entertaining, even brilliant; but its emotional life is on loan from the first sections, the ones that are not universal but personal, right down to the street addresses. Second, the novel is supersaturated with names, allusions, quotations. Claude McKay, Jean Toomer, Chester Himes, Richard Wright, Ralph Ellison—these are some of the more obvious and specific progenitors of the text. Some of the

more unexpected are Gertrude Stein (who supplies the epigraph), William Carlos Williams, Daniel Defoe, Herman Melville and (I swear it) Joyce Kilmer. When a writer loads a book with so many references, the reader is entitled to ask whether he knows what he's doing.

Believe me, Clarence Major knows. He has fashioned a novel that is simultaneously a deception and one great, roaring self-revelation. It has the accent of a black American—of precisely *one* black American, in fact—but its tone should be recognizable to anybody who's ever gotten nervous looking in the mirror. Mason is not the first character to venture into the world playing a role, only to be mistaken for someone playing still other roles. Nor is he the first to try to go home, wearing a mask as self-protection. It is interesting, though, that in his case the mask is a real one, of carved wood, and the home is a hut outside Monrovia.

He has sought first money and fame, then wholeness, then wisdom, and as a result everything that could be amputated from him has been lopped off. Now he has come to the end of his world. Though he should know better, he tamely produces the Magnan-Rockford letter for Chief Q. Tee. He is about to receive the punch line; read it, if you need further demonstration.

"The old man spoke: 'The envelope, please.' Mason pulled it from his pocket and handed it over. The old man ripped it open and read aloud: *'Keep* this nigger!'" (pp. 91-2)

Stuart Klawans, "All of Me," in The Nation, *New York, Vol. 244, No. 3, January 24, 1987, pp. 90-2.*

GREG TATE

In *My Amputations*, Clarence Major goes Ralph Ellison one better, proclaiming invisibility—these days we call it misrepresentation—as not just the black American everyman's fate, but the black American writer's private hell. His protagonist, Mason Ellis, is an extremely literate black ex-con who kidnaps a famous Afro-American writer (Clarence McKay), accuses him of plagiarism, steals his identity, then finances a literary tour of America, Europe, and Africa with the fat grant McKay has received from a prestigious foundation. That hardly anyone notices the switch is Major's blunt way of saying all black writers look alike to an indifferent world.

In this picaresque parody of the literary hustle, Ellis is expected to play a triple role: the black writer as militant activist, cosmopolitan cocksman, and colored plaything. Wherever he turns up, Ellis finds his identity circumscribed by the racial politics of his hosts. White students at Brooklyn College care more about his opinions on liberation movements than his poetry; those at Howard want to know who he writes for, black or white people. In Greece he's invited to an antebellum costume ball; just off the plane in London, he's hustled onto a bill with punk-rock poets; in Berlin, neo-Nazis threaten him with a leadership role in the Fifth Reich; in Ghana, he's interrogated by academics about his love for the Motherland and African literature, then mistaken for a political subversive by government police.

Give or take a wild ballyhoo, such myopic misinterpretations have been Clarence Major's bane since he published *All-Night Visitors,* black literature's answer to *Tropic of Cancer*. But *My Amputations* is no self-pitying exercise in racial farce as the best revenge. Major writes with one of black letters' most experimental fictive voices (as well as its most lyrically unhinged), and the pleasures of this novel come more from the fluid sophistication of the text than from its venting of authorial ire. Although the surface theme of *My Amputations* is the black writer in flight from himself and his public, its true subject is Major's singing and stammering prose. The liberties he takes with narrative suggest his belief that language is the only prison house a writer should ever allow himself to be boxed up in. Major makes Ellis suffer history not as a melodramatic weight but as a rush of literary allusions and poetic ellipses, race memories and memory lapses, sense impressions and existential daydreams. . . .

Major deftly adapts his improvisatory voice to the exigencies of the narrative moment. Less an overt display of styles than a disciplined act of logorrhea, *My Amputations* should easily win Major renown as a prose prestidigitator of the first rank. He handles an encyclopedic range of voices, sensibilities, and zeitgeists (Afro-American, American Jewish, African, Italian, German, English, French) so skillfully that they seem authentic rather than satirical.

In flight from the black writer pigeonhole, Major has become the mythographer of a host of imaginary selves. Yet the confident byplay of folkloric and literary citations in *My Amputations* suggests that Major's alienation from the social fictions about black writers hasn't alienated him from his roots, or his root doctors even. . . . Taking his inspiration from all five senses, a multicultural intellectual curiosity, and a polymorphous tongue, Clarence Major has given American fiction its *Hopscotch*, a cosmopolitan Third World man's guide to ruminating in tongues.

> *Greg Tate, in a review of "My Amputations," in VLS, No. 52, February, 1987, p. 3.*

AL YOUNG

Unlike [Major's] previous fiction, which was unstintingly experimental, *Such Was the Season* is an old-fashioned, straight-ahead narrative crammed with action, a dramatic storyline and meaty characterization. But it's the widow Annie Eliza's melodic voice, by turns lilting and gruff, that salts and peppers and sweetens this story, enriching its flavor and meaning.

While elaborating on what took place last week, when her divorced nephew Juneboy surprised Annie Eliza and the rest of his relatives by coming to Atlanta to lecture at Spelman College, she also reveals a great deal about herself and the Georgia she grew up in—to say nothing of what's been cooking lately around Atlanta and the Georgia that spawned her. And what a stew she serves up! Mayors and ministers, hoi polloi and the ragtag, cops and crooks, scholars and blue-collar scufflers and drunks. . . .

Juneboy—who is also Dr. Adam North, a Yale University research pathologist and sickle cell anemia specialist—has not only broken the vow he made almost 30 years ago when his father, Scoop, was killed, to leave and never again set foot in the South. But the intensity with which he pursues and reas-

sesses information about his roots reminds Annie Eliza of something her sister, Juneboy's mother, once confided.

> Esther told me some years ago that Juneboy wont right in the head. Had something to do with the time he spent in service. The doctors discovered he had some ghosts or something living in his brains. . . . I member feeling real sorry for him and I also member thinking the ghosts got there cause of his sadness due to the way his father died.

As it turns out, Juneboy isn't the only one with ghosts on the brain; Annie Eliza has plenty of her own, and more than a few skeletons in her closet besides. All the characters who figure prominently into this earthy, rambling monologue—including her sons, DeSoto (a police sergeant) and Jeremiah (a minister), Jeremiah's pampered wife, Renee, Mayor George Watkins-Jones, Annie Eliza's lonely widower brother, Ballard, and her niece, Donna Mae, whose husband, Buckle, is a hard-drinking voyeur—end up being something quite apart from what they appeared to be at first.

It is during Juneboy's weeklong stay that Annie Eliza learns how his father, Scoop—a numbers runner who came to a violent, racketeer's end—had secretly helped finance her son Jeremiah's college education. . . .

Annie Eliza has long harbored a virulent resentment of Jeremiah's uppity, aristocratic wife. . . . But Renee is a Wright. "You know the Wrights is one of the biggest and richest Negro family in politics in Atlanta. My boy gets invited to all they big gatherings and most of them go to his church when they bother to praise the Lord at all."

However, after Renee announces her decision to run for state Senate, Annie Eliza's attitude toward her feminist daughter-in-law gradually brightens, and for reasons as complex as they are fascinating. Renee's aggressive, muckraking campaign has barely gotten off the ground when Senator Dale Bean Cooper Jr., her opponent, comes down suddenly with a disease even Juneboy finds mysterious; an illness that the Rev. Jeremiah Hicks has prophesied. After Renee goes public with a statewide scandal Jeremiah is shot and one of his business associates, Cherokee Jimmy, commits suicide. There isn't much that Annie Eliza omits from this folksy, artfully told account of one extraordinary week in Atlanta.

Clarence Major has created a delightfully lifelike, storytelling woman whose candor is matched only by her devotion to truth and her down-to-earth yea-saying to life. . . . It is as if Clarence Major, the avid *avant-gardiste*, has himself come home to touch base with the blues and spirituals that continue to nourish and express the lives of those people he writes about so knowingly, and with contagious affection.

> *Al Young, "God Never Drove Those Cadillacs," in The New York Times Book Review, December 13, 1987, p. 19.*

Hilary Masters

1928-

American novelist, memoirist, and short story writer.

In his fiction, Masters focuses on how the home, the community, and the past interact to shape individual personalities. Like his father, poet Edgar Lee Masters, who is best remembered for his *Spoon River Anthology,* the younger Masters often dwells on melancholy aspects of life. As one critic noted in a review of his first novel, *The Common Pasture* (1967), Masters "demonstrates that he has some of his father's gift of delineating character with a few bold strokes, combining sentimentality with cynicism, and making much, effectively, of minor human tragedies." While setting his works in various locales, Masters often concentrates on ordinary events that converge to profoundly influence his characters' lives.

The Common Pasture covers twenty-four hours in the lives of small-town residents who are preparing a community celebration to honor recent improvements. Tension mounts when certain factions of the townspeople oppose the ceremonies. *An American Marriage* (1969), Masters's second novel, follows the courtship and marriage of a college professor and one of his students. The resulting scandal sends them to Ireland, where they unwittingly become involved with covert activities of the CIA. Martin Levin praised Masters's "verve in shaping and coining language" and his "keen sensitivity to ordinary life." Masters's next novel, *Palace of Strangers* (1971), is written in the form of a journal by a young Congressional campaign manager. Although critics observed that the political aspects of the novel are realistically conveyed, some maintained that the story is marred by the narrator's emphasis on his own sexual exploits.

In his most acclaimed work, *Last Stands: Notes from Memory* (1982), Masters examines the effects of his past in forming his personal identity. He lovingly yet unsentimentally describes the eccentricities of his grandparents, with whom he lived during most of his childhood, and his parents. Although Masters treats his father with respect and expresses an appreciation for his work, Masters's mother, who earned her college degree against her husband's wishes and supported the elderly poet in his last years, emerges as the heroine of this book. Two of Masters's recent novels, *Clemmons* (1984) and *Cooper* (1986), focus on men whose search for an uncomplicated existence leads to greater difficulties in their lives. Masters has also written *Hammertown Tales* (1986), a collection of stories about a small town in New York in the tradition of Sherwood Anderson's *Winesburg, Ohio* and Edgar Lee Masters's *Spoon River Anthology.*

(See also *Contemporary Authors,* Vols. 25-28, rev. ed. and *Contemporary Authors New Revision Series,* Vol. 13.)

of delineating characters with a few bold strokes, combining sentimentality with cynicism, and making much, effectively, of minor human tragedies. *The Common Pasture* is the story of 24 hours in one small American city. Hinton City has a familiar cast of characters: the poor boy who makes it in a big way by marrying the bank president's daughter; the local sweetheart, rejected, who turns prostitute; unscrupulous real estate wheelers and dealers; corrupt politicians; the innocent from the outside world who provides the town with its catalytic moment of truth. There are some contemporary twists and clever gimmicks with Mr. Masters manipulating his people dramatically to illustrate that power corrupts and money does not liberate. This is not a profound novel, it has few emotional surprises, but read as a good straight story of crime and error, sex and suspense, it builds to a resounding climax.

A review of "The Common Pasture," in Publishers Weekly, *Vol. 192, No. 3, July 17, 1967, p. 65.*

PUBLISHERS WEEKLY

In this first novel [*The Common Pasture*], the son of poet Edgar Lee Masters demonstrates that he has some of his father's gift

MARTIN LEVIN

If there were a literary synonym for "painterly," one could say that Mr. Masters has it: a verve in shaping and coining language. This talent, mingled with a keen sensitivity to ordinary life, celebrates the quite untypical marriage of a thirty-ish history professor and his student [in *An American Marriage*].

Patricia Gates is an 18-year-old foundling, an heiress and a wanton, in that order. Hamilton Phillips is a low-pressure academic, who follows the path of least resistance in marrying his pupil, since he finds her irresistible. The two together become a different chemical compound from their single identities, of course, and the author sets them to boil in a damp Irish college, where Phillips has bagged a foundation grant. The foundation turns out to be a C.I.A. cover and the college is a case of mistaken identity, but the honeymoon survives unending anticlimax.

Mr. Masters sees the academic grove with sharp humor, but without bile. It offers a rich backdrop for the counterpoint he develops between the married lovers, as they respond to the rhythm of life.

> *Martin Levin, in a review of "An American Marriage," in* The New York Times Book Review, *April 13, 1969, p. 49.*

AGNES C. RINGER

An American Marriage is a charming book, warm, witty, written in a beautifully controlled style. The story follows the courtship and first months of marriage of Hamilton Phillips and Patricia Gates, a period spent in Ireland where he teaches history at Alclair University.... The narrative cuts back and forth between Ireland and America to chronicle their brief love affair, marriage, and the months spent in Alclair, obviously Dublin, although place names have been altered. The idiosyncrasies of the Irish, the eccentricities of two other visiting American professors, the Phillips' adjustment to marriage, Pat's pregnancy, and a new mode of life, are blended in a sparkling novel that is a delight to read.

> *Agnes C. Ringer, in a review of "An American Marriage," in* Library Journal, *Vol. 94, No. 8, April 15, 1969, p. 1650.*

KIRKUS REVIEWS

In [*Palace of Strangers*] politics become politiks with Russian roulette overtones and with all the backroom gambits where loyalty buys favors and principles are exchanged for proxies. This is Tommy Bryan's personal journal, starting from the time Pug Connors, the Yost County Democratic boss, asks him to manage the Congressional campaign of Howard "Howie" Ferguson, a newcomer candidate.... Howie is a movie star type, with a knockout wife who cleans up his language, takes the mirror down from the ceiling in the bedroom, and manages to say the right thing in the stickiest situations. Until the end when he decides to take on a bunch of threatening, revolutionary students all by himself in a scene that Jerry Rubin might have dreamed up. Unfortunately, Tommy spends a lot of time keeping notes on his own gamey, sexual progress, the characters are political cartoon caricatures and you end up as frustrated as the Democrats at their last convention.

> *A review of "Palace of Strangers," in* Kirkus Reviews, *Vol. XXXIX, No. 13, July 1, 1971, p. 695.*

MARTIN LEVIN

[*Palace of Strangers*] is a round-by-round account of a Congressional primary in upstate New York, seen through the jaded eyes of the candidate's campaign manager. Actually, the election has been programmed in smoke-filled rooms. Candidate A, a bright young millionaire looking for his first hurrah, is a stalking horse to outmaneuver candidate B so candidate C can win. Political scripts, of course, have a way of becoming unstuck, and this one is no exception.

Mr. Masters, a sometime politician himself (he was a supporter of the late Senator Kennedy) describes the maneuvering in the only tone suitable: utter cynicism. High-flown speeches, once again, are a cloak for self-interest; and the rewards of victory are the pork barrel and the gravy train. The narrator's interpretation of democracy at work is low-keyed and credible.

> *Martin Levin, in a review of "Palace of Strangers," in* The New York Times Book Review, *October 24, 1971, p. 57.*

JONATHAN YARDLEY

It is one of those peculiar twists of fate that Edgar Lee Masters, who a few decades ago was one of the best-known poets in America, is likely to be remembered in our day not for his own work but for the portrait of him that emerges in [*Last Stands: Notes from Memory*], his youngest child's memoir. Edgar Lee Masters' poems are rapidly disappearing from the anthologies in which they once had a central place, but he has been given a new life of sorts in his son Hilary's *Last Stands*, a lovely and candid book that is less an autobiography than an effort to understand the legacy its author received from his parents and grandparents....

As a family history that manages—through imagination as well as recollection and research—to connect and interweave the American past, present and future, *Last Stands* deserves comparison with William Maxwell's classic of the genre, *Ancestors*. But though Masters is deeply concerned with the relationship of his family's history to his country's, he is even more deeply involved with attempting, as any serious memoir must, to figure things out—to search for answers to the mystery of identity, to speculate about what it is that brought him to where he is now. Though he tells us little about his present life, we know that he has taught at colleges and that he has published novels; therefore when he writes about his father's struggles to fulfill his expectations as a poet, and his mother's struggles to keep the family afloat through her income as a schoolteacher, it goes without saying that he is describing, in the most intimate way, his own roots.

Edgar Lee Masters' marriage to Ellen Coyne was his second. His first had ended in a bitter divorce the settlement of which had stripped him of most of the possessions acquired in his careers as lawyer and poet; he had three children by that first marriage, though Hilary—the only child of his second marriage—seems scarcely to have known them. Ellen Masters, three decades his junior, admired his poetry almost without reservation and chose to overlook his incessant sexual rovings, yet she declined to tender him mere subservience; she attempted, with some measure of success, to strike a workable balance between the demands of his creative impulse and the needs of his family.

One such effort at balance was the decision to leave young Hilary in Kansas City with his grandparents: the feisty bantam rooster, Tom Coyne, and his ample, motherly wife, Mollie. This was done in order to give Hilary a Midwestern boyhood and to allow his father to write undistracted by the noise and bother of a child, and doubtless it profited both of them. But father and son missed each other greatly, and their summer reunions seem to have contained large measures of happiness and love. . . .

To his immense credit, Hilary Masters neither denigrates his father for choosing this separation nor overrates the work he was able to do as a result of it. In no sense does *Last Stands* attempt a critical evaluation of Masters' father's career, but the book leaves little doubt that the son understands as well as do the critics that apart from the poems collected in *Spoon River Anthology*, the work of Edgar Lee Masters has vanished into the past. Hilary Masters sees his father more as a man than as a poet, and he sees him clearly: a man of enormous energy and passion, unsure of his literary worth yet determined to leave his mark on American letters, in love with his wife yet drawn to other women, self-centered and vain yet unexpectedly thoughtful and generous.

Masters also sees his mother plain. Her portrait is painted more slowly and subtly than that of her husband, but at the end of the book she is its dominant figure. She obtained her master's degree against her husband's resistance and scorn, and the teaching jobs she was able to get as a consequence of having the degree never satisfied him as adequate to his own station. Yet in the last years of his life she supported all three of them; she was able to "make the arrangements and pay the bills," and there was "a freedom in her stride, a sense of moving out of the dark, near tragic times and into the brighter prospect that she had put together." Masters fully understands that it is his mother, more than anyone else, who is the true hero of his tale.

It is a tale that he has told with exceptional grace and artistry. He has not written a narrative but woven a tapestry, in which he moves back and forth in time without any warning to the reader yet without ever creating confusion. He pays loving tribute to his forebears but declines to sentimentalize them. And he never loses sight of the essential truth that we can never know the past, that it can only and always be a mystery, that the most we can hope to do is reinvent it for whatever meaning it offers to the present. This Hilary Masters has done in his small, luminous, consequential book.

> *Jonathan Yardley, "Living with the Legacy of Spoon River," in Book World—The Washington Post, November 14, 1982, p. 3.*

GEOFFREY O'BRIEN

In *Last Stands* Hilary Masters offers not an orderly chronicle of his early doings but a fluid exploration of the way memory shifts and recombines them.

This quiet and rather melancholy book characteristically focuses on life's long intervals of regret, resignation, mere survival, rather than its moments of decisive vigor. The author's father, Edgar Lee Masters, was 60 years his senior and long past the early triumph of *Spoon River Anthology*; his maternal grandfather, Thomas Coyne, was an aged pensioner living on remote memories of his exploits as cavalry scout at Fort Custer and construction engineer on the Panama Canal and the Quito-Guayaquil railway. Hilary, who spent his childhood being shunted back and forth between parents and grandparents, be-

tween Kansas City and his father's rooms in the Chelsea Hotel, has a keen sense of the discontinuities within history and within families. As if to compensate for a painful awareness of absences and dislocations, his book is a formally elegant construction in which near and distant, past and present are reconciled.

The effect is musical. Certain places, certain reiterated phrases and gestures—a hotel elevator, a porch in summertime, a childish nickname, the lighting of a pipe—establish a rhythm in which a lifetime's most commonplace moments are valued as major events. Looming in the background are the great public spectacles: the settling of the West, the Spanish-American War, the Chicago World's Fair. In the foreground, in sharp focus, are the tiny moments of small talk, of restless waiting, of somehow passing time: the decrepit poet listening over and over to *Annie Get Your Gun*, the old soldier wandering over the site of Custer's Last Stand. . . .

It is remarkable that a book which contains so much of death, despair, suicide, failure, should finally convey a kind of muted happiness, the happiness of seeing things clearly and balancing them in the mind. This memoir, free of adulation or bitterness, should be read not merely for the events it records—events such as any family knows—but for what the author has so inventively made of the slippery realm of memory.

> *Geoffrey O'Brien, in a review of "Last Stands: Notes from Memory," in VLS, No. 13, December, 1982, p. 4.*

MICHAEL D. RILEY

[In the right hands], the memoir can deliver the pleasures of art while retaining the sting of actual experience. In his thoroughly satisfying *Last Stands: Notes from Memory*, Hilary Masters achieves just such a blend by making full use of his format's freedoms. *Last Stands* unfolds much in the manner of memory itself, a series of deeply etched vignettes juxtaposed in time yet seamless in effect. That effect is by no means random. Masters develops his material thematically, giving to each episode its full freight of significance before moving on, calculating shrewdly its position in the cumulative effect he seeks. Indeed, *Last Stands* is on all counts the work of a highly conscious writer. Brilliant in its characterizations, unerring in its evocations of scene and historical period, richly poetic in its language, the book's greatest distinction is that it utilizes all of these qualities in the service of interpreting life rather than photographing it.

Irony forms the essence of that interpretation; the quirks, the inconsistencies, the sheer strangeness of experience control the book's episodes just as they define the individual lives of the major characters. Those characters are few but memorable: Hilary, his parents, his maternal grandparents. All find absurdities at the center of life—comic and tragic forces determined to defeat any original purposes to which the characters might hopelessly cling. But as these purposes collapse, the characters manage to blunder into *other* values they had never thought to pursue. Each life examined here is a kind of non sequitur, individually and in interaction with one another; yet the worth and dignity of each life is salvaged and finally affirmed. The book's title supplies a central suggestion, and the lives of Tom Coyne, the author's grandfather, and Edgar Lee Masters, the author's famous father, provide the best examples of the book's perspective.

Custer's Last Stand provides the touchstone for the last stands toward life taken by all the book's major characters, but it applies most specifically to Tom Coyne's tumultuous life. Custer's foolishness achieved the fame denied to Coyne, a man who hungered for it just as much and who pursued it in the same wild way. As a young cavalryman, Coyne was stationed at Fort Custer a few years after the Little Big Horn massacre, and on Sundays he and his comrades would ride out to the battle site, finding at times a piece of leather or spent cartridge. While in the West Coyne had more than his own share of bold and bloody adventures, but his thoughts always returned to Custer's absurd gesture as to a mirror of his own baffled ambitions. (pp. 914-15)

Fierce, indomitable, self-righteous, courageous to the point of foolhardiness, Tom Coyne embodies the values that tamed a continent but could never tame themselves. Scout, Indian fighter, laborer, ranger (he entered the infamous Jackson's Hole singlehandedly to capture and retrieve murderers), civil engineer, railroader, mercenary, entrepreneur (he made and lost several small fortunes), Coyne is the last of his breed. No reader will forget him. But the world he saw as something to use up and discard finally discarded him. (Coyne was renowned for driving his horses till they died; later he drove his automobiles the same way.) His demonic energy alienated the gentle, genteel wife he loved but could never understand, propelling her into premature senility and despair. Like Custer, Tom Coyne ended his life by suicide.

Edgar Lee Masters also hungered for fame; but unlike his father-in-law, Masters found more of it than he ever dreamt of when *Spoon River Anthology* exploded on the literary scene—more, indeed, than he could handle. At the age of forty-seven he suddenly found himself corresponding with Hardy and Yeats, lionized in the press, and surrounded by available women he could not resist. He rode the swell enthusiastically—only to find himself presiding, like Priam, over a life apparently determined to last too long, a life condemned to declining achievement, dwindling reputation, and near-poverty. This is the period that Hilary Masters, born when his father was already in middle-age, recounts in detail. The picture is bleak enough. His father continued to work hard but unselectively. Books, essays, and poems were churned out solely to keep working or to pay bills, and the motivation showed in the results. In poetry he seldom recaptured the terse allusiveness of *Spoon River,* as if that work had been an aberration, a charm or gift he had used up like one of Tom Coyne's horses or automobiles. Instead, he drifted back to the turgid diction and exhausted classicism of the popular poetry he had read and imitated as a young man. In short, he committed stylistic suicide. (pp. 915-16)

Our final impression of Edgar Lee Masters is by no means unmixed. His Olympian lusts and pride coexist in his portrait with his recurrent warmth and his wry self-knowledge. Moreover, he never gives up work or hope. However dubious his choices, habits, and final achievements, he obtains, like Tom Coyne, a complex density of character—one which somehow holds its own against absurdity self-created and absurdity merely found. (p. 916)

Hilary Masters is too mature an observer, too complete an ironist, to manifest either pride or shame in unalloyed form. The odd pleasures and pains of his own upbringing are so obvious in their lived details that no summary comment is needed. But in the end he seems to accept his father's verdict as reflected in these lines from the poem "Silence," which Edgar Lee Masters directed to be read at his funeral: "There

is the silence between father and son, / When the father cannot explain his life, / Even though he be misunderstood for it."

That silence—like the question, "Who knows?"—bends like a horizon not only over Hilary Masters' relations with his father but also over all the richly human ironies that proliferate throughout the book. The author shapes, organizes, implies. He refuses to simplify or to numb these living presences with the grosser conveniences of hindsight. As a result, the reader first notices through the author's eyes the complex patterns of art; but, as with all realized art, the reader next discovers their resemblance to the complex patterns of his own life. He can appreciate all the more fully, therefore, the words with which Hilary Masters closes *Last Stands.* They describe his mother as she observes her husband reading. The aged poet has, by another quirk, fallen into exactly the same pose he struck for the portrait which hangs above him, painted many years earlier. "Her look explores him. It explores her history with him. It explores all that has happened to him and to her because of him and like the portrait behind her, but for a different reason— makes no judgments." One can judge, however, the excellence of *Last Stands* and hope that it finds the wide audience it deserves. It would be a shame if scholars interested in Edgar Lee Masters, whose interest can be presumed, were left alone among such pleasures. (p. 917)

Michael D. Riley, in a review of "Last Stands: Notes from Memory," in The Georgia Review, *Vol. XXXVII, No. 4, Winter, 1983, pp. 914-17.*

HAZEL ROCHMAN

[In *Clemmons*], A. W. Clemmons—successful New England country realtor, sexy lover, self-doubting father—finds that the mess of intimacy interferes with the neat order he'd like to make of his life. His dreams of escape are thwarted by women— wife, lovers, daughters, mother—and by "his feelings hooking him unawares." Masters' ruminating narrative, moving back and forth in time, occasionally has an essaylike quality, but the sharply etched descriptions, as well as the often wryly observed scenes and characters, are part of a complex metaphorical pattern. With neither sentimentality nor easy cynicism, Masters explores ideas of home and community in connection with the past and with one's adaptability to change. Truth holds a "tangle" of contradiction: Clemmons' luminous vision of unity from the roof of the house he is painting is not denied by his sudden ignominious fall and splattering paint.

Hazel Rochman, in a review of "Clemmons," in The Booklist, *Vol. 81, No. 12, February 15, 1985, p. 823.*

JAMES McCONKEY

A major pleasure of Hilary Masters' latest novel [*Clemmons*] comes from the reader's page-to-page involvement in the altering moods of the fiction he has created; he is a deft craftsman, capable of moving from a sardonic insight to compassion, from satire to rowdy comedy, from sexual passion to a wish for, perhaps even a glimpse of, an order or unity beyond our splintered and violent world.

The novel begins with a telephone message to the middle-aged protagonist . . . from one of his roaming daughters that her older sister plans to be married to a rock musician in the field next to the family home in upstate New York, and it ends a few weeks later with a bizarre rehearsal of the marriage. . . .

Such a frame, however, doesn't constrict the scope of the story, for Masters manages to cover a number of decades in Clemmons' life, his movement from theater press agent to country real-estate developer, his marriage to the Southern woman who has more or less left him to assist in various political causes and who is the sister of a governor, and the affairs he has had, or is currently having, with various women, one of them a singer and another a woman of considerable wealth.

The ostensible story line concerns Clemmons and the daughter, Milly, who is to be married and from whom he has become so estranged (because of their similarities) that he tries, unsuccessfully, to flee from that wedding ceremony; it is also, however, the story of his relationships with all the women in his life, including his mother. . . . The conflict with the daughter expands to become the conflict between the sexes; in addition, the conflict between generations. . . . Beyond these matters, the story explores the relationship between past and present in America, at least the past as it is sometimes nostalgically defined; and, though Clemmons wisely makes no pretensions to wide meanings, it does tell us by indirection something about the American condition itself.

Enclosed by its fairly rigid frame, how does the novel manage to include so much? The technique is similar to that of Masters' *Last Stands,* the poignant and much-praised memoir about his maternal grandparents and his parents . . . ; indeed, that biographical and autobiographical work offers a number of parallels to this work of fiction. Though it is perhaps a clumsy way to describe what is an artful structural method, *Clemmons,* like *Last Stands,* seems to me composed of a series of separate globes or transparent bubbles, each of which at its center has a present moment; around that center are arranged memories of past events appropriate to it. These memories avoid the limitation of conventional flashback by being presented directly and dramatically, often by what seems an objective narrator.

It is as if we are being given a series of gestalten, of patterns that show us related but distinct aspects of a whole personality or experience that finally is beyond analysis. I know as I move through the book that I have a series of complex responses to the major character, responses that range from admiration to dislike. Sometimes narcissistic, sometimes petty, he also is compassionate; verging at times toward violence, perhaps even a hatred of some of the women he clearly loves, he is also capable of generosity and selfless acts.

Claire, his wealthy mistress, says to him, "One part of you pretends to be this spirit that cultivates a place of solitude, while the rest of you wants a big campout with all the wickiups," which makes him, I suppose, pretty much like the rest of us, with a desire for spiritual freedom ever fighting the wish for the human community. Stated in other terms, the conflict is between the soul and the body, that old-fashioned antithesis; if Clemmons seems, for his age, unusually horny, his appetite at least makes the conflict more engrossing.

While I was reading the novel, it produced for me several disquieting esthetic moments, for I felt (perhaps wrongly) that it was encouraging me to think of Clemmons as a better human than I felt him to be; but then, I encourage myself in much the same way. I can say with more assurance that the relationship between sexuality and material possession (a link between Clemmons the lover and Clemmons the owner of a town) is a bit murky, leading to a straining of symbols. Ultimately, though, Clemmons stands as he is supposed to, unique and yet Everyman, a human poised between conflicting desires, a collection of opposing wants, a representative of our human state and of our predicament. (pp. 8, 10)

James McConkey, "A Member of the Wedding," in Book World—The Washington Post, *March 17, 1985, pp. 8, 10.*

GEORGE CORE

The village Boston Corners and the metropolis New York City are superbly realized in Hilary Masters's *Clemmons.* . . . Place is an essential element in [this novel] . . . ; so is family, and it is no wonder that marriage is crucial to the action of . . . *Clemmons.* Hilary Masters dramatizes his comedy within the cluttered mind and rambling consciousness of his protagonist, A. W. Clemmons, a public-relations agent who slowly and almost unconsciously buys himself into the little community and becomes its leading citizen and entrepreneur as well as its only real-estate agent. Boston Corners is Clemmons's fief, as his wife and mistresses constantly remind him. But he is a genial and generous lord of the manor, a baron with egalitarian impulses. When one of his two daughters whimsically decides to get married, Clemmons's life becomes hopelessly complicated—and only partly because a movie is to be filmed at the place where the wedding is to occur. . . . Our hero is a restless man, and on the eve of the wedding it appears that he may bolt, leaving not only his wife and daughters but his mother and mistress to manage matters.

The comedy in *Clemmons* is so subtle that at least one reviewer has missed it entirely. Nevertheless the humor of this complex and rich novel is abundantly present from beginning to end as Clemmons muses on all manner of incongruous subjects while his life seems to be drifting into further disorder. Clemmons is a romantic sensibility adrift in a coldly materialistic world who indulges himself in a riot of the senses and an endless speculation upon life's web of complications. (pp. xli-xlii)

Clemmons is [a complex and ambitious novel] . . . : it proceeds by flashback and allusion but never becomes obscure or opaque, just as the action never flags. . . .

Here is comedy of a high order, with little irony and less satire, a comedy that sustains and elevates our sense of life's possibilities. (p. xlii)

George Core, "Procrustes' Bed," in The Sewanee Review, *Vol. XCIII, No. 2, Spring, 1985, pp. xxxix-xlii.*

PUBLISHERS WEEKLY

The better stories in this jarringly uneven collection of [*Hammertown Tales*] . . .—such as **"Foundation"** and **"Success"**—are touching and subtle, executed with a delicate sense of detail and overtone as they approach at oblique angles the gray areas of ambiguous relationships. Others—**"The Moving Finger,"** for example, in which a man passing through Chicago's O'Hare makes the mistake of phoning an old flame—are fragmentary, anecdotal, brittle. The pieces set in the fictive Hammertown, a rural small town in upstate New York, often lapse into a mannered rustic folksiness. In his best passages, Masters shows an authentic, deep-running feeling for the countryside (a compound of awe, nostalgia and regret) and the lyrical and descriptive powers to render it, that help greatly to redeem the weaker pages. (pp. 44-5)

A review of "Hammertown Tales," in Publishers
Weekly, *Vol. 228, No. 24, December 13, 1985, pp.
44-5.*

*Carol Ames, in a review of "Hammertown Tales,"
in* The New York Times Book Review, *April 20,
1986, p. 22.*

KIRKUS REVIEWS

[Fourteen] brief, sensitive, melancholy short stories detailing
the life of a failing village in upstate New York [are collected
in *Hammertown Tales*].

Masters divides his stories of Hammertown (a country village
which has been in slow decline since the freeway passed it in
the early 1950's) into two clear sections: his tales of the people
who were born and raised and are dying with the town, and
the stories of the wealthy professionals who've moved there
to refurbish old houses and live (although not work or, necessarily, feel at home) there. The former are related by a nameless narrator, a formal, rather courteous mechanic and handy-
man with a quiet voice. . . .

The stories about the new inhabitants of Hammertown are generally less successful—Masters stays at a distance, and the
brittle lives he describes are familiar to any reader of modern
literary quarterlies, where most of these were first published.
The people are rich and sophisticated, but with empty marriages, and they find the reality of Hammertown ultimately
depressing. Perhaps the best of these is the blackly humorous
"Here, Daphne!," in which a man confesses to his mistress
that he killed his wife's cocker spaniel—an irritatingly affectionate dog—only to find out that she doesn't miss it, and he
does.

For the most part, though, graceful, thoughtful work from an
accomplished stylist, one with a fine sense of the sorrows of
a disappearing America.

A review of "Hammertown Tales," in Kirkus Reviews, *Vol. LIII, No. 24, December 15, 1985, p.
1348.*

CAROL AMES

This book of fine stories [*Hammertown Tales*] traces its lineage
to Sherwood Anderson's *Winesburg, Ohio* and beyond to *Spoon
River Anthology*; the one masterpiece among the many books
written by Hilary Masters' father, Edgar Lee Masters. Like its
predecessors, the volume focuses on lives in a small town, but
updated by contemporary elements such as the long-distance
commuter and the summer person. Mr. Masters is at his best
showing how these outsiders try to appropriate the town's stories, its collective memory. In the first tale, **"Buster's Hand"**
("Hands" is the first story in *Winesburg, Ohio*), a newcomer
manipulates the town's bicentennial committee into tape recording an old woman's memories, with comic results, while
the old-timers delight in knowing details that will always elude
the outsider. . . . On the other hand, the more someone assimilates into Hammertown, the greater the strain on prior com-
mitments. In the beautiful story, **"A Mechanic's Life,"** a woman
drifts back to the city because her husband is becoming the
spiritual heir to Hammertown's bigoted mechanic. Among the
lesser stories are **"Here, Daphne!"** and **"The Sound of Pines,"**
while the complex **"Success"** has only the most indirect connection to Hammertown. Thus, the book is not Hilary Masters'
best; the leading candidate among his six books so far is his
lyrical autobiographical work, *Last Stands: Notes From Memory.*

PUBLISHERS WEEKLY

[Masters] writes imaginative, perceptive and well-crafted prose.
He deals [in *Cooper*] with people's dreams, flights of fancy
that, in the case of one character, become reality. The story
is seen through the eyes of Cooper, a budding novelist, obsessed with old airplanes and their pilots, who has infused his
retarded but physically powerful son Hal with a similar fancy.
His wife, Ruth, meanwhile, is so obsessed with her desire to
become a respected poet that everything else in her life is
overshadowed. But it is Cooper—who discovers the memoirs
of an American mercenary pilot who fought in the Spanish
Civil War—whose writing career may take off. The veteran's
stories make a pointed contrast with Cooper's life. But Masters's narrative stumbles; there are too many inconsequential
episodes involving Cooper and not enough development of the
veteran pilot's character. His letters as an old man to Cooper
never fully gel with his memoirs as a young fighter to form a
coherent personality.

A review of "Cooper," in Publishers Weekly, *Vol.
231, No. 14, April 10, 1987, p. 82.*

BILL OTT

The protagonists in Hilary Masters' quiet yet resonant novels
are usually perplexed refugees seeking escape from the ca-
cophony of the modern world. They look not just for the tranquility of rural life, but also for ways to simplify the mess of
human relationships—that quagmire of mistaken intentions,
confused loyalties, and misguided loves into which we all fall
so easily. Jack Cooper [the title character of *Cooper*] is the
latest in Masters' line of frazzled individualists hoping to circle
the wagons around themselves and those they love. After moving his family (wife Ruth, a frustrated poet, and son Hal, a
mildly retarded boy with dreams of flying) to the wilds of
[upstate New York], Cooper contentedly burrows into the comforts of home, his used-magazine business, and the adventure
novels about World War I fliers he writes in off hours. Civilization won't stay put for long, unfortunately, as Ruth's infidelities and career dissatisfactions, Hal's obsession with flight,
and a publisher's interest in the war stories all conspire to
confound Cooper's dream. This ruminative, almost elegiac novel
has much to say about dreams—the way they rescue us from
the quotidian, but also the power they possess to make us fall
asleep at the wheel.

Bill Ott, in a review of "Cooper," in Booklist, *Vol.
83, No. 16, April 15, 1987, p. 1249.*

GEORGE CORE

Cooper is the latest of Masters' five novels. The long narrative
sequence, factual or fictive, is his most natural and persuasive
mode. He achieves impressive effects through the steady ac-
crual of detail and image, subtle development of character,
rhythmic orchestration of theme, sure unfolding of plot.

Clemmons, a wonderful comic novel that celebrated life, dramatized intense pathos as well as other matters that prompted
responses far more complicated than a smile or a guffaw. *Cooper*
is forged in a darker spirit. The general situation and scene are

much the same: middle-class domestic life in upstate New York, Masters' Yoknapatawpha County, with occasional forays into Manhattan.

To see *Cooper* in its skeletal form is to realize what unpromising materials Masters has used on this occasion. It is as though he decided to pan gold in a deep raging torrent rather than a slow, shallow current. In any case he has found and refined ore of high yield.

Jack Cooper is a kind and contemplative bookman who sells old magazines . . . for a living. His wife, Ruth, a highly emotional and very fragile person, teaches and writes poetry; her poetry, it is plain to everybody, amounts to very little; and yet she is devoted to poetry, and her very identity depends upon it. Ruth cannot bear children, so she and Jack adopt a child who turns out to be physically and mentally retarded in unpredictable but winning ways. Hal, almost an *idiot savant,* leads a life that is considerably healthier and saner than do most of the ''normal'' characters, especially his promiscuous adoptive mother, whom Jack regularly forgives. Hal is close to his father and to an old cabinetmaker, Clay Peck, who has been deserted by his cranky wife and the wife's frenetic Doberman, which, like Ruth, is perpetually in heat.

All of these characters come fully to life in the unpredictable and rich ways that life—and fiction at its best—always affords. The same applies to the minor figures in *Cooper,* including a World War I pilot with whom Cooper corresponds, Ethel and Ronald Know (Ethel, a dabbler in the arts, kills herself, but her successful husband, an architect, goes on without missing a beat), and Don Jacobs, a smarmy poet and editor with whom Ruth is more than professionally engaged. . . .

By the novel's end everyone has had his flight, especially Hal, the greatest dreamer of all. The metaphors of flying and falling are beautifully sustained throughout the action of a memorable book worth rereading, as I have done with relish.

George Core, ''Flights of a Dreamer,'' in Book World—The Washington Post, *June 28, 1987, p. 14.*

ADAM BELLOW

[In *Cooper,* Hilary Masters] has produced a slight but charming work of fiction. Jack Cooper, a dealer in used magazines, lives upstate in sleepy Hammertown with his wife and adopted son, Hal. Ruth, a poet who teaches English at a rural college, bitterly resents her forced detachment from the urban New York scene and flaunts her infidelities; the more flamboyant these become, the more scrupulously Cooper ignores them. Their mildly retarded teen-age son roams the woods at night, bringing home the skeletal remains of fallen birds which he examines in his room with touching care and concentration. . . . Meanwhile, Cooper—among other things a model plane enthusiast—takes refuge in his reveries. His correspondence with a World War I flying ace inspires him to write a tale about a dashing biplane pilot and his gunner, a trained orangutan, searching for a lovely female flier . . . captive somewhere in the China Sea. . . . Two-thirds through the novel, Cooper's correspondent dies and a new narrative takes over. Mr. Masters' hitherto excessively internal prose becomes dramatic and exciting. The well-realized accounts of open-cockpit dogfights over France and Spain, the boisterous camaraderie of pilots and the rivalry of aces on opposing sides are highly entertaining, and one wishes he had written more in this vein. But the stifling rural reverie returns. Perhaps the message is just that: imaginative freedom is a passing flight; earth's gravity reclaims us in the end.

Adam Bellow, in a review of ''Cooper,'' in The New York Times Book Review, *September 13, 1987, p. 34.*

(Lula) Carson (Smith) McCullers

1917-1967

American novelist, short story writer, dramatist, and poet.

Along with such contemporaries as Tennessee Williams, Eudora Welty, and Flannery O'Connor, McCullers is considered one of the most enduring authors of the American Southern literary tradition. Although McCullers was originally categorized as a Southern Gothic writer due to her portrayal of social misfits and other unconventional characters, most contemporary scholars agree with Louis D. Rubin, Jr.'s contention that her protagonists function as "exemplars of the wretchedness of the human condition," as symbols of psychological isolation and the failure of communication. McCullers's characters are often androgynous, revealing the inadequacy of physical love to fulfill basic human emotional needs. McCullers explained: "Love, and especially love of a person who is incapable of returning, or receiving it, is at the heart of my selection of grotesque figures to write about—people whose physical incapacity is a symbol of their spiritual incapacity to love or receive love—their spiritual isolation."

Born in Georgia, McCullers exhibited musical talent as a child and in 1935 traveled to New York City to study at the Juilliard School of Music. As a result of financial difficulties, however, McCullers never attended Juilliard; instead, she was forced to work part-time while attending writing classes at Columbia University and New York University. In 1937, she married Reeves McCullers, an aspiring novelist, and in 1940 she published her first novel, *The Heart Is a Lonely Hunter*, which established her reputation and was highly praised for its maturity of vision and bleak but lyrical prose style. This book ostensibly revolves around deaf-mute John Singer, a reluctant confidante of four alienated characters who believe that he can comprehend their dreams and frustrations. Critics generally agree, however, that the novel's protagonist is Mick Kelley, an adolescent tomboy whose dreams of becoming a composer are thwarted by sexual discrimination and financial problems. While many reviewers initially maintained that Mick's decision to abandon her ambitions in order to help support her family represents a realistic and appropriate choice, most contemporary scholars contend that her acceptance of a mundane adult life symbolizes the death of her dreams and individuality. Lawrence Graver described *The Heart Is a Lonely Hunter* as "a parable of the human condition, of human isolation, of the craving to communicate and of the impossibility of communication; and also, perhaps, of the inescapable delusions attendant on the inescapable human need to love."

McCullers's marriage was often unstable, and she and Reeves were divorced in 1940 following their involvement in homosexual affairs. McCullers's second novel, *Reflections in a Golden Eye* (1941), is generally viewed as her reaction to the disintegration of her marriage. Set on an army base, the book depicts archetypal characters whose unfulfilled spiritual and physical needs lead to self-destructive, amoral behavior. Captain Penderton, a sadomasochist and latent homosexual, develops ambivalent feelings for an inarticulate private whose inability to initiate human relationships leads him to engage in bestiality. Fascinated by the feminine beauty of Penderton's wife, the private visits her bedside by night; at the novel's conclusion,

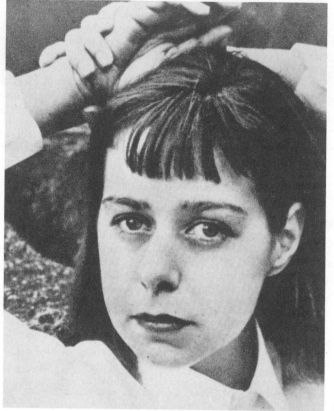

The Granger Collection, New York

Penderton discovers the private leaning over his wife's bed and kills him, suggesting the arbitrary nature of love. Although *Reflections in a Golden Eye* received largely negative reviews due to its unsympathetic characterizations and unorthodox subject matter, several critics maintained that the novel evidences the intensity and candor of McCullers's best writing.

McCullers suffered a series of debilitating cerebral strokes beginning in 1941, but she continued to write and in 1943 published the short novel *The Ballad of the Sad Café* in *Harper's Bazaar*. This piece was later included in *The Ballad of the Sad Café: The Novels and Stories of Carson McCullers* (1951). Often considered McCullers's most outstanding achievement, *The Ballad of the Sad Café* was described by Irving Howe as "one of the finest novels ever written by an American" and by Tennessee Williams as "assuredly among the masterpieces of our language." In this work, McCullers's characters serve to reveal how individuals seek out their opposites, people who embody traits they desire but cannot attain. The story revolves around Miss Amelia, a huge woman whose feelings of freakishness lead her to fall in love with Cousin Lymon, a hunchbacked dwarf. Although Cousin Lymon subconsciously despises Amelia, both for her physical size and for the pathetic nature of her love, his attentions transform her into a warm and caring person, and she opens a popular café. When Ame-

226

lia's handsome ex-husband, a devious criminal, returns following his release from jail, Cousin Lymon falls in love with him, and together the men attack Miss Amelia, destroy her café, and leave town. The novella concludes with Miss Amelia, a physically and spiritually broken woman, closing her business.

The Member of the Wedding (1946), considered McCullers's most accessible and realistic novel, is primarily a coming-of-age story about Frankie Addams, a lonely adolescent who convinces herself that she will discover what she terms "the we of me" by accompanying her brother and his fiancée on their honeymoon and becoming part of their marriage. The novel, which consists largely of conversations between Frankie, her sickly young cousin, and a black housekeeper, encompasses such issues as sexuality, racial prejudice, and death. Frankie's transformation from tomboy to precocious feminine teenager points up society's stifling expectations of what a young woman should be. Spurred by Edmund Wilson's comment that *The Member of the Wedding* contains "no element of drama at all" and encouraged by Tennessee Williams, McCullers adapted the novel for the stage. Retaining its original emphasis on theme, character, and mood, McCullers created a stylistically innovative play noted for being among the few successful dramatic adaptations of a novelist's own work. *The Member of the Wedding* enjoyed a long run on Broadway beginning in 1950 and received a New York Drama Critics Circle Award.

In 1945, McCullers remarried Reeves, but their relationship became increasingly hostile. Frightened by his insistence that they carry out a double suicide, McCullers left her husband in 1953. Shortly thereafter, he committed suicide. Although McCullers did not openly mourn her husband's death and refused to ship his body from Europe to the United States for burial, she was devastated by the death of her mother in 1955. McCullers used both Reeves and her mother as the basis for the central characters of *The Square Root of Wonderful* (1958), a play which many critics viewed as her attempt to reconcile feelings of loss, guilt, and hostility. Although considered one of McCullers's least successful works, this drama is valued for its insights into her life and techniques. In McCullers's last novel, *Clock without Hands* (1961), a bigot overcomes his racist beliefs after learning that he is dying from leukemia. Although critics generally conceded that the book offers McCullers's most optimistic treatment of existence, most agreed that *Clock without Hands* lacks the cohesion of her earlier fiction. McCullers's other publications include *Sweet as a Pickle, Clean as a Pig* (1964), a book of poetry for children, and *The Mortgaged Heart: The Previously Uncollected Writings of Carson McCullers* (1971).

(See also *CLC*, Vols. 1, 4, 10, 12; *Contemporary Authors*, Vols. 5-8, rev. ed., Vols. 25-28, rev. ed. [obituary]; *Contemporary Authors New Revision Series*, Vol. 18; *Contemporary Authors Bibliographical Series*, Vol. 1; *Something about the Author*, Vol. 27; *Dictionary of Literary Biography*, Vols. 2, 7; and *Concise Dictionary of American Literary Biography, 1941-1968*.)

RAY MATHIS

Among other achievements, the ambiguous novel [*Reflections in a Golden Eye*] indicates that modern American man has

religious needs and expressions which often parody Christianity. Because the narrative of *Reflections* contains many symbolic elements, the book's pseudo-realism presents an unbelievable tragedy of bizarre characters who were caught in a universe of materialistic determinism. The novel also has an unconvincing supernaturalism which detours into the mystical or transcendental, thereby confusing the reader and directing him to McCullers' use of symbols. Thus on both the realistic and the allegorical levels, the book is a series of jokes upon the characters and the readers, especially the "Christian" middle class. (p. 545)

In *Reflections* the youthful McCullers, a mere twenty-three years of age, described human behavior which the student of American Christianity might categorize into three basic types—secularism, myth-making, and religiosity. In order to define these terms, it is safe to say that secularism, as McCullers described it, parallels Harvey Cox's definition of it as "the loosing of the world from religious and quasi-religious understandings of itself, the dispelling of all closed world views, the breaking of all supernatural myths and sacred symbols." Thus McCullers' secular characters are those who indicate no need for an assumption of that which has traditionally been called God. Mythicizing, as McCullers described it, is the alienated individual's unconscious and perverted attempt to identify with a person or a group which represents some quality of saviorhood. And her descriptions of religiosity depict man's irresponsible manipulations of a religious faith (in this case Christianity) for his own personal convenience. Alison Langdon and Leonora Penderton are secularists; Anacleto, Private Williams, and Captain Penderton all mythicize ineffectually; and Williams and Major Langdon both show characteristics of religiosity.

Alison Langdon and her youthful Filipino houseboy are the novel's most intelligent characters. They both reveal an unconscious need for traditional philosophical and mythical comforts, but their need goes unmet, and this deficiency contributes to their tragic experience.

Alison was a classicist and perhaps something of a philosopher, who as a young unmarried woman had taught Latin and the works of Cicero and Virgil. . . . Because her husband considered her a morbid female and was impatient with her delicate health, she turned for comfort to the arts and to the friendship of Anacleto. When the Langdon's daughter Catherine was born deformed, it was immediately evident that the infant could not live. After a long, exhausting illness, Catherine mercifully died, but Alison was inconsolable. If she symbolized the West's classical point of view, Alison was probably a Stoic, but hers was the later Roman type because she was pessimistic about the soul and immortality.

After Catherine was buried, Alison was "obsessed by the sharp, morbid image of the little body in the grave. Her horrified broodings on decay and on that tiny lonely skeleton" drove her to have the body exhumed and cremated. Then she scattered the ashes in the snow of Chicago and entered a three-year period of physical and mental disintegration. . . . Now her remaining stability crumbled into disillusionment, spite, and hate, with Morris Langdon's infidelity simply accentuating her own inner deterioration. When the garden shears proved inadequate for suicide, she clipped off her nipples. Although she recovered, at least physically, from that horrible experience, she eventually died of a heart attack, despising her husband and the Pendertons. Ironically, Alison, who was on the verge of insanity, could not compromise her secular materialism to accept the immortality of the human soul or the resurrection of the body. Despite her erudition, perhaps because of it, neither Platonism nor Christian Paulinism was relevant to her crisis.

Seven years before the novel's setting, when he was seventeen years of age, Anacleto had come into the Langdon household during their tour of duty in the Philippines. Alienated from his own countrymen, Anacleto had begged to remain with the Langdons upon their return to the United States. Disengaged from his Filipino culture (the object of significant Christian missionary attack), Anacleto now strived to assume a new identity in the United States (a Christian nation?). Separated from Christianity and other religions, he vicariously imbibed Alison's classicism. If it is too much to view Anacleto as the East whom the West failed to Christianize, he was clearly dependent upon the West's classical culture which failed to make him a man. He learned French, the language of the Enlightenment; he mimicked the ballet; he adored composers and performers of serious music. But most of all he copied his mistress to the point of becoming her double. He was Alison's Platonic shadow and loving nurse, but his devotion was not all selfless; Anacleto was Alison. Because he had to be with her to live, when she died he disappeared and figuratively ceased to exist. (pp. 545-47)

Unconsciously [Anacleto] sought a savior figure with whom to identify, but he aimed too low because Alison was transient. In her, however, he worshiped the Age of Reason, its classical foundation, and its romantic offspring, all of which had combined to free many moderns from the ancient myths of man's identification with the gods. Anacleto identified with a mere mortal and was undone.

In *Reflections in a Golden Eye,* Major Morris Langdon's attitude toward religion is developed with a realism that makes him a stereotype, perhaps the most believable of the novel's unconventional characters.

At one point in the book the major acknowledged a need for religion, but this was a momentary lapse from which he soon recovered. . . . He was a materialist, a sensualist. Twelve months after Catherine's death, following years with Alison's morbid and ailing nature, he had met Leonora Penderton, and within two hours of their meeting each had found the other sexually satisfying. The Major, suffering pangs of conscience at his infidelity, suppressed them as he enjoyed Leonora; but he showed some guilt (for he did not love Alison) in small acts of kindness. (p. 548)

When Alison died and Anacleto disappeared, the Major was visibly shaken. Suddenly he showed a new measure of guilt, and something more. Superficially at least, Langdon repented. He needed to purge himself of guilt-grief for Alison and of self-pity at the loss of Anacleto, who had been a good housekeeper. Being a pragmatist, the Major, with no sense of hypocrisy, activated a thin religiosity to see him through. Now, in addition to his recent practice of praying, he was also "inclined to make doleful platitudes concerning God, the soul, suffering, and death—subjects the mention of which would hitherto have made his tongue grow thick and awkward with embarrassment." In typical loose Protestant fashion, his mind dwelt upon the past for a few days and he grieved privately, except with the Pendertons, who cared for him. Predictably he recovered very soon and expressed the simple ambition of being a good animal and serving his country. With Leonora's gracious nursing, the Major's irresponsible and momentary use of God met the crisis, and his simple sensualism required no more.

As the most "normal" of the novel's cast, his almost unconscious shifts from total secularity to religiosity and back again were made with no evident effect upon his personality. Crisis was not always so kind to the other characters.

Pursuing McCullers' insights into the recent religious temper of Americans, one finds her characters becoming more glaringly symbolic and subsequently more interesting. In the tragedy Private Williams is the southern "redneck" who becomes the murder victim. (pp. 548-49)

Williams had been reared on a one-mule farm by a father who hated women; therefore the household was exclusively male. Conditioned to fear and hate females, the Private had learned at an early age that "women carried in them a deadly and catching disease which made men blind, crippled, and doomed to hell." No wonder the young soldier avoided women and loved horses. Although he [was mentally retarded and] did not think, Williams had had experiences or trances which McCullers left undefined, indicating that they precluded definition. These experiences, however, always preceded actions of his "own accord." The first of these trancelike acts had brought the "sudden, inexplicable purchase of a cow." Milking her tenderly with his head resting in her flank, Williams talked to the cow quietly but urgently, and he drank the warm milk directly from the pail. For him the animal was an unconscious symbol of the mother figure, the unknown female; however perverted, it was mythic appreciation for the source of fertility.

Although the four acts of his "own accord" occurred gradually and arose from basic needs which he did not understand, the second one was more conventionally religious. While Williams' father, a Holiness preacher, expounded on Sundays, the son always sat quietly on a bench in the rear of the church, until one night without warning he made "a sudden, violent declaration of his faith in the Lord." . . . Despite the drama of conversion, Williams' "religion" was undiluted individualism.

Sometime after the church scene and five years before the novel's setting, his third act involved an argument with a Negro over a wheelbarrow of manure. Although the issue was hardly a fighting matter, Williams had stabbed the Negro to death. . . . After Williams' conversion experience, he never knew the spirit again in that way; and in the act of murder his Holiness Christianity conveyed no sense of social conscience, justice, or judgment. While Williams' abnormality renders him a gross exaggeration, it is significant that when he recalled the murder incident he remembered the burning sun of the summer afternoon.

Williams' fourth and last unexplained act of his own accord was to enlist in the army, where he lived a life of surface self-denial. Despite his abstention from gambling, alcohol, tobacco, and women, the Private was a sensualist, savoring his pleasures surreptitiously. . . . During free time he rode horse-back to flee the activities of the base. Riding deep into the camp's wilderness area, he stripped off his clothes to lie in the sun. . . . Naked, he would also unsaddle the horse and ride bareback. During these times the animal and the man underwent mystical transformation, with the army plug rising above his limitations to a "proud, stiff elegance" and the Private showing a "sensual, savage smile on his lips." After these outings Williams returned to the stables in an exhausted state and spoke to no one. In his sun worship and mystical identification with the horse, the Private's religion was far removed from classical Christianity. By weaving fundamentalist Christianity, violence, and paganism so intimately into the personality of Williams, the novel confronts the reader with the unconscious but modern remnants of primitivism.

The Private, however, was open to other religious experiences. Watching through the Penderton's living room window as Leonora undressed, he was struck by the beauty of her body. Now, unthinkingly, he began to reject his father's fanatical prohibitions, and he became a voyeur in order to see and touch the sleeping Leonora. During his nightly vigils at her bed, Williams, without thought or inner conflict, assumed the posture and attitude of a worshiper. In the Private's worship of the sun and Leonora, *Reflections* indicates that some men require their religious experience to continue satisfying the senses, a phenomenon many Protestants have failed to acknowledge.

While the Private is mentally retarded, Leonora's husband, Captain Weldon Penderton, is mentally ill, having symptoms too complex for him to be a convincing character.

Among other difficulties, the Captain suffered from impotence, homosexuality, kleptomania, insomnia, dope addiction, amnesia, and paranoia. On a level of realism Penderton is portrayed as a vain, irreligious dandy who, despite diligent study for his teaching in the infantry school, remained rather shallow. As the novel unfolds, however, the Captain is depicted more clearly on a symbolic level where glimmerings of an ascetic mysticism shine through. (pp. 549-51)

Infatuation with men, particularly his wife's lovers, caused [Penderton] considerable anguish. Although he suppressed that response toward Major Langdon, Private Williams became the focal point of the Captain's frustration. The Private was a beautiful physical specimen, as spare and muscular as a Greek statue. And Penderton, aboard the bolting Firebird, had unintentionally invaded the Private's wooded sanctuary and observed the sun worshiper. But Penderton's love response to Williams was complicated by hate. Already in two minor mishaps the Private had irritated the Captain, but these encounters reflected more of Penderton's perversion than of the Private's carelessness. Therefore Penderton had an ambivalent attitude toward Williams. (p. 552)

Simply stated, Penderton should never have married; he loved no one because he was incapable of love. The reader finally recognizes the celibate Captain as the satirical symbol of a religious monk. At the end of the novel it is evident that McCullers dropped numerous hints to suggest the symbol which she finally defined. . . . Lonely and confused by his ambivalent reaction to Private Williams, Penderton longed for the camaraderie of the enlisted men's mess hall and barracks. His "picture of the life inside the barracks was greatly enriched by his imagination. The Captain was drawn toward the Middle Ages and had made a careful study of European history during feudal times. His imaginings of the barracks were flavored by this predilection." Admittedly, feudalism was political and military, but the Middle Ages also had a basic communitarian institution in the Christian monastery. (pp. 552-53)

Although the symbolism surrounding Penderton's mythicizing satirizes institutionalized religion, Leonora is the novel's supreme blow at America's middle-class readers. The Captain's unfaithful wife was a completely secular individual. A hedonist in every respect, Leonora was nevertheless a very likeable person. (pp. 553-54)

In Leonora Penderton, McCullers created a totally nonreligious character and took considerable pains to demonstrate that facet of her personality.

Leonora Penderton feared neither man, beast, nor the devil; God she had never known. At the very mention of the Lord's name she thought only of her old father [a retired General] who had sometimes read the Bible on a Sunday afternoon. Of that book she remembered two things clearly: one, that Jesus had been crucified at a place called Cavalry Hill—the other, that once He had ridden somewhere on a jackass, and what sort of a person would want to ride a jackass?

Later, wishing to console Morris Langdon on the death of his wife, Leonora quoted scripture, but very badly, when she soothed, "They giveth it and then they taketh it away." Her incorrect use of the Bible was the profane defiling the holy, the secular corrupting the sacred, which in Leonora became a major symbolic theme of the novel.

Yet the least religious of *Reflections'* characters became the potential and ironic symbol of goodness. Leonora was hardly saintly, but she was the most admirable character; she at least attempted to be kind. Furthermore, her roles expressed satirical parallels with the Christian gospel. In the first place, she fulfilled the Pauline theme that the simple are used to humble the wise. While the Apostle referred to God as divine manipulator, McCullers posited no providential guidance. In *Reflections* undefined "forces" used the simple and beautiful Leonora to humiliate the scholarly but impotent Weldon Penderton. And the novel's theme of shaming is broader than this. Obviously Leonora's goodness was not religious in the bourgeois sense; after all, she was an adulteress. But so was the woman taken in adultery, who was used to humble self-righteousness. Although Leonora was an adulteress with no tendencies to religion or guilt or repentance, she was the sole character, including the horse, who did not hate. The patent explanation for her difference is stupidity, and the application of this conclusion to Christianity is not complimentary.

Leonora was also a force for secular reconciliation in that she held the plot together and reached out to manage a balanced tension among the lives around her. There are numerous examples of her "godless" reconciliation. Although she failed to meet the Captain's abnormal needs, she remained his wife and provided a facade of respectability for the military career which was his primary concern. . . . In her "faithful" intimacy with Morris Langdon, with whom she was content, Leonora also balanced the sexual inadequacy of his wife, Alison. (pp. 554-55)

Finally, [Leonora] was the queen of the stables, where the grooms admired her riding prowess and made legend her exploits upon the temperamental Firebird. It was at the stables that Private Williams had first encountered Leonora. Although her demeanor toward him was always above reproach, he had on a particular fall day been assigned to clear a wooded area behind the Pendertons' house. It was dark when the Private completed the task, and as he left the yard he passed an undraped window which revealed a room flooded with light and Leonora in the midst of the disrobing that had horrified her husband. Williams was indeed moved by her beauty, for "never before in his life had this young soldier seen a naked woman."

Now Leonora became the primary object of Williams' attention, his means to a reconciliation which was neither fully recognized nor consummated. In an unconventional way she became his first and only hold, however tenuous, upon the possibility for a normal experience with a woman. But to continue watching her, he became a voyeur, which rendered the relationship illicit. As the Private waited in her room, the sleeping Leonora obligingly exposed herself, and repeated vigils finally gave him the courage to touch her. McCullers implied that on the Private's last visit he would have made another decisive act of his own accord. But the Captain killed him, and the shot aroused Leonora, who only half awake sat up in bed and "stared about her as though witnessing some scene in a play, some tragedy that was gruesome but not necessary to believe." Thus in reality Leonora was the unwitting instrument of forces that moved to tragic conclusion. But in Williams' mind she was the primitive symbol of life, fertility, and hope. She was the mother he had lost, a replacement for the cow, the sweetheart he had never known, and perhaps the object of intercourse he was determined to take. (pp. 556-57)

[In] the experience of Williams, Leonora became "The Lady." Although the name had originated among the stable boys who admired her riding ability, the worshiping Private gave the term a new meaning. In naming The Lady, he concretized *Reflections'* nebulous theme of her person as a source of kindness, reconciliation, and hope—all of which, because she was simple, shamed the other characters.

In the retarded mind of Private Williams, it was a short step from The Lady to Our Lady, and this is another of Leonora's satirical parallels with the Christian gospel. Significantly, McCullers was careful that the symbol be preserved among the novel's morass of deterministic materialism. For example, before her marriage, Leonora had been a virgin and the status continued for some time into wedlock. She combined in her person the qualities of both virginity and adultery, which was not an unusual fusion in the virgins of ancient literature. And on the afternoon before she undressed to spite Penderton and unwittingly inspired Williams to his pilgrimage of death (and justice?), Leonora's face wore the "bemused placidity of a Madonna's." She was a twentieth-century virgin-harlot, the modern mother goddess, the secular anti-heroine. In a world that assumed God but did not know him, she was stupid enough to be untroubled by the lack of teleological or rational meaning. She was the least in religion and intellect; she was also the happiest and the kindest of the novel's cast. In Leonora, McCullers created an ubiquitous figure whose Madonna-like characteristics suggest hope and salvation. But from *Reflections'* angle of vision, the reader may rightly ask, salvation to what?

Unquestionably the novel presents modern human life in a negative light. Man is freed of many myths of the past, but he continues to mythicize in forms that are basically dissatisfying. Given his Western culture, man's unconscious myths and overt religiosity resemble traditional Christian expressions. But the novel's characters are neither churchmen nor Christian, and it is significant that McCullers did not present Christianity as a solution for men's predicament. In fact, traditional Christian forms come in for some subtle yet scathing satire. Yet the novel portrays a vast need for grace, or love, if one prefers the latter term. It also presents the recurring hint or vague assumption that transcendental reality is "out there" somewhere even though it is beyond man's meaningful experience.

Thus, McCullers lampooned several traditional Christian forms and paradoxically revealed a touch of sympathy for an undefined religious need and meaning which pointed implicitly toward Christianity. By inference Alison and Anacleto might have found comfort sufficient for being had they been able to accept Christianity's Platonism and mythical savior. Although McCullers did not label his act Christian, Morris Langdon engaged in a common manipulation of God that often passes under the guise of Christianity; and the fact remains that the performance met his need. By implication Williams and Penderton might have been served by a highly ritualized religion. And Leonora, the secular symbol of animal kindness, unconsciously expressed many traditional virtues of the Christian faith. *Reflections in a Golden Eye* is a strange, troublesome novel that explores several aspects of modern man's religious expressions which have an interesting relationship, however unorthodox, to classical Christianity. (pp. 557-58)

Ray Mathis, "'Reflections in a Golden Eye': Myth-Making in American Christianity," in Religion in Life, Vol. XXXIX, No. 4, Winter, 1970, pp. 545-58.

PATRICIA S. BOX

In *The Heart is a Lonely Hunter* and *The Member of the Wedding,* Carson McCullers examines the problem of spiritual isolation. Both [novels] portray as primary characters young girls who are sexually ambivalent, and *The Heart is a Lonely Hunter* adds a further dimension by including a man who struggles to deny his own sexuality and to become androgynous. These "androgyns," people who embody characteristics and natures of both sexes, uniquely rebel against the loneliness which is the twentieth-century human condition. Significantly, only the androgyns are capable of attempting to escape the isolation of man, whereas distinct sexuality erects a barrier to human interaction and stifles any attempts at unity and understanding between individuals. The androgynous girls of these novels move from adolescent sexual ambivalence to mature womanhood, but as women they fail to experience any hope for escape from isolation. The male androgyn, however, reverses the process: he moves from impotent manhood to an androgyny full of hope.

McCullers' metaphoric medium for expressing the ability to escape from spiritual isolation is music. Only the androgyns are guided by music, and only they are capable of lifting themselves out of the world of superficiality and creating a universe in which people genuinely care about one another. The necessary ingredient for creating this human unity is love, not a sexual love, but a love that denies sex and strives to encompass everyone equally. In these two novels, only the androgyns are capable of giving such love, and consequently any hope for escape from isolation must be hinged on them.

It is no accident that the female protagonists of both novels are given names that are commonly associated with the male sex. Frankie Addams of *The Member of the Wedding* lives up to her name by dressing like a boy and by involving herself in activities which are societally reserved for boys. Although she is sexually confused, she nonetheless recognizes the problem in her existence: she is alone. This perception of the human condition is expressed by Frankie's musing on her exclusion from her peer group: "Yesterday, and all the twelve years of her life, she had only been Frankie. She was an *I* person who had to walk around and do things by herself. All other people had a *we* to claim, all others except her." At this early point in the novel she has not yet seen that all people are actually in the same predicament; she merely knows that she is excluded from the superficial "crowds" and wants desperately to belong to someone or something. She envisions for herself a life with her brother and his bride-to-be, a life that would be rendered complete by the love between the three of them; but that plan has no appeal for characters of a distinct sexual nature.... She wants a life of unity and sharing, a life in which all people would care for each other equally, but such a life denies sex and consequently is rejected by the bride and groom. Only an androgyn is capable of giving the kind of love which Frankie gives.

While Frankie is seeking unity and escape from isolation, she is guided by music. McCullers tells us that "forgotten music... sprang suddenly into her mind—snatches of orchestra minuets, march tunes and waltzes, and the jazz horn of Honey Brown—so that her feet in the patent-leather shoes stepped always according to a tune." The music further foreshadows the incompleteness of her plans by being itself incomplete at times.... (pp. 117-18)

On [one] occasion, when a piano is being tuned, Frankie is stunned by the incompleteness of the scale which the technician plays. She claims that she is saddened and made "jittery" by the abrupt breaking off of the scale; we recognize these feelings as representations of the incompleteness of her dreams of unity. She sees herself in the future drawn into a sexual role which, by the limitation inherent in its definition, precludes the community for which she longs. The sexual nature of men and women prevents them from loving everyone equally; thus when Frankie leaves the world of androgyny, she leaves behind her hopes of escape from isolation. In the third part of the novel, Frankie the androgyn has become Frances the young woman, and the music which pervades the first two parts of the work is significantly absent. No longer can she plan to extricate herself from the monotonous sphere of common people with common plans; no longer can she dream of a universe in which people give of themselves freely. With womanhood comes a friend, a source of identification for Frankie, but the false sense of inclusion which Frankie derives from that relationship makes her renounce her earlier perception of the human condition and consequently give up her plans for a better life. The conclusion is not optimistic; no androgyns remain to give hope to a world in need of selfless love and community.

Following a similar pattern, Mick Kelly of *The Heart is a Lonely Hunter* is an androgynous adolescent girl who finds herself alone in the world.... Although not as distressed by her loneliness as Frankie is, she shares with her fictional counterpart the love of music which serves to partially fill her emptiness. The most revealing passage in the novel explains the function of music as a symbol for the seeking of unification: "But maybe the last part of the symphony was the music she loved the best—glad and like the greatest people in the world running and springing up in a hard, free way. Wonderful music like this was the worst hurt there could be. The whole world was this symphony, and there was not enough of her to listen." The music hurts because Mick recognizes that isolation is the human condition and, moreover, few people seek any escape from that isolation. If more people were able to listen, as Mick is, to the calling of music, a summons to a communal life, then the symphony could be a realistic representation of existence. As it is, the music serves only to remind Mick that people do not seek unification and thus the symphony is a dream fated never to come true. (pp. 119-20)

[In *The Member of the Wedding,* Frankie's housekeeper] Berenice tells Frankie that she recognizes the plight of mankind, but from her limited point of view she sees no alternative. The housekeeper sees the human condition as a trap:

"We all of us somehow caught. We born this way or that way and we don't know why. But we caught anyhow. I born Berenice. You born Frankie. John Henry born John Henry. And maybe we wants to widen and bust free. But no matter what we do we still caught. Me is me and you is you and he is he. We each one of us somehow caught all by ourself."

The androgynous Frankie, however, is not "caught" as are the other characters; she is perceptive enough to realize that through denial of traditional human values, those which dictate patterns of life by assigning sex roles, and through assertiveness and creativity, she can aspire to a better life. The "savior," then, in McCullers' works, is necessarily an androgyn.... (pp. 120-21)

[The androgyny of Biff Brannon in *The Heart is a Lonely Hunter*] has been mentioned by most of the critics who analyze the novel, but many fail to see him as a positive figure. The conclusion of the novel, then, they take as a passive acceptance of the isolation of man, and as such it is hardly optimistic. What is overlooked by that interpretation are the obvious changes which have taken place in Biff and Mick, changes which are signalled by the symbolic music.

Mick's dependence on music is evident throughout most of the novel. The change occurs when she moves from androgyny to womanhood, a shift necessitated by economic circumstances. Significantly, Mick Kelly loses her insights into the human condition at that time; the music in her head disappears and she is resigned to a life of mundane existence and drudgery. (pp. 121-22)

Though this change in Mick signals a pessimistic conclusion, the reader is not left there. McCullers chose to conclude the novel with Biff, for although Mick has lost her perceptivity, Biff is in the process of regaining his. Though he has been an androgyn throughout the novel, he has been forced by his wife to superficially assume the male role. His denial of that role is seen in his refusal to wash below his waist, a symbolic, and practical, method of avoiding sexual contact with Alice. After her death he takes a complete bath, an action which suggests his washing himself of the male role as well as his recognizing that he no longer needs to be physically repugnant. He then becomes even more androgynous, feeling no necessity to hide his sensitivity by conforming to a static sex role.

A character disassociated with music throughout the novel, Biff has been unable to see any hope for change in the human condition. He finds the male role distasteful, but he sees no alternative as long as Alice forces him to provide for them in the traditional manner. He has formerly been a perceptive individual, but marriage has brought loss of his music and his hopes.... Biff grows to love the androgynous Mick, as though recognizing in her the possibility for a community between people; but when she deserts the androgynous lifestyle Biff finds that he himself has become the only person with hope. The old song that he whistles near the end of the novel reflects his slowly returning perceptivity, and it is with this cautious ray of hope that McCullers concludes *The Heart is a Lonely Hunter.*

Both *The Member of the Wedding* and *The Heart is a Lonely Hunter* convey the same message; only androgyns are capable of experiencing the sexless love that can ultimately unite all of mankind and change the condition of humanity from isolation to community. The choice of music as a metaphor for this type of love is particularly appropriate; music connotes harmony, and harmony between people is precisely what a unified life is all about. (pp. 122-23)

Patricia S. Box, "Androgyny and the Musical Vision: A Study of Two Novels by Carson McCullers," in The Southern Quarterly, Vol. XVI, No. 2, January, 1978, pp. 117-23.

MARY ETTA SCOTT

"The greatest danger, that of losing one's own self, may pass off quietly as if it were nothing; every other loss, that of an arm, a leg, five dollars, a wife, etc., is sure to be noticed." Kierkegaard's observation serves as a catalyst to awaken J. T. Malone, the central figure in Carson McCullers' *Clock Without Hands,* a man dying of leukemia, to the realization that only by facing death can modern man find any true meaning in his life. Soon after Malone first encounters the sentence, he wonders "how he could die since he had not yet lived." This awakening in Malone to the emptiness in his life, to the fact that he is lost and that he has never really found himself in his adult life, serves as his moral turning point, enabling him to find himself by placing the responsibility for his life squarely where it belongs—on himself. And in accepting responsibility for his life, he paradoxically is then able to accept his death, not as punishment but as part of the natural course of events that it is. McCullers, I believe, is saying through her presentation of J. T. Malone that modern man can only find meaning in life by facing death. Therefore the disease, the leukemia that Malone thinks is the worst catastrophe of his life, is, in reality, a fortunate accident because it forces him to face death and ultimately to find his salvation.

It is certainly not a concept exclusive to modern literature to find a man grasping some meaning in life only in the face of death; one literary creation of the late Middle Ages, the morality play *Everyman,* already faced its central figure with Malone's very same dilemma. In fact, McCullers seems to have used *Everyman* in a way as an intertext in [*Clock Without Hands*]. Both literary figures have failed to grasp the meaning of their lives until death approaches, and both work out, within the span of their literary framework, their own salvation, using whatever aids they may find available. Significantly for McCullers, man today has in fact fewer aids to salvation and meaning than did fifteenth-century man. Malone's progress through the novel parallels Everyman's progress through the morality play up to the intervention of the Church. However, because the modern Church is too divorced from spiritual matters, matters of faith, to speak meaningfully to man about them, McCullers' modern Everyman can no longer rely on the Church to provide a blueprint for salvation. Hence her modern Everyman, by following his own moral sense, must chart his own salvation.

That task is not easy. J. T. Malone, like Everyman, is a representative figure, but he represents a more negative form. Among the gallery of Carson McCullers' characters, Malone stands out for his pervading *ordinariness,* his complete lack of any distinguishing physical or mental aberration. He is indeed just like every other ordinary person in his world. . . . He reflects the norm in his society as Everyman was designed to reflect his, but Malone represents the emptiness, the negation of individuality in a democratic society. Modern man's task is more difficult not only because he has no effective Church to

aid him, but also because he has farther to go to find himself and his salvation.

It is, then, only in J. T. Malone's confrontation with his own death that he begins to see his condition. Had he not become ill, life might have drained away without his ever having recognized his lack of livingness. So too, the morality figure. Had death not confronted Everyman, he would have continued in his familiar, riotous ways. Hence death is the "fortunate accident" for both. Yet Everyman in the play does far more than die; indeed, his death comes only after he has found an essence of self (soul, if you will) that shows him to be a card-carrying, paid up member of the Christian church. . . . Everyman discovers that the external aids he has relied on throughout his life not only will not, but indeed cannot help him in his extremity. He painfully learns that Fellowship (friends), Kindred and Cousin (family), and Goods (wealth and possessions) actually work to deter him from salvation. Once these externals are rejected for what they are, the dying man is thrown back upon himself to dip deeply into his own store of virtues to mold salvation for himself. Knowledge, Good Deeds, Beauty, Strength, Discretion, Five Wits all come from within the self; it is these attributes that enable the morality figure to save his soul—through the conventional avenues of the Church, of course. So too, it is the internal self, the emergence of Malone as an individual who can speak for himself and stand up for his own beliefs, that saves this modern Everyman—here without the intervention of religious institutions. The difference is significant; Malone relies solely on himself, not on a religious rite like Everyman's Confession and last rites. His victory is truly an existential one.

Malone's confrontation with death begins *Clock Without Hands.* McCullers clearly intended this confrontation and Malone's response to constitute the focus of the novel. The pattern of action, the plot of the novel, follow carefully the pattern of the morality play. Why? Perhaps McCullers hoped by having her Everyman follow the footsteps of the morality figure to invest him with more universal significance. Man's plight, she seems to say, is not unique to this century, but this century provides more roadblocks on the path to salvation than did the fifteenth century. The goal is man's common goal; how he achieves that goal is tied to the society in which the individual man must live.

In the twentieth century, Malone must learn his lessons for himself. When Dr. Hayden confronts him with impending death in twelve to fifteen months, J. T., like the morality figure, denies it at first, refuses to "acknowledge the reality of approaching death, and the conflict led to a sense of ubiquitous unreality." His death becomes real to him only after he has shared his secret knowledge with others. Yet as with the morality figure, friends and family fail to provide any positive answers in his quest for self knowledge and salvation.

Colorful Judge Clane, one of Malone's closest friends, refuses even to believe in the disease. . . . The Judge's denial of the disease enables Malone to deny reality a while longer, but what Malone does not yet understand is that the disease is not the obstacle. Malone needs to find himself, his individual, essential self, and the disease provides an avenue to that discovery, an opportunity to accept reality and perceive his place in it. But the Judge's very nature is to deny reality (as his scheme to restore confederate currency attests). Hence he cannot help Malone to discover his own self. And soon Malone, like Everyman, loses faith in the virtue of the Judge's fellowship. . . .

Malone has now thrown off the first obstacle to understanding his own condition.

Next, Malone approaches his wife to tell her of his disease, even though he dreads the renewal of intimacy that tragedy might inspire with the woman he has ceased to love. His revelation parallels Everyman's approach to Kindred and Cousin. Martha Malone, unlike the old Judge, immediately believes him and accepts the illness as real. . . . Because her response is an acceptance of coming death rather than an affirmation of life, her response also fails to help her husband to find himself. Even her reference to sex ("What can I do?") . . . affirms life in only a mechanistic rather than a real way. It only reveals to him that "not only was he going to die, but some part of him had died without his having realized." Although a measure of love for his wife returns to Malone later in the novel, that renewal of intimacy, his ability to call her "darling," occurs only after he has reached a level of understanding and a vision of his own. Martha is incapable of helping him to find that vision. Hence he turns away from her as well, planning to take a trip North without her to see snow (a symbol of freedom in McCullers' novels). The second obstacle to his finding himself is thus dismissed.

Finally, Malone, like Everyman, turns to Goods, hoping to find himself through his outward possessions. . . . [Like] Goods in the morality play, Malone's possessions only distract him from his real quest for himself. . . . Though some possessions may be necessary props for modern man, a too close attachment to them, says Carson McCullers, will make man lose himself to them. (Cf. Sherman Pew's refusal to leave his beautiful rented furniture and piano even though he has been warned that his house will be bombed and he will be killed.) Malone decides to settle his problem of possessions by making a will leaving everything to his wife—hardly a daring decision. Man cannot find himself through possessions.

Friends, family, and possessions, then, fail the modern Everyman, just as they had failed the morality figure. That figure reaches the nadir of his despair after discovering that no external figure can help him. . . . From here the morality figure quickly sets his sights on eternal life and moves steadily toward salvation through the organized religion of his society. But Malone has yet another external figure to overcome—the very one that ultimately was able to lead the morality figure to salvation—the Church. McCullers condemns the modern church for its failure to speak to modern man about spiritual things. Malone, who attends the First Baptist Church regularly for all the wrong reasons, still feels cheated when Dr. Watson preaches about "the salvation that draws a bead on death." The modern church, so concerned with buildings, choirs, fund raising, and the prestige of its members, has no room left for personal salvation. The church's representative, in the figure of Dr. Watson, speaks of the sacraments as "tanking up" the individual as one would fill a gastank. And on a one-to-one basis, the representative of the church completely falls apart, showing his inability to deal with the issues the Christian Church should be concerned with. When Malone confronts Dr. Watson in the parsonage with his questions about death and the afterlife, all the church's minister can say is, "I don't know what you mean, Mr. Malone."

Only after leaving the parsonage does Malone recall the sentence from Kierkegaard that he had read in the hospital and begin to associate the lines with his own life:

'The greatest danger, that of losing one's own self, may pass off quietly as if it were nothing;

every other loss, that of an arm, a leg, five dollars, a wife, etc., is sure to be noticed.' The incongruity of these ideas, fateful and ordinary as his own life, sounded like the brassy clamor of the city clock, uncadenced and flat.

Through the remainder of Malone's life, these words not only work their spell to show Malone how lost he is, but also spur him to achieve his personal vision of modern life, to stand up for his beliefs in the drugstore meeting, and at last to make a separate peace with himself. The words of Kierkegaard provide the turning point for Malone from despair to hope for personal, individual salvation.

The crucial scene leading to Malone's salvation takes place in his own drugstore, the place where he has spent so much of his dull, ordinary life. Judge Clane has called a meeting for concerned citizens who protest the infiltration of a poor white neighborhood by Sherman Pew, who has rented a house . . . and moved in as a protest against white supremacy. Malone attends the meeting at the request of Judge Clane, but for the first time he is repulsed by the "ordinary" people he meets there. . . . The whisky and the Judge's speech rouse the crowd until someone proposes bombing Sherman. Quietly, Malone suggests talking with "the Nigra" instead and asserts calmly, "Violence or bombing I don't hold with." He is beginning to stand up for what he believes. And when the lot falls to Malone to throw the bomb, he refuses: "But if it's bombing or violence, I can't do it." His reasons given to this group sound rather more selfish than noble—"I am too near death to sin, to murder. . . . I don't want to endanger my soul." But he continues to protest the murder even after the Judge has released him from his lot by suggesting a mob murder. J. T. still refuses to have anything to do with it: "But it is the same thing whether one person does it or a dozen, it's the same thing if it's murder." This final protest, far stronger in wording and tone of voice (McCullers says he "cried out" the words), marks his final turning point. In the very act of standing up and expressing his moral belief in the face of the mob's opposition, Malone has found himself at last, something he has never before done in his entire life.

The effect of Malone's stand is dramatic on his own personal life. That the protest draws only derision from the others at the meeting and utterly fails to deter the bombing (Sammy Lank simply volunteers and throws the bomb, killing Sherman) is of far less importance than the peace, vision, and understanding that the action brings to Malone. He notices more and more the miracles of nature; he finds a renewed love for his wife. And a profound peace settles on his spirit, showing him an "order and simplicity" he has never known before. Malone's vision enables him to see himself in relation to his world and to know himself, an existential discovery that provides his ticket to salvation for himself, a self that was lost and is now found in his dying. It enables him to die without fear, just as Everyman's assurance of salvation through the Church enabled him to descend to the grave fearlessly. Malone's victory seems even greater and more noble because he achieves it alone, with no spiritual guidance.

Thus the course of Malone's dying parallels quite closely that of the morality figure. The internal attributes that sustained Everyman sustain Malone as well until he is on the brink of the grave. The greatest difference between these two literary creations lies in the differing roles the Church takes in their respective societies. Though some doubt is cast on the quality of some priests in *Everyman,* the virtue of the sacraments is upheld. McCullers shows that for her modern Everyman, the church is no longer even a path to spiritual life, for it has become too entangled with earthly interests to speak to the spiritual life. Modern man, McCullers would say, is thrown back on himself alone, with no allies but himself. (pp. 82-7)

Yet paradoxically that very isolation helps man to see and understand himself. The illusion of communication with friends and family, the illusory comfort of possessions, block man from a real understanding of his own moral self, hinder him from acting on the basis of his own moral judgment. Only when stripped of these illusions—so comforting to democratic man—is he really faced with his inner moral convictions. And he is stripped of these illusions only when he faces death. In her earlier novels, McCullers showed that man seeks to end his isolation by finding connections with others through love or even hate. Here she shows that all connections are ultimately dependent on a right relationship with the self, a connection with one's own moral sense. Only after he has achieved his vision, taken his stand, can Malone reestablish his relationship with his wife and feel "a nearer value of her love."

I believe *Clock Without Hands* shows Carson McCullers' view of man to be not nearly so darkly pessimistic as most reviewers and critics would have us believe. Yes, communication fails; yes, love fails; yes, young people are disillusioned as they step into the adult world. But McCullers' final view of man, presented in her final novel, shows a ray of light amidst all this darkness. Like Everyman, J. T. Malone searches methodically for his salvation, his vision of meaning in life. And when he finds it, his vision enables him to make a separate peace with the world. He finds his own self, an existential victory—and that, indeed, according to Carson McCullers, may be the only salvation modern man is capable of achieving. Nonetheless, he is capable of achieving it *alone*. (p. 87)

Mary Etta Scott, "An Existential Everyman," in West Virginia University Philological Papers, *Vol. 27, 1979, pp. 82-8.*

LOUISE WESTLING

During the heyday of Carson McCullers's popular reputation, the tomboy heroines of *The Heart Is a Lonely Hunter* and *The Member of the Wedding* established a type of girlish puberty which the American public could take to its sentimental heart. The success of the dramatic and film versions of *The Member of the Wedding* . . . insured a popular acceptance of the wistful boy-girl which never acknowledged the darker implications of sexual ambiguity hovering around Mick Kelly and Frankie Addams in McCullers's fiction. Some scholarly attention has been paid to the motif of sexual ambivalence in the two novels, but no one seems to have seriously considered the possibility of a relation between that ambivalence and the fact that Mick and Frankie are *girls* who share artistic temperaments and serious ambitions. Mick's longing to become a great composer and Frankie's interest in writing plays and becoming a great poet (or the world's greatest expert on radar) set them apart from other girls in their Southern towns, who spend their time reading movie magazines, primping, and having parties with boys. In Mick and Frankie, McCullers dramatizes the crisis of identity which faces ambitious girls as they leave childhood and stumble into an understanding of what the world expects them to become. The images McCullers associates with the crisis are the images of sexual freaks, supported by an ambience of androgynous longings, homosexuality, and transvestitism.

Such imagery is of course directly related to the tradition of the tomboy so dear to the hearts of English and American fathers since late Victorian times. In childhood, a lively girl can romp with boys, wear boys' clothes, and cut her hair short. She is free to be impish and tough, a pal for her father, a temporary stand-in for a son. . . . But at puberty she begins to feel strong social pressure to conform to conventional notions of femininity. The girl who persists in her boyishness through adolescence becomes odder and odder, as social indulgence changes to disapproval. Dresses must be worn, manners must be learned, behavior must become restrained and graceful. As a girl the tomboy is charming; as an adult she is grotesque.

Ambitions are the psychological equivalents for the physical assertiveness of the tomboy, and again cultural emphasis on submissiveness and graceful restraint operates to discourage pursuit of professional, artistic, or political goals. These pressures exert themselves subtly, woven as they are throughout the texture of adolescent life. But they produce a fear that to be female and to dare to achieve is to venture into dangerous territory, to violate one's gender, to become a kind of freak. The girl who insists on following her ambitions almost inevitably pays the price of shame and guilt as an adult; she must live with a very troubled sense of herself as a woman because she has abandoned the familiar boundaries of her gender. (pp. 339-40)

Understanding these problems of self-definition, we should have no trouble interpreting the psychic paralysis of Sylvia Plath's gifted young writer in *The Bell Jar,* whose talent is rewarded not by serious literary regard but by a summer of luncheons and fashion shows on the staff of *Mademoiselle.* Esther Greenwood's real interests are drowned in a sea of cosmetics, flowers, perfumes, fashionable hats, and piles of flouncy dresses. This conflict between serious ambition and the pressure of conventional femininity is exactly the problem that confronts Mick Kelly and Frankie Addams in Carson McCullers's fiction. McCullers's portrayal of their dilemma is especially valuable because she concentrates on puberty, the time when demands for "femininity" are first clearly recognized, and she allows her protagonists to be more sharply aware of their choices than Plath allows Esther Greenwood to be. Esther is paralyzed because she cannot even look at the contrary impulses within herself. She tries to escape them by blotting herself out, in a sense accepting the verdict implied by *Mademoiselle*'s refusal to acknowledge her identity as a serious writer. Mick Kelly and Frankie Addams have the immense advantage of tomboy self-reliance and a habit of scrappy assertiveness. This "boyish" past makes their passage into adult femininity acutely painful, but it allows them to confront their confusion head-on. Through Mick and Frankie, McCullers provides the most coherent fictional presentation of the problem which warps almost every gifted woman's life.

McCullers's first ambitious tomboy was Mick Kelly in *The Heart Is a Lonely Hunter,* the novel with which she made her debut as a published author. From the beginning of *The Heart Is a Lonely Hunter,* Mick Kelly is presented with a deliberate emphasis on her masculine appearance and her unfeminine ambitions. . . . Rejecting her older sisters' obsession with movie stars and continual primping, Mick dreams of becoming famous by the age of seventeen. She imagines herself as a great inventor of tiny radios and portable flying machines, but her most consistent ambitions are focused on music. She tries to build a violin out of an old broken ukelele, practices the piano in the school gym every day, and attempts to compose music in her secret notebook. At night she roams through the rich neighborhoods of town, hiding in the shrubbery outside the windows of houses where the radios are tuned to classical music stations. In her adolescent fantasies, Mick imagines a brilliant future for herself [as a composer]. . . . The images she projects for her future self waver from masculine to feminine, from evening suit to rhinestone-spangled dress, because there is no tradition of female composers upon which she can model her daydreams.

In fact, Mick's sense of romantic heroism is entirely masculine. The key scene tying her musical sensitivity to her troubled emotions is one in which she listens to Beethoven's *Eroica* symphony in the shrubbery outside a wealthy house. Originally written in Napoleon's honor, that symphony is heroically overblown like Mick's emotions. . . . Her response to the music is ecstasy and terrible pain. To alleviate this pain she resorts to a typically female kind of masochism, turning her frustration back upon herself. . . . Her response to the *Eroica* is shockingly violent. "The rocks under the bush were sharp. She grabbed a handful of them and began scraping them up and down on the same spot until her hand was bloody. Then she fell back to the ground and lay looking up at the night. With the fiery hurt in her leg she felt better."

Mick's reaction to the *Eroica* is clearly no voluptuous sublimation or misplaced pleasure but a frantic effort to release intense emotions which she must feel are forbidden. The circumstances of her musical life are fraught with guilt and the corresponding need for secrecy. Her musical pleasure is illicit, stolen in the darkness from wealthy people by a kind of voyeurism. Mick's own world has no time for her impractical addiction to the arts. Thus there is no constructive outlet for the emotion stimulated by the music, an emotion identified with her ambitions and sense of her own importance. So she turns all the energy upon herself, wounding her flesh to blot out her emotions with physical pain. (pp. 341-42)

Despite her independence Mick lives with profound anxiety. Like the young Jane Eyre, she expresses her fears in childish paintings of disasters, the most telling of them called "Sea Gull with Back Broken in Storm." She is haunted early in the novel by a nightmare which opposes her fantasies of success and prefigures her destiny. She dreams she is swimming through enormous crowds of people, pushing and shoving them out of her way. Sometimes she is on the ground, trampled by the crowds until her insides ooze out on the pavement. Mick's sleeping mind, at least, knows that the world will not allow her to succeed in realizing her dreams of independence and art.

McCullers makes us see that the smothering of Mick's ambitions coincides with her acceptance of adult femininity. The novel opens when she is a twelve-year-old tomboy. At thirteen she starts high school and is thrown into the teenage world of cliques and mysterious, clumsy courtship rites which are initiations into adult sexuality. Confused by the social rules, she feels herself an outsider. Boldly she decides to hold a prom party to end her isolation, and her preparations for the party take on the unmistakable significance of a ritual cleansing. For the first time in the novel, she shucks her khaki shorts, tee shirt, and sneakers and takes a long bath to wash the grime and indeed all vestiges of childhood away. She emerges for the party as from a cocoon, metamorphosed into the conventional female in an adult dress, a hairstyle with spit curls, high heels, and make-up. "She didn't feel like herself at all."

The air at Mick's party fairly crackles with sexual tension as boys and girls in unfamiliar plumage try to act their adult roles as dancing partners. When the party is broken up by a crowd of younger neighborhood ragamuffins, all the guests explode outdoors, finding relief in wild games of chase. The crowd erupts in a dash toward a ditch where the city is digging up the street. Jumping into the ditch, Mick learns with a rude shock how she is physically crippled by feminine clothes. The high heel shoes make her slip, and her breath is knocked out as her stomach slams into a pipe. Her evening dress is torn, her rhinestone tiara lost. Back at home, Mick realizes that she is too old to wear shorts: "No more after this night. Not any more." With her renunciation of these clothes, she renounces childhood and its boyish freedom.

Within a year of the symbolic party, Mick is trapped in a narrow adult world which reduces her to little more than a machine. She has a sexual initiation in the spring and soon after leaves adolescence behind, quitting school to take a job. Her first experience with sex occurs on a picnic with Harry Minowitz, the boy next door. . . . She does not like the sensation, and McCullers's imagery suggests why: sex destroys rational control and blots out the self. In a different way, Mick's job at the dime store shuts out her private world of music and stifles her fantasies. The long days of work leave her feeling exhausted, caged, and cheated, but she can find nothing and nobody to blame. At fourteen she is a grown woman whose life seems to have reached a dead end. There McCullers leaves her.

Mick Kelly was only one of five major characters in *The Heart Is a Lonely Hunter,* but *The Member of the Wedding* focuses exclusively on the figure of the ambitious girl. This time the heroine's ambitions are literary rather than musical: Frankie Addams writes plays and dreams of becoming a great poet. Her ambitions are not blighted as Mick's are, but it could be argued that Frankie's attitude toward writing has changed significantly by the end of the novel. However, the focus of McCullers's attention in this book is not on the protagonist's dreams of fame but rather on the psychological trauma she suffers when required to accept her femininity. (pp. 343-44)

In another work written during the years she struggled with *The Member of the Wedding,* McCullers seemed to be examining the consequences of androgynous identity which she had begun to explore in her first book. The folktale atmosphere of *The Ballad of the Sad Cafe* gave her liberty to create her greatest freaks—the hulking man-woman Miss Amelia and her twisted dwarfish lover Cousin Lymon. The story is a nightmare vision of the tomboy grown up, without any concessions to social demands for sexual conformity. This understanding of the grotesque extreme of masculinity in a female must have contributed profoundly to the undercurrent of fear McCullers creates in *The Member of the Wedding* through the image of the freak show which haunts Frankie's mind and indeed the whole novel.

There are several kinds of freaks which Frankie and her little cousin John Henry West visit at the Chattahoochee Exposition. She is afraid of all of them, but Ellen Moers is right to single out the hermaphrodite as the most important, for it is the quintessential symbol of Frankie's danger. Images of sexual ambivalence are carefully cultivated throughout the novel in the Negro transvestite Lily Mae Jenkins, the Utopias invented by Frankie and John Henry where one could change sex at will or be half male and half female, and John Henry's interest in dolls and dressing in women's clothes. Always such hermaphroditic or androgynous references are placed in a negative frame, for the novel's entire movement is towards Frankie's ultimate submission to the inexorable demand that she accept her sex as female. . . . Children may play at exchanging sex roles, but adults may not, unless they are to be regarded as grotesques fit only for sideshow displays.

This truth begins to force itself upon Frankie Addams in the "green and crazy summer" of her twelfth year. "Frankie had become an unjoined person who hung around in doorways, and she was afraid." McCullers emphasizes the element of fear so rhythmically that the novel's opening pages swim in a fevered, hallucinatory atmosphere. The central setting is the sad and ugly kitchen like the room of a crazy house, its walls covered with John Henry's freakish drawings. Here a vague terror squeezes Frankie's heart. And here she, Berenice, and John Henry constitute a strange family or private world cut off from any other. The real doorway where Frankie lingers in baffled fright is the passage between childhood and the clearly defined sexual world of grown-ups which she must enter, for almost all of the specific sources of her anxiety turn out to be sexual. The older girls who have shut her out of their club are preoccupied with boys and gossip about adult sex which Frankie angrily dismisses as "nasty lies." Yet even she has participated in a secret and unknown sin with a neighborhood boy in his garage, and she is sickened with guilt. (pp. 345-46)

McCullers uses the motif of unfinished music to underline and intensify Frankie's dilemma, suggesting the proper resolution to her confused view of herself. In Part I, Frankie hears a grieving blues tune on "the sad horn of some colored boy" at night. The disembodied sound expresses her own feelings, for she herself is a piece of unfinished music. Just as the tune approaches its conclusion, the horn suddenly stops playing. The music's incompleteness drives Frankie wild, trapping inside her the unbearable emotions it has drawn to a focus. Like Mick Kelly, Frankie tries to find release through masochism, beating her head with her fist, as she will do again several times in the story. When she changes her name to the romantic F. Jasmine in Part Two and waltzes around town in a dress, telling everyone she meets that her brother and his bride will take her away with them on their wedding trip, the unfinished music is resolved in her mind. Her stories about the wedding sound inside her "as the last chord of a guitar murmurs a long time after the strings are struck." Unfortunately her fantasies of the wedding are doomed to disappointment. We know this long before the event because McCullers returns to the motif of unfinished music, this time in the sound made by a piano tuner at work, which embodies F. Jasmine's romantic dream. "Then in a *dreaming way* a chain of chords climbed slowly upward *like a flight of castle stairs:* but just at the end, when the eighth chord should have sounded and the scale made complete, there was a stop" (My italics). (p. 346)

The meaning of the unfinished music is closely linked to Frankie's spiritual kinship with the blacks of her little Southern town. Both are made clear in the person of Honey Brown, Berenice's young, light-skinned foster brother. Too intelligent and restless to live comfortably in the circumscribed world of Sugarville, the black section of town, he periodically explodes. . . . [The] real cause of Honey's problems is the fact that he, like Frankie, does not fit the categories imposed on him by his Southern town.

Frankie shares a sense of entrapment with Honey and Berenice, but hers is not finally as severe, even though it is more vividly realized in the novel. At first she longs to escape from her hot, stultified town to the cold, snowy peace of Alaska. At the end of Part One, however, she fixes on the wedding in Winter Hill as the means of escape. The old question of who she is and what she will become ceases to torment her when she decides to be a member of the wedding and go out into the world with her brother and his bride. This absurd fantasy is a denial of the adult sexuality which Frankie cannot bear to acknowledge, but her attraction to it is obvious in her infatuation with the engaged couple. McCullers associates the returning motif of unfinished music with the imagery of prison to show that F. Jasmine's romantic dream will not bring escape. (p. 347)

Frankie is caught in a blossoming female body which she must recognize and accept. She must also face the fact that grown men and women make love, and that her body makes her desirable to men. As a younger child she had unwittingly walked in on the lovemaking of a man and his wife who were boarders in her house. Uncomprehending, she thought the man was having a fit. Even at twelve she does not understand the nature of his convulsions, just as she refuses to listen to the "nasty lies" of the older girls and tries not to think of her own wicked experience in the neighbor boy's garage. This innocence makes her dangerously vulnerable when as F. Jasmine she wanders through the town looking older and wiser than her years. The toughness that had served her well as a tomboy betrays her now, so that the soldier she meets in the Blue Moon Cafe assumes she is willing to be seduced. F. Jasmine is paralyzed with horror as the soldier embraces her in his cheap hotel room. She feels she is in the Crazy House at the fair or in the insane asylum at Milledgeville. At the last minute she knocks him out with a pitcher and makes her getaway down the fire escape. Not until late the next night, after the disaster of the wedding, does her mind accept the meaning of this encounter and its relation to her veiled sexual memories and anxieties. By then her brother and his bride have rejected her, and she has suffered the humiliation of being pulled screaming from the steering wheel of their car. Back home, she has made a futile attempt to run away and has been recovered by her father in the Blue Moon Cafe where she had felt she was drowning.

The Member of the Wedding ends in a new world, with Frances reborn as a giddy adolescent. The environment of her childhood has been dismantled completely—John Henry has died horribly of meningitis, Berenice has resigned herself to marriage and quit her job, and Frances is preparing to move to a new house with her father. The final scene takes place in the kitchen, now remodeled so that it is unrecognizable, where Frances is making dainty sandwiches to serve her new soul-mate, an artistic girl two years her senior. No longer a frightened alien, she is united with her friend through a mutual infatuation with poetry and art. (pp. 348-49)

The price for this relief from the tensions of strangeness has been high, perhaps too high. Frances is less attractive at the end of the novel than she was as frightened tomboy Frankie. She has become a silly girl who no longer produces her own juvenile works of art—the shows and plays she used to write—but instead gushes sentimental nonsense about the Great Masters. The hard edge of her mind is gone, and all that is left is froth. The struggle against conformity which had identified her with Honey Brown had been a struggle to assert artistic sensibility and intelligence in a world which refused to accept those qualities in a woman or a black man. Honey had expressed his needs by learning French and playing the trumpet, but his music remained unfinished, and he ended up in prison for trying to "bust free" of the narrow limits around his life. Frances avoids such drastic disappointment by giving up and hiding beneath the protective coloration of giddy young womanhood. But if Frances's intelligence is not destroyed, we might speculate that like Sylvia Plath or Adrienne Rich she will some-day feel the old conflict again and awaken to a fearful "sense of drift, of being pulled along on a current which called itself my destiny, but in which I seemed to be losing touch with whoever I had been, with the girl who had experienced her own will and energy almost ecstatically at times. . . ." Without McCullers's two portraits of the artistic twelve-year-old girl and her telling images of sexual freakishness, we could never understand so clearly why "a thinking woman sleeps with monsters" or how those monsters function in the minds of talented girls emerging from childhood. (pp. 349-50)

> *Louise Westling, "Carson McCullers's Tomboys,"
> in* The Southern Humanities Review, *Vol. XIV, No.
> 4, Fall, 1980, pp. 339-50.*

LINDA HUF

Of those who have written about *The Heart Is a Lonely Hunter* only a few have treated Mick Kelly as its protagonist and the frustration of her ambition as a major theme. Most commentators have said that the deaf-mute John Singer is the central character and the loneliness of man the main theme. Although this [essay] treats Mick's story as the primary story in McCullers's novel, it does so in the context of Singer's story, which not only frames and contains Mick's but helps to explain Mick's, the story of an aspiring artist as a gifted but ultimately baffled girl.

John Singer's story, which intersects with several stories besides Mick's, opens at the end of the Great Depression in a stagnant Southern town. There Singer, a gentle and intelligent silver engraver, rooms with another deaf-mute on whom he dotes: a fat, stupid Greek named Spiros Antonapoulos. Singer lives uneventfully with his halfwit friend until one day the Greek begins to do peculiar things—to jostle strangers on the sidewalk, to steal openly from shop-windows, and to urinate in public. When, in consequence of this bizarre behavior, the ungainly Greek is packed off to a state asylum, Singer is left alone and despairing to rent a room by himself in a boarding-house and take his meals in a nearby diner. There, in and about the "New York Café," he encounters four other lonely people, each of whom eventually pours out his earnest heart to him. They are Biff Brannon, the café's watchful proprietor; Jake Blount, a hard-drinking Marxist; Dr. Benedict Mady Copeland, a smoldering Negro doctor; and Mick Kelly, a troubled tomboy.

Hungry for human sympathy, each of the four confides in Singer just as Singer had confided in Antonapoulos. However, each fails to understand that the deaf-mute, although he reads lips, understands little of what he is told. Longing for a sympathetic ear, the four lonely hunters, like their deaf-mute idol, create in their own image what one of them calls "a sort of home-made god." Of course it is an unhearing deity, which, when it fails them as at last it must, leaves them to solitude and despair. Thus, when the Greek dies in the asylum, Singer goes home and puts a bullet through his heart. And when Singer dies in his boardinghouse room, three of his own devotees give up the struggle. The tomboy abandons her dream of going away to study music and takes a job in a five-and-dime store. The radical gives up his hope of moving the mill workers to revolt and drifts out of town. And the Negro doctor leaves off trying to prod his people to purposeful effort and retires ill and demented to the countryside. Only the café owner resists despair, having perceived as if in a vision the heroism of solitary men

and women all struggling in vain to articulate their love to unhearing ears. The novel, its critics say, shows that people remain necessarily lonely and isolated in a world full of people as lonely and isolated as themselves.

Among the five or six stories included within this extended parable of human loneliness is a story of failed aspiration, of deferred dreams shriveling in the hot Georgia sun. Its heroine, Mick Kelly, is a thirteen-year-old tomboy, the fourth of six children in a family that takes in boarders to make ends meet. Like McCullers herself at thirteen, Mick has one grand dream: to become a famous composer of music. But unlike the author at that age, Mick meets with a serious obstacle to realizing her dream: her family's poverty. . . . The Kellys cannot afford a violin, so Mick makes a sad little try at building her own out of a battered ukulele. And piano lessons too are beyond their means, so Mick gives up her school lunch money for rudimentary instruction from a classmate and goes hungry all day.

To realize her dream the heroine plans to finish high school and then go North to study music. However, her parents fall on hard times. Subtly they pressure their youngest daughter to leave school to clerk in a five-and-dime. She turns for advice to the one person she thinks understands her, the deaf-mute John Singer. Unhappily, Singer does not understand her at all, let alone her passion for music, which he cannot hear, for in an uncomprehending attempt to please her he nods his head. Yes, she should take the job. Partly because the deaf-mute has nodded his approval, Mick does take the job, though only to discover a few days later that the man who seemed to encourage her has inexplicably shot himself to death on the floor of his boardinghouse room. By the age of fourteen, then, Mick Kelly has surrendered her dream to spend the rest of her life behind a cash register in a dreary store in a depressing town. It is no longer music she hears coming over the radio but Hitler's voice screeching into the long, dark nights.

Surely nothing could be more obvious than that Mick's life ends in futility at fourteen. Instead of becoming the composer she wanted to be, she becomes only a bitter salesclerk who swills beer every evening in Biff Brannon's café so as not to have to "go home . . . lie down on [her] bed and bawl."

Thus, it is dumbfounding that many commentators on the novel do not see Mick's life as a failure at all. In fact, a number of them suggest that McCuller's heroine, in abandoning her ambition of becoming a composer, does not fail as an artist but succeeds as a woman! One academic writer, Jack B. Moore [see *CLC*, Vol. 12], maintains that Mick's acceptance of a job at Woolworth's is a "necessity, if not [a] positive good," because it shows that at last "she recognizes her true role in the family and community." Another university critic, C. E. Eisinger [see *CLC*, Vol. 12], says that Mick's clerking in a dime store is the "proper" end toward which she, as an adolescent girl, has been struggling all along, as it indicates that she has ceased "to resist the role of woman to which she [was] destined." And a third scholar, A. S. Knowles, says that Mick's acceptance of a meaningless job is not a misfortune but an "opportunity"; that is, a chance to "strike out on her own" after having been immobilized with guilt over her first sexual experience. In effect, the professors are of a mind with the reviewer for the *Greensboro Daily News*, who, attributing to Mick his own satisfaction over her end, insisted that she "aimed at the stars but was happy to land a job in a five-and-ten cent store."

Considering how casually the experts have treated Mick's aspirations as an artist, it is not startling that they have overlooked her primary position in the book. For although Singer is indisputably the focal character in *The Heart Is a Lonely Hunter,* Mick—we may argue—is the foremost character. McCullers herself argued as much when in an outline of the work to her publisher she wrote that Mick is "perhaps the most outstanding character in the book." According to McCullers, Mick is "far more important" than the ostensible hero, John Singer, who is only a "flat character" whose "essential self does not change." If John Singer "is the first character in the book," McCullers said, it is "only in the sense that he is the symbol of isolation and thwarted expression and because the story pivots around him." Mick, on the other hand, "steps out boldly" in the second section and thereafter "commands more space and interest" than the deaf-mute does. (pp. 107-11)

Whether or not we choose to see Mick as the protagonist of *The Heart Is a Lonely Hunter,* we have to grant that she conforms in character and conflict to the type of the creative heroine. She is a tomboy, of course: a rough-and-tumble hoyden with a cropped head and derring-do.... Like other hoydenish American artist heroines who trace their ancestry back to writer Jo March in *Little Women* (1869), Mick Kelly "would rather be a boy any day," or so she tells her primping, boy-crazy sisters, who goad her to take up more feminine ways.

Mick is characteristically an artist heroine also in that she worries she is a freak for failing to conform more to a feminine ideal. Only thirteen and already five-and-a-half feet tall, she fears that she will keep growing until she ends up looking like the eight-foot giant her friend Harry Minowitz once saw at a fair. Although Harry assures her that she'll probably never get that big, Mick, who already towers over the boys her age, will not be comforted.

No doubt Mick would have even more reason to worry if she knew that Biff Brannon, who "likes freaks," has a passionate if innocent love for her. For Biff... is most protective of Mick, suggesting that he too sees the androgynous teenager as belonging among the maimed and misfit who inhabit this anonymous Southern town.

As the type of the artist heroine—that is, as a girl who stands outside everything, including her own sex—Mick should have an ultrafeminine foil, which in fact she does, in Baby Wilson. Although Baby is only four years old, she already has the froth and fluff of conventional adult femininity. Her golden permanent-waved hair makes Mick's straight, straw-colored cowlicks look unaffected by contrast. But most importantly, her tap dancing and acrobatics, when set against Mick's struggle to write serious music, make the heroine's creative efforts look even higher and worthier than they must otherwise.

Although it is clear that Mick has both the boyish character and ultrafeminine foil common to all artist heroines, it is less immediately apparent that she has the inner conflict. Yet at thirteen McCullers's heroine already feels the tug-of-war between her aspirations as an artist and her urges as a woman that fragments other artist heroines. In Mick this divison of self between aspiring artist and developing woman is apparent first in her fantasies, which concern, on the one hand, fame and fortune as a composer and, on the other, love and popularity as a young woman.

Mick's fantasies of fame and fortune reflect both her intensity and her ignorance. In vignettes as naive as they are grandiose she imagines that someday, when she is "about twenty," she will have a whole symphony orchestra to herself and compose all its music. (pp. 111-13)

The second group of fantasies in which Mick indulges features love and popularity, the same motifs that inspire the reveries of many young girls.... Mick is given to secret, hungry infatuations, to daydreaming about "one person after another," although "she [has] always kept it to herself and no person [has] ever known." (pp. 113-14)

Mick also dreams of attracting a clique, or what she calls a "bunch." At her Vocational High School, where she is a first-year student, she struggles to stave off loneliness by schemes of surrounding herself with some "special" group. In high school, however, she finds it impossible to do what she would have done in Grammar School: just go "up to any crowd she wanted to belong with," which would have ended the matter. So now Mick dreams and schemes about joining a "bunch" even as much as she dreams about mastering music. "Those two ideas were in her head all the time."

And that, as it will become increasingly clear, is what leads to Mick's undoing as an artist—that those *two* ideas are in her head all the time.... Mick expends as much energy in dreaming of love as in practicing her piano. She attempts to satisfy the heart's lonely craving as well as the soul's high yearning, and in the end satisfies neither. In the words of Ben Franklin's enduring didact, Poor Richard, she tries to hunt two hares with one dog and returns empty-handed. In short, it is Mick's division of self between "heart" and art which, more than anything else, proves fatal to her as an artist.

Mick's story then is the story of her increasing betrayal of art for heart's sake. As it happens, her first defection from art's solitary struggle comes on her thirteenth birthday, when she throws a big party in the hope of attracting a "bunch." It is at this party that she begins to cast off her boyish dress and dreams and to assume the appearance and prospects of a young lady. For the first time in her life, Mick dons a long dress, silk stockings, and brassiere. She paints her lips and cheeks, combs down her cowlick, and shapes three spit curls around her face. (pp. 114-15)

After her party, which predictably ends in disaster, Mick never again wears her beat-up shorts and T-shirt. In keeping with the feminine role she will eventually assume, she dons a sedate white blouse and blue skirt, albeit the skirt is usually down at the hem.

Continuing in her effort to slake the heart's insatiable appetite, Mick seeks out the affection of specific individuals. Longing to become a *we* instead of an *I*—as the heroine of another McCullers novel puts it—she turns to her younger brother for companionship. (p. 115)

Failing even with her brother to appease the unsatisfied heart, Mick in her need turns to Mr. Singer. Like three other lonely people she takes to visiting the deaf-mute in his room, where he sits over a chessboad remembering Antonapoulos. She pours out her heart to him, talking more than she has ever talked to anyone before. She imagines that if he could speak, he would tell her things he has never told anyone. She is sure there is a "secret feeling" between them. (p. 116)

Then one day she starts to follow the deaf-mute around town.... She follows him home, keeping a long way behind him so that he never knows she is there. "So long as she could see him and be near him she was right happy. But sometimes this queer feeling would come to her and she knew she was doing wrong."

Of course, the only wrong that Mick is doing is to herself in forgetting her dream—for an imaginary friendship. For the only person in the world who she thinks understands her does not in fact understand her at all. (pp. 116-17)

Having failed thus far to satisfy her ravenous heart, Mick at last turns to her family for relief. She throws her life away in an attempt to help her family and thereby secure the affection and understanding she craves. It all happens unexpectedly one June night sometime after Bubber's accidental shooting of Baby Wilson has caused the Kellys to lose their house and go into debt to pay the child's doctor bills. Mick's older sister Hazel comes home from work and announces that a clerkship has opened up at Woolworth's, paying ten dollars a week—enough to buy "fifteen fried chickens" or "five pairs of shoes." After a moment's hesitation Mick, feeling "hot and reckless," offers to take the job.

Her family's reaction is dramatic. "Listen to little Mick," her brother Bill says admiringly. "It would tide us over," her mother muses hopefully. Mick notices that her family, who have before paid little attention to her, are all "talking about her" now, and "in a kindly way." Suddenly she decides that she loves them all very much, and her throat tightens. Ashamed of her initial "scared feeling" about accepting the job, she insists she will take it, despite her parents' halfhearted protests that they want her to stay in school. (pp. 117-18)

In this way Mick Kelly, the adolescent tomboy who has struggled so fiercely against poverty, ignorance, and lack of space, at last succumbs to a craving for love. She throws everything away in an effort to help her family and thereby secure their affection and approval. We are given to understand that Mick's acceptance of a job at Woolworth's is the end of the road for her. Her dreams will never be realized now. (p. 118)

Still in her teens, then, Mick settles down to a life of drudgery in a five-and-dime store. She matures not into an artist but into a sour young woman enduring a tedious dead-end job in the hope of receiving an affectionate crumb from the family table. She has put self-assertion behind her and opted for self-sacrifice. And she feels cheated.

> It was like she was mad all the time. Not how a kid gets mad quick so that soon it is all over—but in another way. Only there was nothing to be mad at. Unless the store. But the store hadn't asked her to take the job. So there was nothing to be mad at. It was like she was cheated. Only nobody had cheated her. . . . However, just the same she had that feeling. Cheated.

If Mick Kelly at fourteen cannot decide who or what has cheated her of a future, she is not alone in her confusion since even Carson McCullers's critics cannot agree. Predictably, Marxist and progressive critics insist that it is capitalism with its inevitable breakdowns which short-changes Mick. And certainly it is true that the Great Depression is partly responsible for Mick's having to leave school to work. At the same time, at least one feminist critic suggests that it is "sexism" that deprives Mick of her birthright. And certainly that too is true, for as Mick tells her friend Harry, "A boy can usually get a part-time job that don't take him out of school. . . . But there's not jobs like that for girls."

Certainly both economic injustice and sexual discrimination contribute to thwarting Mick as an artist. Still, there is something more which prompts Mick to agree (and she does agree) to accept a life of limitation. As we have seen, that something else is her hunger for love, a craving for relationship, which has caught the lonely hunter in a trap.

Young, isolated, half-schooled, Mick can neither name nor explain the trap in which she finds herself captive. Its name, if we would believe another, more sophisticated artist heroine [Jo March], is the "love trap," or, as a contemporary feminist theorist [Carolyn Chesebro] puts it, the "compassion trap." An explanation of how it works can be found in scores of women's artist novels, notably in the last two decades. In fact, if there is a single, central lesson to be learned from the woman's *Künstlerroman* even as far back as Madame de Staël's *Corinne* (1807), it is that for a creative woman, love is a siren song ensnaring her into sacrificing her gifts and goals to give solace and service to others. Mick Kelly is only one of a number of artist heroines who are lured by the promise of affection or protection into throwing away their chances in life in return for obscure and anonymous labor. (pp. 118-20)

[It] is startling how many critics overlook Mick's failure to become an artist and laud her alleged "success" at becoming a woman. To judge from their commentaries it would seem that Mick Kelly has only one ambition: to become a nubile young woman. David Madden sees Mick simply as "an adolescent girl trying to achieve womanhood but fearing to succeed." C. E. Eisinger finds her merely "a typical adolescent struggling blindly toward maturity . . . in the proper preparation for later life." And Alfred Kazin [see *CLC*, Vol. 4] describes her only as a "young tomboy . . . who is too young for sexual love or too odd for it." (pp. 120-21)

In effect, the professors of English, preferring to repeat the commonplaces of myth criticism, ignore not only the text but what Carson McCullers said about the text: that Mick's sexual initiation is not "the most striking thing that happens" to her but is in fact "subordinate" in importance to her struggle against "the social forces" that prevent her from becoming an artist. The truth is, as McCullers depicts it, Mick's uneasy surrender to womanhood-as-usual is not a necessary good but an unnecessary evil. Moreover, her *rite de passage* into adult femininity is not sexual but professional; it is not the resignation of her virginity but the resignation of her ambition, her agreement to accept a life of limitation in the hope of securing love. (p. 122)

Linda Huf, " 'The Heart Is a Lonely Hunter' (1940): Carson McCullers's Young Woman with a Great Future behind Her," in her A Portrait of the Artist as a Young Woman: The Writer as Heroine in American Literature, *Frederick Ungar Publishing Company, 1983, pp. 105-24.*

SAMUEL CHASE COALE

Literary modernism seems tailor-made for the vision and techniques of Hawthorne's romance, thus opening new vistas to that older literary form. The individual self's battle against his/her own consciousness and the primitive world which both surrounds and is embodied within that consciousness rekindles Hawthorne's Manichean vision with a vengeance. Hearts of darkness and haunted minds appear inseparable, just as mythic methods encompass the character's or author's consciousness as the doomed shadow of the past encompassed Hawthorne's. A world of moments produces a literary landscape of scaffold epiphanies, those same episodic tableaux that surface again and again in Hawthorne and Melville, and the poetic spell of language seduces the reader once again into darker "neutral territories'' of fevered minds and distraught souls. Isolation and disconnection, those staples of the failed rescues of Hawthorne's romance, thrive in the often imprisoning banks of the stream of consciousness, and the threat of solipsism lurks within every imaginary rush and turn. (pp. 65-6)

''I suppose my central theme is the theme of spiritual isolation,'' Carson McCullers once said. ''I have always felt alone.'' Her rural South of mill towns and fly-specked cafes, the Columbus, Georgia, of her youth, suggests Hawthorne's Salem in its sense of decay, her vision of alienation and loss more keenly felt, perhaps, in a society which still prized community and tradition. In such a vacuum her characters seem driven inward to a world of private reverie and dream, in her darker fictions into a world of nightmare.

Narcissism plagues McCullers's characters, whether children or adults. An unrelenting solipsism darkens as her people age, the spontaneity of childhood lost in the blind pursuits of adulthood. Sex fuels a gothic world, a place ruled by psychological determinisms, separate selves locked into their fierce habits and obsessions. Her creatures seem possessed by alien forces, the unconscious motivations of lonely, alienated souls, characters fumbling within the primitive mainstream of modernist art. Hence the sense of dread that stalks McCullers's landscape, ''that Sense of the Awful'' that Tennessee Williams described [see *CLC*, Vol. 12], ''which is the desperate black root of nearly all significant modern art.'' Individuals are trapped in a gothic Manichean world that knows no exit. At her best McCullers captures that world, unmarred by the adolescent sentimentalities of *The Heart Is a Lonely Hunter* and *The Member of the Wedding,* where child-heroes thrive in an asexual realm still open to the possibilities of a life lived along a sensitive, vague edge.

McCullers referred to art as a ''flowering dream,'' the reflection of her vision of the world around her. Her best books reflect that dreamworld, the territory of romance akin in kind to Hawthorne's and Faulkner's. That dreamworld also reflects the modernist forms of Eliot's *The Waste Land* with its emphasis on cyclical patterns and its individuals trapped in mythic repetitions in a world that has lost any recognition of the possible liberating visions of ancient mythic rebirths and renewals. The psychological determinism of McCullers's fictional world approaches ritual in its ceremonial scenes and intensities, just as the characters in a romance spill over into the world of allegory, creatures of a metaphoric design that rules their lives and their actions. These often parallel Hawthorne's romantic designs in form if not in style.

McCullers's style for the most part remains objective and concrete in an imagistic manner. The bizarre events and characters in *Reflections in a Golden Eye,* for instance, are reported in an almost clinical manner, as though the writer were viewing her world through a jeweler's eyepiece, with that sharply focused clarity of the imagist poet. Consequently her world ultimately reflects Poe's more than it does Hawthorne's. Any moral sense is replaced by the cold eye dispassionately watching the playing out of events, the setting up of confrontations, the psychic inevitabilities of warring opposites and inner frustrations. The battle between will and instinct rages. The trap of the world is complete in a claustrophobic Manichean manner. And McCullers becomes ''a peacock of a sort of ghastly green. With one immense golden eye. And in it these reflections of something tiny and . . . grotesque.''

Reflections in a Golden Eye, McCullers's second book, reveals that descent into a nightmare world that Frye describes as the dark romance, in which ''life [is] so intolerable that it must end either in tragedy or in a permanent escape.'' Identities crumble; personal actions become restricted, locked into a world of mirrors and self-reflections; sudden metamorphoses—the Captain's passion for Williams—occur; animals, such as Leonora's horse Firebird, become companions and express a kind of freedom human beings cannot; and the whole is represented by a ''symbolic visual emblem,'' like the scarlet letter or in this case the golden eye of the painted peacock. Imprisonment sets the tone of the entire book, and the inevitable demonic recognition leads to ''the realization that only death is certain.'' Faulkner's South falls in upon itself, a black hole absorbing all the light within it.

Of the book, McCullers said that once ''relieved of the moral and physical strain of *The Heart Is a Lonely Hunter* I wrote *Reflections in a Golden Eye* in the spirit of a somewhat ghostly plane. . . . It's really a fairy story—everything is done very lightly.'' Nightmare would be more to the point. The withdrawn setting, the territory of romance, appears immediately: ''An army post in peace time is a dull place. Things happen, but then they happen over and over again. . . . all is designed according to a certain rigid pattern.'' Monotony engenders violent and bizarre action; the rigid caste system with its traditions of rank and service, the Old South in microcosm, breeds hostility and envy, the kind of social protest all romances create against the more conservative, realistic world of the novels Hawthorne described. The emphasis on patterns throughout the book primes the reader to discover allegorical designs, just as McCullers's description of her tale like ingredients in a recipe . . . draws attention to the modernist objectivity and external, dramatic ''reporting'' of her style.

The atmosphere of the book includes intense gloom and explosive light. Captain Penderton's wild ride on Firebird occurs in a dark wood, the same sanctuary from the post where Private Williams suns himself naked. ''Green shadowy moonlight'' haunts the tale, as well as that ''misty lavender glow'' after sunset with ''a hint of darkness . . . already in the air.''

Reflections abound and reverberate. Firebird's name suggests the phoenix, the opposite of Anacleto's golden-eyed peacock. A drugged Penderton feels the presence of ''a great dark bird . . . with fierce, golden eyes . . . enfold[ing] him in his dark wings.'' Penderton glimpses himself as a small grotesque doll, ''mean of countenance and grotesque in form,'' and he resembles a broken doll when he tumbles off Firebird in the forest. Such images reinforce the gothic claustrophobia of the army post, of McCullers's alienated characters, of the world as prison and pit.

But it is the sheer Manichean vision of *Reflections in a Golden Eye* that drives this fictional nightmare. Polarities abound, redouble, repeat, mirror one another. Captain Penderton and Private Williams: a warped aesthetic will and subconscious instinct. Penderton broods on homosexual desires, demands orderliness and rigidity in all his actions, thinks of death and withdrawal. Williams displays the ''strange rapt face of a Gauguin primitive'' and thrives on naked sojourns in the woods. . . . Penderton's wild ride on Firebird, convincing him that death is near, explodes into ''a great mad joy,'' a mystic delight in physical motion on the edge of extinction. His fall and his subsequent vision of the naked Williams, who can soothe and control the wayward horse in a way Penderton cannot, produces that sudden metamorphosis from smoldering ascetic to passionate lover, and he stalks Williams on the post after their return to it.

If Williams is the Caliban of the fable, Anacleto, Alison Langdon's houseboy, is the Ariel, a "rare bird" who ritualizes everything in his delicate Filipino manner and hates the people he must associate with. If Williams suggests unformed natural impulse tainted with violence and voyeurism, Anacleto represents the other pole of consciousness, the too-refined, artificially artistic will. Each is impotent; each is confined in his own world; each suggests the poles of consciousness between which the Pendertons and the Langdons struggle for self-gratification and fulfillment. And each of these couples reflects the Manichean battle between flesh and spirit, a precarious balance and an ongoing war that is "resolved" only by Leonora Penderton's affair with Morris Langdon. (pp. 79-82)

The mind itself is at war with itself: "The mind is like a richly woven tapestry in which the colors are distilled from the experience of the senses, and the design drawn from the convolutions of the intellect. The mind of Private Williams was imbued with various colors of strange tones, but it was without delineation, void of form." Design battles colors; the intellect battles the senses. And in the end, will murders instinct, Penderton kills Williams: "The Captain had slumped against the wall. In his queer, coarse wrapper he resembled a broken and dissipated monk. Even in death the body of the soldier still had the look of warm, animal comfort." Monk and animal: a final Manichean split. The rigid pattern is complete.

In *The Ballad of the Sad Cafe,* perhaps McCullers's masterpiece, the nightmare realm continues, a place where tradition exists only unconsciously as a series of habits and empty rituals. It is a world trapped in a meaningless and therefore grotesque present, resulting in a labyrinth of dark corridors and Manichean gestures. Strange signs and superstitions permeate this world, as they do in old ballads and folk tales: numbers, events, beliefs, a witch's brew. Narcissism triumphs. Lovers love those who love others in a complete circle of disconnection. The imprisonment of *Reflections* conquers all.

"The Twelve Mortal Men" is McCullers's choral conclusion to her ballad. Here the chain gang is working, and yet from them arises a melody that can be heard, and has been heard constantly throughout [*The Ballad of the Sad Cafe*] in the town. "The voices are dark in the golden glare," and it seems as though "the sound does not come from the twelve men on the gang, but from the earth itself, or the wide sky." It is a transcendent harmony of love and despair, mixed "with ecstasy and fright," the essentials of the human condition. It is a lament sung for the inevitable realities of that condition, a song sung by common men bound together by their common mortality, a Hawthornesque brotherhood both black and white. They sing not in spite of their chains but because of them. Unlike the participants in the nightmare which has just been completed, they know they must act together in order to survive the mutual degradation that fate has seen fit to thrust upon them. They can see their chains and acknowledge their common bonds.

The music sinks down, but it can rise again. In the wake of such a cruel and relentless fate, and not in spite of but because of that fate, McCullers captures a faint glimmer of human endurance and brotherhood, even though she can see "just twelve mortal men who are together."

McCullers's vision of the dark labyrinth of the human heart and the brotherhood of all men bound to their separate but equal fates links her to Hawthorne's "truth" of the human heart, but significant differences exist. In McCullers's world, an abnormal fear of adult sexuality permeates everything. This may be linked to her relationship with Reeves McCullers, the man she married, divorced, and later remarried, who eventually committed suicide. It also may reflect the dark side of her sentimental attachment to childhood and children, acknowledging the fact that the South is "a very emotional experience for me, fraught with all the memories of my childhood." Nostalgia breeds paralysis and claustrophobia and leads to such sentimentalized faith, a kind of bastardized Wordsworthian belief (another primitive undercurrent in modernist art, perhaps), in the "poetry in children. It always strikes me that they are so capable of losing and finding themselves and also losing and finding those things they feel close to. . . . Mrs. Roosevelt says, 'Children are the only people that tell the truth.' I agree with her." Here is no charming, enigmatic, demonic Pearl. Southern sentimentality has fallen in upon itself as it does in other ways in Faulkner's work, but here unrelieved by distance and rhetorical exorcism.

McCullers's world remains as Manichean as her vision, an ultimate trap within or beyond which there is no other, save the murky psychological motives of her characters. A quest for moral significance collapses in such a Poe-esque void. Romance can never be delivered from nightmare, since the descent only ends in death. In the final paragraph of *Reflections in a Golden Eye,* still a strange and powerful fiction, Leonora "stared about her as though witnessing some scene in a play, some tragedy that was gruesome but not necessary to believe." Hawthorne sought belief, however fragmented and scattered in his final romances, or at least sought a vision of the world that suggested a morally significant pattern. McCullers like Poe stages gruesome scenes and pursues them to their inevitable conclusions, a mesmerizing, chilling art but one that harbors no tragedy, since there exists no necessity of belief, no moral significance finally. . . . McCullers recreates a modernist dread, itself perhaps the sentimental side of her childhood simplicities and reveries, and stalks it to its Manichean conclusion. But nightmare leads on only to further nightmare, a dark design of momentary stays against confusion that dissolves into the spiritual paralysis of her gothic art. (pp. 82-4)

Samuel Chase Coale, "Faulkner, McCullers, O'Connor, Styron: The Shadow on the South," in his In Hawthorne's Shadow: American Romance from Melville to Mailer, *The University Press of Kentucky, 1985, pp. 63-101.*

David McFadden

1940-

Canadian poet, novelist, short story writer, editor, and journalist.

McFadden is best known as a poet who frequently records observations of domestic life and daily events in his hometown of Hamilton, Ontario. Using accessible language, a conversational narrative style, and both traditional and experimental forms, McFadden views life with exuberance and childlike wonder. Combined with an inventive imagination and wry wit, McFadden's intense fascination with the ordinary often results in surreal and fantastic imagery. In his poems, McFadden also addresses such broader concerns as the definition of poetry, the relationship between art and the artist, and the state of contemporary culture. In his later work, McFadden's tone turns slightly darker, as he attempts to convey a sense of the incongruities and absurdities of modern society.

McFadden began his career by contributing poems to various Canadian literary magazines. His first individually published work, the chapbook *The Poem Poem* (1967), is a meditative piece in which McFadden parallels his process of composing poetry with his wife's pregnancy and the birth of their first child. His next two volumes, *The Saladmaker* (1968) and *Letters from the Earth to the Earth* (1968), contain observations of McFadden's family life and display his interest in children and language. McFadden also addresses such topical concerns as Martin Luther King's death, the policies of Mao-Tse Tung, and songs of The Beatles. With the publication of *Intense Pleasure* (1972), McFadden gained wider critical attention. In this volume, written in the form of a diary, he continues to record the details of daily experience while also including passages of free association, stream of consciousness, and surreal and fantastic imagery.

With *A Knight in Dried Plums* (1975), McFadden began to emphasize such darker elements as violence, death, pain, and anger in his verse while continuing to relate anecdotes about life in Hamilton and the McFadden home. The book-length poem *The Poet's Progress* (1977) is a personal meditation containing random thoughts, feelings, and memories. *On the Road Again* (1978) contains lyrical poems in the Romantic mode, focusing on such topics as love, nature, and emotion. McFadden stated that his next work, the long poem *A New Romance* (1979), "represents a remarkable breakthrough into a purer and more authentic level of my writing life," transcending the more fundamental and immediate concerns of his earlier works. In this poem, McFadden further reveals his affinity for Romanticism by striving for linguistic simplicity and emphasizing humanism, nature, and universal values that are revealed in ordinary life. *My Body Was Eaten by Dogs* (1981) collects representative pieces from six of McFadden's earlier volumes. In *The Art of Darkness* (1984), McFadden continues his celebration of the ordinary while employing black humor and irony to underscore the chaotic nature of contemporary life.

McFadden has also received considerable attention for his fiction. His first novel, *The Great Canadian Sonnet* (1970), is an illustrated satire depicting one man's search for "human

Photograph by Paul Orenstein

perfection" in the superficial popular culture of modern North America. *Animal Spirits: Stories to Live By* (1979) collects McFadden's experimental short fiction written between 1965 and 1977 in which he examines suburban life, presenting by turns its sadness and hilarity, desolation and absurdity. In the travelogues *A Trip around Lake Huron* (1979) and *A Trip around Lake Erie* (1979), McFadden relates humorous anecdotes from vacations he took with his family, his thoughts on various contemporary issues, and his opinions of popular culture. In his recent novel, *Canadian Sunset* (1986), McFadden blends farcical and grotesque elements with offbeat humor to detail the wanderings throughout North America of a weapons salesman-turned-novelist and the bizarre situations and people he encounters.

(See also *Contemporary Authors*, Vol. 104 and *Dictionary of Literary Biography*, Vol. 60.)

PETER STEVENS

Letters From The Earth To The Earth is honest Dave McFadden's family album complete with snapshots, somehow catching moments without killing them off, the poems and the pictures mixing together in haphazard inter-relationship: "honesty in a plastic field". . . . The poems and the pictures involve the reader in the poet's life (which is also his poetry), for the photographs show the reader the poet's wife, his family, places and people he has known and visited: all this he wants to show us and tell us about, so that we can participate in it as well. We become involved in McFadden's world, the "sweet universe of my / waking life".

There are terrifying risks in trying to write this kind of poetry: it can be too private; the trivia of everyday life can seem just too trivial or too inconsequential to be worth recording; the treatment can become too sentimental or nostalgic; incidents insignificant in themselves can be worked up to carry more meaning than they can bear. David McFadden doesn't always avoid these dangers but in this volume he is generally very successful in resolving these kinds of problems. The short poems about his family, the expression of simple incidents and reminiscences cohere around the poet's personality that is presented throughout the whole book.

I think McFadden most successful in his shorter poems. The poems that run to two pages or more are generally too diffuse: the movement of these poems seems less energetic and the meanderings of his reactions lose touch with the reader. He has included an ambitious poem on the death of Martin Luther King but although it is deeply felt, I think it dissipates its sincerity by going on too long, although its last section is perhaps its strongest section. . . .

At times McFadden seems to be attempting a kind of Whitmanesque all-inclusiveness: everything and everybody matter. He is part of that all-inclusiveness and he wants to reach out to include us all. . . . [Although] one remembers single poems, it is the whole book which matters, it is his whole life, which is presented through these *Letters,* "making a masterful sacred whole of it".

Presented as an album of poems and pictures with both blurred and sharp images, with successes and failures, with incidents and simple meditations, this book, like the best letters, reveals the many sides of the poet's character: his resilience and tough-mindedness, his gentleness, good nature and humour and above all his whole-hearted acceptance of life that reaches out from the poetry to touch us all.

> Peter Stevens, in a review of "Letters from the Earth
> to the Earth," in The Canadian Forum, Vol. XLIX,
> No. 586, November, 1969, p. 198.

JOSEPH SHERMAN

Letters from the Earth to the Earth is a composite of poems and photographs, and the latter are non-professional family snapshots, issue of some ten year old Kodak. This combination of one sight-sound medium with another distinct sight medium has an interesting result, for the pictures do not appear to be arranged specifically to complement individual poems. The problem for the reviewer, if not for the paying reader, is to decide whether or not the snaps of wife, kids, relatives, friends, objects, places, and self, distract, help, or do absolutely nothing.

The poems in this fair-sized collection are, by the poet's own admission, from two previously unpublished manuscripts; the poems having been written between 1966-69. If I was not given these dates I would have guessed the same, for the poetry is

permeated by topical observations. Some of the poems can almost be dated precisely. There is, for example, a long poem written just after the death of Martin Luther King; another is concerned with a recent Beatles record; and the universal confusion generated by the existence of Chairman Mao rates two poems.

McFadden deals in distilled poetry; which is to say that he avoids, for the most part, the use of "lofty", excessive metaphor, and/or "ponderous" symbolism; all of which can constitute, for some, a private and workable "music"; for others, chaff. His best poems are clean and even, dealing in subject matter of an immediate nature—his four-part family relationship. He turns in upon himself and this relationship, while maintaining a commendable and enviable objectivity. This poet is an amateur "scientist" (the term is his own), a semi-homespun observer of everythings, and contexts. Couple this with the snapshots and you get a lot. After having come upon countless T-shirted McFaddens and friends in their bare arms and feet and typically unphotogenic faces, you can almost smell the McFadden woodwork.

Mr. McFadden has rare moments of real subtlety, but he works understatement expertly by making full use of fact, as he does in **"Darryl & The Moose."** Here, two separate encounters, of a type too often mishandled and made trivial or maudlin, come off because of close attention to detail. One beautiful, delicate poem is **"Watching Him,"** about vividly painted two year old Gregory:

> He's here
> all day
>
> it's his
> grandfather's
>
> funeral
>
>> Joan & I
>> watching him.
>>
>> walk around
>> exploring things.

McFadden is a discoverer. When he is not exercising his senses first hand, he is doing so vicariously, through those close to him. And there is an attempt, not necessarily sentimental, but rather, functional to his existence as a poet, to retain the thrill implicit in these discoveries. . . . He creates much from recording the reactions of his children to the learning process. He has a share in that learning process and assembles his relatively placid philosophies, augmented by the addenda furnished by his family.

McFadden seems to feel it necessary to define poetry, more than once. He fits these definitions into his best workable relationship. . . . Also, he is not afraid of admitting that what he is writing is Poetry—and he actually calls it by that name. This, in contrast to some modern poets who would rather hear someone else label their work. McFadden's poetry is, for him, neither a weapon, nor even a proclamation, but more a recording of note, or a plain and simple admission. He insists on placing his poetry in its personally-proper perspective. Such is his style, his "simple science poems for all." (pp. 64-5)

Most of the poems in *Letters from the Earth to the Earth* are successful in and out of the context of collection. Some are definitely not. **"Magical Mystery Pool,"** a play upon Beatle lyrics is an improvement upon the original but devoid of any important feeling. (The danger lies in being trivial about another triviality.) McFadden is indeed most effective when he is at home. All forays into other geographical locales are made while attached to a sort of mental elastic arm, bound to be reeled in.

McFadden's poetry has not the flame or vitriol of Layton; the geographical scope of Newlove; the subtle crispness of Nowlan; or ''the honey of Leonard Cohen,'' but he is a good poet. His language is basic and familiar—and this places him in a potentially dangerous position: he is liable to be lost in the crowd. For there is nothing seismic or alarming about the artist or his work, and the occasional slip into poetic mediocrity will not, when all is said and done, be excusable. Meanwhile, praises for a poet who sentimentalizes without being mawkish, and who observes without intruding.

Back to the whole, pictures and all. Despite the questionable abundance of family photos, this is no compleat family album. The poems are not captions, nor are the pictures illustrations. McFadden unites the proverbial picture and the thousand words and emerges relatively unscathed. But poetry must support and substantiate itself, without the use of ''gingerbread.'' For the future, he would do well to remember that. (pp. 65-6)

> *Joseph Sherman, in a review of ''Letters from the Earth to the Earth,'' in* The Fiddlehead, *No. 82, November-December, 1969, pp. 64-6.*

DOUGLAS BARBOUR

The whole of *Letters from the Earth to the Earth* reflects David McFadden's homely concerns, his discovery that poetry is always there, right where he happens to be. Throughout the book, McFadden's poems and photographs of family, friends, picnic sites and vacation spots mix and interact with one another so that no separation is possible even were it desired. The book is a kind of epic, dedicated to the proposition that everything, the prose of life, is really poetry. It's a flawed epic; many segments are flat, barren, and merely prose indeed. McFadden takes chances continually: poem after poem is a high-wire act, with the poet teetering precariously over plain prose. There are very few poets who would even want to try to write poetry McFadden's way: they would be so aware of the possibilities for failure. McFadden appears to be hardly aware of them, however, which perhaps explains the number of his successes. David McFadden is a nice guy, and, although this fact does not argue one way or another for his success as a poet, it does affect one's response to the continuum of poems that is this book. Yet the poems, when they succeed, do so because they bring delight, not because they tell us that he's nice.

There is one poem in this volume that stands out from the rest, for both its length and its subject matter. **''An Hour's Restless Sleep''** was written on the night that Martin Luther King was assassinated. It is a troubling poem because one can't help being moved by it, and yet the poem does not quite work as poetry. It achieves its effects despite itself, and that is not good enough. Some kind of revision is necessary before this poem will achieve a purely formal and aesthetic coherence. Nevertheless, no one can regard as a total failure a poem containing the lines, ''up there waiting to meet him were all the other great Americans / whoever lived—Walt Whitman.'' *Letters from the Earth to the Earth* is a beautiful book.... It also proves a fine introduction to a young poet who has a delightful vision to share. (pp. 122-23)

> *Douglas Barbour, in a review of ''Letters from the Earth to the Earth,'' in* The Dalhousie Review, *Vol. 50, No. 1, Spring, 1970, pp. 122-24.*

RICHARD G. ADAMS

> Hedge protects lawn   Lawn protects
> house Windows chimney porch
> A family at table eating
>
> Let's all have separate houses
> daddy said my daughter
> as she propped a book
> between us

So runs **''Books,''** one typical poem from David McFadden's new collection [*Intense Pleasure*]. I say typical because of the adult's awakening to the child; the sense of family, the elementary comparing, tiny perceptions ballooning. This sort of poem is the starch in Mr. McFadden's poetic meat and potatoes. And, as he has done before, the poet here continues to show how bare-boned kids' perceptions are. (p. 118)

Most of his poems are short; all are pointed, mostly inwards. He attempts, and largely succeeds in striking up a working relationship with the quality of innocence in himself. He desires to be amazed, thus he is constantly amazed. He wastes no time on sympathy when he can empathize. And his uses of imagination, because they are child-like at heart, are at times strained. But fun:

> Chocolate bars can fly,
> a wrapper lying on the ground
>   means a bar is soaring in the clouds
>
> wrapper sadly waiting its return.

When, as he is wont to do, Mr. McFadden reduces the ''coils'' of adult intellect (and all therein) to the level of the wide-eyed child, he fails, and he becomes damagingly puerile, as in **''Hot Coils''**.

And yet the man as poet is engaging. He is not so much a regressive in his child-view workshop as he is a future seeker. He attempts to be and maintain what we all often wish we had never left, and this sort of testimony is always readable. One poem, **''George Bowering''** is retrospective and wistful about human relationships, and we are shown just how close we are all drawn to one another, especially through death. Another poem, **''T. S. Eliot''** (his titles, by the way, are often best put to one side) waxes familial again, but with a sense of history and tradition being redeemed and recycled. And in **''Meaningless Midnight Musings''** McFadden stews thought-association, stream of consciousness, and confession till the whole is nearly completely successful.

I think that I like him because in **''After Thomas Hardy''** he tells me more of himself than I can say of him, in the best of ways:

> After I'm dead
> & time
> continues on without me
> much as it did before I was born
>
> a child will pick up
> a piece of dog shit
> & taste it

& someone will say Look!
McFadden was a man who
would have noticed that.

(pp. 118-19)

Richard G. Adams, in a review of "Intense Pleasure," in The Fiddlehead, *No. 94, Summer, 1972, pp. 118-19.*

DAVID HELWIG

David McFadden's poetry in *Intense Pleasure* is a kind of diary, a set of observations, dreams, reminiscences. His loyalty to the details of daily experience is like that of many fiction writers, and I suppose (to steal an analogy from Hugh Hood) that he could almost be regarded as a kind of superrealist, the analogue of the painter who observes the world with such intensity that the real becomes fantastic. McFadden is also fascinated by dreams and whims (think of Wyeth's *revenant* or Colville's horse rushing toward a train), but his technique is much looser than that of most of the painters I've been evoking. He himself mentions Greg Curnoe once or twice in this book, and certainly there is something in the way Curnoe documents LondonOnt that is like the way McFadden documents Hamilton.

Central to McFadden's poem is a kind of acceptance. . . . He is like [Al] Purdy in his sense that every shape is arbitrary and therefore artificial yet necessary because the poet wants to hang on to whatever is. McFadden reports on wife, children, cars, stores, friends. The epigraph to his book is "These are the days I'll remember when we are dead." His book's title suggests the kind of excitement that allows him to see and record the smallest details without needing to justify them by turning them into art. Artlessness is cunning too, of course, and there are poems where McFadden shows us himself conscious of himself conscious, yet even these seem a kind of tribute to being.

In general, McFadden's poetry [in *Intense Pleasure*] is like that in his previous books, but it seems to me that there is a sense of encroaching darkness now and then, a shadow at the edge of the snapshot. . . . He documents the world of garage mechanics and bank tellers, and these are some of the people who ought to be reading him. But are they? Who is he writing for?

Take some phrases: "the man on the street", "the reading public", "the common reader"; do they create a series of useful referents for placing the poet in our landscape? Purdy and McFadden have both worked at the most ordinary of jobs, both write poems that are sometimes funny and that begin with a clear account of the facts of everyday experience. Yet even Purdy's most popular books reach only a minority of a reading public which is a minority of the population. (pp. 405-06)

David Helwig, "Four Poets," in Queen's Quarterly, *Vol. LXXIX, No. 3, Autumn, 1972, pp. 404-07.*

RALPH GUSTAFSON

Mr. McFadden's verse [in *Intense Pleasure*] left me total and unscathed. Previously I had been irritated. Last year (Mr. McFadden writes a book a year, I gather), in 1971, he presented a book called *Poems Worth Knowing*. The title embodies the unspoken assumption of every poet who publishes, but he usually has the decency to leave the saying of it to the critical reader. "Not again," I groaned. I was already fed up with the colossal inter-adulation carried on by our Little Press groups. "All right, skip the groans," I browbeat myself. "Here might be Canada's Ezra Pound, Canada's John Clare!" Poems worth knowing? Here is one:

> After breakfast
> I listen to music
> or it listens to me
> & watch an airplane flying over—

So. But he might have inadvertently succeeded in hiding his great thoughts. I read another poem; about his little daughter eating her own shit. I persisted; children can be adorable. I read others which say that Kerouac is the author's all-time hero and that Michael Ondaatje is a "living legend", I thought, "Well, the verse in this book does resemble the 'spontaneous prose' Kerouac advocated; it does a hatchet job on almost everything, rhythm, music, the works; but if McFadden gets intense pleasure from playing tennis with the net down, leave him alone with his love match. On the Ondaatje theme, I thought, "Mike will get him off that hook." Then it dawned on me. The book is a put-on! I am a dolt. This is comedy. But no. The author's introduction tells us that the author writes poems seriously,

> with sincere attempts at truthfulness, accuracy,
> meaningfulness & self-discovery.

The self-discovery would eventually take care of itself, I felt; and the guy is truthful—but that's the trouble, therein lies the trouble: he believes that if he tells the truth he has written a poem. Almost as bad, he mistakes domesticity for profundity. (pp. 105-06)

Ralph Gustafson, "Circumventing Dragons," in Canadian Literature, *No. 55, Winter, 1973, pp. 105-08.*

DOUGLAS BARBOUR

A Knight in Dried Plums charts David McFadden's continuing verbal raids on the extraordinary ordinary. If you have enjoyed previous McFadden forays, you will enjoy this one. If you have yet to read a McFadden poem, be warned: the man is charming, comic, strangely affecting when you least expect it, and his poems defy all ordinary modes of classification. Actually, I don't know how McFadden gets away with it: lines, stanzas, even whole poems that shouldn't work, but do. His imagination is rooted in 'normal' living, but it moves far and fast and slippery in just about every piece he writes, touching lightly on a hundred arcane themes and always returning to this nice, ordinary guy with the weird thoughts, David McFadden of Hamilton, Ontario. I would say the poems in this new book are more obviously concerned than earlier ones with the ravages of time, violence and the prospect of death, but these too are a part of everyday life in Hamilton, and so fit right in to his genially explosive poetic universe. There are a number of sly fantasies and dreamvisions here, some moving portraits of people seen and known around the city, and some lengthy surreal philosophic excursions. Personally, I like David McFadden's poems: they appear rather unassuming, it's true, but they are gritty, emotionally real, and they are thoroughly entertaining as well.

Douglas Barbour, in a review of "A Knight in Dried Plums," in The Dalhousie Review, *Vol. 55, Winter, 1975-76, p. 753.*

MARY LUND

The poet of *A Knight In Dried Plums* is open to anything, and he says you might better be, since anything happens all the time. For instance, in a park a boy eats a piece of the pigeons' popcorn and flies away; Siamese twins during a live performance weaken and die. And right along with the things that happen are the things that don't and the things that might. An old apple tree doesn't come when somebody calls it; a "crazy castrated cat called Al" doesn't leap through a brick wall (as expected); someone says "We hope to prove Lee Harvey Oswald knew Joey Smallwood." And a poet might stop writing.

The poems in *A Knight In Dried Plums* are as random as they sound, but their form becomes reliable. *A Knight In Dried Plums* is David McFadden's eighth book of poetry, and the poems in this book have a composure and a concentration that were beginning in the rambling subjective poems of *Letters From The Earth To The Earth* and the more arbitrary sequences and bizarre images of *Intense Pleasure*. The pointblank chaos of subjects in *A Knight In Dried Plums* is steadied by the particular character of the lines. On the page the poems look like poems—neat stanzas, numbered sections—but they don't act like poems.

After reading them, we will remember the medium-length line, speech-like and very plain:

> This is the 20th Century speaking.
> . . . .
> you pulled a kitten from a paper bag in your lap
> . . . .
> Jimmy's intellectual life was shattered . . .

This is the line used in most of the poems, and these statements, usually run-on sentences, are grouped in irregular stanzas which form continuations of the topic in shorter poems and self-contained units in longer poems. A familiar style in free verse. The lines of the poems read like someone talking to someone else. The unassuming diction, ordinary syntax and the distinct rhythms of everyday talk relate the recognizable and the unreal comfortably with no stylistic acknowledgement of this wild mixture. (p. 108)

McFadden's method rushes the extremes of our sensations, acts and motivations into immediate view in the simple words we are reading. The easy habit of our minds that assimilates whatever is said in the same tone in the same sentence goes right ahead: it is then we meet the fracturing of unreason. This certain shock attracts us, makes us laugh in a burst and then work our way back from the fright.

But more possessing is the voice in the poems. This voice is not a persona, it does not take on a subtle dramatic pose characteristic of poetry. In his first lines McFadden anticipates our willingness to move with metre and patterned language and kindly thwarts it. . . . This unevenness, amusing and distracting, sets the manner of the poems right away. But the voice is as guideless as it is deliberate. It is forthright and silly and serious and curious. There is something in the voice in each line that wants to go on talking, keep putting things together in words, in lines, even now—during the poems. In "The Angel" this effort is dramatized:

> and I opened the dusty door of my writing room
> and wrote the above
> then went out and made coffee
> then returned and wrote the following

In "The Golden Treasury of Knowledge" it is said outright:

> & I will continue writing this primitive cycle
> until the final phone rings
> or until I find out why I continue
> in which case I will probably continue continuing
> like a prisoner in an unlocked cell.
> Not that I seriously consider myself primitive
> but I'm no impregnable sophisticate like Robbe-Grillet
> from whom I've stolen an idea here I think.

And in "Nature", a long discursive poem of six sections, the endeavor to include all that is there can be felt in the disparate focuses, the jumps from personal to mystical to abstract: the effect is a constant pursuit of each association that happens to come. Phrases that are repeated and juggled absentmindedly also give the feeling that the poem is being written while it's being read. . . . (pp. 108-10)

The voice in the poems, then, is someone present, someone who refuses to be disguised in the forms or affects of poetry. McFadden claims the voice. He talks outloud in his poems. He interrupts himself to say he is writing this and to say he cannot say why he is writing, what writing is, or what he is. . . . He interrupts again to say how much fun all this is. . . . (p. 110)

McFadden demonstrates the tentativeness of poetry. He insists that the poet be able to speak in his poems to the reader about the act of writing poems. A similar new stance can be seen in current experimental fiction. The "self-conscious narrator" in the fiction of John Barth and Kurt Vonnegut, Jr. steps outside (or inside) his narrative and talks to his reader and comments on the narrative events or techniques. (pp. 110-11)

The tone of McFadden's voice in the poems is the appeal of *A Knight In Dried Plums*. His subjects are ordinary and his concerns are familiar. His impressive feat is the dissolving of the fantastic in and out of the everyday. But his tone draws us into the poems, and this tone is determined and willing. The poet takes on everything, and in the process he laughs and harangues, weeps and dawdles, but he keeps on writing. (p. 111)

> *Mary Lund, in a review of "A Knight in Dried Plums,"*
> *in* The Fiddlehead, *No. 108, Winter, 1976, pp. 108-11.*

GWENDOLYN DAVIES

After reading about disintegration in [Ken] Norris's poems there is something reassuring about the tone and subject matter of David McFadden's *The Saladmakers*. This is not to say that McFadden sees the ills of contemporary society any less clearly than does Norris, but there is a surer sense of control and purpose in McFadden's poems. Poems like "Evening Star," "Bathing in Diabolic Acid," "The Sky and I," and "The Saladmaker" creatively explore the tensions between the artist and his art and the artist and his society. McFadden's poems are relatively free of the abstract, and people (especially his wife, Joan) are important parts of the speaker's world. Yet as poet ("being one with every beating heart in space and time"), he is observer as well as observed in this society. He is never free of the knowledge of his responsibility in time, and thus in "The United Church Observer" he must get it "into my notebook because someday / it will be dead, dead, dead." There is nothing particularly euphonious in lines like this, but when McFadden wishes to lower the knife and slice cleanly as he does in "The Saladmaker," he can create tense, effective impressions. (p. 87)

Gwendolyn Davies, "Something's Happening in Montreal," in Essays on Canadian Writing, *No. 10, Spring, 1978, pp. 82-7.*

DAVID JACKEL

It would be uncharitable to suggest that David McFadden's affection for children, animals, and "ordinary everyday things" is anything but sincere. In **"Small Flowers,"** the concluding poem of [*On the Road Again*], his attitude to life is clearly expressed:

> God
> give me the power to be sensitive
> to the small flowers you cause to
> grow
> in my head
> and to the children and newborn
> lambs
> that surround me
> give me the power not to redeem
> this century
> but to be human
> in the small circle of life
> that surrounds me moment by
> moment. . . .

For McFadden, to be human is to "feel at home" wherever he may be on the road—at a Dairy Queen or a family picnic, riding in a truck or on the Prince George Express, living a fantasy or waking dream ("even meeting by chance / that well-known saviour and holy man / Jesus Christ during a train stop / in Capreol").

Which of us would not join McFadden in asking to be affectionate and sensitive, to be at home, to be human? At least some of us, however, are likely to ask, *from poets,* a good deal more, and these demands McFadden does not satisfy. Sensitive human beings are not necessarily good poets too—because poets not only feel, they write poems. McFadden's poems are in many cases not well written enough to make us share his feelings. It may be true, as he says, "that every day / there seem to be more and more people wandering around / in a lifeless daze, dead, cold, hollow / with all their lights out." Nevertheless, the poet has to turn on the light, through language, not merely assert that he has turned it on.

McFadden's language asserts such a claim, but the assertion is unconvincing. The words do not enlighten; they invite instead stock responses, sentimental displays of emotion inadequately motivated. Lovely, strange, mysterious, majestic, glowing, beautiful, softly, sweetly, delicately, miraculously, curious, magic, thrill: this vocabulary recalls the English Romantics (a recollection encouraged by McFadden's direct and indirect allusions to Wordsworth, Blake and Byron). McFadden fails to bring this vocabulary back to life in the present, and its "poetic" quality does not combine well either with the more prosaic language he uses much of the time ("and she got embarrassed / and said she didn't know much about history") or with such contemporary infelicities as "kind of" (as in "kind of spartan") or "high speed crash."

McFadden's views of poetry and of poetic activity also recall the Romantics: the poet is usually at the centre of the poem, expressing himself ("forever searching / for original ideas and weird experiences") yet reluctant to control the process of expression. . . . (p. 31)

Despite his admirable attempts to write about his world, he ends in most poems by writing about himself and, too often, for himself. In choosing not to be, in his words, "merely mimetic," he rejects the mirror for the lamp, and lights his own darkness, but seldom illuminates ours. (p. 32)

David Jackel, "Sentimental Displays," in The Canadian Forum, *Vol. LVIII, No. 684, September, 1978, pp. 31-2.*

DOUGLAS BARBOUR

David McFadden's *The Poet's Progress* is an exhilarating trip with one of Canada's joyous cosmologists. Like Michael Ondaatje's spider-poet, McFadden weaves his own tightrope as he walks it, the flow of words only what his open mind provides. In some hands this process could result in uninteresting chaos; in McFadden's hands the process of a mind moving as it will, connections occurring freely, is a delight. 'The poet is a token / of the world's magic,' he says, and the belief animates his poem. All its strange twists and turns, the weird and oddly juxtaposed thoughts, feelings and memories, the delight in language playing its games, only serve to signal the world's magic through 'the constant arousal' of both the poet's and reader's curiosity and delight. *The Poet's Progress* is an intensely personal poem; or so it appears at first. All the personal aspects keep shifting into the grand impersonal mode of poetry, however, subsumed to the journey of mind the poem maps. It's not the usual *periplum*, but it's a trip worth taking with this lovable and loving guide.

Douglas Barbour, in a review of "The Poet's Progress," in The Dalhousie Review, *Vol. 58, No. 3, Autumn, 1978, p. 571.*

MICHAEL BRIAN OLIVER

The Saladmaker by David McFadden was first published by George Bowering in *Imago* in 1967; the publication of this new edition perhaps deserves to be considered a minor landmark in contemporary Canadian poetry. In his own unobtrusive, domestic, likeable fashion McFadden has accomplished much the same thing Bowering himself has worked so hard (and awkwardly) at doing for almost twenty years now—that is, composing personal, experimentally "open" poetry that unites the individual consciousness with the vapid, mass-produced, and seemingly meaningless popular culture of the present day. Whereas alienation was the great theme of modernism, acculturation has become the major concern of post-modernism (just as it was for the pre-moderns, though the compass sweeps much wider now). *The Saladmaker* displays an imagination in the process of acculturating, not easily—and certainly not happily—but steadily and almost bravely. As Norman Mailer said of the hipster, more than twenty years ago, the post-modern poet is attempting to "create a new nervous system for himself" so that he might adapt to, include, and re-mythologize all that the modern poets turned away from. This accounts for the accumulation of trivia in post-modern literature and the intensification of the uniquely personal life of the persona, "the life you never lived," as McFadden calls it. Bowering, who is unquestionably the major influence on McFadden's work, calls this method of writing poetry "composition," and it is significant that McFadden says, "my lines / have suffered a certain decomposure" when he describes the effects of passing years on his poetry. These two quotations are from **"Bathing In Diabolic Acid,"** the last—and the only new—poem in the book. In this poem McFadden presents both an apology for the sequence itself and a poetics for post-modernism in general. (pp. 108-09)

The importance of the moment, the necessity to preserve the commonplace in case it may paradoxically yield in time "the big vision," this is the central theme of *The Saladmaker*. Everything the poet perceives may go

> into my notebook because someday
> it will all be dead, dead, dead
>
> and I'll curse myself for not having
> recorded its images
> ("**The United Church Observer**")

Even language itself is subject to preservation or "decomposition," and this explains the post-modernist's fascination with slogans and slang. Bowering, of course, specializes in word play, but McFadden is generally more concerned with happenings than with words, though he does record bits of conversation ("Fortunately for them I overhear"—this might be taken as an axiom of post-modernism), and he does demonstrate a fondness for puns, as when he calls the poetic process "**Bathing In Diabolic Acid**." Appropriately, many of McFadden's poems suggest home movies, both in subject and approach, and his style might even be called poesy verité or whimsical realism. In spite of obvious drawbacks, this method actually works in *The Saladmaker*. McFadden is never overbearing, as Bowering is at certain times, and seldom is he boring, like bill bisset, bpNichol, Victor Coleman and a plethora of other "revolutionary" writers publishing today. The moments McFadden preserves usually do yield vitality when we read them, and sometimes even significance, especially the ones he renders in "**The United Church Observer**," "**Slow Black Dog**," and "**Evening Star**." Towards the end of the book he says, "All I am looking for / is the transformational poem," and, I am happy to say, he occasionally finds it. (p. 110)

> *Michael Brian Oliver, "Lost and Found," in* The Fiddlehead, *No. 119, Fall, 1978, pp. 106-16.*

ROBERT THACKER

David McFadden's *On the Road Again* led me to doubt his editors' judgment because his book of poems is pretentious and trite, and I doubted his publicists' as well because McFadden is in no way western: he lives in Hamilton, Ontario, and always has, apparently.... The putative appeal of McFadden's poetry is that he has traveled the length and breadth of Canada and writes about his experiences. Intrinsically, there is nothing wrong with this but, so far as I can see, these must have been the sole factors leading to a decision to publish. McFadden often begins with promising ideas or angles of vision, as he does in "**How I Came to Understand Irving Layton**," but, because he has little apparent regard for craft—one can seldom understand his arbitrary line breaks—and is constantly patting himself on the back because he is *A POET*, the following lines are woefully representative:

> and oh if only I could know
> where all my energy should go
> I would suddenly become strong enough
> to jump in there and stop that flow
> and by wiggling my fingers to and fro
> could illuminate all of Toronto.

Auden wrote that "Good poets have a weakness for bad puns"; so, apparently, do third-rate ones, judging by McFadden's last line.... McFadden's self-indulgent lines are of little interest, less substance, and ultimately, no real consequence; his book is an example of the sort of poetry "The Canadian Publishers" are bringing forth in the gratuitous hope of salability. Meanwhile good poets go begging. (p. 230)

> *Robert Thacker, in a review of "On the Road Again," in* Western American Literature, *Vol. XIV, No. 3, November, 1979, pp. 229-31.*

JOHN COOK

A finer balance of method and vision may have helped David McFadden's *A New Romance,* a long, rambling poem that gives very little evidence of an imaginative, intelligent mind at work giving shape to the random outpourings of a voice in the wilderness. Out of a pastiche of sound associations, jokes, trite observations, literary allusions, puns, and prosaic diatribes, McFadden tries to create a vision of the beleaguered poet in a world of Kleenex and Scotch tape. The poet sees himself as the prophet of a new religion, "a new romance / that shines through the blackest cloud / that rolls around the world / eternally igniting the purest hearts." This romance will come to us in words that float to the ground on parachutes, says McFadden, and the poet's task is not to organize the airdrop; it is to dispose of those words that don't make it.... The survival of his words seems more the result of the randomness of the Grim Reaper than of the thoughtful, imaginative ordering of expression by the writer. Too high a premium is placed in this poem on a serendipitous similarity of sound either in the form of jingling sequences of end rhymes or in bouncing internal rhymes. The most one can say is that at times the poem does establish a tom-tom beat of like sounds that weave hypnotic spells of a minor sort. The effect brings to mind words such as "cute" or, at best, "clever" to describe the verbal juxtapositions that might occur in the midst of the spell. McFadden admits in a defensive postscript that this book is something of a departure from the sort of poetry he has written in the past, a poetry of the daily round with its ambiguous mixture of trivia and glory. This new direction does not seem at all promising. (p. 39)

> *John Cook, "New Directions and Old," in* The Canadian Forum, *Vol. LIX, No. 697, March, 1980, pp. 38-9.*

GEORGE BOWERING

One does not have to read far in McFadden's verse to find out that he has chosen to be a romantic poet in the line or company of Blake, Wordsworth, Shelley, Whitman, and Kerouac. That choice implies a vision relentlessly connecting metaphysical belief and detailed concern for the quotidian fate of the least powerful people in his society.... McFadden's poems abound with the crippled and ill-used, but the word that shows up most often when desire or appreciation is signalled is "perfect."

The ancient poets believed that perfection existed far from their world. Their Romantic successors wrote about the aspiration to find it, feeling its shadow in the hearts of human fools. Later it became a metaphor in the poets' store of figurative speech. The Moderns have mocked the idea, or rued the loss of its allure. But McFadden sees its gleam still, ready to put the lie to the Modernists' despair. He often follows the word "perfect" with the word "little," to be sure, but throughout his work one reads of perfection as a possibility, a hope, at least a wish—as the positive force that permits such a person as a working poet to seek a worthwhile alternative to the world of trash and murder.

McFadden quite agreeably adopts the Wordsworthian notion of human children arriving in the world as out of perfection, retaining the dream or memory of the divine state. Thus the maimed and oppressed are apt images for his major theme, the dialectic between metaphysical beauty and the trash culture. We see the crippled form divine, and the poet's mercy, pity, peace and love as hope for the redemption of this awful life.

That hope is a very important theme for the lives we have to live after the realized despair of the Modernist era. Can divine hope, back-lit as it is by twentieth-century irony, serve to clean up our trashy world? For a time in the late 'seventies McFadden seemed to be trying to abandon his struggle by entering into a series of long metaphysical poems. But recent short works discover him among the interior mountains of British Columbia, attached again, by personal disruption, to the earth, whose letters he eagerly stuffs into the nearest mailbox. (p. 39)

Somebody with the contemporary sense once did create out of McFadden's vignettes a Hamilton stage production called, I think, "The Collected World of David McFadden." And McFadden has sometimes presented his printed poems as one-page plays. But they are plays, originally, acted for us every day, and the poet presents himself as audience, sometimes interlocutor. He is the twentieth-century artist who allows a lot of light into the poem. He does not, as the normal American or Canadian academic poet does, seize upon a European statue and build a meditation to fill the space. He goes where the true mind bids him. "The open-ended universe opens in the middle," he wrote once, and the play we are watching is the play of air and light and mind around the figures thus discovered.

Such a mode of writing requires subtlety, and McFadden, though sometimes he gives in to a base pun, has from earliest plays shown a subtlety we pick up nicely if we remain tensile of fancy. For one thing, he has always had a deft sense of notation, as for instance in the poem **"God, The,"** in which he makes the most cunning trace of the mind among the quotidian. His is Whitman's ear (though seldom Whitman's mouth; and let me not suggest that I am citing Whitman as a maker of subtle prosody), listening to the world's parts making exclamations in his head. In his best short poems he likes to present narrations without obvious comment, in the faith that his reader also knows where poetry comes from. In fact he often seems to stop the poem before an expected punch line; Robert Frost with a witty pair of scissors. That is why academic Canadianists do not write about his work. (p. 40)

Sometimes the reader will feel herself invited to make conclusions but unsure that she really knows what the "product" should be. The compositional method that makes for such "confusion" or uncertainty is at the heart of McFadden's poetic. Often he will seem to offer implied comparisons of bits of information or events, giving only the implication of the comparison, not the spark that one wants to see leaping across the space between the details, the impulse, say, to settle the order implied in coincidence. It is as if, being the proofreader of God's pages, the poet should proffer only the clarity of the text, not an exegesis of it, not an interpretation. Borges, who proposes just such an occupation, puts it this way: "All poetry consists in feeling things as being strange, while all rhetoric

consists in thinking of them as quite common, as very obvious." You will have noted the aptness of the present participles there.

Thus it is that one comes away from an encounter with McFadden as one does from an encounter with his fellow artist, Greg Curnoe: unable, that is, to feel certain whether the man is determinedly innocent or guilefully parodic. McFadden acts as if fairies on tree-limbs are perfectly ordinary parts of the population, and as if a dog crossing a back yard is magic, as if universal world peace might be reported in tomorrow's paper, while a white hair in a mustache can arrest logic. "There is no difference between Grand Vistas and my everyday body." The world is filled with domestic numen. Thus it is important (see his poem on Thomas Hardy) to write every day, a little in a hurry or more on a long afternoon, to pay for, to use each day.

So to the mind eager for rhetorical instruction, the details seem to declare only their own significances, as in a painting, though in a syntax that we are trained to read for widening meaning. In one of McFadden's poems the colour red shows up all day, and it is with a little conditioned restlessness that the reader will find that the poet does not then make a generalization on the message carried by the colour, as countless university-journal poets would. In my favourite McFadden poem we find a (I almost said "perfect") sly instruction that reads both to and from the McFadden manner:

> Barbara, put down your flute
> and pay attention
>
> A motorcyclist in the high Andes
> has been forced off the road
> and is falling . . .
>
> Quick!
> Do something!

There is a relationship between the poet's decision not to draw conclusions (unless they be transparently preposterous ones) and his interest in little perfections. We cannot be familiar with the perfect, and interpretation makes for familiarity. We cannot be familiar with the perfect unless we are perfect ourselves, and being perfect we would be silent, being perfect we would be saints and therefore still wherever people are moving. In his poems McFadden is always seen as a regarder, moving. In his earliest poems he moves around Hamilton, its corner-stores and buses and bowling alleys. In his second phase he is seen travelling about Ontario, observing people at lake resorts or gas pumps. In more recent times he has taken the whole of Canada (and the odd vacation in the U.S.) as his subject, purposefully making books that collect his little plays set in Nova Scotia or British Columbia. . . . (pp. 40-3)

A name for McFadden's art, observation rather than interpretation, is collage, arguably (Donald Barthelme so argues) the main mode in our century. One critic has noted collage and its effect in the big-little novel, *The Great Canadian Sonnet,* with its left-hand pages by McFadden and right-hand drawings by Curnoe, and in *Letters From the Earth to the Earth,* through which the domestic poems share unnumbered pages with snaps from the McFadden family photo album. But the rest of his books are collage too. If one sets his little plays in a twentieth-century Canadian city such as Hamilton, one has chosen a stage that is itself a collage, where in walking down a street one walks by a Greek pizza parlour, then a Chinese cafe, then a Korean martial-arts gym.

For that reason, because of his interest in disjunction and mind-scatter, McFadden does not employ much rime in his poems (except, again, the obvious ones made for parodic purposes), because they would seem to suggest orderliness that proclaims authorial control of a world. The collage of the visual out there coming in seems to provide a more true imitation of the world so surprising in its multiplicity. Fragments of a city life, as they appear to eyes and ears—at first the poems seem unended or unworthy of beginning, and they do not bring the ease of repeated sounds. They are no more resolved than daily life. They are not a mesh but rather snapshots that form just a collage from what time (tempo) permits. A longer poem, **"Meaningless Midnight Musings"** (from *Intense Pleasure*) brazenly records whatever comes to the poet's consciousness, and admits throughout that a poem is being collected:

> A poem is a hex to prevent repetition.
> Freedom from the cycle of birth & rebirth.
> Her blouse was all undone. Her breasts
> smelled like butter.

From the poem emerges a poetic, not the other way round, emerges a belief that God edits your life and your job is type-setting, proofreading.

In the 'seventies we see in the poems more and more construction of scenes, fewer innocent snaps; the collages are synthesized of outside and inside. At the same time, the vision becomes darker, little lamb replaced by the hungry tiger. McFadden was reading Jung, and mining his dreams, presenting the latter as concretely as possible, trying to pass them off as plain-faced reportage. **"A Typical Canadian Family Visits Disney World"** gives a sense of the new direction in its bipolar title, and throughout illustrates it with a core of the mimetic wrapped in metaphorical exaggeration (elsewhere called a hyperbole) and irony. . . . (pp. 43-4)

"The Spoiled Brat," one of my favourite poems, in which the poet-narrator tricks the title character into a surprise decapitation, is presented as just the latest of many anecdotes about life in the McFadden house. It is delightfully and constrainedly an encasing of wicked emotional fantasy. Such comic malice reappears in **"Houseplants"** (Mrs. McFadden teaches their care), in which the poet tells of the nasty way that he took advantage of the discovery of the plants' sensitivity to human behaviour. In other poems a dream woman turns into a fanged monster, a selfish homeowner dies of shock beside his invaded swimming pool, a stone talks incessantly of its decapitation, enough to make one yearn for ditties of no tone. Yet the sentences are simply declarative, so that we are convinced that their author is yet as he was, staying away from interpretation, quietly and candidly collaging the days. Collage is much more interesting than simile for just that reason, because the latter leads the reader to respond: well, everyone's entitled to his opinion. Opinion? says McFadden, "but I am fearful / of being in error."

It is right that we should still see the enthusiastic, encomiastic young poet, and the gathering of skill, never at the expense of early poetic, through the enclosure of darkness that makes itself appear more authentic on the outside edges of that early light. McFadden has grown to the stature that he displays because he began so openly; he was not just another youngster who equated poetry with the ability to contemplate violence with smug horror.

But if McFadden's plays of experience show a pain that was only posited in his plays of innocence, it is not because he has changed his ideas on what is true. Blake's "Songs of Experience" do not cancel his "Songs of Innocence" any more than the New Testament cancels Moses. We have to die, and we have to grow up, and growing up includes being able to read through newspaper stories instead of just from top to bottom. In his poems of the 'seventies McFadden does not so much speak of his dream of changing history through poems, but rather announces that he does not mind the trash invasion because poetry's work goes on, "the work / of simple people learning how to sing / with the help of the Fairies," so "if you believe as I believe / & have seen strange things you've feared to speak of / please write me care of my publisher." Now that request is loaded with mockery, mainly because the publisher is there in between, but if one did not care, why bother?

Whereas the McFadden over twenty used to speak in Emersonian terms of "error," the McFadden over thirty holds his eyes and mouth open to cruelty:

> for there are mysterious people in the world
> who steal children & kill them
> & stuff them in holes in the ground

And he tells of it with his habituating comic syntax and structure. Now even children partake in what seems natural, inborn cruelty:

> The crazy castrated cat called Al
> sat crouched in front of a brick wall
> as if about to leap
> > through it
> while slowly a crowd of kids
> gathered to watch & jeer
> hoping to see him crack his skull

What McFadden is giving us by his simplicity of view is not a guileful picture of an innocent abroad in a sometimes crummy world—in this later period he offers quite a number of poems that show the lyricist as poorly behaved, too. But he wants to stay away from the narrowed observation of the confessional poets, who tell their readers why they feel as if it is an unpleasant life. McFadden's aim, admittedly futile but gallant for all that, is to compose like the world, not its observer:

> To write involuntarily
> as mountains are formed
> as ice grows on peaks
>
> as forests clothe the slopes
> directly
> > instead of only after
> hasty study of the proper methods
> of producing work merely mimetic
> of the involuntary mind

When he seems to do that his audiences at readings enjoy themselves. McFadden's public readings are more enjoyable than most because they provide relief. Even when he tells stories of murder, evisceration, childhood agonies, listeners smile at one another, laugh till they fall down, nod their sad heads in full agreement. They are hearing a total human person, a cynic who finds life pleasurable, an ascetic who fondly shares his appetites. They are listening to a man who reminds them how two horses stand together in a springtime field, but does not claim that his observation sets him apart. It is as if he is saying: look, the earth gives you all this and it is too easy to forget it. He acknowledges heroes, but no great heroes. He candidly revels in his ability to make poems but he does not ask anyone to interpret his little plays into works of high drama. In one of his earlier poems he said he was happy to recognize his poet-self as "a minor God, but nevertheless God."

Therefore of use. In the 'sixties he averred: "There's nothing for man but art and earth / and no hope but in seeing." The first line echoes medieval division of the world, and the second is a terse and handsome reason for making art in the post-existentialist age. Of his poems from that period the young McFadden advised, "Take them in loaves as for lunch." That is a good line, because it combines the humble with legitimate Christian pretention. It assembles the poet's convictions—bread and poetry are sacramental, but bread is bread, after all, modest daytime fuel.

Thus the title of the book introduced by those three lines: *Letters From the Earth to the Earth.* Loaves, letters. The title refers not just to poems (or to Mark Twain's position), but to human lives as letters that are delivered to their original address. That early, and still today, McFadden is a comic metaphysician, but the working poet reminds us where we live, what our poor bodies are made of and the messages they carry in their transit. Of "poemology," a mystery to his ordinary wife, he wrote, "It grows under her feet / & lines her stomach."

"Infinity needs you, son," he reminded himself then, but the statement is an echo of a line from a western movie, in which a frontier town is trying to recruit a marshall. If John Clare had had a sense of humour he could have been a wonderful early David McFadden. Note the return in these two lines: "the vacuum at the end of the imagination / the amazing ground of laughter." But it is essential to a reading of McFadden that one feel sadness and terror downstairs while one is laughing at one's face in the bathroom mirror. His great preoccupation, children, live in a world of beauty and love, and are closer to death than to poetry. Poetry is an activity derived from experience, *is* experience; it feeds on the innocence of children, keeping itself alive, like a man living on blood transfusions. See **"A Jewel Box"** or **"To Elizabeth Ann Fraser,"** and try to keep laughing. All the poems are indeed love letters to the world, as natural as eating and peeing, but they carry the message of conscious care and the knowledge of probable destruction: "the flower of the world / bullet-riddled."

But as the earth continues to make flowers and children, it does so without mawkishness or misgivings; so one continues to make poems, knowing them to be mortal from the beginning, not knowing how the world is going to use them. There is no market research save in the trash business. "Keep going God," wrote McFadden in the late 'sixties. "You've / got the right idea." Despite the trashing of Vietnam and the shooting of Martin Luther King, sheer plod makes plow down sillion shine. Maybe.

In the context of this kind of place, the best way to read David McFadden's world is to read through it all. You will find "little perfections" from time to time, and they will accumulate, spots in time that happen so often that you will entertain the notion that we *can* be saved. You will see that McFadden often admits a desire to write the perfect poem, but fills his verses with the unavoidable signs of mortality under this earth's veil. Anticipating eternity, he is haunted by time, past and future, his own and the world's. The statue of a knight fashioned of dried plums is a criticism of marble statues, but it is also not food. Cats, dogs, turtles and budgies are invited into the poems to be with the people there. If the world is space, and living a life is time, then David McFadden is, like so many Canadians,

a travel poet. But unlike the others, he does not wind up sitting back in his chair to look and see whether you got the point. In the later and longer poems especially, there is a word that becomes more important than "perfect." It is "and."

"And" is not a word that leads one to dance around a figure; it is, in terms of meaning, concerning the relationship of events in the world, a letter that will never get down to "yours truly," quite correct. It does not allow a "therefore." In the long poem, *The Poet's Progress,* McFadden, on entering the second half of his life, examines his process as a poet, as the formerly neglected arises, and says of his career, as Yeats might: "we / can never know our warm, leafy / surroundings but can only be them." Not imitators but constant creators of the world. (pp. 44-7)

George Bowering, "Proofing the World: The Poems of David McFadden," in Canadian Poetry: Studies, Documents, Reviews, *No. 7, Fall-Winter, 1980, pp. 38-47.*

DOUGLAS BARBOUR

Of David McFadden's three books [*On the Road Again, I Don't Know,* and *A New Romance*], two are small books containing longer poems while the third, *On the Road Again,* is an entertaining collection of shorter McFaddenisms. The wittily allusive title evokes the kind of joyful energy McFadden's best poems generate. Whether he's noticing the invitations or mating rituals of trees, talking to Jesus or some northern workers, discoursing on angels or Hsü Fu, or just enjoying the scenery with friends or family, McFadden projects a persona wholly engaged in the processes of living & loving the life he leads. If his mind often leads him to odd & often fantastical perceptions, well that's just the way things go in the day-to-day life of a working poet. 'There has to be something mysterious about a poem. / No matter how simple it may be / there has to be something about it / that's impossible to understand / that makes you sit there wondering.' Rather prosaic, that, but it points to a key element in McFadden's poetic: his willingness to let the mysterious into his poems, whether it's the white hat 'glowing with a life of its own' which he knows he doesn't own even though a strange man insists he does or the face found in Egypt who now sits on his bookshelf in Hamilton & tells him every nine minutes or so, 'My body was eaten by dogs.'

Not all these poems are equally successful, & some of them fail to achieve the kind of mysteriousness he claims is necessary for a good poem; as well, because he chooses to write such an open lyrical form, he ofttimes gives us somewhat flaccid lines. But at their best McFadden's poems bespeak the magic which participates in the most ordinary of lives, the glow of something mysterious that will lighten the day of all who perceive it. . . . If McFadden is not always as complexly good as he is [in **"St. Lawrence of the Cross"**], he's always aware that such poems are what we reach for, & in *On the Road Again* he hits the target more often than not.

I Don't Know contains two long poems, the title poem & the shorter **"1940."** Both are fine examples of McFadden's postmodern Romantic poetic, cutting every which way through the possibilities his mind can perceive & ramble over, suddenly shifting from one level or theme or form of discourse to another, & filled with a gentle humane enjoyment of the world that is.

Poetry thrives when language is allowed to flow
naturally like a river, brook or creek
and in order to initiate and maintain that flow

the poet must stand aside, keep himself
completely out of it, and once that flow begins
should it wish to carry him or her with it
he or she should not resist.

Though not the finest writing in the book, these lines speak directly to McFadden's purpose as a poet. In fact neither poem quotes easily; the 'flow' is best experienced in the whole composition—basically because there's so much happening in the language & the history (histories) it bears. **"I Don't Know"** moves easily among **"Khubla Khan,"** the Canadian Shield, Ezra Pound & the poet's family. It & **"1940"** (in which he says, 'I wanted to write a poem about the year I was born / and I wanted to keep myself completely out of it') argue McFadden's poetic while beautifully exemplifying its possible successes. They're rich poems, & *I Don't Know* is a fine little book.

In his aforeword to *A New Romance,* which won the 1979 CBC Long Poem Competition, McFadden says it 'represents a remarkable breakthrough into a purer and more authentic level of [his] writing life.' He feels that this new poem transcends 'the more fundamental and immediate concerns' of the earlier books, including the other two under review here. 'The earlier work,' he says, 'always had to be propped up like houses on a flood plain. The props were the conventions of ordinary reality, the conventions of the here and now.' These & other statements in the afterword insist on the mythic & transcendental nature of the imaginative breakthrough McFadden feels the poem represents & lead inevitably to the question: is it so? Well, yes it is. *A New Romance* is not perhaps quite so different from McFadden's other recent poetry as he hints, but if that poetry is moving towards the kind of ecstatic good times *A New Romance* fully expresses, I have to agree with the poet that the latest poem pushes further into glorious *mystery* than anything else he's ever done. Which is not to say that it's hard to get into; just the opposite. It's a joy to read, 'a true work of art lacking nothing / but preconceived notions of what / constitutes a poem,' & somehow McFadden manages to encompass just about everything in it (or rather to convince you that 'the poem' is now capable of encompassing everything, & here are just a few examples of what that means).

At any rate, there's a lot of joy here, though joy won in the recognition, the experience, of all that batters at its possibility. The poem is moving, it's funny, it's human, it's utterly of the world-spirit, & it's tremendously alive in its language, in its awareness of how poetry is fashioned 'from the twenty-six compartments of the heart.' Language & what it can lead us to is one of the core experiences the poem explores. The insistence of repetition has its place here as McFadden circles his concerns, opens them up a bit more each time he touches them, explores their reality & their interactions (I should mention that 'the poet' is present only in the third person, as is everyone else in the poem: it manages to break free completely from the lyric ego, & this is important), so that as you read you're drawn in to the various kinds of mystery **"a new romance"** insists you inhabit. I've called McFadden a Romantic poet, & this poem especially is as Blakean as they come. . . . I can't speak of everything in this wonderful poem, the extraordinary tropes, the gentle comedy of the images, the joyful sense of a loving universe reflecting the possibilities of the human way. They're all there, & *A New Romance* is a poem to celebrate. (pp. 130-33)

> *Douglas Barbour, in a review of "On the Road Again," "I Don't Know," and "A New Romance," in* The Fiddlehead, *No. 124, Winter, 1980, pp. 129-33.*

KENNETH SHERMAN

[*A New Romance*] is a religious book, sharing affinities with the pantheistic works of Wordsworth and the spirit of Zen. In his preface to the *Lyrical Ballads,* Wordsworth tells us he wishes to convey feelings and notions "in simple and unelaborated expressions," while in a note *"To the reader"* which concludes *A New Romance,* McFadden states his poem strives for *"simplicity,"* that the work for him is a *"breakthrough into a purer and more authentic level of my writing life."* It is interesting to note that the most conspicuous word in *A New Romance* is "pure." It, or some variation of it, occurs at least nine times in the poem and twice in the concluding note. Wordsworth also had an obsession with the word ("pure heart," "purest thoughts," "a purer nature"), and in his longing for simplicity condemned the poetic affectation of certain of his contemporaries "as they separate themselves from the sympathies of men, and indulge in arbitrary and capricious habits of expression." So McFadden, in a review published in *Books in Canada,* criticizes Pier Giorgio Di Cicco, a poet of the Neo-Surrealist school, for his "enthralling images" with no power "to enthrall us," complaining there is "no awesome *purity* longing to be born" (emphasis added). And further, in his note to the book under review, states: "In *A New Romance* that which separates human being from human being has been dispersed."

In general, both Wordsworth and McFadden share a generous sense of humanism. To achieve this there is the concern for simple, unelaborate diction. Then there is the love for nature. *A New Romance* is spattered with daffodils, palmettos, kangaroos, and "the innocence of fresh blossoms." According to Romantic theory, if one is after the universal, the humble, as opposed to the particular and perhaps ostentatious, then one heads for the lakes and forests. Also in true Romantic fashion, McFadden sees man as mirroring nature and the universal values. Wordsworth tells us the poet considers man "as naturally the mirror of the fairest and most interesting properties of nature" and in McFadden's book the heart is "a highly polished perfect mirror." In many ways, for NEW ROMANCE one may read NEO-ROMANTIC.

But more interesting than the similarities, are the differences between the two poets' visions. Wordsworth is a poet forever looking backward. His is the more traditional Western vision where man falls from the garden into adulthood, sin, and alienation. The state of grace associated with childhood can only be recaptured at select moments. It is precisely this loss of grace and the attempt to regain it that gives Wordsworth's poetry its sense of tragedy, its nobility, its moral power if you will.

On the other hand, McFadden, in *A New Romance,* seems to be there, to have lost the loss. What falls continually throughout the poem are words, falling from heaven with tiny parachutes, falling like grace for the poet to pick and choose from and make his new romance where the Fall is no more, where the joy of childhood is a continuum in a stream of timelessness. (pp. 224-25)

As in Zen, *A New Romance* is largely concerned with breaking down the subject/object, mind/body dichotomy. No matter how much Wordsworth loved nature, there is always the sense in his work (central to his Romantic theory of the poet's individualism) that he is separate from nature and that the split is something to be perpetually overcome. Zen and McFadden do not see it that way. In section I of the book, we are told "the poet melted like a chocolate bar / in the earth's mouth" and, in section XII, ". . . we are indivisible" from "nature's latest inventions." There is no separation between individuals, nor between humanity and nature. In section VI, McFadden grows even more explicit, praising the innocence of palmettos that

> . . . lack
> even the simplest form of consciousness
> and never mourn their lack
> or even notice it
> . . . .
> for there are forms of consciousness independent
> of the relationship between echo and ego
> and to be truly human does not require
> that we find nothing but ourselves in all we see.

Despite the fact that such theorizing goes against the very grain of Zen which abhors explanation, despite the fact that the language is terribly prosaic, still it provides us with an essential key as to what McFadden is after. Put simply (and I concede probably too simply), Zen Buddhism maintains that our troubles start when we form a subjective idea of self based upon memories, expectations, cultural hand-me-downs. The bind of self-consciousness comes about when we grow aware of the conflict between this idea of ourselves (ego) and the concrete feelings of our true selves. To give up this conflict is to relinquish the ego, to see oneself as inseparable from the external world thus ending the strife between subjective and objective. Thus the poet of *A New Romance* calls for ". . . a mind as pure and neat / as a fresh box of Kleenex . . . / unless we're content to continue writing / egocentric, unilluminated verse." The poet's hope is that ". . . the earth regains the calm / it lost with the birth of ego." As he most unequivocally puts it in section XIII, "Oh what bliss, to be free / of human qualities!", since in Zen, to be free of human qualities is paradoxically a way of becoming most human.

Besides my minor complaint against the intrusion of explanatory phrases and moralistic directives like those quoted above which only detract from the poetry, my major objection is to the cleanliness and purity (pure as a box of Kleenex!) of McFadden's vision. This separates him even from Zen where, by the way, farting is allowed. (pp. 226-27)

I also wonder how in tune McFadden is with our "Age of Uncertainty" (that phrase appearing more and more like a euphemism for something much darker and more ominous). In section XII of the book, McFadden gives us his "rules for writing":

> Be natural, be affectionate

Affectionate? What would Pope or Pound say about that? Pound, after all, had harsh things to say about the Romantics and lived to prove that a Fascist can write exceptional verse: one of the discomfiting facts of the twentieth century that McFadden hasn't noticed. He grins on his lotus leaf as the *zeitgeist* whirls by. (p. 228)

> *Kenneth Sherman, "At the Centre of the Wheel," in* Essays on Canadian Writing, *No. 20, Winter, 1980-81, pp. 224-29.*

DAVID MacFARLANE

McFadden enters the genre [of travel writing] strangely. "I vowed to paint a life-size map of each of the Great Lakes with the flaming brush of my crocus-coloured Volkswagen van." Hardly the stuff of Stanley's search for Livingstone. Mc-

Fadden's home base is Hamilton, Ont., and he and his family are never more than a few days from Upper James Street. Still, his books [*A Trip Around Lake Erie* and *A Trip Around Lake Huron*]—part journal, part novel, part diary—come close to establishing themselves as something of importance to Canadian writing. (p. 28)

It is difficult at times to know how intentional is McFadden's wit, how innocent his naivety, how casual his informality, and how unassuming his design. It is difficult, for instance, to know what led him to write his *Trips*. He's a difficult writer to get a handle on, and one senses that he enjoys that aspect of himself as much as anything.

Both *A Trip Around Lake Erie* and *A Trip Around Lake Huron* are curiosities certainly, but they also have qualities that make them something more. McFadden takes on the ordinariness of a family motor-camping trip—most of which takes place on the American side of the lakes in question—and unapologetically tells us about it. The result is quite unique, and here and there one is reminded of the sly clarity of Heinrich Böll: "We stopped at a K-Mart in Monroe, Michigan. Joan wanted to get some camping supplies. The place was crowded with Americans. I kept wondering if people could tell we were foreigners." The irony is immediately obvious—a Canadian in the States, a writer in suburbia, is not the usual stuff of travel writing. This is not Bruce Chatwin [*In Patagonia*] in a town at the end of the world. But McFadden's sense of that irony maintains the distance required between artist and model. . . . Home and away are not very far apart for McFadden, but he is often funny and perceptive enough to keep them distinct.

There is, however, a great deal that is wrong with the *Trips*, and the fact that there is a great deal that is right makes McFadden's lapses all the more unfortunate. Things start to go awry whenever McFadden loses confidence in his wit and observations, and feels compelled to tell us that really, in case we hadn't noticed, he is a stranger in a strange land, a Chatwin in Patagonia. His references to writing, poetry, Canadian literature, and his own career are obtrusive and clumsy. They are included in order to let us know that he's really not your regular Volkswagen camper, but that job has already been done in more interesting and subtler ways. And things literary are not the only subjects McFadden misuses. He can pin an American personality down with the skill of Nabokov, and then descend to the most self-righteous *and redundant* anti-Americanisms. The books lose their peculiar edge when McFadden ceases to be a dove among pigeons and pretends to be a cat.

If any blame can be cast in failings of this kind, it would seem that McFadden was ill-served by his editors. If a more ruthless pencil had forced McFadden to clarify his intentions, if someone had forced him to defend himself page by page, or had only said, "You don't need this. You've already said that," these two books would have been remarkable, and their comparison to a book as excellent as *In Patagonia* would not be eccentric. As it is, *A Trip Around Lake Erie* and *A Trip Around Lake Huron* are only the precursors of the very good book I hope McFadden will someday write. (pp. 28-9)

> *David MacFarlane, "On/Off/Set," in* Books in Canada, *Vol. 10, No. 7, August-September, 1981, pp. 28-9.*

JUDITH FITZGERALD

The first two volumes of David McFadden's Great Lakes Pentalogy possess their own kind of magic and magnetism. Both

A Trip around Lake Erie and *A Trip around Lake Huron* embrace the smaller things in life, illuminating the everyday, but don't be fooled. They also articulate very precise statements concerning the larger issues. Those issues are never obscured, even though McFadden almost playfully undercuts them in continual succession, in much the same way that the waters of Erie and Huron play along their coastlines. The individual waves may be various and unique, but the overall pattern is a consistent one.

Anyone who has experienced difficulty appreciating the insight and depth of this very talented writer in his earlier works . . . cannot fail to be thoroughly entertained by these flowing accounts of a Hamiltonian family's excursions through Great Lake territory. Both books make great reading. They function on several levels, from the travelogue to the moral treatise, and they're so delightfully written that any kind of reading yields beneficial results.

Despite the publisher's claims, McFadden's family is anything but typical, either in the American or in the Canadian sense of the word. Does a typical Canadian family have a dog named Bruce that spills his recently digested dinner on a cabin floor while the McFaddens visit one of David's closest friends? Or does typical daughter, Jennifer, almost drown because an equally typical American lifeguard was sleeping on the job?

Perhaps McFadden in his quirky accounts of incidents and conversation is simply pointing out that there's a vast difference between typical in Canadian vocabulary and typical in an American sense, taking care to allude to even the basic differences in spelling and alphabets. . . .

McFadden's anti-American sentiments have been overstated. Admittedly, he is not kind to our neighbours to the south, but our neighbours to the south have never been very kind to us, a fact that McFadden continually makes public, in [his] observations. . . .

Both [*A Trip around Lake Erie* and *A Trip around Lake Huron*] are realistic and beautifully concentrated accounts of the way these trips must have been. Along the way, the reader also receives a lot of McFadden's personal philosophy and viewpoints. Art, poetry and Americans continuously crop up in the strangest context. His chapter titles deserve to be remembered for their own poetry (The Smorgasbord of Consciousness, Richard Nixon in Drag, How to Admire Posh Yachts without Envy).

McFadden makes popular culture ominous and mythical in one sweeping gesture. Both novels capture the local color/colour of materialistic manifestations in both countries. Our land is separate from theirs because of our maple leaf on the McDonald's signs, our Dominion Stores, etc.

McFadden has allowed himself the dubious luxury of being the recorder and participant in some of the more jaded aspects of our culture. He functions as the post-modern metropolitan Byronic hero. Here, at the core of both works, is the egoistic rebel, sampling, discarding, never openly damning, but judgemental all the same. His intense pleasures, passions, delights and condemnations are liberally included in both works. Most startling are his almost incommunicable sadness and his equally unrelenting sense of guilt.

There is much in *Huron* and *Erie* that goes beyond the scope of a review; only the attentive reader can savour their delicious plays on language and manipulations of ordinary situations. They chronicle McFadden's adventures in a refreshing way,

proving definitely that Canada is anything but the cultural, emotional and physical wasteland that contemporary critics claim it to be. He deftly shows us that good writers can illuminate the magical, magnetic, curious and mystical aspects of any landscape, merely by "seeing" and "engaging" in it.

Finally, a great deal of insight, sensitivity, pain and joy have obviously gone into the construction of these novels. Their unifying theme, at bottom, is the idea of the quest, and McFadden's journeying is not unlike the medieval knight errant's. He goes forward to redress wrongs committed against himself, his family, his country, every man. It is here that those larger issues mentioned earlier come into focus.

A trip with McFadden and his family around a lake is exactly what it says it is: a trip, an inward and highly controlled tour through both an interior and exterior landscape. McFadden is a master of language and ambiguity in the same breath. Both novels prove this beyond a doubt.

> *Judith Fitzgerald, "An Amazing Trip around David McFadden," in* Quill and Quire, *Vol. 48, No. 2, February, 1982, p. 42.*

ROSEMARY AUBERT

David McFadden is an award-winning and much-published Canadian poet. And judging from *My Body Was Eaten by Dogs,* a selection of his poems . . . , McFadden's work is well worthy of the attention it has received. . . .

The main tool of McFadden's craft is artlessness. His poems move with an apparent spontaneity that is so skillful and convincing that the reader will accept as poetry even a running account of things as they are occurring at the moment the poem is being written. . . .

Another of McFadden's skills is his power of implication. He is neither teacher nor preacher. He merely sets down what he sees as the significant facts of the case, though a strong imagination and a caring sensitivity lie behind the deceptively objective reportage.

The poems of this book are divided into two sections. Poems of The Sixties are characterized by their depiction of a charming domesticity that is capable of projecting the poet beyond his safe and happy home into a consideration of wider realms of human experience. Poems of The Seventies are what Bowering calls "darker". Violence and ugliness occasionally enter the picture. But so does a new strength of vision and craft.

> *Rosemary Aubert, in a review of "My Body Was Eaten by Dogs," in* Quill and Quire, *Vol. 48, No. 3, March, 1982, p. 68.*

SHIRLEY NEUMAN

What *can* be done with the conventions of autobiographical and documentary forms is one of the adventures of David McFadden's *A Trip around Lake Huron,* the second of a projected five-volume *Trips around the Great Lakes.* Notepad on the dash, wife Joan beside him, daughters Jennifer and Alison in the back seat and dog Bruce in the rear of the camper-van, McFadden sets off around Lake Huron on a trip he will turn into a witty "documentary novel" of middle-class America, encased in Winnebagos, on the move back to nature. McFadden places himself and, through himself, his "typically Canadian family" at the centre of his account in a self-confessed egocentrism which, like the position of the camera lens, limits *what* he documents and the angle from which it is seen. The result is situation comedy: it rains; the children clamour for amusement parks and David and Joan try to avoid them; Joan gets angry and thinks poems impractical; Bruce gets ill and bites Jennifer; fellow campers are noisy or dirty or friendly or aggressive; Americans generalize about Canadians and the McFaddens about Americans with about equal prejudice. But as this easy-going, occasionally fumbling, and whimsical narrator (given to rowdy behaviour in restaurants and embarrassment in public washrooms) proves tenacious of his *own* perceptions and very ironic, his "documentary" acquires unusual restrictions and possibilities.

Each "chapter" records an encounter, a stretch of road, a scene, an event witnessed or experienced—records it carefully, paying equal attention to every physical detail, to each nuance of emotion, but never going beyond what McFadden himself noted. The style initially seems journalistic: direct in its statement, impartial in its emphasis, denuded of metaphor. But we soon realize that McFadden's humour and whimsy nudge us out of the passivity "documentary" so often induces (for example, of empty-handed fishermen: "And under the watery flatness we could hear huge schools of fish, giggling"). Each chapter comes with a "title" printed in bold type as a marginal gloss which reinterprets the narrative. The effect is much like that of some of McFadden's poems where a flatly stated observation acquires significance by a sudden turn in the last line. Here the titles stand poised against the descriptions and comment ironically on them; by emphasizing one detail, they alter the significance of all the other details. The act of interpreting and the act of observing illuminate each other in a binary structure that keeps both meaningful and each distinct from the other. McFadden's final restriction of "documentary" is that both acts should signify: they may signify in themselves; the fantasies or memories they trigger may signify; the present act of writing may make them signify. Observation and interpretation become more real by having been alertly, lovingly, exactly seen, thought about, written.

McFadden frequently refers to Greg Curnoe and particularly to his painting of Highway 401. The attraction of Curnoe's subject to the author of **"Travellin' Man,"** *On the Road Again* and *Trips around the Great Lakes* is obvious. But the road and Curnoe's painting fascinate him in other ways. In *Lake Erie* and *Lake Huron* the road becomes a principle of contiguity; it emphasizes position over connection. And just as the objects along Curnoe's 401, because they are presented as contiguous, not connective, and because they are looked at intensely, become super-real, so too do the scenes noted by McFadden. We suddenly notice the hallucinatory quality of a world in which there are girls without arms, men who give away nineteen wheelchairs, husbands who beat wives in public campsites (and wives who defend their husbands' right to do so), lifeguards who insist dogs be kept on a leash and let children drown. The sight that, because of its strangeness or the intensity of its perception, seems like a hallucination merges with the effect of poisonous mushrooms, becomes contiguous with premonitions, dreams, memories, time-warps and déja-vus in a "fabulous" project. In this narrative in which, finally, it is the narrator's *consciousness* that is being recorded so matter-of-factly through his perceptions, things take on new possibilities. Where coincidences were present but not omnipresent in *A Trip around Lake Erie,* during which the Canadian McFaddens accidentally met the American McFaddens, *A Trip around Lake Huron* asserts coincidence as a second binary principle of the

projected series (the dedications of the first two volumes are to two different men who died differently in different provinces, both accidentally, both on January 3, 1979). Coincidence asserts the primacy of contiguity over continuity, of inexplicable meaning over meaningful explanation. Its perception is one of the ways McFadden makes what he observes super-real. The reader is asked to stand back with the writer, to see with accuracy, with concentration, with pleasure. Out of such seeing comes vision. (pp. 127-28)

Shirley Neuman, "Signifying Self," in Canadian Literature, *No. 92, Spring, 1982, pp. 125-28.*

BRUCE WHITEMAN

My Body Was Eaten By Dogs: Selected Poems of David Mc-Fadden is full of the banal details and remarkable coincidences of everyday life, as though a *Bouvard et Pécuchet* had been written by a man with a heart of gold rather than an enlarged spleen. His poems all take for granted that "there is no difference between Grand Vistas / and my everyday body." Nothing is too ordinary or unremarkable for his interest, and thus for his poem-making. He is the *naif* alive to the common and finding in it the extraordinary that only children and visionaries are able to see; but unlike Blake (for example), it is not the world to be found in a grain of sand that interests him, but the fact that there are so many grains of sand in the world and they are all worthy of our attention. . . .

It is appropriate that McFadden should publish a selected poems at this time. His work has recently taken a new path, away from the poem filled with the particulars of day-to-day life, and into a series of long philosophical books. In his introduction to *My Body Was Eaten By Dogs,* George Bowering suggests that this development is rather in the nature of an aberration than a permanent change. But in the postscript to *A New Romance,* published in 1979, McFadden himself noted that his friends had predicted an eventual return to the "reality with a vengeance" of his earlier style, though he himself felt that his new work was finally engaging the poetic concerns with which he had always wanted to deal. Time alone will reveal whether McFadden or Bowering is right. In the meantime, the selected volume allows us to gauge McFadden's work of roughly twenty years. It is *sui generis,* for the most part, inimitable and delightful, and yet unselfconscious to a degree that it manages to rescue all of our lives from the lie of squalor and lack of transcendence. . . . (p. 153)

Bruce Whiteman, "Some Books of Canadian Poetry in 1981," in Journal of Canadian Studies/Revue d'etudes canadiennes, *Vol. 17, No. 2, Summer, 1982, pp. 150-54.*

GARY LENHART

My Body Was Eaten by Dogs has its charms, the title obviously not being one of them. The mind of David McFadden is vigorous, funny, and even at times enlightening. The music of his verse is flatly prosaic; he seems most comfortable with a line that stretches to between eleven and seventeen syllables. Although sometimes given to dreams (as in the title poem), no matter how fantastic the story, the tone of his report is matter of fact.

The book divides into two parts, "The Sixties" and "The Seventies," and the first wins by several laps. McFadden's beginnings as a poet reminds of Tom Veitch, who collected poems under a similarly ludicrous title, *Death College*. Veitch has been described as naif, and one might deal with McFadden likewise. Both poets, however, have the principal materials to hand at the start: wit, spirited vocabulary, and an intensity that must manifest itself comically—humorless it would be painful to bear, too awful for art. The naive tag probably arises from their striking rejection of inherited ways of rounding off poems. They're in fact terrific prose writers who've strayed over into poetry, and you can't figure if they've any idea what they're doing there. Dick Tracy seems more pertinent as influence than John Milton. These are cartoons sketched not like funny comics but with the hard edges of serial adventures. McFadden's work lacks the lucidity and harsh emanations of Veitch's, but in exchange there is a reflective, earnest modesty that enables him to deal tenaciously with the domestic. I don't want to confuse wisdom with melancholia; the verges of McFadden's portraits are sometimes predictably sentimental. . . . The vignette [**"Journey to Love"**] is powerful, clear, and there's not much superfluous (only the unfortunate "sipping at her sweetness"). Concern with form and language is incidental to anecdote, but the anecdote arrests. In other poems, such as **"Sunday Afternoon at Home,"** McFadden rambles on about his kids, the chores, the weather at a football game over 400 miles away. The sketch of impertinence is too convincing, the mimesis wears us down. The narrative is captured by the banter of the omnipresent media. Imagination and will are spent just starting up. We've too many bright adolescents about to be impressed by an ability to chatter like Johnny Carson.

In the poems of "The Seventies" we see McFadden move from the disarming directness that carries the early efforts and attempt to deal with the question, why poetry? Lamentably, he decides for predictable closure instead of profounder interrogations, more attention to music. Not being much of a homebody myself, I admire with undiluted nostalgia his refusal to leave Hamilton, Ontario, but am disappointed by his failure to root in, wait for his restlessness to lead him to decamp for more fertile ground. The disappointing longer efforts collapse into an indolence that costs freshness. One of the best poems of "The Seventies," **"How I Came to Understand Irving Layton,"** a snarl at "puerile Sunday School / steeltrap Christianity," succeeds because we agree, not because we're compelled. (pp. 21-2)

> *Gary Lenhart, in a review of "My Body Was Eaten by Dogs: Selected Poems," in* The American Book Review, *Vol. 5, No. 4, May-June, 1983, pp. 21-2.*

DANIEL JALOWICA

This collection of short stories written between 1965 and 1977 [*Animal Spirits: Stories to Live By*] unblushingly invades the suburban living-rooms, taverns, and greasy spoons of Hamilton, Ontario—McFadden's native city—in an attempt to penetrate the mysteries of Everyday Life in the Twentieth Century (the title of the book's opening story). Evoking sadness, hilarity, desolation, and hope by rapid turns, McFadden's narratives plumb the depths of suburban ennui and bogus intimacy, investigate puppy love's stirrings, and set the record straight about the first moon landings—all in deceptively uncomplicated prose.

Many of McFadden's characters, imbedded in a carefully constructed constellation of sights and sounds, appear to be sleepwalkers at the mercy of ubiquitous, soul-destroying parasites.

He leaves it to the reader to recognize that we are all similarly afflicted.

[Greg] Curnoe's jocose and adventurous pen-and-ink drawings fuse effectively with McFadden's stories to create a provocative ambiguity that opens up new meanings and possibilities in *Animal Spirits*.

"The obscurest epoch is today," wrote Robert Louis Stevenson. David McFadden, with his peculiar, vivifying outlook and bounteous sense of humour, long ago launched a guerrilla assault on our own.

> *Daniel Jalowica, in a review of "Animal Spirits: Stories to Live By," in* Quill and Quire, *Vol. 49, No. 8, August, 1983, p. 33.*

LUCILLE KING-EDWARDS

Reaching back in time, David McFadden [in *Animal Spirits: Stories to Live By*] has come up with a collection of stories from what one might call his early period, the late 1960s and early '70s. (There are two exceptions in the collection that date from the late '70s.) Early McFadden: a touch of whimsy, even madness, to leaven his "suburbs of a typical Canadian city." One wonders why McFadden has not yet won the Stephen Leacock award for his books of humour; they are dark, but then so were Leacock's.

Animal Spirits is set in Hamilton, Ontario, and the stories abound with descriptions of McFadden's native city. They are not, however, all of a piece. The first three conform to the title: a cat with its head crushed like a lightbulb, a dog's lover, and a man who metamorphoses into a cat, all within the commonplace setting of suburban Toronto. The other stories, except for the last, are an on-going saga of one Brownie Bananas, closely related, one would guess, to David McFadden—they share certain biographical facts, and certainly Hamilton.

McFadden's pursuit of the little guy mentality, which takes us through convolutions of sentimentality, sex, egotism, and hard facts—the phone booths are gone from the corner by the ex-Terminal Hotel—is often touching, sometimes dull, and now and then depressing as we see ourselves as Brownie the guilty owner of a beautiful but stolen Indian head-dress, Brownie underpricing a cripple selling Christmas cards, or Brownie praising, then disparaging, his profession of proofreader. There is much that is gratuitous in the Brownie stories, and they lack the wild Bunuel quality of the opening and closing stories of the book, as well as the deft modulations that one finds in McFadden's earlier lake books: *A Trip Around Lake Erie* and *A Trip Around Lake Huron*. It is at the point where he weds realism and surrealism that he is at his best in this volume.

Animal Spirits can't be discussed only in the light of McFadden's stories, for what makes it a truly wonderful book to own are the drawings by Greg Curnoe. . . . Curnoe's visual humour enhances the text while often adding new dimensions, as the drawings, although captioned from the text, don't always follow the plot of the stories. . . . In this play and dissonance between story and picture McFadden and Curnoe have added much to the humour and depth of the book. Brownie, as he is pictured by Curnoe complete with idiot grin, will never dim from the memory. Even so, this collection of stories is definitely not every Canadian's bottle of beer; they are as eccentric as they are sound.

Although he often dips his pen in the stream of prose, David McFadden is primarily a poet, and although his early poetry strikes a similar balance between realism and whimsy, some of his more recent work, notably *A New Romance,* and the long poem **"Night of Endless Radiance,"** catapult him into a different category. . . . (pp. 29-30)

One is tempted, and I think not wrongly so, to put these recent long poems into the same category as Wallace Stevens's "The Idea of Order at Key West" and W. C. Williams's "The Desert Music," for they are about the poet exploring the very source of his own imagination. In **"Night of Endless Radiance,"** night becomes the metaphor for a music that defies understanding and interpretation. It is a poem of and about the imagination, in which the borders of thought and feeling are blurred as the voice of the poet slides through the various keys of creation, from innocence to consciousness, and from music to non-musical singing. . . . It is here that McFadden begins to combine thought, feeling, intelligence, and the deft use of language to make us realize that we are reading poetry in the upper scale. There is little being written in Canada that can touch the quality of this poem. It is a poetry antithetical in many ways to the earlier McFadden, and to the poetry of the '50s that ". . . so much depended upon." It is a poetry not easily accessible to those who have grown accustomed to realism in poetry as well as prose. In some ways it is truly anti-modern, although it does not shirk modern elements in its content. . . .

The two poems in *a pair of baby lambs* are obviously written in a different mood from **"Night of Endless Radiance."** Under the guise of a tall tale, **"The Cow That Swam Lake Ontario"** seems more a continuation of the animal stories of *Animal Spirits.* It takes an outrageous look at our attempts to render animals in a sentimental light, belying our own sentimentality about death, and our hypocrisy when faced with it. The tough ending of the poem comes as a relief. The other poem, which already toys with the phrase "night of endless radiance," is more serious in intent, albeit whimsical in presentation.

These three manifestations of McFadden should remind us of the range of his virtuosity and his deep cunning, for he has, as does the mind of his poem,

> An ability to entertain the night as a
> trained bear entertains the crowd. . . .
>
> > (p. 30)

Lucille King-Edwards, "A Fine Madness," in Books in Canada, *Vol. 12, No. 10, December, 1983, pp. 29-30.*

BRUCE PIRIE

McFadden's *Country of the Open Heart* is another long poem, but with considerably less spontaneous delight [than *A New Romance*], "a poem to sadden the gladdest heart." The mood turns apocalyptic—gibbons "butchering each other at the far end of the jungle"—and the poem presents itself as

> an executioner
> in a black hood full of inexpressible delights
> singing a lullaby to himself while awaiting victims,
> a chronicle of Empty Lives and civilized brutality.

This "lullaby" is in fact a noisy harangue. Individual lines may have "inexpressible delights" but the cumulative effect is of a deluge of scarcely developed images with the ranting voice of a mad visionary. For all the talk about the "open heart," the speaker of this poem masks himself in a sometimes strained affectation of "a heart grown wild and strange." All of this finally alienates the reader, and McFadden may have once again included in the work its own most accurate review:

> even this poem is about to kill itself
> to protest in advance its lack of readers
> and its inability to continue forever
> in a universe of its own destruction.

Three Stories and Ten Poems, also by McFadden, keeps much of that brutality—"you," as a child, punch a pregnant woman in the stomach and torture your friends with a heated screwdriver—but it is delivered in a more seductively prosaic and muted voice. There is no question of sensationalism in this volume (which cannot be said of *Country of the Open Heart*); it is simply that "once you're aware of your capacity for monstrosity / you're less likely to destroy yourself and others." These stories and poems are often apparently rambling and inconsequential, but are always in fact subtly insistent, patiently building up fragments, as in **"Letter to My Father,"** which begins with the confession of an "incredibly trivial" life and proceeds to a fine and moving affirmation of the simple relationship between two people. This collection has a grounding in an everyday reality of bus stops and diners that *A New Romance* shuns. It is nevertheless a reality on the point of astonishing transformations, as when a disease-carrying rat becomes a twelve-year-old girl. Much as we may admire the ecstasy of *A New Romance,* McFadden's technique seems surer and his voice more authentic in *Three Stories and Ten Poems.* At their best, these pieces are transfixing in their power to dip into the unspeakable currents that flow beneath the trivia of our lives. (pp. 123-24)

Bruce Pirie, "Speakable," in Canadian Literature, *No. 102, Autumn, 1984, pp. 121-24.*

ROBIN SKELTON

In his long poem, *Country of the Open Heart,* David McFadden says, "One cannot claim authorship for a vague / intuition that if one continues reading / writing / something wonderful will happen." Unfortunately, for a large part of *The Art of Darkness,* he appears to be making that exact claim. He has a remarkable aptitude for letting free association provide surprising images and fantastic digressions. The result is entertaining in the shorter poems; in the longer ones it is irritating. Moreover, in these longer poems the inventive imagery is often accompanied by phrases of a tiresome banality: "the end of a perfect night", "most beautiful", "the open heart", "peace-loving tribes", "sunset's afterglow", "radiant Nights" are a few of these.

Of course, McFadden is playing clichés and journalistic phrases against more vital and uncommon usages, but all too often the uncommon image is destroyed by the commonplace diction. In the shorter poems the language is usually more crisp, and the combination of fact and fantasy in some of the anecdotes provides us with a world in which the actual may become both ominous and numinous, as in **"Secrets of the Universe",** which ends with the girl walking away, "leaving you to wonder about the part of your life / that is secret even from you". There is true wit in many of these near-surrealist narratives, and in the darker poems a note of pure despair. . . .

McFadden can record the details brilliantly; he can present the black comedies of our days with verve and panache. He cannot yet, it seems, provide a coherent philosophical statement. Perhaps he should not attempt one. Certainly, the long, turgid, verbose poem which opens this collection and the confused and confusing preface lead me to this conclusion.

Robin Skelton, "Borson Shines in the Darkness of New Poetry Collections," in Quill and Quire, Vol. 51, No. 2, February, 1985, p. 39.

FRED COGSWELL

Since, in a reckless moment, T. S. Eliot wrote that "Art should be confused to express confusion," there has been no lack of disciples to further this aspect of his creed. Some distortion of order is, of course, allowable in a world as confused and threatened as our own, and, although I am repelled by it, the use of black humour in David McFadden's **"Pinnochio," "Grease-ball," "The Rat,"** and **"Kitsilano Beach on a May Evening"** is sustained, skilful, and warranted by circumstance. It applies the logic of an earlier, more optimistic time to our epoch ironically, and in so doing illuminates our present disorder by placing it within a logical pattern. What I do object to in McFadden's *The Art of Darkness* is the lack of progression that he deliberately creates in his most ambitious poems, **"Night of Endless Radiance"** and **"Country of the Open Heart."** Here he is careful to follow the advice that in his very fine **"Letter to my Father"** he gives to his creative-writing students:

> The students want to know how to
>   become poets, how to write poems.
> I tell them to think of a line, any line,
>   and write it down.
>   . . . And if
>   these two lines suggest a third put that
>   down too, and a fourth,
>   and a fifth, as long as you're not forcing
>   your mind to be
>   involved in what you're doing.

McFadden not only does not force his mind to be involved in what he is doing, but he actually consults the *I-Ching* as to the length and number of sections the process should take. The result, paradoxically, makes the title of **"Night of Endless Radiance"** very apt indeed. There is "endless radiance" in the lines and in isolated passages, but the direction to which they tend remains as black as nowhere. Since I have devoted my own life—as have generations of writers and scholars before me—to an attempt at ordering chaos, I find McFadden's deliberate refusal to play my game exasperating.

At the same time, however, I must admit that in terms of texture, tonal effect, instinct for the right word, imaginative grasp, and humanity, McFadden is not only my superior but the superior of most of his Canadian contemporaries as well. . . . (pp. 30-1)

Fred Cogswell, "Endless Radiance," in Books in Canada, Vol. 14, No. 6, August-September, 1985, pp. 30-1.

RICHARD STREILING

The narrator [of *Canadian Sunset*], one Walter J. Littlewood, describes himself as "an almost unemployed military armaments salesman trying to become a novelist". . . .

Canadian Sunset is about the narrator's transition from purveyor of destruction to story-teller. Or, put another way, the narrator tells us that his greatest wish is to become a writer and this is the story of his "becoming". It is a process laden with mystical overtones and recorded in typical McFadden style, complete with a constellation of vaguely familiar characters nonetheless made fabulous in the telling. There are moments of magical vision in the book and, for that reason alone, McFadden's fans will not want to miss it. Despite the elevated theme, he retains the self-deprecating comic style that always makes him a genial travelling companion.

Unfortunately, the fact that the novel is yet another mock-travelogue—a McFadden trademark as a novelist—is its greatest weakness. Littlewood wanders all over North America undergoing one mystically significant adventure after another, yet never emerges as distinct from McFadden himself. Since Littlewood has no history of his own, the story of his awakening consciousness is hardly credible. In order for the novel to enunciate its theme, we need to know much more about Littlewood and much less about his travels. A five-day trip around a Great Lake is one thing; wandering aimlessly around North America listening to McFadden try to disguise his voice is another.

Richard Streiling, in a review of "Canadian Sunset," in Quill and Quire, Vol. 53, No. 1, January, 1987, p. 27.

MARK CZARNECKI

Canadian Sunset is full of coincidences . . . , and, like most coincidences, they're not there by chance. In the cosmically integrated world McFadden has conjured up, nothing has meaning unless it is repeated, reincarnated, or reconnected in the golden light of transcendental consciousness. On the spiritual odyssey of Walter J. Littlewood, helicopter salesman and would-be writer, believing is seeing. . . . (p. 19)

The I/eye is an amazing thing. Instant credibility is one of its most reliable virtues, the roving I in the Kerouac tradition especially so. If I document journeys in the [British Columbia] interior, the Toronto subway, and New Mexico in photographic detail, with accurate place names and geographical phenomena, the odds are you'll believe I was *really* there: after all, why spend so much effort imagining something that is real?

Personally I haven't documented travels to these places, but Walter Littlewood has: in fact, they form the only readily visible structuring principle in *Canadian Sunset*. Section I, B.C.: Guided by Zamzam, his steak-loving vegetarian Tibetan guru, Walter and his Japanese artist girl-friend Hiroko visit old buddies, make new ones, and watch their close friend, famous folk-singer George Duckworth, blow his brains out. Walter and Hiroko are breaking up, but they don't quite know it yet. Section II, Toronto: Walter rapidly loses interest in helicopters, wants to be a writer. Hiroko is elsewhere, moving farther and farther away. Walter rides the Toronto subway system, having assigned each station a hexagram from the I Ching ("a device for using chance operations to search the city for mystical and romantic illumination"). At the end he sights a dead anaconda by the lakeshore, but zoo officials claim they are a common optical illusion at that point on the beach. Section III, New Mexico: Blessed by Dixie Moon, an infallible psychic whose spirit guide is Carl Jung, Walter borrows a Maserati, experiences an ecstatic lunar eclipse, resigns himself to Hiroko's absence, and is reborn as a writer. (p. 19)

The overall effect of this high-minded spirituality is strangely light-headed and cuddly. McFadden packs in so much engaging incident that there's never time to get bored, much less decipher what his farrago of attenuated koans is all about. Littlewood is a friendly and impossibly knowledgeable guide, more a cluster of sympathetic attitudes than a human being, but that's all right too. Nothing can be said about *Canadian Sunset* that *Canadian Sunset* doesn't already say about itself, most notably this advice to Walter from a woman into self-mutilation: ''Don't stop writing about the banal, but always make sure your readers will know that you're doing it with holiness.'' Many former helicopter salesmen could do a lot worse. (pp. 19-20)

Mark Czarnecki, ''Believing Is Seeing,'' in Books in Canada, *Vol. 16, No. 1, January-February, 1987, pp. 19-20.*

John McGahern

1934-

Irish novelist, short story writer, dramatist, and scriptwriter.

A controversial and provocative Irish literary figure, McGahern writes traditionally structured fiction in which he challenges many of his homeland's conventional social, sexual, and religious values. Focusing on protagonists for whom life in modern Ireland has become restrictive and repressive, McGahern examines such themes as the failure of love, the erosion of marital compatibility, the difficulty of maintaining hope, and the burden of Irish parochialism and religious conservatism. Often employing religious diction, imagery, and motifs, McGahern presents a vision of contemporary Ireland characterized by symbols of death, darkness, infertility, and impotency. Although McGahern has been faulted by those who consider his portrayal of characters dominated by rural values a misrepresentation of contemporary Ireland's more cosmopolitan identity, critics generally praise his incisive delineation of Irish parochialism and his commentary on the vacuousness of much of modern life.

In his first novel, *The Barracks* (1963), McGahern introduces many of the themes and motifs that recur throughout his works. In this intimate portrait of a middle-aged woman's physical, psychological, and spiritual struggle with cancer, McGahern explores such subjects as alienation and despair, conformity, the search for self, and the transience and apparent meaninglessness of life. His next book, *The Dark* (1965), is regarded as more technically adventuresome than his first novel. Featuring an episodic structure, shifting points of view, and passages of stream-of-consciousness prose, *The Dark* focuses on an adolescent boy's problematic relationships with both his widowed father and provincial Irish society. Concerned with revealing the agonies of growing up in a community that is dedicated to preserving the facade of a rigid social, sexual, and religious moral structure, McGahern depicts a world in which the dreams of youth are consistently oppressed by parents and elders. Due to McGahern's explicit treatment of sexual and religious subject matter, *The Dark* was banned in Ireland. The ensuing controversy, which was further aggravated by the disclosure of McGahern's marriage to a non-Catholic woman, prompted his dismissal from his teaching position at an Irish Catholic school.

McGahern's experiences after the publication of *The Dark* provided him with material for his next two novels, *The Leavetaking* (1974) and *The Pornographer* (1979). *The Leavetaking* is an account of a young teacher's dismissal from a Catholic boy's school because of his marriage to a non-Catholic American woman. This work concludes with an assertion of the power of love to overcome prejudice and rejection. In *The Pornographer,* a young Irish author enlivens his mundane existence by creating autobiographical stories embellished with the erotic escapades of two characters. Utilizing allusion, symbolism, and a conventional narrative style, McGahern focuses on the writer's confrontations with birth, love, and death in his emotionally and morally corrupt milieu.

In his short stories, McGahern pursues thematic concerns similar to those of his novels. In *Nightlines* (1970), the recurring

Photograph by Madeline Green

cycle of life, love, and death is portrayed as a disappointing pattern from which escape is impossible. The stories in *Getting Through* (1978) display some of the guarded optimism McGahern revealed in *The Leavetaking,* although the dominant mood remains bleak. *High Ground* (1985) continues McGahern's concern with relationships between fathers and sons, the banality of conformity and compromise, and sexual and religious conflicts.

(See also *CLC*, Vols. 5, 9; *Contemporary Authors*, Vols. 17-20, rev. ed.; and *Dictionary of Literary Biography*, Vol. 14.)

THE TIMES LITERARY SUPPLEMENT

Mr. McGahern's second novel [*The Dark*] resembles some other outstanding Irish examples in that it is plotless, autobiographical in form and about growing up. The concern with growing up in the Irish novel may be traced to the influence of religion. If you feel that the spirit can be marred for all time in adolescence by a threat-wielding, puritanical, spiritual indoctrination system, or by the abstinences it imposes—or, alternatively, if you feel that you won, single-handed, like Joyce, a victory for the life-wish in those years, it is natural enough to mull them over.

Mr. McGahern well and truly mulls. His title is accurate. This is adolescence in certain conditions as one prolonged ailment, of the body and the soul. His book begins with a scene of parental sadism the pain and horror of which reach the reader even through writing perhaps a little less considered than one has a right to expect from so serious an artist. . . . It continues with a description of a mawkish outing ruined by a parental self-pity; and reaches what might almost be called a climax in chapter 3 with an account of how the father seeks a physical comfort and response from the son while they share the double bed together. It will be seen from the fact that the widower-father and son relationship is of such a dark nature, that the novel is not just an exposition of a typical Irish Catholic up-bringing. This is a merit, undoubtedly; but it is also, in the matter of sheer literary communication, something of a defect, for the two strands are not clearly enough related or distinguished. Over this highly abnormal and ambiguous relationship of a father and son on a small farm in co. Roscommon hang the religious emblems: the crucifixes, the oleographs of the ascension. The son is afflicted with priestly ambitions as well as the frustrations of adolescence. These latter are rather more marked than would again be typical: there is only one conversation, even, with a girl other than a sister. In fact the novel is slightly too repetitive about everything. . . .

These confusions about what is the unappealing product of circumstance and what is a matter of oddity of individual situation are the more marked because of a failure to infuse any real individual character into the hero. He is "good at his books" and he becomes passionately anxious to escape through the medium of scholarships (the grotesquerie of the examination emphasis in a peasant community anxious for escape channels is ferociously brought out). Perhaps partly because of this he remains a bit of a suffering machine—the swotting is also too repetitive. But it should be said in this context that although readers may miss humour and such alleviations of the spirit as are common to all adolescents, let alone exceptional cases like this, and miss them properly again in the interests of a truer art (the writing does not rise to them either) they should not miss Mr. McGahern's irony. We think at times we are reading a story of studious success or failure about which the author is excited. We discover we are reading grim and terrible farce. The writer who is capable of such a double take deserves esteem.

"Swotting Out of the Farm," in The Times Literary Supplement, *No. 3298, May 13, 1965, p. 365.*

VIVIAN MERCIER

The technique for this brief, stripped-down novel [*The Dark*] does not draw attention to itself in the manner of Joyce's *Portrait,* but it is skillful for all that. Not until the end does one realize that the boy's first name has never been used; the father is always referred to by his last name, Mahoney; only one of the numerous other children, Joan, is referred to by name. There are passages of condensed, almost shorthand stream of consciousness. In the final chapter there are no pronouns at all, except in the dialogue: complete objectivity has been achieved.

It is this objectivity-in-the-subjective, constantly growing throughout the book, that sets this novel of adolescence somewhat on a par with Joyce's and separates it sharply from many embarrassingly self-pitying Irish novels whose authors seem to think they are following in the footprints of Stephen Dedalus. No work since Joyce has presented an Irish adolescence with such freshness and objectivity. . . .

Vivian Mercier, "Growing Up in Ireland," in The New York Times Book Review, *March 6, 1966, p. 50.*

JOHN CRONIN

It seems to me that McGahern's first novel, **The Barracks,** a remarkable *tour de force* for a young writer, perfectly achieved his purpose but that **The Dark,** which attempts to present a similar universe in confessional form is, though often interesting and compelling, ultimately much less successful. I do not suggest that Elizabeth Reegan's view of the nature of life is argued more convincingly than young Mahoney's, rather that McGahern makes her predicament vividly credible but fails to repeat this effect in the second novel. The success and the failure depend, I think, on form.

The form of **The Barracks** perfectly suits the writer's purpose. Elizabeth Reegan is thirty-nine years old and soon to die. This life has been lived and its imaginative reality is vividly created for us in a series of capably controlled flashbacks. The boy in **The Dark** is embarking on life—flashbacks are impossible here, the experience must be created chronologically. The second book is, thus, denied one of the earlier work's most powerful ingredients, the moving current of nostalgic regret which rolls through the novel like a dark tide. The middle-aged woman, dying of cancer, trapped in a marriage which has tenderness but no real sympathy in it, is the perfect vehicle for McGahern's purposeful pessimism. Elizabeth Reegan's life is made up of long periods of gallant, dogged silence and occasional moments of visionary joy which blaze like meteors in the darkness of her ordinary existence. Her love affair with a London doctor has both irradiated and ruined her life. . . . The love affair is already over before he kills himself in a car crash but it has served its purpose in the McGahern fictional world. It has awakened Elizabeth to a sense of her own individuality and convinced her of the impossibility of sustained human communication, the inevitability of loneliness. . . . Elizabeth Reegan, mortally wounded by disease but possessed of a tremendous appetite for life and a profound sense of beauty, expresses the novelist's stoic viewpoint admirably. Life has set her on a collision course and McGahern enters her experience at a point where his philosophy gives him complete and convincing command of her destiny and of her doom.

In the second novel, **The Dark,** the philosophy is essentially unchanged but it proves less viable, in literary terms, for an ardent adolescent than it did for a dying woman in middle life. Young Mahoney's stumbling progress through a McGahern universe proves much more difficult for the novelist to chart convincingly. The boy is made to inhabit a fevered and perverted world in which he encounters a series of lonely, frustrated figures: his father; his cousin, Fr Gerald with his epicene house-boy; Ryan, the shopkeeper who tries to seduce Mahoney's sister. All vistas close in sour disappointment. The perfection of the priesthood cannot be his because of his sexual impurity; the university, to reach which he has laboured so terribly, proves a grievous disappointment and he leaves it to take up a job as a clerk. The novel is so determinedly bleak that the novelist runs the risk of finding it impossible to bring it to any kind of convincing conclusion. (pp. 427-28)

Young Mahoney's kind of lonely determination is difficult to achieve in confessional form. The risks are obvious enough. The reader will either cease to believe in an unremittingly Stygian universe or find the main character increasingly a bore. Joyce manages to succeed (to some extent, at least) with Stephen Dedalus in *A Portrait of the Artist as a Young Man* because he employs a high-flown rhetoric which both carries the youthful arrogance and simultaneously undercuts it. The entries in Stephen's diary, for example, multiply the viewpoints. We are not everlastingly trapped inside Stephen's head and the result is that his celebrated declaration that he will 'forge in the smithy of my soul the uncreated conscience of my race' is, at one and the same time, both splendid and absurd, with all the splendour and absurdity of youth. McGahern achieves no such ironies—what comes through is a desperate assertion rather than a realized situation. The puzzlement is the writer's rather than the character's, the philosophy is showing through the fabric of the book and the book is the weaker for it. The closing scene of the novel, where the boy is in bed with his father, is deliberately cyclic and reinforces the claustrophobic feeling of the central character's experience but the ending of this novel is much less satisfactory than the ending of *The Barracks*. In the earlier novel, the closing chapters support and justify Elizabeth Reegan's assumptions about life—this is the sort of place she has believed the world to be, a conglomeration of solitaries brought together by accident and always too late. The book is of a piece and, as it closes, her husband's children are scrambling to pull down the blinds, pulling them down on the day that has died and on the woman who has died and will now fade from their memories, acquiring the dwindling importance which, in terms of this book, is the essential condition of the human being. Ironically, when Mullan, the policeman, rejoices that it is Elizabeth who is under ground and not he, he is clumsily expressing his crude awareness of the vivid life in which she has rejoiced so often throughout the book. The peculiar force and power of this novel is the manner in which it marries a vividly human vision to a philosophy of despair. The artistic triumph consists in the realization of Elizabeth's character and the placing of her in a credible universe. (p. 430)

> John Cronin, " 'The Dark' Is Not Light Enough: The Fiction of John McGahern," in Studies, Vol. LVIII, No. 232, Winter, 1969, pp. 427-32.

THE TIMES LITERARY SUPPLEMENT

John McGahern's first novels, *The Barracks* and *The Dark*, have established his territory and his tone. Both books take a sombre, sufferingly malicious view of contemporary Ireland, both dwell with fond revulsion on the strange, brutal paradoxes that feed on and are fed by the "Irish imagination". Familiar stuff, it might be said, and yet in neither book is there any sense of striving to inject new vigour into stale literary passions—no straining for "creative" novelty, no slumping into shock-journalese. On the contrary, each is distinguished by the only kind of originality that really matters, the kind which insists that we refocus more intensely, more intently, on what we think we know.

Mr. McGahern's piercingly accurate eye for resonant minutiae, his ability to project a world which, though richly darkened by the novelist's imagination, is yet convincingly inhabited and furnished, his very delicate ear for the resources of prose rhythm: these qualities, which place him almost on his own among the younger novelists, are abundantly present in [*Nightlines*], a collection of short stories. In many ways Mr. Mc-

Gahern's gifts, and in particular his unusual concentration upon the internal organization of his prose, are ideally suited to the story form and there are in fact stories here—such as **"My Love, My Umbrella"**, and **"Why We're Here"**—which are structured more firmly and complicatedly than even the most well-made and "finished" passages in either of his novels (and the comparison is not absurd because he does tend in his novels to deal, sometimes a bit self-consciously, in scenes rather than in a single narrative push forward).

One or two of the tales fade out in a complacent haze of inconsequentiality and now and then the language falls into a too lilting, adjectival rut; there is also a weakness in the dialogue attributed to the one or two semi-sophisticates who appear here. . . . But at their best, these stories deepen, and extend, one's admiration for this admirable writer.

> "Ireland Intensified," in The Times Literary Supplement, No. 3587, November 27, 1970, p. 1378.

DAVID PRYCE-JONES

The Ireland of John McGahern's stories is not the country other Irish writers describe. . . . Mr. McGahern is free from the emerald sentiments that have been invested in his native land. He is his own master, and his stories owe nothing to anybody.

If this is an Ireland virtually without a past, it is without a future too. The opening story in *Nightlines* has a young man returning from London to come to terms with his old father, who has remarried. All he can do is to go away again from this country of the aged and the sad.

In their unwisdom and smallness, those who are left behind in Mr. McGahern's Ireland cannot be awakened from themselves, since there is nothing to awaken them to. Their very occupations (like farming and fishing) are coming to an end. Some who persist, such as a country policeman, lose their reason. A carpenter like Lavin, in a poignant story [called **"Lavin"**] . . . , goes crazy with unfulfilled sexuality before he is taken off to the poorhouse. For his characters, the author uses a narrow range of names. One of them is Moran—repeated, one feels, because it sounds so close to moron.

The present, then, is existing in the middle of nothing and its standstill very much interests Mr. McGahern. One of the finest stories in this collection is **"Korea,"** in which a boy is about to leave home, to break the immobilization of his life. For the last time, he is helping his father to fish the nightlines that give this book its title—on the stretch of river from which the family makes a precarious living. The father wants him to emigrate to America, in the knowledge that the boy will be drafted into the Army there. If his son is then killed on active service, the father will receive from the Army more life insurance money than fishing can ever produce. The boy has his would-be murder under consideration as he baits the hooks for his father—and the image of a hook pulling its unknown catch to disturb some dark, still water is a suitable one to apply to Mr. McGahern's work.

In "Korea" the relation of father and son is framed by the box of worms they use as bait. On another occasion, a dead marriage is similarly framed by the smell of a shark rotting on a nearby beach. It is the author's technique, his whole style, to take something from the external world—the wheels of a train, an umbrella, the sea, rain—and to merge into it the components of his story.

Success depends upon picking external symbols apt enough to bear the weight put upon them. In **"Christmas,"** for instance, an orphan is given a present of an unwanted toy airplane: he destroys it, and we are made aware that he cannot fly away from where he is. Such moments of banality are more than compensated by the way Mr. McGahern usually brings together the contrasting elements of his stories. In an irregular but calculated prose he achieves a mood all his own, which is shabby and hurtful and lyrical—"refining our ignorance" in the phrase he puts into the mouth of one of his characters.

Two stories make a particular impact. In **"Hearts of Oak and Bellies of Brass,"** laborers on a building site are waiting for one of their number, Jocko, to turn up to be paid for work he has not done. Jocko is a methylated-spirits drinker; his coworkers have been out to get him and their chance has come. Eight or nine years ago a good many English writers were trying to see the violence of primitive men as something akin to ritual, which was a halfway effort to beautify it. That fashion has passed, but its cruelty is recorded here, as part of what is elsewhere called "the stupidity of human wishes."

"Peaches," the story in which the above-mentioned shark is featured, is the length of a novella. A writer, discontented in his rented house in Spain, works too little and drinks too much and has a protracted neurotic quarrel with his wife. They leave for England the moment a local magistrate (who is also the local fruit-grower and the archetypal Fascist) makes a pass at the wife—but movement will resolve nothing. **"Peaches"** might have been any writer's summer vacation story. Mr. McGahern, using a foreign setting for the first time, shows how well he can extend anywhere he pleases the themes of desolation he has already found at home.

David Pryce-Jones, "Nightlines," in The New York Times Book Review, *February 7, 1971, p. 30.*

JULIAN JEBB

John McGahern's third novel [*The Leavetaking*] is divided into halves of exactly the same length, very different in language and tone—so different that they could be read independently with satisfaction; the relationship between the two parts only becomes fully apparent in the last pages of the book. *The Leavetaking* represents an achievement of a very high order and substantiates the belief that its author is among the half-dozen practising writers of English prose most worthy of attention.

Of prose? The writing in the first and more difficult part of the novel aspires to the rhythms and intensity of poetry. The first sentence announces the images and themes:

> I watch a gull's shadow float among feet on the concrete as I walk in a day of my life with a bell, its brass tongue in my hand, and think after all that the first constant was water.

The chaos of time and its attendant losses or mysteries—shadow, bell and water—are explored in the following eighty-two pages as a young schoolmaster in Dublin recalls, on the day of his dismissal, the grievous facts of his life and above all his mother's death when he was a child. Names and places are arbitrary, and the narrative washes about in an elegy of betrayal, confusion and loss. Sometimes we are in the present with the narrator, his pupils and his as yet shadowy Love who awaits him at eight o'clock in the evening, at the end of his last day

as a teacher. Then, in mid-paragraph, we are taken back to his all-loved mother—to the "first death".

In this section of the book the storyteller is part astronomer and part laboratory assistant, exchanging telescope for microscope with admirable dexterity. Yet however beautifully adjusted the lenses, the reader is always aware of their use. An experiment seems to be taking place: an investigation into grief. The data are presented with uncommon literary skill but the concrete—life outside the narrator's self—is still obscure. Illness and unhappiness are great distorters.

In the second part of the novel it is as if the author has left his laboratory and is looking at the world without the help even of a pair of spectacles. He tells the story of his first consummated love affair, with a widow who eventually rejects him—after which he suffers an echo of his loss of his mother. He takes a year off from his school and goes to London where he meets an American girl, Isobel. The rest of the novel is not so much an account of their affair and eventual marriage as a series of conversations and events in which she tells him about her early life, her father and her previous affairs, including a marriage.... The reality of Isobel entirely alters the style of the novel. In place of reverie within confusion there is the bright evidence of life—of an intricate, suffering, incongruous other person. Meals, streets, clothes come alive and the larger metaphor of the novel begins to be apparent: love is the healing rescue from the watery, shadowy, tolling call of death. A theme so familiar requires the most persuasive and individual handling to give it substance. It is a tribute to John McGahern that while remaining true to the bleak vision of his previous novels, *The Barracks* and *The Dark,* which both deal with loss and sexual repression, he has enlarged his view of the possibilities of life.

Julian Jebb, "The Call of the Deep," in The Times Literary Supplement, *No. 3801, January 10, 1975, p. 29.*

TOM PAULIN

John McGahern's new and very distinguished collection of stories, *Getting Through,* is a fine and interesting development from *Nightlines.* McGahern constantly circles and returns to what Larkin calls "the solving emptiness/That lies just under all we do." In **"Doorways"** the narrator leaves the scene of a recently failed relationship and of past family holidays: "As much through the light of years as through this wet evening the bus seemed to move." Kneeling in church, he reflects, is "more like wandering in endless corridors of lost mornings." And this theme of temporal displacement is developed in **"The Wine Breath"** where a priest feels that he has suddenly fallen through time. He has a vision of a lost life, and feels that he is a ghost, an absence that does not cast a shadow. For one moment in "the showery sunlight" he is bathed in "an incredible sweetness of light", and at the end of the story he imagines a man who is not unlike his younger self: a man who is happy and "immersed in time without end."

This varying sense of timelessness is present in all the stories in *Getting Through,* and there is also a haunting sense of absence, a feeling that something is wrong and missing in the lives of the characters. And at times they recognise that their lives might change if they could only understand or avoid this wronging absence. But they know that it is life itself which is wrong and that it can't change.

This Chekhovian sense of absence becomes a means of exploring the theme of failure which is so deeply embedded in the Irish consciousness. At times, though, McGahern introduces a curiously Scandinavian quality into his accounts of sexual relationships. The couples in **"Along the Edges"** and **"Sierra Leone"** share a sexuality which is mutely guiltless and also somehow sexless. And despite the Flann O'Brienish detail of "The Pint Drinkers' Association" that is formed to fight a rise in the price of a drink in **"Doorways"**, the couple in this story, with their "pale lives here by the sea", read like Bergman in an Irish setting. Imaginatively, this feels right and recognisable, but this Nordic solitude does need to be placed in some relation to society. For despite O'Connor's insistence on the short story's remoteness from the community, there are degrees and kinds of remoteness. And as Gordimer shows, a lyric stasis can coexist with social flux. In **"Oysters"**, a story that pays tribute to Chekhov, there is a careless piece of social detail when a Scandinavian woman meets a poet in a Parisian restaurant: "A once powerful man played an accordion at the door." The French accordion-player might be standing in for the Eiffel Tower: he is a cinematic cliché and should never have been admitted into the narrative.

Running through McGahern's work is a fusion of sex, death and hopelessness. They are the presiding trinity of his imagination and are revealed in a series of epiphanies. In **"All Sorts of Impossible Things"** a bald schoolteacher who is never seen without his brown hat (he wears it permanently when his fiancée rejects him after his hair falls out) watches the alcoholic landlord of his local pub cough after furtively snatching a swig of whiskey.... Here, social detail and lyric feeling are brilliantly combined. This is also true of **"The Stoat"** where a rabbit's cry of pure terror as a stoat drinks its blood is merged with a widower's rejection of the spinster whom he has selected from all the replies to his marriage-advert and who suffers a mild heart attack while they are on holiday.

McGahern's imagination is intimately bound to a terminal condition where "all life turns away from its own eventual hopelessness, leaving insomnia and its night to lovers and the dying", and he writes of this condition in a prose which always possesses an astringent purity and delicacy. The chill beauty of his stories is rather like that of "the bare Scandinavian table" in **"Oysters."** But there is an admonition in this comparison, for although the short story can never be a baggy monster, there are times when a naked, lyric purity of form can seem too distanced from the contingencies of social reality. (p. 70)

> Tom Paulin, *"Evidence of Neglect,"* in Encounter, *Vol. L, No. 6, June, 1978, pp. 64-71.*

MICHAEL IRWIN

Most of these graceful, melancholy tales [in *Getting Through*] are set in Ireland. They deal in love, frustrated or misplaced, and in intimations of mortality. A lonely aging man advertises for a wife, but panics and runs away when the chosen woman suffers a heart attack. A priest, reminded by a trick of the sunlight of a funeral he attended thirty years before, confronts the prospect of his own end. In two of the stories the main character is James Sharkey, a school-teacher, who appeared briefly in John McGahern's novel *The Leavetaking*. Here, as there, he is a sorrowful man, crossed in love, who sees his premature baldness as a first hint of death, and so wears a hat continually, outdoors, indoors, and even in church. In **"Faith, Hope and Charity"** he has to tell the family of one of his

former pupils that the young man has been killed in an accident. In **"All Sorts of Impossible Things"**, perhaps the best-balanced and most moving story in the collection, he is desolated by the death of an old friend.

John McGahern writes with unobtrusive concision. So much of his skill lies in selection, or rather in omission, that his terse narrative seems free and full. He has the Irish gift of being able to move fluently and unselfconsciously between a simple and a heightened style. There are ten stories in this narrow volume, but in each of them he finds scope to create both a situation and an atmosphere. Pace and proportion seem effortlessly adjusted: there is no sense of expository strain....

Mr McGahern's economy is the more remarkable in that he is characteristically concerned not with a single event or mood but with a series of such events or moods. The happening that provides his ostensible subject takes its significance from a previous history that is skilfully implied. The immediacy of the narrative is delusive: the present merges with the past or with the future, "story" dissolves into theme. This habit of imagination is so marked as to become a habit of style.... Within a sentence the reader knows that the meaning of the story will extend well beyond its anecdotal content.

All this is to say that Mr McGahern has his own way of solving one of the obvious problems facing writers of the short story: that of giving imaginative extension to a single episode. Repeatedly he will lead a character towards a moment of stereoscopic vision in which experiences widely separated in time are suddenly juxtaposed by memory and seem to be significantly connected. A colourless life, or a group of colourless lives, can come to display a pattern of pain and loss....

But I must admit to having read this accomplished collection with rather more admiration than pleasure. The tune that is piped is so unfailingly sorrowful that the stories come to seem confined. It is plain that this author will never be surprised out of his own sadness. The end of one of his narratives is often implicit in its very beginning. "Stoat" starts with a rabbit squealing in death. The fate of the animal, like that of the roach mentioned in **"Swallows"**, is already a comment on the human predicament as Mr McGahern sees it. For all its many merits *Getting Through* is a depressing work.

> Michael Irwin, *"Sorrowful Pipings,"* in The Times Literary Supplement, *No. 3976, June 16, 1978, p. 663.*

ALICE ADAMS

[The narrator of *The Pornographer*], a young Irishman living in Dublin, is engaged in three principal activities: first, as a professional pornographer, he writes the raunchy saga of the Colonel and his lady friend, Mavis, a predictably concupiscent couple, sometimes very funny; second, as a dutiful, right-thinking and affectionate nephew, he visits his dying aunt in the hospital, kindly supplying her with the inordinate amount of brandy that she seems to require; and third, what comes to be the most demanding and time-consuming activity of all, he frequents a dance hall, where he encounters various young women, whom he attempts, of course, to take home to bed. He fuels himself for these encounters, as it were, with a stint of writing, a bout with Mavis and the Colonel, and thus he usually arrives at the dance hall in an over-heated state. From the start his life and his work are hopelessly criss-crossed; his fantasies are messier than our own.

Nor does he seem fortunate in his loves. Just as he is recovering from an episode with a woman whom he loved in vain, he meets Josephine, an almost-40, still-beautiful semi-virgin, who would seem to have been saving herself for him. Josephine is as stupid as she is sexually enthusiastic, an almost too-perfect match for a pornographer. John McGahern apparently agrees with Faulkner's remark that women are not seduced, men are chosen; certainly Josephine chooses the pornographer in a vehemently conclusive way. Quite soon, and then often in their relationship, she assures him that she has enough love for both of them. From her first ''O Boy,'' quickly seen to be one of her favorite expressions, we know that things will not work out well, just as we know, when she says that love is ''safe,'' that she will certainly become pregnant, which she does. (p. 14)

Conception probably took place on a boating excursion on the river Shannon, a trip actually taken by the narrator and Josephine; and later by the Colonel and Mavis, in a desperately written pornographic installment whose parodic sexuality compounds the confusion between the real and the secret life.

Once Josephine's pregnancy is established, events go downhill for everyone, including, unhappily, the reader. Just when we should most care what happens we find that we care least, and even the aunt's death is not genuinely sad, because we hardly knew her. And confusion reigns: for a while it looks as though the pornographer-narrator will be let off and that Josephine will marry rich Jonathan (or is Jonathan Josephine's own fantasy?) and that the narrator will go off happily with one of his aunt's nurses. But no, this is a very Irish novel; sins must be punished. At the very end it is not entirely clear just what *has* happened, but because the pornographer is last seen going very fast in a car driven by his very drunken editor, we know that his prospects are not good.

The narrator's chief virtue in life is his honesty: he does not tell women that he loves them when he does not. But that honesty turns out to be not quite sufficient to enlist our sympathies. After all, honesty can occasionally be ascribed to a simple lack of imagination, which in this case would explain the literalness of much of the supposed pornography. ''O Boy, I sure picked a winner,'' is another of Josephine's too-often repeated sentences, and one is inclined to agree with her sentiments and to wonder: why him?—and to wish that the highly talented Mr. McGahern had chosen to write about a more interesting and appealing subject. (pp. 14, 53)

> Alice Adams, ''Mavis, the Colonel and Sin Chastised,'' in The New York Times Book Review, December 2, 1979, pp. 14, 53.

JOHN UPDIKE

[*The essay from which this except is taken was originally published in* The New Yorker, *December 24, 1979.*]

Out of a contemporary Ireland where the production of pornography is still a matter of, if not prosecution, self-reproach, and where a woman can still be concerned for her virginity and a man for his honor, and where the notion can persist in intelligent heads that ''things were run on lines of good and bad, according to some vague law or other,'' and where erotic adventure is still enough freighted with guilt and pain to seem a mode of inner pilgrimage, John McGahern has produced his vivid and involving novel [*The Pornographer*]. His hero, a thirty-year-old unwed male citizen of Dublin, makes a tidy living by penning pornographic chronicles for an old friend, a

frustrated littérateur called Maloney, who has resolved his frustrations by becoming a ''rich and fairly powerful'' publisher of smut in successful defiance of the land's ''obsolete censorship laws.'' For our presumably high-minded delectation, the pornographer narrates the story of a season in his life when death and birth, exhaustion and renewal and momentously conjoin.

While carrying on with the lubricious exploits of his fictitious Mavis Carmichael and Colonel Grimshaw, our youngish man is also dutifully carrying brandy and cheer to his dying aunt in a Dublin hospital, and dealing politely with his other kin and his inherited farm some hours' drive from Dublin. And at the same time, and not so incongruously as he appears to think, he seeks liquid solace in pubs and fleshly consolation in dance halls, which seem still to fulfill a respectable social role in Ireland. At least, our hero finds in one a very respectable pickup, a thirty-eight-year-old semi-virgin (the concept, a new one to me, might also be phrased as demi-deflowered) who with great speed and ease allows him to seduce and—less to his liking—to impregnate her. The pregnancy is mostly at her insistence, for she brushes aside his attempt at contraception with ''It's unnatural. It turns the whole thing into a kind of farce.'' She also finds his pornography a bit much. But her enthusiasm for sex and maternity and marriage, though late aroused, is limited by naught save our hero's surliness; from initial attraction to her ''clean, strong features'' and lust for her body ''lean and strong against my hand,'' he moves through irritation and alarm to loathing, the more intensely she persists in loving him. At the end, we are told, ''The last I remember was striking out at her as she came towards me with outstretched hands.'' With some surliness of his own, Mr. McGahern shows great reluctance to divulge the names of his major characters, but that of the *demi-vierge* is given passingly as Josephine, and that of the narrator's aunt as Mary. Between the two desperately needy women, then, between Josephine's pregnancy and Mary's cancer, our weary pornographer shuttles for the nine and more months that make up his sorry, lyrical tale.

Such a tale of dance-hall seduction, undesired pregnancy, unrequited passion, sickbed visitation, and self-righteously self-imposed solitude, with vistas of slate-roofed rural peace to lend darkening contrast to the moiling urban foreground, might almost be illustrated by Victorian steel engravings. Though located somewhere in our fast-departing decade, it wears a musty timelessness that might strike even an Irishman as quaint. But for the absence of parading British soldiery and horsedrawn streetcars, its milieu could be the well-detailed Dublin of June 16, 1904, with its reek of pubs and rasp of caustic and elaborate jesting among Jesuit-educated idlers. Nor is Joyce's soft-limbed swooningness, in loving echo of the sentimental songs and pious imagery of his upbringing, entirely absent from Mr. McGahern's prose.... His flights of religious-seeming rhetoric fall short of the final clarity they promise.... And the stylist has an overindulged mannerism of running quotes into the next sentence with only a comma.... (pp. 388-90)

But let it be admitted—may, proclaimed—that by and large Mr. McGahern writes entrancingly, with a lively pace and constant melody. Each sentence is tuned to a certain singing tension, the local lilt exploited subtly. ''Way had to be pushed through the men crowded in the entrance at the top of the short steps.'' No American could have composed that sentence, or the echoing sentence that closes the paragraph: ''On the irreversible way, many who loved and married met in this cattle light.'' Visiting his aunt, the narrator begins, ''I caught her sleeping lightly, some late sun on the pillows from the high windows facing home.'' The pornography he writes, and gives us samples of, is rendered chaste by this same dainty magic of phrasing: ''She came with a cry that seemed to catch at something passing through the air.'' Often a single cunning word lifts a description well up from the ordinary: a girl is seen as ''young and healthy and strong, the face open and uncomplicated beneath its crown of shining black hair, a young woman rooted in her only life,'' and a man is ''plainly Irish, from a line of men who had been performing feats of strength to the amazement of an infantile countryside for the past hundred years.'' Without straining, the happy compression of aphorism is attained; of his writing the narrator says, ''Nothing ever holds together unless it is mixed with some of one's own blood.'' Mr. McGahern writes well, and for the usual reasons: he observes well, hears faithfully, and feels keenly.

He is a shrewd psychologist. The distances between people—the jagged rift between the lovers, the gradually widening space the aunt in dying sets around her—are beautifully sketched, in pages of laconic dialogue that are sometimes comic. His portrait, indeed, of the spurned Josephine is so telling that we wind up liking her more than the hero does, and losing sympathy with him; while in some novels this might be a feat of dramatic irony, in this it seems a flaw. The narrator's vacuous response toward her touching eagerness to be married, and then toward the brave act of her moving to London to bear their illegitimate child, never feels justified, though it is often explained. He has earlier suffered a romantic rejection that has left him numbed. He states near the outset of the book, as if in warning, that ''energy is everything, for without energy there can be no anything, no love and no quality of love.'' . . . As Maloney says, it won't do, even though the narrator pleads guilty to ''shameful shallowness'' and finally proclaims that ''there comes a time when you either run amok completely or try to make a go of it. I'm going to try to make a go of it''— i.e., marry the next girl he seduces, a twenty-three-year-old nurse who, like Josephine, is apprehended as a ''strong'' and ''healthy'' female animal. What stuck to this reader's ribs was the hero's deadly coldness, and Josephine's credible, vital, naïve humanity. (pp. 390-92)

Of course, the author has created the character the narrator fails to love, and Mr. McGahern's other works amply include among their aims a wish to display human ugliness. In the short story **''Hearts of Oak and Bellies of Brass,''** the ugliness exists as an end in itself, dreadful to contemplate; in **''Lavin,''** it clashes with a sense of lost beauty in such a way as to become, itself, a kind of beauty. The personal ugliness in the long story **''Peaches''**—one of Mr. McGahern's few portraits of marriage, and a discouraging one—pales beside the political ugliness of the brilliant denouement. These stories all achieve what they grimly set out to do, but *The Pornographer* goes somehow awry. We feel impatience with the hero and a frustrated suspicion that the real story occurred elsewhere.

It is not unusual in fiction for a character to overrespond to a writer's demands and to throw out of balance the moral intended. The rebel Satan makes Milton's God look bad, and Don Quixote's foolishness becomes heroism. Here chin-up, pregnant Josephine makes our narrator look bad, with a badness that taints his narrative. Why is he telling us all this? The question bothers every piece of first-person fiction to a degree, and lays upon it a responsibility to come back with witnessed marvels (*Moby-Dick*) or a clear confessional urgency (*Notes from Underground*). Otherwise, we seem to have bragging

without much to brag about—''conceit,'' to quote Maloney. We would probably judge Mr. McGahern's hero less sternly if we encountered him and his problems in life rather than in a novel. Novel readers are ruthlessly sentimental. We want characters to marry, out of our own need to be done with them, to have them off our consciences. (pp. 392-93)

> John Updike, ''An Old-Fashioned Novel,'' in his Hugging the Shore: Essays and Criticism, *Alfred A. Knopf, Inc., 1983, pp. 388-93.*

TERENCE WINCH

[*The Pornographer*] makes it clear that the Irish are not exempt from . . . failures of love.

The pornographer of the title is the book's unnamed 30-year-old narrator. He lives in an almost anonymous Dublin, where he churns out stories about the sexual adventures of Colonel Grimshaw and Mavis Carmichael for his editor, Maloney, an abrasive character who takes unapologetic delight in the miseries of others. The narrator, emotionally numb because of a recent and final rejection by someone he loved, meets a good-looking, 38-year-old woman at a dance bar. They wind up in bed together. The woman is a virgin once removed (having lost her virginity the year before) and completely inexperienced at affairs of the heart. She quotes her uncle as calling her Josephine. But McGahern keeps the two from ever addressing each other by name. Josephine and the narrator become involved and in a matter of weeks she falls in love with him.

When she tells him that she's pregnant and wants to get married, the narrator is plagued by ''images that enmesh and fester round a life.'' Her dream-come-true is his ''nightmare.'' He feels no love for her, only responsibility.

The other woman in the narrator's life is his (again, nameless) aunt, a crusty, belligerent old woman with a taste for brandy and a distaste for death. For most of the novel, she is confined to the terminal cancer ward of the local hospital. Birth and death become the novel's crucial metaphors as the narrator shuttles back and forth between love-bed and death-bed. For a man comfortable with life in an emotional and moral void, and caught up in ''the nothing that was the rest of our life'' the narrator's confrontation with love, birth and death is especially demanding. That confrontation is the soul of McGahern's book.

McGahern is a poetic novelist. His writing combines ornate prose with a story that depends as much on the development of certain images and metaphors as on anything else. Sometimes the book's language seems overdone: ''Will others be inflamed by the reading, if there is flesh to inflame, as I was by the poor writing? Is my flush the flesh of others, are my words to be their worlds?'' But most of the time McGahern keeps his more heavy-handed tendencies under control. And every once in a while he lets loose with an aphorism or an image that hits home with impact: ''People do not grow old. Age happens to us, like collisions, that is all''; ''Nothing is worse than being stupid''; ''The hearse was parked in front of the church gates, its carriage door raised like an open mouth.''

McGahern writes in the tradition of English Romanticism. There are echoes of Blake (''energy is everything''), Keats (''We have to go inland, in the solitude that is both pain and joy''), and T. S. Eliot (''To find we had to lose: the road away became the road back''). His attraction to religious diction and spiritual motifs is a conspicuous feature of his work. And at times, the novel's techniques seem too contrived: pornographic characters with names sharing the book with "real" people who are nameless; a village with houses that, like the novel's characters, all stand "away from one another at angles and distances of irreconcilable disagreements."

The mix in this novel of allusion, symbolism and conventional technique may seem intrusive and uncongenial to American audiences. But McGahern rescues himself. He can create scenes of hard-edged contemporary reality. . . .

The Pornographer remains a philosophical, melancholy book throughout, although it offers a suggestion of redemption at the end. The narrator begins to reject "the road of reason," and with it, the safe and proper conduct with which he has armored himself. He thinks of proposing marriage to a young nurse he has met and moving back to the country.

But even with its optimistic finish, *The Pornographer*'s real power finds its source in McGahern's ability to write movingly about failure.

> Terence Winch, "*Murmurs from a Troubled Heart*," in Book World—The Washington Post, *December 23, 1979, p. 11.*

TERENCE BROWN

The prose [in McGahern's first published novel, *The Barracks* (1963),] is reflective, expansive, open syntactically and rhythmically to accumulation of event, deed, detail of milieu and to narrative comment. It is a prose untroubled by doubts as to the value of its own movements and procedures as it confidently renders the way of things are in the provincial milieu that is so intimately known. . . . Tone and strategy here are not so distant from the idioms and rhythms of story-telling. (pp. 291-92)

Some of McGahern's best writing is in this assured conventional mode. The implicit, uncomplicated belief in the value of recounting allows for extended passages in which the novelist possesses his world, characters in their settings, landscapes and actions, with the unselfconscious confidence of a story-teller absorbed with his material. In passage after passage in his three novels McGahern concentrates on the particularities of the Leitrim, Roscommon border-country (passages which, extracted from their context, read remarkably like the openings of Irish short-stories). (p. 292)

As with the conventional Irish short stories, those of O'Connor and O'Faolain, this objectivity in McGahern is somewhat disturbed by romanticism, for in his three novels the central character is a sensitive adolescent or young man whose feelings in the midst of a constricted provincial environment are the central points of interest. But the traditional temper, tones and techniques in McGahern's fictions are disturbed in a further much more important way; McGahern is aware of an urban and fragmented culture encroaching upon the stable, provincial, rural world upon which in Ireland the anecdotal, orally-based tale ultimately depends. When the earlier writers took account, as they did occasionally, of the modern urban world it was without any real sense that the encounter with novel experience might require significant aesthetic innovations. They continued indeed to write as if literary modernism had nothing to teach them. McGahern does not.

It is evident even in his most conservative novel *The Barracks* that McGahern, while confident and skilled in portraying the provincial world he knows, recognises a need for modern Irish fiction to meet more stringent demands. It must be attentive to the recent major social changes in the country, in an art that more appropriately reflects the complex psychological currents that stir in its turbulent waters. So McGahern is consciously experimental in his work, welcoming the resonance of image and symbol to the enclosed worlds of rural and small-town Ireland, taking his protagonists away from their childhood farms and fields to the confused cultural settings of modern Dublin and London.

McGahern, as symbolist, is absorbed by the potency of ritual, particularly by the Catholic rituals associated with death, with burial and with Holy Week. In his three novels, imagery drawn from these various rites is employed to ground his fiction in a deeper sense of the way things are, than was the case in traditional Irish short stories and novels. The imagery serves to imply a metaphysical dimension to experience, unknowable except in the mysterious patterns that ritual reveals in life itself, inducing in the participants of ritual an emotional awareness of metaphysical depth. Memory and meaning, myth and mystery, passion and pattern, seem controllable for the protagonists of the novels and for the author himself only through the mediation of rite and symbol. (pp. 293-94)

Such moments, however, run grave tonal risks, dependent as they usually are in the novels on the imagery of a specific church and tradition. For the novelist, writing out of a culture where these images are almost unconsciously understood, must uneasily recognise that in the wider world, where he will most probably find his readers, these familiar properties will suggest not the mystery of ultimate things but the curiosity of the primitive, the exotic. So at times in McGahern's works one senses that the descriptions of rite and custom operate less as symbols than as passages of local colour. There is a note of explanatory insecurity in these passages, a tendency to tonal uncertainty.

It is in his collection of short-stories, *Nightlines* (1970), that we see McGahern attempting to resolve this problem. In this volume McGahern seeks to write short-stories exploiting symbolist possibilities without depending on the traditional metaphors of church and religion. He seeks symbols within the physical properties of his fictional environments, in event and deed. So the symbolism is unobtrusive, tonally contained within the movements of narration, without any sense of the insecurity occasioned when, as in the novels, more explicit symbolism is attempted.

McGahern's short-stories, like his novels, occupy a middleground between the conservative traditionalist mode and modernist experiment. Where O'Connor and O'Faolain wrote their tales of enclosed provincial worlds, McGahern also senses that a short-story must in part depend on such hermetic self-sufficiency. But the social conditions that allowed the earlier writers to explore a stable, self-confident Irish world no longer obtain. So McGahern writes of artificially self-contained worlds. He sets a story in a railway carriage, in a school, on a London-Irish building site, in a guest-house, in a police-station, on a boat in the middle of a lake, in an isolated house on the Mediterranean. In most of them a sensitive central character, so familiar from Irish fiction in general and from McGahern's novels in particular, suffers in an unpleasing milieu. In **"Wheels"** an adult returns to the pain of his provincial origins. In **"Coming into his Kingdom"** a child experiences the discomforts of sexual awakening. In **"Hearts of Oak and Bellies of Brass"** the narrator struggles to anaesthetise his cultural and emotional awareness with back-breaking labour; in **"Strandhill, the Sea"** the narrator is a troubled kleptomaniac; in **"Lavin"** he is an adolescent discovering homosexual feelings and sexual disgust; in **"My Love, My Umbrella"** he is a young Dubliner enduring the agonies of an unrequited passion, in **"The Recruiting Officer"** an alcoholic, failed Christian brother, eccentric and tired rebel.

In *Nightlines* the tone of traditional Irish short-story-telling is not entirely forsaken either. At moments, in fact, one suspects the author's nerves fail him in his literary experimentalism and he falls back on familiar, proved techniques. So in **"Wheels"**, at the opening of the collection, we encounter a very curious blend of prose-impressionism with a structure reminiscent of a much more direct and anecdotal kind of short story.... Elsewhere the anecdotal Irish speaking voice is heard quite clearly, as in so many discursive Irish tales. (pp. 294-95)

McGahern's short-stories are most interesting when these tones and techniques are avoided, when the processes of his prose combine an unsentimental apprehension of the physical world with symbolist resonance and where he manages to generate the symbolic charge of his tales without dependence on the dynamism of a traditional religious or cultural symbol system. In his novels the rituals of the Church provided that charge; in *Nightlines* McGahern turns to imagery of wheel, river, sea. The wheels of the first tale are the wheels of a train bearing a man back through his past across the Shannon and also the "ritual wheel", the repetition of a life in the shape of a story that had as much reason to go on as stop. And the collection ends with a character, who has recognised that life "is all a wheel", contemplating the Shannon as it flows to the sea. Roger Garfitt has suggested that "McGahern sometimes seems more Buddhist than Catholic" and sees the imagery of the Wheel as possibly owing something to that tradition. But, if this is so it functions in a much less obtrusive way than does the Catholic imagery of the novels.

It is in the detailed interrelationship of the facts of McGahern's stories, the blend of event, physical milieu and meaning that McGahern's symbolism is least obtrusive and, I think, most effective. Each story employs one or two central images which, as Henri D. Paratte remarks, "offer a symbolic frame to his vision of reality." That vision is austerely metaphysical but reductively so as the human world of desire and meaning is set against images which suggest iron physical law, machine-like inevitability, cruelty, decay, the ritual wheel which breaks all backs as it turns. The world of these stories is a world of chain-saws, hooks, chains, ice, flame, shovels, metal, shot, coffin-wood, bait, mallets, chisels, rusting tools, iron-bolts, whips with metal tips, glass inseminating plungers, knives, pumps, concrete lavatories, ticking clocks.

The framing images of each McGahern story contain within them accumulations of detail and fact which further serve to symbolise the writer's ambiguous, metaphysically bleak vision of reality, though they do so without any suggestion of overt symbolist technique. It is only on a close examination of these works that a reader realizes how far he is here from the direct, unself-conscious discourse of the traditional tale-taller, how much he is in the hands of a skilled, very self-conscious imagist. For in McGahern the moments of traditional tone distract from the modernist techniques.

"Hearts of Oak and Bellies of Brass" is a sketch of life on a building site in a London summer. The workers are Irish and the central character is a countryman who has sold his sensi-

tivity for the dulled, unfeeling security of life as a wage-slave, which anaesthetises pain and fear of death.... His ambition is, as he puts it, "to annul all the votes in myself". This he does in accommodating himself to the regular, monotonous violence of the building site, its gratuitously violent language, the sexual animality, the sudden eruptions of physical force. Through the story, imagery of machines plays a crucial role in establishing a sense of monotonous dehumanization. A steel hopper, metal buckets, a brass medal bearing a worker's number, the "back of the hopper bright as beaten silver in the sun" and, centrally, the sharp, silver blade of a shovel, serve as metaphors of a dangerous physical violence, a dehumanised instinctual energy in the story. The movements of the shovels further suggest the sexual drives that find release only in violence of tongue and in prostitution.... The wheel of labour turns in this tale. It is sensitivity and human hope that are broken by its mechanical, grinding revolutions. (pp. 296-98)

The longest piece in the collection is **"Peaches"**. It is also the story where the texture of the narrative is most dense with symbolic intimations of the kind I have been identifying. The plot is fairly straightforward. A moderately successful novelist is living in a rented Spanish villa with his Northern European wife. The relationship is in crisis. Creativity is at low-ebb. Neurosis and tension dominate the conversational exchanges, while the smell of a decaying shark on the beach, referred to at various points in the work, suggests the decay of marital compatibility. But there are many other details which embody the story's meanings. The relationship is as infertile as the man's (throughout they are "He", "She") imaginative powers. So there are frequent functionally ironic images of containers being filled to overflowing with liquid. A swimming pool is filled by a pump—"the three started to watch in the simple fascination of water filling the empty pool", water is poured into clay jars, a wine glass is filled "to the brim from the Soberano bottle", peaches in an orchard are sprayed by a "machine on metal wheels". This latter image resonates with another important image complex in the tale—that of machines as artificial and uncreative. The pool is filled by a pump; the woman is obsessed with the possibility of machines replacing people, electric light seems a poor substitute for the religious-sexual mystery of candle-flame, a Vespa scooter is dangerous, risky. The movement of the story in this world of significant patterns of detail can be readily studied in the passage where the couple make love. Section VIII of the piece begins with the image of the decomposing shark; the couple take a swim and in the sea they move to sexual union. But afterwards their lovemaking on the clinical "white sheet of the bed" is crude, acquisitive. Instead of the imagery of sea where they "let the waves loll over them" the man postpones his orgasm by "trying to make up what each gallon cost of the load of water that had been put in the pool that morning". Then he "held her close for her to pump him until she came". The fraught tension of their infertile, uncreative sexual coupling is then suggested in the tense dialogue with its syntactic bluntness:

> "Why do you want?"
>
> Our relationship would get much better.
>
> "But how would it do you good."

The conversation and the section end with the machines, the reductive images of sterility, danger, of cold metaphysical austerity, that are the frightening equivalents of the rotting shark, the ripe peaches proffered as tokens of lust at the story's climax.

> "We'll be happy", the man said.

Later, as he got the Vespa out of the garage,
he heard the clean taps of her typewriter come
from the upstairs room.

The economical skill of passages such as this in *Nightlines,*
with their subtle blend of image, dialogue and action suggest
the degree to which McGahern has moved away from the expansive, anecdotal mode of much Irish fiction to tautly economical stories as metaphysically resonant as his novels, but
without their overt traditional symbolism and techniques.
(pp. 298-99)

> Terence Brown, ''John McGahern's 'Nightlines':
> Tone, Technique and Symbolism,'' in The Irish Short
> Story, *edited by Patrick Rafroidi and Terence Brown,
> Colin Smythe Ltd., 1979, pp. 289-301.*

SHAUN O'CONNELL

Throughout most of his impressive oeuvre—four novels and
two short story collections—John McGahern imagines Ireland
as dark, dank and dour. Ireland is a prison to which his characters are sentenced, from which they are unable or unwilling
to escape. Their lives, turning in a narrow gyre, embody
McGahern's vision of the constricted state of the nation.

However, in his writings of the late 1970s McGahern leads
some of his characters through a door into the light, into a
problematic freedom, out to an open field in which they first
run free, but from which they eventually seek release, so some
return to familiar confines. In *The Pornographer* McGahern
turns his hero homeward, back to the same rural Ireland his
early characters could not wait to leave. Having enacted the
myth of Daedalus, flight past the nets, McGahern's late hero
enacts the counter-myth of Antaeus. ''My elevation, my fall,''
says Antaeus in a Heaney poem. So too might say McGahern's
bright, young men who come home again. Ireland, no longer
a prison, is transformed into a haven. (p. 255)

McGahern's Ireland, its regions and its citizens, is divided by
a deep-running pattern of faults. Yet his divided Ireland, surprisingly, is not political. For all we know from reading
McGahern, the ''troubles,'' which have ripped Ireland apart
for fifteen years, have never happened. Only rarely does he
note in passing that there are two Irelands, North and South.
(p. 257)

McGahern is more concerned with the latent politics of Irish
life: provinciality, family enclosure and Church repression of
sexual expression, an Ireland not far from the starved land in
Kavanagh's *The Great Hunger.* To stay within the circle of
acceptability is, spiritually and sexually, to starve, but to range
outside the province of the predictable in Ireland, particularly
for sexual purposes, is to bring about retribution. ''Either you
toe the line or you get out,'' says the hero of *The Leavetaking.*
Repression is the means by which community is sustained.
This point is clearly made in a scene from *The Pornographer*
in which we trace the sexual adventures of the hero's chief
pornographic characters, Col. Grimshaw and Mavis Carmichael. They . . . travel inland, for a boat trip up the Shannon,
where they assault and rape an Irish yokel while he is in a
drunken stupor. Mavis assures the Col. the lad will remember
nothing when he wakes. ''He'll think he was dreaming. Doesn't
the whole country look as if it's wet dreaming its life away.
He'll want to be no exception. He's a prime example of your
true, conforming citizen.'' Like Joyce's Citizen in Barney
Kiernan's pub, who meets Bloom's plea for love with scorn,

McGahern's citizen is held up for satire, an example of the
thwarted Irish character.

Throughout McGahern's works other sex-driven, yet repressed
citizens appear, though they are treated more sympathetically.
The sexual fantasies included in *The Pornographer* might well
be the dreams of his sad Irish men and women, particularly
those land-locked in the moist valleys of Roscommon-Leitrim.
Pornography is the black mass celebrating Irish repression.
McGahern's sexual politics mock Irish containment: physical
psychic, regional.

His characters are cornered, burnt-out cases. The most moving
of these lost souls is Elizabeth Reegan, heroine of McGahern's
first novel, *The Barracks.* Though she has known some freedom
and love in London, where she served as a nurse during WWII,
she chooses a life of confinement and indifference when she
returns to her Irish village, where she marries a widower, cares
for his children and lives out the rest of her days in seething
conformity.

Married to a police officer who cannot talk to her except to
complain about his barracks supervisor, and caring for children
who ignore her, Elizabeth is trapped inside a quotidian,
''shackled, a thieving animal held at last in this one field.''
Like other McGahern characters, she sees no purpose in her
life. ''She was existing far within the recesses of the dead walls
and gaping out in mute horror.'' Her sense of transciency is
made more poignant by her realization that she has cancer, a
terminal condition which makes her life seem a meaningless
cycle. . . . (pp. 257-58)

In London she had had an affair with an alcoholic doctor,
named Halliday, who initiated her into sex and, after his fatal
car accident, introduced her to death. ''What the hell is all this
living and dying about anyway?'' Halliday would yell, posing
a frequent question for McGahern characters. Surely this torment must have a purpose, they insist.

For Elizabeth, Halliday provided the gift/curse of consciousness: ''it was as if he's put windows there, so that she could
see out her own world.'' However, as her life closes in, Elizabeth sees bars on those windows and wonders at the worth
of a consciousness which sets her apart from others, an awareness which grants her painful attentiveness to her own dete-
riorating condition and presents her with no rhyme or reason
for living.

Finally, as she lay dying, Elizabeth ceases to ask for an Answer;
she accepts her own passing, irresolute condition. ''Nothing
could be decided here. She was just passing through.'' It is
not so much that she has arrived at meaning, but that she can
finally praise life's mystery. ''All the apparent futility of her
life in the barracks came at last to rest on this sense of mystery.'' She chants the rosary at her death, as much for its music
as for its matter.

If McGahern's mothers transmit mystery, his fathers pass along
their own miseries, often with the back of their hands. *The
Dark* opens with Mahoney whipping his son for swearing. Yet
Mahoney is even more eager to inflict psychic than physical
shock, for he brings his strap down on the chair arm, not on
the boy. The effect is even worse, for the boy ''couldn't get
any grip on what had happened to him, he'd never known such
a pit of horror as he'd touched, nothing seemed to matter any
more.'' Since Mahoney is a widower, no woman mitigates his
brutality, so he is an extreme version of *The Barracks*'s stern
father, Reegan. As Reegan had made his children dig turf,

Mahoney makes his children pick potatoes in the lashing rain. McGahern's fathers curse their children with corporal punishment and hard labor. They initiate their children into the stern ways of the world. Mothers hold out a sense of escape into life's mysteries, but fathers know better.

As difficult as paternal discipline is for children, paternal love is worse. Occasionally Mahoney tries to express affection for his children, but he can never wholly give, nor can they ever quite receive. When Mahoney takes his children fishing, the day ends in complaint, his and theirs. However, the real perversion of love is also more psychic than physical. Sometimes at night the lonely Mahoney climbs into bed with his son, hugs him, smothers him in "the dirty rags of intimacy." In a bed of childhood horrors, fleas feed on father and son, mixing their blood in a bond which sickens the boy. He asks: "Why had things to happen as they did, why could there not be some happiness, it'd all be as easy." He includes no question mark, so he expects no answer.

The boy in *The Dark* seeks relief through masturbation and other modes of self-referential dreams. His stark options: either find release from his perverse family thrall or face death, like Elizabeth Reegan. The literary lad determines "It's the same stake as Macbeth's except for the banality of the whole situation. It's fight a way out or go down." However, he finds in Ireland only great hatred, little room. Though he escapes from home, he finds no satisfying alternative place for himself. His vocation for the priesthood and his aspiration to become an educated man are both destroyed by disappointing role-models. Finally the boy's hopes overcast, like an Irish sky.

He is not only disappointed, he is assaulted. When he visits Father Gerald, Mahoney's brother, he is met by death imagery—a burial ground looms outside Father Gerald's residence—and sexual harrassment. Father Gerald gets into bed with him to hug and joke about sex. To underline his point, McGahern doubles examples of sexual assault. The boy discovers that his sister, Joan—for whom Father Gerald had found work in a draper's shop—had been fondled by the draper. Thus the whole male, adult population of *The Dark* is composed of child-molesters. The boy, who misses Father Gerald's faint traces of pathos, rages at all adults: "how your hands hungered for their throats." We see the world from his perspective ("your hands" and "their throats"), a world of adult oppression of the young.

Yet the boy battles on. He will not live his father's life on the farm or his uncle's life as a priest; his is Jude Fawley's dream: self-transformation through higher education. There he would learn and love. Yet this dream also quickly diminishes, for he is too shy to approach women and he quickly decides that university life is a sham. A lecturer throws the boy out of class because he smiled, a gesture the lecturer calls "hooliganism."

McGahern's patterns of adult monstrosity make *The Dark* a stark parable. All elders are killers of the dreams of youth. Ireland's good country people—its priests, its teachers, its fathers—are caricatured. It is small wonder, then, that the Irish Censorship Board banned the novel in 1965, for it seems designed to shock Irish sensibilities through its sexual explicitness and its sustained scorn for Irish culture.

The Dark is a cautionary tale, dramatizing the modern defeat of young Irelanders. In the end the boy does not quite know what he wants out of life. Like Paul Morel or Stephen Dedalus, he dreams of release through art, yet decides to settle for an unadventurous clerkship in Dublin. Neither exile nor native, artist or artisan, the boy is paralyzed in the civil service, an Irish purgatory.

In McGahern's third novel, *The Leavetaking,* a young man is again defeated by narrow-minded Ireland, though he faces defeat with more resiliency than the sad hero of *The Dark. The Leavetaking* portrays a fictionalized version of pivotal events in McGahern's own life, his own difficult passage. McGahern, like Patrick, the novel's central character, was punished for a gesture of independence. After he married a non-Catholic, Patrick, like McGahern, was dismissed from his teaching post at a Catholic boys' school. . . . Patrick follows his author into exile, that wider world elsewhere for so many Irish writers. Like Macbeth, the young man in *The Dark* was unable to fight his way out of his castle keep, Ireland. In *The Leavetaking* he leaps the moat.

It has been argued that McGahern is too much a child of his generation, locked into the problems which faced young men in the 1950s, his decade of coming-of-age. Anthony Cronin, Irish man of letters, has suggested that McGahern, like Edna O'Brien, persists in misrepresenting Ireland—which Cronin sees as urban, open and secular—by portraying characters who are dominated by rural values, taboos and religious repressions. Yet the circumstances of McGahern's life suggest that his Ireland is not fanciful, though the terms in which he portrays Ireland may at times be extreme. After all, McGahern's book was banned in Ireland and he was dismissed from his teaching post. While the rest of the English speaking peoples were discovering sex—"Between the end of the *Chatterly* ban / And the Beatles' first LP," as Philip Larkin put it—Ireland was still preserving its innocence with repression. . . . The hero of *The Leavetaking* certainly seems stuck. He left, but has returned. On his final day as schoolmaster he paces the playground, watching gulls' shadows float on the concrete, his own thought floating in similar hazy circles. Roger Garfitt has described this circularity as McGahern's Buddhist cast, his characters turning on a Wheel of Karma. Certainly Patrick erects a metaphysic out of his immediate circumstances. For him all life turns and returns. He journeyed from rural Ireland to Dublin, where he won his teaching job; to London, where he won his wife; then back to Dublin, where he lost his job. . . . Had the novel ended at that point we would be granted the same No Exit vision we find in *The Dark,* where the boy sinks into a routine job, stuck for life. However, *The Leavetaking* and Patrick (finally a hero worthy of a name) go on to another stage of development.

In a near magical gift of grace—suggesting McGahern's determination to plot in a possibility of relief for his hero—love, in the person of Isobel, an American, walks into the London bar where he works. They match. He has a mother problem: when she died, Patrick's life became meaningless, a mere cycle of regret-nostalgia. She has a father problem: he is managerial, overbearing, another child molester. Patrick and Isobel set out to rescue each other, to build their own separate world. Finally private happiness is possible in a McGahern parable.

Still, the problem of the public life remained to be solved. Patrick returns to Ireland with Isobel—they live on Howth, where Molly said yes to Bloom—and resumes his teaching duties. Here Patrick faces a revealing choice. He knows he cannot hope to retain his position if it becomes public that he married a Protestant, so either he has to lie—say he was married in a Catholic Church in England—or pretend he is not married. He chooses the latter, but Dublin remains a small town, gossip travels fast and soon it is widely known that he is living with a woman on Howth. Then he is dismissed, leaving him where we find him on the opening page of the novel, walking the gull-shadowed concrete of the schoolyard, reverberating in reverie. He did not toe the line, so he is dismissed. The proposition seems confirmed.

Yet Patrick helped to contrive his own dismissal, for he set up a situation which challenged the Irish-Catholic establishment to act and then blamed the power structure when it did exactly what he knew they would. His stage-managed dismissal is his final act of exorcising Ireland. He sets up a situation in which he is forced to choose between his country and his love and, of course, chooses his love at the willing price of exile. Father Curry, an alcoholic who continues to drink despite his ulcer—another Irishman suffering from self-inflicted wounds—meets with Patrick to announce his dismissal and asks why he flew in the face of God. However, Patrick is well-insulated against such taunts; he sees Father Curry as fat, old and bigoted, a horrific version of the priest his mother wished him to be. In engineering his own banishment, Patrick makes his separate peace with all the men he might have become had he stayed. He will not be a policeman, like his father; a teacher, like his mother; or a priest, a role both he and his mother had desired for him. What he will become is uncertain. Like the boy in *The Dark,* he seems to have inchoate aesthetic longings, but as yet has no form in which to translate his impulses. All that seems to matter is that he, unlike earlier McGahern lads, has found his love, a love which constitutes both a profession and a world. The novel ends with a rhetorical flourish which echoes Arnold's "Dover Beach," another land's-end haven where love alone is certain good. . . . (pp. 258-63)

Often McGahern's bright young men and fading women hate the lives they are shown. Through death, self-annihilation in meaningless work, or exile, they fight their ways out. Elizabeth dies; the young man in *The Dark* makes it to Dublin; Patrick, in *The Leavetaking,* will make it again to London, with his wife. Though their lives ease, these novels and stories of McGahern's early career show characters who find Ireland a world well lost.

In the fiction of McGahern's middle forties—*Getting Through* and *The Pornographer*—his characters take new turns: some farther out, some deeper in. Though it never comes easy, some find new ways to live with Ireland. These works constitute a mid-career summing-up, a rounding out of a series of major and minor fictions which embody parables on the state of Ireland, its men and women. What had been bleak and constricting (the dark, nightlines) takes on a faintly optimistic cast (getting through). These works clarify McGahern's revised vision of Irish culture, character and place.

Unlike some of the stories in his early collection, *Nightlines,* which stress separation, the stories in *Getting Through* stress reconciliation. **"A Slip-up,"** for example, describes an elderly couple who left Ireland for London—as though we were picking up the Patrick-Isobel story years later—and their memories of home. Increasingly the husband recollects their days on an Irish farm. Lost, wandering the alien streets of London, in his imagination he walks "safe in the shelter of those dead days, drawing closer to the farm between the lakes they had lost." In **"Faith, Hope and Charity"** an Irish laborer is killed in a ditch cave-in in London. Perhaps, then, London has its own dangers which make Ireland seem more a haven than a trap.

However, themes in *Getting Through* run in several directions. Some stories still feature characters who struggle against ob-

structions which keep them isolated in Irish backwaters. A teacher dreams of "all sorts of impossible things" he might do outside his village, but fears change more. A policeman regrets that he has only a broken fiddle to play to a crone in an isolated village, while others play their fine violins to beautiful women in Galway. Other stories focus not on regions and freedom, but on the perverse contrivances of the imagination to supply counter-realities. McGahern implies that not just rural Ireland is smothering, but that any actuality, any life shown, is enough to set off the imagination in flight for some better place or state of being. **"Doorways"** is about a young man who would rather think than act, so life and love slip away while he stands imagining "all sorts of wonderful impossibilities" in life's doorways; he stands still, though "the day was fast falling into its own night." The imagination soars like Daedalus, but crashes like Icarus. Thus *Getting Through* leaves McGahern's representative men and women in conflicting states of being and ambiguous relation with Ireland. However, his next novel steadies his vision of Ireland.

In *The Pornographer* McGahern brings his characters full circle, back to the moist valleys of Roscommon, the rivers which soak the countryside of Carrick-on-Shannon. McGahern's wheel turns and turns again, yet there is, too, a sense of progression, of moving on past obstructions to a new resolution. At the end of *The Barracks* a woman dies of cancer and her family is land-locked in West Ireland, a bleak fate; at the end of *The Pornographer* another woman dies of cancer and another family is fated to remain in West Ireland, yet optimism buoys the novel. Elizabeth Reegan had little choice, found no exit, but the unnamed narrator, the pornographer, chooses his fate, removes himself from the doorway of indecision and unrealized imaginative possibilities.

The pornographer lives in contemporary Dublin—as much plate glass and disco as it is Georgian and pubs—where he practices his artificial art. He has, it seems, left old Ireland behind. Recovering from a lost love, the pornographer insulates himself from pain by making his appointed rounds: to the hospital to visit his dying aunt; to his room where he contrives more consequenceless sexual acrobatics for Col. Grimshaw and Mavis Carmichael; to pubs where he discusses sexual and literary aesthetics with his publisher, Maloney. The pornographer's doorway is revolving. Between "the womb and the grave," all is an empty cycle, a dutiful dance.

"Dance" is not only a metaphor, but also a site, for at a dancehall on O'Connell St. the pornographer meets a 38-year-old woman, a semi-virgin who jolts him out of his numb cycle. Josephine comes to represent something deeply, darkly Irish to her 30-year-old lover. John Updike was right to note "the hero's deadly coldness, and Josephine's credible, vital humanity," but he misses some of her threat to the pornographer; after creating the illusion of permissiveness, she comes to stand for Irish conformity [see excerpt above].

First she is fertile Ireland. Josephine brings him on a boat trip up the Shannon, where they leave behind the world of contemporary artifice in Dublin and enter a mythic realm: "there was a feeling of a dream, souls crossing to some other world. But the grey stone of the bridge of Carrick came solidly towards us out of the mist around eight." This metaphoric and actual passage ends in Josephine's womb. In a bay above Carrick he enters her, fertilizes her. Finally the McGahern hero unifies geography and psyche, body and mind; he possesses and is possessed by Ireland-as-woman.

But the pornographer will not be so easily netted. Pregnant, Josephine quickly sheds her easy ways: they must marry, settle down; he must give up writing pornography and find a proper job. When he refuses, she moves to London to have her baby, yet still seeks to have him face his responsibilities.

He, however, has other plans, centering upon a 23-year-old nurse who attended his dying aunt. Dancing with her, he feels he is "holding glory," not responsibility. While Josephine represents something grasping in the Irish character, the nurse suggests youthful vitality. . . . His business with Josephine finally settled in London, his aunt buried, the pornographer vows to make a new start with the nurse at his side, deep in the Irish countryside, at a rural farm. The McGahern hero willingly goes home again. "There comes a time when you either run amok completely or try to make a go of it. I'm going to try to make a go of it," he tells Maloney.

Even more than Josephine, Maloney provides impediments to the pornographer's development. (In *The Leavetaking* a character named Maloney, a headmaster, caned boys. In *The Dark* the similarly named Mahoney brutalizes his son. McGahern, who often has no name for his heroes, has found a name for his villains.) In *The Pornographer* Maloney, a publisher of smut, seems at first the least constricting of men. Failed reporter, failed lover, cynic, dandy, aesthete, Maloney's mutability embodies modern Ireland's openness. Yet, McGahern shows, a fierce moral righteousness runs just underneath the skins of Irish men and women, still. Maloney argues the hero is stupid for getting the woman pregnant, so he should be punished with marriage. Josephine argues responsibility; Maloney argues retribution.

Maloney explains that the pornographer must pay because life, unlike art, has consequence. Col. Grimshaw could not get Mavis pregnant, for such things do not occur in pornography. "Art is not life because it is not nature." This Wildean theorizing inspires Maloney with the plan to have the pornographer recreate in pornographic terms, for the Col. and Mavis, the Shannon trip on which Josephine became pregnant. Thus Maloney's "art" is a parody of life. "Life for art," he argues, "is about as healthy as fresh air is for a deep-sea diver." The pornographer carries out his publisher's instructions as though hypnotized. At this point he is caught between high-minded self-sacrifice urged by Josephine and Maloney, who both urge him to marry, and life-defeating artifice, his tawdry "art." At the end of the novel, with the help of the nurse, he rejects both. The hero defines his life in his own terms, rejecting pressures to conform to Irish expectations. McGahern would have us see that life is not all dire consequence, and art is not without such consequence. Further, both art and life should hold glory.

Yeats thought "one's verses should hold, as in a mirror, the colours of one's own climate and scenery in their right proportion." McGahern too seeks such proportion, such balance. The bold clash and colors of his early works has given way to patterns of complexities; revulsion against most things Irish has modulated into a tense truce or a qualified acceptance of the national landscape.

It is an extraordinary turnabout which brings the pornographer to take up his new life and his new wife in the Irish countryside, the trench from which McGahern had previously sent so many of his fictional characters over the top. Of course Ireland has greatly changed since the days of *The Barracks* and *The Dark*—images of solitary confinement, apt for Ireland of the 1950s.

Though still a tight, little island, contemporary Ireland is a place where a freer life is possible. The pornographer can avoid being trapped into marriage, choose his love and still stay on in Ireland. Perhaps McGahern will go on to demonstrate in later fiction the workings out of such an idyll as the pornographer hopes for himself and the dancing nurse in the Shannon valley. (Why would *she* wish for such a life after living in liberated Dublin? Isn't she following the downward spiral of Elizabeth Reegan, another nurse who gave up urban freedom for rural marriage and the family? Or has Irish country life changed sufficiently to make her rustic retreat another form of renewal? Since McGahern does not represent the young nurse's point-of-view, such questions linger.) The glory that the pornographer holds in the nurse's body is the promise of renewal through love and sex, set in an Irish remote field, but the novel ends before we see whether such a new life can be more than a rhetorical assertion.

For all that, McGahern, having made the easy case against Irish parochialism, now brings his considerable talents to focus on the mixed blessings of Irish provincialism, a more exacting challenge. The wall against which the McGahern hero pushes so long and hard has yielded to counter-pressures from Common Market commonality. In the face of such change, McGahern writes parables which suggest, as Edith Wharton once said about another ancient regime in decline, "there was good in the old ways." McGahern's revised version of the Irish pastoral is edged in irony, weighted by expectation and sustained by compelling fictional energies. (pp. 263-68)

Shaun O'Connell, "Door into the Light: John McGahern's Ireland," in The Massachusetts Review, *Vol. XXV, No. 2, Summer, 1984, pp. 255-68.*

PATRICIA CRAIG

[*High Ground*] opens with a broken relationship and ends with a flourishing one, a positive note thereby being struck. In between are some instances of dignified behaviour, and some tests of loyalty—the latter concerning country schoolmasters, young and old, and the choices that confront them. In ["**High Ground**"], to take that example, a boy with a new degree is invited to oust the old master whom drink has impaired. He himself was once the master's star pupil. The prospect of sudden advancement is held out to him by an upstart. Out of these few facts, McGahern makes a poised and resonant tale. As for the need to conduct yourself with decorum—it may be especially pressing if you are an unassertive girl, a maidservant, seduced and let down by the local ladykiller. [The title character in "**Eddie Mac**"] spectacularly abandons, along with his herdsman's post, the woman he has impregnated. This story, like its sequel ("**The Conversion of William Kirkwood**") opposes two qualities, Irish wildness and Anglo-Irish mildness. Or, if you like, Irish unease and Anglo-Irish self-possession.

McGahern isn't after anything so crass as local colour, but locality is important, whether it's a Dublin dance-hall he's envisaging or a Georgian country parsonage complete with walled orchard, lawn and garden. In the first of the Dublin stories, a man is left by his girlfriend and goes adrift for a while in the company of some drunkards. There is another story in which we are asked to accept the peculiarity of an intending nun, in her last days of freedom, accompanying a man to a hotel room (to compound the pattern, he's an ex-seminarist). In fact, McGahern doesn't seem to have a wide range of female characters at his disposal; and this one, typically a nurse, is also typical in being clear-headed, guileless, nerveless and unironic.

A common masculine figure in McGahern's work is the warped Irish father: one or two of these get into *High Ground*, blusterers, grudge-bearers, graceless and glum. They don't loom especially large, however; that's a hell confined to childhood. More agreeable in disposition is the type of old man who ruefully compares himself to Oisin in the wake of the Fenians, the ethnic simile persisting in the face of modern innovations, church bingo, colour television and the like. McGahern, charting social change, notes the disappearance from Irish country roads of bicycles, horses, carts, traps and sidecars. He notes the modernization of the Mass and the advent of the minibus. The newer Irish ways are offered without comment, unless a comment is implicit in McGahern's faintly elegiac tone. He writes, as always, with authority and gravity, and with an instinct for the most appropriate detail.

> Patricia Craig, "Everyday Ecstasies," in The Times Literary Supplement, No. 4302, September 13, 1985, p. 1001.

PAT ROGERS

[In *High Ground*] McGahern confines himself largely to one of two groups: young professional people in Dublin, a little déraciné in outlook, and then the families they have left behind in the provinces. The first set are flat-dwellers, whose local is the Shelbourne and who spend their weekends in the Wicklow mountains, not daring to go home. Back in the country—usually the quiet lakeland of the upper Shannon—becalmed Ascendancy families sink peacefully into oblivion, whilst the true native Irish reflect on their complex fate: 'Only in Ireland is there right time and wrong time. In other countries there is just time.' It isn't true, but McGahern show how these sad myths become self-consolatory.

His previous collections have prompted comparisons with Chekhov, and that's not altogether absurd. But much of the time he seems to be using the data of William Trevor almost as though the setting were Yoknapatawpha county rather than Roscommon. There is the same use of minor characters like the Garda sergeant and the bartender drifting in and out of stories; the same close hold on family trees and private shames; the same sense of a ritualised and inevitable way of doing things. . . . Two stories of Dublin, **"Gold Watch"** and the previously unpublished **"Bank Holiday"**, both take up the rare theme of fulfilled love, and both have the eloquence not to need excitable linguistic gestures. In form and style John McGahern's stories are unmistakably conservative: their freshness proceeds from close observation, a deep inwardness with the milieu, and a willingness to let events and description do their work unmolested by the urge to be wise about human affairs. (pp. 18-19)

> Pat Rogers, "Street Wise," in London Review of Books, Vol. 7, No. 17, October 3, 1985, pp. 18-19.

JOEL CONARROE

John McGahern, the author of such highly regarded novels as *The Pornographer* and *The Leavetaking,* has been called an Irish Chekhov, and one does find in his understated prose a fusion of high seriousness and low comedy, of heartbreak and heartburn, reminiscent of the Russian master. Other writers are brought to mind too by his fine new book, *High Ground,* a collection of stories. When his characters engage in hostile wordplay, the potential violence barely held in check, they sound like Pinter people. The dreamy men and practical women are cousins to Sean O'Casey's strong Junos and inept paycocks. Many of the characters, moreover, paralyzed by convention and habit, are unable to escape their parochial fates; their powerlessness suggests a central motif in James Joyce. . . .

Loss and betrayal are Mr. McGahern's great themes, and several of the stories are calculated to discomfit an attentive reader. (The compressed prose, every rift loaded with ore, must be read as deliberately as lyric poetry.) In **"The Conversion of William Kirkwood,"** one of two especially impressive tales, the man who has taken in Annie May, Eddie Mac's abandoned lover, and raised her daughter to young womanhood is engaged to a woman who suddenly announces that "Annie May will have to be given notice." This prospect sets up the realization that the marriage cannot take place "without bringing suffering on two people who had been a great part of his life, who had done nothing themselves to deserve being driven out into a world they were hardly prepared for." If stories can break hearts, this one will.

A second moving story, **"Oldfashioned,"** treats another of the author's obsessive themes, the conflict between fathers and sons. The tale, rich in characters and plot development, would have emerged, from a less laconic writer, as a novella or even as a full-blown novel. A sensitive working-class lad becomes a kind of adopted son to a wealthy couple who want to sponsor him to Sandhurst, the famous military academy, so he can prepare for a career in the British Army. The boy's real father quickly and violently deflates the dream: "Well, then. I have news for you. You're going to no Sandhurst whether they'd have you or not, and I even doubt if the Empire is that hard up." Much later the son makes a series of documentary films "about the darker aspects of Irish life," even though the people that really interest him are "all dead." It is tempting to find an autobiographical source in this narrative. . . .

In addition to the struggle between rigid fathers and their rebellious sons, these stories invoke other passionate conflicts—between men and women, union members and those who "cross the line," Roman Catholic and Protestant, the older and younger generations, and even between poets and more prosaic folk ("They say the standing army of poets never falls below ten thousand in this unfortunate country"). Only two of the stories strike false notes. In one, **"High Ground,"** a young man who is urged to supplant the benign, hard-drinking principal of his school days—a particularly awful act of betrayal—overhears the old man, at the end of the story, praising his former students. Given the usual credibility of Mr. McGahern's plots, this neat juxtaposition seems contrived. The other unconvincing narrative, **"Bank Holiday,"** treats an idealized affair between a middle-aged Dubliner and a young visitor from America. Unlike the author's plausible depictions of love gone awry, this is not a compelling picture of contemporary life, in Dublin or anywhere else; Mr. McGahern is more persuasive in evoking the moon's dark side than in describing moonlight and roses.

If two stories fail to convince, however, the other eight not only succeed, but even invite second and third close readings. It strikes me, in fact, that with this book, his seventh, Mr. McGahern joins a charmed circle of contemporary Irish writers that includes Edna O'Brien, Seamus Heaney and Thomas Kinsella. . . .

> Joel Conarroe, "Strong Women, Dreamy Men," in The New York Times Book Review, February 8, 1987, p. 9.

Medbh McGuckian

1950-

Irish poet.

In her verse, McGuckian examines themes related to femininity while infusing her language with dense rhythms and erotic images. McGuckian is often linked with Paul Muldoon, Frank Ormsby, and other poets she met while attending Queen's University, Belfast, in the late 1960s and early 1970s. Although these poets do not rigidly adhere to particular topics or styles, their work displays painstaking craftsmanship in rendering a distinct poetic consciousness. McGuckian avoids themes related to the political troubles in Ireland, instead transforming elements of everyday experience into metaphoric representations of the female psyche. She also employs oxymoron to juxtapose concrete and abstract adjectives, imbuing her work with paradoxical and chimerical qualities. The observational and contemplative nature of her poems prompted Anne Stevenson to comment: "Flat, coy, confusing when she fails, [McGuckian's] successes are dazzling, and her contrived syntheses of looking and thinking, fascinating."

McGuckian's early chapbooks, *Single Ladies* (1980) and *Portrait of Joanna* (1980), were praised by critics for displaying inventive figures of speech and sensual evocations. These accolades were tempered, however, by reservations that McGuckian's reliance on tropes often results in obscurity. Similar charges were leveled against her subsequent volumes, *The Flower Master* (1982) and *Venus and the Rain* (1984), in which McGuckian employs the dramatic monologues of an indeterminate persona to focus on love, sex, and the relationship between females of different generations. In a review of *Venus and the Rain*, John Mole described McGuckian as "a fantasist of the everyday" who creates "a thoroughly up-to-date verse . . . which applies many of the symbols of aesthetic romanticism to a thoroughly contemporary exploration of love and motherhood."

(See also *Dictionary of Literary Biography,* Vol. 40.)

ANNE STEVENSON

"Don't think", said Wittgenstein, "look!" Wise council to poets as well as to philosophers. Nevertheless (and this was largely Wittgenstein's point) looking implies seeing, or more specifically, the act of seeing *as*—of seeing shapes and colours as recognizable things which have meanings only in terms of what we know. So the way we look at things comes back, in the end, to the way we think about them. What we think when we look defines what we see.

Thoughts like these are provoked by an extremely interesting, deceptively modest little pamphlet called *Portrait of Joanna* by Medbh McGuckian. Mrs McGuckian is as fine a "looker" as any poet I know. She is as clever (probably) as Craig Raine, as perceptive (possibly) as Elizabeth Bishop. Her eye for the *minutiae* of plant and seed is that of a patient botanist in a high state of emotion. Her sense of the atmosphere of vision is

unique, but it is also curiously upsetting. Where Elizabeth Bishop steadied herself, like her own sun, "on a ripple in the river", calming inner panic with a loving consideration of exteriors, Medbh McGuckian gives the impression that panic itself is exterior. Reading these poems, one senses that thoughts and perceptions make mysterious connections with a hidden terror in the poet's mind—a terror which insists on being visible.

Take, for example, the first poem, called **"Tulips".** The poet begins by describing her human shyness in the presence of more independent, somehow superior tulips which, unlike herself, have "Defensive mechanisms to frustrate the rain / That shakes into the sherry glass / Of the daffodil." In the second stanza, however, the tulips become fallible and more human, "like all governesses, easily / Carried away. . .". They are "ballets of revenge", "an olympic way of earning", necessarily

> . . . sacrificed to plot, their faces
> Lifted many times to the artistry of light,
> Its lovelessness a deeper sort
> Of illness than the womanliness
> Of tulips with their bee-dark hearts.

This, like all the poems in *Portrait of Joanna,* is worth the time spent pondering it. The wealth of exteriors explored by

Medbh McGuckian's poems augurs the flowering of a talent which, fortunately, seems too original—too eccentric, even—to be wrongly directed by over-praise or by critical misunderstanding. She sounds, at times, like a contemporary, Irish Emily Dickinson. Flat, coy, confusing when she fails, her successes are dazzling, and her contrived syntheses of looking and thinking, fascinating.

Anne Stevenson, "With Eyes Open and Closed," in The Times Literary Supplement, No. 4090, August 21, 1981, p. 952.

JOHN LUCAS

In *The Flower Master* Medbh McGuckian shows that she is already a great phrase-maker. But phrases do not make poems and nor, I think, does she. At all events, her transitions are so abrupt, opaque and inconsequential as to be self-defeating. In addition there is a fey whimsicality about her work which some may find appealing but which sets this particular reader's teeth on edge:

This black container calls for sloes, sweet
Sultan, dainty nipplewort, in honour
Of a special guest, who summoned to the
Tea ceremony, must stoop to our doorway,
Our fontanelle, the trout's dimpled feet.

'Sweet', 'dainty': this isn't the new fertilizer, it's merely the same old sterile language that's been around for far too long and that can't be kicked into life by any amount of trout's feet, dimpled or otherwise. (Readers can have fun attaching adjectives of their own devising to the McGuckian run of nouns.) This is not to say that McGuckian lacks talent, but it is to insist that such talent needs to be disciplined, not indulged like a spoilt child. (p. 21)

John Lucas, "Pleading for the Authenticity of the Spirit," in New Statesman, Vol. 104, No. 2682, August 13, 1982, pp. 20-1.

TIM DOOLEY

In his rather condescending poem "A Bookshop Idyll", Kingsley Amis characterized the work of women poets by "the awful way their poems lay them open". Medbh McGuckian's first full collection [*The Flower Master*] demonstrates a determined unwillingness to assume such an undignified position. . . . Repeatedly in her poems an aversion is expressed to hardness and clarity as if they exemplified a predominantly masculine logic which leaves no room for the "curtainings and cushionings" which, in **"That Year"**, she associates with the needs of her own, less will-driven imagination. Tulips, she reminds us

. . . are sacrificed to plot, their faces
Lifted many times to the artistry of light—
Its lovelessness a deeper sort
Of illness than the womanliness
Of tulips with their bee-dark hearts.

"Womanliness"—an assertive quality neither traditionally feminine, nor yet feminist in an ideologically straitened way—is both the source and subject of much of McGuckian's poetry. She takes a particular interest in the historic position of women in the visual arts, whether displayed as models or neglected as craftswomen, and shows how their "narrative secretes its own values" despite attempts to conceal the importance of their

contribution. She takes traditional decorative crafts seriously, rejecting the suggestion that they might be dismissed as self-indulgence or relaxation. . . .

The elaboration of McGuckian's poetry cannot be dismissed as a pointlessly decorative embroidery. The trust she places in instinct and chance collocation is not the result of "guesswork" but of an awareness that a hitherto underpresented view of experience may need radically different forms of expression. By turning on its head Yeats's proposition that "there's more enterprise / In walking naked" and by letting her experience dictate its own private vocabulary, McGuckian achieves the kind of artistic "opening up" and personal liberation that the women described in **"The Seed-Picture"** are only able to "sigh for".

The areas which McGuckian has been particularly successful in opening up tend to be intimate ones, involving sexuality or relations between different generations in a family. Her frequent use of monologue allows her to establish a personal tone which suits these concerns, while her employment of indeterminate first-person speakers prevents a vulgarly confessional identification of poet and narrative voice. This is particularly effective in the family poems where the tensions between a worldly and sceptical generation and their pious and suspicious parents are shown from several angles. . . .

[Distance] is a quality that Medbh McGuckian can overrate—allowing her preference for associations and impressions rather than definitions and names to give her writing a too uniformly soft focus and leading her to idealize a turn-of-the-century "warless world" to the point of sentimentality. That said, *The Flower Master* remains one of the richest and most provocative collections of poetry to have appeared in recent years.

Tim Dooley, "Soft Cushionings," in The Times Literary Supplement, No. 4152, October 29, 1982, p. 1200.

ALAN JENKINS

Ten years ago, in a symposium gathered by *the Review* and grandly titled "The State of Poetry", Peter Redgrove ventured ". . . to me the most encouraging thing in the poetry scene is this relearning and trusting of what used to be called surrealism but which I think is better called 'erotic fluency' or some better coinage, like a lover's language which is not private. . . ." It is hard to say what exactly "erotic fluency" may mean, since, if we sense obscurely that Redgrove's own poetry has it, we also feel that the term could appropriately be applied to the poems of Mallarmé or Valéry; and we might think that it takes yet another form in the work of a poet as different from them as they are from each other, John Ashbery. And now, to confuse the issue, we have Medbh McGuckian's *The Flower Master,* to remind us that it is by no means an exclusively masculine preserve; to remind us, also, that just as it can be a source of poetic vitality and the most seductive of poetic pleasures, so too it can be the natural corollary of an excessively cultivated languor or worse, feyness.

This is all the more noticeable in Medbh McGuckian's poems wherever her language, though certainly that of a lover, becomes a very private one indeed:

In my first sleep, I see in the glass
The man who washed in a southward stream
Where three lands meet, climbing my plaited ladder,

275

And just as socially, dropping out of the picture
Into a dream of cowboy boots—
I should tell the bees, my five pointed stars.

The words "sleep" and "dream" alert us to the presence of something beyond "rational" discourse, may even disarm criticism of a rational kind; but if we take as seriously as Redgrove does—and I think we should—his assertion from the same *Review* article that "dreams (material for 'surrealism') have meaning, deep life-meanings, life talking in its own language about itself", we will look in vain for such meanings, or such a language, in those six lines.

"Erotic fluency", if it is anything at all, is a quality of rhythm and, especially, of syntax; it may partake of "the abstract vitality of speech", "the sound of sense" (as Frost defined it, and as many other poets have independently discovered), or it may aspire to the condition of music (as in Mallarmé and Valéry). Frequently the two nourish each other. McGuckian has surely learnt the trick of producing syntactical "surprises" from John Ashbery: continuity, ("flow") of sound, discontinuities of sense; sudden changes of grammatical subject and tense, shifts in personal pronoun and the consequent indeterminacy of the speaking voice; startling juxtapositions and ellipses; the subverting of expectations set up by the apparent direction of a sentence; qualifying or elaborating phrases proliferating endlessly. Her cadences can, not surprisingly, sound very like Ashbery's as well.

The case against a style can be overdone, though, and the real (or greater) difficulty is that the temptations of a particular kind of lushness and inventiveness lead McGuckian into solemnity and rhetorical posturing, which in poem after poem vitiate a potentially powerful and individual angle of vision. Her predominant theme—an experience of femininity and feminine activities which she characterises, with considerable ambivalence, as "womanliness", in which flower-tending and flower-arranging, handicrafts and arts, but also marriage, domesticity and sex all figure—is central enough, God knows, for us to want to hear about it. But in a poem about desire and self-distrust we get "my tenable / Emotions playing largely with themselves"; elsewhere, we have "your piquancy of dreams", "the shattering excretion of the rose", "their fictions hurt us / Gently, like the nudity of rose-beige tea-gowns. . . ." It's possible that McGuckian is too concerned not to hurt us, or to hurt us only gently. Her own hurt and irony flash out every now and then (she admires, for example, the defensiveness of tulips—"It's their independence / Tempts them to this grocery of soul"—and also respects their "bee-dark hearts"), and persuasively so. Too often, there is a generous quilting of literary self-consciousness—"My books sleep, pretending to forget me"; "the study's brick floor where / My poems thicken in the desk" and, most unforgivably, in an otherwise beautiful and disciplined meditation on home-making and the girls painted by Vermeer, **"The Flitting"** (which won McGuckian the National Poetry Competition three years ago):

> I postpone my immortality for my children,
> Little rock-roses, cushioned
> In long-flowering sea-thrift and metrics. . . .

There may be, behind such lines, the disguised or defended vulnerability of shy intelligence and unencouraged gifts; but the lines themselves strike an unappealing note of the narrowly (and complacently) self-obsessed, almost self-admiring and inviting our admiration. Similarly, it has been claimed that McGuckian's refusal of "conventional" syntax and overtly

logical construction signal a rejection of—even a quiet assault on—traditionally masculine discourse and values. Her own blurring of edges and impressions, however, her softening and rounding-out of images and statements, are too easily caricatured as "conventionally" feminine, and are sometimes disturbingly close to caricature already. Perhaps intentionally so; but there is too little variety or subtlety of tone in the book for such discriminations to be made with any confidence. Apart from a handful of short, direct poems which move away from obviously "personal" themes—**"Gentians"**, **"Fossils"**, **"Power-Cut"**—only two poems, both concerned with the ruses and deceptions of portraiture and female identity, **"The Seed-Picture"** and **"The Witchmark"**, break sufficiently free of the whimsical or the wilfully idiosyncratic to command complete assent. They are stunning poems, and go some way towards justifying the praise and approval—she has been called provocative, original, brilliant—that McGuckian has already received.

To pick up the contrast with Redgrove: is it really that? Redgrove's poems, after all, solicit "the feminine principle"—which McGuckian would find suspect—and submit "masculine" energies to a kind of heroic worship of female properties and propensities; and his work has aptly been called "a kind of inspired domestic science." Should we find all that uncongenial, we can still enjoy his poems for their visionary biologist's attentiveness, their "passionate investigation of nature"—that other continuum, which in Redgrove's poetic world unites the entire chain of creation from the molecular and microscopic to the mountainous. It is this sense of things which gives his work its fluency and excitement, and which he shares with McGuckian to the extent that she sometimes seems to want to lose herself, or her *persona*, in the "dark downward and vegetating kingdom" of plants and flowers. Both show some disregard for expository argument, the linkages of "prose sense", and rely instead on the power of images to see them through. (pp. 56-8)

Alan Jenkins, "Private & Public Languages," in Encounter, *Vol. LIX, No. 5, November, 1982, pp. 56-63.*

CHRISTOPHER HOPE

The Flower Master constitutes a notable debut by a poet of intriguing complexity. On the one hand, Medbh McGuckian's poems are especially well turned out; stylish surfaces and shapely forms show a couturier's love for costume, colour, line, fabric; this is combined with a needle-eye for 'The leaf-patterned linoleum, the elaborate / Stitches on my pleated bodice. / ' (**"That Year"**). Flowers are everywhere; but what strange blooms: 'the sherry-glass / of the daffodil . . .' and the 'tulips with their bee-dark hearts / ' (**"Tulips"**). On closer inspection flowers turn into floral patternings, into fabrics, petals into pleats and tucks; it is beautifully detailed, fine, close work which transforms moths in 'rose-beige tea-gowns', a passionate haberdashery. These disconcerting transformations, like her dubious nature-studies in **"Mr McGregor's Garden"**—'of my favourite rabbit's head, his vulgar volatility / . . . of my resident toad in his flannel box / ', suggest subversive intentions. For what McGuckian is doing with icy skill is not sewing things up, but taking them apart, and the finery with which she decks out her poems initially disguises the real point of her needlework—which is to unstitch, expose, impale. This is mortuary art, her subjects like dressmakers' dummies so tricked out they might almost be alive; all these are aspects of what she calls a '. . .

wholesome curiosity in corpses . . .', a desire to investigate the careers of fossils, to observe how 'Cyanide in the killing-jar relaxes the Indian moon moth' (**"The Butterfly Farm"**), to study the secret afterlives of shells and ghosts. By a kind of full-blooded artifice she contrives to breathe life back into her pinned specimens. McGuckian dwells among such paradoxes in poems such as **"The Seed Picture," "The Soil-Map"** and **"The Flower Master":**

> Our scissors in brocade,
> We learn the coolness of straight edges, how
> To gently stroke the necks of daffodils
> And make them throw their heads back to the sun.

In her strange, oblique love-poems, similarly disconcerting resurrections take place: 'He is like an interim desk I have never got round / to replacing' (**"The Witchmark"**).

And so with studied artlessness McGuckian fleshes out her poems and pricks them into life; by coming at such obscure intangibles as the qualities of sexual tension from unexpected angles she can, as it were, surprise them into disclosing themselves. . . . This is a wonderfully original, bewitching collection. (pp. 106-07).

> *Christopher Hope, "Meaty Flavours," in* London Magazine, *n.s. Vol. 22, Nos. 9 & 10, December, 1982 & January, 1983, pp. 106-11.*

BERNARD O'DONOGHUE

The reviewer of Medbh McGuckian faces in a form more acute than usual the Keats dilemma: the possibility of getting wrong the assessment of a poet of originality who doesn't fit the prevailing literary type. *Venus and the Rain* centres even more insistently than her first volume, *The Flower Master,* on sets of coded ideas and symbols, all of them acting as obscure expressions of sexual feelings and conditions. The female principle is represented by Venus, the Moon, sisterhood, motherhood; the male is the Sun, the Rain and other images of saturation. The two principles meet and conflict in other complexes of imagery: house (associated with furniture and wood) and painting (blue—the dull colour of 'Mars', brown and gold are recurrent value-colours). The hermeticism of the first volume, then, is often even more marked in these poems; but the extraordinary expressiveness of *The Flower Master,* which seemed to emerge in spite of rather than through the words on the page, is also more marked here. The poems, particularly their openings and endings, often have an extraordinary dense evocativeness. . . . (pp. 62-3)

[One] of the most beautiful poems has a . . . haunting opening:

> Your eyes were ever brown, the colour
> Of time's submissiveness.

The same audacity of wit that represented the libido as the hedgehog in **"Mr McGregor's Garden"** is evident here but extended further in a way that can only be called allegorical, rather than symbolist. The 'I' and 'You' of these poems are usually sides of the sexual personality itself; various aspects of it are personified as painter, poet(ess), sister or villain. The most elusive passages are reminiscent of the eccentric poets in the English tradition who are loosely called 'mystical': writers such as Langland or Blake. Sometimes, as in the magnificent last poem of this volume, **"Sabbath Park"**, the 'mysticism' even assumes a more explicit form:

> Sometimes in the evenings
> I would ask, a step not easily taken,
> Whether the bird learns to build its nest
> Like that—a perfect nest from such
> Arthritic wood.

But the elements in the mystical whole remain obscure; it would be less than honest to pretend to know exactly what the nest-building represents in this poem, whatever its resonance. And it is no more critically responsible, even if it is safer, to praise the uncomprehended than to dismiss it on the grounds of obscurity. . . .

[It] would not be true to say that McGuckian's poetry is entirely private in reference. In some ways she is less private than other cryptic modern poets who draw on unshared experience, because she is using that unshared experience not as an end in itself but as it can represent universal experience. The 'I' of each poem has to be examined separately to see what the poem means (for example, the 'half-fatherly' narrator in **"Vanessa's Bower"** is not the same as the voice of female sexuality in **"From the Dressing-Room"**). And just as the speaking persona is not private to the poet, neither is it private to her sex. McGuckian's poems are less politically feminist than, say, Selima Hill's, though, unsurprisingly, they are written out of a woman's experience. The writer whose view of sex she most recalls is D. H. Lawrence. And her best tone of voice (after the ironic one of **"Mr McGregor's Garden"** which is absent here) is an eloquent generalising. . . . In the end only the poet can make poetry of this kind fully accessible to the reader. But its appealing expressiveness suggests that it is not a private code but a public code waiting to be cracked. And McGuckian's sheer originality (no fastidious sucking on the feel of words; no relations coming out of woodsheds; no representations of things as what they are *not* for the fun of it) explains and excuses some of the obscurity. (p. 63)

> *Bernard O'Donoghue, "The Keats Dilemma," in* Poetry Review, *Vol. 74, No. 2, June, 1984, pp. 61-3.*

JON COOK

Venus and the Rain may confirm Medbh McGuckian's reputation as an obscure and esoteric writer. The temptation is to call the poems 'mysterious' and 'erotic' and then use admiration as a form of neglect.

Yet their difficulty is not simply intransigence. The poems possess qualities which connect them to established strengths and traditions and one of those is daring, metaphysical intelligence which is evident, for example, in the first poem in this collection, **"Venus and the Sun"**. Here, the voice of Venus, which recurs in this collection, is transposed from classical mythology into a post-Newtonian universe. McGuckian gives voice to the planet, Venus, held in the gravity of the solar system which is also a world of reversible time and space. . . . The poem ends in an ironic reversal: caught in the world of science, Venus recalls with nostalgia an earlier mythic event in her history, the love affair with Mars. The poem moves out of a mythic frame into a scientific one, only to recombine the two in a way that can recall the capacity of Donne or Empson to make poetry out of scientific theory. Like them, too, the grand scale described in the poem is played off against a deflationary, humanising tone: Venus has grown weary of her place in the universe and yearns for an alternative. The poem becomes an allegory of entrapment.

It is part of the cultural density of these poems that they echo earlier modes. This can be a matter of revisiting traditional poetic sites, as in **"To the Nightingale"**, or of a less assertive repetition as when Keats, again, is echoed in the personification of Autumn which begins the poem **"For the Previous Owner"**. Wallace Stevens is here, too: McGuckian shares his concern with the relations between real and imaginary worlds, notably in **"The Sitting"** which questions whether imagination brings out a potential in the subject or simply imposes a fantasy upon it. There is, as well, a shared delight in poetic invention for its own sake: what Stevens called the 'gorgeous nonsense' of poetry, its capacity for extravagant connections and the creation of a pleasurable language.

But McGuckian's poems are not slaves to precedent. What they echo they also transform and in a way that begins to suggest something of their originality. The poems are everywhere informed by the subject of womanhood. The subject is realised in a way that is complex, richly textured and differentiated. It can be a matter of restoring mythic voices: Venus or the Moon, for example, no longer seen as the mutually exclusive symbols of female lust or chastity but as different phases of identity within the rhythm of a single life. Or it's to do with a knowledge won from experience and given direct and eloquent utterance. . . .

McGuckian's language is charged by a knowledge of sexual difference and, although this knowledge can be held in a political perspective, . . . hers is not a writing fearful of desire. A number of the poems engage quite remarkably with heterosexual love. . . .

The cumulative effect of McGuckian's writing in *Venus and the Rain* is to give the sense of a highly wrought and expanding imaginative world which can give symbolic expression to intimate physical experience without falling prey to the conventions of pornography. The boldness of the writing carries with it certain risks, most notably of a lapse into a merely mannered style, but the book as a whole gives notice of a considerable achievement in the making.

> *Jon Cook, "New Found Land," in* New Statesman, *Vol. 108, No. 2789, August 31, 1984, p. 26.*

MICHAEL O'NEILL

Medbh McGuckian is sometimes described as an "erotic" poet. Certainly her favourite properties—rain, sun, moon, the seasons—are rich in symbolic potential. Yet, in *Venus and the Rain,* she is more compelling as a poet of psychological stresses and pressures. McGuckian writes well, for instance, about antagonisms and doublings within the self, as in **"Isba Song"** or **"The Rising Out"** which starts: "My dream sister has gone into my blood / To kill the poet in me before Easter". A security at which she frets and a freedom she views warily are the opposed points round which other poems spin their verbal webs. In **"Venus and the Sun"**, a quirky monologuing voice charts a series of manoeuvres and recognitions, until, almost wearily, the speaker (Venus) concludes: "with any choice / I'd double-back to the dullest blue of Mars". Elsewhere, the tensions are more overt. **"Catching Geese"** begins: "Dreaming is after I decline to sleep / With you". Through the poem's subsequent mists of invention, it's possible to glimpse the outline of a recognizably human conflict: "You're unhappy / At

my fern-fisted handshake, I'm unhappy / That my fresh hunger doesn't block your throat / Like a person". McGuckian's tone is bracingly unsentimental, yet shouldn't be mistaken for indifference to pain. When the poem ends, "And every sound of you crying could be heard", it catches the reader off balance. Artifice and distress are suddenly brought into disturbing connection. More often, though, her poems seem riddling, blurred or opaque, games played by a sensibility delighting in the gap between words and things. Human qualities are cavalierly and knowingly assigned to "natural" phenomena. The risk of sounding coyly self-regarding isn't one she always avoids, as when she refers to "the art of raining, with its oh-so masculine / Kisses". At her best, metaphors and experience fuse, forming new realities; the visionary opening of **"Sabbath Park"** is an intriguing example. *Venus and the Rain* is a gifted collection, yet it leaves the reader hoping that at some stage in this talented poet's career language will serve less as a screen and more as a torch.

> *Michael O'Neill, "Bidding for Power," in* The Times Literary Supplement, *No. 4261, November 30, 1984, p. 1393.*

JOHN MOLE

The cover illustration for Medbh McGuckian's second collection, *Venus and the Rain,* is a detail from a painting by the 19th-century Secessionist Jan Toorop. It has been well-chosen—a fluid, densely-textured canvas reproduced in shadowy monochrome. The perspective recedes into a forest of prominently-rooted, sinuous trees which gather round a dark, standing pool, and the whole scene is ambivalently enchanting and sinister. In the foreground, a child sits in a high-chair—as if *indoors*, and as if the backdrop of the forest were only a painter's illusion. Immediately behind the child, a young woman is standing in what appears to be a half-opened doorway. Is she coming out or in? Is she choosing the natural world or an elaborate fantasy? Or is she already the victim of a choice made for her in which the child is a crucial element?

To look closely at this picture is to be drawn into a close, teasing world of vital, unanswerable questions which are at the same time about the illusions of art and of domestic experience. To go on, then, to read Medbh McGuckian's poems is to continue the experience in colour. She's a fantasist of the everyday, and hers is a thoroughly up-to-date verse—"retelling the story / Of its own provocative fractures"—which applies many of the symbols of aesthetic romanticism to a thoroughly contemporary exploration of love and motherhood. Often she seems a rather more robust and domesticated *Dame aux Camélias:*

> Each lighted
> Window shows me cardiganed, more desolate
> Than the garden, and more hallowed
> Than the hinge of the brass-studded
> Door that we close, and no one opens,
> That we open and no one closes.

That juxtaposition of the desolate and the hallowed is characteristic, just as McGuckian's tone keeps shifting from the bewildered to the benign. However, it would be quite wrong to suggest that these poems are at all straightforwardly expressive. Self and others are a cluster of images to be arranged and rearranged kaleidoscopically. . . . At one moment the elemental is impinging on the domestic—"a waterfall / Unstitching itself down the front stairs"—and at the next a household prop transforms itself into an emotional strategy—"Except for the staircase that delivers you / Like a jetty into the middle of a lake, / There is no measure of arrival, no / Negotiation. . . .'' This goes on all the time, a considerable poetic confidence at work on an obsessive ground of private enquiry.

Medbh McGuckian's poetry, impressive though it is, does raise the question of how far it's possible to take a coded practice before it becomes a restrictive one. She is in some ways an obscure writer despite the attractiveness of her imagery. Rather too often I feel that I have to take it on trust that, for example, ''the change in your voice when speaking / Is like an orange in a snowdrift'', and it's easy to get lost on one of her extended, metamorphic trails although she seems aware of this and even goes so far as to make it (by implication) one of her credentials when she suggests that ''my longer and longer sentences / Prove me wholly female.'' Yes, but it could also prove her simply rather indulgent. (pp. 58-9)

John Mole, *''From Wave to Cave,''* in Encounter, *Vol. LXIII, No. 5, December, 1984, pp. 56-63.*

CHRISTOPHER BENFEY

Venus is speaking in the title poem of Medbh McGuckian's new book [*Venus and the Rain*]. ''I am the sun's toy—'' Venus says in another poem, ''because I go against / The grain I feel the brush of my authority.'' With such oddly precise astronomical observations—Venus' orbit is the reverse of the orbits of the other planets—McGuckian creates her metaphorical atmosphere. Her poems are as lush and comfortable with astral themes as Elizabethan poetry. . . . McGuckian's poetry, which is often described as hermetic and mysterious, can be startlingly concrete in its images. . . . (pp. 505-07)

But McGuckian is also an inhabitant of Belfast. She was a classmate of Paul Muldoon and she is often numbered among the ''second generation of Ulster poets.'' There was an occasional reference to Ireland in her first book of poems, *The Flower Master* (''Ireland / So like Italy Italians came to film it''), but in these new poems McGuckian is first a Venusian and second—a distant second—an Ulsterwoman. She hasn't followed Seamus Heaney in searching for ways to be true to one's own private experience while registering the public strains of the North, nor has she found, like Derek Mahon, analogues in other artists in other times for her own ambiguous place in society. To scan her poems for allusions to sectarian violence would be as fruitless and naive as to sift Emily Dickinson's poems for references to the Civil War. Of course the reader will find things in both cases, but the reticence is as significant as the revelation. A poet must be faithful to her own imaginative urges; one feels in the poems of McGuckian (and of Dickinson) a powerful inner censor holding the poet to the sources of her own imaginative power. When a Venusian sends a postcard home (to modify Craig Raine's famous title) she writes about love.

There is nothing ''raw'' about McGuckian's treatment of love. It is as though all the conventional discourses of love had been forbidden, declared taboo, so that she must take whatever is at hand—clothes, furniture, flowers, colors, the weather—and fashion love poems out of these. Since this process resembles the machinery of dreams, her poetry is often dreamlike. Love becomes in her poems less taboo than tropical, a topic that can only be approached obliquely, by way of tropes. These tropes provide what she calls ''a sort of hotel / In her voice,'' which is as much a refuge for her as Rilke's ''temple in the hearing'' was for him. . . . Such hermeticism would be merely annoying if it did not have a recognizable (if not easily describable)

authority, and if McGuckian failed to convince us that, as she says in an uncharacteristic disclaimer, ''This oblique trance is my natural / Way of speaking.''

Usually she is as blunt and unapologetic about her obliquity as Emily Dickinson, whose advice was to ''Tell all the Truth but tell it slant.'' A McGuckian poem will often assemble around the sound and connotations of a single word, ''culprits,'' for example. A poet of that title ends with an extraordinary line: ''My curtains skein the cold like culprits of light.'' Sometimes McGuckian confines her slantness to a modest device, for example the coupling of an ordinary adjective with an odd one: ''this gray / And *paunchy* house,'' ''this my / Brownest, *tethered* room,'' ''that smart and / *Cheerful* rain.'' It is a device that Auden explored as well. But obliquity can invade an entire poem. (pp. 507-08)

Christopher Ricks has traced what he calls the reflexive image, or self-infolded image, through the poems of Marvell and the male poets of modern Ulster. In Seamus Heaney's waterfall, ''The burn drowns steadily in its own downpour,'' or, in Marvell's description of a woman crying, ''She courts herself in am'rous rain; Her self both *Danae* and the Showr.'' Ricks suggests that this kind of metaphor may be tied to the experience of civil war, where identity and division of self are constantly in question. But the metaphors McGuckian's poems show off are self-infolded in a different way. Her moods find fit accommodation in the metaphors and similes of houses and furniture. In her first book, *The Flower Master*, McGuckian seemed pleased with the mechanical ease with which the device could bestow the illusion of concreteness on reported moods. . . . In *Venus and the Rain* the still ubiquitous furniture is more mysterious. McGuckian writes of ''a lap-child's sense of chairs' and of ''the overexcitement of mirrors.'' Her groping with chairs and tables and drapery reminds me at times of how victims of adult perversion are sometimes asked to rehearse, with dolls and blocks, what has been inflicted on them. Her poems resemble ''play therapy'' in the ways they fuse eroticism and the furnishings of houses. . . . (pp. 509-10)

McGuckian's rooms and houses are filled with the decor of Victorian sitting-rooms: flowers carefully arranged, letters read and unread, embroidery, lace, silk kimonos. She seems unapologetic about her pleasure in these things. Her procedure in many poems is to rehearse the traditional metiers and meters of women—clothes, men and courtship, sex, child-rearing, and such domestic activities as knitting, sketching, arranging furniture—but to look at them so searchingly that they become strange. (p. 510)

Her poetry, while often courting . . . feminist interpretation, seems more at home in an almost Japanese reticence and reclusiveness. In her first book McGuckian found in the Japanese tea ceremony the model for the mood she wanted in her poetry. She developed, across several poems, her fascination with such ''ladylike'' activities as flower arranging, the tea ceremony, and moon-viewing. . . . *Venus and the Rain* remains, for the most part, in the trancelike mood of the tea ceremony, but the language is denser, weightier, more reclusive. Among American poets Louis Glück probably resembles her most, but McGuckian's richer diction seems to draw from fin-de-siècle sources, the mood of *Pelléas et Mélisande* of Yeats's brief essay, ''The Autumn of the Body.'' (p. 511)

Christopher Benfey, *''A Venusian Sends a Postcard Home,''* in Parnassus: Poetry in Review, *Vol. 12, No. 2 & Vol. 13, No. 1, Spring-Summer & Fall-Winter, 1985, pp. 500-12.*

Ezra (Loomis) Pound

1885-1972

(Also wrote under pseudonyms of B. H. Dias, Abel Saunders, and William Atheling) American poet, translator, critic, essayist, editor, and librettist.

Among the foremost literary figures of the twentieth century, Pound is credited with creating some of modern poetry's most enduring and inventive verse. In such volumes as *Ripostes* (1912), *Cathay* (1915), and *Hugh Selwyn Mauberley* (1920), he expedited the modern period in English and American letters by introducing and elucidating Imagist and Vorticist theories. These works display Pound's efforts to "resuscitate the dead art" and "make it new" by combining stylistic elements from the verse of Provençal and Tuscan troubadours, French and Oriental poets, and the Pre-Raphaelites with Imagistic principles expounded by T. E. Hulme, Ernest Fenellosa, and Ford Madox Ford. Eschewing verbosity and enjambment, Pound sought to employ *le mot juste*—the precise word—which often took the form of foreign phrases, archaic dialects, or technical diction, and he revived the end-stopped line to create self-contained measures of poetry that resonate with independent significance. In addition, Pound's experiments with rhythm are often considered the first substantial twentieth-century effort to liberate poetry from iambic patterns.

Born in Hailey, Idaho, and raised in Philadelphia, Pound made his first visits to Europe with his family in 1898 and 1902. After receiving a philosophy degree from Hamilton College, Pennsylvania, in 1905, Pound pursued graduate work in Romance languages at the University of Pennsylvania and was awarded a fellowship to study the plays of Lope de Vega in London and Madrid. For a short while in 1907, Pound taught Romance languages at Wabash College, Indiana, until relieved of his duties for reputedly sheltering a woman overnight in his rooms. Disgusted with American provincialism, Pound returned to Europe and privately published his first volume, *A lume spento* (1908), in Venice. From there he traveled to London and initiated a period of intense productivity in literary and artistic endeavors. His association with *New Age* magazine over the next several years introduced him to important artists, economists, and politicians and contributed to the development of ideas he would expound upon in his later works. In 1921, having been the key agent in the publication of some of the previous decade's most influential works, Pound moved to Paris, where he continued to assert his literary tastes. Pound left Paris in 1924 to live in Rapallo, Italy, where he endorsed the Fascist government of Benito Mussolini and declared his political beliefs in a series of radio broadcasts during World War II. Arrested by American allies and charged with treason, Pound was briefly imprisoned in Pisa before being found mentally unfit to stand trial and was committed to St. Elizabeths Hospital for the insane in Washington, D.C., in 1946. He returned to Italy upon his release in 1958 and died in Venice.

Pound's early poetry is considered by many critics to emulate the verse of Robert Browning, Charles Algernon Swinburne, and William Butler Yeats. *A lume spento* and the volumes published during his first years in London, *A Quinzaine for This Yule* (1908), *Personae* (1909), *Exultations* (1909), *Provença* (1910), and *Canzoni* (1911), contain such frequently

anthologized pieces as "The Goodly Fere" and "Sestina: Altaforte," in which Pound adopts the voice of a historical persona to narrate the poem. While these books earned him a reputation as a man of letters, they were faulted for Pound's use of archaic diction and medieval allusions, a frequent criticism of his early verse.

By 1911, Pound was immersed in London's intellectual milieu as a critic and poet. The editor of *New Age*, A. R. Orage, regularly published Pound's writings and introduced him to some of the era's most influential and challenging thinkers. Pound's response to this intellectual and aesthetic stimuli was to found Imagism, which involved a group of artists who assimilated techniques of the French Symbolists and Oriental writers. Impelled by essays published in *New Age* by F. S. Flint and T. E. Hulme on modern French poets, as well as the notebooks of Ernest Fenellosa, an American scholar preoccupied with Chinese and Japanese literature, and the work of Provençal poet Arnaut Daniel, Pound developed a verse style noted for encouraging rhythmical variation. He emphasized the "direct treatment of the 'thing' whether subjective or objective" and "the language of common speech, but always the exact word." Pound's poems "The Return," in *Ripostes*, and "In a Station of the Metro" exemplify his Imagist ideal of "an intellectual and emotional complex in an instant of time."

In these pieces, the reader intuits meaning through images, while emotion is conveyed through sound. The impact of Imagism is evident in *Des imagistes,* an anthology edited by Pound which contains works by such other notable twentieth-century authors as Hilda Doolittle, Richard Aldington, James Joyce, and William Butler Yeats. By 1914, Pound perceived limitations inherent within Imagism and disparagingly termed it "Amygism" after Amy Lowell, the poet who edited several subsequent Imagist anthologies and whom he believed devalued the term to connote free verse. With sculptor, painter, and writer Wyndham Lewis and sculptor Henri Gaudier-Brzeska, Pound created Vorticism, a dynamic amalgamation of visual and literary arts. These artists believed the image to be "a VORTEX, from which, through which, and into which, ideas are constantly rushing." While the outbreak of World War I and the enlistment of Lewis and Gaudier-Brzeska ended the movement, much of Pound's later writing displays Vorticism's intolerance, gregariousness, and didacticism.

Pound's remaining years in England were marked by the publication of some of his most renowned work. The poems in *Cathay* (1915) rework Ernest Fenellosa's translations of Chinese verse. Such frequently anthologized pieces as "The River Merchant's Wife: A Letter" and "The River Song" are admired by critics for their refined style and austere beauty. Pound's other volumes from this period are heavily indebted to his readings of such French authors as Theophile Gautier, Jules Laforgue, and Remy de Gourmont, all of whom he admired for their use of formal structures and intellectual content. "Homage to Sextus Propertius," contained in *Quia pauper amavi* (1919), is noted for its stylistic similarities to the heavily ironic verse of Laforgue. In this poem, Pound loosely translated and embellished the work of Roman poet Sextus Propertius with modern references, latinate puns and malapropisms, and scatological language to display his love and learning of history as well as his commitment to the endurance of great art in the modern world. He further explored these themes in *Hugh Selwyn Mauberley,* which is considered his masterpiece by many critics. More reliant on traditional metrical patterns and stanzaic forms, this long poem details Pound's attitudes toward art, public philistinism, World War I, and his earlier poetic affinities. Pound's affiliation with Vorticism is evident in his vituperative description of the destruction of earlier cultural achievements during World War I and his proclamation that the West is "an old bitch gone in the teeth / . . . a botched civilization." Donald Davie asserted: "*Hugh Selwyn Mauberley* remains a very important poem; apart from anything else, it has proved to be the most insidiously and aptly quotable of Pound's poems, and it has very great merit as an Englishing of Gautier."

Before *Hugh Selwyn Mauberley* was published, Pound had already begun work on the *Cantos,* a discursive, multilingual, heavily allusive sequence of poems on which he endeavored for more than forty years. While his concept of the *Cantos* continuously changed, he initially described it as a "cyselephantine poem of immeasurable length." Pound later indicated his epic intentions for the *Cantos* by referring to them as his "*commedia agnostica*"—an allusion to Dante's *Divine Comedy.* In the *Cantos,* Pound draws from the historical and artistic wealth of the ages to depict a cultural and political odyssey through time. While inevitably obscure in parts, these verses reveal Pound's vast and eclectic knowledge and his determination to use the past to explicate the present. The first three pieces, often referred to as the "Ur-Cantos," appeared in 1917 in *Poetry* magazine and were subsequently revised or deleted

from the main corpus of the poem. Later installments, including *A Draft of XVI Cantos* (1925), *A Draft of XXX Cantos* (1930), and *Drafts and Fragments of Cantos CX to CXVII* (1968), were published in unfinished form.

Pound continued to work on the *Cantos* after leaving England in 1921 to live in Paris, where he associated with Dadaists Tristan Tzara and Louis Aragon. Essentially a Europeanization of Vorticism's polemical content and irreverence toward contemporary literary trends, Dadaism actively ignored logic and grammar in favor of random associations. Elements of Dadaism, as well as the influences of Chinese ideograms and James Joyce's seminal novel *Ulysses,* are prominent in *A Draft of XVI Cantos.* By 1924, Pound had left Paris and settled in Rapallo, Italy. Removed from the barrage of cultural stimuli he experienced in England and Paris, Pound composed poetry during this period in a myriad of styles and was unaffiliated with any single literary movement. *A Draft of XXX Cantos, Eleven New Cantos, XXX-XLI* (1934), *The Fifth Decad of Cantos* (1937), and *Cantos, LII-LXXI* (1940) render Pound's impressions of Confucius, American presidents and political theorists John Quincy Adams and Thomas Jefferson, economist Major C. H. Douglas, and Fascist dictator Benito Mussolini.

Following his imprisonment for broadcasting treasonous messages and his confinement at St. Elizabeths Hospital, Pound published *The Pisan Cantos* (1948), his most controversial volume of poetry. The awarding of the Bollingen Prize to *The Pisan Cantos* polarized the American literary community. The Library of Congress panel, which awarded the prize, stated: "To permit other considerations than that of poetic achievement [to sway the decision] would destroy the significance of the award and would in principle deny the validity of that objective perception of value on which any civilized society must rest." The editors of the *Saturday Review* argued: "[Even] if all political aspects, pro and con, are brushed aside, the fact remains that *The Pisan Cantos,* for the most part, seem to us to be less poetry than a series of word games and hidden allusions which, however they may delight certain of Pound's followers, are hardly deserving of an award bearing the name of the United States Library of Congress." The interpretation of several of these verses is also the subject of critical debate. The famous line "Pull down thy vanity," from "Canto LXXXI," for example, is perceived by some critics as Pound's condemnation of his captors and by others as a recantation of his earlier beliefs. Nevertheless, *The Pisan Cantos* marks a transition toward a more personal and elegiac poetry. *Section: Rock Drill, 85-95 de los cantares* (1955), *Thrones, 96-109 de los cantares* (1959), and *Drafts and Fragments of Cantos CX-CXVII* document Pound's resignation to the impossibility of his ideal of a cultural paradise. Although Pound never completed his enterprise and complained, "I cannot make it cohere," *The Cantos* are generally acknowledged by critics as a fascinating display of poetic styles and ideas as well as one of the most ambitious verse projects of the twentieth century. Affirming the importance of the sequence, Archibald MacLeish stated: "The nearest thing we have . . . to a moral history of our tragic age is the *Cantos* of Ezra Pound, that descent, not into Dante's hell, but into our own."

In addition to his poetic accomplishments, Pound is recognized as a formidable literary critic. Along with his essays outlining Imagist tenets and Chinese poetic techniques, Pound contributed three important concepts to literary criticism: melopoeia, phanopoeia, and logopoeia. Each of these terms isolates a method by which poetry imbues language with significance. In melopoeia, meaning is conveyed by the musical qualities of words; phanopoeia is the "casting of images upon the visual imagination"; and logopoeia is described by Pound as the "dance of intellect among words." Pound is likewise acknowledged as a selfless purveyor of other writers' works. His most significant contributions involved securing publication of T. S. Eliot's poem "The Love Song of J. Alfred Prufrock" and editing *The Waste Land*, which Eliot acknowledged in his dedication to Pound as "*il miglior fabbro*," "the greater craftsman." Pound also partially financed the publication of Joyce's *Ulysses*, and he assisted Yeats in developing the style of his later poetry. The numerous periodicals with which Pound was associated in an editorial capacity include *Poetry*, the *Egoist*, *New Age*, the *Little Review*, the *Dial*, the *transatlantic review*, and the *Exile*.

While much of Pound's work has been charged with obscurity verging on meaninglessness, his verse has often been acknowledged for its technical ingenuity and for evidencing his knowledge of a wide range of esoteric subjects. Among contemporary scholars, Pound remains one of the most provocative figures in modern literature, and his importance and influence as a poet have been the subject of constant debate. Summarizing Pound's contributions to literature, Cyril Connolly noted: "Ezra Pound had two very remarkable qualities: he was a poet and, despite his passion for the past, a deeply original one. He was also something rarer than a poet—a catalyst, an impresario, a person who both instinctively understood what the age was about to bring forth and who helped it to be born."

(See also *CLC*, Vols. 1, 2, 3, 4, 5, 7, 10, 13, 18, 34; *Contemporary Authors*, Vols. 5-8, rev. ed., Vols. 37-40, rev. ed. [obituary]; and *Dictionary of Literary Biography*, Vols. 4, 45, 63.)

MICHAEL ALEXANDER

The vitality of Pound's contribution to the arts before the Great War, and the redirection he gave to poetry during his years in Kensington, are acknowledged. His own poetry, however, has received less unanimous recognition, and is commonly not much considered, in Britain at least. It seems that the active English poetic tradition has still to come to terms with Pound's poetic output as a whole. While in America scholars are establishing the detailed references of the remoter Cantos, in Britain a wider appreciation even of his more accessible poetry has not yet arrived. (p. 15)

Indifference and bafflement are today more common than hostility, though for some Pound was simply a Fascist and an anti-Semite, not a poet at all. Academic appreciation has made progress with the studies that followed in the wake of Hugh Kenner. More generally, an opening-up of British poetry to America, to verse in translation, and to its own history in this century make it easier for us to see Pound's poetry. Yet to be ushered into posterity as the greatest literary influence since Wordsworth suggests that Pound's chief interest is to literary historians. Though Pound is said to have altered the course of poetry in this century, most, even among the interested parties, still do not know quite what to make of him. (p. 17)

The anti-Semitic and Fascist sympathies expressed in the middle Cantos cannot be overlooked; these delusions had a destructive effect on the poetry. Pound's treatment at Pisa, the treason charge, the twelve years of 'mental care' and the legal

disabilities and press-ganging which he suffered for the fifteen years that remained to him, were, however, nemesis enough. The strife stirred up has deflected readers from poetry which rewards attention in ways that no other poetry of our time can do.

The poetic output of Ezra Pound is very large. Between 1907 and 1920 he published several small volumes, now collected. During the War he began on 'that great forty-year epic' which he had proposed to himself before 1908 and which was to occupy him to the end. The earlier verse is marked by a change from 'romance' to a concern with contemporary manners which culminates in the two sequences, "**Homage to Sextus Propertius**" and *Mauberley*. The *Cantos* themselves divide into the first thirty (chiefly about the Renaissance); the Cantos of the Thirties (Italian, American and Chinese history); the *Pisan Cantos,* partly autobiographical; and the three last volumes, *Rock-Drill, Thrones* and *Drafts and Fragments*. There are also translations and imitations, most of which are stations on the main line of progress, for example *Cathay* and "**Propertius.**" The *Cantos* themselves contain translations, for example from Homer in "**Canto I**" and from Cavalcanti in "**Canto 36.**" It is often remarked that Pound's poems are translations and his translations are original poems. But most of the later translations appeared outside the *Cantos,* notably *The Classic Anthology Defined by Confucius*, and his version of Sophocles' *Women of Trachis*. Such was the sequence of Ezra Pound's poetic output, revolving from 'romance' to politics and back again to a splintered realization of 'romance'.

A single approach to such a gargantuan body or work cannot be entirely satisfactory. But Pound's true achievement will benefit from an attempt to define it and to discriminate within it; and such an attempt may also help to make Pound's work more accessible to a famished British tradition in need of 'scaled invention' and 'true artistry', of a larger world of ideas and objective reference, and of a more profound self-dedication in her poets. America too, though she has recently paid Pound a more honourable and extensive attention, may need to see him more critically.

As for the Muses, it might be said without anticipating too far, that though one cannot without preamble claim for Pound a major work of unflawed greatness, yet he repeatedly achieved the rarest standards of poetic excellence and invention. Indeed his imaginative writing is so frequently touched with greatness that only Yeats and Eliot seem of a clearly superior order of magnitude among contemporaries. 'Greatness'—even if, as Pound noted, it is a Victorian word—is not an easy one to do without. But poetic courage and largeness, sustained creative enterprise, integrity in his art, the intense reflection of the light vouch-safed, these are not qualities lightly to be despised.

Pound's original sensibility and poetic character preserved a remarkable constancy throughout his career, in spite of the equally constant developments of technique, and in spite also of his changes of fortune, of manner and of subject-matter. (pp. 17-18)

Pound was himself a learned man, though a virtuoso rather than an exact scholar; he did not work in a field. He was, however, very widely, intensely and curiously read in literature and history. 'Curiosity' is perhaps the key word. He was an enthusiastic popularizer as well as savant, and is held in some suspicion by specialists in each of the ten languages that he translated from. Pound was a passionate amateur of literature, a dilettante in scholarship, in old senses of these words, although lacking in the indolence associated with them, and dedicated to the profession of poetry. This pattern used to be common among men of letters—Ford was an example—and even among dons in the days when the Arts at university meant 'humaner letters' and literature meant poetry. An acquaintance with the quotable in European poetry and cultural history could then more confidently have been relied on among the educated than it can in a graduate seminar. Pound's obscurity is thus partly due to changes in what is thought to be worth knowing; he was not, for the lettered reader of his young day, a particularly arcane poet. It must be granted, however, that in old age the poet's allusive obliqueness developed into an elliptical and idiosyncratic manner of reference. Yet, when all the missing information has been supplied, the essence of his poetry remains visionary, mythical or archetypal, and for an appreciation of this kind of poetry, popular in the last century, not so very much learning is initially required, though some literary education is certainly presupposed.

Pound had Donne's 'hydroptic, immoderate desire of human learning and languages', and his version of history is heterodox, but an understanding of his poetic truth relies more on a lively capacity for aesthetic experience and a gift for imaginative affinities than on breadth or depth of learning—he relies rather on quickness, and a willingness to learn. Pound communicates a Rabelaisian enjoyment of literacy and a passionate care for the evolution and direction of Western culture: in this crucial sense he is certainly a poet for the educated reader. (pp. 19-20)

For all their polish, Pound's poems are unfinished; the parts are highly finished, but they require the reader to compose and complete them. The particular instances are so stated that, when taken in conjunction with each other, they project unspoken corollaries, and it is the relation between these unspoken corollaries—in the reader's mind—that brings out the counterpoint. The contemplation of the parts is an aesthetic process; the unfolding of their implications a detective one; the result is catalytic, emotional. Thus a Pound poem is static and may be blank until it is understood, when it becomes dynamic and delivers its charge. There is a tension between the parts, initially palpable, ultimately meaningful. (pp. 42-3)

Pound's condensation undoubtedly makes him cryptic at times, and his ruthless cutting-out of rhetoric leaves the new reader of the *Cantos* without a handrail; but the enigmatic face of his work, seized on early by anthologists of such poems as **"In a Station of the Metro"** and **"The Return"**, is not merely the result of modern technique (or modernized Nineties-ism). Pound's obliquity, though it has to do with his dislike for obvious conceptualization, is the semi-dramatic strategy natural to a sensibility inwardly in awe of life, and the product of a temperament possessed of deep instincts, though normally reticent in their expression. The mysteriousness and refinement in Pound is not an affectation, in spite of his striking of attitudes; it is rather that his inner life was not for direct export. In this he resembles the other 'men of 1914'—Joyce and Eliot, and Wyndham Lewis—if not D. H. Lawrence. As the reader comes to know Pound's poetry, he will increasingly recognize and go beyond the multifarious objects of knowledge that at first dominate the landscape of each poem, and he will become more interested in the poetic character of the presence, seer, protagonist who presents the data. The data are variously instructive, diverting, beautiful or awe-inspiring, and the patterns of emotion and moral value that they create are fascinating or rewarding. Eventually, however, it is the richness and quality of the mind, rather than the *virtù* of the objects it contains and

which it salutes, that continue to fascinate and to instruct. It is only at first that Pound's purism of surface and form seem clinically to exclude the presence of a known human speaker. Not that Pound is often predictable; but he becomes easier to locate. The reader of Pound is forced to develop his senses and his antennae. The art of reading him is, in a phrase he applied to Henry James in **"Canto 7"**, 'drinking the tone of things'. (p. 43)

What to say of a dedicated life? In seeking to make an estimate of Pound's poetic achievements, Pound's own career is itself a warning not to rush to conclusions. To take only the last of its transformations for example, **Drafts and Fragments** significantly softens the impression left by **Rock-Drill** and **Thrones**, and by the **Cantos** as a whole; it has a reintegrative effect on the reader's experience of the poem. The shape the **Cantos** will assume in the minds of poets and readers of the future cannot be predicted, though it is already clear that whereas in the past it has been asked to stand as sponsor at many an unlikely font, in the future it risks becoming a semi-academic institution, at least in the U.S.A. The account given here does not do justice to the overall design of the poem, especially in the later stages, for which much evidence is being produced. It will remain true, however, that this plan is often lost to view, and that for many readers it will be the variety of the *Cantos*, its picaresque explorations and reclamations, that strike and hold the mind. (p. 225)

Certainly his residence in Rapallo and his devotion to the **Cantos** took Pound away from the English language and from the modern world, possibly to his (and their) detriment. Who is to say, however, that the **Cantos**—though a long way round— were a misuse of his gifts, since they clearly remain 'the most important long poem of the century'? For all their wrong-headed politics and confusing form, they present simultaneously an heroic imaginative openness to actual living and to nature, and also to cultural and ideal worlds more various, larger and deeper. This double vision may prove a precious legacy in an age when our own historical culture is becoming alien to us; already, the London, Paris and Provence he knew have gone, and with them certain cultural possibilities that cannot be reproduced. The distinctness and concentration of Pound's mind will not be easily emulated; nor his skills of free-verse composition. (pp. 227-28)

The tendentiousness and unevenness of some of Pound's achievement make it difficult to settle squarely on a tolerable generalization about his place among the poets; he is perhaps the greatest of the moderns, since that term does not exactly fit Yeats, nor the Eliot of *Four Quartets*. However, his Promethean gifts are so original that the process of comparison with others does not seem very productive; perhaps he should not be placed among others. Eliot entitled his first article on Pound "Isolated Superiority."

Unlike many of his readers, I do not exclude any period of Pound's work as without good poetry, from **"The Tree"** to the last sybilline leaf of the *Cantos*; nor do I see significant and decisive developments which lead to radical positive or negative judgements about his career, either in its modernization in **Lustra**, its sophistication in **Mauberley**, its grandiose epic ambitions or its later fragmentation. Like many readers, I do not find the Chinese history fruitful, and find that many of the fragments of politics and history stick in my throat, just as other fragments stick in my head. I share Pound's 'coherent idea'—the idea around which, he said in 1962, his 'muddles accumulated'—that 'European culture ought to survive'; in this enterprise the *Cantos* are perhaps the biggest single effort made by an individual of this century; and may well prove the most valuable. Unlike many readers, I cannot discard the idea that the *Cantos* do form a unity and do record a moral progress both in their content (by design) and in the author. It follows too that I see Pound's whole poetic output as a unity.

Leaving aside the translations, themselves a fresh and distinct adjunct to any bouquet for the Muses, the best of the original work seems to come from six periods: *Lustra* and *Cathay; Propertius* and *Mauberley*; the first seventeen *Cantos*; the *Fifth Decad of Cantos*; the *Pisan Cantos*; and *Drafts and Fragments. Cathay* seems to me the most underrated of his volumes, and I would repeat the suggestion that if the British want to make a fresh start on Pound (and it is about time they did) they could begin with the disciplined free verse of *Lustra* and *Cathay.* 'We will leave it as a test: when anyone has studied Mr. Pound's poems in *chronological* order, and has mastered *Lustra* and *Cathay,* he is prepared for the *Cantos*—but not till then. If the reader then fails to like them, he has probably omitted some step in his progress, and had better go back and retrace the journey. (p. 228)

Michael Alexander, in his The Poetic Achievement of Ezra Pound, *University of California Press, 1979, 247 p.*

ANTHONY WOODWARD

I think one reason why Pound's status is more elusive than that of either Yeats or Eliot is that their work achieves the kind of overall unity of effect which assuages one's natural desire for the synoptic view. To gain such a view of Pound is less easy. The economic issue, if detached from the Confucianism and neo-pagan Illuminism which were the main components of Pound's eclectic religious outlook, is a red herring. Large and over-active, it does credit to his conscience and good intentions but does not, in isolation, help the reader to grasp the elusive coherence of his achievement. Eliot's religious position, by contrast, implicit in *Gerontion* and *The Waste Land,* and gradually unfolding itself in *Ash Wednesday* and *Four Quartets,* gave a unity to his performance by locating his utterances in the still familiar context of Christian sensibility and belief, whereas Pound's more reckless self-exposure to the pressures of his historical moment eschewed any such advantage. Yeats, though having no conventional leanings towards a belief hallowed through time and tradition, still managed to style the conflicting elements of his personality by means of an Occult determinism; and the 'masterful images' of his poetry, clad in a matchless rhetoric, retain even amid the fluctuations of early, middle and late styles a certain noble simplicity of gesture, so that the donning and the doffing of Masks seem contained by a personality with a very firm psychological centre. Moreover, both Eliot and Yeats, not to mention Hardy, Wallace Stevens and Frost, managed their public careers with far greater decorum than did the febrile and ferocious Ezra, whose commitment endangered his reputation and ultimately his life. Yet it is no purpose of mine to give Pound a primacy over such poets as Yeats and Eliot on account of the more dramatically *engagé* quality of his life. It is the poetry that matters, even though I see no reason for such a cleanly surgical severance of poetry from life as purists require. Each of the three poets had his endemic flaw as an artist, a flaw rooted in temperament and hence in life: Eliot's a cerebral monotony, Yeats' a too conscious eloquence, Pound's an allusive incoherence. Each had his exalted poetic flights, and of the three

I myself find Pound's the most moving. But that is no great matter. I aim merely to show where lay Pound's essential greatness and his centrality to his age—a greatness and centrality only understandable in terms of his self-exposure to the disintegrative pressures which the modern age inherited from the nineteenth century and from certain aspects of the Romantic movement.

To link Pound and Romanticism may seem paradoxical, given his vigorous role in the anti-Romantic movement of early twentieth-century modernism, so I shall now venture on a few general considerations which I hope will make it appear less so. (pp. 2-3)

[In his *The Great Chain of Being,* A. O. Lovejoy] has caught two things crucial to our understanding of Pound: historicism, and fascination with the dramas of the self. A concomitant of historicism, as Lovejoy defined it, is the awareness of our own selves as historical beings, fascinated by the interplay of our historical selves with the selves of other times and places. And such concern with the self also engenders fascinated obsession with the nuances, contradictions and, ultimately, the fluidity of that self. The two taken together, historicism and self-consciousness, account for a great deal of what is most relevant to us in nineteenth-century culture and provide perhaps the most vital link between Romanticism and the modern age.

It is possible to suggest, for instance, that Browning's attempt to write a more 'objective' type of poetry in his dramatic monologues, as distinct from the subjective mode he associated with Shelley, was a means of externalising the ambiguous fluctuations and diversities of his own awareness of self, by studying its reflections in the mirror of past historical epochs. It was an early instance of the use of 'masks' or 'personae'. Thus when, in the early twentieth century, sophisticated taste recoiled from the subjective rhetoric of a decadent Romanticism, it was not surprising to find Yeats, Eliot and Pound adopting in their various ways equivalents to the Browning dramatic monologue in order to render what was in essence still the inescapable bequest of Romanticism to modernity: absorption in the fluctuations of the self in a context of historicism.

Furthermore the historical context in which the post-Romantic self found itself was now made both more exciting and more disturbing by the array of historical and prehistorical cultures that anthropological as well as historical research was unfolding. In the absence of any belief in a plan of divine Providence, and, in the writers concerned, of any belief in the surrogate religious notion of Progress, there emerged in some of the great modernists of the early twentieth century an awareness not only of what Eliot called 'the immense panorama of futility and anarchy which is contemporary history' but also of the way in which history might be mastered by calling into service the burgeoning sciences of humanity's past. In the *Musée Imaginaire* of a rootless, eclectic but knowledgeable modernity various compensatory measures could be taken. Attempts to pattern the confusions of modern life by the self-conscious use of ancient myths, fertility rituals and heroic legends were among the most prominent, and they played a part in Pound's *Cantos* as well as in *The Waste Land* and *Ulysses.* Equally prominent not long before Pound began his career—the *The Cantos* were envisaged very early on in that career—was the Symbolist desire to construct through Art the one great Book which would transmute the confusions of historical existence into permanent aesthetic essence: 'tout au monde existe pour aboutir à un livre', as Mallarmé put it. The presence of this kind of Symbolist absolutism is clear enough in Joyce and Yeats, just as the

Symbolist colouring of Eliot's mode of expression is also familiar; yet the fact that Pound dissociated himself from Symbolism should not lead us to underestimate its importance in the background. It was not for nothing that some of his early work was steeped in the languorous imagery of Yeatsian symbolism and cultivated the rare nuances of quasi-mystical self-consciousness; nor was it for nothing that he early (1906) aspired to write an epic thus significantly defined:

> And I see my greater soul-self bending
> Sibylwise with that great forty-year epic

The epic emerged from the poet's quite explicit concerns with the twin problems of historicism and self-consciousness—Romanticism's legacy to the twentieth century. (pp. 3-5)

We should also note, for the sake of its bearing on *The Cantos* proper, the kind of historical experience that obsessed the poet, feeling as he did both its kinship and its tantalising distance: ancient rituals, numinous beings, and stories where the erotic is endowed with a quasi-religious intensity. (Pound's views on the persistence in Troubadour love of an underground mystical tradition stemming from pagan mysteries is well-known from his essay on **"Psychology and the Troubadours".**) It is a modern mind's receptivity to that particular kind of eclectic material from the past which fascinated the poet, along with the elusive relation of present teller to past events and persons. Thus a double nostalgia is distilled by the **"Ur-Cantos"**: a nostalgia for the actuality of past experience seen from one's all too local status in the present, and a nostalgia for certain types of numinous experience that seem to have been more common in the past than in the present. This is what gives an underlying note of loss to much of the **"Ur-Cantos"**, in spite of the occasional Browningesque heartiness of their tone. Pound was indeed, as Wyndham Lewis put it in *Time and Western Man,* 'a man in love with the past'.

The aim of *The Cantos* proper, after the early **"Ur-Cantos"** had been rejected, was to make that love a positive source of analysis and reconstruction: the poet, by means of his imaginative re-creation of certain past instances of *virtù,* civility and sacred vitality, and by means of his radical diagnosis of usury as the persistent flaw in the history of the West since the Renaissance, offers himself as a guide to the future. After all, had not the composition of *Hugh Selwyn Mauberley* intervened, and had not Pound there sloughed off his 'Doppelgänger' aesthetic self, and emerged as the maker of a great constructive epic—the 'tale of the tribe'?

So runs the Authorised Version. I agree that if Pound had not made that effort he would not be the great poet and exemplary figure that he is. Robert Lowell put the matter thus:

> Pound's social credit, his Fascism, all these various things were a tremendous gain to him; he'd be a very Parnassian poet without them. Even if they're bad beliefs—and some were bad, some weren't, and some were just terrible of course—they made him more human and more to do with life, more to do with the times. They served him. Taking what interested him in these things gave him a kind of realism and life to his poetry that it wouldn't have had otherwise.

Yet to read *The Cantos* as if Pound's didactic constructive intentions were the work's true nerve of feeling is to miss a crucial poetic effect, which is one of ironic parody and dis-

integration, shot through with nostalgia for a lost beauty and fierce innocence. *The Cantos* depict, as Richard Pevear has put it, 'the ruin of history', through the eyes of a poet whose greatness lay in the split that existed between his ideals and reality. An eclectic, rootless being, he exposed his imaginative powers to the historicist *mêlée* available to modern culture, but the temperamental bias of the lyric poet was in constant tension with the eager activism of the reformer. Indeed, the vituperative violence of the latter, in the prose and in parts of *The Cantos,* was the symptom of some irritable compensatory drive. Some who knew Pound noted signs of this split in his personality: on the one hand dogmatic, aggressively colourful, a fiery extrovert; on the other an intensely sensitive, tender, even shy being. Fate led him to such wholeness and serenity as can be attained by such a temperament only in the very heart of loss, as can be seen in the culminating Cantos of the Pisan series. And *The Pisan Cantos* are the great modern elegy not only of one man over his individual fate but over a whole civilised order for which he had some claim to speak. (pp. 6-8)

When history defeated the poet-reformer, that failed aspiration towards the worldly realisation of goodness, truth and beauty survived 'now in the mind indestructible', whilst civilisation collapsed around him. In the wilds of that mind alone was there to be an Eleusis, a light of the divine, a glimpsed Confucian harmony.

It would be convenient to claim that the story ended on that note: the poet-seer mystically at peace with Confucian immanence. Yet **"Canto 84"**, the last of the Pisan series, warns us otherwise. Something tragically flawed, an incompleteness either aggressive or semi-despairing, was to be Pound's lot until the end of his life. It is a moving paradox that the greatness of this poet who set so much store by masks and indirections, and who ostensibly rejected the Romantic role of the poet, should in the end touch us most keenly by the interplay between his work and a disastrous yet exemplary life. The Cantos which followed the Pisan series, *Rock-Drill, Thrones,* and *Drafts and Fragments,* cannot in my view be separated from the circumstances of the poet's life during and just after his incarceration in St Elizabeth's hospital for the insane. Moreover the almost total silence that descended on the poet thereafter in his last years in Italy, when taken in conjunction with the disillusioned utterances of a few of the final Fragments, endow the totality of his life and work with a coherence and a grandeur that has something of the cathartic effect of great tragedy. (p. 14)

We must be struck by the courageous persistence with which he continued to attempt a fusion between his intimations of cosmic harmony and the world of practical politics. 'Only connect', Pound seems to be saying. . . . Or, as Octavio Paz puts it: 'Poetry is *paideia.* Those instantaneous visions that rend the shadows of history as Diana the clouds, are not ideas or things—they are light. "All things that are are lights." But Pound is not a contemplative; these lights are acts and they suggest a course of action.' I disagree with Paz—to me the deepest notes of the poet are those of a contemplative—but he puts the opposite point of view extremely well, and Pound himself would undoubtedly, until a very late stage in his life, have seen it as being more loyal to his undertaking. Yet the verdict of aridity and decline which has been passed on some of these later Cantos strikes me as justified. One can be stimulated to learn from them, of course; Pound is seldom less than a teacher. But, as with the 'Adams' Cantos, fragmentation of form seems inappropriate for the constructive didactic purpose, and, fatal to say, lucid expositions of their content (for instance by C. F. Terrell, J. J. Wilhelm or David Gordon) have a tendency to read more interestingly than many of the sections themselves, as they lie scattered over the pages of these last Cantos.

Thus much said, should we not remember the circumstances in which Pound had to write his poetry? A man of extreme though flawed sensitivity confined to a squalid madhouse; disinclined by temperament to sustain a mystical quietism in spite of his contemplative intimations; aware that his own folly, compounding the stroke of fate, had led him to disaster—who can blame him if he turned again toward didactic concerns to sustain himself? I am aware that this may sound condescending. I do not mean it to be so. There are, of course, remarkable things at this didactic level. **"Canto 99"**, for instance, the reworking of K'ang Hsi's *Sacred Edict*, is a *tour de force*. More congruent with Pound's deepest gifts, however, are certain fragments, brief sections, occasionally whole Cantos of a finely etched yet ethereal lyricism. The great things in **Rock-Drill, Thrones** and **Last Fragments** are delicately terse pastoral or myth, punctuated by fragmentary hints of neo-Platonic Light metaphysics, and touched at moments with a piercing sadness. The poet's discovery of the Na-Khi material in the course of composing **Thrones** was of deep significance. There, in the unexpected shape of a great botanist's study of an isolated tribe in South West China, was the vision of a kind of Golden Age perfection that could be played off against surrounding darkness and confusion.

The central part played in the final Cantos by Pound's chance discovery of the customs of this obscure tribe could stand as a symbol of much that we may feel to be typical of his position in twentieth-century culture. An eclectic modern sensibility, exposed to the diversity of the past by a sophisticated historicism, ranges through time fascinated by modes of being very alien to the nature of his own civilisation; and in the course of his time-travelling he is especially drawn to cultures which afford imaginative appeasement to the religious yearnings of a rootless modernity.... A post-Romantic sensibility estranged from the numinous by the hostile pressures of Western civilisation seeks assuagement in primitive religiosity; the chaotic self-consciousness of the modern, by some paradoxical feat, cultivates the rituals of permanence in the wilds of its own mind. The most sustained embodiment in **The Cantos** of this circuitous journey to the sacred is to be found in the Pisan series, which tend at their climax towards a quietistic union with cosmic Process—a union rendered in a fashion curiously oblique and stylised. In the years of strain and suffering that followed their composition, the note of yearning for a lost paradise of religious wholeness persisted throughout the didactic emphases of **Rock-Drill** and **Thrones**. The final version of Pound's 'paradise within' was the versifying of the Na-Khi material, which flutes delicate grace-notes to the growing disillusion of **The Cantos**' last fragments.

Such a conclusion seems logical on the hypothesis that Pound was in essence an elegiac poet, drawn to contemplation. Yet something is wrong, something is missing. For instance, the sheer fun of a good deal of **The Cantos** is missing, their brio and their fighting spirit. Thinking back on **Rock-Drill** and **Thrones,** on the details of the nineteenth-century United States Bank War, tenth-century Byzantine trade edicts, and English medieval charters, one realises that the poem needed these things, though perhaps not always in the shape offered in those later instalments of **The Cantos**. They are undoubtedly more confusing and less enlivening than the historical documenta-

tion, *obiter dicta* and quirky anecdotes of the early Cantos, yet they serve a similar purpose. They direct the mind outwards to the real world of men, to history, to other cultures. Even though the deepest vein and the ultimate effect of **The Cantos** is elegiac—and I persist in thinking so—Pound's decision to risk the epic omnivorousness, the epic diversity, was a great gain. It saved him from the 'damnosa hereditas' of Symbolist introversion and preciosity. And what a relief to turn to the ranging allusiveness of **The Cantos** after dieting on so many small lyric utterances of the twentieth century; tough or tender; all navel-gazing. it was curiosity that did the trick. 'Curiosity—advice to the young—curiosity,' affirms the aged poet in Contino's photographic record of his last years in Italy. The elegiac quality of **The Cantos** would be a minor achievement were it not for the tension generated by the passionate, activist side of Pound's nature, as Robert Lowell well saw. Didactic fury was the needful grain of sand that produced the authentic pearl of contemplation.

The quality of that elegiac contemplation, especially in **Last Fragments,** is something very rare in English poetry. There is sadness, a sense of loss. There is disillusion. Yet the disillusion is of too celestial a simplicity to warrant calling it despair. Pound had never been the type of modern writer who is 'cosmically concerned and terrestrially calm', in Conor Cruise O'Brien's deadly phrase.... Pound knew in the end what the tones of his greatest poetry had been implying all along, that he looked in history for a perfection which can only lie beyond history or in the realm of the imagination.... He had taken on the Great Beast and been worsted. (pp. 14-18)

[Pound's] love of the past, his reverence for all that was vitally beautiful in the natural universe, his admiration for all that was vigorous and pure in certain exemplary characters of human history, had the same source as his crusade for monetary justice, his zeal as an editor, his active devotion to the cause of great friends and contemporaries like Eliot and Joyce. That source was his passion for perfection, as Wyndham Lewis realised earlier and better than anyone else. Such love of perfection, of the ideal, characterised one who in essence was a contemplative, but whose prophetic vigour goaded him to realise his ideals in political action. For that he fought and suffered. If he was wrong in thinking such realisation of the ideal to be possible it was a generous, quixotic error. The violence of some of his writings, and a harshness of one side of his character, were the symptoms of an idealism frustrated. A more attractive expression of that frustration is the vein of sadness and loss that subtly pervades much of his greatest poetry and makes **The Cantos** elegiac in their essence, not epic. Yet that elegiac note arises from so radical a self-exposure to the destructiveness of time that it attains a seriousness transcending any minor connotations which the word 'elegiac' may possess:

> The enormous tragedy of the dream in the peasant's
> bent shoulders

It was the very same urge to perfection which drew Pound towards a *Weltanschauung* in which the universe is posited as a harmonious whole, where there is 'no duality', as he put it in his translation of the Confucian *Chung Yung*; and myths of fertility and light similarly manifest his aspiration towards religious wholeness where all dualities are subsumed by one underlying unity. For all his rejection of the more irresponsible aspects of Taoism, the deepest instincts of Pound's aesthetic and contemplative nature are surely best perceived through the doctrine of the Tao.... And *Chung Yung* (*The Unwobbling Pivot*), Pound's best translation from the Chinese, is significantly that one of the four Confucian classics which is closest in spirit to Taoism.

Yet, without impugning either the sincerity or even the validity of Pound's beliefs, the peculiar expressive poignancy of *The Cantos* can be said to lie in their making us aware of the restless, sophisticated eclecticism which was the necessary medium of this particular twentieth-century religious quest. The poet came to the deep springs of a mysteriously primitive religious feeling without attempting to suppress his ambiguous relationship to such matters. On the one hand this gives a certain abrasive tension to *The Cantos,* and on the other hand perhaps also accounts for the elegiac strain of distance and loss which permeates much of the work. 'And a modern Eleusis being possible in the wilds of a man's mind only?' Curiously enough it is the struggling, exploratory, 'imperfect' nature of *The Cantos* as a whole which may serve to make them germinal for the future, since they do not absorb one totally into their own imaginative self-sufficiency but set one on one's own path of intellectual and imaginative exploration. Viewed in that way even such rebarbative sections of *The Cantos* as deal with American history, for instance, can yield their own ambiguous rewards. Then Pound's greatness as a teacher, an instigator, finds its crowning, paradoxical fulfilment.

To say this is in no way to deny the artistic greatness of many separate portions of *The Cantos.* And of these separate portions *The Pisan Cantos* are perhaps the most notable sustained examples, since the terrible circumstances of their composition were the ideal precipitate of Pound's deepest imaginative powers. In them there is courage, humour, resilience; but ever and again a rhythm, a cadence brings 'the eternal note of sadness in'. If we read them with an ear for their tone, as well as for their rhythms and their cadences, they surely make us feel that the finalities of religion or of a religiously coloured vision of politics can only be realised in the solitude of the imagination—'now in the mind indestructible', as Pound put it in **"Canto 74"**, quite close to a line which affirmed that 'the drama is wholly subjective'. *The Pisan Cantos* will remain his most moving single achievement, since they invest imagined harmonies and remembered perfections with the elegiac dignity of worldly failure. The strange silence which, after much further suffering, took possession of Pound near the end of his life can be seen not simply as remorse, a sense of defeat, but also as an intuitive awareness that what he had sought in life was beyond words as well as beyond realisation in action. Such awareness is desolating for the flesh but inwardly consoling for the spirit. A passage from Cyril Connolly provides the best, most chastening reflection for all who write on Pound, whether to condemn or to praise:

> One would have to have something of Pound's greatness to judge him as he deserves: to assess the mixture of egotism and humility, genius and bigot, wit and warmth; the combination of technical virtuosity with lyrical insight. No poet has written so unfailingly well of water from the pagan springs of simplicity and wonder beneath his clear-eyed gaze.

(pp. 108-11)

Anthony Woodward, in his Ezra Pound and 'The Pisan Cantos', *Routledge & Kegan Paul, 1980, 128 p.*

DONALD E. STANFORD

The revolution in modern poetry, as Eliot and many others have noted, began in 1908 when Ezra Pound settled in London.

Within a few years he became a dominant figure in the London literary scene, where he was discovering and promoting the then unknown talents of such writers as James Joyce, T. S. Eliot, H. D., Marianne Moore, William Carlos Williams, and others. He provided much of the poetic theory behind the poetry of these revolutionists, and he himself was soon engaged in writing what he correctly termed "revolutionist" poetry. Yet Pound's work *as an original poet* is disappointing for reasons which I hope will emerge from this chapter. His career as a translator is another matter. His "translations" (or imitations or paraphrases or adaptations, whatever one wishes to call them), although controversial, have been widely and justly praised.

In his very earliest poetry Pound was extremely eclectic and imitative. As he proceeded, he began to formulate a body of poetic theory which he put into practice in his own work, and he attempted to develop his own poetic style. His poetic theories, like his early style, were not original, being derived from sources as diverse as T. E. Hulme, Dante, Remy de Gourmont, Flaubert, Ernest Fenollosa and the Chinese ideogram, the Pre-Raphaelites, James Joyce, and the empirical scientific method which stresses observation of particulars—to mention a few. He developed his basic theories fairly early in his career and he was consistent in his employment of them. But they contained the seeds of distintegration: excessive emphasis on visual experience, on sensations, and almost complete disregard of conceptual experience; a theory of the structure of a poem which led to extreme looseness, obscurantism, overallusiveness, and an excessive use of quotations. As for his style—he went from a too obvious imitation of the Celtic Twilight Yeats, Browning, and the Pre-Raphaelites in his earliest verse to what can only be called "no style at all" in the last of the *Cantos.* It is ironic then, that the poet who made originality—"Make It New"—his catch phrase may in future years be most highly respected for his free translations of foreign poets. A major cause of his failure as a stylist was this fact: Pound, early in his career, spent a good deal of time trying to master the techniques of Provençal, French, Italian, Latin, Greek, Anglo-Saxon, Japanese, and Chinese poets, but he made little attempt to master the techniques of poetry in English since the sixteenth century. Yet of course English was the medium of his own poetry. He overlooked the simple principle that if one is to write successful poetry in English, one should give priority to the study of English rather than foreign verse. Yet Pound shows an appalling ignorance of English poetry from the Renaissance to the mid-nineteenth century—that is, up to but not including the Pre-Raphaelites, and not including Browning. Although he mastered the intricacies of Arnaut Daniel's sestina and other complicated Provençal forms, he had little appreciation of what has been accomplished and can still be accomplished in blank verse and in all the various kinds of rhymed iambic verse. (pp. 13-14)

It was natural that Pound, who from the very beginning of his career was fascinated by the Middle Ages, should also be influenced by and attempt to imitate the styles of that school of Victorian poets which turned to the Middle Ages for its inspiration in painting and in poetry—the Pre-Raphaelites. In his later *Hugh Selwyn Mauberley* (1920) Pound, in **"Yeux Glauques,"** recalls brilliantly but ambiguously his early admiration for Swinburne, Rossetti, Burne-Jones, and others of the school, but in defending them against the attacks of the more prudish Victorian critics he at times seems to be making fun of them. He appears to be unsure of his own tastes. Be that as it may, there are a number of early poems which are obviously Pre-Raphaelite or Swinburnean. (p. 14)

A more fortunate influence on the very early Pound was Robert Browning. In "**Mesmerism**," suggested by Browning's poem of the same title, Pound addresses Browning thus:

> Here's to you, old Hippety-Hop o' the accents
> True to the Truth's sake and crafty dissector,
> You grabbed at the gold sure. . . .

The poem, partly parody and partly praise, is written in Browning's jocular style. Browning's dramatic monologue, his interest in unusual and abnormal personalities, and his psychological insights also exerted their influence on a number of Pound's early poems, including "**Fifine Answers**" and "**Piere Vidal Old.**" (p. 15)

When Pound arrived in London in 1908 he had a number of things on his mind; one of the most urgent was his desire to re-create for English readers the poetry of the troubadours, which he had been studying since his undergraduate days at Hamilton College where he learned Provençal under William Pierce Shepherd. "**Na Audiart**," inspired by Bertran de Born's "Borrowed Lady" poem, had already appeared in *A Lume Spento* (1908). In his four other volumes of verse subsequent to *A Lume Spento* and prior to the imagist *Ripostes* (1912), he published a number of poems inspired by the troubadours and their period, which fall into two categories—those derived from a specific text in Provençal (and these range from almost literal translations to very free adaptations) and those which have no discernible relation to a specific Provençal poem but make use of the personality of a troubadour poet as a mask or *persona*. This second group of poems shows the aforementioned influence of Browning, and they frequently remind the reader of Browning's dramatic monologues. Many of these experiments are unsuccessful, and in fact Pound eventually rejected most of them in his own selection for the later *Personae* (1926), which contained all the early verse he wished to preserve. Yet the young Idaho-born American in his self-imposed exile abroad deserves our sympathetic respect at this stage of his career, for he was undertaking an extremely difficult task—to make the complicated verse forms of these medieval poets, not to mention their complex social system, relevant to early-twentieth-century London. There are two main reasons for the failure of most (but not all) of the troubadour poems: the remoteness of the period Pound was trying to re-create and, more important, the incongruous mélange of styles Pound had acquired at this time—a mixture, as we have seen, of Browning, Swinburne, the Pre-Raphaelites, the early Yeats, and the fin de siècle decadence of the nineties. And frequently Pound made it worse by deliberately employing archaic locutions which were designed to give a medieval flavor to the verse but instead usually made it artificial and awkward. (pp. 15-16)

In "**Sestina: Altaforte**" (frequently and justifiably anthologized) Pound employs a form invented by Arnaut Daniel, the sestina, a mask or persona derived from the troubadour Bertran de Born, and a style reminiscent of Browning in "Soliloquy of the Spanish Cloister" and elsewhere, together with subject matter that is partly original, yet partly derivative from Bertran's battle poems. The result is curious and interesting. . . . The material for Pound's poem is taken from two or more poems by Bertran and rewritten in the boisterous style of Browning. Pound gives us some of his source material in his verse and prose translations of Bertran's battle verse in *The Spirit of Romance* (1910). . . . Browning is not one of the best

influences on Pound (although a better influence than Swinburne and the early Yeats), but in "**Sestina: Altaforte**" the spirit of the troubadour poet does come through in spite of Browning. Bertran was in fact the kind of man Browning admired and is here presented in a style influenced by, but on the whole superior to, that of Browning himself. (pp. 19-20)

While operating under the heterogeneous influences we have noted and while trying to re-create the troubadours for twentieth-century London, Pound began to develop his theory of poetry, at first implicitly in his poems, sometimes stated in his poems, and then explicitly in his prose. In his earliest poems we find Pound expressing (as we would expect) highly eclectic and inconsistent theories. At one moment, in "**Grace before Song**," he prays that his poems be

As drops that dream and gleam and falling catch the sun

—that is, that they be nothing but pure poetry in the Paterian sense. But in his "**Revolt against the Crepuscular Spirit in Modern Poetry**" he states exactly the opposite, that poetry should be a call to action. There is a similar inconsistency in his early admiration for Walt Whitman, who praised democratic America en masse, and Pound's notion, expressed in "**The Flame**" and elsewhere, that the poet is by his very nature alienated and isolated from normal society—a mystic and a transcendentalist. Similarly in "**In Durance**" (dated 1907) Pound states that

I am homesick after mine own kind,

his "own kind" being an early Yeatsian aesthete striving in a crude commercial society for transcendent beauty.

By 1911, when he began publishing his essays in the *New Age,* under the title "**I Gather the Limbs of Osiris**," Pound (as his title suggests) was making an attempt to pull his heterogeneous ideas about poetry together, and in these essays a few dominant notions emerge which (although Pound's phrasing of them changed somewhat) were to dominate Pound for the rest of his life. Of great importance was his concept of the "luminous detail," first described in the *New Age*, December 7, 1911, in his "**A Rather Dull Introduction**" to the Osiris series in which he formulates "the method of Luminous Detail, a method most vigorously hostile to the prevailing mode of today." He considers the mode of his time to be that of multitudinous detail and the mode of the past to be that of generalization. He goes on to say, "The artist seeks out the luminous detail and presents it. He does not comment. His work remains the permanent basis of psychology and metaphysics. . . . A few dozen facts of this nature give us the intelligence of a period." These luminous details "govern knowledge" as a "switchboard governs the electric current." As Thomas H. Jackson has demonstrated, this notion has affinities with the Pre-Raphaelite and Paterian "charged moment." It also has affinities, I would like to point out, with Joyce's theory of epiphanies, with Pound's theory of the image as an intellectual and emotional complex in an instant of time, and with the later theory of Eliot's objective correlative. Pound's early statements about the luminous detail are also the basis of the theory and method of the *Cantos,* which were considered by Pound himself at one time to be his major life work. The *Cantos* are a series of luminous details giving us the intelligence of a period. The poet has nothing to do with ideas or with generalizations. It is the job of the poet—Guido Cavalcanti for example—to render *emotions* precisely. From Pater to Eliot the basic theory is identical although phrased somewhat differently by each writer. In Pound's case, in the later *Cantos* particularly, we find the theory carried to its illogical conclusion. Rational structure, evaluation of experience, understanding—all are sacrificed to presenting, in a short poem, the luminous detail and in a long poem a series of luminous details. The method led in Pound's final *Cantos* and in Joyce's last work to almost complete obscurantism.

The theory of the luminous detail led directly (with some assistance from T. E. Hulme) to Pound's famous doctrine of imagism, or *imagisme* as Pound named it when he started the movement by sending a few of his friend Hilda Doolittle's poems from a British Museum tearoom to Harriet Monroe of *Poetry*. (pp. 21-3)

The history of imagism has been written, rewritten, and thoroughly documented. Although Pound later denied it, T. E. Hulme probably exerted considerable influence on Pound during the early formative period of the movement. . . . [In] spite of Hulme's claim to being a classicist, his "Lecture on Modern Poetry" appears to me to be a minor manifesto of the romantic movement. In any event, whoever was first in theory, the poetic theories of the early Pound and of Hulme have very close affinities. And it was Pound who put the theories into practice, although Hulme wrote a few minor poems to illustrate his doctrine.

Pound's manifesto, **"A Few Don'ts by an Imagiste,"** as it appeared in *Poetry* in 1913, would have occasioned no surprise to the reader of **"I Gather the Limbs of Osiris"** two years earlier. The imagist doctrine as set forth by Pound here and elsewhere may be summarized as follows—in diction to avoid abstract language, stereotyped "poetic" language, ornamental language, and an overuse of adjectives. *Le mot juste,* the exact word, must be found. In rhythm, the iambic foot should be replaced by the cadence of unrhymed "free verse" so that each poem will have an entirely unique rhythm. Imagery and concentration are the essence of poetry. The image is defined as "that which presents an intellectual and emotional complex in an instant of time." There should be absolute freedom of subject matter. The poem should suggest rather than state.

The immediate result of these theories was a much-needed revitalizing of poetic diction, a new sense of freedom, even permissiveness, in the choice of subject matter, and highly interesting experiments with complex rhythms outside the scansion systems of conventional poetry. Brilliant (but, I think, minor) poems were written in "free verse" by H. D., William Carlos Williams, Wallace Stevens, Mina Loy, Marianne Moore, and Ezra Pound. However, the long-term result was unfortunate. The poetry of the imagist revolution became increasingly obscure and irrational as it was practiced by Pound and others. A kind of freeze set the techniques of all the above mentioned poets except Stevens, so that they never developed beyond the limitations of their early work. And there was a widespread neglect of the efficacy of conventional rhythms to express modern subject matter and an equally widespread neglect of what American and English poets had accomplished before the twentieth-century revolution, although this was offset somewhat by the erudition of Eliot and his admiration for the metaphysical poets.

Pound himself wrote several beautiful poems during his imagist phase, and in some respects he never outgrew imagism, although, as a result of a quarrel with Amy Lowell, he abandoned doctrinaire imagism and for a very brief time became a "vorticist," together with his friend Wyndham Lewis, who edited the short-lived magazine *Blast*. Vorticism was of some importance in the paintings of Lewis. In poetry it was simply a rephrasing of the doctrine of the image with emphasis on the supposed emotional energy concentrated in and liberated by the image or vortex. It was imagism set in motion.

A word here is necessary concerning Pound's so-called ideogrammatic method. Very soon after Pound began publishing the Osiris series of essays with its theory of luminous details in the *New Age,* he met in London the widow of Ernest Fenollosa. She sent him the Fenollosa manuscripts in 1913, the same year that Pound began the imagist movement in *Poetry* with the poems of H. D. The Fenollosa manuscripts contained poems in Chinese ideograms with English transliterations, as well as indications of the Japanese sound of each ideogram (Japanese because Fenollosa was living in Japan and working with Japanese scholars) and also Japanese Noh plays and an essay on the Chinese ideogram as a medium for poetry. From Pound's study of the Fenollosa manuscripts came Pound's *Cathay* (1915), a collection of loose translations and adaptations of Chinese poems; *Noh, or Accomplishment* (1916); *Certain Noble Plays of Japan* (1916); and "The Chinese Written Character as a Medium for Poetry" (1919), this last an essay by Fenollosa edited and perhaps in part rewritten by Pound. In the year 1913, then, Pound was reformulating his theory of luminous details and calling it imagism, and at the same time he was becoming interested in Fenollosa's transliterations and discussion of the ideogram as a medium for poetry. Pound soon discovered that what Fenollosa had been saying prior to 1908 (the year of his death) about the nature of poetry had close affinities with his own theory, which he had formulated under the influence of T. E. Hulme. Pound said of Fenollosa's essay "We have not a bare philological discussion, but a study of the fundamentals of all aesthetics." Fenollosa stressed the concreteness and dramatic qualities of the ideogram. He said that Chinese "brings language close to *things,* and in its strong reliance upon verbs it erects all speech into a kind of dramatic poetry," and he illustrated as follows: "In Chinese the chief verb for 'is' not only means actively 'to have,' but shows by its derivation that it expresses something even more concrete, namely, 'to snatch from the moon with the hand.' Here the baldest symbol of prosaic analysis is transformed by magic into a splendid flash of concrete poetry." The flash of dramatic concreteness was exactly what Pound was looking for in the image and, a bit later, in the *vortex*. He therefore adopted what he called the ideogrammatic method of writing poetry as part of his own creed. "Luminous detail," "image," "vortex," and "ideogram"—all mean about the same thing in Pound's aesthetic. It is interesting to note in passing that Pound, in finding a structure for his poems, opted for a loose association of "images" and abandoned logical structure, which had been used since the Middle Ages, and that Fenollosa too condemned logic as medieval and "discredited." (pp. 23-5)

From imagism and vorticism Pound proceeded, under the partial influence of the quatrains of Théophile Gautier, to write his farewell to London, a series of poems entitled *Hugh Selwyn Mauberley,* published in 1920. The poem is closer to conventional verse than Pound's imagist poetry. In a few instances the iambic foot and slant rhymes are handled with skill. Eliot considered *Mauberley* to be one of the finest poems in English in the twentieth century. Nevertheless, there are typical Poundian difficulties: obscurity, excessive allusions, and, particularly in the final section, an indefensible looseness of structure. *Mauberley* is in fact a conglomerate of separate poems written in various styles. Several of the individual poems are successful, but the work as a whole is not. Besides the looseness of structure there is also an indecisiveness of attitude toward his subject matter and, indeed, an ambiguity concerning the protagonist Mauberley. Who is he? In the first poems he appears to be Pound or a mask for Pound. But in part 2, entitled **"Mauberley,"** he appears to be a sterile aesthete who ends his life on a tropical isle, whereas Pound himself went off to France and then to Italy and became involved, more or less, in politics and economics. Perhaps in part 2 he represents what Pound might have become. Throughout part 1, which has by far the best writing in the series, Pound seems to be indulging in Laforguian romantic irony directed at himself, but he also seems to be blaming his environment, his social milieu, for his lack of success more than himself—that is, the vulgarities of twentieth-century London. Yet, in contrasting his contemporary London with that of the Pre-Raphaelites (whom Pound admired as a young man) and with the decadents of the nineties (who also influenced the early Pound), he seems to be treating them with more irony than approbation. There is, then (as in the *Cantos,* the earliest of which Pound had recently completed), no satisfactory evaluation of himself or of his milieu. There is rather a series of impressions or scenes, ironically described, of the contemporary poet and of literary life in London from the mid-Victorians to 1920. (pp. 26-7)

When we consider the long final effort of Pound's career, the *Cantos,* the problem of point of view, of the attitude of the author toward his material, is ever present. The problem rises directly from his poetic method—the presentation of his material as a series of luminous details which will supposedly give us a sudden subtle insight into a historical situation or a period. As early as 1915 Pound, while explaining vorticism in the *New Age,* wrote, "The Vorticist is expressing his complex consciousness. . . . To be civilized is to have swift apperception of the complicated life of today; it is to have a subtle and instantaneous apperception of it, such as savages and wild animals have of the necessities and dangers of the forest." Will there be any principles, any method by which this series of luminous details can be organized? Pound goes on to say, in the same *New Age* article, "The musical conception of form. . . . that you can select materials of form from the forms before you, that you can recombine and recolour them and 'organize' them into a new form—this conception, this state of mental activity, brings with it joy and refreshment." It is interesting to note that Pound puts the word *organize* in quotes, as if he were embarrassed by it. Years later in **"A Packet for Ezra Pound,"** which Yeats dates March and October 1928, Pound is speaking the same way about the structure of the *Cantos.* Yeats records the conversation with Pound in Rapallo in which they are discussing Pound's first twenty-seven cantos, and Yeats says, "I have often found there brightly printed kings, queens, knaves, but have never discovered why all the saints could not be dealt out in some quite different order." That is, Yeats, like so many early readers of Pound, admired the luminous details but could not discover an overall principle of structure, or for that matter any final purpose or meaning in the *Cantos.* Pound replied that eventually the *Cantos* would have a structure like a Bach fugue. "There will be no plot, no chronicle of events, no logic of discourse, but two themes, the Descent into Hades from Homer, a Metamorphosis from Ovid, and mixed with these, medieval or modern historical characters." And he goes on to speak of the "dream association of words and images, a poem in which there is nothing that can be taken out and reasoned over, nothing that is not a part of the poem itself." It is a clear statement of Pound's intentions and in principle does not go beyond his remarks in the *New Age* article thirteen years earlier. The *Cantos* will be a composition of luminous details organized like a fugue in which two major

themes will be stated and repeated in various ways and minor details added. Pound rejects the traditional methods of organizing a poem: narrative ("no plot"), chronological ("no chronicle of events"), logical ("no logic of discourse"). He uses instead the procedure of "dream association" and the analogy of music. In a poem of medium length such as Eliot's *The Waste Land* or the *Four Quartets,* the employment of motifs repeated with variations may be a fairly successful, although inefficient, way of organizing a poem. But this method is impossible with a poem of over 750 pages and over 100 cantos in length. Of course the original intention of two major themes—a descent into Hades and a Metamorphosis from Ovid—broke down over the years, as did the analogy with a Bach fugue. We are left with a mass of luminous details which, according to Pound himself, should not be extracted from the poem and reasoned over. But because the structure broke down, the only thing one can do with the *Cantos* is to extract details or sections of details—such as the *Pisan Cantos* or the Malatesta cantos—look up the historical background and try to make some sense of them. And this often leads to failure because (as in the John Adams series) Pound does not clearly indicate his point of view. The famous canto against usury (number 45), in which Pound does make his attitude clear, is an exception. In his 1928 conversation with Yeats he said, to repeat, that there would be in his poem "nothing that can be taken out and reasoned over." He is being consistent here with his musical analogy. One can appreciate a Bach fugue as a whole without reasoning over the details, although one should be able to recognize themes and variations. But Pound's *Cantos* of over 750 pages cannot be so appreciated.

Pound, then, as he said himself toward the end of his life, "botched it." There is no structure or overall purpose in the *Cantos,* although heroic attempts have been made to find unity or at least principles of unity in them. Because there is such a mass of material, these various "structures" are always partially successful. The critic (who is in fact imposing his own structure on the *Cantos*) can always find some details here and there to substantiate his argument. But he always has to leave outside his system more material than he puts into it. Each of these structures appears to me to be more the creative work of an individual critic than the demonstrable intention of Pound. (pp. 27-9)

Because of the circumstances of [the composition of *The Pisan Cantos*]—Pound was arrested near Rapallo and thrown into an American concentration camp near Pisa, where he lived and composed his poetry under intolerable conditions—a good deal of sympathy for Pound was aroused, particularly after the passions of the war had subsided. Furthermore, in the widely anthologized **"Canto 81"**, Pound displayed a new humility and (at least for those who admired the *Cantos*), the broken poet who had aimed so high in both literature and politics achieved a kind of tragic dignity. Also, this canto had more unity and coherence and somewhat less obscurity than most of Pound's late verse and it might be expected that this Pisan theme—the fall of a poet whose life had been spent in the search for beauty—would unify and render less obscure the other cantos in the group.

But as we examine the *Pisan Cantos* three decades or so after the event, we find in them most of the same flaws—deriving directly from Pound's method—which we found in the preceding cantos: wide-ranging allusiveness extending now to Chinese as well as to Greek, Latin, and a dozen other literatures, a complete incoherence of texture with a few beautiful images juxtaposed to rags of meaningless (meaningless unless researched and annotated) bits of conversation, and remembered events of significance only to Pound. . . . This is the end of the road which Pound began with his theory of luminous details, formulated before World War I—a poetry of accumulated particulars thrown together without any principle of structure except that of random reverie. They may be fragments composed by the poet himself and therefore of some original literary value—or they may be fragments of art, of music, of almost anything. Their sole value lies in their juxtaposition, and the juxtaposition in the late cantos often appears to be as haphazard and meaningless as the musical compositions of John Cage which are "organized" by pure chance. It is difficult to understand how a number of critics have accepted Pound's irresponsible method without demur. (pp. 31-3)

It is probable, then, that as an original poet, Pound's place in literary history will be that of a minor writer of short impressionistic poems. The method of "luminous detail" which he formulated early in his career and retained until the end—under different labels and phrases—prevented his becoming a major poet, even if he had had the talent to be one. (p. 37)

> *Donald E. Stanford, "Ezra Pound, 1885-1972," in his* Revolution and Convention in Modern Poetry, *University of Delaware Press, 1983, pp. 13-38.*

JOHN TUCKER

In a literate culture, possessed of more effective devices for preserving information, the predictability of poetry comes to be employed to different ends. The expectations of audiences can be thwarted in witty or satiric ways or indulged for authenticating or mesmerising purposes. Pound is to be seen pursuing all of these goals in his early poetry. His first volumes are indeed a record of his assiduous efforts to make himself worthy of this poetic inheritance. As he describes himself in a letter of 1908 to William Carlos Williams, he writes 'To such as love this same beauty that I love somewhat after mine own fashion.' But during the next several years he changed. One might like to think that he began to realise that literacy and more especially the printing press had cut off the roots of poetry, though for centuries no one seemed to have noticed, and that something radical had to be done to revitalise it. He himself more simply acknowledges the influence of Ford Madox Ford, 'the man who did the *work* for English writing' and the 'prose tradition' to which the older writer introduced him.

The prose tradition, which can for practical purposes be reduced to the style of writing perfected by Flaubert, places major emphasis, according to Pound, on *constatation* and *le mot juste*. Pound seems disinclined to translate these terms and perhaps rightly so since they lose much of their charm and potency in English. But both are subsumed in precision and from this period can be dated his conviction that 'The touchstone of an art is its precision'.

The problem is, however, that the kind of precision to which the prose tradition had taught him he must aspire finds its natural expression in, logically enough, prose. In the Imagist writing one sees him struggling towards a new and more precise form of the non-prosaic but unwilling or unable to find any real substitute for the traditional qualities of poetry. This explains the difficulty we have in discerning a practical programme in the ostensibly straightforward, no-nonsense principles of Imagism. Consider, for example, the first—the least dispensable though least definable—principle of Imagism: 'di-

rect treatment of the "thing" whether subjective or objective'. Pound never clearly explains what he intends by this injunction but a study of his criticism reveals that his preoccupation with things and with their direct treatment is related to his complementary beliefs in, to use his own words, 'absolute rhythm' and 'the absolute symbol'. I should like briefly to take up each of these concepts.

Absolute rhythm, the rhythm 'which corresponds exactly to the emotion or shade of emotion to be expressed', can only grow out of a sensitive awareness of 'things'. Thus in his description of the circumstances in which a poet should choose free verse, he states: 'I think one should write vers libre only when one "must", that is to say, only the "thing" builds up a rhythm more beautiful than that of set metres, or more real, more a part of the emotion of the "thing", more germane, intimate, interpretative than the measure of regular accentual verse; a rhythm which discontents one with set iambic or set anapestic.'

The implication here, that the poet will normally use traditional metres, cannot easily be reconciled with the reality of the *Cantos*. Either the poem deals with uniquely non-metrical 'things' or Pound had by 1922 become—in the accusatory words of, apparently, Felix Schelling—a 'confirmed devotee of vers libre'. (p. 40-1)

Pound writes free verse because his commitment to precision allows him no alternative. Direct treatment of the 'thing' insists, at the very least, on the freedom to select the word that most exactly designates the thing. *Le mot juste,* in short. This necessary freedom is incompatible with the requirements of traditional metre, whose demands frequently conflict with those of constatation. The notion of absolute rhythm, then, provides Pound with a perhaps more mystical than practical way of distinguishing between poetry and other language uses without relying on a regularity he has come to reject. In other words, the first Imagist principle entails the third: 'as regarding rhythm: to compose in the sequence of the musical phrase not in sequence of a metronome'.

The other doctrine of absolutes, that of the absolute symbol, depends on a similar sensitivity to 'things', specifically to their symbolic resonances. As Pound expresses it in his **"Credo"**: 'I believe that the proper and perfect symbol is the natural object, that if a man use "symbols" he must so use them that their symbolic function does not obtrude; so that *a* sense, and the poetic quality of the passage, is not lost to those who do not understand the symbol as such, to whom, for instance, a hawk is a hawk.'

On the face of it, this credence seems innocent enough. History required the imagists to define themselves against a largely Symbolist background. But the problematical aspect of the poetic of constatation is just visible here, as we can more easily recognise if we examine Pound's less formal statements on the same theme. Consider his comment in a letter to Iris Barry: 'I think there must be more, predominantly more, objects than statements and conclusions, which latter are purely optional, not essential, often superfluous and therefore bad.' In this, as in the prose tradition's proscription of comment or 'commentation', we see a rejection less of the poet's right to have and to offer opinions (Pound is nothing if not opinionated) than of the predication such opinions necessitate. When in the same letter to the young aspirant poet he speaks of 'a trust in the thing more than the word', he is evidently describing his own attitude.

Perhaps all wise poets experience doubts about language, but, as I see them, the intensity and direction of Pound's distrust do seem unusual. The problem to which he comes back time and again is not the difficulty of expressing himself in words, a pretty standard *topos* after all, but the way in which words inevitably detach themselves from the things they designate and impede where they should facilitate perception. The concern for the semantic bond by which he is haunted makes him suspicious of predication, for in his view when a word is enmeshed in a verbal structure it is pulled away from the thing named. And the less meaning a word derives from the thing it names, the more it depends for its meaning on language and the context to which it belongs. In this vicious circle language tends always to become the vehicle for human reactions to things rather than the medium in which reality discloses itself to the human observer.

Direct treatment of the thing, in short, also entails the second Imagist principle: 'To use absolutely no word that does not contribute to the presentation'. And, to go back to an earlier point, while metre more obviously encourages the poet to add extraneous words, syntax also can be a source of temptation. Syntactically motivated words of secondary importance, that is to say, are as distracting as metrical padding, but they are more difficult to root out. We must realise, for example, that the bracketed insertion in the following haiku, though it makes for 'clarity', is not needed and dilutes its effect: 'The footsteps of the cat upon the snow: (are like) plum blossoms.'

Pound's resistance to the demands of syntax seldom produces disorder in the smaller units of phrase or clause which occupy one or two lines. But his collocations of these units demonstrate the sincerity of his belief that 'abrupt and disordered syntax can be at times very honest, and an elaborately constructed sentence can be at times merely an elaborate camouflage'. The asyntactic tendency of his poetry, in other words, is chiefly apparent in the articulation or 'syntax' of ideas. The words scanted are those whose function is to ensure the cohesion of the text.

This is the Poundian reform. Some may prefer to regard it as, in his own phrase, 'not a revolution of the word but a castigation of the word'. However, a careful consideration of this castigation reveals that it desired and produced a radical change which we may call, according to the circumstances, either a revolution or a mutation. Were the modernists justified in their revolt? Is their mutation viable? These questions remain tantalisingly alive after sixty years of asking. The as yet unborn must make the final judgement, but in the meantime we can try to anticipate their verdict. (pp. 42-3)

The memorability of traditional poetry is a function of the enhanced redundancy which is indeed its constitutive feature. By this means earlier poetry compensated for the 'noise' of defective memory and poor transmission. But Pound's conviction that the poetry of constatation must be condensed (*Dichten = condensare*) causes him to react against such redundancy. His comment in **Antheil**, 'It is redundancy, and therefore bad art, to use [words] where a less conventional humanised means will serve', though it does not address this particular issue, indicates the orientation to which I am referring. Pound's problem is to eliminate redundancy without sacrificing the distinctiveness of poetry. But this dual purpose cannot be achieved by the removal only of the enhanced redundancy of traditional poetry. This would simply produce prose. The logic of his position forces him to the opposite

extreme: Pound's revolution is the redefinition of poetry as language of *minimal* rather than *maximal* redundancy.

The danger faced by traditional poetry, a danger to which in the hands of the unskilled it usually succumbs, is that of fatuous excess. Pound's danger is incomprehensible abbreviation. . . . [Because] Pound had written off his audience as incorrigibly ignorant and backward, he felt no need to take its incomprehension seriously. In his efforts to assess the minimal levels of redundancy needed he turned instead to a theoretical work, Ernest Fenollosa's 'The Chinese written character as a medium for poetry'. (p. 44)

Not surprisingly Pound is infected by Fenollosa's general enthusiasms and specific convictions. That English is an uninflected language and its word order natural becomes an article of faith for him. It explains his attack on 'the mush of the German sentence, the straddling of the verb out to the end', and accounts for his excoriation of Milton. Milton, as Pound would have it, misunderstood the nature of English. 'He tried to turn English into Latin; to use an uninflected language as if it were an inflected one, neglecting the genius of English, distorting its fibrous manner, making schoolboy translations of Latin phrases: "Him who disobeys me disobeys."' (p. 45)

Perhaps we can find a key here to Pound's obsessive antipathy for Milton, the earlier poet whose life and whose ambitions most nearly resemble his own. Is there a troubling awareness deep in Pound that his criticism of Milton is reflexive? Milton may have betrayed English in his decision to dignify his epic style with latinate constructions, but he himself put his language in jeopardy by taking over effects, real or imagined, of a language still more alien. In short, if Milton explores and sometimes miscalculates the thresholds of intelligibility, he is in good company.

As the response to the **Cantos** makes clear, Pound ultimately settles on a level of intelligibility lower than that which most readers find acceptable. In this decision he is encouraged, I think, not only by Fenollosa but by his philological training. The philologist's text, especially a fragmentary one, the product of an ancient culture and in a foreign language, is notably lacking in redundancy. Clearly Pound values the recreative reading that philology attempts and in **"Papyrus"** gives the reader a glimpse of the experience:

> Spring . . . . . .
> Too long . . . . . .
> Gongula . . . . . .

This translation of the first part of a Sapphic fragment may stand as a sort of paradigm for the **Cantos**. The ellipses of the latter merely pre-empt the random deletions of decay and time.

One cannot help noticing, however, that the grammars and glossaries that wait in attendance upon the **Cantos**, as upon a classic text, reintroduce by the back door the very redundancy that Pound has just thrown out by the front. If Pound is troubled by this situation, he gives no sign of it. But then he once wrote to Hardy: 'I am perfectly willing to demand that the reader should read as carefully as he would a difficult latin or greek text.' For this reason he cannot reasonably refuse his reader the tools of the scholar's trade.

To conclude. That traditional and modernist poems cohabit so happily in our anthologies strikes me as peculiar and deserving of comment. If we define poetry simply as significant but deviant language use, this situation will be understandable. But it is worth remembering that the deviations are exactly opposite in nature. The traditional maximisation of redundancy, poetry of double talk as I have called it, is only a distant relative of the contemporary minimalisation of redundancy. The purpose and effects of the two kinds of poetry are surely quite different. And the movement from one to the other kind cannot properly be denied the title revolutionary. Certainly Pound's poetic is revolutionary in the demands that it makes of its readers, although those who have accepted the challenge and studied the *Cantos* with the requisite care seem seldom to have regretted the effort. Nevertheless, it is hard not to feel relief that so few have chosen to follow his radical lead. One would not willingly deny him his lonely eminence. (pp. 46-7)

> John Tucker, "Poetry or Doubletalk: Pound and Modernist Poetics," in Critical Quarterly, Vol. 27, No.2, Summer, 1985, pp. 39-48.

JAMES LAUGHLIN

Pound's memory was more aural than visual. His incredible ear picked up the sounds of words in any language. The number of "original" spellings, particularly of proper names, in the *Cantos* might bear out that theory. When he was in the heat of composing a canto he simply didn't want to stop to do much checking. And reading proofs bored him. Consistency also bored him; he would often make different corrections in his English and American proofs. This presented problems for his editors because his allusions were not often to be found in the usual reference books. . . .

Pound's models for the *Cantos* were primarily the epics of Homer and Dante. How he transformed those models, driven as he was to write a new kind of *personal* epic, is one of the wonders and enigmas of modern literature. Pound's poetic idiom seldom sounds "modern." We can still hear in the *Cantos* overtones of Campion and Waller, Rossetti and Browning, even Whitman. Where he broke with the past, where he became "modern," was in the arrangement of the lines, in his experiments with a collage structure. This making of collages and his practice of weaving into the text words and whole passages from some 13 languages, ancient and modern, including even Chinese characters, perplex many readers.

One of Pound's premises as he began writing the *Cantos* was that an epic was a poem "containing history." But he enlarged his scope as the poem progressed. New ingredients were added, such as the monetary reform theories of C. H. Douglas (Social Credit) and Silvio Gesell. And early on, in **"Canto XIII,"** Pound had added to his master plan the ethics of Confucius.

We find 10 cantos of early Chinese history (LII-LXI), drawn from the chronicles of the French Jesuit Joseph-Anne-Marie Moyriac de Mailla, which show how China prospered when a good emperor followed Confucian principles and what happened to the people when a bad emperor did not. Confucianism tied in with economics—a "Confucian" emperor would have a clean economic system.

The Confucian ethic was not the only gift from Chinese culture to the *Cantos*. Quite as important was Pound's "ideogrammatic method" for structuring poems. This he first derived from the classic Chinese poetry of his little book *Cathay,* which he translated in 1915, working from the notes of the scholar Ernest Fenollosa. . . .

Can we enjoy only what Pound jokingly called the "beauty spots" of the *Cantos,* the simple parts where there are extended passages of sequential narrative or description? Are the rapid collages and the recondite allusions too much for us? Pound seemed to assume his readers knew everything and everyone he did. He provided no notes for the *Cantos*. If we want to know who Gollievski or "old Jarge" was, we must go to Carroll F. Terrell's *Companion to the Cantos of Ezra Pound*. But how much does it really matter who they were if the lines in which they appear are interesting? Did the readers of Dante know who all those people in the *Commedia* were? . . .

Would it help if we stood back to look at the *Cantos* from a distance and asked, "What is really going on here?" Essentially we are listening to a long monologue. Gertrude Stein said Pound was "a village explainer, excellent if you are a village, but if you are not, not." As night wears on in the village square the voice of the *Cantos* is explaining everything except science and technology.

In the early cantos the telling is very lively. Pound is full of excitement about his intellectual and esthetic discoveries—what he learned about the heroes and gods of the Mediterranean world; about Sigismondo Malatesta of Rimini, one of the most colorful of the warrior-princes of the Italian Renaissance; about Confucius; about his blessed Chinese emperors (he liked best Emperor Tang, who had engraved on his bathtub, "Make it new . . . day by day make it new," which became Pound's motto, the goal for his own work); about the American Founding Fathers, particularly Jefferson and Adams. Pound weaves these disparate lives together with ingenuity. Their stories comment on one another; the process becomes a kind of moral criticism.

Later the mood of the *Cantos* changes. Pound's situation has altered for the worse. The broadcasts he made from Rome during the war have brought him to the stockade. Pound's infatuation with Fascism grew out of his hope that he could persuade Mussolini to reform the Italian banking system. The virulent anti-Semitism of the broadcasts may be interpreted as a symptom of paranoia. Winfred Overholser, who was the chief psychiatrist of St. Elizabeths Hospital in Washington, where Pound was kept for 12 years, told me Pound should be judged "medically," not "morally," that the anti-Semitism was a form of paranoia, the need for a scapegoat. . . .

In *The Pisan Cantos* Pound is reflective and nostalgic, less didactic and more humble. . . . (p. 58)

It is in *The Pisan Cantos* that we can approach him most closely as a person. He has had his turn of fortune and he is fearful for his future, but he isn't giving up. Birds perched on telephone wires remind him of notes of music. He enjoys the humor of the prisoners and guards. The gods of Greece are with him in his dark hour. And the goddess Aphrodite. . . . And he calls one of the Carrara mountains he sees from the camp "Taishan," which is a sacred mountain in China. The troubadours whom he had translated are with him. He recalls his good days as a young man in London. In some, though not all, of the three last segments of the *Cantos* the voice changes its tone again. It becomes more subdued, more meditative and speculative. . . . (pp. 58-9)

In the later cantos, Pound is looking back on his life. He is trying to put the pieces together. Dante had always been his model—hence the name *Cantos*. If the early cantos are his *Inferno* and the middle ones his *Purgatorio*, then *Section Rock-Drill* ("I've got to drill it into their beans," he once told me) and *Thrones* (the third order of the angelic hierarchy in Dante) are his *Paradiso*, his ascent to the higher realms of thought and the spirit.

The late cantos are the most difficult to grasp. Readers whom they baffle call them incoherent muttering. The ordering of lines is based on association from memory. These cantos are at first annoying—till we get the hang of them. But if we think of them as music they become clearer. Are they not fugal? There is a hidden structure. There are variations and recapitulations. All the major themes in the earlier cantos are repeated and restated. Fragments are inserted in new conjunctions that give them deeper meaning. And the music of the language keeps pace with the subtlety of form.

The major motifs have now reached their full development. There is love, Amor, in its various aspects, as Pound had found it in the Eleusinian mysteries of ancient Greece and in the love songs of the troubadours. There is nature as it appears in the myth of Demeter and Persephone. There is the ordering of the state as in Confucius and the good Chinese emperors, and in Duke Leopold of Siena and the Founding Fathers. Pound was not a professed Christian but there is religion, or perhaps his own form of mysticism, symbolized in "the great ball of crystal—the acorn of light." This concept is rooted in his understanding of the nature of light, which is both Helios, the sun, and the light that shines in love. And above all there is the dream of the earthly paradise, the *"paradiso terrestre,"* which acceptance of his theories of economic reform might have made possible. (This paradise is figured in his mythical cities of Dioce and Wagadu.) These themes recur, sounding and seen together, for the *Cantos* are intensely visual. Everything is concrete and *shown;* there is very little symbolism and no extraneous rhetoric.

Toward the end of his life Pound worried about the *Cantos.* Had he managed to make them cohere? That is the salient question each reader must answer for himself. Certainly the *Cantos* do not cohere in the way *Paradise Lost* does. They are not tidy. But poetry moves in new ways; that is what insures its vitality from age to age. And if we look at the other personal epics of our century—Eliot's *Waste Land* and *Four Quartets,* Williams's *Paterson, The Bridge* by Hart Crane, Charles Olson's *Maximus Poems,* Louis Zukofsky's *A* and Thomas Merton's *Geography of Lograire*—I think we can say that the *Cantos* do cohere, at least in the frame of modern poetry. In fact, the *Cantos* were the model, in whole or in part, for some of these other great poems.

Are the *Cantos* worth the attention they require? In **"Canto LXXXIX,"** Pound, quoting a 15th-century Dutch scholar, Rudolphus Agricola, defines the purposes of literature as *"Ut moveat, ut doceat, ut dilectet."* Literature should move us, teach us and delight us. Do the *Cantos* meet that test? *"Ut moveat"*—some of us are moved by the fate that the gods, or history, imposes upon us; it's all there in the *Cantos. "Ut doceat"*—except for the sciences, a rich college curriculum awaits us in the poem. *"Ut dilectet"*—there is no finer music or language in the work of any poet of our time. (p. 59)

James Laughlin, *"Solving the Ezragrams: Pound at 100,"* in The New York Times Book Review, *November 10, 1985, pp. 1, 58-9.*

ALFRED KAZIN

If ever man looked The Poet as antagonist of bourgeois civilization (especially in Latin countries, where the beard, the wide-brimmed black hat, the open collar, the walking stick, and the defiant look were familiar at anarchist congresses) it was Pound in the course of a career always full of uproar. . . .

Pound always took all his associations along with him; that was his genius. He was a natural taker-over; when his mind didn't, his will did. . . .

A genius not least in his American gift for appropriating land not his own, gods distinctly not in the Protestant tradition, a language so far out of time that his very need to impersonate it is as impressive as his ability to do so. (p. 16)

[When] Pound is the lyric poet in a state of grace—not repeating the same anecdote in the *Cantos* about Jacques Maritain, not bitching about the failure of the English to appreciate him, not railing at the fall of civilizations that would not have fallen if they had read Confucius and John Adams and the autobiography of Martin Van Buren—you feel . . . that his real genius was to identify with poetry itself, poetry without which men once never went to war, poetry as primal element, kin to nature as prose can never be.

No one of Pound's generation in English, the modernists born in the "failure" of the last century and determined to remake the next, caught so rapturously as Pound did, from within, poetry's genius for summoning up the beginning of things, the archaic as inception, the childhood of the race, the ability to look at the world as Homer did, for the wonder of creation. . . .

Seeing but especially *hearing* such words, one gets charged up, relieved for the moment from the unfelt emotions so often proclaimed in poetry, poetry too often written by people to whom, evidently, nothing very much has happened. The force of Pound's lyricism suggests an extraordinary ability to possess and incarnate his classical reading. From this ability to assimilate, he has imagined as actions words he has taken off the page.

Pound did something amazing: he turned himself into a mythical creature, the poet from ancient times. The bard, the "singer of tales," which Pound in his genius for sound felt himself to be, has an understandable affinity with war as his element. Pound was unable to understand a society that had lost all contact with poetry as its great tradition. It actually declined to credit Pound with the sagacity he attributed to *il gran poeta.* As he grew more isolated abroad, especially after his removal to Fascist Italy in 1924, Pound's talent for seeing life as literary myth augmented each year. He finally understood the vast indifference around him: a malignant conspiracy threatened civilization itself. . . . As he was himself a natural hero-worshipper, so he attracted acolytes by the force of his gift and his total fearlessness in instructing the "bullet-headed many" how to read, what to think.

What spellbound the acolytes were feats of association; they set up reverberations in his readers and replaced contemporary realities with a web of learning. There was an extraordinary energy, a driving impulse; poetry was assuming powers lost in the nineteenth century to the great novelists. The forever bristling Pound style in the *Cantos*—the Browning version he learned early—and his zeal for violent types from Malatesta to Mussolini in the heroic mold, condottieri, reflected Pound's harkening back to martial associations with poetry. These were certainly not in the minds of poets contained by personal anguish like Matthew Arnold and T.S. Eliot. Arnold thought that the future of poetry was "immense" because it would ease the shock of Europe's de-Christianization. Eliot in his journey from Prufrock's conflict of the self to the healing by sacred places in *Four Quartets* practiced poetry as a medium of personal salvation.

Pound never understood such agony. He was no Christian. Poetry could still be primitive because "the gods have never left us." With this he helped to establish modernism as a position marked by fascination with the archaic and the unconscious, disdain for the mass, a view of industrial society as nothing but a matter of mechanization. He was spellbound by the vision of an earlier world, supposedly more charged and radiant than ours, truer to the hieratic world identified with art by conservatives and sought for society by fascists. (p. 17)

Modernism was a summoning up, a way of establishing order, with peculiarly up-to-the-minute tools that were too much in the spirit of the age to be recognized as such by those fleeing Pound's "half-savage country" for "the spirit of romance." Pound's tool he still called poetry. Dante was always in his mind: the unifying figure whose journey through hell and purgatory up to paradise Pound saw as a model for his epic journey in the *Cantos* even when he forgot that it was supposed to make a similar point. Behind Dante was Virgil, behind Virgil Homer. Epic was a book as action (always a hope to Pound) unifying a race through the chronicle of its wars, sacred places, gods.

Did Pound begin the *Cantos* thinking he had the qualifications? Not altogether, but he felt *himself* to embody this affinity with poetry, with its fundamental tonality as a separate medium of speech. *Poetry* was literature. In the novel he could recognize only those who prized style above everything else, had strictness of intention like Flaubert, James, Joyce. The social application of the modern novel meant nothing to him. The great voices were authority. "With a day's reading a man may have the key in his hand." In treating the novel purely as art object, he was projecting poetic epic as the only true history.

This he failed to prove in his inordinate subjectivism. The fascination of Pound's *Cantos* was to lie in its reflection of Pound's mind; not what he brought together but what he was capable of thinking of from line to line. We are never so much in the *Cantos* as we are observing a performance. We join Pound's mental flight even when we don't follow his matter. As for the "matter," his intentions are no help whatever. Pound's mind was not structural in details but assimilative, lyrical, impatient. After some great passage he was always breaking off to introduce something he had read. Early on he told his father that the *Cantos* would constitute a *"commedia agnostica"* as against the *commedia divina.* He liked to stress the work's analogy to musical structure, and its parallels with the "subject and response and counter subject in fugue." There were to be three principal elements: "Live man goes down into the world of the Dead. The 'repeat in history.' The 'magic moment' or moment of metamorphosis, but through from quotidian into 'divine or permanent world,' Gods etc." (I like that "Gods etc.") He hoped that "out of the three main climaxes of themes, permanent, recurrent and casual (or haphazard), a hierarchy of values should emerge."

This was to be a *modern* epic, "a poem including history" that "encompasses not only the world's literature but its art, architecture, myths, economics, the lives of historical figures—in effect, block letters, THE TALE OF THE TRIBE." En route it would take in sixteenth-century Italian architecture, Provençal lyrics, Confucian politics, medieval economic history—almost a dozen languages. Pound was going to show "ideas in action" and "things explaining themselves by the company they keep."

The "quotidian" never got into the *Cantos;* perhaps there was no actual *life* around him for Pound to report. The Bible,

Homer, Dante, even Milton, reflect the day-to-day life of a civilization. The greatest novels of Western civilization, from *War and Peace* to *Ulysses* and *A la recherche du temps perdu,* are easily called epics. Obviously what we get in Pound is something else. Jean Cocteau defined poetry as a separate language. The specialization of consciousness that the Romantics fostered, the journey into an interior world, attains in the *Cantos* the ultimate in self-absorption as the roller coaster of Pound's mind plunges up and down into a world largely of his reading.

Starting from the *Nekuia,* the journey to the dead in Book XI of the *Odyssey,* we go from an ordered universe and comprehensive values to one in which everything coming apart is held together by the names and quotations flashing out of the stream of Pound's references. A sustaining image is always water, that particular Greek medium. . . .Pound's ability to make a frieze out of so many quotations, invocations, imitations, to place an ornamented sculptured band within a cascade, is extraordinary. Who else would have thought of "lynx-purr"? Moving from the sound this makes to the picture, he is so pleased that his lynx is soon "purring" again—and typically for Pound, with less sense but just as much beauty.

From the outset we are in a world of names, great place names—Venice, Burgos, Mount Rokku between the rock and the cedars, Ecbatan, Plantagenet England—and of great names in this culture show of a museum through which an expatriate American is directing us. As Pound said in the *Pisan Cantos* remembering an aunt's travels—and what a commentary on the captivity in which he remembered that—"But at least she saw damn all Europe." Now Eleanor of Aquitaine swims before us, now Henry James—marvelous, marvelous! (pp. 18-19)

Writing about Jefferson and his epoch, Pound sought as always to be the historical dramatist. No one knew better how to pull the best lines from his reading. No one was so adroit at shifting and mixing the great voices of the past. Eliot in *The Waste Land* was haunting when he gave us a collage of actual voices. Thanks to Pound's famous cutting, the poem sustains different moods, builds up to a denouement that leads us to expect the actual fall of civilization. Pound the master critic, the great *practical* critic, cut *The Waste Land* in a way that would have sent him screaming if anyone had proposed equal measures for the *Cantos.* (This would not have worked in any event; the poem is too diffuse.) Pound could only tolerate *Selected Cantos.* In the American History Cantos beginning with XXXI Pound simply cannot tear himself loose from his reading. And with his *idées fixes* about the influence of credit and the dominance of usury in modern economic life, he kept emphasizing every old quote he could dig up that pointed significantly in the direction of his wisdom—Ezra the giant-killer of economics, the Hercules cleaning out the stables.

Pound's genius for the sound and arrangement of words that bring out the *inherency* of poetry did not extend to ideas. In his intellectual rage he was incapable of making the most elementary distinctions. (p. 20)

Allen Tate was unfair when he said that the *Cantos* were not *about* anything. But to "include history," Pound's famous postulate for an epic, is not necessarily to describe it. The fascination of the *Cantos,* circling around golden bits of lyric landscape, lies in the journey up and down Pound's mind, which for great stretches shows mostly his reading. (p. 21)

In St. Elizabeths, talking to Allen Ginsberg and invoking his old friendship with Louis Zukofsky, Pound charmed his audience with the disclosure that his anti-Semitism was "a suburban prejudice.'' Bewitched by words as usual, he also explained that no one named Ezra could really be an anti-Semite. Whether or not he always knew what he was saying—clearly impossible in such a lifetime's flood of words—Pound was dishonest, and so were his defenders, when he finally claimed insanity as a reason for his actions. He got away with it.

Pound was a convinced fascist. The cruelty and death of fascism are an essential part of his epic and cannot be shrugged away in judging his work. Pound recognized his epic hero in Mussolini because fascism, like Ezra Pound, had few abiding social roots and was based on an impersonation, like Pound's, of a mythic personage. Pound was a racist, a defender of racial persecution, indifferent to the obliteration of fellow artists. These were not personal aberrations but part of hierarchic beliefs into which he grew through long years of alienation from his country and from the people around him. Pound was a fascist in a period when everything turned against the humane spirit of pre-1914 Europe in which modernism began.

The growing tendency of our century is against that spirit. Nowhere is it more striking than in the museum of modern literature—where the curators of the modernist classics replay their authors as Pound replayed the epic poets. (p. 23)

The contrast between what History knows and what Pound thought he knew threatens the integrity of literary study if it reduces itself to apologia and to vicarious scorn for what the modernist masters scorned. Ever since modernism became academically respectable, it has threatened to take over the curriculum. Eliot's prescription, that past literature should constantly be assimilated to the taste of the present, has led to a steady omission and distortion of actual history. Modernism must not become the only writer of its history, especially when puffed up with the antidemocratic and racist views of Ezra Pound. Modernism is not our only tradition. The museum of modern literature, like all museums these days enshrining the first half of the twentieth century, cannot show us all that we leave out and even deform in the name of art. (p. 24)

> *Alfred Kazin, ''The Fascination and Terror of Ezra Pound,'' in* The New York Review of Books, *Vol. XXXIII, No. 4, March 13, 1986, pp. 16-24.*

ALAN DURANT

Pound's achievement has always seemed problematic. Few readers would dispute the genius in his ability to render voices, idioms and registers of English. Equally, however, few would be likely to dispute that there are at the very least questions still to be asked about his cultural theories and particular political beliefs. In addition, there remain biographical details to complicate things (Fascism, the trial, madness, the prize); and there are also the changing practices, and fragmentary and incremental character, of the *Cantos* themselves. Could the poem ever have been a coherent work of one hundred cantos, or was it inevitable from the outset it would turn out, as in some of Pound's formulations, an 'endless, leviathanic' poem, of 'no known category', 'cryselephantine', 'of immeasurable length'? Why are the drafts and fragments at first anticipatory, then later retrospective, and does it indicate failure that the poem ends in seemingly the same relation to a paradise to be found as it began in? (pp. 154-55)

Pound, then, has importance in at least two ways: for his cultural pioneering and for his technical innovation and experiment. But it is evidently the ways in which these two domains are interdependent and reciprocally defining which is crucial. The cultural crusade requires the language of literature to be 'made new', but it is that very newness of language which will forge reform at the political or cultural level. This interaction is the real mark of Pound's importance (his work energetically, continually, poses questions about language and its relations to experience and to the world). But it also creates the difficulty over current placings of Pound's achievement or lasting significance.

The difficulty is this. Techniques of imagistic collage displace and dislocate the impression gained from discourse of a central speaking consciousness, or point from which feelings and judgements appear to be delivered. When combined with a counterpoint of dialects, quotations, and registers, this diffraction of a central speaking 'voice' or 'consciousness' into an array of not necessarily commensurate discourses becomes peculiarly prominent, and presses for specific critical explanation. Because of this, the play backwards and forwards of associations and connections experienced in reading Pound's poetry is especially important. Yet for the connections of any one particular reading to achieve the scale of general interpretative importance Pound evidently saw in his own poetry, until very late in his life, it seems necessary to believe that there exists some very exceptional relationship between the associative, concatenating processes of reading and the disposition of objects and processes in the world.

Many people (including Pound) have believed such a special relationship exists. Pound himself, as we know, largely drew support for his beliefs in this area from the small but striking work by Ernest Fenollosa, *The Chinese Written Character as a Medium for Poetry*. But Fenollosa's work—in this respect like much of the discursive or theoretical work Pound invoked in other spheres (e.g. the work of Major Douglas, or Rémy de Gourmont)—is generally considered eccentric to main directions of thinking in the area of concerns it addresses. Clearly, two lines of reasoning emerge from this. Either Pound had an eye for unappreciated genius, and the truths both of his own work and works he revered will finally be vindicated; or alternatively Pound found support for his own very unusual ideas in the equally unusual work of like-minded thinkers, but the most valuable leverage on the issues at stake remains that given by other, often more orthodox forms of reasoning. Both cases, in my view, are worth hearing in full.

Recent psychological and linguistic approaches to Pound's work offer one reasoned challenge to Pound's views. What makes them appear attractive in comparison with more traditional literary criticism of Pound's work is that they *attempt* to analyse the relationship between details of the poetry and the poet's (and subsequent critics') assertions about it. This involves, in particular, describing and assessing what mechanisms and processes—more than intuition—enable a reader to move in any constrained way (as Pound implies we might) from arrangements of words and images on the page into observations about relationships in the world and in experience. Arguably, approaches of this kind should be taken seriously simply because they attempt, in investigating Pound's representations of the unseen and the empyrean, to preclude simply confusing the act of invoking something to be with that of affirming that something is. And exploring processes involved in construing modern poetry seems a valuable enterprise in any case. But such investigation seems nothing less than *crucial* in the instance of a poetry, such as Pound's, which is linked to cultural evaluations and imperatives that range from at their weakest a form of revivalist cultural elitism to at their strongest a virulent racism and practically aligned politics of fascism. (pp. 155-57)

It is relatively uncontroversial . . . that 'ideas' in the *Cantos* are created through sequences of juxtaposed images. This stylistic innovation of modernism—embodied successively in image, haiku, vortex, metaphor, ideogrammic method, and so on—has more than once been called 'paratactic' rather than 'hypotactic' in character (though the precise linguistic accuracy of this is rather dubious). The properties of juxtaposition need, however, to be looked at more closely, if the precise nature of *linkage* between these influential techniques of writing and larger aesthetic and cultural issues of poetry is to be adequately analysed.

Juxtaposition and collage, it might be said, define and explain, producing meaning through images (as facts), and the self-evident force of comparison, rather than through contrived judgement and stated opinion. Yet actual attention to the language of Pound's poetry suggests that the poet's imagistic technique is not one technique at all but at the very least two—with fundamentally divergent properties and implications. Pound appears himself not to have distinguished the two. Yet differentiation between them may begin to account for some aspects of the poet's own sense, in later life, of personal failure and artistic disillusionment. (p. 157)

[The] didacticism of the *Cantos* depends largely on patterns of ideas which are brought together to show what they have in common: the historical rhyme (corresponding events in different periods), the cultural parallel, the unsuspected resemblance. The 'appositive' construction is very suitable for this purpose. The 'listing' construction on the other hand, involves not just superimpositions beneath which lies a single common denominator (the 'topic' or 'meaning' of the passage, ultimately, the 'NOUS, the ineffable crystal:' the end of the poem in truth), but also an endlessly changing Kaleidoscope of perceptions and sensations linked together by what is a purely personal associative itinerary. Where the poetry of equation might be assertive, didactic, metaphysical, the poetry of digression will inevitably be far more individual and impressionistic. Consequently, too, of course, such 'imagistic-associative' poetry will be consistent only with a very different set of claims about poetic process and possible social value for poetry than are appropriate for 'imagistic-appositive' poetry. (pp. 158-59)

Pound's own beliefs may or may not prove to be valuable. What remains most importantly in question about Pound's work is the relationship between the famous literary and cultural opinions and the poetic theories and practices the poet so energetically developed and promoted. It is frequently claimed that Pound's poetic techniques stand as the exemplary means for imprinting his cultural argument; and it is this claim which makes clear Pound's continuing significance. Whether the poet himself held fascist views is a less important issue than whether the *poetics* he laid out is connected with or separable from any specifiable political vision. Pound's writings continue to have a major influence on readers; and new poems continue to be written in response to techniques and ideas Pound did perhaps more than anyone else of his generation to establish. For these reasons, at least, the debate over Pound's work continues to have a wide importance. (p. 164)

> Alan Durant, "Pound, Modernism and Literary Criticism: A Reply to Donald Davie," in Critical Quarterly, Vol. 28, Nos. 1-2, Spring-Summer, 1986, pp. 154-66.

CHARLES BERNSTEIN

The lesson of Pound for contemporary poetry is contradictory and disturbing—for there are elements in his work that give comfort to utopian fantasies of a self-conscious, multivocal, polyvalent, intensely sonorous poetry and also of a repellent, self-justifying, smug, canonically authoritarian, culturally imperialist poetic and critical practice. Attempts to ignore or domesticate this central problematic in Pound fail to appreciate that the irresolvability of the problem is Pound's legacy; for while one may prefer to dwell on the formal innovations of *The Cantos,* the meaning of these innovations can be adequately appreciated only in the context of their fascist roots. If we are to take Pound, or ourselves, seriously, then we must grapple not with "structures themselves" but with the political and historical contexts in which these structures emerge. We must, that is, understand that our poetical practices have political and social dimensions in terms of form over and above content— if we can allow this distinction at all. The sanitized Pound is inert and irrelevant; and it is evident from the remarkably thoughtful new Pound criticism by, for example, Christine Froula and Richard Sieburth, that opening the Pandora's box of "the Pound Error" allows for, rather than precludes, the continuing relevance of Pound's work. ("The Pound Error" is the term Froula devises in *To Write Paradise: Style and Authority in Pound's Cantos* for Pound's inclusion of printer's errors, misattributions, mistranslations, and the like into the text of *The Cantos* so that the "history" that the poem includes is also the history of its groping compositional process. As she uses it, "error" is also errantry, or wandering.) In a similar way, the relevance of Pound for contemporary poetry is to be found most significantly in those works that have confronted the politics of Poundian "textualization" and appropriation and have realized alternatives to it.

The fascist implications of Pound's work can perhaps best be understood by contrasting two compositional techniques, montage and collage. By definition, collage is a more general term of which montage is a type, but I wish to make a different distinction. For Eisenstein, montage involves the use of contrasting images in the service of one unifying theme; collage, as I use it here, juxtaposes different elements without recourse to an overall unifying idea. Pound wished to write a montage but produced something far more interesting in the process. The underlying idea of his montage has been varyingly described by many of the critics who wish to make a claim for the overall unity of *The Cantos.* Suffice it to say here that his appropriation of prior texts (the quotations, citations, and transductions) were intended as an evaluative, "objectively" discriminating—and hence hierarchical and phallocentric—"ordering" of these materials. The "objective" historical synopsis of human culture (what we might call the subtextual curriculum of *The Cantos*) and its claims to ground the poem in an extraliterary reality have made the work especially attractive to many Pound scholars, despite the objectionable and elitist premises of this synopsis and the fact that *The Cantos* implodes the very "objective" and ideological aims it purports to articulate.

Understanding *The Cantos* as montage provides a framework for the poem's implied positivism, which also helps to explain those theoretical statements of Pound's that seem to fly in the face of his actual poetic practice: his insistence, variously, on "the plain sense of the word," on the "direct treatment of the 'thing,' " and on the unswerving pivot whose Imagist distillation was made possible by eliminating any word that did not directly contribute—a poetics commonly taken as a refutation of the artifice of Symbolist and Swinburnian modes as well as a rejection of the excessive verbiage of contemporary conventional verse. Pound vilified fragmentation and abstraction as debasing the "gold standard" of language, yet his major and considerable contribution to the poetry of our language is exactly his rococo overlayings and indirect elusiveness. His fast-moving contrasts of attitudes and atmospheres collapse the theater of ideational representation into a textually historicist, unfinishable process of composition by field—a field of many voices without the fulcrum point of any final arbitration, listening not judging—a *dis*integration into the incommensurability of parts that marks its entrance into the space of contemporary composition. Insofar as contemporary poetry does not wish simply to admire or dismiss Pound's work but to understand it, these competing dynamics must be reckoned with.

It took the arrogance of Pound's supremacist and culturally essentialist ideology to give him the ambition to imagine a work on the scale of *The Cantos,* a poem that theoretically encompasses nothing less than the story—history—of the seminal [*sic*] strains of human culture. That no person has an adequate vantage point to "make it cohere" is of course a lesson *The Cantos* teaches but that Pound never fully learned. It is a lesson *we* need to learn not just from *The Cantos* but from the larger history of geopolitical struggles in this century. While Mussolini's dystopian state failed to triumph, shattering *The Cantos'* objective correlative, the current problematic of imposed order—the United States or the Soviet Union *uber alles*—is too obvious to need reiteration here. It is already constantly reiterated in the eloquent pleas heard from South Africa to Grenada, from Czechoslovakia to New Zealand, for the autonomy of their cultural difference and against integration into an imposed curricular design. So contemporary poetry's response to Pound is to enact a poetry that does not fragment for the sake of a greater whole but allows the pieces to sing their own story—a chordal simultaneity at pains to put off any coherence save that found within its own *provisional* measure. Every grain or strain or swatch has its own claim to truth, not as one of the "luminous particulars"—exemplary types selected by the Agassiz/Fenollosa scientific method and part of what Michael André Bernstein calls a "universally valid, external, narrative structure"—but as part of the democracy of words and cultures and histories, all impossible to exhaust or rank. Pound's historical and ideological tendentiousness is not the problem: indeed, doctrinaire tendentiousness is in many ways a useful corrective to the denial of ideology in the transcendentalist Imagination of Romantic poetry. That is, the failure of *The Cantos* does not entail the necessary impossibility of including history, politics, and economics in a poem, but it does entail the rejection of the positivist assumptions behind these inclusions. So we must now attempt to critique Poundian panculturism with decentered multiculturalism. (pp. 635-37)

The lacunas in Pound's guides to culture have begun to speak. By introducing a form where dialects and languages mingle freely, where "nonpoetic" material—"raw facts," Chinese ideograms, printer's errors, slang, polylingual quotations—are given poetic status, Pound opened the floodgates for what had been left out, or refined out, by precepts such as his own "use absolutely no word that does not contribute." The undigested quality of parts of *The Cantos* gives credence to the further explorations of the unheard and unsounded in our poetry. (p. 638)

Charles Bernstein, "Pound and the Poetry of Today," in The Yale Review, *Vol. 75, No. 4, Summer, 1986, pp. 635-40.*

THEODORE WEISS

[The letter by Theodore Weiss excerpted below is a response to Alfred Kazin's essay excerpted above.]

Like other adverse critics of Pound not altogether unavailable to poetry, Kazin acknowledges Pound's great lyric gifts and quotes some lyrical passages. He tells us that Pound's lyrical power—Kazin seems satisfied with descriptions of it like "silky lines" and "lacy lines"—resides chiefly in his "associations": "he always took his associations with him; that was his genius. He was a natural taker-over." Then, lest we think this unmixed praise, "when his mind didn't, his will did." For he was a literary imperialist, "A genius not least in his American gift for appropriating land not his own, gods distinctly not in the Protestant tradition, a language so far out of time that his very need to impersonate it is as impressive as his ability to do so." Pound was very American, but not entirely—or maybe not sufficiently—so. He should, I take it, have been content to appropriate America and England, not also Greece, Italy, and China. Is it provincialism Kazin is advocating for poets? And was there something wrong or merely unmannerly (un-American) in Pound's forsaking the Protestant tradition? Is there something sacred about it? Yet Kazin calls all this "genius?"

We learn that when Pound avoided obnoxious subject matter and reserved himself to lyricism, his poetry was fine. For his "real genius was to identify with poetry itself, poetry without which men once never went to war. Poetry as primal element, kin to nature as prose can never be." This would seem to be praise indeed. But the reservation asserts itself in the allusion to war. Or Pound as a bloody sort, a theme which is central to Kazin's argument. He never remarks Pound's profound hatred of war, his powerful attacks on it in *Mauberley,* the *Cantos* and elsewhere. And if it would seem attractive of poetry to be kin to nature as prose can never be, we must remember that these are prose times remote from nature.

Kazin acknowledges that no one of Pound's generation "caught as rapturously as Pound did, from within, poetry's genius for summing up the beginning of things, the archaic as inception, the childhood of the race, the ability to look at the world as Homer did, for the wonder of creation." However, lest we take this ability too seriously, Kazin assures us that it was not a direct look after all but mainly out of Pound's classical reading. Or indeed looking at the world through Homer's eyes. So even Pound's lyricism is questionable? Kazin does not seem to realize that Homer was the culmination of who knows how many poets. Yet Kazin admits that "Pound did something amazing: he turned himself into a mythical creature. . . .The bard, the 'singer of tales.' " We might consider this a noble recovery of poetry's great role, but aside from its being archaic (what has a bard from ancient times to do with us now?), Kazin maintains that it was "his genius for sound" that convinced Pound he was such a bard. With him sound overwhelmed sense.

Even as Pound has "an understandable affinity with war as his element," he "was unable to understand a society that had lost all contact with poetry as its great tradition." That loss was, I would say, exactly what Pound did understand and fought heroically against. Furthermore, Kazin fails to notice Pound's success: his influence at least on poets and critics. Even Auden, who little resembled Pound, could say, "There are very few living poets, even if they are not conscious of having been influenced by Pound, who could say, 'My work would be exactly the same if Mr. Pound never lived.' " Nor does Kazin notice Pound's making as much as anyone the vast enterprise of poetry possible today. Now even in the USA, whatever the indifference of the general populace and most of our intellectuals to poetry, one can admit to being a poet without flinching! But here we are at the heart of what concerns me: the relevancy of poetry to our time. Is it, like nature itself, exclusively for a distant age? Does Kazin applaud the inevitability of our society's loss of contact with poetry? Since much of our society is not close to nature why should its language be?

Kazin does admit Pound's impact. But it was suspect, if not pinchbeck. For Pound spellbound "acolytes" (no one, in short, worth taking seriously) by his "feats of association," which "replaced contemporary realities with a web of learning." At least Pound did have something beyond mere "sound?" Kazin recognizes "There was an extraordinary energy, a driving impulse; poetry was assuming powers lost in the nineteenth century to the great novelists." For a moment he seems to appreciate what Pound was trying to do and to a considerable degree succeeding in doing. But, no, his Browning-learned style with his "zeal for violent types from Malatesta to Mussolini. . .reflected Pound's harkening back to martial associations with poetry." Might not Pound's zeal be traced back not so much to the violence of these types but to his respect for them, however mistaken, as vigorous actors who used part of that vigor for the cultivation of the intellect and the arts and for the erection of great monuments?

What Pound apparently lacked was the "personal anguish" of Arnold and Eliot. In short, Pound should have not only stuck to his lyricism but employed it, rather than positively or actively, to express anguish before the troubles and failures of the modern world, especially his own. (So Kazin earlier seemed to regret, "There is very little of Pound's personal life in his poetry; from it you would never guess his relations with Dorothy Shakespeare and Olga Rudge." Whether one agrees or suggests that these relations are present, transformed appropriately into poetry, one might ask whether Kazin thinks the personal an essential ingredient of poetry.)

But Pound's biggest mistake was his "fascination with the archaic and the unconscious." Actually Pound despised the modern absorption in the self and the unconscious and sought to recover something like the unity of being he found in Homer, Dante, and other great poets. He believed in action, not self-defeating introspection.

Kazin stresses the unmodernity of modernism and the basic contradiction in it: "It is funny now to think of how resolutely anti-modern (in spirit) high modernism felt itself to be—while it expressed itself, as Pound did, in telescoped history and in formally disconnected images that were distinctly novel." Must a poet be uncritical of his age? The corruptions of international venture capitalism, our banking system, rampant materialism, conglomerate greed, abject mass society, and all the rest, it is plain what modernism was resolutely antimodern about. But does Kazin believe that Pound and Eliot in all their radical criticism failed to recognize their remarkable new techniques as not only thoroughly commensurate with but emergent from their particular times? What else did Pound mean by Make It New?

Certainly Pound, Yeats, and Eliot were dedicated to restoring some of the grandeur, vision, wisdom of the ancient Greeks, an antidote to the failures of the modern age. . . .[Pound] sees in Daniel and Cavalcanti "that precision which I miss in the Victorians. . . .Their testimony is of the eyewitness, their symptoms are first hand."

Yet Kazin tells us that "The 'quotidian' never got into the *Cantos*; perhaps there was no actual life around him for Pound to report." Is Kazin unaware of the many quotidian poems in *Personae*, the quotidian in *Mauberley*, and in many parts of the *Cantos*, particularly the *Pisan Cantos* and the last, poignant *Drafts & Fragments*? He must be objecting to Pound's successful metamorphosis of "actual life" into the stuff of poetry. As Pound said, "it is not until poetry lives 'close to the thing' that it will be a part of contemporary life." Aside from the frequent splendid picturings of immediate landscape in the *Cantos*, are there not all the portraits in action of friends and not-so-friends as well as of crucial, dramatic moments?

But "Pound's genius for the sound and arrangement of words that bring out the *inherency* of poetry did not extend to ideas." Pound's images, I would say, his metaphors, illustrations and their juxtaposition *were* his ideas. Here Kazin seems to be harking back to critics like Winters, Tate, and Blackmur. They also applauded Pound's music, at least some of it, but deplored his ideas or absence of them, failed the very great ideal he set himself as a poet: the making of a concrete world reflecting the oneness of perception and conception.

Understandably the terror of Pound for Kazin and the rest of us, if we are honest, is Pound's racism, the extremity to which the failure of all his immense efforts in his lifelong passion for improvement brought him, and the ideas that, alas, in his isolation at last prevailed over him. Kazin finds Pound's late renunciation of his racism insufficient, shallow. "Pound charmed his audience with the disclosure that his anti-Semitism was a 'suburban prejudice.' " Kazin rightly says Pound's anti-Semitism "cannot be shrugged away in judging his work." But I would also say that the whole work cannot be shrugged away by Kazin's judgment.

Seeing Pound much too one dimensionally, he is, I think, in danger of oversimplification and its rashness in the very way he accuses Pound. . . . It is one thing to call Pound a racist and even "a defender of racial persecution." It is quite another to declare him "indifferent to the obliteration of fellow artists." With Pound's hatred of war and what it does to mankind, including gifted young artists like Gaudier-Brezska, and especially with Pound's ardent solicitude for the welfare of such artists, Kazin's declaration misses him rather entirely. Who else gave of himself so unstintingly to his contemporaries?

And when one appreciates how crucial the health of art was to him for the health of society, one can well understand his passion. Richard Reid maintains in his recent brilliant dissertation, "It is essential to understand Pound's belief that the correct and accurate word is at the root of justice itself, its fundamental measure, and that the word contains value only because or only inasmuch as it implies the ideal of justice." The mot juste and justice do relate.

Kazin's chief charge is that Pound and modernism had "turned against the humane spirit of pre-1914 Europe in which modernism began." I am not sure what he means by "the humane spirit of pre-1914 Europe," but if I do understand it I would have thought that it was just the best parts of that spirit that Pound and other modernists were fighting for. . . . However much we concede that modernism is not our only tradition, we might wish that Kazin had mentioned other traditions with writers equal to Yeats, Pound, Eliot, and Joyce. But is it not somewhat light-handed, if not light-headed, to propose that

Eliot prescribed past literature's assimilation simply to satisfy the taste of the present?

Now it would appear that Pound and Eliot's interest in the past was, not sentimental nostalgia, but a cover-up of their real designs on us and our time (as well as the past). Surely it is more accurate to say that, like Eliot in "Tradition and the Individual Talent," Pound knew, if the past's accomplishments are profoundly valuable, yet always in danger of being lost, so also the great works of the present are valuable to that past, necessary for its renewal. (pp. 53-4)

For Kazin's fairly wholesale dismissal of Pound I urge that he look again. Whatever their inadequacies, the artists of modernism can, I believe, take their place beside the major poets and artists of other great periods. The work that Kazin questions is, I would insist, larger, richer, much more alive at its best than most of our day's art. We ignore this fact at our own very considerable cost. There are indeed things more important than all this fiddle, especially when the roof is burning. Nor do I believe that Pound's increasingly frantic fiddling could have put out the fire. But it was precisely his concern for these more important things that made him fiddle so frantically. Furthermore, without a fiddler where would Troy be or Odysseus and all the other characters? Artistic celebrations must be performed, essential stories relayed, that the wisdom and so the life of the race be continued. (p. 54)

Theodore Weiss, "An Exchange on Ezra Pound," in The New York Review of Books, Vol. XXXIII, No. 15, October 9, 1986, pp. 53-5.

ALFRED KAZIN

[*The piece excerpted below is Alfred Kazin's response to Theodore Weiss's letter excerpted above.*]

Most of Professor Weiss's lecture is familiar stuff, never more so than in the centenary celebrations. My essay was an attempt, amid the usual tributes to Pound's genius and influence (both acknowledged by me and documented), to show some of the origins of Pound's method and ideas in the history that brought about modernism. I wanted to show Pound as writer, critic, polemicist against the background of the age which he came to dominate in the minds of professors for whom "the modern" pretty much became the curriculum and the standard by which premoderns were accepted or dismissed. I noted the incessant Pound industry and especially, in the case of its "masterpiece," Hugh Kenner's *The Pound Era*, the astonishing defense of Pound's political cruelty.

The "museum of modern literature" exists in the minds of professors who decade after decade keep annotating every last particle in Pound because they are curators, not critics. I don't accuse them of "playing it safe." They just can't see beyond their noses. The *Cantos,* for all their occasional beauty, are in my opinion an essentially disordered work. The violent distortions of history, the scatalogical ugliness of Pound's epithets for English literary enemies, Jews, etc., the idolatry of the murderer Mussolini as a "twice-crucified" Redeemer eaten by "maggots" (the Italian people)—such violations of truth and art, of all that we have left of civilization in this century of totalitarian horror, mean nothing to curator types. And they have so little knowledge of history and of the actual texts Pound was ransacking that they are oblivious to the fact that in Cantos 62-71 Pound transcribes so mechanically John Adams's texts that he includes the misprints in the original edition. And completely omits "the point" when he describes "the Boss" "catching the point before the aesthetes had got there." And distorts actual history in Fascist Italy in the course of celebrating Mussolini's "draining of the muck by Vada."

One point I made about modernism was that while brilliantly "new" in technique, in the concentration of its technical resources, it was often quite archaic in inspiration and reactionary in its resentment of democracy, industrialism, the masses, etc. Professor Weiss reads this as an accusation that I consider poetry inconsequential and peripheral in modern industrial society. Professor Weiss accuses me of not noting "Pound's profound hatred of war, his powerful attacks on it in *Mauberley,* the *Cantos* and elsewhere." Here is a perfect example of the way curators ignore the actual historic circumstances surrounding their sacred object. Pound's horror of the *first* World War in Mauberley and elsewhere did not extend to the Second, in which he was a propagandist for what Churchill called "the worst crime in human history."

Pound's "zeal for violent types from Malatesta to Mussolini" (as I called it) seems to Professor Weiss rather respect for "vigorous actors who used cultivation of the intellect and the arts and for the erection of great monuments." About Malatesta the Poundians know only what Pound tells them. But what "great monuments" did Mussolini erect? Italian Fascists used to celebrate Mussolini exactly the way Pound did in the *Cantos.* Is Professor Weiss now echoing *them?*

Yes, I do believe that with Pound "sound overwhelmed sense"; I offered examples of this in my essay and can offer Professor Weiss many more. Yes, I did "notice Pound's making as much as anyone the vast enterprise of poetry possible today." But I think that Pound's catch-as-catch-can method has been calamitous for people who have nothing to say in "the vast enterprise of poetry possible today." *Enterprise* is just what a lot of it is. And finally, I am amused but not enlightened when Professor Weiss thinks he is refuting me by offering me still more bibliography. I am struck, however, by his failure to say anything about Professor Hugh Kenner's rationalization of Pound's Jew-hatred. And of what followed. (p. 55)

Alfred Kazin, "An Exchange on Ezra Pound," in The New York Review of Books, Vol. XXXIII, No. 15, October 9, 1986, p. 55.

Frederic Prokosch

1908-

American novelist, poet, and translator.

A highly regarded novelist and poet who came into prominence during the 1930s, Prokosch commonly infuses his work with lush vocabulary, evocative imagery, extensive symbolism, and detailed descriptions of exotic landscapes. He has described his style as "a kind of dream-picaresque form" that embodies "certain basic themes of perpetual search, perpetual flight, multiple identities, ambiguities of destiny, and geographical symbolisms." Characterized by its cosmopolitan scope and romantic sensibility, Prokosch's writing features elements of the heroic adventure and spiritual quest while exhibiting, particularly in his early works, a vision of cultural decay that has been described as vivid and authentic. Praised by many respected literary figures, including André Gide, Thomas Mann, Edwin Muir, and William Butler Yeats, Prokosch has received several awards and honors for his work.

Born in Madison, Wisconsin, Prokosch was educated in various schools in the United States, Germany, and England and devoted many years to travel throughout Europe, Asia, and Africa. He began his literary career in 1927 with the publication of his poetry in the *Virginia Quarterly Review*. In his first collection of verse, *The Assassins* (1936), Prokosch draws extensively on his experiences and his reading of travel literature to create poems rich in geographical imagery, symbolism, and allusion. These pieces were compared to the works of such writers as St.-Jean Perse, William Butler Yeats, W. H. Auden, and Friedrich Hölderlin. Imbued with a tense, melancholy mood that has been interpreted as Prokosch's vision of humanity's spiritual state in the years before World War II, *The Assassins* was also likened to Oswald Spengler's writings on the decline of Western culture. Several critics, however, maintained that Prokosch's view in *The Assassins* is ultimately optimistic. John Peale Bishop asserted: "[*The Assassins*] as a whole is filled not merely with dread and longing that, as so many revolutionaries suggest, a particular phase of contemporary civilization may be passing, never to return; there is also the knowledge that over vast tracts and long stretches of time all specifically human endeavor may cease, while men themselves, in countless hordes, survive."

Many of the poems in Prokosch's second volume, *The Carnival* (1938), exhibit a foreboding tone similar to that of *The Assassins*. Highlighted by Prokosch's "Ode," a long piece that weaves the vicissitudes of history and of the author's own life into the events of a single day, *The Carnival* was well received by most reviewers. *Death at Sea* (1940), although often considered less successful than his earlier collections, contains several of his most admired and frequently anthologized poems, including "The Sand" and "The Sunburned Ulysses." Despite high recognition and praise for much of his verse, *Death at Sea* marked the end of Prokosch's career as a poet. Although he continued to issue privately printed chapbooks and published a volume of his selected verse, *Chosen Poems* (1944), Prokosch devoted his subsequent literary efforts to fiction.

Prokosch's first novel, *The Asiatics* (1935), is the story of a young American whose wanderings throughout Asia lead to

brief but intense relationships with several individuals. Employing the picaresque form and lyrical language, Prokosch creates an allegorical story of self-exploration in which the novel's themes and adventures are counterbalanced, according to Richard C. Carpenter, by "a kind of somnambulism that infuses even the most dangerous happening with the atmosphere of dream." André Gide called *The Asiatics* "[an] astonishing feat of the imagination. Poetic in its sensuality, witty in its melodrama, urban in its misanthropy, incandescent in its imagery: it is unique among novels and an authentic masterpiece." In his next novel, *The Seven Who Fled* (1937), Prokosch retains the dreamlike mood of his first book while detailing the adventures of seven Europeans who escape the political chaos of Kashgar, in Chinese Turkestan, and travel to Shanghai. As in his previous writings, Prokosch uses travel and geography as allegorical representations of spiritual quest and psychological landscapes.

Although his work since the 1930s has not received the lofty praise accorded his early writings, Prokosch has continued to write and publish prolifically. *Night of the Poor* (1939), an episodic story rich in popular culture and geographic description, details the nomadic adventures of a young protagonist and his various companions as they traverse the midwestern and southern regions of the United States. *The Skies of Europe*

(1941), in which Prokosch documents international social disorders during the three years preceding the outbreak of World War II, was lauded by Radcliffe Squires as "a vivid, valid portrait of Europe seen as a sleepwalker approaching an abyss." Prokosch's next three novels, *The Conspirators* (1943), *Age of Thunder* (1945), and *The Idols of the Cave* (1946), are his only works to deal specifically with World War II. In *Storm and Echo* (1948), another story concerning transient existence, Prokosch contrasts the exotic setting of Africa with Western civilization. Like *The Asiatics* and the later *Nine Days to Mukalla* (1953), *Storm and Echo* employs the journey experience to symbolize humanity's quest for spiritual enlightenment. *A Tale for Midnight* (1955) concerns events surrounding the death of sixteenth-century Roman nobleman Francesco Cenci, whose alleged brutality and incestuous intentions caused his daughter, Beatrice, to plan and enact his murder. *A Ballad of Love* (1960) explores Prokosch's concerns with the fate of the failed artist. *The Seven Sisters* (1962), which is considered by some critics one of Prokosch's finest achievements, contemplates "what happens to love in a world flattened by socialism and technology," according to Radcliffe Squires. In *The Dark Dancer* (1964), Prokosch explores humanity's paradoxical pursuit of power and its longing for spiritual truth through the symbolic complexities and contradictions of seventeenth-century India. *The Wreck of the Cassandra* (1966) examines the experiences of passengers aboard a shipwrecked ocean liner. *The Missolonghi Manuscript* (1968) is a study of Byron in the form of a journal. *America, My Wilderness* (1971) relates the story of a young man's journey across the United States near the beginning of the twentieth century.

In addition to his collections of verse and his many novels, Prokosch has also translated the poetry of Friedrich Hölderlin and Louise Labé. *Voices: A Memoir* (1983) features Prokosch's recollections and impressions of many of the twentieth century's most celebrated literary figures.

(See also *CLC*, Vol. 4; *Contemporary Authors*, Vols. 73-76; and *Dictionary of Literary Biography*, Vol. 48.)

JOSEPH WOOD KRUTCH

This unusual novel [*The Asiatics*]—if novel it is—begins and ends without explanation. At the top of page 1 the narrator is walking down the streets of Beirut inviting his soul; on page 423 he takes abrupt leave, "feeling very happy" somewhere in China. In between he has scraped an acquaintance with various persons, mostly sinister; he has been a prisoner in Turkey, has smuggled dope, visited a maharaja, been captured by bandits, and has made love to various girls whom he gets rid of with an ease which, life being what it is, seems rather more remarkable than the ease with which the inevitable sweet surrender is made to eventuate. Also—and this is more important than any of the other things—he has smelled Asia at a number of its most odoriferous points.

As is not unusual in tall tales, our hero exhibits a readiness to get into trouble which would verge on the moronic if it affected anyone except the central personage in an adventure story. As a matter of course he throws in his lot with any chance acquaintance who gives obvious signs of being untrustworthy, and he no sooner sees a desire for murder beginning to gleam in a companion's eye than he accepts an invitation to journey into some nice inaccessible spot. He is, according to accompanying publicity, an American youth in his middle twenties and doubtless he will mature—if he lives long enough.

The most remarkable things about the book are, however, that it is vastly entertaining and that, despite all the extraordinary happenings, the tone is lyric rather than dramatic. The author recounts his adventures in a simple, matter-of-fact way as though wandering about Persia with a dubious passport and no money were a usual procedure. What he is really interested in is a poetic abstraction called Asia. What he is out to do is to sense as deeply and as luxuriantly as he can the meaning of a very old, very weary, very corrupt, and very ill-smelling civilization—of a way of life which is ostensibly based upon a determination to be free of desire and of the flesh but which may, perhaps, have only arrived at a state where desire has been reduced to appallingly unadorned manifestations, and where the neglect-born disease makes the would-be ascetic rather more aware of his flesh than the Western sensualist usually is. In the temples they describe the road to Nirvana but around the urinals the despairing perverts gather in miserable company. . . .

Obviously Mr. Prokosch can write. He has an accent of his own. His manner is simple, almost colloquial, and this easy offhand air does much to conceal the essential romanticism of the entire work. The only real question is the question how deeply the thing is really felt, how much of what he has to say springs from anything deeper than a sort of luxurious green sickness. Out of the atmosphere of our times the young author has drawn a Spenglerian despair for the human race. He hints that the deliquescence of the Asiatic is the penultimate phase of all human souls. "The trouble," says one of the characters, "isn't with the West. It isn't with the East. . . . It's with man. He's had his day." But it is difficult not to feel in the almost loving description of human depravity as well as in the easy acceptance of the blackest pessimism a youthful bravado, a more or less individual manifestation of that adolescent melancholy which shocks every thoughtful youth into a pleasurable sense of his own fortitude.

It would be interesting to know how much of the author's wild journey is fact and how much is fiction. From internal evidence it is difficult to say, for the simple reason that the observations and the reflections, boiled down to their solid residue, are really little more than the current commonplaces about Darkest Asia. Possibly Mr. Prokosch did and saw and thought all that his hero does and sees and thinks. But given an ardent imagination, he would not really have needed to do so, and it is a safe guess that before he started he already knew, in a general way at least, what it was that he was going to do and see and think. All of which, however, is no reason against repeating that *The Asiatics* is a very entertaining book written by a man who already knows very well how to write.

> *Joseph Wood Krutch, "'In Darkest Asia'," in* The Nation, *New York, Vol. CXXXXI, No. 367, November 13, 1935, p. 572.*

EDWIN MUIR

The world reflected in [*The Assassins*] . . . is a world falling to pieces beyond repair, the better part of it dead but the worse still surviving. This is the present-day world as Mr. Prokosch sees it; and he sees it without either the instinctive hope of the ordinary man or the willed hope of the reformer. The impression this world produces is of a paralysis or suspension of being, and Mr. Prokosch evokes it by a series of vivid motionless images. As in his novel *The Asiatics,* he brings a great number of scenes before us, but though he moves so freely through space he finds the same time, the same age, wherever he goes. We feel that space is still open to us, but that time is ended, for no matter how far we go we shall always find it fixed at the same point, like a clock which has stopped.

Whether this is a true picture of the world, or of the world of to-day, cannot be examined in a short review. . . . All that we have to consider, therefore, is the power and impressiveness of his picture of it; and here he seems to me to be a very remarkable poet. He has, first of all, that command of sensuous imagery which is necessary to give any picture of life at all, and he has also the organizing power of poetry, the gift of form. His form, indeed, is better than his imagery, which is generally vivid and new, but sometimes relapses into conventionality. His form is seen at its best in the first poem in the book, a poem in short rhymed lines with a rapid impetuous movement which remains throughout perfectly subservient to the theme. Mr. Prokosch seems to have digested modern poetry, but there is no sign that he has been influenced by any particular modern poet, except Mr. Pound in one or two poems; he reproduces none of the clichés which have become current in the last few years; and the creaking sound of the brake, to which one has grown so accustomed, does not sound in his verse at all. His poems have great formal beauty, and they embody a vision of life which is consistent and moving. This vision gives us throughout the impression of being at first-hand and the creation of an original mind; but its effect, like the effect of the verse itself, is eminently natural without being trite, and there is no striving after obvious originality. Mr. Prokosch's greatest fault is facility, but it is not so much a positive fault as a defect of his qualities, and particularly of his unusual gift for sensuous imagery. This is a very remarkable first volume of poetry, and one hopes it will bring Mr. Prokosch the recognition which his gifts deserve.

> *Edwin Muir, "The First Poems of Mr. Prokosch,"*
> in The London Mercury, *Vol. XXXIV, No. 202, August, 1936, p. 365.*

PHILIP BLAIR RICE

[To read *The Assassins*] is to encounter a new creative energy of a high order, expressing itself with a sure dominance of its medium. From his recently published first novel, *The Asiatics,* it was evident that Frederic Prokosch had the sensitiveness to word and image which constitutes poetic receptivity; this volume shows that he can bring to the materials of poetry the formal discipline needed to make a complete poem. The images are brilliantly, even bizarrely colored, and at times unexpected to the point of violence. A less skilful and less serious poet would use them merely to disturb. Here, however, through their power of evocation, their canalization into stately music, and their organization into a unified mood, they not only excite but exalt.

The mood which recurs throughout the book is a reptilian watchfulness and tension, the hushed breathing of a world between two wars. It is conveyed by images of cutting, of fever, of nocturnal fears and sudden whirring wings. The poet's theme is the search, over the exotic places of the earth, for "the concerted will and the quiet heart, and the sure and sharpened spirit." The assassins are "the dead, and the dead of

spirit"; they are preparing to strike, and they elicit visions of falling cities:

> This is the final dreading
> Of history ending, an end to living and terror spreading,
> The dead destroying, the living dying, the dream
>   fulfilling,
> The long night falling and knowledge failing and
>   memory fading.

These lines have analogies with the poetry of T. S. Eliot, yet Prokosch's world, one feels, has recuperative powers that are not present in Eliot's except by hocus-pocus: it is alive with a vital force that is damned, warped, tortured, but full of subtle potencies still. The realm of nature has, for transient moments, generated the realm of grace, and may do so again, after the destruction. Such is, perhaps, the framework of doctrine behind the poems; yet it is not allowed to obtrude. The realization is so consistently in sensuous terms that one must read it several times before perceiving that this is not sheer poetry of feeling.

Frederic Prokosch is an American cosmopolite not yet thirty. If there is immaturity in these poems, it is not to be found in a mechanical echoing of his masters. He appears to have learned from Valéry, Auden, and above all St.-Jean Perse, as well as from Eliot. But he has put what he has learned to his own uses, and his adaptations of Greek metrical and stanzaic patterns have a rigor of form latterly desired but not achieved by many other poets. His shortcomings, such as they are, consist in a tendency to lushness, a reliance upon exotic imagery in some places where quotidian would be more effective, and a substitution of décor for drama. (pp. 398-99)

> *Philip Blair Rice, "A World between Two Wars,"*
> in The Nation, New York, *Vol. 143, No. 14, October 3, 1936, pp. 398-99.*

R. P. BLACKMUR

Mr. Frederic Prokosch puts no [limitations] . . . upon his first volume of verse, called *The Assassins.* . . . He is Faust-like and geographical. The emotions of his poems are universal, dragnets for all experience, and their sites are widely distributed, mostly along the coasts of European seas. His work is, therefore, largely promise and very little performance beyond the measure necessary to establish the promise; but the promise is full, and is his own, with little obvious derivation. It is both welcome and suspicious to find a young poet whose best work is not immediately derivative; welcome for relief and surprise; suspicious because it suggests that he was unaware of his immediate ancestry in living poetry only because he was immersed in the stock ancestry of dead poetry both immediate and remote. With Mr. Prokosch the suspicion is partly gratified: his affective vocabulary is full of snakes and animals and distant places and enormous shores: full, that is, of stock expansive terms which must, without specification, be mostly dead. But the gratification is only partial and the welcome remains: he manages to produce out of each poem an emotional mood only tinted and not controlled by his stock vocabulary; and perhaps indeed his readers could not understand him—nor he understand himself—without the indicative, attention-calling tint. His great virtues are genuine depth and scope of feeling, a sense of the ominous and precarious and infinite, and a talent for phrasing; his defects are looseness of line and a general tendency to allow the number and variety of implications in his words to get beyond the control of his theme. There is an associated quality, sometimes a virtue and sometimes a defect, which rises from the use of a great number of conceptual words and names. He neither specifies his allusions nor certifies his concepts by representation in the actual instance; he rather invokes them. Meanwhile he is readable in the fragmentary scene, for the fragments which are lines and images and for the fragments which are his whole poems. He has more feeling for and has used more of the resources of poetic language—his words show more of the stress and forward rush for meaning and actually come nearer to making idiom—than [many poets]. . . . Being content with the establishment of moods which, isolated, compose themselves if they are composed at all, he has no need for a compositional principle and has made no attempt at a major subject. The title poem ["**The Assassins**"] is the best and presents a dominant mood of our time, rather like the mood of Yeats' "The Second Coming" but without its resource either in language or prophecy; the mood wherein we feel the imminence of chaos and the terrible precariousness with which every value is maintained. (pp. 567-68)

R. P. Blackmur, "The Composition in Nine Poets,"
in The Southern Review, Louisiana State University,
Vol. II, No. 3, Winter, 1937, pp. 558-76.

JOHN PEALE BISHOP

The Assassins is an impressive first book of poems; not all of them are obviously political; in fact, very few of them are. And yet, the volume as a whole is filled not merely with dread and longing that, as so many revolutionaries suggest, a particular phase of contemporary civilization may be passing, never to return; there is also the knowledge that over vast tracts and long stretches of time all specifically human endeavor may cease, while men themselves, in countless hordes, survive. Whether this country is young enough, remote enough, to escape contagion from "these enormous European fevers" is not certain (p. 337)

Mr. Prokosch has traveled widely. Africa is the beginning of his vision and the end Asia. For he has gone beyond the falling cities of the West to "the white death of stagnant centuries." (In these poems, as in Melville, white is the color of dread, ...estruction, of death.) In his voyages he has seen those ...les who have outlived their time of foreboding only to come to a timeless doom. It is this contact, an experience as imaginative as it is actual, which gives to these poems their immediacy.

In more than one poem, but particularly in **"Going South-ward"**, he has set down in a flowing verse, slow but secretly impetuous, steadily mounting, like a torrential stream temporarily halted by a green region of heavy vegetation, the vast supineness of the Asiatics in Siberia, in China, and more especially in India, country of dead cities: the awful surrender of people who, in more than the Spenglerian sense, have passed out of history. . . . For this is the secret of the spirituality of Asia: complete surrender; a meaningless submission to a bleak and crowded impermanence; an endless change, but no significant change; an absence of thought and memory. This is the end, it may be, which is to be reached "by the northern road of doing." It is not thus that the Asiatics have come there, but by suffering and exhaustion; yet there is no doubt that this is the promised end.

The poems of *The Assassins* are not all a sensuous record of thoughts on the present state of the world. This is the trouble of a young man and a poetry of desire. In a sick world, love sickens and acquires the sterile qualities of hate; it becomes

hostile and escapes into solitary or shared perversions. In the old days, through its power, men felt "their thighs cooled in the old tribal water." They were absorbed into the race, to become one with its past and future. It is here that Mr. Prokosch's poetry is least clear; phrases are employed whose implications are too private to be understood. It is only when the particular case dissolves into the common that clarity is completely regained. Through love, the poet is aware of humanity, and with that awareness again comes fear, the prescience of a common doom. The absorption into the race is contemporary, that is to say, it is spatial and not immortal.

All this is traced with considerable power. The verse of *The Assassins* is adroit, fluent and remarkably sustained; it is supported by no small sensuous abundance. The images have that timeless quality which Perse achieved in his *Anabase,* which is also a poem of Asia. Mr. Prokosch has, I think, learned much from Perse, but whether directly, or through Archibald MacLeish, I cannot say. It is unimportant; for though it is clear that Mr. Prokosch has been to school to several contemporary poets, he has learned his lessons. There may be lines that are slightly reminiscent; there is no poem that is not his own. He is a poet to be watched; he is, even now, a poet to be read. (pp. 337-39)

John Peale Bishop, "Final Dreading," in Poetry,
Vol. XLIX, No. 6, March, 1937, pp. 337-39.

MARY McCARTHY

In *The Seven Who Fled,* Frederic Prokosch's Harper prize novel, we find *The Asiatics* elaborated into frozen symmetry. The subject matter, though more rationalized in the second novel, is essentially the same. Asia is Mr. Prokosch's Magic Mountain. To Asia Mr. Prokosch's contemporary Europeans come, not, as one might think, to escape from reality but, as he thinks, to live cheek by jowl with it. On the hot, barren plains and the terrible mountains of Asia life achieves a super-real incandescence; burning as in a tubercular fever it transforms itself more rapidly than in Europe to its ultimate ashes. Decomposition of the flesh and degeneration of the character are in Asia accelerated; yet flesh and character, in their brief lifetime, are more intensely, extremely themselves than in the padded world of the West. For Mr. Prokosch's characters a trip through the interior of Asia automatically becomes a voyage of self-exploration, an excursion into self-consciousness. In *The Asiatics* one introspective globe-trotter, a young American, shoulders the burden of discovery and definition; in *The Seven Who Fled* the weight is distributed among seven Europeans—an Englishman, a Belgian, a Russian, a German, an Austrian, a Spanish lady, and a Frenchman.

To warrant this division of responsibility one would expect a rather sharp and meaningful differentiation of experience. Yet one finds the reverse. The outlines of personality, feeling, and behavior are blurred until the characters seem to dissolve into one another. Even the physical adventures do not differ notably from one character to the next—cold, privation, disease, and compulsive sexual erraticism are the common lot; while on the spiritual plane each person finds in Asia but one thing—heightened sensibility, which is reached via physical hardship, death or its contemplation, and memory. Searching out the meaning of life Mr. Prokosch's people come upon it in the very molecules of existence, in the assaults of natural objects and forces upon the nervous system, or, at second-hand, in the memory of former assaults made in childhood and adolescence, when the receiving apparatus was most highly tuned. Since Mr. Prokosch's characters are mere borderline cases, minor decorative personalities from the fringes of Western society, not actors but sufferers on the Western stage, they have no validity as symbols of either Europe or its respective states; and the novel breaks down into a simple catalogue of sensations, a confession of the meaninglessness of meaning. The characters, indeed, have so little personal identity, so little individual clearness of tone, that the novel in the end reduces itself to a catalogue of the author's sensations, the author's private confession.

The range of the author's sensations is narrow, and for all his admiration of intensity the sensations themselves are not very vigorous. His book is full of "little spasms," "little plans," "little gardens," "little moments." He is a connoisseur of the gentle, the tender, the delicate, the pure, the simple, the sweet, the hesitant; and an academician of the tremor. "Touching" is his favorite designation for the people he likes and the situations he relishes; and the "viciousness" and "corruption" which so much enchant him must always coexist with the gentler qualities. Thus in Mr. Prokosch's novel, for all its cosmic aspirations, its League of Nations personnel, its dedication to violence and the doctrine of extremes, the Magic Mountain becomes a dwarf flower garden, and the terror of the super-real expresses itself in an elegant *frisson*.

> Mary McCarthy, *"The Latest Shudder," in* The Nation, *New York, Vol. 145, No. 12, September 18, 1937, p. 296.*

MARIE SCOTT-JAMES

[With *The Seven Who Fled*] Mr. Prokosch has made another imaginative excursion into the continent of Asia. His seven travellers—an Englishman, a Russian, a Belgian, a Frenchman, a German, an Austrian, and a Spanish woman—are forced by a political crisis in Chinese Turkestan to flee from the town of Kashgar. By describing the experiences of each of them on their devious routes to Shanghai, he has sought to reveal the Asiatic spirit through its impact on the consciousness of widely differing types. His theme is the cohabitation of beauty and corruption—an alliance exhibited in its most startling form in a land where grandeur of landscape throws into startling relief the varied depravities of man.

In all the travellers' reactions, there is a common element—complete abandonment to the fatalism of the Asiatic mind. The self-contained English explorer submits to his impulse to follow the Tibetan road though he knows that it will be his last journey. The simple, giant-like Russian, in his miserable inn at Aqsu, contemplates all winter the murder that he knows he will commit. The sinister Belgian, the narcissist, stands waiting almost joyfully to be killed by his enemy. The bored, weary Frenchman seems detained by some extraordinary magnetism in a cholera-stricken town. The charming Austrian relinquishes himself mindlessly to the experiences of every passing day. The voluptuous, impersonal Spaniard drifts inevitably into the brothels of Shanghai. Even the German disciplinarian, the Nietzschean visionary, is fascinated, in the midst of his fanatical plans for self-perfection, by his awareness of the imminence of death. All of the seven, it is suggested, shedding the rationalism of Europe, discover their essential selves.

Through their reflections and their perilous adventures, Mr. Prokosch exhibits the Asiatic scene—the great snow mountains of Tibet, the parched deserts of Sinkiang, the vicious and dis-ease-infected town of Aqsu, the red-foaming waters of the Yang-tze. Certain scenes are unforgettable.

Mr. Prokosch is a poet and he has attempted to maintain the lyric note throughout—an impossible task. His novel suffers from over-writing, from his refusal to make salutary descents into the valley of plain, straightforward prose. However, at his best, he is an extremely fine descriptive writer. As a student of human nature, he is much more vulnerable. It is not merely that his people are types, each exaggerating the characteristics of a nation. That is permissible in the context. But they are scarcely more than painted figures, distorted into curious shapes; creatures fantastically unresponsive to *human* as opposed to *atmospheric* influences. Clever, imaginative, poetic as this strange novel is, it has a curious air of falseness. Perhaps it is because an epic work demands of the writer a coherent and considered view of the universe—something more than the perception of the canker in the rose which is all that Mr. Prokosch has to offer.

> Marie Scott-James, *"A Poet's Asia," in* The London Mercury, *Vol. XXXVI, No. 216, October, 1937, p. 590.*

DESMOND HAWKINS

[*The Seven Who Fled* traces] the fortunes of a cosmopolitan group of white people in Asia. In its monotonously recurring patter and its lavish embroidery it recalls, as Sinclair Lewis has noted, a tapestry. Personally I don't share the whoopsy enthusiasm which has temporarily united such diverse authorities as Hugh Walpole, Edwin Muir and Hugh Gordon Porteus, though there need be no quibble about Mr. Prokosch's class. As a piece of sheer virtuosity this is a remarkable book; Mr. Prokosch just pulls out all the stops and pedals for hell's delight. It is, in fact, the most luscious piece of literary candy since Sacheverell Sitwell began to cloy. But there is a limit to one's taste for it, and when I had finished the book I was quite certain I should never open it again.

Mr. Prokosch's lust for Drammer is transpontine in its thoroughness. Every character moves in a whirl of baroque frenzy, freely splashed with high colours. The prevailing mood is trance-like, the characters seem to be heavily drugged and gravitate towards their 'fate' with the sightless indifference of somnambulists. The pattern recurs, the flash-back to the days of youth, the sexual initiation, the agonized posture; and eventually it becomes monotonous and suffocating, dulling the mind as the stupendous is heaped on the colossal. The worst of an emotional field-day is that it exhausts the capacity for response. Mr. Prokosch is so ardent in presenting the whole gamut of frenetic attitude that it loses its sting. When the turn of the last character comes, one doesn't care if he is crucified, flogged, disembowelled, cuckolded, swindled, murdered, starved or what-next. And he doesn't care either. The great thing is *sensation;* or as Mr. Prokosch himself puts it, in his hot, rampaging way,

> Danger, danger: the thought of it was tremendously warming. Something deep inside him longed for it; for pain, for torture, for extremity. Captured at last by reality! Ensnared by the will of these hordes, these unpredictable Asiatic hordes, with their beautiful, shining limbs and their eyes flashing with obscene cruelties, all slowly approaching, about to take him to themselves, their ancient and consuming selves.

Isn't that an extraordinarily *feminine* prose? Doesn't it suggest a rabbit's-eye view of a weasel? And isn't the hidden subject of it some form of the way of a man with a maid? Or, since we are dealing with Asiatics and quintessential cruelties, shall we instead say *The Way of an Eagle with a Lady Novelist*? To put it more plainly—if we allow for Mr. Prokosch's greater sophistication and more distinguished style, doesn't he share with Miss Ethel M. Dell the art of objectifying and *disguising* (thinly but sufficiently) a popular social neurosis?

It is in this way, as a symptom, that Mr. Prokosch is most interesting and most valuable. He has produced a phantasmagoria of the feminine psyche swooning and yielding on an absolute battlefield of violence, lust and cruelty. The mood of the white people is one of fatalistic surrender to sensation. Their portrayal is executed largely in the idiom which Auden has skilfully improvised from the clinical psychoanalysis of Freud, Groddek and Homer Lane. The stuff of the book is that segment of life which nineteenth-century liberalism excluded and which now exercises a secret compulsion on our minds. Mr. Prokosch has formulated the new white dream of passion and violence, on a grand scale and in an up-to-the-minute terminology. . . . (pp. 508-10)

I have criticized **The Seven Who Fled** because Mr. Prokosch is sufficiently important to demand an exacting scrutiny. Moreover, his virtues have already had the fullest notice, while his limitations have not attracted much attention. **The Seven Who Fled** is copious entertainment and significant as a furtive dream of our civilization, the dream of possible delights in the act of surrender. As a novel, in spite of Mr. Prokosch's handsome style, I don't think it is much more than a cup of cold Flecker sweetened with the latest Audenisms. I commend it to the author of *Paleface* and shall still prefer Mr. Prokosch's verse, where the invertebracy is less apparent. (pp. 510-11)

> *Desmond Hawkins, "Fiction Chronicle," in* The Criterion, *Vol. XVII, No. LXVIII, April, 1938, pp. 500-13.*

A. C. BOYD

Mr. Prokosch's two novels have won him a reputation on both sides of the Atlantic as an imaginative writer, and when **The Assassins** appeared, he was hailed, and rightly, as a very considerable poet. Here was a new voice of unusual sensibility, sensuous, "romantic" if you will, yet completely contemporary; a poet using more or less formal patterns with sensitiveness and skill, and never becoming boringly conventional. Readers of that first book will remember the poet's eye sweeping from continent to continent and recording a civilization decaying beyond repair, the cities falling—in perhaps too picturesque ruins. The new poems [in **The Carnival**] are just as accomplished as before, though the glowing East has been abandoned, and the glamour of history attracts the poet less.

Of all the younger writers none has a greater command of the sheerly magical phrase, but now the draught of nectar is found to have a slightly bitter aftertaste. Every poem Mr. Prokosch writes is complete, and, although he seldom varies his tone, each has a strange beauty; yet, while one can affirm the poet's immense, if somewhat diffused, grieving over the state of Europe, his need for love, his aching tenderness towards humanity, his nostalgia on observing "the stupid, radiant, lovable Faces of the harmonious," the total result leaves one with a feeling of uneasiness: an exquisite sensibility seems dissolving into patterns of rhetoric rather than passion. Mr. Prokosch is

conscious of his limitations, it appears; in the poet's vision "All men are fragments of a broken dream," and later in this poem he himself dreams of moving towards "some vast belief"; and, indeed, it would be unfair not to record that in the long final poem, **"Ode"**, he is groping towards some integration of his feelings. Yet, for the most part, it is the dream element which prevails, and we move in a highly coloured, exotically beautiful and hypnotic nightmare, in which nothing can be seized, not even the horror of the plight of humanity—which can hardly be what the poet intended. (pp. 279-80)

> *A. C. Boyd, "Mournful Numbers," in* The London Mercury, *Vol. XXXVIII, No. 225, July, 1938, pp. 279-89.*

SAMUEL FRENCH MORSE

In the ordinary, limited sense of the word, Frederic Prokosch cannot be called a prophetic poet, yet the constantly recurring theme of imminent disaster, of darkness, of the disintegration of society, which leads, in the end, to chaos, give his poetry the dominant tone of something very much like prophecy. Again and again, underneath the flowing music of individual poems, one encounters the horror of aimless destruction, the final flooding-over of decay; but this horror, made clear in **The Assassins,** seems to have forced the poet to give way to an "immense despair." In other words, the ruined castle, the broken column, the "Mantuan farm" have assumed a disproportionate importance.

And the dilemma is not to be hastily brushed aside. If one insists that Prokosch is trying to escape the difficulties of affirmation, then one needs a definition of "escape" that will include Henry James, Hawthorne, Eliot, and Conrad Aiken, as well as the more obvious victims of this carelessly handled word. For, one might say, Prokosch has discovered the ruins of Angkor Thom, and like many others, he is bewitched; decay can fascinate as well as repel. Like James, Prokosch acknowledges the artistry and the flaw of the golden bowl; unlike James, he will not have it broken. Neither does Prokosch seem to have any Maggie Verver to resist and foil the rottenness; or at least his resistance has not as yet been called into vigorous play. Love, as a combative force, fails because (as John Peale Bishop wrote reviewing the earlier book of poems) [see excerpt above] it only sharpens the poet's awareness of the general doom. The only other indications of a possible solution lie either in the acceptance of night, or in the scattered statements which appear in **"Ode,"** a kind of spiritual autobiography. . . . (pp. 89-90)

"New Year's Eve" and **"Journeys"** are two poems which suggest, almost exclusively by implication, another solution. But one cannot help speculating a little whether this way out can be found by holding so tenaciously to this single thread, even though the thread gives Prokosch tremendous consistency. For in spite of the insistence that it is better to "be blindly in love Than gloat on the lyric *was* or the lustrous *will be*," the actual images and examples of splendor follow a course that leads back into the past, a one-way street that has all the appearances of eventually revealing itself as a blind-alley. Yet, there is some proof that Prokosch can find affirmation in the present, and that he can see the details of experience very clearly. Now and again, however, one has the curious feeling that something has been left out, not by accident, but deliberately, as if Prokosch were unwilling to risk a temporary misunderstanding for the sake of an immediate response.

When he is writing at his best, these difficulties dwindle into insignificance. The best poems in *The Assassins* are equally as fine as the best of *The Carnival*. Yet there is a great variety within the sphere of reference which Prokosch has drawn for himself, and he manages to use a number of images and symbols over and over with a surprising freshness. Snow, flame, golden fruit, the stars, dark forests, names of places, are all woven into the texture of the writing with great skill. The sense of time is acute. The craftsmanship is obviously the result of more than a little discipline, in spite of some loose joints. . . . It is romantic poetry; the Americas envisioned by Prokosch are distant from the Americas of the other poets of his generation; distant, too, from the ordinary romantic vision. At the same time, it contains a warning not unlike the warning in the work of other younger poets, the threat of a second Middle Ages.

But the calm assurance with which the horror is expected, taken for granted, almost, may well be responsible, in part, for not only the virtues but the vices of this poetry. It may account for the lapse which produces a figure like "our little violins Again will touch our loneliness," for seas which "Enormously dispel Each hour." Inversely, it may be responsible for the haunting **"Hesperides,"** **"New Year's Eve,"** and **"The Castle."** (pp. 90-2)

> Samuel French Morse, "Spectre over Europe," in Poetry, *Vol. LIII, No. 11, November, 1938, pp. 89-92.*

THE TIMES LITERARY SUPPLEMENT

Mr. Prokosch's talent has not gained in translation from Asia to the American Middle West and South, which provide the scene and almost the subject of [*Night of the Poor*]. It is constructed in episodic fashion. Tommy, aged seventeen, leaves the Wisconsin farm where his uncle has died in order to return to his home in San Felipe, Texas. By chance or mischance he does not travel by rail but hitch-hikes in a leisurely way through Illinois, Indiana, Kentucky and Louisiana. Odd encounters and adventures befall him. He starts off in the company of Pete, who is simple in mind and heart, who has a way with women and who involuntarily kills a man in a fight. He continues for a time with Lucy, who is precocious and innocent. After she has abandoned him he comes across Uncle Waldo and the consumptive boy Sandy, in whose company he witnesses a hideously savage lynching. Eventually, when he is a few miles from home, he once more meets Lucy, who by this time is a little depraved, and satisfies the physical hunger that has been troubling him before reaching home.

Mr. Prokosch has an eye for landscape and a sharply individual feeling for words. The principal motive of the story evidently springs from a sense of wonder at the variety of the American scene and the still formative destiny of the American people. Intuitively he pictures the mingling of ancestries and racial memories, from which something new is moulded. . . . This wonder further finds expression in Whitmanesque catalogues of geographical and geological features, in thumbnail sketches of grotesque types, in a variety of moral contrasts. Mr. Prokosch's sympathies are with the dispossessed and the insecure, though he also seems to find room for a philosophy of intellectual detachment. A subsidiary motive of the story is the unfolding of sex in the adolescent mind. Together with sensitive observation, however, there is a degree of brutality or hard-boiled matter-of-factness in several incidents that may be the reverse side of an over-romantic sensibility.

The novel has individuality of style and moments of swift illumination. But it is not very satisfying as an imaginative whole. Besides the lack of organic unity, the human and emotional content is thin. Tommy is a rather colourless figure and the others are even more generalized studies. As for the passages of satire, such as the prolonged dig at the old gentleman with a nose for immorality who had written a work in twenty volumes entitled "God," these are surely more suitable for an undergraduate journal. Mr. Prokosch is not at his commanding best in fiction of this variety.

> A review of "Night of the Poor," in The Times Literary Supplement, *No. 1966, October 7, 1939, p. 578.*

GRAHAM GREENE

The author of *The Asiatics* carries his own Asia with him, and his publishers do wrong to suggest that in [*Night of the Poor*] "he has forsaken Asia for America and has written a far more realistic story." His Asia is not the kind you can easily dispense with—sliding another scene behind the characters: it is a heavy rich romantic mood which has nothing to do with geography, the mood of Mr. de la Mare's *Arabia*, and it absorbs quite blatantly anything which may be of use to it—*Hindoo Holiday* supplied the material for one of the best chapters in *The Asiatics,* just as the commentator of *The River* has helped to write some pages in *Night of the Poor.* One cannot call this plagiarism: some writers use and adapt other men's lives; Mr. Prokosch seems to use and adapt the books he has read. He has immense gusto for literature—there is something very young, very innocent and very greedy about his novels; he doesn't discriminate well between flavours so long as they are spiced enough, and he thrusts in the ruthless gunman out of the films and the motherly prostitute out of how many young men's novels just as they stand, leaving them to be digested by the overpowering juices of the romantic mood. They glimmer oddly and thinly up at us out of his maw, the skeletons of other people's people.

Night of the Poor is the story of a boy, Tom, who was meant to catch a train at Prairie du Sac in Wisconsin for his family home in Texas; his uncle with whom he had lived was dead, and he was leaving one secure way of life for another. But it didn't turn out that way. The old car kept breaking down on the road to the station until it was hopeless to expect to catch the train, so off he went suddenly, like the character in a fairy story, with Pete, a hired man, leaving the other two of his uncle's men fiddling with the car. "To the other two clung the scents of the farmyard; farmyard motions, farmyard calm. But all over Pete hung the sunny, yawning, prowling fragrance of the land itself." So the Odyssey begins, the dangerous tramp through Illinois, Indiana, Kentucky, Louisiana. Pete kills a man over a black girl and they are hunted by the police: Tom loses Pete and picks up other companions—a girl he loves who goes off with a New Mexican and whom he finds again at his journey's end, stray people who are supposed to represent the unemployed migrants of America, but who are curiously undifferentiated. They all have ideas about life, death, "all that immortality crap," philosophy, "that old geezer Aristotle": the background is orientally rich with birds and wild flowers and coca-cola signs; he sees a lynching. . . . The writing is often admirable—the killing of a snake: "It wriggled a moment, then lay still, and began to exude its acid scent of death"; sometimes tiring—because all the people Tom meets (they can be distinguished no other way) are physically monstrous with goitres or sores or just fat. We get a little weary of reading:

"She was the fattest woman he'd ever seen. She bulged, she billowed, she cascaded. Each moment seemed as if it must be her last before bursting. . ." and so on for a paragraph. Nevertheless, this book does not belong to the great fictional morass. It is a genuine imaginative achievement to have made a kind of opium dream out of the burst sandwich-bag, the empty cider bottle, the Cameo cinema and the co-ed girl.

> *Graham Greene, in a review of "Night of the Poor,"*
> *in* The Spectator, *Vol. 163, No. 5808, October 20,*
> *1939, p. 556.*

RANDALL JARRELL

An unsympathetic reader will find Mr. Prokosch a sort of decerebrate Auden, an Auden popularized for mass-consumption; and since Auden himself has been, lately, so successful in the attempt to provide one, it is hard to see in Mr. Prokosch much more than a work of supererogation. But this is a shallow view; Mr. Prokosch's success in the romantic and superficial exploitation of Auden's materials and methods is really incomparable—a triumph unmitigated by the odd intelligence and sensibility that adulterate obstinately even the laxest and most mechanical of Auden's pages. (A person who knows Auden's poetry well will notice his influence in *Death at Sea* many hundreds of times, in tone, form, images, rhetoric and content. Mr. Prokosch's earlier poetry is less singularly derivative.) Mr. Prokosch has sublimated Auden's worst vices and Auden's easiest virtues into a method; it is the mechanical operation of this method that produces the mass of *Death at Sea*—the poems pour out like sausages, automatic, voluptuous, and essentially indistinguishable. The "Love" that is the *deus ex machina* of Auden's worst lapses is the tutelary deity of Mr. Prokosch's poetry: his world-view is too sentimental and palely irresponsible—too *fashionable*—to be valued as much more than an effective romantic pose. He replaces Auden's Freudianism with a psychology that amounts to—*To know anything is to forgive anything;* and for Auden's demi-Marxism he substitutes the *Weltanschauung* of "Manfred" or a Sunday-supplement Spengler. (He has a Shelleyan fondness for the atlas as a bedside book; the argument of many of his poems is virtually, Death and darkness fall over Samarkand, Bokhara, Timbuctoo—fall, in fact, over the great big world.) The list or panorama, a tangle of picturesque details resolved by the blankest of generalizations, is his favorite structural device: *the consumptive cries on the dear Danubian banks, the Senegalese sheds his scalding tears beside the Niger, the Eskimo weeps icicles into Hudson Bay*—*why, they're all crying:* and you have your poem. (You're wrong if you think the *dear Danubian banks* is mine.)

But do not let me give the impression that Mr. Prokosch's poems are failures; the effects are second-hand and second-rate—but oh, so effective! The surface of the poetry has the immediate appeal the able and sensational popularization of a new technique always has; and under that surface bubbles the same old romanticism that infected us all in our cradles. How many ladies' clubs yet unorganized will prickle to the raptures of this verse! Naturally, not everyone will be pleased with such easy and florid romanticism; I read the poems with annoyance and mild pleasure, and thought Mr. Prokosch's obvious gifts childishly misused. But so much glitter and flow and scope have turned better heads than mine. On the dust-jacket of *Death at Sea* are testimonials by Stephen Spender, Robinson Jeffers, Michael Roberts, Edwin Muir and *The Manchester Guardian*—and others by Yeats and Eliot are referred to; I mention these

to bear out my last statement, and to show that my opinion is a dissenting one which the reader should be properly cautious about accepting. (p. 800)

> *Randall Jarrell, "Poets: Old, New and Aging," in*
> The New Republic, *Vol. 103, No. 24, December 9,*
> *1940, pp. 797-98, 800.*

WILLARD MAAS

This season it seems unpopular to like Frederic Prokosch. The passion for praising (and over-praising) only those poets who are represented by first books—to the disparagement of all those who continue to write against time—is, critically speaking, *de rigeur*. It was nearly the unanimous opinion of reviewers that Prokosch wrote "brilliantly" when *The Assassins* appeared. Now *Death at Sea* is called "awkward and prosaic," and less talented poets gain notoriety by attacking him. There are probably as many estimable poems in this new volume as in his former books, but the reviewers are tired of playing nice and have decided to be naughty. Hardly anything about Prokosch pleases them. For my part, I am willing to be impressed again. There is evidence, true, of borrowings, of repetitions of mood and attitude; but in the hothouse of modern poetry, cross-fertilization and inbreeding of the sort is everywhere only too obvious, and Prokosch need not be singled out for special censure.

His virtuoso lyricism, his immense and accomplished casualness, the pryotechnic show of color and landscape, cannot be touched by any of his young American contemporaries. Lush, romantic, baroque, he stands somewhat apart from all those who continue to sell old Eliots at bargain rates. A half a dozen splendid poems by Mr. Prokosch, as good as any he has done, are no mean bargain at any time. This book contains them.

> *Willard Maas, in a review of "Death at Sea," in*
> Accent, *Vol. 1, No. 4, Summer, 1941, p. 252.*

FRANCIS SCARFE

[The essay excerpted below was written in July, 1941.]

[Frederic Prokosch] strikes one as a poet who writes with an immaculate but somewhat fatal ease. He has mastered a limited though satisfactory technique, which in its highly conventional style, its florid diction, its elements of mumbo-jumbo, shall I say a sort of inherited and second-hand style, with fluid, uninhibited rhythms, sets him rather aside from his own generation, and thus helps him to hold a sort of balance between the Ancients and Moderns. This ease is not due to any faulty conception of poetry, nor to his precarious affiliation to the *New Verse* group. He is one of those happy and unhappy people of mixed nationality, a chaos of German, English and Austrian, who has enjoyed what education Germany, France, England and America can afford. This has enabled him to assimilate European culture in a way uncommon to people of his age, though very understandable in a generation which grew up in the shadow of the League of Nations. It can be fairly objected to his poetry that it is too largely cultural and literary, as was the work of Rilke and Mallarmé, which he has obviously read with care but whose concentration he cannot achieve. He has, to balance this praiseworthy fault, a strong lyrical impulse of his own, giving that freshness and enthusiasm which is the peculiar charm of those who write spontaneously. His work is homogeneous, and the same dominant qualities of invention and extravaganza are to be found in his poems as in his novels, *The Asiatics* and *The Seven Who Fled.*

Prokosch's development is another proof of the wisdom of [Geoffrey] Grigson and the *New Verse* policy, for he has developed from floweriness to control, from looseness to dignity, without losing any of his better qualities. *The Assassins* (1936) is not better than, or much different from, what [George] Barker was writing in 1934. Here Prokosch reminisces and resumes pitilessly, serving a laborious apprenticeship to the more lasting poets of the late nineteenth century; his adjectives lusciously accumulated though sometimes primly ordered, his phrases pompously inverted; but with all this there can be little doubt that the book was one of the best first collections which appeared in the 'thirties. On a larger scale there is one serious fault: that some of his poems drift aimlessly, with no clear impulse or direction, the poem achieving no definite centre and therefore having no form to speak of. This is to be seen in such poems as **"The Voyage"** (the too familiar and by now depressing Auden and Spender theme), a poem of five five-line stanzas which forms one very interesting but rambling sentence. The enormous sentence has its legitimate place in the enormous poem—in *Paradise Lost,* for instance, where it is masterfully used—but it is one of the blights of lyric poetry, a trap for the young who can control neither their emotion nor their stanza, and a wicked temptation for the old who have nothing or too much on their minds. Such a poem reminds one of the worst vice of Hugo, Verlaine, Shelley and Wordsworth, in works which are like immense glossy apples, delicious to look at but depressingly watery when bitten. And we find in this same poem one of Prokosch's characteristic devices, which he has repeated so often that I cannot read a poem where this is done without thinking of Prokosch. This is a deliberate and always effective shortening of the last line of each stanza, which gives a pathetic, constricting effect:

> And finally, having come to the world's long boundary,
> We waited, but saw nothing, waited, but no
> Sound broke the huge stillness; and slowly turning
> Saw only stars like snow on the endless prairie
>   And a sea of snow.

Coupled with the numerous negations, heavy internal assonances and the peculiar repetition of the 'snow' image, the pathos here becomes bathetic and recalls the worst of Spender. Prokosch uses this trick in seven or eight of the poems in this book, some five or six in his second book, and seven in his third. Not that it really matters, only he seems to have decided to class himself beyond doubt as a primarily elegiac poet. This is one's first impression, though it might be mistaken. It is certain, however, that his poems which succeed usually have that atmosphere of nostalgia, desolation, frustration and lament which we associate with such names as Dowson. In this first volume the lamentation is rather thin and undirected. . . . (pp. 74-6)

But all his poems have one outstanding quality which defies the cheap trick used above. Prokosch, unlike many of the younger poets, has what is to my mind one of the first requisites of a poet, the gift of a sensitive ear and a feeling for the purely sensual harmonies of words. (p. 77)

I do not propose to analyse the harmonics of Prokosch's poetry: what I mean is that it is not a purely destructive criticism to say that he weeps musically over everything, as well over the (very Audenesque) **"Empty Provinces"**, or the cliffs of Norway, or the world as a whole. . . . He also weeps tunefully

beside **"The Adriatic"**, replays the Byronic Hero or Wandering Jew in **"The Azores"**. . . . And so he continues, weeping at Port Said, in China, in Utah, and between times into the Caspian and the Atlantic. Enough of this: what does it mean? It means, first of all, that Prokosch is as good at what I call 'Psychic Geography' as Auden, or even better because his range is wider. It is said that he wrote a travel-book about the Near East without going there: I am quite willing to believe it, and that the book would be good. I know of no poet, unless we rummage among the great, such as Shakespeare and Milton, in whose poems the child-amazing wonders of the world are so constantly and convincingly present as in Prokosch. This is a fair sign of a poetic disposition, this type of sympathetic and creative imagination which enabled Rimbaud to write his "Drunken Boat" long before he had seen the sea. With such a psychic eye and delicate ear he has all the possibility of being a sort of English Rimbaud, though I should prefer to believe that in Prokosch the English have discovered their own Verlaine (who, it must be remembered, did one or two things which were beyond Rimbaud).

The second meaning of Prokosch's lamentation is, that he has given a purely intuitive interpretation of the mal-de-siècle which weighed so heavily on our poets between the two wars. Perhaps he has been a little wiser than most in refraining from analysing, explaining and apologizing for his nostalgia and tears. His poems are the essence of this feeling, intensified by the psychic geography and by another quality, that sense of mystery which always distinguishes the Romantic poet. Take his flamboyant (and no doubt best-selling) titles to start with: *The Assassins, The Carnival, The Asiatics, The Seven Who Fled, Death at Sea.* These send a thrill down the spine, a thrill sustained by the no less evocative titles of his poems: **"The Masks"**, **"The Tragedians"**, **"The Gothic Dusk"**, **"The Conspirators"**. . . . Prokosch has, before the poem has been read, already managed to excite and hush his reader. And this evocative flair glows throughout his poems. . . . (pp. 78-9)

This gift for suggestive description often leans to the macabre, but Prokosch has instinctively refused to develop fully his gift for the macabre. In his subsequent development he made more sparing but very effective use of the musical, psychic, and what for lack of a better term I must call mysterious methods of suggestion which gave value to his first work.

His second book, *The Carnival* (1938), was on the whole much happier, showing a greater sense of the positive values of life, and a much greater capacity for enjoyment. The book contains one of the best emotional statements of the social crisis of the 'thirties, his eight-page **"Ode"**, which first appeared in *New Verse.*

There is also a greater power of concentration in these poems than was to be found in *The Assassins.* Some of the pieces are slight, but these, perhaps, are those which will never lose their first attraction, poems like **"Evening"**, the **"Songs"**, **"Bathers"** and **"Nocturne"**. His own experience emerges best through these shorter poems, which are moments of intense realization which help us to class him almost as a neo-symbolist. Take, for instance, **"Evening"**:

> Pears from the boughs hung golden,
> The street lay still and cool,
> Children with books and satchels
> Came sauntering home from school;
> The dusk fled softly inward
> Across each darkening sill,
> The whole sweet autumn slumbered,
> The street lay cool and still:

The children moved through twilight,
The village steeple gleamed,
Pears from their boughs hung trembling,
And suddenly it seemed,
     Shaken with such a wildness
     Of terror and desire,
     My heart burst into music
     And my body into fire.

This type of poem should theoretically be easy to write: it is what poets like W. H. Davies spent a whole lifetime trying to write and succeeded only once in twenty years. All the baggage of an outmoded poetic diction is here: 'golden pears', 'dusk', 'sweet', 'slumbered', 'twilight', 'wildness', 'desire', 'music', 'fire'. This looks like a dictionary of clichés, and they are of course words which at once lend themselves to any novice who starts writing poetry. But in this poem they are obviously pardonable and necessary: the whole experience, one of innocence and sensual delight, could only be expressed in this most traditional language because it must be realized that in this poem the poet, so seized by this scene of peace and childhood, speaks *as* a child, identifies the scene with his own childhood, and as a result uses the language which, as a boy, he was accustomed to associate with all poetic expression. Had this not been done, I think the experience could not have been so complete and true as it obviously is in this poem. This very simple experience is paranoiac, having that sense of identification, that transcended atmosphere, created (strange conjunction!) by Dali in his painting and Yeats in some of his poems. It will also be noticed that in this poem Prokosch's familiar nostalgia has now been turned to a creative purpose, in a positive direction, that of participation, and it is this participation, this new social consciousness, which makes *The Carnival* so less literary than *The Assassins*.

The Carnival is the book of an individualist, wrestling as though for the first time with the realities of his social environment. The mystery of *The Assassins,* exotic and obscure, had all the latent horror and fear of the unknown, but this second book portrays the fear and knowledge of the known. (pp. 79-82)

It is obvious that much of this writing springs from purely cultural experience rather than feeling. . . . And the truth is that in the real sense of the term Prokosch, like Eliot and Pound and so many who have tried to understand Europe culturally, through the past, instead of the present, has missed something, and has failed to write any poetry (save the shorter lyrics already mentioned) bearing directly on social matters, which might appeal to any but a very select audience drawn exclusively from the intelligentsia. He belongs, like Rilke and Mallarmé, to a very rarefied and privileged, over-refined caste of poets. Yearning for a 'vast belief', the belief he found was, to my mind, not vast enough. It is a belief in the cream of civilization, unaccompanied by a love of flesh and blood, sweat and toil which go to the making of such culture. This is evident in his magnificent **"Ode"**, which is unpolitical and unsocial in the broadest sense, but otherwise a brilliant defence of cultural and humanitarian values. This **"Ode"** is in many ways like Auden's "Spain", but whereas Auden, in this as in all his poems, always lays emphasis on human activities, and expresses them through motor and social imagery, Prokosch has greater sensual perception, but is much more general, florid and literary. At the same time, his poem is so much more limited that it is more of a personal statement than Auden's, its limitations being those of his own rather intellectual outlook. . . . But once this is said it still remains that, though there is none of that clear definition in which Auden excels, there is a general pleasantness in this writing which is very refreshing. It is because Prokosch has a tender and sentimental attitude to the past (rather like Flecker) that he can write about it in this agreeable meandering way: things happen sweetly and gently for Prokosch which happen brutally and startlingly in Auden. Personally I like this way of dealing with the past, though I feel it is to a degree false; like Banville, whom Baudelaire described as 'The poet of hours of happiness', Prokosch picks out, deliberately, all the plums of his childhood and of his historical sense, omitting the suffering, the slavery and exploitation which lay behind those things. . . . (pp. 82-4)

The justification, on an aesthetic plane, is that all the poem is quotable: this **"Ode"** is perhaps the most intoxicating and sensuous poem produced in the 'thirties. It is the swan-song of Europe, and for that reason, while it is certainly less urgent, less an incentive to action, than Auden's "Spain", less true to the horrible tragedy of modern Europe than Auden's poem, less realistic altogether, the fact that it is a sensual realization of loss, and that the primitive values of poetry are so maintained, makes it *purer* poetry. (p. 84)

It is a long time since we have had a poet who could write so easily, so richly and simply at once. If the poem is written, in a sense, from too great a height, so that the Spanish war which prompted it is quite dwarfed or obscured, this poem is another reminder, to those who ask now for 'war poetry', that the poets of the 'thirties realized very well what was happening long before this war actually 'started'.

The book *Death at Sea* develops satisfactorily in the direction of this broad human feeling which is characteristic of Prokosch's approach to maturity. There is, in these new poems, no sign of any new element, any new interest, any new experiment developing in his mind or technique. It is doubtful whether Prokosch could ever write a long poem, that is to say one longer than his eight-page **"Ode."** He has no need to, for his intuitive grasp of momentary feeling and experience is a quality which debars him at once from any more ambitious or didactic type of writing in verse. At the same time, he seems to have reacted with great sanity to the war, and has not made a fool of himself as many poets who rely less on their feelings have done. His judgment of the matter is, I think, very true to that of his own generation:

Miraculous presences
Whose breath disturbs the silence of ponds at evening,
Now summon forth like a ringing of bells the wildness
In all our hearts: the little hands fade away,
And catching our breath as the vision gathers meaning
And the deafening music quickens, we know that
    somewhere
We shall start again. Though not easily. And not soon.

With so much that is good, these 'miraculous presences', of which we should like to know a little more, this mysterious 'vision', the symbolic 'music', are the old evasions which have beset Prokosch since he started printing his poetry. But such of his war poems as **"Soliloquy"** and **"The Country Houses"** are among the best so-called war poems produced in this conflict. If vices of language persist, his later poems are achieving that firmness of outline which his earlier work lacked. This spoilt child of an over-civilized, or should we say a culture-ridden, Europe has those faults and merits of poetic style which make him something of a modern Keats. (pp. 85-6)

Francis Scarfe, "Frederic Prokosch: An Exotic," in his Auden and After: The Liberation of Poetry, *1930-1941, George Routledge & Sons Ltd., 1942, pp. 74-86.*

THE TIMES LITERARY SUPPLEMENT

[With **The Skies of Europe** Mr. Prokosch has given us] a very considerable work, his most individual to date—subtle, sharply impressionist and charged with an allusive strain of intellectual poetry. His subject is Europe and European tradition in the three years before the outbreak of war. The "I" of the narrative, a very seeing eye, is a young American named Philip, an occasional writer, who wanders from one country to another, always preternaturally sensitive to the genius of place and always taking colour of thought and emotion from the experience of the European society he observes. He is wax on which European civilization writes its symbols of doom. Or, nourished on the poetry of European decay, he is the hero of [Flaubert's] *L'Education Sentimentale* transplanted in the soil of a later and more profound horror.

The argument does not fully develop until towards the end, where in Munich, in the summer of 1939, two shadows walk by the narrator's side in the Englischer Garten and hold fateful discourse—Mr. Prokosch's words are instinct with poetic vision. Until then three principal narrative motives are to be distinguished. There is the cultural sterility, the fake art and intellectual dithering of the motley crowd of advanced spirits at the Café de la Sirène, on the Left Bank; this, in sum, is Paris, the civilization of Europe, freedom, the comic process of disintegration. It is familiar comedy, salty, volatile, verging too narrowly on farce. Then there is the sickness of the German dream, the intoxication of the power to destroy; it spreads, a stifling miasma, over the picture-postcard charm and sentiment of the Austrian Tirol, over the festive joys of a Bavarian Christmas complete with untrodden snow, a Christmas tree, carols, family presents, and a suckling-pig on the table. Finally, there is the personal dream and awakening, the bitter and voluptuous torment of Philip's passion for the Russian or Ruthenian Saskia.

She is Circe, Helen, Isolde, Maya, Thaïs, Dolores, this Saskia—the sensual mask of *das ewig weibliche*. Not so much a person, that is, as an image of beauty and mystery; of beauty that is in the eye of the beholder, of mystery that flows from the impulse of sex. All the same, in this luscious idiom she is very well done, a cool, lovely, enticing creature enslaved and corrupted by her own flesh, a sensualist withdrawn in an alluring inviolability. When Philip first discovers her at the Sirène she is the mistress of a pulsating and fathomless Russian painter. She chatters inconsequent artistic nonsense, temporarily floors the young man with her feminine cleverness, grows more dreamily radiant under his speechless longing and always, with an air of light tenderness, holds him off. From her he betakes himself to Munich and the frugality and cultivation of Frau Meyer's *pension,* where he had stayed as a boy. Here all, it seems, is order, purpose, strength, though with German pride in the result goes an insistent and hangdog craving to be reassured. On to the Tirolean village of Glasenbach, where Mariedl, in her flowered skirt of red and blue, lace sleeves and silver-buttoned bodice almost renews the innocence of lost Eden. Back to Paris, where in an enchanting languor Saskia surrenders at last and Philip, replaced soon after by the virile and visionary destroyer Stefan from Munich, falls under a crueller spell. On to Spain in civil war, with death and the accumulation of suffering numbing mind and sense. Back once

more, by way of extravagant picaresque comedy, to the heartache and despair of Paris.

It is a diverse, deeply studied and original performance, with all the signs of a restless integrity of mind upon it and here and there a passage of soliloquy that sustains a note of high poetic intensity. There are no commonplace humanities beneath these darkening skies; what is not treacherous beauty or impotent defeat is grotesque pathos. Seen in this light, the European rot has a multiplicity of natural causes, and Mr. Prokosch, in his Flaubertian attempt to uncover them all, almost obscures truth by seeking the whole of it.

"Before the Crash," in The Times Literary Supplement, *No. 2085, January 17, 1942, p. 29.*

THE TIMES LITERARY SUPPLEMENT

Mr. Prokosch's new novel [**The Conspirators**] seems more than anything else to reflect a state of mind. As narrative it is inclined to be hollow. The scene is Lisbon, Lisbon in wartime, a window from which refugees and conspirators of every nationality look out on the deluge, the death of an era, the flood of history rushing past, the spectacle (as Mr. Prokosch sees it) of Western Europe rotting away. That idea, repeated with slight variations from beginning to end of a short and oracular novel, is very much in Mr. Prokosch's mind. It twines itself around a simple enough tale of three vaguely mysterious and unhappy refugees, one of them the Mona Lisa-ish female who haunts this author's fiction, the other two—both beloved by her in her capricious and suffering fashion—fellow spirits and ideological enemies condemned by history to be murderer and murdered respectively. For Vincent, who has been betrayed by an unknown associate and who has been daringly rescued from prison, is warned that within a few hours, at one o'clock in the morning precisely, he will meet his betrayer, with a red carnation in his button-hole, in the baccarat room of the casino at Estoril; and the red carnation is worn by Hugo, who was his friend, who takes his orders from Herr Schmidt, who is irresistibly, almost hurtfully, handsome, and who has replaced Vincent in the enigmatical affections of Irina Petrova. So the paper-knife that Vincent has picked up comes into play in a moonlit bedroom, where the victim has been wrestling with a premonition of doom.

Mr. Prokosch, an interesting writer at his best, as in his previous novel, **The Skies of Europe,** is a highly conscious stylist, and his feeling for words, always pronounced, is not without effect here. But his is a cerebral individuality of expression, without warmth or spontaneity of vision. The geographical sense that possesses him, from which stems a truly cosmopolitan sentiment, threatens to become an elaborate mannerism only.... The story evokes very suggestively the atmosphere of Lisbon and has, it must be said, a faintly precious distinction of thought and manner; but the business of the murder is drawn out to tedious lengths of mystification and the hemispherically insular obsession with the death throes of Europe seems a little gratuitous.

"Death of an Era," in The Times Literary Supplement, *No. 2152, May 1, 1943, p. 209.*

HOWARD MUMFORD JONES

Frederic Prokosch's talent for descriptive narrative in romantic prose has led him to create a unique form—the novel of geography touched with nostalgia. Almost uniformly his books are journey books. In *The Asiatics* (1935) the hero wanders from Beirut to Haiphong on the China coast, and at the end is "feeling very happy." In *The Seven Who Fled* (1937) we work our way from the extreme eastern rim of Sinkiang province to the Hoang-Ho—at least the reader does, for most of the seven give out en route. In *The Skies of Europe* (1941) the hero visits the Continental countries just before the storm breaks in 1939. *Night of the Poor* (1939) runs from Tennessee to Texas; *Storm and Echo* (1948) gropes through a jungle of flora, fauna, and primitive tribes in central Africa; and *Age of Thunder* (1945) leads us out of France into Switzerland during the German occupation. Even books like *The Conspirators* (1943), which is staged in Lisbon, and *The Idols of the Cave* (1946), which is laid in New York, do not avoid geography: the characters, who are cosmopolitans, come from the ends of the earth to an international city.

In an introduction to *The Asiatics* Carl Van Doren classifies that novel as an imaginary voyage. I think this is not quite accurate. Mr. Prokosch takes pains to be exact. In *Nine Days to Mukalla,* his latest book, you can follow on a map the fortunes of the four plane-wrecked Europeans from Qmar (Kamar) Bay on the southern Arabian coast to Mukalla (Mokalla), some two hundred miles east of Aden. Three of them die, but the quartet have the usual adventures among picturesque natives, primitive cultures, hatred, fatigue, and love. In this volume, as in its predecessors, casual copulation (which never results in pregnancy), personal bravery, inexplicable psychology of men "closer to Nature," and a kind of weary backward glance at Europe make up the tale. Philosophic discourse unimpeded by linguistic barriers flows on concerning sex, happiness, death, honor, and fatality. As elsewhere, the Europeans do not act, but are acted upon, yet the hero and the heroine mysteriously arouse the loyalty of two natives.

Mr. Prokosch is, of course, a good many cuts above Stoddard's lectures or the travelogues of Burton Holmes. He is often above the level of E. Phillips Oppenheim, and he is sometimes on the level of Conrad, but it is difficult to define the quality of his achievement. It does not especially lie in the creation of character. His hero is virtually anonymous in every book. His women are seldom more than sexual machines. The natives of the several countries are carefully drawn, are picturesque, are probable enough to evoke a suspension of disbelief, but whether they are African blacks, primitive Southerners, or, as in this case, Bedouins, they remain, so to speak, brilliant anthropological pawns.

Nor is the theme especially notable in these stories. . . . In all the books there is a kind of race between love and exhaustion, between primitive vitality and a kind of rich Viennese melancholy that drives Europeans to their doom. But these characters and this attitude are not unique.

What holds these books together is, I think, sheer craftsmanship. Mr. Prokosch is a sort of Berlioz in prose. He has one of the most marvelous descriptive pens now at work. Consider, as an instance, this vignette of an aged French invalid in Teheran, from *The Asiatics:*

> A face like a mask, quite lifeless and expressionless except for the eyes peering with an amazing keenness over the blue-gray pouches which hung above and beneath them. Her mouth was only a scarlet line, her neck a labyrinth of wrinkles, her hands two porcelain claws, her hair an artificial scarlet mass of curls, a great

> wilted peony. But her eyes, as she saw me, grew narrow and brilliant.

This has the clean precision the Imagists sought in their poetry, it has the effortless visuality of Stephen Crane's famous sun, pasted like a red wafer in the sky, and you feel, if the woman does not exist, she ought to have existed.

Unfortunately for us, as soon as she opens her mouth, the mode changes:

> I am still deeply excited by life; it still sets me trembling. You must forgive me. The mere presence of youth, my dear boy, makes my heart beat more quickly. . . Tell me, my pretty friend, what do you think of life?

This is neither realism nor actuality, but the kind of philosophical discourse with which these novels, admirable in so many other respects, are overstuffed.

Nine Days to Mukalla adds little to Mr. Prokosch's stature, however much it may add to his repertory. Yet, it is a better book than, say, *Age of Thunder,* because the philosophizing is held down, and it is a more readable book than *Night of the Poor,* which was just another novel about the poor whites of the South. It is more compressed than *The Seven Who Fled,* quite as picturesque, and somewhat better modelled. Stylistically, it ranks with his best work, filled as it is with virtuoso effects. . . .

> Howard Mumford Jones, "Love and Geography,"
> in The Saturday Review, *New York, Vol. XXXVI,*
> *No. 12, March 21, 1953, p. 15.*

GORE VIDAL

[In *Nine Days to Mukalla,* Prokosch] has produced yet another variation on his central legend: disaster and flight, anticipation and arrival. The plot's construction will be familiar to his readers. Four people, en route from India to Europe, crash in an airplane on an island near the coast of Arabia. They are forced to travel overland and by sea to Mukalla, a town from which they will be able to rejoin their civilization. Before the journey's end, however, two have perished; those who survive die, too, in another sense, since they are changed, demoralized by suffering, by disaster, by encounters with fantastic strangers and unfamiliar powers.

Yet, despite a great deal of superficial excitement, the drama of their flight is essentially unhuman. They are not men and women, but archetypes whose relationships lack immediacy. They are shadows engaged in ritual, their deeds possessing meaning only in relation to the sensuous world, to the natural world at its most implacable—a glittering, heightened place of symbol where shadow-figures cross shining deserts yet leave no single mark of passage upon the sand. As in Prokosch's other books, it is not the people but the design which matters: a vision of human beings shipwrecked and forced to flee through hostile country, harried by a nameless enemy, by that "antique horror prowling across the face of the world . . . half chaos, half intention, half elemental and half human; something which civilized man must battle forever; must be killed by or kill."

And this horror? This enemy? In context, Prokosch means it to be that will to destruction so remarkable in our race. But, in a larger sense, the amorphic evil which provides the tension in all his works is, finally, the fact of death itself, the grim reward of many journeys, the cold truth beyond Mukalla. His voyagers combat their enemy with the only weapon they possess: they live and, living, like Kafka's creatures, they attempt the castle because they must.

Prokosch's gifts, specifically, are lyric not psychological—unusual equipment for a twentieth century novelist. In the one book where he tried for a novel of relationship, **The Idols of the Cave,** he failed because he could not manage the psychological counterpoint which has been the main concern of the post-Jamesian novel. Yet, at his best, as in this work, he writes a rich evocative line with which he creates sensuous worlds he has never seen except with the eye of a superlative imagination. Here, once again, he renders that vision which is obsessively his own: the traveler in strange country, the sunburned Ulysses of his poems, the alien who moves across time, anticipating with a melancholy fascination his last arrival, a private death in some ironically gleaming land.

> *Gore Vidal, "Disaster and Flight," in* The New York Times Book Review, *March 22, 1953, p. 6.*

RICHARD C. CARPENTER

The novels of Frederic Prokosch are domiciled in a small and out-of-the-way province of the world of letters, inhabited by comparatively few other books, with ill-defined boundaries troublesome to the literary traveler. One seldom encounters their curious blend of travelogue, story, philosophy, symobolism, and fantasy—in fact, Mr. Prokosch seems to me the only contemporary familiar with this particular terrain. Other recent writings impinge on his unique genre at various points, but to find close relatives of **The Asiatics, The Seven Who Fled,** or **Storm and Echo** we must go back to The Arcadia, Vathek, Green Mansions, Typee, or Travels in Arabia Deserta. Lost Horizon has more in common with Mr. Prokosch's novels than most other contemporary works, but that novel, too, lacks the peculiar distillation of effect we find in both Prokosch and, say, Hudson. To get the curious compound of such books, a writer must mix poetry and philosophy, exotic scene and lush style, vivid observation and dreamlike fantasy in due proportion. Probably because of these peculiarities, Mr. Prokosch has been little noticed in literary histories and compendia: since he cannot be classified handily with other novelists of the present day—being neither sociological nor psychoanalytic, technically startling nor formally intriguing—he is bundled off into the "minor" category, or simply not mentioned. (p. 261)

Prokosch is both a cosmopolite and a romantic. His better novels are founded on an implicit belief that the primitive, remote, and simple life is more vital and intense than that we ordinarily know. And his best work is set in distant, exotic lands where the civilized surfaces are sloughed off. Unlike most younger American writers he is a spiritual expatriate, creatively most at home when he is farthest away from the United States, finding only a certain kind of stimulant to his imagination. When he leaves Central Asia or Arabia or the Congo, he usually writes a confused, strained, or precious piece that is only occasionally saved from vapidity by the always-poetic, distinguished style of which he is an accomplished master. His reputation, it seems to me, will rest on the four novels which exploit successfully his fascination with strange lands and peoples.

The first of these, **The Asiatics** (1935), is undoubtedly the happiest and most ingratiating, though it lacks structure and fails to sound the deeper note of some others. It can be neatly described as a hitchhiker's tour from Beirut to Hong Kong *via*

just about any place of importance in Turkey, Iran, India, and French Indo-China. On the way, the hero—just a young American—meets assorted natives; Russian, French, and English travelers; beauty, filth, sadness, and ecstasy. He smuggles dope, crashes in an airplane, escapes from prison in the dead of winter; he enjoys a succession of promiscuous loves, talks poetry with a bored rajah, and philosophy with an ancient lama. Since he is just drifting, there is really no need of dramatic structure. He can enjoy his incredible variety of experiences without strain on our credulity.

All of this, of course, can be found often enough in the most hackneyed picaresque novel, as can the precious exoticism of the fabled Orient. But Prokosch effectively saves his book from the sins that bedevil most such romances: motiveless and meaningless adventure and romantic gilding. Counterbalancing the incident is a kind of somnambulism that infuses even the most dangerous happening with the atmosphere of dream, no matter what real peril our hero is in. We never find ourselves merely hopping from one amorous or perilous episode to another. As in dreams, everything has meaning, though it be symbolically ambiguous. This effect is achieved in great part by the "poetic" of the book—its imagery, metaphor, and emotional overtones.

Prosaic and disagreeable scenes and episodes complement the poetry, saving **The Asiatics** from mere prettiness and the puerility of romanticizing Asia, with its filth and disease as well as its silks and sampans. The young American vagabond sees plenty of the seamy sides of Asian life and does not boggle at telling us about them in circumstantial detail. We see beggars with revolting sores and sleep in indescribable hovels; we breathe the manifold stenches of Asian streets and feel the stroke of the Asian sun; we choke down nauseous messes of native food and suffer the "loathsome familiarities of bed bugs." **The Asiatics,** however, would not be the fascinating thing it is without still a third quality. While picaresque in form and poetic in language, it is deeply reflective in theme. Asia is more than a land of many and varied experiences or exotic scenes—it is the "last land" as well as the first. Weary and ancient, it is still the land where people ponder the inscrutable deeper meaning of why we are here and where we are going. The question nearly every Asiatic asks the young American is "Are you happy?"—one he finds difficult to answer, although he thinks he probably is. But this question reveals the focus on human values, on people and how they feel, that is in peculiar and vital contrast to our Western focus on things. It is this he is seeking in Asia—not just new experience but a completely different quality of experience.

In **The Seven Who Fled** (1937) the same emphasis on the unique gifts that Asia presents permeates the experience of the seven Europeans who are forced to leave Kashgar in Central Asia due to a ticklish political situation. As they creep their several ways across the measureless faces of Turkestan and Tibet and Mongolia, they come each one to grips with their inner selves, with the essential meaning of life for them. Prokosch does not tell us *what* they discover exactly, but we feel assured that they *have* discovered whatever they have been seeking and never finding in their previous lives. Layeville, the upper-class Englishman, Goupilliere, the fugitive from France, De La Scaze, a world-weary cosmopolite, all meet death; while Olivia, De La Scaze's wife, becomes a prostitute in Shanghai and Hugo Wildenbruch, the young German, has received his death-sentence from tuberculosis. Certainly not a happy series of destinies. But each one, drawn inevitably toward this destiny, accepts it with what we carelessly call Asiatic fatalism, but which is really insight and acceptance rather than flaccid resignation.

This theme of massive inevitability in our human lot is poised against an even richer background of scene than Prokosch presents in his first novel. There is less of the teeming town life of Asia and more of her vast empty spaces to afford Prokosch opportunities to use his descriptive wizardry. The journey of Layeville, especially, across the blinding wastes of Sinkiang desert and the snows of the Kuen Luen mountains, is portrayed with amazing clarity of scene and evocation of mood. As Layeville is drawn by a mystic magnetic attraction toward the shining pinnacles of the Himalayas, we move with him and the caravan, feeling heat and cold, fatigue and wonder. At the same time we realize what Layeville is gaining from this travail. Like the other six travelers he is not only coming closer to the heart of existence through physical experience—getting at the marrow of life, squeezing it into a corner as it becomes ever more elemental; but he is also getting closer to himself. Long stretches of the novel are basically a *recherche du temps perdu* as each character relives his life in reminiscence and waking dream. The situation provides an intelligible motivation for such nostalgia: Asia is giving these people to themselves.

In these passages of reminiscence, Prokosch's lyricism shows to the fullest advantage. He recreates with astonishing vividness the very immediacy of experience: English university afternoons, green grass and cricket; the love of austerity instilled in German youth; the *Weltschmerz* of Austria; an ugly crime of passion—he manages to strike most notes in the gamut of memory. As in *The Asiatics*, however, the atmosphere of dream permeates these passages, blurring edges, softening contours, so that we would not say that Prokosch's stylistic gift was without concomitant disadvantages. Occasionally our taste is cloyed and we are glad to come back to the filth and bone-chilling damp of the prison at Aqsu or to the description of the cholera epidemic—as graphic as *A Journal of the Plague Year*—that killed De La Scaze.

Yet even in these details Prokosch's romanticism takes hold, sentimentalizing and exaggerating. It is in his natives that he avoids this pitfall most successfully—perhaps because they are in some ways the only true romantics—without self-consciousness or pose. At their best they really come to life, which is something, it must be admitted, that Prokosch's people do but rarely. . . . Although *The Seven Who Fled* is an extraordinarily rich book—in description, event, and reflection—it would quite probably leave most readers bedazzled with its virtuosity but spiritually unfed if it did not present these real people who give the book nourishment.

After writing this second novel in 1937, Prokosch left his Asian settings for an extended fling at other places and subjects, sometimes retaining the virtues of his first work—enough to show that his talent was no flash in the pan—and sometimes suffering sadly from the defects of his qualities. Only in a few places in *Age of Thunder* and *Idols of the Cave* does he manage quite the effects which had elicited such enthusiastic response in the 30's, although when he does bring them off they are indeed the sort of writing that sticks in the mind. In *Age of Thunder* (1945), for example, there are some really wonderful gypsies and superb descriptions of traveling secretly at night across occupied France. He manages to evoke with his usual precision the exact sight, sounds, smells of his setting. And the search-motif provides effective suspense and tension. In *Idols of the Cave* (1946) Prokosch's craftsmanship takes to an urban environment—New York during and directly after the

war—and handles competently some new things for him: social satire on the brittle lives of expatriate society, exploration of intertwined love affairs, and a quasi-dramatic plot structure. Naturally, all these have been completely done by a shoal of young and not-so-young novelists. But in his constant creation of the very stuff of atmosphere, Prokosch shows that very few contemporaries can equal or outdo him in wordmaking. Unfortunately, on more than one occasion he lets words run away with him so that what ought to impress us vividly seems instead only affected, even silly.

Such is not the case with *Storm and Echo* (1948), certainly the most powerful of Prokosch's novels, if not the most effective over-all. The African scene provides sufficient motivation for the novel's poetic, and the undergirding theme of search for an ideal provides a strong forward thrust to keep the story moving. Following his usual practice, Prokosch assembles a disparate group (this time all scientists except the hero, Samuel) but from different national and cultural traditions, and sends them into the heart of darkness, embarked on a dual quest: for Leonard Speght, Samuel's friend and a kind of "Mistah Kurtz," worshipped by the natives, implicitly both a saint and a devil; and for a mysterious mountain called Nagala, which no man has ever climbed and few have ever seen. Their journey, described with Conradian vividness and power, is one of extreme travail, beset with all the torments Africa can devise, but also relieved with moments of beauty and almost mystical joy. Like the travelers in *The Seven Who Fled,* Samuel, Alessandro, Marius, Joshua (their names carry symbolic overtones) come closer to the center of life than they have ever done before though they reach it only through suffering. And like De La Scaze, Goupilliere, and Layeville in the earlier book, Alessandro and Marius meet death. Only Samuel, who is called Sambula by the natives—this indicating his affinity for them and for Africa—succeeds in reaching the top of Nagala with a native. It is a curiously ambiguous triumph, however, for Speght is never found. Evidently he has been killed, and the mountain itself is no great obstacle.

Yet the symbolic import seems clear; though these men have found no clear-cut victory, they have in the course of their journey met *life* in all the savagery and beauty which it can afford. They have escaped from the modern "civilized" world to an elemental one where the most basic values once again apply. They reach no *goal* worth reaching; it is in their pilgrims' progress itself that they find what they are seeking.

Nevertheless, *Storm and Echo* is both more and less than a kind of contemporary *Heart of Darkness*. Its motif of the quest supplies the greater part of its significance, to be sure, but it is the poetry of the book that makes it memorable—its description and evocation of scene and mood.

In *Nine Days to Mukalla* (1953), Prokosch concentrates his efforts on descriptive passages, largely abjuring the symbolism of *Storm and Echo,* with a consequent lightening of the story, a loss of power but a compensating increase in vividness. The plot is as usual loose, picaresque, with a close resemblance in basic situation to *The Seven Who Fled,* but Prokosch avoids a hackneyed repetition of himself, principally through constantly fresh perceptions. The interwoven description and narrative form a shimmering fabric with no thread worn bare though it has often been used before. The Arabian seacoast, towns, and desert stand before our eyes in Van Gogh colors, dazzling and immediate. We follow the fortunes of the four stranded Europeans in a sort of dreamlike indifference to their fate, but the world they move through on their journey to Mukalla is realized for us in all its sensuous intensity. We can almost feel the spray on our faces and the sun beating down on the white-walled towns.

Prokosch's mastery of language is at its most effective in creating Arab life for the reader. The native people of this story are neither the simple and sometimes noble savages of *Storm and Echo* nor the subtle, weary, and wise Orientals of the *Asiatics*. They have their simplicities and their wisdom: they tolerate bedroom spiders because they are protecting spirits; they bear pain and privation without repining since one can do nothing but bear. But they are, above all, *people*—they have a way of life that is not ours but from which we can learn much. Especially do they know how to make the best of everything, to snatch the unforgiving moment of joy—to dance and sing and love—and as well, to endure the endless agonies of a forced march across the edge of the Rub Al Khali, perhaps the earth's most unendurable desert. They are the reason for *Nine Days to Mukalla*'s being more than a mere series of effective descriptions. The contact of the European protagonists with their Arab culture gives the story depth and significance—it opens both the protagonists' and our senses to new dimensions of experience—"freer and more intense," as one reviewer said, "than any they have ever known." The fact that these Arab lives are not mere curiosa for the literary traveler to observe, but are instead profoundly meaningful indicates the way in which Mr. Prokosch differs from the usual writer of fictionalized travel, and attests his legitimate citizenship in his unique literary province. From Hudson to T. E. Lawrence, Prokosch's fellow-citizens have found that in far-off lands the scales of custom are stripped from their eyes and that they can perceive more clearly the essential nature of man's place in the world. The fundamental ambiguity hidden by our prosaic lives becomes apparent. The illumination of this ambiguity is achieved principally through the surrealistic device we have noted before—the waking dream in which all is strange yet impregnated with significance. Prokosch throws reality out of focus so that we may see more vividly the "real reality" behind it. Like the surrealistic painter he creates a world of haunting and enigmatic vistas that speak delphically to us.

Beyond this Mr. Prokosch's motif of the quest enables him to invest his novels with meaning beyond the events of the journey themselves. The search is symbolic: his travelers are not just trying to get to Tibet or Mount Nagala or Mukalla but are, more importantly, trying to make their way toward understanding. . . . I believe that it is even more through this theme than through his imagery or his events that Prokosch manages to make his novels live. In the exotic lands he portrays there is not only a new vision of the real, but also a possibility of finding the self-fulfilment so sadly lacking in our ordinary lives. It is for this reason above all that such works as *The Asiatics* and *Nine Days to Mukalla* belong in the company of *Green Mansions*, *Typee*, and *Travels in Arabia Deserta*.

In his tenth novel, *A Tale for Midnight* (1955), Prokosch has reinterpreted the events surrounding Francesco Cenci, the sixteenth-century Roman nobleman and roué whose purported brutality and incestuous intentions brought his daughter, Beatrice, to plan and accomplish his murder. A tale of suspense and tension, gradually working up to savage executions which ended the whole sordid affair; a tale that explores a tangled web of human relations and motives; and a tale founded solidly on historical research, this is a new venture for Mr. Prokosch. For the first time, his poetic and descriptive ability is complemented by a powerfully dramatic plot and realistic character-

ization. He does not, fortunately, completely abandon his usual technique; besides plot there is a rich background of Renaissance scene and atmosphere. We are treated to sensuous impressions of the Italian countryside and people in all seasons, to the streets and shops of Rome, to flood, plague, and carnival. But the novel is more than a mere rehash of Shelley or Guerazzi, and Mr. Prokosch is as graphic and harrowing in his evocation of murder and torture as he was in description of similar happenings in *The Seven Who Fled* and *Nine Days to Mukalla*.

To be sure, Mr. Prokosch has not simply gained by writing a story of plot based on history. He has lost some of the unique quality which makes his writing stand out from the ordinary, and his abandonment of the quest motif seems to weaken the work. *A Tale for Midnight* drags toward the end, apparently waiting for the inevitable denouement. And no part of the story is quite so effective as the scene of the murder, which comes early. Still, a writer does not make music by plucking the same strings eternally, and Mr. Prokosch has been intelligent enough to realize this. All in all, he is still a forceful and vivid writer. (pp. 262-67)

> Richard C. Carpenter, "The Novels of Frederic Prokosch," in College English, Vol. 18, No. 5, February, 1957, pp. 261-67.

THE TIMES LITERARY SUPPLEMENT

[In *The Dark Dancer*, Prokosch] has taken seventeenth-century India as his subject, specifically, the career of Khurram, who eventually took the title of Shah Jahan, the Lord of the Universe, and who built the Taj Mahal in memory of his chief wife, Princess Arjumand.

India in the seventeenth century, with its massive contradictions—embodied in individuals as much as in the fabric of society—between savage pursuit of power and quietistic life-denying longing for truth, seems an attractive subject for any poet-novelist. The author has not answered any large questions here, but he has succeeded to a remarkable degree in explaining how two such distinctly opposed attitudes can inhabit and activate human beings.

Mr. Prokosch's lushness of style has disturbed readers of his novels—as it used to worry readers of his poems; in the present work it has found a true home. The huge, lurid canvas of seventeenth-century India, perfectly suits his imagination and his talents. He is perhaps less good in depicting the people as they actually were: in Mr. E. M. Forster's terms, they will ultimately be seen as types, discs that vibrate rather than studies in depth. But this is not a true historical novel. It is an allegory of essentially Western conflicts put into an Indian setting, because such a setting is dramatically the most suitable for it. No real effort is made at verisimilitude, nor is much serious attempt made to delineate an Indian psychology: as the author writes in a prefatory note, "An ominous ambiguity hangs over the historical documents. . . .I have taken advantage of this ambiguity and have adapted certain episodes as well as certain settings to suit my own purposes".

If this method is historically questionable it is difficult to see why it is so in the art of fiction. The worst charge that could be made against Mr. Prokosch is one of "working up" his material in a somewhat vulgar manner—of merely using it to create an effect, and of intending nothing more serious. When a writer is as ornate and as technically skilled (for this can have its disadvantages) as he is, such charges are inevitable. It would be a pity, however, if this impressive novel—Mr. Prokosch's best by a long chalk—were ignored or belittled on such grounds. It possesses qualities beyond its great readability and the fascination of its colourful subject.

"India Cover," in The Times Literary Supplement, *No. 3290, March 18, 1965, p. 209.*

PAUL WEST

Alternating between the sick, haunted Byron dying at Missolonghi in Greece and the recollected exploits of the poet who became famous overnight, [*The Missolonghi Manuscript*] is meant to fill some kind of gullibility gap. Ostensibly presented by one T. H. Applebee of Bryn Mawr College, Pa., who wrote a dissertation on Byron at the University of Kansas (!), it doesn't quite square with Byron's habitual ways of spelling and punctuating. T. H. Applebee concedes this ("The thing, of course, may be a forgery"), preferring, however, the notion that "the tight and almost 'modern' phraseology of some of these passages is not so much in conflict with the poet's earlier style as in a subtle and self-developing harmony."

Feeble as the spoof is, it enables Prokosch to vent his embarrassment at having undertaken such a feat of mnemonic possession. Yet need he, after all, be embarrassed or coy at sentencing himself to such an arduous impersonation? The answer has to be, yes: unless he does the one thing we have every right to expect *The Missolonghi Manuscript* to do better than all the biographies, psychoanalytical and critical studies, rolled into one: better, even, than Byron himself does in the brilliant erratic letters and journals we do have. And that is to make Byron—given this chance—explain himself Byronically, see himself whole; or, maybe even more bewitchingly, to show him in the act of trying to do so but failing. Either way, a definitive self-scrutiny by Byron in the first dismal months of 1824, the 36th and last year of his life, would be useful. We could then, on no matter how hypothetical a basis, give up guessing and settle down to read his writings with a new sense of illumination.

But alas, unwilling to stretch his presumption to the limit, Prokosch gives us mostly a repeat of what anyone who's read a biography or two, and dipped into the letters and journals, knows already. I'm not saying he should have concocted "new" data (e.g., Byron suffered lifelong with shingles. Byron ate the clippings from his own toenails. Byron was really Shelly). Prokosch is too scrupulous for that. I'm asking who, if he's got Byron, needs Prokosch? (pp. 1, 3)

Here and there, it is only fair to say, Prokosch does amplify and extend, retrench and imagine. I just feel that, after reading this insufficiently bold exercise, I've not found out about Byron much that I didn't know, whereas I have found a suave, earthy prose virtuoso imposing on Byron an erotic witness which is vividly his own. For the book abounds in curiosa phallic, vaginal, labial, spermatical, pederastical, sodomitical, menstrual, masturbational, fetishistical, fellational, gonoccoccal, but never—unless I've misread the bit about the cheetah—bestial. In short, it's an unashamedly fun book in which Prokosch enjoys his obsession with Byron's obsession. . . .

Apart from Byron in pre-rut, rut, and repining in the sulk of post-rut, Prokosch-Byron gives us a thorough look at Byron as cripple, talker, swimmer, host, dieter, father, connoisseur of curious customs, proprietor of a menagerie, military com-

mander and crypto-Christian. His mind teems with exotic people both ordinary and eminent: but, transcending both the recollected circus of British, European and Near Eastern society and the anti-climactic muddles of Missolonghi, there come numbing hallucinations in which specks in paper turn into tiny orangoutans and heaps of laundry into huge hairy toads. Stark and utterly congruous, these hallucinations—and the distress of mind they evince and aggravate—should have dominated the book. As it is, they appear as mere phantasmagorical items almost lost among the routine recollections. How odd that Prokosch, who has Byron confess a preference for "the strange, the enigmatic, the bizarre, even the repulsive," should have so relentlessly trapped him in the familiar and the commonplace. Even odder, the book tells us less of the processes of Byron's imagination than do things as incidental and as little read as Byron's notes to his own poems. Mr. Prokosch has missed his chance here, I'm afraid: and that's a double pity because he is one of the few writers who could have done concise justice to Byron's last delirium. (p. 3)

Paul West, "A Ghost for Lord Byron," in Book World—The Washington Post, *January 14, 1968, pp. 1, 3.*

EDMUND FULLER

The Missolonghi Manuscript is a novel based on a long study of Byron, cast boldly in the form of three notebooks, supposedly found after his death at Missolonghi, in Greece. Between Jan. 25 and April 18, 1824, the entries take the form of brief comments on the events of the moment, followed by long passages of reflection and recollection ranging across Byron's whole life.

Mr. Prokosch brings off this tour de force with skill and power. . . .

People of Byron's own time, and the Victorians after him, were shocked and titillated by his career. None would have been prepared for some of Mr. Prokosch's pictures of the poet. This supposed intimate journal is sexually explicit often to the point of grossness. Byron is seen as bisexual; someone in the book calls him "amphibious, or 'Janus-headed'." Physical and emotional encounters of varied sorts with both men and women are presented.

"Taste" is not a word of any weight in criticism today. Some of this book will be distasteful to many readers who would like its other aspects. In spite of the changed standards of what is acceptable in print, one can raise a subtle question of propriety here. A writer may attribute any words, thoughts and actions to a character in fiction today. Is it altogether the same to make unrestrained use of this freedom in attributing words, thoughts, and actions to characters who actually lived and about whom they cannot be proved? Is it not, morally, a form of unredressable libel?

This is our reservation about the book—a frankly personal reaction. What Mr. Prokosch presents does not clash with the possibilities, considering what is known of Byron and his associates. Some of this material is justifiable and plausible. Yet we think it becomes excessive, overly insistent, intrusive.

This must not distract from the rest of the achievement, which is impressive and rewarding. The book creates an extraordinary illusion of being Byron from the inside. It is stylistically, intellectually, esthetically and temperamentally persuasive as an interpretation of Byron and his time. . . .

There are splendid discussions of poetry, including penetrating remarks on Shakespeare, especially in conversations with Shelley. The scene of the cremation on an Italian beach of the decaying body of the drowned Shelley is powerfully macabre. . . .

The 1824 Byron at Missolonghi—36-years-old—is waiting for death, which he comes slowly to realize, in the midst of his quixotic involvement with the cause of Greek freedom. In his rapid physical deterioration he has waking hallucinations of a nightmarish sort, some of them being embodiments of evil. He comes to doubt the truth of his memories, as of his present senses. Alone, fighting the self-pity he abhors, he sees himself as "wrong, wrong from the beginning. In everything I thought, in everything I felt." There are subtle inferences, too, that Byron's 1824 is not unlike today.

On the whole, it is a memorable evocation of the image Byron flaunted, "the profligate poet, the notorious *debauche.*" . . .

"My own life has been full of ugly things and full of beautiful ones," Byron writes at the end. That is what Prokosch establishes; it is the reason for what may be the book's excesses. To capture the interior life of genius is difficult. Mr. Prokosch has succeeded at it, dramatically.

> Edmund Fuller, "The Bookshelf: Byron Caught in Fictional Journals," in Wall Street Journal, *January 22, 1968, p. 10.*

THE TIMES LITERARY SUPPLEMENT

[Frederic Prokosch's *America, My Wilderness*] although thoroughly and perhaps surprisingly "modern" in its achievements, reveals many of the best characteristics of his earlier writing. The same cosmopolitan range of interest and influence, the exotic and individual atmosphere, and the theme of loss and exile, are found in his story of a search for the "secret" magical America.

Poncho Krauss, the half-breed orphan hero, travels through America attempting to find a solution to its puzzles and contradictions by turning himself into a passive object, a person who is attacked and raped by men and women, and who witnesses the beauty and grotesqueness of a land which is always "too savage and kaleidoscopic, too vast and elusive and ambiguous to grasp." Within the kaleidoscope, scenes of vicious mutilation, murder and perversity are contrasted with passages of great beauty and tranquillity describing the vivid landscape of this magical country. Mr Prokosch has the rare ability of being able to portray nature without resorting to the tired epithets and limp clichés which generally mark such attempts. In his hands language has a freshness and vitality which reflect the objects he describes, while the newness and purity of this vision only accentuates how irretrievable and lost it is. For Pancho's picaresque adventures and his vision of a sequestered and unrecognized America, a search for the vanished "fresh, green breast of the new world", only lead him to dreams of annihilation.

The loosely episodic, almost inconsequentially linked, structure of the novel turns suddenly in the final chapters into a searing recognition of the waste and violence bred in America. The bright, glittering land of fertile magic and ambiguity which Mr Prokosch creates earlier shatters with the final perception of it as "a nightmare of the unidentifiable, its face covered with clouds and its heart soaked in darkness". America becomes like one of the novel's major figures, a variant Pro-

metheus "chained to a dying body but his soul was like an eagle's"; practising an equivocal magic which mixes the inexplicable and weird with sheer chicanery, combining gratuitous violence with real freedom, finally triumphant though suffering, "too ambiguous to grasp" yet delineated by Mr Prokosch with some skill.

> "American Ambiguities," in The Times Literary Supplement, *No. 3684, October 13, 1972, p. 1235.*

JONATHAN YARDLEY

Though Prokosch would like us to believe that *Voices* is a record of "the essence of other men's lives" and "the echoes of other men's secrets," it is in point of fact an example of that distasteful species of memoir in which anecdotes about the great and near-great are designed to inflate the importance of the memoirist himself, as he basks in their reflected glory. The names drop like flies. . . .

It is a book that begins with promise and charm, as Prokosch recalls his boyhood as the son of cultivated Austrian immigrants to the United States, but rapidly declines into gossipy sighs and twitters. . . .

[The] chatter of all these "voices" is exhausting, especially once it becomes clear that the real purpose of the noise is not to recall Auden and Frost and Forster and Santayana but to celebrate Frederick Prokosch—to get it onto the public record that Lady Cunard thought him "clever" and that Bernard Berenson found him "positively Jamesian." It's a pity that this memoir is so relentlessly self-flattering, for Prokosch is a graceful if mannered stylist and occasionally he catches his quarry in telling, characteristic moments. If one is willing to accept the fundamental premise that these are faithful transcriptions of the words of others, as opposed to embellishments or inventions by the author, then from time to time we glimpse what looks like truth; Thomas Wolfe thundering that "I want to be a Niagara, not a dainty little trickle," for example, or Dame Edith Sitwell complaining of Alexander Pope: "His versification was nimble but he was a horrid little man." . . .

But there are too few such moments to be found in all the clucking of *Voices*. It's a book that means to charm but only repels.

> Jonathan Yardley, "Frederick Prokosch: Eavesdropping and Name Dropping," in Book World— The Washington Post, *April 24, 1983, p. 3.*

PEARL K. BELL

Frederick Prokosch has now written a sort of autobiography called *Voices,* and one turns to it in the hope of unravelling the puzzle of fame and indifference. Perhaps the most touching thing about the memoir is its total lack of bitterness or rancour about his displacement in the literary firmament. Indeed, he alludes to the unpredictability of literary glory only once, and with such subtle indirection that the point is easily missed. . . . There are not many writers who would so serenely forego the chance to brood on the fickleness of fame. Instead, Prokosch has chosen to recollect his life mainly as a series of encounters with the great writers and artists he has known (and at times pursued with rather endearing audacity) and the beautifully wrought nuggets of philosophy, critical judgment, whimsy, malice, pretension and terror they were unfailingly willing to pour, with scarcely any prompting, into the ears of this attentive listener. Not a word, it would seem, has been forgotten; as he remarks at one point, ''I suffer from a malady which is called 'total recall.'''

A zealous traveller, he has been everywhere and known everyone. In adolescence he was privy to the lofty pontifications of Thomas Mann and the polyglot arabesques of Pavlova: they were friends of his father, an eminent philologist, and his mother, a concert pianist. On a visit to Paris during his college years, he did not hesitate to go round to the Rue de Fleurus and ''pay an idolatrous visit'' to Miss Stein and Miss Toklas, who treated him to tea and quirky judgments. On his way to a squash match in Hartford, young Prokosch naturally dropped in on Wallace Stevens at his insurance office, and he has remembered every golden word.

At times Prokosch's unerring ability to divine the presence of the great and the near-great in unexpected places can strain credulity, and one begins to feel a strong craving for the noncelebrity, the obscure. He has only to swim out to a volcanic isle of Capri, and the next voice he hears is Alberto Moravia's, grandly dismissing Hemingway. Who should sit down next to Prokosch on the terrace of a Venetian hotel but Marc Chagall, helpfully full of ''old Hebraic cunning . . . and old Hebraic sorrow''? But if these fortuitous encounters, yielding such a constant harvest of articulate wisdom, after a while seem too worshipful, and less remembered than made up, other voices provide moments of brilliantly sly comedy. . . .

The portrait of Auden, who keeps turning up in these pages like a decaying spectre, is on the whole so devastating that one would suspect some spiteful malice behind it were Prokosch not the generous and compassionate man, altogether free of vengeful emotion, that he reveals himself to be in this memoir. Prokosch revered Auden the poet, pitied ''that self-induced and self-perpetuating Auden unhappiness'', deplored his inhuman arrogance, and tolerated his sadistic mockery with near-masochistic placidity. But as he recounts the gradual disintegration of the man in his later years, ''almost regal in his massive, drunken misery'', it is difficult not to share the sorrow he felt for his one-time hero. The Auden here remembered is unbearable, though it is not at all clear that Prokosch intended the portrait to be this harsh.

It *is* clear, however, that Prokosch has attempted to do more with this autobiography than just render the sound and sense (and nonsense) of remembered voices. Though he reveals nothing about his private life, he is devoted to the kind of abstraction that is supposed to convey a sense of artistic purpose larger and grander than the mundane detail of actuality—though it is precisely such detail that makes his portraits of others so lively. . . . In *Voices,* to his credit, Prokosch has not let himself be sucked into such mystic waters: when a writer abandons the real for the oceanic, he often drowns.

Pearl K. Bell, ''In the Presence of the Great,'' in The Times Literary Supplement, *No. 4212, December 23, 1983, p. 1420.*

Ruth Rendell

1930-

(Also writes under pseudonym of Barbara Vine) English novelist and short story writer.

One of England's most popular and respected mystery writers, Rendell has earned critical acclaim for her complex characterizations and plots and her keen depiction of the criminal mind. She is probably best known for her series of novels featuring Scotland Yard Chief Inspector Reginald Wexford and his assistant, Mike Burden. With Burden, Wexford solves homicide cases by uncovering emotions and motives in his suspects that are overlooked by other detectives. Both characters were introduced in Rendell's first novel, *From Doon with Death* (1964), and have developed and matured in subsequent installments of the Wexford series. Rendell's accounts of the private lives of Wexford and Burden are regarded by many critics as refreshing and entertaining subplots and also serve to counterpoint the mayhem and squalor the characters encounter in their profession. Rendell's recent novels in the Wexford series include *Speaker of Mandarin* (1983) and *An Unkindness of Ravens* (1985).The first book revolves around Wexford's journey to China and his subsequent investigation of the murder of a member of his tour group. In the second book, a slain traveling salesman is discovered by Wexford to have led a double life with nearly identical families. John Gross deemed *An Unkindness of Ravens* "as exciting as anything Ruth Rendell has written, and it shows all her usual mastery of contemporary middle-class folkways."

Rendell has also earned critical acclaim for her works outside the conventional mystery genre. In the psychological thriller *A Demon in My View* (1976), she combines elements of the crime novel with insightful studies of abnormal behavior. This book portrays a mentally disturbed man who "strangles" store mannequins in order to repress his homicidal tendencies. *The Killing Doll* (1984) focuses upon a young man and his disfigured sister whose involvement in occultism brings tragedy to their neighborhood. In *The Tree of Hands* (1984), a chain of terror erupts in the lives of two families when an insane woman kidnaps a child to take the place of her dead grandson. *Live Flesh* (1986) details a bizarre relationship which develops between a convicted rapist and a police officer whom the rapist shot and paralyzed. Joan Smith described *Live Flesh* as "a frightening, resonant novel—an extraordinary achievement." *Heartstones* (1987) resembles *The Killing Doll* in its tale of the occult, while espionage and children's games are cataclysmic elements in *Talking to Strange Men* (1987).

Writing under the pseudonym Barbara Vine, Rendell won the Edgar Allan Poe Award for best novel for *A Dark-Adapted Eye* (1986). In an interview, Rendell explained why she assumed the name Barbara Vine: "I had the idea for the book for a long time, but I never saw myself writing it as Ruth Rendell because it wasn't a Ruth Rendell novel at all." Set in post-World War II England, this novel details events leading to the murder of a woman by her sister. Another novel written as Vine, *A Fatal Inversion* (1987), examines how a murder that was committed in the past affects the present. Anita Brookner commented: "[With] the creation of Barbara Vine [Rendell] reveals that

she is remarkable for being two people. Barbara Vine is a more voluminous writer than Ruth Rendell and a colder one."

Rendell is also an accomplished short story writer. Her first collection, *The Fallen Curtain and Other Stories* (1976), which combines elements of police procedurals and psychological thrillers, won an Edgar Allan Poe Award. *The Fever Tree and Other Stories* (1982) details broken relationships and attempted crimes, while *The New Girl Friend and Other Stories* (1986) explores the dark side of human nature and depicts ordinary people entangled in unusual circumstances.

(See also *CLC*, Vol. 28 and *Contemporary Authors*, Vol. 109.)

JULIAN SYMONS

Ruth Rendell provides the best possible documentary proof of the crime story's dramatic change in the past quarter of a century. She began in 1964 with *From Doon With Death*, a lively and intelligent example of what was still distinctly a Christie-style detective story. Twenty books and 17 years later she is still compared with Christie, and she does retain a liking for the stunning surprise in the last couple of pages, but the differences are much greater than the similarities.

Although her worldly-wise Chief Inspector Wexford and his puritanical sidekick Inspector Burden are stationed in the typical Home Counties town of Kingsmarkham, and often discuss a case over a pint, they are involved in affairs quite alien to Miss Marple or Hercule Poirot. Bodies are found brutally beaten, transvestism is not unknown, rancid family hatreds are common. Unlike Agatha Christie, Ruth Rendell offers no stereotypes. She is not even committed to Wexford and Burden, for almost half of her books are not detective stories at all, but studies of obsessed people whose fantasies and delusions end in violence. . . .

Ruth Rendell's characteristic crime is set in exurbia, sometimes prosperous and sometimes seedy but always commonplace, or in run-down squalid bits of London. She catches the style, the tone, the smell, of people in such places with the feeling Chandler had for parts of California. . . .

It is the frustrations and absurdities of ordinary people that Ruth Rendell notes like an uncensorious Recording Angel. She gives us a woman like a dummy, "realistic but not real, as if made of high-quality plastic", and as a final touch of artificiality adds green fingernails. . . . A man who keeps a life-size window model in his cellar and gets sexual pleasure from strangling her again and again, is shy of being seen to enter the cellar (*A Demon in My View*). These are books about crime and punishment, but also books about taboos and the compulsions by which they are broken.

The Wexford books are puzzles, and *A Sleeping Life, Shake Hands For Ever* and *Some Lie and Some Die* are particularly good, the later books showing an assurance that some earlier ones lack. Wexford himself is a strongly realised character, intelligent but no genius, loquacious, a bit literary, with the strength and weakness of being able to see almost any point of view. His subordinates are almost equally good, and Kingsmarkham is no timeless Christie village but a genuine bustling small town. Wexford's interrogations of suspects and witnesses almost always sound true, and the best of the shock endings are real surprises.

The studies of psychological obsession are more variable. *A Demon in My View* comes off perfectly, with the chances by which the dummy-strangler moves between fantasy and reality carrying total conviction. *A Judgement in Stone,* which begins by telling us that four members of the well-to-do Coverdale family were slaughtered by two psychotic women, and then shows us how it happened, is powerful but a little too much like a textbook account of the criminal psychopath to succeed fully. . . .

[*The Lake of Darkness*] has an idea which gives full play for the Rendell sense of irony. Martin, a well-intentioned but slightly boring middle-class young man . . . wins £100,000 on the pools, and decides to give a lot of the money to individuals who would particularly benefit—a child who needs an operation, a young couple desperate for a house . . . The ironies are suitably exploited—an old man drops dead with shock on receiving his cheque, the young couple think they are being conned—but the book's real subject is Martin's disturbed awareness of a homosexual element in his passionate attachment to Francesca, a young woman whom at first sight he mistakes for a boy. We know that Martin is somehow being tricked, but in just what way is most adroitly concealed until three quarters of the way through the book. It has to be said that the explanation puts

some strain on our faculty for suspending disbelief, but the book contains several masterly portraits, like Martin's father, and the male cleaner of Martin's flat who is unremittingly prickly and sarcastic. Best of all, Martin is made credible as a man who is both good and stupid.

The distinction between Wexford and non-Wexford, puzzle and psychological sex-grill (an accurate word, even though there are no explicit sexual descriptive passages), is not so great as the writer herself may think. The Wexford books often contain studies in criminal psychology, the non-Wexfords can tantalise and baffle. Either way, there is no English crime writer who is so sharply observant of her chosen suburban and exurban world as Ruth Rendell.

Julian Symons, "Paperback Writer," in The Sunday Times, *London, April 12, 1981, p. 81.*

T. J. BINYON

[*The Fever Tree and Other Stories* contains eleven] beautifully written and subtly imagined stories of crimes or attempted crimes. Ruth Rendell charts with artful skill, in the space of a few pages, acquaintance, love, marriage, its breakdown, and murder in "A Needle for the Devil"—a story reminiscent of that divorce case mentioned by Sherlock Holmes, in which the conduct complained of was that the husband "had drifted into the habit of winding up every meal by taking out his false teeth and hurling them at his wife." "The Fever Tree", "A Glowing Future", "A Case of Coincidence" and "Front Seat" also concern themselves with the collapse and disintegration of a marital or extramarital relationship. The microscopic examination of mental fatigue in bonds of this kind is Ruth Rendell's forte, and her stance is objective throughout. . . . [There is] a fascinating treatment of adolescent genius in "Thornapple", and a gruesome account of sibling rivalry, "May and June"; while perhaps the best story of the lot is the ultra-short "The Dreadful Day of Judgement": no crime, just four workmen cleaning up the municipal cemetery together. All in all, a collection to remember.

T. J. Binyon, in a review of "The Fever Tree and Other Stories," in The Times Literary Supplement, *No. 4158, December 10, 1982, p. 1378.*

ROBERT BARNARD

The two foremost practitioners of the traditional detective story today are P. D. James and Ruth Rendell, and it is natural that, when the mantle started slipping from the Christie generation of crime writers and wrapped itself around these two, critics should attempt to define their place in the crime tradition by reference to their predecessors.

P. D. James seemed easy: most critics agreed in labeling her the successor to Sayers. . . . Is Ruth Rendell, then, the natural heir of Agatha Christie? Certainly her novels are meticulously plotted—carefully-worked-out successions of developments that leave nothing to chance. She has, too, a fine eye for the deceptive potential of everyday things, and an instinctive understanding of the reader's inbred assumptions that lead him to jump to predictable conclusions. But Ruth Rendell would not, I think, like the comparison: she has commented on Christie's cardboard characters and the remoteness of her novels from any recognizable social reality. A Ruth Rendell novel is firmly rooted in contemporary life, instinctively reflects current modes of thinking and behavior.

Margery Allingham, then? Rendell certainly admires Allingham, and there are many points of likeness—notably the contemporaneity, the use of characters that can verge on the grotesque, the fascination with evil or perversity. Allingham's gaiety and high spirits, however, are foreign to Rendell, whose sense of humor is blacker, and mostly finds expression in odd conjunctures of personality, or bleak ironies of circumstance. Perhaps, in the long run, we will find these backward comparisons more misleading than helpful, for most of the older generation created an artificial world whose relation to the real one was at best tangential, whereas both Rendell and James bring to popular crime fiction minds that are nourished and nurtured by the social realities of Britain today.

Roughly half of Ruth Rendell's novels are written around the series figures of Chief Inspector Wexford and his deputy Burden; the others center around a crime or a criminal (these are what an American reviewer has called her "chiller-killer" books, which certainly sums up perfectly three or four of her best titles in this mode).... It is important to emphasize, though, that Ruth Rendell has, more than anyone else writing in the field today, the storyteller's gift, without which one is lost in a popular genre. All the Wexford stories are compulsively readable, they are well plotted, ingenious, and fast. Many readers wedded to the traditional type of English mystery will prefer these, and—as a bonus—they will get a sharp and convincing picture of life in the English provinces today.

Undeniably, though, they are less original than the others. The writers of the Golden Age left a highly problematic legacy to their successors. Wexford and Burden are obviously figures in the tradition of the series detective: Wexford is elderly, cranky, a devoted family man, whose tolerance of other people's habits and vagaries (particularly their sexual habits and vagaries) is contrasted with the buttoned-up puritanism of his younger assistant.These are constant features, at least in the later novels.... (p. 146)

The trouble is that, with Rendell's more realistic style of novel, this becomes just a little dull. The Golden Age detectives—Wimsey, Poirot, Campion—have a certain wild panache about them that makes one overlook the thinness of the characterisation and the predictability of their reactions. They are not characters but collections of habits, attitudes, and identifying marks. This is not a criticism of them: they fit perfectly into the world, so stylized and remote from reality, that the Golden Age writers create. But puppets fit less easily into Ruth Rendell's world. She puts into the whodunit convention about as much reality as it will take—the realities of class, the realities of sex, in Britain today—and the element of the automaton in Wexford and Burden consorts uneasily with this. (pp. 146-47)

There is one other drawback to the Wexford novels, and that is the dreaded quotation habit.... Rendell is less prone to this than P. D. James, much less prone than Amanda Cross, who has such a hideous facility in this black art as to render her books virtually unreadable. Still, the habit is irritating, and it invades her titles, which are all too often unmemorable quotes with little or no relevance to the books.... (p. 147)

There is at least one exception to the relative inferiority (only relative, I hasten to emphasize) of the Wexford novels, and it illuminates what leaves one dissatisfied in the other novels. In No More Dying Then, the story centers around the kidnapping of a little boy. Wexford figures comparatively little, and the action is mainly taken up with the distraught mother——a tender, tolerant, slapdash ex-actress—and the affair she has with Inspector Burden, who has recently lost his wife. Burden is revealed as a man of overwhelming, and now repressed, sexuality, and the conflict between his puritan principles and the needs he eventually comes to satisfy with the boy's mother is impressively done. Burden comes over as tormented, passionate, not particularly likeable, but intensely real. But though there are clear enough points of contact between this Burden and the Burden of the other novels, here he is done with a depth and intensity that take him into quite another area of artistic creation. It is significant that we have never, in the earlier novels, suspected that he is a man of such strong sensuality; and though, in the later novels, occasional bows are made to his new tolerance, in essence he reverts to type and becomes the predictable figure he has always been. Under cover of being a Wexford novel, No More Dying Then is really one much closer to her others, to the books which penetrate to an altogether deeper level of psychological insight.

The label "chiller-killer" which has been attached to Rendell's non-Wexford novels is really apt for only four of them, though most of these are among her very best: A Demon in My View, for example, concerns a repressed bachelor who satisfies his sexual urges with a tailor's dummy, until it is removed from the basement where he keeps it and he finds other and more deadly outlets. The recent Master of the Moor, a brilliant and haunting work, also concerns a lonely and inverted man who eventually becomes a woman-killer. Studies of a criminal or misfit occur in many of the others—the weird young man, Finn, in The Lake of Darkness, for instance—but the central interest is usually the crime itself, with the meticulous chronicling of how a certain series of events and conjunctures of personalities lead to a certain conclusion (usually, of course, disaster). (pp. 147-48)

The Face of Trespass is a particularly fine example of this kind of plot, because while the isolated young man, living a bare, hermit-like existence, is being set up as a fall guy by his ex-girlfriend, we are in ignorance of this until the end: each event, insignificant in itself, has to be endowed with interest, even though the reader only later realizes the spider's-web effect each of them has had. It is a stunning example of Rendell's plotting ability. If the novels ever falter, it is because one piece in the structure fails to convince: I can never accept, in The Lake of Darkness, that the young man who wins a small fortune on the football pools would fail to inform the friend who has filled in the form for him—and if the reader is not convinced of that, the structure built on it seems perpetually out of true. Christie, dealing with lightly sketched characters, can make them do what the plot demands. With Rendell's more subtly sketched people, character and plot have to mesh totally.

Though these are far from being whodunits, surprise of one sort or another has a part to play in most of them. But in the book which . . . has claims to be her masterpiece, surprise has no place at all. On the very first page of A Judgment in Stone, we are told what is to happen: "Eunice Parchmain killed the Coverdale family because she could not read or write."... The appeal of this book, then, is far removed from that of a whodunit. Nor has it much in common with the howdunit.... Perhaps the best characterisation we can give of this book is that it is a whydunit—a "how-did-it-come-about" story. (pp. 148-49)

Eunice Parchmain is a middle-aged woman, a spinster, from an unattractive working-class London suburb. She has spent her life nursing her invalid (or deliberately idle) parents, and, due to having shifted schools during the war, and because of her own secretive nature which has prevented her doing anything about it, she has grown up unable to read or write. She lives cut off, in a passive, self-satisfied darkness, gaining obscure pleasure from attempts at amateur blackmail. After the death of her father, whom she has killed, quite casually, it seems, she takes a job with the Coverdales. The Coverdales are four. George and Jacqueline, the parents, have both been married before, and are still very much in love. George owns a factory, but he enjoys playing Lord of the Manor from his substantial and beautiful house. Jacqueline is good-looking, chic, and hardworking, very conscious of her elegance. George's daughter Melinda is at University, going through a phase of mild revolution. Jacqueline's son [Giles] is still at school, an inveterate reader, spotty, dreaming, romantic, almost entirely cut off from the family, to whom he occasionally grunts. (p. 149)

The elder Coverdales are, in fact, play-acting social roles which are things of the past but which give them subtle, guilty pleasure. . . .

All this, and much more, offers us in the course of reading an easy escape route: we can take refuge in instant social criticism, we can adopt an attitude something akin to: "Eunice Parchmain killed the Coverdale family because they were snobs and she was a lonely, deprived, snubbed working-class woman." But as soon as we consider such a position objectively, it immediately is shown to be impossible as an explanation. Not only do we have Ruth Rendell's explicit statements at the beginning, but we also know that, apparently on a random impulse, Eunice has smothered her father. That, for sure, cannot be seen as an engagement in the class war.

For the thing about the Coverdales that brings about their end is not their arrogance (their modern version of old class arrogance), nor their off-hand treatment of Eunice, their ignoring of her as a personality unless something about her absolutely shrieks for their attention. Eunice would have been only too happy to have been ignored for all eternity, safe in front of her television set, watching her American police series. What dooms the Coverdales is that they are a very literate family. Books and writing are in their life blood. . . . It would not have occurred to them for a moment that their servant could not read, and feared to have it known.

Eunice's illiteracy cuts her off in a dumb, heavy, solitary state of darkness. Or is that the wrong way around? We are at least at liberty to believe that Eunice does not *fail* to learn to read as a girl: that subconsciously she *refuses* to, because to read is to become part of the community of men and women of which most people wish to become a part. And Eunice does not want to become part of that community. Her doings with other men and women almost invariably involve an attempt to get some sort of dominance over them. The small-scale blackmailing business she has run in her grimy London suburb seems to involve the only sort of relationship she can understand: mastery allied with contempt. But, mostly, all she asks is to be left in her own dark, dank cocoon.

In this respect, it is the democratic instincts of Melinda, the daughter, which are more deadly than any of the snobberies of George or Jacqueline. True, Melinda's democratic instincts do not go deep. . . . But just now and then she does make the effort to get through to Eunice. And, in spite of the superficiality of her ideas, Melinda does have a brightness, a generosity, an honesty, which shine bright—and threaten to light up the darkness in which Eunice comfortably lives. It is the

cut-offness of Eunice that gives her her coolness, her chill, her forbiddingness. (p. 150)

I said this is a chiller-killer plot, none more chilling. But the book centers around not one murderess but two. Without Joan Smith, Eunice would probably have come and eventually gone without blood on her hands. Joan Smith, after a conventional childhood in which she even showed considerable talent, has had years as a low-class prostitute in Shepherd's Bush, and eventually acquired her meek, helpless husband Norman. She has given up her trade when she acquires an even better stimulus: way-out religion. . . . It is when her husband, driven from his meekness by her supremely aggravating taunts, gives her a mild blow that Joan is driven over the edge into madness.

As the climax approaches, we never get, nor are meant to get, a feeling of inevitability. What we feel is a tension between knowledge and hopeless hope. Even as the Coverdales sit watching the televised *Don Giovanni* in the living room and Eunice and the quite demented Joan Smith pick up the guns from the gun room, it is still on the cards that they will, as they say, only "frighten them." This St. Valentine's Day massacre seems quite as unpremeditated as Eunice's murder of her father. The horrible thing is that this is *not* predestined: it is random, fortuitous, unpredictable. In some of her books, we do see the catastrophe as inescapable, looming ahead. This also looms ahead, but only because we have been told about it. Throughout the book we are told of the many, many occasions when, if someone had acted differently, it would never have taken place. . . . At the beginning of the book, the future is a wide-open road, with side roads leading off to all sorts of possibilities and happy endings. The fascination of the book is to see one after another closed off, as quite harmless and understandable decisions are taken, until only one black road is open: the spectacle of the two demented women bursting into the sitting room and spraying the family with shot.

The book, then, is chilling as well as gripping. There is no possibility of that "cosy read" which many readers claim to get from the English style of crime story. Not that the characters are all "mean"—insignificant in their shabbiness, as is the case in *One Across, Two Down*. Even the elders in the family have fine and generous impulses underneath their snobbery, and the younger generation are positively attractive. It is significant that Giles, who is perpetually buried in a book, or dreaming fantasies of a Byronic, incestuous affair with Melinda, or entering a monastery, is as nearly cut off from the human community as Eunice—a fine ironic touch. (pp. 151-52)

It is a terrible book, but not a horrible one. In its depth of psychological insight, its range of social observation, it takes the crime novel several steps toward the novel proper. It is the compelling plotting, the irresistible storytelling knack, that ensures that it remains within the genre. Dorothy Sayers's argument that the crime story is closely related to tragedy is relevant here, for at the end we do feel something of that purging through pity and terror which is at the heart of tragedy. As in *Macbeth,* there is at the center of this story a character who has free will, one who is not driven by circumstances to evil, but who chooses it. The particular horror of this book is that the choice, when made, seems such a random one—almost, it might be said, a frivolous one.

Ruth Rendell's, then, are unusual crime books for our time. One hesitates to say that she is a pathfinder, a pioneer of new ways. Most of the permutations of popular literary forms have already been tried, and Ruth Rendell does nothing that Dickens, for example, had not aimed to do in *Edwin Drood*. . . . One will only say that Ruth Rendell has a mind unusually attuned to the odd, the menacing, the abnormal; that she seizes on the contemporary forms these assume, and turns them into something unnerving yet oddly satisfying. Like all good crime writers she keeps you turning the pages in bed at night, but Rendell's books are ones that seldom send you happily off to sleep. She has, more than anyone writing today, a talent to disturb. (p. 152)

> Robert Barnard, "A Talent to Disturb," in The Armchair Detective, *Vol. 16, No. 2, Spring, 1983, pp. 146-52.*

MARGARET CANNON

[*The Speaker of Mandarin*] is the 12th in Rendell's series, and there is ample evidence that the author is growing bored. After attending a conference in China, Wexford takes a tour and meets up with the regulars of pulp fiction: the lecher, the drunk and the cynic. Rendell indulges in considerable warbling about Cathay, quotes Li Po's poetry and gives several graphic and technical descriptions of foot-binding. The China trip ends, Wexford returns to Kingsmarkham and is soon investigating the murder of one of the tour members. This coincidental and boring tale is unworthy of Rendell, one of the best of the current British crime writers. The most charitable thing to be said about *Mandarin* is that Rendell must have wanted to write a travelogue.

> Margaret Cannon, "Escaping into Summer," in Maclean's Magazine, *Vol. 96, No. 25, June 20, 1983, pp. 49-50, 52.*

NEWGATE CALLENDAR

There aren't many writers like Ruth Rendell who are highly prolific and yet manage to maintain a consistently high standard. Prolific writers are apt to fall way out, using dialogue that sounds automatic or reflexive rather than really thought through. But Miss Rendell has managed to make most of her books into a fresh experience, even when writing about a series character, such as her Inspector Wexford.

The latest Wexford is *Speaker of Mandarin*. This veteran cop is an unusual man. Well read, he seems at home with Samuel Johnson, Jane Austen, the British poets and anything else that his remarkable memory has ever encountered. He takes this as a matter of course and is mildly surprised that others do not have equal abilities. He is a bulldog on a case but, unlike other cops in his department, does not see everything in black and white. The man has compassion and is content to take people as they are.

Speaker of Mandarin starts in China. Wexford has been sent there on official business and then takes several weeks of vacation time on a tour with a group of compatriots. Some peculiar, even inexplicable, things happen. Wexford wonders if he suddenly has become subject to hallucinations. There also is the death of a young Chinese man, and Wexford wonders about that too; but because he is on vacation and has no official standing in the country, he looks the other way. Miss Rendell (who, one suspects, has made her own visit to the East) has some quiet fun about China in the first part of the book, and her characterization of Wexford's officious guide has its penetrating as well as amusing moments. . . .

Back in England, Wexford broods about his hallucinations and broods even more when a woman who had been on the China trip is murdered. Now Miss Rendell starts writing a proper mystery novel, and an ingenious one it turns out to be. Now you see it, now you don't. Miss Rendell is a plot prestidigitator who has mastered all the tricks of her trade. Including writing.

> Newgate Callendar, in a review of "Speaker of Mandarin," in The New York Times Book Review, *January 29, 1984, p. 17.*

PATRICIA CRAIG

When she isn't writing plain detective fiction, with efficient Inspector Wexford to lay the wrongdoers by the heels, Ruth Rendell specializes in psychotic goings-on in the ill-appointed bedsitters and drab family homes of the inner London suburbs. Her latest novel, of this type [*The Killing Doll*] starts with a memorable piece of hocus-pocus: Pup (Peter), fifteen, whose mother is dying, and whose sister Dolly (Doreen) has a blemish in the form of a naevus on her cheek, sells his soul to the devil in a makeshift ceremony diffidently performed in the sodden tunnel of a disused railway near his home. To Pup, this action is more a joke than anything else, though it's the prelude to an enthusiasm for the occult, which briefly adds interest to his life, before going the way of commoner adolescent obsessions like football or stamp-collecting. It's a matter of greater import to Dolly, who needs to believe in her younger brother's powers; Dolly's increasing battiness leads her to fasten on the supernatural as a source of authority and hope. She starts attending séances, and soon produces a row of dolls—she's a dressmaker by profession—of which one at least is an effigy of an enemy. The usual business with pins ensues, but it isn't until Pup is persuaded to disembowel the doll that an outcome satisfactory to Dolly is effected. Myra, the couple's vulgar young stepmother, is found dead after an accident with a syringe.

The climax of Dolly's career as an exterminator, which began modestly enough with her neighbour's cat, is yet to come. In the meantime, her senses deranged by drink and brooding, she exhibits mannerisms peculiar to the sad and spinsterish, eventually manufacturing a couple of private spectres for herself, her mother and stepmother, who address her exactly as they did in life: "To be perfectly honest, you ought to do it, Doreen." The effect of this pair of comic chimeras is to lighten the atmosphere of seediness and degeneracy in which the characters, like all those devised by Ruth Rendell for a particular purpose, are located. The purpose is to construct a pattern out of converging neuroses, with a deadly occurrence at the point of impact. . . .

Ruth Rendell cannot be faulted in the area of technical ingenuity, and her assurance and boldness are equally remarkable. Her novels are clever and engrossing; however, there is something a little workaday and uneloquent about their narrative style, which hampers the production of a genuine *frisson*, and allows an opening for lurid feeling instead.

> Patricia Craig, "Exterminating Agents," in The Times Literary Supplement, *No. 4224, March 10, 1984, p. 287.*

CAROL KENNEDY

Neither detective story nor psychological thriller of the kind she has made peculiarly her own, Ruth Rendell's [novel *The Tree of Hands*] . . . deliberately sets out to enlarge her range by concentrating on character and the grey areas of behaviour into which it can lead, rather than following the powder-trail of psychopathic crime. The plot does turn on a crime—or the act of a disturbed mind—but the ripples that flow from it, engulfing a series of otherwise unconnected North London lives, are set moving by more sympathetic springs of motive than usually encountered in Rendell's chilling gallery of social and emotional outcasts. . . .

[What] links the principal characters in their chance drift to disaster is a gaping unfulfillment of love, a sense of intermittent hopelessness and deprivation of the affections. It leaps the social divide, from middle-class novelist Benet Archdale and her neurotic mother in bosky Hampstead to anxious young Barry and his older girl-friend Carol, a voraciously sexy single parent with an unruly brood in a bleak working-class estate in Tottenham, and it touches off a chain of fated happenings when a child is apparently kidnapped.

The tree of hands itself, a child's surreal painting in which the branches of a tree sprout upraised hands instead of leaves, symbolises the sad yearning most of the book's people are unable to cope with.

Love and fulfillment of a kind win through in an ending that is both bleak and a hopeful relief, like a winter dawn. The book may leave some Rendell fans mildly unsatisfied, the lack of a 'real' crime depriving it of the cutting edge of psychopathic motive and pursuit. But the narrative strength hooks you swiftly into its current, and not since Ernest Raymond has a writer so powerfully evoked the brooding presence of residential London and the shifting moods of its seasons.

> Carol Kennedy, in a review of "The Tree of Hands,"
> in Books and Bookmen, *No. 353, February, 1985,*
> *p. 33.*

DOUGLAS JOHNSON

We still have a Queen of Crime. For nearly twenty years Ruth Rendell has been hailed as the successor to Sayers, Christie, Marsh and Allingham, perpetuating the old question of why it is that there should be a particularly feminine talent for detective fiction. Her Chief Inspector, Wexford by name, has joined the ranks of legendary police heroes, and although he is Sussex-based he can occasionally, via a nephew, call upon the resources of Scotland Yard. . . .

As Hercule Poirot had waxed moustaches, Lord Peter Wimsey collected first editions and Nero Wolfe wore yellow pyjamas, so Wexford is the sort of man who is always badly dressed and is never certain of having a clean handkerchief. Like Appleby, he has a tendency to quote from literature, but the detective whom he most resembles is Maigret: an aging Maigret, worried about his health. We are repeatedly told what Wexford eats and drinks. . . . There is a Mrs Wexford who, like Madame Maigret, is silent and submissive and to whom Wexford is attached with undemonstrative sentimentality. Just as Maigret, on meeting a widower, reflects on his own good fortune in marriage (see *Maigret et l'Indicateur*), so Wexford, on meeting someone whose wife has been murdered, considers his own happier position (see **Shake hands with a murderer**). At times one wonders whether Ruth Rendell has consciously taken Simenon as a model—for example, when Wexford encounters the pompous solicitors and bank managers of the small towns where crimes have been committed or explores specific

areas of London in search of a murderer, or when he contemplates the weather with studied idleness.

Ruth Rendell has not, however, remained faithful to her successful creation. To the irritation of Wexford's followers, she has written several 'thrillers' that have nothing to do with detection but are concerned with the abnormalities of human behaviour, with madness, delusions, hatreds and obsession. If the ideal detective novel presents us with a world which has been thrown into confusion by a crime, usually a murder, the role of the detective in discovering the author of this act is to end the confusion and restore normality. There is often a final scene where the detective explains all, where the ends are tied together and where the intermezzo of the unusual is declared over. Although Ruth Rendell does not always go in for this studiously coherent ending, she is conscious of the need to keep a normal society going within the upheaval of a story which has begun with the discovery of a corpse. . . . A thriller, however, can have neither beginning nor ending, neither design nor pattern. Its horrors are everlasting, its evils are everywhere.

Ruth Rendell's last two novels are thrillers. In **The Killing Doll** the reader is only gradually made aware of the strangeness of its characters. It begins with the 16-year-old Peter (known as Pup) making a pact with the devil and becoming an ardent practitioner of magic. . . . He lives with his sister Doreen (known as Dolly), who is five years older, and by an oblique reference to a letter in a magazine, we learn that she suffers from a birthmark, or naevus, which disfigures her left cheek. . . . As the novel begins, the mother of these children is dying in hospital, but their father (who runs a typewriter business, as we are eventually told) cannot bring himself to visit her. He spends his time compulsively reading the lives of past royal figures. . . . As if this family did not by itself provide enough melancholy and oddness, we are introduced to an Irishman, Diarmit Bawne, who lives some streets away. . . . The victim of a Northern Irish bombing, he lives in a world of apprehension and is confused about his own identity.

The novel is about non-communication. Dolly hardly speaks to anyone. Pup speaks the ritual language of geomancy which no one can understand; later, when he has lost faith in magic, he invents a mumbo-jumbo with which to deceive his sister. Harold, the father, is invariably too busy reading to speak; later, when he remarries and brings the red-headed Myra into his house, he speaks in portmanteau phrases culled from BBC programmes. The isolated Bawne says as little as possible, even when he goes into a shop, since he does not believe that he really exists. . . . People sit by their windows watching what is going on, but are themselves apart from it, cut off, isolated. The chief symbol of non-communication is the disused railway line which lies at the back of these Late Victorian houses.

It is not clear why the characters behave as they do. . . . Pup, at Dolly's prompting, ritually stabs a doll that has been made to resemble Myra and Myra dies almost immediately afterwards. Dolly becomes convinced of her own magical powers and attempts to win the friendship of a woman by trying to kill the man with whom the woman's husband has established a homosexual relationship: but she makes a mistake—it is the husband whom she pushes under the tube at Hampstead station. In her despair, pursued by the voices of her dead mother and stepmother and haunted by a vision of the dog-god Antrobus, she wanders into the tunnel on the deserted railway line, where she is killed by the waiting Bawne.

In **The Tree of Hands** the successful novelist Benet lives by herself with her infant son James, having refused to marry, or to live with, his father Edward. When her mad mother, Mopsa, comes to stay with her, James is taken ill and dies in hospital. Mopsa then kidnaps Jason, another boy of the same age. We are introduced to Jason's family, where Barry lives with the nymphomaniac Carol, the child's mother. Barry is suspected of having murdered Jason. We are told that when Barry is with Carol sexually he loses himself in a manner that is mystical. A further sub-plot concerns Terence, who fakes the identity of a dead man in order to sell his ex-mistress's house. The novel revolves around these confusions of identity. . . .

In both novels there is violence, but there is no mystery, no detection, no discovery, no revelation and no explanation of behaviour. Because Ruth Rendell is a good writer, she succeeds in creating a certain amount of suspense and in bringing her plots together, but there is little drama in the fact that Bawne kills Dolly and that Benet becomes attached to Jason: these things have come to seem inevitable. The reader is not held in ignorance, no tricks are played, no dazzling displays of logic or of intuition conclude the stories. Nothing could be further from the detective novel than this form of thriller-writing, and one may wonder why Ruth Rendell has moved from the comfortable world of Kingsmarkham where Wexford always gets his man to the lonely, desperate, mist-shrouded world of the Dollys, the Bawnes, the Mopsas and the Benets.

Perhaps there is something logical in the move. Many of the detective novels already had some of the same characteristics as the thrillers. There was, for example, a similar preoccupation with identity. . . . The Wexford stories, like the thrillers, placed unthinkable events within an everyday context, explored confusions that revealed an apparently ordinary person to be abnormal. Both in the thrillers and in the detective novels, Ruth Rendell is meticulous in describing the details of everyday life, the food that is bought from the supermarket, the geography of buses and tubes around North London, the plants and flowers that surround the houses. The precise emphasis on the real and ordinary makes the eruption of the fantastic all the more terrible.

Ruth Rendell's switch from the classical detective story (even with those darker strains of mystery) to the thriller may illustrate some significant developments in the real world that fiction supposedly reflects. What we all wish to know is how Myra Hindley lived her life, surrounded by relatives, friends and colleagues who never suspected anything, or how Peter Sutcliffe went off to work and came home at night, without someone discerning the violence within him. The readers of detective fiction have never cared about morality, and they have rarely been moved by the characters presented to them. Like Wexford's assistant, Burden, who once said that he had never interrogated a single person whom he had liked, they are curious rather than involved. Why not then cut out all the stuff about Wexford and his daughters and his grandchildren and his remorse when he has spoken sharply to an underling? We no longer want to see dedicated policemen or eccentric amateur sleuths defending society. We want to be presented with the violence that lurks within the mundane, we want paranoia to be made plausible, we want to see those who are nourished on hatred, lives that are so suffused with boredom, pain and futility that they become unbearable. This is what Ruth Rendell has written about in her last two novels. It will be interesting to see whether she will return to the detective novel or whether she thinks it a genre that has now become moribund.

Douglas Johnson, "Come Back, Inspector Wexford," in London Review of Books, *Vol. 7, No. 4, March 7, 1985, p. 23.*

JOHN GROSS

[Ruth Rendell] once said that she had made Wexford a man (a thoroughly convincing man, incidentally) because she was still "caught up in the web that one writes about men because men are the people and we are the others," but in the latest Wexford book, *An Unkindness of Ravens,* women are very far from having a secondary role. It is a story where their preoccupations and frustrations are to the fore, and it plays unnervingly on tensions between the sexes.

One of Wexford's neighbors disappears. His wife asks the Inspector for advice, and she is unprepossessing and dandruffy enough for it to seem more than usually plausible that he has gone off with another woman—not that he sounds any great catch himself. It turns out, however, that he had been leading a much more complicated double life than Wexford initially suspected.

Meanwhile, there is a series of stabbings in the neighborhood, attacks on men by women whom they may or may not have been subjecting to unwanted attentions. It also emerges that large numbers of local schoolgirls have formed a red-hot feminist group, under the influence of an embittered physical education teacher who preaches total separatism: their suitably menacing symbol is a raven with the head of a woman. (According to Miss Rendell, an "unkindness" is the collective noun for ravens, as in a pride of lions, although here of course the term has darker overtones as well.)

It is hard to believe that there isn't some kind of link between the disappearance, the stabbings and the militant girls; but the skein of connection that Wexford eventually establishes doesn't fit into any neat, predictable formula. The climax of the story, like much that has gone before, is emotionally unsparing—indeed, my only real complaint against *An Unkindness of Ravens* is that there is something too acrid about it for what is after all basically a whodunit. Apart from that, it can hardly be faulted—it is as exciting as anything Ruth Rendell has written, and it shows all her usual mastery of contemporary middle-class folkways.

John Gross, in a review of "An Unkindness of Ravens," in The New York Times, *August 8, 1985, p. C30.*

PAUL STUEWE

[Ruth Rendell's *An Unkindness of Ravens*] offers her typical mix of realistically observed police work and complex criminal psychopathology, all nicely held together by the detailed social context of an English country town. Rendell is one of the post-Christie generation of writers responsible for transforming the traditional tale of armchair detection into the much more compelling novel of the systematic investigation of character; only Patricia Highsmith rivals her as an analyst of the absorbingly aberrant. *An Unkindness of Ravens* is top-drawer Rendell, and that means another engrossing reading experience for her growing legions of fans.

Paul Stuewe, "The Mercurial Mailer . . . No-Nonsense Cops . . . Build Your Own Robot," in Quill and Quire, *Vol. 51, No. 9, September, 1985, p. 86.*

JANE STEWART SPITZER

[The] 11 haunting, beautifully written stories [in *The New Girl Friend and Other Stories of Suspense*] contain the same suspense, atmosphere, and characterization that are hallmarks of Rendell's novels. In these stories, as in her novels, Rendell explores the dark side of human nature and what happens when ordinary people are thrust into unusual circumstances.

In ["The New Girl Friend"], which won an Edgar Award from the Mystery Writers of America, a young woman's relationship with a friend's husband isn't what it seems to be. This story is the best and the most chilling, surprising the reader right to the very end.

> *Jane Stewart Spitzer, "Two New Mysteries for Suspense Fans," in* The Christian Science Monitor, *April 25, 1986, p. 26.*

JOAN SMITH

[Ruth Rendell] is at the peak of her powers. In *Live Flesh,* she pulls off what is to this reader a dazzling coup—the creation of a rapist who remains, for a large part of the novel, a sympathetic character. The book starts with the shooting of David Fleetwood, a young detective sergeant, by Victor Jenner, a rapist on the run from the police. The obvious way to write this novel would have been to tell it through the eyes of the crippled policeman; Rendell takes the bolder path of getting inside the mind of Jenner. The steps by which he creates a relationship with the man he has condemned to life in a wheelchair are handled with meticulous care, as is his acceptance by Fleetwood's initially hostile girlfriend. *Live Flesh* is a frightening, resonant novel—an extraordinary achievement. (p. 28)

> *Joan Smith, "Whose Eyes?" in* New Statesman, *Vol. 111, No. 2874, April 25, 1986, pp. 27-8.*

JOHN GROSS

[In *Live Flesh*], Victor Jenner is (among other things) a rapist. Interrupted during one of his assaults, he takes refuge in a house, with the young girl he finds there as hostage. The police are uncertain whether the gun he is flourishing is a fake; he warns them that it is real, and then, just before being overpowered, he shoots an officer in the back. Ten years later he emerges from prison. David Fleetwood, the man he shot, has been confined to a wheelchair ever since. . . . David has completed his memoirs, and plans to publish them soon. Marriage? Unlikely, but he doesn't rule it out—and yes, he does have a girlfriend, Clare.

Victor finds himself irresistibly driven to seek the couple out. David is curious, and after Clare has overcome her initial revulsion they befriend him. But the friendship quickly turns into an eerie triangle, and the pressures produce a horrifying climax—not the one you might anticipate, though you can see in retrospect that it is "what all the rapes had been about."

Between its opening and closing bursts of violence, *Live Flesh* is primarily a novel of tension. It turns on the psychology of a psychopath, and if Ruth Rendell's touch were less assured, the result could be merely unpleasant. But as it is she succeeds in making Victor wholly credible, building up a coherent picture out of minor habits and stray memories, and forcing you to follow each detailed step of his sinister progress. She is particularly good on his self-righteousness—above all his conviction that David has done him a great wrong (though he is

willing to forgive it), that when he fired it was the police who were to blame for not listening to his warning.

The atmosphere, too, is perfectly rendered. . . . And even the least of the minor characters make their contribution to the steadily tightening drama.

The book has one marked inconsistency. You feel that for David and Clare to accept Victor so readily, and then positively warm toward him, argues something rather kinky about them, or at any rate something more complicated than anything we are shown. In effect, they are too nice and normal for their allotted roles.

But though this is a weakness, it isn't an unduly damaging one. While you are actually reading *Live Flesh,* Victor's compulsions are enough in themselves to carry you along. . . . Ruth Rendell has written as powerful a book as her admirers have come to expect from her: a troubling book, too, since you are left feeling that Victor is neither mad nor sane.

> *John Gross, in a review of "Live Flesh," in* The New York Times, *August 22, 1986, p. C21.*

NICK KIMBERLEY

Ruth Rendell, writing as Barbara Vine, begins her latest novel, *A Fatal Inversion,* with the discovery of a body on the gunroom floor. Contrary to expectation, it isn't that of a well-heeled aristo, but of an old dog—this is a sly wink at the rigid tradition of country house murders which is so important to British crime fiction, but which Rendell leaves far behind.

Both Barbara Vine novels concern crimes committed long ago; the phrase 'in the far' resonates throughout the first, *A Dark-Adapted Eye.* . . . Rendell re-creates the past so fastidiously that the present becomes a dying echo of 'the far'. Hairstyles, dress lengths, perfumes, flowers: every tiny detail permeates the fabric of memory.

What sets both novels in motion is a guilt born of violence, bending present lives out of shape. There are numerous asides on the state of grace from which the characters have fallen: two are named Adam and Eden; *A Fatal Inversion* makes specific reference to the Garden of Eden, *A Dark-Adapted Eye* to the reappearance of the Mark of Cain. But these aren't so much precise allegorical motifs as fleetingly glimpsed signs. Rendell's concerns are entirely secular. *A Dark-Adapted Eye* establishes that the central villainy lies, not with individual characters, but in the tangled structure of family life. 'The terrible pressure of love' leads people to desperation, but those pressures have little place in *A Fatal Inversion,* where people are barely able to establish links with each other—love and affection are turned inwards. Therein lies the novel's only weakness: there's little of the compassion so important for a humanist like Rendell.

Her world-view may be humanist, but it's hardly optimistic. A dark-adapted eye is one which has adjusted to darkness—like Rendell's own, so focused on gloom that she sees little else. That's no condemnation: crime fiction demands such morbidity. This country has no novelist better than Rendell at suggesting the unpleasantnesses just below civilised surfaces.

> *Nick Kimberley, "All in the Past," in* New Statesman, *Vol. 113, No. 2925, April 17, 1987, p. 31.*

HARRIET WAUGH

Is Ruth Rendell killing the appetite of her readers with her creative largesse? Last year she produced two quite excellent psychological novels [*Live Flesh* and *A Dark-Adapted Eye*], written under her other hat of Barbara Vine. . . . This year, so far, she has produced in very close succession a Barbara Vine novel, *A Fatal Inversion,* just out to excellent reviews, a novella, *Heartstones,* and now *Talking to Strange Men* while lurking in the pipeline is an Inspector Wexford detective mystery. . . . I can think of no other writer, with the possible exception of Andrew Wilson, who sustains at this pace such versatility of subject matter, pleasant prose and psychological insight. The danger is that we might come to take her for granted and not recognise the individual achievement of each novel. It has not happened yet but I can see that it might. (p. 49)

As for *Talking to Strange Men,* it is a very difficult book to describe. The easiest way, probably, is to explain Miss Rendell's stated premise for the novel. She says she has been accused of writing only about psychopathic personalities, so she decided to write a novel about ordinary folk whose actions start a chain of events that ends in violence. Then she was creatively sparked by reading a description of spying as belonging to the closed world of children's games.

Talking to Strange Men combines these two themes in a very curious and complex novel. There are two heroes. The first, John Creevey, is a market-gardener who has had slightly more than his fair share of unhappiness. . . . The other central character is a 14-year-old minor public school boy called Mungo. Mungo's world is that of espionage. He is the director of 'London Central', and his team of 13- and 14-year-old Rossingham boys wage an intense, subtle battle of wits against 'Moscow Central', located in the more progressive public school of Utting. This is not just having fun. 'Spookside', as it is generally known, is a way of life. . . . Ruth Rendell writes about Spookside as John Le Carré writes about Smiley's subterranean world of subterfuge and betrayal. (p. 49)

The two worlds of schoolboy espionage and John Creevey's preoccupation with winning his wife back from her lover start colliding when John, discovering a message-drop, and not realising that he has stumbled on a children's game, eases the obsessive misery he is suffering by trying to unravel the code used by what he thinks is a Mafia-style gang. When in a moment of anger he uses his knowledge of the code for his own ends, he sets in motion a stream of events that ends in violent death.

The main achievement of *Talking to Strange Men* lies not so much in the emotional complexities of John Creevey's life, which are in fact considerable, but in the way that Ruth Rendell successfully involves the reader in the schoolboy world of espionage. This makes it extraordinary.

Miss Rendell is a chilly writer. In general her characters are viewed with acid detachment and the readers' involvement

often comes about through tension, fear and an understanding of the characters' vulnerability rather than through liking. Her flirtation in *Talking to Strange Men* with everyday people and the drama of their lives does suffer slightly from a lifting of this tension, although we are given plenty of surprises, all of which come directly out of the natures of the people in the story. So, although I thought it a stunningly clever novel, it did not have me on the edge of my chair as her other best books have. However, it is another notable example of Miss Rendell's ingenuity and versatility. (pp. 49-50)

> *Harriet Waugh, "From Child's Play to Murder," in* The Spectator, *Vol. 258, No. 8289, May 23, 1987, pp. 49-50.*

GERALD KAUFMAN

Ruth Rendell already has a variety of products to put before her admirers—what with her Inspector Wexford whodunnits, her disturbing psychological thrillers, and, now, her pseudonym of Barbara Vine under which to offer variations on the psychological theme. Even so, in yet two more offerings to succeed her recent and terrifying *A Fatal Inversion,* this dauntingly prolific author has attempted further innovations.

One, *Heartstones,* is a triumph. In this long-short story . . . , she tries a completely new style, that of a self-consciously literary teenage girl—with more knowledge of Gothic novels than is good for her—writing a confidential diary. Elvira's Mozart-loving mother has died of cancer, leaving her, with her plump, confectionery-addicted younger sister Despina, in the keeping of their father, Luke. After the brilliant medievalist whom he chooses as his second wife dies in a fall from the scaffolding of a church whose gargoyles she is inspecting, a despondent Luke shows Despina a suicide letter he has written. Soon he is found with his wrists slit and the note beside him. Elvira, delirious with anorexia, begins to wonder if she has been responsible for both deaths. The final devastating sentence, revealing whether this self-doubt is justified, sent me back to reread this book's 60 pages, replete with clues which I should have been alert enough to note and understand.

Different from anything else she has ever written, *Heartstones* is a deadly marvel. Despite a cunning trick opening, *Talking to Strange Men* is, on the other hand, a stylistic muddle which, unlike Rendell's other work, is often simply unreadable. What was intended as a disconcerting plot device (is Rendell really straying into le Carré territory?) turns out so complex and opaque that I ceased to take interest, only becoming involved when the story reverted to the vicissitudes of one of Rendell's familiar misfits. I welcomed his intermittent re-entry with relief, delighted to be informed of the sharply observed details of his drab life, in which tea consisted of "scrambled eggs on toast with half a tin of fruit to follow and Longlife cream'.

> *Gerald Kaufman, "Something Borrowed and Something New," in* The Listener, *Vol. 117, No. 3014, June 4, 1987, p. 45.*

Gwen(dolyn Margaret) Pharis Ringwood

1910-1984

American-born Canadian dramatist, novelist, short story writer, poet, essayist, and editor.

An important figure in Canadian drama, Ringwood is perhaps best known for her folk plays set in the western provinces of Alberta and British Columbia. During her long and prolific career, Ringwood employed a variety of dramatic forms, including classical tragedy, comedy, farce, and the musical, to focus on characters ranging from common people of the farm and prairie to folk heroes and famous historical figures. In her tragedies, she explored such themes as the relationship between humanity and nature and conflicts between individuals with differing values or ethnic backgrounds. In her lighter plays, Ringwood typically focused upon human foibles. Critics have consistently praised the authenticity with which Ringwood renders the people, landscapes, and conditions of the Canadian West.

In 1937, Ringwood entered the graduate drama program at the University of North Carolina at Chapel Hill. Under the tutelage of Frederick Koch, a noted scholar of folk drama, she wrote *Still Stands the House* (1939), considered by many critics her finest folk drama. Set in a farmhouse in southern Alberta during the droughts of the Depression, this play focuses on a man who must decide between his desire to satisfy the material values of his city-bred wife and his wish to continue farming the increasingly unproductive land he inherited from his father. This conflict is further complicated by his sister, who sees her brother's threat to sell the farm as a betrayal of their father's hopes. Critics attributed the tragic power of this play to Ringwood's strong characterizations, rich poetic language, and her use of symbolism to underscore humanity's struggle with nature. While still at Chapel Hill, Ringwood wrote the one-act play *Pasque Flower* (1939), which she later expanded into *Dark Harvest* (1945). Informed with biblical allusions, this work explores the tragic consequences resulting from a man's fanatical commitment to the land. *The Courting of Marie Jenvrin* (1941) is the first play Ringwood composed outside the drama school environment. A comedy set in the Northwest Territories, this work revolves around a French-Canadian girl and the men who compete for her affections. Critics praised Ringwood's talent for creating colorful characters, realistic comic dialogue, and farcical plot.

Commissioned by the Alberta Folklore and Local History Project in 1944 to write plays utilizing the early twentieth-century history of Alberta, Ringwood created the folk plays *Hatfield, the Rainmaker* (1944), *The Jack and the Joker* (1944), and *Stampede* (1945). *Hatfield, the Rainmaker* relates the true story of a con man who was hired in 1921 by the town of Medicine Hat, Alberta, to bring rain to their drought-stricken farmland. *The Jack and the Joker* is a farce centering on a flamboyant Calgary newspaper editor whose honesty compels him to expose a scandal despite attempts by influential citizens to shut down his paper. *Stampede* concerns the early ranching era of the Canadian West and centers on cowboy "Nigger" John Ware, a hero of Albertan legend. Another of Ringwood's plays with an Albertan setting is *Widger's Way* (1952), considered by some critics her finest comedy. In this work, Ringwood

combines elements of Plautus's *Pot of Gold* and Moliere's *The Miser* to create an ironic but sympathetic commentary on human weakness.

Ringwood wrote several plays focusing upon the immigrant experience in western Canada. These lighthearted comic farces explore the fear and confusion experienced by immigrants as well as the adjustments they were forced to make to assimilate with a new culture. For example, *The Drowning of Wasyl Nemitchuk; or, A Fine Colored Easter Egg* (1946) is a farce centering on a recently settled Ukrainian couple who experience marital discord when faced with the prospect of sudden wealth. The husband goes to extreme lengths to preserve the lifestyle to which the couple is accustomed. Ringwood's other plays featuring immigrant characters include *Chris Axelson, Blacksmith* (1938), *The Deep Has Many Voices* (1971), and *The Magic Carpets of Antonio Angelini* (1976), a prize-winning children's play.

Ringwood also wrote three well-received musicals. The first of these, *Look Behind You Neighbor* (1961), is a historical play commissioned in celebration of the fiftieth anniversary of the founding of Edson, Alberta. Highlighting memorable events in Edson history from 1909 to 1960, this work depicts the experiences of settlers, the opening of the railway, and the effects of World War II. *The Road Runs North* (1967) centers on Billy Barker, a British merchant sailor who prospected for gold in Canada's Cariboo region during the gold rush of the early 1860s. *Mirage* (1979) is perhaps Ringwood's most ambitious musical. An impressionistic epic imbued with symbolism and elements of fantasy, this work relates major events of twentieth-century Saskatchewan history, focusing on the hardships and struggles of settlers and the development of a sense of regional identity and community in the people of Saskatoon.

In her later plays, Ringwood became more concerned with social issues. Three of these works, *Lament for Harmonica* (1959), *The Stranger* (1971), and *The Furies* (1980), explore the myths and culture of North American Indians and concentrate on their conflicts with white society. These dramas incorporate the lore and language of Northern Canadian tribes and make extensive use of imagery and metaphor. Both *Lament for Harmonica*, a realistic work, and *The Stranger*, which is based on the Greek tragedy *Jason and Medea*, center on the tragic consequences of love affairs between Indian women and white men. Other topical plays by Ringwood include *A Remembrance of Miracles* (1975), which addresses the problems of youths during the 1960s, and *The Lodge* (1975), which concerns difficulties faced by the aged.

Ringwood also drew attention for her numerous radio dramas and for several plays for children. In addition, she wrote short stories, essays, articles, and the novel *Younger Brother* (1959). *The Collected Plays of Gwen Pharis Ringwood* (1981) contains twenty-five plays from all phases of Ringwood's career.

(See also *Contemporary Authors*, Vol. 112 [obituary].)

VINCENT M. TOVELL

Among our Western writers, none has written so fondly and interestingly for the theatre of the life and lore of Alberta as Mrs. Gwen Pharis Ringwood. Several of her plays, published and unpublished, deserve wider circulation, for her work is not as well known in the East as in the West. Her colourful one-acter *The Rainmaker* . . . forecast the more ambitious Western story, with its spectacular appeal, which Mrs. Ringwood tells in the three-act play *Stampede.* . . . Juggling facts and dates of history, Mrs. Ringwood portrays the devotion of the popular figure of Albertan legend, "Nigger" John Ware, to the world famous bucking horse Midnight. The play's central characters, "Nigger" John and his partner Shorthorn, who resist the commercialization of the Calgary Stampede, and represent a last vestige of the true old-Western spirit, are sympathetically presented, but the author's regard for them and their way of life softens the play occasionally into sentimentality. While the play has a colourful Western atmosphere, and a spectacular third act heightened by the triumphant (off-stage) ride of Shorthorn on Midnight and the vigorous brawl between the villain and the hero, *Stampede* remains a not yet fully realized work. The emphasis, particularly in the third act, is diffuse and the play's major climax, the parting of the two friends, is not sharply focussed. Certain of the characterizations too, for example the villain Shark and the heroine, are stereotypes and would contribute more to the play if given more individuality. It is important for Mrs. Ringwood to have seen her play staged and to be able to plan its revision in the light of an experience too often denied to our playwrights. (pp. 266-67)

Vincent M. Tovell, in a review of "Stampede," in University of Toronto Quarterly, *Vol. XVI, No. 3, April, 1947, pp. 266-67.*

MICHAEL TAIT

One figure who stands somewhat apart [from the group of Canadian dramatists writing in the early 1930s] is Gwen Pharis Ringwood. Unquestionably she is the most capable playwright of this period. Miss Pharis wrote about ten plays in all, a number of them in connection with the Alberta Folk Lore project. *Stampede,* for example, has to do with the break-up of the old West and increasing commercialism of the annual festivities at Calgary. Only three, *Still Stands the House, The Courting of Marie Jenvrin* and *Dark Harvest,* are readily available. The action of *Still Stands the House* takes place in a farm house in southern Alberta, a region that Miss Pharis knows intimately, during the droughts of the depression. The farm is unproductive and a buyer has offered a good price for it. The conflict arises with inevitability out of the relation of the three main characters: the man torn between a desire to appease his wife and to hold on to the barren soil, the gentle city-born wife who finds the place intolerable, and a crazed love-starved sister (rather overdrawn) for whom the dead father's farmhouse is a sacred thing. Gwen Pharis creates the atmosphere of despair very well indeed and Bruce Warren's anguished identification with his bitter Alberta prairie lingers in the mind as a symbol for all human attachments of this kind. The dialogue is entirely natural without seeming flat. Miss Pharis's infrequent images ("Wheat like gold on the hills," "hair—black as a furrow turned in spring") are always in context and lend an unobtrusive expressiveness to the speech of her characters. The main defect of this, as of so many short plays in English, is a surfeit of well-made plot which tries to go too far, too fast. *The Courting of Marie Jenvrin* tells of a French-Canadian girl and her suitors in the Northwest Territories. It is an unremarkable but well-executed comedy. In *Dark Harvest,* an ambitious three-act drama, Miss Pharis explores again the evil consequence of her protagonist's fanatical devotion to the land. In spite of serious flaws—a gratuitously sensational ending and a style which lacks the necessary vigour to prevent the tragic mood from degenerating into dreariness—the play is powerfully conceived. (pp. 639-40)

Michael Tait, "Drama and Theatre," in Literary History of Canada: Canadian Literature in English, *edited by Carl F. Klinck, University of Toronto Press, 1965, pp. 633-57.*

ANTON WAGNER

Dark Harvest is without question Ringwood's most successful full-length drama to date. Its protagonist Garth Hansen, the land-hungry Alberta farmer attempting to dominate nature and a hostile God, is perhaps Ringwood's only heroic and tragic male figure. At least two of Ringwood's unpublished plays are of similarly high literary merit. Her impressionistic *The Rainmaker* . . . (its title was changed to *Hatfield, the Rainmaker* after the Broadway production of Richard Nash's far better known *Rainmaker* of 1954) is Ringwood's most successful poetic folk play. Based on an actual historical event, the hiring of the rainmaker Charles Hatfield by the town of Medicine Hat, Alberta in 1921, *The Rainmaker* deals with the despair, hope and cynicism with which the inhabitants of Medicine Hat gamble on Hatfield to save their crops from drought. In *Widg-*

er's Way, . . . Ringwood parodies and makes masterful use of melodramatic conventions to create probably her best comedy. Using Plautus' *Pot of Gold* and Moliere's *The Miser* as her basic source material, Ringwood concocts a maddening mixture of characters and fast-paced action resulting in her most farcical and yet humane scrutiny of Canadian character types.

Ringwood's plays produced since 1952, like the Indian problem play *Lament for Harmonica* of 1959 with its realism and social criticism, the historical musicals *Look Behind You, Neighbor* and *The Road Runs North* (1961 and 1967), the neo-classical Indian tragedy *The Stranger* and the multi-media *The Deep Has Many Voices,* both of 1971, are of literary interest in their stylistic experimentation without deviating from the playwright's very personal vision expressed in her earlier dramas. But evaluations of Ringwood's contribution to Canadian theatre have been based far too long on such purely literary considerations. What is equally remarkable about her long theatre career is her ability to create live theatre, theatre traditions and a body of dramatic literature in a near theatrical vacuum. As Ringwood recalls the state of Western theatre in the early thirties in the Prairies, "We didn't have any CBC, any Little Theatre, University Theatre Departments, travelling companies or any money. We had seen very few plays. So we began a kind of Do It Yourself Theatre on the Prairies under the direction of Elizabeth Sterling Haynes." As a student at the University of Alberta from 1934 to 1937, Gwen Ringwood was strongly influenced by Elizabeth Haynes, the founder of the rural community drama movement in Alberta. (p. 64)

Besides Elizabeth Haynes, one of the strongest influences on Gwen Ringwood's writing were her two incredibly productive years with the Carolina Playmakers at the University of North Carolina from 1937 to 1939. *Still Stands the House, Chris Axelson, Blacksmith* and *One Man's House* were written and produced there in 1938, *Pasque Flower* in 1939 and *Dark Harvest,* her M.A. thesis play, written but not produced, also in 1939. . . . Ringwood's two years with the Carolina Playmakers were unique in offering her the possibility of the immediate production of her plays at the Playmaker Theatre, publication in *The Carolina Playbook* and extensive acting and touring before a wide range of audiences. Of equal importance was the constructive criticism of fellow students and professional writers like Paul Green who, in the playwright's recollection, "brought professionalism, a sense of poetry, a feeling for the land and for people to his consideration of our work." Of still greater influence was Frederick Koch's concept of the "folk play" with its regionalism, nature orientation and focus on the "common people" that characterizes so many of Ringwood's works. (p. 65)

The influence of these two concepts of the folk play and popular community theatre on Ringwood's writing cannot be overestimated. *Hatfield, the Rainmaker,* the Western *Stampede* about the ranching era in Alberta and *The Jack and the Joker,* a farce about the journalist Bob Edwards and his muckraking *Eye Opener,* were commissioned under the terms of the Alberta Folklore and Local History Project and produced at Banff in the mid-forties. All three plays reflect the aims of the Folklore Project, its purpose was to record oral historical and traditional material of the region, in their celebration of Alberta history and its early pioneers. Ringwood's playbook for the musical *Look Behind You, Neighbor* was similarly commissioned as a celebration of the 50-year history of the small railroad town of Edson, Alberta. . . . The production of Ringwood's second musical, *The Road Runs North,* for the Centennial Celebrations

in Williams Lake, B.C. in 1967 was achieved with . . . community involvement. . . . From a dramatic point of view, the musical's Billy Barker, the English goldminer pioneer of the Barkerville Gold Rush of the 1860's, is also Ringwood's best developed historical character, an archetypal figure of that whole era of the exploration and settlement of the Canadian North West.

The depiction of the Canadian countryside, its history and the struggles, triumphs and defeats of its inhabitants marks all of Ringwood's dramatic writing. This celebration of her immediate physical environment and its people also has its negative effects, however. Except for *One Man's House* of 1938, a social drama about the political and personal conflicts of a Polish immigrant labour leader, there is little conscious awareness in Ringwood's plays until the 1950's of the role of the dramatist as a social critic. As a result, many of her plays are simplistically optimistic in their outlook and frequently lack strong dramatic conflict. There is, for instance, no direct reflection in Ringwood's plays of the forties of the Second World War in which her husband fought and two of her brothers were killed. There is an anomaly between the romantic and comic innocence of Ringwood's dramas of the forties and ongoing political and social events which she attributes in part to the political naivete of most Canadians at that period. (pp. 65-6)

Ringwood is far from an apolitical writer, however. Despite the pacifying influence of her environment, she has nevertheless attempted to incorporate to some extent the political concerns of her time in her dramatic writing throughout her career. Her satire on racism, the radio play *The Wall* of 1953 is one of her best implicitly political works. (p. 66)

Gwen Ringwood's move to British Columbia in 1953 has brought the local history, physical environment and social problems of Northern B.C. to her writing replacing her previous Alberta setting and setting of the Northwest Territories of her popular *The Courting of Marie Jenvrin* of 1941. In such plays as *Lament for Harmonica, The Road Runs North, The Stranger,* an adaptation of the Jason-Medea myth, and the novel *Younger Brother* of 1959, Ringwood focuses particularly on the plight of the B.C. Indian in conflict with the intruding culture of white society. An unpublished novel finished in 1970, *Pascal,* describes the fight of a young Chilcotin Indian to survive and develop as an artist. Ringwood became familiar with the problems of the North American Indian through her association with Indians as a child in Alberta, as a teenager while working on the Blackfoot Indian reservation in Montana, and her contact with the Shuswap, Chilcotin and Carrier tribes in Williams Lake. One of her unfinished plays at Chapel Hill in 1938 dealt with life on a Blackfoot reservation and incorporated a great deal of Sun Dance lore and rhythmic poetic Blackfoot ceremonial language within the text. Ringwood's contemporary plays about Indians often make this same excessive use of poetic imagery and metaphor. Unlike George Ryga, a former student of hers in a playwriting course at Banff in 1950, who in *The Ecstasy of Rita Joe* manages to create an Indian dialect that is both realistic and poetic, Ringwood frequently opts for poetry alone leaving her Indians speaking out of character like Greek sages. *The Stranger,* like *Lament for Harmonica,* nevertheless succeeds dramatically because of Ringwood's ability to accurately portray the sense of abandonment, rejection and confused cultural identity of her central character.

The increasing social criticism in Ringwood's plays of the 1950's, 1960's and 1970's reflects not only the increased political awareness of their author but also her turning away from the concepts and optimism of folk drama. . . . Compared with her earlier dramas, Ringwood's political plays of the early 1970's are of additional significance for their lack of regional frameworks and the national scope of their political concerns. They indicate an attempt by the playwright to reach a wider national audience. A series of short satiric sketches, *Encounters,* produced in a coffee house in 1971, dealt with political dissent, censorship, pollution, poison gas tests, women's liberation, unemployment among young people and invasion of privacy. Ringwood's belief in and identification with the humanism and idealism of the young is further reflected in *The Deep Has Many Voices,* a complicated multi-media production directed by the author in Williams Lake in 1971. The work is a kind of morality play in which Melissa, the high school valedictorian, hears the sound of trumpets deep in the forest calling her to change the world. (p. 67)

> Anton Wagner, "Gwen Pharis Ringwood Rediscovered," in Canadian Theatre Review, *No. 5, Winter, 1975, pp. 63-9.*

JUDITH HINCHCLIFFE

In her best known play, *Still Stands the House,* Gwen Pharis Ringwood contrasts the pastoral myth with its historic rebuttal, the great prairie drought of the thirties. Her method is to construct a framework of literature, myth and history which locates the characters in a specific time and place, then to let the interaction of the characters provide the incidents for the story. What is potentially a closed world is opened to the universal by carefully placed symbols. When the characters react to the conditions in which they find themselves we see them as victims of their own universal humanity, modified by a particular time and place. Ringwood welds the particular and the universal together to form a new myth native to the new land—a story to be told over dying embers and remembered when the conditions recur.

The particular tone of the play is set by the interaction of the realistic situation, the naturalistic dialogue, and a few symbols which have always represented the struggle for life at a very primitive level—a house, lights, a horse, the weather. The symbols are not arbitrarily attached to the Warrens' situation then, but are naturally found in it. The hard, dangerous life on an Alberta farm is linked to all similar moments in the history of the human race as the common nouns "lamp", "storm", "wind", "cold", etc., bring with them a sense of how they have functioned in other times and other places. The elementary nature of the symbols reminds us that these people are not concerned with sophisticated or very civilized problems, but with the most basic ones of the survival of mind and body.

Ringwood has an extraordinarily strong sense of place. Unlike many Canadian dramatists she eschews the exotic (which they, at best, develop vaguely) for the particular and the familiar. When her characters speak of their land we know they have actually walked on it. The off-stage area becomes a genuine physical environment which moulds their actions and attitudes. She also knows the details of their work. Few writers can convince an audience of the reality of the characters' work when there is no opportunity to display it, but Ringwood convinces us that her characters are actually defined by the labours they perform. They are shaped by the land and their labour.

In *Still Stands the House* Bruce and Hester Warren are left joint inheritors of a farm wrested from the prairie by their father and now threatening to vanish in the face of summer drought and winter blizzard. Hester regards Bruce's failure to make the land fruitful as a sign of his betrayal of their father's trust by marrying. The struggle in the Warren farmhouse between the blonde wife, Ruth, and the dark-haired sister, Hester, for the loyalty of Bruce Warren breaks into the open when a good offer is made to buy the land. Bruce's threat to sell the farm catalyzes a fury in Hester that destroys all three. (pp. 183-84)

Hester blames Bruce for not loving the land, the implication being that, if he loved Ruth less, he could give the land his full attention:

> You have to love a place to make things grow. The land knows when you don't care about it and Bruce doesn't care about it any more. Not like Father did.

By the terms of his father's will, and to satisfy his sister's expectations, he should have wedded himself to the land; great harvests would have been the reward for his dedication. Hester is, in a most primitive fashion, creating a myth to explain the failure of the pastoral aspect of the North American dream. What she forgets is that the construction of a myth implies possession of the magic that makes the myth powerful, and in the Dirty Thirties no one possessed that magic. Love of the land was not enough to save it in the face of history. Myths distance their believers from the actual event and it is Hester's distance from reality that measures her madness. Ruth and Bruce have no such defence against the reality of their world. Hester demands that Bruce love the land more than human society; Ruth wants him to love life more than things and possessions. To idolize the land and serve it without reward seems foolish to her.

In this play the most powerful and important character appears only in a painting. Martin Warren represents a type common enough in novels of the west, a mighty man in life whose energy, in death, is sufficient yet to govern the lives of his children. He is one of those to whom organising a farm becomes an end in itself instead of a means to an end. (p. 185)

Hester goes dutifully on repeating the sacred rituals handed down from her father. But Bruce is less thoroughly indoctrinated, and Ruth's need for a different way of life unsettles his determination to succeed as his father succeeded. (p. 186)

As her father's spokesman Hester dominates Ruth and Bruce. She has much in common with other dramatic heroines, repressed spirits from puritanical societies. One looks at Hester and thinks of Hedda Gabler (and the General's pistols), or Miss Julie (and her father's riding boots) or Lavinia Mannon (and the doors that close at the end of her story). The difficulty with a one-act play is that the characters must be thrust upon us fully developed. The amount of time for explanations is limited, especially when there is a definite action to be accomplished. We are left with the puzzle of Hester, whether her madness is actually brought on by the immediate threat of losing the farm, or whether the strain of sharing the house would, in any case, have driven her to desperate action. Her first appearance is abrupt and embarrassingly rude; it would be a problem for the actress to keep from sliding into the grotesque. But after Hester has explained herself in her conversations with Ruth we understand her nature and what circumstances have done to that nature.

Hester's complete ignorance of her own emotions leads her into all kinds of self-contradictions. Another sacrifice the prairie demanded was childhood, youth, the capacity to see people in a way disconnected from their value to the land. The prairie killed many women early and Hester's story of the little girl, thrust too soon into the responsibilities of her mother's place:

> "We'll have to lean on one another now,
> Daughter."—Those were his words—And that's
> the way it was. I was beside him until—I never
> left him

is not unique in western annals. She absorbed her father's passion for the land, essentially is wedded to it. Her denial of her own sexuality:

> The young men used to ride over here on Sun-
> day, but I stopped that. (A pause) I never saw
> a man I'd let touch me. Maybe you don't mind
> that kind of thing, I do

is as much a dedication of her own creative forces to the preservation of her world as it is a rejection of her humanity. The prairie has demanded her fertility as she thinks it should claim Bruce's. Hester disavows the need to lean on anyone, yet reveals how deeply she has been hurt by Bruce's natural attempts to claim his own independence.

> *Ruth:* . . . It's strange how women feel safer
> when their men are near, close enough to touch,
> isn't it? No matter how strong you think you
> are.
>
> *Hester:* I can't say that I need my strength from
> Bruce, or could get it if I needed it. . . . I loved
> Bruce, but I got no thanks for it. He feels I
> stand in his way now.

Hester saw Bruce, when he was a child, as her possession; she has never forgiven him for growing away from her. It is certain that, after his death, he will return to live in the house with Hester and his father.

Bruce is a dutiful farmer but not, apparently, an instinctively sound one. There is no other explanation for his leaving the black mare in a corral from which she could escape, when he knows it is her habit to seek out the show-shed by the coulee (the valley of the shadow of death) at such times. The colt she carries is one of the few reliable cash crops on the farm, and he has jeopardized it by not ensuring the mare's safety. The playwright manages to show Bruce as a man genuinely torn between alternatives and not merely a weak or indecisive individual. Bruce recognizes the validity of the claims of both women and knows they are unreconcilable. He too feels that he has betrayed the past by his inability to make the soil profitable, yet he feels there is a necessary virtue in the labour itself, even if it is unproductive. When Ruth says: "We can have a garden, and trees growing", he replies, "That's about what those irrigated farms are—gardens." When you have spent a lifetime struggling in the desert, the Promised Land can look a little soft.

Throughout *Still Stands the House* the use of symbols is unusually rich and sometimes paradoxical. Like all farmers the Warrens are tied to the cycle of the seasons which has come into disorder. Drought has made the farm unprofitable (and established the situation which produces the tragedy) but the play is set during a terrible winter blizzard, the paradox being that there is plenty of cold frozen water in winter, but not enough in the warm growing seasons of the year. The natural cycle is twisted. There ought to be an orderly progression of birth, growth, and death, but nature has begun to kill the crops

in summer, and the livestock in winter. If nature herself is crazy can we be surprised if the natural instincts of human beings are distorted by the pressures of living in a disordered world? Martin Warren appreciated the winter snows as "a moving shroud, a winding-sheet." For him, in the seasons of his success, the death was symbolic. But in his son's time the death and madness are literal.

What suffers under these conditions is life itself, for nothing is valued for its own sake, but because it represents prosperity, success, importance, power. Consequently we know that it is impossible for this family to produce a child. The child is doomed like the crops and the hyacinths in the face of a hostile environment. As the crops die before the drought, or the foal in the snows, so the child, a pledge to the future, will die before Hester's rage to preserve only the past. Ruth knows from the beginning that a child raised in the atmosphere of the Warren household would perish from lack of emotional nourishment, just as the crops fail for want of rain. (pp. 187-89)

The final tragedy in *Still Stands the House* is caused by a storm and symbolized by a storm. Man's mastery over nature is like his mastery over wild beasts: he must remain alert. Ruth lacks this instinct of the country dweller. Coming from the town where man, by force of numbers, has tamed winter, she mourns for her past:

> I used to like them [the winters] in town. We
> went skating on the river and tobogganing. But
> out here it's different.

The conversation between Ruth and Manning, the real-estate agent, stresses the fragility of the defences they have built for themselves:

> It's a bad blizzard, alright, but I don't think
> I'll have any trouble. There's a heater in the
> car, and I've just had the engine checked over . . .
> I'd hate to try it in an old car, but this one of
> mine can pull through anything.

This is naturalistic dialogue, but what will kill Bruce and Ruth is the fact that she has delayed "checking over" the lamps for the evening.

The symbols Ringwood counterpoises to the storm, disorder and madness are fire, lanterns, and reason. Here it is, the first half of the twentieth century, and man must still, like the cave man, keep his fires burning high to identify his home place. . . . (p. 189)

The climax of the play depends on Ruth's lack of country-dweller's instinct for [nature's] credibility. After Bruce has decided to sell the farm, and we see signs of Hester's total collapse, Bruce discovers that the mare has fled. The fate of Ruth and Bruce depends on the lamps Ruth has neglected to fill. There is an irony in this because the subject of filling them was raised earlier as Ruth and Hester argued about the sale of the farm and Ruth's inefficient execution of her household tasks. . . . The audience would cheer Ruth on for her show of spirit against Hester's tyranny, but it is a fatal victory. . . .

Ringwood has related the characters to their environment as the Warrens share in the natural disorder. Nature, having neither mind nor will, is neither purposeful nor malevolent, yet its wildness has the same destructive effect as man's madness. The "light" of Hester's reason has been dimmed and the visible effect for us is to see the lights put out one by one, leaving both physical and spiritual darkness to swallow up the Warrens.

Still Stands the House, then, elevates the story of the Warrens from being merely part of prairie history to the status of a myth of a particular time and place. Myths can apparently be either destructive or creative in their power. Motivated by the urge to succeed, the urge to love, the inability to surrender even a lost dream, the Warrens were destroyed by their belief in myths unsuitable to their situation, but the residue of their lives can be seen as part of the mythology native to Western Canada in the nineteen-thirties. (p. 190)

> Judith Hinchcliffe, " 'Still Stands the House': The Failure of the Pastoral Dream," in Canadian Drama/ L'Art dramatique canadien, Vol. 3, No. 2, Fall, 1977, pp. 183-91.

GERALDINE ANTHONY

[What] American regional writers did for their native land, Gwen Pharis Ringwood is doing for western Canada. She responded to her training in [the Carolina Playmaker's School at the University of North Carolina] with a series of Canadian regional plays featuring . . . three types of characters: first, the larger-than-life folk heroes; second, the famous real personalities magnified by time; and third, the fictional common folk of farm and prairie.

She describes her own comedies as: "trembling on the edge of farce." She prefers comedy because she feels more remote and removed from her material. She can then disguise an attitude and express it in comic terms. In *Widger's Way* she parodies and makes use of melodramatic techniques masterfully to create her best comedy in the tradition of such plays as Plautus' *Pot of Gold* and Molière's *Miser.* Widger, the miserly Albertan farmer, is a true native folk type conditioned by his environment—a product of Alberta, that province rich in farmland, oil and geological discoveries of fossils on the Pre-Cambrian Shield. His fellow characters reflect the people of that era from Planter, the goldminer, and his murderous partner, Jake; to Sokolander, the cheap politician; Anastasia the curious widow; Professor Bond, the geologist and his farmhand student, Peter; Garrow, the young American oil technician; Dowser Ringgo, the peddler of strange potions; and Docket the Constable. Together their personalities reflect the land and their conversation is expressive of the folk imagination and folk idiom. Widger's mirror reveals his and their greed, cruelty, fears and ambitions. Rich in humorous dialogue, it expresses a way of life which Widger expounds in these words: "I've lived to myself, don't lend things, discourage children tramping down pastures, don't borrow anything or bother anybody." This small lean man is representative of some native character types bred by the Alberta soil. (pp. 135-36)

Planter leaves Widger his sack of gold for safekeeping against the murderous intents of his partner and there ensues a folk comedy full of misadventures, a maddening mixture of coincidence and fast-paced action resulting in a farcical array of characters. Regional drama it is and strongly Albertan in flavor. Widger, giving with one hand, pulling back with the other, has a Canadian flavor that does not date. *Widger* is rich in dinosaurs, triceratops bones, the exploitation of the land and trial by fire in melodramatic terms—a play people will always understand.

A second type of folk character in the Ringwood plays is the real people whose lives have been magnified by time in western Canadian history: Hatfield, the famous rainmaker of Medicine Hat who brought rain to the farmlands during the depression years of the drought; Billy Barker, the discoverer of gold in northern British Columbia at the turn of the century; Nigger John, the revered Albertan cowboy in the last years of the great ranching era; and Bob Edwards, that indomitable Editor of the weekly newspaper, *The Sheep Creek Eye Opener.*

In *Hatfield, The Rainmaker,* Gwen Ringwood immortalized the character of the con man, Hatfield, before the creation of the American play, *The Rainmaker.* Hatfield, hired by the town of Medicine Hat, Alberta, in 1921, promises to work miracles to bring rain to the drought-ridden Canadian farmland. Rain does come and desperate Canadian couples decide to remain on the land they were about to forsake. Ringwood's impressionistic play deals with the hope, cynicism and despair of the farmers of Medicine Hat.

Stampede evokes the beloved character of John Ware, a great Albertan and a real person, called "Nigger John" by his fellow Albertans. *Stampede* recalls the last years of that great ranching era in a play based on some of Alberta's cowboy legends. Integral to the play is the rich regional background of the Calgary stampedes. Act I takes place at a camp site on a cattle trail leading north to Calgary in midsummer, 1912. Act II occurs a week later at Ma Raybourne's Boarding House in Calgary, and Act III in the enclosure behind the Chutes on the last day of the first Calgary Stampede. The plot involves Shorthorn, the Foreman of Bar XY, wanted for murder, who drives cattle to the Calgary Stampede. Shark, a cowboy, jealous of Shorthorn's abilities, threatens to report him to the authorities. Shorthorn's partner is Nigger John. Together they plan to buy a ranch but Shorthorn is forced to escape the law after saving young Bud's life in the Saddle Broncs Riding Contest. Nigger John is no stereotype black man but a ranch hand no different from the white cowboys. His character is drawn with sensitivity and he appears as an intelligent, kind, experienced westerner whose nickname is a sign of dignity, not opprobrium, in the Alberta of 1912. Regional drama proved him to be a product of the land. The same local idiom used by the white man and the black forces us to see him simply as a man. Nigger John's influence over the other characters is quiet but strong. (pp. 136-38)

Stampede is a romantic evocation of ranching days in Calgary and Ringwood has managed to re-create vividly that era in our imaginations.

Another of her plays dealing with a real person as folk hero is the musical, *The Road Runs North.* Here the legendary Billy Barker becomes her best developed historical character, an archetypal figure of the whole era of exploration and settlement of the Canadian Northwest. The Gold Rush in the Cariboo is depicted between the years 1861 and 1864. The musical is peopled with stock regional figures—the daring gold miners, the heathen Chinese, the faithful Indians, the French settlers, the men from Upper Canada, the Hurdy Gurdy Girls of Barkerville, the tavern-keeper, the Judge, the women camp-followers and finally there is the romantic figure of Billy Barker himself, the British merchant sailor, who gave up the sea to prospect for gold. His successes and failures in this gold rush setting, full of prospectors and desperadoes, is regionalism at its most romantic. Yet the background of fact and character is true to history and once again we see cause and effect in the land and its characters.

Another real person magnified by time was Bob Edwards, the Editor of the *Sheep Creek Eye Opener* (*Calgary Eye Opener*) in Alberta. Ringwood's play *The Jack and the Joker,* set in

1904, is a farce that revolves around the character of the Editor who is honest, pulls no punches but prints the truth in his muckraking *Eye Opener*. He opposes Dudley Carp's dishonest political manoeuvres for a political office. Mrs. Carp forces the owner of the printing press to sell out to her but in the nick of time Bob Edwards obtains evidence that Carp has sold useless land to the owner. Both money and printing press are returned. A slight play, it is nevertheless a tribute to the sense of honesty and justice inherent in the character of Bob Edwards and it was the first work of literature based on this famous Editor.

Gwen Ringwood has also immortalized a town in her regional drama. The people of Edson, Alberta, celebrating its fiftieth Anniversary, commissioned her to write an historical musical. She wrote **Look Behind You, Neighbor** in which the character of Edson with its ordinary people, its births, love affairs, marriages and deaths sets in relief the region and its people. Obviously influenced by Thornton Wilder's *Our Town*, it nonetheless accentuates the Edson people, their coal mining activities, their gardens, railroads, lumbering industry, farmland, streams and rainbow trout, the moose and deer, their oil and other resources, their consciousness of Edson as centre and gateway to the West. The early settlers who came to the locale when it was nothing but forest and wild animals, timber and snow, who had the courage to stay, are celebrated in this musical. The building of the Grand Trunk Pacific Railway from Edmonton to Edson, the opening of the first school, newspaper and jail, Edson's contribution of servicemen to two World Wars makes Edson proud of its status as a town of Alberta.

Gwen Pharis Ringwood has also immortalized fictional characters of the prairies in her regional drama. Hester, the prairie woman obsessed with love of house and land in Ringwood's finest play, **Still Stands the House**; and Garth, the prairie farmer whose angry need to dominate his prairie farmland in the two plays, **Pasque Flower** and **Dark Harvest**, give us a deeper sense of the influence of the Canadian prairies on its people. How simple and how stark life is on the prairies which in turn breed such stoic people! The bitter years of drought are painted vividly in the tragedy, **Still Stands the House**. The play revolves around the struggle to cope with unpredictable weather conditions which has broken the spirit of many farmers and their wives on the prairies. (pp. 137-39)

In **Dark Harvest** Gwen Ringwood again succeeds in melding the prairies and its people. In the same simple, poetic style, she highlights the barrenness and imprisoning quality of the lives of its characters. Although this play does not rise to the dramatic heights of **Still Stands the House**, it does, nevertheless, explore the evil consequences of fanatical devotion to the land. Her one heroic and tragic male figure is Garth, who tries to dominate nature and a hostile God. . . . Garth's passion for the land is not one of love but of anger and a need to conquer. There is something dark and unnatural in his fight against nature. The land which nurtured him has become his opponent and one knows instinctively that he cannot win.

Gwen Ringwood's regional plays also embrace the Indian and his closeness to the land. She attempts to probe his myths and culture. Two young Indian women are symbols of the Canadian Indian tribes. Jana in the play, **The Stranger**, and Maya in **Lament for Harmonica**. In **The Stranger** Ringwood has created a Greek tragedy similar to the *Jason-Medea* story. Jana, the Indian girl, has a baby by Jason, a white man, who rejects her for a white woman. In her grief Jana poisons the woman, kills her baby and commits suicide. The epic quality of the land and its first settlers transcends the plot. The orchestration of Ringwood's poetic language lends depth and richness; her use of classical form provides grace and purity. This is no pale emanation of the stereotyped Indian maiden but an attempt to penetrate to the heart of the Indian and her despair, the Indian's true feelings about the invasion of the homeland by the white man. She uses the traditional Greek chorus to echo her emotional responses to the Indians' plight. . . . These choruses not only express forebodings but also have a healing quality about them.

In **Lament for Harmonica,** Maya, the Shushwap Indian girl, has a child by the white man, Allan, who is unaware of the event. The baby dies and Maya becomes addicted to alcohol and prostitution. Gilbert, an Indian, loves her and attempts to murder Allan whereupon Maya stabs and kills Gilbert. Again Ringwood attempts to probe the inner depths of the Indian's conscience in a play that lacks the power of **The Stranger** but is nevertheless an honest effort to view the Indian in her native ground and folkways and to articulate her puzzlement and confusion in a white man's world.

The last category of regional plays in Ringwood's work concerns the immigrant to western Canada. She explores the love of Canadian girl and Greek boy in her play, **The Deep Has Many Voices**; the Ukrainian's response to life in Canada in **The Drowning of Wasyl Nemitchuk**; the Scandinavian's life in the new land in **Chris Axelson, Blacksmith**; and the Italian's happy abandonment to life in her children's play, **The Magic Carpets of Antonio Angelini**. These four plays are sensitive illuminations of the fears and confusions experienced by immigrants in their efforts to blend with a new land. They are, in fact, the expression of the melding of two cultures, or the inevitable forcing of one culture upon another.

In an overall assessment of Ringwood's regional drama—its creation of folk heroes, its enlargement of historical characters, its development of common prairie people, its Indians and immigrants, one finds running through all the plays a preoccupation with the earth and its manifestations of life. She has tried to penetrate to the very heartbeat of the earth itself in order to find out how people feel about their home which is the earth. She took specifically the western mystique and explored it in its people. Ringwood has a kind of distilling talent for describing the quality and the feel of the land itself. Deep-rooted in man is his adjustment to his own land. He first tries to control it and then to cherish it. It would seem that in her early plays her characters seek to control the land whereas in her later plays they cherish it. There is an epic quality about the open country and the effect of this bigness upon the human being.

Folklore arises out of the common consciousness of the people. It is a feeling for the land and its common people. Ringwood's heritage is definitely that of the land and her language stems from it. Her body of regional drama has a unity in its preoccupation with the land and its people. It is the depiction of western Canada, its history and struggles, triumphs and defeats. The rural crucible of her birth marks all her writing and gives it its larger-than-life quality and its instinctual union with the earth. (pp. 139-41)

Geraldine Anthony, "The Plays of Gwen Pharis Ringwood: An Appraisal," in Atlantis, *Vol. 4, No. 1, Fall, 1978, pp. 132-41.*

MICHAEL BENAZON

Mirage is folk drama at its best. In a tasteful combination of comedy, pathos, mime and music, the play depicts three generations of the Ryland family, from the arrival of the first John Ryland, a Scottish immigrant to the prairies in the first decade of this century, to the present day when John Ryland III returns to the ancestral farm, once again to take up the challenge of the land. The major events of 20th century Saskatchewan history serve not only as backdrop, but also as an explanation of the development of a sense of regional identity in the people of Saskatchewan.

The Rylands face a series of obstacles in their efforts to establish themselves on the prairies. Twice the men part for the battlefields of Europe leaving the farm under the management of the women. But it is the combination of the drought and depression of the 1930's that almost succeeds in severing the connection between the Rylands and the land. These scenes are among the most effective in the play. Increasingly, the Rylands and their friends turn to the co-operative movement and then to the old C.C.F. party for a solution to the economic problems that engulfed them largely as a result of the depression. Ironically it is the success of the second Mrs. Ryland in C.C.F. politics that leads to a job in Regina, and the temporary abandonment of the farm.

However, the wheel turns full cycle with the return, fresh from college, of the third John Ryland. This time the auguries for the future are better. The young, ecologically-aware proprietor will farm the land according to the enlightened principles he has absorbed at college. Moreover, in the emerging friendship between Ryland and an Indian girl from the adjoining reservation, Ms. Ringwood hints that the family has at last sunk its roots into the land. The two friends open the Indian medicine box, the most important symbol of the play, which John's grandmother long ago discovered buried in the soil near her home. In it they find natural objects—the bones of a small animal, a few stones—symbols of the land. Possession of the medicine box, it is suggested, legitimizes the family's moral claim to the land, which their Indian neighbours have always acknowledged. The play is thus pervaded by a poetic, almost mystic quality. (pp. 122-23)

Mirage evokes a strong sense of place, and in this respect it is an expression of the regionalism that has become characteristic of our literature. But *Mirage* is no less Canadian for being regional. It is a play that will appeal to varied audiences all across the country. . . . *Mirage* will probably be around for some time to come. (p. 123)

> Michael Benazon, "Ringwood's Saskatchewan Mirage," *in* Canadian Theatre Review, *No. 24, Fall, 1979, pp. 122-23.*

GERALDINE ANTHONY, S.C.

Gwen Pharis Ringwood is a serious artist consciously aware of her craft, who has sustained and developed and changed her style, her themes, and her vision of life gradually over the forty years of her creative writing. What remains a constant in this development is her sensitivity to poetry, her talent for characterization, and her deep emotional response to life.

It is this passion for life in all its manifest forms that motivates and informs all her work. . . . In her lecture, "So You Want To Be An Actor," . . . she said: "It is time for us to try to interpret the life we know and love to the rest of the world, unless we are content to go down as a people who were blind and inarticulate and afraid, a people who had nothing to say." Ringwood followed her own advice, interpreting the life around

her in artistic forms that indicate a gradual development in style, theme, characterization, and personal vision.

Ringwood's initial style . . . was the traditional folk play as seen in her first dramas . . . : *Chris Axelson, Blacksmith, One Man's House, Still Stands the House, Pasque Flower*, and *Dark Harvest*. In this early period of her work she experimented with comedy, farce, tragicomedy, and tragedy. During these two years of experimentation she discovered that her most comfortable medium in the folk play was a combination of farce and comedy. Hence the second period, her work in Alberta, was one in which she consistently used an interesting blend of farce and comedy, refining and developing it in the farcical comedies: *The Courting of Marie Jenvrin, The Jack and the Joker,* and *The Rainmaker.* She experimented with pure farce in *A Fine Colored Easter Egg,* and culminated this comic period in her writing with the mature and successful farcical comedy *Widger's Way.* This second period in her writing also saw the introduction of music into her comedy *Stampede.* This feeling for rhythm moved her naturally into the third period of her creativity when she wrote her musicals incorporating comedy and farce in an awareness of western Canadian history in the musicals *Look Behind You, Neighbor, The Road Runs North,* and *Mirage.* In the fourth and present phase of her work her style has changed from comedy to the style she had earlier abandoned—tragic drama. Eschewing the folk elements of her initial period, she now experiments with various forms of tragedy, including a serious confrontation play in *Lament For Harmonica,* a use of Greek tragedy in *The Stranger,* surrealism and expressionism in *The Deep Has Many Voices,* a modern morality play in *A Remembrance of Miracles,* and a Chekhovian style in *The Lodge.* During the past forty years, she has thus moved from folk plays to farcical comedy to large scale musicals, culminating today in experimental plays of social protest.

Her use of symbolism remains a constant in her work. From the first superb use of it in *Still Stands the House,* her symbols drawn usually from nature, from animals and plants, have supported and strengthened her style and theme. This is most clearly seen in the use of hyacinths and the unborn colt in *Still Stands the House,* the fragile blue flower in *Pasque Flower,* and the wheat field and the dead tree in *Dark Harvest.* Other animals include Midnight the horse in *Stampede,* the gelded Palomino stallion in *The Stranger,* the moose hypnotized in the car's headlights in *The Deep Has Many Voices,* . . . the golden cougar and the broken legs of the batik horses in *The Lodge.* . . . Ringwood uses many other symbols in her works but those drawn from nature seem to be her dominant symbols.

Ringwood uses poetry and poetic figures of speech, particularly metaphor, simile, and personification, most notably in *Still Stands the House, Pasque Flower, Dark Harvest, The Stranger,* [and] *The Deep Has Many Voices.* . . . All of Ringwood's works contain poetry or poetic prose to some degree. Even her titles are to a large extent metaphors supporting the theme, for example, *One Man's House, Still Stands the House, Pasque Flower, Dark Harvest, The Jack and the Joker, A Fine Colored Easter Egg, The Wall, The Deep Has Many Voices,* and *A Remembrance of Miracles.*

Ringwood's deep emotional response to life is demonstrated most powerfully through her use of language. She is definitely a poet giving voice to her vision of life through symbol, metaphor, simile, rhythm, and the blending of vowels and consonants into dialogue that has the persuasive power of music. Because of this gift her plays become metaphors of western

Canadian life. That she often combines music with dialogue reveals the enrichment she sees in a musical reinforcement of her poetic images. Her poetry catches the attention of the reader and playgoer to the extent that some of her poetic lines have become oft-repeated sayings. . . . Her plays use the rhythms of Canadian speech which differ slightly from American cadences and are very different from British speech patterns. The magic of words captures the reader and playgoer. Another talent is a visual gift for description. She is therefore able to produce an orchestration of language and images. Although she has used this gift in large panoramic dramas and historical musicals, she is at her best in developing subtle shades of feeling in plays that explore the emotions of a few characters only.

In theme her early plays dealt with the isolation and suffering of prairie people and immigrants in western Canada, followed by wry observations on such western Canadians as goldminers, newspaper editors, rainmakers, immigrants, farmers, and cowboys. Ringwood gently exposed human follies and foibles. The musicals examined prejudice in *The Wall* and life in Edson and the Cariboo. Her present period of writing is marked by serious attention to the exploitation of Indians, the violence and confusion of young people, and the self-interest and greed of contemporary society. As Ringwood moves away from the themes imposed by the land on her characters, she confronts human weakness and malice in its bare-faced culpability.

Underlying the surface theme in each of her works is the deeper theme that we are put on this earth to improve conditions, to make life better for others. From her earliest plays, e.g. *Chris Axelson, Blacksmith* (1938), to her latest plays, e.g. *The Lodge* (1975), this idea is apparent. Chris enriches the life of his nephew and his neighbors by considering them first. Ruth looks to the future happiness of her child in *Still Stands the House.* Lisa forfeits her own chances in favor of the happiness of her husband in *Pasque Flower* and he immolates himself for her in *Dark Harvest.* Marie Jenvrin celebrates life as does the community in *The Rainmaker, Look Behind You, Neighbor, Mirage,* and *The Road Runs North.* Bob Edwards preserves truth as his contribution to the enrichment of life in *The Jack and the Joker* and John Ware offers salutory advice on life in *Stampede.* Widger wishes ''to be a bigger fistfull'' of life, and Wasyl seeks real values. The children in *The Wall* destroy bigotry. Maya, Jana, and Merrill are seeking a better life although their quests end in tragedy. Melissa sums up in her person the search of all the Ringwood characters, and Jasmine admonishes her family that it is too late for the land to enrich them. We have come full circle here. Ringwood begins and ends with the land as an enriching factor in preserving and improving life.

In characterization Ringwood has chiefly created female protagonists. One notes the gradual emancipation of women in the roles she assigns them. Originally a traditionalist, Ringwood created her women willingly subordinated to their spouses, bearing the traditional burdens of household and children without any thought of individual careers. Ruth in *Still Stands the House* and Lisa in *Pasque Flower* and *Dark Harvest* are subservient to their husbands, quietly accepting their roles as wives and mothers. But Marie Jenvrin is the exception. She works with one aim in mind—to marry, love, and dominate her husband. The ladies in *The Jack and the Joker* are offensively superior gossip-mongers. Margaret in *The Rainmaker* is easily moved to return to her husband when rain falls on Medicine Hat. Celia in *Stampede* is the stereotyped young romantic in love. Olga in *A Fine Colored Easter Egg* urges her husband,

in traditional style, to capitulate to up-to-date and expensive ways of living. Roselle and the widow Anastasia in *Widger's Way* seek romance and husbands. Mrs. Carmelodeon in *The Wall* is a narrow-minded and bigoted snob. The ladies in the musicals *Look Behind You, Neighbor* and *The Road Runs North* are stereotyped camp followers, husband-seekers, faithful wives, and good mothers. It is only in the present period of her work that Gwen uses what Elsie Park Gowan had long ago urged her to employ—women's liberation. Ringwood today changes her stance in the present and fourth period of her work, creating the characters *Maya* and *Jana,* independent women fearlessly defining their positions in the face of ignorance and opposition; Melissa, a woman with a strong sense of herself as a person seeking the answer to the mystery of life; Merrill, a career woman unsuccessfully defending herself against a bigoted and small-minded community; Laura in *Mirage* leaving with Wilson for the north, without her parents' approval; Jasmine the artist forthrightly confronting her family's selfishness and greed. These women in Ringwood's last six plays are far removed from the old-fashioned concept of women portrayed in her earlier works. Her present protagonists are three-dimensional people struggling with the problems of contemporary life.

Ringwood's personal vision of life has remained constant through the years but her position has radically changed from silent onlooker to articulate critic. Always aware of the world problems of poverty, war, and the enslavement of peoples, she was, in the past, unable to voice her pain but took refuge instead in comedy and gentle satire. Her folk plays were written before the end of the depression and during World War II. She found herself too deeply and emotionally involved in those tragedies to be able ruthlessly and dispassionately to confront the evils they engendered. Although in *One Man's House* she decries social injustice, and in *The Wall* narrow-minded prejudice, these are isolated examples in plays of indifferent quality. It is not until her present period of writing that she seems to be able to attack evil in straightforward manner. Her ability to cope literally with evil in tragic tones which was early evidenced in *Still Stands the House,* once again is manifested in the plays of this present period.

In reviewing the body of her work one is impressed with her insights on human relationships, human conflicts, and human comedy in daily life. Her characterizations of Canadians in the early folk plays, in the Alberta comedies, the musicals, and the present serious dramas, are fine contributions to Canadian literature. Her best work is equal to and in some instances surpasses that of the more prominent Canadian playwrights today. Her language is evocative of the prairie and ranch country of western Canada. To theater in the west she has contributed forty years of dedicated work not only in her own playwriting and directing but also in helping others to realize their creative abilities.

Underlying all her work is the affirmation of man having some control over his destiny, some responsibility for changing the world, making it a better place in which to live. She espouses a philosophy which asserts that human beings can make some choices toward the good. The mystery of life challenges her, and although she has no positive answers on the existence of God she is drawn toward the mysteries of earth, of things that well up from the earth. Her plays include such images as dinosaurs, oil, soda springs, deep forests, and the mysteries they symbolically imply. Through image and word she often uses classical Greek references and Greek choruses, comic and tragic Spanish forms, Irish peasant styles as fitting receptacles to hold her quest for truth. In the final analysis Ringwood is defining those small steps toward growth, growing up, expanding to fit the mold in which a person is cast—the ideal. She is interested in the steps people take "to become a bigger fistful," toward the assertion of the dignity of being human.

Still productive, Gwen Pharis Ringwood is struggling to cope with her own strengths and weaknesses—to find the medium that will today give artistic expression to her vision of life. The international scope of her present political and social concerns is forcing her to seek the form that is best adapted to her particular temperament and talent. The strength of *Still Stands the House* is just that extraordinary combination of form and language, of characterization and symbol, that constituted her total métier forty years ago. Today she seeks this miracle once again. Like Melissa in *The Deep Has Many Voices,* she is on a quest. Whether she achieves her goal, one thing is certain: as she says of Melissa, the search is all. (pp. 164-69)

> Geraldine Anthony, S. C., in her *Gwen Pharis Ringwood, Twayne Publishers, 1981, 190 p.*

MARGARET LAURENCE

Still Stands The House, one of [Ringwood's] early and still one of her best-known plays, was written and first performed in 1938. It was one of the first to explore the Canadian prairie farm experience of those years. The obsessive love-hate that Bruce feels towards his unfruitful land, his half-mad sister's equally obsessive determination that their dead father's house shall not be sold, and his wife Ruth's terrible loneliness and feeling of isolation, all these still exert tremendous force and strength, some forty years after the play was written.

With *Pasque Flower,* written and produced in 1939 . . . , we have the beginnings of *Dark Harvest.* The earlier version is much more naive and derivative than the later. Essentially the same themes and same three major characters are here, but in *Pasque Flower* we can see the influence of Eugene O'Neill and perhaps Robinson Jeffers, 1930s American, out of ancient Greece. The play is written in high-flown oratorical free verse, and plain prairie people talk not in their own idiom but in grandiose language. This play represents a young writer learning her craft, impressed by the giants of American drama, wanting to deal with her own land and people not yet able fully to trust their native speech and her own knowledge.

By the time that *Dark Harvest* appeared in 1945, all this had changed. The borrowed style is abandoned; the characters and feelings are now genuinely those of the people she was writing about. Thereafter her writing was to change and develop throughout the years, but she has never faltered in her ability to portray authentically the people and places she has known so well.

Dark Harvest is a timeless play, even though it is so firmly set in the prairies in the 1930s. As in some of the writing of Frederick Philip Grove, Sinclair Ross, and Martha Ostenso, we have in the character of Gerth Hansen one of those prairie men who worshipped their land, felt bonds of communication with their horses, and starved their wives of affection and love. Unlike Jake Hansen in *Pasque Flower,* however, Gerth Hansen is no brute. He is a complex man who finds it impossible to express his love for Lisa, his wife, and his need for her love. It is not surprising that Lisa finally turns to Gerth's brother, David, a doctor newly returned to the area. The relationship between the two brothers, and the relationship of each of them

with Lisa, is beautifully and subtly portrayed. This is, as well, in some ways a deeply religious play. Gerth sees God as an adversary, and Gerth's own sin is of course that of spiritual pride. But the tragedy at the end is in fact both a triumph of the human spirit and a recognition that no one can live unto himself. Also, in Gerth's words, "Maybe He doesn't want things to die" after all.

In the few years between *Pasque Flower* and *Dark Harvest* the complexity of the characters has grown enormously, as has the playwright's confident handling of her material. The acknowledgement and portrayal of a strong intelligent woman character has also grown impressively. Remember that for Gwen Pharis Ringwood, it must have been initially difficult—as it was for all women writers at that time—to portray women as she *knew* they were, not as they had been presented by generations of male writers. Lisa in *Pasque Flower* is a suffering but essentially passive woman. Lisa in *Dark Harvest* is a strong, intelligent, sexual being who knows she is offering her love to a husband who cannot accept it even though he needs it, and she is not willing to live all her life in that kind of limbo. She also recognizes as morally unjustifiable Gerth's refusal to adopt a child, after their own infant died at birth—"I'll leave no stranger's son the land I've worked for."

Gwen Pharis Ringwood's themes are frequently those of social injustice, the hurts that human individuals give to one another, the love and courage that continues to be a part of the human psyche despite all the terrors. Her people are prairie farmers, the ranch hands of Alberta, the immigrants facing a frightening life in a new land, the native peoples of British Columbia who have been robbed of their land and dignity by the whiteman's culture but who still acknowledge and hear the ancestral voices.

Some of the plays are based on actual events, such as *The Jack And The Joker,* which concerns Bob Edwards of the famous *Calgary Eye-Opener,* or *The Rainmaker,* based on the hiring of a so-called rainmaker in Medicine Hat during a drought in 1921, or *Stampede,* based on the story of "Nigger John" Ware and some of Alberta's legendary cowboys. These plays, as with some of the comedies such as *The Courting Of Marie Jenvrin* seem to me to be good workable dramas but not really in the same class as the plays that are unequivocal tragedies and that come out of Ringwood's own imagination and deep perceptions. (pp. xi-xiii)

The Deep Has Many Voices, written in 1970, indicates very powerfully the playwright's growth, her more intricate sense of staging, her use of poetic and mythic forms to convey the inner truths, but without any of the borrowed styles that marked some of her very early work. In this play, she deals with contemporary society—the violence, the alienation, the materialism, the odd cults that some people cling to out of a feeling of helplessness.

The Lodge, written in the early 70s, reflects the concerns of our times, too, without being in any way didactic. The pollution and destruction of land and forest, the immorality of hunting for sport—these themes occur. Allan and his wife Shelley have bought a rundown lodge in B.C. The family reunion with parents and aunt and uncle, is a disaster. But Shelley's grandmother, the old woman Jasmine, an artist, redeems the situation in her own highly original ways. In this character, Ringwood has created a very memorable old woman. She's no-nonsense, and she isn't about to let her children stick her away in an old folks' home. With her old-time friend, Jimmy, the Band Chief of the local B.C. tribe, she outwits her middleaged children and reassures her grandchildren. It is a play written with anger and with wisdom.

In Gwen Pharis Ringwood's 1971 play, *The Stranger,* there is a coming together of many of the themes and techniques she has used in the past—the chorus, the drumming, the chanting, the mythic quality, the sense of the inevitability of the tragedy. Most of the characters are Shuswap Indians of the Okanagan. The Stranger is the "Chilcotin woman," Jana. As in Ringwood's early plays, there is an echo of the Greek tragedies, but now she has assimilated all such patterns into something that is truly of *this* land. Jana has been dreadfully wronged by her white commonlaw husband, Jason. He wants to take their son away from her, when he is about to marry, with an eye to the main chance, Barbara the white boss woman of the ranch. Ringwood has the bravery to bring the play to its terrible ending. Jana, in her sorrow and grandeur and rage for vengeance, is almost a Medea.

With *Mirage* (1979-80), the tone of the writing is in a lower key, and the speech of the people is the plain idiom of prairie people, as the story traces the lives and sufferings of two Saskatchewan families, one white and one Indian, against the backdrop of history from 1910 to the present. This is a more overtly political play than most of Ringwood's later work, but it is saved from didacticism by its moving portrayal of the fierce devotion of some of these people to a frequently harsh land, and by the presence of the Dowser, a prophet-like figure whose compassion extends to three generations and whose vision recognizes and acknowledges the ancient spirits of the land. *A Remembrance Of Miracles* (1980) is both extremely contemporary and timeless in its treatment of a young high school teacher's dilemma in the face of puritanical and fearful parents who seek to have Merrill's reading list for her senior students in English literature censored, the books banned even from the library, and Merrill herself fired. The title expresses what the teacher has hoped to convey to her students, and has indeed conveyed at least to some of them. I find this play almost unbearably poignant, as I happen to know only too well what the teacher is forced to go through.

For some forty years, Gwen Pharis Ringwood has been writing plays of a very high calibre. She saw, early on, the need to write out of our own people, our own land, and she has remained true to that vision. (pp. xiii-xiv)

> *Margaret Laurence, in a foreword to* The Collected Plays of Gwen Pharis Ringwood, *edited by Enid Delgatty Rutland, Borealis Press, 1982, pp. xi-xiv.*

KEITH GAREBIAN

Gwen Pharis Ringwood will no longer have to remain one of our "lost" playwrights. All her adult plays, with the exception of two long musicals, have been collected together in a massive volume [*The Collected Plays of Gwen Pharis Ringwood*]. . . .

Many of the collected pieces are sketches, but the more substantial works give impressive evidence of her dramatic gifts. Although the Canadian prairie predominates as a setting, and the farmer or Indian as a character, her plays are not the unrelieved flat and bland domain of regional themes. Their plot lines and situations are frequently trite or melodramatic, but their poetic power and moral impulses are strongly apocalyptic. Ringwood's preoccupations are courage, personal and tribal turmoil, and political tyranny, rather than sheer pioneer struggle or native culture. Often her benign moral impulses yield

simplistic stories and resolutions (as in *The Wall, The Jack and the Joker,* and *A Remembrance of Miracles*); but at their best, her plays have remarkable power.

The stage becomes incandescent with her never-ageing passion for social and psychological freedom, and her vibrant sensitivity to common folk who are made magically uncommon by their heroism.

> *Keith Garebian, in a review of "The Collected Plays of Gwen Pharis Ringwood," in* Quill and Quire, *Vol. 49, No. 5, May, 1983, p. 31.*

RICHARD PAUL KNOWLES

[*The Collected Plays of Gwen Pharis Ringwood*] presents, in a chronological arrangement, twenty-five plays by one of Canada's pioneering dramatists, providing the first real opportunity to observe her development and assess her achievement over five decades of playwrighting.

Gwen Pharis began writing plays at a time when there were few Canadian playwrights, few opportunities to *see* plays, and even fewer opportunities to have new plays produced. The earliest play in the collection was written in 1937 at a time "when we had no radio plays, few amateur little theatres, no university theatre departments, and because of the depression the touring companies had stopped coming West." Nevertheless, the plays of the late thirties include some of Ringwood's best-known and strongest work, including *Still Stands the House,* a powerful one-act prairie drama reminiscent of the short fiction of Sinclair Ross; and *Dark Harvest,* a full-length domestic tragedy developed out of the one-act *Pasque Flower* and dealing with the marriage between a strong, intelligent, clearly-drawn woman and a protagonist whose stature, character, and tragic limitations would be familiar to readers of Frederick Philip Grove. It is an impressive piece of work, and it establishes a characteristic and (at the time) revolutionary aspect of Ringwood's best plays: it is firmly rooted in its own time and place. (p. 95)

In the forties Ringwood turned to social comedies such as *The Courting of Marie Jenvrin* which by and large are rather trivial and occasionally are embarrassing. The best of these, *Widger's Way,* dates from 1952. During this period she also wrote a group of one-act plays (based on local material) for the Alberta Folklore and Local History Project. These, including *The Jack and the Joker, The Rainmaker,* and *Stampede,* are more interesting than the comedies, and are, in fact, quite competent, but they never rise to the power or the poetry of the earlier work. It is a measure of the decline that *Stampede,* a cowboy story, is more reminiscent of the Robert Stead of *Dennison Grant* than of *Grain.*

After a hiatus of several years, however, Ringwood returned to playwrighting in the late sixties and seventies with a new seriousness, maturity, and sophistication. Thematically she turned from the humanism of the thirties, with its emphasis on character, to more overtly political plays—plays, as Geraldine Anthony terms them, of social protest [see essay above dated 1981]. In these, the message can occasionally be overstated, but the seriousness of purpose cannot be doubted. At their best they are very powerful, as in *The Stranger,* a reworking of the Jason and Medea legend and the second play in the so-called "Indian Trilogy," and in *The Lodge,* a family drama that deals with ecology, Indian rights, and the role of women.

The plays of the seventies are most notable, perhaps, for Ringwood's increased theatrical sophistication, first apparent in *The Deep Has Many Voices* where the poetry of her earlier work begins to develop its theatrical dimension, extending language to stage picture, and where her experience begins to pay its dividends. The most ambitious and in many ways most powerful play in the volume is Ringwood's last full-length work, the 1979-80 historical epic *Mirage* which follows a Saskatchewan family and its land through three generations of political, social, and personal struggle. The strength of this play and of other late work is a measure of the loss to Canadian theatre that Gwen Ringwood's recent death represents. (pp. 95-6)

The Collected Plays of Gwen Pharis Ringwood is a landmark publication for all those interested in Canadian drama. Gwen Ringwood's was a major voice. She will be missed. (p. 96)

*Richard Paul Knowles, "Ringwood Collected," in
The Fiddlehead, No. 139, Spring, 1984, pp. 95-6.*

DIANE BESSAI

The long-awaited publication of Gwen Ringwood's *Collected Plays* is an important Canadian literary event on two accounts. Ringwood's proper place in the spectrum of western Canadian letters can now be established and her pioneer contributions to modern Canadian letters can now better be understood. . . . We can now recognize that Ringwood has hitherto been a missing link in the chain of western Canadian literary development that extends from Grove through Sinclair Ross, W. O. Mitchell, Laurence, Ryga to a number of younger playwrights. . . .

[What the pieces in this collection] reveal as a whole is a considerable range of style, tone, and dramatic mode: folk comedy, rural tragedy, expressionistic lyricism, historical epic, and social commentary. Ringwood's dramaturgy is not *avant garde;* like her precursor the Merrill Denison of the 1920's and a later successor, David French, her originality lies in the assimilation and development of modern dramatic styles to Canadian subjects filtered through her own particular human sympathies and interests. Unlike the aforesaid writers, she has written for the stage over several decades and her work offers a much greater range of theatrical expression. (p. 100)

To me the early one-act plays bring the short stories of Sinclair Ross to mind, particularly *Still Stands the House* and *Pasque Flower,* the latter the precursor of *Dark Harvest.* The first-named play, in its tight naturalistic structure, presents the destructive conflicts of familial relations bred from the harsh experience of prairie isolation comparable, for example, to Ross' "Painted Door." Yet in *Still Stands the House* there is also an obsessive psychological violence that echoes Eugene O'Neill, reminding us that Ringwood's literary training has been primarily in the theatre.

In 1937 she was awarded a Rockefeller Foundation Fellowship to the Carolina Playmakers School at the University of North Carolina; there, under the supervision of Frederick Koch, she wrote her early, primarily tragic, plays with their strong emphasis on the regional "folk" flavour which, in the tradition of the Irish literary revival, that School encouraged. For Gwen Ringwood this was the right kind of direction for the writing of plays that expressed the qualities of the life she observed in rural Alberta, leading her to become the most serious of the early modern regionalists of the budding Canadian drama.

Perhaps not surprisingly, Margaret Laurence [see excerpt above] expresses preference for the tragic plays of the prairie and the later stark one-act studies of Indian reservation life of the British Columbia interior (*Lament for Harmonica, The Stranger, The Furies*). Yet it is arguable that the dramatic craft of Ringwood's folk comedies is more than merely "workable" for the stage; such plays as *The Courting of Marie Jenvrin, The Jack and the Joker,* and *A Fine Coloured Easter Egg,* for example, bring a much-needed sense of humour to prairie letters, in this respect linking her to W. O. Mitchell and the prairie tradition of the tall-tale. In *Easter Egg,* the intransigent Wasyl Nemitchuk pretends he has drowned in order to frighten his wife from her determination to move to the city should the drillers find riches on their Alberta pig farm; the irascible Bob Edwards of *The Jack and the Joker* gets the last word on Leacockian small town hypocrisy and corruption; the impulsive Marie Jenvrin comes to regret her foolish insistence that the price of her hand must be the importation of a milch cow to the remote reaches of Yellowknife. The comic plays that work the best in Ringwood's *oeuvre* are the ones that combine grassroots particularity with the well-timed combinations of the secrets, reversals, and misunderstandings of skilful farce.

Commissions from the Alberta Folklore Project under Robert Gard at the University of Alberta of the early 1940's encouraged Ringwood to search out the actual stories of her region; in this respect she is a pioneer of the approach to regional material taken by later playwrights such as Ken Mitchell, Paddy Campbell, and Rex Deverell, for example, as well as the collective creators such as Theatre Network and 25th Street Theatre. (p. 101)

One of the striking features of this book as a whole is in the way it reveals Gwen Ringwood's continuing alertness to contemporary themes and styles over the years. *The Deep Has Many Voices,* an experiment in expressionistic lyricism, shows her exploring the potentials of open staging with music and projections to convey poetically and dramatically the perceptions of two young people about to begin their adult lives. *The Lodge* is a romantic comedy that examines current concerns about preserving wilderness environments and associated Indian traditions; its comic characterizations may also be seen as a direct development from Ringwood's earlier folk style. *A Remembrance of Miracles* is a topical examination of the bigotry of high school textbook censorship. *Garage Sale* offers the bemused observations and misunderstandings of an elderly couple as they eavesdrop on their younger neighbours.

Gwen Ringwood has devoted her long writing life to the drama; she began writing for the theatre in the hey-day of the Little Theatre movement and the Dominion Drama Festival. Her work was often performed by amateur organizations and theatre schools (particularly the universities of western Canada and the Banff School of Fine Arts) and over the years she has won many prizes and play competitions. The most valuable point that George Ryga makes in his playwright's Preface to this collection is polemical: without condescension to his subject, he rightly deplores that "a major talent" in the Canadian theatre should still be neglected by the "illiterate theatrical apparatchicks" of our contemporary Canadian theatre establishment. Perhaps the publication of this *Collected Plays* will lead to the correction of this oversight. (p. 102)

Diane Bessai, "Ringwood Recollected," in Canadian Literature, No. 101, Summer, 1984, pp. 100-02.

Michèle (B.) Roberts

1949-

English novelist, poet, critic, and short story writer.

Roberts writes intensely symbolic fiction featuring strong-willed female protagonists who rebel against society's male-imposed values. In her two most respected novels, *The Wild Girl* (1984) and *The Book of Mrs. Noah* (1987), Roberts employs elements of Christian myth and examines historical and contemporary issues pertinent to women as means for providing fresh perspectives on problems of female identity and human relationships. While Roberts's work has been called excessively didactic by some critics, others praise her imaginative exploration of social and individual concerns.

Roberts's first two novels, *A Piece of the Night* (1978) and *The Visitation* (1983), are characterized by recurring images, experimental techniques, and her lyrical use of language. *A Piece of the Night* is a confessional narrative of a young Catholic woman's difficult passage from domination by her parents and her husband to self-discovery as a feminist and lesbian. In *The Visitation,* Roberts symbolically links events in modern London with those in an allegorical Hellenic past. Laura Marcus notes that in this work "[the] classic 'feminine' conflicts—between work and love, autonomy and dependence—are explored in detail." *The Wild Girl* retells from a feminist perspective the biblical story of Mary Magdalene's relationship with Jesus. Roberts expounds her belief that a patriarchal society stifles female expression, and she addresses social and political issues pertaining to women, offering an alternative to the male-oriented interpretation of the Gospels. Emma Fisher observed: "[By] her rich use of symbols and metaphor [Roberts] transforms feminist cliché into something alive and moving." *The Book of Mrs. Noah* is generally considered Roberts's most imaginative work. In this complexly structured novel of ideas, which takes place largely in the protagonist's mind, Mrs. Noah and five sibyls recount the historically repressed status of women. As these characters sail on a metaphorical ark, they discuss the importance of women in determining the destiny of humanity.

In her poems, many of which are collected in *The Mirror of the Mother* (1985), Roberts draws on Greek myth, the Book of Psalms, and seventeenth-century religious poetry to explore archetypes relating to women, particularly mother-daughter relationships. Michael Horovitz observed that much of Roberts's verse "compresses into a musical mouthful of lines the kind of probing psychological insights or metaphysical speculation which are more commonly attempted in prose."

(See also *Contemporary Authors,* Vol. 115.)

Courtesy of Methuen London

lienne—*la mère soupe*, the vegetables mashed by cooking to satisfy men's bellies—certainly has a rough time between a Catholic upbringing, the Warneford Mental Hospital, marriage to an Oxford don, bearing a child, and discovering she's a lesbian. But her story, sadly, remains a runaway chaos of inchoate bits, an incoherence that slumps well short of the better novel it might with more toil have become. The proneness to packaged liberalism about conservation or communes is much too uninspected. So are the oohings and aahings every time a red flag shows up or a flock of sisters appears on stage. I suppose it's credible that Julie should land herself with a historian who fantasises about wrenching women apart. But then Ms Roberts is too much given to a flatly generalised way with people, and language that tends to jargon. . . .

Valentine Cunningham, "Bad News," in New Statesman, *Vol. 96, No. 2485, November 3, 1978,* p. 590.

VALENTINE CUNNINGHAM

Michele Roberts's first novel [*A Piece of the Night*] comes freighted with enough anti-male prejudice to cancel out at least a decade of the male chauvinist milliennia. Julie, a French girl whose name and experience are made to keep harking to Ju-

BLAKE MORRISON

If feminist fiction continues to be met with resistance in English literary circles this isn't just because (as is sometimes said) those circles are "male-dominated", and therefore have a vested interest in frustrating feminist aspirations. The resistance is more deep-seated. Feminist attitudes and aspirations may be tolerated and even acknowledged to be just; what is less easy to take is the confessional feminist mode, a mode conspicuously lacking in irony, humour and open-endedness. . . .

Michele Roberts's *A Piece of the Night* is a good example of a feminist novel heavily reliant on confession. There are passages which make use of a Plath-like, self-aggrandizing "I.". . . Moreover, there are hints throughout the novel that the experiences of the heroine, Julie, have been based on those of the author herself. These hints are confirmed in the novel's final page, which upholds confession as having both therapeutic psychological uses and radical political ones:

> Tell me about your past, Julie begins to urge other women, and they to urge her. The women sit in circles talking. They are passing telegrams along battle-lines, telling each other stories . . . no longer smuggling ammunition over back garden walls, no longer corpses in the church and mouths of men.

It is a strikingly militant (even military) final image—uplifting for those who already share the author's viewpoint, likely further to alienate those who do not. Much of *A Piece of the Night* gives the same impression of a book written under the stern eye of a women's workshop group, and not much interested in winning the hearts of those outside the charmed circle. Such exclusiveness need not be a weakness so long as there is some hard-earned wisdom to show for it. But it is exactly here—in its failure to offer anything new by way of insight—that the novel falls down. The story, to begin with, is drearily unilluminating in its record of a woman's self-realization. Through a series of flashbacks which alternate with Julie's return home to nurse her ailing mother (both the homecoming theme and the flashback technique are strongly reminiscent of Lisa Alther's *Kinflicks*), the heroine traces her gradual emergence into the feminist and lesbian she has now become: how her French parents sent her to England in order to receive a solid convent education; how she then went on to Oxford, and to marriage with Ben, a history don; how, after several years' marriage, she was shown the light by her female friends, and ditched Ben for life in a South London commune. With her raised consciousness, Julie can now see her past life as one of continual subjugation. The convent sought to suppress her sexuality by fitting her for chaste devotion to God. Ben used her as a sexual object (failing to give her orgasms) and treated her as the good little homemaker. Only with her lesbian friends is fulfilment possible. True, there are difficulties: Julie is jealous that her old friend and now lover, Jenny, has relationships with other women, and the temptation to seek a reconciliation with Ben still occasionally asserts itself. But the final image is one expressing defiance of men and solidarity with her own sex.

As if aware of the story's ponderous predictability, Ms Roberts jigs it up with a certain amount of stylistic experimentation. Instead of being divided into chapters (is it the male connotations in this word?), her novel falls into "sections"—"Ninth Section", "Tenth Section", and so on. And there is a fragmentation of time in the novel, not only because of flashbacks, but because Julie's tale occasionally overlaps with the stories set earlier in the century, of Sister Veronica and Great-Great-Aunt Harriet. But in form, as well as content, Ms Roberts finds it hard to escape well-established convention. The opening of the novel, for example, which describes the action (somewhere between rape and seduction) which led to Julie's conception, has an almost Victorian feel.

It is in its descriptions and metaphors, though, that the contradiction of the novel's radical purpose becomes most apparent. The heroine's development is one which is supposed to suggest that she has become more alert and sensitive, more responsive to a world outside daily drudgery. Yet the novel's metaphors consistently reduce and domesticate the wonder of the non-human world. . . . Articulate though Ms Roberts can sometimes be, she fails to suggest that her heroine has won through to growth and vision.

> Blake Morrison, *"In Confessional Circles,"* in The Times Literary Supplement, *No. 4000, December 1, 1978, p. 1404.*

MARION GLASTONBURY

[*The Visitation*] deserves to be approached, like Michele Roberts's poetry, with meditative care. 'One step at a time, duck', as the beloved grandmother warns, 'no good running before you can walk.' And no good galloping through this elaborate lyrical sequence for the sake of finding out what happens next, for it is all richly implicit in the mood of the moment. Memories of childhood—a twin brother, the 11-plus results, holidays in Norfolk, Chartres by night—mingle with the episodic loves of Stephen, George and Robert, and the enduring affection of Beth, to whom the Biblical title obliquely refers, with its invocation of Mary's greeting to the mother of John the Baptist. Both women are pregnant with their own creative promise, their potential for love and revolutionary change.

> Marion Glastonbury, *"Life Class,"* in New Statesman, *Vol. 105, No. 2718, April 22, 1983, pp. 27-8.*

MARION GLASTONBURY

The Eternal Feminine embodied in *The Wild Girl* is mercifully benign. Mary Magdalene proclaims the sanctity of passion following her carnal union with Jesus and strives to promote a girl-friendly version of His teaching in opposition to male-dominated Petrine orthodoxy. Innocence and pleasure make a welcome change from voluptuous cruelty and female succubi, but there are few surprises in this re-told Bible story, and the studied simplicity of Mary's diction as she spells out the new theology sounds infantile rather than child-like. . . .

> Marion Glastonbury, *"Bells of Hell,"* in New Statesman, *Vol. 108, No. 2794, October 5, 1984, p. 30.*

EMMA FISHER

"Novel" seems a strange word with which to classify *The Wild Girl*. It is a Christian feminist testament, in the form of an autobiography or fifth Gospel by Mary Magdalen. Mary appears in all the Gospels as a follower of Jesus who was present at the crucifixion and saw Jesus after his death. The author assumes that she is the same person as Mary of Bethany, sister of Martha and Lazarus, and also as the sinful woman who washes Jesus's feet. This Mary Magdalen becomes Jesus's lover and follows him for the last year of his life. Her dreams and revelations are interspersed with the narrative. She talks to Jesus about some of them, and he preaches on similar themes. Her dreams include new myths of the creation and end of the world, and others personifying processes within the mind, for instance a mystical marriage of male and female as a means of reaching spiritual wholeness. The book ends with a revelation of nuclear holocaust, described in the language of the Apocalypse. . . .

Michèle Roberts says in her introduction that in the process of dissecting the myth of Mary Magdalen, she found herself creating a new one. This new myth tries to tell us how to be happy, how to live, how to save the world, how to solve the problems of relationship between women and men. At the same time, she also gives alternative, non-miraculous versions of many events in the Gospels. Lazarus is not really dead: Mary has put him in the tomb as part of a magical rite to cure his illness. The feeding of the five thousand is a "miracle" of Martha's good housekeeping. Most important of all, Jesus did not rise from the dead. His preaching about resurrection is replaced by a quite different idea: spiritual rebirth during life by entering eternity through the body, or knowing God by being fully human. He preaches this doctrine most fully to Mary alone. Mary sees Jesus in the garden after his death, but acknowledges it to be an inner vision; the male disciples—it is suggested—claim falsely that Jesus has appeared to them too, this time in the body. It is the culmination of their quarrel with Mary. Led by Simon Peter, who is anti-women and anti-sex, they have all along resented her closeness to Jesus and her stepping out of women's traditional role. In claiming the physical resurrection of Jesus, they reject Mary and his true teaching, and set the course for a male-dominated Christianity, in which God is only Father and not Mother, and women are subservient to men and cannot be priests.

At least, I think this is what happens. Like all the best revelations, the book is obscure. Its obscurity is part of an intentional complexity. Some feminists will find in it a convincing message for their new religion. Michèle Roberts is intelligent and passionate; by her rich use of symbols and metaphor she transforms feminist cliché into something alive and moving. Her poetic gifts, which turned the screw of intensity rather uncomfortably in her two semi-autobiographical novels (*A Piece of the Night* and *The Visitation*), are seen to better advantage here. The shadow of the author speaking about herself and other women is often felt, especially in the description of Mary laboriously writing her book, but when she is more oblique Roberts says more about women's condition without seeming to wallow in self-pity.

> Emma Fisher, *"New Myths for Old,"* in The Times Literary Supplement, *No. 4256, October 26, 1984, p. 1224.*

KATE FULLBROOK

The Wild Girl is a feminist version of the gospel, with Mary Magdalene as the liberated lover of a sexually delicious Jesus who has as much time for the metaphor of God as Mother as for the more usual concept of a Father-God. The first Christian schism is portrayed as one between Simon-Peter, an anxious paternalist jealous of his opponent's closeness to Jesus, and Mary Magdalene, a brave feminist who has undergone all the degradations and joys of womanhood in her career as prostitute, free woman and, finally, mother of Jesus's daughter. Needless to say, Mary loses to Simon-Peter, and the false masculinist pattern is established for Christianity. The split that denies validity to half of humanity leads directly to Mary's apocalyptic vision of a holocaust of nuclear fire that consumes the world. The sentiments that animate this novel are fine, even noble. But the fiction itself never comes alive. Mary Magdalene remains nothing but a committed feminist of the 1980s; Jesus

becomes nothing but a simple archetype for the non-sexist male; Simon-Peter stays stiff and lifeless; the dreams and visions that pepper the book seem textbook exercises. The whole production is eminently predictable—an allegory that scarcely invites interpretation. (pp. 49-50)

> Kate Fullbrook, in a review of *"The Wild Girl"*, in British Book News, *January, 1985, pp. 49-50.*

LAURA MARCUS

In *The Visitation,* Michele Roberts incorporates female figures which patriarchy has attempted to destroy, literally or otherwise, because their power is threatening: the witch, the spinner/spinster, the parthenogenetic goddess, the wisewoman. The radical feminist philosopher Mary Daly would seem to be an influence here, but whereas Daly spins off into a matriarchal cosmos, Roberts contains her mythical figures within the dreams and fantasies of her central character, Helen. Helen is a writer, but the voice of *The Visitation* is not quite hers, nor is it that of an omniscient narrator. This disembodied voice transforms scenes of contemporary London life . . . into their counterparts in a mythical Hellenic past or in the ritual-dominated world of Africa, blurring the distinctions between reality and fantasy in a prose which is full, resonant and at times over-charged.

Without this linguistic and mythical apparatus, the novel would be a fairly conventional female *künstlerroman,* as Roberts traces her heroine's progress through childhood, convent school, Oxford and London. The classic "feminine" conflicts—between work and love, autonomy and dependence—are explored in detail. . . . The strengths of the novel lie in its incorporation of a dream text into a realistic framework, in the portrayal of relationships between woman across generations, and in its structure: flashbacks to earlier periods in Helen's life are effectively made by means of recurrent images and objects.

> Laura Marcus, *"Feminism into Fiction: The Women's Press,"* in The Times Literary Supplement, *No. 4304, September 27, 1985, p. 1070.*

PETER PORTER

The poems in *The Mirror of the Mother: Selected Poems, 1975-1985* have the manner of improvisations, of statements and metaphors directed straight at an audience, with no attempt at . . . elaborate contrivances. . . . The present tense and the active mood predominate. Many of the properties are traditional, however—there is a sequence devoted to the sojournings of Persephone. Ms. Roberts stakes a great deal on her instinct and when this is in good order she writes with power and conviction. **"Levelling with Death"** may seem crude in its effects but it is in many ways the legitimate heir to Donne's Holy Sonnet. . . .

> Peter Porter, *"Over-Egging the Pudding,"* in The Observer, *March 9, 1986, p. 27.*

MICHELENE WANDOR

[The poems in *The Mirror of the Mother: Selected Poems 1975-1985*] encompass a range of ways in which the woman's voice searches for its own identity, through friendships with other women, through male lovers, through a sexuality inscribed in landscape and drawing on a lush and dense imagery. . . . Mostly the voice is assured and plush, with straight expressions of loss and quests for new forms of friendship and heroism, without irony. Occasionally the imagery becomes overblown, like a flower allowed to remain too long on its stalk, and occasionally the legacy of Sylvia Plath is a little too evident. But these are only moments when the high tone dips; by and large it is a strong and assured collection, which suggests ways in which a modern verse form can still be used to create a new romanticism, spoken by a female voice.

> *Michelene Wandor, in a review of "The Mirror of the Mother: Selected Poems 1975-1985," in* British Book News, *April, 1986, p. 246.*

MICHAEL HOROVITZ

The Mirror of the Mother is subtitled *Selected Poems 1975-1985*, and shows a steady maturation of feelings, thought and technique. [Robert's] iconoclastic novels, especially *The Wild Girl* (i.e. Mary Magdalene), have attracted a certain amount of public notoriety, and much of her verse compresses into a musical mouthful of lines the kind of probing psychological insights or metaphysical speculation which are more commonly attempted in prose.

At its most glaringly polemical, her language risks the stodginess Keats dreaded—"poetry that has a palpable design"—but only infrequently in this highly selective edition.

At her most relaxed, Ms Roberts is at once intellectually passionate and passionately lyrical. (p. 80)

> *Michael Horovitz, "Daughters of Albion," in* Punch, *Vol. 291, No. 7612, November 12, 1986, pp. 78, 80.*

HELEN BIRCH

The Book of Mrs Noah is Roberts' most ambitious and carefully conceived novel to date. Through the character of Mrs Noah, the nameless wife, the not-man, she refracts her themes—of women and writing, motherhood as cultural symbol and as social pressure/enigmatic desire—taking her on a voyage into a lost history of the feminine.

Mrs Noah is a librarian; she classifies information, tries to find order. She also wants a child. Her husband demurs, arguing the irresponsibility of bringing a child into this 'poisoned place'. In Venice, the floating city of dreams, she has a vision of an ark, filled with women: outcasts and amazons who want to write. Joined by five sibyls, prophetesses of the future—mothers, wives, lesbians, a Black woman, mourners—she creates a *'salon des refusées. Des refusantes'*. Together, they discuss the problems of writing as a woman, rehearse old arguments about feminism and creativity, and exchange stories. The ark becomes Protean, a womb, the mother's body, containing the history and dreams of all the women. God puts in an appearance too, as male Author and maker of canons; the women call him The Gaffer. His Bible is the Word which holds theirs in place, the ego which defines theirs as alter/Other. The sibyls' struggle for a language to tell their own stories takes the narrative back into mythology, to the original Mrs Noah, to the servant raped by her master, to sexualities denied and punished. (p. 27)

The novel's structure is intricate: debates are picked up, dropped, re-woven with another theme. The effect is somewhere between symphony and cacaphony; the writing is sometimes too clotted with images, too self-conscious to be really rich. Yet Roberts' refusal of a stable subjectivity allows her to explore psychological as well as literary terrain, and to dissolve the borders between the two. She is one of a very few contemporary feminist novelists who engage with and reform the theories of the academy in her work. Her ideas can be set in play with Freudian and Lacanian psychoanalysis, the theories of Julia Kristeva. The women on the ark re-experience what Kristeva calls the 'semiotic': the pre-Oedipal moment before language. They are bound to the body of the mother—to rhythm, movement and melody—yet paradoxically left wanting, barred from any stable signification or meaning. The ark is a 'long twist of words spun out of loss'. Women exist as lack. Men appear as children, fixed to the mother's breast. Yet all the voices in the novel are bound together through the idea of Everywoman, the Other of Christian myth; what is psychoanalytically true about sexual difference is turned into a universal, *lived* truth. Difference is a condition of gender alone.

The Book of Mrs Noah is playful, allusive and challenging. But, for all the splitting, the debunking of dualistic thought, there's a circularity about Mrs Noah's journey, a desire for unity. There are no lived diversities left in the novel; everything is pared down to the dream of a common language, a collective history, where plurality has no place. At the core of the novel, there's a whole Woman, a self who can be alienated, cut off, can still fall from grace. Despite itself, the floating city of dreams remains bound to the heavenly idea of its own creation. (pp. 27-8)

> *Helen Birch, "Women at Bay," in* New Statesman, *Vol. 113, No. 2930, May 22, 1987, pp. 27-8.*

VALENTINE CUNNINGHAM

The eponymous heroine of Michèle Roberts's *Mrs Noah* . . . encounters the madness sploshing about in old libraries. But [she] stays sane because she has seen through the distorting stories about women catalogued in that great dementing depository of male consciousness, the British Museum Reading Room.

Readers as mindful of Virginia Woolf as Ms Roberts's Mrs Noah will recognise here a revamp of certain central Woolf themes. Still, the redoing of *A Room of One's Own* is admirably energetic, as Mrs Noah abandons Mr Noah in Venice for a jaunt in a feminist Ark. The craft's chief passengers are a bunch of less renowned sibyls—all gender discontents and marital victims. These women want to reauthorise the world, to reinscribe it as the product not of father-gods but of mothers, queens of heaven, single-parent madonnas. Above all, they've got it in for the hapless Gaffer, a version of Judaeo-Christian divinity and male authorship.

All of which is familiar stuff to followers of feminist theory. Nor is this novel easily let off charges of narcissism and narrowness simply by having a few bubble-pricking voices point out that Mrs Noah's shipmates are all bourgeois and hyperliterate and therefore aloof from the problems of working-class women. Sensibly, however, the sibyls all get returned at the end to the real banalities and compromises of the quotidian world. And that, agreeably, is quite a distance from the feminist *Narrenschiff*'s rather self-condoning time-capsule.

> *Valentine Cunningham, "Skulls Beneath the Skin," in* The Observer, *May 24, 1987, p. 25.*

CLAIR WILLS

In Michele Roberts's work, the use of natural metaphor does not imply a privileged relation between woman and nature.

The Mirror of the Mother, a selection from her work of the past ten years, includes a sequence of lyric poems, constructed round the myth of Demeter and Persephone, in which "woman" is examined through the imagery of the seasons. Here, language is not a simple reflection of experience, but the mirror of a myth through which experience is mediated. . . . Roberts plays with duplicitous language, uncovering possibilities hidden in even the most mystifying metaphors.

> *Clair Wills, "Driving a Tradition to the Wall," in* The Times Literary Supplement, *No. 4397, July 10, 1987, p. 748.*

ANNA VAUX

The Book of Mrs Noah is a story about women's writing—the unwritten parts of old and well-known tales, hidden or silenced voices—and the visceral world of a subculture. It is also concerned with repossession and reclamation, a submerged world reasserting itself, and with "rival versions of the truth". Michèle Roberts's most fantastical novel so far, it begins with a dream of Mr Noah's death, and ends with Mrs Noah's anticipated pregnancy, a new life, or at least a promise of such. What happens in between takes place in Mrs Noah's unconscious. Not that this is a personal domain: her inner world is of the collective sort, though it is also almost exclusively female. Re-termed her "Ark", or, more tellingly, her "Salon des Refusées", it is both an erotic Utopia—which promises a better world with woman at its centre—and a savage terrain overwhelmed by sadists, where everyday actions are twisted into signs that something is drastically wrong. Nuclear holocaust is used as the ultimate indictment. But Mrs Noah's fantasies, and those of five companions (Roberts calls them "Sibyls"), stand as the only alternatives.

The novel strives, however, for this sort of imbalance. Language, literature, the canon, the Sibyls complain, are what is wrong, have excluded women, denied them a voice, an idiom and a set of references. What gives the book its peculiarly blank atmosphere is its replacement of narrative at every point by argument and counter-argument. Characters are introduced and arranged not so much to tell a story as to elaborate a thesis or to demonstrate a method. . . .

One of the larger paradoxes here is that the concentration on theoretical device is developed to ensure the importance of domestic trivia and experience. Indeed, theory has become a way, not of explaining, but simply of demonstrating an inner life. . . . The Sibyls invent semiologies of food and create whole grammars out of household objects, and their own stories and reflections circle around an abundance of personal and incon-

sequential detail. It has predictable results, too. Mrs Noah, following the feminist injunction to "write your body", is unable to distinguish between books and bodies, reading and sex, the bibliophile and the expert lover, and the completion of her book coincides with her looked-for pregnancy as the expected metaphor for self-expression.

The motivation for Mrs Noah's experimental text comes with her recognition that "here on the Ark, in my Arkive, I can connect I *want* with innumerable other words". The novel's suppression of the third person, and its focus on a demanding, pleasure-seeking and confessing self, may answer Roberts's questions and endorse the egotism she feels is necessary to restore the status quo, but it is the male, and minor, characters who stand out, sympathetic in their alienation: Mr Noah arguing about not having a baby, or a character called God, immeasurably depressed when told he has died twice over, once as omnipotent ruler and again as omniscient narrator. It is during these moments and on this level that *The Book of Mrs Noah* can be warm and witty. For the most part Roberts's devices are so dry that they fail to inspire warmth, and generate a language so private and confessional that it rarely extends beyond self-indulgence or wishful thinking.

> *Anna Vaux, "From the Archives," in* The Times Literary Supplement, *No. 4399, July 24, 1987, p. 801.*

JENNIFER McKAY

I've always avoided novels in which bowels are apt to melt. *The Book of Mrs Noah* convinces me I'm right, though not because it's run-of-the-Mills & Boon romantic fiction. No, it's a serious novel about a broody librarian whose husband, Mr Noah, doesn't want children. She could do the decent thing and throw away her Pills without telling. Instead she jumps naked into the Grand Canal and has visions about a floating ark full of women writers or sibyls.

This ark represents the solution to the problems peculiar to women writers and isolated by Virginia Woolf in *A Room of One's Own*—problems of privacy and time. During the ark's voyage the sibyls consider these and other aspects of women's lives, such as motherhood, sexual exploitation and the prevalence of flashers wherever women choose to walk alone.

There are many other themes, such as religious experience, and the inevitability of suffering. The trouble is that as a novel of ideas *Mrs Noah's* ideas are not especially novel and they form too heavy a load for the fragile narrative.

> *Jennifer McKay, "'I Am Not a Story'," in* The Listener, *Vol. 118, No. 3028, September 10, 1987, p. 23.*

Budd (Wilson) Schulberg

1914-

American novelist, scriptwriter, nonfiction writer, dramatist, short story writer, editor, and memoirist.

An acclaimed author of social realist works, Schulberg is perhaps best regarded for his screenplay for the American cinema classic *On the Waterfront*, for which he received an Academy Award in 1954. In his novels and film scripts, Schulberg addresses what he termed "the prime American theme"—destructive national ideals related to success and materialism. Through his trenchant critiques of corruption within the entertainment industry and organized labor movements, Schulberg examines such topics as the conflict between social responsibility and financial prosperity and the disintegration of personal integrity and moral values. Although some reviewers contend that Schulberg's terse, often vulgar prose style and stereotypic characterizations detract from his powerful subject matter, many commend his social insight and his incisive, unsympathetic portrayal of American society.

The son of Benjamin P. Schulberg, one of the most powerful motion picture producers of the 1920s, Schulberg experienced life in Hollywood as an insider. His childhood adventures, together with early assignments as a reader and junior contract writer for producer David O. Selznick, provided material for many of his early novels. *What Makes Sammy Run?* (1941), a mordant examination of the materialistic axioms of the Hollywood film community, depicts a lower-class Jew who engineers his rise from newspaper copy boy to prestigious Hollywood producer through such practices as plagiarism and betrayal. Although several critics faulted the novel for anti-Semitic implications and stylistic lapses, many praised *What Makes Sammy Run?* as an honest and poignant examination of Hollywood corruption. *The Harder They Fall* (1947), detailing the rise and fall of an unskilled immigrant who is promoted as a talented boxer by opportunists seeking to manipulate his career for their own ends, was acknowledged for capturing the atmosphere of the brutal Chicago prizefighting circuit as well as for its condemnation of boxing as an exploitative industry.

Schulberg's next novel, *The Disenchanted* (1950), chronicles the demise of Manley Halliday, an alcoholic American novelist who is forced by financial debts to write plot scenarios for an overambitious film producer. Although many critics suggested that Halliday is modeled after F. Scott Fitzgerald, with whom Schulberg collaborated in 1939 on a film scenario entitled *Winter Carnival*, Schulberg insisted that the character is a composite of many alienated writers he knew in Hollywood during the 1930s. The book received largely favorable notices and is regarded as among Schulberg's most ambitious works. Schulberg collaborated with Harvey Breit in adapting *The Disenchanted* for the stage in 1959, but the drama received mixed reviews and is generally considered of lesser importance than the novel. *Waterfront* (1955) expands on the sociological and historical background of Schulberg's screenplay for the film *On the Waterfront*. Like the film, this novel offers a realistic exposé of union corruption and brutality on the New York harbor from the perspective of Terry Malloy, an amoral longshoreman and former boxer whose brother is associated with the harbor mob. Pressured by his girlfriend and a local priest,

Malloy decides to testify against union grafters, but when his threat results in his brother's death, he is driven to a futile stand against the mob. Although the novel did not attain the status of Schulberg's screenplay, James Kelly called *Waterfront* "the best of Schulberg, a full-fledged performance by a gifted American writer."

Schulberg's later novels have received largely mixed reviews. *Sanctuary V* (1969) was written after a fourteen-year hiatus during which Schulberg wrote exclusively for stage and screen. Set in a fictitious Latin American country, this work traces the downfall of a socially committed political figurehead who flees his country following the ascension of a tyrannical dictator only to encounter further persecution in a neighboring nation. Although faulted for vague social views, Robert J. Shea called *Sanctuary V* "an intelligent, humanistic examination of Cuban-style revolution as well as a vivid portrayal of deterioration in captivity." Schulberg's next novel, *Everything That Moves* (1980), features corrupt unionist Jerry Hopper, whom many critics interpreted as a thinly disguised caricature of former Teamsters Union president Jimmy Hoffa.

In addition to his screenplay for *On the Waterfront*, written in collaboration with director Elia Kazan, Schulberg has authored such film scripts as *A Face in the Crowd*, also written with Kazan, and *Wind across the Everglades*. Schulberg's early short stories collected in *Some Faces in the Crowd* (1953) offer satiric sketches on such topics as Hollywood and boxing. Schulberg's nonfiction works include *The Four Seasons of Success* (1972; revised as *Writers in America: The Four Seasons of Success*), a collection of essays about the changing literary fortunes of such authors as Nathanael West, John Steinbeck, and Sinclair Lewis; *Loser and Still Champion: Muhammad Ali* (1972), a candid portrait of the flamboyant prizefighter; and *Moving Pictures: Memories of a Hollywood Prince* (1981), a memoir of Schulberg's early experiences in Hollywood. Several of Schulberg's novels have been adapted for film.

(See also *CLC*, Vol. 7; *Contemporary Authors*, Vols. 25-28, rev. ed.; *Contemporary Authors New Revision Series*, Vol. 19; *Dictionary of Literary Biography*, Vols. 6, 26, 28; and *Dictionary of Literary Biography Yearbook: 1981*.)

JAMES KELLY

Unless there is to be a radical change in dramatic values or public taste, the violence and venality of a seamy situation like the New York waterfront will always yield more reader magic than the idyllic placidity of a vine-covered cottage. Which explains in part why reporter Malcolm Johnson was asked to do his Pulitzer prize-winning newspaper pieces on the New York harbor. Which explains why a knowing professional like Budd Schulberg gladly undertook to translate this material into the prize-winning film. And why Mr. Schulberg's sibling novel, aptly titled *Waterfront*, now provides a fitting cap for the pyramid.

Johnny Friendly, the hamhanded boss of Bohegan's I.L.A. Local 447, had a saying: "We got a couple of the fattest piers in the fattest harbor in the world. Everything that moves in and out, we take our cut." Using limitless graft, trigger happy hoodlums, chain-reaction political influence, and the discipline of brutality, Johnny misses few bets—from extortion and loansharking to murder. But one little mistake was made in the routine rub-out of a troublesome young progressive named Joey Doyle. The mistake was to involve Joey's friend and pigeon-racing colleague, a fuzzy-headed, half-vicious former fighter named Terry Malloy. Stirred to dim rebellion by Joey's schoolgirl sister Kate and egged on by Father Barry..., Terry is fingered by the mob. And when, as a little reminder, they dump his mobster brother's body at his feet, something flares up in the punch-battered brain. It's an all but unbearable sequence of climactic scenes as Terry fights back, defies Friendly, sparks off hearings of the State Crime Commission—and pays up.

Characters in *Waterfront* are studied from the inside out, passionately and with no attempt at impartiality. They wake up each other. There's an inevitability about their actions, identified in a poetic way with rhythms of the great liners moving down river and the grace of wheeling pigeons above the tenements. The author's ear for high-octane language and his ability to transcribe it without spurious literary flourishes, evidenced in earlier novels and stories, tie up the package. Demurrers, if there are any, will be based upon the note that Mr. Schulberg's indignation and desire to expose all dimensions of the waterfront web run neck and neck with his story, occasionally threatening to beat it under the wire....

One can regard this story of members of the International Longshoremen's Association "pistol local" at work on the blood-stained, corruption-clouded piers of a North River town as creative journalism. One can also think of it as intensely personalized, white-hot fiction with all the menace, suspense, narrative flow, fresh characterization, and social message anybody could reasonably expect in a novel. Either way, it's the best of Schulberg, a full-fledged performance by a gifted American writer.

> *James Kelly, "In a Harbor of Greed and Violence,"* in The New York Times Book Review, *September 11, 1955, p. 5.*

W. R. BURNETT

It is very difficult for me to write a fair review of Budd Schulberg's new novel, *Waterfront*. Like millions of other Americans, I saw the movie version, and so I find it impossible to read the book freshly and judge it merely on its merits as prose fiction. Owing to an excellent screen play by Schulberg, top direction by Elia Kazan, and superb acting by Marlon Brando, Eva Marie Saint, and Karl Malden, [*On the Waterfront*] was to me one of the finest movies of this generation. It had everything: suspense, heart, pity, and terror. I'm sorry that I can't quite say the same for the novel. Maybe if I'd read it before seeing the movie version my feelings might have been different....

I had the feeling at times in reading the book that Mr. Schulberg's heart was not in it, as it was in *What Makes Sammy Run?*; that it is just the result of research in a district and in a milieu completely unfamiliar to him. And then he has difficulties with his style. Some books are written in one style, some in another; but Mr. Schulberg switches from style to style. Sometimes it is just plain tough, when the characters are talking and the action is moving of itself; at other times, when the author is explaining a character or a scene, the reader comes upon words like "dichotomy," which do not belong in a story like this.

And then Mr. Schulberg never seems quite at home with his leading character, the young Irish ex-fighter, Terry Malloy. Terry is shown in conversation with a "nice" girl. "Terry paused, shaken by her frankness, by her—the word eluded him—purity." The word would have eluded him entirely.... You can hear the adroit mind of the author groping—and in vain.

On the other hand he hits Terry off to life further along in the story. Terry has just found his brother, a dressed-up hoodlum—murdered by gangsters—hanging from a docker's hook in an alley. Says Terry: "Look at the way the sonsabitches got his coat all dirty." This speech has the anguished irrelevance of life itself.

And so it seems to me that this very fine novel goes by fits and starts. Budd Schulberg is one of the most competent novelists now writing and this is a very interesting and hard-hitting book, make no mistake about that; but I think it was a task he set himself to perform and that it was not a book that just begged to be written. However, there is at least one respect in which it is superior to the movie version. It is more honest at the end. What happens to Terry Malloy in the novel is exactly what would have happened to him in actuality.

W. R. Burnett, "Dockers' Dilemma," in The Saturday Review, *New York, Vol. XXXVIII, No. 39, September 24, 1955, p. 17.*

BERNARD D. NOSSITER

Reversing the usual order, Budd Schulberg has fleshed out his commercially successful scenario to produce a novel [*Waterfront*]. Most of the scenes and large chunks of dialogue that mesmerized movie audiences are here reduced to the printed page. The book, like the picture, hurries from event to event, almost as if Elia Kazan were peering over Schulberg's shoulder muttering, "Make it move, make it move." . . .

The picture at least caught for us the sight, smell, and taste of the longshoreman's setting. The novel lamely tells us most Americans don't live in railroad flats.

At a time in our literature when most talented young men are concerned with intimate dissections of fragile psyches, the gentler reader waits impatiently for novels of three-dimensional characters interacting with a real world. But Schulberg offers us outsized screen figures. The great naturalists awakened our understanding of life with fresh insights into the human condition; perhaps today writers are afraid to describe a social reality unless it is a state-sanctioned aspect.

Can anyone believe a priest in a dockside parish could know nothing of the way his parishioners live and work until a young girl taunts him? Is Terry, the fighter who finally tells all to the crime commission, man or Marlon? Does Schulberg really think Terry acquiesces in waterfront violence and extortion because his "inability to look into himself or experience anything other than immediate pleasure or pain was nothing but sloth?" Equally improbable is Katie the virgin's literal Catholicism being fired into militant revenge by the murder of her brother.

To be sure, the author of **What Makes Sammy Run** is a polished technician with a knack for taut, dramatic dialogue. There is a poignancy and tense understatement in the duet between Terry and his brother, the fast-talking henchman of the racketeer unionist, as they ride to the brother's doom. Father Barry's moving speech to the longshoreman, "Christ stands alongside you in the shapeup," is a stunning piece of imagery and polemic.

Schulberg, too, has a reporter's eye. He reproduces accurately the dock worker's sense of being outside the pale and his solidarity against even well-intentioned intruders. His novel exploits some of the freedom that taboo-ridden movies are denied. . . .

But underneath this skin lie some very brittle bones. Father Barry looks to a Christian revolution to rescue the docks from communism and the International Longshoremen's Association. In an age when organized religion is a vestigial institution, manipulated by other, more powerful social and economic forces, the Barry-Schulberg mystique is singularly fanciful. . . . When it comes to political science in the raw, uneducated waterfront workers could tell Schulberg a thing or two about the nature of the state and whose side it is on. If, in his Hollywood youth, Schulberg had visited San Francisco and other West Coast ports, where a rotary hiring hall and stiff contracts have been routine for a generation, he might have written a different book.

Bernard D. Nossiter, "Unsuccessful Reverse," in The Nation, *New York, Vol. 181, No. 14, October 1, 1955, p. 288.*

WILLIAM PFAFF

[*Waterfront*] is the story of the movie [*On the Waterfront*], as the movie was the story of the book—each says the same thing in its own terms. Schulberg's original story and characters created the film, but I think it is clear that the direction of Elia Kazan and the acting of Marlon Brando had a good deal to do with the re-statement of the story in the novel. This is particularly evident in the scene where Terry's brother tries to convince him not to go to the Crime Commission, and then pulls a gun on him. The scene in the novel is more than it was on the screen, but I do not think it could have been written in this form without Brando having first acted it. There is something in it that seems outside the limit of fiction, an element of the instinct and presence of the actor's art.

This novel stands up as an independent creation; it is not Schulberg's best book, but it is a good, solid one. It suffers in the beginning from an affected toughness in narration, but that soon disappears. The toughness in dialogue is right. And in Terry and the priest, Schulberg has two really valid characters, and he explores them superbly. (p. 101)

William Pfaff, "On the Docks," in Commonweal, *Vol. LXIII, No. 4, October 28, 1955, pp. 100-01.*

KENNETH TYNAN

[With *The Disenchanted*], Budd Schulberg and Harvey Breit have done something that is rare in the history of the theatre: they have collaborated on the story of a collaboration. In 1939, Mr. Schulberg was invited by a Hollywood producer to work on the script of a campus musical with F. Scott Fitzgerald, who accepted the job because he needed the money to pay off his debts and to support his wife and child. The assignment involved a trip to New York, in the course of which Fitzgerald tumbled off the wagon he had been on for many months and, in the upshot, got himself peremptorily fired. Out of this experience Mr. Schulberg wrote a novel [*The Disenchanted*], on which the present day play is loyally founded. . . . Since the hero of both novel and play is called Manley Halliday, it cannot fairly be objected that he bears little resemblance to Scott Fitzgerald. Even so, our interest in the piece depends on our accepting the authors' assurance that Halliday is a great writer wrecked by his playboy past. And here . . . our otherwise willing suspension of disbelief [is damaged]. . . . Messrs. Schulberg and Breit have put into Halliday's mouth very few words that suggest greatness, however ruined or vestigial. Bumping into his wife-to-be at the 1918 armistice celebrations in Paris, he observes, "You're my eternal jazz baby, Lorelei." And he indulges, twenty-odd years later, in a paean to the twenties that pays tribute to everyone from Jack Dempsey to T. S. Eliot and is phrased so lushly that it might, given adequate orchestration, pass unnoticed into the musical version of *Gentlemen Prefer Blondes*. The only scene that conveys a hint of Halliday's putative stature is the one in which he defends his contemporaries against the charges of his irate young collaborator, a child of the depression who sees the twenties as nothing more than a breeding ground of elegant, evasive ostriches. Historically, the young man may be right, but dramatically the scene makes Halliday eloquent and strong. (pp. 107-08)

Kenneth Tynan, in a review of "The Disenchanted," in The New Yorker, *Vol. XXXIV, No. 43, December 13, 1958, pp. 107-09.*

NEWSWEEK

No matter how sternly Budd Schulberg and Harvey Breit insist that they were writing about half a dozen other people, the doomed hero of *The Disenchanted* is clearly F. Scott Fitzgerald in the encircling gloom of his last years. By calling their hero Manley Halliday, the authors (who used Schulberg's novel for their source) were allowed the freewheeling of fiction. Nevertheless, in all its gaiety and sadness, this is the Fitzgerald story; and with that identification the play becomes a truthful and deeply moving study of a great writer in the final stages of disintegration as man and artist. . . .

Time was when Manley Halliday, bursting with talent, and his bewitched, bedeviling wife . . . "danced in a champagne haze on the rooftop of the world." That was back in the '20s when Halliday was the golden boy of American letters, the Meistersinger of the jazz age, and the Pied Piper who defied the depression by throwing "parties to end all parties." . . .

These frivolous days of champagne and the Charleston are caught up in flashbacks. The grim present finds Halliday a defeated champion who sells ten weeks of his few remaining months to collaborate with an admiring young hack on a Hollywood spectacular called *Love on Ice*. In the end, despair and disillusion and the fading image of a vanished world, with an assist from the bottle, leave him at peace, but not before . . . the authors have achieved a complete and compassionate portrait of a fallen idol in distress.

> "*A Hit with Champagne*," in Newsweek, Vol. LII, No. 24, December 15, 1958, p. 63.

HAROLD CLURMAN

[*The Disenchanted*] is presumably the story of Scott Fitzgerald's collaboration on a silly movie with a young scenarist who watches the famous writer's tragic decline with frustration, anguish and compassion.

The play is weakened by the fact that the character of Fitzgerald or whoever the writer in the play may represent, exists on the stage by reputation only. We know—or are supposed to take for granted—that he is an important writer, but the figure we are presented with is a generalization. He has no real individuality, no personal identity. Nothing that happens to him therefore can really be significant or moving. The same is true of the lady who is supposed to be the writer's wife (ostensibly the now fabulous Zelda). She too is a cliché. . . .

The play states a point: the artist who deteriorates does so, not because he "sells out" at the end of his career, but because there has been a flaw in integrity from the beginning. This is interesting and probably valid, but a point does not make a play.

> Harold Clurman, in a review of "The Disenchanted," in The Nation, New York, Vol. 187, No. 22, December 27, 1958, p. 501.

RICHARD HAYES

To that meager chronicle of art's high world of concepts and of life translated itself into art, *The Disenchanted* must be said to add only a melancholy statistic. Ironically, there would have seemed every precedent for hope: Mr. Budd Schulberg, upon whose novel of splendor in decline the play rests, is an unillusioned writer, copious and seasoned in experience; the wis-

dom, literary and human, of his collaborator, Mr. Harvey Breit, is as various as his sensibility is infallible and just. What is more, the substance they so earnestly search—those notoriously missing second acts in American lives—has become a specter of cultural anxiety. That the whole event should come off, then, so mildly, with no more stir than a morose disappointment, is perhaps less a comment on the authors than on the hazard of subduing to the uses of drama experience which may seem more accessible than the shock of investigation will prove it to be.

In a vehement note to the text, Mr. Breit, refusing to admit Manley Halliday of *The Disenchanted* as more than a dazzling prototype of Scott Fitzgerald, insists on the "absolute difference" between works of imagination and the marvels of reality; by the tests of the former only would he have the play judged. It is the artist's honorable position, but fatal, for the only honorable response to such a demand must be that imagination but lightly brushes this piece for the theater, and that its evocation of reality is most tenuous indeed; ghostly and bodiless, vagrant with old griefs, *The Disenchanted* is like some silent film played without titles or score. Some of this absence may derive from stage transmutation, which denies the play that factuality which often sustained it as fiction, and has imposed a dramatized remembrance of things past too poetically stylized for its strictly realistic structure. . . .

At the last, however, I should trace the fault to the nature of the experience Mr. Schulberg explores. Protest as he may, *The Disenchanted* derives its ultimate value from a particular amplified comment on Fitzgerald and the myth of the twenties. . . . Mr. Schulberg brought us grittily up to date, but as the Fitzgerald literature subsided to its just and high estate, it became evident that the *specific* conditions of his decay were hardly symptomatic, were indeed "only personal," as Gatsby said of Tom and Daisy; that the Fitzgerald *exemplum* fascinated, in any significant sense, only because of his talent, and that the problem, psychological and cultural, which divided him and which has variously afflicted Melville and Poe, Hawthorne, James, Miss Dickinson, Willa Cather, Twain, Hemingway, Mrs. Wharton, *everybody*—that this remained as much a mystery as ever. I cannot think that *The Disenchanted*, novel or play, penetrates it; to do so would compel a more intricate and laborious search than the authors seem prepared to make.

We are led, finally, to an intuition ever more obvious and driven in: that the consciousness, glory and lament of the artist, as verbal or theatrical substance, is of its nature intractable, and close to the Greek conception of *obscene*. There may be a place for such images in literature, which itself feeds on the ideas, artifacts and theories of culture, but to hear this Manley Halliday speak of his grief and his pride is to have a sense of interior violation. One knows now why artists, well met, will talk of boxing, of cuisine, of cats or money or the iniquities of their fellows, but will tell so rarely of their art. "We work in the dark," Henry James said, "our passion and our task"— and if this event of *The Disenchanted*, so sincere, so rigorous and ineffectual, may bring down the happy grace of darkness on what is at once sacred and unavailable, it will be remembered gratefully.

> Richard Hayes, "The Lesson of the Master," in Commonweal, Vol. LXIX, No. 15, January 9, 1959, p. 386.

THEATRE ARTS

Mr. Schulberg, who dramatized his own novel [*The Disenchanted*] with the aid of Harvey Breit, has always been a handy man at providing fabulous characters and surrounding them with a colorful milieu. In *The Disenchanted* he is dealing with the most glamorous literary hero of one of the most glamorous ages, the twenties, when, presumably, every night was Halloween without the formality of false faces. Although the primary action of the play is set in 1939 and deals with the painful disintegration of the great man amid the sinful vistas of Hollywood and memories of his past glories in the East, there is still plenty of the aura of the earlier age of Manley's triumphs, provided by means of flashbacks—and even the movieland of the thirties is not without its own high color. Atmospherically the play is first-rate.

Dramatically it is somewhat less admirable. In the novel, Manley's descent from hero to Hollywood hack (and a completely ineffectual one, at that) was a nightmarish and grotesque excursion that could be laughed at, or wept over, without reference to big scenes. The implications of the story were enough to sustain us when the writing was vivid, the narrative was fascinating, the comic sequences were hilarious and the central character was much larger than life. In the more exacting medium of the theatre, it becomes necessary to exteriorize all of that, and the difficulty is increased by the split nature of the text: the hard realities of the thirties juxtaposed with the glitter of the preceding decade. Even with . . . the assistance of flashbacks, it is less easy to accept Manley as such a creature of the gods. We actually see him on the toboggan, for the most part; we must constantly be reminded that there were better days, and we must also be content with a skeleton representation of how his downfall came about. It is just possible that Manley Halliday, like Sherlock Holmes and archy and mehitabel, is the sort of creation who exists best in the minds of individual readers; represent him on a stage and some of the magic disappears. More important, the theatre demands a dramatic high point—in the present case, Manley's confrontation with the powers of the Eastern college being celebrated in the film script he is writing. In the novel it was merely a crowning episode. In the play it becomes the climax, and the build-up proves too great for the scene's eventual impact. Suspended uneasily somewhere between bitter, ironic comedy and genuine tragedy, the climax seems merely ineffectual. (p. 11)

> A review of *"The Disenchanted,"* in Theatre Arts, *Vol. XLIII, No. 2, February, 1959, pp. 11, 20.*

JOHN LEGGETT

The Four Seasons of Success is Budd Schulberg's gallery of fellow-novelists. He wrote four of the portraits, those of Scott Fitzgerald, Thomas Heggen, Sinclair Lewis and William Saroyan, a decade ago for *Esquire,* and more recently has added miniatures of Nathanael West and John Steinbeck, but there is no dust on any of these canvases. The Schulberg recollection is clear and his hand goes instinctively to the telling incident.

The chain linking his six mid-century novelists is a common compulsion toward American-style success. Each in his way acknowledged that article of American faith which relegates any of our public figures to the championship or else skid row. Each had a different turn with fortune, sometimes starving for its gifts, sometimes drowning in them. Often the experience was not just painful but threatened his will and ability to write. None, however sure of his talent, was immune.

It is clear at once that the maxim "Nothing succeeds like success," does not apply. "Nothing fails like success" is more like it. (p. 30)

In each of his six portraits I suspect that Budd Schulberg is making some kind of self-discovery; that they offer him accurate reflections of himself in the toils of the bitch-goddess. Bucking up a melancholy Tom Heggen, Schulberg told him that he need not top his first success, that a writer should think of himself as a mountain range, not worry if every peak isn't a new Mt. Whitney. His reputation may rise and fall, even drop away, and in the end, hopefully, he'll "throw some sort of shadow against the sky." Hearing this sound advice, I was certain that Budd Schulberg was actually reassuring himself and, for that matter, all of us.

It is this very personal urgency and sense of shared fate pervading these pages which gives a modest collection of literary profiles so keen an edge. It is both a grave and an exuberant little book. The rivet at its center is hard truth about our worship of fame and fortune, how it has poisoned some of the best American artists. (pp. 30-1)

> John Leggett, *"In the Toils of the Goddess,"* in The New Republic, *Vol. 167, No. 19, November 18, 1972, pp. 30-1.*

JOHN COLEMAN

In a highly suspect introduction [to *The Four Seasons of Success*], which drops more names than notions, it is proposed that too much is asked too soon after an initial success, that writers lack the old in-built warmth of the sort of salon that Madame de Stael and the Algonquin round table provided, that Americans labour under the delusion that there has to be a Number One. Some truth in the last, if one thinks—as Mr. Schulberg does—of those literary pugilists, Hemingway and Mailer. . . .

Schulberg's subjects are Sinclair Lewis, Saroyan, Fitzgerald, Nathanael West, Thomas Heggen and Steinbeck. Most he sought out, with a freshman's enthusiasm: Heggen, who wrote *Mister Roberts* and died prematurely in a bath—causes uncertain—came after him, seeking advice on where to go next. Here one might unkindly recognise a failure to communicate: Schulberg, on this record, talks horse-sense to him for several pages. There is, in effect, an overdose of the compiler everywhere. His excited prose . . . spreads a wash of vulgarity over the cast he has assembled: he is omnipresent, as the possible 'young Ivy league leftist' hero of Lewis's germinating novel, as the fellow whose wife slipped Saroyan a friendly dollar, as the man who gave Fitzgerald much of the material for the unfinished *The Last Tycoon.*

A pity the occasions didn't happen to a better writer less committed to self-aggrandisement by association. The longest chapter, basically an account of a frightening trip with Fitzgerald (they were supposed to be concocting a script for Walter Wanger on their drunken way to Dartmouth), catches true echoes and even finds itself written more simply: yet another postscript to that sad life.

For those capable of fending off scruples about style and unburdened intimacies, there are inevitable scraps of interest in Schulberg's assembly. 'Red' Lewis was blacker than painted,' Steinbeck has his death-bed angers, Saroyan is shown traumatised by the war. But if there is a hard core to this ostensible study of big men falling down, it is Mr. Schulberg at the centre, watching and taking notes: no more. An alternative title might have been *Nipped in the Budd.*

John Coleman, "Walking Wounded," in The Observer, March 3, 1974, p. 36.

PHILIP FRENCH

[One] cannot in all honesty claim that Schulberg's fuzzy musings on success and failure among modern American novelists [in *The Four Seasons of Success*] can be discussed on the same level as Kazin's [*Bright Book of Life*]. His style is often embarrassingly vulgar and sometimes barbarous, something I find easier to accept in his vigorous study of Muhammad Ali, *Loser and Still Champion,* than in *The Four Seasons of Success.* However, if you can get beyond the first few pages without gagging there are some interesting and affecting glimpses of American writers *in extremis,* including Sinclair Lewis, Nathanael West, Steinbeck, Thomas Heggen, and above all Scott Fitzgerald. . . . This particular essay [on Fitzgerald], an extended version of a 1961 *Esquire* article, is much more valuable than Schulberg's Fitzgerald novel *The Disenchanted* and throws an odd light upon the way the younger writer was pumped as source material for *The Last Tycoon.* Fitzgerald told him that 'I sort of combined you with my daughter Scottie for Cecilia' (the narrator), and Schulberg recalls the shock of reading the opening chapters in manuscript: 'It was almost as if I had written the book and then Scott had filtered it through his more tempered and sophisticated imagination.'

Yet for all his protestations of concern for true artistic merit and disinterested endeavour, Schulberg is really obsessed with success as measured by sales, money, public adulation and celebration. Railing against fickle critics and blaming American society for the fluctuations in authors' reputations, he seems unable to understand that most writers consider themselves fortunate if they are held even in moderate esteem in their lifetime. He himself might do well to remember his own short story, **"A Note on the Literary Life,"** in which a once celebrated novelist loses his vast popular and critical reputation to such a degree that he gets into the reference books only as the one-time employer of his ill-treated secretary, a posthumously acclaimed poet of alleged genius. (p. 364)

Philip French, "Thirty Years On," in New Statesman, Vol. 87, No. 2243, March 15, 1974, pp. 364-65.

STANLEY ELLIN

The publication of a new novel by Budd Schulberg should be a happy event, but the appearance of *Everything That Moves* is anything but that. I am old enough to have been around when the dazzling *What Makes Sammy Run?* heralded Mr. Schulberg's arrival on the scene; I have been a devoted fan ever since. Judging by past performance, all that can be said about *Everything That Moves* is that it misfires, one of those books which every writer must be allowed in the course of a long and noteworthy career. It is a noisy, hollow replay of the Jimmy Hoffa story, written in stilted prose and presented in third-person present tense so that it emerges more as an attenuated screen treatment than as a novel. (pp. 15, 31)

Stanley Ellin, "Criminals at Play," in The New York Times Book Review, July 13, 1980, pp. 15, 31.

ROB EDELMAN

Moving Pictures is, on one hand, the story of an Everyboy who loves racing pigeons, playing Halloween pranks on a neighbor, attending the Friday night fights with his dad and identifying with the Jewish fighters. He experiences the rigors of a high school freshman, feels anguish at his parents' separation, undergoes a growing social awareness as he observes the world around him. For instance, he writes with compassion about the dilemma of Wilma, his light-skinned nurse, a black woman alone in a lily-white world.

But young Buddy is no ordinary American boy. He is the boss' son, the privileged child of Hollywood nobility. And that boss is B. P. Schulberg, film pioneer and vice president in charge of production at Paramount Pictures; his mother Adeline, "Ad," built the first house in Malibu and later became a successful movie agent. As a boy, Schulberg played in the studio backlots, living in a "world of date palms and klieg lights." . . .

Thankfully, however, **Moving Pictures** is not yet another sordid, salacious, self-serving Hollywood memoir, with sex passages on page 3. Schulberg does not brag about his Tinseltown conquests, youthful sexual exploits both real or imagined; he was, after all, a prince, not a playboy. Indeed, throughout his childhood he was a chronic stammerer and wallflower. . . .

While he obviously loves and favors his parents, Schulberg paints them intricately, with a knowingly realistic, three-dimensional brush. His father was a genius (he dubbed Pickford "America's Sweetheart"), more humane than other studio heads, but he was insecure, with a penchant for drinking, gambling and womanizing. Ad, more self-assured than her husband, was always right but always nagging, a culture maven and self-described socialist who was nonetheless a practical, practicing capitalist.

Schulberg offers delicious observations about Hollywood and its populace. He describes film as "the only art to become an industry and the only industry to became an art"; director Edmund Goulding was "half artist, half charlatan (the ideal Hollywood mix)." . . .

[Schulberg] is particularly fascinated by the famous who topple into obscurity, most specifically Hollywood celebrities and boxers, a theme which runs throughout his other work (chapters in *Moving Pictures* could be titled *The Harder They Fall*). Last year's glimmering stars dim today and burn out into anonymity tomorrow. Most memorably, Schulberg describes gum-chewing Clara Bow, "an adorable, in fact irresistible, little know-nothing" who grew up poor and abused on the streets of Brooklyn, became the It Girl, a national institution, and was washed up at 26; hulking, thick-headed George Bancroft, star of *the* original gangster movie, *Underworld,* who was consumed by pretention, made unreasonable salary demands, and ended up a supporting player, a footnote in film history; and an obscure, one-shot director named Marcel DeSano who eventually committed suicide.

Schulberg may be forgiven for his occasional lapses in spelling and fact. Joan Crawford was originally Lucille Le Sueur, not Laeseur or Laseur; John Wayne was born Marion Michael (not Marshall) Morrison; Pat O'Brien played Knute Rockne in *Knute Rockne—All American,* not *The Spirit of Notre Dame*; Theodosia, not Theodora, Goodman became Theda Bara. And he sometimes is annoyingly redundant, as when he notes his youthful disdain for girls, gambling and gin for the umpteenth time.

Some of what Schulberg describes has been oft-told—the Fatty Arbuckle case, for instance, or bullying parents abusing their pint-sized movie star offspring, or Von Stroheim ordering silk underwear for the extras in *The Wedding March*. But he writes from memory, from his parents' recollections, from the vantage point of an insider; he recalls Arbuckle from a personal perspective, remembering his impression of the fallen Fatty from the eyes of a 10-year-old.

Rob Edelman, "What Makes Hollywood Run?" in Book World—The Washington Post, July 26, 1981, p. 4.

JANET MASLIN

[Schulberg's *Moving Pictures*] isn't the usual Hollywood memoir, because the reputation he seeks to protect is not his own. Mr. Schulberg proudly recalls the triumphs of his father, B. P. Schulberg, a studio executive whose fortunes rose and fell markedly during Budd's childhood. He also marvels at his mother, Ad, who patiently remained loyal to her husband long after he had ceased wanting or warranting her trust. He remembers early film pioneers, unsung heroes and movie queens who took the trouble to befriend a small boy. But most of all Mr. Schulberg celebrates Hollywood itself, and he celebrates something more than movieland glamour. To him, it remains "Home Sweet Hollywood, a lovely place to play with lions and alligators, to ride my bike down lanes of palms and pepper trees, and to make lemonade from my own lemon tree."

Mr. Schulberg's candor serves him well, especially when his reminiscences overlap with those of countless other Hollywood raconteurs. He may not be the first to note Clara Bow's flirtatiousness, but he can describe how embarrassed, pleased and suspicious he felt, as a small boy, to have her fuss over him. Like many an actor or actress young Budd met, Clara Bow offered attentions to the child that were really meant for his father.... The son's opinion of his father's accomplishments is mixed. And the mixed emotions are intense ones—pride and shame....

Fifty years after the fact, Mr. Schulberg still writes with tremendous bitterness of his father's affair with Sylvia Sidney, an affair that he says caused irreparable damage to his parents' marriage. He remembers, as a teen-ager, going to Miss Sidney's house and demanding that his father come home. He also remembers watching Miss Sidney in the movie version of Theodore Dreiser's *An American Tragedy* and thoroughly savoring the scene in which she drowns....

The most interesting anecdotes in Mr. Schulberg's rambling memoir are those that make the best use of his unique vantage point. Many people have shared their recollections of Louis B. Mayer, Jack Warner and Harry Cohn, but Mr. Schulberg remembers their fathers, who with his own grandfather banded together to establish the first Hollywood synagogue. He remembers seeing a child star named Baby Richard Headrick play a fountain-dunking scene over and over again. Six-year-old Baby Richard looked up at Budd, teeth chattering, and asked "Are you an actor too?" Budd said he was only there watching because his father was B. P. Schulberg. "Gee, you're lucky," the wet little child star told him. (p. 9)

Moving Pictures is an uncertain mixture of homely anecdotes like these and airy, self-important excesses. The sections of the book are called "Genesis," "Exodus," "The Promised Land" and "Kings," and the prose is often comparably overblown....

Mr. Schulberg has a tendency to intertwine his own history with that of the movies to an unreasonable degree. "While I was teething, this Motion Picture War of Independence was seething," he declares at one point. Later he says: "Often, when I am asked if I was born in Hollywood, I have to pause and think because Hollywood's growing up and my own are inextricably bound together."

So Mr. Schulberg appoints himself a keeper of the flame, and one of the things he accomplishes is to revive the reputations of those who he feels have been, like his father, unjustly overlooked. There is Edwin S. Porter, the pioneer director for whom B. P. worked as scenario editor.... Another ghost is Marcel DeSano, who had such great success with his first movie, *The Girl Who Wouldn't Work*, that he couldn't work again."

He recalls George Bancroft, star of gangster films, who traveled to Europe with the Schulbergs, telling the press he wanted to meet "the underworld" wherever he ventured, and using his favorite word, "facsimile," even though he didn't quite know its meaning. "You know, Buddy," he told the author, "this trip to Europe is a facsimile of the wonderful relationship I have with your father. And that I'm going to have with you as you grow older. An absolute facsimile." (p. 22)

Janet Maslin, "Home Sweet Hollywood," in The New York Times Book Review, September 6, 1981, pp. 9, 22.

FRANCIS KING

It was no doubt because [*On the Waterfront*] mounted so devastating an attack on labour racketeers that, in 1960, Robert Kennedy selected [Schulberg] to write the script of a film based on *The Enemy Within*—the American best-seller in which Kennedy described how, as chief counsel to a Senate committee, he had taken on both Jimmy Hoffa of the corrupt Teamsters union and the Mafia, with which the union had mutually lucrative contacts. That film was never made—abandoned, so it was rumoured at the time, as a result of Teamster and Mafia pressure. Now, 20 years later, Mr Schulberg has turned his script into this perfunctorily fictionalised account of the meteoric rise and mysterious death of a man who, in his early years, seemed genuinely to care for the welfare of the rank and file of his union and to have no personal ambitions for himself. Even the name that Mr Schulberg has chosen for his central figure, Joey Hopper, is so close to Jimmy Hoffa as to invite immediate identification.... [Schulberg's *Everything That Moves*] often reads as though he were summarising a script to some money-men either too illiterate or too busy to assimilate it from the page. The tense is the present. When a character appears ('Enter Allie Hotzer' we read at one point, as though it were a stage direction), Mr Schulberg roughs in an outline to be fleshed out later by an actor. 'A chunky ex-football player from Columbia with a taste for cheap cigars'; 'a quiet pipe-smoking Virginian'; 'a tough-minded black intellectual from Dartmouth'; 'a paunchy accountant of fifty who wears thick glasses': in each case, the money-men can visualise precisely the kind of actor required and, if they cannot, then the casting department can....

Mr Schulberg shows little psychological subtlety in his drawing of his characters. There is Hoffa/Hopper himself, first seen triumphant in a bowling-alley when he is still a simple trucker, who cunningly realises that the way for him to win power is to appear to despise all its appurtenances of luxurious cars, large mansions, expensive suits, beautiful women and extravagant entertaining, and so to present himself to the electors as a rough man of the people. In truth, of course, he is as greedy as any of his rivals. . . .

Hoffa/Hopper has a pathetic working-class wife who, neglected and out of place, spends her time drinking gibsons and reading trashy magazines. He also has a former buddy, his ally in his early struggles against management, whom he ruthlessly has his henchmen blind with sulphuric acid, when it seems probable that the buddy will give hostile evidence to the Senate Committee. (p. 21)

The message of the book is, firstly, that those who are the most vociferous about the sweeping away of corruption are often themselves the most liable to corruption; and, secondly, that it is only the courage of the 'little man', defying an unholy alliance of union bosses and Mafia crooks, that can safeguard American freedom.

To date, in England, we have produced no union boss with the power or the ruthlessness of Hoffa/Hopper; but when, for example, the novel describes how a picket beats up a schoolboy going to work at a filling-station during a strike, it acquires a disconcerting relevance for us too. Similarly, the kind of conspiracy between unions and management at the expense of workers and public alike, which Mr Schulberg describes so graphically, is not something of which we can say that we know nothing.

Though it lacks literary grace and psychological depth, this novel does have the merit, by no means to be despised, of continuously holding the attention. The story is a good one; and it should make an even better film. (pp. 21-2)

> *Francis King, "Unholy Union," in* The Spectator, *Vol. 247, No. 7992, September 12, 1981, pp. 21-2.*

MARK ROYDEN WINCHELL

At the same time that Fitzgerald was writing his last novel [*The Last Tycoon*], a Hollywood native named Budd Schulberg was writing his first. It is a noteworthy irony that Fitzgerald the outsider seemed to have greater affection and respect for the film capital than did Schulberg the hometown boy. *What Makes Sammy Run?* (published in the same year as *The Last Tycoon*) is a cynic's version of the decline of Hollywood, a theme Fitzgerald had approached as tragedy.

Not only were Fitzgerald and Schulberg writing at the same time, but each was aware of the other's work in progress. (Indeed, in creating the character of Cecilia Brady, Fitzgerald relied greatly on Schulberg's inside knowledge of Hollywood.) In both novels, an old-guard producer with the taste and integrity of Irving Thalberg fights a losing battle against a sleazy opportunist. The main difference is that Fitzgerald's focus is on the fall of the producer, whereas Schulberg's is on the rise of the opportunist. The contrast between these two novels becomes even more pronounced when we consider that both Monroe Stahr [of *The Last Tycoon*] and Sammy Glick rose from poverty and obscurity in the Jewish ghetto of New York to achieve fortune and fame in Hollywood. Stahr did so as an Horatio Alger figure, Glick as a Flem Snopes.

In *What Makes Sammy Run?* Schulberg employs a first-person narrator whose primary function in the novel is to try to understand its protagonist, (a function emphasized by the question that serves as the novel's title). In this regard, *Sammy* is similar to *The Last Tycoon, The Great Gatsby,* and quite a few other major works of twentieth-century fiction. In the hands of a Fitzgerald or a Conrad such a technique can result in a subtle tale of moral education. Schulberg's narrator Al Manheim is, however, an essentially static character who serves as a fairly unambiguous surrogate for the author. (pp. 153-54)

There are . . . a few places in *Sammy* where Al Manheim is genuinely excited by the aesthetic possibilities of the motion picture medium. Like Fitzgerald and quite a few others, Manheim is essentially a writer of words who must learn how to tell stories in pictures. At one point, the Thalberg-type producer Sidney Fineman tells Al of the time he brought a famous Broadway playwright out to Hollywood. Given the assignment of writing an opening scene which would establish that a husband was tiring of his wife, the playwright came back fifteen thousand dollars later with a twenty-page scene filled with brilliant dialogue but way over the length for the start of the picture.

Fineman gave the scene to his director, Ray MacKenna, a veteran of the Mack Sennett days. MacKenna reduced the scene to half a page of wordless action in an elevator. The husband and wife are in evening clothes, when a "classy dame" enters. The husband removes his hat with a flourish, as his wife glares at him. "Mac couldn't write a complete sentence," Fineman says. "But that was great writing—for the screen." (p. 154)

Such paeans to the magic of movies, however, are few and far between in Schulberg's novel. As the wheel of fortune turns, the Finemans are on their way down and the Glicks are on their way up. In the process, men with real talent experience Hollywood as Destroyer. This is true of Sammy's ghostwriter Julian Blumberg and, on a grander scale, of the lyric poet Henry Powell Turner, a former Pulitzer Prize winner who has degenerated into an alcoholic hack.

Of course, what makes this novel memorable is not Al Manheim, Sidney Fineman, or Henry Powell Turner, but the obnoxious social climber Sammy Glick. If Sammy is in many ways the obverse image of Monroe Stahr, he is also a cynical perversion of other Fitzgerald heroes. In his maniacal pursuit of social prominence, he vaguely resembles Jay Gatsby—even to the point of changing his name. The main difference is that Gatsby seeks to rise in the world in order to win the golden girl, whereas Sammy seeks the girl as confirmation that he has already risen. Sammy's bride, the blue-blood Laurette Harrington, is a variation of the Fitzgerald coquette—kin to Daisy Buchanan, Nicole Warren, and Judy Jones. Indeed, the only time that Sammy is not in control of his life is when Laurette cuckolds him on their wedding night. The one thing that his gall and his money cannot buy him is entrance into the aristocracy. To achieve that level of decadence requires several generations. Instead, he simply ends up as Gatsby with horns.

If Sammy represents the wave of the future in Hollywood then vulgarity has indeed triumphed. . . . Unfortunately, Schulberg's liberal social philosophy will not allow him to present Sammy as a culpable villain. Toward the end of the novel Al discovers that it is Sammy's ghetto background that has made him into an aggressive little punk who runs over everyone who stands in his way. Thus, what is ostensibly an anti-Hollywood novel turns out to be an indictment of the New York slums.

Midway between the extremes defined by Monroe Stahr and Sammy Glick is Victor Milgrim, the producer in Schulberg's 1950 novel *The Disenchanted*. Lacking the genuine taste and integrity of Thalberg or Stahr, Milgrim is essentially a more sophisticated and benign version of Glick. Although he is a man of intellectual pretensions who lusts after an honorary Doctor of Humanities degree, he is capable of referring to himself as an "omnipotent reader." He hires the once-great writer Manley Halliday not because he wants to elevate the literary quality of the cinema, but because he wants to promote his own image as a man of culture. (pp. 155-56)

Milgrim, however, is at best a peripheral figure in *The Disenchanted*. The focus of the novel is on two of his screenwriters, the youthful Shep Stearns and the aging Manley Halliday. Because Stearns and Halliday are so obviously fictionalized versions of Budd Schulberg and Scott Fitzgerald, much criticism of *The Disenchanted* has concentrated on the book's biographical veracity. This is understandable when one considers that Schulberg is probably more responsible than any other individual for our popular image of Fitzgerald in Hollywood. . . .

And yet to read Schulberg's novel solely as *roman à clef* is to miss the point. Like Monroe Stahr, Manley Halliday is a fictional character inspired by a real-life prototype. . . . Schulberg

[was] more concerned with symbolic reality than with biographical verisimilitude in *The Disenchanted*. . . . [It is] possible to read *The Disenchanted* for what it is—a powerful and touching work of fiction.

Manley Halliday and Shep Stearns represent different generations. Halliday is still living in the carefree 1920s, while Stearns is an earnest, socially conscious product of the 1930s. These different perspectives are reflected in their contrasting attitudes toward Hollywood: Halliday sees screenwriting as a quick means of getting out of debt so that he can return to serious fiction, whereas Stearns sees the motion picture medium as potentially a folk art. The conflict of generations provides a social context for the action of the novel; however, Schulberg does not simply stack the deck so that his own alter ego emerges as morally superior to Fitzgerald's. Instead, the novel traces the development of Shep's understanding of the older writer. (pp. 156-57)

Mark Royden Winchell, "Fantasy Seen: Hollywood Fiction Since West," in Los Angeles in Fiction: A Collection of Original Essays, *edited by David Fine, University of New Mexico Press, 1984, pp. 147-68.*

(Julian) Randolph Stow

1935-

Australian novelist, poet, author of children's books, librettist, and editor.

Regarded as one of Australia's finest contemporary writers, Stow is praised for his lyrical prose, authentic rendition of dialect, and haunting evocations of his country's diverse landscapes. Rich in allegory and mythical allusion, Stow's works explore such themes as the effects of misguided pride and love, the beauty and cruelty of nature, and the individual's alienation from society. S. A. Ramsey remarked: "To read any Randolph Stow novel is to embark upon a tortuous and harrowing journey into the heart of the human predicament."

Stow's first two novels, *A Haunted Land* (1956) and *The Bystander* (1957), are written in a naturalistic prose style and focus on the emotional tribulations of a rural Australian family searching for stability and attempting to cope with death. Although some critics faulted these books for melodrama and underdeveloped characterization, most lauded Stow's poetic language and descriptions of nature. In his third novel, the highly symbolic *To the Islands* (1958; revised, 1981), Stow probes deeper into the emotional states of his characters, blending realism and allegory in a story of an elderly missionary's quest for identity. After attempting to kill an aborigine who challenges his religious work, the missionary undertakes a journey to a remote island which the aborigines believe to be inhabited by the dead. On the island, he seeks to regain his spirituality and confront the self-doubt and evil that led him to attempt murder. Granville Hicks observed: "[Stow's] style, never merely pretty and never lush, is truly poetic and perfectly suited to his theme. 'Universal' is a large word but if it can ever be used, it can be applied to *To the Islands,* which reaches down to the basic stratum of human nature." Stow again employs allegory and symbolism in his next novel, *Tourmaline* (1963), a tale of a stranger's fraudulent promise to deliver rain to a drought-stricken Australian town. With *The Merry-Go-Round in the Sea* (1965), Stow returned to the naturalism of his first two novels. Drawing upon events from his own adolescence, Stow recounts a boy's coming of age during World War II and his relationship with his older cousin, a soldier who spent time in a Japanese prisoner-of-war camp. Anthony J. Hassall called *The Merry-Go-Round in the Sea* "the definitive account" of "the Australian childhood experience of a generation."

Following a fourteen-year hiatus, Stow published his sixth novel, *Visitants* (1979), an account of an inquest into the death of an Australian official on a Melanesian island. Three colonists and two aborigines describe the events leading to the man's death, offering insight into the effects of colonialism and the conflict between European and indigenous cultures. Although several critics noted similarities between this book and Joseph Conrad's classic novella, *Heart of Darkness,* Bruce King considered *Visitants* "a remarkable achievement in narrative technique, characterization, and the re-creation of a foreign culture through a style which in English reproduces Melanesian language and vision." Stow also uses multiple narrators in *The Girl Green as Elderflower* (1980), in which he chronicles an Australian writer's recovery from a nervous breakdown. The protagonist

Courtesy of Randolph Stow

of this novel incorporates his friends and relatives into his renditions of medieval English legends as a means of therapy. In *The Suburbs of Hell* (1984), Stow manipulates the conventions of crime fiction to comment upon modern humanity's fascination with horror and misfortune. Using epigraphs that celebrate death and destruction from Elizabethan and Jacobean dramas, Stow depicts a seaside English village plagued by several grisly murders. Critics praised Stow's skill at rendering the terror and suspicion among the tightly-knit townspeople. T.E.D. Klein called the novel an "elaborate literary joke" that "masquerades as a murder mystery but which is in fact a parable on . . . The Human Condition, The Fallibility of Man, and The Supremacy of Death."

Stow is also an accomplished poet whose verse is collected in *Act One* (1957), *Outrider* (1962), and *A Counterfeit Silence* (1969). Displaying many similarities to his fiction, Stow's poems center on such topics as childhood, nature, love, death, and redemption. Stow has also written a book for children, *Midnite: The Story of a Wild Colonial Boy* (1967), and librettos for the musicals *Eight Songs for a Mad King* (1969) and *Miss Donnithorne's Maggot* (1974).

(See also *CLC*, Vol. 23 and *Contemporary Authors*, Vols. 13-16, rev. ed.)

LUCY HUGHES-HALLETT

In his preface to the revised edition of this 24 year-old novel Randolph Stow admits to the grandeur of the ambitions of his youth. *The Lyke-Wake Dirge, Everyman* and *King Lear* were his literary models for *To The Islands* 'which in retrospect' he writes, with the sad circumspection of his 47 years, 'makes me realise how horizons narrow in middle age'. (p. 23)

[*To the Islands*] was first written [in 1958] with the conscious intention of drumming up support for the missions, in particular for one where Randolph Stow had himself worked as a ration-store man. There is a certain amount of discussion about the role of such settlements (shortened in this revised version but still substantial) and five additional white characters are introduced chiefly for the purpose of this debate. One of these comes to life by virtue of his touchingly described loneliness, saved, in a rather jolting little happy ending, by his marriage to the nurse. None of the others are more than shadowy figures and while the novel lingers over their rivalries and anxieties it feels slow and awkward. The dialogue sticks and the narrative meanders while great trouble is taken over the description of scenes which seem to tell one little.

Whenever the focus switches to Heriot, though, the novel lives up to its publisher's boast. It is indeed 'a classic Australian novel'. Stow conjures up a landscape of mythic suggestiveness and grandeur and places in it a character whose combined frailty and courage perfectly complement the setting. Traversing the grassy plains and sun-scorched plateaux, Heriot acts as a highly sensitive receiver, our perceptions being mediated through his. The beauty and desolation of the landscape play on him. He perceives his surroundings with the hallucinatory vividness peculiar to states of extreme physical exhaustion and, outcast as he feels himself to be, he examines every object and every detail of his own and Justin's behaviour with the bemused concentration of an alien. Lear-like, he begins to see better.

The journey, as is made explicit (too explicit for my taste—the youthful Stow's artistic virtues did not include subtlety) is a spiritual one. Heriot is exploring his own soul. As he, or rather Justin, hunts for food he learns that life inevitably attracts violence. He encounters two other men in the wilderness, a murderer and a demented recluse, each one a horribly distorted reflection of himself, and he leaves them both behind him. (pp. 23-4)

It is a measure of Stow's skill that his account of these emblematic encounters and actions can be read without any sense that the narrative is being manipulated for the sake of the symbolism. Stow has something of William Golding's gift for actualising the mythical. Heriot is a three-dimensional naturalistic character. From the opening of the first chapter, when he is discovered waking bad-tempered to quote Baudelaire to a lizard, to the movingly irascible moment when, before parting, he begs Justin to address him by his Christian name and break the enclosing fence of white supremacy which makes him a perpetual foreigner, he is an entirely credible, consistent, idiosyncratic person. At the same time he is a conventionally perfect realisation of a mythic archetype—the dethroned king who must lose all he ever had and sojourn in the wilderness a while before he will be wise enough to die. The juxtaposition of such a figure with the vast and savage landscape which Stow evokes makes this a haunting, impressive novel. (p. 24)

> *Lucy Hughes-Hallett, "An Australian Classic," in* The Spectator, *Vol. 248, No. 8016, February 27, 1982, pp. 23-4.*

NORMA JEAN RICHEY

For the newly revised edition of the modern Australian classic, *To the Islands*, . . . Stow has written a preface discussing the devastating effects on Aborigines jettisoned by a world they never made. The symbiotic relationship between the Aborigines and the whites who distribute food and Western civilization's dictums upon them is nonfulfilling for both races. The leading character, Heriot, has devoted his life to a mission station but finds its relationships and structure inadequate for what happens within himself as he reaches the end of his life. After having struck and, he thinks, possibly killed a returned rebel, Heriot heads for the outlands, the perimeter of our charted world. He is followed by Justin, an Aborigine who loves him and wishes to be able to help him. Heriot's paradigmatic odyssey leads to an inner reconciliation out on the edge of the world, where only his heart can help him.

Faulkner said in his Nobel Prize acceptance speech that "the problems of the human heart in conflict with itself . . . alone can make good writing because only that is worth writing about." For both Stow and Faulkner, racial divisions reflect an intrinsic inner division of the self, and for both writers the record of that inner struggle is the dominant theme of individuality. *To the Islands* reflects a respect for individuality so profound that all else is secondary. (pp. 684-85)

> *Norma Jean Richey, in a review of "To the Islands" and "Tourmaline," in* World Literature Today, *Vol. 57, No. 4, Autumn, 1983, pp. 684-5.*

BRUCE KING

Using the underpopulated, distantly separated towns of western Australia, where the decaying aboriginal culture remains highly visible, for mystical allegories of the soul's journey toward spiritual and interracial communion, Stow's early novels concern attempts at rebirth in an emotional wasteland. In *To the Islands* Heriot, an aging missionary, tries to kill an aboriginal who has consistently challenged and threatened to destroy his work: the confrontation, representative of the colonialist's relation to the native and the land, results in Heriot's search for the aboriginal islands of the dead. During the journey he confronts his personal, racial, and historical guilt before embracing native gods. The novel concludes ambiguously but strikingly with the missionary kneeling among the bones and skulls of a shrine on the edge of a cliff, staring into the light, searching sun and sea for the islands while he whispers "My soul is a strange country."

The preface to the first edition aggressively began: "This is not, by intention, a realistic novel." Stow now says this was an expression of irritation with the tyranny of social realism in the Australian 1950s, when novelists were expected to "concern themselves with Statistically Average Man." Instead in *To the Islands* Stow was making "propaganda" on behalf of Christian mission stations for aborigines, where he had worked, a cause soon lost as by the late 1960s the missions were abandoned. This revised edition is supposedly "slightly abridged" by removal of passages concerning the problems of the missions; but the new preface does not indicate the extent of such deletions, nor warn of the inclusion of new paragraphs and material. With the elimination of some poeticism and propaganda, the texture of the opening of the novel has become thinner, making the exposition direct, creating an imbalance to the later sections. The first sentence—"A child dragged a stick along the corrugated-iron wall of a lot, and Heriot woke"—

originally continued: "and found the morning standing at his bed like a valet, holding out his daylight self to be put on again, his name, his age, his vague and wearying occupation." The deleted half-sentence reveals Heriot's alienation, lack of roots, and loss of faith. The deletion of later remarks defending Heriot's use of a whip as "necessary" in the past to get "results" avoids the historical context of his guilt; the missionary's overbearing rightcousness is part of what must be expiated by his journey of spiritual and racial reconciliation.

Stow's novels, for all their surface realism, are dramas of the soul: their actions are slight, but the prose is charged with symbolism. The rocks, barren landscapes, dried streambeds, and decaying towns of western Australia typify the spiritual drought which resulted from the imposition of foreign order on the region. Part of Stow's attractiveness is that in his writing the complexity and depths of the modernists slide into a green quietism and Third World sympathies closer to post-1960 sensibilities than to the great writers of the first half of this century.

Tourmaline, also set in western Australia, concerns a former garden paradise now infertile and dry, where a water diviner brings promise of renewal but finds only gold. In a novel where characters have such names as The Law, Rock, Mary, Agnes Day, and Gloria Day, an analogy is suggested between the Old and New Testament, with the diviner Michael, a Christ figure, replacing the aged Law, historian and jailer. Symbolism from Revelation implies the time is ripe for a restoration of Eden and the start of a new order—an assumption furthered by Stow's prefatory note saying that the action of the novel takes place in the future. But *Tourmaline* unexpectedly treats its own analogies critically, skeptically acknowledging its own methods; it is as if a very late work of the High Christian phase of modernist literature were transitional, being also an early instance of self-referential postmodernist writing.

Stow has been influenced by Eliot's poetry (to which the novel alludes), and he has argued in favor of the missions; but he ironically uses religious analogies here to criticize the role of Christianity and western culture in Australia, especially among the aborigines. The criticism is subtle, as a highly visible, dominant, vigorous, self-deceiving activity is contrasted to the silent, barely perceptible inactivity which Stow sees as suitable to Australia's place in the Pacific. (pp. 137-38)

A concern with peace and nonaggression is a general theme of Stow's work; and [Helen] Tiffin, a strongly nationalistic critic, argues that the contrast of Taoist indifference, humility, and compassion to western Christian dualistic concepts of good and evil, truth and falsehood, with their patterns of aggression and guilt, is implicit also in *To the Islands.* Whereas the land seems to western Christians something to be overcome, used, and dominated, Stow's work shows that Australians should be aware that the land's meaning is that it will endure, silently, nonaggressively, and will reign in the end, after man and his cities have returned to dust. Tiffin's essay is a good starting-place for American readers seeking enlightenment about Stow. But *Tourmaline* remains impressive, puzzling; that it is in a colloquial Australian makes it even more unusual. Although quirky and at times a bit unsubstantial, Stow's early books continue to grow in stature. His recent novels are more technically dazzling and avoid clumsy poeticisms, but they are not necessarily better. (pp. 138-39)

Bruce King, "Two Commonwealth Novelists," in The Sewanee Review, *Vol. XCII, No. 3, Winter, 1984, pp. 136-40.*

FRANCIS KING

Randolph Stow's is so idiosyncratic a talent that it is both surprising and disconcerting to find the framework of [*The Suburbs of Hell*] to be that of a conventional whodunnit. In the East Anglian port of Old Tornwich, with its desolate saltings, its narrow streets, its ancient houses and its population of fisher-folk, there occurs a succession of motiveless murders, seemingly the work of a psychopath. The first to be shot is Paul Ramsay, the sort of bearded schoolmaster whom one would assume to be a Morris-dancer. The next is an elderly barmaid, Eddystone Edna, living alone in a disused lighthouse situated in the middle of the town. After her, Commander Pryke falls victim to the mysterious assassin, to be followed by Linda de Vere, pallidly enervated wife of sinister Frank, who collects firearms and deals in drugs, and by jolly, tough Harry Ufford, a fisherman turned labourer. In addition, Paul's brother, Greg, goes mad as the result of the tragedies; and a black taxi-driver, Sam Boskum, kills himself.

A baffled search for the key to these multiple killings can be guaranteed to hold the reader's attention; but any expectation of the kind of denouement that closes a conventional whodunnit with all the mechanical neatness and efficiency of a zip-fastener is certain to be disappointed. (pp. 27-8)

But the epigraph from *The Duchess of Malfi* that gives the book its title—'Security some men call the suburbs of hell, Only a dead wall between . . .'—and the subsequent quotations from *Beowulf, Titus Andronicus, The Jew of Malta* etc at once make it clear that Mr Stow is as much concerned with the metaphysical, as with the physical, dimensions of the horrid events that crowd so thick and fast on each other. . . .

Although born in Australia, Mr Stow depicts Old Tornwich and the flat countryside around it with the skill of some master water-colourist of the East Anglian school. In accurately rendering the local speech, he does not always make it easy for the reader, with sentences like 'I fought I'd have a house-warmin, but I dint get back here till late' and 'I'm off, I've got a randy-voo.' The comic oddity of the way in which his characters thus express themselves contrasts piquantly with the horrific oddity of the way in which they meet their ends.

The succinctness of Mr Stow's narrative style evokes one's admiration; but an unfortunate result of it is that the characterisation suffers. Harry Ufford, with his 'rebellious law-breaking boyhood, truculent adolescence and man's life of loving and feuding', is perfectly realised, and the finest chapter in the book is that in which he swims for over five miles with 'a heart like a bull' before finally sinking to his death by drowning. But most of the other victims—Paul Ramsay, Commander Pryke, Eddystone Edna—are treated as though they were peripheral to the story, although in fact central to it.

There is much to admire here: the evocation of life in the small East Anglian town and the countryside around it; the acute ear for the speech of its inhabitants; above all, the depiction of how, inexorably, the infection of suspicion spreads. . . . But there is also a curious unease about the whole undertaking, as though intermittently an author usually so assured had lost confidence in his task. The result is an always interesting and sometimes absorbing novel but one that, in the canon of Mr Stow's work, is unlikely to come to be regarded as one of the finest of his achievements. (p. 28)

Francis King, "Highly Suspect," in The Spectator, *Vol. 252, No. 8126, April 7, 1984, pp. 27-8.*

D. A. N. JONES

[*The Suburbs of Hell*] deals with the deeds of a murderous maniac, and we are encouraged to suspect eccentric old ladies and retired naval officers, Harry the fisherman and his small-boy pal, Killer, while feeling mildly compassionate toward the innocent, the potential victims and suspects. But the author has tried to make the book more challenging than Agatha Christie's yarns. Randolph Stow, we are told, is of Australian birth and has worked among the aboriginal people of his homeland, as well as assisting the Government Anthropologist among the subject peoples of Papua New Guinea. After spending many years in East Anglia, he now seems to take an almost ghoulish interest in the possibilities of savagery among the comfortable people of Suffolk. He frames his story with Jacobethan verses—murderers like Barabas the Jew and Aaron the Moor expressing evil desires—and his last page offers a Tarot-card drawing of Death scything off mortals' heads.

Facing this *memento mori* is a page made up of headlines from the Suffolk newspaper Stow has invented for the purposes of his fiction. Most of these headlines are World News, starting with '1,000 Bengalis massacred in Assam' and 'Belfast pub holocaust', concluding with 'Headless corpses in El Salvador' and '"I am not a cannibal"—Ex-president.' Tucked among these items is a paragraph of local news: 'The Coroner was told that De Vere had been drinking heavily on that day. Death was due to inhalation of vomit.' The story that Stow neatly tells is about the events leading up to that coroner's verdict: but his way of displaying it suggests that he is attempting, as well as a skilful whodunnit, a stern comment on the reader's appetite for bad news and juicy murders.

Turn back to *The Merry-Go-Round in the Sea* and we find the little boy touching, 'with pleased interest', the scars on his cousin's ankles, souvenirs of his imprisonment by the Japanese. 'Gee, you *did* get tortured, then,' says the boy. The released prisoner replies 'in a small, strained voice', looking at his little cousin with apparent hatred: 'You'd have been disappointed if I hadn't, wouldn't you? I bet none of your bloodthirsty little mates has got a cousin who was tortured.' He tells the boy that the scars came from a red-hot bayonet and the boy feels sick. . . .

The writing of *The Merry-Go-Round in the Sea* seems to have been heartfelt; but *The Suburbs of Hell,* despite its portentous decorations, is surely little more than a game, a puzzle for unsentimental readers. So, it would be best not to spoil the game by discussing the plot and characters here, but rather to commend Randolph Stow's skill in recording the customs and speech patterns of modern Suffolk.

> *D. A. N. Jones, "Doctor, Doctor," in* London Review of Books, *Vol. 6, No. 7, April 19-May 2, 1984, p. 23.*

NORMA JEAN RICHEY

One can almost hear the footstep in the back of the mind, the silence of fear, the rustle of terror as Randolph Stow explores the infinity of mortality in *The Suburbs of Hell*. The setting for death is timeless; but in the contemporary urban sprawl there are no perimeters for defense against intrusion, and death comes anonymously and invisibly in the form of serial murders in a small fishing village, Old Tornwich. Stow had considered calling this latest work *Someone Is Mad among Us,* which conveys the strain of living with the knowledge that anything

can happen. . . . The omnipresence of death pervades this setting of a world on the fringes of hell in which Stow has created a modern-day *Everyman,* where the rituals of human encounters fail to provide a safeguard against death that comes willy-nilly, "like a thief in the night." (p. 315)

On the surface *The Suburbs of Hell* might seem like an exceptionally well-written mystery or detective story, but only on the surface. Like all of Randolph Stow's novels, its structure brilliantly suggests its theme—in this case, that labyrinthine overlappings make the edges of one kind of reality (mind, place, knowledge) merge with other edges until all boundaries disappear. The similarly labyrinthine motion of the action and the spiraling of the characters' thoughts and actions all repeat themselves within the surrounding, enveloping presence of death in a world where everyone is literally living on the edge of life. On the edge of awareness, on the perimeter of society, outside the boundaries of our recognizable world, death waits in the spaces between the known and the unknown, between one heartbeat and the next. Man is caught in the richness of life and its beauty and passes like a sound heard at a distance. . . .

Stow is one of the most extraordinary and gifted stylists of our time. It is an inexcusable offense against intelligence that his novels should be summarized as plots and his gift neglected by lack of recognition that his is indeed a unique voice. *The Suburbs of Hell* is another step in the evolution of an artist of world stature whose novels are open doors to new stylistic creations for everyone fortunate enough to read his work. (p. 316)

> *Norma Jean Richey, in a review of "The Suburbs of Hell," in* World Literature Today, *Vol. 59, No. 2, Spring, 1985, pp. 315-16.*

D. KEITH MANO

The Suburbs of Hell has been shoehorned into a gothic / whodunit genre. It will essay more than that, but, foot-bound by convention, never really attain flank speed. And, as though gone spiteful from restraint, it also twits the expectation of your gothic / whodunit constituency. Yet, somehow, in between, Stow has managed to make a taut, gorgeous, swirling heat devil out of this bastard thing. (p. 45)

The Suburbs of Hell, I'd hazard, isn't typical Stow—more a genre-fit. He writes economically, yet he doesn't nickel-nurse his prose. First-chop dialogue, plotting tighter than a Denver boot. Somewhat overcute with assonance / alliteration—"trees . . . holding in their black coral boughs black shocks of rooks' nests"—but that isn't an actionable offense. Good, I mean to say.

Several inexplicable murders occur in Old Tornwich, your standard gothic soundstage-with-fog-machine English seaside town. Murder will ignite madness, suicide, and surplus murder. More plot the *Miranda* decision saves me from having to disclose. But there is something scandalous and chatty, fun even, about abrupt death in a small middle-class place: everyone suspects everyone else. Stow has meant to convey the village-wide degeneration of character and relationship. He is just half successful: genre requirements pressure him in turn. . . . In general, the book has an ambivalent attack: neither time nor space enough for thorough psychological examination. And, when you foreshorten truth, it tends—good prose or not—to sound pretentious.

More vexing still is the inadequate presence of a first-person speaker that may be Death or Fate. Initially this dramatic figure serves to decoy attention.... But this Death or Something soon decays into just another, not very informative, omniscient point of view. And at the end it will say, "He lies on the floor in his vomit. He stares up into my face. He sees me in my own likeness, without disguise. For flesh is a disguise. He cannot speak or breathe. Yet he speaks to me, with his blazing eyes. I can read his eyes. I have read many." Hum ... You have to expect sententiousness, I suppose, from anyone or anything in so high an ambassadorial post. Myself, I do hope for some more engaging, wittier exchange at the end. Moreover, Stow's device is maddeningly inconsistent, often plain apathetic. The serious novelist trying, without much conviction, to impregnate a spayed genre.

Even more stagy and vain, though, is Stow's wrap-up. He has pasted together a headline collage: HEADLESS CORPSES IN EL SALVADOR. 1000 BENGALIS MASSACRED IN ASSAM. And so, grimly, on. This plus an engraving of the Tarot card for death. Throughout, too, there have been chapter-head quotes from mostly Jacobean literature, celebrating pure evil—the senseless, native force of it. As a human position this is both pessimistic and defeatist. I prefer to consider it Stow's retaliation against the genre. Whodunits should provide perpetrator and reasonable motive. Stow, maybe in pique, will withhold that informational courtesy. His title, note, has been lifted from John Webster: "Security some men call the suburbs of hell, / Only a dead wall between." No one is or should be secure: nor will the executioner of those headless Salvadoran corpses be found by Hercule Poirot. Intellectual *haute couture* all this: it paints on an acrylic coat of High Intention not really earned.

Yet the book is snap-rolling aerobatic entertainment.... As for who dunit: the author isn't above suspicion. I'd have him detained for questioning. (pp. 45-6)

D. Keith Mano, "Strait-Genred," in National Review, *New York, Vol. XXXVI, No. 10, May 31, 1985, pp. 45-6.*

ANTHONY J. HASSALL

If *The Girl Green as Elderflower* marks the end of a period in Stow's writing, *The Suburbs of Hell* (1984) marks something of a new beginning. Part thriller and part medieval morality, the book is compulsively readable. The writing is tight, there is more vigour and less anguished personal involvement, and the pace is expertly controlled. Stow has described the book as a modern version of *The Pardoner's Tale,* and like that tale it is a good deal more unsettling than the average murder mystery. The web of literary allusion throughout the book attests to the relentlessness with which death pursues life, and to the reckless enthusiasm with which men cooperate by killing themselves and one another, and this dual pattern is echoed in the narrative. Like *The Pardoner's Tale, The Suburbs of Hell* is both a rattling good yarn and a searching exploration of the curious mixture of fear, fascination and indifference with which death, especially if it is violent, is commonly perceived. The result is a powerful meditation on this most abiding of human concerns.

Stow has always been an ambitious and adventurous writer, driven to remake conventional forms to accommodate his contrary and divided vision. In his most recent work he combines, like Chaucer, a gripping narrative and a chilling theme, though the greater length and detail of *The Suburbs of Hell* prevent it

from imitating closely the profound, uncluttered parable at the centre of Chaucer's tale. Stow's unusual combination of a naturalistic "whodunit" with a moral tale about the visitations of death makes this a particularly *scriptible* book, one which denies the reader the pleasures and the security of a closed form. The greatest contrasts occur at the beginning and the end of the book. At the beginning the bible-laden reflections of Death, precise, world-weary and yet excited, sit uneasily beside the snug, unpretentious cosiness of Harry Ufford at home. And the ending disregards the reader's desire to be told "who done it", a desire normally satisfied in crime fiction, though not so often in the factual world of police investigation. Stow has always avoided tidy endings—his vision of human experience precludes them—and even the death which closes *Visitants* is a beginning as well as an ending. The difficulty this imposes on him when he writes a thriller is that he is bound to disappoint the expectations of his readers, and the challenge he faces is to persuade those readers that their shock of disappointment is also a shock of enlightenment. The denial of closure in *To the Islands, The Merry-go-Round in the Sea, Visitants* and *The Girl Green as Elderflower* expresses powerfully a vision that remains unresolved. In *The Suburbs of Hell* the success is less complete. It is unsettling not to be told the identity of the murderer, and not to be able to deduce who it is from the inconclusive and contradictory evidence provided. If the moral is, as the title suggests, that no man is secure from sudden and inexplicable death, and that we should therefore so live that we are always ready to die, then the "whodunit" clues and suspicions create false expectations in the reader. And the realization that identifying the killer will not slow the march of death, and may only induce a false sense of security, does not entirely compensate for the reader's sense of frustration.

The insinuating first-person reflection with which the book opens unnerves and intrigues the reader partly because, like the openings of other Stow books, it is not quite consonant with what immediately follows. On the first day of winter Death has returned to Old Tornwich, anticipating a spate of killings which will feed his desire to see inside the lives of those who will die. He quotes with approval the biblical descriptions of death as a thief in the night, defining a thief as:

> a student of people ... I have stood in a pub and seen a face, heard a voice, and slipped out and entered that man's house, calm in my mastery of all his habits. But then—ah, the thrill then, after my many studies; to find his things, his self, lying opened before me, all his secrets at my fingers' ends.... It is the intoxication of inside.

While these might be the thoughts of a human thief, an outsider voyeuristically looking in, coveting the lifestyle of his victims, they might also be the thoughts of a novelist insatiably curious about the secrets of other people. Like the thief, the novelist can invade his characters' privacy, and kill them off violently if he wishes. And if the perfect "whodunit" has the reader as the murderer, then one in which the writer is the murderer is not without its attractions. The reader is thus involved in the roles of killer and victim, and as these metafictional possibilities echo in his mind, Death goes on to other descriptions of his motives: "It is not envy or anything of hatred ... No; it is never hostility or malice. Simply, it is correction, a chastising". He seems morally to disapprove of his victims for forgetting that they are mortal, that they owe God a death. He identifies the murderer's first victim as the teacher Paul Ramsey. And he ends as he began with the bible: *"Thou fool, this night thy soul shall be required of thee"*. This mixed set of motives offers the reader a typically enigmatic insight into the story which follows. Death strikes randomly, without apparent reason, thereby reminding his subjects that they must answer to him, and chastising their forgetfulness. Human killers, however, usually have motives which, while they may be arbitrary and even bizarre, are also understandable.

The flourish of epigraphs and allusions with which the book begins reinforces the metafictional dimension of the first section. . . . Stow has used epigraphs from Jacobean drama in many of his books, clearly seeing an affinity between his own work and the grim world of senseless violence depicted by Webster and his contemporaries. The epigraph to the first section of the book is from *Beowulf* and it reinforces the image of death as a Grendel-like monster, seeking whom he may devour:

> But the demon, a black shadow
> of death, prowled long in ambush,
> and plotted against young and old.

Grendel, like the "Nedlands Monster" referred to in the dedication, and like the killer in *The Suburbs of Hell,* is inhuman in his seemingly motiveless thirst for blood. And yet it is paradoxically true that it is both human and inhuman, natural and unnatural to kill, as the bloody history of human affairs, and the long list of those who have gorged death's insatiable appetite, bear eloquent witness. (pp. 165-68)

The irruptions of the murderer break in on the reader, however, as they break in on the citizens of Tornwich, reminding both that their worlds are not inviolate. Each of the murderer's appearances is preceded by a bloodcurdling epigraph:

> *Barabas.*
> As for myself, I walk abroad o' nights,
> And kill sick people groaning under walls:
> Sometimes I go about and poison wells . . .
>
> *Ithamore.*
> One time I was an hostler at an inn,
> And in the night time secretly would I steal
> To travellers' chambers, and there cut their throats.

The effect of these epigraphs, and of the switch to first-person narration for the sections which follow them, and which describe Death "at the shoulder of the gunman, looking down the gun-barrel", is to interrupt both the illusion and the narrative method to which the reader has become adjusted. The *frisson* of terror which accompanies the gunman's appearance is thus reinforced by literary devices which extend the fictional world in two directions: back through literary parallels to a medieval tale of death; and out—through Brechtian alienation—into the reader's own, extra-fictional world, which is not allowed to remain as comfortably separate from the fictional mayhem as is usual in the murder mystery genre. Stow also uses other means to blur these boundaries. The only person to report a possible sighting of the murderer, for example, is a boy nicknamed "Killer". . . . While the main purpose of this early scene is to introduce the Tornwich Monster as dramatically as possible, it also illustrates, through the ironic naming of the witness, the curious mix of fear and fascinated admiration with which killers are condemned and celebrated, both within fiction and outside it. (pp. 168-69)

The enigma of the human gunman is not resolved in the later sections of the book. Each of three initial murders he commits is preceded by a short section in which Death reviews the life of the victim and takes pleasure in knowing him or her at the moment of death, when change becomes impossible. But there is no indication why Death's human accomplice chooses the people he does, and this makes the accomplice seem more like an extension of Death itself, and less like a human, motivated killer. Death describes and imagines the victims like an omniscient novelist viewing his characters and able to enter their private worlds. . . . Death thus occupies a fictional dimension separate from the rest of the narrative, and to which the reader has only limited access. We do not get to know him as he gets to know his victims, and see him only as a shadowy figure of mystery and fear.

The central "character" in the novel is Harry Ufford, whom we first see in his middle years, in "the privacy of his own special place", surrounded by the possessions which reflect the man and his interests. Harry is a devotee of real-life murders—as well as ships and horses—and his copy of *The Murderer's Who's Who* is to be instrumental in the death of Frank De Vere at the end of the book. . . . [Harry] has L-O-V-E and H-A-T-E tattooed on his fingers. But he is not psychically riven as Cawdor and Random are, and he does not contribute to his own destruction, as a number of Stow's earlier protagonists do, though he does let himself go down to death at the point of rescue. Nor do love and hate oppose one another in *The Suburbs of Hell* as starkly as they do in *The Girl Green as Elderflower.* Harry is occasionally pugnacious when provoked, but on the whole he is remarkably even-tempered, tolerant, and comfortable in his middle years, as few of the young / old characters of Stow's earlier books have been comfortable. His death therefore seems arbitrary, tragic in the medieval not the Shakespearian sense. His destiny is not his character. . . . The death of Harry, and the depredations of the Tornwich Monster, serve as grim reminders that any appearance of comfort and security is deceptive. And as the headlines from *The Tornwich and Stourford Packet* at the end of the book reveal for those who take it in, the world of the late twentieth century is little removed from that of *Beowulf,* with its constant killing and struggle for survival, or from the macabre dance of death played out so despairingly in Webster's plays. (pp. 169-71)

The second half of *The Suburbs of Hell* is both less disturbing and more exciting than the first. The already hectic pace increases and the suspense is heightened further. The killings in this part of the book have detectable human motives, and the thrill of the chase is added to the mystery of the first half of the book. Sleazy characters like Frank De Vere and Dave Sutton, who make their money from drugs, move into prominence, while the harmless victims like Sam and Greg, who are characterized more fully, disappear. Harry, who has been the centre of interest, and the moral centre of the book, moves into the midst of the action. He tries to rescue Dave, the son of an old friend, from his involvement with drug-peddling. Dave repays this good-natured concern by arranging Harry's "accident". The description of Harry's struggle to survive his drowning is both intensely dramatic and movingly lyrical. . . . The spare narrative . . . is reminiscent of Conrad, while the sense of an entire life caught in a moment of poignant reflection recalls Virginia Woolf. Stow, like Woolf, is often a poet of death, but nowhere more strikingly than in this powerful climax.

While it is Dave who arranges the accidental drowning, Harry's real opponent is Dave's boss, Frank De Vere. Frank dislikes the likeable Harry from the beginning, for reasons that are never explained, but which may be no more than the inevitable dislike of the bad for the good. The two men share a drink in the Speedwell on the night that Paul Ramsey is shot—the first night of the book—and their hostility is evident. Frank accuses the genial Harry of being "half-cut":

> When scenting an offence Harry's face took on an odd expression, mild yet grim. Not moving his head, he said: "Psychologically speakin, young Frank, you're a sort of a Peepin Tom. What the Frogs call a *voiture*."
>
> "*Voyeur*, you tool," Frank murmured.
>
> "Is that it? Where did I get *voiture* from, then?"
>
> "Off the car-deck on the *Felix*, I should imagine."

If Frank wins the verbal exchange here, Harry wins the moral exchange. And it is apparent that the sparring between them is in earnest, despite Frank's jokey attempt to pass it off. Harry's later comments that Frank's associate Dave has never shown much interest in women, and that he has a surprising amount of money for "a young fella on the dole" are shrewd and prophetic. We later learn that Frank may have supplied his wife Linda with drugs in lieu of sexual satisfaction, and that he is more interested in "firearms and bladed weapons" than women. His relationship with his business associate Dave is hardly one of friendship, but it may be that he prefers to deal with someone who shares his own sexual disinclinations. Frank's nastiness, evident in this early scene, sets Harry thinking about him more deeply than before.

Frank becomes directly involved with the killings when his wife finds a message in lipstick on her sitting-room window:

> NOT TONIGHT:
> SOON
> The Os of the last word had irises and pupils.

If this is a message from the Tornwich Monster—and there is no other explanation for which there is any evidence—then it is the first and only time that he has warned, and so terrorized his victims. And the message raises further questions. Why is there a warning in this case, and is it intended for Linda, or Frank, or both? Is it intended that Linda should misinterpret it as a message from Frank, as she does, at least to begin with? Linda is later shot, though not immediately killed, and Frank is shot at, without being hit. Is the gunman losing his aim or his nerve? The narrations by Death which precede these two unsuccessful attempts to kill are comparatively detached and impersonal—there is, for example, no first-person reference in Linda's—and there is less of the pleasure of getting inside Frank's character, or Linda's room and possessions. Death, it seems, can only get "inside" at the moment of death, and is therefore not so interested in near misses.

The attempt on Frank's life is the last recorded attack by the Tornwich Monster, and it leaves the reader no closer to finding out who the Monster is. Much of the early evidence in the book points to Frank as the murderer. His rifle appears to be the murder weapon—one assumes the police later check it— he dislikes Harry and Harry's friends (the first three victims), and he is nasty and self-interested enough to kill his associate Dave after persuading Dave to kill Harry. But Frank's thoughts in "A Riposte" contradict this evidence and indicate that he is himself desperately trying to identify the murderer before it is too late. Frank thinks it must be Dave, who has motive

enough to dislike Linda and to hate him. And it would be a nice irony if Dave, who is dubbed the Monster after Frank arranges his "suicide", were indeed guilty. But the scene in which Frank shows Dave the rifle hidden in Harry's backyard shows Dave to have been unaware of the rifle's existence, and therefore to be innocent. Dave's puzzlement leads him to advance the theory that someone, "a nut-case", was looking out of an attic or a bathroom window when Frank first hid the rifle, and that this unknown person is the murderer. This theory, which is reinforced perhaps by Stow's original title for the book, *Someone Is Mad Among Us,* and by the reference to the Nedlands Monster in the dedication, has at least the virtue that it is not disproved by the evidence—or lack of it—in the book. It would also be ironic if the killer were Killer, but the boy seems genuinely frightened at the beginning of the book, and, unless his hypocrisy is precociously accomplished, his deductions at the end with Frank are genuinely a couple of guesses behind those of Frank and the reader. So the reader is left to share the uncertainty and suspicion which are tearing Tornwich apart. Is it one of the obvious suspects, or is it an inexplicable nobody like Eric Edgar Cooke, the "Nedlands Monster"? The author himself is not saying: "if it stays like *Edwin Drood*, I don't mind . . . the urge to 'solve' it, and so sweep it out of mind, is one which Death, sardonically, would understand very well. That is part of the moral".

Frank's death at the end of the book, which is brought about with an irony reminiscent of *The Pardoner's Tale,* does leave the reader with some satisfaction. Frank's earlier suspicion that Harry is the Monster is too much even for the pliable Dave to believe; but Frank still thinks that Harry was capable of poisoning a birthday bottle of whisky, and his fear that he has inadvertently drunk most of that bottle chokes him to death. The sweetness of the poetic justice does not belie the moral that the fear of death can be lethal, but it does give a partial sense of closure to the end of the narrative. The identifiable villain gets his just deserts. What happens to the Monster is another question.

In its final pages then *The Suburbs of Hell* deconstructs itself as crime fiction. The morality theme remains, however, and it is Death who has the last word. . . . Death is thus finally portrayed, in filmic manner, as the Grim Reaper, and his omnipresence is attested to by the catalogue of headlines from *The Tornwich and Stourford Packet* which follows, and which chronicles the violence of death throughout the world. The reader is left to ponder the moral that after death he too, whether killer or victim or observer, may be judged at last. Finally there is the tailpiece: the Tarot Card XIII—Death—and underneath it the thirteenth-century distich:

> All too late, all too late,
> when the bier is at the gate.

The story of Harry Ufford and the Tornwich murders is thus finally embedded in a medieval context, a time when the bier at the gate was an all too familiar summons.

Death belongs to no single time, however, and Stow expands his picture of a small and close-knit community in trauma into a general meditation on the frailty, the impermanence of life. It is a perennial theme of literature, and Stow echoes works as diverse as *Beowulf* and *The French Lieutenant's Woman* as he creates a book as multilayered as Old Tornwich. As *Tourmaline, The Merry-go-Round in the Sea, Visitants* and *The Girl Green as Elderflower* all testify, Stow likes to explore the rich presence of the past in the communities he portrays. Unlike these books, however, ***The Suburbs of Hell*** does not have a major character especially sensitive to history, and it is therefore the author—and Death—who take the longer view. The author's voice in this last book is less personal and more dispassionate. The writing of ***The Girl Green as Elderflower*** seems to have freed Stow from his intense concern with the personal crises of 1959-60 which form the basis of that book and ***Visitants***. ***The Suburbs of Hell*** remains haunted by fear and death, as these books were, but it is more fully projected into the central narrative of murder and suicide. The result is both a loss and a gain: there is less anguish; and there is also less of the fierce intensity which has illuminated Stow's books from the very beginning. If, like Harry Ufford, he is becoming a little more comfortable in his middle age, he remains aware that comfort is illusory, and he still hears clearly behind him the steps of the Grim Reaper. (pp. 174-79)

> *Anthony J. Hassall, in his* Strange Country: A Study of Randolph Stow, *University of Queensland Press, 1986, 213 p.*

Ronald Sukenick

1932-

American novelist, short story writer, critic, editor, and non-fiction writer.

Sukenick is regarded as an eminent practitioner and theoretician of American postmodern literature. In his fiction, Sukenick rejects representational and mimetic forms of realism to focus on the fictional process itself. His writing emphasizes spontaneity, improvisation, and the primacy of imagination in rendering experience through language. Sukenick's fiction is marked by humor, self-reflexiveness, protean characters, equivocal plots, unconventional typography, and disjointed narratives. While primarily concerned with the relationship between fiction and reality, Sukenick's works also address social, cultural, and political issues.

Sukenick's first novel, *Up* (1968), established him as an important figure in American experimental fiction. Ostensibly an account of a group of New York intellectuals and bohemians, this work primarily traces the progress of a novel being written by a character named Ronnie Sukenick. The writer and other fictional and nonfictional characters fade in and out of the story in a series of fantastical, disconnected vignettes that playfully mock the literary and academic environments. Jerzy Kutnik noted: "*Up* is for Sukenick in the most literal sense a process in which the writer tries to get at the truth of his experience by imaginatively recording his thoughts and perceptions occurring during and because of the composition of his novel." Sukenick's next work, *The Death of the Novel and Other Stories* (1969), is a short fiction collection which retains the improvisational style of *Up*. Featuring such techniques as side-by-side dialogue, marginal remarks on the text, and taped conversations, many of these stories are preoccupied with the problem of organizing reality into fiction. Sukenick's second novel, *Out* (1973), concerns a seemingly purposeless westward journey across the United States by an obscure group of characters. This novel represents Sukenick's attempt, as his fictional alter ego states, to "write a book like a cloud that changes as it goes." As the book progresses, the amount of text on each page diminishes, the narrative becomes increasingly fragmented, and the plot loses coherence. Most critics interpreted *Out* as an exploration of the experience of writing fiction and the nature of meaning.

In *98.6* (1975), Sukenick shifts his emphasis from artistic matters to social and political issues. "Frankenstein," the first section of this novel, depicts through a collage of newspaper articles a fictional United States embroiled in decadence and meaningless brutality. The second section, "The Children of Frankenstein," recounts an attempt by refugees to escape the insanity of the modern world by founding a commune. A character named Ronald Sukenick tries in vain to write a novel about this experience as a means for imposing order in a chaotic society. The final section, "Palestine," portrays an imaginary Israel where the contrasting values of the communards and the citizens of Frankenstein are reconciled by The Mosaic Law, which offers suggestions for coping with a fragmented world. *Long Talking Bad Condition Blues* (1979), Sukenick's most technically radical work, consists of one long, unpunctuated sentence, in which blocks of text are separated by spacing

Photograph by Sarah. Courtesy of Ronald Sukenick.

according to the rhythms of blues music. This novel focuses on the existence of young exiles who have difficulty adjusting to the post-industrial era. Through a series of random incidents, Sukenick conveys the horror and aimlessness beneath the veneer of contemporary life.

In *The Endless Short Story* (1986), Sukenick synthesizes his social interests with explorations into the relationship between imagination and reality. Lois Gordon observed: "[Sukenick's] quest is to get to the truth of perception *preceding* language, to convey feeling and sensation in fresh metaphors that will release the visionary potential latent in language." In *Blown Away* (1986), Sukenick uses a tawdry Hollywood revision of Shakespeare's *The Tempest* to investigate the art of storytelling. Sukenick has also written *In Form: Digressions on the Act of Fiction* (1987), a collection of "digressions" that advocate nontraditional forms of writing, and *Down and In: Life in the Underground* (1987), a personal history of the counterculture and artistic community of New York City from the 1950s to the 1980s.

(See also *CLC*, Vols. 3, 4, 6; *Contemporary Authors*, Vols. 25-28, rev. ed.; and *Dictionary of Literary Biography Yearbook: 1981.*)

IRVING HOWE

Ronald Sukenick . . . can do just about anything with words. He can turn out a parody, a burlesque, a pastiche, a bit of genre realism, a modernist set piece; he has a fine gift for mimicry; he knows literature backward and forward—imagine, in 1968 a young writer modeling the structure of his *Up* on Laurence Sterne's *Tristram Shandy*!; he has absorbed the lessons of Joyce and the influence of Bellow; he has done just about everything except write a good novel.

Seldom has so much literary knowingness . . . been brought together with a setting, a group of characters, an intellectual terrain, all calculated to stir memories of high school. Weaving, Sterne-like, time future and time present into a skein of vignettes, *Up* presents a promising lad named Sukenick, prisoner of Brooklyn, lover of the recalcitrant Nancy, future author of *Up,* and soon a teacher of English. The grubbiness of lower-middle-class Jewish life is again put on display; the once enchanting schoolmates sink into dismal employment; and somehow Strop Banally, a pop-cult fantasy figure, weaves his way in and out of *Up* with feats of manly sadism. (pp. 85-6)

It really ought to be great fun, an exuberant outpouring of comic genius, mocking the banalities of the age and the pretensions of the young. But alas, no. *Up* cannot rise very high above the level of its materials; effective satire cannot be written about a world that is silly rather than evil, characters who are pipsqueaks rather than ominous. (p. 86)

> *Irving Howe, "First Novels: Sweet and Sour," in* Harper's Magazine, *Vol. 236, No. 1416, May, 1968, pp. 83-8.*

THOMAS LASK

Ronald Sukenick's [*Up*] seems to be the kind of work that only needs sorting out to become a novel. It spins its own form as it goes along; it is busy all over; it is full of color, energy, life; an action painting in words, it sometimes dribbles a sentence here and there. It contains fragments, exaggerations, parodies. Yet when it is finished, it has a unity of its own. More, it is something of its own kind and not something else.

To be obvious, it is not a conventional novel. The author doesn't even like the term. He prefers "book," for he contends that he has tried not to tell a story but to tell the truth. And in spite of everything that appears haphazard, directionless or disconnected, the book does strike the reader as right.

The boys and girls and later on the young men and women who swirl around in these pages are recognizable aspects of our society. . . . But the author never lets you forget the kind of citizens they are.

Any summary of the contents of the book will place an artificial order on a work that is best described by a reading. But generally it is about Sukenick, teacher and author, his growing up in Brooklyn, his difficulties at home with the devouring love of the uncle and aunt he lives with, the adolescent clashes with his young cousins, the trials and fate of his many friends, his work in the maternity ward of a hospital, his teaching and his writing, his knotted and convoluted sex life.

Perhaps the substance of the book is not new and Mr. Sukenick reminds us that he hasn't forgotten any of the authors from Homer to Joyce he has read. But he has at least refused to play it safe and made something fresh and crisply readable from matter that could have been tired and jaded.

> *Thomas Lask, "Making Their Way," in* The New York Times, *June 22, 1968, p. 31.*

RAYMOND A. SOKOLOV

When he reviewed this modish verbal romp [*Up*] for Harper's, Irving Howe [see excerpt above] grumbled that the young author had "done just about everything except write a good novel." After fifty-odd years of living with modernity and the awareness that the center no longer holds, that the golden bowls are all broken and the well-wrought urns in shards, we apparently still hanker after classics, shapely masterpieces. Something very different is going on, and it had better be dealt with on its own terms, not Jane Austen's or even William Faulkner's. Plot, character and verisimilitude are no more. Without them, the novel has veered, in France toward *cinema verité,* in this country into put-ons and the picaresque.

Ronald Sukenick knows this and a great gaggle of other freshly minted commonplaces. A product of the graduate schools and a Wallace Stevens mystagogue, his mind is stuffed with the jargon and the superfine esthetics of Eng. Lit., which he abandoned to write *Up.* Not surprisingly, his first "novel" is a compendium of sly jokes on literature.

Though it pretends to be autobiographical (and is to a certain extent), *Up* is really a work of literary criticism in, very loosely speaking, novel form. For those in the know, it will be a picnic of assorted delicacies, nearly all to be eaten with tongue in cheek. The author delights in gratuitous segues between "fiction" and "reality." His time sequence is baroque, not to say chaotic. . . .

Though he certainly thought it out carefully beforehand, *Up* does read like a long improvisation with episodes strung hectically together. Some of these mosaic bits are not shiners, but the author's hypertrophied imagination seldom falters from "adventure" to "adventure." He, or do I mean the character of the same name, is an urban, literary, Jewish Don Quixote of our time.

> *Raymond A. Sokolov, "Ga-Ga-Ga-Gug," in* The New York Times Book Review, *July 14, 1968, p. 34.*

TOM JOHNSON

The use of language [in *Out*] is even more virtuosic than in Sukenick's first novel, *Up,* and his way of structuring the whole thing works very well.

"I want to write a book like a cloud that changes as it goes," he says at one point, and the metaphor seems apt for the novel he did write. . . .

It is really the imagery which holds the book together, and it holds together very well, despite the absence of logical threads, social messages, character development, and other conventions. Stick-ups and seductions occur with fair regularity. Fuses and sticks of dynamite occur throughout the book, usually as phallic symbols. Countdowns, numerological symbols, cryptic messages, pig Latin, tongues, and spy-story references are scattered through the book. The many characters frequently change their names and seldom stay around for more than a chapter, though they often turn up later in some form or other.

Occasionally the movements of Sukenick's changing cloud are interrupted by the voice of the author himself, and these rare intrusions turn out to be one of the most interesting elements of the novel. Most of the book is in the third person, but when Sukenick comes across a character or a situation he particularly identifies with, he shifts to the first person. (p. 29)

Sukenick is a master of rhythm, and the rhythmic structure of *Out* is one of the most enjoyable aspects of the book. The only punctuation he uses is the period, and often even this is avoided, so that the prose speeds down whole pages without a breath. On other pages periods are sprinkled all over, and the prose slows way down, breathing every few words.

Superimposed on the rhythm of the prose itself is a rather strange design idea. On each page the text is divided arbitrarily into three equal clumps. These clumps become smaller and smaller as the book progresses. So by the end we are rushing along at the rate of only 30 words a page, and the author begins pointing the "way out," meaning, of course, the end of the book, which is the only exit, the only way to get out of the book.

This is not only one of the nicer metaphors of the book, it is also absolutely true. Once we become involved with Sukenick's unique style and his many fleeting characters, we have no choice but to finish his captivating book, and to experience the whole countdown. (p. 30)

> Tom Johnson, in a review of "Out," in The Village Voice, Vol. XVIII, No. 47, November 29, 1973, pp. 29-30.

RAYMOND FEDERMAN

[*Out* is] a stubborn novel. It progresses with total disregard for credibility, and with a kind of determination that negates the logic of continuity because "when ya gotta go ya gotta go," and here anything goes! Those novels written in a state of anger, anguish, or serene reflectiveness perpetuate their fake fiction along the lines (the straight lines) of a temporal dimension which allow the elements of the story to be organized in a meaningful manner.

OUT stubbornly refuses to make sense—to make sense out of itself, and out of the past. Indeed, as one of the characters in the story says of his own unpredictable predicament: "It makes deep nonsense of my trivial sense."

Stubbornness, in fact, rejects the possibility of reflective perception. If one reflects, logically, calmly, obediently, reasonably, on one's course of action, then it is not possible to be stubborn about it.... *OUT* (by Ron Sukenick) is the most obstinate, the most perverse, the most unreasonable story I've ever read. It obstinately maintains its (hopeless, perverse, hilarious) course of action without ever looking back at its point of departure. It progresses with total disregard for coherence and credibility.

Stubbornness, moreover, functions outside and beyond temporal justifications. *OUT,* therefore, does not set itself in motion on the basis of an occasion which lies OUTside its fiction (in some distant place and some remote time). *OUT* is an occasion! An occasion of the present—of the HERE and NOW! *OUT* refuses to expand, progress, move, out of the past. It refuses to project its fiction from a specific point in time. *OUT* begins in a kind of unreal present, and moves further into that unreal present, thus abolishing that temporal dimension which gives traditional fiction (the angry, anguished, tranquil novels) a fraudulent space into which it can write itself. *OUT* uses REAL space to perpetuate its contours, detours, and move-

ments (its "plots and counterplots"). *OUT* uses the REAL space of the pages upon which it is written. *OUT* wriggles its way OUT of a closed and intricate formal pattern which has no antecedents outside of itself—no point of departure in the past, before the book, and beyond the covers of the book. *OUT* writes itself OUT of the corner into which it has cornered itself from the beginning.... The fiction then sneaks OUT of the page into empty space—blank space: the blank spaces essential to the layout of the book, blank spaces which augment in whiteness as the fiction empties itself into the blank pages at the end of the book. Or, as Sukenick (not the author, but the mythic character in the novel) tells us: "I want to write a book like a cloud that changes as it goes." (pp. 138-39)

OUT, then, stubbornly goes OUT of itself. Empties itself rather than fulfills itself (like most novels). Rather than augmenting as it progresses, rather than establishing its purpose with each new sentence, each new paragraph, each new page, and with each additional complication (as is the case with most traditional fiction), *OUT* juggles away its purpose and its complications. *OUT* improvises its events and occasions before the reader's eyes, and does so by using techniques of the movies, the comic strips, the slapsticks, as it is explicitly stated in the pages of the fiction: "Wake up. Everything up to here has been a movie." (p. 139)

Obviously, then, *OUT* makes a shamble of traditional fiction. It brings fiction to the brink of playful disaster. As such, *OUT* is a remarkable piece of fiction—a tour de force—because it fucks up all preconceived notions of what fiction should be. *OUT* fucks up the whole conventional way of reading a story. And above all, *OUT* fucks up the English language. No one, as far as I know, as yet so successfully, so brilliantly, so deliberately messed up the English syntax. *OUT* is written in a most unpredictable syntax: half-finished sentences run into other half-finished sentences to make new unfinished sentences: "the rumpus room picture windows on both sides leather armchair card table foldup ping pong table this is where we store the bicycles here's the bar that's the gallery the bridge is up ahead captain's quarters two TVs one here one in the crew's quarters aft are you a veteran." The punctuation dances among the words and the words bounce between the white space. It's beautiful to look at. It moves all over the place. It's full of energy! Full of surprises!

When ya gotta go this is the way to go!

And yet the novel is readable, very readable. And very funny too, but unpredictable. That's for sure.

But for those who still read books (novels?) for the story, the plot, the action, the so-called dramatic development, let us sum up. *OUT* is the story of a conspiracy, a plot. And since everyone in the novel carries a stick of dynamite, everyone therefore is part of the plot (and/or the counterplot). *OUT* is also the story of a trip. It's a trip! From East to West—from the big messy metropolis (New York, if you wish, or to be exact, Brooklyn: the El, the BMT, Coney Island, etc.) to the "blue gold orange sky" of decadent California.... It's a trip—an escape from the plot, from the big city, from the present, from the burden of social life, from the illusions of reality, but since everyone is involved in the plot (or the counterplot, as you wish), there is no way OUT! No way OUT for the Kids (that's what the characters are called) who, like comic-strip figures, struggle to find their way OUT of the frames into which they have been drawn. All of them are interchangeable.... Anything goes. And the fiction goes on, playing its game toward its end: point zero. But it's very serious too. For instance, for those who like mysteries, *OUT* is also full of mysterious (tragic!) events. Dynamite. Holdups. Stickups. Secret agents. Secret messages. Riots. Cops. Tear gas. Guns— lots of guns! (pp. 140-41)

Unlike most traditional fiction which tells its story by starting from a point in the past (the beginning) and moves toward another point in the past (the middle) to finally reach a point closer to the present (the end), *OUT* begins in the present (at the end) and constructs itself on the spot in the present (beyond its own end). Therefore no time is spent—just space: the space of the pages into which the fiction writes itself. The space it takes for the kids to move around, and move OUT.

It is in this nonmovement (except the movement of its pages) that *OUT* not only changes our reading habits, but also changes (improves rather) our perception of the world.

To change the level of perception one has of social reality, one must change the psychic mechanism which makes the writing of fiction possible. It is a matter of releasing a burst of creativity which shakes the real world (the classified world, the named world, the known world), and consequently releasing a true hallucinatory energy.

OUT releases such energy!

Indeed, if art (and I am using this useful word to designate all unfunctional activities) had as its only goal to make us see the world better, it would be nothing else but a technique of analysis, an ersatz science (and it is indeed what realistic art has been all about). But in seeking to produce the something else which is in the thing, it is an entirely new epistemology which is created. This unlimited, unrestricted work frees us of all accepted notions of hierarchy: true perception, fixed nomination, credible association. *OUT* is such a work which changes our perception of the world. *OUT* gets rid of social reality as a stable, organizable, recognizable entity. *OUT* demolishes any pretention we may have of perceiving the world as being rational, safe, and apprehensible. (pp. 141-42)

> Raymond Federman, *"In,"* in Partisan Review, *Vol. XLI, No. 1, 1974, pp. 137-42.*

ELIZABETH INNESS-BROWN

98.6 is a book without commas, question marks, exclamation points, colons, semi-colons, slashes, quotation or punctuation marks of any kind except for a few periods. Despite this, the novel is an enigmatic but perfectly comprehensible statement: incisive, sorrowful, humorous, and fascinatingly complex. The combination of an intense personal sensitivity, some literary game-playing, and an adroit, almost poetic use of language makes *98.6* both hard to define and wonderfully reasonable, both serious and somewhat satiric, both sad and funny; in short, human.

The book is about love: love of language, self-love, sexual, nationalistic, and scientific love. In three parts it explores love in a fashion not unlike that of the Russian novel, with its characters (or caricatures, as Sukenick would have it) living out their idealistic philosophies and slowly discovering either the difficulty or the impossibility of conquering illogical human emotion with cold logic: "Love conks all." In the first part Sukenick sets the scene with a collage of thoughts, images, experiences, and newspaper "clippings" that conjures up the late sixties in the United States. Violence and science invade

the homes and even the bedrooms of ordinary people; the search for something to believe in and to trust becomes more and more frantic; society becomes a "Frankenstein," out of control and uncontrollable. The need to escape this leads inevitably to "dropping out," and the first part of the novel leads to the second, which is the narrative of the experiences of ten people, "The Children of Frankenstein," who leave their mother-society to attempt to create a society of their own. . . . The third part of the novel, called "Palestine," is set more or less in Israel, to which Sukenick has made a pilgrimage of sorts. Read this part especially carefully: it draws in the loose ends of the novel, all the ideas that are at first difficult to understand, and ties them in rather neatly.

What Sukenick does with language has great impact on the texture of the novel. By leaving out all commas and question marks and other punctuation, and by sometimes not separating thought and description from speech, he allows the statements to have infinite combinations and permutations of meaning. . . . As in poetry, the author controls the attention certain images and statements receive by maneuvering, juxtapositioning, and isolating them; a beautiful and peculiar taste is the result. (pp. 163-64)

Sukenick uses language magically and maneuvers form, ideas, and the reader to fit the world of thought that he so skillfully creates. (p. 164)

> *Elizabeth Inness-Brown, in a review of "98.6," in* fiction international, *Nos. 4-5, 1975, pp. 163-64.*

CARLL TUCKER

98.6 is witty, worthy, intelligent. Most of the way, that is. The first of the three parts, "Frankenstein" (his name for America), is a satchel of fragments, a collage portrait of a nation going "flat"—mechanical, violent, dead. The second part, "The Children of Frankenstein," details the assembling and disintegration of a commune, the hope and inevitable disillusion of a Utopian.

Blessed with an artist's green thumb, everything Sukenick touches grows to metaphor. In "Frankenstein," the sodomist who "colonializes" images the mechanization of society. The father who strikes a bargain with some besieging Mafiosi stands for all of us who try to compromise gracefully with helplessness. By juxtaposing news clippings about the Manson murders, the Hell's Angels, prison atrocities, sadomasochistic crimes, with ritual slaughters in 16th-century Mexico, Sukenick forces us to wallow in the perverse madness of our age.

After 60 pages of this, the reader is grateful to escape into the optimism of the utopian clearing by the sea. Here there are characters and good humor and landscape painting worthy of Faulkner. . . . The building of "the Monster," the communal home, makes one smile sadly, knowing that internal relationships and external pressures are certain, soon, to disrupt the dreams. Irony prevents the author from embracing any optimism entirely. Yes, he says, the outside world is frighteningly "flat," but flatness cannot be routed by wishful thinking: it is our nature.

Sure enough, the bikers and the truckers and a Mr. Stamp, the local authority, combine to destroy the commune's peace. The Utopians retreat farther and farther into their private world by changing their names. But there is no salvation. The commune shatters, one member taking a job as a go-go girl, others converting "the Monster" into a commercial statement.

And when Utopia fails, where next? A sadder man but wiser, Sukenick ought perhaps to have returned to brutish civilization. Instead, he continues his pilgrimage—to Palestine, where he meets a purported prophet who spouts 20 pages of gibberish. The theme is "Interruption. Discontinuity. Imperfection . . . Failure." The effect is exasperation and, once again, boredom. If the preceding pages weren't so excellent, one wouldn't care—but Sukenick could have written, almost did write, a masterpiece.

> *Carll Tucker, "Failed Utopia," in* The Village Voice, *Vol. XX, No. 26, June 30, 1975, p. 44.*

PAUL D. McGLYNN

98.6 is a novel in three sections, whose titles—"Frankenstein," "The Children of Frankenstein," and "Palestine"— perhaps reveal the basic, though not at all fatal, flaws. I refer to an occasional tendency to archness and an urge to thump the reader over the head with a Myth. Sukenick's strengths, however, outweigh his weaknesses. His prose style is fast, nervy, exciting, like Mailer and even Kerouac at their best, the comedy nearly always works, and it is interesting to see a writer in 1975 identify himself with the venerable form of the anatomy, in the tradition of Sterne, Swift, and Burton. Sex and violence, instead of being mere juvenile exhibitionism, create the narrative rhythms and character, in turn, creates the sex and violence. The process is as old-fashioned as Aristotle even if the effects are "modern." Sukenick's recurrent images are the sea, spouting whales, motion and stasis, very appropriate to the creation-redemption-apocalypse structure and the omnipresent birth-copulation-death cycles. . . . The vision is genuinely universal. The central section, set in a spaced-out commune, reveals a satiric potential that we should hope to see Sukenick develop more fully. (p. 77)

> *Paul D. McGlynn, in a review of "98.6," in* The Southern Humanities Review, *Vol. XI, No. 1, Winter, 1977, pp. 76-7.*

LARRY McCAFFERY

Ronald Sukenick's ability to create and control a wide range of literary styles is given free reign in *98.6,* an apocalyptic, poetic novel. . . . The plot of the book concerns a band of refugees who have escaped from a destructive society and are desperately attempting to put the pieces of their lives together again by creating a utopian home in the wilderness of Northern California. The first section of the book, entitled "Frankenstein," is a disjointed series of prose fragments created out of Sukenick's most hallucinatory rhetoric; taken as a whole this first section presents a mosaic of ugliness, chaos, and sexual despair—elements which have produced the "Frankenstein" that the United States has become. The solutions which offer themselves, such as dope, joyless sex, murder, limitless but pointless freedom, are clearly insufficient, and so in the second section, "Children of Frankenstein," a commune is formed in which the members collectively attempt to reshape their fragmented lives via the process of the imagination. As in Sukenick's earlier novels, *Up* and *Out,* struggle with the threat of chaos is depicted on three levels: the societal, the personal, and the fictional. Thus as we watch the commune attempt to create a healthy unity, we focus our attention on the book's main character, novelist Ron Sukenick, who is also struggling with self-creation within the novel we are reading; but we are also aware of the "real" Ronald Sukenick and *his* efforts to put together a meaningful text. In effect, all of these processes mirror each other and suggest different aspects of the problems created by "The Mosaic Law": "the law of mosaics or how to deal with parts in the absence of wholes."

The efforts of the commune predictably fail; greed, sexual duplicity, and violent encounters with a rival commune are demonstrated not to be the proper elements out of which a stable, fully realized "fiction" can be formed. In the third section, "Palestine," the character Ron remains to create an eschatological fantasy land of pure harmony (Bobby Kennedy is alive, there is peace between the Jews and Arabs). Although even this last effort of the imagination eventually fails, Sukenick's point about the way in which the imagination can *create* reality has been embodied not only in the action within the novel but in our own confrontation with the text itself. This book, like the commune, is spawned out of raw, chaotic elements which constantly threaten to decompose themselves. But the process of imaginative composition (our own and Sukenick's) which result in the novel before us provides an exemplary, magical act of the imagination, for it has created a new reality; this process is exactly the sort of divine creation that the commune members were striving for, but failed to achieve. As Sukenick tells us in all his fiction, life is like a novel—you have to make it up. (pp. 104-05)

> *Larry McCaffery, in a review of "98.6," in* Contemporary Literature, *Vol. 19, No. 1, Winter, 1978, pp. 104-05.*

PETER QUARTERMAIN

Long Talking Bad Condition Blues consists of a series of speech "routines" in a variety of forms: continuous flow of words, the prose solidly filling the page (for the character who sees the world as a flowing), breaking up in the second section into units (as, in Spring, the six main characters "resolve into emerging units")—a page of type at a time, with holes which in the third section become blank paper separated by chunky blocked single paragraphs roughly the same size. And so on. The second half of the book uses the same forms in reverse order, so that the book ends as it began, a solid flow of unpunctuated prose. There is minimal story: a bunch of young exiles on a nameless island, "figures on the ground of nothing", staving off with a mask of indifference the deep panic and aimlessness they feel (the world is full of holes, emptiness), pass time as they can, and at the end of the book are visited by their parents who, instead of offering hoped-for rescue, turn out to be more hopeless and helpless than their dislocated offspring.

Sukenick has a lively sense of comic irony, and the language of the novel is a *tour de force;* this is a brilliant book. Patterns are woven of abstractions and particulars, of sentences patterned by length—two-words, foursomes, then sevens—and syntax, patterns of voices for the ear and on the page for the eye. The range of Sukenick's writing is quite extraordinary, and this is that rare thing, a novel entirely without punctuation which is racy, colloquial, comic, readable; it is a prose in which the reader feels instantly at home, and at which he laughs, and in which on reflection he finds himself homeless— like the people in the book.

Detached from the world of experience by an inadequate conviction of their own reality and by the conviction that it is only through the insubstantiality of language that the world acquires reality, the people in this book have no aims, no hopes, no expectations, and cope by talking . . . : the world, for each of them, is *noise,* and is dominated by "the stale directionless tone of the official structure," by "new conditions" which "were not jumping to any conclusions," by Power, Superpower, and Absolute Power ("seediness in power", says one). It is a world where knowledge has been supplanted by information which comes in fragmented indigestible computer-ready binary bytes, where the disoriented young struggle with meaningless language, and find comfort or even glee in stupendous and utterly hilarious routines of gobbledygook explanations tenable only in a time of confusion. The confusion is of public and private, real and fantastic, pain and joy, sex and love, language and thing, religion and astrology, information and knowledge. A world of collage-reality, where an incompleteness in the landscape matches an incompleteness in consciousness, and the world-language is full of holes/emptiness. A provisional world, held together by "attitude" rather than by action or thought. The book is a vision of hell, very funny, highly readable, and at the same time deeply moving: people caught in inertia, hanging around waiting for something to happen, like teenagers in a suburban shopping mall. (pp. 71-3)

> Peter Quartermain, *"Trusting the Reader,"* in Chicago Review, *Vol. 32, No. 2, Autumn, 1980, pp. 65-74.*

RICHARD PEARCE

Like Hawthorne's wandering Jew and Melville's confidence man, Sukenick is an outlaw and trickster who reveals a world where senseless movement is all there is, draws us in, and compels us to take responsibility for it. (p. 123)

In such a world fiction does not imitate life; therefore such well-established canons as the imitative and intentional fallacy are fallacious. All canons, hierarchies, purposes, and meanings are called into question. Or, as Sukenick argues: "Reality doesn't exist, time doesn't exist, personality doesn't exist. God was the omniscient author, but he died; now no one knows the plot. Everything has been leveled, but everything is on the level. After a relatively conventional *Up,* Sukenick's confidence man contributes to the leveling. Everything is there, on the page, where the author, his characters, his story, their stories, fragments of the contemporary world, figments of the imagination, and the text itself—all equally responsible and irresponsible—create the surf and ride it. The surf, exhilarating and threatening its riders as it challenges their skill and cunning, is in constant motion. Sukenick makes the motion itself the subject of *Out* and *98.6.*

"This is the start of a journey," says the protagonist of *Out.* "I don't known how long it will be or where it takes you no one ever does. All you do is keep track". The journey, impossible or purposeless, across expanses of empty space, is archetypically American. Thoreau dignifies the "saunterer" by inventing his etymology and tracing him back to the "idle people who roved about the country in the Middle Ages . . . under the pretense of going *à la Sainte-Terre,*" to the Holy Land. Melville's Moby Dick and Faulkner's Old Ben realize their power and mystery from their ceaseless, indeterminate motion, which Ahab and Ike try to constrain. Huckleberry Finn must light out for the territory. Whitman celebrates "Nature without check" and expresses it in the unchartable movement of "Song of Myself," and Henry Adams gives ambiguous testimony to its manifestations in the dynamo. Senseless movement dominates the novels of Dos Passos, Hemingway, Fitz-

gerald. Kerouac inspired a generation with *On the Road.* But it took Pynchon to reveal the demonic power of movement for its own sake, recalling Melville in the confidence woman of *V.,* and realizing this movement not only in his subject but in the dynamic structure of his novel. In *Out* Sukenick confronts the reader even more directly with this movement. (p. 125)

Sukenick's confidence man, addressing the reader in the second person, draws us into a world where everything is senselessly connected, or part of a senseless plot. Even more, he reduces the world of the sixties to sheer plot—that is, conspiracy and movement from event to event without agents, goals, or ends. And finally, without ending, he empties the world of all content, drawing the reader into empty space.

The movement of the novel, besides following what turns out be a journey from the east to the west coast, takes two forms. The first is in the characters, who, not trusting anyone, have aliases, change names, and continually meet characters with their names. (p. 126)

The second and more essential form of movement is in the very form of the novel, which drives the reader to read faster and faster. The reader is told that he too carries a stick of dynamite and "the countdown starts with nine". What this means is that the second chapter is headed 9, then 8,7,6,5,4,3,2,1. The reader's momentum increases because each chapter has successively less print and more space—chapter 9 is composed of nine-line blocks separated by one line of space, and so on down to chapter 1 where each line is separated by nine lines of space. Compelled more by the violent momentum than by the violence of the story, the reader leaps across more and more space; and the momentum increases as some sentences run on without punctuation within a block and some sentences complete themselves across a space. Due to Sukenick's fine ear for the idiom and mastery of the printed line, we are able to keep on the track. (pp. 126-27)

After riding the swift surf of the novel, the reader is swept *out.* The novel and the reader are emptied of all words and all thought. Now—fully awakened and moving on his own—the reader continues into the empty space, facing nothing. Or facing what Sukenick describes in his next novel as "the gap. The blank space the clean slate. Where the terror is. And where dreams condense like clouds in an empty sky"

While *Out* moves westward to the open sea, *98.6* moves eastward to the hol(e)y land. "Who knows what salvations we might pluck from circumstance if we were open to the unknown". The novel begins with a plucking from circumstance, moves through a period of being plucked by circumstance, and ends with the salvation of wholeness in the holey land. "Frankenstein," the first part, is a series of disordered and discontinuous diary entries, plucked from the past of an anonymous third person. It counterpoints a journey across a sea and through a desert to the Ancient Caja with a return to his country "racing like a wheel". The second section, "Children of Frankenstein," turns into a continuous third-person narrative describing the formation and dissolution of a commune in California. Dissolution is inevitable because the commune cannot withstand the pressures from without—the law, the anarchist hippies, and the terrorist motorcycle gang. Dissolution is also inevitable because of its members' natural impulse toward violence. But, more important, it is inevitable because its seeds are sown in the very act of forming: in its rejection of society's norms but also in its construction of the building that they call "The Monster". . . . In the end the dissolution is reflected in the very language that Ron is using to write a novel about the commune. (pp. 127-28)

But the language, which continues nonsensically and poetically . . . , is also a new beginning, or a new opening to the unknown. "Palestine," the final section, is a short, fast, first-person monologue set in Israel (Is-real). Israel is the holey land and the promised land. It is holey with the promise of wholeness, for it continues the kibbutz or ideal commune; indeed, it contains the kibbutz where surfing is practiced, giving "every man and woman direct access to that union with nature so sought after by the sages" . . .

The disordered and discontinuous diary entries of "Frankenstein," the third-person narrative of "Children of Frankenstein," and the language of The Missing Lunk are finally brought together in "Palestine." We finally become attuned to the Mosaic Law—"the law of mosaics or how to deal with parts in the absence of wholes". And we finally become attuned to the voice and consciousness of the novel—plucking salvation from circumstance as it reaches into the unknown, constantly moving forward as it attempts to embrace the parts and the holes, the facts of the past and present, personal recollections and reactions, imagined fears and possibilities. It also reaches for wholeness in the holey land, attempting to see, grasp, and say everything at the same time. . . . (p. 128)

Out is an experience of emptying. *98.6* is an experience of collecting. Both are novels of pure motion—of language on the printed page moving forward, creating and destroying, creating in its own destructions, fashioning connections out of its disconnections, carrying the known into the unknown. In *Out* the unknown is empty space or nothing. In *98.6* it is everything at the same time. If the empty space at the end of *Out* contains infinite possibility and infinite terror, so does the wholeness that climaxes *98.6* for it contains the holes. The holy land contains the chamber of horrors—a memorial to the concentration camps. It also contains Dr. Frankenstein, "whose researches have unlocked the secrets of life itself," who "has taught us how to create ourselves in finer and finer harmony with the rhythms of the cosmos," and who may be planning to "promote the kind of neoindustrialism with which [he is] identified in Europe and America". Moreover, the movement of *98.6* has an ambiguous direction. It moves to the holy land, which houses the Ancient Caja. But we should remember that in the beginning of the novel, the protagonist had traveled across a sea and through a desert to see the Ancient Caja before returning home—that is, "Palestine" may lead to "Frankenstein."

Sukenick's confidence man has created or exposed the surf of modern experience—the continually changing surface, which includes fact and fiction; historical events, imaginative events, and events on the printed page; the author, his characters, and his readers. He rides the surf with skill and cunning, drawing us in with him till we see and feel the movement of the surf as all there is. (pp. 129-30)

Richard Pearce, *"Riding the Surf: Raymond Federman, Walter Abish, and Ronald Sukenick," in his* The Novel in Motion: An Approach to Modern Fiction, *Ohio State University Press, 1983, pp. 118-30.*

MARCEL CORNIȘ-POP

When, as in his recent collection of essays *In Form: Digressions on the Act of Fiction* Ronald Sukenick makes it the "duty of interpretation to avoid hierophantic complications and to render itself unnecessary as it extends our experience of the poem," he is not—one earnestly hopes—wishing criticism out of existence, but rather redefining it as part of the writer's *textual experience*. What Sukenick has in mind here is a kind of "writing on writing" and thinking "in form" which completes the writer's "ongoing conversation with himself that may be overheard in a poem, a story, an essay or an interview. One can start at any point on the periphery and arrive at the center." Still, we should expect this self-conscious, critical voice to mark itself out in the conversational rumor and advance beyond the limited exercise of "metafiction." It is true that Sukenick's early narratives contributed their share to that trendy species that "assimilates all the perspectives of criticism into the fictional process itself" (according to Robert Scholes's classic definition of "Metafiction," *Iowa Review*, I, 4, Fall 1970); but the very fact that he now felt the need to bring together his "theoretical" pronouncements and "digressions" proves that contemporary fiction has been seeking (and finding) a working theory *outside* its narrative world. . . .

With the very notions of "underground," "avant-garde," "experiment" now slipping away, "pasteurized and homogenized" by the publishing industry, what is needed is some new form of *artistic resistance*, a new poetics of composition. This is Sukenick's theme in his introductory essay, **"Art and the Underground."** . . . The message is hopeful: "There is an underground about to make its presence felt" in such forms as the new innovative fiction or the deformalized, digressive critical thinking. Sukenick traces their roots back to an American tradition of "resistance," extending from Emerson to Wallace Stevens, Henry Miller and Charles Olson. The fateful disregard of this tradition is responsible for creating that "schizoid split" in contemporary culture between conventional art and avant-garde, between art and life, pop-cultism and experimentalism, pattern and process. A return to Emerson means a return to improvisation and freedom of thought, to literary discourse as "composition." (p. 66)

Sukenick translates his ideal of "a thinking about art based upon the way it is composed rather than how it is interpreted" in terms of a *generative theory* of fiction. In simpler terms this means that the literary text is generated by the activity of composition, in the absence of any *a priori* idea of form and in disregard of any concept of imitation/representation. The immediate models for this generative, antimimetic approach (the same ones discussed by Sorrentino in his early *Kulchur* reviews) are action painting, Williams, Frank O'Hara or Olson's ideas of composition as an "open field," as "a nexus of various kinds of energy, image, and experience." Sukenick's overall method, opposed polemically to the parody-of-exhausted-forms approach (as represented by Barth) aims "to push out to the edge of culture and form and work always with open forms, which can in the language of some of the painters allow more reality into the work. I'm always working with collage and tape recorders, or the unpremeditated. I like forms which do not allow me to know what's going to happen next, even formally." . . . The other techniques in Sukenick's bag of tricks: improvisation (a kind of "mental jazz"), narrative flow and blockage, collage and cutting, metamorphosis (of names, identities, places, images). Such methods, treating art as *process* and form as an emanation of experience have little to do with the "cul de sac" formalism of early metafiction. . . . Sukenick . . . shows interest in artificial forms and arbitrary sequences (of numbers, narrative situations) to the extent he can take advantage of their (culturally) "empty space," or can transgress their meaningless frames. "Through puns or through arbitrary devices," he explains in [an] ... interview, "through the imposition of odd schemes, non sequiturs, even through improvisation" one can crack the protective shell of language and release its hidden energies.

Such ideas (illustrated in fact with the work of Raymond Roussel) recall the best of the avant-garde traditions. Sukenick's compositional theory (and often his practice) aim at a radical readjustment of fiction to "reality," at a break through the line dividing "art" from "life" (this also an avant-garde goal). . . . For Sukenick . . . fiction is a "beneficial form of counterfeit," one in fact that strives to escape its own condition. "Its truth is poetic: a statement of a particular rapport with reality sufficiently persuasive that we may for a time share it." Depending upon its persuasive authority, fiction can become an important experiential medium, "no longer an imitation of life, but rather . . . an illuminating addition to its ongoing flow," "simultaneously part of life and about it." (pp. 67-8)

Sukenick successfully avoids many of the pitfalls of the writer-writing-a-novel-about-a-writer-writing-a-novel-that-never-takes-shape formula. Besides the various aborted, mock-novels and stories that his books contain and review critically (as in *Out,* 1973) there is always a framing outer story, a novel that *does take place* eventually, rescuing its author (real Ronald Sukenick) from his many inside fictional avatars experimenting with failure. Especially *98.6* (1975) illustrates the cohesive force of *writing,* yoking together mock-autobiography, non-fictional material, newspaper clippings, history and symbolic generalizations according to what "Cloud" (another authorial alter ego) calls the "law of mosaics": "a way of dealing with parts in the absence of whole," of completing a narrative through the sheer energy of composition. . . .

There is a very clear *anti-interpretive* and *anti-transcendental* orientation in the essays of Sukenick. . . . Sukenick's . . . radical version of anti-Aristotelianism is most evident in **"The New Tradition"** article-manifesto (1972), in the presentation of the "Bossa Nova style" of "no plot, no story, no character, no chronological sequence, no verisimilitude, no imitation, no allegory, no symbolism, no subject matter, no 'meaning' . . . The Bossa Nova is nonrepresentational—it represents itself. Its main qualities are abstraction, improvisation, and opacity." This *opacity,* he theorizes in the conclusion, "should direct our attention to the surface of a work, and such techniques as graphics and typographical variation, calling the reader's attention to the technological reality of the book," to "the truth of the page."

Still, Sukenick's fictions have gradually gone beyond the *surface* mechanics of writing. The spatial structures, useful to him at the beginning in breaking up the illusionistic flow of the story, have been more recently returned to motion, dissolved in the textual process that unfolds its own "story" again in time.

"The petty iconography of the quotidian" or the early sallies into a spectacular but superficial "Erotic Autobiography" have (especially in *98.6,* but also in *Long Talking Bad Condition Blues,* 1979) become part of a larger movement of cultural exploration and of (in Sukenick's own words "invention and even prophecy." (p. 68)

Sukenick's generative theory of composition has ultimately little to do with Chomsky or Derrida, placing a greater stress on the experiences of the writer and reader than on the self-generating energies of the text (though the latter are not neglected). Finally, his "working theory" of composition is . . . a direct emanation of his own fiction, a kind of ongoing "report" on a passionate "struggle with the angel of form" and a necessary gesture of artistic resistance against the "Disneyland" approach of the dominant, mass-marketed fiction. (p. 70)

> *Marcel Corniş-Pop, "Working Theories of New Fiction," in* The North American Review, *Vol. 270, No. 3, September, 1985, pp. 66-70.*

TONY TANNER

For the most part these pieces [in *In Form: Digressions on the Act of Fiction*] were written in the 1970's. They hardly add up to a theory of fiction; rather they contain a continuing manifesto, creed, polemic—fitting, perhaps, for a teacher of creative writing. . . . Mr. Sukenick's "digressions"—the term is by courtesy of Laurence Sterne—tend to reiterate certain basic propositions and assertions. He is against the "fairy tale" of the "realist text" and against any notions of transcendence. Art is an "activity" as well as an "artifact."

The key recurring words in Mr. Sukenick's essays are "participation," "improvisation" (jazz is often invoked), "energy" and "flow"—fiction should be an addition to, an extension of, the "experiential flow." The aim is always to "stay within experience," to establish "contact with experience," to invent "more experience," to participate in "process" and avoid "stasis." Art should be "unpremeditated," a "game" that is constantly being made up. Plot and story are superfluous—what matters is the "flow of energy." Experience is to be rescued from the appropriations of history, politics, commerce, theory, even language itself. Mr. Sukenick wants to break with the "hermeticism" of the great moderns, to elevate "spontaneity" above craft. The only tolerable structure for him is the "structure of the arbitrary."

The canonical writers in this tradition, often invoked though rarely examined here, are Henry Miller, Rabelais, Sterne, Jack Kerouac, and the egregious Raymond Federman. . . . Whitman should be there but, oddly, isn't. Backup names are William Burroughs, Frank O'Hara, Allen Ginsberg, Gilbert Sorrentino; and from France, Raymond Roussel, Céline, and Jean Genet. The point about all this is that it now reads so predictably.

The advice he apparently gives his students is good. "If you don't use your own imagination, somebody else is going to use it for you." But for a writer who attaches so much importance to flow, motion, generation, improvisation and so on, the attitudes and prescriptions expressed in a series of recorded interviews (entitled **"Cross Examination"**), as in the essays, are disappointingly static, reiterative. "I'm like a fisherman with a fast boat that keeps pulling in fish and throwing them overboard, I like to travel light." The trouble is, it is invariably the same fish he pulls in. Arguably Mr. Sukenick travels rather *too* light.

One of Mr. Sukenick's more recent essays in this book, **"Narrative Authority"** (1984) continues the attack on "consensual reality," and notes that the so-called "underground" has been "merchandised away" and the notion of the "experimental" becomes "a meaningless label." The "autonomous text" that simply allows language to speak itself seems to command some of Mr. Sukenick's support, though he does seek to maintain a kind of moral function for fiction—"to help uncreate the forged consciousness of the mass market."

In his introductory essay, **"Art and the Underground,"** Mr. Sukenick predictably cites Emerson's central stress on the possibilities of endless "metamorphosis," and refers approvingly to Emerson's insistence that the "intellectual man" must "shoulder considerable public responsibility and power." How actually to *do* this was an endless and unsolved problem for Emerson, and it is not yet clear that Mr. Sukenick has any new suggestions to offer a contemporary novelist on how to profitably heed the injunction. However, he intimates a potentially new dimension of social—or antisocial—commitment in his thinking about fiction. But basically he holds to an established and familiar posture. . . .

There are a couple of pieces in the book of some interest. **"The Politics of Language"** revealingly engages the actual publishing and market difficulties confronting new writers in America, and a **"Film Digression"** offers some interesting thoughts about the results of "growing up in the electrosphere" and its possible effects on the culture of the future. Mr. Sukenick is a highly intelligent and interesting writer with real imaginative gifts. But he would have done better to have let most of these "fish" stay in the sea of the 1970's and instead "pulled in" another fiction.

> *Tony Tanner, "Throwing the Fish Overboard," in* The New York Times Book Review, *September 22, 1985, p. 26*

LOIS GORDON

Once again Ronald Sukenick's peripatetic hero, Ronald Sukenick, is on the road, revisiting his childhood kingdom of Brooklyn, as well as the more exotic landscapes of Paris and California. The postromantic Mr. Sukenick . . . still yearns for imaginative transcendence in a world grown violent and banal. *The Endless Short Story,* however, unlike his other books, is a more interiorized journey, and Mr. Sukenick's inquiries into the relation of imagination to reality are now fully integrated into his social and cosmic concerns. The ESS (his abbreviation) is a beautiful and poetic work, funny, intellectually challenging and unexpectedly moving.

Early on, Mr. Sukenick stands at the peak of the Colorado Rockies, reflecting with a certain equanimity on the "endless short story" of his life. Disparate sequences, in diverse styles, convey his preoccupations with birth, death and the deterioration of love; he is, above all, committed to his art. Puns, parodies, word games and cartoon antics also convey Porfessor (sic) Sukenick's bemused encounters with his critics. . . .

The key episode in *The Endless Short Story* is the apocalyptic sequence "Bush Fever" (a biblical burning bush sequence), where Mr. Sukenick confronts the human condition and responds with a gospel of his own making. The setting is a collage of jungle tales, and the narrator's assignment is to translate "the heart of darkness." In so doing he locates a messianic Jim Jones type who has the verbal potential to choreograph a mass suicide.

The narrator is compelled to understand the power of language and its relationship to death and salvation, and he formulates his own "In the beginning *is* the word." Rhythm "wells up out of the darkness," and writing involves "a tuning of the nerves to the score of life in all its irreducible twists and possibilities contained in the prophetic multiplicity of language in the wisdom of its evasions our only salvation."

Having accepted his condition, Mr. Sukenick commits himself to the solitary life of the nomad (pun)-fisherman, aboard a refurbished marble slab (see Moses, Huck Finn), set apart from the social currents around him. He returns to the humdrum life of the city, in the trinitarian persona of three Brooklyn "princes of foolishness, boogalooing to the unboogalooable."

The Endless Short Story is Mr. Sukenick's most lyrical fiction. It lacks the violence and defiance of, say, *Up, Out* or *98.6,* although it retains the author's favorite visual effects and disjunctures of language and punctuation. Like an Abstract Expressionist painting, the book invites the reader into the act of creation. If one trusts and identifies with Mr. Sukenick's language, as it stretches and metamorphoses, appears and reappears in new contexts much as a character in traditional fiction, one may indeed discover "a Kingdom coming . . . a Kingdom come."

Typically, Mr. Sukenick provides his own self-criticism: "at times the intention is puzzling the discontinuities inexplicable." A few sequences require too much study, and some of the block passages are too long. More importantly, one or two of the shorter episodes lack a thematic or linguistic connection with the rest of the book. These are, however, minor reservations about an impressive achievement.

> *Lois Gordon, "Unboogalooable," in* The New York Times Book Review, *November 16, 1986, p. 37*

GERALD JAY GOLDBERG

The self-declared omniscient narrator [of *Blown Away*] is the mind reader and astrologer Dr. Boris O. Ccrab, who was once cheated by a crooked movie director, Rod Drackenstein. Though his pretext is thin, Ccrab promises to give us love and death in a tale of revenge that moves crablike "sideways into the future," but in fact events in this novel samba back and forth in time. The instrument of retribution is a beautiful U.C.L.A. student, Cathy June Grunion, whom Ccrab transforms into the starlet Clover Bottom. . . . But before a screenplay (loosely based on Shakespeare's *Tempest*) can be completed for her, Drackenstein's writer is murdered. Ccrab predicts that the deceased's unfinished work, which "turns out to be not the story in the film, but a story about the production of the film," will be published as *Blown Away.* Mr. Sukenick has elsewhere gone on record as being antiplot, anticharacter, antiverisimilitude. In this work he gives the reader a large order of verbal playfulness and a side dish of moral pique. . . . Truth, he implies, can be found in discontinuity too. Whatever conceptual merit there may be in his method, the result here is a lethal loss of fictional energy. One looks in vain for a compensating resonance.

> *Gerald Jay Goldberg, in a review of "Blown Away," in* The New York Times Book Review, *March 15, 1987, p. 16.*

STUART KLAWANS

Down and In by Ronald Sukenick is a lovely book, deserving of thoughtful consideration. . . .

Sukenick's guided pub crawl begins in 1948, when he was fresh out of Brooklyn's Midwood High School. In search of real life, he joined his sister Gloria at the San Remo, Greenwich Village's hippest bar. Bar? "An actual Village-Bohemian-literary-artistic-underground-mafioso-pinko-revolutionary-subversive-intellectual-existentialist-anti-bourgeois café.'' Yes, they really did exist—bars where you could run into John Cage, Miles Davis, Merce Cunningham, Jackson Pollock, Julian Beck and Judith Malina, Dorothy Day, Allen Ginsberg, Gregory Corso and the sainted Jack Kerouac himself. Later, the scene shifted to the Cedar Tavern. . . . [And at] the Five Spot, the hippest writers and artists came to hear the hippest jazz musicians—Charlie Mingus, Thelonius Monk, Sonny Rollins, Cecil Taylor, Ornette Coleman.

Into the 1960s, the scene moved to the East Village and Stanley's on Avenue B. Stanley's was such a dive that when characters like Ed Sanders and Tuli Kupferberg started hanging there, the bedazzled owner thought he was stepping into the middle class. And then came Max's Kansas City, ''where the transition took place from artist as outsider to artist as insider, from Jackson Pollock to Andy Warhol.'' Suddenly the uptown, high-fashion crowd and the downtown bohemians were brought together. (p. 276)

Gone, all gone, including the owner of Max's, Mickey Ruskin, who died of a drug overdose in 1983. The final chapter of **Down and In** records the period of the Mudd Club and the punks (who receive Sukenick's blessing) and their opposite numbers, ''the new Hipoisie going south of the Village to SoHo and Tribeca.'' To a mind less clear than Sukenick's, this final phase might be occasion for mourning or, worse, nostalgia. . . . Sukenick knows those were glorious days; his book is, among other things, an oral history full of wonderful stories, wonderfully told. But Sukenick also knows about the violence of underground life, the passivity and self-destruction and self-delusion and waste. ''Yeah,'' his sister Gloria comments, ''Iris Brody jumped off the roof, Sonya OD'd, Marilyn also jumped off the roof.''

Thus, like any truly satisfying pub crawl, **Down and In** combines autobiography with the confidences of friends, high times with 4:00 A.M. despair. The final ingredient, of course, is an argument, which should flare up periodically and be left unsettled when day finally breaks. **Down and In** has that, too: a debate on the nature of adversary culture, moderated by Sukenick with rare intelligence.

The culture in question grew out of cold war politics and cold-water flats. When Sukenick was young, he couldn't stomach the dominant culture—the piety, the greed, the sexual repression, the smell of the Rosenbergs frying. But he didn't believe the left was an alternative, partly because he was wise to Stalinism and partly because he couldn't abide folk-singing. Old-style bohemianism, with its high European culture and political activism, seemed a false contrary; *real* opposition was a matter of hanging out on Bleecker Street, which was possible because in those days you could get a three-room apartment for $18 a month. ''The misunderstood genius starving in the garret was the role model for artists of all kinds at the time,'' Sukenick writes. ''I myself could hardly wait to start going hungry.'' But with rents so low, bohemians didn't have to go all *that* hungry.

In fact, material and political conditions were so favorable to the formation of an underground that at least two of them arose: On the one side (or so it seemed at the time) stood Allen Ginsberg, with his ''angelic and lamby politics.'' On the other stood Norman Mailer and the White Negro. The choice, Sukenick explains, ''was between two different kinds of withdrawal.'' . . . Sukenick himself believed in a ''third course''

of hopeful participation. . . . At the time it simply wasn't a realistic option.'' Now, he believes, it is.

> ''The truth is that in this country the myth of the genius in the garret, flaunting an impoverished purity, was always a middle-class soap opera. . . . Its unrecognized message is that genuine art deserves rejection—as if it were not bad enough that it is often in fact rejected.''

Sukenick believes the evolution of the last four decades has resulted in a new underground that is not self-destructive. . . . ''For subterraneans who don't turn out to be closet Yuppies, and of course many do,'' Sukenick comments, America now offers the possibility of an idea of purity ''purified of defeatism and hypocrisy, envy and contempt.''

I agree with all my heart and don't believe a word of it. As Sukenick himself admits, it took him years ''to desentimentalize the underground, differentiate the interesting from the merely seedy, and begin to acknowledge its darker, unredeemed, infernal aspects.'' Can that demonism really be purged? At one point, Sukenick seems ambivalent on whether he wants it to be. ''It might be argued that tapping the infernal is necessary to release the darker powers of consciousness that energize art,'' he says. The real problem, apparently, is that ''not everyone is an artist and not everyone can handle it.''

For Sukenick, then, adversary culture is a culture by and for artists; its violence and self-destructiveness grow uncontrollable only in the presence of the ''floaters'' who mingle with the underground—the hordes of young people, for example, who flooded into the East Village in the 1960s with no clear idea of why they were there or what they wanted to do. The problem here is the assumption that artists are different from everybody else. No doubt they are, for those few hours of the day when they're actually at work. But artists, Sukenick included, are not portrayed at work in **Down and In**. They're shown drinking, which puts them in a larger New York community that existed through the mid-1970s because it could scrape by without much money. In that context, it was an act of solidarity with the ne'er-do-wells for Pollock to refuse success, an act of imagination for Warhol to play with fame. Whichever side you chose in the dialectic of holy losers and sell-outs, the scufflers' community remained the standard of judgment. No more. (pp. 276-77)

In today's circumstances, few people, artists or not, can sustain the necessary level of self-delusion for them. It's true, of course, that the Lower East Side has seen previous struggles for turf. Sukenick documents quite unsparingly the battles that took place in the 1960s between the older community and the new youth culture. But he doesn't offer much explanation for those conflicts, other than to suggest that folk music was to blame. In other words, he sees them as a clash of cultures more than of classes, which may be a fair reading of the 1960s. When he gets to the 1980s, though, Sukenick doesn't even address the immediate, material cause of the breakup of the community. For that, you'd have to go to Yvonne Rainer and her film *The Man Who Envied Women,* which is, among other things, a reaction to the moment when downtown artists realized they were competing for space with impoverished and angry Puerto Ricans, and that both sides would lose.

Now, if you understand why the community broke up, you will have a somewhat different attitude about Sukenick's main point, that the artists' ideal of failure is dead. It's dead because the younger artists (or older ones who didn't grab a rent-controlled apartment) have to hustle in the straight world now, and they can no longer count on the approbation of a low-rent, leisure-time community. Some of the most adversarial artists I know have taught themselves word processing and are working the graveyard shift on Wall Street. In order to reach the other word processors who might appreciate their art, they must spend the rest of their time begging for a mention in *The Village Voice,* a weekly newspaper run for the profit of a catlitter tycoon.

And a good thing, too. The bums have been pushed out of the business. Only the committed remain, such as Sukenick himself, whom I salute for his four decades of accumulated wisdom and disagree with only on matters of cause and effect. His third course of hopeful participation is now the only course since, like it or not, we've all got to participate. The violence of the underground now can be seen as part of the violence and self-destructiveness of American culture as a whole, neither to be praised for its artistic possibilities nor evaded as the work of the Other. The artistic productions of the underground now can be seen simply as artistry, when they're any good; and when they're not, they no longer have the barflies' applause. Best of all, artists and nonartists alike now can express their opposition to American yawp and twaddle *even if they don't live in lower Manhattan.* At last, we may be able to erase the line between hip and square. (pp. 277-78)

> Stuart Klawans, "Hip and Square," in The Nation, New York, Vol. 245, No. 8, September 19, 1987, pp. 276-78.

LARRY RIVERS

Choosing *Down and In* as the title is telling us down is not out. "Down" in the cliché is only the middle class's expression of its antagonism for the place where the "other life" is bound to bring you. "Down" are the schmoes, which is as close as I can come here to what Ron actually calls them, back in Brooklyn or whatever suburbia, small town or neighborhood block you come from.

For Ron down is in, and great. Down is reserved for bohemia, its floundering soul and the arena in which its citizens play out the much more idealistic and exciting possibilities of existence. It is these subterraneans and their underground he studies and treats affectionately and with heart dedicates his book to. Like a lot of other bohemia-mappers, Ron concludes that the underground situates itself near and often touches the world of schmoes above ground if only to observe the shock waves it causes. Making this book was more than bar-hopping down memory lane. It is a collaborative cross-cultural construction with a star-studded road gang helping Ron find the way to his own history. And more. (p. 3)

A schmo is "somebody with a certain way of thinking, a combination of caution, conformity, and mercenary values. An idolater of Things, a consumer at the feet of the Golden Calf." He thinks if we were without the word and the notion of a schmo, most of us could never cross a river, or a state line, take a bus, plane or even walk to the grace and salvation waiting for us in the underground of Greenwich Village. Twenty pages past my difficulty with the use of "the schmoes" for what I guess in Europe was simply the bourgeoisie, I realized I was in the presence of a rolling energy, pouring information and serious ideas on this information with the abundance of a good working shower head. It is illuminating both for those who

were there and who think they know what was happening and for those not born or too young or who were somewhere else. It is an amateur historian's history. Its scholarship consists of Ron looking into his own bohemian experience and finding there some of the aging, by now successful citizens of that old country who appear in the book, plying them with his anecdotes to pry loose some of theirs. The listing of these old snow-tops, yesteryear's bohemians, gives name-dropping a moral lift.

The hallways of their past have become quite long. Looking down them at moments gets serious and makes life in the underground, a little inaccurately, into a symposium on esthetics and soul-searching. Gregory Corso, for example, a rare bird any way you look at him, is a Greenwich Village native whom I saw more of in the 60's. He is still an enjoyable, easy-to-love and easy-to-forget man. Here he is telling us if you chose to be a poet it's enough, you're saved. Later, as he keeps going, he is happy to hear that a poet he knew was rejected by the National Academy of Arts and Letters. Gregory is "not . . . an evil man," he is just against ambition.

From Gregory Corso's reflections on salvation you can shift to the pile of information Ron pokes into. It feels enormous, so much so that he needn't dwell on anything for too long. He may be too serious but he's very smart. He knows the real subject matter is about not boring you. You are continually surprised by the things he's offering for your observation—not for their importance, but for the pleasure you get from his bringing to you things you knew but forgot and perhaps see in a new way. (pp. 3, 31)

We look at Bleecker Street, travel to Paris—hear a lot from an artist, Ted Joans, black with a strong Midwestern twang, who was paid by the minute in the early 60's for showing up at parties as a beatnik. We also hear from him with some lightheaded conversation he remembers having with Jackson Pollock in the Cedar Tavern. We even get to the Cedar, and when Ron deals with Abstract Expressionist paintings and painters it is almost silly. He brings in quite a few artists to help him but they suddenly have no names. We will have to go through the drug department and quite a few bar scenes—from how Louis's was founded to the White Horse and Dylan Thomas—over a few years to the far east to Stanley's, Max's Kansas City and up to One University Place and Mickey Ruskin's O.D. Even the infant maneuvers and movement of disco outlined in the electric circus are gone into. Ron is quite unrelenting in his cross-cultural reflections on these various phenomena. He also picked up truckloads of stuff from people whose conversation or ideas never make his pages.

In the end the book is worth the three or four hours you need to finish it and it will probably stand as the best work of its kind. But I don't like his knee-jerk respect for the beatnik ambiance or the church he puts them into. Hardly anyone without a pretty strong ambition and work ethic has left us anything to think well of outside its behind-the-scenes melodrama. It's one of the lip-biting acceptances of life to realize the effect of the media on versions of history. All I can say, Ron, is that there is more between Allen Ginsberg's "Howl" and a woman saying "You name it, I'll do it" at the bar of Max's Kansas City than is contained in your *Down and In.* But not much more. (p. 31)

> Larry Rivers, "Where Has All The Floating Energy Gone?" in The New York Times Book Review, November 1, 1987, pp. 3, 31.

R(onald) S(tuart) Thomas

1913-

Welsh poet, nonfiction writer, editor, and autobiographer.

Thomas is considered one of the most important contemporary Welsh poets writing in English. Admired for his attention to detail and unsentimental approach to his country's people and landscapes, Thomas imparts themes related to Welsh nationalism and his personal search for modern empirical proof of the existence of God. The latter concern is underscored by Thomas's use of religious allusions and by frequent references to his vocation as an Anglican priest. Although his poetry displays affinities to the work of William Wordsworth in its evocation of rural life, Thomas eschews a romantic treatment of nature. He instead presents rural farm life as impoverished and uncivilized, commenting on the encroaching industrialization, urbanization, and materialism that has resulted in a diminishing national identity. The thematic tension of Thomas's works is further emphasized by his use of short, terse lines that result in poems noted for their clarity and rhythm.

Since his ordination as an Anglican priest in 1936, Thomas has served in a succession of rural parishes, some of which figure prominently in his verse. The hardships of an agrarian lifestyle are depicted in his first book, *The Stones of the Field* (1948). This volume contains "The Peasant," the first installment of an ongoing sequence centering on Iago Prytherch, an archetypal Welsh farmer who voices Thomas's belief in the provincialism of the Welsh people. Many of the poems in *An Acre of Land* (1952), reflecting elements of nationalism, assert that Wales is becoming increasingly alienated from its history and traditions. Poems from these two collections, as well as Thomas's radio play *The Minister* (1953) and previously unpublished verse, appear in *Songs at the Year's Turning: Poems, 1942-1954* (1955), a collection which firmly established Thomas's reputation as a gifted lyric poet.

In several volumes following *Song at the Year's Turning,* Thomas adopts a more despondent tone and a sparser style. In *Poetry for Supper* (1958), he laments the abandonment of farms by Welsh families seeking urban employment and examines the demise of poetry as a mirror of the commoner's views. *Tares* (1961) includes irregularly metered Petrarchian sonnets in which Thomas observes that his parish has replaced the worship of God with more temporal concerns. *The Bread of Truth* (1963), *Pietà* (1966), and *Not That He Brought Flowers* (1968) are marked by an increasing concern with the nature of religious faith. These books are also noted for their compassionate portrayal of Iago Prytherch and other Welsh characters. *Selected Poems, 1946-1968* (1973) reprints little of Thomas's early work, favoring instead his later, more direct poems. In his collections of the 1970s, *H'm* (1972), *Laboratories of the Spirit* (1975), and *Frequencies* (1978), Thomas attempts to intellectualize Christian faith rather than blindly accept biblical evidence. Thomas's other works include *Neb* (1986), an autobiography written in the Welsh language, and *Later Poems* (1983) and *Poems of R. S. Thomas* (1985), which combine selected and new verse. Affirming Thomas's technical and thematic achievements, Colin Meir commented: "From the beginning [Thomas's] hallmark has been the unity of manner and meaning; and this is as true for the lighter lyric verse, which shows

© Linda Bartlett

a highly developed skill in language and tone, as it is for the urgent and tortuous questionings of the mind about the spirit."

(See also *CLC,* Vols. 6, 13; *Contemporary Authors,* Vols. 89-92; *Contemporary Authors Autobiography Series,* Vol. 4; and *Dictionary of Literary Biography,* Vol. 27.)

R. GEORGE THOMAS

R. S. Thomas is the finest living Welsh poet writing in English: this fact in itself is an ironic comment on the nature of the cultural life of Wales in the twentieth century and the poet would be the first to appreciate and savour the irony of the situation. For he, more clearly than any of his contemporaries, is specifically concerned with one small area of recognizably Welsh life and, more sharply than they are, is motivated by a desire to capture the essential quality of the national voice. Like them, he is compelled to use the English language for this purpose—a hard fact of linguistic experience that he seems continually to regret and that is expressed in numerous disguises in his poems—and, like them, his reputation has flourished among English readers outside Wales. In this hard soil his poetry continues to grow and, like his own characters who scratch a bare living from the agricultural Welsh wilderness, he returns again and again to his task, patching the gate and turning the stiff clod. The harvest, in terms of quantity is a bare but adequate one; its quality improves with each year's tillage, for

> the heart's roots
> Are here under this black soil

at which he labours.

Since the publication of his early selected verse in 1955, R. S. Thomas has published five slim volumes of poetry: *Poetry for Supper* (1958), *Tares* (1961), *The Bread of Truth* (1963), *Pietà* (1966) and *Not That He Brought Flowers* (1968). . . . [Thomas] claims that 'the poet of the new age may already have been hatched in some incubator or other. For myself I cannot boast even a guitar. I play on a small pipe, a little aside from the main road. But thank you for listening.' Here in prose, with a warning touch of irony, is the essential quality of the poet: deliberate withdrawal, severe concentration, clearsighted purpose, ironic detachment, a half-concealed pride in his chosen role, absolute truth of bare statement, and a grateful awareness of his growing audience. But the verse texture contains an additional quality—the poet's humility before his self-imposed and self-impelling task:

> I have failed after many seasons
> To bring truth to birth,
> And nature's simple equations
> In the mind's precincts do not apply

and yet

> the old lie
> Of green places beckons me still from the new world,
> Ugly and evil.

His reputation as a poet rests securely on the force and power with which he follows this uncompromising quest.

Not That He Brought Flowers, with its ambiguous and wavering title, has forced me to review his poetry of the last decade and to clarify my own attitude to it. I find this a most difficult undertaking, chiefly because the poet refused to stand still while critics, reviewers and publicists (myself among them) have neatly pigeon-holed his achievement, saving themselves the effort of close reading while they patted him on the back for being so ruthlessly and successfully his old uncompromising self. Nothing could be further from the mark: this poet, who pries for truth as much into his own heart as into the real or imagined lives of his parishioners, rejects falsity, posturing, and clichés—even those he has himself inspired. The open-eyed stance he offers to the late twentieth century may be as inflexible and old-fashioned as W. G. Grace at the wicket, but his 'eye' is not self-deceiving. Unlike those who have talked of the earth . . . his belief, like ours, must be dipped

> Not in dew nor in the cool fountain
> Of beech buds, but in seas
> Of manure through which they squelch
> To the bleakness of their assignations.

The actors in this poem ("**Look**") are two cronies who stand aside from modern science, modern medicine and a welfare society, but the poem is not a simple knocking exercise. The poet offers no easy dogmatic textbook answer; repeatedly he hammers on the door of his faith. . . . Some years ago it seemed to me that the voice of compassion and belief was less apparent

in R. S. Thomas's poetry than the exclamations of satire, hungry insufficiency, and despair. Latterly, successive volumes have laid bare the uncompromising wrestle with faith that gives these hard-seeing poems their skeletal rectitude and spare force. . . . In this latest volume there is a widening of interest, both in imagery and in themes, and a greater flexibility of rhythm and tone without any slackening of grip on 'the truth' that is central to all his verse.

Not That He Brought Flowers is especially remarkable because it contains no poem about Iago Prytherch. This is a significant omission. Iago made his first appearance in Thomas's poetry a quarter of a century ago and he has stayed on. In all previous volumes the Iago poems recur almost like the 'sure touch' of a professional beggar: the poet returns constantly to this well-worn patch—the fixed life of the hill-farmer—in search of some assured certitude about his own attitudes to mid-twentieth century urban civilization. The plight of Iago is the plight of the decaying depopulated Welsh hillside farms; he is an uncertain repository of a way of life that, stated explicitly in political terms, could become the cradle of an enduring Welsh way of life which, the poet believes, should be maintained and extended against the false values of an invading English culture. In some subtle way Iago has become part of the poet's mind, an *alter ego:* the peasant is tied to his soil and animals; the priest is tied to his faith and his parishioners; the poet is anchored to his craft and cannot let go. Not surprisingly, then, Iago is valued for his capacity to endure and to accept. . . . [Prytherch] is many-faceted and, in Coleridge's sense, he is a true poetic symbol. (pp. 55-7)

Some years ago I wrote a short study of R. S. Thomas's poetry based on his first three collected volumes. At that time I was puzzled by the absence, so I thought, of the spirit of compassion that one could expect to find in the poems of a Christian priest. I glimpsed its presence most securely in the developing figure of Prytherch, especially in two fine poems in *Poetry for Supper:* in the one the poet denies that he had made fun of Iago's gaunt figure and unlovely habits—

> My poems were made in its long shadow
> Falling coldly across the page;

in the other poem ("**Absolution**) the poet makes magnificient amends for the errors of his own tone and the blindness of his readers. . . . Surely it is in the clear yet humble tone of such poems that Welshmen must learn to detect the sincerity with which R. S. Thomas castigates our national faults. He is under the lash himself, both as poet and priest, as two poems like "**Service**" and "**They**" make quite clear when read in their entirety. In like fashion, one could elaborate the newly emergent themes of the family unit in the last three volumes: the family as an agency of disruption as well as a key to self-knowledge. The pattern of development of this slowly maturing poet becomes clearer with hindsight: the priest and his parishioners, the father and his family, the peasant and his earth, the birds' conflict with nature, the poet's wrestle with himself and words, the believer's renewed struggle with his faith; these are the concentric circles that surround the far-from-still centre of R. S. Thomas's poems.

Slowly the voices through which he speaks are multiplying and the *personae* of his verse are showing a protean quality. I detect, too, a loosening of the texture of the verse. Until recently R. S. Thomas seemed to favour two kinds of structure. One was a short sharp burst of a poem, frequently of sonnet form with an octosyllabic line and the merest hint of an assonantal rhyme, and with a clear-cut antithesis between octave and sestet: this was a favourite form for the Iago poems and the sharp protests of his peasants. The other frequently used structure was a longer wavering poem of short lines, throughout which fairly long sentences were broken up by taut, jerky phrases, frequent questions, and vitriolic phrases that were offered to the reader in the tone of a calm un-Welsh litotes. These two structures are still the norm of his latest volume, but one detects a new form that replaces some earlier experiments with dialogue. Poems like **"After The Lecture"**, **"The Priest"**, **"That"**, **"Tenancies"**, **"Concession"** (that gives the volume its title), and **"A Grave Unvisited"**, are based on a longer line-unit and although they still present a thesis and an antithesis, their tone is more relaxed, the meditative ideas dominate over the visual images, and there are fewer last lines that clap a resounding finish (a merely verbal synthesis?) on the inner movement of the progressing argument that usually forms the core of each poem. Illustration would be tedious, however necessary, especially quotation in print, because R. S. Thomas is essentially a poet to be read aloud; all I can suggest is that interested readers should take down these poems and judge for themselves.... There is much in R. S. Thomas's poetry that cuts across the easy, *fin de siècle* optimism of Yeats in 1900, but the wavering, meditative, organic rhythms are a pronounced feature of this latest volume in which the poet seeks to open, unambiguously for the first time, a small window into the inner sanctum of his hardly-won faith. Such poems add a new dimension to his poetry and one that sympathetic young listeners will readily understand. Such poems, born of a 'willed gentleness,' are like parables that are as candid as any of Edward Thomas's poems and as cautiously insistent on the need for faith as the verse of George Herbert. Their most welcome explicitness of the poet's frequent cry in all his poetry, that he is a man like us, comes through his poems on the migrant martins:

> It is I they build
> In and bring up their young
> To return to after the bitter
> Migrations, knowing the site
> Inviolate through its outward changes.
>
> (pp. 60-2)

R. George Thomas, "Humanus Sum: A Second Look at R. S. Thomas," in Anglo-Welsh Review, *February, 1970, pp. 55-62.*

JAMES F. KNAPP

Although he was not a member of the Movement, R.S. Thomas was always admired by Movement poets for the qualities of clarity and economy which his verse had displayed as early as 1946, when his first volume of poetry was published. Like many of the Movement poets, Thomas saw his role as that of an intelligent and responsible member of a community, and the very themes of his poems reflect that concern: he writes about peasants who have let themselves become blind to all things of the mind and spirit, about an inhumanly metallic modern world, and about a Wales which has sold its heritage in exchange for English factories. The poetic world which emerges from the verse of R.S. Thomas is a world of lonely Welsh farms and of the farmers who endure the harshness of their hill country. The vision is realistic and merciless, and while Thomas is aware of the possibilities for picturesque nature poetry in his subject matter, he scorns that romanticism, even parodying the tradition from time to time.... The glazed

eyes, the wasting disease, the grim acceptance of fate, the silence: these are almost stock elements in the human portraits which emerge from Thomas' verse.

The Welsh hills provide a rather grim setting for his poetry, but it is far more than simply setting. The grey, barren farms and their equally grey inhabitants represent a particular vision of the human condition, a kind of vision with which the poet finds himself forced to struggle. The children in Thomas' verse are thrust into this alien world unaware that they will simply perpetuate the long round of suffering.... The child is "dropped," like an animal, into this hostile environment, and the only suggestion of cause lies in [the] word "luckless"— the endless suffering of which he will become a part seems very often to be a kind of joke. If the general tendency of Thomas' verse is not so fatalistic as this might suggest, we must not, however, ignore the fact that many of his poems offer an unsparingly bleak view of man and that even in those cases where hope seems clearly offered, the elements of the drama are still exceedingly grim.

The basic postulate is a kind of minimal man, struggling to endure in his little universe.... Occasionally there are scenes in pubs and beside warm hearths, but mostly the visual aspect of the poetry concerns lone figures, working the stony fields, walking along the roads. Very often the poem focuses on one of these figures, using the farmer, or perhaps his wife, as an object for the poet's contemplations. It would be hard to imagine a verbal description more suggestive of those terrible, stark figures of Giacometti, chipped down to sheer bone and eye, than this:

> Nothing is his, neither the land
> Nor the land's flocks. Hired to live
> On hills too lonely, sharing his hearth
> With cats and hens, he has lost all
> Property but the grey ice
> Of a face splintered by life's stone.

It is with men like these that Thomas begins to shape his vision of how the world goes.

However, if the lives of the hill farmers sometimes seem fated to end in sterility and despair, the cause does not lie for Thomas in the nature of things. The material which he finds around him is stubborn in its apparently inevitable grimness, and yet as he explores the lives of these people, the spring of evil is variously seen in social, and psychological, and spiritual terms. For all the thatched roofs, the sheep, and the apparently dateless peasants, Thomas' verse is clearly written in our age, and the poetic world which he creates must be witnessed within the context of history. Thus the question of the intersection between the modern world and this old Welsh country becomes a significant theme. A good example of this concern is the poem **"Cynddylan On A Tractor,"** where the poet's judgment of what is happening to man's soul in the machine age is clear.... The notion that man can too easily become a part of the machines which ostensibly serve him is not a new one— Charlie Chaplin made the point in *Modern Times,* to say nothing of Blake and Wordsworth. What is more significant here though, is the distinction between this new, gear-oriented man, and the natural world which his tractor assaults—the poem describes Cynddylan riding to the fields in complete self-satisfaction, but "emptying the wood" of all its animal life as he passes. The pride with which Cynddylan rides to work "as a great man should," is perhaps related to the religious sense of pride as primary source of sin, and even in purely secular terms, it is clear that Cynddylan has damned himself just insofar as he has broken all connection with the natural world. "The old look that yoked him to the soil" refers to that bond of empathy through which the farmer could formerly become one with the natural world he cultivated; but for Cynddylan, that possibility no longer exists, and when he rides off on his tractor he is, in a very real way, a man alienated from the living earth.

In a poem entitled **"Too Late"** Thomas considers this problem through his character Iago Prytherch, who represents the Welsh peasants in all their aspects throughout the poetry. In this poem, Prytherch has been transformed into one of the "new" Welsh men, like Cynddylan, and the poet contemplates the consequences of this change:

> But look at yourself
>   Now, a servant hired to flog
> The life out of the slow soil,
> Or come obediently as a dog
> To the pound's whistle. Can't you see
> Behind the smile on the times' face
> The cold brain of the machine
> That will destroy you and your race?

The destroyer may sometimes be seen in obvious manifestations—the noisy tractor, smashing its way through the peaceful farm country—or, as in this poem, it may be a more subtle "machine": the entire society, hard, quantitative, concerned solely with the greatness of its economical soul. In either case, the effect is disastrous for man's life because the machine works to dim his consciousness of the nature of living things, offering instead a mechanistic and meaningless world view. And Thomas does not simply ask the reader to draw his own conclusions from this situation. Addressing Prytherch (a common technique with Thomas) he makes his judgment explicit: "I would have seen you poor and in rags, / Rather than wealthy and not free." The bitch-goddess of the machine age would enslave her followers, and she is uniquely dangerous to the men of Wales, coming as they do from the harsh, lonely farms. (pp. 1-4)

A very simple, and dramatic, treatment of these crucial questions, posed by the changing nature of man's world, occurs in **"Tramp,"** where Thomas presents an encounter between an undefined householder, and a tramp begging for food. . . . The poem asks a question which it does not explicitly answer:

> I sleep in my bed,
> He sleeps in the old,
> Dead leaves of a ditch.
> My dreams are haunted;
> Are his dreams rich?

For Thomas, this is the question which must be asked when we consider the consequences of our increasing commitment to technology. Salvation, however, is not simply a question of going out into the countryside and waiting for the dew to cover one's hopeful body like a blessing. One of the primary concerns of Thomas' verse is why man fails so often to find this "earth's charity" that can preserve his life. . . . The last three lines of this poem pose one of the crucial questions: is there any spirit, any love, any sense of beauty or mystery within this flint-hard old man? Crushing the plants like the wheels of a tractor, this man does not even have that obvious mechanical scapegoat, although his sensitivity to the natural world is approximately that of a gasoline engine.

Thomas questions this imaginative poverty more explicitly in a poem called **"Enigma."** Pointing out a man in the fields, he

asks that we try to see the world through his eyes. . . . The man hears the birds singing, but to him they only represent a threat to his seeds, and he refuses to accept their "rich crop of music" as payment for his loss. . . . The man is indeed blind to beauty, but the crucial question has to do with his essential nature: does he in fact bring with him a kind of unfallen, Edenic purity, or is there simply sterility and nothingness in his undeveloped heart? The latter would imply that man's humanity is not something "natural," but rather a way of being which man must seize and shape through his own intelligence and effort. The peasant is indeed an enigma, and a threatening one for any poet who is concerned with how he might save his people from such a deadness of the spirit.

It is easy enough, however, to create a fictive world of men and women who urgently call for the kind of salvation which poetry can offer them; but if this calling for help is to be more than an element of plot structure, then there must also be, within the poet's imaginative world, some more specific vision of what might constitute that salvation. In a poem from *Poetry For Supper,* entitled **"Age,"** Thomas considers a man's failure to realize the possibilities of being, here in the form of his relationship with his wife. The farmer had been young once, he had married a woman who was warm like the soil he fondled in the spring, and she had given him four strong sons. But somehow he had been too blind or insensitive to cherish her properly, and now their life was grey and sterile. . . . The poem "means" that a man has ruined his own life, and that of his wife, through his harsh insensitivity—but the really crucial element here lies in the poem's central metaphor. Throughout the poem the farmer and his wife are compared to the earth and its plants—the wife is warm soil, but she becomes dry and "fallow"; her sons are "like corn in June," while she withers to a "dry stalk"; the husband is finally "an old tree." There is an insistence here that the flowering we seek must have its beginning in the warm earth and in man's body, and the poem's final image is a description of this farmer's failure to make that vital connection.

A poem which more clearly defines Thomas' attitude toward the green world is **"The Garden."** The poem begins by viewing the garden as a symbolic act of order, shaping the natural chaos: "It is a gesture against the wild, / The ungovernable sea of grass." The garden is described as a place where man can go for solitude, for regaining his spiritual bearings, and for a temporary release from his cares. And then returning to a more symbolic description in his last stanza, Thomas sees the garden as a vestige of Eden, where the flowers still bear within them the old power that was man's, but without sharing his sin. . . . Thus the assumptions become clear: Man is a fallen creature, but the power and mystery of original creation still remain in the world of growing things, which therefore may serve as a place of rest and healing for "one querulous human." This poem illuminates both those poems where earth is viewed as redemptive to man and those where man is seen as inevitably burdened by his flawed nature.

In poems such as **"The Garden,"** Thomas reveals most clearly the mythic power of his poetry. The end of myth, and that of art, has always been, in Joseph Campbell's phrase, "the reconciliation of consciousness with the preconditions of its own existence"—that initiation, deeper than any of the practical problems of living a life, into the terrifying mystery of birth, and growth, and death. . . . R.S. Thomas posits a kind of minimal man, hewn and hardened by the seasons, and revealing a truth which is "archetypal," a truth which goes as near as possible to the heart of human experience. (pp. 4-7)

[It is the] wholeness of body and soul together, sensitive to beauty and the things of the spirit, and yet instinctually in touch with the dark power of trees and flowers to endure through the seasons, that emerges as Thomas's vision of the ideal. Often the affirmation is a negative one, as he describes the tragedy of men who are merely brutalized by the soil they work, but always there is the vision of a better way, an awakening of the "shy soil," which would permit not only full realization of man's potential in individual cases, but the rebirth of an entire Welsh nation.

This reawakening will not happen of itself, however, but only if those men who still remember the old greatness can find a way to communicate their vision, and it is here that the poet must acknowledge his responsibility. Throughout his verse Thomas is working to define and reveal his vision of Wales's shame and its potential salvation—he moves through history and myth and through the brutal ugliness of the present, and his role is nowhere better defined than in a poem called "**Taliesin 1952.**" Taliesin was an ancient Welsh bard, and for Thomas he becomes a symbol of the poet's long struggle to learn the truth, and finally to communicate that truth to men who continue to suffer in darkness, to heal them, if he can, by showing them what he has seen:

> King, beggar and fool, I have been all by turns,
> Knowing the body's sweetness, the mind's treason;
> Taliesin still, I show you a new world, risen,
> Stubborn with beauty, out of the heart's need.

As Taliesin, poet and seer, R.S. Thomas would seek a new myth for his people. And he knows well that "a new world, risen" will be found nowhere but "out of the heart's need." Focusing relentlessly in on his peasants, on their gaunt faces and vacant eyes, and on the green, living world all unseen around them, he writes of people who are out of touch with their world, and with themselves. The power of myth in Thomas's poetry derives from just this insight into the deep levels of man's need, and from his capacity to convince us that in those barren hearts there is a new world waiting, "stubborn with beauty." (pp. 8-9)

James F. Knapp, "The Poetry of R. S. Thomas," in *Twentieth Century Literature, Vol. 17, No. 1, January, 1971, pp. 1-9.*

C. A. RUNCIE

The reputation of R. S. Thomas as a regional poet has kept his work from travelling; and so whatever may be said now in Australia of Thomas's work may be said by way of introduction. Born in Cardiff in 1913, Ronald Stuart Thomas is a Welshman and a parson, a tidy, boney man with a thin face rutted by severity. And the poems are the man. Austere and simple and of repressed power.

What gives his work this power, this life, is that it comes forth, unwillingly, sparingly, without manner, from a deep secret wound. It comes forth not from love of man alone nor of God alone, but of both man and God; and not from love alone, but from hurt love. A sense of betrayal, a bitter tenderness for everything proud that has hoped and now sorrows, makes its way through Thomas's poems—a fierce compassion for the young girls stealthily ageing at their country chores; for the young men who can't regret their lust; for the old men who have forgotten theirs; for the fox or the bird caught in flight,

for all those creatures that are in harsh league with "the stones of the field", the title of his first volume in 1946.

Like Robert Frost, but without his whimsy, Thomas is the poet of the countryside and his countryside is Welsh. Gaunt sunless skies, owls and foxes in the dark woods and an unwilling earth patched with starved farms—this is his landscape; and set in its midst are a few silent figures, the very elements of humanity, which the poet, by what he admits was a "slow charity", has come finally, in just these last two decades of his work, to understand. He repudiates his "bland philosophy" of nature and confesses "Earth / Has of itself no power to make men wise". As he understands, with an eye on the cruel landscape, so he forgives. It is this understanding and forgiveness that makes Thomas not just a regional poet, but one of both deeper and wider significance. (p. 56)

His farmers and labourers and hillmen, unlike Frost's, are not philosophers. Thought has been worked out of them year after year. Only life and a little, obtuse, silent feeling remain. . . . But these few figures against the landscape Thomas sees not just through a poet's eyes, but through a parson's as well. The elemental world he sees presses upon him certain knowledge that he can neither forgive nor forget: "You are betrayed by wilderness within, / That spreads upward and outward like a stain." This stain that stains all life and love, the flaw inherent in the very nature of things, is the parson's and the poet's source of grief and the reason for his bitter compassion. (pp. 56-7)

Reiterated in various forms throughout the poems this is Thomas's deepest concern, Job's knowledge. But his actual subjects are more various than this suggests and go beyond the borders of Wales and the daily chores of its people. In fact, Thomas often writes what one may call occasional poems and his subjects range from the landing on the moon to the temptation of Saint Anthony, from poems about Kierkegaard and Coleridge and Wallace Stevens to poems about poems.

Whatever the subject though, the technique is largely the same; and Thomas rigorously protects this technique. Except for Yeats, he will not read any poetry that has regular phonetically stressed syllables or rhymes. He keeps the purity and constancy of his technique—simple verbs and short nouns, nouns of such authentic meaning that they rarely need modifiers, moving as beats at a controlled place in stress accent metre—a constant technique to effect a constant tone, his own inexhaustibly haunting tone that lingers like sounds in a darkness. It's Thomas's only tone, and the only tone suitable for what he writes of.

There have been some few failures, however. The earlier poems show a harshness, a "pulpiteering" as one Welsh critic says, and Thomas recognised this himself in a severe winnowing for his first collection, *Song At The Year's Turning* of 1955; and even though his most successful work is that after his 1955 stocktaking, there have been some failures since. (p. 57)

But the failures are only relative and rare, and scarcely touch Thomas's reputation, a reputation not among coteries, for Thomas is too pure and urgent in feeling to be a fashionable experimenter. His reputation is among those of us who are "common readers". Matthew Arnold once said of Thomas Gray that he was our frailest and scantiest classic; and frail and scanty as Thomas's slim volumes are they have something of the classic in them. This is not to suggest that his work is not modern, only that the style is not 'moderne'. The poems themselves are the work of a Christian who is a modern Christian, one who sees about him, no, not vanity, vanity, but vain suffering, and who has the unquiet memory of the promise of the new covenant. (p. 58)

C. A. Runcie, "The Poetry of R. S. Thomas," in Poetry Australia, 1972, pp. 56-8.

A. E. DYSON

R. S. Thomas's poems usually begin in a very distinctive manner. The first line does not appear to be the logical start of a particular thought, or even of a particular experience or event, but to be the moment when some profoundly meditated anguish, or image, forces itself into words. Immense silence of the hills, in the background. History, waiting still longer, for its dead centre. The Virgin, surely not weeping as she receives the Body. A man, brooding on life, and focusing on a brilliant lyrical or dramatic image, or startling statement, as some long notion intensifies and compresses itself towards form. The poem is precipitated, with unusual and brooding power, into the ambiance where it then exists: language, submitting after long struggle, to will. (p. 5)

Many of R. S. Thomas's poems home in upon a vivid image which is characteristically in, but not of time. Some perception, arrested in time and space, acquires tragic or elemental colouring for the reader, momentarily before he senses also, the consolation ('Dear parents, I forgive you my life'; 'Yes: that's how I was'; 'It will always win'; 'I want you to know how it was'). The consolation, coming as it does from some region of consciousness or creation wholly different from the often savage insight, is hard to pin down. Some long built-up or pent-up force is precipitated, and the poem as a whole seems to be precisely the right weight, and length, to bear it. Only once or twice, as in the beautiful **"The airy tomb"**, does Thomas take a longer flight, floating more serenely above his sombre tale.

All of Thomas's readers recognise this tone—which one calls Welsh, or laconic, or lacerating, or ironically detached, or bitterly compassionate, or rarely empathetic, or universally human, for all these apparent contraries meet in it—only, it is never despairing, though the word 'despair' sometimes rings out unforgettably. There is pared down linguistic austerity, always reaching towards some apparent simplicity—though when Thomas encounters other people's attempts in this direction, they may wryly amuse him:

> Rose Cottage, because it had
> Roses! If all things were as
> Simple. . .

Yet this search is also pre-eminently his own, the endlessly sought-after illusion of his kind of art. Kingsley Amis has written of it perceptively in words which, recognising the note of linguistic sparseness, draw attention also to the complex and vivid imagery that accompanies this:

> His imagery, thickly clustered as it frequently is, and made to proliferate and interconnect with great brilliance, is built upon a simple foundation of earth, trees, snow, stars, and wild creatures. To describe the effect of his work it is enough to say that he often moves to tears, and that certain lines of his impress themselves instantly, and perhaps ineradicably on the mind.
>
> (pp. 5-6)

[Thomas's Iago Prytherch poems have] their concrete lucidity, which for habitual readers is, more than anything, a distinctive tone. Thomas is one of those poets who is always and immediately recognisable, whether we chose to use the term 'poet' or 'persona' to describe this seal of his power.

We could say, that Iago is certainly a victim, cut off from culture and poetry, and cut off too (but here is a *real* problem) from religion—or from the religion, at least, of a highly literate priest. We could say too, with some certainty, that Thomas does question his own 'refinement', and ours, if this runs to elitism—which he is honest enough to see as unavoidable temptation, and likewise as part of a truth.

Yet Iago has an elemental reality and power in his life which is in part to be envied; 'the machine' comes, to hill farmers, at best as a dubious friend. We might decide that this is not unlike Gray's ambiguous feelings for the 'unlettered dead' of his *Elegy:* he pities yet envies their ignorance, their solitude, their very unfulfilment—the mute Miltons, and the guiltless Cromwells alike. Yet the pity is tinged with guilt—what do his letters do for him? And, the paths of glory lead but to the grave. As for the envy, it may come from his heart, or it may come rather from weariness; it may be an envy as much for the death of these simple folk as for their once death-in-life. The poet more than half identifies with them, or wishes to, in their simplicity; yet draws back from the thought of really being unlettered and uncouth himself. Such conflicting reactions can be sneered at (and are, by some critics), but art of Gray's power, and still more Thomas's, evades such attack. The poems are after all (one returns to this) images, and stand or fall by their fidelity to the experience evoked.

The startling aspect of R. S. Thomas may be his deliberate refusal of the egalitarian challenge, which looms so much more directly in our time than it did for Gray. It is central for many great artists, at least since Dickens, and Thomas will not be forgiven, by some, for keeping it at the periphery of his vision, and his art. Should Pip have stayed at the forge, and avoided snobbery; or was he right to accept the great expectations, with their social risks? Should young people today accept grants, and go to universities; or should they keep their 'working-class culture', or its myth, beautifully intact? The case of Iago and his like may seem still more urgent, since if we believe in art, how can we be reconciled to such a condition of life? If we believe in social justice, there is another strong challenge; which may (or may not) point in the same direction as the first. But if we are seeking the image of man, the image of God, the meaning of existence, then are the implications not bound to be of another kind? What has education to do with virtue, civilisation with resilience? Where shall we find the truest images of man's cosmic plight?

R. S. Thomas is not only concerned with poetic fidelity to mixed love-and-hate relationships (though the psychology of this is endemic in the depiction of his peasants, his parishioners, his country, his religion, and not least of himself). He is concerned still more basically with the present and future destiny of the poor forked creature, who might be a god in exile as well. Thomas has his great hatred of hedonism, garishness, vulgarity, modern urban culture—and the barren Wales of the hill farmers could have for him some touch of the gospel blessing of poverty, however disguised. It could equally be the place where religion has its deepest reality—as much in Iago Prytherch, Evans, Job Davies even ('Live large man; and dream small') as in the priest on his knees in long, bare vigils by the untenanted cross.

In the later poems, the religious questions are directly confronted, and perhaps *Pietà* and *Laboratories of the Spirit* are best texts for the discussion of these. But in the early poems, from the first in fact, we are aware that the poet who might choose to ignore or despise much of the specifically 'modern', cannot evade our modern religious crisis of doubt. If our most serious need is for identity, meaning, apprehended divinity, then we all start today with the apparent absence of God. We cannot evade the findings of Darwin, Freud, Einstein, and their questions, we cannot evade the failure of discursive reason, and dogma, to satisfy the religious need. Perhaps in the end, this may prove to be a blessing, and the recovery of doubt will be looked back upon as necessary prelude to the recovery of religion in its deepest sense.... And, again in these early poems, R. S. Thomas faces the possible consequences of an empty universe more directly than many more consciously intellectual moderns have always done. If intellect leads nowhere, and sensitivity debilitates, is Iago not a more viable, as well as accurate image than, say, the poet and his readers, of 'man himself'—alone with the visible world? And what right have we to think that virtue and beauty are in any sense 'natural'? (But—if we cease to think them so—then the mystery of what they portend *may* again appear.) (pp. 12-14)

Thomas is not a Wordsworthian poet, and his 'nature' is not Wordsworth's; it is history, rather than divinity, which he responds to most, in the bleak beauty of Wales. In Christian terms, Thomas is not a poet of the transfiguration, of the resurrection, of human holiness: despite **"Farm wife"**, **"The country clergy"** and one or two poems where supernatural grace may be hinted at, he more usually sees 'nature' spelled out in the peasants we have been considering and their like. He is a poet of the Cross, the unanswered prayer, the bleak trek through darkness, and his theology of Jesus, in particular, seems strange against any known traditional norm.

But, equally certainly, he is not a determinist poet, but a believer in the free acceptance of life, whatever its offered terms. He always avoids the naivete of those who imagine that contact with nature, or with culture or art or education or religion or any other single influence, has an automatic power to ennoble, or even make good. By the same token, R. S. Thomas is saved from the equally fatalistic pessimism which may set in when those who start from this view come to a point of disillusionment—as they surely must sooner or later, for one experiential reason or another. Thomas's view, I take it, is the more normal Pauline and Christian one, which is that things that are good, true, pure, lovely *tend* to work for good, if one chooses to be open to their influence and celebrate them, but that the choice whether to accept, or reject, the influence remains open. The mystery of good and evil is after all central; and in Thomas, it is all the more impressive for not being identified with partly faked or superficial dilemmas such as pre-modern versus modern, civilised versus uncivilised, or even urban versus rural, but rather found·in the inner tensions of the people he knows best.

It seems then that in finding in the Welsh peasants a 'prototype' of man, Thomas is making a universal statement, which may chime in with modern doubt, yet which equally has its roots in Christian paradox. This pared-down existence, in a land of ruined beauty belonging to the past, is more human than any educated sophistication. Or perhaps one should say, it is more truly symbolic of the human predicament, as educated sophistication now often understands it to be, than such educated sophistication is itself. Some such paradox does, I think, underlie the other complexities; and explains why the social challenges do not emerge in any simpler form.

So we may turn to the poet; or at least, to the poems where he seems to present himself most directly; or where we feel we have most directly tracked him down. I have already touched on the problems involved in this, particularly with a poet so rooted in his own country, his own situation, and his own tone. Of course R. S. Thomas *does* speak to us directly, and is not obsessively concerned to plead artistic detachment and disappear. On the other hand, he is a complex and—paradoxically in a poet, perhaps—a reticent personality, whose lucidity is clearly the product of highly wrought art. Often, he seems to be surveying his people, his themes, himself from an immense distance, even when remarkable empathy is also achieved. We recognise also that in poems so notably selected, distilled, refined, both in language and in evoked experience, any self-revelation must be very directly controlled by artistic form. R. S. Thomas is nothing like a 'confessional' poet, either in intention or by accident, and is not—I suspect—beyond laying false clues, with wry amusement, when in the mood. There is the further factor that, in recent volumes, he has become notably more experimental, so that it becomes increasingly difficult to regard any statement as unequivocally 'his'.

Among the earlier work, **"Twentieth century pharisee"** should not be forgotten, as a piece of apparent self-satire which no one will swallow whole. We might next remember **"Sick visits"**, a wonderfully accurate description of a geriatric ward, with a pastor visiting, where it is easy to believe that 'They keep me sober, the old ladies' is a statement fairly directly related to his own work.... Without them, he ends, 'I would have gone wild, / Drinking earth's huge drafts / Of joy and woe'. The Blakean echo here ('Man is born for joy and woe') seems highly personal; and we recall that Thomas quite often mutates well-known Christian formulae in a way which takes us close to his own sensibility. In **"A blackbird singing"**, for example, the resounding 'It seems wrong' of the opening records a feeling that total dualism would be almost more appropriate than the actual mingling, in the bird's song, of black and beautiful; and the phrase 'Love, joy and grief', describing the song itself, would *be* the fruit of the Spirit, as listed by both St Paul and St John, were it not for the substitution of 'grief' for 'peace'. (pp. 15-16)

Thomas is not a poet of transfiguration, of the coming of the Spirit and the witness of holiness, in any obvious sense—his poems have few saints, though it is possible to believe, as I have already suggested, that the anguish and brokenness of the Welsh peasants is indeed a witness to the divine, if one has eyes to see in the great darkness of life. No: Thomas is now, as always, a poet of the Cross; and the Cross without the exegesis or piety of the ages to help it—more than ever facing us with its own starkness, as God's side of the dialogue. **"Poste restante"** opens with the possibility that the Cross itself might grind 'into dust / under men's wheels', just as it might shine 'brightly as a monument to a new era', and with this huge possibility open, his poem is a bleak record of the anguish of a priest *now*, compressed between its first line 'I want you to know how it was', and its last, 'you, friend, who will know what happened'. Many poems, such as **"Emerging"**, **"The hand"** and **"The combat"**, conduct a kind of imaginary dialogue with God—in which possibilities are faced such as God's own surprise, and challenge, by 'the machine'; God's possible impotence or unwillingness as the explanation of unanswered prayer; God's dismay at his creation, or almost demonic laughter in the face of it. (p. 24)

A. E. Dyson, "The Poetry of R. S. Thomas," in Critical Quarterly, Vol. 20, No. 2, Summer, 1978, pp. 5-31.

COLIN MEIR

Over a period of some forty years of writing, R. S. Thomas has published fourteen volumes of poetry and two selections, *Song at the Year's Turning* (1955) and *Selected Poems: 1946-1968* (1973). None of the separate collections is very large, but each uncompromisingly defines the poet's attitude to his subject matter. And it is the subject matter which counts with R. S. Thomas; it is what the poems draw attention to: not to the poet nor the poetry, but to the scrupulous concern to record faithfully what has been thought, seen or experienced in a language which, though not foregoing change or development, preserves throughout a distinctiveness gained remarkably early in the poet's career. The most striking change from one volume to the next occurs between *Not That He Brought Flowers* (1968) and *H'm* (1972), but the latter volume's emphasis on the definition of man's relationship to God had already been prepared for in the context of two of Thomas's preoccupations of the preceding years.

One of these, and perhaps the most compelling for the general reader, is that which has to do with Welsh hill-farming life as it is epitomized in [the figure of Iago Prytherch]. . . . Prytherch has a 'half-witted grin', his clothes are 'sour with years of sweat'; yet, even though the poet declares 'there is something frightening in the vacancy of his mind', Prytherch is seen as embodying man's fortitude. But R. S. Thomas did not begin with such poems. His distinctive stance is identifiable only from the moment when, under the influence of Patrick Kavanagh's *The Great Hunger* (1942), Thomas turned from merely descriptive verse like **"Cyclamen"** (published in the *Dublin Magazine* in 1939 and collected in *The Stones of the Field*, 1946) and found both subject and theme in his native Wales. While the impact of Kavanagh's poem, which Thomas readily acknowledges, has not gone altogether unnoticed in Ireland, it has been overlooked by Welsh and English critics alike. Kavanagh's slap in the face of Yeatsian idealism about the Irish peasant was in places couched in terms that were intended to shock, and perhaps the debunking of that myth called for extreme measures; it is, however, the less sensationally ironic aspects of Kavanagh's peasant farmer, Maguire, which impressed the Welsh poet. (pp. 1-2)

Thomas's poetry about the Welsh peasantry swings from the sympathy expressed in **"Affinity"** (*Stones of the Field*) to the almost vindictive attack in **"Valediction"** (*Song at the Year's Turning*). Here he is less generous to his Welsh farmer than Kavanagh had been to his Irish counterpart: 'Unnatural and inhuman, your wild ways / Are not sanctioned; you are condemned / By man's potential stature'. This characteristic method of pushing each line of enquiry and response to the limit may risk the tedium of mere repetition, but it intimately prepares the reader for whatever resolution of the extremes is achieved.

The most significant move towards such a resolution occurs in *Poetry for Supper* where in two poems Thomas asks forgiveness of Prytherch, (that '. . .dark figure / Marring the simple geometry / Of the square fields with its gaunt question'), yet at the same time points out that his words sprang neither from mockery nor mere compassion. In **"Dark Well"**, the opening poem of the next volume (*Tares*), the poet recognizes that his emphasis on the animal vacancy of the peasant's mind was a

necessary exaggeration in order to imply spiritual need. . . . In both **"Absolution"** (*Poetry for Supper*) and **"Servant"** (*The Bread of Truth*) Thomas concedes that the peasant's struggle with the land represents a fidelity of purpose and identity, in bone and blood, which the poet's mental strivings after truth have failed to achieve. (pp. 3-4)

A second persistent theme throughout Thomas's work concerns the lonely and often barren predicament of the priest, who is as isolated in his parish as Prytherch is on the bare hillside, 'Ploughing cloudward, sowing the wind / With squalls of gulls at the day's end'. . . .

The priest's frustrated desire to serve requires the sustenance of solitary meditation, and this subject becomes increasingly prevalent throughout the published work up to *Frequencies* (1978). (p. 4)

If there were any doubts before about whether R. S. Thomas should be called a religious poet—though there should have been none—they must have been resolved during the past decade with the appearance of *H'm* (1972), *Laboratories of the Spirit* (1975), *The Way of It* (1977) and *Frequencies* (1978). There are some beautiful love poems to be found here, and each volume continues, though sometimes in a new style, some of the subjects of the poetry published up to 1968. The main preoccupation, however, is with questions concerning the nature of spiritual reality; and the territory to be explored is no longer the natural setting of the Welsh hills but the mind itself. . . . The outcries of dismay with which many of Thomas's faithful readers greeted *H'm* were . . . not so much caused by a failure to see the development of themes as by the change of form that volume represents. In the early poems the shift from what is observed to what is felt by the poet requires that the peasant in the field, or the parishioner in the street or at prayer, be seen by the reader, whether the description carries metaphoric meanings or not. When, on the other hand, the poet turns from observation to introspection, from what can be seen (as so often in the early volumes we are enjoined to see) to what cannot, the language becomes more abstract; concepts replace images. (pp. 5-6)

[An] element in both [*Laboratories of the Spirit* and *Frequencies*] which gives the reader pause is the poet's view of 'the machine' as an evil force obliterating man's relationship with God and even having the power to challenge God himself. This attempt at a kind of mythologizing is a large step from the anger directed against the constraining effects of mechanization in many of Thomas's poems about Wales; and it fails not only because it is unrealistic to imply that man would be better off in a pre-industrial civilization, but principally because the threat of 'the machine' is never made vividly real. (pp. 7-8)

Thomas's evocation of 'the machine' as responsible for the break in what should be a natural link between man and God invites comparison with Ted Hughes's recent work. The picture of mockingly destructive energies in *Crow* (1970) and of a world governed solely by sexual aggression in *Gaudete* (1977) constitute an attempt to create a mythology as negative as Thomas's. . . . How far Thomas is able to go beyond Hughes thematically is demonstrated by **"The White Tiger"** (*Frequencies*). In this poem, with an exactness of physical description which Hughes might envy, and a profound irony Hughes has not yet shown he can match, Thomas at the same time reveals the unavoidable limitations of man's view of the eternal, and recognizes what restrictions are thereby imposed on God.

After *Laboratories of the Spirit* Thomas drops the features which temporarily identify him with Hughes. One of the many distinctions between the two poets over the period from 1970 to 1975 is that while the latter's mythologizing relies on rhetorical tricks which soon become boring (and whatever else myth may be, it cannot be that!), Thomas constantly refers to the topography of a Christian imagination. And although he fails to create a new myth out of 'the machine', he revitalizes the old one by his insistence on the enormous gaps in man's understanding of spiritual reality.

The difficulty has precisely to do with language, with the means of communication. . . . Whereas the irony and compassion of the Prytherch poems came from the linking of man and nature through interdependent images of the physical world, the exactness of Thomas's new vocabulary provides not so much for irony as for the religious paradox of 'this great absence / that is like a presence' which is defined in **"Absence"**, from the 1978 volume whose title takes as metaphor those frequencies which load the invisible air with language. But there is no diminution of compassion: the poet makes it clear that although the terminology of science (see **"They"**, *The Way of It*) may be the means of defining this 'God of form and number' (**"Emerging"**, *Laboratories of the Spirit*), it does not explain the predicament of the sentient man in a universe beyond both his control and his understanding. . . . [The] tentative hope that God may not be indifferent to man who cannot live without the concept of his existence represents an attempt to articulate the nature of belief. Inevitably it involves a conflict between reason and imagination which can only be resolved in either faith or doubt, and Thomas's poetry explores both states, but in very different ways. The theme of doubt often takes the form of a series of questions which at times run the risk of being just rather turgid prose. . . . (pp. 8-11)

None of the books published since 1970 lends itself to a reading through at one sitting because the poet's method is to exhaust all the avenues of enquiry into a particular topic. Since Thomas does not revise a poem once it is finished, the various approaches to the same subject are in a sense rewritings; but the fact that there is never a revising of exactly the same material may in part explain why there are few poems which are perfectly wrought throughout. When Thomas's subject matter was visually identifiable, a change in the way of seeing it brought pleasurable familiarity; when, however, the poetry is largely conceptual, as in the 1972 and 1975 volumes, the repetition of theme can be stultifying to the point where subtle differences of method and purpose are missed. But *Frequencies* clearly shows that the experiments of *H'm* and *Laboratories of the Spirit* have been worked through to a more assured handling of the new forms and mode. References to 'the machine' are dropped; there are fewer abstractions and a greater integration of metaphor and allusion with the new vocabulary; there is, too, a wider list of subjects, some of which hark back to the poet's earlier concerns but are expressed more succinctly than before.

The last thing R. S. Thomas's poetry does is draw attention to itself as poetry: from the beginning his hallmark has been the unity of manner and meaning; and this is as true for the lighter lyric verse, which shows a highly developed skill in language and tone, as it is for the urgent and tortuous questionings of the mind about the spirit. His basic limitations have to do with narrowness of range and style, but the choice on Thomas's part is deliberate. It is his conviction that one of the important functions of poetry is to embody religious truth, and

since for him as poet that truth is not easily won, his poems record the struggle with marked honesty and integrity, thereby providing the context for the necessarily infrequent moments of faith and vision which are expressed with a clarity and gravity rarely matched by any of his contemporaries. (pp. 12-13)

> Colin Meir, *"The Poetry of R. S. Thomas,"* in British Poetry Since 1970: A Critical Survey, *edited by Peter Jones and Michael Schmidt, Carcanet Press, 1980, pp. 1-13.*

J. D. VICARY

The publication of *H'm* in 1972 marked a change of direction in R. S. Thomas's work. Despite continuities between the earlier and later poetry, the sense of a radical break has been noted by those who welcome and by those who regret his recent development—and indeed by Thomas himself. The change has been partly a change of subject matter. The country (in both senses) in which he has lived, and its population, are no longer the major stimuli. In an interview on Radio Cymru, broadcast in 1983, he said that, while feeling 'more of a Welshman, a straightforward Welshman' than before, he no longer felt the need 'to write like a Welshman'.

Instead, his religious concerns, always evident, have come to dominate his poetry. Problems of Christian belief, the complexity of religious experience, and their particular contemporary forms, preoccupy poems which range from explorations of states bordering on a blank despair to speculation, in a language that can be traditional but also restlessly modern, on the nature of God. Not all his poetry can be characterised in this way, the main exceptions being the short (twelve poems) *What is a Welshman?* (1974) and the sequence of poems relating to impressionist paintings that make up the first part of *Between Here and Now* (1981). But it is the religious poetry that forms the central and distinctive body of work. It is interesting to note that Thomas's most recent selection, *Later Poems* (1983), includes only one poem from *What is a Welshman?,* and two from the first section of *Between Here and Now.*

R. S. Thomas has always been a religious poet. He has written about the role of the priest in relation to his parishioners, and he has tested his beliefs against his perceptions of those who feel no need to share them. His sense of the 'spiritual' has been made to confront the insistent pressures of the 'natural' and 'material'. (p. 41)

In the earlier poetry particular observations of people and places provided the occasions for Thomas's religious reflections. Even his most introspective poems tended to be given a local habitation. One thinks of poems which feature the priest in his church, and of the importance of the church as building, where 'the dry whisper of unseen wings' comes from 'Bats not angels, in the high roof' (**"In a country church"**).

In the later poems these mediating contexts and occasions frequently drop away, and the subjects of Thomas's meditations are abstracted from any tangible surroundings. The extent of the change can be gauged from the terms that have been used to describe Thomas's earlier work. Calvin Bedient, for example, writing about the poetry that precedes *H'm,* praises Thomas for his 'passionate naturalness', for 'the grateful dependence of his senses on the world'. For Bedient, Thomas is a 'natural poet' who 'never tires of speaking of what is around him' [see *CLC*, Vol. 6]. . . .

By giving 'mind' its head and by relegating 'nature' (in one sense at least) Thomas has divided his readers. He has placed himself in a tradition of meditative and speculative religious poetry, claiming, in **"Groping"**, a poem from *Frequencies* (1978), that 'The best journey to make/is inward. It is the interior/that calls'. (p. 42)

Thomas's scepticism about language has become one of the central subjects of his poetry, and is closely connected to his religious concerns. If the poet cannot be confident about the naming of things, how much less confident must he be about the naming of God? The naming of God is a difficult matter. Thomas occupies a position where the name precedes him, 'ubiquitous / in its explanations', as he puts it in **"Waiting"**, a poem from *Frequencies*. It is these explanations that have to be unpicked so that the poet can get behind the name, not to the 'thing' itself, but to the gap that separates name and thing.

The word 'God' is an empty space waiting to be filled with whatever meanings the poet projects into it. At the same time it necessarily comes laden with the weight of past associations. The poet is both free and constrained, and it is the acceptance of this dilemma that gives Thomas's later poetry its particular character. (p. 43)

A negative title seems appropriate for much of [Thomas's] work since *H'm*. His poems frequently announce their 'true nature' by their 'ability to be in hell', the place where God is absent. They remain 'religious' because this absence implies, elsewhere, a presence. It is a theological absence they explore, one that only has meaning because of the tantalising proximity of its opposite term. (p. 44)

Thomas's later poetry has made . . . distrust of the imagination into a central theme, while at the same time allowing itself considerable speculative scope. The pull of imaginative freedom and the restraints of scepticism become the actual material of the poetry. His poems only rarely exhibit . . . confidence in 'the unifying power of the imagination'. . . . (p. 45)

[The] sense of a denial which is occasionally redeemed in ways that are not explicable by reference to a rational understanding of belief dominates much of Thomas's later work. The theology of his poetry from *H'm* onwards could appropriately be given the title of one of the poems from that volume, **"Via negativa"**. The title refers to the Christian mystical tradition which is based on a sense of the inadequacy of human attempts to give expression to the experience of encounter with the divine. (p. 47)

A reading of **"Waiting"** and **"Via negativa"** brings us close to the central subject of much of Thomas's poetry of the last decade. This subject is the complex relationship between faith and doubt, between a theology of presence and a theology of absence. His exploration of this area is, in his best poems, neither didactic nor abstract, but depends heavily on paradox and ambiguity. **"Waiting"** and **"Via negativa"** are situated, typically, in the gap between affirmation and negation. In the vacated footprint, absence and presence are intimately connected. (p. 51)

> *J. D. Vicary, "Via Negativa: Absence and Presence in the Recent Poetry of R. S. Thomas," in* Critical Quarterly, *Vol. 27, No. 3, Autumn, 1985, pp. 41-51.*

GWYNETH LEWIS

'Some day on the beach in Hoylake his father directed his attention to a ridge of mountains a long way over the sea to the West "There's Wales," he said in English.' This childhood memory is itself recounted in Welsh in R. S. Thomas's autobiography *Neb* ('Nobody') and is an ironic reminder of the complexity of this poet's Welsh identity. The man who made his name as a major Anglo-Welsh poet by writing tortured poems on Welsh themes has slipped out of the reach of the English literary 'establishment' by writing his autobiography for Welsh speakers only. Although he now lives in a Welsh-speaking community on the Lleyn peninsula, Thomas was born in Cardiff and brought up in Anglesey speaking *yr iaith fain* ('the thin language'). (p. 116)

Like Henry Adams, Thomas uses the third-person singular in his autobiography, as if he were already dead to himself— 'R.S. was *like* that' is a recurrent phrase. Thomas plays up to his stern poet-priest 'image'. A short autobiographical essay published in Welsh in 1972 and covering his early childhood is a more cheerful document than *Neb*. In the later version, Thomas has deleted passages about childhood friends and even a sweetheart, making himself into an isolated figure.

He is never shy about his love of the Welsh landscape. Descriptions of various scenes are clearly informed by a lifetime's observation. He writes, 'If there is a life after this, and if it does not contain things similar to those which are so dear to him in Wales, the streams, the moorland, the birds, the flowers, he has no desire to experience it.'

Thomas writes enthusiastically about birds, and tells of being arrested for espionage during an ornithological holiday in Spain. For all this, he comes across as a rather joyless character. He confesses that he is prone 'to the temptation of every old man, that is, despair'. What Thomas chiefly despairs about is the state of Welsh culture. His brand of nationalism is implacably hostile to English capitalistic urban culture: 'He always tended to look back and see the past as better. A long time ago the Welsh language was safe. There was brotherhood and neighbourhood here. Heavy industry hadn't reached South Wales to spoil and ruin it, making the nation sluggish. Architecture was better, more compatible with the beauty of the environment; and the craftsman still took pride in his work. One other blessing was that the country was comparatively free of the harmful presence of the English. He [R.S.] always saw the industrial revolution as Wales's greatest disaster.' Because he blames external factors almost exclusively for the Welsh decline, Thomas succumbs to the myth of the 'golden' Celtic society, one which was wholly hospitable to the values he now espouses.

However, Thomas is honest enough to realize the implications of this idealization for his work. (pp. 117-18)

The most interesting passages in the book are those which throw light on Thomas's work as a priest. He has always been unconventional in Church matters. As a pacifist, he was horrified by the Church's support of the Second World War, and he has also been critical of its lack of interest in Welsh culture. He has often been asked whether he sees any conflict between the rôles of poet and priest. He says that 'he denied this by insisting on seeing Christ as a poet. But what confused people was his use of the word metaphor. In a television programme he said that the Resurrection was a metaphor. So he didn't believe in it? But of course, what he had in mind was a question of language. . . If we have not received a vision of the risen Christ, we have to accept the verbal testimony of the evangelists. But language is a symbol, a description of one thing in terms of another. And that, to R.S., was the meaning of metaphor.'

Experimenting with an Amen, Thomas's most recent volume of poetry, is a far less interesting book than *Neb.* Many of the poems read like paraphrases of earlier Thomas poems. At its worst, Thomas's metaphysical meditation can sound like the sentiments written inside religious greeting cards but as always, Thomas's self-scrutiny is disarming. For example, 'I fasted / at import's table, so had // an appetite for the banal, / the twelve baskets full left / over after the turning / of the little into so much.' But this honesty is not endearing and, on this occasion, doesn't redeem his determined dourness. (p. 118)

Gwyneth Lewis, "Unconventional Priest," in London Magazine, *n.s. Vol. 26, Nos. 9 & 10, December, 1986-January, 1987, pp. 116-18.*

JAMES FINN COTTER

In [*Poems of R. S. Thomas*], R. S. Thomas, like his Celtic predecessor W. B. Yeats, looks back on time to cast a cold eye on life, on death. The Welsh minister finds little comfort in sectarian Christianity and even less in our current industrialized society. Art, in the Impressionist painters, a parishioner's piano-playing, and one's own poetry, embodies a search for meaning in ways religion often fails to achieve. In his one-act play, *The Minister,* Thomas has the narrator call Protestantism "the adroit castrator / Of art" and "the bitter negation / Of song and dance and the heart's innocent joy." Ironically,

"In Church" asks: "Is this where God hides / From my searching?" The darkness inside the church, in shadows cast by "an untenanted cross," represent the dark night of the modern soul. God no longer or so readily reveals himself in nature as to poets of the past: "He is such a fast / God," Thomas observes in **"Pilgrimages,"** "always before us and / leaving as we arrive.". . . In these poems, the pilgrim waits in silence, "somewhere between faith and doubt." Just as a poem emerges from morphemes and phonemes and the sculpture comes from the stone, so in everyday life "it is the plain facts and natural happenings / that conceal God and reveal him to us / little by little under the mind's tooling" (**"Emerging"**). The mind's tooling is too often in evidence in these lines, however, and the homiletic tone at times becomes overbearing. Even the flowers, bright spots on this bleak poetic landscape, wilt in the didactic atmosphere. Although Thomas always offers himself as a forthright and humble witness in his quest for meaningfulness, his presence grows impersonal and stony, like the hills he treads in loneliness and cold. Here the public voice sounds a sour note, while the private voice hesitates to affirm anything more than a hint of what it might discover. **"Suddenly"** is one of the rare poems that throw off their inhibitions and sing "in the vernacular / of the purposes of One who is." (pp. 153-54)

James Finn Cotter, "Public and Private Poetry," in The Hudson Review, *Vol. XL, No. 1, Spring, 1987, pp. 149-55.*

James Tiptree, Jr.

1915-1987

(Pseudonym of Alice [Hastings] B[radley] Sheldon; also wrote under pseudonym of Raccoona Sheldon) American short story writer, novelist, and critic.

Among the most acclaimed authors of science fiction to have emerged in the early 1970s, Tiptree combined the tight narrative style and aura of amazement generally attributed to literature of the ''Golden Age'' of science fiction with the moral and psychological emphasis often associated with the genre's ''New Wave'' movement of the 1960s. Tiptree, whose major themes encompass psychological, anthropological, and feminist concerns, often stressed the need for individuals to achieve wholeness by integrating such stereotypical masculine attributes as aggression and competitiveness with feminine qualities like pacifism and protectiveness. Although Tiptree's novels have not received the consistent acclaim awarded her short stories and novellas, most critics commend her witty, acerbic style and convincing examinations of alien and human psychologies.

In the late 1970s, Tiptree was revealed to be the pseudonym of Alice B. Sheldon, a perceptual psychologist who adopted the masculine pen name, according to Robert Hunt, because it ''gave her professional anonymity, protection from the more intolerant [science fiction] fans, and (since about 1972) considerable freedom in dealing with themes sexual and violent.'' The daughter of Herbert Bradley, a renowned explorer, and Mary Hastings Bradley, an author of travel books and journals, Sheldon became acquainted with a variety of foreign cultures and beliefs through her travels with her parents in India and Africa. She established a reputation as a graphic artist and painter during the 1930s and also served as an art critic for the *Chicago Sun* from 1941 to 1942. During World War II, Sheldon became the first female photo-intelligence officer in the United States Army Air Force; this distinction led to a position with the United States Central Intelligence Agency from 1952 to 1955. In 1967, Sheldon received her doctorate in experimental psychology from George Washington University. She engaged in scientific research for several years before devoting herself to science fiction in the late 1960s.

Tiptree's first book, the short story collection *Ten Thousand Light-Years from Home* (1973), features standard science fiction suspense tales as well as farcical pieces. In ''Beam Us Home,'' an American boy's feelings of estrangement lead him to believe that he is stranded on an alien planet on the television show ''Star Trek.'' Tiptree established her literary reputation with *Warm Worlds and Otherwise* (1975), a collection of short fiction addressing psychological and feminist concerns. ''Love Is the Plan, the Plan Is Death,'' which won the Nebula Award for best short story of 1973, is narrated by a spider-like extraterrestrial who confronts the aggressive instincts of his race before offering himself as food to sustain his mate and offspring through their planet's long arctic winter. This story implies that life and death are not opposites but inextricable parts of the same natural process. In *The Girl Who Was Plugged In*, for which Tiptree received the Hugo Award for best novella of 1973, a deformed girl named P. Burke is electronically attached to Delphi, a female cyborg who is used as a model

Photograph by Patti Perret

in television advertisements. Delphi soon attains her own consciousness; both characters fall in love with a handsome male model who unintentionally kills them while attempting to disconnect Delphi from what he presumes to be mind control. Commenting on the story's wider implications, Lillian Heldreth asserted: ''Both P. Burke and Delphi suffer and die as victims of a society that uses women as disposable objects, neither of them perceived as human beings by the manipulators who use them.''

In her first novel, *Up the Walls of the World* (1978), Tiptree uses nonchronological structure and shifting narration to examine three disparate racial intelligences. In this book, a human expedition makes telepathic contact with the Tyrenni, a race of alien creatures who embrace radical notions of masculinity and femininity. Both humans and Tyrenni are consumed and incorporated into the body of a lonely alien consciousness they label The Destroyer because of its tendency to extinguish stars. The two races discover, however, that The Destroyer's true purpose is to eradicate specific suns, thus preventing a chain reaction with stars exploding at the center of the galaxy. Although several critics deemed *Up the Walls of the World* overambitious in scope, others praised the novel's structural and thematic complexity.

The stories in Tiptree's next collection, *Star Songs of an Old Primate* (1978), address the relationship between sexuality and violence. In "Your Haploid Heart," a conservative race of asexual beings known as Esthaans attempt to exterminate a rival race, the Flenni, out of disgust for their sexual habits. The Esthaans learn, however, that the Flenni are merely an alternate, diploid generation of their own race. *Houston, Houston, Do You Read?*, for which Tiptree won the Nebula Award and shared the Hugo Award for best novella of 1975, concerns three astronauts stranded in the future who encounter a spaceship of female clones. Learning that all male humans have died from a viral plague and frustrated by their own sexual aggressions, the astronauts unsuccessfully attempt to take over the ship. Although the women initially consider the men dangerous to the freedom and autonomy of their society, the story suggests that they may lack the competitive instincts associated with masculinity that are critical to human progress and survival, thus reinforcing the theme of reciprocity prevalent in many of Tiptree's works. Tiptree's next collection, *Out of the Everywhere and Other Extraordinary Visions* (1981), contains *The Screwfly Solution*, for which she received the Nebula Award for best novelette of 1977. In this work, extraterrestrials attempt to take over the earth by manipulating the hormonal system of human males so that they will rape and murder their female counterparts and subsequently destroy one another. Carol Page maintained that *The Screwfly Solution* offers "the disturbing thesis that the male sexual urge is on the same spectrum with, but slightly below, the urge for violence."

Tiptree's later works attracted less critical attention than her early short stories. Her second novel, *Brightness Falls from the Air* (1985), concerns an intelligent race of insect-like extraterrestrials who were nearly exterminated by humans for the euphoric glandular secretion that is extracted by torture. Set fifty years after the atrocities, the novel addresses new threats to the aliens and, according to Noel Perrin, reveals to readers "the human in the alien, and the alien in the human." *Tales of the Quintana Roo* (1986) is a collection of three surreal novellas set on the Pacific coast of the Yucatan Peninsula that draws upon the Indian legends of the region. Bob Collins described this volume as "neither fantasy nor science fiction, but expressions of a strangely populous and multi-layered alien history." *The Starry Rift* (1986), billed as a novel by Tiptree's publishers, was considered by many critics a collection of novellas linked by their setting—a starless void known as the Great Rift, where time and space undergo strange transformations. D. Douglas Fratz called *The Starry Rift* "probably the least successful of Tiptree's books to date; but the worst of James Tiptree, Jr. is still very good indeed."

(See also *Contemporary Authors*, Vol. 108, Vol. 122 [obituary] and *Dictionary of Literary Biography*, Vol. 8.)

P. SCHUYLER MILLER

[James Tiptree, Jr.'s] first collection of short fiction [is] *Ten Thousand Light-Years from Home*. Only one of the fifteen stories—"**Birth of a Salesman**"—was published in *Analog*, but that's all the more reason you should acquaint yourself with one of the finest talents to appear in the field in some time.

Tiptree is apparently a lineal descendant of the Sumerian who discovered that that same old barley mush would make beer as well as bread. He uses plots, themes and formulas that the critics have assured us were given the *coup de grace* by Doc

Smith and converted them into dazzling new science fiction— "hard" SF, farcical SF, moving SF, whatever kind of SF amuses him at the moment. At the same time, perhaps with tongue in cheek, he concocts titles that are part in the current "in" wave in literature—the wave that produces films with titles like *I Could Never Have Sex with Any Man Who Has So Little Regard for My Husband*. Is he riding the wave? Is he ridiculing it with titles like "**And I Awoke and Found Me Here on the Cold Hill's Side**" or "**I'll Be Waiting for You When the Swimming Pool is Empty**"? Tiptree knows. And maybe the Shadow.

"**Birth of a Salesman**" is one of four farces which may owe something to their author's reputed association with the Pentagon. Their message—and they have one—is that however confused your personal corner of bureaucracy may be, you ain't seen nothin' yet. What's worse, when you look past the stage business, is that the snafu is logical. In "**Salesman**," the unbelievable complexity of interstellar export. In "**Faithful to Thee, Terra, in Our Fashion**," the axiom that all's fair in war and sport. . . . And in two stories, one Max, a CIA agent (and a rather perceptive one) copes with galactic invasion—in "**Mama Come Home**," by raunchy giantesses from Capella, come to Earth on a slaving raid, and in "**Help**" by huge blue dinosaurs and little butter-colored missionaries in a used spaceship. (pp. 152-53)

About as different as they can get are the "straight" or "hard" SF stories. They're the ones I starred when I took notes.

"**The Snows Are Melted, the Snows Are Gone**," takes us into a post-holocaust world in which defective but intelligent mutants must send their girls—and wolves—out to seduce sound genes among the barbarians. "**The Peacefulness of Vivyan**" takes us to a seaworld and a pitiful programmed "traitor." "**Painwise**" explores another aspect of official pragmatism— a man sent out to explore other worlds after he has been revised so that pain isn't pain. "**Mother in the Sky with Diamonds**," the first Tiptree I ever read, which packs all the clichés— asteroid miners, drug peddlers, corporate inhumanity, a great lost ship from ancient times, and more—plus some ingenious biological architecture, into a completely believable story.

You may have picked up the feeling that these are not just gimmick and gadget stories, ingenious as some of them are. Hobie, in "**Beam Us Home**," is a boy whom Earth and people rejected, but whom Space accepted. The mutant girl in "**Snows**" . . . the old woman in "**Mother in the Sky**" . . . they're all people clubbed by their world. And so is the red-haired man in "**Cold Hill's Side**," with its savage message that "Man is exogamous."

I have a few stories left that are so-so, and one that I should have included with the comedies—"**When the Swimming Pool is Empty**." It's a ruthless lampoon of war and orgies and do-gooders, but it's also a little lesson in cultural diffusion and a warning against starting something you can't stop. "**I'm Too Big But I Love to Play**" is a slight thing about the space-thing (really only an organized drift of plasma) who tries to play with the little people on Earth. "**The Man Doors Said Hello To**" has to be fantasy—somewhere between Pangborn and Lafferty in mood. . . .

Why [*Ten Thousand Light Years from Home*] isn't in hard covers, I'll never know, but even if you're the fussiest of collectors, don't let that stop you. Get it. (p. 153)

P. Schuyler Miller, in a review of "Ten Thousand Light-Years from Home," in Analog Science Fiction/

Science Fact, *Vol. XCII, No. 5, January, 1974, pp. 152-53.*

GERALD JONAS

If it made any sense to talk about a successor to Cordwainer Smith among contemporary S.F. writers, the most likely candidate would be James Tiptree Jr., author of the stories recently collected in *Warm Worlds and Otherwise*. Tiptree is the current mystery man of science fiction. He keeps to himself, does not show up at S.F. conventions to receive the awards that he wins, and is rumored to work for a Government agency in Washington. No one knows whether the name he signs to his stories is his real name or a pseudonym. And Tiptree, like Smith, does things in his stories that seem to stretch the medium without any sense of strain. For example, he writes about aliens in a way that makes the extra-terrestrial creatures in most S.F. seem like little children in Halloween masks. There are no human beings at all in **"Love Is the Plan, the Plan Is Death,"** which won a Nebula Award for Best S.F. Short Story of 1974. Tiptree always works on a grand scale; the theme of this story is nothing less than the unequal conflict between free will and biological necessity, and by the last page, one can almost feel the tides of evolution lapping at one's feet. (pp. 31-2)

> *Gerald Jonas, in a review of "Warm Worlds and Otherwise," in* The New York Times Book Review, *March 23, 1975, pp. 31-2.*

JAMES HAMILTON-PATERSON

On the whole, James Tiptree has two modes [in *Ten Thousand Light-Years from Home*], whimsy-whimsy and serious-whimsy. The whimsy-whimsy mode produces stories like **"The Man Doors Said Hello to"**, which is about a man being continually greeted and addressed by lavatory doors, wardrobes, and one of the minute but perfectly formed girls who live in his own clothing. The serious-whimsy stories have titles like **"I'll be Waiting for You when the Swimming Pool is Empty"**.

There is, however, a recurrent theme which can be glimpsed in several stories and finds full expression in the last, **"Beam us Home"**. This is a preoccupation with people lost in space or time desperately trying to regain Earth or the present. **"The Man who Walked Home"**, which has appeared in numerous anthologies, is about John Delgano, a scientist involved in a laboratory explosion who every year reappears for a split second at the site of the explosion in almost the same frozen attitude. . . . **"Beam Us Home"** concerns an apparently ordinary American boy who has been fed on weekly instalments of "Star Trek." His feelings of alienation from modern American life lead him to the inescapable conclusion that he is actually taking part in an episode of "Star Trek" and, as a member of an exploration party on the surface of the planet Earth, is merely waiting for Scotty to beam him back up to the starship Enterprise. It is a very neat blending of reality and myth, and it makes one despair for the tiny grain of seriousness swamped by Mr Tiptree's facetiae.

> *James Hamilton-Paterson, "L'intrigue c'est l'homme," in* The Times Literary Supplement, *No. 3830, August 8, 1975, p. 903.*

GERALD JONAS

As the back-cover photograph [of *Up the Walls of the World*] coyly suggests, the name "James Tiptree" is a pseudonym for a woman who has chosen not to reveal her identity when she writes science fiction. Whatever her reasons for concealment, as James Tiptree she has written some of the finest s.f. short stories of the last decade. Now she has tried her hand at a novel.

Anyone familiar with the previous work of James Tiptree will not be surprised to find that *Up the Walls of the World* is thematically ambitious. At the heart of the book is a clash between representatives of *three* different races: human beings, the Tyrenni (giant, squidlike telepathic creatures who "swim" in the atmosphere of their wind-blown planet) and a supremely odd being known to the Tyrenni as the Destroyer. The Destroyer may or may not be alive; it roams the interstellar void, eating stars and feeling lonely. The reason for its curious diet becomes apparent only after it devours the sun that lights the home planet of the Tyrenni. A handful of survivors find sanctuary in the Destroyer's "body," along with some neurotic "sensitives" from Earth who have gotten mixed up with the Tyrenni during an abortive attempt by the latter to take refuge in the minds and bodies of Earth-dwellers.

If all that sounds complicated in synopsis, I assure you it is even more complicated in the telling. But Tiptree treats it all with the utmost seriousness, and there are numerous fine touches of characterization. Each of the sensitives is a wounded soul who is restored to health through (literally) cosmic travail. It seems that exploding stars in the center of the galaxy have triggered a kind of chain reaction, which is spreading outward; the real function of the Destroyer is to create a "fire break" to contain the conflagration and save at least some suns from otherwise-certain destruction.

As befits such a vast theme, the book starts slowly. At first, I had trouble visualizing the Tyrenni on their home planet, just as I had trouble sympathizing with the problems of the human sensitives or with the inner anguish of the Destroyer. But when destiny throws the three races together, the pace picks up. The scenes in which human, Tyrenni and the Destroyer take one another's measure have a persuasive solidity that is all the more remarkable considering that none of the creatures at this point possesses a body in the usual sense of the term.

To say that *Up the Walls of the World* is only partly successful is to state the obvious. Novels that deal with the mental gymnastics of superminds, or with concepts like eternity and infinity, are doomed to fall short of the mark. But Tiptree's misses are more exciting than the bulls-eyes of less ambitious authors. As Browning said, "A man's reach should exceed his grasp, or what's a heaven for?"

> *Gerald Jonas, in a review of "Up the Walls of the World," in* The New York Times Book Review, *February 26, 1978, p. 28.*

SPIDER ROBINSON

[*Up the Walls of the World*] is a rather long novel, a whole different kind of writing than anything . . . [Tiptree] has done before, and a clear triumph on anybody's terms.

You know the lovely device of telling two apparently unrelated stories side by side, in alternating chapters, and then bringing them together suddenly at about Chapter Twelve? Sure you do;

the best example that comes to mind is William Goldman's brilliant *Marathon Man*. Well, Tiptree . . . decided, for pure swank, to start out with three major threads, apparently *unrelatable* at first, and then tie them together into a mind-boggling package. She pulls it off with the breathtaking ease of Fred Astaire making an anatomically implausible step look simple. Three different typefaces are used to help avoid confusion, but Tiptree is so good a writer that they are actually superfluous. Two lines into any chapter and you know just where you are—and what was happening on this channel when you left it last.

And what you have here are not just three subplots, or just three different worlds, or even just three different (literal) species of protagonist—but three different planes for existence. Channel One brings you a being, an "evil presence," so vast that it steps on solar systems, yet so subtle that it can perceive individual electrons, vagrant thoughts. Channel Two brings you a sort of aerial jellyfish named Tivonel, a telepathic female whose race lives high above the surface of a far distant planet, and is being threatened with destruction by the baddie on Channel One; she is utterly alien, and one of the warmest, noblest characters I've ever seen. (Don't ask *me* how Tip does it.) Channel Three brings you Dr. Dan Dann, an MD attached to a parapsychology research project funded by the US Government: shattered by personal trauma, Dann is addicted to his own drugs and plagued by an unwanted and inescapable talent for empathy. (I should mention that the villain on this last channel is one of the nastiest and most economically sketched I have ever seen.)

The level of excellence on all three channels is Master Class, and when they all come together they heterodyne. By that point I was exhausted, and I was only halfway through the book. From there, by God, she accelerated sharply and built to a climax! . . . I don't think *tour de force* is too strong; frankly, I'm stunned.

Oh, all right, it's not perfect. It could have been polished some; once or twice I got the feeling that a given chapter contained maybe one sentence worth of plot advancement and indeed was an entire chapter only because symmetry required a chapter of that Channel in that slot. The seams showed once or twice, is what I'm saying, only I'm being a little more unnecessarily redundant than is called for by strict necessity—which is *Up the Walls*'s other occasional problem. Then again, redundancy is an excellent way to minimize confusion with a complex plot. (pp. 172-73)

So okay, toward the end I did maybe once or twice reflect that it certainly did go on. But then there was no law saying I *had* to read it in a single sitting.

The hell with picking critical nits. [*Up the Walls of the World* is] probably the best thing Tiptree has published so far, which more than means it's Hugo material. And I was impressed by the tastefully underplayed wit with which editor Hartwell made no mention of Tiptree's sex in the blurb copy, avoiding all sex-specific pronouns—and then ran Alice Sheldon's picture big as life on the back cover.

A gem, just barely flawed enough to make it bearable. (p. 173)

Spider Robinson, in a review of "Up the Walls of the World," in Analog Science Fiction/Science Fact, *Vol. XCVIII, No. 6, June, 1978, pp. 172-73.*

ALGIS BUDRYS

[Readers may] be wondering whether *Up The Walls of The World*, the first Tiptree novel, is worth reading.

Yes and no. It is intensely overcomplicated, in the sense that a great many major plot-points and overwhelming internal discoveries are constantly being made by the principal characters. A new wonder arrives on every page. This wouldn't be so confusing if we understood *where* the characters are, exactly, and which of them is lurking behind Tiptree's less than expert use of pronouns. To understand the story, it is sometimes necessary to back up a few paragraphs, or occasionally half a chapter, and carefully chart out who the "he" or "she" in a crucial scene is, and just where they last were within "it." The story also apparently does not proceed in a straight line, chronologically. There are a great many characters, moving on separate tracks, and when they intersect from time to time it turns out that what had seemed to be simultaneous activities were, in fact, not.

Tiptree has chosen to use one very old SF convention—the interpolated passages which always go: "It moved, woke, thought, looked about itself. Unimaginably vast, greatly ancient, it sent out the gigaparsec-scanning mentations of its kind. . . ." Tiptree puts them in capital letters where Murray Leinster put them in italics, but the effect is the same. Tiptree has also chosen a fairly recent SF invention. The entire book is written in the present tense. . . . (p. 33)

Tiptree consistently maintains present tense, even in the conventionally orthographed passages concerning the human characters and the inhabitants of the giant planet Tyree. This consistency makes the device useless as an aid in unscrambling the chronology of events, and reduces it to its usual form, which is that of an interesting curiosity all other fields of literature had pretty much abandoned by the time SF readers began praising it for its originality. It must be said that Tiptree handles it well; in no time at all, the reader's mind is automatically translating it into past tense and so learning to ignore it.

Given all that for evidence of an intelligent, talented person trying to make something special out of her first novel, and making a series of honest mistakes in the process, we are also given a story of considerable power, characters whose internal dimensions frequently exceed the ordinary, and pictures, pictures, pictures of landscapes mundane and landscapes alien which are not readily forgotten.

The essential situation in the story is simple. The capital-letter creature is a vastly diffuse organism, part of a tribe of such sentient beings which are forging through the galaxy extinguishing suns. Its crime is in abandoning its task. (It's not very bright.) It is withdrawing from the remainder of its kind and their area of action. Wandering away, it is causing suns to flare and die. It is attracted to suns which broadcast psychic emanations; its attempts to communicate with them are what destroys them. (I think.) It has (I guess) no idea that there are such things as planets or that life might have attained intelligence—and psychic ability—on them.

On the planet Tyree, . . . the intelligent life form is a sort of half-squid, half manta-ray which perpetually rides the mighty winds of its home world. This race naturally and readily uses what we would call ESP to manage its affairs. It is now dying of exposure to increasing radiation from its star, which I'm pretty sure is not Sol. On Earth, meanwhile, a CIA-sponsored ESP experimental task group accidentally comes into contact with Tyree's people, and some of the Terrestrials half-accidentally exchange bodies with some of the personalities from Tyree.

After that, the story begins to complicate. Eventually, a number of diverse and interesting characters, human and alien, are taken up as disembodied personalities within the interstellar creature. They are in contact with varied aspects of the creature at varied times, and their contacts among themselves are at various levels of reliability. Finally, in a welter of characters abandoned by Tiptree as loose ends, some of the principals achieve good ends, and incidentally the galaxy is saved.

Reading the book is an at times frustrating, at times highly rewarding experience. The story told straight out would have been more than sufficient to establish this book's credentials as a major piece of SF. As it is, it is an ambitious and very large effort, but one which tried to do too many things, with the usual results. (pp. 33-4)

> *Algis Budrys, in a review of "Up the Walls of the World," in* The Magazine of Fantasy and Science Fiction, *Vol. 55, No. 3, September, 1978, pp. 33-4.*

DOUGLAS A. MACKEY

Ursula Le Guin introduces this new collection of seven stories [*Star Songs of an Old Primate*] originally published between 1969-1976. These are powerful and provocative tales, giving impressive testimony to Tiptree's "star" reputation. The relativity of sexual categories is one of Tiptree's main themes, and woe to the character who loses touch with the values of the opposite sex within him or herself. The novella *A Momentary Taste of Being* ranks with the best of Le Guin, interweaving sexual and philosophical themes in the tradition of *The Left Hand of Darkness*. It's a First Contact situation in which a starship crew is infected with a quasi-religious passion to encounter the alien. Only the ship's doctor maintains the scientific objectivity necessary to remember safeguards. But he must struggle to keep his sense of being "human" against the allurements of the alien, as embodied in his sister—with whom he'd formerly had an incestuous relationship. Tiptree's compassion allows her to handle psychosexual subjects with uplifting results.

The Hugo- and Nebula-winning **Houston, Houston, Do You Read?** has three men on a modern space mission getting zapped into the future, thereby encountering a shipful of female clones. The clones appear more refined and humane than the male barbarians. But it subtly emerges that they also lack something in individualistic and emotional values, in the vital energy that has destructive as well as creative potential, without which humanity cannot progress. Here, as in Wilhelm's *Where Late the Sweet Birds Sang,* the dynamic balance between such opposites as male/female, individual/society, and subjective/objective awareness must be maintained for psychic well-being.

These two works constitute the greater part of the book, but the five shorter stories are also well worth reading, particularly **"She Waits for All Men Born,"** in which a gentle mutant girl in a post-holocaust world becomes the Death Mother of myth and legend. . . . [The] stories in [*Star Songs of an Old Primate*] are especially strong in mythic resonances and psychological insight. [Tiptree's] tales are balanced in wholeness of vision, inspiration, craftsmanship, and appeal to both heart and mind.

> *Douglas A. Mackey, in a review of "Star Songs of an Old Primate," in* Science Fiction & Fantasy Book Review, *Vol. 1, No. 1, February, 1979, p. 5.*

FRED NIEDERMAN

In her first novel [*Up the Walls of the World*], Tiptree creates a masterful, panoramic adventure story spanning three separate worlds, integrating characters in a subtle and thought-provoking tale describing their quests for health, wholeness, purpose, and wisdom. Dr. Daniel Dann, a somewhat cynical but loving physician, is the nucleus of a shabby group of psionically-gifted gentle-people. Their band is created by and endangered by clandestine government agents, who herd them to a remote testing station to seek new ways to communicate with deployed submarines.

Tivonel lives with her people in another part of our galaxy, in the Great Wind. Her people are physically much like large earthly undersea creatures, but are shrouded in a communication mantle which uses colors to reveal their thoughts. Tivonel and her male, child-bearing partner, Giadoc, are caught up in attempts to save their civilization from the radioactive force of an entity so awesome that it is called only "The Destroyer." . . . Tiptree moves from world to world, introducing essential information with grace and ease. The evidence of a long apprenticeship in shorter fiction can be seen in the tight writing style and attention to detail. The novel remains fresh and alive, even as Tiptree returns to familiar themes: individuals whose gentleness and honesty set them apart from their immediate society; truly alien worlds and creatures; exploration of the identity between mental and electrical/mechanical function, and of the relationship between male and female within a society. [*Up the Walls of the World*] displays the same care, attention, imagination, and science background that has earned Tiptree numerous accolades from the science fiction community. (pp. 62-3)

> *Fred Niederman, in a review of "Up the Walls of the World," in* Science Fiction & Fantasy Book Review, *Vol. 1, No. 5, June, 1979, pp. 62-3.*

ROBERT HUNT

For some nine years "James Tiptree, Jr." was the impenetrable *nom de plume* of clinical psychologist Alice Sheldon. The masculine pseudonym gave her professional anonymity, protection from the more intolerant SF fans, and (since about 1972) considerable freedom in dealing with themes sexual and violent. Since the revelation of her identity in late 1976, her output of stories has slackened. Her first novel, *Up the Walls of the World* was disappointing, in its ectoplasmic vagueness, to readers accustomed to the author's incisive short fiction. . . .

[*Warm Worlds and Otherwise*] (from the period 1968-73) shows Tiptree at the height of her powers and in command of several styles. The jaunty, elliptical mode of **"All the Kinds of Yes"** (in which a polymorphous alien meets and mates with four flower children) and several shorter *jeux d' esprit* has worn least well: the satiric Tiptree is delightful, but distanced, her targets rooted in the early '70s. In **"The Milk of Paradise"** and especially *The Girl Who Was Plugged In* this fragmented style is wedded to savagely distasteful themes. In the latter story (winner of the 1974 Hugo for Best Novella), a hideously misshapen girl lives vicariously the life of a jet-setting cyborg; the narrator's slangy asides to his "zombie" reader enhance the horror they pretend to sneer at.

Impressive in a different way are the sober, subtly building narratives of **"And I Have Come Upon This Place by Lost Ways," "The Last Flight of Doctor Ain,"** and the extraordinary **"The Women Men Don't See."** To describe this last as a UFO/alien encounter story would reduce it to the level of the cover illustration; it is a masterful exploration of the full implications of the word "alien." Tiptree's skills are most devastating in the depiction of men and beasts destroyed by the blind drives of an indifferent nature. The Nebula-winning **"Love Is the Plan, the Plan Is Death"** is a *tour de force* in its first-person glimpses of a non-human consciousness overruled by hormonal destiny. The despairing **"On the Last Afternoon"** pits human aspirations against a crushing alien sexuality; its description of the mating sea monsters is one of the most horrifying scenes you will ever read. (p. 93)

There are two other Tiptree collections: *Ten Thousand Light Years from Home* (1973) has fifteen fine, if more conventional, stories from 1968-72; *Star Songs of an Old Primate* (1978) contains seven stories, most from the mid-'70s, including **"Your Haploid Heart,"** the award-winning *Houston, Houston, Do You Read?* and the long, apocalyptic *A Momentary Taste of Being.* Both *Star Songs* and *Warm Worlds* belong in every collection of modern science fiction—or of the contemporary short story. (p. 94)

> *Robert Hunt, in a review of "Warm Worlds and Otherwise," in* Science Fiction & Fantasy Book Review, *Vol. 1, No. 7, August, 1979, pp. 93-4.*

DEBBIE NOTKIN

[*Out of the Everywhere and Other Extraordinary Visions*] includes the four published Raccoona Sheldon stories, a few Tiptree stories that have appeared since her last collection was published, and two brand-new novellas.... **"We Who Stole the Dream,"** a story I didn't like at all when I first encountered it, improved quite a bit this time around. (There are certain authors whose works should always be reread; if you didn't like them, it's probably something *you* missed, not something they left out.)

The highlights of [*Out of the Everywhere and Other Extraordinary Visions*] are one of each: one Raccoona Sheldon story, one reprinted Tiptree story, and one of the previously unpublished works. **"Your Faces, O My Sisters! Your Faces Filled of Light!"** appeared under the Sheldon by-line. This is a grippingly lovely, painful story which functions equally well on two entirely different levels. If you choose to read it as a contemporary story of madness, it works; if you would rather read it as a complex science fiction story of time travel and world skipping, it works just as well. Sheldon didn't patronize her readers by forcing us into one mode or the other. I haven't decided which one I like best (or which one she likes best).

On the other hand, *The Screwfly Solution* is science fiction at its most literal, grounded in the pheromone research of the last decade, and absolutely terrifying. I find the ending, a rather gimmicky twist which Tiptree is very fond of, far too weak for the story—but I just pretend that it ends a page and a half earlier. I've heard this story criticized on the grounds that it gave the reader nightmares, but I think that's a compliment. If by any chance you missed this Nebula winner you are in for a (rather unsettling) treat.

With Delicate Mad Hands, one of the two new stories, echoes two favorite science fiction themes: the misery of the outsider and the loneliness of the long-distance space voyager. In this case, the outsider is not one of the voyagers themselves, but their sexual release valve. The story is strongly reminiscent of both Sturgeon's underexposed *The Pod and the Barrier* and Tiptree's earlier *The Girl Who Was Plugged In.* These are both excellent stories, and this one is a worthy successor, tribute and extension rather than repetition.

A Tiptree collection is always an event, and *Out of the Everywhere . . . ,* despite one or two weaker stories, is no exception. (pp. 26-7)

> *Debbie Notkin, in a review of "Out of the Everywhere and Other Extraordinary Visions," in* Rigel Science Fiction, *No. 4, Spring, 1982, pp. 26-7.*

ALEXANDER J. BUTRYM

All the stories [in *Out of the Everywhere and Other Extraordinary Visions*] reflect [Tiptree's] characteristic interest in encounters between humans and aliens, and as always the strength of Tiptree lies in her ability to evoke the alien. She does so here by imagining strange looking creatures whose life processes are based on odd vital principles, whose sensations are to us synesthetic and whose social systems reflect their odd physiologies and psychologies. But most of all she puts her aliens in relationships with her readers and lets the awe and wonder develop. Tiptree is also good at conjuring visual images that seem to have concrete physical effects. **"A Source of Innocent Merriment," "Beaver Tears,"** and the novella, *With Delicate Mad Hands,* evoke the physical sensations of swooping, twisting, gliding, plunging, and falling in orbiting, landing or cruising space ships. In addition to this "kinetic" impression, the visual details form powerful sentimental and emotional effects, as in **"Slow Music."**

Tiptree's favorite motif seems to be human-alien encounters, especially as in five of the stories the aliens manipulate whole human populations. **"Angel Fix"** has the lightest tone in the collection, but its comic-inept central alien isn't characteristic of Tiptree, and the story is not really successful. This fact suggests the weakness of the collection: Tiptree's humans are generally uninteresting; she relies on aliens to carry the story, and where they can't, the story doesn't work. **"Time Sharing Angel"** is another example of a story that seems finally pointless for this reason. It's an exercise in the mathematics of population control; the alien is merely a *deus ex machina* to get the narrative going. *With Delicate Mad Hands* succeeds because although it focuses on a human, Tiptree describes the main character as insane, and therefore by definition alien.

The main thematic concern of the collection is best expressed in both the reprinted Nebula winner, *The Screwfly Solution,* and *With Delicate Mad Hands.* These stories describe primal human brutality in gruesome detail that might force a wince from readers with sharp sensitivity to pain. Two other stories are also concerned with the brutality that lies beneath the human skin. They are the very short **"Beaver Tears,"** which neatly ties the alien motif to the brutality theme, and **"Your Faces, O My Sisters! Your Faces Filled of Light!,"** in which the alien motif is expressed as insanity, a variation on *Delicate Hands.*

[Of the] novellas, *Out of the Everywhere* is the least satisfying. The relations between humans and aliens in it are purely mechanical and accidental in the philosophic sense. The story uses an old-fashioned kind of pulp wish-fulfillment plot that would have point only if the aliens were better realized and more intimately and actively involved than they are.

[*Out of the Everywhere and Other Extraordinary Visions*] is an important collection in spite of my reservations. Its stories span the main range of Tiptree's motifs and themes and illustrate her strengths and weaknesses. It should be in any SF collection. (pp. 19-20)

> *Alexander J. Butrym, in a review of "Out of the Everywhere and Other Extraordinary Visions," in* Science Fiction & Fantasy Book Review, *No. 5, June, 1982, pp. 19-20.*

ADAM J. FRISCH

The Quintana Roo, a primitive area in the eastern Mexican Yucatan, serves as the setting for several of the short stories by science fiction writer James Tiptree, Jr. A stark, empty land sparsely inhabited by ancient Mayan peoples, the Quintana Roo provides a sharp contrast to modern western civilization; it suggests the vast, unorganized turbulence lying beneath our twentieth century's technological identity. Thus, it provides an excellent landscape from which Tiptree can explore her central concern as a science fiction writer: the psychological consequences of the war between contemporary logical thought and primitive mythical thought and between the patterns of science and the patterns of fiction, which characterize the modern human condition. (p. 48)

Perhaps the most dominant theme in Tiptree's works is the psychological pain and the lack of personal fulfillment human beings experience when they allow themselves to remain isolated in limited patterns of behavior. Tiptree's fiction particularly focuses upon two such behavioral models, one of which has historically been associated with "male" conduct and the other of which has traditionally been labeled as typically "female" behavior. Tiptree identifies the male behavior pattern as involving psychological drives for survival and for order in the environment, goals customarily linked with "unemotional" systems of logical thought. Conversely, her stereotypical female figure is the overly protective, loving mother, actively concerned about the welfare of others but always passive about her own well-being. For Tiptree, an exclusive preoccupation with either of these traditional sexual models will lead not only to a severe retardation of an individual's development but also to pain, stagnation, and possibly death for members of that individual's society.

The three male astronauts in Tiptree's story *Houston, Houston, Do You Read?* offer excellent illustrations of the dangers of an overly masculine orientation. The astronauts have been on a circumsolar space mission when their capsule was caught in a gigantic solar flare and hurled forward in time. They emerge into a world where Earth's only inhabitants are cloned females, the other half of the population having been destroyed by a global plague. The spacemen are rescued from their cramped capsule, which lacks sufficient fuel for a return to Earth, by the female crew of the spacious, ecologically self-sufficient explorer ship *Gloria*. But the women discover that even a year-long journey back to Earth is not adequate time to wean the males away from the patriarchal patterns of thought that constitute their only meaning in life. Engineer Bud Geirr, driven by severe penis anxieties, pursues the women aboard *Gloria* to the point of an attempted rape. Commander Norman Davis displaces his sexual drives into a religious authoritarianism that

eventually causes him to attempt a takeover of the rescue craft. And even the story's likable and well-meaning narrator, ship scientist Doc Lorimer, cannot escape behavioral anxieties stemming from a traumatic childhood incident in a girl's lavatory, which force him continually to prove to himself that "I'm not a girl. I'm a boy." The women aboard *Gloria* conclude that, while male aggressiveness may once have been necessary to "save society from the crazies," it now has little to contribute to their civilization. . . . In a world where "what males protect people from is largely other males," masculinity in the historical sense can only be considered a "disease," and the women aboard *Gloria* eventually administer to the astronauts what they consider the only possible "antidote." (pp. 49-50)

But although Tiptree rejects the historical role of the male as an aggressive patriarch, she also cautions against an exclusive acceptance of traditionally female behavior patterns such as intellectual noncompetitiveness or personal passivity. Tiptree believes that excessive emphasis on either sexual stereotype will retard the development of both the individual and his or her society. If males have been history's "guerillas," then women have been the "opossums . . . living in a toothless world," according to Ruth Parsons in the story **"The Women Men Don't See."** This work, narrated by hunter-fisherman Don Fenton, tells the story of a quartet marooned in the Quintana Roo by an airplane crash. As Don Fenton and Ruth Parsons hike through the wilderness seeking fresh water or human aid, Ruth gradually reveals the extent of her alienation from and sexual frustration with the twentieth-century, male-dominated world. "Men," claims Ruth, "live to struggle against each other; we're just part of the battlefield. It'll never change unless you change the whole world." The problem with maintaining this attitude, as Ruth discovers, is that it tends toward self-fulfillment, as its adherent becomes a passive survivor whose responses further reinforce the very alienation originally causing the problems. Indeed, so "alien" does Ruth become to Don that at a critical moment he wounds her rather than one of the extraterrestrial beings who have discovered the pair. Ruth Parsons escapes her victimization by some shrewd bargaining that secures for her and her pregnant daughter passage off Earth aboard the alien vessel, but this option hardly seems viable—even symbolically—to her fellow victims of twentieth-century masculine mistreatment. . . . Although Tiptree may ultimately be more sympathetic toward female passivity than toward male aggressiveness, she never endorses the "opossum" approach to life advocated by women characters such as Ruth Parsons.

Tiptree rejects all unibehavioral attitudes toward life because for her they invariably lead both the individual and his or her community to that form of psychological stagnation known as narcissism or selfishness. . . . [**"Her Smoke Rose Up Forever"**] clearly demonstrates the dangers inherent in any "me only" approach to life. Peter, the story's narrator, discovers through a series of painful flashbacks that he has always been so concerned with his own personal tragedies that he has never truly loved another person. . . . Peter finds that this powerful selfishness has changed each moment of possible life triumph into a bitter-tasting personal defeat, until at last his personality has become locked into an alien-invoked energy pattern in an eternity he most desperately longs to escape. Clearly, Tiptree insists upon the elemental need for getting beyond one's singular self.

Yet, somewhat paradoxically, Tiptree condemns the complete abandonment of that self. Her stories emphasize that it is the very incompleteness of the individual, his or her "haploid" condition, that produces human creative vitality. Just as Freud identified the pulse of life as originating from the irreconcilable struggle between order-loving ego and death-desiring id, so Tiptree sees our traditional male/female role divergences as symbolic of the life/death dialectic whose potential sparks all that we find meaningful in existence. Thus, Tiptree's fiction continually warns the reader away from any reductionistic solution that would destroy human potential simply by abandoning self-concern.

For example, Tiptree's short story **"She Waits for All Men Born"** depicts the final, fatal merging of the life and death forces that have powered human evolution from its beginning. Snow, a blind but immortal mutant girl with pale-white eyes, is born into a postholocaustic world where a slowly diminishing band of civilized humans battles a growing number of cannibalistic fliers who seek children for food. . . . Snow automatically reacts when threatened by telepathically destroying the danger with her blank, silver gaze. But since all living beings, whether friends or enemies, inherently pose a potential danger to her immortality, Snow finds herself eventually destroying all life within her immediate vicinity, until she finally becomes "the last human . . . wandering and waiting alone through the slow centuries for whatever may come from the skies." Through this figure of the eternal child, Tiptree warns the reader of the cold, lonely stasis that will result should humanity ever learn to reconcile its life-oriented and death-oriented impulses. (pp. 50-2)

If exclusive adherence to male or female behavior patterns is considered by Tiptree to be inevitably destructive and if she also believes that their distinctness is crucial to vitality in a species, what sort of behavioral ideal does Tiptree favor? How should the individual who wishes to develop physically, morally, and aesthetically proceed? Tiptree's answer seems to lie in a kind of pluralistic union of human sexual patterns. She favors a psychological synthesis in which both sexes retain their behavioral identities while simultaneously learning to appreciate and incorporate selectively the most important goals and attitudes of their sexual counterparts. Tiptree is not advocating some kind of bland, best-of-both-worlds abstraction; rather, she is seeking to delineate the kind of individuals who can be comfortable with their own sexual identities yet who can call upon the power arising from their own incompleteness to develop even in times of crisis. Perhaps the best illustrations of Tiptree's pluralistic ideal appear as the main characters in her longest work, the 1978 novel *Up the Walls of the World*.

Tiptree's novel takes place in three distinct locales. The first and most imaginative of these settings is the wind-swept planet Tyree, whose telepathic inhabitants live amid the turbulences of their world's upper atmosphere. . . . [Tiptree] gives the Tyrenni a highly developed aesthetic sense, appropriate to creatures who must be sensitive to the slightest wind variation, and this keen perception leads to many synesthetic reversals of human sensory experience. For example, the Tyrenni perceive all light as sound, and all emotions as combinations of colors and sounds, so that their sun is called "the Sound" and fear is always manifested as "a green squeal." Even the sexual act itself is reversed by Tiptree. Intercourse on Tyree involves a pair's achieving the utmost distance from each other while still maintaining contact, as opposed to our human desire for a close embrace. All these reversals spill over into behavioral modes, which was the primary reason Tiptree created them. For example, the women on Tyree are "naturally" considered their

race's explorers and providers, whereas the males are physically dominant enough to be "capable" of controlling and educating the children. Thus, the main Tyrenni character, the young lady Tivonel, considers her desires for freedom and adventure intrinsically feminine traits. . . . Conversely, Tivonel feels somewhat guilty about her "masculine" impulses to cherish her child or to pursue "domestic" tasks, such as logical speculative thought. . . . Tivonel's beloved, Giadoc, similarly combines a Tyrenni male mind of scientific discipline with a "motherly" desire for adventure and travel. Even as such mixtures of human behavioral norms encourage the reader to posit alternative possibilities for his or her own twentieth-century culture, they propel Tivonel and Giadoc into the only possible survival responses when crisis faces their planet.

A second set of chapters in Tiptree's novel takes place on present-day Earth, where Dr. Daniel Dann is providing cursory medical service to a small group of psychological "misfits" involved in an extrasensory perception project. . . . Dr. Dann, driven to drug addiction by a past failure to be "masculine" enough to rescue family members from a burning building, at first considers himself a complete failure as a human being since his only asset seems to be the rather worthless ability to sympathize with patients' pain and isolation. He longs for the scientific detachment to regard others as numbers rather than as persons, as his fellow doctors can. It is not until Dr. Dann can accept himself as both a powerful person and a sympathetic human being that he comes to understand the link between the pain of isolation and the joy of love. His is the universal personal predicament, as one of the poems he quotes to himself suggests: "What else, when chaos turns all forces inward to shape a single leaf?" Like many of his "misfit" patients, Dann eventually finds his apparent emotional liability a survival factor when cosmic rather than terrestrial perspectives become involved. A similar reversal also happens to the main female character on Earth, the computer analyst Margaret Omnali. . . . It is precisely her mixture of paternal logic and matriarchal protectiveness that eventually allows Omnali to assume control of a gigantic alien gas cloud apparently threatening both Earth and Tyree.

The third group of chapters is set within the huge gas cloud itself. And it is here that Tiptree most fundamentally posits the need for all life forms to maintain their pluralistic behavioral structures. The Destroyer, as the cloud is named by the Tyrenni, has a primitive form of self-consciousness that allows it to drift apart from synchrony with others of its kind. Feeling a profound guilt at this separation, the giant being searches through space, seeking a logical alternative to the task for which it feels it was formed but destroying whole worlds in the process. Eventually, its duty/guilt "intolerable stress" and its inherent "great contradiction of underlying realities" compels it to make itself vulnerable to the spirit of Margaret Omnali. She teaches it in turn never to allow the potential gradient of energy known as life to "fall to zero," and she eventually finds it a task worthy of its immense powers.

Tiptree's novel *Up the Walls of the World* is significant not only because it delineates thematically and individually the author's beliefs about the necessity for behavioral mixes but also because its use of stylistic devices such as synesthesia and multiple points of view forces readers to create within their own minds the kinds of psychological syntheses the book's own themes endorse. As a prelude to examining the ways in which Tiptree achieves these effects, let us first consider the following imagistic description:

We emerge dry-mouthed into a vast windy
salmon sunrise. A diamond chip of sun breaks
out of the sea and promptly submerges in cloud.

This colorful passage, which might be picturing the windy
world of Tyree but in fact is describing a sunrise over the
Quintana Roo in **"The Women Men Don't See,"** does a precise
job of externalizing the fragmented emotional feelings of its
narrator, Don Fenton. The description is torn between images
of sterility (such as "dry-mouthed," "windy" and "chip of
sun") and images associated with wetness and fecundity (such
as "salmon," "sea," and "cloud"). . . . These internal tensions within the short description mirror the internal strife Fenton feels as he suddenly finds himself isolated in a wilderness
and alienated from his sole female companion.

It is not an exaggeration to claim that the majority of Tiptree's
descriptions depend for their effect on a similar kind of internal
polarization of imagery. . . . [A] black-versus-white dichotomy
permeates the award-winning story, **"Love Is the Plan, the
Plan Is Death,"** in which a male alien creature confronts his
own and his race's aggressive impulses while he searches for
his destined mate. Tiptree will also employ other color contrasts. For example, the boy Timor in **"The Milk of Paradise"**
is continually torn between the pale pinkness of his human
ancestry and the drab grayness of the beings he has come to
admire on the planet Paradise, a conflict highlighted by the
emotional coldness of the pink world as opposed to the tender
warmth of the gray. But whether Tiptree employs a prominent
color contrast or a more subtle internal polarization of imagery,
her descriptions serve to externalize the tensions every individual faces by virtue of his or her incompleteness. Some
characters, such as Peter in **"Her Smoke Rises Up Forever,"**
never manage to resolve that incompleteness and hence remain
trapped in their "black-and-white" worlds forever. Others mistakenly select one pole of the dialectic only, such as Timor in
"The Milk of Paradise," who opts for the gray world of total
love but in the process gives up his inheritance as a civilized
human being. But the truly successful characters manage to
attain a plurality of color in their world visions. (pp. 53-7)

The job of science fiction authors is a difficult one, for the
very nature of this genre forces them to unite the power that
lies in scientific truth with the emotional wisdom that abides
in a fictional vision. By using the insights of psychology, which
combine the penetrating accuracy of science with the archetypal
significances of myth, James Tiptree, Jr., continues to form
imaginative creations that show us who we are as modern,
sexual, and human beings. (p. 59)

> *Adam J. Frisch, "Toward New Sexual Identities:
> James Tiptree, Jr.," in* The Feminine Eye: Science
> Fiction and the Women Who Write It, *edited by Tom
> Staicar, Frederick Ungar Publishing Co., 1982, pp.
> 48-59.*

NOEL PERRIN

When did science fiction become respectable? Was it in 1932,
when Aldous Huxley published *Brave New World*? Was it not
until the 1960s, when a whole constellation of major writers
appeared, such as Ursula Le Guin and Walter Miller (he wrote
A Canticle for Leibowitz) and, in Russia, Boris and Arkady
Strugatsky? Was it only in the late '70s, when the once-lowly
sf story began to appear in such august settings as the *New
Yorker*?

Or has it not happened even yet?

I think it has not happened even yet. Science fiction thrives—
millions read it—but it has not become fully respectable. There
are two quite different reasons. One is that most English professors continue to stand aloof, and it is they who in the long
run decide what counts as literature and what doesn't. (p. 1)

The other and much more important reason is that science
fiction, when it is most itself, disdains respectability. That is,
it prefers ideas to technique, practically anything to "art." If
it keeps an eye on the future, this is not for its own sake (will
I still be read in a hundred years? every poet asks anxiously)
but out of curiosity about the universe, concern for the world.

The work of James Tiptree, Jr., is a case in point. Tiptree is
a major science fiction writer. She looks more major all the
time. . . . Her work is odd and brilliant and occasionally sentimental; at no time is it safely respectable.

Take the first work of hers I ever encountered. That was a
novella called *A Momentary Taste of Being*, back in 1975. It
occurs on a spaceship called *Centaur*. For 11 years *Centaur*
has been in flight, looking for a habitable planet to which some
of the 20 billion people on earth can emigrate. Naturally there
are tensions on board: personal, political (the United States,
the Soviet Union, and China all have teams on board), even
physical. I found it utterly gripping. I *believed* in that voyage,
as I don't in the usual space odyssey. Yes, I kept saying; yes,
there would be psychosis like this; yes, these are real people—
and Tiptree's PhD in psychology shows in her incredible understanding of them, I would have added if I'd known then
that she had one. Yes, only a master writer handles language
so unerringly.

And then I came to the ending, and was shocked almost out
of my mind. The voyage of *Centaur* turned out to have a
purpose unknown either to the governments on earth which
had sent it, or to the 60-person crew. Put simply, the 60 human
beings are giant sperms, rushing to meet equally large ova on
the planet they have found. Crazy! Definitely not a respectable
idea. Bellow wouldn't use it, or Joyce Carol Oates, either.
And yet . . . one puts the novella down, not feeling that here
is a trick ending, but that here is an unusually daring metaphor
for the life force, or the evolutionary drive, or whatever it is
that uses human beings, that causes there to be so many billions
of us, so eagerly pushing outward.

Brightness Falls From the Air is Tiptree's second novel and
sixth book. It is just as odd as *A Momentary Taste of Being*,
and nearly as successful. Why only nearly? Chiefly, I think,
because Tiptree tends to do her best work in the middle range:
long short stories and short novels. *Brightness* runs to almost
400 pages. That provides room for a few more convolutions
than some readers will prefer.

The scene opens on the planet Damiem just as a ship is arriving.
The time is many thousands of years in the future. (pp. 1, 13)

Damiem is a planet with a terrible history. It is inhabited by
a winged race called the Dameii. They are not human or humanoid in ancestry—like most life forms on Damiem they
evolved from insects. But they *look* somewhat like human
beings with two sets of wings, and they are an intelligent and
gentle race, loving as parents, skilled as artisans.

One of their peculiarities—from our point of view—is that
emotion stimulates a set of glands on their backs. For each
emotion they secrete a slightly different exudate, much as for
each emotion we mostly assume a different facial expression.

Long ago, an early exploration party discovered that if a human being tastes the tiniest amount of this exudate, it produces sensations of bliss. They did not tell their government that, or even that they'd found a new planet; they simply went into business. Over the years they discovered that the sensation of pain gave the best variety of the liqueur which was now famous on many planets under the name Stars Tears. They and their successors devised wonderfully ingenious tortures for the Dameii, eventually discovering that agony mitigated with just a trace of joy produced the finest vintage of all.

Now wings happen to be Tiptree's own symbol for whatever is best about life, and pain for what is worst. In an early and wonderful story called **"Angel Fix,"** an alien visitor to earth defines a good person as one "to whom pain felt by others is real." . . .

The production of Stars Tears is thus about as criminal as something can be. When the Dameii are nearly extinct, a small warship happens to touch down, and its crew discovers what is going on. Most of them are killed in an impulsive rush to stop it—but reinforcements are sent, and the trade *is* stopped. That was perhaps 50 years before the time of the book.

Now the planet is a protected place, with a human administrator, a handsome middle-aged woman named Cory Estreel. The Dameii have made a comeback. Limited tourism is permitted. The ship that arrives in the first chapter brings 13 wildly assorted visitors, and launches five or six different plots. One, you can be sure, is an attempt to resume production of Stars Tears. One involves racial revenge. The third is Cory Estreel's own bizarre story, and so on. To my taste there is at least one plot too many.

And yet . . . Tiptree writes with so sure a hand that the book still succeeds. She can show you the human in the alien, and the alien in the human, and make both utterly real. By sheer narrative power she can *force* you to suspend disbelief and stay up half the night reading, as I did. And yet there are a thousand subtle touches, beginning with the triple play in the book's title, taken from a 17th-century poem. . . .

Brightness is not the book I'd advise a newcomer to commence Tiptree with. It's too big a mouthful. I'd start a beginner with her early collection of stories **Ten Thousand Light Years From Home** or perhaps with **Warm Worlds and Otherwise.** But then I'd unhesitatingly send him or her on to **Brightness,** as one might have sent an early European visitor on to Niagara Falls. Me, I finished reading it at 3:30 on a night when I had to be up at 7 the next morning. There are not many books I'd do that for. (p. 13)

> Noel Perrin, "James Tiptree Jr. and the Pleasures of Science Fiction," in Book World—The Washington Post, *February 24, 1985, pp. 1, 13.*

TOM EASTON

What a delight it is to turn to **Brightness Falls from the Air,** by that brilliantly warm writer, James Tiptree, Jr. . . . Here we have the world of Damiem, home of the winged Dameii, whose bodies exude a substance that can be processed into a marvelously euphoric drug. Unfortunately, the prime exudate appears only under emotional stress, especially pain, and most especially the pain of parents watching their children tortured.

Fortunately, the Federation military cleaned out the goons who were exploiting the Dameii. They also set up a small base for two people and a doctor to serve as protectors of the Dameii and hosts for the occasional visiting fireman. As the story opens, a party of such visitors is landing, come to watch the light show that will result when the wave of particulate radiation from a nearby nova strikes the atmosphere. The party includes . . . a disguised alien from the novaed system, seeking revenge on the humans who had done the deed to end a war, and a trio of baddies who plan to incapacitate everyone else and torment Dameii for the sake of the wealth they can gain.

Tiptree deftly portrays her characters and the forces that shape their various goals. She falters slightly only in that her villains are too much symbols of pure evil, and her Dameii are too much symbols of good. The latter symbolism she weakens to excellent effect when she draws a curious threat from the nova that illuminates her story, but the former she leaves intact. The rest of her people she draws more in the round, a little good, a little bad, the whole illumined with a most sympathetic eye.

Tiptree does indulge herself in one stylistic rarity, for she tells her story in the present tense. The effect is to distance the reader from the story, which is presumably why writers are so often warned against using it. But it works very nicely here.

I loved the story. May you also. (pp. 182-83)

> Tom Easton, in a review of "Brightness Falls from the Air," in Analog Science Fiction/Science Fact, *Vol. CV, No. 9, September, 1985, pp. 182-83.*

KEITH SOLTYS

[The plot of **Brightness Falls From the Air**] could be a summary of Agatha Christie's *Death on the Nile:* ten tourists are visiting a remote resort to witness a rare natural phenomenon. The natives are friendly but restless. Some of the tourists seem to have motives that are mysterious, if not illegal. Then there is a murder.

Now change the setting. The remote resort is the planet Damiem and the tourists are there to witness the passage of a nova wave front, a result of war between humans and the Vlyracochan. Cory Corso, proprietor of the resort, fought in that war and was a witness to the ghastly extermination of the aliens. . . .

Tiptree weaves a complex plot around this background. As the story progresses, it becomes clear that none of the characters are what they first seemed to be. Even the passage of the nova front, an event of great beauty, has unforeseen qualities. Tiptree strips away layers of illusion until what remains, at the heart of the novel, is a story of compelling power and pathos.

Tiptree uses an elaborate, baroque style appropriate to the involved story. Despite complexities the narrative is compelling and the book is more enjoyable than her first, **Up the Walls of the World.**

As good as the best of Tiptree's short stories, **Brightness Falls From the Air** is very good indeed.

> Keith Soltys, "Complex But Compelling," in Fantasy Review, *Vol. 8, No. 12, December, 1985, p. 22.*

BOB COLLINS

Three tales set on the easternmost coast of the Yucatan Peninsula, an area "officially but not psychologically" part of Mexico, are gathered [in **Tales of the Quintana Roo**] with a note from the author about the Maya Indians, descendants of the great native American culture destroyed by the Spaniards back in the sixteenth century, who form the dominant cultural influence in the tales. (p. 24)

"Most of the matter of the stories set down here is simple fact," says the author, and her evocation of life along "these jungly beaches" where flow "tides and ancient currents of great power" is both naturalistic and broodingly atmospheric. Dazzling sun and feverish heat easily concoct a veil of nostalgia: vanished glories, ancient passions, sensed rather than seen. All three tales concern the sea, all contain narratives within narratives—Tiptree supplies evocative settings in which tall tales may be rehearsed to great effect. Though something like a time warp operates in two of them, and nature's adaptive mimicry rises to terrifying extremes in a third, these tales are neither fantasy nor science fiction, but expressions of a strangely populous and multi-layered alien history, "four-thousand-year-old voices that whisper and murmur in the nights of the Quintana Roo." The book is a delicate pleasure, preserving a swiftly passing bit of exotic Americana. (pp. 24-5)

> Bob Collins, "A Master of Maya," in Fantasy Review, Vol. 9, No. 3, March, 1986, pp. 24-5.

JOHN CLUTE

[*Tales of the Quintana Roo*] has all the flavor of Tiptree but little of the meat, little of the tightrope-walking complexity of her more extended work, where one plot is never enough, nor one climax, nor one neat message. Generally, Tiptree is a writer of fiery acumen, psychologically acute, sharply compassionate. In *Tales of the Quintana Roo*, all set on the Caribbean side of the Yucatan Peninsula of Mexico, and all narrated by a protagonist who is clearly herself, this acumen and edge fade into a perfectly respectable—but slightly cloying—earnest piety. Her love for the area does come amply across, as do her ecological fears for its survival now that roads penetrate and gringoes surfboard its remotest reaches; but she has chosen to couch these concerns through three didactic fables in which the supernatural aura of the Quintana Roo raises warning ghosts and signals to the world above. The book is nakedly decent but mediocre as art. Compare the story **Beyond the Dead Reef** with **"The Last Flight of Doctor Ain"** (1969), and see the difference between immortal art and sermonizing.

> John Clute, "James Tiptree Jr.," in Book World— The Washington Post, April 27, 1986, p. 10.

D. DOUGLAS FRATZ

Since entering the field in 1968, James Tiptree, Jr. . . . has become one of science fiction's best authors, known for her hard-science sense of wonder as well as her humanistic sensitivity. A new novel by Tiptree is clearly an event worthy of note.

The Starry Rift, however, despite its billing as "the long-awaited sequel to *Brightness Falls from the Air*" (her brilliant novel published in early 1985), is neither new nor a novel. It is, rather, a collection of three novellas (all published elsewhere in the past year) set at later times in the same universe as *Brightness Falls from the Air.* All three are set in the great rift, an area of no stars and strange space-time distortions. Tiptree's attempt to make the book a novel takes the form of a frame around these novellas which has an alien librarian recommending the stories to aliens of yet another race to assist their

studies of human psychology. This frame adds little and is indeed somewhat distracting. *The Starry Rift* is best seen as a collection of three loosely related stories.

The first is *The Only Neat Thing to Do,* one of the best novellas of 1985. The protagonist is an intelligent and precocious teenage girl, a likeable and believable character. (Why are precocious, highly intelligent juveniles a mainstay in SF and almost totally absent in all other fiction?) This girl's first less-than-fully-authorized travels in her new spacecraft into the frontiers near the rift uncover a strange new alien species, leading to heroic tragedy.

The second story [*Collision*] is a fine suspense thriller featuring a very different protagonist—a hardened, middle-aged loner who spends most of his time in his spaceship in cold-sleep making a living in deep-space salvage and rescue. His efforts to outwit and subdue a group of "Blackworld" pirates who threaten him and the occupants of a luxury ship he has rescued . . . make for a tense and gripping tale.

The final story [*Good Night, Sweetheart*] is highly inventive space opera, once again involving first contact with a new alien species, this time from beyond the rift. The primary characters are a group of researchers in the first ship to cross the rift, and, as in *The Only Neat Thing to Do,* they must save mankind from the disastrous misunderstandings that first contacts may produce. This final story is marred somewhat by pulp science, some of it extraneous (long-range infrared readings used to detect aliens in cold-storage aboard a ship), and some crucial to the plot (the human heart stimulant digitalis just happens to work on an alien species with a totally non-aqueous biochemistry).

One would expect these three works with a common background to benefit from being read together in one volume, but such is not the case. For one thing, there are discrepancies which become more noticeable when they are read sequentially. For another, all three are written in present tense, which becomes annoying and distracting at book length. Overall, the sum is slightly less than its parts.

This is probably the least successful of Tiptree's books to date; but the worst of James Tiptree, Jr. is still very good indeed.

> D. Douglas Fratz, "Exploring the Rift," in Fantasy Review, Vol. 9, No. 7, July-August, 1986, p. 36.

GERALD JONAS

As one might expect from the woman who signs her science fiction James Tiptree Jr., *The Starry Rift* is a tricky piece of work. On one level, it presents itself as a latter-day space opera, replete with daring heroes, plucky heroines, nasty villains, inscrutable aliens, nonstop interstellar action, life-saving (and life-threatening) technology and a general air of wide-eyed wonder at the vast playground we call the universe. At the same time, the author has placed all this familiar material in a series of narrative boxes within boxes, so the space operatics are viewed through layers of distancing devices, fictionalized reports of transcribed tapes of official debriefings and so on.

Curiously, this apparatus serves an entirely different purpose in science fiction than it does in contemporary experimental fiction. Instead of drawing attention to the story as linguistic artifact, it adds verisimilitude by solving one of the oldest problems of far-future narration—how to fill in the reader on indispensable background information without cluttering up the telling with facts that the characters already know. Mr. Tiptree is aware that when people talk into machines, they not only speak more slowly and formally, they typically rehearse familiar knowledge, as if to make sure that the doubly distanced auditor (removed in time and in space) doesn't miss anything. Reading *The Starry Rift* is like listening to a long message left on an answering machine, telling you what someone did on an action-packed trip to the other side of the galaxy.

> *Gerald Jonas, in a review of "The Starry Rift," in*
> The New York Times Book Review, *August 10, 1986,*
> *p. 29.*

TOM EASTON

Dr. Alice B. (aka Raccoona) Sheldon (aka James Tiptree, Jr.) is well known for her many superlative SF stories, including several set on the Yucatan Peninsula of Mayan Mexico. Three of those stories appear in Tiptree's *Tales of the Quintana Roo*: *What Came Ashore at Lirios, The Boy Who Waterskied to Forever,* and *Beyond the Dead Reef.* The second is a tale of time travel via waterski and serendipity. The others express an environmentalist's dream of the sea's yearning for revenge against the humans who have despoiled and polluted its waters and reefs. All are memorable tales. . . .

[In *The Starry Rift*] Tiptree gives us three more tales (without credits), the excellent *The Only Neat Thing to Do,* in which a Podkayne-type (precocious) girl takes off for the Rift in her new starship, finds a species of strange and dangerous aliens, and must save the human realm; the only slightly less excellent *Good Night, Sweetheart,* in which a solitary driver of an interstellar towtruck must save his one-time darling, and the young clone of her clone, from pirates; and *Collision,* in which a naive crew of explorers finds the Ziello Harmony and must convince the aliens of human trustworthiness and peacefulness despite their bitter experiences with the Black Worlder pirates. I am half inclined to call *Collision* the best of the three, but it is marred for me by Tiptree's strange Ziellan biology; they breathe our air, with added carbon dioxide, and they respond to human drugs, but water is corrosive anathema, even though it rains on their world.

Tiptree and TOR pretend that *The Starry Rift* is a novel by giving the stories a frame set far in their future. University students visit the library to learn something of the human emergence into galactic civilization, and the genial librarian has dug out these three "gems." It fails to convince, the more so because it echoes a hundred similar pretences. I preferred *Tales of the Quintana Roo,* for though it offers fewer pages per dollar, it is a more honest book. It lets its stories stand alone.

> *Tom Easton, in a review of "Tales of the Quintana*
> *Roo" and "The Starry Rift," in* Analog Science Fiction/Science Fact, *Vol. CVII, No. 1, January, 1987,*
> *p. 183.*

LILLIAN M. HELDRETH

Ten years ago the works of James Tiptree, Jr., began to be widely published, and surprised and delighted readers encountered a fey new talent. . . . Tiptree's identity was a mystery: no such name was listed in either the Manhattan or the District of Columbia telephone directories, and one critic's only certainty was that Tiptree could no more be a woman than Jane Austen could have been a man. (p. 22)

Beginning to win top awards in the field and being essentially an honest person, he finally revealed himself to be Dr. Alice Sheldon, experimental psychologist. The faces of many who had been thoroughly fooled were distinctly red. Ursula Le Guin wisely admonished readers that the Tiptree phenomenon should make them think "about all our arguments concerning Women in Fiction, and why we have them; and all the panels on Women in Science Fiction . . . and all the stuff that has been written about 'feminine style,' about its inferiority or superiority to 'masculine style,' about the necessary, obligatory difference of the two. All the closed-shop attitudes of radical feminism. . . ." Not only should we think about these stereotyped literary attitudes, but also about our own attitudes and why they so completely mislead us.

Tiptree's style certainly helped us believe the masquerade. Witty, outrageous, and pungent, with the double cover of masculine narrators and a masculine pen name, the stories overwhelmed our better judgment. The dazzling style led readers to perceive the author as male, even when the subject matter was more extreme than Erica Jong's, the feminism more radical than that of Joanna Russ. In fact, the skill and invention in the narratives often obscured more serious themes. Huge, furry Moggadeet, hulking about and singing little songs to his lady love [in **"Love Is the Plan, the Plan Is Death"**], was charming, and the idea of humanoids who were diploid in one generation and haploid in the next [as in **"Your Haploid Heart"**] was fascinating. One tended to remember the delights of the extrapolations and forget that Moggadeet's mate devoured him alive, while the haploid humanoids were systematically exterminating their diploid fellow beings without realizing they were killing their own parents and children. The threads that thematically bind the stories are usually bloody. (pp. 22-3)

Another theme pervades all of Tiptree's work but is a major plot element in only five or six of them—feminism. Cloaked in the various masculine personae of her narrators, it is a feminism at once so bitter and so radical that it may be the root, or at least the beginning, of Tiptree's pessimistic worldview. Tiptree's women suffer. In her much-praised *The Girl Who Was Plugged In,* she gives us as protagonist a deformed girl who is persuaded to have her gross body made more ugly with electronic implants. Poor P. Burke then becomes the remote operator of a beautiful but brainless cloned body, sweet Delphi the model, who is used in advertising films. Vicariously, Burke becomes a beautiful person, playing opposite an actual handsome playboy, with whom she falls in love. At the same time, Delphi begins to develop a consciousness of her own and falls in love with the same man. The results are disastrous, as the playboy, who did not know his lover was a remote-control unit, kills them both in an effort to free Delphi from what he thinks is mind-control. Both P. Burke and Delphi suffer and die as victims of a society that uses women as disposable objects, neither of them perceived as human beings by the manipulators who use them.

The world is intolerable for women, Tiptree seems to say. They are victims of man's drives and desires, tools for his manipulation. (p. 23)

[In *Houston, Houston, Do You Read?,* a] genetic disease has resulted in no men being born; the women who survive the upheaval of those times have learned to reproduce themselves by cloning. They are a world of perhaps fifteen hundred individual genotypes in all. They have no central government and no wars. . . . [They exist as] a society of women, gentle, cheerful, and cooperative, making scientific progress in easy, humane stages. It is a utopia of sorts, but a very practical, earthy one, complete with its in-jokes, its music, and its legends.

Into this quiet world are hurled three male astronauts from the late twentieth century, thrown out of their place in time by a massive solar flare. They are rescued by a spaceship full of women, who do not tell them anything about their society, or even that the men have been long gone from it. So skillfully does Tiptree build the story from the point of view of one of the astronauts that the reader is in danger of sharing his reaction to what he can see of this society. David Lorimer finds the women interminably chatty, commonplace, and non-competitive. . . . By increments he learns the truth about his rescuers, and he is grieved and shocked, even though he, as the scientist on the mission, is not nearly so steeped in the masculine mystique as his captain and navigator. He is, in fact, considered more human by the women—but when he realizes that there are no more men at all, he, too, mourns the demise of all the competition and aggression that have made his life worthwhile. The story climaxes when the other two astronauts also learn that they have emerged into a world of women. Bud, the navigator, high on a truth-serum he has been given, attempts rape in zero-gravity, while one of the women films the performance and the victim tries to get a sperm sample in a baggie. The scene is both tragic and hilarious, with Bud fantasizing about the sexual delights of being the last man on Earth, until the captain appears with a pistol, ready to take over the ship in the name of God the Father. With regret, Dave Lorimer helps the women to subdue his leader. . . . (pp. 24-5)

The denouement is chilling. Dave accuses the women of having caused the crisis by giving the men a drug which disinhibits their normal aggressive fantasies. Lady Blue, the ship's senior person, points out wearily that aggressive fantasies do not exist in her society. . . . It is then that Lorimer realizes that he and his colleagues will not return to a delighted and welcoming Earth. They are superfluous, even dangerous. . . . Males, with their aggressive drives and their biologic need for dominance, have no place in a truly free and equal society. At the end of the story, Dave still does not know his exact fate. The drink he is given tastes "something like peace and freedom, he thinks. Or death." (p. 25)

[Tiptree] sees the plight of twentieth-century women to be both grave and frightening because the facts of human biology preclude real equality, not because women are inferior to men, but because sex is so tightly linked to violence for human males.

Tiptree writes several variants of the sex-violence theme. In some of them, there is merely a juxtaposition of sexual activity and violence or death; examples would be **"The Milk of Paradise,"** in which the mating at the end crushes a spectator to death, or **"Amberjack,"** in which a lovers' quarrel results in the woman's being pushed over a balcony to her death. . . . In **"Your Haploid Heart,"** [Tiptree] suggests that difference alone can be a basis for violence; the asexual phase of her humanoid aliens finds the sexual beings of the alternate generation so disgusting that the asexual people are engaged in extermination of the sexual ones. They have built a mythos which totally denies the fact that they are alternate generations of the same species. Their revulsion can be seen as paralleling the human male's perception of the female as filthy and evil, because her body functions so differently from his. But perhaps alienation can be overcome; Tiptree lets an expedition from Earth begin a process of reconciling the two races.

However, the violent ending of **"Love is the Plan, the Plan is Death"** is the result of more imperative causes. The protagonist-creature, Moggadeet, who is something like a cross between a woolly mammoth and a tarantula, must die as part of his reproductive cycle. He is portrayed as a being with a higher consciousness than most of his fellows, who have their whole being rooted in an instinctive following of "The Plan" of their lives. Moggadeet struggles to learn, to live as an individual, to act on his own initiative. But finally he mates with his beloved Lilliloo, only to become the food which sustains her through the winter of her pregnancy. In his last words, he accepts the Plan, and yet tries to pass on an observed warning. . . . Not only does Moggadeet perish: in all likelihood his race may perish too, for Lilliloo, caught in her own imperative of motherhood, may not pass on the information that their planet's climate is changing. Unless the individuals of the race can modify the Plan or go against it, they will be wiped out by the coming ice age.

Tiptree indicates repeatedly that biological imperatives, outlived or destructively modified, are deadly. Specifically, the human link between sex and violence may be a fatal natural law. *The Screwfly Solution* is a story which strikingly parallels Georges Bataille's assertion, in *Death and Sensuality,* that there is an "elemental violence which kindles every manifestation of eroticism," and also his belief that physical eroticism signifies "a violation bordering on death, bordering on murder." The title of the story refers to the practice of controlling insect pests by biological manipulation. It is possible to deplete whole populations by releasing hordes of infertile males to breed the females, or by spraying synthetic hormones which cause the insects to mate at an infertile phase of their growth cycle. In Tiptree's variation of the technique, aliens, who want to occupy Earth without destroying the environment, manage to release a hormone that modifies the human male sexual urge, turning erotic aggression to actual homicide. The result is an epidemic of rape-murders and an outbreak of religious fanaticism which glorifies cleansing the race of its filthy females. (pp. 26-7)

The aliens' "screwfly solution" works very well; when no women are left, the human males begin raping and killing each other. Move sex and violence just a bit closer together, make "snuff flicks" a reality and the extermination of the race results.

Tiptree seems to see no hope for feminist equality, no release from the bondage of violent sex, and no hope for the human race. In one story, **"The Last Flight of Dr. Ain,"** she implies that the race does not deserve to survive. Dr. Ain, a mild-mannered scientist, spreads a fatal plague, 100 percent effective, over the world because he wants to save the life of his true love, Earth herself. As he sees it, there is no need for the race's inevitable self-destruction through pollution or atomic holocaust to take with it all the other plant and animal lives. He dies happy, of his own plague, knowing he has saved the bears.

At least he succeeds in saving *something*. Tiptree protagonists who try to save their races usually fare worse, although their efforts are sometimes heroic. Mysha, in **"On the Last Afternoon,"** struggles [unsuccessfully] to save his stranded human colony from being crushed by sea monsters, for if their machines and computers are wrecked, the people will regress to stone-age ways or die off. . . . Added to the futility of his dying is his chilling realization that if he *could* save his people, he would preserve them only for more breeding and dying. (p. 28)

Sex equals death. Life equals death. In Bataille's words, "In the long or short run, reproduction demands the death of the parents who produced their young only to give fuller rein to the forces of annihilation." Tiptree devotes **"She Waits for All Men Born"** to exemplification of this principle, interweaving into the narrative long, italicised prose poems. . . .

Between parts of the prose poem, Tiptree traces evolutionary struggles: pelicosaurus, clawing its way to becoming a primate; early humans murdering their less-evolved brothers; the death-bred warriors of Europe, skilled in killing, decimating the Native Americans; Hitler exterminating Jews; the bombing of Hiroshima; the waging of full-scale nuclear war. At last we read the story of Snow, a radiation-mutated girl-child, whose white eyes radiate death. Beautiful and utterly deadly, Snow kills the last survivors of the atomic wars. She is reminiscent of Coleridge's "Nightmare life-in-death" as Tiptree describes her: "In her flesh the eternal promise, in her gaze the eternal doom, she will absorb all." She is "the final figure of humanity," life and death joined in "one imperishable crystal shape." (p. 29)

[Two] years after the publication of **"She Waits for All Men Born,"** Tiptree produced a novel, *Up the Walls of the World.* A full discussion of it is beyond the scope of this article, but in it Tiptree goes beyond the triumph of death to the existence of disembodied consciousness. In *Up the Walls of the World,* Earth and the planet Tyree are destroyed by cosmic forces; both Tyrennian and Terrestrial consciousnesses persist inside a great energy-being who sails between the stars. Shorn of bodies, and therefore of the sex roles that divided them, these beings become part of the energy creature, beginning a great task of exploring the universe. The entity they comprise is described at the novel's end as "A PROTO-PRONOUN, AN *IT* BECOMING *SHE* BECOMING *THEY,* A *WE* BECOMING *I* WHICH IS BECOMING MYSTERY."

The operative word is "mystery," for however intellectually unsatisfying the concept may be, the only way off the wheel of existence, the only direction beyond the angst, is through mysticism to that farther intangible state where certainty ends and "maybe" begins. It is heartening to know that Tiptree, who has the courage to look straight into the darkness of the human condition, has also the greater courage to look beyond it. At the same time, for those of us who would like to build utopias, feminist or otherwise, Tiptree's answer seems to be "not in this world." (p. 30)

Lillian M. Heldreth, "'Love Is the Plan, the Plan Is Death': The Feminism and Fatalism of James Tiptree, Jr.," in Extrapolation, *Vol. 23, No. 1, Spring, 1987, pp. 22-30.*

Frederick Turner

1943-

English-born American poet, novelist, critic, editor, and non-fiction writer.

Turner is noted for his use of a wide range of traditional poetic techniques through which he presents an English perspective of the positive and negative aspects of American culture. Many of his early poems collected in *Between Two Lives* (1972) document Turner's attempts to identify renaissance qualities of North American society for British audiences. Turner's later book-length narrative poems, *The Return* (1981) and *The New World* (1985), are composed of irregularly accented meters that display his agility with sprung rhythm and enjambment and have elicited comparisons to the work of Gerard Manley Hopkins. These pieces also mark Turner's efforts to create twentieth-century verse epics. In *The Return*, an American journalist is imprisoned by opium smugglers in Southeast Asia. He escapes and journeys through Indochina, nostalgically reminiscing throughout his travels about his native country. In *The New World*, Turner employs science fiction elements to depict the social structure of the United States in the twenty-fourth century.

In addition to his poetic accomplishments, Turner has written a critical study, *Shakespeare and the Nature of Time* (1971), and a science fiction novel, *A Double Shadow* (1978). *Natural Classicism: Essays on Literature and Science* (1985) reflects Turner's preoccupations with philosophy, linguistics, natural and biological sciences, and literature. Turner also served as editor of the *Kenyon Review* from 1978 to 1982.

(See also *Contemporary Authors*, Vols. 73-76; *Contemporary Authors New Revision Series*, Vol. 12; and *Dictionary of Literary Biography*, Vol. 40.)

PETER COOLEY

[Frederick Turner's *Between Two Lives*] speaks from a voice which is more the poet's own than any place he came from or finds himself in, much as he makes of the importance of location. Turner maintains a difficult balance on the axis of the two-life dichotomy which magnifies his perspectives as the volume proceeds: England-America (especially California), body-soul, artificial vs. organic life, microcosm-macrocosm. His best poems (and here I speak of the majority of the poems in the book) are extended mediations not on subjects but in pursuit of them: there is little of the set-piece here.

The dust jacket tells us Turner has published a critical work, *Shakespeare and the Nature of Time*; temporality and transcendence are among his poems' obsessions. Some of his formulations are intriguing ("compromise, after all, need only be incarnation" or "All that / which properly occupies us, takes a second and a half"), but here and there strain appears: the context can't support the questions thrown to it and Turner's wonder seems Wordsworthian in the worst sense: *faux naif.*

Courtesy of Frederick Turner

However, the poems at the end of *Between Two Lives* are especially noteworthy: **"The Frontiersman," "The Search for Tom and Lucy," "Libbard's Last Case."** Each of these long works avoids occasionalness by playing with reality-illusion. Turner becomes the Prospero-like arranger of phenomena or, as an actual character, the detective of the last poem. Here, in the causality of life, not art, we begin with knowledge of the characters; then they are depleted for us at the poem's end, folded up like Thackeray's marionettes or the elements in *The Tempest*.

> Peter Cooley, "Turning, Turning: 7 Poets Moving In and Moving Out," in Michigan Quarterly Review, Vol. XIII, No. 1, Winter, 1974, p. 82.

LEROY SEARLE

[*Between Two Lives*] refers to the fact that Turner, born and educated in England, has been living and teaching here for several years; but the quality of "between-ness" is not confined to the duality of cultural experience. The poems themselves are composed with subtle blendings of verse and prose, as in **"Poem"**, in confessional and almost hortatory stances as in **"The Birds"**; there are biographical, almost documentary meditations, together with delightful run-away narratives. All of this leaves a lot to straddle; and Turner is acutely aware of the demands of craft, crafty though he sometimes seems. One is aware of a nervous tuning of different styles, and a penchant for pursuing metaphors into kinky mixtures of social comment, metaphysics, and self-conscious fantasy. (pp. 356-57)

These tense poems show time and again that Turner understands the mind to be far from gentle, whether it is seen in the privacy of meditation or in collective outcroppings of "gross power"; and the mind is never more than a millimeter or a word away from violence. The underlying "between-ness" in these poems is an intuition that poetry comes from visions of the monstrous, whether seen or unseen, that must be warped away from terrible consequences by acts of imagination. "There are some things in us, very deep down, that we look at sometimes in horror, but which contain the seeds of what we most truly are", he says in **"Poem"**; and there too, he sees that even the act of writing poems can be monstrous. . . . But in a poem like **"The Birds"**, Turner arcs between visions of savage violence and an earnestly tender desire for peace, trying by means of poetry to learn not to be trying so hard.

The tensions of this book are manifest, frequently uncomfortable; and it is not an easy book to like. But it is one that imposes an uneasy vision important to look at. When one remembers the last few poems, especially **"The Actor to the Audience"**, **"The Cave"**, or **"Libbard's Last Case"**, where Turner is riding high with interesting personae, delightful narrative and fantasy, and then looks back at the marvellous opening poem, **"Deep-Sea Fish"**—"This devil we have drawn up / Will not let us go unless we bless / And bestow what kindness we can feel upon it"—what is in between seems far less uncomfortable to read. One would like to think that the next book will be more comfortable on the ground level. (p. 358)

> Leroy Searle, "Craft and Vision: Six Poets," in Poetry, Vol. CXXIII, No. 6, March, 1974, pp. 356-58.

THE TIMES LITERARY SUPPLEMENT

Perhaps the American quarrel between poetry and eloquence receives a flickering illumination from the example of Frederick Turner [in **Between Two Lives**]. Except in fantasy, Mr Turner provides little violence or barbarism and does not limit his language to colloquial idiom. He is a cosmopolitan young Englishman, educated at Oxford, who has settled down in Ohio. As a poet he shows an acute sense of the cliché, in word and gesture, and an agreeable attention to smells. His best poems are short, and in them he illustrates what distinguishes his literary tribe from that of most American poets. This is the location of his voice as a poet in the evolution of his character.

In an expansive mood, Mr Turner dwells on the freakishness of a poet's vocation. But the way he himself speaks still goes back to the landscape, smells, and sounds of his childhood. In the States he naturally finds the exotic where few Americans have seen it. Chicago for him means a bar in the Greek quarter—"the / heat of the tomcat, furry, gentle drunken night / moist air from the deep gulfs of the Midwest / the steaming gullies, the moist hilltops / a smell of moussaka and chemicals". This is hardly how David Wagoner remembers Chicago. For Mr Turner, Santa Barbara is "a strange city, built on the western seaboard of a / continent, under a foreign light of blue / weather one would never expect of a familiar place". Precisely because he is a stranger, the poet feels akin to the strangeness of the place.

But even while he surveys the mores he has abandoned, Mr Turner is willing to echo Keats and Arnold. The impulse that drove him to write poems was not destructive of his inherited culture and language. For many Americans, to be a poet is to bury one's own history in universal history, or to substitute for a shaping vision the features of a place one has moved to. They try to cleanse their language of the culture that nursed it, to make it discontinuous with their origins. As poets they wish to be at home elsewhere, in the subliterary, the primitive. For Mr Turner, art and personal history are deeply connected.

> "Poetry by the Yard?" in The Times Literary Supplement, No. 3760, March 29, 1974, p. 339.

GEORGE STEINER

The Return is a gripping tale of adventure, of broken pontoons and ice-fields, of hunters and fatigue. With the authority of obviousness, Fred Turner reclaims for poetry its antique privilege of heroic action, its right and, perhaps, primal compulsion to tell a story more sharply, with more economy than can that later idiom which is prose. **The Return** has the uncanny spectral concreteness, the high mountain light passing through objects yet giving them a vibrant presentness, which marks Turner's science-fiction. But it is, of course, far more than a concentrated epic of search and of homecoming.

It is a poem about radical politics, the politics at the root of our western condition. It is a critique, none the less poignant for its wryness, of 'the barbarians who don't see themselves as barbarians', of the massacres which inhabit our jaded imaginings. **The Return** is a poem about the leaps of new sensibility, of logic transcended or made playful, which, paradoxically, may be found both in the ancient disciplines of meditation (the Orient in the mind) and in the newest zones of biology and of physics. And **The Return** is, for all its pain, a celebration, an attempt to involve its reader in "the full gaiety of their art of belief" which the narrator experiences in the high cold air and gong-strokes of his venture. Finally, **The Return,** is, in the richest, most traditional sense, a prothalamion, a song sung before and in honour of a nuptial (its points of contact with Spenser are real). It is an account of an education to love. There is no richer schooling.

Wanted: the reader's trust. Reward: a new guest in the house of one's own being and awareness. (pp. v-vi)

> George Steiner, in a preface to The Return by Frederick Turner, Countryman Press, 1981, pp. v-vi.

WILLIAM LOGAN

Science fiction is a version of pastoral, more dependent on Theocritus than space travel. Like pastoral, its simplicities are deceptive. The attractive ease with which complex social ideas can be inserted into simple characters has ensnared many authors. In **The New World**, Frederick Turner has conceived a grand and grotesque ambition, an epic poem that fuses science fiction with medieval romance, finding in the future the grim corruptions of the present and from those corruptions forging an idyll.

The poem opens four centuries in the future, in the year of the sexcentennial of the United States. The oil and gas reserves, the uranium deposits and the mineral resources have been exhausted. The world has been depopulated by immigration to distant planets and the slaughter of the middle class. The great nation-states of the 20th century have been whirled into the vortex of history, the Union of Soviet Socialist Republics collapsing into its ethnic groups, Japan into its company families, Europe into the catchment areas of its soccer teams. In the United States, now called the Uess, the cities have become Riots, lawless matriarchies that feed off the slave labor of the suburbs. Outside are only Mad Counties and Free Counties— the former, fundamentalist theocracies, constantly warring against the latter, Jeffersonian democracies. (p. 14)

The conventions are familiar but, however ingenious the adaptation of American geography to epic mythology, an epic relies on the telling more than the tale. Mr. Turner . . . has a theory of prosody, though the practice has proved considerably more difficult than the preaching. The difficulty of the long poem in our century has been to fashion a verse line adequate to the diversity of incident and tone such a poem demands. When the verse of *The New World* is confined to the luxuriance of nature or the special effects of battle, it has the texture and visual attention derived from its particular details. Given the poet's philosophical and literary ambition, the practice elsewhere produces a line indistinguishable from prose and therefore almost incapable of subtlety as a poetic medium. The opening invocation implicitly announces the limits of invention that elsewhere afflict the work:

> I sing of what it is to be a man and woman in our time.
> Wind of the spirit, I should have called upon you long
>   ago
> but you would have me gasp, draw dust for breath,
> weep without tears, spoil the tale in its telling,
> wander an emigrant where no garden grows
> before you'd take me back into the bosom of your
>   word.

Mr. Turner's real epic interests are not in what his talent can manage, but in the ethics and social organization of his new world. After the first sweep of narrative, the poem stalls to allow long tracts of genealogy and the complete college education of Ruth Jefferson McCloud, the heroine. The lengthy lessons in future legal history, economy, religion and art are introduced with all the literary suggestiveness of a sociology text. . . . Few poets can successfully versify a legal code. Mr. Turner has failed to understand the essence of both epic and science fiction: their worlds are called into being in response to dramatic action. The drama provides the social detail with its necessity and suggests an entire world of which narrative reveals only a part. Mr. Turner is so enamored of his fanciful contrivances that he cannot bear to leave any of them out. For all the effort and text expended on the complicated social foundation, it is of remarkably little concern to the tale. The elaborate caste system of the Free Counties proves almost irrelevant. No one is inconvenienced by it; no battles are lost because of it. (pp. 14-15)

The New World thieves shamelessly from many sources, including *Beowulf, Burnt Njal's Saga, The Odyssey,* the story of Abraham and Isaac, virtually the whole range of myth and romance. Kingfish, the hero's black mentor who inhabits the old subway system beneath Hattan Riot, is of course the Fisher King with his secret wound, and [James Quincy] is the Perceval who must relieve him by asking the proper question. His homely philosophy is rendered arcane by an accent not much employed since the casual racism of dialect novels. . . . The ludicrous effect of this clash of dictions suggests the high comedy to which Mr. Turner's epic is accidentally subject.

The New World is of course only our own culture drawn and distorted. Science fiction ages gracelessly because its projections are helpless and automatic. Transient contemporary phenomena, not current so much as *au courant,* are blown into the social organizations of the future, and a reader can everywhere trace today's concerns in tomorrow's guises. Mr. Turner has the original theory that the mere imagining of this romance guarantees or at least influences a better future. The science fiction of the 1940's and 50's did not guarantee us a better present, and there is little reason to suppose current science fiction will have much effect on the future. Science fiction is wish fulfillment of the most nakedly adolescent sort and, although the best of it has wit and intelligence, to imagine that it has serious cultural or literary consequences is wishing beyond fulfillment. Unfortunately, Mr. Turner seems to have created, not an epic that will "serve as an opening to a postmodern creative era," as he says, but a classic of camp literature. (p. 15)

William Logan, "In the Medieval Future," in The New York Times Book Review, *October 27, 1985, pp. 14-15.*

ALFRED CORN

Frederick Turner's *The New World* calls for a special welcome at the very least because it attempts something unusual. Contemporary poetry is overwhelmingly a matter of the short lyric, usually written in the first person and the present tense. A talent as restless and challenging as Turner's wouldn't have been content with that limitation for long. Although he has written lyrics, he is also the author of a science-fiction novel, *The Double Shadow,* and *The Return,* a book-length narrative poem about drug traffic in Cambodia. . . . Despite all this, *The New World* comes as a surprise. Turner's subtitle describes it as "an epic poem," and in fact what we get is a six-part science-fiction poem running nearly 200 pages. (p. 38)

[Turner explains] why he has chosen to cast his narrative in verse rather than prose. In fact, I did wonder why it wasn't written as a novel, considering the success enjoyed by post-Armageddon works like Russell Hoban's *Riddley Walker* or Denis Johnson's *Fiskadoro,* or even the Mad Max movies. Turner says that he needed the resources of "meter, image, symbol and allusion; the poetic freedoms offered by figurative language and compression; the mysterious affective forces of dream and vision; and the poetic power to change the very ground rules of the game." Except for meter, all these are available for contemporary fiction (even meter: whole paragraphs of *The Waves* are written in iambic). In any case, Turner's metric is a special variant, an accentual line based on five main stresses, the unaccented syllables falling as they may. I think I can scan most of the stresses as he intends, even though the longer lines leave room for doubt. But the overall impression the poem makes is not metrical. Though meter is "legally" present, it doesn't help decipher the meaning or enhance what the text is saying, except as a faint background drumbeat.

The most engaging aspect of the poem is its story and its invention of a future. We're to imagine a globe that has exhausted its fossil fuels and metallic ores; an America with no central government but instead local dominions, falling into four categories—the Riots (lawless urban matriarchies with an idle, drug-addicted populace), the Burbs (middle-class communities enslaved to the Riots), certain Mad Counties (agrarian theocracies based on fundamentalist Christianity), and Free

Counties. . . . I suppose it's this last group that Turner holds out as a hopeful alternative to our fears of the world that may be in store for us; otherwise, his portrait of the future is appalling, a sardonic exaggeration of some present-day ills.

Of course Turner knows that his audience will identify with the Free Countians. When we read medieval romances, do we ever fail to assume that we would belong to the knightly classes rather than the peasantry of the world into which we fancifully transport ourselves? In the case of *The New World,* prospective Free Countians must be prepared to defend themselves with electronic swords and "resinite" shields, sometimes with lasers, and always with bodily agility and native cunning. The Mad Counties are known for proselytizing at swordpoint, and in fact, much of the poem is taken up with battles in the Mad Counties' latest jihad against the Free. Turner is no more compelling at the depiction of warfare than most other poets; and we may decide, as we glide along, to handle the battle scenes as we do the *Iliad*'s when we reread it. But Turner could have hardly dared to call his work an epic without them, and they play a creditable role in the unfolding narrative. (pp. 39-40).

Most of the trappings of quest romance can be found in the narrative, at least if we are adept at recognizing archetypes. Example: the wise old centaur or mentor who sets the young hero on his path is, in this poem, an extra-large black sage named Kingfish, who speaks in a dialect not heard since the old "Amos & Andy Show." Archetypes for Turner often take the form of stereotypes. James Quincy's Mercurial road companion turns out to be one Maury Edsel, a traveling salesman who, with his streetwise patter, white shoes, wiliness, and double knits, represents what some people think of as being typically Jewish. Here's some of "Skip's" speech:

> No shit. You're in a whole heap of trouble.
> Take my advice and go back. They won't
> mess with you here, but further out west
> it's a sick elephant's toilet.

This doesn't so much bring on future shock as a sense of banality. Turner had led us to expect more from the year 2376.

No romance can operate without a fair lady, and *The New World* offers us Ruth McCloud, a sturdy young lawyer and political candidate. It is through marrying her (after some trials of strength and wit) that young James wins back his status in Mohican County. But the marriage doesn't solve everything. A subtle but ruinous barrier separates them even in wedlock. During one of her campaigns Ruth encounters an old flame and—but this should be enough to give an idea of the plot of Turner's romance. It *is* a romance, not an epic. Not that the distinction actually makes a difference to any page-by-page reading of the text. The intrinsic value of the descriptions, character analyses, and battle scenes is in no way altered by the rubric placed over the poem.

Naturally anyone would like to be the author of an epic; but perhaps Turner's poem is more likable if we come to it without large-scale expectations. At some level he seems himself aware that he has written an entertainment in verse and not a great epic. (p. 40)

Alfred Corn, "Post-Armageddon Romance," in The New Republic, *Vol. 193, No. 22, November 25, 1985, pp. 38-40.*

ROBERT B. SHAW

Subtitled "an epic poem," [*The New World*] takes place in the sadly altered United States of four hundred years in the fu-

ture. . . . It's curious how old-fashioned the future is made to sound. Women and blacks especially will find Turner's conception more retrograde than futuristic. His new world is one in which women accept in marriage men who kill wild boars for them. It is also one in which an oracle called Kingfish holds court in the ruins of the New York subway system, uttering pseudo-profundities in a language like that of his namesake in "Amos 'n' Andy." "Love de game, boy," he tells the hero, a youth even more vapid than Luke Skywalker. "De flesh be de life / ob de spirit, an' de spirit be all a game." Four hundred years, evidently, haven't brought philosophy forward very much.

Turner's plot is spasmodic, and his characters, who are meant to recall the heroic scale of figures in epic and myth, have rather the glaring unreality of people in Robinson Jeffers. What really makes *The New World* hard going, though, is the verse. Reading it is like slogging through quicksand. For long stretches it is barely distinguishable from prose, and it features throughout some of the most ill-considered enjambments lately seen in print. (pp. 47-8)

There may be a certain mandarin pleasure in identifying the *topoi* Turner has so freely helped himself to. Oh yes, we say, there's that speech from *The Battle of Maldon,* or whatever. But the use made of these nuggets is so facile that his adaptations seem more a travesty of their grand originals than a tribute to them. In the twenty-fourth century, Turner tells us, "the old distinction between art and technology's gone, / and so too that between poems and advertisements." That a university press should have published this hapless farrago will be taken by some as a sign that such esthetic confusions are already far advanced. Meanwhile Homer, Virgil, and Milton continue to await further company on the upper slopes of Parnassus. It must be getting lonesome after all these centuries— and never yet a chance for a game of bridge. (p. 48)

Robert B. Shaw, in a review of "The New World," in Poetry, *Vol. CXLVIII, No. 1, April, 1986, pp. 47-8.*

MARK JARMAN

Daryl Hine and Frederick Turner have given us two book-length narrative poems that say a lot about how narrative poetry is currently conceived. Besides the fact that both are, in the end, quite readable, they also have historical importance.

For all its science-fiction prose and phoney behavior of characters (an over solicitousness for feminine propriety, for example, especially with regard to obscene language), for all its space opera and pseudo-medieval mores, which we are to assume we will return to after the apocalypse and the oil wells run dry, for all its pretentious mixing of traditional myths and legends, including Siegfried and Brünnhilde, Sohrab and Rustum, Arjuna and Krishna, Odysseus and Nausicaa, Arthur and Modred, Adam and Eve, and finally even the Jonestown mass suicides, for all this machinery to present us a single warrior-savior, an Oedipus as Christ, Frederick Turner's epic poem [*The New World*] is quite a read, absorbing and atrocious, tasteless and tactless, bloodcurdling and inconsistent (the invented language and coinages of the recent post-apocalypse novel *Riddley Walker* are more successful). There are moments that make a reader wince, but times, too, when one is in the presence of real epic poetry and feels what the first auditors of Homer may have felt.

Yet the adrenalin that gets pumping through the vascular reader at the climactic end of *The New World* is no different than that secreted by reading a fast-paced potboiler. The so-called prosody Turner claims to be following really isn't demonstrable. The characterizations are often ludicrous, especially the retro-Nigger Jim speech of the Kingfish, the Krishna-like presiding deity over the poem's final internecine battle. Still, if we are to have a resurgence of narrative poetry, then a work like this should have a place in it, just as science fiction has a place more and more in serious fiction. I don't really believe Turner's intention is to capitalize on the *Star Wars* hokum that James Merrill refers to in a cover blurb, nor is it to write a kitsch epic, taking the risk others like Turner Cassity and Peter Klappert have of turning kitsch into culture rather than reducing culture to kitsch. Too much in Turner's poem is in earnest, too little is humorous, the entire enterprise is solemn. As one who watches recent developments in narrative poetry, I read Turner's poem with chagrin, asking myself if this is, in fact, what one thinks of when one considers a contemporary epic? Must the dim past return as science fiction? Must the narrative poem of epic length be resurrected as pulp? It could very well be that a poem like Turner's, in which action and character are of heroic dimensions, is where it all has to start, again. (pp. 343-44)

Mark Jarman, "Singers and Storytellers," in The Hudson Review, *Vol. XXXIX, No. 2, Summer, 1986, pp. 343-44.*

TOM EASTON

Poetry is foreign to my usual tastes. . . . But some things transcend taste and the distinction between prose and poesy. I have before me a piece of science fiction so marvelous that if it were a novel, it might well cop the Hugo and the Nebula both. However, though it was published in 1985, none of us heard of it in time for the voting. We need a special award for such occasions.

What am I talking about? It's Frederick Turner's *The New World.* It's an epic poem, of all things. And it may be the first volume of poetry in many decades to warrant mass market publication. Bluejay, Bantam, NAL, TOR, take note. I can't believe you could lose by grabbing the paperback rights.

We usually think of epic poetry as in the style of *Beowulf,* the Norse sagas, Tolkien, and their ilk. They are set-pieces for archetypes, oral comic strips, akin to grand opera, their background replaced by thunderous music. Their lines are strongly rhythmic, their stories painted in bold primaries, their villains unmistakable, their heroes golden.

Turner has chosen a more modern verse form, "an enjambed long line divided by a caesura," of which the classic iambic pentameter is a special case. As a result, it is difficult to read his lines aloud in the sing-song so easy with the *Aeneid* or *Beowulf.* The rhythm is almost that of prose.

Turner improves on the classics in other ways as well. His characters are as boldly drawn as any of the past, but he fills in much more of the background, as perhaps he must if he chooses to write an SF epic. . . .

Turner has given himself some grand material. There are conflicts of ideology and of personality, of good and evil. There are echoes of myth, of Homer, of Beowulf. There is high heroism, and love, and sacrifice. And there is beauty—I think of a lyrical paean to the seasons in Mohican County. There is . . . There is poetry as poetry should be, but too rarely is.

I recommend this book as heartily as I possibly can. You are criminally remiss if you deprive yourself of the experience it offers.

Tom Easton, in a review of "The New World," in Analog Science Fiction/Science Fact, *Vol. CVI, No. 12, December, 1986, p. 178.*

Tarjei Vesaas

1897-1970

Norwegian novelist, short story writer, dramatist, poet, and scriptwriter.

A prominent figure in Scandinavian literature, Vesaas was one of Norway's most celebrated contemporary novelists. In his fiction, Vesaas combined realistic details with abstract, often symbolic imagery and characterizations to explore questions of personal guilt and ethics. His most acclaimed works, written in a lyrical, pictorial prose style, examine such themes as humanity's relationship to nature, the damaging effects of psychological isolation, and the need for human companionship. According to Kenneth G. Chapman, Vesaas does not "tell a story in the traditional sense of the word, but presents, for the reader's intuitive acceptance, an image, or series of images, which expresses his impression of a life situation." Although occasionally faulted for obscure mysticism, Vesaas is praised for his evocative language and his ability to examine universal concerns within a distinctly regional context.

Vesaas spent much of his youth and early adult life in Telemark, a southern region of Norway where traditional folk legends and rural art have flourished. Myth and folklore are evident in Vesaas's early allegorical novels, which reflect the influence of both romanticism and realism and address such Christian concerns as penance, sacrifice, rebirth, and salvation. In *Menneskebonn* (1923), a woman relinquishes her love for one man in order to save the life of another. When the woman dies in a blizzard, the two men share their grief by erecting a cross in her honor. Sacrifice and salvation are again prominent issues in *Sendemann Huskuld* (1924), in which a man seeks a child to give meaning to his life but instead decides that his purpose is to communicate universal love to humanity. *Dei svarte hestane* (1928) is an uncharacteristically melodramatic novel about a young boy's withdrawal from reality due to the marital disputes of his parents. Vesaas attained significant critical recognition in Norway with *Det store spelet* (1934; *The Great Cycle*), a lyrical work in which a young man attempts to flee the farm life he associates with death before resolving his fears through an understanding and appreciation of the natural cycle.

Many critics contend that Vesaas responded to the forces of Nazism and Fascism threatening Norway and other European countries at the advent of World War II by rejecting the rural, personal themes of his early works to examine ethical conflicts. His novels composed during this period utilize a straightforward, poetic prose style and approximate Norwegian dialect through such techniques as parataxis and ellipsis. *Kimen* (1940; *The Seed*), a surreal novel inspired by the Nazi invasion of Norway, transforms the story of a young girl's senseless murder and the resulting mob execution of her mentally unstable killer into a concise study of individual responsibility and group violence. *Huset i mørkret* (1945; *The House in the Dark*) is an allegorical novel that reveals the varied reactions, ranging from escapism to opportunism to covert resistance, of Norwegian people to the Nazi occupation of their country.

Following World War II, Vesaas retained his emphasis on symbolism and allegory but favored a more abstract blend of expressionism and realism. In *Vårnatt* (1954; *Spring Night*),

an adolescent boy is forced to mature both psychologically and emotionally when a circle of social outcasts invades his family's home after he is left alone with his sister. *Fuglane* (1957; *The Birds*) explores the mind of Mattis, a retarded man who is cared for by his sister in a rural village. Although Mattis finds happiness through his relationship with nature, he recognizes the burden he represents to his sister when she falls in love with a young lumberjack, and he sacrifices his own life to insure her future happiness.

Vesaas's later works again examine conflicts involving emotional maturity and personal responsibility. *Is-slottet* (1963; *Palace of Ice*) centers on Siss, an extroverted girl whose shy friend, Unn, is ostracized by her classmates. When Unn disappears, presumably trapped in a cavernous frozen waterfall she is known to frequent, Siss finds herself unable to accept the situation until she forgives her fellow students and accepts their sympathy and understanding. In *Bruene* (1966; *The Bridges*), a young couple discovers a dead infant in the woods and decides to take responsibility for locating the child's mother. Vesaas's last work, *Båten om Kvelden* (1968; *The Boat in the Evening*), follows the emotional growth of an unnamed character from adolescence to adulthood. According to Joseph Meledin, Jr., the details of this novel "are sharp though lyrical, telling though evocative, clinical though mysterious. . . . [Vesaas] reduces the interplay of man and man and of man and nature to their bare metaphoric and symbolic essentials.''

Vesaas also authored poetry, dramas, short fiction, and scripts for radio and television. His verse, which examines such topics as individual responsibility and humanity's interaction with nature, is contained in the volumes *Kjeldene* (1946), *Leiken og lynet* (1947), *Løynde eldars land* (1953; *Land of Hidden Fires*), and *Ver ny, vår draum* (1956). Vesaas's best-known play, *Ultimatum* (1934), anticipates his fiction written during World War II in its examination of the different responses of Norwegian youths to the imminence of war. Vesaas's stories, which correspond thematically and stylistically to his novels of various periods, are collected in such volumes as *Klokka i haugen* (1929), *Leiret og hjulet* (1936), *Vindane* (1952), and *Ein vakker dag* (1959). *Collected Short Stories* (1966) showcases translations of representative tales from throughout Vesaas's career.

(See also *Contemporary Authors*, Vols. 29-32, rev. ed. [obituary].)

JAMES WALTER McFARLANE

From the point of view of style, Vesaas's work from his début at the age of twenty-six with a short novel entitled *Children of Men* (*Menneskebonn,* 1923) up to the present day offers the record of one who has sought unremittingly to discipline his style. He made his mistakes early, and profited by them; his first novel was refused by the publishers and was thrown on the fire, presumably along with some of the bad habits that had contributed to it; nor was it his only rejection in these early years. But the year after his début, he published *Messenger Huskuld* (*Sendemann Huskuld,* 1924), a novel which, in spite of its digressiveness and sentimentality, was not without power to move. The adverse criticism that greeted his next three works (two dramas and a novel) perhaps convinced him that some things might be written too easily, for his next work did not appear until 1928, a novel *The Black Horses (Dei svarte hestane),* where the tighter control over the composition and the language is at once apparent. It is only now, however, at this distance in time, that one can see not merely that this was the beginning of a process, but also *how* it was; how it was a *point de départ* in the sense that the road Vesaas subsequently followed meant a steady departure from the realistic style it affected rather than a following up; it was, as it were, an exercise that required to be completed before the author could move on. From this point he followed a quest for new ways of adding to the allusiveness and suggestiveness of his words without destroying (and indeed where possible enhancing) the terse economy of his methods; his task was to fine everything down in the greatest possible degree, to increase the efficiency of his communication in a kind of engineering sense by improving the power-to-weight ratio, by giving it a super-charged power of intimation and cutting away everything superfluous; the result was to combine strength and lightness in a way reminiscent of some of the best of modern architecture, to give an audacity of range to his seemingly frail constructions that is altogether amazing.

His work in the 'thirties is dominated by two separate but chronologically overlapping groups of novels: the one, a group of four novels dealing with the career of Klas Dyregodt . . . ;

the other group, with Per Bufast as its central figure, consists of the two novels *The Great Game* (*Det store spelet,* 1934) and *Women Calling Home* (*Kvinnor ropar heim,* 1935). . . . And already here there is a hint of what has in time come to be recognized as the current ethical theme traceable in and through so much of Vesaas's work, above all in his works of the 'thirties: the theme of the 'helping hand' offered, sometimes unknowingly and sometimes deliberately, to a man who has reached the very flash-point of despair, and the inscrutable ways whereby a whole personal destiny can be changed by a readiness (or sometimes no more than a hint of readiness) to make sacrifices for others. Thus alone, he suggests, can man sustain himself and others in a world of disintegration and dread and hidden menace. (pp. 183-85)

A change came with the war, a turning-point where the technical progress in his art followed naturally upon what had been achieved in the previous decade, but where the direction changed. Allegory in the service of mysticism, the symbol as the weapon of the visionary, these are the things of which the novels of the latest years give testimony: *The Seed (Kimen,* 1940), *The House in the Dark (Huset i mørkret,* 1945), *The Bleaching Ground (Bleikeplassen,* 1946). . . . *The Seed* appeared in the first autumn of the Occupation, *The House in the Dark* in the autumn immediately following the end of the war; and each of them in an oblique but intimate way expressed something of the deeper feeling of these years. One must understand that just as, shall one say, the Inflation was to one generation of Europe, or the Depression to another, or the War, so the Occupation was to a whole generation of Norwegians an ordeal of a very special and testing kind, a regional mutation of war's hideousness. That it should inspire the country's artists and writers was natural and inevitable; that it should encourage such excessively literal and repetitive treatment as one finds for example in the mural paintings of Oslo Town Hall is unfortunate; but here in Vesaas it is the very lack of realism that makes everything so real, there being no report of what took place but instead a reconstruction of how it was—[*The Seed*] demonstrating in its indirect way the spread of evil passion through a community, and [*The House in the Dark*] in its superbly fantastic way taking in the whole atmosphere of the domestic war years under the roof of its capacious and intricately contrived symbol. The novels of the war and of the post-war years explore the nature of decay and sickness and frustration as the earlier ones had that of the living and the vital; and with *The Bleaching Ground,* Vesaas produced one of the most remarkable novels of the present age.

Vesaas is primarily a novelist and short story writer, but not exclusively. In 1946 he published his first volume of lyric poetry *The Springs (Kjeldene),* which he has followed up with three other volumes of verse. Of his ability as a dramatist, opinion in his own country is still uncertain; but it is of some interest that in recent years Vesaas has given careful attention to the technical demands of the radio play, and several pieces by him written specially in his idiom have been broadcast since the war. It is, however, as a narrative writer that his chief contribution has been made to Norwegian literature, and upon which his international reputation is basing itself. (pp. 185-86)

James Walter McFarlane, "The Literature of Nynorsk," in his Ibsen and the Temper of Norwegian Literature, *Oxford University Press, London, 1960, pp. 169-88.*

EDVARD BEYER

[The essay from which this excerpt is taken was originally delivered as a lecture at the Universities of Stockholm and Uppsala, December, 1963.]

Tarjei Vesaas comes from Telemark, one of the richest parts of [Norway] as far as rural art and folk poetry is concerned. Most of the Norwegian ballads and folk songs were written here. And the tradition lives on in Vesaas—*not* in the trappings of folklore, and only in the first books as an element of pastiche; it lives on in the background and the undertones. Several of the tales have the simplicity of legend: this applies particularly to the wanderer novels, *Messenger Huskuld* (*Sendemann Huskuld*) and *The Sandalwood Tree* (*Sandeltreet*). And now and again in the metaphors there is an echo of folk song and ballad. (p. 99)

But Vesaas's prose style has its deepest roots in the oral narrative tradition which has long flourished in Telemark. A major development can be demonstrated in his style, but it is a development from a more literary, sentimental and romantic lyricism to a more and more concentrated spareness, employing and cultivating features of the spoken language—parataxis, asyndeton, ellipsis. In his later books he leaves out not only superfluous minor words, but can allow even the principal words—the subject or the verb—to be implied. He does not build on a discursive spoken style, but on the laconic, confidential communication that shuns all superfluous talk. The dialect of Telemark provides the basis for many characteristic traits in his style. But he does not use rare or strange words. He makes use of dialect with artistic intent, to create a suggestive concentration or an intimate mood. But he never becomes its slave. (pp. 99-100)

[It was] with *The Seed* that Vesaas seriously went in for the symbolical and allegorical type of writing that has made him known all over Scandinavia. However, right from his first books we can see a tension and oscillation between earthy realism on the one hand, and on the other fairy tale, myth and expressionism.... Both tendencies are induced above all by an ambiguity in the writer's own make-up: a strong and immediate feeling for reality, sensitive powers of perception, an impetuous delight in the senses, an enjoyment of life's teeming multiplicity on the one hand, and on the other strong powers of imagination and a keen eye for the general in the particular. And again we can link this with an ambiguity in his feeling for life itself: a strong tension between the need for roots and the desire for freedom and escape, between the longing for security among known and familiar things, and a violent urge to break away from them, a restless, searching disquiet and an apprehensive awareness of the world. We can discern this duality in his own life, in the changing phases in his writing, but above all as the basic theme in central portions of his work.

The first book, *Children of Men* (1923), is a sentimental, romantic love story in traditional style; it is in the main the descriptions of nature's moods that reveal the presence of a poet. However, as early as in his second book, *Messenger Huskuld* (1924), we find a tendency towards a form of writing with elements of legend and symbolism. Huskuld sets out on his wanderings to find a child he can live for, but deep inside he—and the reader—divines that he is really out on another mission; he is a messenger, bringing tidings of "an age of greater love and goodwill among mankind". And the ending has a completely legendary ring: One night when frost threatens the corn in the field he spreads over it all the clothes he pos-

sesses; thus he sacrifices his life for the crops. Here, too, we have a central theme in Vesaas's early work, the idea of sacrifice.... (pp. 100-01)

The books that followed—[*Grindegard: Morgonen* (1925) and *Grinde-Kveld, eller Den gode engelen* (1926)], and several others—are weaker, but provide pictures of childhood and youth, nature's moods, and a distinctive earthy poetry of the backwoods that points far ahead in his writing. In *The Black Horses* (*Dei svarte hestane*) (1926)—which first won him a wider circle of readers—the romantic, lyrical, sometimes sentimental element that was so strong in the first books, is suppressed in favour of a more realistic description of people and their surroundings, and more dramatic action. It is partly a novel about marriage, but the most captivating thing is the picture of *the child*, little Kjell, who is being poisoned and destroyed in the conflict between his parents. Here Vesaas takes another step forward in his portrayal of children—with the help of an older master in that sphere, Hans E. Kinck. But we also find other themes central in Vesaas's work. In Kjell's father, Ambros Førness, we meet *the man possessed*. He runs a posting-station, and because of his unhappy marriage develops a passion for horses and racing and gaming that drives him to ruin. This rootlessness is set in relief by the earthbound countryman on the neighbouring farm. His son Leiv is also on the way to being possessed by horses and gaming, but he is saved in a way characteristic of Vesaas: by a young girl's love and by work on the land.

For all its powerful realism, *The Black Horses,* as the very title suggests, also contains an element of symbolism.... [The horses] become a symbol of the dangerous forces in man himself, the irrational powers, the wildness that kicks out blindly, kills and desolates. They embody the tension that is the underlying theme in the novel.

Later the horse becomes one of Vesaas's most important symbols, most often as an expression of warmth, harmony with the soil, and secure, resilient strength. As a rule, the destructive forces find other symbols.

The series of novels *Father's Journey* (*Fars reise*), *Sigrid Stallbrokk, The Unknown Men* (*Dei ukjende mennene*) and *The Heart Hears Songs of Home* (*Hjarta høyrer sine heimlandstonar*) appeared in the years 1930-8.... The books tell of Klas Dyregodt's long and difficult way as boy and man through loneliness, fear, even thoughts of suicide, to an aim, a responsibility and a meaning in life. While still a young boy he must help his father to guard the dam that threatens to burst and lay the valley waste—and more than that: he has to guard his father against the powers that threaten to burst the dams in his own mind. The symbolism is powerful and striking. This applies no less to the rotting houses and barns that lie at the bottom of the dammed-in lake and that become visible when the water level is low. They are like old half-forgotten sins. Here Klas means to seek death, out of desperation and unlucky love. But at the last moment he is restrained by an inscription on the wall: "You are your own master, Klas" which halts the avalanche in him. He understands not only that he must act on his own initiative, but also that there is someone who wishes him well; there is someone who has understood him and written the words that call him back to life. And again we come to one of Vesaas's central themes—*the helping hand*, the help from one man to another just when things are worst, the help that breaks through the wall round the enclosed, isolated mind, saves it from destruction, awakens new courage and kindles new warmth. (pp. 101-02)

The sense of catastrophe that is expressed in many instances in the first volumes of the Dyregodt series pervades the play *Ultimatum*.... It is a play about young people's reactions under the threat of an imminent outbreak of war. Its form is influenced by the contemporary European theatre, especially German expressionism. When it was recently broadcast, in a revised form, it showed that it still had significant suggestive power, but little dramatic force.... In the same year that *Ultimatum* appeared—1934—Vesaas achieved his break-through with the reading public with the novel *The Great Game* (*Det store spelet*), in many ways a contrast to the play. It is a work about the good powers in life, the unity of all things, about earth and man and the steady rhythm of farm-life. The narration of Per Bufast's childhood and youth belongs to the best Vesaas has written in one of his special fields. But it is a far from idyllic and harmonious development that Per under-goes. On the contrary, the central theme of the novel is the tension between the urge for freedom and the desire to break away on the one hand, and on the other, all that ties him to the soil. "You shall live on Bufast all your life," Per's father tells him. But the father himself belongs to those of Vesaas's characters who are possessed.... The words he says to the boy, Per feels as a merciless judgement. For there is so much that frightens him on the farm—above all *death*, death as he meets it from the first years of his childhood. And there are strong forces in him that want to escape far away from this fear and oppression. Not until, as a grown man, he has himself to take the life of the old horse, and in a trembling, ecstatic moment he experiences death as an inextricable part of life's wholeness, does he find his place in "the great game". Per's life is continued in *Women Calling Home* (*Kvinnor ropar heim*) (1935), where fertility, luxuriance, the smell of the soil and prosperity are portrayed with true exuberance. Closely con-nected with these books, both in style and content, is the col-lection of short stories *The Clay and the Wheel* (*Leiret og hjulet*) (1937) and ... [*The Heart Hears Songs of Home*], the last volume in the series on Klas Dyregodt.

Realistic and symbolic elements are combined in all these nov-els. Their relative strengths may change, but the symbolic elements are always deeply anchored in the action and in the surroundings. The effect of the symbols lies above all in the aura that surrounds them, and less in the plane of thought. Things warn and threaten, entice and call; again and again they announce their presence and so acquire suggestive power and often undertones, as from some greater and deeper context. The author develops this technique from work to work—the suggestive repetitions that give a deeper significance to con-crete phenomena and expand them into symbols without break-ing the realistic frame-work. (pp. 103-04)

[In *The Seed*], a large number of the threads we have been able to trace through [Vesaas's] writing are gathered together. Here the view of the destructive tendencies in man meets with the faith in man's dignity and ethical responsibility; wildness and humiliation stand against the will to regeneration and the quiet sustaining help from mind to mind. (p. 104)

The work creates a new and distinctive unity from old themes; it also contains new ones. It tells of collective madness, of mass psychosis and the infectious lust to kill, and it gives a glimpse of the involved motives that can lead to murder when the opportunity is there—escape from one's own defeats, thirst for revenge disguised as holy rage. But it also gives stronger expression to the belief in ethical regeneration, the will to conciliation and the power of self-renewal—"the seed in the

dust"—than any of his earlier books. And *The Seed* has a clear and powerful message: "Wildness must not be tolerated"—strong and courageous words against the background of the contemporary situation.

In form *The Seed* unites old tendencies and develops them further. The tendency towards simplification and concentration which can be noticed early in Vesaas has given the language and composition here a compressed power of expression and conciseness. Unity of place and time is effected, and the action follows simple, clear lines. And here the characteristic Vesaas style has attained full maturity. All unnecessary words are pruned, and the sentences are short, taut, forceful with mean-ing. But all the omissions compel the reader to fill in the gaps. The words gain time to take effect. The conciseness makes room for an abundance of associations. And the strict artistic economy gives the suggestive repetitions, that heighten the atmosphere and create symbols, a special emphasis. Here Ve-saas steps right into symbolism, without violating the descrip-tion of solid reality. There are admittedly elements in *The Seed* that could scarcely be considered in the elementary plane of reality, but they are for the most part realistically motivated; they are not forced on the material from outside. Symbol is reality and reality is symbol, and together they create a unified fiction.

The Seed tells of mass psychosis, collective madness. In *The Bleaching Place* ..., it is a question of individual madness, delusions that run wild and assume control in an isolated mind, driving it on to insanity and murder, of complex motives, of the thirst for love, beauty, and purity that becomes entangled with the delusions and makes them the more dangerous, but that also makes the man possessed by them receptive to the sacrifice of love, the helping hand, the inscription on the wall.... In this novel the outer and inner action, symbol and reality, are even more closely united than in *The Seed*. The action takes place entirely in the wash-house and at the drying-place where the white linen shines in the night, and these surroundings provide at one and the same time a realistic setting and an expressive symbolism which broadens the perspectives.

In *The House in the Dark* (*Huset i mørkret*)—written during the last winter of the war and published in the first autumn of peace—Vesaas creates a framework of a purely allegorical kind. The house in the dark does not create the illusion of a house, but it gives a concentrated image of Norway during the occupation.... The clipped style, the suggestive repetitions, the expressive symbolism that expands within the allegorical framework—all this re-creates the mood of the occupation with an intensity that strikes home even today. The allegorical struc-ture also provides room for a delicate and expressive treatment of vital problems, individualized, intimate characterization, and deeply gripping episodes. While the fundamental vision in *The Seed* was pacifistic, the heroes in *The House in the Dark* are active resistance fighters; but the problems of the end and the means, pure or impure motives, guilt and atonement, are central in this work as well.... We feel justifiably pleased that this broad-visioned and deeply humane work should stand as the chief literary monument to the years of occupation in Norway.

The simple, compact composition, the clipped style, the styl-ized picture of a milieu, the focusing round a central symbol which sometimes acquires a purely allegorical nature—all this characterizes in a varying degree Vesaas's post-war books. In book after book he circles around a collection of deeply per-sonal, topical, but also timeless and general, basic themes: the threat of catastrophe, the dangerous forces in the mind, delusions, isolation, crippling guilt, but also life's primary healthiness as it is revealed in plants and animals, in children and in young love, the secret attraction between human beings, the longing and the gentleness that flow in deep undercurrents, the feeling of responsibility, the will to sacrifice, the power in a word or a helping hand when all is at stake.

In *The Tower (Tårnet)* (1948), as in *The Bleaching Place*, the symbolism is founded in the actual surroundings and in the main characters' spiritual states, while *The Signal (Signalet)* (1950) continues the allegorical line from *The House in the Dark*. Just as the house was "bewitched", so he describes here a "bewitched" train, a train that remains standing in the station, waiting for a signal that never comes. In this image we recognize the world situation itself, and the feeling of crippling guilt, irresoluteness and powerless passivity that may plague any one of us. . . . The allegory may sometimes seem forced and far-fetched—more so than in *The House in the Dark*—and the deep abstractions get the upper hand. It is, however, not allegorical parallels that give the work value but the atmosphere and lively details.

In several of the short stories in the collection *The Winds* (1952), in the action-packed and richly lyrical novel *Spring Night (Vårnatt)* (1954) and in *The Birds* (1957), Vesaas leaves allegory and approaches poetic realism.

The Winds is one of the richest books in all his production. Here, and in a later collection of short stories, *A Fine Day (Ein vakker dag)* (1959), he plays over the whole register. . . . Many of Vesaas's most prominent characteristics—his conciseness, concentration, simplification—make him an excellent short-story writer, and the short stories provide a good approach to his writing.

Several of the later novels also approach short-story form. This applies to *The Birds,* one of the most beautiful and perfect of all his books, with its simply and deeply moving story of "Tusten", the handicapped village misfit, and his secret, fear-filled inner world, doomed to overthrow and yet rich in beauty. But *The Birds* is something more than the intimate tale of a village half-wit's life and dream and sacrifice. The very intimacy in the description forces us to see other perspectives. Are we not all related, in one way or another, to Tusten? Do we not all fight dumbfounded and helpless against destructive powers that are deeply rooted in us? And do we not all bear some responsibility for Tusten in one another? (pp. 104-07)

[*The Ice Palace,* a novel published in the United States as *Palace of Ice,* is] a continuation of the line followed by *Spring Night,* and *The Birds.* As a description of children and young girls it has roots far back in [Vesaas's] production. Like all the postwar books it has a central symbol, which is named in the title itself. But rarely has the central symbol been motivated with such certainty, such simplicity, and at the same time such expressiveness and so full a meaning. So I will be careful in interpreting it, only saying that it stands in every sense central to the work and that this novel is a variation on important themes of Vesaas's: loneliness and the desire for friendship, love of life and a longing for beauty, madness and delusion, the quiet liberating help from man to man. In its monumental simplicity *The Ice Palace* belongs to the most intimate and at the same time the most universal Vesaas has written. (p. 108)

Edvard Beyer, "Tarjei Vesaas," in Scandinavica, *Vol. 3, No. 2, November, 1964, pp. 97-109.*

HEDIN BRONNER

Tarjei Vesaas, hitherto known beyond his homeland only in Germany and a handful of other European countries, is one of the "new" generation whose work has been awaiting discovery on this side of the water. His use of the synthetic language *Landsmål* (*Nynorsk* if you will) has not barred him from the literary majority in Norway, where his praises are sung in rare unison. There are several reasons for this. His use of rural characters and settings, his leaning towards true dialect, and his originality of style, all combine to rescue him from that which users of standard Norwegian (*Riksmål*) find bookish and mechanical ("departementalt") in *Landsmål*. His implied treatment of the German occupation theme in *Huset i Mørkret* (*The House in Darkness,* 1945) has insured him a sympathetic reception since the war. His independence in pursuing new forms is true to the best national tradition of nonconformity. And his restless concern with human conscience demonstrates a deep and harmonious identification with the intellectual spirit of the North.

It is high time that the work of such a writer be placed before American and British readers. There is no small selection to choose from, and Rie Bistrup was not entirely facetious when he recently asked, "Is Tarjei Vesaas author, poet or writer?" This rugged man from the Telemark mountains, now 68, was only 17 when, as he puts it, he first "sat writing under the kerosene lamp." Which of the thirty-odd volumes that have appeared since then would serve as a proper introduction to him? Which would best represent him as an individual, as a product of the national soil, and as part of the literary tides and currents of Europe?

I suppose many Norwegians would favor *Huset i Mørkret.* They identify its stark symbolism with a theme that remains close to their hearts, the ethical problems of confrontation with a wartime aggressor. . . . In his struggle away from existing literary forms, Vesaas has here placed himself very nearly in a relationship with an ancient one—the medieval dream allegory. This represents only one side—an extreme side—of his richly varied production, and I think it is a salutary thing that it was not chosen to become the "first Vesaas in English."

Unfortunately, however, the same holds true of the two short novels *Kimen* (*The Seed,* 1940) and *Vårnatt* (*Spring Night,* 1954) which now have been made available [in translation]. . . . There will, of course, never be unanimity in any choice of contemporary works of literature. While a novel like *Dei Svarte Hestane* (*The Black Horses,* 1928), for example, might be recommended by those who enjoy the color and human warmth of Vesaas the Realist, it would be decried by those who admire Vesaas the Romanticist, or Vesaas the Impressionist, to say nothing of Vesaas the Expressionist! A reasonable solution might have been to translate first one of his short story collections, like *Vindane* (*The Winds,* 1952). These present many aspects of Vesaas; they entertain; they whet the appetite; and they are identifiably Norwegian. Among them is that little gem called **"Tusten"**, the wistful tale of a parish dimwit whose boldest wish is to be addressed by his real name.

The present translation is characterized by a ruthless adjustment of the original to the tastes of the unrefined. Gone are the terse and incisive sentences of Vesaas; gone his whimsical ellipses, his impulsive leaps of mood and tone. Gone, too, are the original names of some of the characters, leaving Hill for *Haug,* Dale for *Dal,* Lee for *Li,* and—of all things!—Olaf for *Hallstein.* Gone is an entire chapter of *Seed*—the sixth one—liquidated without a word, and all evidence concealed under new chapter numbers. (pp. 168-69)

[*Spring Night*] should have been a milestone in the progress of Norwegiana on this side of the Atlantic. Instead, its inaccuracies, interpolations and stylistic inferiority may leave it lying by the wayside, sadly unmarked. I am very sorry to say that we still have far to go before we reach the real Vesaas in English. (p. 170)

> *Hedin Bronner, in a review of "The Seed" and "Spring Night," in* Scandinavian Studies, *Vol. 38, No. 2, May, 1966, pp. 167-70.*

KENNETH G. CHAPMAN

As so much of his best writing, [Vesaas's *The Ice Palace*] is a very simple story, delicately and lyrically told, but one which delineates very accurately the conflicts and stresses within the human psyche. A new girl, Unn, comes to school, but keeps out of contact with the other children, whose leader is Siss, a girl of Unn's own age (eleven). But despite her aloofness, an unexpressed rapport develops between the two girls, leading finally to a request from Unn to meet Siss after school.... Though Unn, lonely as she is, desperately needs the contact such a friendship would give her, she is also frightened by the demands it must make on her and by the revelation of her true self which it would involve. She skips school the next day and goes walking by herself. She wanders into the depths of a frozen waterfall, is trapped and frozen to death. Siss feels the need of remaining true to Unn, and withdraws from her circle of friends, threatening to seal herself off from them. She searches for Unn, several times stopping by the mass of ice in which Unn is imprisoned, but never finds her. Her health and sanity are threatened by the experience, but when spring finally comes she is able to regain her faith in life, helped by the understanding and concern of the other children. Vesaas makes the conflicts and resolutions in this story convincing by the use of a style highly lyrical even for him (indeed, one of the chapters consists of a poem, set in verse form, but many other passages, though set as prose, are difficult to distinguish from verse.) Woven in with this highly lyrical style is some very beautiful nature imagery, of which the frozen waterfall—the ice palace itself—is the central image. (pp. 80-1)

> *Kenneth G. Chapman, in a review of "The Ice Palace," in* Scandinavian Studies, *Vol. 39, No. 1, February, 1967, pp. 80-5.*

THE TIMES LITERARY SUPPLEMENT

The characters in Tarjei Vesaas's novels grow out of the landscape. They are seen not in relation to nature but as part of it. He achieves this effect, which gives his writing a rare inward stillness, because his vision of the Norwegian countryside is close and undeviating. The way he notices the shapes of clouds, the colour of the moon, the footprints of woodcock in a forest marsh, the smell of the lake at evening, is not as a botanist but as a receptive inhabitant. Contemporary events and the pressures of the city do not touch even remotely the isolated lake and forest landscape he describes in his latest book, *The Birds*. The age of his human figures can be measured as one can calculate the age of a tree, but like trees they are timeless; they could belong to another century.

The brother [Mattis] and sister [Hege] who are central to his narrative are cut off from the village community because Mattis

is simple-minded.... The novel attempts to explore the slow, fearful, blundering mind of Mattis, which is occasionally lit by flashes of insight and delight in nature which he can only half express.... When a lumberjack comes to lodge with [Hege and Mattis] the pattern of their relationship inevitably alters, and Mattis is incapable of adjusting to change.

Less dazzling than *The Ice Palace* with its frozen waterfalls, *The Birds* is a more rounded, sympathetic novel which projects Mattis's struggles humanely, without sentimentality.

> *"Untimely," in* The Times Literary Supplement, *No. 3465, July 25, 1968, p. 775.*

JOHN COLEMAN

This very subtle story [*The Birds*] must have been a swine to carry through and I don't know how to make it sound as attractive as it is. Mattis, a 37-year-old mental defective, lives with his slightly older sister in a small Norwegian village by a lake. The sister gets a kindly lover one day and Mattis, obscurely, suffers. The narrative is communicated through his consciousness, for the most part. If this sounds daunting, I had better add that areas of the translation leave something to be desired. 'Jolly well' crops up as an epithet and the tree-felling lover disburdens himself thus: 'What I thought I'd do was walk along by the lake till I reached habitation.' Mr. Vesaas's feat is to break through such unhappy webs of language into a feeling interpretation of a limited understanding. He makes you live along with Mattis.

Evidently some of the occasions that excite an idiot are similar to what excites technically normal people. The book doesn't make an issue of this, although it implies it. Where it is so powerful is in its devotion to the awfully abrupt and tenuous contours of nuttiness. Mattis senses that a flight of woodcock, straight over the home chimney-stack, spells a riddle and its answer: later, two holidaying girls are nice to him and they become another solved puzzle. His principal enigma, which is about what happens when his mothering sister belatedly finds a life and satisfactions of her own, is accorded its mad, woefully logical solution. Fashionable discussion of schizophrenics has it that they know more than we do. Mr. Vesaas almost convinces you of it.

> *John Coleman, "Black Sea Bubble," in* The Observer, *August 4, 1968, p. 23.*

MARSHA McCREADIE

[*Palace of Ice*'s] serene, yet stirring narrative centers around only two major characters and one incident. And yet, somehow, questions of utmost importance evolve and thread in and out of a primordially simple structure....

Emanating from this simple structure is Vesaas' vision. He senses the ambiguous needs of both isolation and companionship. He pits the fear and horror of the unknown against the irresistible and unavoidable nature of knowledge.

There are pitfalls in Vesaas' simplicity, especially when the climax—Unn's death—occurs near the beginning, and the remainder of the novel seems, at least, somewhat foreseeable. Sometimes the narrative and dialogue degenerate into parable, and if there's one thing that can put off the modern reader, it's old-fashioned didacticism.

But any momentary irritation felt by the reader of *Palace of Ice* doesn't mar the book's effect. It is still something of a marvel to read a new book that attempts to deal with large and great themes (amazing enough) in a traditional manner (even more amazing).

Marsha McCreadie, "Nordic Prizewinner," in The Christian Science Monitor, *December 19, 1968, p. 7.*

ANTHONY WEST

We are informed by authoritative European voices [on the dust cover of *Palace of Ice*] that [the novel] is a work of "immense concentration," that it is "relentlessly beautiful," that it has an "austere poetic clarity," and so forth and so on. It is about two little girls, unpromisingly named Siss and Unn. And because they are so very little they talk to each other and much of their doing and thinking is described in "Run, John! Run!" language. Perhaps it is less drearily prattling in the original Norse. (p. 145)

[What *Palace of Ice*] seems to be in aid of is the not very profound thought that death is a frightening idea but once you get used to it you can go ahead and live with it; and if one wanted to be precise one would say that the book gives an overwhelming impression of the intellectual poverty of the Nordic culture that has adopted the slogan "Less is more" as its battle cry. *Palace of Ice* is indeed a manifestation in literature of the aesthetic of design, vulgarly known as Swedish, which evades all major problems of choice and preference by scraping everything down to the rudimentary minimum. Siss and Unn aren't little girls with the complexities of surface, interior, reaction, and interest that real little girls possess. They are two polished "Swedish modern" egg shapes labelled Siss and Unn that have been placed against a neutral gray homespun backcloth with a boringly monotonous surface called winter and enshrined in the bleak gallery of Tarjei Vesaas's prose. His novel is exactly like some ghastly provincial museum in which a tiny collection is surrounded by an excess of space and an atmosphere of reverence, and in which one's spirit faints from lack of nourishment—a formalist tomb in which the interaction that gives art its meaning is suspended. To accomplish his work of museum, or mausoleum, art, Tarjei Vesaas has abstracted everything from his two little girls that constitutes the reality of an individual personality and that establishes a claim to our interest. We are offered children reduced to something negotiable in place of the exploration of developing awareness that makes children worth writing about. What is negotiable is precisely the simpleton—the conception of a child that gives rise to the pejorative use of the world "childish"—that the average adult philistine puts in the place of any real child he may have to deal with, in order to evade the difficulties that follow on the recognition that its as yet uncysted sensibility may be even more penetrating and perceptive than his own. The difficulties arise from the fact that the child's unanswerable questions dissolve the fabric of lies men weave in order to protect themselves from their experience of a pointless and amoral universe. As no adult wants to have his feet kicked out from under him by a child, we get "beautiful" stories like *Palace of Ice* that equate innocence with idiocy and spare us the truth that we have no power to protect true innocence, or to protect ourselves from it. (pp. 145-46)

Anthony West, in a review of "Palace of Ice," in The New Yorker, *Vol. XLV, No. 11, May 3, 1969, pp. 145-46.*

KENNETH GRAHAM

[It is] only in the last year or two, through the translations of *The Great Cycle, The Seed, The Ice Palace* and *The Birds,* that [Vesaas's] name has become known to English readers as a Norwegian symbolist, pastoralist and fabulist of possibly the very first rank. Like these others, . . . [*The Bridges*] is lapidary, pared down to the bone, yet filled with the sombre glow of feeling for people and for their landscape.

Aud and Torvil, girl and boy in a village by a bridge, come upon a crisis in their inner lives when they find a dead baby in a wood. They become involved; the girl of their own age who has given birth comes between the two of them, then goes away; and Aud and Torvil are left as before, only different. The main issues I take to be those of human contact (always, hands are touching) and of growth into adulthood, both being symbolised by the bridge. And much that is not so easily interpretable can still be responded to with some vividness: experiences of terror, longing, bewilderment and nightmare are directly re-created in us by stark dream-imagery, by the highlighting of isolated phrases, by understatement, and by the formally simplified dialogue that implies depths: words handed from character to character like carved pebbles.

Yet eventually I found the sustained, astringent mysticism obscure and wearying. All these intense perceptions grew disembodied after a bit: who owned which? At this level of vision the sense of personality falls away, even though the book is *about* personality. What remained was, in part, Scandinavian wind and shadow—together with an uneasy awareness in me that the simplicity of great artists in their old age has often fooled critics.

Kenneth Graham, "Wind and Shadow," in The Listener, *Vol. 81, No. 2094, May 15, 1969, p. 686.*

THE TIMES LITERARY SUPPLEMENT

"She's not grown-up, any more than we are", says Aud to Torvil, the boy next door, about the strange girl who has erupted into their lives. It emerges [in *The Bridges*] that all three are in fact eighteen, and although this may be the age of swinging consent in London, in Tarjei Vesaas's Norway it is still a satchel-carrying, transitional time between innocence and experience. Aud and Torvil are old enough for their families to hope for their marriage but too young themselves to have been marked by any emotion other than that of friendship.

The simmering quality of their relationship and the simplicity of their upbringing is nicely caught by the spare, concentrated style of the book. . . . This tight writing is also a good foil for the essentially melodramatic story of how Aud discovers a dead new-born baby in the woods. . . . The trouble with the novel is that the message, the imagery, the symbolism, the nightmares, the similarities and the contrasts are all spelt out far too clearly. . . . Aud and Torvil certainly had to learn how to communicate but need they have done so by holding hands with Valborg in silence under the dripping trees? Like some lesser Bergman film *The Bridges* is gripping but slightly ridiculous.

A review of "The Bridges," in The Times Literary Supplement, *No. 3513, June 26, 1969, p. 677.*

HOLGER LUNDBERGH

This tense and highly dramatic story [*The Birds*] is less a novel than the anatomy of a troubled mind. As such, often painful, even harrowing, it is a little masterpiece, carried to its logical conclusion by the author's skill and wisdom. In Scandinavia, where he is acclaimed a major writer, Vesaas's readers are accustomed to the raw nerve-ends he invariably exposes, to his muted, lyric descriptions of nature, to the mysticism and allegory that are intrinsic to his work. All these are present in *The Birds* ..., but its main character, Mattis, is undoubtedly one of the most memorable he has created in the many books he has written since his first was published in his native Norway, back in the early 1920's.

Mattis, almost 40 years old, lives in a small cottage beside a lake in Norway with his older sister Hege, a mousey, prosaic woman who provides for them both by knitting sweaters. (p. 4)

One night a woodcock from the neighboring forest flies over the house. It has changed its usual path and Mattis, mystified and filled with excitement, tells Hege. She fails to find any significance in it. Every night, for nearly two weeks, it passes overhead. Mattis is entranced. Then, one day, a fowler shoots the bird; Mattis's world rings with despair as he buries it.

He has one other love: an old, much-repaired dory. He is a strong oarsman, and Hege, desperately trying to find something for him to do, suggests he become the ferryman on the lake. Docile and proud, he enters hopefully on a new career: he has a full-time job. . . . One day he is hailed by a man who wants to be ferried over to Mattis' side. He is a lumberjack, looking for a place to stay. "Stay with us," Mattis urges. "We have an extra room." The inevitable conflict quickly builds up. Hege and the newcomer fall in love, and Mattis, at first incredulous at what he senses more than sees, soon finds his fears and suspicions confirmed. . . . With a sudden lucidity, brushing hesitation and doubt aside, he understands that he must disappear, and carefully lays his elaborate and desperate plans.

Vesaas's superb description rises to an almost explosive climax in the final pages. It is a searing end that echoes all the moods and intricacies of Mattis's stunted, bewildered, searching nature. The mystery of the woodcock's flight adds a familiar, haunting Vesaas touch, as does the tragic irony that it is Mattis who ferries the lumberjack across the lake—his only passenger—thus unwittingly seals his own fate.

Vesaas has, with clear design, I am sure, reduced Hege and her lover to secondary characters. In fact, Hege emerges only once with full clarity when, early in the story, she asks Mattis in chill despair, "Why am I living?" The lumberjack, regrettably, is even more two-dimensional, if not shadowy. In contrast, Mattis stands out vibrantly alive. It is, after all, very much his story—and Vesaas's portrait of him will not easily dim in the reader's mind. (pp. 4, 29)

> Holger Lundbergh, "Soul-Searching beside a Lake in Norway," in The New York Times Book Review, September 14, 1969, pp. 4, 29.

ROLF FJELDE

For some years preceding his death this past spring. Tarjei Vesaas was the Norwegian author most seriously considered for the Nobel Prize in Literature. If this brief novel [*The Bridges*] is too slight to substantiate his claim to that high honor, its classically spare story with its intaglio of powerfully evocative symbols would be sufficient to establish him as a writer of rare imaginative vitality and perception. . . .

Two events propel the story into motion. First Torvil, standing on the bridge, dreaming of Aud, is almost run down by a speeding truck. Shaken by the sudden intimation of death—"the shadow of a stone," in Vesaas's poetic style—Torvil seeks out Aud and finds her unexpectedly, not at home, but deep in the nearby wood, weeping heartbrokenly. Beside her in the failing light, half hidden under blackening twigs, is the source of her grief: the body of a newborn lifeless child.

The remainder of the novel traces the radical consequences of this discovery in changing three lives. Torvil and Aud debate whether to report the infanticide to their parents or the police; and it is Aud, with the words "someone needs all the miserable help we can give," who decides they must, on their own, involve themselves in the torment of the unknown mother.

The action thus comes to exemplify one of the author's recurrent themes: man's necessity to move out into life. . . .

Paralleling the story, the form of the book as well moves out beyond narrative. Interpolated chapters are sunk, like vertical shafts, into the depths of life, into the blind, instinctual forces of nature, a Roethke-like world of minute, creeping things and flowing waters and nightmare images of horror. These passages are often obscure and, one suspects, at times escape the writer's control; but they contain some of the most impressive language in the book. . . .

As Vesaas increasingly gains recognition in the English-speaking world, it can only be hoped that more of his works will be made available on the same general high level as this latest confirmation of his singular talent.

> Rolf Fjelde, "A Need to Move Outward," in The New York Times Book Review, November 1, 1970, p. 50.

KENNETH G. CHAPMAN

The general nature of [Vesaas'] early writing is well, though perhaps a bit too harshly, described in his own judgment of his second published novel, *Huskuld the Herald (Sendemann Huskuld,* 1924): "so romantic that it is unreadable." This novel, and most of Vesaas' early writing, is most certainly romantic, at times even sentimental, but if one first accepts its romantic nature, there is a great deal of readable material to be found there.

We do not have to search long to find the sources of this romantic approach. About a volume of prose poems which was rejected for publication (perhaps fortunately) in 1922, Vesaas has written that they were "short prose poems such as the great Tagore in India wrote, with phrases like those used by my idol Knut Hamsun, and full of romanticism in the style of my other idol Selma Lagerlöf." . . . And at this stage in Vesaas' development it was certainly Knut Hamsun's early neo-romantic novels (especially *Pan* and *Victoria*) which had the greatest influence on his style.

Despite the heavy dose of romanticism in both style and content, however, Vesaas' early writing displays a highly original, though frequently unbridled, talent. Early reviewers were almost unanimous in predicting a brilliant, if unusual, writing career for him, even when they criticized him in the same breath for the excessive and transparent influences evident in his writing.

In addition to its heavy overlay of romanticism, Vesaas' earliest writing is characterized by frequent, often rapturous and even sentimental, expressions of religious belief reflecting traditional Christian attitudes. (pp. 27-8)

This tendency toward religious sentimentality in Vesaas' early writing is closely connected with its overall romantic flavor, and can undoubtedly be at least partially ascribed to the same literary sources, but in addition there were probably some environmental influences at work on Vesaas from the strongly pietistic attitudes common at the beginning of the twentieth century in Norwegian rural communities, of which the township of Vinje is quite typical. As in the case of the romantic influences, these influences from traditional religious attitudes were not lasting, and the excesses to which they led soon disappeared from his writing.

Closely related to the romantic and religious strains in Vesaas' early novels, plays, and poetry, is the highly unrealistic attitude toward women in these works. There is an ethereal, madonna-like glow to most of these early Vesaas women. Liv Myrejard in *Children of Man* [*Menneskebonn*] is even referred to as "Madonna" by the two men who love her. Lis in *Evening at Grinde* (*Grindekveld*, 1926) is time and time again referred to as Toremun's "good angel" and the novel is subtitled *The Good Angel*.... Only Tuve in *The Dwelling Places of God* [*Guds bustader*], who bears the child of one brother while married to the other, shows any tendency to behave in a non-angelic fashion, but even her behavior and its consequences serve primarily as a vehicle for moralizing on the part of the author. In this respect, too, Vesaas showed rapid changes in attitude, and in his later books, although women are still looked upon as a primary source of all that is good (due to their close connection with the creative processes of birth and regeneration), his early uncritical, romantic portraits of women give way to more rounded, realistic ones.

The basic themes of these earliest works are also derived from traditional Christian attitudes: the will to sacrifice oneself for others, and the will to do penance. (pp. 28-9)

[In *The Farm at Grinde* (*Grindegard: Morgonen*)], Toremun, the central character of the Grinde novels, throws an innocent lamb (!) into the rushing outlet of a mountain pond. He does this in a fit of depression and anxiety, though imagining that he is doing it for the sake of Brit, a girl he has grown up together with and with whom he is falling in love. He is then overwhelmed by remorse and longs to make good his misdeed. He goes into the mountains, looking for lost lambs to save, longing to "take the lamb on his shoulder and carry it and do penance." He spends the summer in this way, and "when he finally returned home to Grinde he had found consolation and help, had won out, even if the agony might someday come back." And the "agony" does come back. In the final section of *The Farm at Grinde*, Toremun accidently kills Brit during a trip across the mountains in a blizzard, and once more he is obsessed with the desire to do penance, although he is totally innocent of any misdeed: "Oh, to suffer, that's what I must do from now on...."

Evening at Grinde opens with Toremun in jail, doing penance for a crime he did not commit, and even after it has become quite clear to the authorities that he is innocent (from hearing his feverish babbling when he lies ill in the prison infirmary), he still refuses to admit his innocence and to leave. The infirmary nurse, Lis, also tries to persuade him of his innocence, but in vain. She is falling in love with him, and leaves her job

when she sees it is impossible to convince him. The rest of the novel tells of Toremun's decision to leave the prison and return to Grinde, and of the struggle in his mind between remaining true to the memory of Brit and giving in to his awakening love for Lis, his "good angel," who has devoted her life to trying to win him back to life. The book ends melodramatically, with Toremun being killed when he protects Lis from injury by a blasting charge, without Toremun's conflict really becoming resolved. (pp. 30-31)

These earliest plays and novels cannot be said to have been successful, despite occasional well-written nature descriptions and a few passages here and there which reveal true poetic talent. The religious themes which they contain, and the characters in terms of which they are presented, are in general treated much too superficially to be either interesting or enlightening. The characters are for the most part figures rather than living people, and the religious and romantic clichés which are frequently used to describe their situations frustrate any attempt on the part of the reader to understand them and their plight. What makes these books interesting, and is the reason for discussing them in such detail, is that their central themes, however unconvincingly presented here, serve as a background for an understanding of the resolution of modern ethical conflicts which Vesaas arrives at in his later works. (pp. 31-2)

Kenneth G. Chapman, in his Tarjei Vesaas, *Twayne Publishers, Inc., 1970, 180 p.*

ROBERT GARIOCH

Tarjei Vesaas's *The Boat in the Evening* comes through in translation from the Norwegian with the intensity of major poetry, in a form of its own. It has the appearance of a novel, but its 16 chapters are very different in kind. Some are short stories of a quality that magazine editors long for, some are short or very short dramatic monologues, and others mingle prose and verse. Instead of named characters we find 'the stern man' and 'the drifter' and 'the girl on the road'. There is a continuity of artistic effect, but not of action; the unity is of a kind that does not depend on the simple meanings of words, though words do retain their simple meanings as well as their overtones—this is literature, not music. The author is extremely alert; his power of invention is quite extraordinary and he allows it a fantastic liberty, so we may think, but he bumps it hard on the ground at the artistically correct moment.... [*The Boat in the Evening*] is the last work of the author, who died last year. He spent most of his 73 years in the Telemark district of Norway, in surroundings, we suppose, that have little consideration for human perplexity, loneliness and anguish. That provides the unifying force of this book: the author's nearly, but never quite, frantic attempt to become one with his surroundings of high rock and deep water. Made out of such a rude, remote environment, the book is good enough for the libraries of the world.

Robert Garioch, "Telemark News," in The Listener, *Vol. 85, No. 2182, January 21, 1971, p. 89.*

THE TIMES LITERARY SUPPLEMENT

This elusive, poetic book [*The Boat in the Evening*] ... helps to explain why the Norwegian writer [Vesaas] was so often (three times) a candidate for the Nobel Prize but never won it. ...

In strained, tense phrases and sentences Vesaas evokes from the deepest recesses of his memory, one feels, a boy helping his stern father clear a road in a pitiless snowstorm. All the unspoken embarrassments of childhood are somehow summed up in the inability of this unnamed boy to produce some urine to wash the wound of their lamed horse. The several lonelinesses that can exist within a family, the physicality of close relationships, the effect on the emotions of the living presences of grass, trees, water, the half-understood nature of the adult world to a child: all these Vesaas conjures brilliantly from the sombre north.

In some of these pieces, however, the imagery takes such complete possession that Vesaas seems to be relating uninterpreted dreams. Then his touch is less sure. It is possible to understand what he feels when he talks of being between walls of stone, or of the timeless rivers that flow beneath the earth, but it is more difficult to divine with any precision what he wants us to conclude. It is a pity that when he was so good at conveying the meaningful details of life these attempts to measure its cosmic forces seem to meander into confusion.

> A review of "The Boat in the Evening," in The Times Literary Supplement, No. 3598, February 12, 1971, p. 173.

R. R. DAVIES

[*Spring Night*] is virtually a domestic melodrama, as overloaded with emotion as the stickiest bits of Ibsen, but narrated with such cool sparseness that events seem to sink, even as they happen, into the soft, yielding texture of life.

It is clear from the start that when Sissel and her young brother Olaf settle down to mind the house for their absent parents, they are in for one of those character-building sleepless nights. Their peace is disrupted by the arrival of a woman in labour, with her distraught family: the short-tempered husband Karl, who has 'been in the war'; his young sister Gudrun, the startling embodiment of the Gudrun who has been Olaf's fantasy-world companion; and their father, whom they call 'The Butterfly' on account of his fluttering hands and perpetual agitation. Outside in the car is The Butterfly's second wife, who for the past year has feigned paralysis, to which she has now added dumbness, in vengeful protest against the ceaseless, nagging chatter of her pathetic husband. . . .

There is much here that could be preposterous, but Vesaas shows no signs of strain in making it acceptable. Explanations are not attempted, for everything is seen through the eyes of the boy Olaf. Adult neuroses burst forth and die away as he watches; he begins to understand something of their origins, and to realise that the systems of emotional interdependence soon to start making their claims upon him can breed sickness and strife. He is called upon for the first time to give back some of the strength he has derived from his own family life. . . .

Vesaas's story deals in sensibilities as yet quite unliberated by the notion that self-confidence is roughly equivalent to self-awareness.

> R. R. Davies, "Midwinter Spring," in New Statesman, Vol. 83, No. 2129, January 14, 1972, p. 53.

D.A.N. JONES

Tarjei Vesaas is said to write a very bare simple prose in his native Norwegian. Unfortunately, the American translation of *Spring Night* is in jejune, impoverished English. It is, perhaps, a surrealist novel, playing with our ideas of reality not, like the French, through worried word-play, but contriving to suggest dream-like pictures. An adolescent brother and sister, left alone in their house, are visited by a car-load of inexplicable adults, including a pregnant girl, a woman pretending to be dumb and immobile, a flapping butterfly of a paterfamilias and his stern, military son. It recalls the neurotic car-load in Bergman's *Wild Strawberries*, and might possibly have influenced that film. The reader won't remember a word—but will probably remember the pictures summoned up, like shots from an intriguing movie.

> D.A.N. Jones, "Oh Montreal," in The Listener, Vol. 87, No. 2234, January 20, 1972, p. 90.

THE TIMES LITERARY SUPPLEMENT

[*Spring Night*] confirms the impression Tarjei Vesaas gave before he died in 1970 of writing with particular power and sensitivity about adolescence against a background of the Nordic countryside. . . .

This is not the kind of story that can be swallowed with aplomb even by those used to the chance but fateful meetings of symbolic Scandinavian films. Vesaas's skill is therefore the greater in that he manages to convey a sense of reality as well as subtlety in all the relationships. Particularly clever is his treatment of involvement, the way the boy is drawn into the complicated, menacing lives of the troubled, demanding people who have suddenly brought both light and dark into what had promised to be a special night.

> "After Lights Out," in The Times Literary Supplement, No. 3649, February 4, 1972, p. 117.

VICTOR HOWES

[In *The Boat in the Evening*, Vesaas depicts] people who nourish within them a spark of individuality, an openness to experience, against the odds. Who'd expect a hardworking Norwegian farmer to read up purposefully about the Khirgiz steppes and the herds of horses that roam there? Tarjei Vesaas, that's who. . . .

[*The Boat in the Evening*] is a prose-poem of evocative images, each chapter a separate sketch, yet each joined by recurrent motifs, fragmentary revelations, floating themes.

Vesaas is half visionary, half naturalist. If his personages have hidden, impassioned depths, so do his objects. He dreams a dream of vast upright plateaus of stone: "I believe that these great expanses of stone have echoing cries within them. The cries are silent within the walls." He hears small beetles send obscure signals. His "boat in the evening" is no real boat, it is a human heart, fastened in a storm, but bumping to be free.

At times Vesaas is graphic, clear as the crystalline Nordic air. At other times snow-clouds of mysticism obscure his text. Dark logs, swirling rivers, shining stampedes, mirrors that smash and vanish along a water's edge, these are the traps of his impressionistic style. Too often we are told, "There are no limits out there. One can imagine distant shores. Great thoroughfares, and harbors in the unknown.". . .

[Vesaas] is to be prized, not for his wild and whirling symbols nor his mystical transparencies, but for his sharp focus on the local citizenry, the actual angelica growing in the fields, the visible, tangible cranes.

The riverboat oarsman, for example, who fishes a half-drowned boy from the shallows of a river with the words, "I expect you'd rather come home with me instead of lying here."

Now there's a laconic Norseman for you.

Victor Howes, "'Visible, Tangible Cranes'," in The Christian Science Monitor, *March 16, 1972, p. 16.*

JOSEPH MELEDIN, JR.

The Boat in the Evening is a disconnected, impressionistic rendering of a lifetime, maybe Vesaas' own, but also standing as an artistic representation of the universal. Its episodes trace the subjective, emotional development and maturity of one unnamed character from boyhood to adulthood, touching on his growth in terms of such relationships as son to father, son at mother's death, adolescent and first love, and young man experiencing nature.

In fact, in describing nature scenes and man's emotional conflicts within them, Vesaas is characteristically Norwegian and at his strongest as a writer. His details are sharp though lyrical, telling though evocative, clinical though mysterious. Even more important, however, is the subjective depth of feeling he draws in his ability to see man as more than just a reasoning being. He reduces the interplay of man and man and of man and nature to their bare metaphoric and symbolic essentials. Like Ingmar Bergman at work in film, Vesaas can tell a good story while reducing that story to its skeletal, though rich, symbolic and thematic threads of life-stream and emotion, thereby questioning and challenging the essence of existence itself.

The effect of a universal life is heightened by the lack of specific character identifications, and fragmented episodes often cloud straightforward plot. Yet the richness and beauty of a total, advancing work of art synthesizing a vision is there.

Impressionism and plot are often at odds, as many frustrated readers often discover, but in *The Boat in the Evening* Tarjei Vesaas manages to reconcile both without compromising either. This novel won't be a top seller in America, but still deserves a spot as a minor classic of fiction. (pp. 438-39)

Joseph Meledin, Jr., in a review of "The Boat in the Evening," in America, *Vol. 126, No. 16, April 22, 1972, pp. 438-39.*

R. G. POPPERWELL

At first *The House in the Dark* might seem to be one of those novels characteristic of the immediate post-war period in Norway, and well represented in the work of many of Vesaas's contemporaries, where the genesis of the traitor and the motivation of the hero are scrutinized with the fundamentalism endemic in much Norwegian literature. Here, however, the individual psychology of the characters is of secondary importance: Vesaas has sought instead to depict, partly in allegorical terms, the psychological impact of the Occupation on the whole community. At the time of its appearance *The House in the Dark* evoked, almost unbearably, the claustrophobic, menacing atmosphere of the Occupation. Today one can look at it more dispassionately.

The house in the darkness is a metaphor for Norway during those years. . . . In the cellars the resistance is burrowing away in the darkness seeking to blast the Centre, the headquarters of the occupying forces, where the Arrow men have their being and from where they conduct their terror. When they go out the members of the underground cling closely to the walls in dark side-streets: the way to the centre, by contrast, and the Arrow men themselves, gleam with light from shining arrows.

[The house] is a setting which could be thought to have a touch of science fiction about it: robot-like figures manipulate the switches that open the steel door to let in and out the vehicle (*vogn*—its translation as *van* is far too utilitarian) which scours the streets sucking in victims. There is melodrama too—an invisible finger traces a message on the table of the informer. However, the setting also provides a common background which throws into relief the reactions of the characters and their human qualities: Stig (the Home Front leader) and his associates; Martin, the stamp collector; the Arrow Polisher who works for the Arrow men. Neither the terror of the Arrow men nor the iron discipline of the underground can prevent the human from breaking through. . . .

It is implicit, however, that the "house" has an overriding right to the loyalty of its inhabitants and that when that is lacking normal virtuous effort may be a perversion. Thus the Arrow Polisher prides himself on doing an honest job and being a good father. Martin the philatelist, an expert on perforations and watermarks, tries to practise non-involvement, shutting himself up and getting on with his "own work". The forced labour of the concentration camp is a perversion of the work of the hands. The darkness of the cellars becomes the light of virtue, the brilliantly lit corridors of the Arrow men the black night of inhumanity. There is no doubt that at times the heavily symbolic mode of presentation becomes unnecessarily obfuscatory, though it is the obliqueness of the novel which gives it validity beyond its "local" setting—a setting which never receives specific mention.

R. G. Popperwell, "Occupational Hazards," in The Times Literary Supplement, *No. 3885, August 27, 1976, p. 1060.*

STEPHEN TROMBLEY

[*The Bleaching Yard*] is a deceptively simple and elegantly structured work which demonstrates great economy of language. . . .

The simple tale which the novel relates principally involves five characters: Johan Tander, proprietor of the bleaching yard, or laundry; his wife, Elise; Vera, a young girl employed by Tander; Jan Vang, a forester who is in love with Vera (both of them have rooms in the same house as Tander); and Krister, an old man for whom no one seems to have any use. Tander becomes infatuated with Vera, whom he adopts as a symbol of purity. . . . [He develops a] profound hatred of Jan Vang, who loves (and is loved by) Vera. Tander, intending to kill Vang and so protect his fantasy, introduces a palpable sense of evil into the quiet village.

In one sense, the novel is an essay on the evil which can result from lack of understanding among people obliged to live together. Tander's wife has an intuitive grasp of his obsession with Vera, and thinks she might jolt him out of his silent brooding by writing on a village wall, under cover of darkness, "NOBODY CARES FOR JOHAN TANDER". Tander assumes this to be the work of Vang, whom he proposes to kill that evening, announcing his intention to Vang the same afternoon. Meanwhile Krister is drawn to the bleaching yard, sensing that this evening he too will die. He would like a clean white shirt, but none of the villagers will oblige him. Krister, in his need, turns to Tander, who repulses him.

Tander also discovers that his wife was responsible for the writing on the wall. This comes as a revelation; Tander rescues himself from hatred, and seeks to explain himself to Vang and Vera. Vang and his friends, meanwhile, have banded together against Tander, and, fortified by a bottle of wine, they frog-march him to his death in the laundry.

Read as myth or fable, the events in the bleaching yard, and the novel as a whole, are an exploration of salvation in a social context; their tragic power lies in the frustration of individual efforts towards redemption. Vesaas's implied resolution seems to be a variation on the Great Commandment: if you cannot love your neighbour, at least be generous.

Stephen Trombley, "Dirty Linen," in The Times Literary Supplement, *No. 4103, November 20, 1981, p. 1374.*

Richard (Nathaniel) Wright
1908-1960

American novelist, autobiographer, short story writer, nonfiction writer, essayist, scriptwriter, dramatist, poet, and editor.

Best known as the author of *Native Son* (1940) and *Black Boy: A Record of Childhood and Youth* (1945), Wright was one of the first American writers of his generation to confront readers with the dehumanizing effects of racism. In his graphic, often brutal accounts of victimized blacks, Wright reveals the physical and psychological torment produced by segregation and discrimination. His stories usually center on alienated, impoverished black men who have been denied freedom and personal identity. In order to overcome racial barriers, Wright's protagonists frequently resort to brutality. Although some critics fault Wright for his preoccupation with violence and his ideological digressions, he remains a seminal figure in twentieth-century American letters and has influenced such prominent contemporary black authors as James Baldwin and Ralph Ellison. According to William Peden, "Wright's stories of helpless or long-suffering Blacks victimized by societal and individual White brutality mark the beginning of a new era in Black fiction and even his least important pieces contain unforgettable scenes and characters that burn their way into the reader's consciousness."

Much of Wright's fiction draws upon his impoverished childhood in the South and his early adulthood in the segregated communities of Chicago. His first published work, *Uncle Tom's Children: Four Novellas* (1939; revised as *Uncle Tom's Children: Five Long Stories*), attacks the racial discrimination and bigotry Wright encountered as a youth. Writing in a naturalistic, straightforward prose style reminiscent of the work of such authors as Theodore Dreiser and John Dos Passos, Wright graphically depicts brutal confrontations between southern whites and blacks. "Down by the Riverside," for instance, chronicles the tragedies that result when a black man takes a white man's raft to transport his pregnant wife to the hospital. After killing the owner of the raft in self-defense, the black man himself is killed as he flees the scene of the murder. While some reviewers objected to Wright's stark, unsympathetic depiction of whites, many praised his ability to capture the fear, humiliation, and anger experienced by blacks in the Jim Crow South. Edward Margolies remarked: "[These] are stories whose sweep and magnitude are suffused with their author's impassioned convictions about the dignity of man, and a profound pity for the degraded, the poor and oppressed who, in the face of casual brutality, cling obstinately to their humanity."

Wright's first novel, *Lawd Today* (1963), was completed during the 1930s but not published until after his death. Also written in the naturalistic tradition, this book unsparingly details a day in the life of Jake Jackson, a violent and ignorant black Chicagoan whose squalid environment offers little opportunity for advancement. While critics considered this a book of minor distinction, they recognized qualities and concerns that would surface in Wright's more powerful work, most notably his highly acclaimed novel *Native Son*. Considered both a psychological melodrama and a protest novel, *Native Son* candidly exposes the pent-up hatred and bitterness of the oppressed black American. In this book, Bigger Thomas, a poor

young black man who has been deluded by the myths and stereotypes of a racist society, accidently murders a wealthy white woman. At the end of the novel, imprisoned and sentenced to death, Bigger gains self-awareness, realizing that his life has meaning and that although he is black he is no less human. Critics immediately hailed the novel as a penetrating indictment of racial persecution. Irving Howe commented: "A blow at the white man, the novel forced him to recognize himself as an oppressor. A blow at the black man, the novel forced him to recognize the cost of his submission." *Native Son* became the first novel by a black American writer to achieve widespread critical and popular success; it was later brought to the stage under the direction of Orson Welles and was adapted for film on two occasions, the first of which featured Wright as Bigger Thomas.

Black Boy is regarded by many critics as Wright's masterpiece. An autobiography structured in many ways like a novel, the book recounts Wright's experiences as a youth in the South. In this work, Wright attacks both white victimization and the predatory nature of members of his own race. He rebukes his strict religious upbringing and reprimands blacks for their servile response to racial subjugation. While some reviewers contended that *Black Boy* offered a bleak, one-sided viewpoint that failed to delineate the complexity of the situation, Raymond Kennedy dissented: "This, with few exceptions, is precisely how race relations are in the Southern States: clean-cut black and white. The Negroes must either surrender and allow themselves to be spiritually stunted and deformed, or they must get out of the South." The posthumously published *American Hunger* (1977), a sequel to *Black Boy,* traces Wright's migration to the North and his early years as a writer in Chicago, during which he became a member of the Communist party.

Wright gradually became disillusioned with the efforts to improve race relations in the United States. He subsequently abandoned communism as a plausible solution to social inequality and moved to France in 1946. Wright's literary output during this period is generally considered inferior to his early work. Many critics attribute Wright's creative decline to his newfound interest in existentialism, which they believe stripped his work of its urgency and power. Gloria Bramwell declared: "Wright, an emotional writer, could paint a stunning picture of the Negro's plight but when he attempted to intellectualize it he embraced it from the wrong angle, from the inside out rather than in terms of his own characters." *The Outsider* (1953), the first novel Wright produced after leaving the United States, was one of the first existentialist novels written by an American author. Avoiding racial issues in this work, Wright recounts the story of a black man who joins the Communist party and kills several of its members in his search for identity and meaning. Critics generally dismissed *The Outsider* as an ambitious but unsuccessful work in which Wright was unable to smoothly assimilate his philosophical theories into the narrative.

Wright's next novel, *Savage Holiday* (1954), is a psychological thriller involving a white insurance salesman who becomes a symbol for modern alienated humanity. Few American critics reviewed this book, and those who did deemed it Wright's least effective work. Wright followed *Savage Holiday* with *The Long Dream* (1958), a novel that returns to his early thematic concerns. Set in Mississippi, this book depicts the psychological growth of Fishbelly, a middle-class black youth who must come to terms with his father's amoral business practices and the racial conflicts ravaging the South. After serving a prison sentence for a crime he did not commit, Fishbelly leaves for France, fleeing the violence and oppression of his past. *The Outsider* generally received unfavorable notices from reviewers, many of whom argued that Wright had lost touch with the black American experience. *Eight Men* (1961), a posthumously published collection of short stories, contains "The Man Who Lived Underground," which is often regarded as Wright's most important fictional work of the 1950s. Reminiscent of Fedor Dostoevski's *Notes from the Underground,* this story concerns a black man who attempts to escape punishment for a crime of which he is innocent by hiding in the city sewer system.

In addition to his novels and short stories, Wright produced several nonfiction works. *12 Million Black Voices* (1941) is a textual and photographic history of the racial prejudice to which black Americans have been subjected. In *Black Power* (1954), Wright records his reactions to a visit to Takoradi, a British colony in Africa where a black man had been appointed prime minister, and in *The Color Curtain: A Report on the Bandung Conference* (1956), he reflects on a conference held in Indonesia by the free nations of the Third World. *Pagan Spain* (1957) recounts Wright's bitterness over the poverty and corruption he observed while traveling in Spain. Joseph G. Harrison commented: "While *Pagan Spain* is patently written from an outlook that stresses the bad and largely ignores the good, few neutral observers would deny that a great deal of what the author says both is true and urgently needs saying." *White*

Man, Listen! (1957) collects four lectures Wright presented on racial relations.

(See also *CLC,* Vols. 1, 3, 4, 9, 14, 21; *Contemporary Authors,* Vol. 108; and *Dictionary of Literary Biography Documentary Series,* Vol. 2.)

In this volume commentary on Richard Wright is focused on his novel *Native Son.*

RICHARD WRIGHT

[*The essay from which this excerpt is taken was originally published in* The Saturday Review of Literature, *June 1, 1940.*]

I am not so pretentious as to imagine that it is possible for me to account completely for my own book, **Native Son.** But I am going to try to account for as much of it as I can, the sources of it, the material that went into it, and my own years' long changing attitude toward that material. (p. vii)

The birth of Bigger Thomas goes back to my childhood, and there was not just one Bigger, but many of them, more than I could count and more than you suspect. But let me start with the first Bigger, whom I shall call Bigger No. 1.

When I was a bareheaded, barefoot kid in Jackson, Mississippi, there was a boy who terrorized me and all of the boys I played with. If we were playing games, he would saunter up and snatch from us our balls, bats, spinning tops, and marbles. We would stand around pouting, sniffling, trying to keep back our tears, begging for our playthings. But Bigger would refuse. We never demanded that he give them back; we were afraid, and Bigger was bad. We had seen him clout boys when he was angry and we did not want to run that risk. We never recovered our toys unless we flattered him and made him feel that he was superior to us. Then, perhaps, if he felt like it, he condescended, threw them at us and then gave each of us a swift kick in the bargain, just to make us feel his utter contempt.

That was the way Bigger No. 1 lived. His life was a continuous challenge to others. At all times he *took* his way, right or wrong, and those who contradicted him had him to fight. And never was he happier than when he had someone cornered and at his mercy; it seemed that the deepest meaning of his squalid life was in him at such times.

I don't know what the fate of Bigger No. 1 was. . . . But I suspect that his end was violent. Anyway, he left a marked impression upon me; maybe it was because I longed secretly to be like him and was afraid. I don't know.

If I had known only one Bigger I would not have written **Native Son.** Let me call the next one Bigger No. 2; he was about seventeen and tougher than the first Bigger. Since I, too, had grown older, I was a little less afraid of him. And the hardness of this Bigger No. 2 was not directed toward me or the other Negroes, but toward the whites who ruled the South. He bought clothes and food on credit and would not pay for them. He lived in the dingy shacks of the white landlords and refused to pay rent. Of course, he had no money, but neither did we. We did without the necessities of life and starved ourselves, but he never would. When we asked him why he acted as he did, he would tell us (as though we were little children in a kindergarten) that the white folks had everything and he had nothing. Further, he would tell us that we were fools not to get what we wanted while we were alive in this world. We would listen and silently agree. We longed to believe and act as he did, but we were afraid. . . . Bigger No. 2 wanted to live and he did; he was in prison the last time I heard from him.

There was Bigger No. 3, whom the white folks called a "bad nigger." He carried his life in his hands in a literal fashion. I once worked as a ticket-taker in a Negro movie house . . . and many times Bigger No. 3 came to the door and gave my arm a hard pinch and walked into the theater. Resentfully and silently, I'd nurse my bruised arm. Presently, the proprietor would come over and ask how things were going. I'd point into the darkened theater and say: "Bigger's in there." "Did he pay?" the proprietor would ask. "No, sir," I'd answer. The proprietor would pull down the corners of his lips and speak through his teeth: "We'll kill that goddamn nigger one of these days." And the episode would end right there. But later on Bigger No. 3 was killed during the days of Prohibition: while delivering liquor to a customer he was shot through the back by a white cop.

And then there was Bigger No. 4, whose only law was death. The Jim Crow laws of the South were not for him. But as he laughed and cursed and broke them, he knew that some day he'd have to pay for his freedom. His rebellious spirit made him violate all the taboos and consequently he always oscillated between moods of intense elation and depression. . . . He had no job, for he regarded digging ditches for fifty cents a day as slavery. "I can't live on that," he would say. Ofttimes I'd find him reading a book; he would stop and in a joking, wistful, and cynical manner ape the antics of the white folks. Generally, he'd end his mimicry in a depressed state and say: "The white folks won't let us do nothing." Bigger No. 4 was sent to the asylum for the insane.

Then there was Bigger No. 5, who always rode the Jim Crow streetcars without paying and sat wherever he pleased. I remember one morning his getting into a streetcar . . . and sitting in the white section. The conductor went to him and said: "Come on, nigger. Move over where you belong. Can't you read?" Bigger answered: "Naw, I can't read." The conductor flared up: "Get out of that seat!" Bigger took out his knife, opened it, held it nonchalantly in his hand, and replied: "Make me." The conductor turned red, blinked, clenched his fists, and walked away, stammering: "The goddamn scum of the earth!" A small angry conference of white men took place in the front of the car and the Negroes sitting in the Jim Crow section overheard: "That's that Bigger Thomas nigger and you'd better leave 'im alone." The Negroes experienced an intense flash of pride and the streetcar moved on its journey without incident. I don't know what happened to Bigger No. 5. But I can guess.

The Bigger Thomases were the only Negroes I know of who consistently violated the Jim Crow laws of the South and got away with it, at least for a sweet brief spell. Eventually, the whites who restricted their lives made them pay a terrible price. They were shot, hanged, maimed, lynched, and generally hounded until they were either dead or their spirits broken. (pp. viii-xi)

[Why] did Bigger revolt? No explanation based upon a hard and fast rule of conduct can be given. But there were always two factors psychologically dominant in his personality. First, through some quirk of circumstance, he had become estranged from the religion and the folk culture of his race. Second, he

was trying to react to and answer the call of the dominant civilization whose glitter came to him through the newspapers, magazines, radios, movies, and the mere imposing sight and sound of daily American life. In many respects his emergence as a distinct type was inevitable.

As I grew older, I became familiar with the Bigger Thomas conditioning and its numerous shadings no matter where I saw it in Negro life. It was not, as I have already said, as blatant or extreme as in the originals; but it was there, nevertheless, like an undeveloped negative.

Sometimes, in areas far removed from Mississippi, I'd hear a Negro say: "I wish I didn't have to live this way. I feel like I want to burst." Then the anger would pass; he would go back to his job and try to eke out a few pennies to support his wife and children.

Sometimes I'd hear a Negro say: "God, I wish I had a flag and a country of my own." But that mood would soon vanish and he would go his way placidly enough.

Sometimes I'd hear a Negro ex-soldier say: "What in hell did I fight in the war for? They segregated me even when I was offering my life for my country." But he, too, like the others, would soon forget, would become caught up in the tense grind of struggling for bread. (pp. xiii-xiv)

It was not until I went to live in Chicago that I first thought seriously of writing of Bigger Thomas. Two items of my experience combined to make me aware of Bigger as a meaningful and prophetic symbol. First, being free of the daily pressure of the Dixie environment, I was able to come into possession of my own feelings. Second, my contact with the labor movement and its ideology made me see Bigger clearly and feel what he meant.

I made the discovery that Bigger Thomas was not black all the time; he was white, too, and there were literally millions of him, everywhere. The extension of my sense of the personality of Bigger was the pivot of my life; it altered the complexion of my existence. I became conscious, at first dimly, and then later on with increasing clarity and conviction, of a vast, muddied pool of human life in America. It was as though I had put on a pair of spectacles whose power was that of an x-ray enabling me to see deeper into the lives of men. Whenever I picked up a newspaper, I'd no longer feel that I was reading of the doings of whites alone (Negroes are rarely mentioned in the press unless they've committed some crime!), but of a complex struggle for life going on in my country, a struggle in which I was involved. I sensed, too, that the Southern scheme of oppression was but an appendage of a far vaster and in many respects more ruthless and impersonal commodity-profit machine. (pp. xiv-xv)

As my mind extended in this general and abstract manner, it was fed with even more vivid and concrete examples of the lives of Bigger Thomas. The urban environment of Chicago, affording a more stimulating life, made the Negro Bigger Thomases react more violently than even in the South. More than ever I began to see and understand the environmental factors which made for this extreme conduct. It was not that Chicago segregated Negroes more than the South, but that Chicago had more to offer, that Chicago's physical aspect—noisy, crowded, filled with the sense of power and fulfillment—did so much more to dazzle the mind with a taunting sense of possible achievement that the segregation it did impose brought forth from Bigger a reaction more obstreperous than in the South. (p. xv)

There is in me a memory of reading an interesting pamphlet telling of the friendship of Gorky and Lenin in exile. The booklet told of how Lenin and Gorky were walking down a London street. Lenin turned to Gorky and, pointing, said: "Here is *their* Big Ben." "There is *their* Westminister Abbey." "There is *their* library." And at once, while reading that passage, my mind stopped, teased, challenged with the effort to remember, to associate widely disparate but meaningful experiences in my life. For a moment nothing would come, but I remained convinced that I had heard the meaning of those words sometime, somewhere before. Then, with a sudden glow of satisfaction of having gained a little more knowledge about the world in which I lived, I'd end up by saying: "That's Bigger. That's the Bigger Thomas reaction."

In both instances the deep sense of exclusion was identical. The feeling of looking at things with a painful and unwarrantable nakedness was an experience, I learned, that transcended national and racial boundaries. It was this intolerable sense of feeling and understanding so much, and yet living on a plane of social reality where the look of a world which one did not make or own struck one with a blinding objectivity and tangibility, that made me grasp the revolutionary impulse in my life and the lives of those about me and far away.

I remember reading a passage in a book dealing with old Russia which said: "We must be ready to make endless sacrifices if we are to be able to overthrow the Czar." And again I'd say to myself: "I've heard that somewhere, sometime before." And again I'd hear Bigger Thomas, far away and long ago, telling some white man who was trying to impose upon him: "I'll kill you and go to hell and pay for it." While living in America I heard from far away Russia the bitter accents of tragic calculation of how much human life and suffering it would cost a man to live as a man in a world that denied him the right to live with dignity. Actions and feelings of men ten thousand miles from home helped me to understand the moods and impulses of those walking the streets of Chicago and Dixie.

I am not saying that I heard any talk of revolution in the South when I was a kid there. But I did hear the lispings, the whispers, the mutters which some day, under one stimulus or another, will surely grow into open revolt unless the conditions which produce Bigger Thomases are changed. (pp. xvii-xviii)

All Bigger Thomases, white and black, felt tense, afraid, nervous, hysterical, and restless. From far away Nazi Germany and old Russia had come to me items of knowledge that told me that certain modern experiences were creating types of personalities whose existence ignored racial and national lines of demarcation, that these personalities carried with them a more universal drama-element than anything I'd ever encountered before; that these personalities were mainly imposed upon men and women living in a world whose fundamental assumptions could no longer be taken for granted: a world ridden with national and class strife; a world whose metaphysical meanings had vanished; a world in which God no longer existed as a daily focal point of men's lives; a world in which men could no longer retain their faith in an ultimate hereafter. It was a highly geared world whose nature was conflict and action, a world whose limited area and vision imperiously urged men to satisfy their organisms, a world that existed on a plane of animal sensation alone. (p. xix)

From these items I drew my first political conclusions about Bigger: I felt that Bigger, an American product, a native son of this land, carried within him the potentialities of either Communism or Fascism. I don't mean to say that the Negro boy I depicted in *Native Son* is either a Communist or a Fascist. He is not either. But he is product of a dislocated society; he is a dispossessed and disinherited man; he is all of this, and he lives amid the greatest possible plenty on earth and he is looking and feeling for a way out. Whether he'll follow some gaudy, hysterical leader who'll promise rashly to fill the void in him, or whether he'll come to an understanding with the millions of his kindred fellow workers under trade-union or revolutionary guidance depends upon the future drift of events in America. But, granting the emotional state, the tensity, the fear, the hate, the impatience, the sense of exclusion, the ache for violent action, the emotional and cultural hunger, Bigger Thomas, conditioned as his organism is, will not become an ardent, or even a lukewarm, supporter of the *status quo*.

The difference between Bigger's tensity and the German variety is that Bigger's, due to America's educational restrictions on the bulk of her Negro population, is in a nascent state, not yet articulate. And the difference between Bigger's longing for self-identification and the Russian principle of self-determination is that Bigger's, due to the effects of American oppression, which has not allowed for the forming of deep ideas of solidarity among Negroes, is still in a state of individual anger and hatred. Here, I felt, was *drama!* Who will be the first to touch off these Bigger Thomases in America, white and black?

For a long time I toyed with the idea of writing a novel in which a Negro Bigger Thomas would loom as a symbolic figure of American life, a figure who would hold within him the prophecy of our future. I felt strongly that he held within him, in a measure which perhaps no other contemporary type did, the outlines of action and feeling which we would encounter on a vast scale in the days to come. Just as one sees when one walks into a medical research laboratory jars of alcohol containing abnormally large or distorted portions of the human body, just so did I see and feel that the conditions of life under which Negroes are forced to live in America contain the embryonic emotional prefigurations of how a large part of the body politic would react under stress. (pp. xx-xxi)

But several things militated against my starting to work. Like Bigger himself, I felt a mental censor—product of the fears which a Negro feels from living in America—standing over me, draped in white, warning me not to write. This censor's warnings were translated into my own thought processes thus: "What will white people think if I draw the pictures of such a Negro boy? Will they not at once say: 'See, didn't we tell you all along that niggers are like that? Now, look, one of their own kind has come along and drawn the picture for us!'" I felt that if I drew the picture of Bigger truthfully, there would be many reactionary whites who would try to make of him something I did not intend. And yet, and this was what made it difficult, I knew that I could not write of Bigger convincingly if I did not depict him as he *was:* that is, resentful toward whites, sullen, angry, ignorant, emotionally unstable, depressed and unaccountably elated. at times, and unable even, because of his own lack of inner organization which American oppression has fostered in him, to unite with the members of his own race. And would not whites misread Bigger and, doubting his authenticity, say: "This man is preaching hate against the whole white race"?

The more I thought of it the more I became convinced that if I did not write of Bigger as I saw and felt him, if I did not try to make him a living personality and at the same time a symbol of all the larger things I felt and saw in him, I'd be reacting as Bigger himself reacted: that is, I'd be acting out of *fear* if I let what I thought whites would say constrict and paralyze me. (pp. xxi-xxii)

Another thought kept me from writing. What would my own white and black comrades in the Communist party say? This thought was the most bewildering of all. . . . How could I create such complex and wide schemes of associational thought and feeling, such filigreed webs of dreams and politics, without being mistaken for a "smuggler of reaction," "an ideological confusionist," or "an individualistic and dangerous element"? Though my heart is with the collectivist and proletarian ideal, I solved this problem by assuring myself that honest politics and honest feeling in imaginative representation ought to be able to meet on common healthy ground without fear, suspicion, and quarreling. Further, and more importantly, I steeled myself by coming to the conclusion that whether politicians accepted or rejected Bigger did not really matter; my task, as I felt it, was to free myself of this burden of impressions and feelings, recast them into the image of Bigger and make him *true*. (p. xxii)

There was another constricting thought that kept me from work. It deals with my own race. . . . I knew from long and painful experience that the Negro middle and professional classes were the people of my own race who were more than others ashamed of Bigger and what he meant. Having narrowly escaped the Bigger Thomas reaction pattern themselves—indeed, still retaining traces of it within the confines of their own timid personalities—they would not relish being publicly reminded of the lowly, shameful depths of life above which they enjoyed their bourgeois lives. Never did they want people, especially *white* people, to think that their lives were so much touched by anything so dark and brutal as Bigger. (pp. xxii-xxiii)

But Bigger won over all these claims; he won because I felt that I was hunting on the trail of more exciting and thrilling game. What Bigger meant had claimed me because I felt with all of my being that he was more important than what any person, white or black, would say or try to make of him, more important than any political analysis designed to explain or deny him, more important, even, than my own sense of fear, shame, and diffidence. (p. xxiii)

I don't know if *Native Son* is a good book or a bad book. And I don't know if the book I'm working on now will be a good book or a bad book. And I really don't care. The mere writing of it will be more fun and a deeper satisfaction than any praise or blame from anybody.

I feel that I'm lucky to be alive to write novels today, when the whole world is caught in the pangs of war and change. Early American writers, Henry James and Nathaniel Hawthorne, complained bitterly about the bleakness and flatness of the American scene. But I think that if they were alive, they'd feel at home in modern America. True, we have no great church in America; our national traditions are still of such a sort that we are not wont to brag of them; and we have no army that's above the level of mercenary fighters; we have no group acceptable to the whole of our country upholding certain humane values; we have no rich symbols, no colorful rituals. We have only a money-grubbing, industrial civilization. But we do have in the Negro the embodiment of a past tragic enough to appease the spiritual hunger of even a James; and we have in the oppression of the Negro a shadow athwart our national life dense and heavy enough to satisfy even the gloomy broodings of a Hawthorne. And if Poe were alive, he would not have to invent horror; horror would invent him. (p. xxxiv)

Richard Wright, "How 'Bigger' Was Born," in his Native Son, *Harper & Row, Publishers, 1966, pp. vii-xxxiv.*

JAMES BALDWIN

[*The essay from which this excerpt is taken was originally published in* Partisan Review, *June, 1949.*]

[The] avowed aim of the American protest novel is to bring greater freedom to the oppressed. They are forgiven, on the strength of these good intentions, whatever violence they do to language, whatever excessive demands they make of credibility. It is, indeed, considered the sign of a frivolity so intense as to approach decadence to suggest that these books are both badly written and wildly improbable. One is told to put first things first, the good of society coming before niceties of style or characterization. Even if this were incontestable—for what exactly is the "good" of society?—it argues an insuperable confusion, since literature and sociology are not one and the same; it is impossible to discuss them as if they were. Our passion for categorization, life neatly fitted into pegs, has led to an unforeseen, paradoxical distress; confusion, a breakdown of meaning. Those categories which were meant to define and control the world for us have boomeranged us into chaos; in which limbo we whirl, clutching the straws of our definitions. The "protest" novel, so far from being disturbing, is an accepted and comforting aspect of the American scene, ramifying that framework we believe to be so necessary. Whatever unsettling questions are raised are evanescent, titillating; remote, for this has nothing to do with us, it is safely ensconced in the social arena, where, indeed, it has nothing to do with anyone, so that finally we receive a very definite thrill of virtue from the fact that we are reading such a book at all. This report from the pit reassures us of its reality and its darkness and of our own salvation; and "As long as such books are being published," an American liberal once said to me, "everything will be all right."

But unless one's ideal of society is a race of neatly analyzed, hardworking ciphers, one can hardly claim for the protest novels the lofty purpose they claim for themselves or share the present optimism concerning them. They emerge for what they are: a mirror of our confusion, dishonesty, panic, trapped and immobilized in the sunlit prison of the American dream. They are fantasies, connecting nowhere with reality, sentimental; in exactly the same sense that such movies as *The Best Years of Our Lives* or the works of Mr. James M. Cain are fantasies. Beneath the dazzling pyrotechnics of these current operas one may still discern, as the controlling force, the intense theological preoccupations of Mrs. Stowe [in *Uncle Tom's Cabin*], the sick vacuities of *The Rover Boys*. Finally, the aim of the protest novel becomes something very closely resembling the zeal of those alabaster missionaries to Africa to cover the nakedness of the natives, to hurry them into the pallid arms of Jesus and thence into slavery. The aim has now become to reduce all Americans to the compulsive, bloodless dimensions of a guy named Joe. (pp. 31-2)

In *Native Son*, Bigger Thomas stands on a Chicago street corner watching airplanes flown by white men racing against the sun and ''Goddamn'' he says, the bitterness bubbling up like blood, remembering a million indignities, the terrible, rat-infested house, the humiliation of home-relief, the intense, aimless, ugly bickering, hating it; hatred smoulders through these pages like sulphur fire. All of Bigger's life is controlled, defined by his hatred and his fear. And later, his fear drives him to murder and his hatred to rape; he dies, having come, through this violence, we are told, for the first time, to a kind of life, having for the first time redeemed his manhood. Below the surface of this novel there lies, as it seems to me, a continuation, a complement of that monstrous legend it was written to destroy. Bigger is Uncle Tom's descendant, flesh of his flesh, so exactly opposite a portrait that, when the books are placed together, it seems that the contemporary Negro novelist and the dead New England woman are locked together in a deadly, timeless battle; the one uttering merciless exhortations, the other shouting curses. And, indeed, within this web of lust and fury, black and white can only thrust and counter-thrust, long for each other's Now, exquisite death; death by torture, acid, knives, and burning; the thrust, the counter-thrust, the longing making the heavier that cloud which blinds and suffocates them both, so that they go down into the pit together. Thus has the cage betrayed us all, this moment, our life, turned to nothing through our terrible attempts to insure it. For Bigger's tragedy is not that he is cold or black or hungry, not even that he is American, black; but that he has accepted a theology that denies him life, that he admits the possibility of his being sub-human and feels constrained, therefore, to battle for his humanity according to those brutal criteria bequeathed him at his birth. But our humanity is our burden, our life; we need not battle for it; we need only to do what is infinitely more difficult—that is, accept it. The failure of the protest novel lies in its rejection of life, the human being, the denial of his beauty, dread, power, in its insistence that it is his categorization alone which is real and which cannot be transcended. (p. 33)

James Baldwin, *''Everybody's Protest Novel,''* in his The Price of the Ticket: Collected Nonfiction 1948-1985, *St. Martin's/Marek, 1985, pp. 27-33.*

KATHLEEN GALLAGHER

That in a racist society blacks become criminals by virtue of their very existence is a predominant theme of Richard Wright's fiction. His criminals run the gamut from Big Boy and Mann to Cross Damon—from the illiterate victim of oppression, who acts in explicit self-defense, to the intellectual ''ethical criminal,'' who acts to reshape the world to meet a self-definition. (p. 293)

Wright implies that whether his characters become convictable criminals or not is largely a question of luck, context, and semantics. In the eyes of the dominant society, they are guilty and not to be proved innocent. . . . As Robert Bone has said, Wright, like his fictional heroes, knows that the crime for which he will be punished is ''the crime of being black.''

In *Native Son*, Wright develops most explicitly the metaphor of potential criminality that haunts much of his work. The crime for which Bigger Thomas is condemned to death, the killing of a young white woman in her bed, is a metaphor that represents the meaning of Bigger's life. Lest the point be missed, Bigger's Communist lawyer, Boris Max, will say with emphasis at the trial: *''His very existence is a crime against the state!''* (pp. 293-94)

Native Son might be said to be about Bigger's perception of images. It is about his struggle to understand and control the metaphor of his own life. Bigger, who begins by refusing to confront the terrible reality of his life, at the end glimpses the truth: ''I didn't want to kill!. . . But what I killed for, I *am*!'' He comes to a comprehension of the metaphor as a result of his growing understanding of the partial and false images that have defined his being. Images at first cloud the truth for Bigger, but his growing ability to understand and control them launches him toward a deeper understanding of reality. By the end of the book, he will make the great leap from the literal to the figurative.

In Book One of *Native Son*, Bigger is dominated by images that he cannot control. Because of the false images or stereotypes that govern whites' perceptions of blacks, he is offered no acceptable image of who he is or what he might become. Because of his own partial image of whites, he lives in continual hate and fear. He fragments the reality of both worlds, keeping the painful truth of his own world at bay and creating a fantasy white world which he peoples with his own cast of stereotyped characters. (p. 294)

By the time we meet Bigger he is a full-blown juvenile delinquent of age twenty. . . . He is as close as possible to being that unthinkable child that not even a mother can love. [His mother] says, ''Bigger, sometimes I wonder why I birthed you.'' Because the reality of his world is too frightening to confront, Bigger filters it through a mental curtain: ''He knew that the moment he allowed himself to feel to its fulness how they lived, the shame and misery of their lives, he would be swept out of himself with fear and despair. So he held toward them an attitude of iron reserve; he lived with them; but behind a wall, a curtain. And toward himself he was even more exacting.''

It is, of course, the white world that has set the narrow limits of the black world and forced Bigger to retreat behind his self-protective curtain. Bigger's notions of the white world are derived primarily from the mass media and are the stuff of one of his sustaining modes of escape. White men, to Bigger, are presidents, generals, and corporate executives. When he and his friend Gus ''play white,'' they mimic the voices and manners of men of power. White women are promiscuous ''rich chicks,'' like the featured character in a movie Bigger sees, *The Gay Woman,* who floats between ''scenes of cocktail drinking, dancing, golfing, swimming, and spinning roulette wheels.'' (p. 295)

By sending Bigger into the Dalton household as a live-in chauffeur, Wright plunges him swiftly and dramatically into the heart of the white world. Here the stereotypes loom more menacingly. Bigger can ''play white'' with Gus and be entertained by the whites in the movies because he restricts the white world to a comfortable cast of well-defined stock characters. Since these stereotypes are images of his own creation, he can control them. His perception of the real white world, however, is more closely represented in the vague, gothic whiteness of the blind Mrs. Dalton and her ubiquitous, Poe-like cat. Later, he perceives her as a white blur, a white blur that will terrify him throughout most of the book. For Bigger, the white world is a ''looming mountain of white hate.'' At the trial, Max will describe the distortive barriers set up between races and classes by stereotypes and false images. Rather than people facing people, he says, ''They feel that they are facing mountains, floods, seas: forces of nature. . . .''

In their misguided attempt at improving race relations, Mary Dalton and her Communist boy friend, Jan Erlone, succeed only in magnifying the color-line for Bigger. Mary and Jan use Bigger to fill a role that they are defining for him: they simply change the role from black servant to black proletarian. Their presumption is little more than a variation on Mr. Dalton's refusal to rent housing to blacks in white neighborhoods because "Negroes are happier when they're together." (p. 296)

Mary and Jan force a further conjunction of the black and white worlds by insisting that Bigger accompany them to a black restaurant on the South Side. As Dan McCall has noted, Jan and Mary regress further into stereotypes as they become more drunk. Mary becomes a self-parody as she coaxes Bigger to help her sing a spiritual and, after Jan has left, flirts with Bigger and puts her head on his shoulder. When Mary passes out trying to climb the stairs of the Dalton house, Bigger finds himself in a rather traditional servant's role after all; having had their fun, Mary and Jan have left Bigger to protect both them and himself by cleaning up the mess. Quietly he carries Mary upstairs and locates her room, thinking, "Well, all they could do was fire him. It wasn't his fault that she was drunk."

Bigger suddenly has been dragged further into the No Man's Land between the black and white worlds than he ever has been in his life. He smothers Mary on her "white bed" with a pillow in "hysterical terror" when he hears the door creak and turns to see Mrs. Dalton, like a "white blur . . . standing by the door, silent, ghostlike." Bigger has no thought of killing Mary; his intention is to keep her quiet so that Mrs. Dalton will not come over to the bed and discover him. (p. 297)

Wherever one turns, it is ultimately because of the racism of the white world that Bigger kills Mary. Bigger does not for a moment consider his course of action rationally. . . . Bigger is "intimidated to the core by the awesome white blur floating toward him." Although he knows that the white blur is Mrs. Dalton, it is not until Mary has stopped struggling that he can "see Mrs. Dalton plainly." Over three hundred years of conditioning tell him the implications of his being found in the unconscious Mary's room, and he acts in response to a racial prototype rather than to the specifics of the situations. Mrs. Dalton is a white blur; Mary is a white body to be silenced; Bigger himself is a quivering black mass of terror and taut nerves.

In terms of the essential, almost archetypal, conflict Bigger is a victim of his environment: the killing is an accident, and Bigger is innocent. Without denying the truth of this view of events, Wright shows that reality is considerably more complex and even ironic. Mrs. Dalton is not really a blur of white vengeance. In his terror, Bigger forgets his earlier opinion that she would always judge him fairly. He has no way of knowing that Mary has caused trouble for her parents before, that the Daltons dislike Jan, that there is a very reasonable possibility that Mrs. Dalton would believe the truth and that Mary herself probably would confirm it. With good historical reason, Bigger has feared all along that the Daltons somehow would hold him responsible for the entire evening. All along, he has known that because he is black he is guilty. (p. 298)

The crime has two effects on Bigger: it gives him an identity for the first time in his life, but it also drives him to such a frenzy of fear and guilt that he quickly brings on his own destruction. Not once does Bigger consider shirking responsibility for murder. As soon as he realizes that Mary is dead, he accepts the image of himself that he knows society will see:

"The reality of the room fell away from him; the vast city of white people that sprawled outside took its place. She was dead and he had killed her. He was a murderer, a Negro murderer, a black murderer. He had killed a white woman."

As he accepts the role society has assigned him, he comes from behind his wall of indifference. He now has a way to act, an image with which to conform, and he acts like a murderer. . . . With a definite role to play, he feels that he can control himself and other people, even white people, for the first time. What actually has happened is that, without understanding fully, Bigger has sensed that the symbolic truth of the image is greater than the literal truth of what has occurred. . . . (pp. 299-300)

In Book Two, Bigger learns to manipulate the images. With his wall of indifference down, he is able to look directly at both the white and black worlds for the first time. At home with his family the morning after the crime, he begins to see things that he has never permitted himself to see before. He sees the shabbiness of their lives and the passivity of their response to it. He also begins to perceive another metaphor that permeates *Native Son* to the saturation point, that of blindness. Mrs. Dalton's physical blindness, without benefit of which Bigger could not have killed Mary, is symptomatic of the mental blindness that handicaps everyone in the book. Bigger now sees that his family, like everyone else, "wanted and yearned to see life in a certain way; they needed a certain picture of the world . . . and they were blind to what did not fit." (p. 300)

The practical implication of Bigger's awareness of everyone's blindness is that he can use it to make himself invisible as a criminal. He assumes that people will see what they want to see; whatever does not fit their preconceived image will be discarded. Bigger has always known what whites want to see. The role works in two directions, pleasing them and permitting him to disguise his real feelings. His entire manner changed when he first entered the Dalton household; the surly, sassy Bigger became obsequious and soft-spoken. His lack of practice with the role made him play it nervously, but he did it well enough to pass inspection. . . . (pp. 300-01)

Now Bigger is able to use the stereotype consciously. If he conforms well enough to the preconceived image, no one will suspect him of being anything else. . . . Living has become a great game for Bigger, a game to which only he knows the rule: "[A]ct like other people thought you ought to act, yet do what you wanted." He has done that all his life, he thinks, but now he sees it "sharply and simply."

Bigger has become a conscious dealer in stereotypes. He has made rapid strides in his ability to perceive and analyze. But his vision is only partial. He does not see that while he is manipulating the "obsequious servant" stereotype, he is being manipulated by another stereotype which he has chosen to assume, that of the "bad nigger." Although he has acted like a "bad nigger" for much of his life, even with his family and friends, now he seizes the role with a vengeance. In the supposed rape and murder of a white woman, the image is fully realized. Bigger thinks, in effect, that if that is what society thinks he is, then that is what he will be; if he has wished and felt these things, then he will do them; if he will be judged guilty anyway, then he will be guilty. He will be the quintessential "bad nigger," all the while acting the role of "timid Negro boy." Because he controls one stereotype, he thinks he controls the situation. It is only on an emotional level that he knows that he is still a victim, and it is his emotions that will do him in. (pp. 300-02)

The rape and murder of Bessie are a mirror image of what Bigger is thought to have done to Mary. He becomes as nearly the animal that the whites assume him to be as is possible: the rape is a completely irrational act, and he bashes Bessie's skull with a brick, much as he had killed the rat [in the first chapter]. These deeds are superfluous to the plot, since it is the supposed rape and murder of the white woman for which Bigger will be condemned, not the known rape and murder of the black woman. Bigger already has accepted responsibility for raping and murdering Mary because he sees in those acts an objective correlative for his violent mental response to the white world. Of the murder, he thought that he had killed many times before, even though there were no corpses to show for it. When Bessie first points out to him that because he has destroyed Mary's body, the whites will assume that he raped her, he at first reacts with shock but then embraces this crime too. Again he sees that the symbolic truth carries greater weight than the literal. . . . (p. 303)

With his capture, at the close of Book Two, Bigger is temporarily thrown back into passivity. His brief reign as the King of No Man's Land having ended, he rejects reality once again and retreats further behind his mental curtain than he ever has before. In Book Three, as he awaits his trial and execution, he must start from scratch in defining the reality of his life. He begins to see that in embracing the false images he has succeeded only in playing himself further into the hands of the white world. As the stereotypes crumble, he sees that he has let himself be used as a piece in someone else's image pattern.

One set of images that Bigger has rejected steadily throughout the book is that offered by Christianity. His mother's singing of hymns and spirituals while she works had been a continual source of annoyance to him. While he was in flight in Book Two, he overheard singing from a black church. The music was full of "surrender, resignation" and the belief that "all life was a sorrow that had to be accepted." When he is visited in prison by his mother's minister, the Reverend Hammond, he is again briefly drawn toward this ordered view of reality. Although he loathes the preacher's message, he responds to the configuration of images which the preacher presents. . . . (pp. 304-05)

Jan Erlone visits Bigger next, and this encounter proves more significant. Because he had attempted to frame Jan for Mary's disappearance, Bigger is "galvanized by fear" at the sight of him. But what Jan has to say quickly startles Bigger out of his fear. Jan says that although he was angry at first, now he understands why Bigger killed. Now he wants to break the pattern of racial vengeance by helping rather than hating Bigger, and he has a friend, a lawyer, who wants to help Bigger, too.

The impact Jan has on Bigger is unique and irreversible: he offers Bigger an escape from No Man's Land through a transcendence of the boundaries of the black and white worlds. (p. 305)

Where religion has failed Bigger by its rejection of humanity for another world, humanity itself offers him redemption. That Jan's forgiving nobility is not entirely credible is less important than it might be because of the emphasis Wright places on Bigger's role in the experience. Bigger is not just the passive recipient of the white man's enlightenment. Wright describes a reciprocal process that gives responsibility and control to Bigger. Because Jan sees that Bigger is human, Bigger is able to see that Jan is human. It is Bigger's recognition of Jan's humanity that breaks the color-line for him, that makes him feel remorse, and that offers him the chance to stop being a "No Man" and join the human race. Through Jan, Bigger begins to see through the image of the white mountain.

Despite its importance, what has occurred is only the beginning of an idea for Bigger, and he soon is confronted with other people and events that sweep him back into shame, despair, and hate. He is intimidated by Buckley, the swaggering, cigar-chewing state's attorney. He is terrified at the appearance of the Daltons and mortified by the behavior of his family and friends. While the public story marches to its foregone conclusion, Bigger continues his attempt to find a center of stability. (p. 306)

The emotional fluctuation that has been part of Bigger since the beginning of the book has become a vortex that spins faster and faster. With his capture, he entered a new spiral between the hope suggested by his brief feelings of kinship with Jan and the despair engendered by Buckley and the whites who want to destroy him like a "black lizard." As he has become more aware, he also has become more susceptible to pain. Having decided that he will trust no one, he is dragged into this last major cycle through a conversation with Max.

Max comes to talk with Bigger in order to prepare his defense. Their talk is quite unremarkable, so unremarkable that Max later forgets that they had it at all, and the tremendous weight that it carries for Bigger can only be an index to his desperation for human contact. Max asks Bigger about the crime and about his life. Some of his questions and reactions seem insensitive; he says nothing brilliant or terribly perceptive. What is remarkable from Bigger's point of view is that for the first time someone has sat and listened to him talk about how he has felt about his life. (p. 307)

[Bigger] begins to wonder whether other people, even those who hate him, have the same kinds of feelings that he has. He senses the possibility of "a supporting oneness, a wholeness" to life that he had not perceived before. Relating this conversation to his earlier one with Jan, he sees the possibility of relationships "that he had never dreamed of": "If that white looming mountain of hate were not a mountain at all, but people, people like himself, and like Jan—then he was faced with a high hope the like of which he had never thought could be, and a despair the full depths of which he knew he could not stand to feel."

Bigger is unable to follow all these tantalizing new thoughts on his own. He is pressured into a frenzy by the shortness of the time he has left. Max, who is utterly unaware of what has been wrought, is too busy with the trial to talk with Bigger. When the judge hands down a death sentence, Bigger falls into a new despair, since "life was over without meaning, without anything being settled, without conflicting impulses being resolved." He longs to talk with Max, yet he has no idea what he will say when he has the opportunity: "He could not talk about this thing, so elusive it was; and yet he acted upon it every living second." He struggles to bring the words, the images, and his life together.

Max finally comes to the prison on the day Bigger is to be executed, having failed in his last appeal to the governor to save Bigger's life. Bigger has anticipated this meeting so much that at first he is unable to verbalize anything at all. . . . (pp. 307-08)

What Bigger really wants to know is whether the insight that was born of his earlier conversation with Max is valid: is it true that despite their destructive isolation from one another, people all feel the same way and want the same things? With much stuttering, he tells Max that what he did was not reflective of what he had wanted, and he asks if that is also true of the people who want to kill him. This question is a weighty one for Bigger. It is his ticket into the human community; if he is right, his needs and longings will receive the validation of universal experience. If he is right, it also will mean that he understands the people who hate him, demolishing for good the image of the white mountain that began to shatter when he first recognized Jan's humanity. (p. 309)

Instead of answering Bigger's question directly, Max takes the opportunity to give a speech. His answer ultimately is "yes": he says that everyone wants the same things in life but that some men (capitalists), in their fear of losing what they own, force others (workers) to suffer. Their acts, like Bigger's killing, are wrong, but there are alternative ways for people to fulfill their needs without oppressing others. He says that Bigger should have faith in himself and in his own feelings.

It is at this point, mid-conversation in the last two pages of the book, that Wright abruptly and disturbingly abandons Bigger's point of view, giving the reader no more information than he gives Max and throwing the action into some confusion. Bigger says that Max's words make him "kind of feel what I wanted. It makes me feel that I was kind of right." He goes on to say that he had not wanted to kill but that "when I think of why all the killing was, I begin to feel what I wanted, what I am." He says, "What I killed for must've been good!" and "I didn't want to kill! . . . But what I killed for I *am!*" Max is horrified. Staring with "eyes full of terror," he says, "Bigger, not that." He leaves the cell with his face averted and with tears in his eyes. Before Max leaves, Bigger asks him to tell his mother that he is all right and to tell Jan "hello." Bigger is last seen smiling "a faint, wry, bitter smile" and grasping his cell bars with both hands. (pp. 309-10)

In the last hours before his death, Bigger confronts reality directly. He sees what his life has meant and that he has no savior but himself. What Wright seems to have been trying to do in the last scene is to shift the action to a more abstract level. Bigger becomes for a moment the distillation of his own idea, and when he does he leaves Max behind. In **"How 'Bigger' Was Born"** [see excerpt above], Wright says that he intended to show Bigger "living dangerously, taking life into his hands, accepting what life had made him." That is precisely what Bigger does—no more, no less, no hate, and not even a value judgment except of his own being. He does exactly what Max told him to do. He separates his action, which he had not intended, from the feelings and desires that brought on the action. It is the feelings and ideas which are Bigger: he perceives what he is when he thinks of "why the killing was"; he says that it is "what he killed for" that must have been good and that it is what he killed for that he is. He shakes himself loose from the metaphor just long enough to perceive the relationship between who he is and what he has done, affirming himself but denying the senseless crime that society made of his life.

Bigger has moved in the novel from what Wright describes as "bare sensation" toward conscious thought. At first, he only responds to the stereotypes and vague images through which his reality is filtered. Then he assumes the stereotype and acts out the metaphor: the crime is his life, and he takes upon himself the "crime of being black." He uses the stereotype and the metaphor for his own ends, without understanding that it is still the image that is controlling him. Through Jan and Max he begins to see through the stereotype. The white mountain begins to crumble, and he catches a glimpse of a human community. At the end, he breaks through to a comprehension of the metaphor of his life. Max does not separate the figurative from the literal: all he sees is Bigger accepting the crime, but what Bigger accepts is the only life he has been given. As a white man, however sympathetic, Max cannot see Bigger's life as Bigger himself sees it. Nor can Bigger explain it to him; he can only reassure Max, saying "I'm all right. For real, I am." (pp. 312-13)

[Bigger stands alone at the end because] that was the only way he could confront his life. As an individual, Bigger finds that he must answer his own questions and supply his own definitions—the kind of existential solution that Wright would use more consciously in his later work. As a black, Bigger stands alone as well. Despite the undeniable gifts that two white Communists have given him, he cannot depend on their vision unless he makes it his own. Bigger never believes it when Max tells him that society hates "Reds" and other working people as much as it hates blacks, and neither do we. Marxism cannot save Bigger any more than Jan could give him humanity; he must take responsibility for his own salvation.

Wright does not condemn the Communist vision in Max. His attitude is the more benign one he expressed in retrospect after he left the party: ". . . they had missed the meaning of the lives of the masses, had conceived of people in too abstract a manner. . . . I would tell Communists how common people felt, and I would tell common people of the self-sacrifice of the Communists who strove for unity among them." In *Native Son,* he goes one step further. In Jan he portrays a Communist who breaks through the abstraction to some understanding of Bigger's life. And in Bigger he demonstrates that for blacks a process of self-definition must precede specific political action. He tries to capture the pre-revolutionary Bigger at the moment of his first comprehension of the meaning of his oppression, an attempt more universal, more radical, and more ambitious than a propaganda statement. Max is deeply disturbed by the potential he sees in Bigger for two events that he dreads: a violent revolution or an irreconcilable split among the workers. But Wright freezes Bigger at the moment of comprehension, with a wry, bitter smile on his face. He leaves unanswered the question Max seems to answer: he asks what will happen when Bigger—a human being, a black, an oppressed proletarian—comprehends the metaphor and, in so doing, takes his life into his own hands. (pp. 313-14)

Kathleen Gallagher, "Bigger's Great Leap to the Figurative," in CLA Journal, *Vol. XXVII, No. 3, March, 1984, pp. 293-314.*

LOUIS TREMAINE

It is time to put *Native Son* together again. What is most characteristic of the text, from first to last, and which therefore cannot be ignored, is precisely that which "offends" the reader's expectations of it as a serious work of fiction. By looking at, rather than away from, Wright's handling of character, plot, and narration, one discovers that these elements point directly to a dissociated sensibility lying at the heart of Bigger Thomas. They are, in fact, the effective means by which the book as a whole functions as a formal projection of Bigger's struggle toward self-expression.

A number of critics have observed already that there exists a "split consciousness" in Bigger and have analyzed the various ethical and perceptual conflicts that plague him. What needs further attention in order to understand the kind of dissociation that Bigger suffers, however, is the specific consequences of these conflicts for the character. In *Native Son,* these consequences are described repeatedly and forcefully and constitute a highly consistent pattern. Bigger's essential dilemma is not simply his ethical hesitation between social values and self-interest, not simply his perceptual confusion of concrete reality and abstract symbol, but his inability, in his daily functioning, to express his emotional experience in ways that make its meaning accessible both to his own consciousness and to the consciousness of those around him. It is this dissociated sensibility, this conflict between experience and expression where there should be complementarity, that makes of Bigger a mass of unsatisfied urges, that creates "the rhythms of his life: indifference and violence," that defines Bigger's very existence. . . . It is his longing somehow to bring these dissociated parts of himself together and thereby "explain" himself, create a true image of his feelings, that causes him to cling so desperately to life though condemned to certain death. . . . (pp. 63-4)

This hunger for self-expression is due in part to socio-economic conditions that deny Bigger access to conventional modes of communication, to the tools of language and culture systematically reserved for the use of the dominant race and class. This is clear to most readers and is made explicit in Max's courtroom speech. But what Wright is most concerned with is the ways in which an individual's experience is distorted by these conditions. It is true that Bigger lacks words, audience, and forum, but the primary reason for his failure of self-expression is his fear of what he has to express, a characteristic and generalized fear that repeatedly blocks any efforts to integrate his own sensibility.

Partially responsible, of course, is a fear of whites, which not only motivates his fight with Gus but prevents him from understanding the nature of that motivation:

> His confused emotions had made him feel instinctively that it would be better to fight Gus than to confront a white man with a gun. But he kept this knowledge of his fear thrust firmly down in him; his courage to live depended upon how successfully his fear was hidden from his consciousness.

But the willful suppression of awareness described in this passage operates in many other areas of his life as well and accounts for the imagery of barriers (walls, curtains, veils, and related images) which is so often commented on by critics. . . . [A] failure—or refusal—to delve into his own experience affects the operation of Bigger's consciousness with respect to religion as he knows it, to his marginal legal status, to the threat of betrayal in human relationships, and to other areas of Bigger's fear-ridden life from which he seeks instinctively to protect himself. Such situations are repeatedly presented in language that emphasizes this process of suppression: "Not once . . . had an image of what he had done come into his mind. He had thrust the whole thing back of him . . ."; "there appeared before him . . . images which in turn aroused impulses long dormant, impulses that he had suppressed and sought to shunt from his life''; "A strong counter-emotion waxed in him,

warning him to leave this newly seen and newly felt thing alone.'' Bigger is thus caught between his deep need to make his own experience manifest to himself and his equally deep fear of doing so.

Bigger, in fact, yearns to make himself understood not only to himself but to those with whom he shares the world. He fears, however, that any attempt to establish such an understanding is futile and will only confirm his sense that he is different—different not only as a black but as Bigger. This longing for connectedness is at times directed toward "his people" (a term he fails to understand when it is spoken to him by the Daltons), "but that dream would fade when he looked at the other black people near him. Even though black like them, he felt there was too much difference between him and them to allow for a common binding and a common life." (pp. 64-5)

His need is to communicate, and yet his instinct, an instinct he overcomes only with Max, is to dissemble. This becomes a recurring motif in Bigger's interactions with others throughout the book: he gauges how he is perceived, calculates what is expected of him, and then acts (in both senses of the word) to direct attention away from himself as he is and toward a more desirable image of himself. His fight with Gus, for example, is an effort to hide his fearful and irresolute nature from his poolroom friends and from Doc. . . . With Peggy, he adjusts his table manners and tries to express the sympathy for the Daltons that he thinks she expects of him. He "distrusts" and "hates" Jan and Mary because he cannot read their expectations and act accordingly. . . . Even with Max, he is initially wary and gradually makes his first ineffectual attempts to express himself to another only in response to a concerted—and professional—effort on Max's part to elicit Bigger's confidence. Max's repeated question "How do you feel, Bigger?" is no mere formulaic greeting.

Bigger yearns to understand his own feelings by expressing them both to himself and to others, but his fear both of himself and of others is an obstacle to such expression. (p. 66)

A considerable case is made in the novel, and accepted by many critics, for the murder of Mary as Bigger's one successful expressive act. He insists to himself that the crime was no accident, that he "had killed many times before, only on those other times there had been no handy victim or circumstance to make visible or dramatic his will to kill," that in this act the "hidden meaning of his life . . . had spilled out." Even Max, in court, refers to the need of black people for self-expression and then characterizes Bigger's crime as "an act of creation." These remarks concern the killing of Mary in particular, but she and Bessie and the rat in Bigger's apartment are merely the most obvious, not the only, murder victims portrayed in the book. For in his mind, Bigger actively fantasizes killing Gus, Mr. Dalton, Jan and Mary, Peggy, Britten, Jan again, Bessie before her actual murder, a reporter, a black couple he overhears, the men searching for him, and all the people at the inquest and at the trial. (p. 67)

That is a lot of killing—but its function is not necessarily expressive. If one examines these killings, both real and imagined, in context one finds that each of them is in fact an instinctive response to fear, a means of escape from a physical or psychological threat, a survival strategy in the most direct sense. It is true that Bigger attempts to turn the killing of Mary to account after the fact, to attach expressive significance to the act in his memory. The act itself, however, is motivated by no such intention. In the page or so of text that recounts the first murder, Bigger and his feelings are described in the following terms: "hysterical terror," "fists clenched in fear," "afraid" (used twice), "fear," "frenzy," "frantically," and "intimidated to the core." These or similar terms accompany each of the accounts of Bigger's killings, real or imagined. Killing, in other words, is not a consciously chosen form of self-expression for Bigger but rather an involuntary consequence of his failure to express his feelings, his failure to understand and communicate his own fear and thereby to disrupt "the rhythms of . . . indifference and violence" that rule his life.

The question still remains whether Bigger discovers any mode of expression capable of reunifying his dissociated sensibility and rendering him a whole human being. The answer is that the book itself, as a self-reflexive work of art, accomplishes that function. This success is a highly qualified one, however, for it is achieved only in the shadowy realm of virtual reality, of projected desire, and not in the realm actually inhabited by Bigger. As a human being, Bigger fails utterly to resolve the conflicting terms of his existence. What resolutions he achieves, he finds only by turning himself into a character and his life into art. This is not to imply that Bigger is somehow the author of the book—he emphatically is not. It is to say, rather, that the book is written in a manner consistent with an imaginative reality which Bigger struggles to create. (pp. 67-8)

[Wright] gives the reader not the world Bigger lives in but the world Bigger lives. He presents the world as Bigger feels and experiences it. . . . It is the projection of this being and consciousness onto the world, and not what "really happens," that finally matters to Wright, to the reader, and especially to Bigger himself.

This technique of projection is most readily apparent in the depiction of characters. Wright acknowledges that he "gave no more reality to the other characters than that which Bigger himself saw," and Bigger sees only what his fear allows him to see. Bigger's interactions with others are conditioned by his efforts to meet expectations by conforming to type. . . . The characters of the novel, apart from Bigger, are stereotypes because they are stereotypes for Bigger. They are individuals who have been reduced to what Bigger fears, needs, desires, and struggles to understand, and a different part of Bigger swings into action to meet the threat or, less often, the opportunity that each offers. (p. 69)

But all of this typing, both of self and others, takes its toll. Bigger longs for genuine acceptance and understanding, though he continually frustrates this longing by the barriers he erects. His need to be something different to each is in tension with his need to be himself to all. This second and deeper need, long suppressed, eventually takes precedence, and the turning point depends upon a most improbable manipulation by the author: the scene in which a dozen characters all crowd into Bigger's jail cell. . . . What happens in that cell is that all of the distorted versions of Bigger represented by all of the characters in his life come together at once, and in the process a psychic critical mass is reached and exceeded. He must be several different Biggers at once, and he cannot do it. . . . After this scene, his conscious energy no longer focuses on maintaining his many outward guises but rather on the search for his own inner reality. (pp. 69-70)

The element of plot has the same function in the book as that of character, to project images that express Bigger's emotional experience. Plot, in part, supports character in this respect, for not only does it bring all the important surviving characters together in the crowded-cell scene, but it brings Bigger into contact in the first place, against all likelihood, with precisely those forces that he most fears and that most challenge his self-understanding, forces represented by the Daltons, Mary, Jan, Buckley, and Reverend Hammond. More importantly, it parallels the element of character in creating and arranging events which pose fundamental threats to Bigger at the same time that they serve his need to see his life as he really feels it. Like the characters, the events in the novel are "typed" events. They consist not of complex concatenations of forces and circumstances but of experience reduced to single emotions projected onto reality and objectified, haunting fantasies become real. The murder of Mary thereby becomes a concentrated, particular experience of fear, the disposal of her body one of dehumanization, the capture of Bigger on the water tower one of utter isolation and victimization, and so on. Bigger feels excluded from the conventional "picture of Creation" which, in his emotional core, he has "killed" and in its place "created a new world for himself." This "new world" is reflected in the book and its extravagant plot. (pp. 70-1)

Like the characterization and plot, the narrative voice in *Native Son* serves as more than simply a technical support to a work of fiction. It too functions more particularly as an expressionistic projection of Bigger's sensibility. It not only expresses Bigger's dilemma, but in its particular mode of expression it concretely embodies that dilemma as well.

Broadly speaking, Bigger suffers from an inability to communicate a conscious understanding of his own emotional reality. In a narrower sense, Bigger lacks words and feels this lack as a potent form of alienation from others. James Nagel, commenting on "images of 'vision' in *Native Son*," suggests a similar insight, that only at the end does Bigger realize "that his real tragedy is not death; it is rather the fact of never having been clearly seen by anyone." This is spelled out most clearly when Bigger attempts to express himself to Max, the one person who has come closest to understanding him. . . . The long-felt need to explain himself becomes at last, in the terms of the plot, a matter of physical survival, for he can finally do nothing to save himself but plead his case to the court, and yet "he knew that the moment he tried to put his feelings into words, his tongue would not move." (p. 73)

If Bigger cannot speak for himself, however, others can and do speak for him and in the process take from him a large measure of control over his own destiny and over the satisfaction of his own needs. . . . [The] most significant figure in this respect, of course, is the lawyer, Max, who promises Bigger, "I'll tell the judge all I can of how you feel and why," and who stands up in court before the assembled representatives of the world Bigger fears but needs, and announces, "*I* shall witness for Bigger Thomas." Max has been characterized by various readers as a mouthpiece for the Communist Party. In fact, he is much more importantly a mouthpiece for Bigger, a fantasy come true: he possesses a vast audience, commands the language (words, imagery, frame of reference) of that audience, and stands in a privileged forum from which to address it. In every sense of the word, he *represents* Bigger to the world in a way that Bigger could never represent himself.

What Max is to Bigger's fictional life, the narrator is to the artistic image that is projected out of that life. The narrator's facility with words and propensity for extended abstract analysis and complex syntax compensate—indeed, *over*-compensate—for Bigger's stance of mute incomprehension before his own experience. As the novel proceeds, Bigger acts and feels while the narrator reasons aloud about these actions and feelings. The relationship is precisely the one described (by the narrator) between the two parts of Bigger as he lies in his cell awaiting trial: "Blind impulses welled up in his body, and his intelligence sought to make them plain to his understanding by supplying images that would explain them.". . . Because Bigger cannot "reach out with his bare hands and carve from naked space the concrete solid reasons" for his actions, the narrator is created to carve those reasons from language, an equally resistant material for Bigger. There is nothing subtle about the narrator of *Native Son:* his comments are obtrusive, overwrought, and tendentious. He lacks sophistication. He is a literary cliché. And he is precisely the narrator Bigger would create, if he were able, to tell his story for him.

An enormous imaginative structure of characters, events, and narrative devices has been elaborated not merely to describe but to *express,* in the full sense of that word, the emotional experience of Bigger Thomas. The question which remains is whether this structure has been adequate either to repair or to circumvent Bigger's dissociated sensibility. There is a certain sense of failure implicit in any recourse to an expressionistic mode of writing, a despair at one's inability to make sense of experience that is fundamentally hostile to certain human needs or values. In *Native Son,* there seems to be a recognition of that failure or inadequacy built into the very terms of the work itself. In the first two sections, Bigger's persona expands to fill the world as he perceives it, and an extravagant sequence of characters, events, and commentaries provides him with images of his own experience. In the last section that sequence slows and eventually shuts itself off, leaving Bigger immobilized and forced—or free—to contemplate those images. Such contemplation is, in Bigger's terms, the function of the entire procedure. The original movement of expansion does not merely halt, however, but reverses itself as Bigger's persona collapses in on itself. As the trial plays itself out, Bigger's active experience becomes increasingly restricted and the *images* of his past experience take up exclusive and fixed residence inside his consciousness. His last hope for contact with others is cut off as Max backs away in terror from Bigger's dawning sense of "rightness." Gone too is any hope of escaping execution. All that is left in Bigger is a solipsistic acceptance of his own feelings, now beyond explanation or justification:

> What I killed for must've been good. . . . I can say it now, 'cause I'm going to die. I know what I'm saying real good and I know how it sounds. But I'm all right. I feel all right when I look at it that way. . . .

Not only does Bigger have "the last word" over Max, as Irving Howe has so often been quoted to say, but over the narrator as well, who drops away at last because Bigger "can say it now" and knows what he is saying "real good." This final pathetic utterance, so triumphant in Bigger's mind, isolates him forever and leaves him clinging with a kind of desperate joy to the fear and hate that have destroyed his life. (pp. 74-5)

> Louis Tremaine, *"The Dissociated Sensibility of Bigger Thomas in Wright's 'Native Son',"* in Studies in American Fiction, *Vol. 14, No. 1, Spring, 1986, pp. 63-76.*

JAMES A. MILLER

Critical commentary about *Native Son* has invariably focused on the meaning of the final section of the novel, particularly Max's impassioned speech to the judge in his vain attempt to save Bigger Thomas's life and the final encounter between Max and Bigger at the end of the novel. Max's appearance in the novel has been regarded by many critics . . . as an ideological intrusion which disrupts the artistic unity of *Native Son.* To the extent to which Max speaks for Bigger Thomas and, by implication, for Richard Wright—so the argument goes—Wright succumbs to his own ideological (i.e., political) impulses at the expense of his literary artistry. One important consequence of the centrality some readers and critics confer upon Max's role in *Native Son* is that it inevitably leads to the conclusion that Bigger Thomas himself is inarticulate, incapable of negotiating the conflict between "thought" and "feeling" which defines his emotional life for a great deal of the novel, incapable of telling his own story and, therefore, of defining himself. To be sure, Bigger's story is presented from the perspective of a third-person narrator who is clearly more politically informed and verbally articulate than Bigger himself, and, within the novel itself, readers are confronted with a variety of voices—ranging from Buckley, the State's Attorney, to Max—which seek to define Bigger's reality. Nevertheless, the concluding scene of the novel clearly belongs to Bigger and his recovery of his voice at this crucial moment in *Native Son* not only undermines the argument that Max functions as a spokesman for Wright's political views but also challenges the view that Bigger himself is inarticulate. (p. 501)

Bigger is sullen, brooding, brusque, and sometimes violent in his attitude towards his family and immediate community, but he is definitely *not* inarticulate. If we define the pattern of call-and-response in the Afro-American community as a dynamic exchange between speaker and audience, one which elicits responsive speech from the audience and encourages the audience to respond with its own variation on the performer's song or story, there are numerous examples of Bigger Thomas's participation in this pattern in *Native Son.* (p. 502)

[Bigger] belongs to a specific speech community within the larger black community, one which is governed by its own norms and values: the world of the black, urban, male *lumpenproletariat*. Not only is Bigger articulate in this world, he exercises considerable power within it. Bigger realizes, perhaps more fully than Gus, Jack, and G. H., that fear and shame are the dominant forces in the world he inhabits; and, by successfully manipulating these emotions, externalizing them—as he does when he pulls his knife on Gus in the pool-room—he gains power over this world, or at least manages to keep it at bay.

Bigger Thomas's quest for voice and audience has therefore little to do with his relationships with the black community, tension and conflict-ridden as they may be, but is inextricably connected to his perceptions of the white world. In other words, Bigger's quest for voice and audience is essentially Other-directed, defined by his need to struggle with externally determined definitions of the self. (p. 503)

It is within [the white] world of "authoritative discourse"—symbolized by the billboard of the State's Attorney in the opening pages of the novel, the distortions of African reality at the Regal Theatre, the liberal pieties the Dalton family, the inflammatory rhetoric of the press, and the blatantly racist arguments of the State's Attorney—that Bigger must struggle to discover his voice and, presumably, an audience which will give assent to his testimony.

But what is the nature of the dialogue Bigger Thomas seeks, and with whom? As readers of *Native Son,* we know the sense of elation Bigger experiences in the aftermath of Mary Dalton's accidental death, the ease with which he accepts responsibility for his action and confers meaning upon it, the way in which his secret knowledge establishes further distance between himself and his family, the sense of power he temporarily achieves over a white world trapped smugly in its own assumptions of racial superiority; yet, one of the questions which has always intrigued me as a reader is: why doesn't Wright allow Bigger Thomas to escape, say somewhere between the first and second books of *Native Son*? What would be the imaginative and ideological implications of Wright exercising such an artistic choice? The text of the novel provides us with a clear answer:

> He wanted suddenly to stand up and shout, telling them that he had killed a rich white girl, a girl whose family was known to all of them. Yes; if he did that a look of startled horror would come over their faces. But, no. He would not do that, even though the satisfaction would be keen. . . . He wanted the keen thrill of startling them, but felt that the cost was too great. He wished that he had the power to say what he had done without the fear of being arrested; he wished that he could be an idea in their minds; that his black face and the image of his smothering Mary and cutting off her head and burning her could hover before their eyes as a terrible picture of reality which they could see and feel and yet not destroy. He was not satisfied with the way things stood now; he was a man who had come in sight of a goal, then had won it, and in winning it had seen just within his grasp another goal, higher, greater. He had learned to shout and had shouted and no ear had heard him.

Bigger will not be satisfied, in other words, until his actions are recognized by the world whose attention he seeks. And it is here that we see how completely Bigger's quest for voice and audience are determined by his fascination with the white world.

For Bigger, in fact, *does* achieve recognition for his actions from his girlfriend, Bessie. . . . Like Gus, Jack, and G. H. she participates in Bigger's world and understands its terms. Bessie knows Bigger so well that she realizes fairly quickly that he has murdered Mary Dalton and elicits a confession from him. Enlisted by Bigger as an unwilling accomplice in his inept kidnapping scheme, Bessie articulates the pain of her life with all of the passion of a blues singer, a testimony to which Bigger nods his head and assents, but a song which he clearly does not want to hear. And when Bigger rapes and murders Bessie, he effectively severs his ties to the black community. From this point in the novel until its conclusion, Bigger functions essentially as a soloist.

It is in this context that Max emerges in *Native Son* as an intermediary between Bigger Thomas and the white world. . . . [The] difference between Max and the other white characters Bigger encounters is that Max addresses Bigger as a human being rather than as a social type. This is clearly the kind of human encounter for which Bigger has been yearning throughout the novel, one which has been presumably missing up until this point, and Bigger instinctively and immediately places his trust in Max. Nevertheless, while Max and Bigger communicate reasonably well in their private conversations, Max's defense of Bigger in the public sphere reveals that Max, too, suffers from some of the limitations of the white world.

There is, first of all, the problem of the legal strategies Max chooses to pursue in his defense of Bigger Thomas. In his review of *Native Son* for the New York *Sunday Worker,* Benjamin Davis, a leading black official in the American Communist Party during the 1940s, correctly pointed out that Max's defense of Bigger is seriously flawed and, in fact, atypical of the kind of legal defense the Communist Party would conduct. Max does not challenge the false charge of rape against Bigger Thomas, he pleads Bigger guilty to both the rape and murder of Mary Dalton, even though it is clear that the murder is accidental. Finally—Davis concludes—"Max should have argued for Bigger's acquittal in the case, and should have helped stir the political pressure of the Negro and white masses to get that acquittal."

Secondly, there is the question of whether Max fully understands Bigger Thomas. It is true that Max's probing questions awaken Bigger to a sense of his own reality which he has not experienced before, but it is also clear—as Donald Gibson has pointed out—that Max is primarily concerned with the social and symbolic implications of Bigger's situation while Bigger is concerned with his personal fate. (pp. 503-05)

[Throughout] the third book of *Native Son,* Bigger Thomas remains curiously detached from the action; he functions as a witness, an auditor to the public debate which rages about him, but not as a participant in the dialogue. The public exchanges between Max and the State's Attorney, Buckley, represent two attempts to define, in opposing ideological terms, the meaning of Bigger Thomas's actions—and, by extension, his existence—in the public sphere of "authoritative discourse." In the final analysis, however, Bigger repudiates both arguments—as we see in the concluding conversation between Max and Bigger, when Bigger blurts out: "What I killed for, I *am!*" and Max backs away from him, groping for his hat like a blind man.

Max does not speak for Bigger Thomas, nor does he speak for Richard Wright. He attempts to *represent* Bigger, in both a legal and linguistic sense, and fails. Nevertheless, Max's presence in the novel does have an important bearing on the development of Bigger's consciousness. Through his relationship with Max, Bigger Thomas is able to further de-mystify the power of the white world over him, a process which has been unfolding since the accidental murder of Mary Dalton. And even though Bigger does not understand Max's language, he nevertheless appropriates it for his own purposes.

"The word in language," [Mikhail] Bakhtin observes, "is half someone else's. It becomes one's own only when the speaker populates it with his own intentions, his own accent, when he appropriates the word, adapting it to his own expressive and semantic intention. Prior to this moment of appropriation, the word . . . exists in other people's mouths, in other people's contexts, serving other people's intentions: it is from there that one must take the word, and make it one's own," seizing it and transforming it into private property.

This is precisely what Bigger Thomas does in the concluding pages of *Native Son*. Having shaken the "authoritative discourse" of the white world to its foundations and triggered off an ideological debate which seeks to define his place in the public sphere, Bigger Thomas, partly inspired by Max's rhetoric, chooses a position that places him decisively outside of the existing social framework.

Nevertheless, Bigger Thomas's achievement of the voice he assumes at the end of the novel has not been without its price. In cultural terms, the strategies Bigger pursues to evade white society after Mary Dalton's death—particularly the gratuitous murder of Bessie—only serve to isolate him from the black community. In social and political terms, Bigger's actions not only invite the wrath of a racist society but confirm his place within popular mythology. In personal terms, Bigger seems to achieve a level of human recognition—of sorts—through his relationships with Jan and Max, accepting Jan's offer of comradeship by, for the first time in his life dropping the use of "mister" in front of a white man's name. But Max—as we have seen—recoils from Bigger's final speech, and the call which Bigger issues in his assertion "I Am" does not receive responsive testimony from Max. Rather, we are left with the final image of Bigger Thomas facing his impending death in proud and lonely isolation, a soloist listening to the sound of his own song. (pp. 505-06)

> *James A. Miller, ''Bigger Thomas's Quest for Voice and Audience in Richard Wright's 'Native Son','' in* Callaloo, *Vol. 9, No. 3, Summer, 1986, pp. 501-06.*

DAVID BRADLEY

I first began Richard Wright's *Native Son* in the winter of 1971, when, as an undergraduate at the University of Pennsylvania, I was taking a course called "Readings in Black Literature." (p. 68)

Although I had never read *Native Son,* I had long been aware of it. . . . And I had occasionally run across references to *Native Son.* I knew, for example, of Irving Howe's declaration that "the day *Native Son* appeared, American culture was changed forever" [see *CLC*, Vol. 3], and I had seen the contents page of David Littlejohn's *Black on White: A Critical Survey of Writing by American Negroes,* which had sections headed "Before *Native Son:* The Dark Ages" and "Before *Native Son:* The Renaissance and After." Also, since I wanted to be a writer, I was acutely aware that *Native Son* was the first book published in America to make a black author a lot of money. I therefore opened it with great expectations. Like Dickens's Pip, I was terribly disappointed.

Put simply, I hated *Native Son.* Put more accurately, I hated it with a passion. Hated it because it violated most of the principles of novelistic construction I was struggling to master. The plot was improbable, the narrative voice intrusive, the language often stilted and the characters—especially that silly little rich white tease Mary Dalton and her stupid, gigolo Communist boyfriend, Jan—were stereotypical beyond belief. At first I tried to rationalize these flaws as precisely the "ineptitude" and "unfitness" that James T. Stewart had written about. But I couldn't get around what I hated with a passion: Bigger Thomas.

It wasn't that Bigger failed as a character, exactly. I had read Wright's essay **"How Bigger Was Born"** [see excerpt above], and therefore knew that Wright had set out to write a book "no one would weep over." In this, for me, Wright succeeded. I shed no tears for Bigger. I wanted him dead, by legal means if possible, by lynching if necessary. (The only difference between me and the mob that pursued him was that I hated him not because he had accidentally killed Mary—I *understood* that and would have preferred it to have been intentional—but because he had intentionally murdered Bessie, a woman who loved him and would have done almost anything for him.) But

I knew, too, that Wright had intended Bigger to be a flat character, so he could serve as a "meaningful and prophetic symbol" of the black masses. In this, for me, Wright failed. I did not see Bigger Thomas as a symbol of any kind of black man. To me he was a sociopath, pure and simple, beyond sympathy or understanding. The truth is, my first reading of *Native Son* ended at the passage in which Bigger, after practically raping Bessie, bashing in her face with a brick and tossing her body down an airshaft, thought that "he was living, truly and deeply." This, I thought, is sick.

I said so in class. . . . I silently endured my classmates' charge that I had been so brainwashed by the dominant culture that I was "not black enough" to appreciate *Native Son.* I did not even protest (though I thought about it) that it was the dominant culture which had declared *Native Son* a work of brilliance. (pp. 68, 70)

[James] Baldwin expressed eloquently the things I had tried to express in class. In "Everybody's Protest Novel" [see excerpt above], he charged that the works belonging to the sub-genre known as the protest novel, such as Harriet Beecher Stowe's *Uncle Tom's Cabin* and Wright's *Native Son* were unreasonably forgiven "whatever violence they do to language, whatever excessive demands they make of credibility. It is, indeed, considered the sign of a frivolity so intense as to approach decadence to suggest that these books are badly written and wildly improbable." In "Many Thousands Gone," Baldwin criticized *Native Son* in particular. "A necessary dimension," he wrote, "has been cut away; this dimension being the relationship that Negroes bear to one another. . . . It is this which had led us all to believe that in Negro life there exists no tradition, no field of manners, no possibility of ritual or intercourse. . . ." Aha! I though triumphantly. Who is going to tell James Baldwin *he* isn't black enough?

But Baldwin did something more significant than rescue my claim to racial identity in arguing that the flaws in *Native Son* were common to novels distinguished not by the race of the author but by the form of the work. Baldwin, in effect, was challenging the black esthetic. This made me realize that although a course in black literature had made it possible for me to read works by black authors which were otherwise absent from the curriculum, the assumptions behind the course had made it impossible for me to see those works as part of an American, as opposed to Afro-American, literary tradition. I wondered if I would have a different reaction to *Native Son* if I considered it in a new context. So I went in search of a copy.

My reaction was indeed different. Put simply, *Native Son* infuriated me. Put sequentially, it bemused, astonished, horrified and then infuriated me. And then it frightened me out of my wits. (p. 70)

[The] original edition of *Native Son* . . . included an introduction by Dorothy Canfield. It seemed curious that a contemporary novel would require an introduction at all. But especially *that* introduction. For, while Canfield said things you would expect an introducer to say, testifying that "the author shows genuine literary skill in the construction of his novel," and comparing him to Dostoyevsky, she also said things you would expect an introducer *not* to say—for example, that she "did not at all mean to imply that *Native Son* as literature is comparable to the masterpieces of Dostoyevsky. . . ." What was horrifying was what she thought Wright's novel *was* comparable to.

"How to produce neuroses in sheep and psychopathic upsets in rats and other animals has been known to research scientists for so long that accounts of these experiments have filtered out to the general public," she began, and went on that "our society puts Negro youth in the situation of the animal in the psychological laboratory in which a neurosis is to be caused." *Native Son*, she said, was "the first report in fiction we have had from those who succumb to these distracting crosscurrents of contradictory nerve impulses, from those whose behavior patterns give evidence of the same bewildered, senseless tangle of abnormal nerve reactions studied in animals by psychologists in laboratory experiments."

Suddenly I realized that many readers of *Native Son had* seen Bigger Thomas as a symbol in 1940 when *Native Son* hit the shelves, they, like Mary Dalton, had probably never come into enough contact with blacks to know better. God, I thought, they think we're all Biggers.

I found myself wondering how many of the attitudes of 1940's whites toward blacks may have been confirmed, influenced, if not totally shaped by such a tremendously popular "report." Had *Native Son* contributed to the fact that in 1947 less than half of all white Americans approved of integrated transportation facilities, and that only about one in three approved of integrated schools or neighborhoods? And, if they believed *Native Son* was an accurate "report," who could blame them for those attitudes? I myself did not want a nut like Bigger Thomas sitting next to me on a bus or in a schoolroom and certainly I did not want him moving in next door.

Still, I thought, while Canfield's characterization may have seemed credible to the general public, it seemed incredible to me that literary critics would have accepted it. So I sought out Irving Howe's essay, "Black Boys and Native Sons," from which the "changed the world" quote had come. In Howe, I thought, I'd surely find someone who knew that a novel is not a report.

But Howe was just as bad. True, he praised *Native Son* for having changed our culture, but he also wrote of

> all its crudeness, melodrama and claustrophobia of vision. . . . The language is often coarse, flat in rhythm, syntactically overburdened, heavy with journalistic slag.
>
> *Native Son,* though preserving some of the devices of the naturalistic novel, deviates sharply from its characteristic tone: a tone Wright could not possibly have maintained and which, it may be, no Negro novelist can really hold for long.

At that moment, I saw how *Native Son* could be a classic according to the black esthetic and still be loved by white critics: the whites did not view it as literature, except in the sense that scientific journals or polemical pamphlets are literature. (pp. 70, 72)

My second full reading of *Native Son* filled me with a terrible sorrow. Not for Bigger Thomas—I still did not give a damn about him—but for Richard Wright himself. For when I read the passage in which Mary Dalton tells Bigger how she had long wanted to enter a ghetto house "and just see how your people live," I heard the echo of Dorothy Canfield's introduction. And in the passage in which Jan tells Bigger that it was really O.K. that Bigger had killed the woman he, Jan,

loved, because "You believed enough to kill. You thought you were settling something, or you wouldn't've killed." I heard Irving Howe's blithe waiver of the esthetic standards that he, as a critic, had to hold dear. And when Bigger, at the end of his life, reiterates that piece of dialectic insanity, I saw Richard Wright letting somebody tell him where his life logically ended.

And I realized that previously I had done *Native Son* the injustice of trying to fit it into my America. . . . Richard Wright's America was a very different place, a place where a black who hoped to survive needed a sense of humility more than a sense of dignity, and where Bigger Thomas's story was no more melodramatic, crude or claustrophobic than the times themselves.

In Richard Wright's America, a novelist could—as Wright did—base descriptions of lynch mobs in the streets of Chicago on reports taken directly from newspapers. In Richard Wright's America, a best-selling, financially independent novelist—if he was a Negro—could not lunch with his agent in a midtown Manhattan restaurant, could not buy a house in Greenwich Village and could only rent an apartment there if he found a landlord willing to defy half the neighborhood. In Richard Wright's America, a critically acclaimed, Guggenheim Fellowship-winning Negro novelist would hesitate to use the surnames of his agent and his editor in the dedication of a book because he was not sure they would want to be so closely associated with a black. In Richard Wright's America, they didn't have black literature courses: a black boy who wanted to be a writer could remain tragically unaware of the writing of black people, and could say, while explaining the origins of his characters, that "association with white writers was the life preserver of my hope to depict Negro life in fiction, for my race possessed no fictional works . . . no novels that went with a deep and fearless will down to the dark roots of life."

And so I came to realize that *Native Son* was not as inaccurate as I had thought, and that, in a sense, Dorothy Canfield was not entirely wrong. Not that there was great validity in Wright's use of Bigger Thomas as a type. Nor is there any validity in reading any piece of fiction as "a report" of general social conditions. But fiction *is* a report of specific conditions, that is its value. *Native Son,* I realized, shows the vision one black man held of his people, his country, and, ultimately, himself. And I thought, Dear God, how horrible for a man to have to write this. And, Please, God, let no one ever have to write this again.

It is the autumn of 1986. I have just finished reading *Native Son* for the fourth time. I have been invited to write an introduction to a new edition. Put simply—and frighteningly, to me—I have been asked to step into the role of Dorothy Canfield, and dared to do a better job.

I am not sure I can do a better job. For while what Canfield wrote still infuriates me, she was a part of her time, as I am a part of mine. Still, I have had the opportunity—as she did not—to read *Native Son* over a span of years. And I find that I can be kinder toward *Native Son* than I have been in the past.

Not that I think *Native Son* has suddenly become artistically brilliant. But I have realized, belatedly, that *Native Son* is a first novel. Its flaws are typical of first novels, no more severe than those found in most. And now I can see beneath the shroud of politics and accept that *Native Son* is, in fact, a valuable document—not of sociology, but of history. It reminds us of a time in this land of freedom when a man could have this bleak and frightening vision of his people, and when we had so little contact with one another that that vision could be accepted as fact.

But despite that, I find that Wright, after all these years, has failed in an ironic way. He wanted *Native Son* to be a book "no one would weep over." With me, he once succeeded. He no longer does. *Native Son* is an ineffably sad expression of what once were the realities of this nation. We have not come as far as we ought. But I hope we have come far enough by now to read *Native Son* and weep. (pp. 74, 78-9)

David Bradley, "On Rereading 'Native Son'," in
The New York Times, *December 7, 1986, pp. 68-79.*

Appendix

The following is a listing of all sources used in Volume 48 of *Contemporary Literary Criticism*. Included in this list are all copyright and reprint rights and acknowledgments for those essays for which permission was obtained. Every effort has been made to trace copyright, but if omissions have been made, please let us know.

THE EXCERPTS IN CLC, VOLUME 48, WERE REPRINTED FROM THE FOLLOWING PERIODICALS:

Accent, v. 1, Summer, 1941.

Agenda, v. 25, Summer, 1987 for "One Barker to Another" by Jonathan Barker. Reprinted by permission of the author.

America, v. 126, April 22, 1972; v. 134, May 29, 1976. © 1972, 1976. All rights reserved. Both reprinted with permission of America Press, Inc., 106 West 56th Street, New York, NY 10019.

The American Book Review, v. 3, March-April, 1981; v. 4, September-October, 1982; v. 5, May-June, 1983; v. 8, September-October, 1986. © 1981, 1982, 1983, 1986 by *The American Book Review.* All reprinted by permission of the publisher.

The American Poetry Review, v. 9, November-December, 1980 for a review of "Collected Poems" by Valerie Trueblood; v. 11, January-February, 1982 for "Some Recent American Poetry: Come All Ye Fair and Tender Ladies" by Dave Smith; v. 12, November-December, 1983 for "Pictures from Borges" by Mary Kinzie. Copyright © 1980, 1982, 1983 by World Poetry, Inc. All reprinted by permission of the respective authors.

The American Spectator, v. 18, February, 1985. Copyright © *The American Spectator* 1985. Reprinted by permission of the publisher.

Analog Science Fiction/Science Fact, v. XCII, January, 1974 for a review of "Ten Thousand Light-Years from Home" by P. Schuyler Miller. Copyright © 1973 by the Condé Nast Publications, Inc. Reprinted by permission of the Literary Estate of P. Schuyler Miller./ v. XCVIII, June, 1978 for a review of "Up the Walls of the World" by Spider Robinson. Copyright © 1978 by the Condé Nast Publications, Inc. Reprinted by permission of the author./ v. CV, September, 1985 for a review of "Brightness Falls from the Air" by Tom Easton; v. CVI, December, 1986 for a review of "The New World" by Tom Easton; v. CVII, January, 1987 for a review of "Tales of the Quintana Roo" and "The Starry Rift" by Tom Easton. © 1978, 1985, 1986 by Davis Publications, Inc. All reprinted by permission of the author.

Anglo-Welsh Review, February, 1970 for "Humanus Sum: A Second Look at R. S. Thomas" by R. George Thomas. Reprinted by permission of the author.

The Antioch Review, v. 38, Spring, 1980; v. 42, Summer, 1984. Copyright © by the Antioch Review Inc. Both reprinted by permission of the Editors.

The Armchair Detective, v. 16, Winter, 1983; v. 16, Spring, 1983; v. 20, Winter, 1987. Copyright © 1983, 1987 by *The Armchair Detective.* All reprinted by permission of the publisher.

THE EXCERPTS IN CLC, VOLUME 48, WERE REPRINTED FROM THE FOLLOWING BOOKS:

Alexander, Michael. From *The Poetic Achievement of Ezra Pound*. University of California Press, 1979. © Michael Alexander 1979. Reprinted by permission of the publisher.

Andersen, Richard. From *William Goldman*. Twayne, 1979. Copyright 1979 by Twayne Publishers. All rights reserved. Reprinted with the permission of Twayne Publishers, a division of G. K. Hall & Co., Boston.

Anthony, Geraldine, S. C. From *Gwen Pharis Ringwood*. Twayne, 1981. Copyright 1981 by Twayne Publishers. All rights reserved. Reprinted with the permission of Twayne Publishers, a division of G. K. Hall & Co., Boston.

Baldwin, James. From "Everybody's Protest Novel," in *Notes of a Native Son*. Beacon Press, 1955. Copyright 1949, renewed 1976, by Partisan Review. Reprinted by permission of Beacon Press.

Barnard, Robert. From *A Talent to Deceive: An Appreciation of Agatha Christie*. Dodd, Mead & Company, 1980. Copyright © 1980 by Robert Barnard. All rights reserved. Reprinted by permission of Dodd, Mead & Company, Inc.

Brown, Terence. From "John McGahern's 'Nightlines': Tone, Technique and Symbolism," in *The Irish Short Story*. Edited by Patrick Rafroidi and Terence Brown. Colin Smythe Ltd., 1979. Copyright © 1979, by Presses Universitaires de Lille (C.E.R.I.U.L.) and Colin Smythe Ltd. All rights reserved. Reprinted by permission of the author.

Chapman, Kenneth G. From *Tarjei Vesaas*. Twayne, 1970. Copyright 1970 by Twayne Publishers. All rights reserved. Reprinted with the permission of Twayne Publishers, a division of G. K. Hall & Co., Boston.

Coale, Samuel Chase. From *In Hawthorne's Shadow: American Romance from Melville to Mailer*. University Press of Kentucky, 1985. Copyright © 1985 by The University Press of Kentucky. Reprinted by permission of the publisher.

Dathorne, O. R. From *Dark Ancestor: The Literature of the Black Man in the Caribbean*. Louisiana State University Press, 1981. Copyright © 1981 by Louisiana State University Press. All rights reserved. Reprinted by permission of the publisher.

de Garcia Barrio, Constance Sparrow. From "The Image of the Black Man in the Poetry of Nicolás Guillén," in *Blacks in Hispanic Literature: Critical Essays*. Edited by Miriam DeCosta. Kennikat Press, 1977. Copyright © 1977 by Kennikat Press. All rights reserved. Reprinted by permission of Associated Faculty Press, Inc., New York, NY.

Dobbs, Annie-Claude. From "Reality and Dream in Julien Gracq: A Stylistic Study," in *Twentieth Century French Fiction: Essays for Germaine Brée*. Edited by George Stambolian. Rutgers University Press, 1975. Copyright © 1975 by Rutgers University, the State University of New Jersey. Reprinted by permission of the publisher.

Ellis, Keith. From *Cuba's Nicolás Guillén: Poetry and Ideology*. University of Toronto Press, 1983. © University of Toronto Press 1983. Reprinted by permission of the publisher.

Frisch, Adam J. From "Toward New Sexual Identities: James Tiptree, Jr.," in *The Feminine Eye: Science Fiction and the Women Who Write It*. Edited by Tom Staicar. Frederick Ungar Publishing Co., 1982. Copyright © 1982 by The Ungar Publishing Company. Reprinted by permission of the publisher.

Hart, Francis Russell. From *The Scottish Novel: From Smollett to Spark*. Cambridge, Mass.: Harvard University Press, 1978. Copyright © 1978 by Francis Russell Hart. All rights reserved. Excerpted by permission of the publishers.

Hassell, Anthony J. From *Strange Country: A Study of Randolph Stow*. University of Queensland Press, 1986. Reprinted by permission of the publisher.

Huf, Linda. From *A Portrait of the Artist as a Young Woman: The Writer as Heroine in American Literature*. Frederick Ungar Publishing Company, 1983. Copyright © 1983 by Linda M. Huf. Reprinted by permission of the publisher.

Jackson, Richard L. From *Black Writers in Latin America*. University of New Mexico Press, 1979. © 1979 by the University of New Mexico Press. All rights reserved. Reprinted by permission of the publisher.

King, Lloyd. From "Nicolás Guillén and Afrocubanismo," in *A Celebration of Black and African Writing*. Edited by Bruce King and Kolawole Ogungbesan. Ahmadu Bello University Press, 1975. © Ahmadu Bello University Press, 1975. Reprinted by permission of the publisher.

Kirstein, Lincoln. From "On Edwin Denby," in *Edwin Denby: The Complete Poems*. Edited by Ron Padgett. Random House, 1986. Copyright © 1983, 1986 by Lincoln Kirstein. Reprinted by permission of the author.

Klinkowitz, Jerome. From "The Self-Apparent Word: Clarence Major's Innovative Fiction," in *Studies in Black American Literature: Black American Prose Theory, Vol. 1*. Edited by Joe Weixlmann and Chester J. Fontenot. The Penkevill Publishing Company, 1984. Copyright © 1983 by Jerome Klinkowitz. Reprinted by permission of the author.

Laurence, Margaret. From a foreword to *The Collected Plays of Gwen Pharis Ringwood*. Edited by Enid Delgatty Rutland. Borealis Press, 1982. Copyright © by Borealis Press Limited, 1982. All rights reserved. Reprinted by permission of the publisher.

Márquez, Robert. From an introduction to *¡Patria O Muerte! The Great Zoo and Other Poems*. By Nicolás Guillén, edited and translated by Robert Márquez. Monthly Review Press, 1972. Copyright © 1972 by Robert Márquez. All rights reserved. Reprinted by permission of the publisher.

Matthews, J. H. From *Surrealism and the Novel*. The University of Michigan Press, 1966. Copyright © 1966 by J. H. Matthews. All rights reserved. Reprinted by permission of the Literary Estate of J. H. Matthews.

McFarlane, James Walter. From *Ibsen and the Temper of Norwegian Literature*. Oxford University Press, London, 1960. © Oxford University Press, 1960. Reprinted by permission of Oxford University Press.

Meir, Colin. From "The Poetry of R. S. Thomas," in *British Poetry Since 1970: A Critical Survey*. Edited by Peter Jones and Michael Schmidt. Carcanet Press, 1980. Copyright © 1980 Carcanet New Press. All rights reserved. Reprinted by permission of the publisher, Carcanet Press.

Pearce, Richard. From *The Novel in Motion: An Approach to Modern Fiction*. Ohio State University Press, 1983. © 1983 by the Ohio State University Press. All rights reserved. Reprinted with permission of the publisher.

Robinson, Christopher. From *French Literature in the Twentieth Century*. David & Charles (Publishers) Limited, 1980. © Christopher Robinson 1980. All rights reserved. Reprinted by permission of A. D. Peters & Co. Ltd.

Scarfe, Francis. From *Auden and After: The Liberation of Poetry, 1930-1941*. George Routledge & Sons Ltd., 1942.

Stanford, Donald E. From *Revolution and Convention in Modern Poetry*. University of Delaware Press, 1983. © 1983 by Associated University Presses, Inc. Reprinted by permission of the publisher.

Steiner, George. From a preface to *The Return*. By Frederick Turner. Countrymen Press, 1981. Preface © 1979 by George Steiner. All rights reserved. Reprinted by permission of the publisher.

Tait, Michael. From "Drama and Theatre," in *Literary History of Canada: Canadian Literature in English*. Edited by Carl F. Klinck. University of Toronto Press, 1965. © University of Toronto Press 1965. Reprinted by permission of the publisher.

Updike, John. From "An Old-Fashioned Novel" and "Borges Warmed Over," in *Hugging the Shore: Essays and Criticism*. Knopf, 1983. Copyright © 1979, 1982 by John Updike. All rights reserved. Reprinted by permission of Alfred A. Knopf, Inc.

Wagoner, Mary S. From *Agatha Christie*. Twayne, 1986. Copyright 1986 by Twayne Publishers. All rights reserved. Reprinted with the permission of Twayne Publishers, a division of G. K. Hall & Co., Boston.

Winchell, Mark Royden. From "Fantasy Seen: Hollywood Fiction Since West," in *Los Angeles in Fiction: A Collection of Original Essays*. Edited by David Fine. University of New Mexico Press, 1984. © 1984 by the University of New Mexico Press. All rights reserved. Reprinted by permission of the author.

Woodward, Anthony. From *Ezra Pound and "The Pisan Cantos."* Routledge & Kegan Paul, 1980. © Anthony Woodward 1980. Reprinted by permission of Routledge & Kegan Paul PLC.

Wright, Richard. From *How "Bigger" Was Born*. Harper & Brothers, 1940. Copyright 1940 by Harper & Row, Publishers, Inc. Renewed 1967 by Ellen Wright. Reprinted by permission of Harper & Row, Publishers, Inc.

☐ Contemporary Literary Criticism Indexes

Literary Criticism Series
Cumulative Author Index
Cumulative Nationality Index
Title Index, Volume 48

This Index Includes References to Entries in These Gale Series

Contemporary Literary Criticism

Presents excerpts of criticism on the works of novelists, poets, dramatists, short story writers, scriptwriters, and other creative writers who are now living or who have died since 1960. Cumulative indexes to authors and nationalities are included, as well as an index to titles discussed in the individual volume. Volumes 1-48 are in print.

Twentieth-Century Literary Criticism

Contains critical excerpts by the most significant commentators on poets, novelists, short story writers, dramatists, and philosophers who died between 1900 and 1960. Cumulative indexes to authors, nationalities, and titles discussed are included in each new volume. Volumes 1-28 are in print.

Nineteenth-Century Literature Criticism

Offers significant passages from criticism on authors who died between 1800 and 1899. Cumulative indexes to authors, nationalities, and titles discussed are included in each new volume. Volumes 1-18 are in print.

Literature Criticism from 1400 to 1800

Compiles significant passages from the most noteworthy criticism on authors of the fifteenth through eighteenth centuries. Cumulative indexes to authors, nationalities, and titles discussed are included in each new volume. Volumes 1-8 are in print.

Classical and Medieval Literature Criticism

Offers excerpts of criticism on the works of world authors from classical antiquity through the fourteenth century. Cumulative indexes to authors, titles, and critics are included in each volume. Volume 1 is in print.

Short Story Criticism

Compiles excerpts of criticism on short fiction by writers of all eras and nationalities. Cumulative indexes to authors, nationalities, and titles discussed are included in each new volume. Volume 1 is in print.

Children's Literature Review

Includes excerpts from reviews, criticism, and commentary on works of authors and illustrators who create books for children. Cumulative indexes to authors, nationalities, and titles discussed are included in each new volume. Volumes 1-14 are in print.

Contemporary Authors Series

Encompasses five related series. *Contemporary Authors* provides biographical and bibliographical information on more than 90,000 writers of fiction, nonfiction, poetry, journalism, drama, motion pictures, and other fields. Each new volume contains sketches on authors not previously covered in the series. Volumes 1-122 are in print. *Contemporary Authors New Revision Series* provides completely updated information on active authors covered in previously published volumes of *CA*. Only entries requiring significant change are revised for *CA New Revision Series*. Volumes 1-22 are in print. *Contemporary Authors Permanent Series* consists of updated listings for deceased and inactive authors removed from the original volumes 9-36 when these volumes were revised. Volumes 1-2 are in print. *Contemporary Authors Autobiography Series* presents specially commissioned autobiographies by leading contemporary writers. Volumes 1-6 are in print. *Contemporary Authors Bibliographical Series* contains primary and secondary bibliographies as well as analytical bibliographical essays by authorities on major modern authors. Volumes 1-2 are in print.

Dictionary of Literary Biography

Encompasses three related series. *Dictionary of Literary Biography* furnishes illustrated overviews of authors' lives and works and places them in the larger perspective of literary history. Volumes 1-67 are in print. *Dictionary of Literary Biography Documentary Series* illuminates the careers of major figures through a selection of literary documents, including letters, notebook and diary entries, interviews, book reviews, and photographs. Volumes 1-4 are in print. *Dictionary of Literary Biography Yearbook* summarizes the past year's literary activity with articles on genres, major prizes, conferences, and other timely subjects and includes updated and new entries on individual authors. Yearbooks for 1980-1986 are in print. A cumulative index to authors and articles is included in each new volume.

Concise Dictionary of American Literary Biography

A six-volume series that collects revised and updated sketches on major American authors that were originally presented in *Dictionary of Literary Biography*. Volumes 1-2 are in print.

Something about the Author Series

Encompasses two related series. *Something about the Author* contains heavily illustrated biographical sketches on juvenile and young adult authors and illustrators from all eras. Volumes 1-51 are in print. *Something about the Author Autobiography Series* presents specially commissioned autobiographies by prominent authors and illustrators of books for children and young adults. Volumes 1-5 are in print.

Yesterday's Authors of Books for Children

Contains heavily illustrated entries on children's writers who died before 1961. Complete in two volumes. Volumes 1-2 are in print.

Literary Criticism Series
Cumulative Author Index

This index lists all author entries in the Gale Literary Criticism Series and includes cross-references to other Gale sources. For the convenience of the reader, references to the *Yearbook* in the *Contemporary Literary Criticism* series include the page number (in parentheses) after the volume number. References in the index are identified as follows:

AITN: *Authors in the News*, Volumes 1-2
CAAS: *Contemporary Authors Autobiography Series*, Volumes 1-6
CA: *Contemporary Authors* (original series), Volumes 1-122
CABS: *Contemporary Authors Bibliographical Series*, Volumes 1-2
CANR: *Contemporary Authors New Revision Series*, Volumes 1-22
CAP: *Contemporary Authors Permanent Series*, Volumes 1-2
CA-R: *Contemporary Authors* (revised editions), Volumes 1-44
CDALB: *Concise Dictionary of American Literary Biography*
CLC: *Contemporary Literary Criticism*, Volumes 1-48
CLR: *Children's Literature Review*, Volumes 1-14
CMLC: *Classical and Medieval Literature Criticism*, Volume 1
DLB: *Dictionary of Literary Biography*, Volumes 1-67
DLB-DS: *Dictionary of Literary Biography Documentary Series*, Volumes 1-4
DLB-Y: *Dictionary of Literary Biography Yearbook*, Volumes 1980-1986
LC: *Literature Criticism from 1400 to 1800*, Volumes 1-8
NCLC: *Nineteenth-Century Literature Criticism*, Volumes 1-18
SAAS: *Something about the Author Autobiography Series*, Volumes 1-5
SATA: *Something about the Author*, Volumes 1-51
SSC: *Short Story Criticism*, Volume 1
TCLC: *Twentieth-Century Literary Criticism*, Volumes 1-28
YABC: *Yesterday's Authors of Books for Children*, Volumes 1-2

Author Index

Author Index

Author Index

Author Index

O'Grady, Standish (James)
    1846-1928 . . . . TCLC 5
    See also CA 104

O'Hara Family
    See Banim, John and Banim, Michael

O'Hara, Frank
    1926-1966 . . . . CLC 2, 5, 13
    See also CA 9-12R
    See also obituary CA 25-28R
    See also DLB 5, 16

O'Hara, John (Henry)
    1905-1970 . . . . CLC 1, 2, 3, 6, 11, 42
    See also CA 5-8R
    See also obituary CA 25-28R
    See also DLB 9
    See also DLB-DS 2

O'Hehir, Diana 1922- . . . . .CLC 41
    See also CA 93-96

Okigbo, Christopher (Ifenayichukwu)
    1932-1967 .CLC 25
    See also CA 77-80

Olds, Sharon 1942- . . . . . . CLC 32, 39 (186)
    See also CANR 18
    See also CA 101

Olesha, Yuri (Karlovich)
    1899-1960 . . . . .CLC 8
    Scc also CA 85-88

Oliphant, Margaret (Oliphant Wilson)
    1828-1897 . . . . NCLC 11
    See also DLB 18

Oliver, Mary 1935- . . . . . . CLC 19, 34 (246)
    See also CANR 9
    See also CA 21-24R
    See also DLB 5

Olivier, (Baron) Laurence (Kerr)
    1907- . . . . .CLC 20
    See also CA 111

Olsen, Tillie 1913- . . . . CLC 4, 13
    See also CANR 1
    See also CA 1-4R
    See also DLB 28
    See also DLB-Y 80

Olson, Charles (John)
    1910-1970 . . . . CLC 1, 2, 5, 6, 9, 11,
                                                              29
    See also CAP 1
    See also CA 15-16
    See also obituary CA 25-28R
    See also CABS 2
    See also DLB 5, 16

Olson, Theodore 1937-
    See Olson, Toby

Olson, Toby 1937- . . . . : . . . . . .CLC 28
    See also CANR 9
    See also CA 65-68

Ondaatje, (Philip) Michael
    1943- . . . . CLC 14, 29
    See also CA 77-80
    See also DLB 60

Oneal, Elizabeth 1934-
    See Oneal, Zibby
    See also CA 106
    See also SATA 30

Oneal, Zibby 1934- . . . . .CLC 30
    See also Oneal, Elizabeth

O'Neill, Eugene (Gladstone)
    1888-1953 . . . . .TCLC 1, 6, 27
    See also CA 110
    See also AITN 1
    See also DLB 7

Onetti, Juan Carlos 1909- . . . . . . CLC 7, 10
    See also CA 85-88

O'Nolan, Brian 1911-1966
    See O'Brien, Flann

O Nuallain, Brian 1911-1966
    See O'Brien, Flann
    See also CAP 2
    See also CA 21-22
    See also obituary CA 25-28R

Oppen, George
    1908-1984 . . . . CLC 7, 13, 34 (358)
    See also CANR 8
    See also CA 13-16R
    See also obituary CA 113
    See also DLB 5

Orlovitz, Gil 1918-1973 . . . . .CLC 22
    See also CA 77-80
    See also obituary CA 45-48
    See also DLB 2, 5

Ortega y Gasset, José
    1883-1955 . . . . TCLC 9
    See also CA 106

Ortiz, Simon J. 1941- . . . . .CLC 45

Orton, Joe 1933?-1967 . . . . . . CLC 4, 13, 43
    See also Orton, John Kingsley
    See also DLB 13

Orton, John Kingsley 1933?-1967
    See Orton, Joe
    See also CA 85-88

Orwell, George
    1903-1950 . . . . .TCLC 2, 6, 15
    See also Blair, Eric Arthur
    See also DLB 15

Osborne, John (James)
    1929- . . . . CLC 1, 2, 5, 11, 45
    See also CANR 21
    See also CA 13-16R
    See also DLB 13

Osceola 1885-1962
    See Dinesen, Isak
    See also Blixen, Karen (Christentze
    Dinesen)

Oshima, Nagisa 1932- . . . . .CLC 20
    See also CA 116

Ossoli, Sarah Margaret (Fuller marchesa d')
    1810-1850
    See Fuller, (Sarah) Margaret
    See also SATA 25

Otero, Blas de 1916- . . . . .CLC 11
    See also CA 89-92

Owen, Wilfred (Edward Salter)
    1893-1918 . . . . TCLC 5, 27
    See also CA 104
    See also DLB 20

Owens, Rochelle 1936- . . . . .CLC 8
    See also CAAS 2
    See also CA 17-20R

Owl, Sebastian 1939-
    See Thompson, Hunter S(tockton)

Oz, Amos 1939- . . . . . . CLC 5, 8, 11, 27, 33
    See also CA 53-56

Ozick, Cynthia 1928- . . . . CLC 3, 7, 28
    See also CA 17-20R
    See also DLB 28
    See also DLB-Y 82

Ozu, Yasujiro 1903-1963 . . . . .CLC 16
    See also CA 112

Pa Chin 1904- . . . . .CLC 18
    See also Li Fei-kan

Pack, Robert 1929- . . . . .CLC 13
    See also CANR 3
    See also CA 1-4R
    See also DLB 5

Padgett, Lewis 1915-1958
    See Kuttner, Henry

Padilla, Heberto 1932- . . . . .CLC 38
    See also AITN 1

Page, Jimmy 1944-
    See Page, Jimmy and Plant, Robert

Page, Jimmy 1944- and
    Plant, Robert 1948- . . . . CLC 12

Page, Louise 1955- . . . . .CLC 40

Page, P(atricia) K(athleen)
    1916- . . . . CLC 7, 18
    See also CANR 4
    See also CA 53-56

Paget, Violet 1856-1935
    See Lee, Vernon
    See also CA 104

Palamas, Kostes 1859-1943 . . . . TCLC 5
    See also CA 105

Palazzeschi, Aldo 1885-1974 . . . . . . .CLC 11
    See also CA 89-92
    See also obituary CA 53-56

Paley, Grace 1922- . . . . CLC 4, 6, 37
    See also CANR 13
    See also CA 25-28R
    See also DLB 28
    See also AITN 1

Palin, Michael 1943-
    See Monty Python
    See also CA 107

Pancake, Breece Dexter 1952-1979
    See Pancake, Breece D'J

Pancake, Breece D'J
    1952-1979 .CLC 29
    See also obituary CA 109

Papini, Giovanni 1881-1956 . . . . . . TCLC 22
    See also CA 121

Parker, Dorothy (Rothschild)
    1893-1967 .CLC 15
    See also CAP 2
    See also CA 19-20
    See also obituary CA 25-28R
    See also DLB 11, 45

Parker, Robert B(rown) 1932- . . . . . .CLC 27
    See also CANR 1
    See also CA 49-52

Parkin, Frank 1940- . . . . .CLC 43

Parkman, Francis 1823-1893 . . . . . NCLC 12
    See also DLB 1, 30

Parks, Gordon (Alexander Buchanan)
    1912- . . . . CLC 1, 16
    See also CA 41-44R
    See also SATA 8
    See also DLB 33
    See also AITN 2

Author Index

CLC Cumulative Nationality Index

Nationality Index

CLC-48 Title Index